NEWBERRY COUNTY, SOUTH CAROLINA:

Historical and Genealogical Annals

By
GEORGE LELAND SUMMER, SR., A.B., A.M.

CLEARFIELD

NOTICE
This work was reproduced from the original edition. A characteristic of this copy, from which the printer worked, was that the image was uneven. Every effort has been made by the printer to produce as fine a reprint of the original edition as possible.

Reprinted for
Clearfield Company, Inc. by
Genealogical Publishing Co., Inc.
Baltimore, Maryland
1992, 1995, 2002

Copyright © 1950
George Leland Summer, Sr.
Newberry, South Carolina
All Rights Reserved
Reprinted by arrangement with
Mrs. George Leland Summer, Jr.,
With an added table of contents,
By Genealogical Publishing Co., Inc.
Baltimore, 1980
Library of Congress Catalogue Card Number 79-67869
International Standard Book Number 0-8063-0872-9
Made in the United States of America

PREFACE

The purpose of this book is to set forth much of the history of Newberry County, South Carolina that has not been heretofore published.

Originally, the author was interested in researching his own family of Summer and other pioneer families, and in publishing a genealogy, together with genealogies of other pioneer families of the county. Then he became interested in the general history of the county, and he thereupon undertook additional research. Hence the work in its present eclectic form.

The sources in which the data have been located, in addition to early histories, include church minutes, family Bibles, courthouse records, cemetery markers, and family traditions that have been substantiated through family records. The biographies include some that have not been heretofore published, or are incomplete in other published records.

The genealogical data include family sketches by descendants' and by the author, who used the following general sources in his researches: wills, intestate files, judgment files, equities, and deeds in the courthouses; and records found in public libraries, family Bibles, and cemetery markers. The names and dates are definite—a few dates are closely approximated, as based on information obtained—and the relationships definitely given. Many pioneers and their sons fought in the early Indian Wars, in the Revolutionary War, and in later wars. Names of the soldiers from this section were found in the State departments, though they are incomplete in some instances.

Most of the material in this history was published by the author previously in daily and local papers, and in magazines. In rewriting for this history, little revision has been made. This seemed necessary in order to give all history pertaining to each subject, hence some overlapping has resulted.

It is hoped that this history will be of service and interest to the many families in our city and county, and to the many descendants of these early pioneers who are now living not only in Newberry County but also in other counties of the State and in other States. Many are living in the southern States, in the northwestern States, in the West and in the North who are descendants of these pioneers who fought in the Indian Wars, the Revolutionary War, the Seminole Indian Wars, the Mexican War, the War of Secession, and the Spanish-American War.

G. Leland Summer

Newberry, South Carolina
June 20, 1950

CONTENTS

Preface	iii
Topography	1
Natural Resources	2
Origin of the County's Name	2
Early Pioneers and Their Settlements	4
Early History—Indians—Anthropology	6
Ethnology	7
Soldiers of Early Wars	9
Newberry County Court House and Jails	14
Early County Government	18
Historic Sites in City and County	22
Notable Citizens and Public Figures	27
Economic Developments	33
Social Development	49
Newberry Companies in the Spanish-American War	65
Education	67
Communities and Towns	88
Churches	100
Newberry County Women	145
Street Names	153
Some Reminiscences by the Author	155
Family Folklore	160
Historic Old Homes	164
Some Biographies of Newberry Citizens	176

Genealogies of Some Pioneer Families ... 193

Anderson ...193	Leitner ...255
Barre ...194	Lindsey ...256
Boozer ...195	Lyles ...257
Boyd ...197	Mayer ...259
Burton ...202	Mayes ...262
Caldwell ...202	Nance ...263
Cannon ...204	O'Neall ...264
Chandler and Gilbert ...205	Pearson ...265
Chapman ...207	Pope ...265
Counts ...209	Quattlebaum (Quaddlebaum) ...266
Cromer ...212	Ramage ...267
Eichleberger ...217	Ruff ...267
Epting ...217	Rutherford ...268
Feagle ...219	Satterwhite ...272
Floyd ...220	Schumpert ...273
Folk (Fulk or Foulque) ...222	Sheppard ...276
Gary ...225	Singley ...277
Gillam ...226	Stark ...278
Gilliam ...228	Stewart (Stuart) ...279
Glenn ...229	Suber ...280
Goggans ...230	Summer ...281
Goree ...231	Summers ...298
Gray and De Walt ...232	Waits (Wait) ...299
Griffin ...238	Waters ...299
Houseal ...240	Werts ...301
Kibler ...245	Wicker ...303
Kinard ...246	Wilson ...304
Kuhn ...248	Worthington ...305
Lake ...250	Wise and Wyse ...306
Langford ...253	

Other Colonial Pioneers and Their Families   310

Some Old Cemetery Markers   402

Abstracts of Old Wills   453

Bibliological [Bibliographical] References   467

Index—Abstracts of Old Wills   471

General Index   473

TOPOGRAPHY.

When old Ninety Six District, South Carolina, was divided into several counties about 1782, Newberry County was formed near the eastern edge of the Piedmont Plateau. It was given area of 623 square miles or 298,720 acres of land,(this has been increased by an addition from Lexington County on the Southeast). According to Robert Mills' statistics (page 641), the average extent of the county was equal to twenty four miles square, containing about 368,640 acres. This latter acreage may have included the territory formerly ceded from Lexington County after the original formation of the counties from Ninety Six District; and was later given back to the county.

Newberry County is bounded on the North by Union County, the line running Southeast on Broad River to Dawkins Ferry, then South on Broad River to the North of Buffalo Creek, on Saluda River, with Fairfield County on the East, Richland and Lexington Counties on the South; thence, the line runs Northwest by Saluda River, with Saluda County on the Southwest, to the Island Ford; thence, West to O'Dell's Ford above Whitmire, on Enoree River, with Greenwood County on the West and Laurens County on the Northwest; thence, Northwest near the highway to Gordon's Bridge, on Tyger River, and then to it's junction with Broad River. The meridian line runs from about Kempson's Bridge on Saluda River to Tucker's Bridge on Enoree River, passing North and South directly through the City, and is about twenty sixmiles.

The small hills in different sections of the county, with occasional flat surfaces, give the impression of gently rolling areas and good drainage generally. In a small area, though, from the Dead Fall section South to below the town of Prosperity, on Bush River, and a larger area around the site of the old village of Maybinton, near Broad River, are large soil erosion wastes From Maybinton to the town of Whitmire, in the northern section, are large gullies and small ravines showing the effects of erosion, especially nearer the rivers and creeks. This condition is not so apparent further into the southeastern section, except near Little Mountain where is seen a succession of hills, a series of hills, the most prominent of which is Little Mountain which rises about 200 feet above the surrounding area.

The highest altitude in the county is 780 feet, the general level in the northwestern section, in the western section about 675 feet, and in the southern and southeastern about 500 feet. The general slope being to the Southeast, except the part North of the so-called " Back-bone" ridge, or plateau edge, which slopes to the Northeast. These conditions give different drainages, the southern section to Saluda River, and through it's tributaries, and the northern section to Broad River, through it's many streams that reach well back into the county. Practically all farms are served by streams that are fed by good rains. The remains of old grist mills along the banks of the rivers and creeks indicate the full, even flows of the waters.

The rain-fall and other conditions vary little during the seasons—few extreme weather changes. About the average or mean temperature is 40 in the Winter, 60 in the Spring, 80 to 85 in the Summer, and 60 in the Fall. A mean average rain-fall is about 48 inches, and is distributed during the seasons, about 13 inches in Winter and about 10.5 inches in Spring, 14.5 inches in Summer, and about 10 in the Fall. A fair indication of the average rain-falls in Newberry is shown by a period from 1904-1930, by months, which gives an arithmetic mean of 3.88 inches, distributed as follows: January 3.98, February 4.45, March 3.99, April 3.25, May 3.66, June 4.16, July 4.71, August 5.21, September 3.45, October 2.78, November 2.61, and December 4.32.

The soils in each section of the county vary some, but may be divied into three natural divisions, viz: Upland or residual, terrace or old alluvial, and first bottom or recent-alluvial. While the color of the sub-soils are not so different, there are much differences in the content of both surface soils and sub-soils. The differences are mainly the percentages of sand, gravel, silt, and clay. Near the central area, for instance, is mostly the Appling sandy loam, having a gray or grayish-brown surface, with a yellow sub-soil. In this area are intermingling of other types of soils, as the Congaree type and others, generally fine sandy loams. In the northern section the hills are more noticable, and here the soil is more of the broken phase type, withfew small sections of silt loam near the streams. This silt loam has a grayish or whitish surface and is silty and floury in structure; and the sub-soil a yellow, friable, heavy silt loam to silty clay loam. The trend from the northern to the western section is to a greater variety of types, including the Appling loam. ....

In Stoney Battery section, near Saluda River, about two or three miles wide, a streak of rough, rocky land extends across the county to Broad River, near Peak. Large numbers of rocks and boulders are seen on the surfaces. Above Little Mountain, where the condition is wider, there is included, too, much mica and chist that diminish in quantity with depth. North of the town of Pomaria the rocks are less numerous but is in an area of trap and porphyries. The horse blende chist is developed between Prosperity and Saluda River, and in the sections around Whitmire and Maybinton.

In the Stoney Hill or Stoney Batter section, in the region North of the slate belt, is seen clay containing thin veins of quarts. South of Little River and as far West as Camping Creek are slate formations that contain some talc; but more of the quartz is nearer Little Mountain.

North of Peak, on Byoad River, between Clayton's Ferry and old Asford's Ferry, extending South to the town of Newberry through Caldwell township, are large areas of granite, where many outcroppings are seen, especially between the headwaters of King's Creek and Prosperity. On Crim's Creek, too, are large outcroppings of granite, mostly seen in the creek beds. In the North section are seen few granite formations.

(Ref: Soil Erasion Surveys, U. S. Dept. of Agri., and The Annals of Newberry, Part 1.)

NATURAL RESOURCES.

The natural resources of the county have not varied from the time it was formed in 1782. There are several large rivers and creeks, that in early times were used as beds for small fisheries, which the early settlers developed. At that time dams were not permitted to be built because they stopped the migration of fish up-stream. At a later time, when small power mills were built on the streams by planters to grind their own and their enighbor's wheat and corn, dams were built to give this water power; and not much objection to them was made since local fisheries on a large scale became unprofitable.

The forests consist, mostly, of short-leaf pine timber, though there are, too, much of the oak, hickory, and walnut and other kinds to be seen. There was much long-leaf pine timber in the southern part of the county up until about 1870-80, but it was cut so fast that this kind of pine tree is now exhausted.

Large rock formations—gray stone—have in recent years afforded good incomes to granite producers. Much of it has been and is yet being cut into stone blocks and shipped to large cities. A streak of this quartz stone stretches about a mile wide wide near Saluda River, and joins the area across the southern section of the county.

There are springs that are said to have medicinal qaulities. A few years ago Spearman's Spring above Jalapa, was developed, but only for a short time. (See other part of this book for data on the mineral springs).

The large rivers, Broad and Saluda, have afford opprtunities for constructions of large power dams, as the Parr Shoals Dam on Broad River, Lexington Power Company Dam on Saluda River.

ORIGIN OF THE COUNTY'S NAME.

Newberry got it's name, according to tradition, from the fact that a beautiful new kind of berry was found growing near Vanduslah Spring, on the hill above which was the tavern used by all who traveled through this section. (See reference in another part of this book).

Another tradition is there was an American soldier in the Rev. War, in General Sumpter's Brigade, whose name was Newberry, and the village received it's name for him. This reason is apparently far-fetched, as there was no reason for naming the place for him. He never lived in Newberry and never visited here, as anybody has ever learned about, and nothing occured to associate him with the community; hence, little or no credence is given to this idea.

Wild Flowers in The County—

Many flowers, common to this section, grew in and around Newberry, particularily along the small streams and meadows and in scattered wooded areas. Many are yet seen.

On the banks of small streams, at the first dawn of Spring, can be seen many wild violets, and wild phlox, the pink which retains it's lovely background from early Spring until September. Under dead brown leaves in the woods may be found blooms of the trailing arbutus, which sometimes come out from under their cover. The woodbine and the wild geranium may be found or a fragrant sweet-shrub.

In the open fields, on terraces or waste places, the poppy, Jamestown weed, or the may-pop show their varied colors; when sometimes the chigger weed (known as the " devil's paint brush") stands as a sentinental . In the sandy loam sections are the milk-weed, poverty grass, and popsissiwa; or, perhaps, the yellow and light red cactus, (prickly pear).

Spring and Summer flowers along the edges of meadows are the white dog-wood, generally prolific in thick patches, with , very infrequently, the red-bud or Judas tree. Maybe a meadow lilly is seen in the lower marshes. Further up, on higher grounds, the spearmint sometimes grows, and the sarsaparilla which was grown much by the settlers for it's curative powers, as well as the saxifrage and the yellow eyed grass.

Along the road-sides or the edges of the fields during the Summer months a variety of blooms, sometimes inordinately situated, may greet the tourists' eyes. Generally, the daisies, yellow wood sorrel, and dandelions are seen in the fields; but the sun-flower is seen mostly in the yards of some rural homes. Sometimes a field of blue vetch stretches it's beautiful covering; and the larkspur appears near the edges of the woods or fields, or a wild carrot in bloom, or Queen Anne's lace. Large patches of blooms of the blackberry bush, the plum trees, and other smaller plants are seen; and the dewberry which appears earlier is less often seen.

When Summer begins to fade, and at the first sign of Autumn, the golden-red blooms on the banks of streams, the elder with it's beautiful clusters, the rose-acacia and others still show themselves. Some rare Summer flowers are the white astor, gardenia, ladies-slipper, pennyroyal, helenium, and virbunum. Many of these are now culyivated.

Scattered over the county are many kinds of plants and trees, to some extent indicating the range of the streams. In thick patches along streams or in the meadows are the cane, elder, alder, trumpet vine, yellow jessamine, wisteria and rabbit weed. Nearer the woods or within their borders are the muscadine, the privett, sometimes the souppernong(originally cultivated), the woodbine, cross vine, southern smilax, ampelopsis, or the Virginia creeper. Sometimes the ivey and the mullion are seen in moist places.

In the fields and orchards are now seen many cultivated fruit trees or plants, as the pear, peach, apple, figs, plums, and locusts trees. Around the edges of farms or nearer the woods can be seen the crepe myrtle, cedar, sugarberry, mulberry, chinaberry, sycamore, persimmon, wild cherry and holly trees.

In addition to the pine trees named above, and the oaks and hickory trees, are found, also, beech, elm, base-wood, birch, ash, walnut, and the small dog-apple tree. Willows are nearer the banks of streams; though the weeping-willow is seldom seen except in the backyards of homes, being cultivated.

Some types of trees are said to be poisinous. The green burrs of pine trees are poisonous to animals, also the sheep laurel, wild cherry leaves that form a prussic acid when beginning to wither. Others that are poisonous to both people and animals are the sumac, ivy, rhododendron, the Carolina cherry which is kind of evergreen; the buck-eye, larkspur, and Jamestown weed.

The edible berries are mostly the blackberries, raspberries(originally cultivated), dewberries, wild strawberries, gooseberries, huckleberries, sparkelberries, and sandberries.

EARLY PIONEERS AND THEIR SETTLEMENTS, OLD FORTS.

Early pioneers who settled in the territory of what is now Newberry County were, mostly, Irish, Sotch-Irish and Germans, mingled with English and French in a smaller degree. The Irish and Scotch-Irish settled in the northern and western sections while the Germans and Dutch settled in the southern and southeastern sections. The Stoney Hill settlers were mostly Irish, and, like their German neighbors, received grants of lands from the English King; the number of acres to each depending on the size of the family or specific public services performed by him. They brought with them from the old country many old customs that were peculiar to their native lands. At a later period, another influence began to show in dances and songs, some of which were brought from Virginia by the slaves. Predominantly Christian peoples who fled their native countries on account of religeous persecutions or to seek better economic advantages, the new country soon fell into the order of good government under the English laws, the parent of our American legal procedure and institutions.

There were two religeous sects that were particularily opposed to slavery, the Friends and the Covenanters. The Friends, or Quakers, who had come from Pennsylvania and settled on Bush River, about three and one-half miles from Coats's Shop,(site of old church and the cemetery can yet be seen), many stopping in western North Carolina, were distinctly peculiar in their dress and habits; ceremonbous in habits. (See another part of this book for sketch of the Quakers).

Anthony Park, an Indian trader, moved to the Alleghany mountains to ply his trade, then came back to Newberry or the section of what is now Newberry County. He was one of the first Indian traders in this section, and had traveled over wide areas.

John Lyles, another Indian trader, had come from what is now the territory of North Carolina, though from a Virginia family. He settled on Broad River, near a place afterwards known as Lyles Ford. His brothers, James and Williamson Lyles,followed him to this section. All of them, and also several of their sons, served as patriots in the Rev. War.

Adam Summer came from Pennsylvania, and was said to have been the first settler in the upper Dutch Fork, though tradition is that John Lyles and John Adam Epting were in that area about the same time. (Sketch on Adam Summer in another part of this book.)

John Duncan, a native of Aberdeen, Scotland, came to the northern section of what is now Newberry County, and settled on the creek which now bears his name. He died early, but left several sons. The section in which he located was known for it's density of forests, with wild shrubbery and fruits that grew on the banks of the streams.

Other pioneers in the section between Duncan's Creek and Enoree River were, William Calmes, Benjamin Hampton, John Caldwell, Col. David Glenn, Peter Brazzlemann, and others. Further East, near Tyger River, were William Gilliam (from Virginia), Jacob Geiger, John Henderson (from Virginia), and William Maybin, and others.

West of Little River the first family of Caldwells had settled, coming from Virginia. James, William and John Caldwell, who were active patriots in the Rev. War; and their younger brothers, Robert and David.

Southwest of the town of Prosperity were such pioneers as Archibald Boyd (from Pennsylvania), James Lester, Samuel McQuerns, Nathan Hunter, and others, Where is now Black's Bridge,Col. Philemon Waters lived. He was a native of Virginia. It was said of him that he served with General George Washington in the French and Indian Wars in Virginia, before coming to South Carolina.

Rev. Joseph Summers came from Maryland or Deleware, and settled within five miles of where is now the County Court House, just beyond the Hartford section.

On the old " Belfast Road" leading to the Laurens County line, the old Griffin grave-yard is seen, where a Rev. War patriot is buried. On the way to that place, passing old Bush River Baptist Church cemetery, where are several graves of Rev. War patriots, are the sites of other settlars's homes.

Robert Gillam, Sr., one of the first County Judges, and a Rev. War patriot and officer, is buried on Page's Creek, not far from where is now the town of Chappells.

(See family sketches elsewhere in this book).

Early Business Men in Newberry—
Daniel Brooks, Thomas Pratt, Phillip Schoppert, P. B. Waters, Samuel Lindsey, John Speake, David Gunn, James Fernandez, Robert Stewart, Y. J. Harrington, Alexander Chambers, Ker Boyce, Abram Gilbert, John McMorries, Elisha Hammond, John S. Carwile, John B. Carwile, John Johnstone, Robert Boyce, Robert McCollough, Marmaduke Coate, John Coate, James Coate, John Holman, Hiram Hutchinson, John I. Gracey, E. Y. McMorries, Vincent Pope, Joseph Mooney, G. T. Scott, Samuel Pearson, Joseph Coppock, and others.

Early Physicians in Newberry and Newberry County—
Thomas Thompson, P. B. Ruff, Thomas Long, John Caldwell, William Harrington,...... Pratt, ... James, Joseph Waldo, Thomas Shall, ... Dodson, Burr Johnstone, M. T. Mendenhall, Freeborne Adams, William Summer, William Berley, James K. Chapman, Hugh H. Toland, Samuel Myrick, and others.
Later physicians in town were: John A. Berly, J. E. Berly, Thomas C. Brown, James McIntosh, Robert Campbell, David A. Cannon, James Coffield, David E. Ewart, Samuel Fair, George W. Garmany, James H. McIntosh, John K. Gary, Elijah Gates, Eli Geddings, James K. Gilder, William M. Hatton, John Foote Johnstone, Thomas B. Kennerley, Jacob H. King, Wylie K. Lindsey, John Long, O. B. Mayer, Sr., O. B. Mayer, Jr., James A. Renwick, M. A. Renwick, Benjamain Worthington, B. T. Yarborough, Thomas R. Gary, J. Marion Sease, and others.
Within the past twenty five or thirty years the following are some of the physicians who practiced in Newberry: W. G. Houseal, James M. Kibler, P. G. Ellesor, Robert L. Mayes, E. M. Moore, Robert W. Houseal, Frank D. Mower, Thomas H. Pope, J. Claude Sease, W. C. Holloway, William A. Dunn, William E. Pelham, Jr., E. G. Abel, Thomas Nealy, Hugh B. Senn, Robert E. Livingstone, Elbert J. Dickert, Jr., A. J. Katzberg, V. W. Rhinehardt, Raymond Lominack, and others.

Business Men in Newberry from about 1880 to 1900, and later—
George McWhirter, James N. Martin, Foster N. Martin, William G. Mayes, Sr., William G. Mayes, Jr., Robert L. McCaughrin, William T. Tarrant, Thomas Tarrant, Edward R. Hipp, Charles E. Summer, John H. Summer, George W. Summer, G. M. B. Epting, Mrs. Cynthia Mower, Duane Mower, John M. Kinard, Dr. James McIntosh, Robert H. Wright, John W. Chapman, Leland M. Speers, Robert Y. Leavell, Fred H. Schumpert, Walter H. Hunt, Z. F. Wright, Thomas J. McCrary, J. Marion Davis, John W. Kibler, Arthur Kibler, M. A. Carlisle, William J. Lane, Thomas M. Lake, Calhoun F. Boyd, Dr. Peter Robertson, John C. Goggans, Sr.,William R. Smith, John P. Fant, Frank Z. Wilson, John C. Wilson, R. H. Greneker, J. Thomas Mayes, James A. Crotwell, Dan B. Wheeler, Thomas M. Neel, Thomas V. Wicker, L. W. Floyd, H. H. Folk, G. Fred Long, Tench C. Pool, C. C. Davis, E. B. Wilbur, P. C. Scott, Charles J. Purcell, W. F. Pratt, W. H. Webb, B. H. Lovelace, Marcus L. Spearman, Henry L. Parr, Jesse Y. McFall, James Y. McFall, J. D. Cash, A. C. Jones, Burr F. Goggans, James F. Todd, Samuel P. Boozer, O. H. P. Fant, William A. Fant, C. M. Harris, Wallace A. Cline, J. R. Green, Robert Smith, R. D. Smith, Sims E. Brown, O. M. Jamison, E. H. Kingsmore, William T. Wright, J. William White, A. J. Sproles, James A. Mimnaugh, Otto Klettner, Thomas Q. Boozer, Edward Scholtz, John L. Ramage, Paul Johnstone, Luther Riser, William A. Kinard, J. D. Davenport, C. L. Havird, Joseph Mann, Osborne Wells, " Jew" Mittle, John A. Eddy, William H. Eddy, " Jew" Brown, D. M. Ward, Julius Smith, W. J. Duffie, E. S. Bailey, ... Twonsend, S. J. Wooten, John O. Peoples, William Johnson, Thomas P. Johnson, W. C. Peoples, ... Gary, W. F. Pratt, ...Motte, C. T. Summer, Edward Y. Morris, Dr. W. K. Griffin (druggist), Dr. L. A. Rast (druggist), R. H. Land, J. D. Bruce, W. W. Houseal (onetime Sheriff), M. J. Jenkins, Andrew Wicker, M. Barre, Robert Moorman, Alex Singleton, J. B. Fellers (onetime Probate Judge), Junius E. Chapman, James M. Crawford, ... Girardeau, L. R. Marshall, Shockley Brothers (Contractors), Thomas H. Cromer (Contractor), J. L. Aull, I. M. Suber, William H. Dickert, W. D. Goggans, E. S. Coppock, W. C. Wiseman (photographer), Richard H. Wearn, P. W. Chick, R. S. Chick, J. Z. Salter (Photographer), Henry H. Blease, Thomas F. Harmon, E. M. Evans, H. H. Evans, A. M. Bowers, John W. Taylor, C. M. Jones, Sam B. Jones, John Montgomery, Summerfield Montgomery, F. J. Moses, C. B. Buist, W. T. Livingstone (Contractor), E. Livingstone (Contractor), L. A. Wilson (Contractor), G. L Summer, O. L. Long, R. M. Fellers, E. Hugh Summer, Holland Fellers, and others.
The tailors in Newberry were, Patrick Scott, James Guy, ... Golding, Burrell Raines (col), "Swede" Carlson, and others.

EARLY HISTORY-INDIANS-ANTHROPOLOGY.

Charleston was settled at first by colonists from England, with some scattered French, German and Irish settlers; later, by Germans and French; but it was many years before the upper part of the State was settled. After the first Charleston and other coastal settlements were made, a Proprietary form of government was established by the King of England. In the year 1665, John Locke, the English writer and philosopher, helped in framing the first State Constitution. The Rights Lords Proprietors, English noblemen and friends of the King, were given this first charter on March 24, 1663, and a second charter on June 30, 1665, which formed the basis for the new government. This form lasted until 1720, when the Royal government took over until 1776, when the Declaration of Independence was signed. All of this effected the people in making settlements in the upper section.

The colonists near Charleston were reluctant to advance into the interior as much as they would have liked to explore it, because of the Indians. Eventually, an expedition was sent among the Indians, subduing them, and a peace treaty was signed. However, the French explorations in the interior caused animosity against the white people, especially the English. Warfare started, and peaceful settlers in the southern section were unable to trade among the Indians. They refused to accept help from the English in having timber cut down and new fields opened up for cultivation.

The Cherokee Nation, with it's many tribes, stretched from across South Georgia through South Carolina, up to the central and northwestern part of the State. There were many hunting grounds between Broad and Saluda Rivers. One tribe, the Salutah, lived on the river which now bears it's name, near what was later known as "Old Town". They were a less ferocious tribe, and soon afterwards moved up into Pennsylvania, the remaining ones, with other tribes, gradually migrating to the mountains of East Tennessee. It is said that an old Indian mound, of which there were many, could be seen plainly within recent years near the West bank of the Saluda River, between Chappells and Old Town. Another mound is above the town of Chappells, near the highway which leads to Greenwood. There are other indications of their habitat, as the old flint rocks of various sizes and kinds are found on the river and creek beds in the county. A mound can be seen on Mudlic Creek, on lands of the late John D. Williams.

The rivers and creeks have, many of them, Indian names, with their significant meanings. Broad River was called by the Indians, "Eswawpuddeneh", meaning line river between the tribes. Saluda River got it's name from the Salutah tribe that lived on it, meaning "corn river". Tyger River was called "Amoyescheck", which originated from an Indian story that a bear and a tiger once fought on the river bank and the tiger killed the bear, though both animals were unable to leave the ground. Indian Creek got it's name from a Cherokee village located on it, and where the last wild-cat was killed within the territory. Enoree River meant a river of "muscadines". Keowee River meant a river of " mulberries".

The Cherokees were adept in the art of carving stone and wood. A month's work for a warrior to carve and fashion his ornamental pipe was required.

An old map of the coastal section of the State and of the western interior, made by one George Hunter about the time of the settlements, gives the original Cherokee trail from the coast up the Santee River to the Congaree River, (near Columbia), thence traversing Saluda River, which correseponds with statements made by older people living around or close to the present Lexington Power Dam, where the trail crossed the river, and followed a course up Camping Creek, just South of where the town of Prosperity is located. From there it appears to have joined the Keowee trail leading up to the mountains of the northwestern section of the State.

In 1735 there were 6,000 warriors in the Cherokee tribes, which was reduced in 1775 to 2,500 by wars, epidemics, rum. Many drifted North, while the Congarees who lived in the central section drifted to below the Savannah River, and finally formed part of the tribes of Seminoles in Florida.

The Cherokees of the southern section were a light, copper-colored, or reddish tinged race, with straight black hair and black eyes. They were medium in height and generally heavy built, and typified many features of their earliest recorded ancestors of the extreme Northwest, the Esquimos.

ETHNOLOGY.

Racial Elements in South Carolina-in Newberry County—
Races differ according to their locality, darker people having come from the southern regions where the quality of the air is the primary cause of color. This dominant characteristic is further emphasized by heritage—groups or tribes that had no chance for assimilation with other races.
Similarity, therefore, is preponderant evidence of race heritage; and changes of physical character is made only through new invironments of peoples of different race groups. New social activities and developments of new works are determining influences for obliterating differences. However, in America the same invironments, the same climates and the same social institutions have not proven sufficient to obliterate differences between Indo-European races. In England and in France there have been several distinct ethnic elements, where, during the past centuries, new races were formed by amalgamation of the races that were origininally distinct.
In the crossing of types of two different elements the persistence of race characteristics and the unification of different factors in a complex social life tend to perpetuate those differences that are best suited to them.
Thus, an ethnical background of the early settlers of South Carolina, and in the area of Newberry, is first considered in order to ascertain some facts regarding the types or races from which they came. In this section or County the most numerous elements were the Scotch-Irish and Irish who settled in various sections of the State and County; and the Germans with intermixture of Dutch and French of the upper Rhine. All of these belonged to the strict Teutonic element of North and Central Germany. In the third numerical order were the French Huguenots who were a mixture of the Swiss, South Germans, and Italians, with prior elements of the old French Empire that had an infusion of both Spanish and Italian.
The early settlers of three nations were not really distinct races, and for this reason they became easily assimilated after a short period of group or tribal exclusiveness. In the short time since the first settlements in America there is little perceptible change in ethnic types on account of assimilation, yet a common invironment has been causing some differences that may be best suited for all to be perpetuated in a common social order.
The Scotch-Irish, like the Germans, were mostly blond types, both being descended from Saxon ancestors of earlier senturies. The French Huguenots were originally French Lutherans, and took the name "Huguenot" from the Protestants of Tours, in France, who used to assemble by night near the gate of King Hugo, whom the people regarded as a ghost because he went out at night. A monk said that the people should be called "Huguenots", a name that had been used since the year 1650.

The Germans and Dutch Saxon Settlers—
The Germans of the Dutch Fork section of the State were mostly from the regions of Hiedleberg and were Palantines. They had fair or light colored hair and blue eyes; but there was, also, some evidence of an earlier amalgamation with French Huguenots who had fled from France into Germany and Holland, then sought refuge or moved into England; due to the French King's order to banish all Protestants. A mixture of German and French constituted mostly the types of people from Alsac-Lorraine from which came many settlers in colonies of Germans and Dutch to America, sailing from Rotterdam. They, as well as the English and Scotch-Irish, brought with them early customs, habits and dress peculiar to their countries.

Common Type Among Settlers—
When the settlers came, the country was occupied by Indians, the Cherokee tribes in the district between the Savannah River and the Broad River. "They were tall, with regular features, high cheek-bones, nose aqualine or hooked, eyes small, black and full of fire." ....
They tore out their hair on their faces so that they did not shave. "Their women were tall and slender, and smaller than the men." ...."They were comely,........................"
The white traders who lived among the Indians had their own private homes, and they frequently employed Indian squaws to cook and look after their homes. Many of these squaws became wives of the traders, others were mistresses, and they became mothers of half-breeds who,

many of them, grew up and became Chiefs of Tribes, and some became amalgamated with the white families.

There is slight evidence of Indian ancestry among the people of this area, the percentage so small that little or no consideration being given it. The few half-breeds remained Indians and married Indian squaws, so that there was little or slight amalgamation of the two races. The tribes disappeared soon, and moved West. However, some of the Indian influence is seen in certain ingenious arts, in cooking, dances..........The early settlers brought with them their own customs, dress and habits, but many of the Indian customs were used, also.

The Negro Slaves to America—

The negroes who were sent to America as slaves, beginning to come into the State about the year 1818 in material numbers, always remained a distinct race. There were not then, and not at this time, intermarriages among the negroes and other races. Their very distinct physical character and disproportionate population have been causes of maintaining this condition. The numbers of negroes increased so much that by the end of the War Between the States there were in the South four million of them suddenly emerged from a slave system. Even this could not effect any change in social conditions.

Prior to the War Between the States the slave system, with probably a larger number of negro women than negro men, caused some of the white landlords to use slave girls as concubines, from which came a mulatto type of negro. These mulattoes married with the black, distinctly regarded as negroes, from which have appeared by further processes of marriages, a race of negroes not as black as the original African type but much darker than the mulatto type. There is a tendency, therefore, towards the establishment of a new negro race, gradually obliterating the original black type, thus carrying out an expressed sociological theory.

In the year 1880 one-third of the negroes in the United States had an infusion of white blood, one-third had less, and one-third had so little it was hard to determine how many had none. Since that time, smaller numbers of mulattoes have been seen, absorption among the negro race gradually obliterating them.

Negroes in the South recognize race distinction; they have a tendency to work well with white people; and the recognize the white man's inherent geniousness and initiative, and are, apparently, happy and content.

Since the females perpetuate the race, and where there is real distinctiveness between two races, the things that are best for all will be best pepetuated through non-assimilation and process of absorption in a new type. According to scientific theories the white race will always be white, while other races may change it's physical characteristics. Hence, there are bilinqual districts in all towns and cities, races of peoples preferring to live among themselves or among their own. Where there are scattering families of less distinct races and no material numbers among them in a town or community, such as the Jews, the Greeks, or the Italians, they live among native white Americans.

SOLDIERS OF EARLY WARS FROM NEWBERRY COUNTY.
(A partial list)

Cherokee Indian Wars of 1759-62—
Names of some from area now comprising Newberry, Laurens, and Lexington Counties:
In the first draft for the company of Captain Lewis Colsan, Regiment of Col. John Chevilerre, were, John Folmor, George Cromer, Frederick Cromer, Jacob Cromer, George Leitzey, George Rhiddlehuber. In the second draft were those who were on duty at the Congaree Nov 14, 1759, including John Miller, Sgt., Barnett Seigler, Henry Gallman. In Col. George Gabriel's Regiment of militia, from October 11, 1759 to January 15, 1760, were, Thomas Burton, Adjutant, Thomas Conner, Captain. In Captain Kolb's Company, same Regiment, were, John Hamm, Jacob Ham, William Wise. In Captain Butler's Company were, David Cannon, John Holloway. In Captain James Leslie's Company, of Col. Richard Richardson's Regiment, were, Ephriam Lyles, John Lyles, David Henderson, Joseph Brown, William Busby, Solomon McGraw,..................
In Captain John Pearson's Company, same Regiment, were, John Busby, Andrew Cromer, Henry Anderson, Samuel Anderson, Isom Busby, Richard Strawther, James Myrick, ...

Rev. War patriots—
Officers: Captain Jacob Roberts Brown, Major Jacob Barre, Major John Caldwell, Captain James Caldwell, Major William Caldwell, Captain John Caldwell, Brig. Gen. Levi Casey, Captain John Coate, Rev. Giles Chapman (Chaplain), Captain Thomas Cureton, Major.Jonothan Downs (later in Laurens District), Lietenant David Dixon, Col. Thomas Dugan, Captain Benjmain Eddings, Major Robert Gillam, Captain Robert Gillam, Jr., Col. Daved Glenn, Major Thomas Gordon, Captain John Griffin, Major Frederick Gray, Captain John Floyd, Captain Micajah Harris, Captain David Henderson, Col. Benjamin Herndon, Captain William F. Houseal, Captain Thomas Jones, Lieutenant James Kelly, Lieutenant Henry Kuhn(later signed, "Koon"), Major Michael Leitner, Lieut. Col. John Lindsey, Captain John Lindsey, Jr., Lieutenant Colonel James Lyles, Captain John Lyles, Captain Ephriam Lyles, Captain Williamson Lyles, Col. Aromanus Lyles, Major Spencer Morgan, Major Samuel Otterson (moved to Union County), Captain Anthony Park, Captain James Spence, Major Thomas Starke, Major Adam Summer, Captain John Adam Summer, Jr., Lieutenant Henry Summer, Captain Oliver Towles, Lieutenant Colonel Philemon Waters, Major Thomas Waters. Col. James Williams (later in Laurens County),
Privates: Mercer Babb, Frederick Boozer, John Boyce, David Boyd, John Boyd, Noah Bonds, Adam Bedenbaugh, Jacob Boozer, Elisha Brooks, John Buchanan, John Brown, Sims Brown, Stephens Bowers, Jacob Anderson, Abram Anderson, Henry Anderson, Gabriel Snderson,Isaah Anderson, Jacob Chandler, William Coate, Charles Crenshaw(in a Va. Reg.), Cornelius Cox, Jacob Crosswhite, Mordecai Chandler, James Chandler, John Clarke, Henry Counts, John Counts, Aaron Cates, Benjamin Conwell, Zacariah Gawrile, Samuel Cannon, John Cole, Sr.,William Calmes in Va. Reg.), James Creswell, George Cromer, Martin Cromer, Frederick Cromer, Jacob Cromer, Thomas Duckett.(later in Laurens County,), John Duncan, Benjamin Duncan(said to have joined the Tories), James Duncan, James Dugan, Robert Dugan, Chesley Davis, Henry Dominick, John Dominick, George Eichleberger, John Eichleberger, John Edwards, William Eddins, Edward Finch, John Ford, Daniel Goggans, Joseph Goodman, Sashal Grasty, John Goree, Thomas Goree, William Greer, James Galbraith, Charles Griffin, James Griffin, Caleb Gilbert, Thomas Gilbert, William Gilliam, George Goggans, Thomas Gary, Sr., Thomas Gary, Jr., William Gary, Charles Gary, John Hampton, Peter Hair, Peter Hawkins, Matthias Hentz, Maximillan Haynie, William Houston, John Kinard, Martin Kinard, Edmund Kelly, John Kelly, Samuel E. Kenner, Charles King,John Kibler, Michael Kibler, Benjmain Long (from Union to Newberry), Ephriam Lyles, Jr., John Lyles, Jr., William Lyles, Henry Lyles, Charles Littleton, Charles Littleton, Jr., Mark Littleton, James Lindsey, Samuel Lindsey, Thomas Lindsey, Levi Manning, John Means, Robert Maffett, William Maybin, Matthew Mybin, Robert Moore, Samuel Newman, William O'Neall, John O'Neall, Jacob Pennington, Charles Lester, Peter Lester, James Lester, George Ruff, Christian Ruff, George Rsier, Martin Riser, Caleb Pitts, John Pitts, William Pitts, James Sheppard, John Satterwhite, William Stephens, Henry Steddam, George Adam Summer, Nicholas Summer, Francis Summer, William Summer, John Speake, John Spence, Robin Spence, William Spence, Samuel Teague, Elijah Teague, William Turner, Benjamin Taylor, James Tinsley, Golding Tinsley,Jacob Ulmer, Charles Vessels, Shadrack Vessels, Samuel Waldrop, John Waldrop, William Waldrop, Joseph Wright, George Wheeler,John West, William Wilson, James Wilson, William Wadlington, Benjamin Worthington, Nicholas Vaughan, Abram Young, Sr.
(Some of the above privates may have also served as officers)

Other privates were: Jacob Aaron, John Adams, James Anderson, John Atkins, George Ashford, (probably near Broad River in Fairfield District), Michael Bates, James Beard, John Beard, John Belton, Samuel Belton, Peter Boseman, John Boland, Patrick Bowers, Henry Boozer, Peter Braswell, Jesse Brooks, Grissell Brown, William Buchanan, Charles Bundrick, Aaron Burton, William Burton, Thomas Burton, Adam Byerley, Robert Campbell, Ephriam Cannon, David Cannon, John Cannon, Alexander Chambers, Thoroughgood Chambers, Samuel Chapman, Giles Chapman, Joseph Chapman, John Chappel, Joseph Clapp, Thomas Clark, John Clark, Thomas Coate, John Coate, Jr., Marmaduke Coate, John Cook, Jacob Cook, Allen Cox, William Cox, Benjamin Collier, William Cooper, John Cunningham, William Crow, John Dalrymple, John Darby, Richard Darby, Daniel De Walt, Chesley Davis, Harmon Davis, James Davis, John Davis, John Dennis, Michael Dickert, John Dickert, Jeremiah Dial, James Duncan, Edward Edwards, Isaac Edwards, John Eichleberger, John English, Stephen Elmore, Adam F. Epting, Jacob Epting, John Enlow, Jacob Felker, John A. Felker, James Finley, John Finley, Reuben Flannagan, Henry Folk, William Folk, Jacob Fulmer, John Fulmer, Israel Gauntt, John Galbraith, Peter Galloway, David Gilbert, Gilbert Gilder, Henry Gilder, Robert Glasgow, John Glenn, Anthony Golding, John Golding, Timothy Goodman, John Goodwin, John Gordon, Nathaniel Gordon, James Goree, Josiah Goree, Cladius Goree, Harris Gillam, Joshua Gillam, James Grayham, John Graham, James Graves, Thomas Green, James Griffin, William Griffin, Joshua Griffith, Matthew Hall, Andrew Hallman, James Ham, John Hardy, Thomas Hardy, Jacob Halfacre, William Henry, James Henry, Benjamin Hampton, Joseph Hampton, John Harmon, Burr Calvert Harris, Nathaniel Harris, James Hawkins, Thomas Hawkins, James Hayes, Joseph Hayes, Thomas Herbert, Francis Higgins, John Hipp, George Hipp, James Hodges, John Hogge, Lewis Hogge, Isaac Hollingsworth, David Harper, Thomas Harper, James Houston, John Houston, Daniel Horsey, John Howard, John Hughey, Alexander Hutchinson, John Hutchinson, William Hutchinson, Jacob Houber, Benjamin Inman, David Jenkins, James Johnson, John Johnston, Sr., John Jay, William Jay, Jesse Jay, James Jones, John Jones, Thomas Jones, George Keller, Joseph Keller, Samuel Keller, Henry Key, Michael Kinard, Matthias Kinard, Jacob King, John Knox, John Langford John Lark, Robert Leavell, John Leavell, Jacob Lominick, Michael Lominick, Thomas Long, Mrs. Mary Letssey(widow of George), Casper Leophardt, Jacob Lewis, Stephen Lewis, Richard Lewis, Andrew Lee, Frederick Le Gronne, John Le Gronner, John Livingstone, Michael Livingston, John Lohmer, William Malone, Sr., John Malone, John Mangum, John Mann, John Marrs, Solomon Martin, James Massey, William Massey, Sr., Robert Maxwell, Sr., Benedict Mayer, Ulrich Mayer, James Meadors, John Meadors(lived later in Laurens District), Samuel Miles, Jacob Miller, Robert Mills, Sr., John Mills, Thomas Mills, Isaac Mitchell, William Moore, William Moore, Jr., John Moore, Thomas Morgan, John Morgan, Joshua Morgan, John Morris, William Montgomery, Sr., David Montgomery, William McClelland, John McClelland, James McClintock, John McClintock, James McCollom, John McCollom, William McConnell, James McCrackin, Robert McCrackin, William McDaniel Patrick McDowell, James McGill, Thomas McKie, James McNeill, James McMaster, John McMorries, William McTeer, John Neal, John Newman, William Nimmons, Audrey Noland, John O'Dell, James Oliver, William Owens, John Parrott, William Page, Sr., Daniel Parkins, James Patterson, James Patty, Enock Pearson, John Pearson, Isiah Pemberton, Thomas Perry, Henry Pitts, Thomas Pitts, John Price, Matthias Quaddlebum, James Ramage, John Ray, Thomas Ray, Reagan(John), William Reagin, Joshua Reeder, Amos Richardson, Daniel Richardson, George Rhiddlehuber, Michael Rhiddlehuber, Elisha Rhodes, John Richey, John Rikard, Michael Rikard, John Robertson, James ross, Thomas Ross, Andrew Russell, Peter Ruble, John Ruff, John Riley, Frederick Schaffer, John Carrol Seigler, Bartlette Satterwhite, Matthias Senn, George Adam Setzler, Peter Setzler, William Sheppard, Sr., David Sims, Sr., John Sims, Phillip Sligh, Sr., William Speers, David Speers, Daniel Stewart, Robert Stewart, John Stewart, Joshua Stewart, Alexander Stewart, Henry Stockman, John Stockman, George Strother, Conrad Suber, Matthias Suber, John Suber, Ulrick Suber, George Suber, John Summers, James Summers, John Swann, John Swinford, Everhardt Swittenberg, Elijah Teague, Mrs. Alce Teague (widow of Elijah), William Taggart, William Taylor, Jonothan Taylor, Joshua Teague, Stephen Thomas, Joseph Thompson, Charles Thompson, John Thompson, James Thompson, William Thompson, John Towles, James Toland, John Toland, Joseph Tucker, James Turner, Thomas Turner, James Vardeman, John Voluntine, George Wadlington, James Wadlington, William Wadlington, Joseph Walker, William Wallace, Henry Wertz, John Wertz, Peter Wedsman(pensioned), James Weeks, William Weeks, George Wells, Benjamin West, George Whitmore, Frederick Whitmore, Ambrose Whitten, Mrs. Mary Wicker (widow of Simon Wicker), Daniel Williams, John Williams, Stephen Williams, Joseph Williamson, Robert Williamson, John Wilson, George Wilson, James Wilson, Thomas Wilson, John Wood, Samuel Wood, Thomas Wood, John Workman, Robert Workman, John Wright, Alexnander Wright, George Young, James Young (pensioned).   (some of above may have also acted as officers—uncommissioned officers. and the widows named furnished supplies to the army).

SOLDIERS OF EARLY WARS FROM NEWBERRY COUNTY.
(A partial list)

Cherokee Indian Wars of 1759-62—
Names of some from area now comprising Newberry, Laurens, and Lexington Counties:
In the first draft for the company of Captain Lewis Colsan, Regiment of Col. John Chevilerre, were, John Folmor, George Cromer, Frederick Cromer, Jacob Cromer, George Leitzey, George Rhiddlehuber. In the second draft were those who were on duty at the Congaree Nov 14, 1759, including John Miller, Sgt., Barnett Seigler, Henry Gallman. In Col. George Gabriel's Regiment of militia, from October 11, 1759 to January 15, 1760, were, Thomas Burton, Adjutant, Thomas Conner, Captain. In Captain Kolb's Company, same Regiment, were, John Hamm, Jacob Ham, William Wise. In Captain Butler's Company were, David Cannon, John Holloway. In Captain James Leslie's Company, of Col. Richard Richardson's Regiment, were, Ephriam Lyles, John Lyles, David Henderson, Joseph Brown, William Busby, Solomon McGraw,....................
In Captain John Pearson's Company, same Regiment, were, John Busby, Andrew Cromer, Henry Anderson, Samuel Anderson, Isom Busby, Richard Strawther, James Myrick, ...

Rev. War patriots—
Officers: Captain Jacob Roberts Brown, Major Jacob Barre, Major John Caldwell, Captain James Caldwell, Major William Caldwell, Captain John Caldwell, Brig. Gen. Levi Casey, Captain John Coate, Rev. Giles Chapman (Chaplain), Captain Thomas Cureton, Major. Jonothan Downs (later in Laurens District), Lietenant David Dixon, Col. Thomas Dugan, Captain Benjmain Eddings, Major Robert Gillam, Captain Robert Gillam, Jr., Col. Daved Glenn, Major Thomas Gordon, Captain John Griffin, Major Frederick Gray, Captain John Floyd, Captain Micajah Harris, Captain David Henderson, Col. Benjamin Herndon, Captain William F. Houseal, Captain Thomas Jones, Lieutenant James Kelly, Lieutenant Henry Kuhn(later signed, "Koon"), Major Michael Leitner, Lieut. Col. John Lindsey, Captain John Lindsey, Jr., Lieutenant Colonel James Lyles, Captain John Lyles, Captain Ephriam Lyles, Captain Williamson Lyles, Col. Aromanus Lyles, Major Spencer Morgan, Major Samuel Otterson (moved to Union County), Captain Anthony Park, Captain James Spence, Major Thomas Starke, Major Adam Summer, Captain John Adam Summer, Jr., Lieutenant Henry Summer, Captain Oliver Towles, Lieutenant Colonel Philemon Waters, Major Thomas Waters. Col. James Williams (later in Laurens County),
Privates: Mercer Babb, Frederick Boozer, John Boyce, David Boyd, John Boyd, Noah Bonds, Adam Bedenbaugh, Jacob Boozer, Elisha Brooks, John Buchanan, John Brown, Sims Brown, Stephens Bowers, Jacob Anderson, Abram Anderson, Henry Anderson, Gabriel Snderson, Isaah Anderson, Jacob Chandler, William Coate, Charles Crenshaw(in a Va. Reg.), Cornelius Cox, Jacob Crosswhite, Mordecai Chandler, James Chandler, John Clarke, Henry Counts, John Counts, Aaron Gates, Benjamin Conwell, Zacariah Gaxwile, Samuel Cannon, John Cole, Sr., William Calmes in Va. Reg.), James Creswell, George Cromer, Martin Cromer, Frederick Cromer, Jacob Cromer, Thomas Duckett.(later in Laurens County), John Duncan, Benjamin Duncan(said to have joined the Tories), James Duncan, James Dugan, Robert Dugan, Chesley Davis, Henry Dominick, John Dominick, George Eichleberger, John Eichleberger, John Edwards, William Eddins, Edward Finch, John Ford, Daniel Goggans, Joseph Goodman, Sashal Grasty, John Goree, Thomas Goree, William Greer, James Galbraith, Charles Griffin, James Griffin, Caleb Gilbert, Thomas Gilbert, William Gilliam, George Goggans, Thomas Gary, Sr., Thomas Gary, Jr., William Gary, Charles Gary, John Hampton, Peter Hair, Peter Hawkins, Matthias Hentz, Maximillan Haynie, William Houston, John Kinard, Martin Kinard, Edmund Kelly, John Kelly, Samuel E. Kenner, Charles King, John Kibler, Michael Kibler, Benjmain Long (from Union to Newberry), Ephraim Lyles, Jr., John Lyles, Jr., William Lyles, Henry Lyles, Charles Littleton, Charles Littleton, Jr., Mark Littleton, James Lindsey, Samuel Lindsey, Thomas Lindsey, Levi Manning, John Means, Robert Maffett, William Maybin, Matthew Mybin, Robert Moore, Samuel Newman, William O'Neall, John O'Neall, Jacob Pennington, Charles Lester, Peter Lester, James Lester, George Ruff, Christian Ruff, George Rsier, Martin Riser, Caleb Pitts, John Pitts, William Pitts, James Sheppard, John Satterwhite, William Stephens, Henry Steddam, George Adam Summer, Nicholas Summer, Francis Summer, William Summer, John Speake, John Spence, Robin Spence, William Spence, Samuel Teague, Elijah Teague, William Turner, Benjamin Taylor, James Tinsley, Golding Tinsley, Jacob Ulmer, Charles Vessels, Shadrack Vessels, Samuel Waldrop, John Waldrop, William Waldrop, Joseph Wright, George Wheeler, John West, William Wilson, James Wilson, William Wadlington, Benjamin Worthington, Nicholas Vaughan, Abram Young, Sr.
(Some of the above privates may have also served as officers)

Other privates were: Jacob Aaron, John Adams, James Anderson, John Atkins, George Ashford, (probably near Broad River in Fairfield District), Michael Bates, James Beard, John Beard, John Belton, Samuel Belton, Peter Boseman, John Boland, Patrick Bowers, Henry Boozer, Peter Braswell, Jesse Brooks, Crissell Brown, William Buchanan, Charles Bundrick, Aaron Burton, William Burton, Thomas Burton, Adam Byerley, Robert Campbell, Ephriam Cannon, David Cannon, John Cannon, Alexander Chambers, Thoroughgood Chambers, Samuel Chapman, Giles Chapman, Joseph Chapman, John Chappel, Joseph Clapp, Thomas Clark, John Clark, Thomas Coate, John Coate, Jr., Marmaduke Coate, John Cook, Jacob Cook, Allen Cox, William Cox, Benjamin Collier, William Cooper, John Cunningham, William Crow, John Dalrymple, John Darby, Richard Darby, Daniel De Walt, Chesley Davis, Harmon Davis, James Davis, John Davis, John Dennis, Michael Dickert, John Dickert, Jeremiah Dial, James Duncan, Edward Edwards, Isaac Edwards, John Eichleberger, John English, Stephen Elmore, Adam F. Epting, Jacob Epting, John Enlow, Jacob Felker, John A. Felker, James Finley, John Finley, Reuben Flannagan, Henry Folk, William Folk, Jacob Fulmer, John Fulmer, Israal Gauntt, John Galbraith, Peter Galloway, David Gilbert, Gilbert Gilder, Henry Gilder, Robert Glasgow, John Glenn, Anthony Golding, John Golding, Timothy Goodman, John Goodwin, John Gordon, Nathaniel Gordon, James Goree, Josiah Goree, Cladius Goree, Harris Gillam, Joshua Gillam, James Grayham, John Graham, James Graves, Thomas Green, James Griffin, William Griffin, Joshua Griffith, Matthew Hall, Andrew Hallman, James Ham, John Hardy, Thomas Hardy, Jacob Halfacre, William Henry, James Henry, Benjamin Hampton, Joseph Hampton, John Harmon, Burr Calvert Harris, Nathaniel Harris, James Hawkins, Thomas Hawkins, James Hayes, Joseph Hayes, Thomas Herbert, Francis Higgins, John Hipp, George Hipp, James Hodges, John Hogge, Lewis Hogge, Isaac Hollingsworth, David Harper, Thomas Harper, James Houston, John Houston, Daniel Horsey, John Howard, John Hughey, Alexander Hutchinson, John Hutchinson, William Hutchinson, Jacob Houber, Benjamin Inman, David Jenkins, James Johnson, John Johnston, Sr., John Jay, William Jay, Jesse Jay, James Jones, John Jones, Thomas Jones, George Keller, Joseph Keller, Samuel Keller, Henry Key, Michael Kinard, Matthias Kinard, Jacob King, John Knox, John Langford John Lark, Robert Leavell, John Leavell, Jacob Lominick, Michael Lominick, Thomas Long, Mrs. Mary Letssey(widow of George), Gasper Leophardt, Jacob Lewis, Stephen Lewis, Richard Lewis, Andrew Lee, Frederick Le Gronne, John Le Gronner, John Livingstone, Michael Livingston, John Lohner, William Malone, Sr., John Malone, John Mangum, John Mann, John Marrs, Solomon Martin, James Massey, William Massey, Sr., Robert Maxwell, Sr., Benedict Mayer, Ulrich Mayer, James Meadors, John Meadors(lived later in Laurens District), Samuel Miles, Jacob Miller, Robert Mills, Sr., John Mills, Thomas Mills, Isaac Mitchell, William Moore, William Moore, Jr., John Moore, Thomas Morgan, John Morgan, Joshua Morgan, John Morris, William Montgomery, Sr., David Montgomery, William McClelland, John McClelland, James McClintock, John McClintock, James McCollom, John McCollom, William McConnell, James McCrackin, Robert McCrackin, William McDaniel Patrick McDowell, James McGill, Thomas McKie, James McNeill, James McMaster, John McMorries, William McTeer, John Neal, John Newman, William Nimmons, Audrey Noland, John O'Dell, James Oliver, William Owens, John Parrott, William Page, Sr., Daniel Parkins, James Patterson, James Patty, Enock Pearson, John Pearson, Isiaah Pemberton, Thomas Perry, Henry Pitts, Thomas Pitts, John Price, Matthias Quaddlebuam, James Ramage, John Ray, Thomas Ray, Reagan(John), William Reagin, Joshua Reeder, Amos Richardson, Daniel Richardson, George Rhiddlehuber, Michael Rhiddlehuber, Elisha Rhodes, John Richey, John Rikard, Michael Rikard, John Robertson, James ross, Thomas Ross, Andrew Russell, Peter Ruble, John Ruff, John Riley, Frederick Schaffer, John Carrol Seigler, Bartlette Satterwhite, Matthias Senn, George Adam Setzler, Peter Setzler, William Sheppard, Sr., David Sims, Sr., John Sims, Phillip Sligh, Sr., William Speers, David Speers, Daniel Stewart, Robert Stewart, John Stewart, Joshua Stewart, Alexander Stewart, Henry Stockman, John Stockman, George Strother, Conrad Suber, Matthias Suber, John Suber, Ulrick Suber, George Suber, John Summers, James Summers, John Swann, John Swinford, Everhardt Swittenberg, Elijah Teague, Mrs. Alce Teague (widow of Elijah), William Taggart, William Taylor, Jonothan Taylor, Joshua Teague, Stephen Thomas, Joseph Thompson, Charles Thompson, John Thompson, James Thompson, William Thompson, John Towles, James Toland, John Toland, Joseph Tucker, James Turner, Thomas Turner, James Vardeman, John Voluntine, George Wadlington, James Wadlington, William Wadlington, Joseph Walker, William Wallace, Henry Werts, John Werts, Peter Wedsman(pensioned), James Weeks, William Weeks, George Wells, Benjamin West, George Whitmore, Frederick Whitmore, Ambrose Whitten, Mrs. Mary Wicker (widow of Simon Wicker), Daniel Williams, John Williams, Stephen Williams, Joseph Williamson, Robert Williamson, John Wilson, George Wilson, James Wilson, Thomas Wilson, John Wood, Samuel Wood, Thomas Wood, John Workman, Robert Workman, John Wright, Alexander Wright, George Young, James Young (pensioned).   (some of above may have also acted as officers—uncommissioned officers_ and the widows named furnished supplies to the army).

SOLDIERS IN WAR OF 1812

A Partial List of Newberry County Soldiers—
Henry Anderson, Jr., Peter Black, Thomas Brooks, Charles Bulow, Samuel Busby, James Butler, John Caldwell, Jr., William Chalmers, David Charles, Albert Cromer, George Cromer, Jr., Samuel Crow, Edward Crow, James Dunlap, George Eigner (Agner), Thomas Felker, James Graham, John Geen, Hardy Hancock, William Hancock, Thomas Hardy, James Hargrove, William Harper (Hopper), Lacey Harvard (Havird), John Henderson, Jr. (Corp.), John Herndon (Corp.), John Hix, John Hill, John Howard, William Howard (Sgt.), David Houseal(Sgt.), Joseph Hunter, John Hutchinson William Jenkins, John Knox, John Law, Thomas Linsey, Jr., James Lyles, Thomas Lowery, David Martin, Edmond Martin, John Martin (Sgt.), James McGraw, John Miller (Capt. in Militia), John Montgomery (Capt. in Infantry), Benjamin Moore, Isaac Morgan, John Morgan, Isaac Palmer, Ephriam Prescock(Priscock), John Richardson, John Reid, Ezekiel Roebuck, John Roebuck, Ranley Roebuck, Michael Schaver, John Sims (Second Lieut.), Gilbert Smith, John Smith, James Spence, Robert Spence, Samuel Spence, Benjamin Taylor (Corp.), John Taylor, Joshua Teague, James Thompson, Daniel Thornton, Charles Tucker, Jeremiah Dail, Jeremiah Walker, Stephens Welch, Daniel Wheeler, Elisha Williams, John Wilson, James Wright, John Wright, Jonothan Wright.

Captain Pearson Holloway's Company of Militia, which included mostly those from Edgefield District—
James Sheppard, Sgt., George Quaddlebuam, Musician,George McCreless, Solomon Haynie, William De Vore, William Sheppard, John Coleman, George Alewine, Elijah De Vore, John Chappell, Thomas Chappell, Berryman Bledsoe,...................

WAR WITH THE SEMINOLE INDIANS IN FLORIDA.

Companies from Newberry County—
Two companies went out from Newberry to Florida, which may have included few names of soldiers from nearby counties. They were commanded by Captain S. C. Hargrove and Captain Mathis.
On page 799, Part 11, "The Annals of Newberry", the following are listed in the company of Captain Hargrove: S. C. Hargrove; Captain; James T. Sims, 1st Lt.; James V. Lyles, 2nd Lt. Robert Dugan, Ensign; G. Ashford, Sgt.; Nicholas Summer, 1st Sgt.; H. T. Clark, Sgt.; E. F. Williams, Sgt.; H. Martin, Corp.; J. K Jenkins, Corp.; D. Lewis, Corp.; L. Suber, Corp.; and privates, J. Hunter, J. M. Henderson, T. J. Stewart, J. L. Kenner, James Caldwell, John Summer, D. Simmons, H. Oxner, E. Prewitt, R. Coates, D. Jenkins, H. Roberts, M. McClure, B. Whitmire, A. Aughtry,W. McCrackin,C. Boyd, S. Stark,J. F. Williams,J. McMorries, L. Lane, M. Ruff, J. Miller, G. Harris, R. Dawkins, J. Floyd, W. Adams, D. Alewine, A. M. Newbil, B. Felkman, M. Goree, I. Davidson, M. Chambers, I. Prewitt, O. Simmons, ...Walker, Oliver Towles, M. Motes, N. Johnson, J. Baker, T. Livingstone, G. Smith, T. D. Chalmers, H. Suber, P. Suber, ...Stribling. S. Vessells, E. Harris, J. W. Bird, J. O. Bedsil, W. H. Allen, W. Smith, L. E. Horton, P. Phillips, L. Culbreaith,Harvey Suber, B. Durrett, T. Morris, ...

WAR WITH MEXICO.

Newberry County Company—
This company was organized by James H. Williams January 29, 1846, who became Captain. At that time , or just previously, he served as Major in the 38th Regiment of South Carolina Militia. His Company for Mexico was Company L., Palmetto Regiment. They took part at the siege of Vera Cruz. The Company was one of the first to enter Mexico City, after their advance from Pueblo to Mexico City. Captain Williams was wounded in battle at Garita de Belen.
A story of George Gusmann, a German Music Teacher in Newberry, who was a member of the Company is told in Carwile's " Reminiscences of Newberry". He died while aiding wounded soldiers in Mexico, and was buried in that country.

Members of Captain James H. Williams' Company—

George H. Abney, Thomas Anderson, William Anderson (died in service), C. W. Armstrong (died in service), Ferdinand Bartee, George Boone(died in service), John B. Brooks, David J. Brown, Abner Bundrick (died in service), William Calkin (died in service), Thomas Callahan (died in service),Richard C. Carwile (died in service), Thomas Chapman, James H. Clanton, Levi H. Clodfelter (killed in service), Martin Clopton, Joseph Culbreath,Second Lieut., David M. Cole (died in service), John Dean (died in service), James Denson, 2nd Lieut.(killed in service), Israel P. Detter (died in service), John W. Downing (died in service), John C. Enlow, 1st Sgt. (died in service), A. Ennis (died in service), Adam Feagle, William P. Feltman, Thirs Corp.(died in service),Thomas Ford (died in service), V. R. Gary, John E. Graham, Larkin D. Griffin (died in service),George Gusmann (died in service), Matthias Hair (died in service), Julius Harris (died in service), John C. Higgins (promoted to 2nd Lieut. in Aug. 1847), Hugh Hilburn (died in service), William Hilburn (died in service), Thomas Hogge, Hollis Livingstone, Joseph W. Holt (died in service), John Howard (died in service), William Hutchinson (died in service), J. P. Jackson(died in service), Andrew J. Kerr (died in service), James J. Lane (died in service), Thomas Lindsey, Allen Little, Reuben B. Lyles, Benjamin H. Mathis, William Meek (died in service), Ferdinand Morris, Forgus McClelland, William McClelland (died in service), John McFarlane (died in service),Samuel McGill (died in service), Rutherford Nance, Sampson F. Nance, Jesse Nates (died in service), John Belton O'Neall (killed in service), John Pitts, Zadoc Pitts, Charles P. Pope, 1st Lieut., Vincent P. Pope, Henry P. Pratt, 3rd Sgt. (died in service), Jacob Presnall, William Qualls, David M. Riser, John S. Sheely (killed in service), William Shepard, William D. Smith (died in service), John A. Spears, 3rd Cpl. (killed in service), James Spence (died in service), L. B. Stancil (died in service), John W. Stewart, 2nd Lieut.(died in service), Hiram Saber, Henry H. Summers, Jacob P. Summers (died in service), William Summers (died in service), James D. Teacle, M. M. Thomas, Theodore Thompson, 4th Sgt., Wallace R. Waldrop, George Warner (died in service), George W. Warner, Henry Warner, Jacob Warner, Harrison D. Watson (died in service), ... Watts, 4th Cpl. (died in service), Owen Weatherbee (killed in service), Elijah F. Williams, 2nd Lieut. (died in service),Charles Wood (killed in service).

REV. WAR BATTLE SITES IN NEWBERRY COUNTY
OR IN ADJOINING COUNTIES.

Blackstocks—

Battle here in 1780, near Tyger River, now in Chester County. Col. Tarleton crossed the Broad River and was marching towards Ninety Six, but came in contact with General Sumpter's troops who had retreated towards the Tyger River.

Hays' Station—

This battle occured in 1781, just across the Newberry County line(where is now the line), and at a place that is now in Laurens County. The place was formerly called Edge Hill. Some of the Tories attached Col. Hays who had barricaded his troops in a small house. The fire that burned the house, set by the Tories, almost burned the soldiers who came out and offered to surrender. The Tory Colonel, "Bloody" Bill Cunningham, received them but later hung them and mutilatedtheir bodies.

Clark's Ford—

This site is in Newberry County, on Enoree River. The land was originally owned by John Clark, the settler. The Americans were under Captain John Jones. John Clark was shot in the leg as he attempted to escape in order to get help; then stopped at his home for his mother to dress the wound; and started to Ninety Six, but was captured and put in prison. Captain Jones was killed.

Battle of Mudlic—

This skirmish was fought in the Summer of 1781 by a remnant of garrison of militia under Col. Benjamin Roebuck, that were stationed at Williams Fort.

WAR BETWEEN THE STATES.

Newberry Companies—

A good list of the names of these companies are given in the " Annals of Newberry", Part 11, though not complete enough to include all names of soldiers in some of the companies.

Captain Basil Manly Blease, said to have been the first volunteer from Newberry, is buried in the old Village Cemetery. The first Company was formed by Captain Whitfield Walker, who volunteered January 5, 1862, to enter as Colonel of a Regiment in the West. This first company was formed under an oak tree in the front yard of home of F. B. Higgins (more recently in the backyard of the late J. Y. McFall), and close to Johstone Street. This was Company B., First Regiment of S. C. V.

Other companies are listed in The Annals of Newberry, with the names of their Captains and other officers and men.

Some Newberry Officers who were Killed in Battle—

Col. W. D. Rutherford was killed at the battle of Strasburg, Virginia, October 13, 1864. He had been promoted to Colonel after Col. James D. Nance was killed at the battle of the Wilderness on May 6, 1864. After Col. Rutherford's death Captain John K. G. Nance was made Captain.

Captain John C. Summer was killed at the battle of Fredericksburg, Virginia. Col. Robert C. Maffett, who was made prisoner at Union Prison, Fort Delaware, died there. Captain James M. Maffett died at Lockhart, Miss., in 1864, while on his way back to Newberry to assume the duties of sheriff of Newberry County, to which he had been elected. Captain John M. Kinard, who volunteered as First Lieutenant in Company F., had been made Captain when his uncle, John P Kinard, resigned as Captain. Captain Philander Cromer, who was promoted from Third Lieutenant to Captain of Company D., the 13th Regiment, was killed at the battle of Gettysburg. Captain Jacob Warner was killed at or near Petersburg, Virginia. Captain William L. Leitsey was killed at the battle of Deep Bottom, Virginia.

Some Officers cited for bravery—

Major J. F. J. Caldwell, Major Isaac Hunt, and others. Col. James H. Williams, who had served in the Mexican War, was made Colonel of the Third S. C. Regiment of Volunteers, one of the ten regiments that were organized under a bill passed in the South Carolina Legislature on December 17, 1860. His Regiment went to Virginia in June, 1861, and was at the battle of Bull Run. Her served in other battles including the siege of Charleston, S. C.

General A. C. Garlington , a lawyer in Newberry, served as Major awhile in the Holcombe Legion; later, in the Adjutant General's office.

(Ref: " The Annals of Newberry", Part11).

General Beauregard's March Through Newberry—

In May, 1865, General Beauregard passed through Newberry, on the 5th of the month, with his men. He stopped here and dispersed them, telling them to go to their respective homes and their families. They refused to leave him, and insisted on going with him until he was safe at his home. However, he prevailed upon them, explaining there was no danger; so they reluctantly yielded to his wishes. The troops passed through Charlotte, N. C., and Rock Hill, S. C., then to Newberry, and on to Edgefield and Hamburg, S. C., and arrived at Augusta, Georgia.

NEWBERRY COUNTY COURT HOUSE.

The new Court House is modern in style of architecture, which combines a picturesque mixture of the old Romanesque design and the Grecian Ionic columns that give it a colonial appearance. The trend from the style of the old court house to that of the new shows no change in public appreciation of attractiveness; but rather, it gives an impression of a deeper appreciation of the classics among earlier leaders. This dimming interest among modern students may be due to modern sociological conditions.

On the marble tablet with the hall of the new Court House is the following inscription:
Members of General Assembly,
1906,
Senator: Cole L. Blease,
Representatives:
Francis W. Higgins,
John W. Earhardt,
John M. Taylor,
Court House Commission:
George S. Mower, Ch'r.
Otto Klettner, Sec'y.
J. Monroe Wicker,
J. A. Sligh,
C. H. Shannon,
J. R. Perdew,
W. D. Senn.

History of First Court Houses—
The old court house stands as a landmark on the site of one of the first court houses in the upper part of the State, which was constructed under the American government. With it's typical Doric style of architecture, manifested by it's large columns, single wide roof and exterior work—a plain, stern design, representative of a house of justice—much of which was used in Eighteenth Century architecture; it signifies, too, with the symoblic design on the front the southern spirit that prevailed after the War Between the States.

During the time of "reconstruction" in South Carolina just after the war, the Court House was repaired under a contract with the late Osborne Wells. At that time he concieved the idea of adding the symbols on the front gable. The explanation of the design, which was often repeated by Mr. Wells to some of descendents, is that the palmetto tree (this tree being a part of the South Carolina Court of Arms), signifies an uprooted State government which is being held in the beak of the American eagle, as the Federal government, who weighs in the " scales of justice" the people of the State, as represented by the crowing cock which stands on the base end in an attitude of being not conquered even though down; and on the other end among the branches and leaves is the "dove of peace", with the olive branch in it's mouth, an emblem which is ever significant among an enlightened people.

A brief history of the earlier court houses or the court sessions in Newberry may be interesting. The first sessions of court were held at the home of Col. Robert Rutherford, one of the first County Judges, about ten miles Southeast of the present court house. This was in 1785. Though the county was formed out of old Ninety Six District in the year 1783, the first court house did not hold sessions until 1785. Continous meetings were held there until June 4, 1787. In 1786 John Coate who owned much of the land on which Newberry is built offered two acres to the county on which to build a court house and other public buildings. This offer was not immediately accepted because some of the County Commissioners wanted to locate the court house at another place. The division of opinion as to the best leoation prevented coming to a definite decision until 1788 or 1789.

The first settlement was just below the present old village cemetery, and near what was then known as " Cedar Spring", which was the home of John Coate. A survey of the county to find a place that would be central did not result in any definite decision. It was not until court convened in March, 1789, that the offer of two acres by John Caote was accepted. When the deed was made in September, 1789, a valuable consideration was given the Commissioners, with a clause that the two acres should be always used for a court house or other public buildings. The court which was held at the home of John Coate on June 5, 1787, was held in a small frame building which stood for many years across from the rear playground of Boundary Street School, on a lot of the late Robert H. Wright.

John Coate owned and operated a blacksmith shop on a lot where is now the Bazhardt Furniture Store or the Chapman-Hawkins Hardware store. He, no doubt, built this shop when the first public road leading from Charleston through Columbia and Newberry was built. It appears that the courts held in the Fall of 1788 and in the Spring of 1789 were held " at Coate's Shop".

In 1789 or 1790 the first court house was built on the two acres (now the public square), a small frame building which was removed in 1799, probably to the corner of Boyce and Nance Streets (West side), and used as a tavern. A new brick court house was erected that year. Thomas W. Waters was the contractor, who employed an expert carpenter from Virginia, named George Schoppert, a German, as his supervisor. The work began in 1799 but was not completely finished until 1801. The new building, according to John B. Carwile in his " Reminiscences of Newberry", was "a more attractive building than the present one" (the old court house).....
" Before the main entrance which was in the eastern end of the edifice, there was a portico supported by four large Tuscan columns resting upon a brick floor; beneath this there was a vestibule. Through this vestibule you entered an arched hallway, upon which the offices of the county officers opened. The floor of the portico was reached by a semi-circular flight of granite steps on each side. From the portico you passed through a spacious doorway into a hall, on both sides of which were stairways leading to the spectators gallery above."....

In the office of the Newberry Observer is an oblong brown tablet which was taken out of the corner stone of the first brick court house at the time it was torn down, in 1850, to make way for the newer court house. On one side of this tablet is the following inscription:

" The Cornerstone of Newberry Court House; Laid Jan. 18, Anno Lucis 5827, (Ann. Dom. 1823).
By
Job Johnstone, W. M. of Lodge No.
11, A. F. M. S. C.
And
A Number of Other Brethern,
Acting
Under a Dispensation
From
John S. Cogdell, Most Worshipful
Grand Master, 0f the Ancient Free
Masons of South Carolina."

And on the other side of the tablet is the following inscription: " Defend the Poor and Fatherless, do Justice to the Afflicted and Needy, Deliver the Poor and Needy: rid them out of the hand of the Wicked."—Psalm 82-3 and 4.

This court house stood over twenty years without a cornerstone; and the idea of building one, which was recommended by the Grand Jury, was carried out in the year 1823.

In the rear of this first brick court house was built a two-story stone gaol. The present stone terraces on the sides of the Confederate monument contains the stone blocks that were a part of the foundation of the old gaol. A door of the gaol opened about twenty five feet from the rear door of the court house, which made it convenient to take prisoners to their trials.

Construction of the present old court house began in the Fall of 1850, after the old building had been torn away, some distance from the stone gaol. The architect was Jacob Graves, and the contractor, Wallace A. Cline.

During it's construction, the General Sessions courts were held in the Newberry Methodist church and in the Newberry Baptist church. The Spring term of court, in 1851, was held in the Methodist church for which the county paid the church rent of $75.00. In the Fall term of 1851, and the Spring and Fall terms of 1852, they were held in the Newberry Baptist church, for which the county paid a rent to the church of $50.00 for each session. Equity court was held in a house owned by James Bond, a former sheriff of the county. The new building (the present old court house) is located little further back than the old building was located. The old mile-stone in the middle of the square, directly in front of the steps, was considered the exact center of the town, from which the number of miles in any direction was determined.

NEWBERRY COUNTY JAILS.

The present jail building, a large red-brick, two-story structure, was planned by J. Ernest Summer, Architect, and built by Henry L. Parr, the Contractor, in the year 1918. It's Corinthian styled columns, wide porch and colonial effect, together with it's long extension in the rear enclosing many steel cells, make, indeed, " the best jail in the State", using a Chamber of Commerce slogan.

In a brief history of the first jails, it is recorded that the first Sheriff was Major Thomas Gordon who received his appointment from the governor. He kept his prisoners in a small cabin on his place on Enoree River, where he lived. When some of his prisoners escaped he was fined for neglect of duty and ordered to keep them in a more secluded and secure place, near the village.

Tradition is that the prisoners were kept for a short time in the old "Rock House", about four miles Southeast of town, until the completion of the first jail.

The first jail built was in the rear of the present old court house building. One account states that it was built between high stone walls that stood on the North and West sides of the first brick court house, the rear end of the court house basement or the enclosures between the walls and the building used for cells. In 1826 these walls were torn down and the stones were used to erect a two-story gaol in the rear. The walls were four inches thick, forty feet high, sixty feet long, with a breadth of sixty feet. A portico on the first floor of the stone gaol reached from the gaol to the court house. In 1853 the gaol was condemned by the Grand Jury, and new building ordered to be erected at a more suitable place.

In 1855, when the first brick jail was built, at it's present location, parts of the old building were torn away; but most of the walls stood until the stone terrace now around the Confederate monument square, was built about 1878. (See Sketch of Court Houses, above).

The first brick jail was two stories high, the upper floors being cells. The Contractor was Thomas W. Blease.

ADDRESS OF HON. JOHN BELTON O'NEALL
ON
THE DEATH OF HON. JOB JOHNSTONE.

At a meeting of the Newberry Bar, held at Newberry, on Tuesday, the 15th. of April. 1862, Chief Justice John Belton O'Neall was called to the Chair, and L. J. Jones requested to act as Secretary—Chief Justice O'Neall upon taking the Chair addressed the members of the bar as follows:

Gentlemen of the Bar—

The occasion which brings us together this morning is one of peculiar sadness. We meet to express the feelings, which as Lawyers and neighbors crowd upon us, upon the remembrance of the death of Hon. Job Johnstone. To you, gentlemen, I have no doubt it is an occasion of much feeling; to me it is more so. We were early associates. The Deceased studied law with me—For eight years he was my partner for Newberry District. I can hardly realize his death—For near two months he was my junior, yet it has pleased God to cut him down and spare me. It is my duty to realize the sad event, and to profit by it.—To you, Gentlemen, I may possibly beneficially recall the incidents of his life. He was born .... day of June, 1793. He received a good classical education under the direction of the Rev. Mr. Reid.— He entered the South Carolina College in the year 1808, when he was a little past 15 years old. He graduated in December, 1810, ranking with several others as third.—He embarked immediately in the study of Medicine. He was licensed to practice—The profession did not suit his taste— He studied law with me, and was licensed to practice law and Equity in December, 1818—He practiced law and Equity with great success, with me until 1828—He had in the meantime, in November, 1826, been elected Clerk of the Senate which office he filled, with unusual satisfaction until 1830, when he was elected Chancellor. This office he filled in all the successive changes of our Judiciary until December, 1859, when he was elected an Associate Judge of the Court of Appeals—This office he accepted and discharged it's duties in the midst of ill health until Tuesday evening the 8th day of April instant, about 7 P. M. when he was called from

Earth to give an account of life, and all it's trials before his merciful Judge, and Creator. He suffered long and most painfully and we are permitted to hope and believe that he has parted with this body of pain and trials for happiness beyond the Grave—

He was unquestionably a man of talents. He wrote beautifully. Some of his decrees in Chancery will be read and admired as long as time shall last. He prepared in January, 1860, an article for Bouvier's Law Dictionary entitled, " South Carolina", which, when it shall be published, will testify to his unrivalled powers. But I need enlarge no farther, you all know him.

The Hon. F. B. Higgins then introduced the following resolutions, which were unanimously adopted:

Resolved, that the death of an eminent man calls for some notice, more especially by his associates, who have known him as a Lawyer and a Judge for many years.

Resolved, that the death of Hon, Job Johnstone, an associate of the Court of Appeals, has made a great void in the social circle of Newberry and deprived the Judiciary of one of it's brightest ornaments.

Resolved, that while we all deplore the sad event of his death, yet as Christians we are bound to bow to the event as a chastening from our Mighty Master, Judge and Creator.

Resolved, that we sincerely sympathize with his widow and cildren, but we trust that they will be consoled by Him, who alone can dry up tears and pour consolation into the hearts of the afflicted ones.

Resolved, that the above resolutions and remarks of Chief Justice be furnished to the family of the deceased, and published in the Newspapers.

John Belton O'Neall, Ch.
L. J. Jones, Sec.

It is ordered that the above minutes of the proceedings of the Bar be entered on the record of the Court of Chancery for Newberry District.

John A. Inglis.

June 14, 1864.

CONFEDERATE VETERANS LIVING ON APRIL 2, 1931,
IN NEWBERRY COUNTY.

William Y. Fair, Newberry, died 1932.
J. N. Feagle, Little Mountain, died ....
W. D. Hardy, Slairs, died 1932.
J. J. Hipp, Pomaria, died 1931.
J. R. Irvin, Chappells, died ....,
W. T. Jackson, Newberry, died 1932.
W. P. Koon, Pomaria, died.................
Robert Y. Leavell, Newberry, died ....
A. A. Nates, Prosperity, died 1932.
J. G. Rikard, Newberry, died.............
J. H. Riser, Newberry, died ....
P. H. Shealy, Pomaria, died.............
W. F. Suber, Pomaria, died ....
H. Pink Summer, Peak, died 1932.
J. William Summer, Pomaria, died Jan. 1933.
G. P. Werts, Pomaria, died 1932.
J. M. Werts, Prosperity, died...........
Elijah Whitmire, Whitmire, died ....

EARLY COUNTY GOVERNMENT IN NEWBERRY.

The present county government of Newberry and that of the city vary but little at the present time, with their different departments and factors in control; manifesting a slight distinctiveness in some details of law procedure. However, it is interesting to note from 1785 to 1832 all county laws, created under State legislative Acts, and all government operations in the county included the village of Newberry, which was subject to the administrative offices of the diffpent commissions. This form was preceded by similar forms during Colonial times, that were, of course, the principles of the old Common Law of England. At this time there are several different features in the city government that are different from those in the the county government, even though by these same principles there are some similarities and enlarged overlapping forms in court procedure.

A review of the first forms under the Proprietary and the Royal governments, with references to a few of their laws, shows the handicaps the people had to undergo in the beginning. These governments, under English control, had their Judges, Sheriffs, County Clerks, and Commissions--a system of old England--with the usual authority attached to certain Commissions. The most powerful was the Commission on Roads and Bridges, which had charge of all the finances, and were continously busy developing new roads, building new bridges, and keeping watch on all public affairs pertaining to the county. They issued all licenses to businesses, those being most subject to license having been keepers of taverns, distillers, liquor shops, billiard tables, and other forms of remunerative amusements.

The State government had control of real estate trasnfers, with State Commissioners who exeduted all titles in the districts, and made records at the State capital which, at that time, was at Charleston. All real and personal property under the Proprietary government were vested, at first, in commissioners, who, under the Royal government, became empowered to confiscate old landed estates--landgraves--and divide them into smaller tracts of land of not over 500 acres each, and granted them to settlers who qualified for bounty or who would make purchases.

In 1762 the Indian Commissioners were empowered to carry on trade with the Indians at Keowee, the central place of trade for the upper section of the State. This law was rescinded after the American Revolutionary War.

The first sessions of courts were held at Charleston, under the Colonial government. Most of the population of the State was in the section around Charleston or in the southern section; but when grants were given settlers, under the Royal government, the upper section became more populated. From it's beginning all of the section above Charleston had much trouble attending court sessions, with the bad roads and poor conveyances. However, every cause had to be tried at Charleston, and "great oppressions and inaccuracies were felt by the people living in the remote sections from the seat of justice." Often delays and bad results from " the insolence of office", and cruelly exacted court costs were imposed on the people. The Association of Regulators was formed among the best planters of the outlying sections to enforce certain laws in their communities--in many cases the lash was used, but which became very unpopular. This finally brought a change in the laws in 1769, when the first Circuit Courts were established.

Under the Circuit Court system, sessions were held at Charleston, Orangeburg, Beufort, Ninety Six, and Cheraw. It continued until 1778, when a new State Constitution was adopted and new laws formed for the districts. Justices of the Peace, Justices of the Quorum, that had existed under the former law, were given powers to hold trials in each district. The Judges of the General Sessions Courts and of the Common Pleas Courts had charge of the District Courts; while Justices of the Peace had power to try smaller cases or those involving smaller amounts, and misdemeanors. The Justice of the Quorum, in a group, passed on the difficult local cases that involved litigations of larger amounts, but less than those of a criminal nature which were required to be tried by district or circuit Judges.

When Newberry County was formed out of old Ninety Six District, in 1782, the county courts were held at Ninety Six District Court House until 1785, when the County Court Act was passed. The author of this Act was Henry Pendleton, Judge, for whom the county of Pendleton was named. In that year the government was organized by the appointment of Justices of the Peace, then called County Judges, by the county delegation. The first members of the legislature were

Dr. George W. Glenn, Major Michael Leitner, and George Ruff, Esq. The first County Judges appointed were, Robert Rutherford, Robert Gillam, Sr., George Ruff, Levi Casey, Levi Manning, Philemon Waters, and John Lindsey.
At the meeting of the court held on September 5, 1785, the County Judges present were: Robert Rutherford, Robert Gillam, Sr., George Ruff, Levi Casey. Major Thomas Gordon, a Rev. War patriot and officer, was appointed the first Sheriff, and at this meeting he produced his commission which was signed by the governor for a term of two years. William Malone was appointed the first County Clerk, who appointed as his Deputy Clerk, Thomas Brooks Rutherford. At the same meeting the Court appointed the following Grand Jurors, the first Grand Jurors under the new government, as follows: Edward Finch, William Wadlington, Edward Wadlington, Braswell Robertson, Bartlette Satterwhite, John Swetenberg, James Caldwell (of Little River), Thomas Harbert, James Williams, John Adam Summer, Jr., Francis Summer, Jeremiah Williams, Levi Manning, Abner Casey, Ephriam Cannon, John O'Dell, Williamson Iyles, David Edwards, and John Lindsey. At this court the following County Road Commissioners were appointed for the purpose of constructing a new road from Hogg's Branch on the Charleston Road to Harbert's Ferry on Broad River: Thomas Harbert, Nathan Busby, John Adam Summer, John Love, George Swygert, Francis Summer, William Ballentine, John Edwards, William Woodward, John Swetenberg, John Ammons, Victor Harris, and Micheal Mints (Monts).
In 1786 Jacob Roberts Brown was appointed the first County Attorney.
In the beginning the Judges were required to make trips to Charleston to make appeals, motions for new trials, and other motions before the State Court, pertaining to their respective counties. Under the Act of 1791 they were required to go to Columbia and meet in order to hear appeals and to take up other court matters.
Under the County Court Act of 1791, the number of Judges for Newberry County was reduced to three, when the legislature elected the following: James Mayson, Jacob Roberts Brown, and George Ruff. In July, 1792, George Ruff resigned, and Levi Casey was elected in his place.
When the Constitutional Court was started at Columbia, in 1799, officers of the court, as the Sheriff, the Ordinary, the Tax Collector, the Master in Equity, the Commissioners on Locations, and the Commissioners of Roads and Bridges were filled by elections by both houses of the general assembly. Many of the same powers were retained by these officials. The sheriff was to hold office for four years in place of two, and was not eligible for a succeeding term which succeeded the term he served. Justices of the Peace were nominated by the State General Assembly and appointments made by the governor. Certain Commissioners about this time were appointed to superintend slopes and sluices in the rivers, to prevent dams from stopping passages of fish up streams. Commissioners on Locations had been appointed in the Cirucit Court Districts under an Act of 1784; and they were regularily appointed or reappointed for several years.
While a form of Equity Court law was in force prior to 1799, the Equity Court in South Carolina was not instituted under the new government, practically, until that time; and became effective in most of the counties from the year 1812. This court was established at Newberry under a special Act of the State Legislature passed December 17, 1817. It was in force until about 1868-70; and stood for many years a bulwark for many difficult cases that could not be determined or settled under the laws as existed unde the Common Law form.
Up until the time this new system came into use, no real progress had been made in improvement of government forms under the laws. Various new Commissioners were appointed by the General Assembly: Commissioners of the Schools, of the Poor, of Public Buildings, of Roads and Bridges, each functioning as seperate units and with distinctive powers.
Under the Act of December 15, 1815, methods of chosing certain county officers were changed. Ordinaries, Court Clerks, Commissioners on Locations, were chosen by popular vote. In the year 1820 Ordinaries were Justices of the Quorum, with authority to try certain cases within the work of the Ordinaries' offices. In cases of partitions of Lands, in equity, those involving small amounts or values were settled by the Ordinaries.
New County Court Acts were passed by the General Assembly, effective January 1, 1800, with County Judges who acted under the Associate Judges of the State or District Courts. These courts of general sessions or common pleas had the same powers as the old circuit or district courts. A prosecutor or solicitor was appointed for each district. Under this Act the old Ninety Six Court was abolished, and new Equity Districts were formed. The district of this area included the counties of Laurens, Greenville and Newberry, and called division two of the

Western District; and the courts held at Laurens which was the central town in the division. The first record of the Ordinary (much of whose duties are now devolved on the Judge of Probate) is that of Samuel Lindsey, who negan service in the year 1800. Prior to that year the duties of this office were in the hands of the Equity Commissioners or the Justices of the Quorum. It was not until 1868 the office of Probate Judge was established, taking over the work of the Ordinary and some of the work of the Commissioner in Equity. The office of Master in Equity was established to carry on part of this work, and it was not until recent years this office was consolidated with that of the Judge of Probate.

The Clerk of Court, the first county office established, along with the Sheriff's office, in 1785, was held by Major Frederick Nance (he was said to have been the first settler within the village) from 1794, for several terms. The duties included then, as now, the register of mesne conveyances, as well as that of other work within the scope of the office.

Newberry County had a Tax Callector from 1800 to 1868; all finances of the county being in the Treasury of the Commissioners of Public Roads and Bridges, who had power to receive and pay out county funds under the direction of the County Judges. In 1868 the County Treasurer's Office was established, which took out of the hands of the Commissioners of Public Roads and Bridges the funds of the county, and also took over the TaxCollector's duties, eliminating that office. In that year a County School Commissioner was added, and a new office created, called the County Road Commissioner. The duties of the former were similar to what they are at the present time, except at this time they work more directly under the State Department of Education.

In 1841 the office of magistrate was started, which assumed many of the same duties as the county Justices of the Peace. The following year the office of Coroner was created.

All of the county (which includes the city)was at first under the same government, until December 20, 1832, when Newberry village received it's first charter as an incorporated town. This charter was issued under a special Act of the State legislature. It gave the people who lived within a radius of one mile each way from the court house, the privilege of establishing their own town government, with the authority of electing an Intendant and four Wardens. The county delegation appointed them, to serve until the second Monday in September of the following year, at which time an election should be held, and on each succeeding second Monday in September thereafter, to elect them by popular vote.

The Intendant and Wardens were given the same powers as those of Justices of the Quorum, and the town Commissioners of Roads and Bridges were to have the same powers as those of the State Commissioners of Roads and Bridges, within one mile radius. They were, also, given powers to issue licenses to keepers of taverns, retailers of liquors, operators of billiard tables, all within the town limits, and turn over all monies to the town's Commissioners of Public Roads and Bridges. They were given the power, too, to appoint patrol men (policemen), any citizens they should see fit, and on any occasions, and to appoint regular constables for the town. All men within the age limit of 16 and 60 were required to help work the roads and streets in the village when their services were needed. This system operated in the town until several years after the War of Session.

After a few years, the power of handling the town's funds was given over to a town Clerk and Treasurer, a new office, who under the direction of the town council had the power to receive and pay out town funds.

The city government has, at present, a Mayor and six aldermen, a city recorder, and clerk and treasurer, with a Board of Health department. Functioning under these departments are active patrol officers (policemen), a fire department, a street supervisor, a public utilities department (this last department operates under a Board of Commissioners of Public Works).

The City and County is divided into six magistrates' districts, with one magistrate in each, who is elected by popular vote of the people. Their duties are similar to the old justices of the peace, but restricted to smaller cases of theft, larceny, breach of trust, and other causes that involve amounts of fines not over $100.00 or imprisonment of not over thirty days. the larger cases are handled by the Circuit Courts. The City Recorder has charge of cases coming within the jurisdiction of the city limits, that do not conflict with the causes that are handled by the District Magistrate; confined to small cases.

Slave Laws—
In order to give freedom and justice to the slaves in their daily lives, and to give them justice in the courts, the old slave laws were passed. Most southerners looked upon slaves as humans, and upon slavery as an institution that had been established by pioneers. The first slaves were Indians who were captured by the French and Spaniards.

In a report on the many indictments in South Carolina, from 1842 to 1860, only seven are recorded for Newberry County, and of these, only two were convicted, but carried no penalties.

According to the late Judge John B. O'Neall, in a court which closed in 1859, a number of cases on the docket were for "trespass for hitting or beating a slave". A white person who was charged for beating a slave of another , when no white person could qualify as witness, was judged guilty if he refused the plead.

Public Hangings—
Executions by hangings were done out of doors, as a public occasion, when hundreds of people would congregate to witness it. Low, flat places were usually selected as places of execution; and wodden platforms built, with two sills. In the village, near Scott's Creek, was a place for public hangings, just before and after the War Between the States. Several hangings were held at a public hanging place then located where is now the Thomas and Howard warehouse, near the railroad.

Public Nuisances—
About the period from 1852-1858 the Grand Jury of Newberry County condemned operations of "grog shops", "cock pits", and "ten-pin alleys" as public nusicances, and recommended that the owners be indicted. About this time many small places or villages had taverns being operated without licenses, and were given large penalties.

County Commissioners of Public Buildings in 1842—
At a meeting of the Commissioners held February 5, 1842, the following were present: Major Peter Hair, Chairman; Phil Schoppert, N. A. Hunter, J. J. Sloan, J. H Hunt, John Holman, and John S. Carwile.

Copy of a report of the Grand Jury about 1842, to Governor Scott, and signed by John R. Spearman, Foreman— In Re: report that one Robert Riser had been lynched.
The report reads: " We the Grand Jury of Newberry County, have had the letters of his Excellency, Governor R. K. Scott, or his private Secretary, under consideration. Col. Chapman who is one of our number and lives at Pomaria, had this day called upon Robert Riser who was said to have been lynched, and he states that he was not lynched or hurt in anyway whatever. And he, also, states that he called on Mr. C. Suber who it was said could give him evidence or information that would implicate certain parties, who stated that he knew nothing in regard to the matter referred to. Col. Chapman further states that if there is any organized body of lawless men in that neighborhood he knows nohting of it."

" We have also had Mr. G. G. De Walt before us who states that sometime in January last a party of men visited his premises at night and fired several rounds into his house, and he returned the fire. He also said that he was able to defend himslef. We got no names of parties from him."

J. R. Spearman, Foreman.

HISTORIC SITES IN CITY AND COUNTY.

Old Court House—on the public square, built about 1858; the prevous building having been on the same site, which was erected about 1799.

Site of the first court sessions—in a small house on a lot where is now the Wright property, across Coate Street from Boundary Street School. This house was used from 1789 to 1790; then court was held in a small house at Coat's Shop, where is now the Buzhardt Furniture Store, or within that area; until the court house was completed in 1799.

Helena—the town where the first Southern Railway Shops were located (then known as the Columbia & Greenville Railroad).

Springfield—site of the home of Judge John Belton O'Neall, located about two miles Northwest of the Court House.

Vanduslah Spring—site of an old tavern which was used during colonial days and after the Rev. War as a place of loafing for the first judges and first lawyers who came to Newberry to attend court sessions. The springs furnished water for the village and was said to have been of value as a mineral spring. It was then a place of loitering during the Summer days. Around it grew much shrubbery; and a new kind of berry which grew in the vicinity, which suggested the name of the town, called a "New Berry".

Site of Malone's Meeting House—the house was built about 1804, on the road leading to Henderson's Ferry on Broad River.

Mendenhall's Mills—the site of the mills that were owned first by Hugh O'Neall, then by Dr. Mendenhall, and more recently known as Langford Mill. It is located just beyond the old Quaker Cemetery.

Benjamin Evans Home—the site of this place is Northwest of the Court House, on a road to Trinity Methodist Church. The house was owned in 1850 by John G. Davenport. Benjamin Evans was the inventor of the screw augur which later he manufactured in large quantities.

Beth Eden Lutheran Church—this church is located about six miles North of Newberry Court House on the old Whitmire public road. It was here that the first association to defend the country against black Republicans was formed, which were being worked by the Abolitionists.

Goggan's Old Store—a Rev. War site. It is located opposite to where the old Longshore store once stood, above Bush River. A few miles North of that place was the original home of Captain John Floyd, a Rev. War patriot and officer.

Hartford Old School—located about three miles South of the city. Site of the first settlement of Universalists in the county, and site of their church.

Tunker Graveyard—site of church, and near to old Paysinger home, about four miles South of the Court House, on old Hartford School road.

Zack Herndon home—site of old home is on Little River, the place owned by the late Henry Burton. He was son of Col. Benjamin Herndon, a patriot officer in the Rev. War.

William F. Houseal home—and his grave—site of these places is just South of Pomaria, where a gin house was built over his grave, according to tradition. He was a patriot officer in the Rev. War.

Col. Thomas Dugan home—site of his home is just across Gilder's Creek, above the Long Lane settlement.

Col. John Lindsey home—site of his home on Indian Creek, in the Long Lane settlement; though the precise spot is not known. He was a patriot officer in the Rev. War.

Mill Creek—site of home of Mrs. Rebecca Caldwell, mother of three sons who were patriot officers in the Rev. War, John, William, and James Caldwell.

Capture of Bill Cunningham—site of place where he was captured is near mouth of Duncan's Creek on Enoree River. He was a Tory officer of bad repute, and was captured by Lieutenant Levi Casey and his men; and all of the tory gang captured. The Tories had made an attempt to capture another patriot, John Boyce, in the same vicinity, but failed to carry out their plans.

Caldwell Rock—the rock is located near the right of the old public road going towards "Belfast", where the road turns off going to Mt. Zion Church. The rock on which Major William Caldwell fed his horses with shelled corn that his troops had carried in their bags.

Robert Gillam home—site of this old home is on Page's Creek, in the vicinity of Mill's Creek or Mill Creek. Nearby was the home of Captain John Satterwhite. Both were Rev. War patriot officers. Major Gillam's home was destroyed by fire in 1781, by the Tories.

Adam Summer home—site of old home in the upper Dutch Fork section, where, in 1775, the election to decide adherence to the patriot cause or to join the British, was held, with Major Michael Leitner as manager of the polls. The result was to join the patriots. Major Summer and Major Leitner were, both, patriot officers in the Rev. War.

Griffin Old home—site of this home is near "Belfast". Also, site of the first old church and old cemetery.

Gum Springs—about two miles North of Newberry Court House, on highway to Laurens. The first graduate of the State Medical College of Charleston was born and reared in his parents home located there. He was Dr. Eli Geddings. After his father's death, his mother married Major Frederick Gray, a Rev. War patriot and officer, and moved to Abbeville District. Dr. Eli Geddings practiced awhile at "White Hall" in Abbeville District, but it is thought that he later moved to Charleston and practiced, and where he died.

Site of Parkins Ford—Captain Parkins, a Quaker, was assaulted by a part of whigs there because of his neutrality; probably a party of young whigs from the Indian Creek settlement. At Bush River, nearby, was the place where Captain Parkins made a heroic rescue of a team and wagon of Mrs. Mary O'Neall, that had been washed down stream after a heavy rain. He swam to the team and with great difficulty, barely was able to unhitch them and bring them to shore. (From O'Neall's Annals of Newberry).

Liberty Hill—first residence of Col. Robert Rutherford, near Broad River, about nine miles East of town, and where the first county court was held. The old residence has been destroyed. It is probable that the first court was held at a house which was once nearer to the old family graveyard, where Col. Rutherford first lived when he came to the section from North Carolina.

Water's Blockhouse on Saluda River—where Col. Phil Waters, a patriot and officer of the Rev. War, erected a blockhouse, after the battle of Eutaw, to get young tories of the settlement to come and be instructed on the ideas of Liberty. Many were converted.

Site of Home of Col. David Glenn—located on Enoree River, later becoming known as Brazzleman's. Col. Glenn was a Rev. War patriot and officer; a member of the South Carolina Legislature after the War.

Site of Home of Major Adam Summer—located on Crim's Creek, near Pomaria. He was the first permanent settler of the upper Dutch Fork; he brought the first colony of Germans, Swiss, Dutch and Welsh to that section about 1745. Major Summer is buried in or near the family graveyard which contains markers over the graves of his eldest son, Col. John Adam Summer and wife. This was his home-site.

Site of Brazzelman's Mills on Enoree River—here Lord Rawdon's British troops camped, near home of Col. David Glenn, when they were in pursuit of General Greene's troops on their retreat from Ninety Six. In this vicinity, but nearer the fork of Enoree and Tiger Rivers, lived the father of Emily Geiger, the brave heroine who made a heroic ride with a message to General Sumter to warn him that the British were marching in that direction.

Lyles Ford—on Broad River, where the first settler of that immediate vicinity came. He was John Lyles, a fur trader. There is where Lord Rawdon crossed the river into Fairfield District then known as part of Camden District.

Henderson's Place—located on Broad River, near where General Dawkins and Col. Means were quartered for the night on their march from Spartanburg, Union, to Charleston.

Ferguson's Camp—located on Heller's Creek, South east of Newberry, about three miles East of Pomaria. The seventy-first British Regiment on their march from Camden camped there, near the home of one Hentz. They had crossed Broad River, thence marched to the plantation of Col. James Lyles and camped on Broad River.

Site of Bobo's Mill—located on Bush River, about five miles from town and three miles from the old Friend's Church. It was afterwards known as O'Neall's Mill. Also, there were tories scouting and several skirmishes in that community.

Site of old Henderson's Home—located near Broad River. Where Theodocia Burr, daughter of Aaron Burr, spent the night when she was on her way by way of coach to Charleston, where she was to take a boat to New York. She had been spending awhile in the mountains. She had an appointment to meet her father in New York, who was returning from a trip to Europe. Her boat never arrived in New York; but was supposed to have been wrecked at sea, probably off Cape Hatteras, where a hurricane struck them.

Newberry Baptist Church—site of the first Baptist Church built in Newberry, located where is now the First Baptist Church parsonage, the parsonage when built later occupied the site where is now the church building.

Newberry Lutheran Church—site of first Lutheran Church in the village located on Boundary Street where is now the dwelling on the right of A. H. Dickert's home, the Dickert home being rebuilt from the old parsonage home. The first church was built in 1854.

Newberry Methodist Church—site of first Methodist Church in town, which was built in 1833. Located on Johnstone Street where is now the new Sunday School building.

A. R. P. Church—site of first church on corner of Main and Thompson Streets, built in 1854. Frank Lominacks Hardware Store is the exact site, the yard being in front and on both sides of the building.

Mount Bethel Academy—site of first school located on Kings Creek. The first school of high standard in the county was established here by the Crenshaws and Finches. Ex-Governor Hammand attended this academy before entereing South Carolina College, as did Anderson Crenshaw who was the first graduate of South Carolina College in the year 1806.

Newberry Academy—first academy was organized in 1806 and stood at "Halycon Grave", about where Dr. J. K. Wicker's home is and the home at present occupied by the descendents of late John H. Wicker. This first school was attended by John B. O'Neall and Job Johnstone. Later the building was used as a Female Academy, when a Male Academy building was erected about where is now the Newberry County Jail; the school moved when the first jail was built to a lot on Harrington Street, in front of the Dr. W. G. Mayes old home.

First Jail in Newberry—site where is now the Confederate Memorial Monument, behind the old Court House building.

Site where Calvin Crozier was executed—between the Farmers Oil Mill and the Bowers home which faces Boundary Street.

Site of first county Fair Grounds—in rear of old Bowers home, at "Halycon Grove", the old academy building being used for displays.

Hayes Station—Battle of Rev. War occured there in October or November, 1781, just across Laurens county line. Place was once known as "Edge Hill". There the tories attacked Col. Hayes and his men who were in the barracks. Tories set fire to the house and forced the Americans out, then killed them, or hung them, those that were not shot, including Col. Hayes, Captain Daniel Williams, (son of Col. James Williams of Rev. War fame at battle of Kings Mountain).

Clark's Ford—located on Enoree River. Land here was originally owned by John Clark, Sr. It was a site of a Rev. War skirmish or battle between American troops and a large band of Tories. Captain Jones, head of the American company, was killed. A yound lad, John Clark, Jr. son of John Clark, Sr. was wounded.

Old Fair Grounds—after the War Between the States—located at the end of Main Street, in rear of Davis home or the two blocks between Main Street, and Johnstone Street and between Hunt Street and......Street.

The "Old Locust" tree—this old tree was on the corner where is now the South Carolina National Bank Building. It stood on the North side of the public square.

The tree was cut down in 1853, when it was thought to be over one hundred years old. During the early part of the century many young men assembled under it's shade in the late afternoons, and discussed the various topics of the day, in law, literature and government, etc. From these meetings was organized the Locust Club of Newberry, which met and functioned for many years afterwards, meeting in an upstairs room.

Cannons Creek A. R. P. Church—located about three miles Southeast of the court house, and Kings Creek A. R. P. Church, about ten miles North of the court house. Graves of many early immigrants are in their cemeteries with markers. These are the two oldest A. R. P. Churches in the county.

Old Ebenezar Methodist Church—located near Maybinton. The church was organized about 1784.

Home of Edward Finch—site of this home is near King's Creek A. R. P. Church; it was there that the first Methodist Conference was held in upper part of the State, in 1794. It was there too, that the Mount Bethel Academy was organized.

Mount Tabor Methodist Church—located near Whitmire, Newberry County; it was organized in 1820.

St. Paul's Lutheran Church—located above Pomaria; was organized in 1761, or not later than 1764. The first pastor was Rev. Joachim Bulow, the second was Rev. Frederick Joseph Wallern, who is buried in the church cemetery.

Bethlehem Lutheran Church—located above Pomaria, near Cannon's Creek. It was organized in 1816.

St. Luke's Lutheran Church—located a few miles below Prosperity; was organized in 1828.

St. Matthews Lutheran Church—located near Broad River; was organized in 1827.

Smyrna Presbyterian Church—located about five miles West of town, on old "Belfast Road". It was organized in 1838, by Rev. Ketcum and Rev. Frazer.

Village Cemetery—located near the railroad in town of Newberry, at the end of Coats Street. Many early settlers are buried there.

Old Town—located at the site of ford crossing on Saluda River. The ford was used (formerly an Indian ford) to bring shipments of goods from up country to the lower section of the State. Across the river is site of an old Indian Mound.

Chappells—site of home of a pioneer named James Chappell, merchant and ferryman before the Rev. War. It is on Saluda River.

Quaker Cemetery—located at site of old Quaker Church, near Bush River.

Site of First Giles Chapman Home—located on left of old road leading East to Crotwells old place, and Matthews Fish Pond, on left of road near branch of Cannons Creek, Giles Chapman was a native of Wales.

Chancellor Job Johnstone Home—this home is on Johnstone Street, at the end of Calhoun Street was known in early times as "Coatswood". It has recently been renovated by his grandson, Alan Johnstone, Jr., but the house has kept most of it's original size and design.

Tarleton's Tea-Table Rock—located about four miles North of Newberry Court House, to left of old road to Whitmire, about two hundred yards behind some woods. It was there that the British officer, and his men, Col. Tarleton, camped several weeks while on their march to Ninety Six to help Lord Cornwallis. Here they ate, and were served tea on the rock by some neighborhood young women who were instrumental in delaying their March; as the result of which his regiment could not contact Cornwallis in time from preventing the latter suffering a defeat from the hands of the Americans.

G. B. Summer Store building—this is the site of an old building which was once used as a theater, the players being local talent, and where the Newberry Harmonic Society was organized.

Gray Graveyard—located about five miles South East of the court house, on old Pomaria road. There is where is buried a pioneer, Frederick Gray, said to have been a Prussian soldier of the King's Guards in Saxony; but no marker is shown to his grave. His son, George Gray, Sr., is buried there, he being the father of the patriot officer, Major Frederick Gray.

Pennington's Fort—located on Enoree River, where the Pennington family lived. Another fort....Pennington constructed as protection against the Tories was on Indian Creek.

Site of first Banking institution in upper part of State—located on square in Newberry, where is now the office of J. Dave Caldwell, Realtor.

The old Buncome Road below Pomaria was the line of March of the Kilpatrick raiders, a part of Shermans troops.

Mower Home—said at this time to be the oldest dwelling in Newberry. It was built about 1810-15. It is located at the end of Johnstone street, at the corner of Johnstone and McKibben Streets.

Speer Street Grammar School—the original building, (same except small addition in rear) was the home of Col. W. D. Rutherford, Confederate Officer, and it was built by his father-in-law, Col. Simeon Fair, a lawyer of Newberry.

Crotwell Hotel Building—now known as the Hotel Wiseman, is located on College Street, the site of the large colonial home of Dr. Freeburn Adams, an eminent physician and surgeon who came South from Newburyport, Massachusettes. He left no descendents now living.

Dr. Houseal Clinic—was originally a red brick building which was the old Newberry Female Academy. Later, it was served as the Newberry Graded School, at its first years opening, 1888-89, until the present Boundary Street building was built.

John Rogers Home site—located near Maybinton, remains of which can be seen in the form of two stone posts at the gateway entrance, on which are carved designs of orange blossoms; hence the home was known as "Orange Hall".

Henderson's Island—located on Broad River, a place for early fishers.

King's Creek Cemetery—many early settlers are buried there, with markers. They represented the first Presbyterian congregations of that community. Rev. John Renwick and his wife have markers.

Head Springs Cemetery—located about four miles North of town. Some early covenanters or their descendents are buried there.

Pagesville Academy Site—located about one mile from old Gary's Lane, to the right of main highway going towards Greenville. This is about fourteen miles Northwest of town. Once a school of high standard, which included two large buildings, professors home and the academy building. One hundred acres was owned by the school board.

Turner's Blockhouse—site of this place is near the site of the home of William Turner, one of the first settlers of Little River. His house was used as a refuge for himself and his neighbors during the Indian uprising in 1762. Then, for himself and his neighbors he erected a blockhouse with stockade, which they all used. The old house was used later by Benjamin Long as a home; then it became a school house.

Central House—site of place where Major Frederick Nance, who later became Lieutenant Governor of South Carolina, had built a home for his daughter.

Nesley Home—the first home on this site was built by Mrs. Dorothy Nance Pratt.

C. L. Havird Home—this home was built by Erasmus Nance, a nephew of Major Frederick Nance. Located about two hundred yards in rear of home, is the old Nance family graveyard.

Hornsby Home—this house was built by one William Caldwell and occupied by his son, Patrick Caldwell, a prominent lawyer of the town. Patrick Caldwell married Frances Nance.

Site of old McCkintock Home—located in front of the Houseal Clinic. It was once owned and occupied by Wm. G. Mayes, Sr. and family, before the Civil War; before which Robert Dunlap, a lawyer, lived in it; and after his death his widow marrying John K. Griffin, United States Congressman, lived awhile there until their retirement to the Griffin farm near "Belfast".

Robert Wright home—located across Boundary Street School grounds on Coats Street, owned by Z. F. Wright, son of Robert Wright. The house was built and owned, first, by Mrs. Abigail O'Neall, then sold to John Caldwell, a lawyer in Newberry.

J. W. White Home—located on Caldwell Street in front of Central Methodist Church. It was built by Judge O'Neall for his daughter, the wife of Dr. W. H. Harrington.

Thompson House—located on the corner of Caldwell and Johnstone Streets, has been torn away since writing this, was the old DeWalt house; later owned by the Thompson family.

Eichleberger Home—site of one of the first German settlers home; located about two miles North of Pomaria. It is said that the first Lutheran Theological Seminary was organized at St. John's Church and the sessions held in this old home. The present old house, however, represents a part only of the original house. A renovation of the old house having been made about 1866-67.

Home of John A. Summer (now Mrs. Herman Huggins)—just South of Pomaria. This was the site of the Pomaria Nurseries which were owned by one William, a noted horticultruist in his day. Also, it was here in the yard the first Post Office was established in the stage coach days.

St. John's Lutheran Church—located on Crim's Creek, said to be the oldest church congregation in Newberry County, having been organised in 1762. Present old church built about 1809.

Site of Home of Captain Adam Mayer—located on the road going from Pomaria highway to Peak. He was son of the Rev. War patriot, John Benedict Mayer. He was one of those who, with his company of guards, (State troops), escorted General LaFayette through that section the State to Columbia, when the French General visited America, and was on his way to Charleston.

Site of the first Presbyterian Church in Newberry village—located about one and one-half miles East of the court house, near the old cut-off road.

LAWYERS IN NEWBERRY
(1936-1946)

Lambert W. Jones, Eugene S. Blease, Steve C. Griffith, Thomas H. Pope, Jr., John F. Clarkson, Frank L. Bynum, Fred H. Dominick, T. William Hunter, R. Aubrey Harley, B. V. Chapman, Henry C. Holloway, C. E. St. Amand, Felix B. Green, J. O. Havird, Frank Jordan(1948).

Some Lawyers in Early Times—
From 1800 to 1810 the lawyers in Newberry were, James McKibben, P. E. Pearson, William Pearson, Samuel Thee, David T. Milling, and Anderson Crenshaw. Those who lived in other places and practiced in Newberry were,Peter Carnes, William Shaw, William Tate, Robert Stark. Some of these lived in Newberry between 1784 and 1790. Anderson Crenshaw, son of Ordinary Charles Crenshaw, moved from King's Creek section of the County. Then, moved to Alabama where he became an able Jurist of his day.

John Caldwell was practicing in Newberry in 1809. John B. O'Neall started in 1814; James J. Caldwell in 1812; Robert Dunlap in 1820; Patrick C. Caldwell in 1822; Simeon Fair in 1824; Thomas H. Popein 1825; Dennis Moon in 1827; Job Johnstone in 1818. Judge John B. O'Neall was Chancellor from 1828 to 1850, and Chief Justice from 1850 to his death in 1863. Job Johnstonewas Chancellor from 1831 to 1852. James J. Caldwell was Chancellor from 1846 to 1850. Y. J. Pope was Judge from1865 to 1868; elected Associate Justice of State Supreme Court in 1891 and elected Chief Justice in year....... Some of early Solicitors were, James J. Caldwell, Simeon Fair, and O. L. Schumpert. Col. Schumpert was succeeded by Thomas S. Sease who later served as Circuit Judge at Spartanburg, S. C. Judge Sease's nephew, C. C. Wyche, a native of Prosperity, Newberry County, practiced in Greenville, S. C.; and afterwards became Judge of the Federal Court, Western District, of South Carolina.

Ira B. Jones, native of Newberry, practiced in Lancaster, S. C. He was a member of the S. C Legislature from that County; later became Associate Justice, then Chief Justice of the State Supreme Court.

Other lawyers in Newberry were, Francis B. Higgins,Drayton Nance, Spencer C. Harrington, Silas L. Heller(he later moved to Texas), Nicholas Summer (admitted to the bar in 1830; killed in the Seminole War of Florida in 1836), E. Y. Fair,(he moved to Alabama, and became U. S. Minister to Belgium in 1857, serving until 1861). Henry Summer was admitted to the bar in 1833; moved to Alabama, but returned to Newberry before the War Between The States. John Pearson was admitted to the bar in 1838. Lambert J. Jones was admitted to the State Bar in 1839. Col. James H. Williams, admitted in1843; served as Captain of a company in the Mexican War; :sometime after the War he moved to Arkansas. General A. C. Garlington was admitted to the bar in 1844; James M. Crosson in 1846, then moved to Texas where he served as Circuit Judge. James M. Baxter admitted to the bar in 1849, practiced in Newberry until his death in 1861. Some lawyers of a later generation were,Silas Johnstone (son of Job Johnstone), Christian Suber, Howard H. Caldwell, John A. Chapman, and others. Some during the War of Secession and afterwards were, Adam G. Summer, John C. Higgins, George F. Epps, Charles W. Montgomery, J. Elvin Knotts, and others.

Carl C. Jaeger, native of Germany, was admitted to the bar after the War Between the States. A well educated man, being able to read and translate in fifteen different languages, and to speak in seven of them.

Thomas M. Moorman, Y. J. Harrington, James K. P. Goggans, and others were in Newberry just after the war .

Some of lawyers of late years were: Harry Blease, James B. Hunter, James Y. Culbreath, George Johnstone, Colie Blease, G. G. Sales, R. G. Watts, John Harrington, Robert H. Welch, Dr. George B. Cromer, Walter H. Hunt , Isaac H. Hunt,George S. Mower,Neall W. Workman.

There were three brothers whose father or grandfather moved from Newberry to Abbeville District before the War Between the States, Frank B. Gary, Eugene Gary, Ernest Gary. They practiced law in Abbeville, S. C. All became distinguished Jurists. Eugene B. Gary was Chief Justice of the State Supreme Court, (father of Mrs. Marie Gary Pope of Newberry).

MEMBERS OF THE GENERAL ASSEMBLY OF S. C.

Early Members of the State Legislature—
In the year 1781 the county was formed from part of old Ninety Six District, and the first members of the South Carolina General Assembly from the county were the following: Levi Casey, State Senator; Benjamin Kilgore, Mr. Montgomery, Dr. Ross, and Captain........., for the House of Representatives; for the District of Little River; and for the District of the lower section, between Broad and Saluda Rivers, were: Major Thomas Gordon, State Senator; Representatives, David Glynn, Major Michael Leitner, George Ruff, and Philemon Waters.

Members of the General Assembly from 1893 to 1946—
1893- W. D. Hardy, John T. Duncan, Wm. Young, Representatives; George S. Mower, State Senator.
1894- same as above—1895-96- W. D. Hardy, Arthur Kibler, Dr. C. T. Wyche, Representatives; and George S. Mower, State Senator.
1897-98—John F. Banks replaced W. D. Hardy. 1899-1900- John F. Banks and Arthur Kibler were replaced by Cole L. Blease and H. H. Evans. 1901-02- Fred H. Dominck, Arthur Kibler, John F. Banks were Representatives; and George S. Mower, State Senator.
1903-04- E. H. Aull replaced Fred H. Dominick. 1905-06- F. W. Higgins, John W. Earhardt, Sr., John M. Taylor, were Representatives; and Cole L. Blease State Senator.
1907-08- Alan Johnstone, Sr., E. H. Aull, C. T. Wyche, were Representatives; and Cole L. Blease, State Senator. 1909-10- Representatives: Dr. C. T. Wyche, Arthur Kibler, Godfrey Harmon; State Senator, Alan Johnstone, Sr. 1911-12- Representatives: Arthur Kibler, George S. Mower, Dr. C. T. Wyche; Srate Senator, Alan Johnstone, Sr.
1913-14- Same as above- 1915-16- Representatives: B. V. Chapman, George S. Mower, and Neal W. Workman; State Senator, Alan Johnstone, Sr. 1917-18- Representatives: H. H. Evans, W. B. Boinest, T. A. Dominick; State Senator, Alan Johnstone, Sr.
1919-20- Representatives: H. H. Evans, Dr. J. William Folk, George S. Mower; State Senator, Alan Johnstone, Sr. 1921- Representatives: Dr. E. N. Kibler, George S. Mower, and William A. Counts; State Senator, Alan Johnstone, Sr. 1922- Same as above, except Eugene S. Blease for George S. Mower. 1923-24- W. R. Watson replaced Wm. A. Counts.
1925-26- Representatives: A. P. Coleman, Dr. John J. Dominick, I. H. Hunt; Alan Johnstone, State Senator.
1927-28- Representatives D. Liyther Booser, A. J. Bowers, Jr., and Dr. E. N. Kibler; with Alan Johnstone, Sr. as State Senator. 1929-30- Representatives: Arthur Kibler, W. B. Boinest, Z. H. Suber; State Senator, Tabor L. Hill.
1931-32- Representatives: A. J. Bowers, Jr., Dr. E. N. Kibler, Z. H. Suber; with Tabor L. Hill, State Senator. 1933-34- Representatives: Marvin E. Abrams, Dr. John J. Dominick, James P. Setzler; with B. V. Chapman, State Senator.
1935-36- Representatives: M. E. Brams, J. Kess Derrick, Z. H. Suber; with B. V. Chapman, State Senator. 1937-38- Dr. John J. Dominick, J. Claude Senn, Thomas H. Pope, Jr., as Representatives; with M. E. Abrams, State Senator.
1939-40- Representatives: J. Kess Derrick, Thomas H. Pope, Jr., T. Aubrey Harley; with M. E. Abrams, State Senator. 1941-42- Same as above, except Thomas H. Pope, Jr. in Army service and Julian H. Price elected in his place (Mr. Price resigned in 1942). 1943-44- Representatives: R. Aubrey Harley, J. Kess Derrick (he died before end of the term), Steve Griffith (appointed to fill the unexpired term of Mr. Derrick); with M. E. Abrams, State Senator.
1945-46- Representatives: R. Aubrey Harley, Thomas H. Pope, Jr. (elected to fill the unexpired term of Steve C. Griffith who was appointed Circuit Court Judge); with M. E. Abrams, State Senator. 1947-48- Same as above—
1948-49- Same as above, except R. Aubrey Harley not having run again, was replaced by Walter Lake.

PHYSICIANS IN NEWBERRY.
(1936-1946)

Dr. Robert W. Houseal, Dr. Hugh B. Senn, Dr. Robert E. Livingstone, Dr. Thomas H. Pope, Sr., Dr. Frank D. Mower, Dr. E. G. Abel, Dr. J. Claude Sease, Dr. A. T. Neely, Dr. E. H. Moore, Dr. A. J. Katsberg, Dr. V. W. Rhinehart, Dr. Rayburn Lominack, Dr. J. H. McCollough, and Dr. A. W. Willing, Dr. Elbert J. Dickert(1948); and Dr. J. E. Grant (colored).

Newberry has had some very able physicians not only in the present,but also in the past. Within the past thirty years such men as the following have served the community as physicians and surgeons: Dr. William E. Pelham, Jr., Dr. O. B. Mayer, Sr., Dr. O. B. Mayer, Jr.,Dr. J.B.Setzler, Dr. Robert L. Mayes, Dr. James M. Kibler, Dr. W. G. Houseal, Dr. William E. Lake, Dr. P. G. Elleser, and others.   At Prosperity,Dr. Ira Bedenbaugh, Dr. C. T. Wyche, and others, At Pomaria, Dr.Pinner, and others. Dr. J.H.McCollough who was reared between Prosperity and Newberry practiced in Newberry.

DENTISTS IN NEWBERRY.
(1936-1946)

Dr. E. H. Kibler, Dr. R. M. Kennedy, Dr. Young Brown, Dr. F. A. Truett, Dr. John Boozer, Dr. B. G. Qualls (colored). At Prosperity were: Dr. E. N. Kibler, Dr. George Harmon, Dr. Godfrey Harmon, and others.

Fifty years ago, Dr. E. C. Jones was a Dentist in Newberry ; and others of equal talent.

OPTOMETRISTS
(1920-1946)

Dr. G. L. Connor, Dr. H. M. Bigby, Dr. A. T. Neely, Dr. T. M. Rogers, Dr. ..... Rones,(1947), and others who have recently located in the city.

EARLY MAYORS IN NEWBERRY.
(Data incomplete—from old newspapers and biographies)

1832-...................   1848-52- Col. James H. Williams.   1852-60- William G. Mayes, Sr. 1860-66 ....   1866-70- James M. Baxter. 1871-76- Y. J. Pope.   1876-79- Jordan P. Pool.   1879-83-................................ 1883-86- J. Malcome Johnstone.

Early Aldermen in Newberry-
1878- L. M. Speers, George S. Mower, Peter Rhodlesperger, Alan Johnstone.
1879- L. M. Speers, E. H. Christian, J. Malcome Johnstone, George S. Mower.

Clerk and Treasurer, 1878-79:   C. B. Buist.   1879-1885 ....

City Officers 1886-1948—
Mayor: George B. Cromer; Aldermen: Eduard Scholtz, James K. P. Goggans, C. J. McWhirter, W. A. Cline; Chief of Police, John Henry Chappell; Clerk and Treasurer, John S. Fair; Members of the Board of Health, Alan Johnstone, Dr. J. M. Kibler.   Year 1886.
1888- Mayor: George B. Cromer; Aldermen, Eduard Scholtz, James K. P. Goggans, C. J. McWhirter, and E. C. Jones.
1889- Mayor: George B. Cromer; Aldermen, George A. Langford, Eduard Scholtz, L. M. Speers, T. E. Epting; Clerk and Treasurer, John S. Fair.
1890- Same as above, with Wm Johnson taking place of Eduard Scholtz.
1891- Election held April 14, 1891, resulted as follows: Mayor, James K. P. Goggans;

1892- Mayor, L. W. C. Blalock; aldermen, James M. Kibler, D. B. Wheeler, Charles E. Summer, and Otto Klettner; Clerk & Treasurer, John S. Fair; Cheif of Police, H. H. Evans; Lamp Lighter, Rial Bates (colored).
1893- Mayor, Dr. E. C. Jones; aldermen, James M. Kibler, D. B. Wheeler, Charles E. Summer, and George A. Langford; Health Officer, C. W. Bishop;Clerk & Treasurer, John S. Fair.
1893-Dec12, 1893 (date of election changed)for year 1894- Mayor, Dr. E. C. Jones; aldermen; John W. Taylor, E. Cabiness, William F. Ewart, John H. Wicker; Clerk and Treasurer (elected January 10, 1894), Charles A. Bowman; March 1, 1894, G. M. B. Epting made a member of the Board of Health, with H. C. Hunter as Health Officer,
January 31, 1895, no change from 1894 except Proctor Todd was elected alderman in place of John W. Taylor.
December 16, 1895 election- Mayor, H. H. Evans; aldermen, J. B. Walton, R. D. Smith, William F. Ewart, John H. Wicker, and W. B. Timmerman. (Five wards from this time). Clerk & Treasurer, Charles A. Bowman. December , 1896- no change from previous year, except Bedenbaugh elected alderman in place of Timmerman.
December, 1897- Mayor, H. H. Evans; aldermen, John W. Earhardt, J. J. Lane, Thomas E. Epting, John M. Taylor, and .... Young. Clerk & Treasurer, Charles A. Bowman.
December 1898- Mayor, Dr. O. B. Mayer; aldermen, John W. Earhardt, E. Cabiness, William F. Ewart, J. C. Meyers, T. S. Hudson. Clerk & Treasurer, John C. Goggans(elected January 2, 1899); J. C. Meyers resigned and J. W.White elected to serve the unexpired term.
1900- Mayor, Dr. O. B. Mayer; aldermen,E. Cabiness, William F. Ewart, J. J. Langford, John W. Earhardt, T. S. Hudson. Clerk & Treasurer, John C. Goggans.
1901- Mayor, Otto Klettner; aldermen, E. A. Carlisle, E. C. Jones, Eduard Scholtz, J. J. Langford, R. J. Brown. City Attonery, Cole L. Blease; Clerk & Treasurer, W. Smith Langford.
1902- Mayor, Otto Kelttern; aldermen, Eduard Scholtz, J. J. Langford, H. K. Blats, E. C. Jones, S. K. Bouknight. Clerk & Treasurer, W. Smith Langford. H. B. Wells elected alderman in place of Blats who resigned on March 4, 1902.
1903- Mayor, John W. Earhardt; aldermen, Henry B. Wells, Julius J. Langford, Dr. Van Smith, R. J. Brown, and .... Guin. Clerk & Treasurer, Thomas O. Stewart. City Attorney, Cole L. Blease. Commissioners of Public Works: Charles E. Summer, Dr. James McIntosh, and T. C. Pool.
1904- Same as previous year, except.... Hutchinson who takes the place of .... Guin.
1905- Mayor, George B. Cromer; aldermen, L. C. Pitts, William Johnson, Dr. Van Smith, J. J. Langford,J. B. Leonhardth. Clerk and Treasurer, Thomas O. Stewart. Thomas O. Stewart resigned and Eugene S. Werts elected in his place.
1906- Mayor, A. T. Brown; aldermen, J. H. Hair, William Johnson, L. W. Floyd, J. J. Langford, E. L. Rhodlesperger. Clerk & Treasurer, E. S. Werts.
1907-08- Mayor, J. J. Langford; aldermen, P. F. Baxter, J. R. Green, S. K. Bouknight, John A Senn, E. L. Rhodelsperger. Clerk & Treasurer, E. S. Werts.
1909-10- Mayor, J. J. Langford; aldermen, G. C. Evans, George W. Summer, C. H. Cannon, P. F. Baxter, J. R. Green. Clerk & Treasurer, Ulin Bushardt.(Served in 1909) Mayor, Cole L. Blease; aldermen,P. F. Baxter, R. B. Lominack, Gregg C. Evans, C. H. Cannon, E. L. Rhodlesperger. (Served in 1910). Clerk & Treasurer, John R. Scurry.
1911- Mayor, Cole L. Blease; aldermen, R. B. Lominack, E. L. Rhodlesperger, G C. Evans, P. F. Baxter, Clarence T. Summer. Clerk & Treasurer, John R. Scurry.
Council met February 7, 1911, present: Mayor, J. J. Langford; aldermen, John W. Earhardt, R. B. Lominack, C. T. Summer, E. L. Rhodlesperger, O. S. Goree.. Clerk, John R. Scurry.
February 6, 1912, Mayor, J. J. Langfordy; alderman, H. H. Abrams, W. H. Shelly, C. T. Summer, E. L. Rhodlesperger, O. S. Goree. Clerk & Treasurer, John R. Scurry. O S. Goree resigned April 16, and J. P. Livingston elected to fill out his term.
1913- Mayor,Z. F. Wright; alderman, W. H. Shelly, H. H. Abrams, C. T. Summer, E. L. Rhodlesperger, J. P. Livingstone. Clerk and Treasurer, John R. Scurry.
1914- Mayor, Z. F. Wright; aldermen, P. F. Baxter, J. R. Green, C. T. Summer, E. L. Rhodlesperger, W. H. Hardeman. Clerk & Treasurer, John R. Scurry.
1915-16- Same officers as pervious year. John R. Scurry died in 1915.
Council met December 14, 1915, with new council, same except John A. Senn in place of J. R. Green. Resolutions adpoted and page reserved to the memory of John R. Scurry.
1917- Same as pervious year. New Clerk and Treasurer, John W. Chapman.

1918- New Council same as previous year, except Thomas K. Johnstone in place of E. L. Rhodlesperger. 1919- Same as pervious year, except H. D. Whitaker in place of C. T. Sumner.
1920- Mayor, E. S. Blease; aldermen, W. H. Hardeman, John A. Senn, R. C. Sligh, W. B. Wallace.
1921- Mayor, E. S. Blease; aldermen, (Same as previous year).
1922- Mayor, Wm. W. Cromer; aldermen, R. C. Sligh, W. B. Wallace, H. D. Whitaker, W. H. Hardeman, John A. Senn.   1923- Same as pervious year.
1924- Mayor, Walter B. Wallace; aldermen, W. H. ardeman, E. B. Purcell, John A. Senn, J. Ernest Summer, H. D. Whitaker. 1925- Same as pervious year.
1926- Mayor, Z. F. Wright; aldermen, W. H. Hardeman, John A. Senn, M. O. Surmer, L. A. Wilson, E. J. Dickert. E. J. Dickert resigned March 9, 1926, and Dr. E. E. Stuck elected in his place. 1927- Same as pervious year.
1928- Mayor, J. Marion Davis; aldermen, John A. Senn, W. H. Hardeman, Dr. E. E. Stuck, Marvin O. Summer, and L. A. Wilson. 1929- Same as previous year.
1930- Mayor, J. Marion Davis; aldermen, A. H. Clark, C. W. Douglass, C. A. Shealy, John A. Senn, L. A. Wilson. 1931- Same as pervious year.
1932- Mayor, John W. Earhardt; aldermen, A. H. Clark, Charles W. Douglass, C. A. Shealy, Mo. O. Summer, L. A. Wilson. 1933- Same as pervious year.
1934- Same as pervious year, except H. D. Whitaker elected in place of L. A. Wilson.
1935- Same as pervious year. 1936- Same as pervious year, except J. T. Hayes in place of M. O. Summer.   Acting Secretary at meeting held in January, J. T. Hayes.
February 25, 1936, resignation of John W. Chapman as Secretary , Clerk and Treasurer.
March 3, 1936 Drayton L. Nance elected Clerk and Treasurer.
1937- Mayor, John W. Earhardt; aldermen, A. H. Clark, C. W. Douglass, J. T. Hayes, C. A. Shealy, and H. D. Whitaker. Clerk & Treasurer, D. L. Nance. 1938- Same as pervious year, except R. C. Floyd and M. K. Wicker elected in places of J. T. Hayes and C. W. Douglass.
1939- Same as pervious year. 1940-41- Mayor, John W. Earhardt; aldermen, C. A. Shealy, Raymond Blair, M. K. Wicker, Leland Wilson,....... Shealy.
1942-34- Mayor, Herman Lagford; aldermen, Leland Wilson, C. A. Shealy, Raymond Blair, ... Shealy, M. K. Wicker. 1944-45- Mayor, E. B. Purcell; aldermen, Metts Fant, C. A. Shealy, M. K. Wicker, Leland Wilson, and .... Shealy.
1946-47- David L. Hayes, Mayor; aldermen, Edward McConnell, Metts Fant, M. K. Wicker, Leland Wicker, and ..... Shealy.   Clerk & Treasurer, D. L. Nance.
1948- Mayor, A. P. Salley; aldermen, ...
The City Manager form of govern ment started in 1949.

COPY OF LETTER WRITTEN FROM COUNTY ANTRIM, IRELAND,
IN YEAR 1818.

To Maxwell McCormick,
   Dear Brother:
I take this oportunity of writing to you to Let you know that we are all in good Health at present, (Thank God for it), hoping this to find you in the same. I am Very Glad to hear that you are well as I have no overt Since the Year 1801. I have Wrote Several times But has Rec'd No answer, But find my mistake not knowing how to Direct—Before the Letter you sent to Wm. Man, therefore I would Be very happy in having a Letter from you. I am in a very hard way of Earning my Bread. Iam Labouring with one Mr. John Montgomery Casement which I have been with him since I was able to take a man's work upon me. Labourer's and tradesman's wages is Reduced very Low and provisions of all kinds are very high. I would be very happy to be near you If I was in ability to come But times is so bad and wages so Little that all that a man can Doe in this County will doe Very Little for him, therefore my Dear Brother, If you will let my uncle David Reed know my Desire I think if it is in his power he will Doe somethin for me in the Case while my family is not Verylarge and thank God I am in Ability to work If I rec'd anything for it, and I understand furthing well I have wrote Several times to my uncle and has not Recd No answer. Therefor, you will let my Uncle know that the Acct. that he transmitted over to—James Walket to pay my father when he was over with him in the year 1801 that he Denyed payment and never proved one penny of it.Therofore If there was any means of Recoovery I would be happy in pushing him for the Same as he is in possession of all his Uncle

Doctor Willson's property, my Mother is in a Very Good State of health, thank God for his Mercies to us. I have three Children, two sons and One Daughter, the oldest 10, the youngest 3 year of Age. Sister Ann is Married to a Man the Name of James Grey and Lives in the Clougher within 1½ Miles of Ballymena. Sister Jerry is married to A James Alen and Currier to trade. Nancy's husband's Name is James Lock, he is Weighmaster in Larne and they have Both familys of children, James Man and family is well, William Man and family is well. Let uncle David Reed know that my Mother Desires to be Remembered to him and his family and all her friends especially Sister Margaret. My sister's kind love to you and you family and I give my own Love to all our friends not knowing how to write to them Seperately. I beg you will write to me the first Opportunity and Cause mu Uncle to write and Give me proper Dirictions that I may know where he is and how to Direct to him. No more at present But Remains you Loving Brother and Sister to Death.

John and Ann McGermick.

Larne, July the 5th, 1818.
N. B. When you write Direct to the Care of
John M. Casement, Inver Larne,
County Antrim,
Ireland.

COPY OF OLD SUBPEONA.

The fact that Major Spencer Morgan, one of the Rev War patriot Officers, once lived within sixty miles of Newberry Court House, is shown by the following copy of a subpeona:
Lewis Hogge and Charles Crenshaw, Admrs.   Benjamin Johnston and Edmond Gains, Decd.
Estate of Richard Strother, Decd.   VS.
Personally appeared before me Major Spencer Morgan and being sworn saith that he attended Court as a witness in this case, two days being legally subpeoned at Nov. Term, 1805; that he lives sixty miles from this place, that his ferriage coming and going amounted to twenty five cents—

Signed: Spencer Morgan.

Sworn to before me this
13th day of Nov. 1805.
Fred. Nance, J. U. Q.

ECONOMIC DEVELOPMENTS

History of agriculture and industrial growth-
When the white man first came to this section he came as a trader among the Indians. (The Cherokee Tribes occupied all that section between Broad and Saluda Rivers). He made treaties with them so that some kind of trade could be had with them. Then settlers came with their families and built log cabins not far from the trading posts.
The first enterprise may be that of "Cow-drivers" or "Cattle-drovers", who built their huts and surrounded them with high fences in which to drive the cattle. All of the upper part of the State was inhabited by wild animals, such as buffaloes, deer, bears, wolves, panthers, wild cats, and others; also, by many wild turkeys. The animals furnished valuable skins for shipping, and meat, most of which went to Charleston, South Carolina, to be exported, and some to the North.
The animals grazed on a variety of grasses and canes that grew in abundance. The cane, at the present time, is scarcely seen; but it onetime grew in abundance along the banks of creeks and on the hillsides; it was especially abundant around Ninety Six section. Around Newberry a greater abundance of wild peas and pea-vines grew. All of these furnished natural food supplies for the animals.
Animals were caught by the "Cow-keepers" who, usually, were owners of the huts and enclosures, and employed the "Cow-drivers" with the aid of paid Indian guides. The locations of these places were near pastures, or within the pastures, to which the herds were driven and held for marketing. Often settlers would appear around the fences and select their animals for purchases; many were shipped or driven to market.
Horse-raising soon became a favorite profession, and South Carolina became noted for it's high quality of horses, so much so that a statute of the Provincial Congress of South Carolina forbade the introduction of inferior horses from Virginia and from other northern plantations.
For many years wheat and Indian corn or maize were exported from the Province. Hemp, particularily, grew in large quantities between Broad and Saluda Rivers. Tobacco was grown, but it was largely restricted in being marketed for export on account of it's bulky package. Hay and bermuda grass were grown, and in scattered sections the vine, which was very successfully cultivated. This latter product grew around the French settlements in upper Ninety Six District (Abbeville County).
The settlers cultivated their own crops and attended to their own work, until the importation of negroes began, who were shipped as slaves from Virginia and from the lower section of the State, this latter group having been sent at an earlier time from the Barbadoes, to which place they had first been shipped from Africa.
The people built and cared for their own roads in each community. The first road built was in 1768, and extended from Orangeburg across the Saluda River to Newberry, thence to Laurens. In 1770 a road was built from Orangeburg to Ninety Six through Abbeville to Pendleton, about one hundred and ten miles.
Since the first roads were rough and lacked any kind of top soil or smoothness, oxen were used to haul cotton and produce to markets. Sometimes cotton was put in river boats or flats and allowed to drift down stream to or near a market place. Many bales were shipped this way to the village of Hamburg, one of the cotton centers. A few canals were built, but it was not until later that they received more attention. When the railroads came, they were stopped.
Early settlers located lands from grants given them under the Royal government. The farms were small, but the up-country settled rapidly. Each family received one hundred acres to the head of a family (and his wife), and 50 acres for each child. These were known as " head rights" under the English law, and were called bounty grants.
The farms produced grain, foodstuffs, cattle in large numbers; with beef, bacon, flour which was made from crude mills; and shipped to Charleston. There were good foreign markets to which they were shipped from that city.
The plantations had their blacksmiths and woodshops, flour and grist mills, gins, with skilled workers, including, too, wagon-makers, rope makers, basket makers, and others, including spinners and weavers. Sometimes the workers were trained slaves, or white men who operated their own business. Raising their own meats and vegetables, barter and exchange was common. One Dutch Fork farmer concieved the idea of running water uphill from his creek to his mill wheel by means of a specially built wooden pump, and then back again—the first attempt to execute the idea of the force pump. During the cotton-ginning season, when cotton was baled

by means of the wooden " Screw", pulled by mules or men, it required a whole day to gin one or two bales of cotton. The blacksmith usually had a full day's work to perform, in keeping repairs to gins, wagons, and other handmade tools.

History relates that a Newberry County man invented the old-time screw augur, a wooden affair which was used for many generations afterwards, until supplanted by the steel augur. His name was Benjamin Evans and lived up on Little River, near Beaver Creek, in Newberry County. He sold his interest in his shop where he made them, at his home, to his partner, John Edmundson, when he, too, got the "western fever", and removed to Ohio.

The early plantations had their own distilleries; made whiskey mostly for their own use and their slaves' consumption. One of the cardinal principles of neighbors in those days was to help one another when it was needed; so that it was often seen that night socials were held to which neighbors were invited to help in corn-shucking, pinder-pulling, quilting, log-rolling, the latter of which was generally done in the day-time. Clothes were made by slaves or clothesmakers in the neighborhood, from thread made from the wooden spinning wheel and cloth from the wide wooden loom which required a space under some tree or in the back room of the house. Shoemakers had their duty to perform on the farm. If one of them worked for himself he enjoyed the patronage of all who lived in the surrounding section; and he could make soles that were cheaper than tanning his leather. Hat-makers could weave most any style from straw grown in the fields. If the family desired to make a trip in their high, heavy buggy or wagon, shaped like a row-boat, either the husband or the wife could drive if there were no slaves dressed in a high hat and long-tailed coat.

All the families had cows, bee-hives; and milk and honey were plentiful. They knew nothing about ice; but kept the milk fresh by placing it in jars down in the branch or spring, enclosed , frequently, with milk houses. The people often had " spring fever" which was cured with root teas or boiled leaves. The hand- made hickoryplaited baskets were of different sizes for cotton picking and for other useful purposes. Another custom which still prevails among the negro women in the rural sections is that of picking blackberries, plums, and selling them at the homes in the towns.

After the introduction of the burr stone, many grist mills began to be built along the banks of streams by the larger farmers who, generally, served an entire section. In the mills they ground their own wheat and corn, made their own flour, which was produced on their own farms, and ginned their own cotton. These old watermills, the remains of some can yet be seen, were interesting sites. When the steam-engine was introduced small engines were put on many farms to produce power necessary to operate the mills, and gradually the water-mill disappeared. Most of the flour and grain now used in this section are shipped from the western area which seems more able to produce and make it at less expense than in this section.

After the War of the Revolution, iron works became common in the up-country, where iron was extracted from the ore. Many plantations had their shops and blacksmiths that made their own tools and emplements, and repaired them. This method was used for many generations, until the advent of new inventions and the establishments of new factories.

Some idea as to land and commodity values may give an idea of the basis for the upward trend in price values during this period of early economic development. The main influence, of course, in determining prices of fixed resources, intangible property, food-stuffs, and any commodities, is the supply and demand. This supply and demand is in turn influenced by an available circulating medium. In the earliest period, with lack of transportation facilities for large shipping and trading centers, necessarily saw much of " Barter and Trade", or exchange of goods; until a gradual improvement in social benefits began to appear in the form of railroads, new towns, and local market centers.

Land values were determined upon the basis of location and quality of soil; and probably, as at this time, the proximity of markets had a large bearing on fixing prices. But unlike the present time the prices were not influenced by local centralised government systems nor by speculations through specifccally organized efforts. Prices of farm lands varied according to locations; good farms sold at $1.00 to $3.00 an acre, the highest at $7.00 an acre, about the year 1805. The State monetary system during and after the Rev. war was the English pound-sterling, and continued in use until about 1800, when the American dollar began to be used.

Prices of many early articles of personal property and farm produce may show some of the determining influences for gradually increased values. There seemed to have been, as it is much the same to-day, an influence for determining prices from what may be called a general or public concept of money valuation, which is the foundation on which normal or fixed valuations are determined. Since that time the gradual increase in this normal Valuation has resulted from growths of populations, new commercial centers, new markets, and individual accumulations of wealth that give or make necessary this larger concept of this normal valuation. The value of gold which has determined the purchasing power of money did not have the attention of the government during the country's early development; hence, the trend of prices over the years has not been as consistent in one direction. The reason, therefore, for many of the price changes was a lack of control of normal values of money.

Some of the early settlement returns of estates as shown in county records, disclose old sales bills and appraisals that show prices often varied, which had no definite determining influence. About 1800 to 1820, prices of good cattle ranged from $7.00 to $10.00 a head, horses from $50.00 to $60.00 a head, mules from $50.00 to $80.00, hogs from $1.00 to $2.00, sheep $1.50 to $2.50; and pork sold at two cents to three cents a pound. About 1845 to 1850, there were slight increases in values: cows $10.00 to $12.00 each, steers at $8.50 to $10.00, mules $70.00 to $90.00, hogs from $2.00 to $4.00. The increased prices were comparatively slight during a period of about forty years. After the War of Secession, when an unnatural inflation of values had covered the country as a result of the war, and the reactionary depression had subsided, normal prices of goods were larger than the pre-war period, and continued to increase, reacting periodically as the result of unbalanced production and consumption, and exports. The same effect was produced as the result of the first World War, a new normal valuation coming out of a post-war depression, influenced, no doubt, by a new concept of the intrinsic value of money

There were many other crops in Newberry County during early times, but they were not especially noticeable until about 1830 to 1840. In the year 1840, there were 168,000 acres of land in cultivation in the county, with a population of 18,360. Of this population, there were 8,446 white people and 9,904 slaves or negroes, of which 300 lived in the village of Newberry. The production of cotton in that year, according to the United States Census, was 3,105,107 pounds, and the grain crops ranged as follows: wheat, 57,350 bushels; barley, 1,129 bushels; oats, 73,185 bushels; rye, 708 bushels; corn, 635,634 bushels; making a total grain crop of 768,006 bushels.

In the year 1850 there was produced in the county 19,894 bales of cotton, of about 7,957,600 pounds, and with a population of 20,143. This shows a slight increase in population in ten years, and the cotton produced during that period was more than doubled. Grain crops in 1850 were: wheat, 79,375 bushels; barley, 1081 bushels; oats, 99,798 bushels; corn, 664,058 bushels; rye, 696 bushels; making the total grain production that year 845,008 bushels.

In the year 1858, approximately 10,000 acres were in cultivation in the county, while nearly 100,000 acres were in waste land and 100,000 acres in forests. Thus, apparently much of the land had been abandoned by farmers or left idle due to the conditions in the South just before the outbreak of the War of Secession.

In 1880, in the Piedmont section of the State, there were 6,672,000 acres of land, of which fifty per cent were in woodlands, twenty-eight per cent tilled, and twenty two percent waste lands. There were in that year 38,591 farms, an increase of eight per cent since 1870; which indicates the manner in which the people came out from the post-war depression. About fifty-six per cent of these were worked by renters, and forty-five per cent worked by owners. In this section about ten per cent more land was rented than in any other section of the State. Of the increased land tilled, forty-eight per cent was in grain and twelve per cent in gardens or truck. These figures apply largely to Newberry and Abbeville Counties (then included the present county of Greenwood) that were considered the most thriving areas of the up-country at that time.

In Newberry County, in 1880 the average production of cotton to the acre was 188 pounds. Farm supplies raised in the county for the ten years preceding 1880 increased much during that period, and the county led in cotton production, over the counties in the Piedmont section in that year.

The tenants on the farms at this time were mostly negroes who worked the farms on shares, one-half of the proceeds from sales of crops to go to the tenant and the other one-half to the landlord. This sytem has been extensively used since that time. The landlord usually furnished all the fertilizers. The renters, however, who contracted for a specified number of acres, purchased their own supplies and fertilizers, and paid the landlord an amount for rent or a certain number of bales of cotton. Much of this system has been changed within the past few years, under the more recent government loan agencies.

A gradual increase in population since 1880 has shown at each tenyear period large productions of farm crops, more increased interests in farm co-operatives or farm units, resulting in the establishment of Clemson College, in South Carolina,and an agricultural estension department...... A brief glance at the production period from 1850 to date shows that very large reductions in crop productions have come about since that year. Corn, oats,and rye decreased to a marked degree from 1850 to 1882; according to State Agricultural statistics, there have been like proportional reductions in grain crops and many other of the smaller crops. This, no doubt, has been caused by the development of grain growing in the Northwest and the establishment of large flour mills in that area, who, it is stated, can ship these products into South Carolina at less expense than the cost of producing them here. On the other hand, cotton, dairies, cows, hogs, and cattle increased during the same period. The production of grain in Newberry County in 1882 was as follows: corn, 412,140 bushels; oats, 376,152 bushels, wheat, 131,472 bushels;............ In 1920, the grain crops were: corn, 76,800 bushels; oats, 30,000 bushels; wheat, 84,000 bushels; and small productions of rye, barley, vetch, cowpeas, and other grasses including burr clover which is grown, principally, as a soil builder though used as feed for cattle. The average production of cotton in 1920 was a little over one-half bale per acre, which is not a great improvement over some of the prior years. The large reductions in grain crops, however, show to what extent this section of the country has drifted in not meeting competitive markets of the Northwest; and what result may be expected when properly organized market facilities are not available.

However, more interest has been shown in dairy cattle in the county. This indicated by the growth of the Newberry Creamery since it started in 1922. Prior to it's establishment the few dairies then in the county shipped milk and butter to Columbia and elsewhere, so that from 1910 to 1922 the number of dairy cows increased from 3,735 to 6,700.

The increased crops in recent years, a tendency towards more diversification, show that under a natural growth and expansion and a growing population even greater diversification and an increased crop productions may be on the way.

NEWBERRY COUNTY FAIRS

The Newberry County Fair held on October 13 to 18, 1947, showed more than $2,000.00 offered in cash as prizes for that year. In addition, a midway wasshown on the grounds. The Board of Directors that year were the following: James W. Johnson, T. E. Davis, H. O. Long, J. F. Hawkins, Y. T. Dickert, J. W. Bremer,John F. Clarkson, John C. Epting, and Claude G. Gilliam. Officers: J. F. Hawkins, President; Henry T. Cannon, Secretary; J. W. Johnson,Vice-President; James D. Brown, Treasurer. Superintendents of the various departments were: A. M. Miller and Burton Sease, of General Farm Crops; Miss. Ethel Counts, 4-H Girls Club Work; Mrs. C. C. Wallace, Flower Department; Mrs. J. W. Danning, Fancy Work Department; Yancey T. Dickert, Superintendent, P. E. West, Manager, and W. C. Huffman and W. O. Stone, Asst. Supts. of the Poultry Department; Mrs. B. M. Scurry, with Mrs. William Hunter, Mrs. T. B. Amis, and Mrs. Edgar Hart, of the Art Department; T. B. Amis, with D. Govan Sease and Ellerbee Sease, of the Beef Cattle Department; S. C. Paysinger, with J. W. Abrams and A. W. Atkins, of the Dairy Department;....

Located on the main highway to Columbia, about two miles from the County Court House, the fair grounds are wide and deep, with three large buildings having an L-shaped design, which gives the appearance of six buildings. The poultry building, swine and cattle, the stables for horses that were originally designed for thirty six stalls, and the dsiplays for agricultural, commercial and domestic arts products. All are one-story buildings, following the same architectural lines, and are well ventilated. The race track, and a keeper's home, with office.

History of Early Newberry County Fairs-

The idea of public displays of home-grown products was born in the minds of the early settlers who raised a large variety of products on their farms, and brought them to market to sell or exchange. Their products were shown in wagons, many of which were oldtime covered wagons, which remained for several days in a market place. The principle market place for this section was Columbia, South Carolina, where many people from different sections met and exchanged friendly greetings, casually disposing of their goods. Later, the farmers of this county brought their goods to Newberry; with a gradually increased population in both the town and the county, they soon established a fair market, continuing to barter and exchange as well as make sales. The early plantations, too, in some sections became market places, mostly for barter and trade.

The few villages then established, with rough roads and burdensome traveling, soon gave way to more villages and better roads; and all roads led to the county seat.

Each community in the county had it's different kinds of specialties, in crops, and had it's specialists in work-jobs, as the shoe-maker, the hatter, the saddler, the tanner, the blacksmith, the silver-smith, the rope-maker, the cabinet maker, the weaver, dyers, tailors, and distillers.

Cattle at that time included hogs and sheep, mostly, with few cows for sale. Hogs were profitable to raise for both home use and for the market. The hogs roamed the fields or woods all day, grew fat on the waste lands after the crops were gathered. Sheep were profitable both as a meat crop and as a means of supplyig wool for home operated card and spinning methods. The wool was mixed with cotton, about one-half each, which made the yarn to be used in Winter clothes. Cows were more expensive to raise for beefs, unless they had good pasturage, even then the cost being comparatively high; but each farm had it's milk cow for family use.

When the farmers began bringing their products to town in larger quantities, popular interest began to be manifested in some form of institution that would help to create demands for the goods and stimulate interest in raising products on a profitable basis. From this idea came the formation of the first agricultural organization in the county, the Newberry Agricultural Society.

In the year 1838, when the old Newberry Academy had moved from it's building in Halycon Grove, then located in a large grove some distance in the rear of where is now the old Bowers home on Boundary Street(the small house just this side of the Wicker brick home), the building was used for meetings of the society. After 1841, there were regular meetings each year. In the Fall they would have a variety of displays, along with horses, cattle, poultry, wines, all kinds of knittings, paintings, canning products, and home-made clothes.

The first Officers of the society were: President, Judge John B. O'Neall; First Vice-President, Dr. George W. Glenn; Second Vice-President, Simeon Fair, Esq.; Treasurer, H. H. Kinard; Recording Secretary, Lambert J. Jones, Esq. Later, Mr. Kinard and Mr. Jones resigned and W. B. D'Oyley became Treasurer and Silas Johnstone became Recording Secretary. (Ref: Annals of Newberry.)

Nearly all the people of the county and town attended these annual fairs. Some of them were prominent merchants, like Robert Stewart and Robert Moorman, who were very active; and William Summer, the horticulturist, of Pomaria, S. C., and Thomas W. Holloway, the latter of whom served many years as Secretary of the State Fair Association. Even the lawyers took an active interest. Of course, the farmers were there each year with their products.

Newberry County was benefited to a great extent by having these annual displays that continued over a period of over twenty years. From 1856 to 1859 interest began to weaken and the work went down; due largely to political unrest in the South; and the association disbanded in 1859. In the Fall of that year Col. James M. Lipscomb tried to revive public interest in the meetings; again in 1860 another attempt was made to create new interest, but the fear of war prevented it's reorganization.

Throughout the period of the War Between the States, and just afterwards, during reconstruction times, no attempt was made to organize a fair association. But in 1878, after Wade Hampton became Governor of the State, the Newberry County Agricultural and Mechanical Association was organized. It was made a joint stock company, and it's officers elected August 19, 1878, as follows: President, John C. Wilson; First Vice-President, Thomas W. Holloway; Second Vice-President, John McCarley; Third Vice-President, John R. Spearman; Fourth Vice-President, W. D.

Hardy; Secretary & Treasurer, George S. Mower; Executive Committeemen, Alan Johnstone, J. A. Sligh; Andrew J. Kilgore, Nathan A. Hunter, Michael Werts.

The first exhibits were held on November 20-21 in the building on the Northwest corner of Main and McKibben Streets (old Salter Studio building), and now used as an auto supplies store. The second fair was held the next Fall at the new fair grounds at the East end of Main Street, about one mile from the court house. (The grounds occupied the whole block, just beyond the Charles E. Summer home.) The new buildings and the conveniences were largely responsible for the one thousand entries that appeared in this second annual exhibit. The grounds included what is now the two residential blocks, front and rear, on which is the home of J. Marion Davis, and that of Allen Murray on the next block. At that time there were no side streets,(the street running by the side of the lot of C. E. Summer, and the street dividing the two blocks.) The ticket office was about where is the entrance to the present street, by the Marion Davis home. The office had two large rooms, a front piazza, a side exit from the porch to the grounds. The grounds were enclosed with high, wide boards, closely fitted.

In the center of the present residential block on Main Street, was a two-story round house, called the " theater", with narrow winding stairway. This was used by the Judges in the contests, who watched from the second story as the cattle and horses were driven around the grounds; and also for watching the horse-races. South of this building, for exhibits and displays was located the main building near the edge of the grove (now the street dividing the two residential blocks). This large two-story building had only two rooms, one upstairs and the other downstairs, with small cloak room at West corner of each large room. The roof was supported by large square columns in the middle of each room. In front of the building, and facing the "theater" stand was a wide and long piazza extending the entire length of the building, both upstairs and downstairs, with high heavily built bannisters that, no doubt, kept many people from being pushed off. This building stood many years after the other buildings were torn down and the fair had ceased to operate; the last fair having been held there in October, 1885.

The old " Fair Grounds" were afterwards used for many years for picnics, barbecues (in the grove), and rabbit hunting by the local boys.

In the early 1890's when bicycling became the fad of the day a race track was built around the round house. It covered all of the front ground. Many bicycle tournaments, State and District, were held there; and people came from many parts of the State.

After bicycling began to lose it's popularity, the track was used for local horse races, and the center of the track as a ball park ,(the round house having been torn down), where local junior teams would play as well as some of the teams of the grown-ups.

The main building was the last to be torn down; after a period of usefulness as a ten-pin alley, it had to give way to the gradual expansion of Newberry's residential districts.

The present Fair Accosiation has functioned for several years, sometimes through difficulties; but by earnest efforts of those interested it has continued to give the people annual County Fairs, which is a recognized asset of a community.

EARLY RAILROADS THROUGH NEWBERRY.

The railway lines that pass through Newberry, the Southern and a branch of the Atlantic Coast Line, each has a background of methods of constructions that varied much. The Southern Railway which was first known as the Columbia and Greenville Railroad, was built about forty years before the Atlantic Coast Line road (then the Newberry, Laurens and Columbia Railroad—the C. N. & L.) was built. It is noticable that in this period of time many improvements in rapid executions of mechanical constructions had come about; though it was, no doubt, due to original unexplored sections and the usual freshets that prevailed at the time that first road was built, which required much longer time in completing.

The " Annals of Newberry", Part I, by Judge J. B. O'Neall, gives an extensive sketch of the first railroad construction, and in Part II of the same book, by John A. Chapman, Esq., is given some history of the building of the second railroad; which agree with many traditions and information as disclosed by old newspapers. Hence, it is not necessary to give any extensive details as to these first two railroads; but just a brief account of their progress and incidents connected with them.

The Southern Railroad-

The first effort to build a railroad was in 1847, when William Spencer Brown, a West Point graduate, was sent South to aid in developing the railroads of this section. He was a structural engineer, an energetic worker. He came about 1847, and in June that year he helped to make the first survey for the first railroad through Newberry, from Columbia to Greenville. He succeeded the Chief Engineer in 1849; and though the road had been started in 1847, he had to endure many hardships due to crude methods of transportation, bad roads and bad weather conditions. So that, it was in 1852 that the road was completed. In that year, Col. Brown was drowned in Broad River, in an effort to cross the swollen stream to get to Columbia and examine the bridge at that place. He had just returned from Laurens where he located a site for a depot for the branch road from Newberry to Laurens, called the Newberry and Laurens Railroad, the construction of which Col. Brown, also, supervised.

When the Columbia and Greenville Railroad was organized, a Newberry man, Judge John B. O'Neall, was elected President. When the tracks were laid from Columbia to Newberry, being about the half-way point to Greenville, a decision was made to have the railroad shops at Newberry. Accordingly, a surburban site was selected, and called the place, "Helena," in honor of Judge O'neall's wife, Mrs. Helen O'Neall.

The first engine to run over the new track after it was laid a few miles out from Columbia was called the "Abbeville", as it was supposed to have been furnished by the Abbeville Railway shops, the end of the line of the old South Carolina Railroad. This was done to try out the tracks. It was a small engine, with large smoke-stack that had a small scooped-shaped top; and burned two-foot wood. It puffed very loudly trying to make it's twenty miles an hour.

The tracks reached Newberry in March 1851, nearly four years after beginning construction; but greater strides were made from that time on. At Newberry a great crowd of citizens gathered to greet the first train as it arrived at the depot which then was near where is now an old wooden building directly across the tracks from the water tanks. The people shouted and waved as it came up the track; and the few slaves that were there thought it was some live thing coming, and hastily ran away. A similar incident occured at Ninety Six when the train reached there sometime later, the negroes even holding open prayer meetings.

The next depot at Newberry was the front part of the present Southern Railway freight office, the rear end of the warehouse being added later. It was at this place that an unfortunate tragedy occured, when a well-known Methodist minister, Rev. Samuel Dunwoody, was accidentally shot and killed by the night-watchman who thought he was a burglar.

The small frame passenger depot which was built afterwards stood many years on the spot at the South end of the present cement walk at the untion station.

The first plan was to build the road through the town of Anderson; but, later, it was decided to run from Belton to Greenville. The people in that district were extremely disappointed, and after several meetings they offered to subscribe to all the stock for a branch line from Belton to Anderson, and pay for it by their own labor or cash. It was so agreed, and many stockholders paid for their stock by laboring on the railroad. The point of stop of the road to Greenville was named Belton in honor of Judge O'Neall whose middle name, Belton, is from his Irish ancestors.

Since one train a day was run in the beginning, to Greenville and return, perhaps no anxiety was felt as to collisions. The first telegraph line was constructed in 1871. On July 5, that year, the first dispatch over the wires was sent by the President of the road to the Newberry County Sheriff, Thomas M. Paysinger, congratulating the citizens on it's completion. Prior to this time an effort had been made to construct a line from Newberry to Columbia, by a local newspaper in order to get quick news; but the line failed after it had been put up a few miles out from town.

Atlantic Coast Line Branch-
(C. N. & L. Ry.)

The first effort to organize a new railroad from Columbia to Greenville by way of Newberry failed. This was prior to the year 1884. Then some interest was shown in building a road from Augusta, Ga. to Newberry, and extending it on to Blackburg to join the main line of the C. C. & C. Railroad. The grading was done during the latter part of 1884 and 1885; but due to certain political pressure, according to tradition, the project fell through and the tracks were never laid. Remains of this old grading can be seen at West End, in Newberry. However, in the year 1885, the matter of building a railroad from Columbia to Greenville by way of Newberry and Laurens was again discussed; whereupon a number of Newberry citizens met at the town of Prosperity. A tentative organization was made there, and authorized. In the year 1886 the State Legislature amended an Act authorizing the construction of a road. The first meeting of the stockholders was held at Newberry, when plans were made for going ahead with the work. Another meeting was held a little later in Columbia, when fifteen directors were elected to the Board, Mr. H. C. Mosely, of Prosperity, S. C., elected as the first President.

The next step was to secure stock subscriptions, and in order to facilitate this part of the program, the suggestion was made to secure them by what was called, " ownership subscriptions," each township being allotted a certain number of shares for which they were to pay. Much opposition to this method was shown, and an appeal to the State Supreme Court was made which was held by them to be unconstitutional. The State Legislature then passed an Act to validate the issuance of bonds. Then, in 1889, a company was organized for the purpose of building the road.

Mr. Mosely resigned as President in 1889, and W. G. Childs, of Columbia, S. C., was elected President, and served for several years. The road was completed from Columbia to Newberry in July, 1890, in little over one year, and then to Clinton and Laurens in 1891. The first train to run over the tracks was in charge of Captain P. C. Gaillard, the Conductor, and who several years aftewrads served Assistant Freight Agent at Newberry.

When the old Newberry and Laurens Railroad was discontinued, about 1891, the track was taken up; and in 1896 the old road-bed was made into a bicycle track; where many people on Summer afternoons could be seen engaged in their fashionable sport of bicycle riding.

The first depot was in the present warehouse, the Southwest corner; until a small frame structure was put up near Friend Street crossing, on the West side of the tracks. After the Union Station was built this small building was bought by Henry ("Bud") Kinard who moved it to a lot near his present residence and made it into a comfortable dwelling house.

HISTORY OF COMMERCIAL AND INDUSTRIAL GROWTH.

The present large business and industrial enterprises of Newberry are but the results of many years work among people who have been awake to opportunties. The three large textile mills in the city, and the one at Whitmire, in the county, are the fruits of that one factor, American ingenuity. In the inventions of new machinery, new processes and methods, a community goes forward in proportion to the average integrity and industry of it's citizens. There are many smaller industries, too, in the city, that have been started—some short-lived— giving good pay-rolls to the community. If one could vision some of the early methods of enterprise since Newberry was founded in 1789, he could wonder that so great a change has come about.

The present economic and social conditions as compared with those of about one hundred fifty years ago, is astoundingly different. The earliest settlers were planters, chiefly, and received large land grants from the King of England. There were few if any villages then, until after the Revolutionary War. Villages began to form in various sections, and the village of Newberry was under the same county government as the other villages, until 1832, when Newberry Village was surveyed one mile each way and incorporated under the State law, receiving it's first charter that year, under a new form of government.

The necessity for concentration of trade at the county seat may have been on account of the court sessions that were frequently held, and which was a natural result when the court houses were built. The logical central place for high standard schools so that all could have an equal chance. The old overland stage coaches brought new roads, though rough and hard to travel over; so, when the old Charleston Road passed " Little" John Coats' shop, there was started the town's business.

Even as the plantations made all they needed at home, they sometimes represented a small community to which they furnished supplies. Such a community was "Little" John Coats' place in 1789, at his blacksmith shop. Moving his shop down on the Charleston Road, just before the location of the court house, and previous to which his donation of two acres land for a court house and jail, started others to move to the community. Homes and stores were soon built, so that in 1805 Abram Gilbert and his brother, Lovinski Gilbert, had built the first brick store, at that time there being only one or two other stores. The Gilberts sold out in 1825, and Abram moved to South Georgia, while Lovinski went to Spartanburg District. In 1825 there was hotel on the corner where is now Hal Kohn's Book Store. A long wooden building, on the porch of which loafers could be seen sitting on chairs, and the weather-boarding behind them filled with bill heads, tacked on the wall, advertising a circus coming to the village, or maybe a cock-fight to be held on a certain day.

The stores that were started prior to 1830 were mostly wooden one-story structures, and the general store sold everything needed in the area. The Post Office was in the corner of a store, the propreitor being the Post Master. Robert Stewart, descendent of a Scotch family who settled on Enoree River, owned and operated such a store. It's location was where is now the Ten-Cent store on the corner of Caldwell and Main Streets. His store was always packed with anything a customer wanted; he had many credit customers.

Some of the stores kept fresh beef in a small one-room hut in the rear of the store. Not having ice the beef was killed the evening before and brought to the market before daylight next morning, and sold out during the early forenoon. Customers were notified when fresh beef would be sold.

Plantation workers began to move to town to try to make more money in their trades. Shops started, such as harness shops, blacksmith shops, hat-making and clothing shops, and shoe-shops. The cabinet-maker combined his services with making small pieces of furniture, chairs, boxes, chests; coffins. Many years after the War Between the States a Confederate veteran named Monroe Harris kept such a shop near the railroad, at end of Friend Street. He invented the first automoatic railroad coupler, which invention was afterwards stolen from him. He made many curved handled walking sticks for the well-dressed sports of the town.

Some of the early shoe shops operated after the War Between the States were those of Jesse D. Hornsby, W. H. Blatz, William H. Dickert, and Peter Rhodlesperger. They repaired shoes and harness, and made harness. Before that time, John Boyle and B. M. Blease operated saddle and harness shops at different times. Some of the early wagon and buggy makers were C. M. James, Stiles Hurd; and later John Taylor who kept a shop near where is now the Newberry Creamery.

Early Industries—
Newberry Handle and Shuttle Factory—located where is now the Newberry Lumber Company plant. It's first officers were: T. C. Pool, President, Charles E. Summer, Vice-President. They manufactured farm emplements, such as hoes, handles, shovels, and wooden shuttles. they operated about two years, from 1895 to 1897, and then liquidated.

Cline's Shop—once operated near Southern Railroad, at the street crossing where is now the Newberry Lumber Company plant. It was owned by W. A. Cline, a contractor, who made his own finished material.

Newberry Steam Roller Mill—a two-story brick structure which was located about two miles North of Newberry, on Greenville Road, between where is now Guy Whitener's home and Forest Summer's home (this was the old Aull home). The plant was built and operated by John P. Aull prior to the start of the War Between the States; during the war, stopped; and about 1865 was operated until Mr. Aull's death in 1879. His son, James H. Aull, took charge of the plant, operated it until his removal from the county about 1895. It was continued a short time thereafter, by leases. Later, it was sold, but not operated as a grist mill.

Newberry Knitting Mill—this plant was organized about 1895, operated few years, then liquidated. The building still stands, a brick structure just across the South fork of Scott's Creek on Caldwell Street; later was occupied by A. F. Bush for his roofing business.

Newberry Cheese Factory—located about two miles East of town, to the left of the highway at Charles Suber's store. It occupied a one-story wooden building; concieved, owned and operated by the late Smauel P. Crotwell and his friends. After six or seven years it liquidated. Some years afterwards, Mr. Crotwell invested in large land holdings in South

Georgia; and later moved with his family to that section.

Wells's Match Factory—located in rear of home of the late Osborne Wells, a well-known brick contractor in his day. The plant was near where is now the A. C. L Railroad, North of his home.

Newberry Box Factory—was organized not so many years ago; located about two miles North of Newberry Court House, near Greenville Highway. The plant makes wooden strips for making shipping cartons or boxes.

Prosperity Oil Mill—was located in the town of Prosperity, Newberry County; operated several years, then discontinued. The late Dr. J. S. Wheeler was President.

Hunter-Saner Lumber Company—was located near the Southern Railway in the town of Prosperity. They dressed and planed rough lumber which was furnished them by the saw-mills in the surrounding section. After years operations it was sold to local interests.

Little Mountain Oil Mill—was located in the town of Little Mountain, Newberry County; in a one-story brick building. After a few years' operations the plant closed down. Later, the building was occupied a short time by Matthews Bros as a milling plant, then owned and operated by the Locke Construction Company.

Pomaria Oil Mill—was located in the town of Pomaria, near Southern Railway. They, also, ginned cotton. The plant was sold after a few years' operations.

Pomaria Lumber and Paner Mill—was located for a short time near the town of Pomaria. It was started by North Carolina lumber saw-mill people who had located in the community.

Crotwell Brick Yard—was located for several years one and one-half miles East of Newberry on the old Pomaria road. It was first owned and operated by the late James A. Crotwell. After his death the plant discontinued operations, except for a brief period by some of his children.

Pool' Brick Yard—was located about one mile North of town, on left of highway across from Rosemont Cemetery. The reamins of the plant operations can be seen in the form of deep excavations in the earth. It was owned by the late T. C. Pool.

Spearman's Springs— is located about eight miles Northwest of Newberry Court House, between the Greenville Highway and the road right of Jalapa. At one time a popular resort for travelers andothers. A typical mineral spring; around which was a roundhouse and pavilion.

Chick's Springs— was located about twelve miles North of Newberry, near Indian Creek. It was a popular place for travelers seeking it's water. Like Spearman's Spring, it was never develpoed commercially, except in,a small way by some recent purchasers of the place.

Walton's Harness Shop—Jerry B. Walton who operated a harness shop made many sets of harness and collars. Later, he became associated with the Newberry Hardware Company, which was under the management of Frederick H. Scumpert,(this business was bought by others and then managed by L. G. Eskridge for many years).

Thompson Tanyard—located across from where is now the home of Dr. T. Boyd Jacobs, (lately owned by Jeff Lane), on "Tanyard Hill". It furnished much tanned leather for local shoe shops and also shipped much of it away. The shoe shops then used wooden pegs in the shoes, and did only hand-sewing. Some of these shops were located in back of small stores.

Early banks in Newberry—

The first bank started in Newberry about 1852 was called the Newberry Bank. They built the present one-story brick building which is now occupied by J. David Caldwell as a real estate office. The style of front with it's small Doric columns, supported by stone bases, indicate that even in that day this popular form architecture was used for financial institutions.

The great strides in business and industry in Newberry has been due to a recognition of community needs; and this period of expansion may be said to have been most apparent from about 1880 to 1916. Large scale co-operative methods have become necessary to meet the demands of a rapidly growing population.

This first bank had a capital stock of $300,000.00, which was increased to $400,000.00 in 1856. The only President was B. D. Boyd, who, after leaving Newberry, went to California. The Cashier was Thomas W. Holloway, who was for several years Secretary of the State Fair Assoc iation. Robert L. McCaughrin succeeded Mr. Holloway. When the War Between the States started the bank suspended business.

Newberry National Bank- was organized in Newberry in 1871 by Robert L. McCaughrin, who had served in the Confederate Army, He was the bank's first President, with John B. Carwile, Cashier, and Thad. S. Duncan, Assistant Cashier. The following were the other directors: G. T. Scott, John T. Peterson, Robert Moorman, J. N. Martin, W. H. Webb, J. B. Palmer, and Y. J. Pope. Mr. Carwile resigned as Cashier in 1864 and was succeeded by Thomas J. McCrary who was at that time the Assistant Cashier. The orginal capital stock was $100,000.00, which was increased in 1872 to $150,000.00 . The bank liquidated few years ago, about the time of the depression following the end of the First World War.

Newberry Savings Bank—
Organized in 1891, with the following officers: Dr. James McIntosh, President; Robert H. Wright, Cashier. They started on a Capital of $15,000.00 which was gradually increased to $50,000.00.

The Commercial Bank—
Organized in 1896, with the following Officers: John M. Kinard, President(he was the Clerk of Court for several years); Z. F. Wright, Cashier; Dr. O. B. Mayer, Vice-President. When Z. F. Wright was elected President of the Newberry Cotton Mills, Jesse Y. McFall (then the Assistant Cashier) was elected Cashier. The bank sold its business to the South Carolina National Bank few years ago, when J. Y. McFall (then Vice-President and Cashier) continued as Manager of the bank, after the death of John M. Kinard; and Floyd Bradley, the Assistant Cashier, became the Assistant Manager. More recent changes in the bank show: Pick Salley as Manager, after whose death, John T. Norris became Manager and J. L. Keitt, Jr., Assistant Manager.

The Exchange Bank—
Organized after the Commercial Bank was in operation a few years. The first President was Edward R. Hipp. a well-to-do merchant in Newberry, with Marcus L. Spearman as Cashier. After the death of Mr. Hipp, Henry L. Parr became President and M. L. Spearman was elected Vice-President and Cashier, with Walter B. Wallace as Assistant Cashier. The bank was sold to the Peoples State Bank of South Carolina (prior to this it was consolidated with the Newberry Savings Bank); and not long afterwards it was liquidated. (Note: J. D. Davenport, of Newberry, was the organizer and first President, and not Mr. Hipp who succeeded him).

Industries in Newberry.

The Newberry Cotton Mills —
This plant was incorporated December 21, 1882. The incorporators met on May 7, 1883, and elected directors and officers as follows: Robert L. McCaughrin, President and Treasurer; George S. Mower, Secretary; with others as directors(including them), James McIntosh, D. H. Wheeler, J. N. Martin, James H. McMullin, M. A. Renwick, Robert H. Wright, William Langford, James A. Crotwell, and William T. Tarrant. In 1887, H. C. Robertson came from Charleston, S. C. and became the Treasurer and Manager , and served until his death in 1892.
There have been many increases in the size of the plant since it's organization. Starting with 10,000 spindles, in a few years the building was enlarged to double it's size, with increased machinery. Later, another building was erected in the rear of and adjoining the original plant, increasing the spindles to 44,000 and the looms to 1,296.
For many years the late Thomas J. McCrary served as Treasurer, after the death of Mr. Robertson. After the death of Mr. McCaughrin, Mr. J. N. Martin was made President, then after his death, Mr. McCrary succeeded him as President, being made both President and Treasurer. The mill thrived under Mr. McCrary's leadership. After his death, Z. F. Wright was elected President and Treasurer, and Frank Z. Wilson, Vice-President. The Superintendent after the death of Mr. Robertson, was J. Higgins, who was succeeded by E. B. Wilbur who had come South from some New England State. When Mr. Wilbur resigned to go to Gaffney, J. Marion Davis was promoted to the Superintendency from that of Boss-weaver. In that capacity he served many years; and was recognized as a capable man. After Mr. Davis's death, Jesse Y. Jones was made Superintendent, and served until the plant was sold to northern interests.

The Mollohon Manufacturing Company—
This company was organized in 1901, the prime movers in it's organization being the firm of Summer Brothers (Charles E., John H. and George W. Summer), and Walter H. Hunt, Dr. O. B. Mayer, John M. Kinard, E. B. Wilbur,   The directors were: E. B. Wilbur, Z. F. Wright, G. W. Summ Dr. James McIntosh, Walter H. Hunt, S. M. Milliken, Charles E. Summer, John M. Kinard, and Dr. George Y. Hunter. George W. Summer was elected President and Treasurer, in which capacity

he served until the plant was sold a few years ago to the Kendall Mills Corporation.
E. B. Wilbur was made Vice-President and Superintendent, and Z. F. Wright, Secretary.
After the resignation of Mr. Wright who was elected President of the Newberry Cotton Mills,
G. Leland Summer, who had served as Executive Accountant and Office Manager, was promoted to
Secretary and Assistant Treasurer, a member of the Board of Directors.

The plant was enlarged in 1907 and the capital increased from $200,000.00 to $500,000.00,
and the plant increased from 10,000 spindles and 400 looms to 48,000 spindles and 1,000 looms.
The architects for the first building were Lockwood, Greene & Company, of Boston, Mass., and
the contractor was Granby & Sons, of Greenville, S. C. For the second building, or the
addition, the architect was J. E. Sirrene, of Greenville, S. C., and the contractor, C. C.
Davis, of Newberry.

For many years the class of goods made were light weight sheetings and prints, then fancy
goods. When Kendall Mills bought the plant the change was made to surgical gauze, as well as
at the Oakland plant which they, also, bought.

The Oakland Cotton Mills—

The company was organized and constructed the plant about 1916, the prime mover being Col.
Walter H. Hunt, who was the first President and Treasurer, until his death; and the first
Vice-President being George W. Summer, who was succeeded by John M. Kinard, who was succeeded
by James N. McCaughrin, then the Secretary. The Superintendent was T. J. Digby, until the plant
was sold.

The first capacity of the mill was 10,000 spindles and 542 looms. Later, this was increased
to 20,160 spindles, when the building was doubled. Both the Kendall plants in Newberry now
have a capacity of 70,000 spindles and over 1,800 looms. Henry P. Kendall, of Boston, Mass.,
is President and Treasurer. The first Manager at Oakland under the Kendall control was A. S.
Paine. After his resignation, he was transferred to Mollohon plant as Manager. After leaving
Mollohon plant, Wilton Todd succeeded him, who when being transferred to another city, was
succeeded by William Tedford.

Whitmire Mills—

This mill which is located about seventeen miles North of Newberry Court House, on the
Spartanburg highway, was organized about 1900 by William Coleman, it's first President, with
a capital stock of $500,000.00. It was known as the Glenn-Lowery Manufacturing Company.
It started with 25,000 spindles and 650 looms, in a large, four-story, brick building. In
fifteen years it more than trebled it's capacity; now having over 70,000 spindles and over
1,400 looms. Mr. Coleman was succeeded as President by Mr. Childs. Later, the plant was
sold to the Aaragon-Baldwin Cotton Mills Company. R. E. Henry, of Greenville, S. C., became
President, R. G. Emery, Vice-President, and C. B. Gaines, Secretary, with John G. Barnwell,
Assistant Treasurer. They manufacture shades, prints, and broadcloths. The company owns
a community building near the mill, which was originally the home of the local Y. M. C. A. and
the Y. W. C. A., and the gymnasium.

The Southern Cotton Oil Mill—

This plant was bought from the Newberry Cotton Seed Oil Mill and Fertilizer Company which
was organized in Newberry on July 8, 1890. The following were their first Board of Directors:
Thomas V. Wicker, George W. Summer, G. Fred Long, Thomas M. Neel, Dr. O. B. Mayer, L. W.
Floyd, H. H. Folk, J. M. Johnstone, George S. Mower. J. M. Johnstone was elected President and
L. W. Floyd, Secretary and Treasurer. They built a two-story brick edifice near the junction
of the two railroads. Their capital stock was $30,000.00. After operating few years the
plant and equipment(which then included, also, a ginnery) were sold to the Southern Cotton Oil
Company, in the year, 1901.

The new owners retained L. W. Floyd as Manager, who served until his death in 1922, and
was succeeded by Harry W. Dominick who was, at that time, the Cashier. Mr. Dominick operated
the plant under a lease from 1924 to 1927. After a short close-down of the plant, J. C. Team
was sent to Newberry from Camden to take charge of the plant as Manager, which resumed
operations. The plant operated until 1931 under Mr. Team's managership; then S. A. Williams
was sent from Abbeville to take charge of it.

The Farmers Oil Mill and Fertilizer Plant—

This plant was organized by the late John H. Wicker, with the aid of Wilbur K. Sligh.
At the first meeting of the stockholders the first Directors elected were the following:

H. H Folk, H. H. Evans, I. H Doulware, Dr. W. D Senn, J. M. Suber, J. S. Dominick, M. A. Coleman, George C. Glasgow, and Ben F. Cannon, and John H. Wicker. The first Presidents in order of their services were, W. K Sligh, H. H. Evans, Alan Johnstone, A. L. Coleman; while John H. Wicker was elected as Manager, and served in that capacity for over twenty five years, until his death. Alan Johnstone was elected a member of the Board of Directors, probably before the election of the second President. After Mr. Johnstone's death, Z. K. Suber of Whitmire, S. C., became President and served several years, until the plant was sold to the Spartan Mill and Grain Company, of Spartanburg, S. C., who now operate the mill as a branch plant.

L. A. Wilson & Son, contractors, operate a lumber and storage plant, which is located near the A. C. L. Railroad, in "High Point".

E. T. Mayer, contractor, has been operating in the city over twenty years. He constructed the large concrete bridge on Boundary Street. He was associated for sometime with his son, E. Boyd Mayer.

The Newberry Hatchery—

This business was organized and operated by Yancy T. Dickert, of Newberry. The plant is located on South Main Street, and the poultry farm located about three miles from the city. They make large shipments of poultry and small chicks to various sections of the State and to other States. They have recently built a dresser plant near the outskirts of the city.

Neville's Ice Plant—

This business is located in the Newberry Creamery building, on South Main Street. A small packing plant was built and operated a short time in their building. It is owned by D. W. A. Neville who has recently branched out into the bottled gas business.

The Newberry Garment Factory—

This is a branch of the Greenwood factory. They manufacture garments for men. The plant is up-to-date, with all modern machinery.

Whitener Lumber Plant—

This plant is owned by Guy Whitener, who operates it. It operates a modernly equipped planer mill, and ships large car-loads of finished lumber to other sections. It is located just without the city limits, on the Greenville Highway.

Hotel Wiseman—

This business is owned and operated by J. E. Wiseman, which opened up on January 1, 1937. Previous to that time, Mr. Wiseman was Manager of the Newberry Hotel. Formerly known as the National Hotel, prior to which it was the Crotwell Hotel, the Hotel Wiseman has been renovated and finished throughout the interior, with a new lobby. Mr. Wiseman at this time (1949) is serving as Mayor of Newberry.

Newberry Hotel—

The hotel has been known as hostelry for many years, under many different Managers. It is located on the site of the first hotel operated in town, before the War Between the States. Before the war it was a wide frame building with large front porch; and when it burned up just after the war, a new brick building was erected, which in recent years has been renovated and improved with all new equipment.

The Gulf Refining Company—

This company was established in 1924, and name changed to Gulf Oil Corporation, by E. M. ("Buddy") Lipscomb who was the Manager for many years. They maintain well-trained personnel and well equipped trucks for deliveries to dealers and service stations. They have recently moved into their new building on College Street, near Scotts' Creek.

Palmetto Cotton Company—

This company was organized at the time of the purchase of the Oakland Cotton Mill and the Mollohon Manufacturing Company by the Kendall Mills Corporation. It is centrally located, on Friend Street, near the Standard Warehouse Company plant. This was started in 1928, and J. D. French was sent to Newberry to act as Manager; and P. M. Fant and R. W. Kirkland were employed as buyers. They buy raw cotton for several spinning mills of the Kendall group.

Newberry Creamery—

This company was organized in 1922, as a stock company. In 1923 James W. Johnson was made Manager. The plant has been successful from it's beginning, with increases of butter production. Most of the cream comes from the county, and the product is shipped to other cities, as well as a large sales output in Newberry and vicinity. At the retirement of Mr. Johnson, a full-time supervisor has been employed.

Newberry Steam Laundry and Dry Cleaning Company—
This business first started operations in 1928 under the direction of E. E. Langley and H. W. Mabry as owners, in a building just below where is now the present plant. J. Dean was sent to Newberry as Manager, until his transfer to another town, when William M. Summer acted as Manager. D. D. Pitts purchased the plant in 1933, and sold it in 1936 to Clem Youmans.

Since that time the plant has been increased in size, and new machinery and other equipment installed.

The Sanitary Dairy—
This plant was established four miles from the city by George W. Summer who employed Jesse Frank Hawkins as Manager, in the year 1923.

The first dairy in Newberry was operated by Peter Hare on the hill across from the old knitting mill. This site is now a part of the Mollohon Mill village, to the left from Caldwell Street. A large two-story home was in the middle of this section, which was later occupied by Silas McCaughrin who operated a dairy there, and who, too, was a horse-fancier with several fine race-horses.

Before the Sanitary Dairy started, Joe Williams, a colored man, operated a dairy about one mile out on the Greenwood highway.

A modernally equipped plant was installed at the Sanitary Dairy, including one of the first concrete silos in the county. Then a milkhouse was added. Mr. Summer sold the dairy to Jesse Frank Hawkins in 1932, who took charge in 1934. They have registered Guernseys.

Other modernally equipped dairies in the county are the Dennis Dairy, the Barre Dairy, the Neel Dairy, and the Senn Dairy. They are all at this time, with the Sanitary Dairy, members of the Cooperative Dairy Plant which have constructed a new brick building in the city.

Coco-Cola Bottling Company—
This plant is located on College Street, just across Scott's Creek. The first plant was started in Newberry in 1907, owned by Captain W. Smith Langford (now of Witchita Falls, Tex.), and was operated by his brother, David Langford, who later bought a partnership interest. After the death of David Langford, W. Smith Langford operated it until 1917.

L. F. Fischer came to Newberry and bought the plant about 1917 or soon thereafter. In 1934 a new brick building was constructed.

The Chero-Cola Bottling Company—
This plant is operated by Horace O. Swittenberg, and it is now located in a new brick building in the rear of his home on Nance Street. A twostory building, with storage rooms, and modern eqipment.

Southern Bell Telephone and Telegraph Company—
The outcome of a small, original plant in Newberry, called the Newberry Exchange, which was organized in 1892, is the present business. This exchange operated three years, and was sold to L. W. Floyd who operated it until October 24, 1902, when he sold it to the Southern Bell Telephone Company. J. Epps Brown, of Atlanta, Ga., an official of the company, (he was a native of Newberry County), negotiated the deal. Sometime later Mr. Brown became the President of the company, in which capacity he served until his death.

The first telephone directory printed in Newberry was in 1915.

Duke Power Company—
This company constructed it's branch plant in Newberry in 1911. Being a necessary asset to any town or city, it has increased it's service materially since that time.

The Fish Hatchery—
The hatchery is located about two miles from the city. It was built in 1937 on lands bought from Otis Whitaker. Financial aid was given the project by the Federal Works Progress Administration, amounting to about $24,000.00. It was sponsored by the State Department of Game and Fish, and supplental contributions by the county and by the local people interested.

The hatchery is maintained to furnish fish for Lake Murry, and includes in the area the counties of Newberry, Lexington, Richland, and Saluda.

The plant consists of one main resevoir, ten pools, and also two holding pools, a hatchery shed, a spring house, a keeper's dwelling, an assistant's dwelling, a work-shop, garage, a cooking shed built with furnace and oven for preparing food for fish.

Wholesale Companies—

R. D. Smith & Son, located on South Main Street, are wholesale distributors groceries. Formerly, the firm included the father of the present senior member of the firm; the business established in 1909. After the death of his father, he took over the business as Manager; in 1935, he purchased the business and admitted his son into the firm.

The oldest grocery wholesale firm in Newberry was the J. W. Kibler Company, whose warehouse was located on the Atlantic Coast Line Railroad, near the end of Friend Street. About 1899 three brothers, John W. Kibler, William Kibler, and Arthur Kibler, organized the business; and operated it successfully for many years. Then, in 1911, they sold the business to Clary Brothers, consolidating their own business which had been started a short time prior to that time with that of the Kibler Company, and continuing under the name of The J. W. Kibler Company. The officers of this new firm were: John W. Kibler, President; Arthur Kibler, Secretary-Treasurer; and M. W. Clary, General Manager. William Kibler in 1917. John W. Kibler retired in 1919, and his brother, Arthur Kibler, retired in 1924, when W. C. Wallace came into the firm. M. W. Clary became President, and W. C. Wallace, Secretary-Treasurer.

The firm sold all of it's assets and business to the firm of Thomas & Howard Company in 1935, whose local branch had just been established by the purchase of the business of Baker Wholesale Company.

Insurance and Investment Companies—

Bowers Insurance Agency, located in it's own building, the old National Bank of Newberry, was started in 1917 by A. J. Bowers, Jr. The organization has handled life, health, fire, and casualty insurance, and represents at this time some of the largest organizations in New York City and London.

In 1929 the business was incorporated, known as the Bowers Insurance, Realty and Investment Company, with the following directors and officers: A. J. Bowers, Jr., President & Treasurer; E. A. Carpenter, Vice-President; and in 1925 Miss. Pearl Hamm was elected Secretary. The other directors were: Z. F. Wright, I. H Hunt, and S. C. Paysinger.

The R. E. Summer Insurance Agency was started about 1932. They handle all general insurance, including fire, casualty, tornado, and other lines. They are associated with several of the large and leading insurance organizations in New York City and other places.

The Security Loan and Investment Company was incorporated in 1905 by the late Walter H. Hunt, who became it's first President. Since that time three other Presidents have served, as follows: Dr. O. B. Mayer, Wm. A. McSwain, and J. H. West. Mr. McSwain served, actively, for many years as Secretary-Treasurer, then was elected Vice-President, after which he was elected State Insurance Commissioner and removed to Columbia. Mr. West served, actively, for many years as President during which time the business grew in strength and influence. They have engaged in the automobile finance business for over twenty years, insurance of all kinds, real estate, and other investments. Thomas L. Hicks was Secretary & Treasurer of the company during Mr. West's life, and after his death, Mr. Hicks was elected President.

Newberry Federal Savings and Loan Company was organized in 1934, as the result of an Act of the U. S. Congress placing the government in position to aid in making loans to local people and organizations; which is under an insured plan providing equal responsibility up to a maximum amount between local investors and the government. The local organization received it's charter in Newberry in 1935, and since then has grown in service and value to the community.

Baker's Finance Company, owned by Ralph Baker, former owner of the Baker Wholesale Company, was started few years ago.

Farmers' Mutual Insurance Company, who has offices in the Turner Building, was started by a few farmers few years ago, to provide insurance protection to farmers at a minimum premium rate, covering houses, crops, and personal property. At this time, Robert Hunter is Secretary & Treasurer. The company functions as an assessment and cooperative concern, and not primarily for profit.

The Newberry Hospitalization Insurance Company was organized by John F. Clarkson, of Newberry, who was the first, and the only, President. The directors have lately changed the organization to a life insurance company, extending it's services into the fields of life, sick and accident insurance.

The Newberry Insurance and Realty Company was started from the agency of the late Samuel P. Boozer of Newberry, who operated an insurance office in the building which stood where is now the Turner Building, the one-time old Post Office Building. Mr. Boozer's Secretary was his daughter, Miss. Ethel Boozer.

When Mr. Boozer died in 1910 his Agency was purchased by James A. Burton, one-time Freight Agent of the Southern Railroad in Newberry. Miss. Boozer continued with him as his Secretary. Later, Miss. Boozer resigned and moved to North Carolina, and was succeeded by Miss. Lenora Broadus who resigned after one year and was succeeded by Miss. Lucy Hill (later she became Mrs. Robert Park). Then, Mr. Burton's son, Richard Burton, became Secretary. In 1912 Miss. Maggie Thomasson became Secretary.

Mr. Burton built up his business quite extensively, including stock investments in the textile mills, loans to large organizations, and represented several large insurance companies. **He died 1925 and Miss. Thomasson was continued** in the office, with the assistance of John A. Lindsay who had been the assistant of Mr. Burton. In September, 1927, the business was sold to C. E. Monts and A. H. Counts, of Little Mountain, S. C. They operated a short time; and in 1929 the Spearman and Wallace Agency bought the business, when it was moved to the first floor of the Exchange Bank Building. It was then incorporated under the name of Newberry Insurance and Realty Company, with William R. Reid, Sr., as President, W. B. Wallace, Vice-President, and Miss. Maggie Thomasson, Secretary & Treasurer.

In January, 1930, E. B. Purcell bought the business, or an interest in the business, and was made President, with Jospeh L. Keitt, Jr., Vice-President, and Miss. Maggie Thomasson, Secretary-Treasurer. At that time they included automobile financing in their services. In 1938, Miss. Thomasson resigned, and was succeeded by Eva Jane Davis, and afterwards by Mrs. Wyche Dickert. At this time, Mr. Purcell has with him in his office, his son Keitt Purcell, and Mrs. Eva Jane Wherry, and Mrs. Trolle Senn.

NEWBERRY CHAMBER OF COMMERCE.

The Chamber of Commerce is located in the old County Court House building, on the public square, occupying one corner of the first floor. They have an active Secretary, L. C. Graham.

The following composed it's Directors and Officers in 1945-46: J. N. Beard, President; A. P. Salley, Vice-President; R. B. Baker, Treasurer; L. C. Graham, Secretary, Dr. J. N. Burgess, R. Wright Cannon, Z. F. Wright, A. W. Murray, C. C. Hutto, John F. Clarkson, E. M. Lipscomb, George K. Dominick, E. B. Purcell, John W. Earhardt, Jr.

The Officers and Directors elected in 1946 were: A. P. Salley, (he was elected Mayor in 1947), President; George K. Dominick, Vice-President; later became President); R. W. Cannon, Treasurer; L. C. Graham, Secretary. Directors: Dr. J. N. Burgess, J. Dave Caldwell, R. Wright Cannon, John F. Clarkson, George K. Dominick, John W. Earhardt, Jr., Dave Hayes, E. M. Lipscomb, A. W. Murray, Thomas H. Pope, E. B. Purcell, A. P. Salley.

History of Chamber of Commerce—

The first organization was made about 1912-15. After functioning a short time, and having no full-time Secretary, the organization was disbanded. In 1920 a new organization was started, with Dr. S. J. Derrick as President (he was at that time President of Newberry College). They employed Loyd A. Maxwell, of Georgia, as a full-time active Secretary; after having elected a Board of Directors. Other Presidents of the organization were: James W. Johnson, in 1922. Mr. Johnson was succeeded by L. G. Eskridge. Mr. C. P. McDaniel, of Camden, S. C., succeeded Mr. Maxwell who resigned. In April, 1923, James B. Hunter was elected President, and served until April, 1924, when B. C. Matthews (then President of the National Bank of Newberry) was made President. He served until 1925. Then, the following served as President, in succession: P. D. Johnson, M. L. Spearman, A. S. Paine, Dr. James C. Kinard, Jesse Y. Jones, Gordon Blackwell, and others. James P. Moon had been active Secretary for several years, when he resigned.

In 1939, the organization had become weak in numbers and in interest; so that in that year a reorganization was necessary.

A Junior Chamber of Commerce has been organized, and now functioning successfully.

SOCIAL DEVELOPMENT

There were several early organizations in Newberry that helped in the social progress of the County.

The Newberry Auxiliary Bible Society, a branch of the American Bible Society, was founded by Rev. Charles Strong in 1808, who had come to Newberry just after his graduation from the South Carolina College. (An account of this organization is given by Judge J. B. O'Neall in the Annals of Newberry, Part 1).

The Newberry Total Abstinence Society was organized in Newber y, in the old Odd Fellows Hall on September 22, 1859, with the following as it's officers: John A. Chapman, President; Col. Whit. Walker, Vice-President; Henry H. Blease, Second Vice-President; W. G. Glenn, Treasurer; B. S. Buzhardt, Secretary. It is not known how long the society functioned, but evidently the influence of this organization was felt, the outcome of which, at a later time, was the organization of the Woman's Christian Temperance Union in Newberry, and throughout the State.

The first W. C. T. U. in Newberry was organized by Mrs. Cynthia Mower in the early 80's. Mrs. Mower was woman of good business talent, and possessed "true Christian piety and benevolence". The local society grew and several branches were started in the smaller towns or communities in the county. At one time they had accumulated as many as four or five hundred volumes in their library. After the death of Mrs. Mower, her niece, Mrs. Sophia Mower Redus, continued the work for several years. (See Biog. section).

There were, too, several fraternal organizations in Newberry in early times, including the Masons, the Odd Fellows, and others.

When Newberry College started back in 1856, a Young Men's Christian Association was started with it, which allowed men who were not students to join, also; and they received many outside members. It was not until co-education started at the college that a Young Woman's Christian Association was formed.

The substantial colored people of Newberry, being ambitious to improve their race, in the 1878 organized the Future Progress Society. They had already built two or three churches in town. The purpose of this organization was to improve the general intelligence, stimulate good morals, and elevate them. Also, there was connected with the society an insurance feature on the mutual plan.

Another organization was the Farmers' Alliance, a State organization which was formed in 1881, the Newberry branch having been started in the year 1888. The first Newberry officers were: W. D. Hardy, President; W. C. Cromer, Vice-President; John F. Banks, Secretary; W. B. Boinest, Treasurer; J. W. Scott, Lecturer; F. N. Calmes, Assistant Lecturer; Jeff. Quattlebaum, Chaplain; H. S. Knight, Doorkeeper; J. M. Werts, Assistant Doorkeeper; P. H Koon, Sargeant-at-Arms; ...... (An account of this organization is given in Part 11 of the Annals of Newberry).

There were granges in Newberry County from just after the War of Secession. An old Almanac which was printed in 1874 gives the Newberry County Granges for that year, as follows: Pomaria-Master, John L. Derrick; Secretary, E. J. Lake; Prosperity (Frog Level)-Master, A. H. Wheeler; Secretary, S. J. Hiller; Beth Eden-Master, H. H. Folk; Secretary, John P. Kinard; Belmont-Master, L. E. Folk; Secretary, H. D. Booser; Silver Street-Master, J. B. West; Secretary, J. W. L. Spearman; New Chappell-Master, Frank Moon; Secretary, M.J. Boyd; Liberty Hill-Master, J. W. Anderson; Secretary, Thomas Duckett; Bethel- Master, J. K. G. Nance; Secretary, F. W. Higgins; Jalapa-Master, S. O. Welch; Secretary, ... ; O'Dell's-Master, R. P. Briggs; Secretary, J. W. Hill; Cannon's Creek-Master, David Halfacre; Secretary, Henry Halfacre; St. Matthews Church-Master, E. S. Keitt; Secretary, S. J. Wood. The State organization in 1874 had officers: Master, Thomas Taylor, of Columbia, and Col. D. Wyatt Aiken, of Cokesbury, Secretary.

In the year 1878 there was an Old Men's Club, also a Young Men's Club, the Newberry Sporting Club, and a unit of the State Palmetto Guards.

The Sporting Club would meet at some place to try out the members' skill in trap shooting. With two spring traps and some glass balls, the traps about twenty feet apart, hollow, two-inch balls placed one in each trap and swung simultaneously, the shooter standing about eighteen feet from the traps. Not knowing which trap would be sprung first, until he saw the ball flying in the air, his alertness and aim were tested.

Members of the club that year were the following young men: Frank W. Fant, Charles A. Bowman, James K. Gilder, George W. Garmany, John R. Thompson, J. C. Myers, John Mayzick, D. Sampson

Pope, and I. W. Walters.

The Palmetto Guards were organized sometime presvious to 1878; but after they stopped functioning, they were reorganized on August 14, 1878, with the following officers: Munson M. Buford, Captain; J. C. Duckett, First Lieutenant; H. W. Cromer. Second Lieutenant; Wallace C. Cromer, Third Lieutenant; L. D. Abrams, First Sargeant; J. T. Mayes, Second Sargeant; P. B. Sligh, Third Sargeant; J. W. Folk, Fourth Sargeant; J. C. Hargroves, Fifth Sargeant; W. P. McCullough, First Corporal; John Smith, Second Corporal; T. R. Glasgow, Third Corporal; P. M. Denson, Fourth Corporal; J. C. Abrams, Color Bearer.

The Newberry Guards who were a part of the State Troops in the year 1897 had the following officers: W. Smith Langford, Captain; Richard H. Wearn, First Lieutenant; Ben M. Aull, Second Lieutenant; John A. Eddy, First Sargeant; Lawson B. Kibler, Second Sargeant; Henry B. Wells, Third Sargeant; E. L. Watson, Fourth Sargeant; Thomas H. Pope, Fifth Sargeant; Thomas H. Pope, also the Color Bearer; M. P. Hornsby, First Corporal; Hugh T. Renwick, Second Corporal; Moses D. Hulett, Third Corporal; James S. Renwick, Fourth Corporal; Rev. Junius B. Fox, Chaplain; Dr. W. G. Houseal, Surgeon; C. D. Weeks, Secretary-Treasurer; G. G. Jones, Quartermaster; John W. Daniels, Armorer; Julian H. Kinard, Drummer.

The local Chapter of the Red Cross was organized during the First World War. It has grown in membership, in it's services, and financial aid. Many volunteer members were employed during each World War to make supplies for the soldiers. Other services were in making contact, families's sons who were in service, either in this country or across the oceans. The special methods used were based on coordinative systems used throughout the world.

Spanish-American War Veterans, General Joseph Wheeler Camp—

There were two companies that went out for services from Newberry in the Spanish-American War. One was commanded by Captain W. Smith Langford, and the other by Captain Silas J. McCaughrin.

The camp was organized by the Department Commander, L. J. Schaefer, of Charleston, S. C. The following officers were elected: James C. Duncan, Commander; Vance V. Pearsall, Vice-Commander; Thomas Rowland, Vice-Commander;J. Longshore, Quartermaster; and Trustees, Thomas O. Stewart, J. E. Edwards, J. Longshore. The Ladies's Auxiliary was organized under the direction of Mrs. Louise Knox, of Charleston, S. C.; and the following were selected as officers: Mrs. Annie S. Duncan, President; Mrs. Eunice S. Stewart, Vice-President; Mrs. Eleanor Johnson, Vice-President; Mrs. Mary Pearsall, Chaplain; Mrs. Bessie Edwards, Patriotic Instructor;..... Jacob R. Wise, county service officer for World War veterans, was appointed service officer for the camp.

American Legion Auxiliary—

In 1945 the American Legion Auxiliary had the following officers: Mrs. C. A. Dufford, President(elected to succeed Mrs. Mae Tarrant Stuck); Miss. Grace Summer, Vice-President; Mrs. Frank Sutton , Second Vice-President; Mrs. Randolph Kirkland, Third Vice-President; Mrs. Henry T. Fellers, Chaplain; Mrs. O. H. Hatchett, Assistant Chaplain; Mrs. Thomas M. Fellers, Sargeant-at-Arms.

The auxiliary was first organized in 1921, with Mrs. L. W. Floyd as the first President. In that year the following Newberry ladies were made charter members: Ruby Goggans Brown (Mrs. Wm T.), Leila Bullock (Mrs. W. W.), Kate Summer Caldwell (Mrs. J. Dave), Miss. Sara Caldwell, Virginia H. Caldwell (Mrs. R. T.), Miss. Agnes Chapman, Ellen Becser Cromer (Mrs. Berley), Miss. Sudie Dennis, Geneva T. Dickert Workman (Mrs. Neal W.), Mary P. Fant (Mrs. J. P.), Ola Clark Floyd (Mrs. L. W.), Miss. Sadie Goggans, Charlotte J. Herbert (Mrs. W. W.), Susan C. Herbert (Mrs. W. J.), Leila Kennedy Johnstone (Mrs. Alan, Sr.), Anna Coe Keitt (Mrs. J. L., Sr.), Anna Coe Keitt Hart (Mrs. Edgar), Anna W. Keitt (Mrs. Thomas W., Sr.), Margaret Land Kinard (Mrs. John M.), Verna Summer Kohn (Mrs. Hal Kohn,Sr.), Hassie Livingstone (Mrs. D. A.), Ida Cromer McCarley (Mrs. S. C.), Miss. Georgia Porter, Trent Keitt Purcell (Mrs. E. B.), Helen Smith Reid (Mrs. William R., Sr.), Lavania Eleazar Summer (Mrs. Oscar R.), Mamye Swittenberg Summer (Mrs. J. H.).

The President, Mrs. L. W. Floyd, was appointed in 1922 by the State Commander to organize thirteen chartered units into a State organization; and Mrs. Floyd was elected the Department President, with Miss. Sadie Goggans as Secretary. Three Newberry women have served as officer in the State organization, viz: Mrs. L. W. Floyd, as President; Miss. Sadie Goggans, as Secretary, and Mrs. J. H. Summer, as Vice-President and as Chaplain.

Their principle work has been in helping needy families, in rehabilitation and child welfare; also, in serving the families of war veterans. They aid in the Armistice Day programs, and on "poppy" days. They have furnished and cared for a local room at the Newberry County Hospital. There are many other services of the organization.

In 1931 a Junior organization was formed, which help the senior organization in much of it's work.

In 1929 the local unit first sponsored the Christmas Seal sale, with Mrs. B. V. Chapman as Chairman; and they sold a record number of seals, amounting to $823.94. Another energetic worker at that time was Mrs. Strother C. Paysinger who won the Individual Member Getter award for obtaining a large number of new members. The McKissick Cup, given for the best kept history was won in the years 1930, '31, '32 by Mrs. Henry T. Fellers, who was historian for the local unit.

The following members have served as President since it's organization: Mrs. L. W. Floyd, Miss. Sadie Goggans, Mrs. C. W. Sanders, Mrs. E. J. Dickert(now Mrs. Neal W. Workman), Miss. Cornelia Mayer, Mrs. M. C. Caldwell, Mrs. Butler Holmes, Mrs. J. H. Summer, Miss. Sarah Caldwell, Mrs. S. C. Paysinger, Mrs. G. R. Summer, Mrs. L. G. McCollough, Mrs. P. B. Ezell, Mrs. O. J. Wilson, Mrs. J. R. Stewart. (This list was made in 1939). (Ref: Newberry Observer, April, 1938, and data furnished by members).

The Eagles Club—

This club was organized in February, 1929, for the young men of the community. The first President was James E. Summer, (afterwards Second World War soldier, Sargeant in Base Depot Company, serving three years in France). The other Presidents in their order were: George D. Way (also a World War soldier in the Second World War, serving in Europe), Pete Coleman (another soldier of the Second World War),C. M. Smith, Jr., Downs Wright (a Second.World War soldier, of the Army Air Corps). Others who have served as President at different times were: Johnnie Swittenberg, Griffin Langford, Frank Sanders, J. H. Clary, Jr., and Dave Caldwell.

A State Charter was obtained in 1931; and the location changed to the Masonic building.

Newberry Woman's Club—

This club was organized on Februray 13, 1901, with thirteen charter members. During the first year it became a federated club. From it's organization it has been a study club, maintaining a high standard in it's progress.

The club first used for it's programs the Bay View Reading Course. Later, the courses were those outlined by the extension division of Winthrop College, the University of North Carolina, and the University of South Carolina; which were adapted to the club's needs and studies. Programs arranged by local members included the study of biography, great Cathedrals of Europe, the drama, art, music, books of travel, and others.

County Council of Farm Women—

This organization was started in 1922, formed from seven Home Demonstration Clubs of the County. The constitution, by-laws, and creed, which were first adopted by the State Council, in 1921, was offered to the clubs forming the county council. At the first meeting, held on November 16, 1922, at the home of J. J. Sease, in "Tranwood Community", they were adopted.

In 1922, Mrs. J. W. Denning (then Miss. Daisy Berrie), helped materially in making the organizations, at which time she was the County Home Demonstration Agent. The first President was Mrs. Clarence A. Matthews, of the Tranwood community. Mrs. Sims W. Brown was President in 1923; Mrs. James Caldwell, and others, have served the Council as President.

Prosperity Community Leage—

This organization was first named the School Improvement Association. Their object was to improve the school grounds of the town of Prosperity; which they did with much success, includ- the purchase of new equipment.

Newberry Red Cross—

An active organization in Newberry, with Mrs. Jordan Pool and Mrs. Thomas J. Abrams as directors.

Newberry County Farm Agents—
In 1945-46 the following were head of this department: P. F. Ezell, County Agent; W. A. Ridgway, Assistant County Agent; T. M. Mills, Extension Work; Miss. Ethel Counts, Home Demonstration Work; Miss. Jane Winn, Assistant Home Demonstration Work (she was appointed in 1947).

The Emery Circle—
Charter members were: Mrs. James A. Burton, Mrs. W. H. Hunt, Mrs. George Johnstone, Mrs. John M. Kinard, Mrs. O. B. Mayer, Miss. Fannie McCaughrin, Miss. Lucy McCaughrin, Mrs. J. O. Peoples.

The Fortnightly Club—
Charter members were: Mrs. Charles A. Bowman, Mrs. W. H. Carwile, Mrs. L. W. Floyd, Mrs. O. McR. Holmes, Mrs. E. C. Jones, Mrs. S. B. Jones, Mrs. J. N. Martin, Mrs. J. T. Mayes.

The Emery Circle and the Fortnightly Club were organized for both services and social purposes. They did much good work, primarily of a literary nature.

Daughters of The American Revolution—Jasper Chapter—
The Daughters of The American Revolution was organized in Newberry in 1910, known as Jasper Chapter, D. A. R. The plan was started by Mrs. O. B. Mayer. The founders and charter members were: Miss. Mary L. Burton, Mrs. Sarah Wheeler Harms, Mrs. Lucy Baxter Hunt, Mrs. Gena Merriman Jones, Mrs. Margaret Land Kinard, Miss. Frances Baxter McCaughrin, Miss. Lucy Williams McCaughrin, Mrs. Elizabeth Land McFall, Mrs. Caroline Lee McSwain, Mrs. Harriet Jones Mayer, Mrs. Caroline Mayer Mayes, Mrs. Elizabeth Wheeler Sligh, and Mrs. Caroline Mayes Summer.

Regents of the Chapter from 1910 to 1936 were the following: Mrs. O. B. Mayer, 1910-1913; Mrs. L. W. Jones, 1913; Mrs. J. T. Mayes, 1913-1916; Mrs. J. L. Keitt, 1916-1918; Mrs. G. Leland Summer, 1918-1920; Mrs. Walter H. Hunt, 1920-1926; Mrs. C. L. Trabert, 1926-1929; Mrs. Walter H. Hunt, 1929-1932; Mrs. J. Y. McFall, 1932-1935; Mrs. James C. Kinard, 1935-1936.

Chapter officers for 1935-36 were: Mrs. James C. Kinard, Regent; Mrs. L. W. Jones, Vice-Regent; Miss. Grace Summer, Vice-Regent; Mrs. W. H. Carwile, Chaplain; Miss. Mary Schumpert McClure, Recording Secretary; Mrs. W. H. Hunt, Corresponding Secretary; Mrs. John M. Kinard, Treasurer; Mrs. O. B. Mayer, Registrar; Mrs. G. Leland Summer, Genealogist; Miss. Sudie Dennis, Historian; Mrs. ...., Librarian.

The Chapter was named for Sargeant William Jasper who was born in South Carolina in 1750, and died in 1779 in the service of his country. He was enlisted as Sargeant in the Second S. C. Regiment in 1775. On June 28, 1776, he distinguished himself at Fort Moultrie by recovering, through an act of personal bravery, the American colors which had fallen outside the walls. For this act, Governor Rutledge offered him a commission as Lieutenant, but he modestly refused it because of his lack of education. He was commissioned , however, by Governor Rutledge to make scouting trips through the State to harass the British outposts, and he became the hero of many adventures. During the assault on Savannah on October 9, 1779, he fell mortally wounded while trying to fasten his regimental colors on the parapet.

Many members of Jasper Chapter have been honored with State offices. Some were: Mrs. John M. Kinard, State Genealogist; Mrs. Walter H. Hunt, State Vice-Regent; Mrs. J. Y. McFall, State Vice-Regent and State Registrar; Mrs. W. H. Hunt, Mrs. J. Y. McFall, Mrs. Frank R. Hunter, and Miss. Mary McClure, as State Chairmen. Those who have served as pages at both the State Conference and the Continental Congresses at Washington, D. C., were: Miss. Grace Summer and Miss. Mary S. McClure.

The Chapter maintains an Educational Fund from which it contributes towards the preservation of historical places and the placement of monuments. Also, it has a Human Welfare and War Relief Fund. It is a contributor to the American Red Cross and other charitable organisations. It has given financial aid to the Martha Berry Mountain School in Georgia, to the Willard School of South Carolina, to the Schaeffer Training School, and the American International School, Springfield, Mass.; and to the Tamassee D. A. R. School in Oconee County, being one of the first founders of that institute, and building and equipping one of the rooms there. Donations, also, have been given to the Memorial Continental Hall, Washington, D. C. During both World Wars, the Chapter gave funds to the United War Work Relief; performed many acts of service by it's members, as knitting garments, sending clothes to war refugees.

Sons of The American Revolution--Philemon Waters Chapter--

This Chapter was organized in Newberry in 1924, with the following charter members: Arthur Kibler, Joseph L. Keitt, Sr., Frederick H. Dominick, Thomas K. Johnstone, Joseph L. Keitt, Jr., Jesse Y. McFall, John M. Kinard, Sr., John M. Kinard, Jr., George W. Summer, Sr., Dr. James M. Kibler, J. Ernest Summer, G. Leland Summer, Sr., A. J. Bowers, Sr., A. J. Bowers, Jr., Dr. Wilson C. Brown, J. Claude Dominick, Harry W. Dominick, and James N. McCaughrin.

The first officers elected were: Arthur Kibler, President; Joseph L. Keitt, Sr., Vice-President; John M. Kinard, Jr., Secretary-Treasurer; Dr. James M. Kibler, Historian. Later, the following new members were added: J. F. J. Caldwell, Z. F. Wright, E. B. Purcell, R. H. Wright, C. F. Wertz, and Charles E. Summer.

United Daughters of the Confederacy--William Lester Chapter--

This Chapter was started November 30, 1906, with sixteen members, in a meeting at the town hall in Prosperity, Newberry County.

The Chapter was named for Col. William Lester who was the first Captain of Company G., 13th Regiment, S. C. V.; and was promoted to the rank of Colonel after a short time in service.

The services of the Chapter include work on Memorial Days, placing flowers on graves of Confederate soldiers and on Memorial monuments. Also, to collect old records of World Wars veterans who are of Confederate descent; they plant trees on school grounds, and help improve the school surroundings; they visit the sick and wounded veterans. At the business and social sessions, that are held each month in the home of some member, historical programs are given, in which papers are read and basic subjects outined for the yearbook.

The following are some of the members who have served as President: Mrs. Carrie De Walt Hunter, Miss. Effie Hawkins, Mrs. Ruby Wallace Harmon, Mrs. Kitty Schumpert, Miss. Annie Lee Langford, Mrs. Minnie Lee Bowers, Mrs. Juliet Boozer Wheeler, Mrs. Corrie Black Price, Mrs. Ethel Sana Wheeler, Mrs. Gertrude Bobb Hamiter, Miss. Sallie Pugh, Mrs. Addie Werts Bedenbaugh, Mrs. Rosa Duncan, Mrs. Carrie Griffin Crosson.

United Daughters of The Confederacy--Drayton Rutherford Chapter--

This is the oldest U. D. C. Chapter in the county; was organized in 1897 by some of the real daughters of the Confederacy. The members then were: Kate Rutherford Johnstone (Mrs. George), Fannie Baxter McIntosh (Mrs. J. H.), Mamie Pool Schumpert (Mrs. O. L.), Margaret Land Kinard (Mrs. John M.), Kate Ewart Bowman (Mrs. Charles A.), Mattie McCaughrin Gist (Mrs. Nat), Fannie Baxter McCaughrin, Lucy Williams McCaughrin, Elizabeth Weir Glenn, Laurens Weir Glenn.

The name of the Chapter was suggested by Mrs. Ellison Capers, then President of the South Carolina Daughters of the Confederacy; Col. Rutherford being the father of Mrs. George Johnstone who was only one year old when her father was killed in battle in Virginia.

The first President was Mrs. George Johnstone (Kate Rutherford Johnstone), the first Vice-President, Mrs. John M. Kinard, the Second Vice-President, Mrs. Mattie McC. Gist, Secretary-Treasurer. Some of the older women who came in as members soon after organization were, Mrs. Y. J. Pope (mother of Mrs. Johnstone). Mrs. Laura Ewart (mother of Mrs. C. A. Bowman), and Mrs. O. G. Stewart.

The general objective of the organization, like others of it's kind, are to honor the memory of those men who served their country, to protect and preserve , and mark, places of historical interst, to collect material for history of the war Between the States, to record the part taken by the brave women during that period. Also, to make contributions to all worthy causes pertaining to Confederate Veterans and veterans of other wars.

The following members have served as President (up to 1939): Mrs. George Johnstone, Mrs. R. D. Wright, Miss. Fannie McCaughrin, Mrs. O. B. Mayer, Mrs. W. H. Hunt, Mrs. J. A. Burton, Mrs. J. E. Norwood, Mrs. L. W. Floyd, Mrs. J. H. West, Mrs. Frank R. Hunter, Miss. Nora Long, and others.

The State Division, U. D. C., has drawn from the membership of Drayton Rutherford Chapter several women to serve in the division, some of whom were: Mrs. James A. Burton, Division Registrar; Mrs. J. H. West, First Vice-President; Mrs. J. Y. McFall, Secretary; Mrs. S. B. Aull, Mrs. John M. Kinard, both as Secretaries; Mrs. J. H. Summer, Recorder of Crosses; and Mrs. R. D. Wright, as Vice-President and Honorary President.

United Daughters of The Confederacy—Calvin Crozier Chapter—

This Chapter was organized in May, 1909, as Calvin Crozier Chapter, No. 1191, U. D. C., by Mrs. R. D. Wright, then the President of the South Carolina Division. There were thirteen charter members.

The first officers were: President, Mrs. R. H. Wright; Vice-President, Mrs. Henry De Vega (then Carrie J. Pool); Recording Secretary and Corresponding Secretary, Mary Carwile Burton (Mrs. Clarence Reneker); Treasurer, Camille Evans (Mrs. J. N. Stone); Historian, Adeline Johnstone (Mrs. Walter Rountree); Registrar, Martha Johnstone (Mrs. W. W. Coleman); and of those who were the other charter members were, Ethel Bowers (Mrs. Raymond Fellers); Florence Bowman (Mrs. T. Roy Summer); Bess L. Gilder (Mrs. O. H. Johnson); Maude Langford (Mrs. L. G. Eskridge); Sarah Pope (Mrs. Paul Anderson); Lalla Rook Simmons (Mrs. Alan Johnstone, Jr.).

The name given the Chapter was in honor of a Confederate soldier form Texas, who, on his way home from the war, gave his life in Newberry in the defense of a southern woman. (The story is given below).

The services of the Chapter have been many. They were the first Chapter in the State to furnish a room at the Old Soldiers Home, Columbia, S. C. In 1912, a gift scholarship was established at Newberry College by the Chapter. In 1914, it was supporting three scholarships at this college. The Shiloah and Arlington Funds that were completed in 1916, received substantial contributions from the Chapter. In 1917 the Chapter formed an auxiliary to the Red Cross; made hospital supplies, knitted sweaters and mufflers, and made cash donations, sent Christmas gifts to the soldiers; helped support one hospital bed in France; and did other work.

In 1920 another scholarship was added to Newberry College by the Chapter, making a total of five.

In 1925, the Chapter furnished a room at the Newberry County Hospital. In 1928, it gave a generous contribution to the County World War Memorial.

Story of Calvin Crozier, Heroic Texan Soldier—

On a Wednesday, September 8, 1865, "the sound of drums and marching could be heard in the town; Federal soldiers going towards the depot". Among these soldiers were several negro companies, of the 33rd U. S. Regiment, under command of Col. Trowbridge. They had come on the train from Greenville, while about the same time a train going North had arrived from Alston. Among the passengers in the latter train were two young ladies, with a young Confederate from Texas, named Calvin Crozier, on his way home. He had left the ladies in the coach when some negro soldiers intruded themselves in the car and became very unpleasant towards the ladies. Crozier, coming into the car, requested the negroes to leave. Upon refusing one of the negroes in an encounter with Crozier was wounded. The negro soldier reported the difficulty to his command. Not knowing Crozier, they seized one Jacob Bowers, section master of the railroad, despit protestations of his innocence, and were about to lynch him. Crozier, hearing of the capture of Bowers, gave himself up to them, declaring Bowers to be innocent and admitting his own guilt in wounding the negro soldier.

Crozier was afterwards carried to a spot not far from the depot (a place about one hundred yards behind where is now the Farmer's Oil Mill); he was stood over a newly dug hole in the ground, there shot, his body falling into the hole, when they covered his body. Later, when the soldiers had left the community, friends went to the spot, dug up the body, and buried it in a coffin in a grave in the old Village Cemetery. There it remained about thirty years; the the U. D. C. Chapters sponsored an idea of again disinterring the body and burying it in Rosemont Cemetery, which was done; and a large monument was placed over his grave.

Newberry Civic League—

The organization was started in February, 1905, by the late Mrs. L. W. Floyd, who served as it's first President. Others who served were: Mrs. Walter H. Hunt, Mrs. R. H. Wright, Miss. Blanche Davidson, Mrs. Butler Holmes, Mrs. Margaret Hunter, Mrs. Everett Evans, Mrs. J. H. Summey, and others.

They have a large memnership; several women who give much of their time and skill to the improvement of the city. The construction and development of Margaret Hunter Memorial Park and the swimming pool is one of their accomplishments. Their other works are the World War Memorial, Standard Milk Ordance, The Rest Room, Cemetery Piers, beautification of grounds in

World War Memorial Square, the Confederate Memorial Square, New Court House grounds, the Newberry College grounds, Newberry County Hospital grounds, Newberry County Fair grounds, and other places.

Masonic Lodges in Newberry—

The Masonic Lodges in Newberry, from time to time, and other fraternal lodges, have grown in strength and numbers of members. Besides the Blue Lodge, there are now the Royal Arch Chapter, Knighst Templars, and a local Club of Shriners.

The first lodge was organized over one hundred twenty five years ago; for we find that in the old cornerstone of the second brick court house laid in 1823 (this was about twenty five years after the court house was built, when it was decided to add a corner-stone , when the old goal in the rear was torn down), was found the following inscription: " The corner-stone of the Newberry Court House Laid January 18, Anno Lucis 5857—Anno Dimini, 1823, Job Johnstone, W. M. of Lodge No. 11, A. F. M. of S. C., and number of the brethern under a dispensation, from John S. Cogdill, Most Worshopful Grand Master of Ancient Free Masons of South Carolina."

There was another Lodge which was organized at the time of the laying of this cornerstone, known as No. 44, and stood by to assist in the services.

In later years, both lodges were disbanded; and in the year it was found that no lodge was in Newberry, was 1850. Another lodge, the Newberry District Lodge of Ancient Free Masons- York Masons- No. 53, was located at Hogg's Store, in the county, near Enoree River; which later changed it's number to No. 27.

In 1825, lodge No. 44 had the following officers: James J. Caldwell, W. M., Francis B. Higgins, S. W.; Burr Johnstone, J. W.; with Past Master members, James J. Caldwell, Hiram Hutchinson, Birt Harrington, James Fernandez, Robert Dunlap, Job Johnstone.

From Mackey's History is the following: " In 1807 there was a York Lodge at Newberry, the number as 43 had become extinct before 1817. March 16, 1821, the Grand Lodge granted a warrant for it's revival, with a new number 11. In 1823, an application of the lodge changed the number from 11 to 44. This lodge No. 44 made no returns after 1826, and was suspended in 1830. The Lodge was revived in 1853, with the following new officers: E. S. Bailey, W. M.; W. B. McKellar, S. W.; J. M. Phillips, J. W.;....." In that year it became Lodge No. 87.

During the War Between the States the Lodge stopped functioning. After the war, a revival was made under the leadership of William G. Mayes, Sr. who became it's first Worshipful Master. Since that time the lodge has been served by many officers.

Newberry Country Club—

The Newberry Country Club was organized in 1920, the first officers elected having been the following: Z. F. Wright, President; L. G. Eskridge, Vice-President; W. B. Wallace, Secretary-Treasurer. The first Directors elected were: Dr. George Y. Hunter, Welch Wilbur, T. Roy Summer, L. G. Eskridge, W. M. Sherard, C. W. Fant, Thomas K. Johnstone, W. B. Wallace. Mr. Sherard resigned after a year and George W. Summer was elected to fill out his unexpired term of two years.

About the year 1922 the swimming pool was constructed. M. Q. Chappell was elected as Keeper of the Club premises. Temporarily the members used tents in which to dress when going in swimming. In that year a nine-hole golf course was made, all the lands covering several acres that were bought from Welch Wilbur. The location is about two miles Northwest of the city, to the end of and to the right of the extension of Nance Street.

The first club house was erected in 1925. The architect was J. Ernest Summer, of Newberry; and the supervisor of construction was John H. Wicker, of Newberry. Later, it burned; it was constructed mostly of granite, with a row of archways around the sides, and having stone columnr adjacent to the swimming pool. Stone steps with concrete led up to the entrances from the side which was near the pool and from the front side. On the first floors were showers, baths, and private lockers. Also, there was a dining room and a kitchen.

The new building is much like the original house, with baths and showers on first floor, a large reception room for members; and in the rear of the reception room being a dining room and kitchen.

The keeper's home was built in 1935. The first keeper, M. Q. Chappell, died about that year or the previous year.

In 1938 the following served as Directors: J. D. French, L. G. Eskridge; C. Foster Smith, A. J. Bowers, Jr., Z. F. Wright, P. D. Johnson, J. W. Johnson, L. F. Fischer. Officers that year were: J. D. French, President; A. J. Bowers, Jr., Vice-President; C. Foster Smith, Secretary-Treasurer; ...... The membership that year was 125.

In 1945 the following Directors and Officers were elected: H. H. Setzler, President; Guy V. Whitener, Vice-President; A. J. Bowers, Jr., Secretary-Treasurer; R. L. Baker, Alan D. Barron, E. A. Carpenter, L. F. Fischer, S. C. Griffith, Dave L. Hayes, James W. Johnson, Dr. E. H. Kibler, (Dr. Kibler died in 1946), Joseph L. Keitt, Jr., E. B. Purcell, J. L. Welling, and C. I. Youmans.

Service Clubs in Newberry—

The Rotary Club was organized in 1920. Some of the charter members were: Z. F. Wright, President; B. L. Dorrity, Secretary; Hal Kohn, Treasurer; George W. Summer, James P. Moon, T. Roy Summer, Walter H. Hunt, and others. Some Presidents who have served since 1920: 1920-Z. F. Wright; 1921-22-Dr. George B. Cromer; 1922-23-Dr. E. H. Kibler; 1923-24- Dr. S. J. Derrick; 1924-25-Rev. Earl Babb; 1925-26- Henry B. Wells; 1926-27-Dr. James C. Kinard; 1927-28- Hal Kohn, Sr.; 1928-29- Harry W. Dominick; 1929-30- John M. Kinard, Sr; 1930-31-Charles L. Trabert; 1931-32-James P. Moon; 1932-33-J. Dudley French; 1933-34-Z. F. Wright; 1934-35- Ralph Baker; 1935-36-Fred H. Dominick; 1936-37-Clarence C. Hutto; 1937-38- Jesse Y. Jones. ....

The following Directors and Officers for 1945-46: Frank Sutton, President; Pick Salley, Vice-President; Hal Kohn, Secretary-Treasurer; J. Dudley French, James C. Kinard, Hal Kohn, Don Rook, Pick Salley, Frank Sutton, being the Directors. Chairman of the Service and Program Committee was W. Fulmer Wells.

The Lions Club was organized in 1928, with the following charter members: Wilson C. Brown, John F. Clarkson, John W. Earhardt, Jr., T. E. Epting, L. F. Fischer, P. K. Harmon, H. H. Hedgepath, E. M. Lipscomb, J. C. Longshore, George Rhodelsperger, H. O. Swittenberg, R. G. Wallace. Rev. M. C. Dendy was the first President; some of the other Presidents were: John F. Clarkson, P. K. Harmon, John W. Earhardt, Jr., E. M. Lipscomb, George K. Dominick, L. F. Fischer, T. F. Cooley, D. O. Carpenter, R. G. Wallace, John Epps, and others.

The Kiwanis Club was organized in 1920, with the following charter members: Eugene S. Blease, A. J. Bowers, Jr., H. M. Bryson, D. J. Burns, E. A. Carpenter, J. C. Caldwell, O. B. Cannon, O. O. Copeland, W. W. Cromer, Frank G. Davis, J. M. Davis, F. R. Fellers, L. B. Friday, P. F. Gilder, O. McR. Holmes, I. H. Hunt, J. B. Hunter, T. K. Johnstone, T. E. Keitt, Joseph L. Keitt, Jr., John B. Mayes, James N. McCaughrin, William L. Matthews, Edward B. Purcell, John B. Setzler, J. Edwin Stokes, Patrick E. Scott, E. E. Stuck, Oscar R. Summer, Elmer S. Summer, John H. Wicker, Clarence R. Wise, Herbert A. Workman, Thomas M. Seawell.

Some of the Presidents were: William L. Matthews-1920; W. W. Cromer-1921; Rev. J. W. Carson-1922-23; Rev. Charles A. Freed-1924; Olin B. Cannon-1925; J. M. Davis-1926-27; A. J. Bowers, Jr.-1928; Rev. John Peery-1929; F. R. Hunter-1930; S. C. Paysinger-1931; S. A. Black-1932; A. W. Murray-1933; O. B. Cannon-1934; Rev. E. B. Keisler-1935; A. J. Bowers, Jr.-1936; F. D. McLean-1937; J. N. Beard-1938; Dr. J. C. Sease-1939; .... Directors and Officers in 1945 were: Houseal Norris, President; Rev. H. C. Ritter, Vice-President; J. C. Pruitt, Secretary-Treasurer; Seth Meek, Second Vice-President; Allen Murray, Willton Todd, Richard Lominack, Robert Marshall, Howard Turner, and Grady Donaldson. President, 1948-49, G. Leland Summer, Jr.

The American Legion—

A charter was granted to the American Legion in Newberry in September, 1919, and became known as the Newberry County Post 24. The following ex-service men were some of the first signers for membership: Dr. E. E. Stuck, D. A. Livingstone, T. Roy Summer, Carl E. Epting, Benedict Z. Burn, Francis E. Fant, Huiett C. Caldwell, Thomas A. Hair, Charlie J. West, Fred F. Scurry, Marvin O. Summer, Carol M. Dennis, Thomas E. Bullock, A. J. Bowers, Jr., and Holland Sligh. The following were elected the first officers: Post Commander, Hal Kohn; Vice-Commander, Dr. John B. Setzler; Adjutant, J. Dave Caldwell; Historian, J. L. Keitt, Jr; Finance Officer, B. M. Scurry.

Their first quarters was the old court house, upstairs, the large room having been renovated and quarters made for that purpose. Within the past few years a new building has been erected, located out on the Columbia Highway, near the entrance to Memorial Park.

The following members have acted as Post Commander at different times: Hal Kohn, Sr., Dr. John B. Setzler, J. L. Keitt, Jr., Henry T. Fellers, P. K. Harmon, John M. Kinard, Jr., Roy Elam, Tom M. Fellers, Paul B. Ezell, Duane A. Livingstone, F. E. Adams, Tabor L. Hill, Jacob R. Wise, Strother C. Paysinger, T. Roy Summer, Frank Sutton, and others at later time.

Newberry Electric Light and Water Plant—

The plant was constructed in 1897, the contracting engineer then being P. J. Voss, of Athens, Georgia. Mr. Voss was made the first Superintendent of the plant.

An artesion well was bored with a depth of 293 feet, of which about 243 feet was bored through solid blue granite. The location selected, on Scott's Creek, is about two blocks below the old Opera House building, on Nance Street. The first building was put up by W. T. Davis & Company, Contractors, of Newberry, who used brick from the plant of T. C. Pool, in Newberry.

The stand-pipe was located in rear of Boundary Street School, on Coate Street. (It was torn down in 1948).

The first Board of Commissioners were: Dr. James McIntosh, Tench C. Pool, Dr. James K. Gilder, P. J. Voss. After a few years, Mr. Voss resigned as Commissioner and Superintendent. He was succeeded by Fletcher M. Boyd who, too, after few years, resigned. Homer W. Schumpert was elected Superintendent who served over thirty years ; under his administration a new modern brick station was built, the old station being used as a storage house. In place of water from the two wells then in operation, water is pumped from Bush River, about three miles away, into a new reservoir which is equipped to have the water sterilized under improved methods. The architect and engineer for this new plant was Paul Norcross.

Surrounding the premises is an attractive park, with green terraces among large shade trees, and an attractive scattering of shrubbery.

The following are names of some local business men who have served on the Board of Commissioners: F. M. Boyd, Charles E. Summer, W. Smith Langford, Thomas O. Stewart, William F. Ewart, Eugene S. Werts, Homer W. Schumpert, O. L. Bushardt, M. L. Spearman, H. O. Fellers, Harry W. Dominick, C. F. Werts, E. B. Purcell, John W. Earhardt, Sr.. Robert G. Wallace, Robert M. Lominick, Wilbur Long, Jr., and others.

The officers during 1945-46 were the following: Homer W. Schumpert, Superintendent; J. K. Willingham, Robert M. Lominick, William R. Reid, Jr., Commissioners. (Mr. Schumpert retired in 1948, and was succeeded by William Wise, of Newberry, who had been serving as Assistant Superintendent. They are both graduates of Clemson College).

In 1949 the city government was put under a City Manager form of administration, coordinating all the departments of the city, including the Water and Light plant.

Margaret Hunter Park—

This park is located near the corner of Chapman and Nance Streets; occupies several acres of land, a small stream traversing the center of the plot. The name given it was in honor of the late Mrs. Frank R. Hunter (Margaret H.), as a memorial. She was the head of the Newberry Civic League, a public spirited worker , and did much for the beautification and improvement of the city.

Under the sponsorship of the Newberry Civic League, the swimming pool, the building, and the park were constructed by the local branch of the then Federal Works Progress Administration at a cost of over $22,000.00. The pool is concrete, with concrete floor, and slopes to various depths so that it is adaptable for both children and grown-ups. A diving ladder, safety rods and lines, are shown; and the water is kept clean and fresh by the city from which the water is obtained.

The building is a long frame structure, with stone corners and foundation; there are many dressing rooms, showers, and other conveniences.

The park is landscaped; has many varieties of trees and flowers, well arranged, with shrubbery surrounding the park. On the left the land gently slopes to a small stream, shaped so as to form a natural amphitheater that may be used for openair plays. Across the stream are natural terraces. The rustic bridges over the stream are in the midst of large trees. The bandstand across the stream is an open pavilion where many bands are used; and where many speakers deliver their talks or campaign speeches. In the back part of the park is a picnic ground where there is an open-air oven for preparing foods and barbecues.

Willowbrook Park--

This park is located at the corner of Crosson and Drayton Streets, in West End, on both sides of Scott's Creek. It covers several acres, has a attractive lawn which extneds the entire site. A large pavilion is used for dancing, suppers, skating, and for other entertainments. Nearby is a round band-stand. Rustic bridges over the creek are seen. On one side of the creek is the childrens's playground with swings, toboggans, and other amusements; and a Boy Scout cabin on the other side. Much shrubbery is seen on the grounds.

Newberry Fire Department.

Within recent years a new fire truck was installed , a new fire house constructed. Improved water force and services has resulted, with new combination ladders, base-wagon, pumpers, and boosters. These are known as the "Quad". Many of these new features embodied the ideas of the late Chief, Henry B. Wells, Sr. The present fire chief is Sam Beam.

In the building are quarters for the men, a dining room, kitchen, workshop, (the last named room being in the basement, as also the dining room and kitchen). On the ground floor are motot trucks, with capacity for instant action in case of an alarm. Living quarters are on the top floor for the families of drivers or other drivers's quarters, two in front and two in the back.

History of Newberry's Early Fire Department--

It was back in the pioneer days that, as a small village, with only a few frame stores and homes, the fire squads consisted of three or four young men, volunteers, who would run with buckets of water from the nearby wells or springs, or keep large casks filled for an emergency, and endeavor to put out the fire.

At a later time, the squads worked in a more systematic form. They had leather buckets that were kept in public places and ready to be used in case of a fire. When an alarm was given, they ran with buckets to the nearest water places, filled them, and with ladders ran to the scene. The ladders were placed on the burining building, each ladder having several hooks in it to hold about twenty buckets. The men lined up the ladder, and from the ladder, as fast as the men on the building could empty them and throw them back to the end of the line to be filled again. This team was called the " hook and ladder team."

The first regularily organised fire company was started in 1873, when some young men in town met and formed the Excelsior Steam Fire Engine Company, with George S. Mower as the first President, and M. Foote, Jr., as Secretary-Treasurer. A list of the names of the first members is not available; but a year or two later the following are named members: George S. Mower, President, Mordecai Foote, Jr., Walter H. Hunt, William Walters, J. W. White, Harry White, John W. Taylor, E. H. Kingsmore, W. S. ("Billy") Mann, Harry Blease, Jesse Prince, Brice McCarley, Ben Lane, Frank Lane, W. T. Jackson, George Gillilland, who was the engineer. Sometime later I. H. Hunt was elected Secretary-Treasurer.

A fire engine was bought about the time the fire company was organized, or soon thereafter. They used an old hand-pump which was operated by men on each side. This pump was used after the coming of the new fire engine, by the young negroes of the town, who started a company which the called the " Eagles", and who sometimes helped the engine pump frpm the old cistern when large fires were in progress. The first water that was pumped from an old hole which was about fifteen feet square, was on Scott's Creek, on Nance Street. Nance Street had been extended from the corner of Harrington Street to the Wells' old home in " High Point". The engine was a small one, with a large smoke-stack, and with equal dimensions from front to back. It was called " Young John", for the later Young John Pope who was Mayor of Newberry about that time. It would burn either wood or coal; but four-feet pieces of wood were used most of the time.

The first quarters of " Young John", and the reels, was in the Foote building which was located where is now the filling station on corner of Harrington and College Streets. Here M. Foote, Sr. (he was a Jew), kept his dray horses and permitted the fire company to use them when they were in their stables, in the adjacent section of the building, to haul the engine to Scott's Creek. The horses were sometimes used, too, in monthly contests and at fire tournaments, and were arrayed in colors fitted for the occasion.

Soon therafter a large cistern was built on lower public square, near the side-walk, (the present side-walk since widening of the street was where the cistern was located.)

At that time there were large mulberry trees on the edge of the side-walk, under whose shades many folks would stand or sit on chairs watching the work of the fire-fighters who frequently practiced shooting water over the Opera House steeple, which was accomplished after many trials. The roar of the large engine and pumping of water was most interesting to younger boys. When the cistern was being dug the workers found many large rocks that had to be blasted, and at one time a large stone was thrown over to where is now the C. L. Havird store, knocking out a small piece of stone from the window sill, the gap of which can be seen. The late Warren Jones, known to many as "Hogge" Jones, was sitting on the window sill and was almost hit by the flying rock.

When the cistern was completed, cemented on bottom and sides, it was covered with wide boards, level with the ground. The square at that time was used as a public parking place for wagons and buggies, but they were not allowed to park near the cistern.

Soon thereafter, another cistern was built on Harrington Street, it's board covering being used as a bridge over which vehicles passed. This was over the small branch or ditch that was just below where is now the home of Mrs. C. D. Weeks, corner of Harrington and Thompson Streets. This branch was formed from the sources of three springs some distances above it. One was in the yard of late Henry H. Blease who operated a hotel on Main Street, another in the front yard, left side, of the Associated Reformed Church, and the third in the yard of the old Kinard home (later the flower garden of Henry ("Bud") Kinard.

The fire company changed it's name, later, and was known as the Excelsior Hose Company, and had two hand reels, working as two seperate companies, No. 1 and No. 2, each with about twenty volunteer members. Annual races were held on Main Street, foot races and hand-reel races. They were considered friendly competitions, and the winning team would receive a medal, it's Captain being required to wear it until the next annual races when the winner would wear it for a year.

After the death of M. Foote, Sr. new quarters were obtained, various temporary places being used. One was in the rear part of the Opera House building (now used as offices of the City government), where the equipment stayed for several years, until newer quarters were provided in it's present locality.

When the water works system was started, and hydrants placed on street corners, local drills and races were held monthly. Local competitions and State tournaments became popular. These became regular events when competitors would come out in full regalia, being distinguished by their different colors and waving banners. Prizes and medals were awarded the winners. At that time, " Young John" was placed in discard, and horses were purchased; first, one horse, then two horses, and placed in the fire house, standing near for instant use. The horses had dropharness hanging over the front of the trucks, so that when an alarm sounded the harness would drop quickly on the backs of the horses and quickly hitched up. It was a few years ago that they were superceded by the present motor truck equipment.

Newberry County Health Department.

This department was organised on July 1, 1920. ..... The personnel, at that time, consisted of Dr. Roy P. Finney, County Physician, and Miss. Theresa Leightsey, County Nurse, and Jacob R. Wise, Sanitarian, and Miss. Julia Johnstone, Clerk and Secretary. At that time there were many cases of typhoid fever, with many deaths in the county. On July 1, 1921, Dr. Finney resigned and entered general practice at Gaffney, S. C.

Dr. Kneece was elected County Health Physician, and remained one year, resigning to accept work in the Canal Zone. He was succeeded by Dr. Paul E. Knotts, formerly health officer at Orangeburg, S. C. On April 1, 1924, Dr. Knotts resigned to enter the field of private practice at Denton, Maryland. Dr. H. G. Callison was appointed Director in his place.

On January 1, 1930, funds became available for the employment of a Clerk-Secretary, in which position Miss. Bennetta Dorrity (Mrs. Alan Johnstone, third,) worked for two years.

On June 1st, 1932, Dr. Callison resigned to accept a similar position with the Richmond County Health Department and the City of Augusta, Georgia. Dr. Hugh B. Senn was made Director, being transferred from Beaufort, S. C. Dr. Senn resigned January 1st, 1934, to enter the field of private practice of medicine, in Newberry.

On July 1, 1934, Dr. J. C. Sease, the present Director, was appointed to fill this position. Dr. Sease had previously practiced medicine at Little Mountain, Newberry County, for eighteen years. On August 15, 1934, through funds provided by the Federal Government, the department was enlarged, and Miss. Pauline Willingham was assigned as a nurse in the health unit. Other nurses were assigned at different times after miss. Willingham resigned.

By an Act of the State Legislature on January 1, 1939, the County Health Department and the City Health Department were combined. R. D. Bradley was assigned as City Sanitary Inspector under this new system; but he held the position only a short time, succeeded by others at different times.

The present personnel includes Miss. Theresa Leightsey, County Nurse and State Health Dept. Nurse, Jacob R. Wise, Secretary and Sanitarian, with Dr. J. C. Seaso, as physician. Miss. Leightsey and Jacob Wise have been with the office since it started.

Newberry County Hospital.

The Newberry County Hospital is located about one mile East of Newberry Court House, facing Hunt Street, and the land on which it is built extending to Kinard Street, thence to Mayer Avenue. There are two buildings, the main hospital and the nurses home; but just recently, a new building has been constructed for the colored people. The main building was erected in 1925. The architect was J. C. Hemphill, of Greenwood, S. C., and the contractor was W. T. Livingstone, of Newberry. .... The electric equipment was isntalled by the Webb Electric Company, of Anderson, S. C. The plumbing and heating by A. F. Bush, of Newberry.

The site covers three and one-third acres land that was bought from Olin B. Cannon, of Newberry.

The main building is a two-story brick structure. It has a cement terrace in front, extending the width of the building; high roof, with squared ends near top, similar to much of the early American architecture.

The entrance to the hall shows an office on the right, and the left a reception room, which leads into a long hall. On the first floor are two operating rooms. The main operating room is completely equipped with all modern fixtures and furnishings, which were donated by Captain W. Smith Langford, of Newberry (now of Wicita Falls, Texas), as a memorial to the members of his company in the Spanish-American war, the names of whom are on a large bronz tablet over the door of the room. Each door on this floor has a small bronz tablet on it, given by local organizations as memorial, who gave all the furnishings and equipment in the room. Some of these organizations are: Jasper Chapter, D. A. R., Drayton Rutherford Chapter, U. D. C., Newberry Commndary, No. 5, (in memory of the late George S, Mower, Esq.), and Mr. and Mrs. Walter B. Wallace (in memory of their infant daughter, May Reid Wallace). On this floor are, in addition to the two operating rooms, the nursery, childrens' ward, obstretics department, sterilizing room, and the delivery room.

On the second floor are two wards, with twenty five or more beds; also, the X-ray room, the utility room, a diet kitchen(one also on the first floor), a chart room, and a sun-porch. The bronz tablets on the doors of these rooms are represented by the following organizations: J. F. J. Caldwell Chapter, Children of the Confederacy; all U. D. C. Chapters of Newberry; Winthrop Daughters; Newberry College Co-Eds; Signet Chapter, No. 16, R. A. M., (in memory of Curtis Burr Martin). The Mary Frances Wright room, the Elizabeth Bacon McCollough room, the Calvin Crozier Chapter, U. D. C., the American Legion, and the Kiwanis Club.

At the first meeting of the organizers, held December 11, 1928, the following were elected members of the Board of Directors: George B. Cromer, S. J. Derrick, W. H. Hunt, John M. Kinard, B. C. Matthews, George W. Summer, Z. F. Wright, Mrs. Henry L. Parr, and Mrs. R. H. Wright. The Board elected the following officers the same day: President, Dr. George B. Cromer; Vice-President, Z. F. Wright; Treasurer, B. C. Matthews; Assistant Treasurer, Mrs. R. N. Bryson. The terms of the members of the Board were made rotating, three expiring each year; the first being determined by drawing slips.

A charter was granted December 27, 1923, with a Capital Stock of $80,000.00............. The first Medical Advisory Board included Dr. W. G. Houseal, Dr. James M. Kibler, Dr. Thomas H. Pope, Dr. Frank D. Mower, and Dr. Robert L. Mayes. The Medical Department included all physicians in the city and county, members of the Newberry County Medical Society, in good standing. Also, the charter included the establishment of a training school for nurses.

The hospital is operated strictly as an eleemosynary institution, the capital stock having been turned in by the stockholders; a community or public service enterprise, though self-supporting; any surplus revenues to be used in buying new equipment, and meeting other expenses.

In 1945 the following were Directors and Officers: George K. Dominick, Chairman; Dr. S. J. Derrick, Vice-Chairman; J. L. Keitt, Treasurer; Z. F. Wright, A. W. Murray, E. S. Rlease, E. A. Carpenter, Mrs. J. N. McCaughrin, Mrs. R. H. Wright, Jacob R. Wise, Secretary.

In 1948, D. O. Carpenter was elected on the Board in place of E. A. Carpenter; and A. W Murray was made Vice-Chairman in place of Dr. S. J. Derrick who died in that year.

Libraries.

Newberry College Library—

The library is located in the top floor of Keller Memorial Hall, on the College campus. It occupies the entire top floor. In it's collections of books and papers, it includes all the popular classics, histories, old and new; State, County, Church histories; biographies. Among them are The Oxford-English Dictionary, Encyclepedia Brittanica, new edition; The American Encyclopedia, new edition; The New International Encyclopedia, new edition; The Dictionary of American Biography; The Cambridge Modern History; The Cambridge History of English Literature; The Cambridge History of American Literature; and many others, including all of the old and modern histories of the County and State and of other Counties; also, works on genealogical history. There are many old newspapers, and other old papers.

Miss. Carolyn Cromer is the Librarian, who has been with the library many years. She is a daughter of the late Dr. George B. Cromer, one-time President of the college.   Mrs. S. J. Derrick, (widow of the late Dr. S. J. Derrick) is the Assistant Librarian.

Newberry County Library—

This library is located in the first floor of the old court house building. It was organized by the local Womens' Club. The following sketch regarding it's organization is taken from the Newberry Observer, April, 1938: " On the afternoon of February 10, 1904, by invitation of the Womans Club of Newberry, forty ladies assembled in the parlors of Central Methodist Church, to meet Mrs. Martha Orr Patterson, then President of the State Federation of Women's Clubs, and to hear her speak on the subject of club work, especially that phase of it pertaining to libraries.

" At the conclusion of Mrs. Matterson's address a Library Association was temporarily organized, with Mrs. J. E. Norwood, as Chairman Pro Tem.

" A Constitution Committee composed of Mrs. O. B. Mayer, Mrs. S. B. Jones, and Mrs. R. D. Wright, was appounted to draft a constitution and by-laws to be submitted to the next meeting to be held on March 8th." The following officers were elected: President, Mrs. J. E. Norwood; Vice-President, Mrs. W. H. Hunt; Secretary, Mrs. R. D. Wright; Treasurer, Miss. Helen Mower (later Mrs. F. N. Martin).

The first home of the library was a large room on the second floor of the building then owned by Hon. George S. Mower, (now Carpenter's Store).

The library at first was supported by private subscriptions and with some aid from the town. Among the first Librarians were, Mrs. W. E. Belcher, Miss. Gertrude Carwile, and Miss. Alice Hornsby.

When the library had outgrown the room it was occupying, above Mower's Store, the County Commissioners agreed to the request of the Association for the use of two lower rooms on the left of the old court house building; but having use for only one at that time, the other was given over to the Chamber of Commerce. Miss. Lois Fant was Librarian here several years.

Under the Works Projects Administration, many old books were reconditioned.

The number of books has gradually increased so that at this time it is well-filled, and occupying three rooms.

Some of the other women who served the Association in the past , as President, were: Mrs. O. McR. Holmes, Mrs. A. T. Brown, and Mrs. R. D. Wright.

Literary.

Early Publications in Newberry—

" The Mirror", a weekly newspaper, was established in Newberry in 1853 by Joseph S. Reid, publisher and editor. In 1854 Mr. Reid made the paper a tri-weekly; and a year after, Gen. A. C. Garlington was appointed Associate Editor. In 1856 "The Mirror" was sold to William F. Nance and John C. McLemore, the name of the paper being then changed to "The Conservatist."

In most of the early newspapers nothing much of human interest is seen printed. They had articles of a general nature, pertaining to current events of a political nature, with some personals, and frequently copied events that occured in distant States or larger towns.

There seems to have been an attempt at some earlier time to operate a newspaper in Newberry. In 1849 the Newberry Sentinental had it's inception; but operated a short time. In 1852 came the "Weekly Newberrian"; in 1853 the "Mirror"; in 1858 the "Rising Sun"; in 1856 the "Conservatist"; in 1865 the " Newberry Herald". All were short-lived, except the " Herald". In 1873 the " Progressive Age" started, but lasted a short time. In 1878 the " Newberry News" was established, which was sometime later consolidated with the " Newberry Herald" and was known as the " Newberry Herald and News".

The "Lutheran Visitor" was started in Prosperity in 1880, and was moved to Newberry in 1881. In 1885 the " Reporter" started in Prosperity, which was in 1886 changed to the " Press and Reporter", published at Prosperity a short time, closing down.

The " Newberry Observer" was established in 1883 by the late William H. Waalace, of Newberry, the Editor and Publisher. Mr. Wallace was Publisher and Editor for many years, until his death; having kept up with his paper during the time he was Superintendent of the City Schools.

A small paper called " The Midget" was operated in Newberry in 1920, for about three months.

Newberry College published " The Stylus" about 1900-1915; later it was stopped, and then the " Newberry College Indian" was started.

Authors of Newberry—native or resident—

John B. O'Neall, author of the " Annals of Newberry", Part 1, " The Bench and Bar of S. C.", and other works.

John A. Chapman, Esq., whose works were Part 11 of the " Annals of Newberry", " A School History of South Carolina", and a Book of Poems.

James Wood Davidson, (died in Florida in 1905), whose works were: " Living Writers of the South", " History of South Carolina", " Dictionary of Southern Authors"; and several articles in daily papers and magazines.

James F. J. Caldwell, author of " History of McGowans Brigade", and several contributions to papers and magazines.

Duncan D. Wallace, author of " History of South Carolina," " Constitutional History of South Carolina"; also, articles in daily papers and magazines.

David Augustus Dickart, who wrote the " History of Kershaw's Brigade".

Howard H. Caldwell (died at Columbia, S. C.), wrote many poems and other articles in papers and author of " Poems-Oilatts and Other Poems".

John B. Carwile, who was author of " Reminiscences of Newberry".

James Henry Hammond, author of " Cotton is King", and other short sketches. He died near Augusta, Ga., at "Radcliffe."

James A. B. Scherer, (born in Virginia), was President of Newberry College, died in California; was author of " Japan To-day", " Young Japan," " Four Princes" " The Holy Grail", " Japan, Whither?" " The Japanese Crisis", " The Nation at War", " The First Niner", " The Romance of Japan". He wrote other sketches in daily papers and magazines.

Vivian M. Moses, lived at Sumter, S. C., author of poems.

Dr. O. B. Mayer, Sr., some of his works were: " Malladoce, the Briton; his Wanderings from Druidism to Christianity," " The Music Girl of The Silhouette,"and others, including several historical sketches in daily papers and church papers.

Rev William L. Seabrook (born in Virginia), pastor of the Lutheran Church of the Redeemer, of Newberry, was the author of " Immortality".

Rev. Thomas Frean, (born in Ireland), died in Newberry, was author of " Ten Years in The Treasury".

Miss. Mary Fowles, author of " The Golden Fence", " The Sequence of Songs", A Heroes Last Days". (Fiction).

Mrs. L. M. Sale, author of a novel entitled, " The Saddest of All is Loving".
Paul Johnstone, author of law manuals, " Equity Digest."
William B. Seabrook (born in Virginia), author of works, " Adventures in Arabia", " The Magic Island", " Jungle Ways", " Air Adventure", " The White Monk of Timbuctoo", and " Asylum".
Dr. James P. Kinard(born in Newberry) was author of " Old English Ballads", " English Language and Literature", " Our Language", " English Grammar for Beginners", and other sketches.
Rev. Paul Scherer (born in Virginia) died in California. He was author of " When God Hides", a book of sermons.
Dr. Hugh Huger Toland, (died in California), was the author of ".Works Pertaining to Surgery", in pamphlet form.
Edwin Boinest Setzler, of Newberry College, was author of " Notes on English Grammar", " On Anglo-Saxon Versification".
Other authors and writers who have been contributors to daily papers and magazines were: John Kinard Aull, (he died in Columbia, S. C.), who was born in Newberry; William P. Houseal, born in Newberry and died in Columbia, S. C.; George Leland Summer, of Newberry; Miss. Blanche Davidson, of Newberry.

Art and Music in Newberry.

Early Musical Organizations—

Musical organizations in Newberry before the War Between The States included, primarily, the Philharmonic Society. Among it's concerts in that day were many popular numbers of the time. It was organized in what was then known as the Simeon Pratt Hall. Some of it's concerts were given in Thespian Hall, where, too, many celebrated musicians performed.
One of the great violinists of his day, Signor Jos. Borra, was a performer there in 1854, when he gave a new style imitation of all kinds of animals upon his violin; also, the grand Julien Waltz, and several other numbers.
Here, also, appeared many dramatists of that day in popular stage plays, including some Shakespeare's plays.

The Newberry Music Club—

This club was organized in 1923 under the direction of Maurice Mattison, of Columbia, S. C. The charter members were: Mrs. Ben Anderson, Miss. Goode Burton,(now Mrs. Brice Waters), Miss. Maizie Dominick, Miss. Janett Freed, Gus Houseal, Miss. Juanita Hitt, Miss. Julia Johnstone, Miss. Marion Jones (now Mrs. H. B. Wilson), Miss. Julia Kibler, Miss. Teresa Maybin (now Mrs. H. W. Boozer), Miss. Vivian McNeill (now Mrs. Fred Gilbert), Dr. John B. Setzler, Miss. Carobel West (now Mrs. Clem Youmans), Miss. Marion Jones was elected President at the first meeting held June 8, 1923.
Since the club's organization , several have served as President, including, in addition to Miss. Marion Jones (Mrs. Wilson), the following: Miss. Julia Kibler, Miss. Juanita Hitt, Miss. Margaret Farrow, Mrs. P. K. Harmon, Mrs. J. D. French, Mrs. Henry T. Fellers, Miss. Rose Hamm, Mrs. Paul Ensrud, and others.
Several public concerts have been given by the club, under the direction of Miss. Maizie Dominick and Miss. Frances Jones. In 1927 music memory contests were give in the City Schools.under the direction of Miss. Rose Hamm, who was the Director of Music in the City Schools and a member of the club. In 1928 a lyceum course was sponsored at Newberry College with the help of the club.
The South Carolina Federation of Music Clubs met in Convention at Newberry in 1935, as guest of the local Club. Miss. Mary Frances Jones was elected Second Vice-President of the State Federation; she has been, also, contest chairman, student advisor, and junior counselor.
Some of the other music clubs in Newberry are the following: Newberry College Singers, The Junior Music Club, Newberry College Music Club, Newberry High School Glee Club, and the Newberry Textile Mills Band.

Some of the Music Teachers or Studio Directors in Newberry are : Miss. Pawnee Jones, Mrs. Hal Kohn, Sr.(Verna Summer), Mrs. Harry McDonald (Hattie Leavell), Mrs. J. P. Moon, Miss. Vivian Ellis, Miss. Mary Frances Jones, Mrs. J. W. Haltiwanger(Susie Summer), she later moving to Columbia, S. C.

Art-Portrait Painters —
The earliest known portrait painter who lived in Newberry was C. H. Kingsmore. He painted the portrait of Judge Butler, which was shown at the State Fair held at Charleston, S. C. Albert Guerry who opened a studio at Newberry, at the Newberry Hotel, during the early part of the last century, painted the portrait of well known and prominent people of his day; among them were, Dr. J. W. Butler, P. W. Chick, Duane Mower, William W. Rice, Col. W. D. Rutherford, Gen. Martin Gary, and others. The portrait of Gen. Gary was presented to the State General Assembly and hangs in the hall of the House of Representatives in Columbia.

Williams Welch, an artist of ability, produced many portraits; but he was best known for his general sketches. He was born and reared in Newberry, a brother of Mrs. R. D. Wright of Newberry.

Theaters—
The Newberry Opera House was once a popular place for stage drama and other plays. It is located on a lot at the corner of Boyce and Nance Streets, which was once owned by a tavern keeper; then bought by John R. Leavell who operated the tavern awhile, then sold the lot for the Opera House building. Mr. Leavell's home was just behind the building, facing Boyce Street.

The Opera House was erected by Contractors, Wells and Cline; Mr. Cline having the construction contract while Mr. Wells did the brick work. This was in 1881; the dedication ceremonies of the building being held February 20, 1882. At this time, a German linguist, Dr. Jaegar, the Professor of Music at the Newberry Female Academy, wrote a poem describing the building. Dr. Jaegar was later head of the Music Department of the old Cokesbury Institute (then called Academy), and of the Laurens Female College.

The style of the Opera House building is Gothic in design, with it's tall steeple and wide gable on the front side. The parcade is sloping; the balcony wide and sloping.

Prior to it's erection the Thespian Club (1876-1881) gave shows in the rooms of the second story of the building at corner of Boyce and Caldwell Streets(now occupied by G. B. Summer & Sons). Here were many high-class shows during theatrical seasons. The Ethiopian Troup gave productions here (1870-71); and were said to have been members of the Ku Klux Klan with their faces blackened.

The Opera House before the advent of motion pictures was the scene of many high class dramas and musical comedies, and the old minstrel shows. It is now used exclusively for motion pictures, since larger auditoriums have been built in the city.

Ritz Theater— located on Main Street, is a large structure of gray stone blocks. The front entrance has a shed with the usual lights and electric signs. In the center of this entrance is small ticket office . From the front entrance to two double doors leading into a wide vestibule, then to the lobby, shows the entire interior to be covered with large soft rugs On each side of the lobby is an open entrance to the auditorium, with it's sloping floors that lead to the stage.   At right of the lobby is a mens' dressing room and at the left a ladies's dressing room.

R. T. Albrecht is Manager and William Darby is Assistant Manager.

Wells' Theater—located on Main Street, South side from the old Court House building. There H. B. Wells, Sr. owned and operated the theater at the Opera House for many years, and after his death it was taken over by his widow and son, W. Fulmer Wells. Later, they built the new theater on Main Street.

The theater has an open entrance on the right side of which is the cashier's office. Two swinging doors lead into the lobby which extends the width of the building; with a door at each side leading into the auditorium; with gradually sloping floors to the stage. Soft rugs cover the floors . The Ladies dressing room is on the left, and the mens' dressing room upstairs. There are two entrances to the balcony, one on the outside of the building, the other in the lobby.

Drive-In Theater— located about two miles from the Court House, started about 1947, by R. K. Brown, a native of Alabama, and who married a Newberry girl, Miss. Rook Purcell. It is well constructed, with ample room for automobiles.

NEWBERRY COMPANIES IN SPANISH-AMERICAN WAR.

Company B, First Regiment—
William Smith Langford, Captain; Richard H. Wearn, First Lieutenant; Thomas O. Stewart, Jr., Second Lieutenant; George F. Wearn, First Sargeant; George F. Smith, QM Sargeant; Alonzo J. Cook, Sargeant; George P. Boulware, Sargeant; John F. Langston, Sargeant (from Clifton); William E. Blats, Sargeant; Milton C. Lancaster, Corporal (from Clifton); David E. Sheppard, Corporal (from Colemans); Robert Norris, Corporal; John H. Davis, Corporal (from Swain); William W. Farrow, Corporal. (from Greenwood); Richard J. Fuller, Corporal; John P. Cannon, Corporal (from Prosperity); Lany Wood, Corporal (from Milleys); Silas L. Medlock, Corporal (from Poverty Hill); John A. Foster, Corporal (from Brannon); Earle Sanders, Corporal (from Cowpens); Andrew J. Kilgore, Corporal(from Tacoma Park); Charles P. Mims, Pvt.(Clifton); William B. Werts, Pvt.; Casper C. Stewart, Pvt.; John E. Outz, Pvt.;John W. Abrams, Pvt. (from Whitmire); Walter Allen, Pvt.(from Pelzer); William M. Best, Pvt. (Whitney, N. C.); John A. Blats, Pvt. ; Middleton S. Bodie, Pvt.; Joseph E. Boyd, Pvt. (Clinton); Alsa D. Brown, Pvt. (Clifton); John L. Brown, Pvt. (Clinton); John H. Bruce, Pvt. (Spartanburg); Walter B. Bullington, Pvt. (Clifton); John O. Bright, Pvt. (Spartanburg); Ed. R. Caldwell, Pvt.(Clifton); Jeff D. Chapman, Pvt. ; Robert T. Cockerel, Pvt.; Joseph B. Cooley, Pvt.(Columbia); Charles O. Cannon, Pvt. (from Ellis); John P. Cannon, Pvt. (Prosperity); James M. Cassidy, Pvt.; John D. Cooley, Pvt.(Clifton); William O. Copeland, Pvt. (Clintpn); Charlton T. Cromer, Pvt.; Julius G. Daniels, Pvt.; Edward A. Davis, Pvt.(Hickory, N.C.); Robert R. Dawson, Pvt.(Clinton); Jesse L. Denson, Pvt.; John E. Dreher, Pvt. (Selwood); Joseph L. Edwards, Pvt. (Colemans); George C. Ezell, Pvt.(Cowpens); Robert Finger, Pvt.; Levi E. Folk, Pvt.; Thomas N. Folk, Pvt; Rowland H. Garrison, Pvt. (Clifton); Jesse T. George, Pvt. (Spartanburg); Frank P. Gray, Pvt. (Atlanta, Ga.); John E. Griffith, Pvt.(Saluda); Elijah S. Grise, Pvt. (Spartanburg); Henry H. Hinson, Pvt.; Malcom B. Hipp, Pvt. (Whitmire); Clayton F. Holmes, Pvt. (Clifton); James E. Hopper, Pvt. (Spartanburg); Pope Duncan Johnson, Pvt. (Jalapa); Joseph H. Keith, Pvt.(Bath); David V. Kirkpatrick, Pvt. (Union); William T. Livingstone, Pvt. ; James J. Longshore, Pvt. (Mudlic); Lois S. Lovelace, Pvt.; James S. Lyons, Pvt.(Clifton); Clarence E. Matthews, Pvt. (Saluda); John Mayer, Pvt. (Peak); Samuel P. McCarty, Pvt.; Thomas S. Mitchell, Pvt. (Dennys); George Moore, Pvt.; James W. Nelson, Pvt. (Clinton); John C. Nicholson, Pvt. (Harridsville); Samuel H. Paysinger, Pvt.; Vance V. Pearsoll, Pvt.;Thomas J. Pearson, Pvt. (Clinton); Samuel D. Potter, Pvt. (Spartanburg); Eddie P. Redish, Pvt.(Williams); Ernest M. Reeder, Pvt.(Chas.); William C. Reeder, Pvt. ; Richard L. Roberts, Pvt. (Bridgeton); Thomas M. Roebuck, Pvt.; William M. Roberson, Pvt. (Union);Aumerle Schumpert, Pvt.; Henry L. Simmons, Pvt.; Edwin B. Sligh, Pvt.;Theodore Spehl, Pvt.; George B. Suber, Pvt. (Pomaria); Thomas W. Swindler, Pvt.; William O. Swindler, Pvt.; William A. Tilson, Pvt. (Pacolet); Jefferson Tribble, Pvt.; George Wall, Pvt. (Spartanburg); Miles A. Wallace, Pvt.; James K. Weeks, Pvt.; Thomas Griff Williams, Pvt.(Helena); Carleton Williams, Pvt. (Anderson); William B. Wise, Pvt. (Prosperity); William S. Wix, Pvt. (Whitney); William P. Yarborugh, Pvt. (Dennys); Perry M. Martin, Pvt. (Clinton); Thomas C. McGahee, Pvt. (Augusta, Ga.); Marvin Yeargin, Pvt. (Laurens); Miles Stevenson, Pvt. (Spartanburg); Robert A. Morrison, Pvt. (Chester); John A. McCafferty, Pvt. (Spartanburg); Harry T. White, Pvt. ; Herbert Hughes, Pvt. (Peak); John M. Kinard, Pvt.; Robert Aldridge, Pvt.; Frank J. Clapp, Pvt.; Andrew T. McGee, Pvt. (Clifton); James L. Henderson, Pvt. (Spartanburg); Zack. R. Henderson, Pvt. (Spartanburg);Herbert A. Ross, Pvt. (Spartanburg);

Company G, Second Regiment—

Silas J. McCaughrin, Captain; Edwin C. Horton, First Lieutenant(Clinton); Robert F. Dukes, Second Lieutenant,(Branchville); Caldwell E. Fant, First Sargeant; George S. Noland, QM Sargeant; Harman P. Aull, Sargeant; Andrew B. Stoudemire, Sargeant,(Peak); George H. Ballentine, Sargeant, (Laurens); William J. Miller, Sargeant, (Newberry); Leonard B. Cummings, Corporal,(Oswego); George F. Turner, Corporal; Oillie O. Eargle, Corporal (Peak); Jackson J. Abrams, Corporal, (Whitmire); Snyder J. Parrott, Corporal (Clinton); Wilbur C. Hipp, Corporal, (Pomaria); Robert L. Kiblera Pvt.; Watson M. Connor, Pvt. (Branchville); William J. Sloan, Pvt. (Laurens); James N. Sligh, Pvt.; James S. Chalmers, Pvt.; Kemble P. Bailey, Pvt. (Laurens); Arthur J. Bair, Pvt.(Branchville); John J. Barrs, Pvt. (Branchville); William A. Barrs, Pvt. (Branchville); William A. Boyd, Pvt. (Laurens); Elmore G. Bramlett, Pvt. (Laurens); Charles H. Broughton, Pvt.; Frank J. Byrd, Pvt. (Branchville); Samuel B. Cauble, Pvt. (Salisbury, N. C.); Kisler Collins, Pvt. (Branchville); Julius J. Connelly, Pvt. (Branchville);John C. Connor, Pvt. (Clinton); George B. Cook, Pvt. (Prosperity); John Davis, Pvt.; Ransom DeWitt, Pvt. (Branchville); William DeWitt, Pvt. (Branchville); William D. Divver, Pvt. (Helena); Frank W. Fant, Pvt.; Claude P. Finley, Pvt. (Madden); Giff H. Finley, Pvt. (Madden); John L. Finley, Pvt. (Madden); James Flake, Pvt. (Orangeburg); John D. Glynn, Pvt. (Clinton); William M. Glynn, Pvt. (Clinton); Edward Groves, Pvt. (Clinton); Arthur Haney, Pvt. (Winston, N.C.); Patrick H. Hargrove, Pvt.; James F. Hinton, Pvt. (Lykesland); Armand P. Hinton, Pvt.; William Huiett, Pvt.; William O. Jordan, Pvt.(Clinton); David Malone, Pvt. (Laurens); William D. Maybin, Pvt. (Maybinton); Madison D. Milam, Pvt. (Clinton); James G. Miller, Pvt.; William McGravey, Pvt. (Laurens); George A. McKinney, Pvt. (Spartanburg); Leon M. Myers, Pvt. (Branchville); Henry Pitts, Pvt. (Laurens); Ford Roper, Pvt. (Laurens); Owens P. Saxon, Pvt.; William J. Smith, Pvt.; Hugo S. Spehl, Pvt. (Branchville); George J. Spotts, Pvt.; Edgar W. Teague, Pvt. (Laurens); John H. Todd, Pvt.; James R. Tucker, Pvt. (Clinton);Thomas F. Turner, Pvt. (Clinton); James A. Watson, Pvt.(Branchville); James B. Watson, Pvt. (Branchville); Thomas H. Watson, Pvt. (Branchville); Hugo W. Weathers, Pvt. (Branchville); John H. Whitsell, Pvt. (Branchville); George J. Wilson, Pvt. (Newark); James M. Wilson, Pvt. (Branchville); Thomas Woodall, Pvt. (C;inton); Walter A. Syfrett, Pvt. (Reevesville); John L. Goff, Pvt. (Wilkesborough, N. C.); Charles E. Glenn, Pvt. (Clinton); James W. Hawkins, Pvt. (Pleasant); Morgan T. Mooney, Sgt.(Branchville); Jasper Ulmer, Pvt. (Elloree); Dugan Hargrove, Pvt. (Laurens); Abe Pearlstine, Corporal, (Branchville).

EDUCATION

Newberry County Education Association—1947-48-
James D. Brown, County Superintendent of Education.
Mrs. Mae E. Aull, Secretary to Superintendent of Education.
Mrs. Sudie Crump Wicker, County Attendance Teacher.
Mrs. Ruth Longshore, County Lunch Room Supervisor.
Mrs. Catherine Hawkins, Secretary to Lunch Room Supervisor.
Members of the County Board of Education: Thomas E. Epting, R. C. Lake, James D. Brown.
General Officers: Mrs. Mary E. K. Griffith, President; F. P. Hill, Vice-President;
Mrs. J. W. Lominack, Jr., Secretary.
County Teachers: Newberry High School, No. 1, Newberry, S. C.—P. K. Harmon, Supt.;
J. V. Kneece, Prin., D.O., Math.; Mrs. Carl Amick, Home Ec.; Miss. Myra Boozer, Lib.;
George P. Boozer, Hist., Sci., Phy. Training; Miss. Mittie Bryan, Home Ec., Sci.; Miss. Louise Buzhardt, Eng.; Mrs. John W. Clark, Eng., Glee Club; Miss. Sudie Dennis, Math.; Harry Hedgepath, Coach, Phy.Training; Miss. Claire Henry, Sci.; Mrs. Venessa Holt, Math.; Miss. Dorothy Lee, Biol., Phy. Training; Miss. Julia Kibler, Latin, French; Mrs. J. V. Kneece, Eng.; Mrs. P. M. Nichols, Social Science; Miss. Margaret Paysinger, Eng.; B. H. Phillips, Metal Work; Mrs. Julia M. Tindall, Math.; Social Sci.; E. E. Westwood, Ind. Art; Mrs. H. B. Wilson, Math., Bkp.; Charles E. Bowers, Spanish.
Junior High School—B. L. Frick, Prin.; Mrs. Arlie Johnson, V11; Mrs. Georgia H. Welborn, V11;
Mrs. Elise P. Bowler, V11; Mrs. Nina G. Brown, V1; Mrs. Elizabeth R. Graham, V1; Mrs. G. L. Summer, V1; Miss. Georgia Porter, V1; Miss. Bertha Gray Gallman, Lib.
Boundary Street School—Miss. Gertrude Reeder, Prin., 1; Miss. Lila Summer, 11; Miss. Ruth Feagle, 111; Mrs. Ruby R. Abrams, 1V; Miss. Sarah Boozer, V; Mrs. Naomi Epting, V; Mrs. Eva F. Bullock, Lib.
Speers Street School—Miss. Ethel Jones, Prin.,111; Mrs. Beale H. Cromer, 1; Miss. Annie Abrams, 11; Miss. Rosabel Thompson, 1V; Miss. Juanita Hitt, V; Mrs. Gloria A. Parks, V.
Mollohon School—Miss. Sarah Caldwell, Prin.,1V; Mrs. J. Frank Browne, 1; Miss. Carolyn Lane, 11; Miss. Lucile Eleazer, 111.
West End School—Mrs. F. R. Fellers, Prin., 1; Mrs. Maude Matthews,11; Mrs. C. W. Sanders, 111; Mrs. Josie O. McAlhany, 1V.
Oakland School—Mrs. Bertha D. Boylston, Prin., 1V; Miss. Helen Nichols, 1; Miss. Katie Shealy, 11, 111.
Mt. Bethel-Germany, Dist. No. 2, Newberry County—Mrs. Marie F. Mills, Prin., 1, 11, 111, 1V; Mrs. Evelyn S. Langford, V, V1, V11.
Long Lane, Dist. No. 4—Miss. Aurelia Mayer, Prin., 1V-V11; Mrs. Gladys T. Haile, 1,11,111.
McCollough, Dist. No. 5, Whitmire—Mrs. John Riser, 1, 11, 111, 1V, V, V1, V11.
Hartford, Dist., No. 11—Mrs. Elizabeth P. Fulmer, Prin., 1V, V, V1, V11; Mrs. Richard McWhirter, 1, 11, 111.
Johnstone, Dist. No. 12—Mrs. Annie M. S. Cromer, Prin., V, V1, V11; Mrs. Kate N. Wilson, 1, 11, 111, 1V.
Stoney Hill, Dist. No. 13, Prosperity, S. C.—R. H. Amick, Supt.,Math; B. A. Long, Agri.; Mrs. J. W. Lominack, Jr., Eng., Soc. Sci.; Mrs. Sudie Wicker, Eng. and Sci.; Charles E. Wise, V, V1; Miss. Myrtice Lee Counts, 111, 1V; Miss. Rosa Dreher, 1, 11.
Prosperity, Dist. No. 14, Prosperity—F. P. Hill, Supt.; Sci.; H. B. Hendrix, Agri.; R. M. Monts, Sr., Math. and Sci.; Grady Lee Halfacre, Social Sci.; Mrs. Willie Mae Young, Eng., Tch.-Lib.; Mrs. Lucile Hancock, Math and Fr.; Miss. Edith Dill, Home Ec.; Miss. Rosalie Wheeler, Comm. and Eng.; Miss. Mary Langford, V1; Mrs. Nan B. Hill, V; Mrs. Annette Brooks, 1V; Miss. Clara Brown,111; Miss. Susie Langford,11; Mrs. Julia Wessinger, 1.
O'Neall, Dist. No. 15, Prosperity—W. R. Lominick, Prin., V1, V11; Mrs. Isadore Ruff, 111, 1V, V; Mrs. Gladys H. Hipp, 1, 11.
Fairview, Dist. No. 18, Prosperity—Mrs. Elberta W. Pugh, 1, 11, 111, 1V.
St. Phillips, Dist. No. 22—Mrs. Nina Cromer Price, Prin., V1, V11; Miss. Martha C. Bouknight, 111, 1V;V; Mrs. Frances K. Harmon, 1, 11: Mrs. Sara B. Rucker, Piano.

Pomaria, Dist. No. 26, Pomaria, S. C.—R. H. Setzler, Supt., Math.; G. S. Glymph, Agri.; Mrs. Marvin Rucker, Music; Mrs. Fred Gilbert, Home Ec. and Sci.; Miss. Juanita Felker, Eng.; Miss. Mary Elizabeth C. Koon, Comm. and Geo.; Mrs. Jennie Byrd Hentz, Hist., Sci., Eng.; Mrs. Martha Hatton Dominick, Vl; Mrs. Mary Hentz Britton, lV, V; Mrs. Elizabeth Sease Lominick, lll; Miss. Julia Kate Sease, ll; Mrs. Marie Summer Huggins, l.

Little Mountain, Dist. No. 30, Little Mountain, S. C.—Rev. E. B. Heidt, Supt., Math., Chem.; C. S. Glymph, Agri.; Miss. Lucile Derrick, Fr., Wng., Tchr. Lib.; Mrs. Elizabeth Crowell, Social Science; Miss. Stella Wessinger, Music; Miss. Eula Epting, l, ll; Miss. Myrtle Matthews, lll, lV; Mrs. B. M. Wise, V, Vl; F. E. Metts, Vll.

Chappells, Dist. No. 39, Chappells, S. C.—Miss. Lillie Mae Workman, Prin., V, Vl, Vll; Mrs. Irene D. Parnell, lll, lV; Mrs. Rebecca S. Boozer, l, ll.

Bush River, Dist. No. 43—J. H. Bedenbaugh, Supt., Math., Hist.; S. P. Harris, Agri.; Otis N. Gibson, Math. Hist,; Mrs. Margaret Stone, Comm., Sci.; Mrs. J. E. Kinard, Home Ec., Sci.; Mrs. George P. Boozer, Eng.; Miss. Bera Glenn, Vl; Mrs. Grace H. Bedenbaugh, V; Mrs. Edna W. Ringer, lV; Mrs. Mildred L. Fulmer, lll; Mrs. Edith Walker, ll; Miss. Jessie Mary Derrick, l; Mrs. Louise C. Appling, Music.

Kinards, Dist. No. 49, Kinards, S. C.—Miss. Ola Mae Miller, Prin., l-Vll.

Silver Street, Dist. No. 58, Silver Street, S. C.—J. G. Long, Supt., Math., Bus. Sci.; L. B. Bedenbaugh, Agri.; Mrs. Mary E. Griffith, Eng., Hist.; Mrs. Harriett H. Sligh, Home Ec., Chem.; Miss. Bessie Campbell, Comm., Sci.; Miss. Clifford Coleman, Vl, Vll; Miss. Ruth Martin, lll, lV; Miss. Sara Folk, ll, lV; Mrs. Mattie L. W. Blackmon, l, lV; Mrs. Mary B. Coleman, V, Vll.

Whitmire, Dist. No. 52, Whitmire, S. C.—High School—R. C. Lake, Supt.; Woodrow Dixon, Sci.; Miss. Jeanette Tolbert, Biol., Comm.; Miss. Allene Hawthorne, Math., Chem.; Miss. Rebecca Liminack, Social Sci.; Miss. Eleanor Mayfield, Home Ec.; Miss. Gertrude Bell, Eng., Math., Health; Miss. Edna Frazier, Lib., Fr.; Miss. Frances Shealy, Eng., Latin.

Whitmire Elementary School—Miss. Pearl Stockman, Prin., Vll; Miss. Emmie Wright, Vll; Miss. Martha Creekmore, Vl; Miss. Virginia Dufford, Vl; Miss. Leonora Neel, Vl, Vll; Miss. Doris Mayer, lV, V; Miss. Marjorie Gossett, V; Miss. Rosa Payne, V; Miss. Julia Milam, lV; Miss. Garrie Wightman, lV; Miss. Rachel Neil, lll; Miss. Lucile Leslie, lll; Miss. Evelyn McGraw, ll; Miss. Mamie Lou Shealy, ll; Miss. Lila Kimbrell, l, ll; Miss. Lottie Cumalander, l; Miss. Mae Plumley, l; Miss. Elizabeth Weeks, Bible; Miss. Emmie Stewart, Public School Music.

Well known educators in Newberry in the past, some of whom were born and reared or lived in Newberry, and who did much to build up the educational system of the State, including a theory of education which had it's inception in Newberry—the study of the English language from original sources. They were: Dr. George W. Holland, D. D., Dr. James A. B. Scherer, D. D., Dr. John H. Harms, D. D., Dr. George B. Cromer, LL.D., Rev. Theophilus Stork, D. D., Rev. J. P. Smetzler, Dr. S. J. Derrick, LL.D., Dr. James C. Kinard, LL.D., Dr. James P. Kinard, LL.D., (former President of Winthrop College, Rick Hill, S. C.), Dr. Duncan D. Wallace, (formerly with the Dept. of History, Wofford College, Spartanburg, S. C.), Dr. E. B. Setzler, Litt. D., Ph. D., (formerly in the Dept. of English, Newberry College), the author of the new system of English study; and Dr. A. J. Bowers, Sr.(formerly with the Dept. of Anc. Languages, Newberry College), DR. A. G. Voight, D. D.(late Dean of the Southern Lutheran Theological Seminary, of Columbia, S. C.); Dr. C. A. Freed, D. D. (late President of the Southern Lutheran Theological Seminary, and former pastor of the Lutheran Church of the Redeemer of Newberry), Dr. Samuel P. Pressley, former President of the Newberry Female Academy, Dr. O. A. Busby, formerly Prof. at Newberry College, Dr. Julius D. Dreher, (formerly President of Roanoke College, Salem, Va.), Dr. Frank Evans, (late Supt. of Spartanburg City Schools, formerly Supt. of Newberry City Schools).

Earley Schools in the village and the county—

Prior to 1800 there is no record of any school, though there were a few private schools in parts of the county, including the village, usually taught by some person on his own account. He was known as the " school master". One tradition is that the first private school started about 1767, near King's Creek. Another was near Little River; and another about one-half mile from where is now the court house, on the road leading to Saluda.

First Village Academies-

The first academy building was a large two-story, frame structure, the first floor being used for school purposes and the upper floor for the Masonic Hall. The first floor, according to a statement by Silas Johnstone, was used, sometimes, for school plays, and was called "Thespian Hall" The great religous revival of 1830 disorganized the society and caused it's discontinuance; many of the Thespians becoming converted and joining the church, which was against some of the public plays and variety entertainments they had on the stage. Soon after the church revivals, and as one of the fruits of them, the Baptist Church was organized in Newberry and a church building erected.

Others who taught in this old academy were, Mr. McGuinnis, Rev. James W. Alexander, Samuel Pressley, Solomon Pope, John Pressley, and Jefferson Fair. In 1828 James Divver was the Master of the school. Henry Summer, a lawyer in Newberry, also taught there.

In 1834 the male academy (the section of the old school for boys) was transferred to a building on the ground where is now the jail building, and incorporated in that year with the following Trustees: John B. O'Neall, Major Frederick Nance, Job Johnstone, Y. J. Harrington, James Fernandez, Thomas Pratt, William Wilson, Esq., Burr Johnstone, and Francis B. Higgins.

The old building continued as the female school until a new building was put up about 1835-36, and was called the Female Academy. The first teacher was a Miss. Boyd, who was assisted by a Mrs. Saxon, the music teacher. In 1839 the female academy was moved to a house on Pratt Street (now known as Main Street), on Dr. Thompsons lot, and the building reconverted to the purposes of a male school under the charge of Rev. Wiley, an Episcopal minister.

Others who taught in the male school were Leonard Williams, James M. Baxter, James M. Crosson, Major George James, Jospeh S. Reid, William Hood, W. J. Duffie, and Thomas Duckett.

In 1870 a lot on the corner of Harrington Street and Crenshaw Street was bought and a new male academy was started. (This is the same house now used as a dwelling, next to the home of Miss. Mary Burton). The following taught in this school until the graded school system started in 1889,or a few years just prior to that time: James C. Hardin, William M. Brooks, R. H. Clarkson, James P. Kinard, John P. Glasgow, Miss. Willie Cozby.

The Female Academy continued in it's one-story building which was built before the War Between the States, on College Street—originally constructed with brick— located on College Street, across from where is now the Central Methodist Sunday School. The building has been renovated by Dr. W. G. Houseal who used it as a clinic until his death, and now used by his son, Dr. Robert W. Houseal.

Among the early teachers in this school were, William Berley, William Hood, Mrs. Susan Anderson, Capt. A. P. Pifer, and Miss. Octavia Garlington (she became later Mrs. Wm Y. Fair).

The names of pupils at the Female Academy under Capt A. P. Pifer, the Principal, during the years 1871-72-73, were: Jennie Anderson, Leila Blease, Corries Blease, Laura Blease, Mamie Barr, Lucy Baxter, Sue Boyle, Bessie Blease, Jessie Blodgett, Lila Boozer, Maude Boozer, Sallie May Boozer, May Boozer, Lucy Bowers, Jennie Brown, Sallie Brown, Mattie Brooks, Kate Bruce, Lulie Baxter, Eva Calmes, Willie Calcote, Sophia Carson, Lizzie Campbell, Minnie Chalmers, Anna Chalmers, Mary Chappell, Alice Cline, Carrie Cline, Fannie Cline, Fannie Chapman, Cornelia Coppock, Sibbie Coppock, May Chappell, Florence Cromer, Emma H......., Lucia ...., Sue Daudry, Addie Duckett, Kate Ewart, Sue Fair, Eula Floyd, Leah Foote, Rachel Foote, Tulla Gallman, Lillian Glenn, Lula Greneker, Sallie Greneker, Tama Greneker, Minnie Harman, Sallie Harrington, Emma Havird, Mattie Houseal, Alice Hornsby, Alice Hunter, Julia Hunter, Chicora Johnson, Alice Johnson, Clara Johnstone, Carrie Jones, Iula Jones, Maggie Jones, Rosa Jones, Alma Kibler, Gussie Kibler, Lilla Kibler, Lizzie Kibler, Alice Kinard, Kate Kinard, Angella Langford, Emma Langford, Lula Langford, Nannie Lark, Beta Leavell, Brantley Leavell, Maggie Livingstone, Kate Mayer, Pauline Mendenhall, Lula Mendenhall, Mamie Mood, Maria Mood, Addie Moorman, Bettie Moorman, Tilly Montgomery, Sallie McCants, Mattie McCaughrin, Mattie McIntosh, Emma McKellar, Alice Mayer, Kittie Mazyck, Sue Mazyck, Carrie Moon, Mamie Moon, Polly Mittle, Minnie......., Marena........, Fannie Paysinger, Mamie Paysinger, Carrie Peoples, Mamie Peoples, Mattie Piester, Lilly Pool, Lula Pool, Mamie Pool, Mary Pool, Minnie Pratt, Elvira Ramage, Sarah Ramage, Sue Rawlinson, Mamie Riser, Hennie Richie, Mamie Rhodelsperger, Sue Robinson, Kate Rutherford, Lizzie Schumpert, Fannie Sill, Mamie Sill, Ella Sligh, Fannie Slider, Emma Simmons, Cora Smith, Florence Smith, Hattie Smith, Kate Summer, Minnie Summer, Sue Teasly, Tena Tucker(?), Helen Wardlaw, Hattie Wells, Mary Wells, Gertrude Welch, Maggie Webb, Ora Webb, Andrena Werber, Marian Werber, Bessie Wheeler, Mallie Wheeler, Mamie Whaley, Mary Whaley, Lizzie White, Olivia White, Katie B. Whites, Mamie Whites, Clemence Wilson, Bessie Wright, Dosia Wright, Sallie Wright.

A copy of record of pupils at the old Female Academy, as taken from an old book of Captain A. P. Pifer, for the years 1878 and 1879. The pupils then were: Talu Aull, Mollie Anderson, Lelia Aull, Nettie Austin, Rowena Aull, Lula Baxter, Leila Blease, Lucy Bowers, Sallie Brown, Jennie Brown, Alice Boyle, Kate Cline, Cornelia Coppock, Nellie Chapman, Fanny Cunningham, Carrie Cline, Sibbie Coppock, Mamie Dickert, Addie Duckett, Della Duckett, Ella Duncan, Igora Duncan, Kate Fair, Leah Foote, Silena Foote, Lillian Glenn, Sallie Greneker, Julia Hunter, Nora Harmon, Lily Herbert, Alice Hornsby, Lilly Harris, Emma Havird, Kittie Havird, Carrie Hentz, Clive Johnson, Iula Jones, Lilly Kibler, Alma Kibler, Gussie Kibler, Tilla Langford, Nannie Lark, Nannie Livingstone, Mattie McIntosh, Mamie McCaughrin, Carrie Mayes, Emma McKellar, Flora Meridith, Polly Mittle, Mamie Mangum, Mattie McCaughrin, Janie Martin, Sue Mazyck, Kittie Mazyck, Lila Mathews, Lula Pool, Katie Parker, Mamie Paysinger, Bessie Perkins, Kate Rutherford, Mamie Rhodelsperger, Sarah Ramage, Sula Robertson(Rawlinson ?), Sallie Stoddard, Fanny Setzler, Laura Schmidt, Julia Shirey, Mamie Sill, Carrie Setzler, Helen Vaughan, Alam Werber, Eliza Wilson, Docia Wright, Mariam Werber, Mallie Wheeler, Mamie Whites, Alma W......., Helen Wardlaw, Mamie Whaley, Laura Whaley, Mamie Wells, Hattie Wells, Bessie Wheeler, Nannie Wilson, Nannie Wicker, Helen Ward, Sallie Wright, Katie White. Other names included the following: May Boozer, Bertha Blease(?), Lizzie Bryson, Martha Brooks, Janie Bowers, Kate Brice, Mary Boland, Maude Boozer, Lucy Boozer, Bessie Blease, Clara Blease, Laura Blease, Sue Chapman, Lilly Clark, Alma Clark, Lizzie Campbell, Minnie Chalmers, Anna Chalmers, Mamie Chappell, Alice Cannon.

Names of some patrons who are listed in the old record, who paid tuition fees from time to time, as follows: Thomas Blease, Mrs...... Brooks, Henry Blease, S. Barre, Foster Blodgett, S. P. Boozer, ... Boozer, John Boyle, John Brown, J. D. Bruce, S. B. Calcott, John Chapman, Richard Chapman, W. A. Cline, Major Crooks, Mrs. ......, Davis, ... Duckett, M. Foote, Jeff Gallman, R. H. Greneker, Thomas F. Harmon, Jesse Hornsby, Nathan Hunter, Ed. Jones, L. J. Jones, William Johnson, Malcome Johnstone, ...Jacoby, Jacob Kibler, W. J. Lake, William Langford, Dr. O. B. Mayer, Sr., L. Marshall, McD. Metz, Dr. James McIntosh, Mrs............ Montgomery, Col. R. Moorman, Frank Moon, Rev. Mood, ...McCants, Nathan ...., J. O. Peoples, J. P. Pool, B. J. Ramage, ... Pratt, ...Schumpert, A. W. T. Simmons, T. P. Slider, William Summer, Jean Ward .... Webb, Frederick Werber, Dr. .... Whaley, Zeb. White, W. G. Wright.

The idea of popular education began to spread over the South, free schools for every child; and for several years it was vigorously and strongly debated, both by the people and by the press; whether every child should be given free schooling. Finally, the growing demand for popular education won out, and as a result, on December 23, 1869, a charter was granted for the Newberry Graded Schools. The schools were opened soon thereafter, the following Board of Trustees having been elected: J. F. J. Caldwell, George B. Cromer, William H. Wallace, James K. P. Goggans, J. S. Cozby, George S. Mower, L. M. Speers, N. B. Mazyck, Alan Johnstone, William E. Pelham, and Dr. James K. Gilder.

The following is part of an article in the Newberry Herald & News about the new schools: "In the year 1900 these men were on the Board of Trustees, F. N. Martin, Dr. W. G. Houseal, John M. Kinard, William T. Tarrant, G. M. B. Epting, and George W. Summer."...............

"The Charter of the graded school provided that tuition should be absolutely free to the children of all citizens living within the Newberry School District, which district was made coterminus with the city limits. The graded school for the white children was carried on the first year in the one-story brick building which was used as the Female Academy, the building now occupied by Dr. W. G. Houseal as a home and clinic."

"Boundary Street school, the first of the present system, was built in 1890, corner of Boundary and Coates Streets." .... In that year Newberry had a population of 3,030 people."

"The enrollment for the year 1870, was: Whites-369; colored-297; total- 666. For the session of 1899-1900, the enrollment was: whites-511; colored- 328; total-839.".........

" The teachers in 1899 were: Mrs. O. E. Fair, Miss. Rachel B. McMaster, Miss. Mary L. Burton, Miss. Nellie G. McFall, Miss. Maggie W. Daniel, Miss. Carrie E. Aull, Miss. Mary Elizabeth Dominick, Miss. Eloise Welch,............ At a meeting of the Board in June, 1900, Miss. Lalla Martin was elected an additional teacher and Prof. Burr H. Johnstone was elected Superintendent."

"The next Superintendent elected was W. A. Stuckey, who served until 1910,...............
During his administration the old home of Judge Y. J. Pope was purchased, remodeled, and made into a new grammar school."

"In 1910, a new school bond issue was made for the purpose of erecting a high school building. This building is now the present Junior High School, on Martin Street. A two-story brick building, which at this time takes care of the sixth and seventh grades. Henry Lee Dean succeeded W. A. Stuckey in 1910, and served three years as Superintendent.".....

"Prof. Ernest Anderson succeeded Prof. Dean in 1913. About this time a Domestic Science department was established in the high school, also Botany and German."

"In 1916 Dr. James P. Kinard was elected Superintendent, and after one year's service, he resigned to accept the chair of Education and Psychology at Winthrop College, Rock Hill, S.C. Soon afterwards, Prof. O. B. Cannon was elected Superintendent."

" The following have served as Principals of the High School, from 1911 to 1940: J. B. O'Neall Holloway, C. F. Wertz, Wallace Pryor, L. K. Hagood, J. M. Bedenbaugh, Prof. Fairey, J. L. Keitt, Jr.,P. K. Harmon. Prof. Harmon was elected Superintendent after the death of Dr. O. B. Cannon. During Dr. Cannon's administration the Oakland Grammar School was taken over by the city system, as well as that of the Mollohon Grammar School.

"In the year 1921, under the administration of Dr. Cannon, a new High School building was constructed. A special issue of new bonds enabled the Board to improve both the Grammar schools and the high school which was made into the Junior High school, also the Colored school, Hoge School, on Drayton Street, which was bought after the old school building on Caldwell Street was sold. The new Drayton Street buildings were constructed about 1926; which,in 1938, were made additions, the manual training department and the gymnasium."

"Some of the Trustees since 1900 were: Otto Klettner, John H. Wicker, Dr. Van Smith, William A. McSwain, J. Marion Davis,George S. Mower, W. S. Langford, L. W. Floyd, Arthur Kibler, J. L. Keitt, Sr., Dr. William G. Mayes, J. Y. McFall, T. Roy Summer, P. D. Johnson, and others."

The present Board of Trustees (1948) are the following: A. J. Bowers, Jr., Wright Cannon, A. W. Murray, J. L. Keitt, Jr., D. O Carpenter. Teachers that year: P. K. Harmon, Superintendent; .... Beck, Principal of Junior High; J. V. Kneece, Principal of High School.

NEWBERRY COLLEGE.

Newberry College is located about three-fourths of a mile from Newberry Court House, on College Street. The President is Dr. James C. Kinard. The buildings are on an eminence overlooking the city, on a gradually sloping hill, on lands formerly owned by the late Col. Simeon Fair, Esq.

The College is owned and controlled by the three Synods of South Carolina, Georgia-Alabama, and Florida, of the United Lutheran Synod of America. There is a rotating Board of Trustees, eighteen members from the South Carolina Synod, four from the Georgia-Alabama Synod, and two from the Florida Synod.

The grounds, equipment and buildings are values at about $450,000.00. Total assets amount to about $850,000.00

The College was organized to give complete training in the liberal arts. Two degrees are at this time (1938) offered. In addition to the regular liberal arts courses, the College provides special training in the Departments of Music and Business Administration, and courses leading to Law, Medicine, Theology, etc.

History

The Rev. John Bachman, President of the South Carolina Synod before the War Between the States, became interested in establishing an institution in South Carolina as early as the year 1828. The outcome of this idea was the founding in 1832 of the Classical and Theological Institute of the Synod, at Lexington, S. C.

The institute at Lexington was in operation about twenty five years. About 1853, owing to the conditions prevailing at that time, and the languishing condition of the institute, an effort was made to remove the school. About 1855 it was moved to Newberry, and named Luther College and Theological Seminary.

In 1856 the name was changed to Newberry College, a charter being granted from the State Legislature in that year. At a meeting of the Board of Trustees, January 13, 1857, the Rev. John Bachman was elected President of the Board. Plans and specifications were made for a building which was erected in 1858. In December, 1858, Rev. Theophilus Stork, D. D., of Philadelphia, was elected President of the College, the first President. One hundred and fifty students enrolled the first session.

At the outbreak of the Civil War, the College was effected in that many students volunteered for service in the Confederate Army, and some of the Professors resigned and returned to their homes. The enrollment in 1863 was forty five; when it had to discontinue, stopping work in early 1865.

On account of the invasion of General Sherman's troops of the State, the Confederate purveying establishment was removed from Walhalla to Newberry, and used the College building, which was forced to move out when the United States troops came through and camped in the building. The Federal troops remained several months in the building, doing much damage to the property, tearing away parts of the structure, knocking down fences, and carrying away many valuable books from the library.

After the war, the College having become heavily involved in debt, a financial offer from Walhalla was received, in 1868, to which town the College was moved. But in 1877, after several citizens in Newberry had made responsible offers of financial help, amounting to about $15,000.00, the College was brought back to Newberry, and a new building erected in place of the old one which had almost fallen down. This new building was completed in 1878. It is now known as Smetzler Hall, and used as a girls' dormitory. It is a three-story brick building, and recently renovated. It has three sections, the North, South, and Middle dormitories, seperated by partitions, with arched door entrances. (Ref: " Herald & News", March 30, 1925)

In the Presidency of Dr. George W. Holland (1878-1892) Keller Memorial Hall was erected at an approximate cost of $55,000.00. The contractor was C. C. Davis, of Newberry, S. C. This is a two-story building of red brick, with high Gothic style steeple and gables. The Laboratories of Physics and Chemistry, and Biology, occupy the first floor and the library the entire second floor.

Holland Hall, a memorial to Dr. George W. Holland, was built during the Presidency of Dr. George B. Cromer (1895-1904). In this building are classrooms, the administration offices, on the first floor, and on the second floor literary society halls and the auditorium. It was during the administration of Dr. Cromer that the College was able to secure from the Federal Government $15,000.00 as part compensation for the damage done the original college buildings by Federal soldiers in 1865. This amount was applied to the construction cost of Holland Hall. The approximate cost of the building was $75,000.00.

Co-education was instituted in 1898.

Carnegie Hall was erected during the administration of Dr. James A. B. Scherer (1904-1908), with funds contributed largely by Andrew Carnegie. A technilogical department was housed in the building, but the department was discontinued in 1917. The building is a three-story structure. On the first floor are the dining hall and kitchens; on the second floor, the Department of Business Administration and the matron's quarters; and on the third floor, the men of the Freshman class have dormitory quarters. The cost of the building was $50,000.00. The building was completely remodeled in 1920 at a cost of $20,000.00, the architect being J. Ernest Sumner, of Newberry, S. C., and the contractor, P. C. Corn.

The men's dormitory for upper-classmen was erected a few years ago at an approximate cost of $40,000.00, the architects and contractors being L. A. Wilson & Son, Newberry, S. C. This is a three-story building, with halls running the entire length of each floor, and baths are conveniently arranged.

The gymnasium was built in 1925 with funds contributed in part by the citizens of Newberry. The total cost was $40,000.00. The contractors were L. X. Wilson & Son. This is a two-story building. The first floor is provided with offices, showers, and a place for a swimming pool. The second floor is given over to a basket-ball court and space for either indoor games or other amusements.

The athletic field is at the rear of the gymnasium and is named "Setzler Field", in honor of Dr. E. B. Setzler, head of the English Department many years and Chairman of the Faculty Commitee on Athletics.

(References: "Annals of Newberry", " Rem. of Newberry", by Carwile; Newberry Observer, Apr. 1938).

RURAL SCHOOLS

Prosperity High School-

During the early times there were several rural schools in the vicinity of what is now the town of Prosperity. A good school was at the place of the town, near old Prosperity Church (the community later became known as "Frog Level"),.

When the village began to grow several years later, about 1875, a school was organized by the citizens, and the first session was held in an old two-room cabin near the village cemetery. In this cabin J. B. Lathan had a private school before the organization of the school.

A new building was erected near the old A. R. P. Church, and in 1879 the citizens met and elected a regular Board of Trustees or association, with Patrick E. Wise as President. The members of the Board of Trustees elected were: Rev. James C. Boyd, and Rev. Jacob Hawkins, Major G. G. DeWalt, Henry S. Boozer, and B. L. Dominick. In 1880 the number of Trustees was increased to nine, and in the Fall of that year they elected Professor C. W. Welch, as Principal, and Mrs. Jane Long as Assistant Principal.

There have been several changes in the school's curricula since it's beginning, increasing from six to nine grades, then in the year 1901 the tenth grade was added. A brick building was erected in 1905, but a few years later it was necessary to add three more new rooms to the building.

They became part of the State High School system in 1907. In 1924 the eleventh grade was added. In 1925 the Mt. Pilgrim School consolidated with Prosperity School. In 1927 the present building was erected, which has five class rooms, a laboratory, a library, a large auditorium, with a seating capacity of about five hundred, and a stage and gymnasium combined. The building has all modern conveniences, with water, lights and steam heat. Each class room is equipped with individual steel lockers.

A modern farm shop and an agricultural class room were added to the high school building in 1937. Large bulletin boards then were placed in each class room. In 1937 tables and chairs were installed in each class room of the higher grades, as well as in the library.

In the grammer school building many new improvements have been made. Electric lights and many sanitary facilities have been put into the building.

A Home Economics and a Commercial Course have been started in the High School. Also, a department of Music.

All sports and playground activities are clean, and include every kind. Basket-ball, baseball, foot-ball, are the principle games played.

Some of the teachers who have served in the past according to the Annals of Newberry, Part two, were:

In 1881, Professor D.C. Lake, who was Principal; other Principals being J. C. Perrin, 1882-83; J. C. Cork, 1883-84; J. A. Hubbard, 1884-85; A. S. Scheetz, 1885-87; A. J. Bowers, 1887-88; J. E. Brown, 1888-89; F. E. Dreher, 1889; J. T. Moore, 1890; E. O. Counts, 1891-92; and others.

In 1938, the records show that the following teachers served: Superintendent William R. Watson; teachers, Miss Juanita Swindler, Miss Rachel Kennedy, Miss Clara Brown, Mrs. Annette Brooks, Miss Bertha Ruff, Miss Mary Langford, Miss Corrie V. Morgan, Mrs. L. C. Derrick, Miss Willie Mae Wise, Miss Adeline Stuckey, J. S. Luther, J. A. Bedenbaugh, and S. C. Brissie. The Board of Trustees of that year were: J. A. Price, W. L. Mills, and J. P. Cook.

Smyrna School-

The first free or government school to operate at Smyrna was about 1872. This school was located about five miles West of Newberry, on the old Belfast Road, and on land owned by David Boozer.

This was a one-teacher school, the building being a one-room log building, and the equipment being rough slab benches and tables. The State paid for a three-month period term, and the patrons making up the balance to extend the session.

Some of the first teachers in the school were: Wm. Reeder, John R. Spearman, Gage, McKittrick, W. H. Wallace, (he was later editor of the Newberry Observer), Then, Miss Sallie Boozer taught there awhile, being the last teacher in the building.

About 1879, the school was moved for a year to an old abandoned tannery, the Joblin House, on land later owned by Miss Mary Burton. One of the teachers there was Miss Carrie Aull, who later was one of the efficient teachers of the Newberry City Schools for several years.

The school was then moved to a small house on property owned by Smyrna Presbyterian Church. Some of the teachers there were: Miss Maggie Jones, Miss Nora Cofield, Miss Della Anderson, Miss Emma Wilson, Miss Lula Wertz, and others.

In 1893, the school was moved to a one-room building which was built for them, on land of Mrs. Caroline Boozer, and now owned by Dr. Hugh B. Senn. Some of the teachers there were: Mrs. Helen Clary, Misses Fannie Johnston, Minnie Wallace, Lucy Whaley, and W. D. Senn (Dr. W. D. Senn).

In 1894, a larger building was erected, and some of the teachers were: Misses Lillian Wertz, Lula Blackwell, Janie Chalmers, Bertha McClure, Carrie Spearman, Agnew, Winton, and Howe Ligon, and Moody Bedenbaugh.

In 1914, the district bought two acres of land from George P. Boozer, Sr. and built a modern two-story structure. A library was added, and other needed equipment. Two teachers were employed, one for the grades and one for the high school department.

Long Lane School-

Lone Lane School is a new modernly equipped, brick building, located about ten miles North of Newberry, on the highway leading to Whitmire and Union. It is a well-modeled school, with several teachers of ability. It was the outcome of two smaller schools within the community, the old Beth Eden Church School and old Kings Creek Church School.

The history of the schools go back to before the Rev. War, as this is one of the oldest sections of the county. Many families whose names are seldom heard of to-day in the county were some of the first settlers and patrons of the schools. The Kenners, McMorries, Brazzlemans, Gilders, Kings, Davis, Dugans, Glenns, and others are not now living within the community.

The name originated from an early road of the Colonial period. That part of the old Buncombe Road traversing Kings Creek, then to Gilder's Creek, was fenced in to keep cattle out of whence the name, which soon afterwards came to apply to the community. This was before the year 1769.

Several schools were built from time to time at different places within the community, usually small one-room huts, on land given by some patron.

The first deed made to the school was in 1899; then, in 1910 a larger building was put up, and later an addition, making it a two-teacher school.

In 1922, 4.13 acres were bought from Henry P. Baker, then living in Florida, and on this the present new building was erected. It contains three class rooms, a library, cook room, dining room, and an auditorium. With a large playground and facilities, it gives to the pupils plenty of recreation. It now has four teachers. Some of its teachers were: Mrs. Ellerbe Sease, Miss Ruth Lominack, James D. Brown, and others, The Trustees (in 1939) were: C. M. Folk, L. E. Rikard, W. S. Hentz, E. C. Folk, and H. T. Carlisle.

Fairview School-

This school is located in District No. 18, Newberry County. It was organized in 1884, in a small one-room frame structure, on the Calk Ferry Road about seven miles South of Prosperity.

A one-teacher school, with an enrollment of about fifty, it thrived under the public school system; so that in the year 1894, one acre of land was given to it by Burr Connelly, and a one-room building was erected. The name was then changed to Fairview School.

This building later was burned, and a two-room structure was erected at the same place. In the year 1917, the building was moved away and a new one built, with modern equipment. Later, it was remodeled and the building wired for electricity.

In 1926, another acre of land was purchased from Burr Connelly to be used as a playground. Since about the year 1917 the school has employed two teachers.

For the past ten years the high school students have been transported by school bus to the high school at Little Mountain.

Some of the first teachers of this school were: Thomas S. Sease (now Judge Sease), Thomas Mills, Dr. J. I. Bedenbaugh, Miss Sally Pugh, and others.

St. Johns School-

An early bounty grant to St. John Lutheran Church, in 1760, shows that one hundred acres were given for religeous and school purposes; so that there seems to have been a school there as early as that time.

The first church building which was abandoned for a better building, was used for school purposes. This was back before the year 1808, when the present church was erected. Like many of the earliest schools, private subscriptions made possible the operations of many of the schools, and the same applied to St. Johns School.

Hartford School-

Located three and one-half miles South of Newberry. It has been within that same vicinty since its organization. One of the first men to settle in that community was John Paysinger, and afterwards two of his grandsons, Lawson and Ben, lived on lands on which the school was built.

A Universalist Church in that section, the outgrowth of an earlier church of like denomination in the same section, was built in 1823. Services were held in the church until about 1870, after which the church being abandoned, the building was used as a school. In 1870 the enrollment was eighty-five, and all of the pupils were taught by one teacher.

School was carried on in this building until 1924, when the present building was constructed, a large frame building with four class rooms, a library, a cook room and an auditorium seating about two hundred. At present the enrollment ranges from seventy-five to one hundred pupils, with three teachers.

Kinards School-

Sharon Methodist Church at Kinards having its first pastor about 1875, a school was organized that year, and held its sessions in a one-room cabin on the Gorse estate, the location being within a few yards from the railroad depot, where it now stands.

In 1882, the school was moved into a cabin belonging to Henry Hinson, closer to where the church now stands.

The first building owned by the school district was a one-room house on land of J. D. Smith, built in 1894, and used as the school until 1916, when the property was turned back to Mr. Smith's estate.

In 1916, the school district bought two acres of land opposite to the depot, from J. A. Dominick. On that land they built a two-room house, the present building now used as a two-teacher school.

Tabernacle School-

The first building was erected on land given by Dr. M. P. Johnson, the building and land to be returned to Dr. Johnson's estate when no longer used for school purposes.

The first school built was about 1880, a one-room cabin built of logs, with narrow strips over the cracks between the logs. With its one window and one door it was easily kept warm during the Winter months. With it's roughly built benches and one long plank to serve as desk for all the pupils the slates were placed in a long row. There were no blackboards and no writing paper. A large open fire-place furnished the heat.

Some of the first teachers were: Pink Jones, Miss Joe Jones, Miss Susie Jones, Miss Sallie Langford, Miss Lula Workman, and Miss Janie Chalmers.

In the year 1902, a one-room building was rented from John Miller. Built with lumber and ceiled, with two windows with glass panes, it was an improvement over the old building. Some of their first teachers were: Miss Lena Glenn, Miss Pearl Sullivan, Miss Emma Longshore, Miss Annie Lou McMillan, Miss Lucy Wheeler, Miss Carrie Lee Buford, Miss Ola Miller, and Miss Vera Parrott. The sessions were held here until 1918.

In 1919, a new and more modern structure was completed, on the Dr. Johnson property. Though with just one room, it was furnished with better equipment. In 1926, the school was abandoned and the pupils were transported to Jalapa and Newberry. Later Bush River School consolidated with them and Jalapa School and James High School which received many pupils.

Union School-

Organized about the year 1895, under the consolidation of two old schools, the Gallman School and the Ridge Road School, it was called Union. The first Trustees of this new school were: J. K. Gallman, Thomas J. Wilson, W. M. Bobb. The location was made at a point which is the exact distance between the two old schools.

Many children have gone out from the school, who lived in the community, from families of Epps, Fellers, Quattlebaum, Wilson, Gallman, Kinard, Livingstone, Bobb, Long, Griffin, Enlow Dominick, and others.

Some of the first teachers were: Miss Bessie Dominick, Miss Cora Dominick, George Mills, John Kibler, Miss Lillie Wertz, Miss Vick Crosson, Miss Ollie Feagle, Miss Teddie Maybin, Miss Eunice Halfacre, and others.

The school now operates with two teachers.

Rutherford Academy-

The school was first established about 1888, located near Keitt's Cross Roads. It was located on lands of George S. Hower who deeded to them 2.66 acres; the school being named for the late William Rutherford.

The house was erected in 1890, with the following as the first Trustees: John A. Cromer, John A. Graham, and J. L. Keitt. Other Trustees elected later were, Thomas W. Keitt, Thomas Hutchinson, F. W. Higgins. On resignation of Mr. Higgins, J. Owen Turnipseed was elected in his place.

The first teacher was Thomas W. Keitt, with an Assistant, Miss Ellen Suber. Mr. Keitt afterwards being elected County School Commissioner, Mr. J. O. Turnipseed was elected teacher in his place. Some of the first teachers who served later were: Mrs. Minnie Caldwell, D. A. Kleckley, Miss Annie Higgins, Miss Janie Chalmers, Miss Joe Caldwell, Miss Ola Brown, Miss Maude Epting, Charles Ballentine, Murray Rikard, Miss Essie Suber, Mrs Dovie Rutherford.

Others who served as teachers were: Miss Pearl Lominick, Miss Mattie Cromer, Miss Emmie Brownlee, Miss Lula Lominick, Miss Marie Sease, Miss Mary Brown, Miss Roberta Lominick, Miss Lois Long, Miss Ethel Stoddard, Mrs. J. B. Kinard, Miss Ethel Seybt, Miss Mamie Crooks, Mrs. Bessie Crisp, Miss Lillian Brownlee, Mrs. Ray Feagle, Miss Madalene Savage, Miss Annie Laurie Harmon, Miss Rosa Lee Anderson, Miss Beatrice Graham, Mrs. Mae McDonald, Miss Nina Cromer, Miss Rose Mae Mitchell, Grady Lee Halfacre, and Miss Elizabeth Ruff.

In 1934, the school was consolidated with the Pomaria High School.

Broad River School-

Not so far from the site of old Rutherford School was the Broad River School, organized through the efforts of the late Col. D. A. Dickert (he was a Confederate Officer and later author of the "History of Kershaws Brigade").

The school was served by many able teachers.

Bush River Private School (Before 1867)-

The school was first started before the War Between the States, at a place near where is now Wm. Schult'z home. Later, about the year 1867, it was moved to a site now occupied by the Bush River Church parsonage. A small one-teacher school, in a frame building. Some of it's first teachers were: Drayton Smith, Eb. Chalmers, Tom Workman, Kemper D. Sonn, Sallie Cleland, W. M. Purifoy. The school becoming too large, the trustees started two schools called Bush River and Reederville.

A new site for Bush River School was a few miles south of the Church, on Cleland's land Some of the teachers who taught there were: Nera Lake, Fannie Johnston, Mary Burten, Ola Bramlett, Joe Jones, Douglas Pitts.

The school was moved a few years later, on land now owned by Elmer Rikard. Some of the teachers there were: J. E. Johnston, Laurence Glenn, Lillie Ferguson, Essie Wise, Mamie Clary, Nannie Simpson, Nettie Epps, Rebecca Wideman, Bess Wallace, Louise Anderson and Lina Glenn, Cora Culbertson, Dollie Cleland, Annie Herbert, Irene Adair, Sybil Marshall, and Ethel Anderson.

In 1920 the school was moved to a location between M. M. Satterwhites home and Bush River Church. A modern, well-equipped two-story building, with kitchenette in rear, was used. The first teacher here was Miss Beulah Smith, and with an enrollment of about fifty pupils other teachers were added for the next session, who were Miss Agnes Monts and Miss Lera Livingstone. Some of the other teachers who taught there were : Misses Jummie McNinch, Rhoda Dominick, Louise Asbyl, Olivia Kyzer, Mayme Hill, and Mabel Johnson.

In 1921, a school improvement association was started in the school district. They earned money to equip the school, including a gas stove, a piano, and started a library. The Presidents of the assoctiation were: Mrs. R. H. Burris, Mrs. Hayne Buford, Mrs. R. E. Livingstone.

In 1926, the school joined the other districts in organizing a Consolidated School.

Stoney Hill Schools-

The first school in that community was started about 1850, first as Pine Grove School. Then, about 1870, the Hunter School was started, then the Post Oak School, all within the same community. Some of the first teachers at Post Oak were: Thomas Boozer, Miss Bertie Hillhouse, and Cornelius Boozer.

About 1872, a school was built at St. Lukes Lutheran Church, which later was torn down and a new two-story building erected. In 1880 a school was conducted at Nebos Methodist Church site.

Big Creek School was built in 1890. Some of the first teachers were: J. Ed Black, Forest Stilwell, J. I. Bedenbaugh, Robert Abrams, Mike Monts, Professor Joseph Hunter, Miss Sallie Pugh, L. W. Bedenbaugh and wife, Robert C. Hunter, Miss Estelle Dominick, Miss Olga Foster, Forest Bedenbaugh, Gurney Nichols, Miss Helen Nichols, Miss Ethel Sawyer, Miss Claudia Shealy, Miss Lera Livingstone, Mrs. Fannie Mills, Mrs. Ola Kohn.

In 1924, Big Creek and St. Lukes were consolidated, and the name Stoney Hill given the school

About seventy-five years ago there were two or three schools within the Post Oak Grove district, one being located in front of where is now Horace Boozer's place. Daniel Moore taught here. Later, the father of Mrs. Esther Lester gave a small piece of land on which a larger building was put up. The school was later abandoned.

All of the schools of that vicinity have been abandoned or consolidated with the Stoney Hill School organization

Johnstone School-

Located about three miles South of Newberry, on the highway leading to Prosperity, is a large brick structure, with five class rooms, a large auditorium, a library room and a sanitary lunch room. This building was erected in 1924.

Some of its teachers have been the following: Mrs. Margaret Fellers, Miss Juanita Hitt, Miss Annie Banks (Mrs. Sligh), Earl McCullough, Gladys Hipp, Kate Wilson. The Board of Trustees in 1939 were: P. B. Banks, Frank Miller, W. C. Norris.

The first school started there was in a small one-room frame cabin in the year 1886; named for the late Chancellor Job Johnstone, who owning much of the timber in that section, gave the lumber for building it. The lot was donated by Jake Perkins. A few years later, John C. Neel gave three acres adjoining the lot so that an addition could be made to the building. It is on this land that the present building stands.

The first teacher in the Fall of 1886 was Matthew Henry. A pay school then, and among its first students was : H. A. McCullough (afterwards Rev. H. A. McCullough, of Columbia). Students could be prepared for college at the school since its curriculum was raised. The organizers and first Trustees were: Andrew Kilgore, John C. Neel, and McDuffie Sligh.

After Matthew Henry resigned, Mrs. Jane Long became the teacher, and continued the one- class room until 1899, when the building was enlarged, and an assistant teacher, Miss Joe Langford, was added.

Some of the teachers have been: Mrs. Jane Long, Joe Reid, Mamie McGraw, Hattie Caldwell, Mattie Brown, Nannie Livingstone, Rosa Kilgore, William McMorries, Helen Ray, Miss Pettgrew,

D. A. Kleckley, Hattie Leitzey, Gertrude Bobb, Blanche Davidson, Anita Aull, Thomas E. Wicker, Belle Kay, Pearl West, Adam Cole, Mamie Crooks, O'Neall Holloway, Sarah Caldwell, Mrs. J. E. McFadden, Elizabeth Neel. Other teachers were: Sarah Houseal, Mildred Abrams, Mrs. Bertha Boylston, Nannie Wheeler, Kate Neel, Ethel Saner, Annie Halfacre, Dolly Lominick, Azile Parr (afterwards Mrs. Ralph Baker), Elizabeth Renwick (afterwards Mrs. Graham), Rosa Walpole, Bonnie Neel, Willie Mae Culbertson, Margaret Fellers, Corrie Lee Friday, and others.

Garmany-

About eighty-five years ago John Garmany owned much of the land in the section where is now Garmany School, about three miles East of town. He gave seven acres to the community for religeous and school purposes; hence, came the name of the school. He is buried near the County Home in a family burial plot.

Some time before the Confederate War a small house was built on the original plot for school purposes which would accommodate about twenty or twenty-five pupils. The names of the teachers nor the names of any of the pupils of that school could be had for this history. During the war very little interest was taken in education as all interest was centered on winning the war. The little old school rotted down. It is thought that no school was held in the community for a period of ten or twelve years.

About 1875 a school was started again in a tenant house on the old Billy Caldwell place. The first teacher of this school was Miss Addie Cannon, who afterwards, became Mrs. T. W. Gallman. J. E. Buzhardt, a brother of Mrs. John T. Norris of Newberry, was one of Miss Cannon's pupils. He continued under other teachers of this academy until Mr. Henry Boyd was teacher. He then won a scholarship by competitive examination at the Citadel and graduated from that College in 1890 with second honor. He helped organize and taught in the first summer school for teachers in South Carolina.

He was professor of Mathematics in Texas and in this state from the time of his graduation to his death in 1904.

As Mr. Caldwell needed his tenant house in 1876, the patrons decided to build a log building farther up the road on land furnished by a Mr. Livingston, the grandfather of Mrs. T. W. Folk, who now lives on some of the land owned by her grandfather. Miss Callie Cannon, an aunt of Professor O. B. Cannon of Newberry City Schools, was the first teacher in this building.

This school was not in the center of the district so in 1879 or 1880 it was decided to go back to the old Garmany site again. Jonathan Martin was secured as the first teacher. He taught for sometime, but as he had a desire for going west, he left for Texas, where he became a successful lawyer. Other teachers following him were: Miss Alice Barre, Mr. Ned Brown, Mrs. Cyrilla Rutherford, Miss Janie Chalmers, Miss Emma Havird, Miss Mary Boyd and Mr. Henry Boyd. None of these teachers received a salary of more than twenty-five dollars per month and their school term was about five months.

Professor O. B. Cannon, superintendent of the Newberry city schools, had his beginning in this school under the above teachers.

As there was unrest among the patrons about the location of the school, a new survey was made of the district about 1893 and 1894. Many patrons wanted the school to accommodate centrally the school population. To do this two acres of land were bought from Leonard Sease near where Mr. Hubert Smith now lives. A large building was erected. It was considered one of the nicest country schools of the time. Mr. B. F. Cannon, Mr. Caleb Buzhart, and Mr. Antoine Bushardt were trustees at that time and continued so for some time. These trustees secured the services of Mr. W. L. Motes for 1893-94, Miss Unie Gibson for 1894-95 and the Rev. W. W. McMorris for 1895-96. At this time the salary of the teacher began to go up. Rev. McMorris received a salary of forty dollars per month and possibly the term was six or seven months. Mrs. Jane Long taught the sessions of 1896-97 and taught 1897-98. It is not known who taught next but Mr. O. B. Cannon was the teacher for sessions of 1899-1900 and 1900-01. He was followed by his brother, Mr. H. T. Cannon, who taught three sessions. Both of these men had attended Garmany.

For the school term of 1904-05 the trustees, Mr. Caleb Buzhardt, Mr. T. B. Leitzsey and Mr. J. J. H. Brown secured the services of Miss Willia Jones. Following her were: Miss Mildred

Simmons, one year; Miss. Carrie Hunter, one year; Miss. Dollie Cleland, one year; Mr. J. B. Buzhardt, a former pupil, taught two months. His unexpired term was finished by Miss. Sadie Bowers, who now works in the Newberry Post Office. In 1909-10, Miss. Mary Brown came as teacher for one term, and was followed by Miss. Mary Cannon, for the next two sessions. ......
For several years J. L. Mayer, J. J. H. Brown, and M. T. Oxner served the school as Trustees. In 1911 Mr. Mayer resigned and B. B. Leitsey was elected. J. H. Brown served until 1915, then J. E. Sease succeeded him. These Trustees held office the consolidation with Mt. Bethel School.

In 1911 Miss. Mary Brown was again elected teacher and taught for the next four years. On May 7, 1915, a tornado demolished the building. Two teachers, with thirty four pupils, were in the building; but they all came out alive, with just a few scratches and bruises. It was due to the thoughtfulness of Miss. Margarete Burton and Miss. Nina.Gibson(the latter then substituting for Miss. Mary Brown) that all lives were saved.

The next school session of 1915-16 was held at D. A. Livingstone's house, now owned by W. C. Brown, and the eccupants being Charlie Ruff and wife. Miss. Olive Feagle and Miss. Mary Brown were the teachers for that term..........

In the school year of 1916-17 the Trustees decided to go back to the old Garmany site. A few repairs were made on the old building that had been discarded for years. Miss. Olive Feagle and Miss. Felicia Koon were the teachers that session. The next year Miss. Marie Sease was added as a teacher, to take the place of Miss. Koon.

In the Summer of 1918 the citizens of Mt. Bethel, Garmany, and McCrary School Districts, being of one mind to have better school facilities, united the three schools into one with the name, Mt. Bethel-Garmany. McCrary School had been organized from part of old Garmany and St. Phillip's School land. Upon consolidation, the land reverted to the former school district. The Trustees of the comsolidated school were: Dr. W. C. Brown, S. W. Brown, B. B. Leitzsey, J. E. Sease, and J. T. Oxner. These, with M. T. Oxner, C. H. Alewine, M. R. Brooks, and L. I. Feagle, constituted the building committee. The land was bought from B. H. Wilson. In order to secure certain State aid at that time, a building designed as recommended by the State Superintendent of Education had to be adopted. A two-story frame structure was completed for the school term of 1918-19. Miss. Olive Feagle was elected as the first Principal of the new consolidated school. Misses. Marie Sease and Mattie Cromer were her assistants.

During the next school session Miss. Mattie Cromer was made Principal, with Misses. Ida Young and Mary Nichols as assistants.

The session of 1920-21 was taught by Misses. Mattie Cromer and Mary Brown, and Margaret McIntosh. For the next session, only one change was made, Miss. Mary Wheeler being selected to succeed Miss. Maragert McIntosh.

Since that time there have been many able teachers in the school.

Dominick School-

This school was the outgrowth of the first school in that community, about 1809, known as the Milton School. It was located near Goggans's Old Store, on the old Belfast Road. Later, a small one-room cabin near where is the Brehmer place was used as a school each Winter.

About 1875 Fred H. Dominick (grand-father of U. S. Congressman, Fred H. Dominick), bought the Moses Anderson place, with a large palatial home, about two miles from Goggans's Old Store. After moving into the neighborhood from the Dutch Fork, Mr. Dominick realized the necessity for a better school building, and offered to donate a lot of land for a school. His offer was accepted and a new school building erected. This building was standing in 1940, being used by negroes in the community as a school.

The school joined the Bush River Consolidated School, then abandoned as a school building. The Trustees at that time were, John N. Livingstone, and William Brehmer.

Whitmire High School-

This school is located in the town of Whitmire, about seventeen miles North of Newberry Court House. It is a large one-story brick building, with modern design and structure; with wide extensions and plenty of ventilation. The main entrance is about the center of the building.

The grammar school is, also, constructed with brick, two stories, and was formerly used as grammar and high school. They are operated under the State High School system. The Superintendent is Prof. R. C. Lake, who has many well-trained teachers.

A history of the schools of Whitmire go back many years, the first being a one-story one-room private school. (See sketch of town of Whitmire for more history of schools)......

The Old Crosson Field School-

The origin of the work that is annually commemorated, known as the Crosson Field School, was supervised and sponsored by J. T. P. Crosson. Mr. Crosson was a capable and sterling man. He was a graduate of Erskine College in the class of 1855. He served four years in the Confederate Army, in General McGowan's Brigade, 13th S. C. Regiment; was present at the surrender at Appomatox, and walked part of the way from Virginia to his home in South Carolina.

Just after the war of secession, and in close proximity with Sherman's march from Atlanta to the sea; when our forefathers had come back to reestablish their families and homes, the best methods of progress was foremost in their minds. Mr. Crosson favored a public school system, which was beginning to be spoken of. He said, "it is a model after the Prussian system; it is not the best, but the best we can reach at the present time."

He, seeing the needs of his own, and his neighbor's children, succeeded in having a public school located on his own farm. With the hands on his farm, a log cabin was built for the purpose. Mrs. Jane Agnew Long---nee Miss. Jane Martin---who was a Junior at the Woman's College at Due West, S. C. when the Confederate War began, was employed as the first teacher. This was the first public school opened in Newberry County.

When the time for opening came he took his little son, D. M. C.(later, Dr. D. M. Crosson, State Senator) , in a buggy and drove to Mr. Jacob Singley's. " The school will open next Monday morning if no other children are there but my own," he told him. Fifteen children were eventually enrolled from these families. Thirteen children by the name of Singley came to this school. The name was one of three families that was never absent from a roll call.

The school grew until 113 pupils were enrolled (54 girls and 59 boys). Sixteen girls and twenty boys are still living (1938). The little log cabin was used until the school outgrew it's capacity. It was then moved about one hundred yards South on the same farm to a house with three rooms and two porches, known as the Maffett house, but this house had been, originall built by some of the ancestors of the Longs.

Free text books were furnished, for two years under the Republican regime. Acting not upon a domineering basis, but supported by the confidence of the people, in which they were placing him. He did not favor some of them; the people all being Democratic in their principles The teachers were all educated in leading colleges in this State (Wofford, Newberry, Erskine), one from a distant business college, and one from Virginia.

The names of the teachers were, Miss. Martin, Rev. H. G. Wingard, John B. Lathan, Miss. Laura Gaulder, Rev. John R. Edwards, J. E. Perrin, Chris. Welch, Miss. Drucie Aull, John Schumpert,(he was from a business college), who was identified with the school about three months one Summer. A man by the name of Harrerood, whose penmanship was beautiful, taught penmanship a short term at night. The names of some of those who were helping to build up the vicinity and whose children have gone out to fill all lines of avacation were, Kiblers, Wickers, Kinards Singleys, Werts, Wheelers, Counts, Shealys, Cooks, Moore, Stone, Sligh, Livingstone, Neel, Griffins, Dominicks, Sease, Aulls, Stockmans, Taylors, Nates, Wilson, Mathis, Cannon, Long, Bobb, Schumpert, Hawkins, Quattlebaum; and the names of some of those parents who sent their children from town were, Bowers, Cureton, McFall, Boozer, Hussey, Wise, Berge, and Bridges.

It's pupils have filled all lines of occupations: farmers, teachers, ministers, merchants, physicians, docots of divinity, State senator, and last but not least the home-maker. This school was run about eight years, from 1868 to 1876.

About this time railroad traffic began to improve and business to loom up. The people of Prosperity had more children of school age, and wanted to build up a school nearer to themselves. They solicited Mr. Crosson's influence. He considered it, and said, "everything seems to be drifting toward common centers and railroads are the centers. It will be cheaper for me to send my two oldest to Due West and keep a buggy and horse for the younger ones."

To show their appreciation they made him Chairman of the Trustees in this movement of the first public school in Newberry County. The present High School in Prosperity is the offspring of the opening of this first public school in Newberry County. It was about twelve years (1868) before there was one in the city of Columbia, S. C. (1880). After this, Mr. Crosson and his wife continued to take an interest in school matters. Their home was a rendezvous for speakers and teachers. Once they entertained for a night, one the speakers(Miller), who was afterwards governor of Alabama. John C. Hope, of whom it was said he aided in keeping off the war of seccession for two years, was a frequent visitor to their home.

Roll of pupils at old Crosson Field School-

Preston Cannon, Willie Cannon, Minnie Cannon, Sallie Long, Abram Long, Simon Long, Hilliard Long, Ellen Long, Polly Long, Sallie Wertz, Bettie Wertz, Annie Sease, Carrie Sease, Ella Sease, Texanan Wicker, Laura Wicker, Jane Wicker, Tommie Summer, Natta Summer, Callie Summer, Jack Summer, Lula Matthews, McFall Matthews, Sondley Matthews, Adeline Shealy, Tirzah Shealy, Andrew Shealy, Samuel Shealy, Lawson Shealy, Julius Counts, Louisa Counts, Edward Aull, Adam Aull, Fannie Aull, John Cook, George Cook, Fletcher Bowers, Dedrick Boozer, Pink Hawkins, John Cureton, Sallie Cook, Texana Cook, Nannie Cook, Drayton Cook, Ebbie Cook, Josie Buzhardt, Mollie Buzhardt, Sallie Singley, Birge Singley, Roda Bolin, Bettie Neel, Ida Stockman, Jacob Wheeler, Thompson Wheeler, Alice Wheeler, M. M. Kinard, Sallie Kinard, Lizzie Kinard, James Kinard, Hampie Kinard, Henry Kinard, Calvin Singley, Gussie Singley, Alice Singley, Carrie Singley, William Singley, James Singley, Lee Singley, John Singley, Ned Singley, Mary Neel, Lizzie Cureton, Carrie McFall, Fannie Bridges, William Berge, Mary Berge, Drayton Crosson, Allie Crosson, John Crosson, Willie Maffett, Bobbie Maffett, Lula Maffett, Drayton Wilson, Toni Wilson, Crayton Dominick, Mary Dominick, Maggie Dominick, Nannie Livingstone, Robert Taylor, Jack Taylor, Maybin Long, Tirzah Kibler, Chellie Kibler, John Kibler, Henry Kibler, Jennie Singley, Eliza Nates, Calvin Long, John Long, Alice Long, John Stone, Jennie Stone, Jeff Wicker, Pink Wicker, Luke Cook, Tom Kinard, Alice Sligh, Lawson Wise, Allen Wise, James Wise.

(From a sketch in the Newberry Observer, Apr, 1938, and written by descendent of J. T. P. Crosson).

Jolly Street School-

The first school in this community was about 1845, in a little one-room cabin, and the first teacher was Mathias Wicker. It is said the pupils first used goose-quills for pens. They sat on a long bench in front of a wide open fireplace; but they first had to gather the wood in the surrounding woods with which to make the fires.

The next teacher was a Mr. Dukes. Then, several different teachers served the school. Some of the later ones were: George Hough, a Mr. Brooks, D. L. Livingstone. The location of the houses being changed from time to time, as the private teachers choose, it was difficult for them to know just where or in what cabin each of them taught; but they worked within the same community. Other teachers were: Henry Stone, Burr Livingstone, Miss. Sophia Seybt, Miss. Ida Seybt.

About 1875, the first money from the public school funds were received, when the teachers were paid $25.00 a month salary for three months in the session, and occasionally, when the school ran longer, the difference was made up by the patrons.

Then Mrs. Wright taught the school, and G. A. Mills, Miss. Minnie Willinghan, Miss. Mary Norris; and Rev. R. E. Livingstone, J. W. Stone, Miss. Lilla Werts, and others.

Pomaria School-

Pomaria School was founded about 1869; could well go back for it's origin to the old St. John's Church School. The old Bethel Academy near Pomaria may, too, be called the parent of the present high school.

When St. John's Church was established in 1763 a school was taught on it's premises, under the bounty grant provision of the church. Not until 1921 did a school stop operating there, and then for the purpose of consolidating with Pomaria School. Back in the reconstruction days a school here was taught by a Miss. Love; then, about 1876, Mrs. Alice Efird Summer (wife of John A. Summer), who lived nearby, taught the school in a building on the Summer property.

Bethel School which was established in 1869 had many teachers who were well trained and with college education. The school soon established itsself with a high standard.

Several of the teachers at Bethel School were: Miss. E. A. Souter, John F. Banks, D. B. Busby, J. M. Alewine, J. B. O'Neall Holloway, Mrs. S. M. B. Wright, and Miss. Hattie Steck (she later became Mrs. Jaynes, of Walhalla, S. C.); Miss. Hennie Boozer (she was later the wife Dr. W. D. Senn, of Newberry County), Rev. W. K. Sligh, (he was later a professor at Newberry College), Miss. Alma Kibler(she was later the wife of R. F. Bryant, of Orangeburg, S. C.), Prof. Burr Johnstone (later professor at Clemson College), W. B. Boinest, Miss. Lula Teague, Miss. Ella Belle Spirey, and others.

(Refernces: The "Annals of Newberry," Newberry Observer, Apr. 1938).

This school sent out many students who after completing their college courses have become prominent ministers of the Gospel, teachers, physicians, college professors, lawyers, and in other professions.

The present high school building is constructed of brick, with two-stories, and has many modern conveniences for the students.

Peak Station School-

The nearest school to that community about 1890 was the one called the "Counts School". The first in the village was held in an old store building, near the railroad station, with Mr. McLaughlin as the first teacher.

The next year the school was held in the town hall, taught by William Sharpe. The classes were held upstairs, which later was needed for the meetings of the local Masonic Lodge.

Then, a school house was built, about 1889, with the following elected as Trustees: George M. Stuck, Jackson Counts, J. L. Dominick, John C. Swygert, and F. B. Lucas. Mr. McLaughlin was again elected the teacher.

Later, the teachers elected were women.

The same building was used for several years, until 1924, when it was moved to a newly erected building, with two rooms, an auditorium, cloak room, and other added facilities. The old school building was given over to the school for the colored children.

The Trustees in 1925 were: H. L. Suber, Olin Lindler, R. V. Eargle. The first teachers in the new school were: Mrs. J. T. Judy, from Neeses, S. C., Mrs. O. H. Swygert, of Peak.

For the past few years the high school pupils have been transported by bus to a neighboring High School, at Pomaria. (Ref: Newberry Observer, April, 1938).

Little Mountain High School-
Mount Tabor Church Academy-

The present High School at Little Mountain, Newberry County, is the offspring of the old Mt. Tabor Academy which was located about two miles North of the town, and was the first school started in that neighborhood, about the time the first Mt. Tabor Church was built.

Realizing the need for a school of higher learning, the patrons met in the church in 1885, and decided to organize a school of high standard. The school became known as the academy, with a ten months session each year, or 200 days the first term, from October 1 to June 1, and the second term from July 1, to run two months. A Board of Trustees was elected, with seven members; then a Principal and one assistant teacher elected. They decided to increase the salaries of the teachers by charging the pupils for the studies they pursued. Those taking reading, writing and spelling, each paid six cents a day, and those who added history and arithmetic were charged eight cents a day, each; and those taking the further additional studies of Latin and Greek and Literature were charged eleven cents a day, each.

The first Trustees were: The Rev. J. A. Sligh, A. N. Boland, George N. Shealy, D. C. Boland, W. C. Shealy, B. F. Shealy, and John A. Shealy, Sr. L. C. Boland was elected Secretary at the meeting.

In 1891 a small school was started in a one-room house near the I. V. Matthews home, taught by Rev. S. L. Nease, then the pastor of Trinity Lutheran Church there. Then, A. N. Boland gave one acre land near the mountain for a new school, which was erected thereon (site of the present high school), and the two schools were considated with this school.

E. O Counts taught at Mt. Tabor School, as Principal, with Miss. Maggie Monts as assistant. Miss. Monts resigned after three months work, and Miss. Ella Sease was elected to fill out her term; but she, too, resigned, after a month's service; and Miss. Kamie Whites was elected.

Little Mountain school started with Prof. Thad. Dreher as teacher, in a one-room building. Afterwards, W. A. Counts took charge as Principal. A large two-story building was erected, and two assistant teachers were added to take care of the increased enrollments. Ed. Boland succeeded Mr. Counts, then came J. R. Unger, J. W. Ballentine, in 1905. In 1907, the State High School system was established in Little Mountain.

In 1908, a new brick building was constructed, two stories, and Virgil Sease took charge as Principal, in 1908; then came F. O. Black, J. B. O'Neall Holloway, J. W. Mack, G. H. Ballentine, A. F. Pugh, Ernest Cannon, Miss. Mamie Swittenberg(now Mrs. J. H. Summer),Miss. Lizzie Neal, Price K. Harmon, and Ben Eleazar, and others.

In 1929, a large auditorium and two class rooms were added to the building. Virgil Cannon was elected Principal that year; then, R. H. Miller, C. W. Riser, W. L. Epting, J. W. Ballentine, Dan Epting, and others.

Eleven teachers are now (1938) employed in the school. The Trustess in 1940 were: B. M. Wise, L. C. Derrick, R. O. Shealy,.... Other leaders of the community who have served as Trustees were: A. N. Boland, Dr. J. M. Sease, Joe B. Derrick, W. B. Shealy, James Wise, W. A. Counts, J. K. Derrick, A. Z. Stoudemire, and others.

Cross Roads Old School-

This school was located about half way between Little Mountain and Pomaria, on the site of the old John Summer home. It began probably before the year 1870.

J. William Folk taught the school about 1871. One of his old day books gives data pertaining it's operations at the time he was the teacher. It is dated January 9, 1871, the time he began teaching there, " which is the second year taught by Willie." March 7, 1870 was the beginning of the first year of his teaching. " Saturday night, the 12th of February, 1870, will never be forgotten", the book reads. He gives some of the " Rules of the School", which he instituted, which are as follows: "First, scholars must obey the teacher in all things; second, scholars disobeying the teacher must suffer; third, scholars shall not be allowed to carry fire-arms of any kind; fourth, the boys and girls shall not be allowed to play together; fifth, the boys shall not sit with the girls; sixth, no liquors shall be allowed at school, nor boys under the influence of it; Seventh, good order and behavior is expected from all; eighth, no scholar shall call each other nick-names of any kind; ninth, no whispering shall be allowed in time of school; tenth, no telling each other in time of recitation; eleventh, no fighting shall be allowed at any time; twelfth, no swearing or cursing at any time; thirteenth, no lying or telling an untruth at any time; fourteenth, no laughing in study hours, nor in class; fifteenth,no scholar shall be allowed to go out of the house, unless having permission from the teacher; sixteenth, the scholars shall not go out of sight of the school house; seventeenth, no cutting or marking the desks or benches; eighteenth, perfect obedience to the above rules is expected; ninteenth, no playing cards at school or on the school ground."

List of subscribed scholars in 1871 whose parents were as follows: D. D. Long, A. Shealy, Thomas Summer, George Stoudemire, John Fulmer, Mrs. Martha Summer, George Epting, Joseph Summer, John Swittenberg, Mrs. Martha Stoudemire, Tarsey Stuck, Francis Clark, John Farr, John Epting,Lang. Sease, Henry Cumalander, J. J. Derrick, A. A. Guise, William Martin, Jacob Epting, Sr., Joseph Shealy, Jack Addy, L. Lem Chapman, Susannah Koon, Henry Miller, Sallie Swittenberg, Noah Sease, Luther Mayer, O. P. Fulmer.

Record of attendance: Walter Long, Noah Summer, Andrew Shealy, Luther Miller, Pressley Shealy, George Fulmer, Sidney Clark, Paul Addy, George Summer, Charlie Summer, Charlie Stoudemire, Jack Shealy, Johnnie Epting, Bluford Stoudemire, Charlies Swittenberg, George Farr, Solomon Martin, Robert Stuck, Mike Stuck, Florence Stuck, Nora Long, Dora Epting, Cummings Sheely, Janie Stoudemire, Annette Clark, Brinhill Clark, Dora Summer, Elby Guise, Bettie Swittenberg, Alice Long, Mary Farr, Mahalla Martin, Beauregard Bundrick, Walter Addy, William Chapman, John Swittenberg, Pink Summer, Gussie Summer, Mary Summer, Elmira Summer, Ella Hipp, Alice Sease, Walter Derrick, Bach Swittenberg, Mattie Derrick, Mary Stoudemire, Emma Sease, John Cumulander, Walter Miller, Elliot Huffman, Katie Huffman, John Boland, Luther Mayer, Hack Summer, Jacob Koon, Milas Koon, Laura Stoudemire, Cummings Stoudemire, Jimmie Clark, Perry Fulmer, Jessie Koon, Mary Chapman, Kaus Epting, Olivia Epting. Johnnie Long, Mary Huffman, Boyd Epting, Jackson Counts, Johnnie Chapman.

The record gives a detailed statement of each patrons contribution, the humber of days' attendance of each pupil, both 1870 and 1871, and amounts collected from the patrons.........

Since that time, several teachers taught the school, until it was discontinued , among them S. J. Derrick who was later President of Newberry College.

O'Neall Consolidated School-

The following is an extract from an article in the Newberry Observer in April, 1938, regarding the O'Neall Consolidated School:

Through untiring efforts of Col. Elbert H. Aull, County Superintendent of Education, Saluda, O'Neall, and Monticello schools were consolidated in 1925 to form O'Neall high school.

The construction of the building was started in the spring or early summer during Col. Aull's administration and completed in the fall after Mr. D. L. Wedaman took office.

Mr. N. E. Oxner of Saluda, was the contractor, and Messrs. J. A. Bowers, W. H. Long, and P. W. Counts were trustees.

The building was not completed in time to start the 1925-26 session. School was held for two months in the large "Harmon House", now the home of Mr. J. P. Fellers.

1925-1926 the school was a two-teacher three year high school. R. C. Hunter was Superintendent, and A. G. Pugh, Sr., was the other high school teacher. The grammar grade teachers were Mrs. R. E. Sharpe, Mrs. Estelle Boozer, and Miss Sarah Alice Koon. During the session Miss Mary Ellen Rampey was added.

In the fall of 1926, P. Clyde Singley was added to the high school faculty and F. N. Culler taught agriculture. Misses Eula and Chloe Epting took the places of Mrs. R. E. Sharpe and Miss Rampey who had resigned.

During this session the eleventh grade was taught. Seven completed the work and received high school diplomas. Fairview high school students also attended O'Neall this year.

1927-1928, the faculty remained the same except Miss Koon had resigned, and Miss Violet Lester filled this place.

Mother Walker of Winthrop College planned and supervised the laying off and planting of the school ground. Mrs. R. C. Hunter cared for the shrubs, with the aid of the children. Six boys and girls graduated and received high school diplomas.

During the 1928-1929 term, D. Feldon Ruff taught in Miss Lester's place, she having resigned. Twelve students finished the required four year high school course and were the first class to receive State High School diplomas.

During the past four years the high school had steadily grown from about forty-two to sixty enrollment. Much credit is due to Superintendent R. C. Hunter who contributed his time, and means to making O'Neall a successful and prosperous school.

There were several faculty changes in 1929-30. Mr. Javas Black was elected superintendent and Miss Elvelyn Halfacre, (now Mrs. John Sanders), and Mr. D. F. Ruff were high school teachers. The grammar school teachers were: Misses Eula and Chloe Epting, and Mrs. Javas Black, Mrs. Bennie Wicker taught music, and Mr. F. N. Culler, agriculture.

1930-31 the faculty remained the same as the past year.

1931-1932, Miss Rebecca Kibler, (now Mrs. J. W. Lominick), and Miss Rosalee Wheeler took the places of Misses Eula and Chloe Epting. Mr. Virgil Cameron, now a Lutheran Minister, succeeded Miss Evelyn Halfacre. Miss Floride Pollard taught music.

The school session 1932-1933, the high school faculty remained unchanged. Mr. H. O. Frick was elected to fill the vacancy by Miss Wheeler's resigning. Miss Luva McDonald was the music teacher during this session.

1933-1934, Mr. H. O. Frick was elected Superintendent. Messrs. Clyde Bedenbaugh and B. R. Nichols were the other high school teachers. The grammar school teachers were Misses Sarah Harmon, Rebecca Kibler, (now Mrs. J. W. Lominick), and Katherine Long, (now Mrs. Ligon Kimball)

In the fall of '33 the teachers' home was erected on the school ground. Mr. and Mrs. Frick were the first to live in this brick-veneered home.

1934-1935. Only two changes in the faculty were made. Mr. Claude Lawson taught in the place of Mr. Bedenbaugh, who resigned, and Mr. Herman Shealy filled the vacancy left by the resignation of Miss Harmon.

1935-1936. Mr. G. A. Lindler was elected Superintendent, and the remaining teachers were: B. R. Nichols, Miss Rose K. Hallman, R. H. Amick, Misses Prema Lever, Ruby Arant, and Myra Bowers, (now Mrs. L. C. Fellers). Miss Lever taught the fifth grade and music.

The following year Miss Lever filled the vacancy left by Mrs. Fellers' resignation, and music was no longer taught at the school.

Helena School-

The first schools in that suburb of Newberry were ones taught at different times by different teachers at their own homes or their own locations.

One of the first schools was at the time, before the War Between the States, conducted to furnish facilities for the children of the families who were connected with the old Southern Railway Shops that were located just beyond Helena, or just beyond the "grove". Some of these, there, were: Miss Maybry, Miss Flora Meredith; later, Mrs. Ann Milligan taught in a house that stood where now lives J. R. Wood. Some of her pupils were from the families of Coats, (Jesse Coats and his sister, Nellie who later married a Davis), Shockleys (Mrs. Daisy Wilbur, Mrs Eunice Stewart), the Welches (Mrs. Elois D. Wright), the Zobels (Mrs. Elizabeth Melton, and Mrs. Burns).

When the Southern Railway shops were moved to Columbia, South Carolina, a school was started in the old shop office where Miss Beulah Greneker taught (later became Mrs. Baxter Julian).

Later, the school was moved to the Huntington house, where the following taught at different times: Arthur Kibler, Robert Norris, Miss Beulah Greneker, Miss Lillian Glenn, (now Mrs. Austen, of Laurens, South Carolina), Miss Emily Scott (later became Mrs. J. Henry West), Miss Bessie Wheeler (later became Mrs. W. K. Sligh), and Rev. John W. Speake (who later was President of Lander College, Greenwood). Some of the pupils in these schools were children from the families of Dobbins, Leonhardth, Wilson, Salter, Summers, and others.

At the last school the following were some of the teachers: Miss Julia Brown, (later Mrs. George Epps), Miss Alma Bishop, Miss Elizabeth Dominick, Miss Minnie Wallace, Miss Blanche Davidson, Miss Lucile Wallace (later Mrs. Jesse B. Mayes), Miss Corrie Lee Havird.

The Trustees, J. C. Abrams, Luther Cousins, and Oscar Bouknight, sold the building and the school was discontinued, as arrangements were made to transport the children to the Newberry City Schools where they could receive the advantages of high school standard.

Silver Street Consolidated Schools-

When the schools of the Silver Street section were consolidated, there were several small schools in the different outlying districts, Mount Zion, Trinity, Utopia, Silver Street, Reagan, Ridge Spring, and probably others.

Most of these schools were private ones that grew out of the need for facilities for local children of each community. They were small one-room cabins with one teacher each. Dead Fall was the first school established, not far from the village of Silver Street. At Utopia the school was called the "Crab Orchard" school, being situated near the old George Schumpert place and the Boulware place, where were said to have been apple orchards. Another private school, called the Burton School, was not far from J. S. Floyd's home.

The school at Silver Street grew out of a private school which was located at the Willie Spearman place (now owned by the Richard C. Neel estate). The first school grounds were bought from Mrs. Fannie Maffett and H. C. Lake.

The enrollment in the consolidated school in 1939 was over two hundred pupils, and they were transported daily to and from the school in five buses.

The buildings have been enlarged, renovated, and the grounds extended and landscaped, with new plants and trees planted. The library is large for such a school.

The first seven grades have five teachers. In the high school there are two teachers in addition to the principal. They have several good organizations among the students, as, the Literary Society, the Future Farmers of America, the Glee Club, the Better Speech Club; and sports, as, the Basket-ball Teams, Base-ball team, dramatics, ets. The graduating class usually takes a trip each year, that is of educational value. Some of these have been to Columbia while State Legislature was in session, to the State University Library, and to points in Charleston, and other places.

A Parent-Teacher Association is formed, who help in distribution of books, etc.; free lunches, etc.

1937-1938. Mrs. L. C. Fellers was elected to succeed Miss Hallman, who had resigned. Mr. A. A. Webb taught Agriculture.

Mr. Roston Hare was elected Superintendent in 1938. Two other new teachers were in the faculty. They were Miss Sarah Pitts and Clifford Coleman to succeed Misses Lever and Arant.

In 1930 the pupils from Corinth district in Saluda County were transported to O'Neall. These pupils were transported here six years. Later the high school students from Pleasant Grove, Delmar and Verona were transported here, and they are still attending O'Neall school. The high school enrollment at present is around sixty, and there are three teachers in grammar school.

Mt. Bethel Academy-

Bishop Asbury, like a true philosopher, knew that the hope of the country depended upon the proper education of the young; and like a wise builder in the erection of the Christian edifice he was fully impressed with the fact that the hope of the church, as it regarded, symmetry, beauty and strength, depended upon the rising generation.

As early as 1780 he invoked the council and aid of John Dickens, who was educated at Eton College, England; and they agreed to establish a system of Christian education, embracing a central institution with a school in each district of the conference. The system was endorsed by Dr. Coke. In pursuance of this plan he organized Mt. Bethel Academy in Newberry District, South Carolina.

The Finches, Crenshaws, and Malones were the most prominent Methodists in that district.

When the subject of the school was proposed they entered into the project heartily and with liberal subscriptions. Edward "Needy" Finch gave thirty acres of land as a site for the institution. Subscriptions were raised and the building finished and formally dedicated by Bishop Asbury, March 20, 1795. The school was for six years under the rectorship of Rev. Mark Moore, assisted by two other teachers, Messrs. Smith and Hammond. At the close of the sixth term Mr. Moore then resigned and took a charge of a school in Columbia where he materially aided in the permanent establishment of Methodism in that city.

Mr. Hammond, father of Ex-governor Hammond, took charge of the school and taught it with signal ability for many years.

Mt. Bethel and Willington Academy in Abbeville District, afterwards taught by Mr. Moses Waddell, were the only schools of higher learning in the interior of the state for many years. John C. Calhoun attended Willington Academy.

Mt. Bethel Academy was largely patronized by students, from South Carolina, North Carolina and Georgia. The first and second classes which graduated in South Carolina college received their training here. Mt. Bethel was the nucleus of the University of South Carolina. William Harper was the first to matriculate at Carolina. He stopped to teach a year and Crenshaw was the first to graduate. Both of these became noted jurists: one in Alabama and one in South Carolina. Wesley Harper graduated in the second class. He died soon afterwards. Other noted men who received their training at Mt. Bethel were: John Caldwell, Chancellor James J. Caldwell, Dr. G. W. Glenn, Governor Manning, Dr. Tom Brown, Davis Smith and Glover.

The main building of this academy was twenty by forty feet, divided by a partition, with a chimney at each end, constructed of rough unhewn stone. The upstairs was used as lodgings for the students. Mt. Bethel Academy was located twelve miles ortheast of Newberry on a lofty knoll in front of what is now known as the Dr. Tom Brown place.

Edward or "Needy" Finch, who gave the land on which to locate the school, boarded many of the pupils in his home, located where the Dr. Tom Brown place is today. One of his daughters married Dr. Adams. He died and she then married Dr. Atwood. Their daughter married Captain Jack Henderson. Dr. Finch, son of "Needy" Finch, went to Columbia to see Wm. Henry Drayton inaugurated governor. His horse ran away and killed him

Later several comfortable cabins were built and served as residences for the teachers and as boarding houses.

About one hundred yards distant at the foot of the hill ran a bold spring of pure cold water. It had sufficient volume to supply all the wants of the resident population at Mt. Bethel.

The money with which to build the academy and to sustain it was obtained by annual collections in aid of which Bishop Asbury sent out written appeals.

The salary of the rector, three hundred dollars a year, was pledged by the South Carolina Conference. Bishop Asbury raised the funds to pay expenses as he traveled about.

Some evidences of the old Academy may still be seen but all the buildings have been torn down and a traveler who might visit it could hardly conceive of its former glory and usefulness.

Nearby is a large graveyard in which many of the original settlers and some of the students quietly sleep in death. The noted remains of Rev. John Harper, who established Washington Street, M. E. church in Columbia, lie here in modest seclusion. A rude stone six or eight inches above the ground bearing the letters J.H. marks his grave. The stone cannot be seen now.

Bishop Asbury says that after holding the seventh conference in Charleston, he went to Georgia and accompanied by Hardy Herbert and Hope Hill to Finches in Newberry to hold the eighth session of South Carolina Conference. And to connect it with the Georgia Conference, on January 1, 1794 about thirty preachers of South Carolina and Georgia, including members and those who had business with the United States Conference attended. We were straightened for room, having only twelve feet square in which to confer, sleep and for the accommodations of those who were sick.

The Bishop says, "we removed Br. Bruce, who was attacked with dysentery into a room without a fire. We hastened the business of our conference as fast as we could. After sitting in a close room with a very large fire, I retired into the woods for nearly an hour to pray and was seized with a severe chill and an inveterate cough, a fever and sick stomach. With difficulty I sat in the conference the following day and that night I could get but little rest. Brother Bruce's moving so often and the other brethren talking, all disturbed me. Sick as I was I had ordained four elders and six deacons. Never did I perform such a burden. I found that I must go elsewhere to get rest. The day was cloudy and threatening snow, however, Brother Reuben Ellis and myself made out to get seven miles to dear Brother Yeagin's. The next day came a heavy fall of snow which continued two days and was from six to ten inches deep. A total membership of six thousand, six hundred and sixteen was reported at that conference."

Bishop Asbury continued annually to visit Mt. Bethel Academy until 1815 when old age and infirmities contracted the field of his labors. A marker should be placed on the road going from Whitmire to Columbia by Pomaria, so that passers-by may know how to go out to where this sacred spot is located.

Said John Wesley, "I am not afraid that the people called Methodist should ever cease to exist, either in Europe or America; but I am afraid that they should exist as a dead sect having the form of religion without the power."

Rev. John Harper gave the land for the building for Washington Street Methodist Church, one of the earliest if not the first church erected in the state capital.

Mt. Bethel closed about 1820 superceded by Tabernacle Academy in Abbeville County. This Academy, after, grew into the Cokesbury school, and out of this Cokesbury school Wofford college, or perhaps better said, Wofford College was established and that meant the death of the school at Cokesbury.

(Note: The above sketch is copied from an old sketch—Author unknown).

COMMUNITIES AND TOWNS IN THE COUNTY.

Pomaria.

Pomaria may be considered the center of the upper Dutch Fork section, located about eighteen miles Southeast of Newberry Court House, near Crim's Creek. The name was first given the Post Office over one hundred years ago. The highway crosses the railroad at the town and follows, practically, the old stage-coach road which extended from Charleston, S. C. to Buncombe County, North Carolina. If a stage-coach or wagon could pull up the long red hill at this point, called in early times the " Folk Hill", it could pull up any hill on the route.

Where is now the old " Summer Home", about three-fourths of a mile further down, which was originally built by John Summer, William Summer, a son, lived and operated a large nursery The nursery became widely known throughout the State and in other States, to which many rare plants were shipped. He imported many rare specimens from Europe and this started in this country many species that were not native to this country. It is thought, too, that in some instances he gave new plants through some grafting processes.

William Summer built the first post office in that section, the old building which still stands in the yard of the old home. He was the first Post Master under the stage coach regime. He named the place " Pomaria", from the Latin word,"Pomus" or " Pomaria", meaning plants or trees, using the feminine adjective which is spelled , " Pomaria".

When the Columbia and Greenville Railroad was completed as far up from Columbia as Pomaria, about the year 1850, and a station built near the railroad, the post office was removed to it's present location. William Summer was appointed the first Post Master at it's new location, and Thomas W. Holloway as Assistant Post Master. It was first operated in the corner of one of the general stores that had been built, owned and operated by John A. Folk. Mr. Folk operated this store until 1855, when he was succeeded by Thomas W. Holloway with his brother-in-law, H. H. Folk. They continued the business until the War Between the States, which compeled them to quit.

After the war, Thomas W. Holloway and Hayne D. Reid carried on the business, in partnership, until Reid was murdered by a negro robber one night, Mr. Reid then living in the rear of the store.

The next firm to start business was David Hipp and William Dickert, in partnership. They were succeeded by D. Hipp & Company (Edward R. Hipp, a nephew, being the company). When this firm dissolved, David Hipp's son-in-law, William Hatton, came into the business as a partner.

It was not before other stores began to be built, that the town showed some progress. Thomas W. Holloway had built a store in 1878, and operated it with his son, John B. O'Neall Holloway. The son having married in Orangeburg, he and his family removed to that county, his interest being sold in 1889 to Edward R. Hipp, son—in-law of Thomas W. Holloway; but the business was short-lived, as the store and all it's goods were burned in 1891.

There have been many changes in a business way. At the present time, there are several stores, a post office, a frame hotel, and one time a bank thrived in the town, until it was closed at the time of the depression after the first World War.

There are good schools and churches in the town and in the nearby area; a large brick school building in town, nice homes, and in addition there was once a large oil mill and ginnery, and a lumber plant.

The surrounding area felt the effect of General Sherman's march in 1865, when they marched from Columbia towards Broad River. Kilpatrick's Raiders, as they were called, caused many homes to be destroyed by fire, barns and gin-houses, much stock and other valuables stolen. Among the many instances may be mentioned that of the home of Major Henry Summer, a lawyer of Newberry, who had retired to his plantation during the war times. All his valuable law library was destroyed. (Reference is made to this in another section of this book).

The raiders then stopped at two Epting homes, one that of Captain George Epting, then at his brother, John Epting's, home. They were about to set fire to the first home, when Epting gave the leader a Masonic sign. The leaders then stopped the raiders and requested Epting to get his pistol or gun and bring it to him, which was done. Many of the raiders wanted to burn the home anyway but the leader pulled the gun and dared them to molest the home. They were then given something to eat and drink, thereupon they left but took with them all of the food in kitchen and all the live-stock.

At John Epting's home they stopped and gathered food and drink, which was given them. They were about to hang Epting from a tree when an old negro slave approached the leader and asked he be sacrificed in place of his master. When asked why he wanted it done that way, the slave replied that " Mars' Epting" had been so good to them, had never whipped or harmed them, his slaves, had taken care of them when sick as if they were his own children. The slave got on his knees and begged the Yankees not to harm them or barn the home. The leader seeing much attachment, said that so good a man should not be harmed, and they left, not even stealing a thing.

The raiders marched into the upper section, above Pomaria, and continued looting, taking stock and other valuables on their way. They stopped at Thomas V. Wicker's home and were about to raid the house, after ordering food. Mrs. Wicker gave them so many good things to eat, including many delicacies that they would not raid the home. On their way out, however, they stole several fine mules and horses from the barns, and marched towards Broad River; but a a company of young men, hearing of it, soon got behind them, and captured them near the river, bringing back most of the stock.

South of Crim's Creek, near Pomaria, lived Major Micheal Leitner, a brave American officer during the Rev. War, a Justice of the Peace, Justice of the Quorum, and a member of the Second Provincial Congress. None of his descendents of that name are living in the Dutch Fork at this time.

On all sides of the town lived many early Germans, Swiss, and Welsh or English; the most of them having come from Pennsylvania in the colony of Adam Summer about 1750. They were opposed to changing their native language from German to English, until about two generations; and when they began to change, they changed, too, the spellings of many surnames using the easy phonetic form, some of which are the following: Koon (Kuhn), Eigner (Agner), Suber (Zuber), Summer (Somer and Sommer-German, and Summer-Swiss), Swygert (Zweighart), Berly(Byerly), Cromer (Krommer), Wicker (Weisker), Counts (Kountz), Epting (Eplin), Lester (Leister), Bedenbaugh (Peterbaux), Werts (Wirtz), Singley (Single), Hare or Hair (Haire), Folk (Faulk), Sheely (Scheale), Houseal(Haushl), Kibler (Keibler), Wedaman(Wydemann), Livingston (Levistein), Kinard (Kynnard), and others.

Prosperity.

The town of Prosperity, located about seven miles South of Newberry Court House, is a place of about 900 population, with many good stores, churches, schools, and modernly equipped with water and lights. It has a mayor and a board of aldermen, being incorporated.

The first store at it's present location was started in 1830 by Matthew Hall, Sr., where he lived. A school was started about 1831, and a church built nearby. On Account of the low land the place gained the name, " Frog Level", according to tradition, as many frogs were in the ponds in the vicinity; the incident leading to the name having occured while a young couple were riding, horse-back, from church one Sunday. It appears that while they were watering their horses nearby they heard many frogs croaking, when the young lady exclaimed, " Hello, this must be frog level".

Another store was built nearby by David Kibler, and others later; so that the town then began to grow. Good churches were built in the town, a large school which took the place of the one-room school building that was built in 1831.

In 1873 a large fire destroyed most of the business section; several of which were replaced with large brick stores.

After the two railroads came through (Southern Railroad in 1858 and the Columbia, Newberry, and Laurens Railroad in 1890), enterprises started. The Southern Bell Telephone Company came about 1900; and the city water works completed in 1936; new banking buildings; and a large planer mill. The Commissioners of Public Works (1936-38) were: Dr. J. I. Bedenbaugh, Dr. George W. Harmon, and J. A. Sease. J. Frank Browne, Clerk, and James Lee Counts, Superintendent.

There are several mens's and womens' organizations and fraternal orders. Among them were, and still are, the Womens' Bridge Club, the Dutch Club, Masonic Lodge, Woodmen of the World, Community League, Literary Sorosis, Garden Club, the United Daughters of the Confederacy. For the young people there is a Music Club and an Honarary Beta Club.

The physicians practicing in the town are Dr. J. I Bedenabuag, Dr. John J. Dominick, Dr. Von Long. The late Dr. C. T. Wyche who had come from North Carolina, practiced several years, then operated a large drug store in the town.

Some other industries not mentioned above, that have been established, are the following: Prosperity Ginnery, the Ice and Fuel Company, the Prosperity Depository (taking place of the banks that have been discontinued), two motor companies, hardware stores, groceries, dry goods and clothing stores, new drug store, and a fertilizer business.

About 1940 the following were the officers of the town: Robert P. Luther, Mayor; Councilmen, P. C. Singley, D. H. Hamm, Sr., H. E. Counts, and C. Barnes. The Commissioners of Public Works were: Dr. J. I. Bedenbaugh, Dr. George W. Harmon, J. A. Sease, and J. L. Counts, the latter being the Superintendent.

Silver Street

Silver Street, a town of about 300 population, is located seven miles West of Newberry Court House, on the Columbia and Greenville branch of the Southern Railroad, on Highway No. 22, between Newberry and Greenwood. It is incorporated, with an Intendent and Wardens. The town was incorporated in 1910, with B. M. Havird, Intendent, and Wardens, D. L. Hamm, W. V. Bledsoe, S. H. Paysinger, and J. C. Berry.

A tradition is that it's name was given because of the fact that a profusion of silvery looking flowers or plants once grew along the sides of the road. Another tradition is that it's name came from Indians, or that the name may have been derived from the Latin word, Silva, meaning forests.

The first post master after the railroad came was Thomas J. Maffett, who was, also, a merchant in the place. After the death of Mr. Maffett he was succeeded by B. Mayer Havird as postmaster. During Mr. Havird's administration the first rural route was established in 1904, with Mott G. Sheppard as the first rural carrier.

One of the first physicians was Dr. Pitts; then came Dr. Julian, Dr. Longshore, Dr. Kinard, Dr. Martin, Dr. E. H. Moore, Dr. Hugh Senn, and others later.

The industries are , a ginnery, a lumber plant, several stores, and shops. The first store was started several years prior to 1900. The first ginnery was owned by B. Mayer Havird, and later operated by the Silver Street Warehouse Company which was established in 1907. The first officers of the warehouse plant were the following: Henry O. Long, President, B. Mayer Havird, Vice-President, and D. L. Hamm, Manager. The plant was operated until 1922 when it was discontinued. Richard C. Neel operated ginnery for several years. Then, Richard Floyd started one in the old warehouse and installed electric power. Through the present Rural Electric Authority many stores, homes, and other places are now using electric power.

At one time the Farmers' Dead Fall Telephone Company constructed a line, and operated it until sometime later. This was in 1908, the year it began operating. Their first officers were: J. Fred Schumpert, President, D. G. Livingstone, Vice-President, H. O. Long, Secretary, and James F. Stephens, Treasurer. They had a 100-drop switchboard which was located in the home of D. G. Livingstone at Dead Fall.

A large brick school building is now in the town, with a standard curriculum.

Several churches are withing the immediate community, including the Zion Baptist, the Lutheran which was constructed in 1908 on land donated by Henry O. Long, and their first pastor being the Rev. Samuel P. Koon, who, also, acted as the first school principal. The present Methodist Church was erected in 1936 on land given by B. Mayer Havird and H. C. Lake. The Pentescostal Church was built about 1915 on land given by Jacob Crouch; it has never had a regular pastor.

About a mile from Silver Street, at the end of a straight road to D. G. Livingston's house, is known as the Dead Fall community. It is said to have gotten it's name from an accident which occured at the end of the road. Frequently horse races were had on this mile strip of road, and at one time a horse fell dead at the end of the road; hence, the name. Another tradition, which seems more logical, is that at this place traps were set for wild animals; the traps being called " Deadfalls", as they fell when the animals entered it.

(Above data from Newberry Observer, April, 1938.)

Mollohon

This is a community located near Indian Creek, or above that creek and including the section around Duncan's Creek. It is not on a railroad.

During the early days of the Rev. War period, a family, according to tradition, lived in the section, the wife and mother of the family being named Molly. It seems that Molly liked to blow the plantation Horn. (These horns used on early plantations were made from cow's horns) Molly's horn became quite famous in the neighborhood; so that name got the name, " Molly's Horn". Afterwards the spelling was changed to Mollyhorn, then to Mollohon.

Liberty Hill

Liberty Hill was another old community which was not on a railroad, but included a small neighborhhod between Whitmire and Clinton. It got it's name from the fact that a muster ground was nearby, where the soldiers of the Rev War were trained, of that section.
It was a popular place in later times for meetings, picnics, and barbecues.

Jalapa

Jalapa is located about seven miles Northwest of Newberry Court House, on the A. C. L. Railroad and the main highway from Greenville to Columbia.

It has a large general store, a ginnery, that were at one time operated in connection with a large plantation. Though one store has taken care of the customers for many years, at one time there were two or three stores. During the life-time of Dr. Clark, who lived in the large two-story white house on the left of the railroad, he operated a store. Also, the late William H. Eddy, Sr., a native of New York State, who settled there several years before the War Between the States, and served the Confederate cause, had a store. The Eddy home and store was was located on the right of the road, opposite of the Clark home. At one time, Dr. J. W. Folk operated a store, as did George Campbell. Each of them burned down. The ginnery was built within the past few years; owned and operated by the firm of Summer Bros at the time they owned and operated the old Clark plantation.

The name " Jalapa" was given the town on account of the fact that many young men of that section volunteered for service in the Mexican War of 1847; and all were killed or died in Mexico, at the battle of Jalapa.

While there have been good churches and schools in that community, most of the history centers around old Tranquil Church. (See history of Tranquil Church in another section of this book).

Kinards

Kinards is located about two and one-half miles South of Goldville and about one and one-half miles North of Gary's Lane; it is close to the Laurens County line. On the Columbia, Newberry and Laurens Railroad(now branch of the A. C. L Ry), and on the U. S. Highway with buses running between Greenville and Columbia.

The name of the town came from a pioneer settler of that Community, Martin Kinard, who moved from the upper Dutch Fork several years before the War Between the States. He became a large landowner, owning all the plantations around the town in both counties. One of his daughters married Jacob Summer who built the present Jack Smith home over one hundred years ago.

Gary's Station , just South of the town, was the home of Thomas Gary, a descendent of the Rev. War patriot, Charles Gary, who is buried at old Bush Rover Baptist Church Cemetery. Thomas Gary's son, Dr. Thomas R. Gary, moved to Cokesbury, in old Abbeville District, and was the ancestor of the late Chief Justice Eugene B. Gary , Judge Ernest Gary, and Judge Frank Gary.

Between Kinards and Garys, about one mile to the right of the main road, was once a large school of high standard, the Pagesville Academy. Many graduates from this school entered the South Carolina College, at Columbia, S. C. The school was established in 1848. One hundred acres of land was granted to the Trustees who were elected by the patrons. In addition to the main academy building there was a four-room house for use of the professors, and other buildings.

At the beginning of the War Between the States the school closed and never resumed work.

Goldville, just North of Kinards, in Laurens County, was also a flag station. It was first called Martins Station, for the late Martin Kinard who owned most of the lands around or between Kinards and Goldville.

Helena

The surburban village of Helena was once largely populated, when the old railroad shops were located in it, the shops of the first Greenville and Columbia railroad.

The town was named for the wife of Judge J. B. O'Neall, Mrs. Helena O'Neall, who was the daughter of Captain Sampson Pope and Sarah Strother Pope of Edgefield District, S. C. Judge O'Neall was the Attorney, then the President of the Columbia and Greenville Railroad. The shops were built about 1850-52.

The village streets are narrow, and the few side-walks un-paved, which indicates it's early beginning. The few large trees that are left in the once large, shaded grove, where not so many years back were held picnics, barbecues and campaign meetings, are but relics of this once industrial village.

The site of the old Union Church which stood for many years after the War Between the States was just beyond the village, about two hundred yards to the right of the railroad near the edge of a grove of pine-trees. The old graveyard there contains many early markers.

There were private schools in the community, taught at different times by men and women of " the old school", cultured and well-educated instructors; until the graded school system started in the town of Newberry.

Some early families of village were Bowers, Coats, Leonards, Scruggs, Summers, Zobels, and others whose children attended the schools.

The Leonards and Zobels came directly from Germany, while others came from other sections of the county or from other counties. The late Mrs. Kate Coats was a native Wales, coming to this section when quite a young girl. Jacob Bowers, an employee of the railroad, a Section Master, lived in the village. (See another section of this book for the story of his capture by the Yankees just after the war).

Another Civil War story is related by Col. D. A. Dickert concerning a young man from Helena named Zobel who volunteered for service in the Confederate Army, though he was a German. It appears that at the battle of Knoxville, Tenn. while serving as a private in the company of Captain James D. Nance, young Zobel was captured and taken prisoner, to the " Bastile" prison, " a reputed loathsome den in New Jersey." While there he was visited by the German Consul, who, learning that he was not yet naturalized, endeavored to get him freed. The only condition upon which the Consul was able to get him his freedom was that he join the Union forces. Young Zobel's reply to this proposal was that he would rather died in that hell-hole than desert his friends and comrades and betray the flag under which he was serving.

An incident is related in the " Annals of Newberry" about the time when the wife of President Jefferson Davis passed through Newberry with her sister on their way home in Alabama. They stopped at Newberry while the train was being repaired at the Helena shops. Then the railroad company gave them a special car from the shops in which the continued their journey through Georgia.

After the War Between the States many families moved to the village. Allen Scruggs who was famous as a maker of good wines and brandies, may have come just before the war. Many farmers brought their apples, peaches and grapes to Scruggs to be bottled, which they took back home with them. After the War, and Allen Scruggs death, his son-in-law, H. Clinton Summers, continued the business awhile, and also operated a pool-room and store, in a two-story building on the corner.

Dr. S. G. Welch lived in the village awhile. He was a Confederate surgeon.

B. A. Julien operated a grocery store on the corner opposite to the Summers place. His son, Carl Julien, became known as a color photographer.

The other old places or sites of a once thriving community, like many other places, are but ghosts of other generations.

Chappells

Chappells, located about nineteen miles West of Newberry Court House, on Saluda River, has several stores, filling stations, a lumber plant. Within the vicinity are nice homes, good churches, and a large school building. The new concrete bridge over the river, over State Highway No. 22, has taken the place of the old steel bridge below it.

The population is about two hundred people. Recently incorporated, it now has it's intendent and board of aldermen.

The town was started about one hundred years ago when the pioneer of that section located there and started a store, whose name was Thomas Chappell. He had lived in the locality since 1756. One of his sons, John Chappell, became the first merchant and owner of a ferry boat on the river.

When the Columbia and Greenville Railroad was built (now the Southern Railway), one store had started, then another, and in 1884 there were three stores. In that year all the stores and other nearby buildings were destroyed or damaged by a cyclone which swept across the country. Five people were killed and several injured.

In later years Chappells was visited by other storms; then a big fire occured; which at each time damaged or destroyed much valuable property.

There are some very old historical places near Chappells. On Mudlick Creek where once "Bloody Bill" Cunningham, and his tories sometimes organized for plunder. One of his attacks was prevented by Col. Washington at Hammond's Old Store, who defeated the tories and scattered them. The Mudlick tribe of Indians lived there; hence the name of the creek.

Some of the early settlers before the Rev. War in that immediate locality were Foster Wells and Nicholas Vaughn. They lived near the present community known as "Vaughnville". In this neighborhood was the route of General Greene in his retreat from Ninety Six by way of the Island Ford.

Since the War Between the States William B. Smith operated the ferry. Later, he gave his right in the property for a free bridge across the river. The first bridge was a narrow, crude, wooden bridge, which was soon afterwards replaced by a longer and better constructed one, of steel, which stood the elements for many years; until the construction of the present concrete bridge.

Below Chappells, a few miles to the South, was once a store on the river, the place being known as "Saluda Old Town". It got it's name from the Salutah tribe of Indians, which belonged to the Cherokee Nation. The name was afterwards changed to "Old Town", about the time the town of Saluda about ten miles away was started. Old Town is within site of the old Indian village on Saluda River. Once trading wagons forded the river at this point, before the ferry at Chappells was started. Now nothing is left of the place except the railway station, sometimes used as a flag station.

Little Mountain

Little Mountain was founded about 1890, at the time the Columbia, Newberry and Laurens Railroad was built. It is about seventeen miles South of Newberry Court House. The town is located within the radius of the old quartz zone which stretches from Saluda to Broad River. It was incorporated in 1930.

Some of the first active men in the town were the late A. N. Boland, J. N. Feagle, John B. Lathan and others. At a later time, were the Sheelys, Stoudemire, Wise, Derricks, all active business people there. The home and place of business of the late John K. Derrick who represented the county in the State Legislature for several terms; also, the home place of Dr. Sidney J. Derrick who served for many years as both Professor and President of Newberry College.

Some of the earliest settlers, however, who were there in the community before the town started, were the families of Houseal, Ruff, Epting, Sease, Sheely, Wheeler, Feagle. The background of the community started when the Dutch Fork began to be settled nearer Pomaria about the year 1752. The Ruff family owned the mountain which was then called "Ruff's Mountain", which was then the scene of many early socials, "dances under the light of the moon", at the foot of the mountain. In recent years this same spot has been used for many picnics and barbecues, and campaign meetings.

Peak

Peak Station was started about the time the Columbia and Greenville railroad was built about 1850. Mr. H. T. Peak was the first Superintendent of the railroad and aided in building the first bridge across Broad River from Alston. Alston was the site of the construction camp later, when a flood washed away parts of the bridge, and repairs were made on it.

Starting with only one store, the town now has several stores, many good homes, churches and a high school. They also have a Post Office and several lodges. It is a good trading center, surrounded with small, productive farms, owned and operated by industrious folk who generally live within their means.

Before the building of the railroad this section was inhabited by many early pioneer families, many descendents of whom still reside thers, as, Mayer, Hope, Hobbs, Eichleberger, Swygert, Stoudemire, Chapman, and others; the names Eichleberger, Hope, and Hobbs are about extinct in that section. Many have moved to other sections and other States, and have served as physicians, ministers of the gospel, merchants, educators and in other lines of work.

Maybinton

Maybinton is not an incorporated town; located about sixteen miles Northeast of Newberry Court House on the county highway.

Once a thriving village with several stores, a good school, churches, and several good homes, it has dwindled down to only one store, about two or three homes and no school within it's community. Founded by Col. Benjamin Maybin, an energetic business man of his day; son of the pioneer, William Maybin, who settled in the neighborhood in 1771, and gave his life in the service of his country during the Rev. War.

In this vicinity lived Emily Geiger, with her parents, who was one of the Rev. War Heroines, having carried alone through tory settlements a message from General Greene to General Sumter.

Col. Maybin started one of the first stores there and built and operated the Buck Hotel, which being a well-known stage-coach route, became a popular resort for tourists or travelers. Tradition is that the name "Buck" was given the hotel or inn, on account of the wild animal hunts at that time, many inns being named for some wild animals.

Maybinton became the center of a flouishing section of the county; grew in industry and enterprise; as large quantities of cotton were shipped by flat-boats down Broad River to Columbia, thence by boat to Charleston. Some of the stores were brick buildings. A tannary and a brick-yard were established. There was a Masonic Lodge and Hall.

Not far away, Ebenezer Methodist Church was built, close to it's present location, which is said to be one of the oldest Methodist Churches in the county. A Baptist Church was built, and a lot set aside for the erection of a Presbyterian Church, which was never built on account of it's limited membership.

In 1836, there were two academies in the village, male and female. The male school was situated in a remote, elevated part of the village, while the female was in the center. They were both schools with high standards of study, teaching English, Higher Mathematics, Latin, and the other classics. The girls school had a course in music. Each had it's own board of trustees. The principal of the male academy was Professor Chancey Stone while his daughter, Miss Sarah Stone, had charge of the female academy.

In a few years the village began to wane, the two schools stopped work. Later a single school was established for both boys and girls.

In the year 1886 an unique plan was adopted by the board of trustees, under the sanction of the County Superintendent of Education. The school at that time was under the direction of Miss Helen Hodges. There were two schools that were about two or three miles apart, The law allowed a three-months free school term for each school; and in order to get a six-month school term, one three-month term was held in one building and another three-month term held in the other building.

Though the one-time village has the appearance of a "ghost-town", many descendents of it's earliest settlers still live there or within the surrounding section. Some of these are the following: Lyles, Maybin, Hardy, Henderson, Douglass, Thomas, Henry, and Cornwell. The pioneer of the Whitney family came from Charleston about the time of the stage-coach days, since the Rev. War, when many people from the lower country frequently sought temporary resorts in the up-country.

Whitmire

In presenting a history of Whitmire, the following is part of an interesting sketch written by Mrs. Ann E. Lewis, of that town in 1938:

"Whitmire owes its early beginning to the fact that near where the town now stands the old Buncombe road from Buncombe County, North Carolina, crossed the Ninety-Six road which led from Fishdam Ferry on Broad river across the country to the old Starr Fort at Ninety-Six. As early as Revolutionary days George Frederick Whitmire, a German emigrant coming to Carolina from Pennsylvania, built his log cabin home and soon afterwards a trading post at this cross roads, which from then until now has been called after his name. That the town is today a prosperous and thriving community is due to the facts that in 1890 the Georgia-Carolina and Northern Railroad, now the Seaboard Airline, was built through this section; and some ten years later a cotton mill was built by the late William Coleman".

"The first settler in this section of the country, according to Robert Mills, was a Mr. John Duncan, native of Aberdeen, Scotland, who came here in 1752 from Pennsylvania and settled on the creek that now bears his name. His nearest neighbor was Jacob Pennington who lived on Enoree river, and was the only man at this time who had either negro, wagon or still in this part of the world."

"Following Braddock's defeat in 1756 a number of emigrants from Pennsylvania came to this place seeking homes and farms safe from the French and Indian menace of the Pennsylvania frontier The names of some of these first settlers were McCreary, Green, Hannah, Abernathy, Miller, Beard, King, Mitchell, Wells, Coffee, Grisham, Barton, Yount, M'Clure, Adams, M'David, Prater, Bright, Barns, Oglesby, Hoskins and Holstien.. In this immediate vicinity the earliest settlers were the Whitmires, Duncans, O'Dells, and Ducketts. It must be remembered that in those early days homes were far apart, and today little remains to show their locations."

"Just outside the incorporate limits of Whitmire, are still standing the early home of the Whitmires and across from it the trading post that served also as post office for a wide area during the days of stage coach. If these old buildings could tell their story of the scenes they have witnessed it would be interesting indeed. Facing the old Ninety-Six road, they witnessed the passing of General Greene's soldiers hurrying to the defense of old Star Fort at Ninety-Six."

"Down the old Buncombe road came the mountaineer traders, driving their turkeys and rolling their hogsheads of tobacco to Charleston, returning with salt and sugar and tinware, and stopping to tell their stories."

"According to the Annals of Newberry this section was sorely afflicted by opposite political factions, from which sprang the bitterest strife. Neighbor was arrayed against neighbor, until the excess into which they were led was truly shocking to every sentiment of humanity. And gruesome accounts of Tory outrages followed by Whig vengeance tell of the execution of several Tories on the gallows at the cross roads near the residence of Mrs. Henry Whitmire, and thus received in part a just penalty for this and other crimes committed."

On another occasion, eleven or twelve tories who had attempted the life of a neighbor, Captain Boyce, were run down and captured on the banks of Enoree river near the mouth of Duncan's creek.

"They were conveyed," the Annals relate, "to the place where the Charleston road crosses the Ninety-Six road, now Whitmire, and there a 'short shift', a strong rope, and a stooping hickory applied speedy justice to them all. A common grave at the foot of the tree is their resting place for all time."

"Little has been recorded of the life of the country-side during the period following the Revolution and the succeeding years. Large families were reared and the sons and daughters married and moved away, many to other parts of this state and a large number also joined in the general westward movement."

"About 1820 Mt. Tabor Methodist church was built on a site about four miles south of Whitmire. The Lower Duncan's Creek Church had been organized earlier in 1787, and in the cemeteries around these two old church-sites are to be found many interesting old graves.

"Among the large landowning families of this period in addition to those already mentioned were the Abrams, Scotts, Risers, Subers, Andrews, Herndons, Hattons, Shells, Setzlers, MacCarleys, Epps, Spearmans, Hargroves, and across the river in Union county, the Colemans, Rices, Jeters, Sims, Cofields, Nances, and others. During the Confederate War, these families made their loyal contribution to the cause of Southern independence and suffered the common lot of the South!

"During the chaotic days following the war came two men, David R. Phifer and Charles Tidmarsh, both traders, the latter a teacher also. Both established families here.

"By the year 1890 there were six families, living within the radius of the present town limits, and in that year the Georgia-Carolina and Northern Railroad was completed, the century old trading post was abandoned for a site facing the railroad and the town of Whitmire had its birth, with the depot, its heart, and the new "iron road" its backbone, with straggly, muddy and crooked streets winding about the hills and gullies and pine thickets."

"From that day to this the town has grown, very much as many a human baby has done, by leaps and bounds, too fast for its own good at times, with many a spell of colic and mal-nutrition and broken bones. But progress has been made."

"Mrs E. C. Briggs, known as "L" Briggs, a cotton buyer of Clinton, gave the right of way to the railroad and quite a number of valuable lots in the business section. He also gave the land for the streets of Whitmire and a lot for the Baptist church (where the Baptist parsonage now stands) and a lot to the Methodist church where the post office building stands. He had four wooden store buildings put up and rented them. A land sale was held and many new homes were built. Families moved in from the surrounding country-side."

"The charter of incorporation for the Town of Whitmire was granted on December 18, 1891, and was renewed December 2, 1919. The first charter forbade the sale of intoxicants, set the limits of the town as one square mile, with the depot as the center, and the following men were named commissioners to hold the first election of officers: John P. Fant, E. C. Briggs, and Charles Tidmarsh. At the election held on January 14, 1892, S. A. Merchant was elected mayor, Dr. R. R. Jeter, Charles Tidmarsh, H. E. Todd and B. F. Morrow were made alderman."

"The Methodist church was organized during the first year, 1892, and a small wooden building erected with lumber donated and hauled by the late J. D. Tidmarsh, then only a boy. In the following year, the organization of the old Lower Duncan's Creek Baptist church, established in 1787 and located about three miles from Whitmire, and was transferred to Whitmire. Until a building could be erected, services were held in the depot and Setzler's store. The Presbyterian church was organized in 1905 and the building erected in 1908. In 1916, the Wesleyan M. E. Church was formed and building erected in 1919. A detailed account of the growth and development of these churches and also of the public schools of Whitmire is to be found eleswhere in the columns of this section."

"The first school of ten pupils was taught in a one room log house, and later moved into the house that is now the residence of Mr. and Mrs. Rion Gilliam. After the mill was built, the number of pupils increased more rapidly than the facilities for caring for them. For awhile classes were taught in the Methodist church. In 1905 the grammar school was built, only to be doubled in size when the mill doubled its capacity in 1911. In 1924, after the coming of Mr. R. C. Lake, a sixty thousand dollar bond issue was voted and the present high school building erected. Both buildings are filled to capacity at the present time and the problem of future expansion will have to be faced soon. (1938)."

"It would be interesting to trace in detail the changes of business partnerships, the building of residences and the moving in of families and the leaving after a time of many families who lived for a while and left their mark on the community that has grown in less than fifty years from a population of twenty to more than three thousand, from four stores to fifty business firms, including one industrial plant employing one thousand, four hundred people with a weekly payroll that would have bought out the town and its surroundings at the time of its beginning. But that cannot be done here."

"The first merchants operating within the new town of Whitmire were J. C. Abrams and S. P. McCrackin, in a wooden building where Berelowitz is now located; Summer Brothers on the corner where Abrams-Riser is now, Spearman and Tidmarsh and John P. Fant occupying buildings on Railroad avenue. Dr. Marion Setzler built a store on the site where his son, J. G. Setzler now does business and next to it Dr. Joe H. Hamilton and Dr. R. R. Jeter built a drug store. B. F. Morrow of Mecklinburg County, North Carolina, put up a wooden store building on the corner where the cafe is now. He later added to it making the Morrow Hotel."

"In 1900, Wm. H. Rasor and John Miller came from Cross Hill and established a general mercantile business in the corner building first occupied by Summer Brothers. Three years later the store was burned and the partnership dissolved, with Mr. Miller beginning anew on Railroad avenue in partnership with his brother, Henry and Hassell.

In 1911 they built a fine double store on Main Street in their present location, only to be burned out again in the fire of 1916. The firm of Miller Brothers, now devoted to furniture and hardware and that of J. G. Setzler, a grocery store, are the two oldest businesses operating continuously in Whitmire.

"As has been said, Whitmire would probably have remained a straggly country crossroads, had not the late William Coleman bought a large tract of land from the Spearmans and Whitmires and on it built a cotton mill and village. Disappointed in failing to get the property he wanted near Carlisle at the price he was willing to pay, he decided on Whitmire as the location for the mill he wished to build. In 1902 the mill, called the Glenn-Lowry Manufacturing company, began operation with thirty-three thousand spindles and three hundred looms. Mr. Coleman was President and Treasurer, Dr. R. R. Jeter, general manager; Thomas H. Watson, Secretary; E. E. Child, Assistant Treasurer; Thad W. Coleman, Superintendent. And from that day to this and for years to come the condition of the mill has been and will continue to be the barometer of the welfare of the town."

"Mr. Coleman built a home here for his family and with his wife, who was before her marriage, Miss Evelyn Kamback Coleman of Ashville, North Carolina, took a personal interest in the development of the community. How great a debt of gratitude is due this family for the part they played in building the town of Whitmire cannot be estimated."

"In 1911, the Glenn-Lowry Manufacturing company let the contract for an addition, doubling its capacity. New homes for the operatives were built, the school was increased in size. A local newspaper, edited by Albert Young, made its appearance, making the plea for "a long pull, a strong pull and a pull together" to the end that a new county with Whitmire its county-seat be demanded. Advertising in this paper were Miller Brothers Department Store, listing everything from ladies' dress goods and laces to fancy groceries and coal; the C. H. Cooper, Company, Duncan's Bargain Store, the Whitmire Hotel, J. G. Setzler, Whitmire Pharmacy, A. J. Holt, opposite the depot; John G. Holder and Dr. Hilton, dentist; and Blackburn's Drug Company."

"In May 1916, a disaster of no small order befell the town, A fire starting in the livery stable owned by the late P. B. O'Dell located where the Whitmire Motor Company is now, swept up the street behind the stable and garage to Wall Street, and on down to Main Street, and back again to Railroad avenue, burning everything in the block, except a little smithy stand. Twenty-six business establishments went up in flames, and with them the handsome trees that lined both sides of Main Street. The Glenn-Lowry Company Store, the C. H. Cooper Company, Miller Brothers, the post office, then located where the Whitmire Pharmacy is now (the late David Duncan, postmaster), the Tidmarsh building, then a picture show, the pool room and barber shop operated by J. G. Holder; a market owned by W. D. Suber; M. Berelowitz who had moved to Whitmire only a few months before; J. G. Setzler and P. B. O'Dell's stable, garage and undertaking establishment, including a new hearse, the first in town, all was burned. The loss from this fire has been estimated at two hundred and fifty thousand dollars, and as someone has said, there wasn't enough food left to feed the people of Whitmire for a day. And that was one day when the school children got an extra holiday."

"There was then a row of cotton seed warehouses down on the railroad tracks, and into this shelter the merchants set up temporary quarters to carry on what business they could and to supply the necessary demands of the community. And by the time the Ashes were cold they began to rebuild the town."

"At the call of M. E. Abrams, a mass meeting was held the following night and the Town Council passed an ordinance establishing a fire zone with the usual regulations governing the type of buildings allowed within the business area; and so, progress on the heels of disaster, led to the building to today's modern and neat appearing business houses."

"The next few years saw many changes in Whitmire. The mill passed into the possession of J. P. Stephens & Company, selling agents of New York, and many changes have taken place."

"Back in 1903, a small two-story brick jail was built, the upper story serving as mayor's office. In 1923 a handsome town hall was erected. This building houses the jail, the offices of the mayor and town council and fire department. Up-stairs is an auditorium that is used occasionally for town meetings, and frequently for religious meetings. Charles Wilson was the architect and Robert McClure the contractor. The first jail has been variously used as a shoe shop and a smithy stand."

"A fire department was organized in 1922 with Frank Sinclair as chief and L. W. Cody as assistant. In 1924 it was reorganized and made a member of the South Carolina Firemen's Association. They used to blow the mill whistle as a fire alarm, but in recent years a siren has been installed in the town hall. Joe H. Simpson is chief of the department."

"About 1919 a pumping and filtering plant was built and a waterworks system installed to serve both the mill and the town. A bond issue was floated to finance the project. The water is obtained from Duncan's Creek and every analysis has shown it to be pure. J. L. Miller served on the Water Works Commission, which controls the plant, from its beginning to the last election when he did not offer for reelection. G. R. C. Gary, J. W. Gary and Frank Sinclair are the present commissioners."

"Until the water works system was installed, wells throughout the community were used and the well on Main Street had the distinction of being mentioned by the late and ever-famous O. Henry (Sidney Porter), in one of his best known short stories, "The Rose of Dixie". Mr. Porter's wife frequently visited her sister here, Mrs. William Coleman."

"The Aragon-Baldwin Mill is running at full tilt, giving employment to about fourteen hundred persons. Another addition has been built and new machinery was installed a few years back. The plant now operates approximately seventy thousand spindles and eleven hundred looms. A number of kinds of cloth are made. In addition to sheetings and fancy broadcloths, striped shirtings, voile, bedford cord, twill, rayons, and special purposes are made."

"There are more than four hundred homes in the village. All have modern conveniences and are kept in repair by the company. Every house has recently been painted white, with green roof, making a very attractive appearance. There are five big cow barns and pastures provided for those who wish to keep their own cows. The majority of homes have both lawns and space for flowers and vegetable gardens."

"Much interest is taken in athletics. A large gymnasium is provided, as well as tennis courts and a ball park, both lighted."

"There is an active Girl's Club and Mother's Club. Mrs. S. B. Pruitt, the mother of thirteen children, is president of the Mother's Club."

"R. E. Henry of Greenville has been president of this mill since 1928, and R. G. Emery, also of Greenville, is general manager. J. G. Barnwell is assistant treasurer and C. B. Graves is secretary. J. T. Crawford is superintendent of it and the following are overseers of departments: F. J. Campbell, carding; J. E. Stone, spinning; Glenn Kingsley, twister; H. W. Campbell, warping and slading; J. J. Frier, weaving; W. L. Moss, cloth room; A. I. Jackson, master mechanic; Sam Gary, shipping and warehouse; I. M. Thomas, yard and village; George Donnan, paymaster."

"The old cemetery, started again a number of years ago by the late P. B. O'Dell and owned for many years by M. E. Abrams, was bought recently the Town of Whitmire at a cost of one thousand and three hundred dollars. It was in an unsightly state of neglect, covered with broom-straw and brambles, with a great number of unmarked graves. A committee was appointed by the council to begin the work of beautification and a splendid start has been made. Mrs. George Young is chairman and has worked untiringly on its behalf. Other members of the committee are Mrs. J. D. Tidmarsh, Mrs. W. S. Suber, W. H. O'Dell, Sam Young, Tom Abrams and J. G. Barnwell."

"Three years ago, an Historical Association was formed for the purpose of restoring the old trading post, first in this section, located just at the edge of town on the Z. H. Suber property, and given by Mr. and Mrs. Suber. The building is used as a museum, of local history and has in it a number of interesting articles that have been given or loaned. A library was started in connection with it but on account of insufficient funds and interest, is not kept open regularly."

"There are three fraternal orders in Whitmire, the Masons, Junior Order of United American Mechanics, and Red Men."

"One troop of Girl Scouts has been formed under the leadership of Mrs. C. B. Graves and there is much talk of a Boy Scout organization, but as yet no definite step has been taken."

Among the Women's organizations, the Biographical club organized by the late Mrs. Coleman, is the oldest and the only literary club. Mrs. Coleman also formed a social club that met bi-weekly for many years and played rook. A contract club was organized several years ago and meets weekly.

The business women formed a club called the "Idle Women's Club" which meets in the evenings. The Mothers' Club meets in the community house and the members carry on a number of activities, serving banquets for other organizations, and doing some welfare work. The Parent-Teacher Association is a member of the National Congress of Parents and Teachers and is a very active unit. This years membership is the largest in its history, being two hundred. Mrs. J. T. Crawford is President, Mrs. W. H. Miller, Vice President; Mrs. J. C. Lee, Secretary, and Mrs. Joe Eason, Treasurer."

"Each church has an active Woman's Auxiliary and the fine record of their work will be found in the respective church histories."

"Whitmire has had two citizens in recent years to serve the county and state as members of the legislature. Z. H. Suber served three terms in the house of representatives, and M. E. Abrams, after serving two terms in the House is now senator from Newberry County."

"The town has had the following mayors: S. A. Merchant, John P. Fant, J. K. S. Ray,....McNeil, S. H. Matteson, A. J. Holt, S. T. Sims, Dr. Van Smith, John Duckett, W. F. Howard, W. J. Atchison, S. A. Jeter, W. G. Duckett, C. G. Gilliam, J. W. Gary and J. T. McGregor. Mr. Gilliam is now serving his sixth two-year term. Dr. R. M. Duckett has served as alderman for years."

"The following men have served as magistrates: Jim McCarley, F. W. Fant, A. J. Holt, R. M. Aughtry (served nearly twenty years) and W. G. Puckett, J. H. Wilson, J. W. Riser and J. G. Watts.

"Serving as Clerk and Treasurer have been the following: A. M. Watson, M. E. Abrams, W. J. Hackman, S. A. Jeter (served twenty years) and H. B. Riser."

"The following men have policed the town: K. F. Jones, Will Lyles, John Morse (for about fifteen years), E. L. Street, Jim Brock, Wm. Stuart, ...Peterson, D. H. Waddell, L. W. Cody, Tom Kinard, R. R. Gilliam and Bill Evans."

With Dr. Marion Setzler and Dr. Joe Hamilton serving as the country doctors for this section of Newberry county and nearby Union county at the beginning of the town, Whitmire has had the following doctors: Drs. R. R. Jeter, George Douglas, H. K. Boyd, Van Smith, James H. Moore, W. E. Brackett, E. G. Able, F. L. Webb, and the now practicing physicians, Dr. H. B. Thomas and Dr. W. R. Norville. Dr. S. H. Trotti practices dentistry."

"(The writer is indebted to Mrs. S. A. Jeter for the above listing of names. Mrs. Jeter, who taught for many years in the Whitmire schools has preserved much historical data and is considered the authority on matters of local history. She wrote a very interesting series of articles on "Whitmire, Town and Citizens" for The Whitmire News which was published here in 1934 and 1935)".

(Sketch in Newberry Observer, April, 1938)

CHURCHES

Some Old Churches Now Gone.

There are several references to these old churches in Howe's History of the Presbyterian Church, in The Annals of Newberry, and in other church histories.

The old Presbyterian Churches were Grassy Spring Presbyterian Church, Indian Creek and Gilder's Creek Churches.

The first Presbyterian preacher in the county preached the first sermon to be given in this county to a Presbyterian congregation in year 1758 at the home of Jacob Pennington on Indian Creek. From this first meeting came the Indian Creek Presbyterian Church which was established and the church building located nearby, in the year 1768. A short time later, Grassy Spring Presbyterian was organized, shortly before the year 1773. The Reverends Roe, Close, Campbell, and Diffield preached at these two churches at different times until 1773. Afterwards, Dr. Jospeh Alexander served at intervals.

In 1785 the Rev. James Templeton served Indian Creek church; in 1786 the Rev. Robert Hall and Rev. Robert Mecklin served; in 1787 the Rev. Thomas McCaule and Rev. Robert Hall ; in 1788 the Rev. James Templeton again; and in 1789 the Rev. James Wallis and Rev. Francis Cummings. Rev. Robert McClintock served as regular pastor of Indian Creek Church from 1785 to 1805, the year of his death.

Major Samuel Otterson was an Elder in the Grassy Creek Church. He married Ruth Gordon, a member of the same church. He served in the Rev. War as a patriot officer, Captain of a company of militia.

Rev. William Williamson preached at Grassy Spring church until 1802. Rev. Daniel Gray was pastor from 1806 to 1811, when he was dismissed on account of ill health; he died in 1816, in Spartanburg District. The church was supplied in 1811 and 1812 by Rev. John B. Kennedy and then by Rev. Hugh Dickson. About the same time the church ceased to function and the congregation disbanded.

In 1799 Indian Creek was unable to support a pastor, but supply pastors preached there occasionally, until 1815, when it , too, was disbanded.

When the first and second Presbyteries were formed in 1799, a new church came out of these two churches, which was called the Gilder's Creek Presbyterian Church, located near Gilder's Creek, just North of Indian Creek. The members first called it " McClintock's Church", first using the old Indian Creek church building, in honor of Rev. Robert McClintock who was instrumental in having the new congregation organized. In 1839 a new building was erected a little further away. The pastor in 1839 -from 1820 to 1840- was Rev. John B. Kennedy who served, also, Rocky Spring Presbyterian Church in Laurens District. In 1860, Gilder's Creek Church had sixty members. Rev. John Renwick preached at the church before or just after the term of Rev. Kennedy. In 1845, the Rev. E. F. Hyde became pastor, and served , also, at Aveleigh Presbyterian in Newberry and Smyrna Presbyterian Church about four miles from Newberry Court House, Northwest. Gilder's Creek Church was disbanded when many of it's members moved away, some to near the Court House or in town and others to other States, and still others moved their memberships to Cannon's Creek and King's Creek Churches, that were Associate Reformed Presbyterian congregations. The old building has disappeared, but many old grave markers can be seen in the old church cemetery near the site of the church.

Coate's Old Metting House was located on the road from Newberry to Long's Bridge on Little River(this old bridge has long since been gone, after the construction of the new highways that changed the courses of the roads.) It was said to have been built before the Rev. War, of huge logs; and stood for many generations, being used as a school house after the congregation was disbanded. Originally, it was known as " White Lick", and used as a Quaker Meeting House.

Rev. Russell was the first preacher at Coate's Meeting House, and the school was directed by Captain Ross Byrd, who was succeeded by Prof. Evans. Prof. Evans was a " Monomaniac" on the subject of grammar; he boarded around among the families of his pupils and made it a point to lecture on Grammar every night. In this way he got the name of " Big Syntax". He was a great ladiesman, and tried to court every woman with whom he came in contact. The result was, he became quite unpopular and was compeled to leave the school.

Prof. A. R. Able taught the school for several years, and proved to be a good teacher. Later, the church was disbanded and the school stopped, many members becoming affiliated with other churches. (Ref: The Annals of Newberry; Newberry County Court Records.)

CHURCHES ESTABLISHED IN NEWBERRY BY THE COLORED PEOPLE.

St. Matthews Baptist Church is located West of Newberry, about one and one-half miles from the court house. It was organized several years ago by the colored Baptists in the neighborhood.
Their first meetings were held in a small house in the neighborhood, until the completion of the new building, which was in 1937. The new building is a large frame structure.

Bethlehem Baptist Church is located on College Street, in Newberry, near Scott's Creek. It is, probably, the oldest established church for colored people in the city. Their first meetings were held in a small house near the Columbia, Newberry & Laurens Railroad Freight office. The first building that was put up was on Caldwell Street, just in rear of the present church but on the South side of the creek. Later, a building was erected on College Street, South side of the creek and a parsonage erected by it, which was used for many years. The land for these two buildings was given by J. D. Scott, a white citizen of Newberry. Many of the white citizens helped, financially, to pay the costs of the buildings of both the first church and the second church building.
The present building, on the North side of the creek, is a large, substantial structure of frame, which has been improved from time to time. It has stained windows, most of which are memorials, a large steeple, and two front entrances.

Miller's Chapel African Methodist Church is located in what is known as "Graveltown", in the southern section of the city. It was organized about the year 1869, by members of the Central Methodist Church of Newberry and the negro Methodists in the city.
The first meetings were held under a "Brush Harbor", which was put up at or near where is now the old knitting mill building, near "Vanduslian-Spring". Later, the present building was erected; and improvements from time to time has made it an attractive structure. It's new window's, new painting both inside and on the exterior, and new equipment, are some of it's improvements.

PENTECOSTAL HOLINESS CHURCH.

This church is located in "High Point" in Newberry. It was organized about 1918 by Rev. J. C. Smith who became the first pastor. The first meetings were held in a vacant store near where is now the church building.
The present building is the only one which has been built, which was in 1920 or 1921. It is a neat looking frame structure, painted white. It has been served by several pastors since it's beginning. It has been visited by Rev. J. H. King, who was then the General Superintendent of the Association in the United States. Also, the States Superintendent, Rev. W. F. Bramlett, has visited it and preached there on several occasions.

CLAYTON MEMORIAL CHURCH.

This church is the only one of the Universalist faith in or near Newberry. It is located five miles East of the court house. It is said, however, there was at one time a Universalist church about five miles from the court house, Southwest of the City, near Hartford Community. This was about one hundred twenty-five years ago; and it was located in the vicinity of the old Tunkard Cemetery (near the Paysinger home).
Clayton Memorial Church was organized in 1905 by Rev. J. M. Rassake. The first building is the one that is now used, which is a frame structure, painted white, and well arranged on the inside.
The Rev. D. S. Halfacre was their pastor for several years, until his retirement a few years ago. About that time, a State conference was held in the church when the State Superintendent of the South Carolina Association of Universalists preached. Also, Dr. Shinn, of Massachusetts then acting southern Superintendent of the Universalists of the South, preached there.

THE QUAKERS OF BUSH RIVER

Their characters and customs, site of old church and cemetery, anecdotes, superstitions.

About three and a half miles Southwest of Newberry, near Bush River, and one mile this side of old Langford's Mill (once called Mendenhall's Mill), can be seen among a patch of small oaks and hickories the old Quaker cemetery. Here is silence, ever as a quiet reminder of a once large community of Friends, and their church which once stood by its side. Here the members that included many families within a radius of several miles, as far as Saluda river and Little river, would come on Sundays, spend the day, and with customary quiet humility and feelings of strict adherence to their religion, worship God in their own way.

Tradition is that nearly a thousand Friends are buried in the cemetery, most of them without markers. The first monument which attracts the visitor when he enters is the very tall, tapering monument in the family plot of Rev. Thomas Frean, who though he married in a Quaker family, lived among them, became a Methodist minister; and later changing his views as to his concepts of the Bible became a Baptist, and began preaching in about 1772 in that denomination. He served several years as pastor of the Newberry Baptist church.

Some of the large land owners in that community during the early periods were: Jacob Chandler, Israel Chandler, Timothy Pugh, Isaac Jenkins, Sr., Isaac Kirk, John Kelly, Samuel Kelly, David Jones, Hugh O'Neall, Joseph Coppock, and others. Over the graves of some of these are large markers. The first Quaker settlers also included William Coate, William Miles, John Furnas, Robert Evans, David Jenkins, William O'Neall, Enos Ellemon, William Wright, John Embree, Moses Embree, Benjamin and Joshua Inman, and Thomas Pearson.

The cemetery and church included five acres, conveyed by John Embree on March 26, 1772, to David Jenkins, William Wright, Moses Embree and Enos Ellman, as trustees for the Society called Quakers. It appears that at the time of conveyance a church was already on the land, indicating that John Embree gave the use of a plot of land for the church, probably between 1760 and 1770. The old church, first a log hut, was superceded in about 1772 with a larger building; and in 1798 a new church was built a little farther away from the cemetery, about one hundred yards distance. This last church stood for many years after the late War Between the States, a deserted place after the removal of the Friends to the Northwest.

The Friends, as the name typifies and represents the real name of the organization, were from Pennsylvania, the Quaker State, which was given, first settled by William Penn, a Quaker. The name "Quaker" was given them in derision by outsiders before they left the old country, a name which clung to them ever after. Their early manifestations of religious fervor were by a form of trembling and quaking of the body in humbleness in God's house; hence came the name.

Some of the Quaker colonies from Pennsylvania first settled in Western North Carolina and on Bush River in South Carolina before the Revolutionary War. The old Quaker Meeting House on Bush River became a central point for meetings.

About 1796, some members living in the neighborhood of Rocky Spring branch organized the Rocky Spring Meeting, and built there a small church on two acres of land which was given by Thomas Pearson, a well-to-do Quaker. The trustees were Samuel Miles and Samuel Teague (the latter was a small boy during the Revolutionary War, but having seen his father shot in the back by Tories, joined the American forces as soon as they would receive him, to take revenge upon them). In 1800 another crowd organized the White Lick Meeting, near a place called White Lick, on Little River. John Inman gave six acres in 1800 for a church and any other buildings they saw fit to erect. Neither of these churches made any headway and soon discontinued services.

Unique in their customs, having staid qualities of character, strict adherence to their church views, they were nevertheless citizens possessing much patriotism. Opposed to war they largely remained among themselves during the period of the Revolution, but some of their young men became American soldiers after the war started. At a later time, during their monthly meetings their ministers preached against war, and at one meeting which was held at Wrightsborough, Georgia, in 1803 one Rev. Zacariah Dicks, an evangelist, predicted a great internecine war would come in the distant future. He said that the child was then born who would see it, and the civil war came fifty eight years later. A few years after this meeting in Georgia the Quakers sold their lands, manumitted their negroes, and moved to Ohio, from where many removed to the state of Indiana and other Northwestern states.

The site of Judge John Belton O'Neall's home, "Springfield", is just beyond Neel's dairy, on the left of the highway where are some trees and a small house. No part of the old home is left, however, it having burned down many years ago. Samuel Kelly, grandfather of Judge O'Neall, owned the place originally, and left it to him in his will. A store on the same place, known as Kelly's Store, was once a place of popular resort for Friends. Across the road, in the rear of a small house now standing there, is the old spring which was walled with solid stones.

The Quaker styles of clothes indicated much of their character, habits and thoroughness. The men wore broad-brimmed hats, with low crowns, straight-breasted with collars, coats, knee-breeches without suspenders of the plainest colors, held up by large buttons, plainly visible on the shirts or bodice. The women wore white beavers having mere indentations for crowns, brims about six inches every way, and secured on the head by plain white ribbons, passing through loops; or the plain silk bonnets called hoods, long waisted gowns or petticoats that spread out in wide circles, and touching the ground. Their language was "thou" or "thee" in place of "you".

Their religious customs being very strict, many of their ceremonies were necessarily elaborate and methodical in church affairs They considered it as part of their business life. There were meetings to worship and meetings for the transactions of business, that were held on certain days of each month. When entering their church they would sit down covered, in silence for an hour until the spirit moved some Friend to speak. The Friend who spoke would uncover himself and then kneel if he prayed, but the congregation always stood up.

Marriage ceremonies were very strict. A couple that wished to be married presented their purpose to a monthly meeting, when a committee would be appointed to inquire into their fitness for marriage and ascertain if there were any objections. At the next monthly meeting if the reports were favorable and the Friends present assent to it, on the succeeding fifth Thursday the marriage took place. They were married by taking each others right hand and repeating the whole ceremony. After the ceremony they would sit down, the clerk would read the certificate of marriage which was then signed by all Friends present.

The Quakers were not a very superstitious people, much of this having been attributed to other sections. However, some of it was absorbed among them, as many old stories would indicate.

An old Revolutionary war story has been related about a young Quaker girl whose sweetheart joined the American forces. After they had become engaged, rather than seem a slacker, he volunteered along with some other men for service in the army.

He was reluctant to go and leave her but he would not hold back. He told her, though, he would return to see her each night at the same time he had been in the habit of calling on her, whether he was alive or dead, nothing could keep him away. He returned each night and at the same time for several months, returning on his horse from his camp, sometimes being required to ride as far as a hundred miles. Suddenly he stopped coming, and not having heard from him she became worried, and finally one day a peculiar feeling came over her that her sweetheart was killed. One dark night while sitting in her door waiting for him, a habit she had each night, a dark cloud came up, with much thunder and lightning, and eventually the rain forced her to go inside and shut the door. She could not sleep, and about twelve o'clock she heard a horse galloping; opening the door she caught a glimpse in a flash of lightning of a large steed on which was a man in a long black cloak under a large tree. Three times they suddenly appeared in the light made by the flashes of lightning. There was peculiar light about the apparition; and no sooner had she seen it than it galloped away. She knew then that her sweetheart had been killed and had come back to her as he said he would. On each night at the same time thereafter, she would sit in the door and watch, each time the dark steed appeared, the rider clothed in a long black coat. The young lady grew to middle age, her father died, and she was left alone. She continued to live in the house, and nothing could induce her to sell her place. The neighbors thought she was peculiar in hermit life. She grew old, and died in the same house, never lax in her vigil of sitting at her door at a certain time each night.

There were many superstitious stories about the old church after the Quakers left, and the deserted building in later years became the scene for many amusing ghost stories.

On one occasion several young men from town had gone seining in the old mill pond nearby. It was always considered the best time to take a drink of whiskey, while standing in the water; hence they drank freely. On the way back home one of the young men having drunk too much for his good, was forced to go to sleep, and went into the old Quaker church and lay down on a bench. After about an hour he was awakened by a loud and mournful sound under the floor almost directly under him. Of course, the place was reputed to have ghosts, and when he heard the sounds he ran out, and ran all the way to town without stopping or slackening his speed. The next day he related his experience to some others in town; but the incident was soon explained when it was learned that an older man who had drunk more than was good for him, on his way home passing the church had stopped in to sleep off his stupor, and had crawled under the church, going to sleep under the place where the young man was sleeping inside the church.

Another anecdote is related about two of the Quakers before their removal to Ohio. It seems that one Thomas Hasket while at O'Neall's Mill on Bush River was standing near an outdoor fire getting warm, when David Jones came to the fire. Crossing the mill pond Jones had fallen into the water, and wishing to be funny he said to Hasket, "Mr. Hasket, you see I'm a Baptist but I suppose you are a Quaker." "Yes," said Hasket, I believe in going to the fire this cool morning, but thee believes in going into the water." Thomas Hasket and his brother, Isaac, were expert carpenters, and built the Quaker church in 1793.

It was a Quaker, Benjamin Evans, who invented the screw auger, which was used for many generations over the country. He sold his rights to another Quaker, John Edmondson, who had associated with him one Joseph Smith. Smith very soon after gave up his interest in the business and Edmondson continued it for many years, his place of operations being near his home on Little River. He sold many screw augers in other states, and some were shipped to Charleston, thence to Europe. Sometimes later he sold out his business and he, too, moved to the Northwest.

When the Friends moved to Ohio, other colonies moved to that State from Wrightsborough, Georgia, and from Guildford Court House, North Carolina, about the same time. Apparently they all had some agreement or understanding in regard to their leaving.

Very few Quakers remained in Newberry but those that remained were gradually absorbed by other churches of other denominations. One of those remaining was the late L. J. Jones, who became a lawyer and commissioner in equity in Newberry and never missed attending a term of court during fifty years or more of his practice.

Many Quakers, descendents of the colony that left Bush River for the Northwest became distinguished citizens in their respective communities. Among them may be mentioned Robert Furnas, grand son of Joseph Furnas, who became governor of Nebraska. One of the O'Neall family settled in Indiana (a small town in that state was named Newberry, for their native town in South Carolina); and the Honorable John H. O'Neall became a distinguished lawyer and a member of the United States congress from that state. Other descendants became noted ministers, physicians, and teachers. Though they were mostly farmers they succeeded well in their new territory, having taken with them a heritage of strong religious characters.

ST. LUKE'S EPISCOPAL CHURCH.

The beginning of St. Luke's Episcopal Church in Newberry was in the year 1845, when a meeting was held in the town of Newberry in the old court house and Bishop Gadsden preached. The meeting was for the purpose of organizing a congregation, which was completed in the early part of 1846.

Services continued in the court house each month until 1853, when they were held in the old Female Academy building on College Street, until 1855. A lot having been bought on the corner of Calhoun and Main Streets, the present church was constructed that year on this lot, and consecrated by Bishop T. F. Davis on August 26, in the same year.

Mr. Chapman, in his Part II of the "Annals of Newberry", described the building as a "handsome little Gothic edifice, with supporting roof, stained glass, and tasteful interior design and finish."

When the church was built there was a high symmetrical tower on top of the roof, on the North West corner, but owing to defective work it had to be taken down after a few years. Then, a cross was built at the front top of the roof.

The first Episcopal missionary to Newberry was Rev. R. S. Seely, in 1845, and the first minister officiating in the church was Rev. E. T. Walker, in 1855. The first officers elected that year were: E. S. Bailey, and Stiles Hurd, Wardens: Norman Brunson, William B. D'Oyely, William S. Johnson, G. H. Kingsmore, and Albert C. Garlington, Vestry.

As a mission church many pastors served the congregation since it's organization, generally living in another town and serving the churches in two or three towns. Rev. C. R. Haines, in 1859-60, and others; but only one minister served as resident pastor, from January 1882 until the close of that year, the Rev. W. F. Dickenson. For several years the Laurens minister served Newberry, and more recently, Rev. Bennett, of Columbia.

Though the building retains it's original design, improvements have been made on the interior, including a pipe organ, and other new equipment.

AVELEIGH PRESBYTERIAN CHURCH

As early as 1822 there was a Presbyterian church in Newberry, with an organization, and occasional preaching services in the court house. This was the earliest church organization in the town, but with its small and scattered membership and its irregular and insufficient ministry of the Word, it soon fell to pieces and was no more.

Under its present name, and as a permanent institution, Aveleigh Church was organized May 30, Saturday, 1835, by Rev. Moses Waddell and Rev. S. B. Lewers.

The following is a copy of the congregational covenant entered into by the church on the day it was organized, and the names of the thirty-two persons who signed it:

"Believing that the true God is justly entitled to the reverential and social worship of all intelligent creatures, and that their social homage is conductive in the highest degree both to the present comfort and future happiness of mankind, we, the undersigned inhabitants at Newberry district, S. C., residing near the court house, have felt a strong desire to associate and unite ourselves together in the capacity of a religious society for the purpose of improving ourselves in the knowledge and practice of our duty to God and man and of exciting ourselves to love and good works, and believing that the doctrine and discipline approved and adopted by the General Assembly of the Presbyterian church in the United States of America, as set forth in their Confession of Faith, conforms most nearly to the system of faith and order taught in the Gospel, we profess our desire and design to unite with and place ourselves under the pastoral care and direction of that ecclesiastical body, so long as they adhere to that confession. In testimony of which we have voluntarily attached our names to the above, this thirtieth day of May, 1835.

"Signed, (Aveleigh's original roll of members) John Garmany, Jr., David Griffith, Andrew Spence, Sr., Joseph Y. Hunter, David Clary, Matilda M. Saxon, Eliza M. Johnson, Sarah Boozer, Margaret Piester, Sarah B. Caldwell, Mary Welch, Rachel Keller, Sarah Glasgow, Sarah K. Foote, Elisabeth Clary, Mary Garmany, Maria Garmany, Isabelle Foote, Elizabeth Gilliam, Catherine Johnstone, Isabelle H. Chambers, Mary Marrs, Barbara Boozer, Williams Welch, Isaac Keller, Sarah Belton, Mary Griffith, Job Johnstone, Alexander Chambers, Thomas J. Brown, Mary Sligh."

The first ruling elders were Issac Keller and Alexander Chambers. In March, 1839, Chancellor Job Johnstone and Dr. George W. Glenn were ordained and added to the number of ruling elders.

A goodly number of the descendants of the original members are in the church today.

The origin of the name of the church is as follows:

Chancellor Job Johnstone, because of his leadership in the organization of the church, and in the building of the house of worship, and being the practical founder of it, was asked to give it a name. He named it Aveleigh for the church to which his parents belonged in Ireland, before they came to this country.

During the first three years after the organization, services were held occasionally by Rev. Moses Waddell, Rev. S. B. Lewers, Rev. E. Holt, Rev. Joseph Johnson, Rev. Isaac Waddell, Rev. James Lewers, and Rev. R. C. Ketchem.

Five acres of land were donated by Mr. Robert Boyce for Aveleigh's first organized church site. It is understood that the church building stood about the location of Mr. Bishop's present garden. Near this place may be noted the vaults in the old cemetery lot. Legible markers show to be buried here, Mr. David Boozer (1788-1850), Mrs. Sarah Boozer (1786-1840), his first wife; John H. Garmany, a one year old child; George B. Suber, a ten year old boy; Asenah Lane, wife of Wm. B. Lane and daughter of Jacob H. Hunt; a child of Wm. B. Lane and a Moon child.

The lot here containing about one-eighth of an acre of ground is considered still the property of Aveleigh church. The high stone wall enclosing the tombs of Mr. and Mrs. David Boozer, the Garmany and Suber child, is the wall built with funds when Mr. David Boozer's will for that purpose, back in the nineteentieth century. The wooden cover has completely disappeared, along with many markers of other graves. This location is on the North side of the east extension of Main street, about two hundred yards from the intersection of Main street and the highway cut-off, joining Mr. Bishop's place . (Note: The church stood across the road, facing the Pomaria road, the present road in front of Bishop's dwelling, not being in existence, the rear of church stands about where the road runs).

"The trustees and members of Aveleigh Church believing that it would be to the interest of the church to remove their original place of worship (which was about a mile and a half from Newberry Village) have disposed of the old building, and in the course of the year 1852 erected a new church in the said village, which is to retain its original name Aveleigh. On the seventeenth of December of the present year, a meeting was appointed for the purpose of dedicating the church. By invitation of its present pastor, Rev. W. B. Telford, the Revs. Messrs. Gaillard, by request, preached the dedication sermon on Friday, and Rev. Mr. Wills preached on Saturday and Sabbath". Mr. E. Y. McMorris donated the lot on which the building stood. This church was enlarged in 1892 at a cost of $3,500. On March twenty-ninth, 1907, this structure was completely destroyed by fire, along with manse and outbuildings. At the time of its erection in 1852 its membership consisted of about twenty-seven communicants.

Immediately after the fire of 1907 a new church was built at a cost of $6,500. The building committee consisted of Messrs. Alan Johnstone, F. Z. Wilson, W. A. McDwain, and John W. Chappell. The manse was built at the same time at a cost of $3,027.00.

In 1930, under the leadership of Rev. M. C. Dendy, Aveleigh's pastor at the time, the church was remodeled and the Sunday School building annex was built at a cost of $17,000. The building committee consisted of Mr. R. D. Smith, Jr., chairman; Mrs. F. D. Mower, Mr. James Smith, Mrs. E. B. Purcell, Mr. B. M. Scurry, Mr. A. S. Paine, Rev. M. C. Dendy and Mrs. R. D. Smith, Jr. The present indebtedness is something over $5,000.00.

Rev. Claude A. Calcote came to Aveleigh church in February, 1932, and is now the present pastor.

Complete List of Aveleigh's Pastors:
Occasional supplies-1835-1838.
Rev. R. C. Ketchum-1838-1839
Rev. John McKittrick-1840-
Rev. E. F. Hyde-1845-
Rev. W. B. Telford-1850-
Rev. A. D. Montgomery-1856-
Rev. E. H. Buist-1862-
Rev. R. A. Mickle-1866-
Rev. R. A. Fair-1874-
Rev. John S. Cosby-1886-1894-
Rev. R. P. Pell-1895-
Rev. J. L. Williamson-1896-1907-
Rev. S. L. Wilson (S. S.)-1908-
Rev. J. E. James-1908-1911-
Rev. E. D. Kerr-1912-1927-
Rev. M. C. Dendy-1928-1931-
Rev. C. A. Calcote-1932-present-

COLORED PERSONS RECEIVED INTO AVELEIGH
(Authentic from original records)

"May."-The servant of Phillip Metts, received on examination and baptised March 31, 1839.
"Patsy"-Servant of John Wilson received on examination September 22, 1839, and baptized July 26, 1840. The servant of Job Johnstone, Esquire, received on examination July 26, 1840.

The particular historical documents of Aveleigh covering the period from 1853-1904 were presumably destroyed by the fire of March 29, 1907, which also destroyed the church and Manse.

Chancellor Job Johnstone is considered the founder of Aveleigh Presbyterian church, and was from the beginning a leading elder in the church, and the chief supporter. He was born January 7, 1793, in Fairfield county, and died April 12, 1862. He and Mr. George Glenn were ordained and installed elders in Aveleigh on March 14, 1839.

SESSION OF ELDERS IN 1938:

Rev. C. A. Calcote, Moderator; R. D. Smith Jr., Clerk; H. M. Boozer, O. F. Armfield, Dr. Hugh Senn, D. W. A. Neville, B. M. Scurry, George Davenport and S. A. Williams.

BOARD OF DEACONS:

E. B. Purcell, chairman; James Smith, George Hunter, Treasurer; William Hunter, C. F. Smith Warren Abrams, J. D. French, W. R. Reid, and Theodore Neely.

SUNDAY SCHOOL.

D. W. A. Neville, Superintendent.
S. A. Williams, Assistant Superintendent.
R. D. Smith, Jr., Secretary.

WOMAN'S AUXILIARY

Presidents from the time of beginning in 1921 :
Miss Fannie McCaughrin, Mrs. J. M. Workman, Miss Minnie Gist, Mrs. W. H. Carwile, Mrs. E. B. Purcell, Mrs. James Smith, Mrs. A. T. Neely, Mrs. E. B. Purcell, the present president.
Miss Fannie McCaughrin has been the treasurer since 1925. The present Auxiliary has four circles.

YOUNG PEOPLE'S LEADERSHIP

Mrs. Hugh Senn, leader of Senior League, Miss Constance Armfield, leader of Pioneer Young People.
In 1935 Aveleigh celebrated its centennial.

OLD MINUTES OF AVELEIGH PRES. CH. NEWBERRY, S. C., R. D. SMITH, CLERK.

Members who signed the covenant at formation of church in 1835, as Charter members:

John Garmany, Jr.	Mary Welch
David Griffith	Rachel Keller
Andrew Spence	Sarah Galsgow
Joseph Y. Hunter	Sarah K. Foote
David Clary	Elizabeth Clary
Matilda W. Saxon	Mary Garmany
Eliza M. Johnstone	Mary Griffith
Sarah Boozer	Job Johnstone
Margaret Piester	Alex Chambers
Sarah B. Caldwell	Thomas J. Brown
Maria Garmany	Mary Sligh
Isabella Foote	John Garmany, Sr.
Elizabeth Gilliam	
Catherine Johnstone	
Isabella H. Chambers	
Sarah Belton	
Mary Marrs	
Barbara Boozer	
Williams Welch	
Isaac Keller	

A Sacramental Meeting was held May 30, 1835; congregation organized; and the following first Elders were elected: Isaac Keller and Alexander Chambers, ordained; sacrament of Lords Supper administered to about sixty people. Rev. Moses Waddell and Samuel B. Lewers were officiating ministers.

Rev. Joseph Johnson labored part time, preached one day.

July 1837: Rev. Isaac W. Waddell and Rev. James Lewers from Charleston, Union Presbytery, with R. C. Kitchen, a licentiate, (Rev. Kitchen was pastor at the church of Harmony Presbytery) preached, November 1837, fourth Sabbath: Rev. R. Colden Ketchin; Alex Chambers, Clerk. January, 1838, Fourth Sabbath: The services commenaldon Friday, through Saturday and Sunday. Rev. Isaac W. Waddell preached, and Rev. S. B. Lewers delivered the charge to the pastor and to the congregation. June, 1840, Fourth Sabbath: Sermon by Rev. Hugh Dickenson, and John McKittrick, a licentiate attended. August 29, 1840: Rev. John McKittrick was called to be pastor of the church and also to serve Smyrna Church. April 7, 1843: James Fleck applied for membership; certificate good standing in the Larne and Inver Presbyterian Congregation under General Assembly of Pres. Ch. in Ireland, which was signed by Rev. H. W. Molyneauz. September 1845: Sessions Meeting held at home of Chancellor Job Johnstone, sessions of Aveleigh, Gilders Creek, and Smyrna Churches (full meeting except David Clary, who was absent); Judge Johnstone in the chair-call was made in writing, which sent in hands of the Comrs. Isaac Keller, George Boozer, and Wm. Mars, who were appointed to attend the meeting of South Carolina, Presbyterian at Laurens the first week in October, call made to Rev. Mr. Hyde and he accepted.

Peter Gray left a legacy to the Aveleigh Presbyterian Church.

March 28, 1847: Baptism of the children of James Fleck, held to be in his home, because of illness of his wife. The child was named Eliza Stewart.

Rev. E. E. Hyde, pastor, of the Baptism of Eliza Stewart.

October 25, 1849: Alan, child of Job Johnstone, was baptised at home, on account of child's sickness, too ill to be carried out of house.

Born 8-12-1849--Present at the baptism were: Mrs. Rebecca DeWalt, Misses Catherine, Rebecca and Caroline Dewalt, Mrs. Dr. Thompson, Mrs. Mathias Miller, Miss Ann Gary, Mrs. Spence and her daughter, Mrs. Williams Welch, Mr. George DeWalt, Paul Johnstone, and the parents of the child.

June 8, 1850: Meeting of Presbytery at Greenwood, call was made to Rev. Wm. B. Telford, a licentiate of the Presbytery.

New church was erected in Newberry in 1852, and dedicatory service with sermon by Rev. S. S. Gilliard, on Friday, and on Saturday and Sabbath by Rev. Mr. Mills. Lords Supper administered on Sabbath when two new members joined: Dr. John Long by examination, and Edward Douglas by certification; Rev. Wm. B. Telford, Pastor.

Negroes were admitted as members of the church, slaves and probably one freeman. They were baptised in the church, were allowed to sit in the gallary or in the rear of the church downstairs. (Source: from Newberry Observer, 1938, suthor unknown).

DUNCAN'S CREEK PRESBYTERIAN CHURCH

Duncan's Creek Presbyterian Church is located in the southeastern part of Laurens County, about five miles east of the town of Clinton, South Carolina.

The church building now standing was erected about 1848, of solid square granite, a plain, simple design, much like the rural churches of old England. It has one large roof, with entrance at one end of the building. On one side is a large cemetery containing many old markers over graves of early settlers of that community, among them being those of American patriots during the Revolutionary War. There is, also, a marker over the grave of Rev. John B. Kennedy who once served the congregation as pastor, and a marker over that of his wife. A tablet in the church which commemorates the memory of the Revolutionary War patriots was placed there by the Daughters of the American Revolution, and reads as follows:

"Memorial to Men of this Congregation
who served their country
1775-1781.

Joseph Adair, Sr., Jospeh Adair, Jr., Thomas Logan, Robert Long, Leonard Beasley, John Copeland, George Young, Sr., Jospeh Ramage, Thomas McCrary, Thomas Holland, Robert Hanna, John Craig, James Craig, J. Bell, James Adair, Sr., William Woodward. Erected by Musgroves Mills and Henry Laurens Chapters, D. A. R., 1928.

The settlement in this community was made by Scotch-Irish immigrants from Pennsylvania ans some from Ireland, about 1752. They formed a religious society soon after, and in 1763 or 1764 built a small house which was put up by Jospeh Adair, Thomas Erving, William Hanna, Andrew McCrory and his brothers. The people conducted their own meetings until 1768 when the Rev. Hezekiah Balch, of Pennsylvania, visited them and preached to them. He advised them to elect elders of their congregation, and the following were elected: Andrew McCrory, Joseph Adair, Robert Hanna, and probably Thomas Erving, who were ordained by Rev. Balch. (Ref: Jones-Mills Hist of Pres. Ch in S.C., p 999). Two others, James Pollock and Thomas Logan, who had just moved into the community were elected elders; and, after the congregation had had the time to investigate their standings in the Communities from which they came. At this meeting there were about 60 communicants. Many of the men came dressed in the fashion of that day, with hunting shirts on, with splits and leggins and moccasins that had buckles and beads; and the hair clubbed up and tied on the head with deer-skins. The women came with long-eared caps or Virginia bonnets, some sort of short or long gowns; with high wooden heels on their shoes.

From 1770 to 1780 the church was served by Rev. James Creswell as supply pastor, and then by Rev. John Harris and Rev. Jospeh Alexander who served through the period of the Rev War. In the year 1789 the church was visited by Rev. Humphrey Hunter, who served them as supply pastor and also at Little River Presbyterian Church. Then came the Rev. James Templeton, later came Messrs. Williams, Hunter, Wilson, A. Brown, and John B. Kennedy. About this time a call was made to Rev. John B. Kennedy, in September, 1795, and he accepted the call at a meeting in April, 1796. He was ordained September 8, 1796, the ordination sermon having been preached by Rev. William Williamson, and the charge delivered by Rev. James Templeton. Then came differences of sentiment among the members of the congregation as to certain uses of old versions or songs. The pastor introduced changes, even hymns, and for this he was criticised by a few of them. The early members had used Rause's Version of the Psalms, and never Watts's Versions or hymns, until August, 1788, when John Springer, then a teacher at the chool at Cambridge, had the 91st hymn of the second book of Watts' sung in the congregation.

After 1823, Rev. John B. Kennedy and others served the church at various times. The record of the church dates back to 1844, since when many able ministers have served as pastors. The membershop has not materially increased, having been from 25 to 40 for the past decades. (Source: article in Newberry Observer, 1938, author unknown).

LITTLE RIVER PRESBYTERIAN CHURCH.

Little River Presbyterian Church—site of first church which was organized in 1764 not exactly located—was the first church of that denomination which started in Newberry County, or what is now Newberry County. Presumably, it was near the head waters of Little River; for such men as Col. James Williams (who fell at Kings Mountain), James Burnside, and Angus Campbell were the first Elders of the congregation; and Major William Caldwell, Rev War Patriot, who donated the land for the church building, an orginal grant of twenty acres being reduced to five acres, as the Elders returned to Major Caldwell fifteen acres since there was no use for that much land. The church building which was standing in 1837, was built with the same framing timbers that were in the old church or the first church.

Rev. W. Tannant preached there in 1775, and after two and one-half years service, Rev. William H. Drayton came, who stirred the people to resistance to British dominance (Ref: Howe's Hist. of the Pres. Ch).

Rev. John B. Kennedy served the church as pastor from 1896 until about 1836, a period of forty years.

Some other Ruling Elders prior to 1841 were: Dr. J. W. Simpson, John Black, Robert Gray, and John Burnside. In 1841 were Benjamin Williamson, Dr. Anthony F. Golding, and William W. Horan. About this time the church was supplied at various times with Father H. Dickensen and Rev. Alexander Kirkpatrick as preachers. During these days, two sermons were always preached, one in the morning and other in the afternoon.

The church was also supplied at different times by Rev. Johnstone, the Rev. Whimpy who preached the new school doctrines, and the Rev. John McKittrick, who served before 1840. In 1841, the pastor was Rev. W. McWhorter, and in 1843 and 1844 the church had no pastor.

In the years 1855, 1856, and 1857, and again in 1863, 1864, and 1865, the church was supplied by the Rev. Samuel Donnelly. In 1859, 1860 and 1861, by the Rev. Robert McLees.

About that time the church was removed from it's original site to about three or four miles away, in Laurens County, on the left side of the road that leads from Newberry to Laurens, and near the residence of David Vance (where he was living in 1873).

The church was dissolved in 1932 by the Presbytery of South Carolina, but continued as an outpost Sunday School for two years, when the church was re-organized with about thirty-five members. In 1938, it was emerged with Dominick Church which had been organized just across the county line, in Newberry County, in 1913. Then, a new building was constructed of brick near the site of the old Little River Church and named Little River—Dominick Presbyterian Church.

The building is substantially constructed, the architectural style being unique. The front entrance leads into a small vetibule, on one side being a long hat and coat rack and on the other a bronz tablet with the following inscription:

Little River Church
1762
Dominick Church
1916
Erected in 1938.
Rev. Curtis Matthews,
Pastor.

SMYRNA PRESBYTERIAN CHURCH.

Smyrna Presbyterian Church is located about five miles from Newberry Court House, on the county highway leading towards " Belfast". It was organized September 25, 1838, by Rev. R. C. Ketchum, with seventeen members, with George Boozer and David Clary as Ruling Elders. The members were: George Boozer, and his wife Sarah (Wilson) Boozer, David Boozer and wife, John Senn and wife, David Clary and wife, Mrs. Harriet Coppock, Mrs. Elizabeth Boozer, Mrs. Christiana Senn, Mrs. Mary Boozer, Mrs. Permelia Burton, Miss. Caroline Boozer, Miss. Mary Boozer, Mrs. Sarah (Boozer) McKittrick, Mrs. Rebecca Hendrix.

Soon after organization a church building was put up, the services being conducted, meanwhile, under an arbor brush.

In November, 1840, Rev. John McKittrick was ordained and installed pastor, along with Aveleigh Church, serving both churches until the year 1844 when he moved to Greenville County, S. C.

On September 21, 1844, Aveleigh, Smyrna, and Gilder's Creek Churches made a joint call to the Presbytery for the Rev. E. F. Hyde (or Hide), who accepted and came in November, that year. David Clary was elected a delegate to the Presbytery in October, which met at " Little Mountain" Abbeville District, Presbyterian Church. On November 17, 1844, Smyrna Church session was held and elected George Boozer as a delegate to the Synod of Georgia and South Carolina, which met the Second Sunday , December 12, 1844, at Columbia, South Carolina. A session of the three churches was held in Newberry on September 18, 1845, and a call to Rev. Hyde was made that he continue his labors with the churches. October 7, 1846, Dr. George W. Glenn was elected by the three churches a delegate to the Synod of South Carolina to meet at Charleston, S. C. on November 12, 1846.

Rev. John McLees preached at Smyrna Church on the second Sabbath in February, 1849. Rev Hyde having resigned, the Rev. Z. L. Holmes supplied Smyran Church until January 1, 1855, after which the church had no pastor. On December 3, 1854, three additional Elders were elected, viz: James M. Senn, Charles A. Teague, and David B. Piester. Since the Fall of 1855, Rev. Robert McLees supplied, with joint pastorage in Smyrna, Bethel, and Gilder's Creek churches.

On May 2, 1857, a session at Smyrna Church was held, when the several names were presented for membership. Also, letters of dismissal were given to Dennis Senn and his wife, Mary, from Hopewell Presbytery, Georgia, and were received by Smyrna Church Presbytery.

The Rev. John I. Boozer was made commissioner to the meeting of the general assembly held in Augusta, Georgia, on December 4, 1861, when the Southern Presbyterian Church was born.

In the early days, the old session books contain names of many negroes who sat in the back of the church, and were faithful and regular attendents.

George Boozer and his son, Henry D. Boozer, held the offices of Elder and Clerk of the Sessions for a period of eighty years.

Aveleigh Church withdrew from Smyrna and Gilder's Creek, and Mount Belthel was added. When these dissolved, Morris Church was added.

In 1916 the church building was remodeled, and the old building retained as a Sunday School building. In December, 1934, the church was destroyed by fire. In 1935 a new brick and stone structure was erected. Trees were planted to commemorate the work of the following who have served as Elders: O. H. Abrams, V. C. Wilson, W. O. Pitts, J. V. Clary, George P. Boozer, Henry D. Boozer, J. S. Boozer, George A. Boozer, Henry Hendrix, Dr. W. M. Dorroh, Charles C. Teague, David Boozer, George Boozer, Thomas R. Wilson, John Senn, James Senn, D. B. Piester.

According to one record the following pastors have served the church: Rev. John McKittrick, 1838-1844; Rev. E. F. Hyde, 1845-1849; Rev. W. B. Telford, 1850-1853; Rev. Z. Holmes, 1853-1855; Rev. Robert McLees, 1856-1860; Rev. A. D. Montgomery, 1860-1865; Rev. Samuel Donnelly, 1866-1868; Rev. W. R. Atkinson, 1868-1869; Rev. M. Young, part of 1869; Rev. Hugh Strong, 1869-1871; Rev. J. B. Hillhouse, part of 1871; Rev. T. C. Ligon, 1872-1882; Rev. A. M. Hassell, 1883-1887; Rev. J. W. McClure, 1888-1893; Rev. Cutina Smith, 1894-1897; Rev. J. D. Blackwell, 1898-1901; Rev. R. C. Ligon, 1902-1905; Rev. R. S. Latimore, 1906-1912; Rev. T. C. Crokar, 1912-1920; Rev. A. H. Key, 1920-1924; Mr. Meeks, supply in 1925; Rev. J. N. McCord, 1926-1930; Rev. Cockran Preston, 1930-1932; Rev. Curtis Matthews, May, 1933- after 1938; and ....

(From Sesqui-Cent Edition Newberry Observer, April, 1938)

CANNON'S CREEK A. R. P. CHURCH.

This church is located about three or four miles Southeast of Newberry Court House, on the highway leading to St. Paul's Lutheran Church and the Pomaria section. It was formerly a part of the pastorate with old Kings Creek Church, the two oldest A. R. P. Churches in the county. It was organized about 1772, and the first pastor was Rev. John Renwick, Sr. who had come from Ireland with others of the same faith(Covenanters) about the year 1767.

Their first building was a log-house which was built in 1772; later a larger frame building being put up; still later a newer building; all on the same site.

Three able ministers went out from this church: Rev. A. S. Sloan, who preached in Tennessee; Dr. H. T. Sloan, and Rev. John Bushardt (he preached for sometime at Troy, in Greenwood County, S. C.).

In 1872, a Centennial celebration was held at the church; the principle address was made by Hon. J. F. J. Caldwell, of Newberry, which was then under the pastorate of Rev. James C. Boyd. A meeting of the Presbytery was held in the church on November 10, 1831.

A large cemetery is nearby, in front of the present church, where are many very old markers, including several graves of American pioneers and soldiers in the American Army during the Rev. War, and of Confederate soldiers.

KING'S CREEK A. R. P. CHURCH.

This church is located about twelve miles North of Newberry, on or near King's Creek. The congregation was organized in 1772, first with Cannon's Creek church, with Rev. John Renwick as pastor. Later, some of the members withdrew from Cannon's Creek church and started King's Creek congregation.

The first building of King's Creek was near the old cemetery. The building was torn down to build a new and larger one on the main highway leading to Whitmire (the old main highway which has been changed in recent years).

There are many old markers in the cemetery, including those of early pioneers and American patriots of the Rev War.

NEWBERRY ASSOCIATE REFORMED PRESBYTERIAN CHURCH.

The Newberry A. R. P. (first known as the Thompson Street A. R. P. Church), was organized in 1850. Services were held in the Methodist church and in the court house for three years until a church building was erected on a lot donated by Dr. Thomas W. Thompson. When the church was organized, Dr. William McMorris and Dr. Thomas W. Thompson were elected and ordained as Ruling Elders, and shortly thereafter Prof. William Hood was added to this number. Thompson Street church and King's Creek church united in a call to Rev. H. L. Murphry, who was installed in 1853; and labored earnestly as pastor until the close of the War of seccession in 1865. At that time conditions were very discouraging; consequently Mr. Murphry resigned his pastorate and moved to West Tennessee. Dr. McMorris was now the only Ruling Elder; and later J. N. Martin was elected Ruling Elder and was a leader reviving this desolate place in our beloved Zion. During the next few years the church was irregularly supplied. Dr. W. M. Grier preached one year as stated supply.

In 1870, Rev. E. P. McClintock began preaching at Thompson Street church and at King's Creek church. He accepted, in 1871, a call to the joint pastorate and was installed the same year. Twelve years later, however, Dr. E. P. McClintock, pastor, moved to Newberry, relinquishing his charge of King's Creek church, and devoted his whole time to Thompson Street church. The officers were: Rev. E. P. McClintock, D. D., Pastor; M. A. Carlisle, George S. Mower, LL.D., C. F. Boyd, John C. Wilson, and James F. Todd, as Elders; and Dr. E. C. Jones, S. B. Jones, F. N. Martin, and Edwin A. Carlisle, as Deacons.

The membership at the time of organization was nine. In 1906 the membership was one hundred and twenty. On March 17, of that year, on account of failing health, Dr. McClintock resigned.

The church was well organized, with an active Ladies's Missionary Society, started November 22, 1885. Dr. McCintock presided at the meeting when it was organized, and Mrs. George S. Mower acted as Secretary. A letter was read from the Board of Foreign Missions, stating the design of sending out a lady at any early day to cooperate with Rev. Neil E. Pressley as missionary to Mexico. Nine names (all deceased at this writing), were enrolled, and in three years the membership had increased to twenty three. The minutes of August 13, 1891, reveal that contributions were made to home and foreign missions and to a new church fund. Gradually the new church fund was increased, until it came to $4,000.00

In November that year Dr. McClintock resigned as pastor, and Rev. D. G. Phillips, former pastor of an Atlanta, Georgia, A. R. P. Church was installed as pastor. Rev. O. Y. Bonner addressed the congregation and Rev. H. B. Blakely adressed the minister in the installation services.

The church building was completely destroyed by fire on Friday March 28, 1907. The St. Luke's Episcopal church kindly extended the use of their church for services until definite plans could be formulated for church worhsip. In June, P. E. Scott, of Newberry, offered the use of his hall building until a new church could be built on the lot which had already been bought for that purpose; which offer was gratefully accepted. One year later the new building was completed and services were held in it for the first time in June, that year. The Young People's Society bought and gave to the congregation the lot for the building. The name of the church was changed from Thompson Street A. R. P. Church to the Newberry A. R.P. Church.

The able ministry of Dr. D. G. Phillips expired when he got a call from the Chester

A. R. P. Church, and resigned from his Newberry pastorate on May 23, 1909. For the next sixteen months the church was without a pastor, but regular prayer meetings were conducted by the Ladies's Missionary Society. They were active in carrying on their own meetings, also. The need of a pastor was greatly felt.

On October 5, 1910, Rev. J. W. Carson became pastor of the Newberry Church. But in 1925, he was appointed Chairman of the Forward Movement by the A. R. P. Synod, in which field he rendered valuable service.   As Dr. A. J. Ranson was not able to return to India as a missionary because of ill-health, he was available at this time , and accepted the call to the Newberry church.   Bryson College elected Dr. Ranson as President, and for a few months the Newberry Church was again without a pastor. After two years, however, Dr. Carson having completed his work as Chairman of the Forward Movement, accepted a second call to the Newberry Church to serve as pastor. .... (Dr Carson recently resigned to accept a call to a North Carolina Church).

The Newberry A. R. P. Church has been, and is, a liberal supporter to all causes of the A. R. P. Synod, at home and abroad, and is an influence for good in the town of Newberry.
(Source: The Newberry Observer, 1938, and author, Mrs. H. L. Parr).

PROSPERITY A. R. P. CHURCH

Prosperity A. R. P. Church, composed of Irish settlers in the town of " Frog Level", was organized by Rev. Thomas Clark in the year 1802,.......... His body lies buried in the Cedar Springs Cemetery.

Thomas Clark was born in Scotland, educated in Scotland, at Glasgow, studied under Ebenezar Erskin, and after being licensed to preach the gospel he received several calls to come to America.

He set sail from Newere or Batleby, Ireland, May 10, 1768, in company with eight hundred of his associates and landed in New York July 28, the same year. Part of his company settled in Salem, N. Y., while the others came to South Carolina with their pastor, and settled in old Abbeville District. They founded what is known as Cedar Spring community and church.

Later, he came to Newberry District, settleing at Prosperity. When the citizens were selcting a new name for the town they decided on the name Prosperity in honor of old Prosperity Church, the first church of the community.

The first church building was situated on what was now the South side of the town of Prosperity.   The land was deeded to the chucrh by James Young, a Rev. War patriot, on May 3, 1802. Rev. James Rogers was the first pastor.   Samuel McQuerns, Robert Drennan, and James Young were the first Ruling Elders.

About the year 1843, a new building was erected on the same ground. This building continued to be used until the year 1889, when the present building was erected. near the center of town. The lot for this building was given by Rev. James C. Boyd, who was pastor of the congregation for thirty four years. He occupied his own home on a lot adjoining the church lot. At this time, the congregation owns a very neat, two-story parsonage on the same street.

When the church was moved to within the town limits the lot for a parsonage was given by Mrs. Elvira Kibler as her share of the contribution. A substantial building was erected , but in January, 1908, the building was accidentally burned down.   The insurance on it and other contributions enabled the members to build a better and more modern church.

Brown and Mosely, two enterprising business men of the town, and members of the congregation, (both now deceased), gave the lumber for the present church building. The old building was sold and the proceeds placed in the hands of a united people; then they built a nice church building, a neat parsonage and grounds.

In the past century and nearly one-half the congregation has been served by the following pastors: Rev. James Rogers, 1802-1815; Rev. Charles Strong, 1816-1824; Rev. S. P. Pressly, 1825-1832; Rev. Jonothan Galloway, 1835-1855; Rev. J. C. Boyd, 1855-1889; Rev. G. D. Phillips, 1891-1892; Rev. T. W. Sloan,(supply), 1893-1894; Rev. H. R. McAuley (supply), 1895-1896; Rev. J. B. Hood (supply), 1896; Rev. A. G. Kirkpatrick, 1897-1900; Rev. J. M. Boyd, 1902-1905; Rev. I. S. Caldwell, 1906-1912; Rev. O G. Davis; Rev. C. H. Nabors; Rev. J. Meek White; Rev. J. A. McKeown; Rev. R. I. McCowan; Rev. Roger Echols; Rev. Frank B. Edwards; Rev. Murray Griffith; Rev. Charles Edwards; Rev. Murray Love; Rev. F. W. Sherrill; Rev. R. D. Ryrd.

CENTRAL METHODIST CHURCH.

Central Methodist Church of Newberry is located on corner of Caldwell and Johnstone Streets. It is surrounded by a large, wide lawn, with a stone terrace in front. At the entrance to the church, which leads up wide, stone steps to the porch, with a church entrance on each side through a small vestibule.

The interior presents an amphitheatrical form of seats on a sloping floor; in rear of church an elevated pulpit, and to the right, a large pipe-organ. Chimes have been installed recently.

The building is constructed of beautiful white pressed brick. The architectural style is Gothic, with tall steeples and high gables, with steep roof. The arched effect is carried out in it's porch entrances and it's memorial windows of varied colored designs. It was erected in 1900.

The new Sunday School building is in the rear of the church, on corner of College and Johnstone Streets, facing Johnstone Street; on the exact spot that the old church stood, while the present church is on the site of the old parsonage. A two-story brick building which was built in 1929.

The church has been served by many able pastors, the present (1947) pastor being the Rev. H. C. Ritter. In 1938, Rev. A. E. Holler was the pastor and Honorable John F. Clarkson, Superintendent of the Sunday School.

The history of the Methodist Episcopal Church in Newberry began in 1820, when the first circuit in this area was started; and the first pastor of that circuit was Rev. Coleman Carlisle. He served the few congregations in the county at that time.

It was not until 1832, that the first congregation in town was organized, and the first frame building was built in 1833, which served them until 1873 when that building was enlarged and renovated throughout. The enlarged church was used until the year 1900, when it was torn away after the erection of the present building.

Newberry was established as a station in 1854, the pastor of the church (then called Newberry Methodist Church) at that time being Rev. John R. Pickett.

A Centennial celebration was held in the church on November 13, 1932, presided over by Honorable Eugene S. Blease, at that time the Chief Justice of the South Carolina Supreme Court. It was, also, a memorial meeting, commemorating the following members who were active in helping to build the new church: Former Chief Justice, Honorable Y. J. Pope, Honorable Z. F. Wright, Rev. W. I. Herbert, (one of the former pastors of the church and Presiding Elder), Mrs. R. D. Wright, and former Governor Cole L. Blease.

In 1928, the Womens Missionary Society celebrated it's fiftieth anniversary, the first Womens Missionary Society of the South Carolina Conference having been organized in this church in 1878. (Sources: Early newspapers, history of Methodists in South Carolina, and Newberry Observer, April, 1938).

EPTING MEMORIAL METHODIST CHURCH.

This church is located in Mollohon Mills village. It was organized in the year 1905, by the then pastor of Central Methodist Church and other Methodists of the community.

The first building used by the new congregation was the old Mollohon Mill School House, as an union church for both the Methodists and the Baptists of that community. Later, a building was erected for the union church with the help of the mill company. It was as an union church until the building of this one, the Epting Memorial.

The new church is a red brick structure which was erected sometime prior to 1936, the year in which it was dedicated. Bishop Paul B. Kern was the principal preacher at it's dedication.

The pastor in 1938 was Rev. W. H. Lewis.

O'NEALL STREET METHODIST CHURCH.

This church is located at West End, in the city of Newberry. It was organized about 1890 by some of the Methodists in the community, mostly as a result of a revival tent meeting held in a nearby grove.

Prior to building the church, the congregation held meetings in a one-room school building in the village, in which also the Baptists held meetings prior to building their Church.

It's first name was the Second Methodist Church of Newberry; but in 1895 the name was changed to O'Neall Street Methodists Church. A new church was built in 1897, while Rev. John W. Speake was pastor. A few years later the building was destroyed by fire, while the Rev. J. H. Graves was pastor. Soon thereafter, another new building was erected; and some years later the building was renovated through out with modernly designed windows and other improvements. In the summer of 1937, other outside repairs were made and the building repainted.

The pastor in 1938-40 was the Rev. M. M. Brooks.

It has been served by many able pastors during its existence. The fiftieth anniversary of its organization was held in the church in 1937. At this time (1946-47), the Rev. C. Frank DuBose, Jr., is the pastor.

NEW HOPE METHODIST CHURCH

This church is located about four miles North of Pomaria, in Newberry County. It was organized about the year,1795. In the year 1800, Salem Methodist Church on Second Creek was organized. The two churches were merged in the year, 1835. New Hope was organized by the Rev. Nathan Boyd, son of John Boyd, of Union District,(a Revolution War patriot and soldier).

The first building was a small cabin which was on a site about two miles from where the present church stands. A new frame church was built in 1831, on the present lot. Later, the building was renovated, painted and improvements made inside.

Rev. Nathan Boyd lived within the community; he had married in the neighborhood. He and his wife were of the old time Methodist type, and the influence of their home resulted in three of their sons becoming influential Methodist Ministers.

In the year 1895, an anniversary service was held in the church, a form of Centennial celebration. Several of the Ruling Elders were present.

A church cemetery is near the present church. Also, it is said there are some graves near the site of the first church.

OAKLAND METHODIST CHURCH.

This church is located in the village of Oakland Cotton Mills, in the city of Newberry, or just without the city limits. It was organized in 1913, by several of the Methodists ministers of the city and section.

The first building used was a small cottage, used as a union church by both the Methodist and the Baptists of that community. Later, a new union church was erected by both congregations; but in 1937 both decided to have their own church building. Accordingly, the union church was taken over by the Baptists and the Methodists erected a new building.

Several pastors have served the church, the Rev. W. H. Lewis, in the year 1937-40, when the new church was built, was the pastor.

There is no cemetery by the church.

WIGHTMAN METHODIST CHURCH
Prosperity, S. C.

In 1877, Rev. Thomas G. Herbert of Newberry Circuit, in his first quarterly report said that he had hopes of organizing a church at Prosperity to take the place of Capers Chapel, which had been cut off from the circuit. A few weeks later Rev. Herbert and his junior preacher, Rev. J. W. Arial, obtained permission to hold services on the first and third Sundays of each month in a building in Prosperity, called the Wheeler & Moseley Hall. On October 21, 1877 a candle light service was conducted by Rev. T. G. Herbert.

The minutes of the secretary, David B. Kinard, showed that these meetings were well attended, and the few Methodist believers realized their hope of organizing a church. The first roll of members was as follows: Louisa M. Counts, Mary Jane Abney, George S. Chapel, B. Haradora, (a Spaniard), S. J. Riley.

B. E. Kinard and L. J. Counts were elected stewards. A Sunday school was organized with J. L. Counts as superintendent. The church was taken into Newberry circuit under Rev. Manning Brown as presiding elder and Rev. T. G. Herbert, preacher, in charge, and Rev. J. W. Ariail, junior preacher.

After the annual conference held in Columbia in 1877, the presiding elder and the preacher in charge were returned to the work. W. P. Meadows came as junior preacher. Appointments in Prosperity continued on the first and third Sabbath evenings at "early candle light" in the Wheeler & Moseley Hall. In 1879 with Rev. C. H. Pritchard as presiding elder, Rev. J. W. Kelley came on this circuit as preacher in charge, Rev. W. P. Meadows returned as a junior preacher.

During this year, as the Wheeler & Mosley Hall was no longer available services were held in the old Birge school house, and later in the Masonic Hall over a grog shop, at which the members discussed plans for building a church.

Bethesda, one of the near by churches on the Newberry circuit, seemed about to be discontinued. At the third quarterly conference in 1879, a motion was made and carried that Bethesda be asked to sell her property and donate the proceeds toward the erection of a church at Prosperity. This plan was not agreeable to Bethesda. Later, its membership divided and part came to the Methodist Church in Prosperity, Bethesda being discontinued.

Rev. C. H. Pritchard was returned in 1880, as presiding elder of Cokesbury district, with J. W. Kelly preacher in charge and J. S. Porter as junior preacher. During the next four years services were held in charge, with T. M. White and J. W. Neely serving as junior preachers.

The second quarterly conference in 1882 adopted resolutions to the effect that plans for the erection of the house of worship at Prosperity should be considered immediately. A. J. Kilgore and J. L. Counts were appointed a building committee to which the membership gave enthusiastic support. A small lot in the town of Prosperity was given by Dr. J. R. Langford and D. M. Langford to be used for church purposes. W. H. Hodges, the junior preacher during the year 1883, gave his devoted and untiring efforts to the work of building the church. A report for the year 1885, shows that the building had been finished and furnished, and was valued at $800. It was dedicated by Dr. W. D. Kirkland, as Wightman Chapel.

From 1885 through 1889 the following preachers served this charge:

1885—W. D. Kirkland, presiding elder; Manning Brown, preacher in charge; G. H. Waddell, junior preacher.
1886— R. D. Sinart, presiding elder; M. M. Brabham, preacher; J. M. Steadman, junior preacher.
1888— A. W. Cauthen, presiding elder; M.M. Brabham, preacher; A. W. Attaway, junior preacher.
1889— A. J. Cauthen, presiding elder; M. M. Brabham, preacher; H. C. Mouzon, junior preacher.

During the session of the fourth quarterly conference in 1889, A. J. Kilgore made a motion that Newberry circuit be divided as follows:

Prosperity, Zion, Mt. Pleasant, and New Hope to be known as Prosperity circuit, and Trinty, Ebenezer, Lebanon, and New Chapel to be known as Newberry circuit.

After the division of the Newberry circuit, the following preachers served the Prosperity circuit.

1889-1892— J. B. Traywick; 1892-94, D. D. Dantzler; 1894-97, Dave Tiller; 1897-99, E. G. Price; 1889-1900, J. W. Arial;1900-01, W. P. Wharton; 1901-03, G. R. Schaeffer; 1903-05, J. K. McCain; 1905-09, H. W. Whitaker; 1909-13, S. C. Morris.

In 1913, the Prosperity charge was divided, Prosperity and Zion forming the Prosperity charge and Mt.Pleasant and New Hope, with others, forming Broad River Circuit. Rev. E. P. Taylor served the new charge for four years. He was succeeded by Rev. J. L. Stokes, D. D., who served only one year, leaving to take the chair of Religious Instruction at Columbia College.

In 1918, Rev. J. D. Griffin came to the charge and remained until 1922. During this pastorate there was organized an Epworth League, which has remained active. Rev. R. W. Sharp served as pastor from 1922 to 1926. At this time, the question of a new building was agitated, and Dr. J. R. Langford and D. M. Langford gave to the church a title in fee simple for the reverting title of the church property, in order that the property might be sold and the proceeds applied to the erection of a new building.

Rev. A. Q. Rice came to the charge as pastor in 1926. At the second quarterly conference of 1927, Mr. and Mrs. D. M. Langford offered a plot of ground for a site for a new church.

The oifer was accepted, and the following building committee was appointed: W. P. B. Harmon, H. C. Dominick, W. T. Gibson, D. M. Langford, W. L. Mills, Mrs. D. H. Hamm, and Mrs. W. C. Barnes. Later the first four above named resigned and J. M· Bedenbaugh and W. C. Barnes were placed on the committee.

In the fall of 1928, the first worship service was held in the new church, which is a modern brick building, with Sunday school rooms necessary to meet present and future requirements.

(The above sketch was written by Miss Mary Boulware Langford at the request of her pastor, Rev. A. Q. Rice., for Sesqui-Centennial of 1938, edition of Newberry Observor).

1928-32 George H. Pearce served this charge as pastor.
1933-36 G. F. Clarkson was pastor.
1937-38 T. L. Bryson served.
1938-M. E. Boozer.

EBENEZER (MAYBINTON) METHODIST CHURCH.

"Ebenezer Church was organized in 1784, or soon after. This being the celebration of Sesqui-Centennial of Episcopal Methodism, it is most fitting to observe the anniversary of Ebenezer."

Methodism was not introduced into the State by immigration from Europe, as in the case of Lutheran and Presbyterian Churches, but by itinerant preachers, who were usually changed annually, and who served large numbers of preaching places. The early church had no records except classbooks for societies; hence much of the valuable history of Methodism in the first half century of its existence in this county was lost.

It is quite probable that the first Methodist Society in Newberry county was organized in the house of Edward Finch. Bishop Asbury held a quarterly conference here in 1788. This is near where Mt. Bethel academy was built and dedicated by Bishop Asbury in 1795. This school continued until about 1820, when it was superseded by Tabernacle Academy.

Ebenezer (Maybinton) according to the records is the oldest continuously organized Methodist church in Newberry county. Bishop Asbury's Journal records four visits to this community, and mentioned stopping at Thomas Hardy's and George Clark's and Casey's.

We have records of three church buildings. Of the first little is known. It was used as a school building. The second building was on land donated by Dr. Burwell Chick on Casey's branch. Two acres of land of this site still belongs to the Methodist church. Among those connected with the earliest buildings are mentioned Herron, Hardy, Caldwell, Cofield, Brazzleman, Clark, Chandler, Davis, and Harris, and later, Moorman, Chick, Maybin, Douglas, Lyles, Oxner, Glenn, Worthy, Bishop, Goudlocke, Murtishaw, Hodges, and Sims.

Tradition says that Casey's Spring was used by the Casey family as a looking glass to arrange collars, ties, etc., before going to church.

Appointments that were made in 1792, at Charleston, this being the only district in the conference:

Presiding Elder-Jonathan Jackson.
Charleston and Georgetown- Benjamin Blanton, J. W. Jones, and James King.
Edisto-James Simmons, N. Williamson.
Broad River- Rufus Wiley, Alex McCaine.
Saluda-George Clark, Samuel Douthit.
Bush River- Richard Posey.
Santee, Catawba and Camden-Tobias Gibson, Josiah Cole, Isaac Smith, Mark Moore.
Union-H. M. Gaines, Mose Wilson.

At this time Ebenezer must have been on the Broad River Circuit. The first mention of the two districts in the general minutes is in 1802 when Old Saluda is named with George Dougherty, presiding elder. The following appointments were embraced in Old Saluda district: Broad River, Saluda, Keowee, Edisto, and Orangeburg, and Charleston. The other district being Camden district, James Jenkins, presiding elder. In 1803, there were no changes save in the increase of appointments. In 1808 Union was left out of Camden district, doubtless transferred to Saluda.

In 1802, 1803, 1804, the eldership was the same. The first mention of Enoree Circuit, of which Ebenezer Church was a part, is in Saluda district in 1804. In 1804 the two circuits, Enoree and Sandy River and Bush River and Keowee, took in all the country above Columbia from Catawba to the Savannah River.

In 1804, the appointments for Enoree and Sandy River, William Cassaway, Hanover Donnan, Daniel Asbury (after three months).

The second building was superceded by the present building in 1848. The ground was given by Rev. George Clark, a local preacher, who traveled some years in the conference, but located and lived in this community. A plat of this location that was made by Williamson Clark, is still in existence. A sketch of George Clark in the minutes of 1874, among the memoirs of local preachers: "George Clark admitted in 1792, located in 1801. Mr. Clark had quite respectable preaching talents, and was esteemed by his neighbors and the public generally. Sociable and pleasant in his manners all were at ease in his company. He was plain in dress, though a man of considerable wealth. He resided on Enoree river, Union district, South Carolina. The cause of Methodism in that county was much aided by his influence and talents. He lived to an advanced age, (and he died), is all the church generally knows"

In 1878, the church was remodeled and enlarged. In 1889 it had its first coat of paint. Rev. E. T. Hodges went out from Ebenezer in 1870. Rev. Melvin Kelly lived within the bounds of this charge and applied for license to preach at Ebenezer. He preached here often before admission to conference, assisting Rev. J. M. Fridy. Rev. T. G. Herbert was then presiding elder.

The first mention of Sunday school in the district was at Rogers meeting house in 1802. The earliest Sunday school at Ebenezer that we know about was in 1848, superintended by Col. Robert Moorman, with Mrs. Louisa Worthy, Mrs. Francis Douglas and Mrs. Nancy Oxner as teachers. A grandson of Mrs. Oxner, Rev. J. W. Lee, Missionary to Brazil, once lived here and attended Ebenezer.

The parsonage was located at Maybinton in the Dr. Holmes residence, but was used only for that purpose during the pastorates of Rev. S. W. Martin, and Rev. A. W. Walker, when the preachers's home was moved to Santuc on South Union circuit. During this period a parsonage aid society was formed.

In 1900, the first Woman's Missionary society was organized. During the pastorate of Rev. J. F. Lupo, Ebenezer was again repaired and painted- 1926.

When Central of Newberry celebrated its centennial in 1932, the membership of Ebenezer, as the mother church, was invited as special guests. Rev. J. W. Lewis, pastor, extended greetings.

Only one marriage is known to have taken place at Ebenezer. This brings the history up to 1934, with Rev. J. W. Lewis, pastor, serving the fourth year, and who is responsible for the celebration of the one hundred and fifieth anniversary.

(This sketch was contributed concerning Ebenezer by a former resident of Maybinton. She attended Ebenezer in her youth and said she, "heard grandmother often speak of Rev. Jesse Lee and of the wonderful sermon she heard him preach at Ebenezer one Christmas" Distressed by much drinking and dancing among the people he skipped on the platform and said in a loud voice, "Whoopee, boys, let's go! Apple cider persimmon beer, Christmas comes but once a year"!

Jesse Lee was closely associated with Bishop Asbury, entered the ministry in 1783, and transferred to Virginia in 1800.

Rev. W. F. Harris followed Mr. Lewis and served four years, 1934-1938.

Ebenezer changed from Greenwood to Rock Hill district in 1935.

Rev. J. A. Carter, present pastor, is serving his first year, (1938).

(From Newberry Observer, April, 1938, Sesqui-Centennial Edition).

LEBANON METHODIST CHURCH.

This church is about six miles East of Newberry Court House, in Newberry County. It was organized in 1872. About 1870 and 1871, two meetings were held by the Methodists in the community to hold services and discuss the advisability of building a Methodist Church.

The organizers in that year were: Rev. J. C. Counts, who was the first Pastor, and D. H. Bushardt, and Benjamin McGraw. This was the outgrowth of the old Pleasant Grove Methodist Church which was organized in 1838, near Cannons Creek, by the late Col. Samuel Cannon, and a building erected in 1840; but a few years later the Church was disbanded.

The second church built at the same place was also superceded by a larger one which was built in 1924.

The congregation has given several sons to the ministry, some of whom were : Rev. G. A. McGraw, Rev. Walter S. Henry, and Rev. J. Matthew Henry, the last named having served in a southwestern State for many years as a Ruling Elder.
The cemetery is near the building.

NEW EBENEZAR METHODIST CHURCH

Located about four miles East of Newberry Court House, left of the county highway leading from Mollohon Mill plant.
The congregation was organized before 1814, and for several years known as Watson's Camp Ground, then Ebenezer Camp Ground, which was organized by the late Dr. James Kilgore.
The first building erected in 1814, on old camp ground; then, in 1837, a new frame building, much larger, was put up, under the leadership of Dr. Kilgore and Jacob Sligh. This served the congregation until 1880 when the present larger building was erected.
The Rev. John B. Kilgore was a son of this church.
A cemetery is near the side of the church building.

NEW CHAPEL METHODIST CHURCH

The church is located about ten miles West of Newberry Court House, on a road leading from the county highway across Bush River to old ferry on Saluda River.
It was organized in 1800 by some of the Methodists in that community. The first building was put up, a very small cabin, in the same year, probably a log hut. However, in 1830, a new frame building was erected on the same site. In 1879, another building was erected, about two miles away from the old site. This last one is it's present church. A large donator towards the building of this church was Isaac Herbert, a leader in the church. He was the father of two well-known Methodists ministers in the State, viz: Rev. Walter I. Herbert, Rev. Thomas G. Herbert.
A special service was held in the church in 1900, a kind of Centennial celebration.
There are two cemeteries, one at old site and the other near the church.

MT. PLEASANT METHODIST CHURCH.

The church is located about twelve miles East of Newberry Court House, near Broad River, and near or within the Maybinton section.
It was organized in 1822, by Dr. Thomas Rutherford, Micajah Suber, and others.
It's first building was a small frame one, built about 1822.
The present building was erected about 1862, displacing the older one, on the same site. There have been many improvements on the church since it's erection. Two very liberal contributors to the church were Dr. Thomas Rutherford and Rev. Dr. McCants.
A cemetery is near the church.

TABERNACLE METHODIST CHURCH

This church is located in the northern part of Newberry County, near Indian Creek.
It was first organized in the year 1842, one of the leaders in it's organization having been John B. Richie.
The first church building was erected in 1842, which was a small frame structure. In 1856, a new building was built, a much larger one, on land donated to the church by the late Nathan Johnson, a leading Baptist in that community.
The church edifice has no memorial windows.
A cemetery is near the building.

SHARON METHODIST CHURCH

This church is located in the town of Kinards, in the county. It was organized about 1850, by Jacob Summer, who moved into the community from "Little Dutch Fork", of the county, and had married a daughter of Captain Martin Kinard, Jr.

The first building was frame, which was built in 1854, meetings previous to it's completion having been held in the homes of it's members. In 1869, need for a larger building was apparent, and a new one was erected in that year, which is the building now used, with some later remodeling having been made.

One of the young men who went out from this church into the field of ministry was the late Rev. Walter Summer, son of Jacob Summer.

In the rear of the church is an old cemetery.

OLD TRANQUIL METHODIST CHURCH.

This building was destroyed or removed to near Jalapa Station about the year 1890. Later, it was used as a school house.

The first congregation was organized about 1799, and the first building erected with logs in that year. The site of this old church is adjacent to the present cemetery which contains many old markers over the graves of many first settlers of that community. The organizers of the church were: Zaccheus Wright, Dr. Thomas Shell, and Robert Gilliam. In 1832, a new building of frame structure replaced the log house. In 1859, a much larger frame church was erected.

The first Sunday School organized in the county was started in this church, about the year 1827, by Zaccheus Wrright, with the help of a local Presbyterian named Absalom Glasgow. They thought there was much need for a school of religious instruction for children in that section.

ZION METHODIST CHURCH.

This church is located West of the town of Prosperity, in Newberry County. It was organized about 1813, some of the organizers having been Thomas T. Cureton and Dr. George Lester.

Their first building was erected in 1829, a larger frame structure than the original building which was on the present church lot. In 1880 another larger building was erected under the pastorate of Rev. J. W. Kelly, which is the building now used. A few years ago furnishings were installed, a bell tower built, and other improvements made.

Several young men have gone out from this church into the ministry.

Tradition is that some form of anniversary or centennial was held in the church in 1913; but no record of these services are available.

A great revival was conducted in the church in 1853 under the direction of Rev. G. W. M. Creighton, a well-known Methodist minister of that day.

No memorials are in the windows.

There is a church cemetery near it; also, a small family grave-yard not far away, at site of the old church.

MT. TABOR METHODIST CHURCH.

This church is sixteen miles North of Newberry Court House, near the town of Whitmire, in Newberry County. It was organized in 1820 by Col. Benjamin Herndon, a patriot Officer in the Rev. War, and Rev. John B. Glenn, William Shell, John Epps, Anderson Hipp, and David Epps.

The first building was erected in 1821, a small frame structure, which was used until 1845, in which year five acres of land not so far away was given the church by Allen Shell. The congregation was later merged with the Methodist Church in Whitmire. Then, in about 1892, a large brick building was constructed in the town of Whitmire. It was dedicated in 1893 by Bishop W. Duncan.

TRINITY METHODIST CHURCH.

This church is located about six miles Northwest of Newberry Court House, in Newberry County. It was organized about 1831, and first called Kadesh Methodist Church. In 1836 Kadesh Church was combined or merged with Moon's Methodist Church. At that time Moon's Church and Kadesh were located on either side of the present Trinity Church, about two miles either side. Shortly thereafter old Shady Grove Methodist Church which was located about one mile above the present town of Silver Street, merged with Trinity. Old Shady Grove Church has been torn down many years but the old cemetery is still seen with several markers.

Organizers of Trinity Church were, principally, Henry Cromer, a leader in old Kadesh Church, and Daniel Stewart, a leader in old Shady Grove Church. It is said that Henry Cromer was often inspired to both preaching and leading the prayers of his church. A few years later he moved with his family to Georgia, and there he acted as an itinerant preacher in his community.

The first building of Trinity Church was erected in 1836. This building was discarded in 1888, in which year a new one was built. This latter building is the present church used, and has had several improvements made on it from time to time.

Trinity Church has given several young men to the ministry, among the earlier ones having been, Rev. V. Martin, Rev. James H. Martin, Rev. M. E. Boozer.

A large cemetery is near the church with many old grave markers.

THE LUTHERAN CHURCH OF THE REDEEMER.

It was in 1852, when the population of the village of Newberry was only about 1,400, that the first steps were taken to establish a Lutheran Church in this community. Conscious that among that small population there was a goodly number of families of the Lutheran faith without a convenient church home, the Rev. T. S. Boinest, at that time pastor of Bethlehem Church, Pomaria, ministered to the spiritual needs of the local Lutherans and led them in the organization of a congregation. It was on Sunday, July 10, 1853, after a service held in the old court house, that the congregation was effected. The charter membership consisted of twenty-one, " all of whom were regular communicants of various congregations in the Dutch Fork of Newberry and Lexington counties." The name was chosen," Luther Chapel."

On Wednesday, August 10, just one month after the congregation was organized, the cornerstone was laid for the house of worship which was being erected on Boundary Street, near the terminus of McKibben Street, the lot having been donated by a citizen of the town. The Rev. Mr. Boinest became the first pastor and for him is named the most used room in the present church building. Another 10th of the month is significant in the life of the congregation. It was December 10th, 1854, that the church was dedicated. The dedicatory services were conducted by the Rev. John Bachman, D. D., LL. D., pastor of St. John's Church, Charleston, S. C., for a decade the President of the South Carolina Synod, and the leading figure in that body, being assisted in the services by Pastor Boinest and other Lutheran ministers.

While the original church building was of frame structure, it was of superior workmanship and was beautiful Gothic architecture. The cost of it's erection was $4,000.00, all of which, with the exception of $900.00 was provided in cash on the day of dedication. Largely through the liberality of one of the charter members, Matthias Barre, the $900.00 indebtedness was removed within less than three years.

During several pastorates and for decades the building on Boundary Street met the needs of the congregation. But during the pastorate of the Rev. William C. Schaeffer, D. D., 1887-92, a movement to erect a better house of worship was begun. Through subscriptions and two bequests on the part of members of the congregation a building fund of about $5,000.00 was gathered. It was during Dr. Schaeffer's pastorate, too, that the matter of changing the location of the church was agitated. During the pastorate of the Rev. Junius B. Fox, D. D., Ph. D., 1893-99, a large lot bounded on Boundary, Wilson, and Johnstone Streets, was bought. It was on this lot that the cornerstone of the present building, in it's original form, was laid on October 20th, 1896. At that time the name was changed from"LutherChapel", to " The Church of The Redeemer". The new edifice, including the lot, cost $14,500.00, and was occupied for the first time on the first Sunday in October, 1897. After all indebtedness had been liquidated, the new church was dedicated on February 28th, 1904, during the celebration of the semi-centennial of the congregation. It was during that celebration, too, that the Rev. W. L. Seabrook was installed as the new pastor. During his pastorate a commodius parsonage which is still in use for that purpose, was erected on a lot adjacent to the church. Pastor Seabrook resigned in 1907. In March of 1908, the Rev. Edward Fulenwider took up the duties as pastor of the congregation and continued until October, 1920. During this pastorate notable gains in church membership were enjoyed. Especially worthy of note is the fact that during the Easter celebration of 1909, 108 new members, twice as many as had been received during the first twenty years of the congregation's existence, were added to the church roll.

In April of 1921, the Rev. Charles A. Freed, D. D., became the pastor. During his pastorate necessary enlarged facilities were provided and improvements made. Dr. Freed relinguished the work in the Spring of 1925. On the first of September, 1925, the Rev. J. C. Peery, D. D., President of Lenoir-Rhyne College, became pastor and labored faithfully and effectively until illness in the Summer of 1930, made it necessary for him to give up such duties. His resignation became effective on December 31, 1930.

September 1st, 1931, the Rev. E. B. Keisler became pastor, which time a substantial indebtedness, incurred by the renovating and enlarging program, was removed. Rev. Keisler resigned in year 1946; and Rev. Paul E. Monroe, Jr., became the pastor.

It would, perhaps, be impossible to find another congregation in which there are represented so many professional and industrial interests. Among it's members are cotton mill employees, farmers, merchants, clerks, mechanics, contractors, publishers, lawyers, dentists, physicians, three ordained ministers, besides the pastor, almost half a hundred public school teachers, and more than a dozen members of the faculty of Newberry College—all working and worshipping harmoniously together.

Except a Brotherhood, all the organizations ordinarily found within the Lutheran congregations are doing efficient work with and in the congregation. The Men's Bible Class, a third larger than any other in the county, is doing much of the work for which the Brotherhood exists.

The following is the list of pastors who have served the congregation and the dates of their pastorates: Rev. T. S. Boinest, 1854-56; Rev. William Berley, 1856-68; Rev. Theophilus Stork, 1859-60; Rev. J. P. Smetzler, 1861-68; Rev. Jacob Hawkins, D. D., 1869; Rev. H. S. Wingard, D. D., 1870-72; Rev. H. W. Kuns, 1873-78; Rev. S. P. Hughs, 1879-81; Rev. J. Steck, D.D., 1882-83; Rev. A. M. McMackin, 1885-87; Rev. W. C. Schaeffer, D. D., 1887-92; Rev. Junius B. Fox, D. D., Ph. D., 1893-99; Rev. M. G. G. Scherer, D. D., 1889-91; Rev. W. L. Seabrook, 1902-07; Rev. E. Funenwider, 1808-20; Rev. Charles A. Freed, D. D., 1921-25; Rev. J. C. Peery, D. D., 1925-30; Rev. E. B. Keisler, 1931-46; Rev. Paul E. Monroes, D. D.(the present pastor).

Especially because of it's strategic position in connection with Newberry College it has been the good fortune of the congregation at different times in it's history to enjoy, during vacancies, the services of distinguished ministers who, in connection with their teaching, were regular supplies of the congregation. Among those are the following: Rev. Prof. J. A. Brown, D. D., the Rev. Prof. George W. Holland, D. D., the Rev. Prof. A. G. Voight, D. D., LL. D., the Rev. Prof. W. K. Gotwald, Ph. D., the Rev. Prof. R. A. Goodman, D. D., Rev. Prof. A. J. Bowers.

Among the family names found in the early congregational rolls whose representatives have been, and in many cases still are, active and prominent in the work of the congregation should be mentioned especially Barr, Bowers, Cline, Dickert, Hipp, Houseal, Kibler, Long, Mayer, Schumpert, Summer, Swittenberg, Zobel.

(From sketch in the Newberry Observer, 1938, Sesqui-Cent Edition).

POMARIA LUTHERAN CHURCH

This church is located in the town of Pomaria, Newberry County. It was organized by the Lutherans of that section in the year 1910, which year the present church building was erected. Since that time, however, many new improvements have been made on the building. The church has been served by many able ministers.

The membership was made up, mostly, by those who had been members of St. Paul's Lutheran Church and of St. John's Lutheran Church, both about two miles distant from the town.

MT. TABOR LUTHERAN CHURCH.

This church is located about two miles North of the town of Little Mountain, Newberry County. It was organized about 1880, by the late Rev. J. A. Sligh, D. D., who became it's first pastor.

The first building was erected in 1880, a very small frame one, on the site of the present building. A short time before the year 1930, while Rev. J. L. Cromer (son of Rev. J. A. Cromer), was the pastor, a new brick building was erected; also, a good Sunday School room; and a large parsonage built. Both of it's buildings had appropiated dedicatory services the year in which they were built. It was said that the pastor and many of the members worked continously by making sales of farm products and performing other work to pay for the church when it was completed; which was accomplished, with no debt on the church.

The cemetery is near the church.

ST. JOHN'S LUTHERAN CHURCH.

This church is said to be one of the oldest, if not the oldest, church in the county. It goes back to a time when a small group of settlers from Pennsylvania, mostly, to the Dutch Fork section of Newberry and Lexington Counties about 1750; and having brought their Bibles, (they were Germans and Swiss who had left their native countries on account of lack of religeous freedom and to seek better oppprtunties in the new world), and their pastors in each colony, they were a religeous lot.

They seemed to have been educated in the German language, for all could sign their names legibly, even though they used the German forms; for this reason they adhered to their language for several generations before giving it up for the English language, but retained much of their phonetic spelling. The following is part of an extract from the Newberry Observer in year 1938 pertaining to the church and it's founders; " The group, about 1750, under the guidance of Adam Summer, accompanied by their pastor, Rev. Lutz or Luft, had brought their Bibles and hymn books, and together they organized St. John's Church, building first a log hut in which to worship. It remained a primitive house of woship during more than fifty years, when in 1808 they built the present substantial frame structure." (There may be some error here, for it is said the new church was built just after the end of the War of Secession; but this may have been a complete remodleing of the old one). " It has since been in constant use some interior changes having been made with the installation of more modern pews to replace the highback equipment which must have been designed for churches of that period so that the individual worshipper should not be disturbed in his meditations as he enetered the sanctuary. Likewise, the sounding board,which had it's place above the pulpit, was removed.......... The sounding board was presented to Newberry College about fifty years ago as a historic souvenir of a period of primitive simplicity."

" Another feature of historic interest in St. John's Church is it's communion service of six pieces which was brought from Germany, with the exception of the small wafer plate, made by a member of the congregation named John Setzler, the only tools he used being his hammer and an anvil as he fashioned the plate out of silver coins. He was known in the community as the " Wizard Gunsmith." (One reference to him is that he was a"silversmith".)

" The hinges and nails were made likewise locally, in his blacksmith shop by John Summer, in year 1808, the great-grand-father of several members of the present congregation..........."

" The church having been located in an original forest of 100 acres."....... " Seventy acres of it yet remains in oak and hickory,........ " However, the virgin pine has since disappeared, and the line of demarcation dividing it from the hardwood is easily apparent.........."

" Standing in the northeastern portion of the 70 acres, the church fronts the roadway,....."

" The Royal Grant of one hundred acres is preserved in the State Archives of History, at Columbia, S. C. , though a copy or the original being held by a member of the church, bears date October 5, 1763, under the seal of King George lll, King of Great Britain. The grant assigns the tract of one-hundred acres to John Adam Epting and Peter Dickert, as the proper officers of the congregation, their heirs and assigns forever, the land on Crame's Creek (now spelled Crims) between Broad and Saluda Rivers, for a glebe and church building, and a 'meeting house for the time being. A peculiar provision of the deed, considering it is a proviso at this period, is that the crown reserved the right to any minerals that might be found on the land, for none has ever been found or discovered to this day"... (this form of proviso was usually used in all sections)...

"Formerly, the congregation maintained a school, but within the past fifty years it was discontinued and the building now used for Junior grades of the Sunday School"............

"The church has been served from time to time by many able pastors; and many young men have gone out into the ministry from this church, as well as many able physicians, and others in various professions, including lawyers who lived in the city of Newberry and in other places."

The old church cemetery is nearby, containing many old markers; but the families, generally, during the earliest times buried their dead in private family graveyards near their homes.

GRACE LUTHERAN CHURCH
Prosperity, S. C.
by
Rev. George E. Meetze, Pastor

Grace Lutheran Congregation, Prosperity, S. C., came into existence in 1859, the exact date not being known. The Sesquice-Centennial year of Newberry County is the eighteenth anniversary of the organization of Grace Church. The name of the Congregation was first "Newville Evangelical Lutheran Church," organized when Prosperity was Frog Level.

THE CHURCH EDIFICES:

Through the generosity of the Bridges family the lot was given to the congregation on which three church buildings have been built. The first building was a neat wooden structure, erected the year the congregation was organized and dedicated on the fourth Sunday in August, 1859, with the Rev. W. W. Berley officiating. For a number of years, this building was adequate, but the growing congregation realized a larger church must be constructed. In 1878, during the administration of Rev. G. W. Holland the old church building was torn down and a larger one erected at a cost of $850. This building was dedicated October 2, 1878 and the name changed to Grace Church. But as the congregation grew, a still larger building was needed. In 1907, under the guidance of Rev. M. O. J. Kreps, the present stately edifice was started. The cornerstone was laid November 21, 1907, but the building was not dedicated until May 1910. Early in this year, (1938), the work of renovating the interior of Grace Church was begun, and this Spring in the eightieth year of her life, the present church will be rededicated with appropriate services. In this connection it is interesting to note that the bell in the Church tower (and still in use) was purchased during the early years of the Church's existence and that one hundred dollars in gold was paid for it.

THE PASTORS OF GRACE CHURCH

From the best authority on the subject the Rev. W. W. Berley organized Newville Evangelical Lutheran Church A. D., 1858, (according to some records) and proceeded to build a house of worship. The Rev. S. E. Smithdeal was the first regularly called pastor after the organization. The Rev. J. H. Bailey succeeded the Rev. Smithdeal some time during the War Between the States (1861-65); Rev. H. Eichelberger, also served during the war.

After this time the Rev. J. A. Sligh preached for some time (length of time unknown). Mr. H. S. Wingard, while a student at the Theological Seminary preached for a while, as did the Rev. J. P. Smeltzer, D. D. The Rev. J. Hawkins, took charge in 1871 and served one year when he left for Virginia. Rev. H. S. Wingard took charge in 1873 and served six years. In 1878 steps were taken to build a new church. Dr. G. W. Holland was again called to supply in 1882. The Rev. J. E. Bushnell was called in the winter of 1882 and took charge January 1, 1883. In a letter he says he served as pastor until December 1, 1885, during which time he received a salary of $450. per annum. The Rev. C. A. Marks was called and took charge in March 1886. He found the congregation building an addition to the church for Sunday School purposes. He also succeeded in having a new site purchased for a parsonage on which a nine-room house was built. He served until March, 1890.

On June 1, 1890, the Rev. T. O. Kiester took charge and served until April 5, 1895. He said in a letter, "I found the people fruitful in good works and attentive to my wants".

The Rev. S. T. Hallman was called and entered upon his service December 1, 1895. He served Mt. Tabor in connection with Grace, preaching there on the second Lord's day at 11 a.m. and on the fourth Lord's day at 4 p.m. He says "I was zealous in the promulgation and defense of the truth and condemned error and sin fearlessly. I found the people very kind and the Church Council prompt in the payment of my salary. I resigned my work in order to give more of my time to the Lutheran Visitor of which I was editor."

The Rev. W. H. Hiller, was the next pastor. He took charge June 1, 1900 and served the pastorate for eighteen months. He says, "I found the people very kind and appreciative of my services." He resigned, effective January 1, 1902.

The Rev. W. A. Lutz, succeeded to the pastorate and served from March 17, 1902, to May 1, 1905. He himself wrote, "On January 10, 1902, I received a unanimous and urgent call, unexpectedly, to become pastor of Grace and Mt. Tabor congregations on a salary of $600. per annum. I was at that time President of North Carolina College and hence could not act either to accept or decline the call. I held the call for forty-five days, waiting to see the guiding hand of God. I feel that I was led lovingly by the hand of the Great Shepherd to see my duty plainly. On February 25, I accepted the call subject to the approval of the board of trustees. The board on March 4, accepted my resignation and left me free to take this work. I moved here on the eighteenth of March, 1902, and took charge of the work fully determined to know nothing but Christ and Him crucified. My first work was to conduct services every evening during passion week and administer the Lord's Supper on Easter Sunday to a very large number. The parsonage had been renovated at a cost of $200. and is in first class condition. The first year passed very pleasantly. We observed the church year and the congregation follows the rubrics in worship. It became necessary to use discipline for the reclamation of some offending members. Intemperance and indifference have destroyed the usefulness of a number of members. During the second year developed intemperance and public dances and wordly pleasures for the weak and unstable members. This called for plain and earnest sermons against these soul destroying evils. God owned and blessed my efforts so that the intemperate have been reclaimed and public dancing and dances are a thing of the past. An effort was made to administer Christian discipline but it was opposed by those wedded to worldly pleasure. This caused a little friction. A few designing men fanned this into a flame of opposition, intended to render the pastor unpopular and force his resignation. After repeated efforts to accomplish their end and God frustrating their plans they failed because of the large majority of noble and faithful and pious members who stood by the pastor and held up his hand. I offered my resignation to the joint council of twenty-seven members, November 17, 1904, when of this number only six voted to accept it. I again resigned peremptorily February 2, 1905, to take effect May 1, 1905. The work has been very pleasant and the friends loyal."

The Rev. M. O. J. Kreps, who was pastor of Holy Trinity, Augusta, Georgia, was called and accepted and entered upon the work October 1, 1905. It was during this administration that the present handsome church was built.

The Rev. E. W. Leslie was called from the Bote Court Charge, Bote Court County Virginia, and entered upon his duties as pastor of Grace and Mt. Tabor churches January 8, 1911.

On November 1, 1914, Grace Church was constituted as a pastorate at their own request and Rev. E. W. Leslie was retained as pastor. Mt. Tabor, Mt. Pilgrim and Mt. Olivet were constituted a pastorate April 16, 1915, at a meeting of the Joint Council of the three churches, Rev. Leslie presiding.

Rev. Charles J. Shealy was called from Macon County Charge, Oglethorpe, Georgia, and entered on the first Sunday of September as pastor of Grace (1916) and served the church about five years.

The Rev. S. W. Hahn followed Pastor Shealy about the year, 1922, and served two years, and he in turn was followed by the Rev. Charles A. Philips, who accepted the call extended him on October, 1925, taking charge of the work January 1, 1926. In the fall of 1927, Pastor Philips resigned the pastorate to accept the work of St. Mark's Mooresville, North Carolina, his resignation taking effect November 30, 1927.

Mr. Fred E. Dufford was called during February of 1928. He was in his senior year at the Seminary at Columbia, South Carolina, when he received the call sometime in March, 1928. He preached twice each month from the time he was called until his graduation from the Seminary in May, 1928. He took full charge of the parish on May 18, 1928. Pastor Dufford served Grace Church until August 15, 1933, resigning to accept work near Greenville, Tennessee.

The Rev. Carl B. Caughman accepted a call and assumed charge December 1, 1933, coming from Grace, Rock Hill, South Carolina. Rev. Caughman served until Easter of 1937.

A unanimous call was extended to the Rev. George E. Meetze, then pastor of St. Barnabas' Church, Charleston, South Carolina, in March. The call was accepted and Pastor Meetze assumed charge of the Parish on May 17, 1937.

(Since the resignation of Rev. Meetze, Rev. Counts and Rev. W. D. Haltiwanger have served as pastors). (From sketch in Newberry Observor, April-1938.

BETHANY LUTHERAN CHURCH

At different times after the settlement of the Oakland Mill community, the advisability of conducting services for the Lutherans was discussed, but nothing definite was done until the summer of 1935, when the Rev. Gilbert B. Goodman, then a Theological student, by authority of the Mission Committee began holding services in the Oakland School House. When he returned to the Seminary in the fall to resume his studies, the services were continued by the Rev. E. B. Keisler, D. D., until the spring of 1936, when the Rev. J. C. Perry, D. D., took charge. Under the capable leadership of Dr. Perry the congregation was formally organized on June 10, 1936 with a confirmed membership of thirty-five. He supplied the newly organized congregation until November 1, 1936. After its organization this congregation was united into a pastorate with Summer Memorial, Mollohon.

For the pastor of this pastorate the services of the Rev. J. B. Harmon were secured. He took charge November, 1, 1936, and he still continues to serve as pastor. (Rev. Harmon recently retired,—Author).

For over three years the congregation worshiped in the auditorium of the Oakland School House; but during the latter part of the year 1938, the members of the congregation, with the aid of the Kendall Mill company, the congregations of the Newberry Conference, the Newberry District Brotherhood, the Women's Missionary Society, of South Carolina, and other friends in the County and State erected a beautiful flint rock veneered building on a lot given by the Kendall Mill Company on the corner of Third Street and the Extension of Nance Street leading to the Country Club. The first service was held in this new building on December 25, 1938, and the public opening service was held on January 1, 1939.

The first members of the Church Council were: H. L. Goff, E. B. Hite, D. B. Going, O. L. Kinard, J. Simeon Miller, James O. Miller, Claud Mize, W. M. Shealy, Joseph Snipes, John C. Suber and Homer E. Schumpert, This congregation rotates its officers, and the members of the Church Council at this time (1938) are: Eugene B. Hite, O. L. Kinard, J. J. Slice, J. R. Timmerman, Herman O. Graddick, Ernest Morris, B. L. Turner, W. O. Stone, Joe Price, Miller, J. C. Snipes, Claud Mize and Homer E Schumpert.

All the auxiliary organizations are functioning reasonably well with the following leaders: Eugene B. Hite, Superintendent of the Sunday School; Mrs. E. B. Hite, President of the Women's Missionary Society; Miss Azalee Graddick, President of the Luther League; and Mrs. W. O. Stone, Secretary of the Children of the Church, with Mrs. Homer E. Schumpert as assistant.

The teachers in the Sunday School are Mrs. H. L. Goff, Miss Azalee Graddick, Miss Alda Rae Boland and Mrs. W. O. Stone.

The enrolled membership of the congregation is eighty-four, and the Sunday School enrollment is eighty-six.

(From the sketch in the Newberry Observer, April-1938).

History of
MAYER MEMORIAL LUTHERAN CHURCH

This congregation was organized on Sunday afternoon, October 15, 1899, by the Mission Committee of the South Carolina Synod, Dr. M. G. G. Scherer, Rev. W. K. Sligh, and Dr. O. B. Mayer, Jr. There were twenty-five charter members. The first edifice was erected during the summer months of 1899 by the late Dr. O. B. Mayer, Jr., who was a recognized leader of Lutheranism in the South Carolina Synod. His life was one of the unremitting effort to do good and promote the interest of the church as his manifold activities indicate. This church building, which cost over two thousand dollars, was a gift to the new congregation as a memorial to his father, the late Dr. O. B. Mayer, Sr., who was long an officer in Luther Chaper Congregation (Redeemer) and who during all his useful life was prominently associated with the religious and educational work of Newberry County.

A part of the lumber of the Luther Chapel Church was used in the erection of this (daughter) church. The lot (on Drayton Street) was given by the Newberry Cotton Mills, also the mill company gave $500. for the pews and the electric lights. The first church was a frame building thirty-six by seventy-two feet, including the pulpit recess and vestibule entrance.

Mayer Memorial was placed in a pastorate with Colony and Beth-Eden. The joint council met on Saturday, December 2, 1899, and extended a call to the Rev. Charles H. Armstrong, Ph, D., of Greenford, Ohio. Dr. Armstrong accepted the call and entered upon the work February 1, 1900, and served until April 1, 1902. The church made splendid progress. Sunday School was organized with Mr. Frank E. Addy, superintendent. He served about two years, then Mr. Andrew W. Eargle assumed these duties and served several years. In the fall of 1906, Mr. J. D. Kinard, was elected superintendent and has served most efficiently and faithfully to the present. The Sunday School began with about twenty-five pupils and has grown steadily, almost reaching the three hundred mark.

The first church building was dedicated on May 20, 1900 when the first pastor, Dr. Armstrong, was installed.

When the congregation was organized there were twenty-five members. The growth was slow for quite a number of years. This was possibly due to the recent change of pastors and pastoral relations. But in these later years there has been a rapid growth and development. On January 1, 1921, the church became independent of Synodical aid, and in the fall of 1929, assumed the support of the pastor and withdrew from the pastorate with Summer Memorial. Sunday school rooms were built in the summer of 1929 at a cost of $1,100.

On the second Sunday in January (January 12), 1919, the first church edifice was destroyed by fire. Immediately the congregation set to work to rebuild, and by the help of friends and neighbors the present building was erected during the summer months. Mrs. O. B. Mayer gave the insurance which her late husband had kept up on the building from the beginning, a sum of $1,500. This, together with other gifts besides the self-sacrificing efforts on the part of the congregation, enabled them to rebuild without any debt. The first service was held in the new church on the first Sunday in October, 1919. The pews were given by Mr. Z. F. Wright and the altar furniture by the Women's Missionary Society of the congregation. The large memorial window is a gift of a friend to the memory of the late Dr. O. B. Mayer, Jr. (1853-1918). This is a grateful recognition of the financial support given the congregation during his life.

Sunday, October 24, 1937, was a memorable day in the history of Mayer Memorial church. On that day the church, remodeled during the summer, was rededicated. This happy event was made more impressive by the publication of a Memorial Number of the Parish Review. The pastor conducted the service and the Rev. E. Z. Pence, president of Synod, preached the sermon which was listened to with marked interest. The preacher spoke on the subject: "God's House". "Let your interest and life hang around the House of God's", said the speaker.

A special anthem was rendered by the choir and called forth many favorable comments. The concluding exercises were held at the evening hour and consisted of greetings from the Conference by the Secretary, Rev. M. L. Kester, and addresses by Messrs. Z. F. Wright and A. J. Bowers, Jr. All spoke of Dr. Mayer, Sr. who for several years practiced medicine in Newberry, and then pursued further study in medicine and surgery in France and Germany. Upon his return in 1847, he did general practice in his home town. The joy of the occasion and the gratification of the congregation at the successful completion of a work which had engaged their attention for two years. These addresses were appropriate and were much appreciated.

A few days before the dedication, the Women's Missionary Society received and placed on the Altar a new set of Chancel Paraments. These added so much to the appearance of the Church. The interior of the church is handsome, ceiled with masonite, wood work painted and new light system installed. For these services the church was beautifully and attactively decorated by the flower committee. Throughout there was a live, warm and personal interest manifested by the members as a whole. The committee in charge was faithful and their efforts were gratefully appreciated.

CHRONOLOGY

May to October, 1899, building operations of first church edifice by Dr. O. B. Mayer, Jr.
October 15, 1899-Organization of the congregation by the Synodical committee: Rev. W. K. Sligh, Dr. M.G.G.Sherer and Dr. O. B. Mayer, Jr.

November 18, 1899- First Joint Council Meeting: A call was extended to Rev. W. K. Sligh, Rev. Sligh declined. (Churches in the Charge: Beth-Eden, Colony and Mayer Memorial).
December 2, 1899- Second Joint Council meeting. Rev. Charles H. Armstrong, Ph, D., called. (Accepted several weeks later).
February 1, 1900-Rev. Charles H. Armstrong takes charge of the work.
May 20, 1900-Dedication of the church and the installation of Dr. Armstrong. Sermon by Dr. Schaeffer.
Spring, 1905-Church building enlarged, a vestibule with two rooms and belfry added.
January 12, 1919-Church destroyed by fire.
February to October, 1919-New church building erected.
October 5, 1919- First service held in the new church.
Spring of 1928-Sunday school rooms built and other improvements made.
October, 1929-Mayer Memorial withdrew from pastoral relations with other churches and assumed full support of the pastor.
October 23, 1934-Present pastor took charge of the work.
October 13, 1935-Dedication services and thirty-sixth anniversary observed. Rev. W. H. Dutton preached the anniversary sermon.
Rev. T. F. Suber, president of the South Carolina Synod, preaching the Dedicatory sermon. The pastor conducted the Dedication service.
Summer, 1936-Church painted and other improvements made.
Summer, 1937-Interior of church renovated, receiled, painted and new lighting system installed.
October 24, 1937-Rededication and observance of the thirty-eight anniversary. Historical Bulletin published.
Present (1947) pastor: Rev. V. L. Fulmer.
(From sketch in Newberry Observer, April-1938).

History of
SUMMER MEMORIAL LUTHERAN CHURCH

When the Mollohon Mill began operation a community church was built in which all people could worship regardless of denomination or creed. Occasional services were held there for the Lutherans by different ones in the Newberry Conference, but no special arrangements for Lutheran services there were made until 1909. Then at a meeting of the Newberry Conference at Beth-Eden it was decided to give $100. towards regular preaching services to be held there, and the services of the Rev. P. H. E. Derrick were secured.

Following this the Rev. J. D. Shealy took charge of the work in connection with the Mayer Memorial Lutheran Church and formally effected an organization on July 24, 1910 with twenty-six confirmed members. Eight of this twenty-six are still members of the congregation.

The first officers of the congregation were: J. Willie Shealy, H. Cromwell Shealy, Joseph A. Derrick, A. P. Boozer and Thompson Addy. The first and last mentioned of these are still members of the congregation.

This congregation was highly favored by being given a house of worship by Messrs. Charles E. Summer, J. H. Summer and George W. Summer in loving memory of their parents, George W. and Martha D. Summer. The building stands now as it was erected in 1911.

The following pastors have ministered to this congregation since its organization: Rev. J. D. Shealy, J. B. Harmon, E. C. Witt, S. W. Roof, J. A. Shealy, A. J. Bowers, D. D., S. P. Koon, D. D., W. H. Dutton, J. C. Wessinger, W. D. Wise and J. B. Harmon, (the second time, and the pastor at the present time-1938).

The members of the Church Council at this time are: O. O. Shealy, Eugene Shealy, Quinton Shealy, Homer E. Addy, E. S. Fulmer, Ira Fulmer, Alvin Fulmer, Monroe Bickley, J. J. Kibler, L. F. Price, Eddie Reeves and E. Berley Hawkins. Mr. L. A. Boozer is a Life Member of the Church Council.

The following are the officers of the auxiliary organizations: Eugene Shealy, Superintendent of the Sunday School; Mrs. E. Marvin Harmon, President of the Woman's Missionary Society; E. Marvin Harmon, President of the Brotherhood; J. B. Harmon, Jr., President of the Senior Luther League; Miss Anna Margaret Kibler, Superintendent of the Intermediate Luther League; and Mrs. Kenneth Swygert, Secretary of the Children of the Church.

BETHLEHEM LUTHERAN CHURCH.

This church is located just North of the town of Pomaria, in Newberry County. The first Lutherans in this community met about 1784 at Wicker's Camp Ground, about two miles Northeast of the present church. Here they organized a congregation of a few members in the year 1784. Later, a small log hut was put up near the grounds, which they used until a church was erected at it's present site in the year 1816 under the influence and pastorage of Rev. Godfrey Dreher. Rev. Herman Aull laid the foundation of the church and John Carr completed the building. Since then it has been remodeled and improved.

Rev. Godfrey Dreher served as pastor until 1824. Rev. Michael Rauch then came and served until 1830. Some others who have served as pastors were the following: Rev. J. C. Schwartz, who is buried in the church cemetery, from 1830-31; Rev. J. C. Hope, 1832-37; Rev. William Berley, who acted as supply a short time, as did, also, the Rev. George Haltiwanger. Rev. Schwartz had died while pastor, when quite young, on August 26, 1831. Then came Rev. J. B. Anthony, Rev. Thaddeus S. Boinest, Rev. George W. Holland, Rev. S. S. Rahn, and Rev. H. S. Wingard. Rev. Dr. S. T. Hallman served awhile, then the following: Rev. J. H. Wyse, Rev. J. D. Bowles, Rev. John J. Long, Rev. J. D. Sheely, Rev. I. E. Long, Rev. J. A. Linn, Rev. R. H. Anderson, Rev. S. C. Ballentine, Rev. Enoch Hite, Rev. H. A. Kistler, Rev. J. B. Haigler, and others whose names not available.

It is noted that the above pastors served several Lutheran Churches at a time, in the same area.

The large church cemetery contains many markers, some over the graves of Rev. War patriots, some of whom are: Adam F. Epting, David Cannon, John Eichleberger.

A centennial celebration was held in the church in 1915, the anniversary of it's second organization.

COLONY LUTHERAN CHURCH.

Colony Lutheran Church was organized in the year 1845 by Rev. William Berley, and dedicatory services were held in the new building in August, 1846, the sermon preached by Rev. J. C. Hope.

The church is located about five miles South of Newberry Court House, on the right of the highway leading to Prosperity. It's first building was a small frame edifice, erected in 1846. It was not until after the War Between the States that the present building was erected on the same site; since then many improvements having been made.

The original membership was made up of people in that community who were members at that time of St. Paul's Lutheran Church and of St. Luke's Lutheran Church. Rev. J. C. Hope said in his report to the State Synod that "they are indeed a colony;" hence, the name which they used for the church. One of it's charter members was the late Mrs. Julia Aull, who died in Columbia few years ago at the age of one hundred years.

Some of the pastors who have preached in the church were: Rev. William Berley, Rev. J. C. Hope, Rev. T. S. Boinest, Rev. J. P. Margart, Rev. J. H. Bailey, Rev. J. A. Sligh, Rev. Jacob Hawkins, Rev. J. D. Bowles, Rev. George W. Holland, Rev. W. K. Sligh, Rev. Charles H. Armstrong, Rev. John J. Long, Rev. R. E. Livingstone, Rev. A. J. Bowers, Rev. J. D. Kinard, Rev. P E. Sheely, Rev. L. P Boland, and others in later years.

Some of the sons of this church who have gone out into the ministry are: Rev. H. A. McCollough, D. D., of Columbia, S. C., and Rev. I. E. Long, and perhaps others.

In the church cemetery are many markers, including soldiers of the late wars; also, that of the late Rev. J. D. Bowles.

ST. MATTHEWS LUTHERAN CHURCH.

This church is near Broad River, about eight miles North of Pomaria, in Newberry County. It was organized in 1827 by Rev. J. D. Scheck who became the first pastor. Some of the other pastors who have served were: Rev. Jacob Moser, Rev. John C. Hope, Rev. S. R. Shepperd, Rev. William Berley, Rev. Thaddeus S. Boinest, Rev. J. Hungerpeler, Rev. Jacob Hawkins, Rev. J. A. Sligh, Rev. J. D. Shiery, Rev. Z. W. Bedenbaugh, Rev. William A. Julian, Rev. J. H. Wyse, Rev. J. D. Bowles. Rev. John J. Long, Rev. J. D. Sheely, Rev. I. E. Long, Rev. J. A. Linn, Rev. R. H. Anderson, Rev. S. C. Ballentine, Rev. Enoch Hite, Rev. H. A. Kistler, Rev. J. B. Haigler, and others.

On February 18, 1884, the church was destroyed by a cyclone. It was rebuilt under the pastorage of Rev. Z. W. Bedenbaugh in 1885, and the dedicatory sermon was made by Rev. J. D. Shiery on May 17, 1885.

A new Sunday School was added in 1937. In 1927, a centennial celebbratoon was held in the church.

Rev. Thomas F. Suber, of Columbia, S. C., is a son of this church. There may have been others who went out from this church to the ministry whose names are not known.

The new church was remodeled; it stands out in a grove of large oaks and other trees. A cemetery is near the church.

BACHMAN CHAPEL LUTHERAN CHURCH.

This church is about six miles South of Newberry Court House, on the old county road leading on the left from the main highway to Columbia, by way of " Jolly Street".

The church was organized on April 17, 1887, by Rev. J. A. Sligh, D. D. who became the first pastor. The first services were held in the old Ridge School house, and the first congregation was known as the Ridge Road Church.

The first building was erected about ½ miles away, it's present site, in 1889; on October 13, 1889, the Rev J. D. Bowles visited the church and preached the dedicatory sermon, the services being conducted by Rev. J. A. Sligh. It was then that the name was changed to Bachman Chapel Lutheran Church, in memory of Dr. John Bachman, a prominent Lutheran minister in the State and who preached in Charleston, S. C.

Some pastors who have served the church were the following: Rev. J. A. Sligh, Rev. W. A. Julian, Rev. C. P. Boozer, Rev. J. D. Bowles, Rev. H. P. Counts, Rev. P. H. E. Derrick, Rev. J. C. Wessinger, and others in recent years.

In the year 1909, the church was combined with St. Paul's Church pastorate, and the Rev. J. A. Sligh served both churches; but on account of advanced age he was given an assistant, the Rev. Y. Von A. Riser. In 1911, the Rev. Sligh resigned and Rev. Riser became the pastor. Rev. Riser served until 1915 when he accepted a pastorate in North Carolina. Others who have served the church were, Rev. J. B. Harmon, Rev. S. P. Koon, and others in recent years.

ST. JAMES LUTHERAN CHURCH.

This is a comparatively new church; it is located seven miles North of Newberry Court House, near Jalapa.

The first congregation in that immediate community of the Lutheran faith was, probably, that of old Liberty Hill Lutheran Church, whose members then lived in or near the Mollohon section of the county. These were instrumental in the church's organization.

The first building was a log building, built in 1848, near Indian Creek, which is about four miles from the present church of St. James. Then, in 1869, a new building was constructed at the same place. In 1890 the building was discarded and a new one erected at it's present site, four miles away. This was done mainly through the efforts of the late Rev. Wm. C. Schaeffer D. D. who was then the pastor of the Lutheran Church in Newberry. Rev. Schaeffer preached the dedicatory sermon on December 31, 1890, and the name then changed to St. James Lutheran Church.

In 1937 improvements were made on the church building.

Some of the early pastors who served the church were: Rev. Herman Aull, Rev. John C. Hope, Rev. G. H. Brown, Rev. William Berley, Rev. E. A. Bowles, Rev. W. H. Finck, Rev. J. B. Anthony, Rev. R. J. Hungerpeler, Rev. Stanmore Sheppard, Rev. Jacob Moser, Rev. Jacob Hawkins, Rev. James M. Schreckhise, Rev. J. D. Shirey, Rev. W. K. Sligh, Rev. A. G. Voight, Rev. A. J. Bowers, Rev. J. D. Sheely, Rev. James D. Kinard, Rev. P. E. Sheely, Rev. L. P. Boland, and others in later years. Some of these were Newberry College professors who preached to the congregation while they performing their duties in the college, others held pastorates in other churches at the same time, joint pastorates.

The congregation has steadily grown to an enrolled membership of about two hundred and thirty, fifty of whom have moved to different sections of the State. Preaching services are held on the first and third Sundays in the morning and on the second and fourth Sundays in the evenings. The attendance is usually very good.

A great deal of interest is taken in the Sunday School. There are nine classes with an enrollment of nearly two hundred. Every class has a teacher and an associate teacher.
(From sketch in the Newberry Observer, April, 1938).

ST. PAUL'S LUTHERAN CHURCH
(By W. P. Houseal)

St. Paul's Lutheran Congregation, located near Pomaria, in Newberry County, in celebrating the second anniversary of the opening of the new church, Sunday, March 20, had held special services on the corresponding date last year, March 19, 1938, when the first service was held in it. So when the city of Newberry is celebrating the 150th anniversary of its incorporation, St. Paul's congregation is observing the 178th year of its organization, and is thereby the oldest church of any denomination in the county, and at least a decade older than the oldest of all others. Newberry County, being first settled by the Germans, who were all Lutherans, in the Dutch Fork, in 1740.

While different dates between 1761 and 1764 are given when St. Paul's congregation was organized, it must be said when an estimate of the German character is analyzed, it is realized that they do not enter into any enterprise without due consideration of accomplishing its success. Therefore, in making any research of the actual year of its organization, it must be said that much preliminary work was done before they established the first congregation of any religious denomination in the county. Tradition places the organization during the administration of Governor Joseph Boone of South Carolina, which fixed the date between 1761 and 1764.

The land belonging to the congregation is a tract of sixty-eight acres. It must have been granted by George III, and it may have been a portion of the tract of two hundred acres on Crim's Creek, which was owned by the Rev. Joachim Bulow, who organized the congregation and became its first pastor. The Rev. Mr. Bulow owned a mill on Bush River and thereby was enabled to furnish supplies to the American army during the Revolutionary War. The records of these transactions are on file with the historical commission in Columbia, the latest date being in 1783. All records of the Rev. Mr. Bulow disappear after the above date. Tradition says his body was buried under the first church which the congregation erected. This church was destroyed by fire. Mr. Bulow's only son lived in Charleston, where he died, and his tomb is there to this day.

REVOLUTIONARY WAR INCIDENT

The first church of the congregation was built of logs as it stood near the spring on the church property, and served the congregation as a house of worship about twenty-five years, when it was destroyed by fire.

The second church, a frame structure, was erected on the East side of the road, and served the congregation about forty years until the third church was built in 1830. It had, first, doors in the rear and one on either side. The vestibule and recess were since added.

Dedicatory services of this church was performed by the Rev. Michael Rauch, the pastor, assisted by the Rev. John G. Schwartz, home missionary of the synod (the only Lutheran Minister of the synod who was an alumnus of South Carolina College) and became the first professor of the Lutheran Theological Seminary when it was established that year in the home of Col. John Eichelberger, as the house still stands on the Columbia road near Pomaria.

It is, coincidentally, mentioned that the mother of the writer attended the dedicatory services as she was wont to recall that event, which occurred when she was in her eighth year; the daughter of Matthais Barre, who aided in building the second church as well as the church of 1830. Likewise the maternal grandfather of the mother, Henry Werts, Revolutionary patriot, was among the founders of St. Paul's congregation in 1761, and the latter was ancestor of six Lutheran ministers, descendants of members of the congregation; while descendants of Henry Werts became liberal supporters of the causes of the Lutheran church, like Aaron and Hurs, as it were, who upheld the hands of Moses in this respect in the contest of the Israelites with the Amalekites.

A very significant event connected with the history of St. Paul's church is the fact that the forty-fourth convention of the South Carolina Synod held there November 15-21, 1868, it was decided to remove Newberry College to Walhalla, and on December 1st. of that year the removal took place.

FOURTH CHURCH FINE GRANITE STRUCTURE

Preliminary to the erection of the fourth church, breaking of ground took place with suitable ceremony August 10, 1936, with laying of the cornerstone in November following, the members faithfully giving their services during the winter and spring of the next year in sawing lumber from the forest of the church property, when much of the material of the third church being used, other portions being sold, for it was in a fine state of preservation.

Uncut granite, used in construction of the new church, was generously donated by C. E. Lominick of Pomaria. It was quarried six miles distant from the church and hauled there by members and friends of the congregation. The new church, crucifix in design, is distinctively Lutheran in arthitectural character; native granite is used in its structure, making it one of the handsomest churches in the Synod of South Carolina, with its main dimensions eighty by forty feet. Six Sunday School rooms are included in the balcony. Its windows are all placed as memorials to families of the congregation. The pulpit is the gift of the Rev. Thaddeus Bowman Epting, who was one of the sons of the congregation, who is now (1938) pastor of a Lutheran congregation in Springfield, Illinois. The church is lighted by electricity furnished by the Rural Electrification Authority.

The cost of the church is estimated at $15,000. in cash and gifts in kind-material and labor. However, if built by contract, for the entire work of construction, it could not be erected for less than $35,000.

SPECIAL SERVICES OPEN NEW CHURCH

When the new granite church was opened March 19, 1938, and the history of the congregation was read at the morning services by the Rev. S. P. Koon D. D., former pastor, of Lone Star, as he had made diligent research, thus this account is based mainly on his compilation. Doctor Koon was on the program for an address in like manner in the afternoon.

The service was in charge of J. A. C. Kibler, who introduced the speakers. He was the leader in the new church enterprise, and as member of the church council, his enthusiasm enlisted the hearty support of his co-workers, together with the women of the congregation, who deserved great praise for their faithful service. The program of addresses in the afternoon included former pastors, the Rev. Y. Von A. Riser, of Pomaria, the Rev. Glenn S. Ekard, Lexington, the Rev. J. S. Keisler, and the Rev. E. Z. Pence, president of the Synod, the Rev. E. Bryan Keisler of Newberry and William P. Houseal of Columbia.

SECOND PASTOR TAKES CHARGE

The Rev. Frederick Joseph Wallern succeeded the Rev. Mr. Bulow in 1787, as the second pastor, at the age of twenty-eight, serving until 1818. Upon his death that year he was buried at his home. However, in 1919, his body, together with that of his wife, was removed and interred in the cemetery at St. Paul's church, the original tomb bearing the inscription: "Sacred to the memory of Frederick J. Wallern, who was born April 6, 1759, and departed this life October 6, 1818, aged fifty-eight years and six months. He was a preacher of the Gospel in the Lutheran church, and we hope is removed to the rest prepared for the servant of God."

Another of the pioneer pastors was the Rev. Mr. J. Yost Meetze, who followed the Rev. Mr. Wallern, and was preaching at St. Paul's Church when the South Carolina Lutheran synod was formed in 1824.

The Rev. Mr. Meetze was followed by the Rev. S. Hersher, whose pastorship was of short duration.

RECORD OF PASTORS:
DURING CENTURY

The record shows the following pastors have served the congregation since the Lutheran synod was organized in 1824:

The Rev. Michael Rauch, 1825-27; the Rev. Jacob Wingard, 1828-29; the Michael Rauch (second pastorate), 1830-33; the Rev. John C. Hope, 1834-38; the Rev. W. G. Harter (following a vacancy of two years), 1840-41; the Rev. William Berley, 1841-50; the Rev. J. B. Anthony, 1851-53; the Rev. J. S. Stingley, 1853-55; the Rev. J. P. Margart, 1855-58; the Rev. D. M. Blackwelder (following a vacancy of a year), when clerical members of the faculty of Newberry College supplied services, 1860-65; the Rev. J. A. Sligh, 1865-1912, with the Rev. Y. Von A. Riser as assistant, 1911-12, the Rev. Y. Von A. Riser, 1912-16; the Rev. S. C. Ballentine, temporary supply pastor during portion of 1916; the Rev. S. P. Koon, 1916-34; Rev. J. A. Koisler, Jr., 1934-37; the Rev. J. W. Roof (after a vacancy of about a year) now the pastor since April, 1938.

LONGEST PASTORSHIP SOUTHERN CHURCH

The longest pastorship of any church in the Southern Lutheran synods, at the time was served by the Rev. Jefferson A. Sligh, D. D., when he took charge of St. Paul's congregation in 1865 and served until 1912, a period of forty-seven years, when he retired on account of impaired health. His body rests in St. Paul's cemetery. The Rev. Y. Von A. Riser was his assistant pastor, beginning in that respect in 1911 and serving until 1912, when he became the regular pastor. The cemetery was started in 1865 when Doctor Sligh became pastor.

The new and commodious parsonage was built at a convenient location during the pastorship of the Rev. S. P. Koon, D. D., at a cost of more than $5,000. Assistance in building the parsonage was rendered by the congregation of St. Paul's and Bachman Chapel, which now (as then) are connected with St. Paul's congregation in a pastorate. The first parsonage was built in 1855 during the pastorship of the Rev. J. S. Stingley.

GIVES THIRTEEN SONS AS MINISTERS:

Thirteen sons of St. Paul's congregation have become ministers of the Lutheran Church, as follows: Herman Aull, William Berley, Elijah Elmore, J. Eusebius Berley, M. D., Monroe J. Epting, Sidney T. Riser, George A. Riser (brother of the former), Robert E. Livingston, Wilbur K. Sligh (son of Doctor Sligh) Henry P. Counts,* Thaddeus B. Epting, E. K. Counts, Lewis Koon (son of Doctor Koon).

Besides the above group there are others who became members of other congregations who have likewise entered the ministry of the Lutheran Church. Likewise quite a multitude of laymen have gone from St. Paul's church far and wide to enrich other congregations with spirit of liberality in the progress of the Gospel. St. Paul's is thus the mother church of all the Lutheran congregations in Newberry County except Bethlehem Church and one or more to the number of a dozen or more. It has been liberal in support of the educational institutions of the Lutheran Church, and many of her sons are listed among the graduates of Newberry College and quite a number of the Columbia Theological seminary.

(From sketch in Newberry Observer, April, 1938)

* Rev. T. B. Epting was in 1948-49 an Associate Pastor of an Episcopal Church, Atlanta Georgia.

G. L. S.

ST. PHILIP'S LUTHERAN CHURCH

St. Philip's church was organized by Rev. H. S. Wingard in August, 1881, while he was pastor of Bethlehem charge. The organization was perfected in the home of Mr. Philip Sligh and the church building was erected in the same year. The building was dedicated November 5, 1882. The pastor was assisted in the dedicatory services by Rev. J. Steck, D. D. Rev. Mr. Wingard was succeeded as pastor by Rev. S. T. Hallman, December 2, 1883, who was succeeded by H. F. Scheele, theological student, June 6, 1888, who served as supply pastor, Rev. J. H. Wyse was called and became pastor February 2, 1890, and served the congregation two years. Rev. J. A. Sligh began work as supply pastor the first Sunday in December 1892, for one year. Rev. Dr. Sligh was assisted in the work by his son, Rev. W. K. Sligh. Rev. J. D. Bowles succeeded Rev. J. A. Sligh, December 9, 1893, and served as pastor to October 2, 1898. Rev. J. J. Long was called as supply pastor and served until October 1900. Rev. Dr. Hallman was again called and served St. Philip's together with Mt. Olivet and Bachman's Chapel as a pastorate, until January 1901. Rev. H. P. Counts was called to become pastor of St. Philip's and Bachman's Chapel and took charge February 3, 1901. He was succeeded by Rev. P. H. E. Derrick, in March 1902, and he served until 1905. Rev. Mr. Derrick was succeeded by Rev. J. C. Wessinger, November 26, 1905, and continued as pastor until March 28, 1909. Rev. J. J. Long served from April 11,1909 to October 16, 1910.

At this time a new Pastorate was formed, composed of St. Paul's, St. Philip's, and Bachman's Chapel. This Pastorate called Rev. J. A. Sligh, as pastor and Rev. Y. Von A. Riser as assistant. Dr. Sligh, having retired from active ministry, Rev. Mr. Riser became pastor. During his term as pastor the old church building was removed and the present one erected, in 1914.

Rev. Mr. Riser served until January 1915, when he was succeeded by Rev. A. J. Bowers, D. D., whose services embraced a period of one year. Rev. S. P. Koon, the next pastor, entered upon his work December 10, 1916. Under his administration the debt on the new building was paid off
  (The first church was named "Phillip's Church", for Phillip Sligh, who gave the lot and money for erecting it).
  (Sources: Hallman's History of South Carolina Lutheran Synod, Newberry Observer, April, 1938).

ST. LUKE'S LUTHERAN CHURCH

St. Luke's Evangelical Lutheran church, Prosperity, S. C., (Route 2) was organized in 1828 by Rev. J. G. Schwartz, who was then on a missionary tour for the South Carolina Synod. Worship was first held in a log building known as the Baptist meeting house, which was located on Johnny Bedenbaugh's place about two and one-half miles southeast of the present location. In about 1830, a building was erected near where the church now stands, and Rev. J. G. Schwartz was the first pastor.

In 1845, the first building was torn-down and the material sold to the Colony Lutheran Church between Prosperity and Newberry, and in the same year a new church building was erected. That building is a part of the one that is now used. In 1886, this building was remodeled and new pews were installed. In 1904, while Rev. S. P. Koon was pastor, the church was repainted both inside and outside.

In 1916, while Rev. B. W. Cronk was pastor a Sunday school room was built adjoining the main part of the church. New church furniture was placed in the church in 1924.

The regular pastors have been as follows: Reverends J. G. Schwartz, William Berley, J. Moser, J. C. Hope, J. P. Margartt, T. S. Boinest (assisted by Rev. J. D. Smithdeal), J. Hawkins, D. D., J. D. Bowers, J. Hawkins, D. D. , M. J. Epting, J. Hawkins, D. D., (third term served until his death, July, 1895), George Bearden, H. J. Mathias, S. P. Koon, B. W. Cronk, W. H. Roof, E. H. Seckinger, J. B. Harmon, J. Virgil Long, the present pastor. (1938).

The following are sons of this congregation: Reverends Stanmore R. Shepherd, Levi Bedenbaugh, Wilson Bedenbaugh, J. S. Elmore, Jacob Hawkins, I. P. Hawkins, Z. W. Dodonbaugh, W. E. Pugh, P. E. Shealy, C. P. Boozer, J. A. Shealy, and others.

(Sources: Hallman's History of South Carolina Lutheran Synod; Newberry Observer, April,1938).

HOLY TRINITY LUTHERAN CHURCH

Holy Trinity Evangelical Lutheran church, Little Mountain, was organized January 1, 1891, with the Rev. J. K. Efird as its first pastor.

The first building was a frame structure thirty-five by fifty-six by sixteen feet with a fifty foot tower over the entrance. The building committee was composed of A. N. Boland, David Boland, G. M. Shealy, Jr., and W. E. Miller with Shockley Brothers as the contractors. The pews, altar and pulpit were made by them also. In 1902, a Sunday School room was added.

In 1917, this house of worship was supplanted by a more commodious brick building with a churchly interior nicely furnished and with its basement fitted for church school purposes. There are fifteen class rooms. This building was dedicated June 18, 1922.

With more than four hundred members and property valued at $16,000.,Holy Trinity is recognized as a progressive and efficient congregation. All of its educational departments are well organized and graded and auxiliary societies are maintained for all members from the youngest to the oldest. The congregation strives to meet its financial, educational and spiritual responsibilities one hundred per cent.

Superintendents who have founded and maintained the progressive church school are: A. N. Boland, Dr. J. M. Sease, J. H. Wise, W. A. Counts, George B. Derrick and W. B. Shealy.

Pastors who have guided the spiritual welfare of Holy Trinity throughout the years are the Reverends J. K. Efird, A. G. Voight, D .D.,(supply), S. L. Nease, H. P. Counts, O. B. Shearouse, J. J. Long, J. B. Harmon and E. Z. Pence.

Sons of the congregation who have entered the ministry are the Reverends L. P. Boland, H. D. Chapman, J. V. Long, and J. O. Kempson.

(From sketch in Newberry Observer, April-1938).

MT. HERMON CHURCH
Peak, S. C.

On March 3, 1889, there was a called and authorized meeting at Peak,(then Lexington County), Newberry County, for the purpose of organizing and establishing a Christian Church. At this time the constitution and by-laws were framed and adopted.

Rev. Junius B. Fox, of Newberry, South Carolina, entered upon his duties as pastor on December 2, 1888, having received a call from many of the Lutherans in Peak and the surrounding community to begin the work of organizing and establishing a Lutheran church in this place and to become the first regular pastor of the congregation.

A Sunday School was organized on Sunday, January 6, 1889, with Mr. Brooks Swygert as superintendent.

The congregation was organized on Sunday, February 3rd, 1889, with the names of thirty-three persons who signified their willingness to enter into the organization. A constitution and by-laws were adopted and officers elected and installed. Subscriptions were commenced for the erection of the church.

The first Communion Service of the congregation was held on Sunday, May 5, 1889. On Sunday, June 2, 1889, the congregation by a unanimous vote decided to make application for admission into the South Carolina Synod.

On the 13th of May, 1889, Brooks Swygert was elected the first secretary of this congregation and H. W. Whites the first treasurer.

The cornerstone of Mt. Hermon church was laid on the sixth day of March 1890, Rev. J. B. Fox officiating.

Mt. Hermon E. L. Church was dedicated on the fifth day of October, A. D., 1890, Rev. J. B. Fox officiating.

The first sermon preached in Mt. Hermon church was by the Rev. W. C. Schaeffer of Newberry, on the third day of October, 1890, from Isaiah, sixtieth chapter and first verse.

Newberry Conference met at Mt. Hermon church April 26, 1893.

The first officers elected were: Elders, Brooks Swygert, A. M. Sease, J. H. Shell, P. E. Bargle, A. G. Dickert and Jno. C. Swygert.

Deacons: F. B. Lucas, W. Pink Summer, H. W. Whites, Jackson Counts, Jno. W. Summer and L. P. Stoudemayer.

(From sketch in Newberry Observer, April-1938).

BETH EDEN LUTHERAN CHURCH.

This church was organized about 1843, by the Rev. G. H. Brown, who was graduated in 1842 from the Lutheran Theological Seminary, then at Lexington, S. C. At the Convention of the South Carolina Lutheran Synod in November. 1846, Rev. George Haltiwanger, Sr. was selected as pastor. Later, came Rev. J. F. W. Leppord in 1848. Rev. J. B. Lowman served from 1849 to 1864, and again from 1867 to 1870. Rev. William Berley served from 1871 to 1873. Since then several different pastors have served the church at various times.

The church has been the central meeting place for many public meetings of the peoples of that section. It was the place of meeting of the early organization against the abolition of slavery in the State.

(Ref: Hallman's " Hist. of Luth. Synod of S. C."; Oneall's " Annals of Newberry", Part 11, by John A. Chapman.)

BUSH RIVER BAPTIST CHURCH

This church is located about ten miles Northwest of Newberry Court House, near upper branch of Bush River. It is the oldest Baptist Church in the county, having been organized about 1765, and constituted in 1771 by Elders Phillip Mulkey and Samuel Newman, with nine members. Elder Newman was appointed the first pastor— a custom since then for many generations to select their pastors from among the members of the congregation. Rev. Newman died 1773; and then Elder Norris was chosen pastor, and was licensed to preach from the Baptist settlement on Little River. He was ordained in 1773 by Elders Phillip Mulkey and David Reese. Pastor Norris visited his people at their homes frequently, and his custom was, when entering a house, to say, " peace be to this house".

Pastor Norris served during the Rev War, and his doctrine was non-resistance; and for this boldness in his preaching he was jailed at Ninety Six. His liberty was offered him several times on condition he would stop preaching such dostrines, but he always refused to accept his freedom on such conditions. He was finally released without condition. He continued to preach until 1780 when he died.

In 1781, John Cole, a member of the Church, was chosen to be their pastor, and in 1783 he was ordained by Elders Joseph Burton and John Webb. Under him the church grew, and in 1791 the church was first represented in the Bethel Association. From this time a regular record of the church began to be kept, by the first Clerk, Michael Landers. Rev. John Cole died in 1816.

In 1802 a great religious revival started over the country, and here the Baptists used such methods of showing their religeous spirits by spasmodic actions or " jerks", which sometimes accompanied their fervor. Many persons were received in the church and baptised from August 22, 1794 to October, same year; and from this congregation came their first missionary to foreign fields, Charles Crow.

In 1804 Stephen McGraw was appointed Clerk, Michael Landers having died. About this time, Charles Griffin was received in the church and baptised. He was a member of the State Legislature; and one of his sons, John K. Griffin, at later time represented his district in the United States Congress.

In 1807 Charles Crow and James Teague were ordained as preachers by Elders Palmer, Shakleford, Lilly, and King. Here, too, John S. Carwile, a long-time member, became Clerk when Mr. McGraw moved to Alabama. Mr. Carwile was the father of the author of " Rem. of Newberry".

On October 6, 1831, John S. Carwile and James Divver were dismissed at their requests so that they could organize the first Baptist Church in the village of Newberry, to which place they had moved. The early families of Thomas Gary, of West Gary, and of Lewis Jones, and others were among the church's first members.

The fourth pastor, Charles Crow, served from 1816 to 1825, and then moved to the Southwest.

Rev. Daniel Mangum and Rev. David Peterson were pastors at different times, both having at first been Elders. Rev. Mangum served twenty six years, from the year 1826; and he is buried in the church cemetery. He, also, supplied at Cross Roads, Rocky Springs, and Mt. Zion Church and acted as supply at the Newberry Baptist Church for two years. He was a member of the Newberry Baptist Society, and it's Vice-President. As a friend of temperance he took an active part in temperance organizations.

The church has been served by several able preachers since the War of Secession. It has had built a large substantial building and parsonage. They have a membership which includes many substantial citizens in the upper section of the county.

(From Townsend's " South Carolina Baptsist", and O'Neall's " Annals of Newberry".)

HELENA COMMUNITY CHAPEL

The church started at Helena about the year 1935. It is located in Helena, Newberry County, about one and a half miles from Newberry County Court House. It was first organized by Rev. C. A. Calcote, who was at that time the pastor of Aveleigh Presbyterian Church in Newberry. The meetings have been held since in a small one-story frame building, once a dwelling.

BETHEL BAPTIST CHURCH

Bethel Baptist Church is on the old Holly's Ferry Road, about six and one-half miles South of Prosperity. It was organized September 29, 1840, by Rev. Daniel Mangum and Rev. Thomas Frean. (Rev. Frean had been converted from the Quaker faith to that of the Baptists).

The church was supplied by Rev. Mangum and others until 1852, and in that year Rev. A. W. Asbill was called as the regular pastor. He served sixteen years. Since 1867 it was served by various ministers, among them being the following: Rev. John Barry, Rev. W. T. Farrow, Rev. N. N. Burton, Rev. J. M. Morris, Rev. Lewis O'Neall, (he, too, was the first Quaker), Rev. M. D. Padgett, Rev. W. B. Elkins, Rev. R. W. Seymour, Rev. Joab Edwards, Rev. N. B. Williams, Rev. J. D. Higgins, Rev. H. T. Smith, and others.

The first church building was a small frame structure, erected about 1841. Later, a new one was built on the same lot. Several young men of the community have gone out from the church and entered the ministry. A cemetery is near the chucrh.

MT. ZION BAPTIST CHURCH.

Mt. Zion Church is located on the West of the highway leading to Beaver Dam Creek, about one mile North of Silver Street. It was organized in July, 1832, the officiating ministers being Rev. Daniel Mangum and Rev. N. W. Hodges, aided by laymen from the Bush River Baptist Church and the Cross Roads Baptist Church that are in the same area.

The first building was erected in 1832, a small frame edifice. The second building, the present one, was built just after the War of Secession.

Rev. Mangum preached to them once a month, and served as pastor for eighteen years. The next pastor was Rev. James F. Peterson, who served fifteen years, during which time one hundred and thirty eight members were added to the church roll. Rev. Peterson died on June 10, 1881, aged eighty five years. The next pastor was Rev. James K. Mendenhall, who served from 1865 to 1870, during which time he baptised sixty six people. In 1871, the Rev. A. W. Lamar was called, and ordained on Janury 15, 1871. After one year he left to become Secretary and Treasurer of the Baptist State Convention of South Carolina. In 1872 the Rev. T. W. Smith and the Rev. William Williams preached, alternately, once a month.

In 1873, Mt. Zion Church and Bush River Baptist Church united in calling W. D. Price to serve both congregations. Rev. Price served until 1879 when he was succeeded by Rev. James C. Furman, D. D., of Greenville, S. C.

In 1880, the church called Rev. William B. Elkins to take charge as pastor of the one church; but after three years he resigned on account of bad health.

In December, 1883, Rev. W. J. Langston was called, and was installed in June, 1884, when he completed his theological course. Meanwhile, the Rev. Luther Broadus, then pastor of the Newberry Baptist Church, filled the pulpit until his return. Rev Langston served until 1892. Since that time several able ministers have served the church.

A cemetery is near the church.

SALUDA BAPTIST CHURCH.

This church is located in the town of Chappells, Newberry County, near Saluda River. It was organized on December 27, 1892, by a Council of representatives from Cross Roads, Bethabara, Bush River and Prosperity Baptist Churches

The charter members were: J. R. Irwin, Mrs. J. R. Irwin, J. J. White, T. B. Starnes, D. F. White, Mrs. D. F. White, Mrs. Jane Starnes, Miss. Leila Starnes, Bessie Starnes, Anna Starnes, W. H. Betts, Mrs. H. M. Betts, Mrs. Hampton Betts, S. G. Carter, Mrs. M. C. Carter, Miss. Leila Carter. Eight of these were from Cross Roads, and the remaining seven from Sister Springs and Bethabara Baptist Churches.

The first and only building was erected in 1892, and dedicated November 5, 1893, debt-free. The Rev. Thomas K. Bailey, D. D., a native of Ireland, then living in South Carolina, preached the dedicatory sermon.

There are no memorials in the church, except pages dedicated to the memory of the following: Nannie Andrews, A. Parks, J. G. Holloway, Mrs. F. E. Bozeman, Mrs. J. R. Irwin, Mrs. W. J.

Holloway(Vicie Jennings), Dr. W. J. Holloway, J. L. Watkins, A. P. Coleman, J. R. Irwin,.....
Mr. J. R. Irwin was Superintendent of the Sunday School for fifty eight years.
The only cemetery near the church is that of the old Bozeman-Scurry graveyards, both of which
are enclosed with strong iron picket fences.

ENOREE BAPTIST CHURCH

Enoree Baptist Church is located near Keitt's Cross Roads, about twelve miles East of
Newberry. It was organized in 1768, and was known at first as Bauskett's Church. One of
the first pastors was Rev. Jacob King. The first church was a log hut until their membership
grew when they built a new church.
The new building was erected in 1822 on the same lot where the log building stood. It was
dedicated in the same year by Elders Thomas Ray and J. Davis, and a Mr. Alexander. The
written records begin in 1832 when Rev. E. Lindsey was the pastor, who was assisted by
Rev. Thomas Frean and Rev. G W. Brooks from time to time.
In 1838 Rev. G. W. Brooks became the regular pastor; he served ten years. In 1849 Rev.
J. A. Hill took charge as pastor. In 1850, Rev. Brooks again was called. There was no
regular pastor from 1851 to 1852; but Rev. E. Lindsey returned in 1853, then Rev. Brooks again
in 1854. In 1855 and 1856, the Rev. F. C. Jeter served as pastor; and in 1857 the Rev. G. W.
Brooks; and in 1858-59, the Rev. W. H. Martin, who assisted the Rev. R. P. Vann.
Later, the church building was discared; and in 1859, the present church building was erected
and the name changed to the Enoree Baptist Church. It is located a few yards to the right of
the old church site. Rev. J. J. Brantley preached the dedicatory sermon in the church in
that year.
In 1860, the Rev. W. D. Mayfield became pastor, assisted by Rev. Mullinax. In 1861, the
church was supplied by Rev. Mullinax. In 1861, again, the church was supplied by Rev. Mayfield
and Rev. Brooks. In 1862, the Rev. James K. Mendenhall was called to be pastor. In 1864,
Rev. Jeter was called and served one year. In 1865 Rev. Mendenhall served as pastor.
During the year that followed the War of Secession, the church was served by several different
pastors, among them having been Rev. B. F. Corley, Rev. Thomas H. Pope, Rev. W. H. Leavell, and
others.
A Sunday School was organized in the year 1877, with W. W. Johns as Superintendent.
Many improvements have been made on the last building from time to time. In 1938-40 the
Rev. C. C. Vaughan was pastor.
A large cemetery is near the church containing many old markers. Also, a small grave-
yard is near the site of old Bauskett's Church, called the Wadlington graveyard, which adjoins
lot of Enoree Church.

BAPTIST CHURCH
of
Prosperity, S.C.

The Baptist State Mission Board was established as a Mission Church at Prosperity, S. C.,
the year 1880. The station was supplied with preachers from 1880 to 1884, including Rev.
Paugh, Rev. Seymour, and Rev. Elkins.
The organization of the church was made on the fourth Sunday in April, 1884, with a membership of eleven, with the Rev. Wilson as pastor. At a meeting one month later it was decided
to erect a concrete building. Mr. Hussa gave the land for the building. Many people
outside of the denomination donated to the cause. Most of the rocks that were used in building the Church were hauled from B. Lindsey Dominick's place, about six miles away.
In March, 1885, the church building was begun, and continued under many difficulties.
Much damage was done to the building by excessive rains and winds, so that the work was delayed
The Rev. W. B. Elkins took charge of the work January 20, 1887. The building was completed
in 1889.
It was one of the first concrete buildings in this part of the State. It's success was due
largely to contributions made by Dr. E. C. Ridgell of Batesburg, Mr. B. Lindsey Dominick, and others
(From sketch in Newberry Observer, April, 1938).

FIRST BAPTIST CHURCH

The first Baptist church was the first church in Newberry. Up to 1831, there was no church organization and no house of worship in the city. In the summer of 1831 a group of men gathered at the home of John S. Carwile and discussed plans for holding a meeting here to be conducted by students of the Furman Theological Seminary. Sometime in September of 1831 four young men: N. W. Hodges, J. M. Chiles, Josiah Furman, and John M. Barnes, came to Newberry and held a series of meetings, some outdoors and some in the old court house. As a result of this movement, the Newberry First Baptist church was organized on the thirtieth day of September, 1831, with forty-two members. At the first meeting of the church the constitution was adopted and John S. Carwile was named deacon and John M. Barnes, pastor. Barnes served, however, only three months.

On October 15, 1831, at the first meeting of the church after its organization, Y. J. Harrington, William Wilson, M. T. Mendenhall, and Thomas Pratt were appointed to aid the deacon in his duties. At the next meeting Harrington and Pratt were elected deacons.

Rev. N. W. Hodges was called as pastor in December of 1831 and began work the first of the next year.

The first church building was completed in 1832 and was used until 1907 when the building that is now in use was erected. When the first church was torn down it was re-erected at the Mollohon Mill village where it stands today. The site of the present church on Caldwell and Boundary streets was given by Y. J. Harrington and John T. Young.

While the second pastor, the Rev. Hodges, was in charge, the church grew rapidly and the membership at the end of 1833 numbered one hundred and thirteen members.

In 1833 the church was received into the Reedy River Baptist Association of which it is still a member. Three more deacons, J. B. O'Neall, M. T. Mendenhall, and Drayton Nance, were added in March of 1834. Chief Justice John Belton O'Neall continued deacon until his death in 1863.

Rev. Daniel Mangum succeeded Rev. Hodges in 1835. He served only a short time, however, as Rev. Hodges returned in 1837 to supply the pulpit once a month during a part of 1837 and 1838.

Rev. Thomas Frean, and Irishman, became pastor in 1839 serving until 1842. Next was Rev. Samuel Gibson of Greenville who came to Newberry twice a month to hold services. In 1846, the church secured the service of Rev. J. G. Landrum, pastor of the Spartanburg Baptist church, who like Rev. Gibson rode down once or twice a month to conduct services.

Rev. M. C. Barnett, also of Spartanburg Baptist church, succeeded Rev. Landrum in 1848, and preached here until the end of 1849.

In 1850, the church called Rev. J. J. Brantley as its pastor and he served sixteen years proving very popular with members of all the city churches. Under his ministry the church underwent many changes. Y. J. Harrington, treasurer of the church since its origin, died November 11, 1850. He was succeeded by deacon Drayton Nance. In 1852 G. T. Scott was elected deacon and later the same year the church suffered another loss when John S. Carwile, first deacon of the church and for years church clerk, died. The vacant deaconate was filled by W. H. Harrington. In September of 1856 deacon Nance died. He was succeeded in a few months by John B. Carwile, and at the same time deacon W. H. Harrington was named treasurer. In 1861 J. D. Nance succeeded Harrington as treasurer.

The Baptist church struggled through the trying days in the South during the War Between the States under the leadership of Rev. Brantley who resigned soon after the war, January 6, 1866.

Rev. J. T. Zealy succeeded Rev. Brantley in 1867, resigning in 1868. In this year John R. Leavell and W. T. Wright were named deacons.

Rev. Richard Furman was called to the pastorate in 1868 and served until 1869, his health failing him. During 1870 the church was supplied by students from the Southern Baptist Seminary.

In 1870 Dr. John Stout took charge of the church, resigning in 1873, and he was followed by Rev. F. W. Eason who served well until 1878. During his term, G. T. Scott died and James McIntosh became deacon.

Rev. Luther Broaddus was called in 1878 and served until his death in 1885, being one of the church's outstanding pastors. The present parsonage was built during his time, being completed in 1883.

Following the death of Rev. Broaddus, Rev. C. P. Scott of Richmond, Virginia, was called and he served here until 1890. It was during Rev. Scott's years here that the First Baptist church was called upon and assisted in organizing a Union Church at West End. A committee met with mill officials and organized the Baptist church at West End in 1887.

Rev. George A. Wright succeeded Rev. Scott in 1891 and served the church faithfully for twenty-one years, the longest term of any pastor in the history of the church. Many changes were affected during his service here. Among the faithful church members who died were: Chief Justice Y. J. Pope, J. R. Leavell, J. K. P.Goggans and John B. Carwile. Among the deacons ordained during Rev. Wright's ministry were R. Y. Leavell, W. H. Hunt, John M. Kinards, E. B. Wilbur, W. H. Shelley, J. H. West, W. O. Wilson, and M. Werts.

In 1912, Rev. E. Pendleton Johes was called to the pastorate and in 1915, Rev. Earl V. Babb came to serve as pastor, serving until 1925. Newberry College bestowed upon Rev. Babb the degree of Doctor of Divinity. In 1919, James McIntosh, a deacon and treasurer in the church for many years, passed away. New deacons in Dr. Babb's ministry included: J. H. Clary, J. A. Burton, B. L. Dorrity, M. W. Clary, and others.

Upon Dr. Babb's resignation the church called Dr. Charles E. Burts. It was during his years here that the church was remodeled and enlarged and the Sunday school rooms added. New deacons at this time, 1926 and 1927, included Floyd Bradley, I. H. Hunt, M. L. Spearman, and T. E. Epting. In 1927,Dr. Burts resigned.

In 1927, Dr. F. O. Lamoreux was called and at the present time (1938) he is still serving, being one of the city's outstanding ministers.

Members who died in Dr. Lamoreux's first years here included: Walter H. Hunt, superintendent of the Sunday school for many years, and M. L. Spearman, deacon and treasurer for many years.

The Sunday school has long been a valuable factor in the work of the First Baptist church. Among its outstanding workers and superintendents were: John B. Carwile, Walter H. Hunt, John M. Kinard, James P. Kinard, E. B. Wilbur, M. L. Spearman, B. L. Dorrity, C. F. Wertz, and the present superintendent, W. C. Wallace.

Another important organization of the church is the Woman's Missionary Society which was formed in May 1871, by the Rev. John A. Stout. The first officers were: Mrs. John B. Carwile, Mrs. Elizabeth H. McIntosh, Miss Fannie Leavell, and Mrs. Margaret Leavell Tarrant. Today, Mrs. Walter H. Hunt is president of the Society. She has served capably in this office for a number of years.

An impressive feature of the Sunday school is the obervance of the White Christmas service each year, a custom of over thirty years standing. Miss Mary Burton has been in charge of the decorating of the church and of the program which consists of music, songs, and recitations by the children of the Sunday school since it first started.

The present membership of the First Baptist church is five hundred and fifty. The Sunday school enrollment is two hundred and eighty-five,(year 1938).

Betty Jean Toohey, a small daughter of Mr. and Mrs. E. H. Toohey of Greenville, recently joined the First Baptist church. She is of the sixth generation of descendants of John S. Carwile, the first deacon of the church.

Present members of the board include two life members, J. H. West, Chairman, and Floyd Bradley, Vice-chairman. Other members are T. E. Epting, W. C. Wallace, R. E. Blair, R. G. Wallace, M. W. Clary, James R. Leavell, S. C. Paysinger, Neal W. Workman, George Bodelsperger, Frank Sutton, James W. Johnson, and Paul B. Ezell.

(Sketch in Newberry Observer, April, 1938).

EAST SIDE BAPTIST CHURCH

East Side Baptist church was organized in the Mollohon Mill community on March 15, 1903, and is located on the corner of Montgomery and Glenn Streets. The following officers were elected: J. D. Galloway as Clerk and Treasurer, and C. A. Dickert, J. H. Rhodes and J. S. Galloway as deacons. The church was then called a chapel, with the following denominations meeting there: Baptist, Methodist and Presbyterian.

On April 5, 1903, in a church conference, the people called their first pastor, who was the Rev. N. N. Burton.

In a church conference held on September 6, 1903, the church voted to send delegates to the Reedy River association to make application for entry into the association.
The following pastors have served the church:
Rev. N. N. Burton, April 5, 1903—September 4, 1910.
Rev. W. C. Dudley, September 4, 1910—January 28, 1912.
Rev. Garrett, January 28, 1912—January 9, 1914
Rev. W. D. Hammett, January 9, 1914—May, 1915.
Rev. J. M. Culbertson, May, 1915—December 3, 1916.
Rev. W. C. Baxley, December 3, 1916—January 31, 1918.
Rev. E. P. Driggers, January 31, 1918—November 24, 1919.
Rev. W. E. Furcron, November 24, 1918—June 27, 1920.
Rev. J. P. Carter, June 27, 1920—October 22, 1922.
Rev. W. H. Whaley, October 22, 1922—September 26, 1926.
Rev. S. J. Morgan, September, 1926—October, 1931.
Rev. E. G. Ross, October, 1931—February 2, 1936.
Rev. C. M. Johnson, February 2, 1936—June 6, 1937.
Rev. James B. Mitchell, June 13, 1937—.
The following pastors have received licenses from this church:
Rev. T. B. McEntyre and Rev. E. P. Driggers.
In June, 1907, the church, which was the original first church, was moved from up town (Newberry Baptist) to the corner of Lee and Glenn Streets. Some of the timber now in the church is over one hundred years old. The lumber was built in the original church in 1831—1937.
Present officials of the church are Deacons, R. J. Willingham, chairman, G. W. Marin, treasurer; H. A. Ruff, H. L. Reeves, Lee Boozer, Claud Hanby, David Brown, Jack Matthews, E. A. Howard.
(Sketch in Newberry Observer, April, 1938).

HUNT MEMORIAL BAPTIST CHURCH, OAKLAND VILLAGE.

Since 1913, Baptists have had an organized church at Oakland, going under the name of the Oakland Baptist church. It was not until 1938, that the congregation changed the name from Oakland Baptist church to Hunt Memorial Baptist Church. It was also in 1938, that the building which the congregation now occupies was built. Through the years the Methodists and Baptists shared a building, erected and owned by the mill company. A Union Sunday school was the order, while the times or appointments for worship and mid-week prayer service were shared between the two churches. Under that arrangement much good resulted and naturally that one building was the center of all community activity. However, as the congregations grew and enlarged their organizations and increased their activities, the one building became quite inadequate to meet the needs of the two congregations, and it became evident that there must inevitably be an additional building constructed.
It was in 1937, that under the leadership of the pastors working in conjunction with the management of the mill that plans were worked out whereby the Baptists were to build the new building and the Methodists were to retain the one then in use.
The present building which has thirteen class rooms, an auditorium with a seating capacity of three hundred and fifty, and cost approximately $16,000., including equipment, was occupied in May, 1938.
The Hunt Memorial congregation is not one of the large Baptist churches (two hundred and ten) members but is one of the most active. With its Sunday school enrollment of two hundred and thirty-eight, the B. T. U. with an average attendance of more than one hundred per Sunday; the W. M. U. which is fully organized; the mid-week and Saturday evening prayer services, the church is seldom without some meeting of one or more groups each day.
The officers of the church are: Pastor Emeritus, Rev. E. G. Ross; Pastor, Rev. C. M. Johnson; deacons, C. H. Kirby, C. J. Swindler, J. T. Thompson, R. M. Bolton, A. N. Brown, W. E. Holsonback, G. B. Wilhite, J. W. Wofford, and S. H. Abrams. Roy Cochcroft is superintendent of the Sunday School; F. H. ("Preach") McConnell, director of the Baptist Training Union; Mrs. F. H. McConnell, president of the W. M. U.

The pastor, Rev. Clyde M. Johnson, has served since March, 1936, succeeding Rev. E. G. Ross, who was taken ill while serving the Oakland and Mollohon churches. He is now residing at Hendersonville, North Carolina.

(Sketch in Newberry Observer, April, 1938).

WEST END BAPTIST CHURCH.

On April 10, 1887, a council consisting of Pastor C. P. Scott, and brothers, J. R. Leavell, John B. Carwile, Dr. James McIntosh, John S. Carwile, J. K. P. Goggans and A. A. Killian, from the Baptist Church of Newberry, South Carolina, and the Pastor, Rev. W. J. Langston and brothers A. P. Davis and W. P. Johnson from Bush River Baptist Church, Newberry County, South Carolina, met in the afternoon at 4:00 o'clock in the Union Church building which was located on O'Neall Street, where the O'Neall Street Methodist parsonage now stands. This building was on the grounds of the Newberry Cotton Mills and was owned by the Newberry Cotton Mills of Newberry, South Carolina. At the request of a company of believers in Christ, connected with the Newberry Cotton Mills, who wished to organize themselves into a Baptist Church, brother J. R. Leavell was elected moderator and Brother John S. Carwile, secretary of the council. The following then presented letters of dismission from various Baptist Churches: From the Baptist Church of Piedmont, South Carolina, John E. Crosby and Ardella Crosby; Good Hope Baptist Church, Edgefield, South Carolina, S. B. Tompkins and Ella Tompkins; Saludaville Baptist Church, Basheba Koon; Williamston Baptist Church, Williamston, South Carolina, Sarah Tempie Thoxton; Vaucluse Baptist Church, Aiken County, South Carolina, John M. Foster; Unity Foster, Hazel Floyd, Amanda Floyd and Elizabeth Floyd; Bethel Baptist Church, Newberry County, Stuffle Gruber, Marion Gruber, and Lucinda Gruber; Graniteville Baptist Church Graniteville, South Carolina, Rev. John C. Rhoden, Nancy Rhoden, Robert E. Rhoden and L. W. Redd; Bush River Baptist Church, Eliza Dobbins; Newberry Baptist Church, C. W. White, Jane White and J. T. Setzler.

The church was named the Second Baptist Church of Christ. The church then elected brothers J. E. Crosby and L. W. Redd as deacons. Robert E. Rhoden was elected as church clerk. Rev. W. J. Langston read the second chapter of Ephesians, the hymn "I Love Thy Kingdom Lord" was sung. Rev. Langston preached the sermon from second chapter of Ephesians, verses 20-22. Brother John R. Leavell lead in prayer. Rev. C. P. Scott then delivered the charge and extended the right hand of fellowship to the church, the hymn "Stand Up, Stand Up for Jesus," was sung and Rev. Langston pronounced the benediction.

The meeting place at this time was the chapel which was used by the Methodist and Baptist churches, alternating Sundays. It was also used for school purposes and social affairs. On May 22, 1887, the church in conference elected Rev. John C. Rhoden its pastor for the remainder of the year. A committee of three, consisting of C. W. White, L. W. Redd and W. R. Jones was elected to investigate the income of the members of the church so the financial affairs of the church could be arranged. Brother J. E. Crosby was elected treasurer of the church and Brother Hazel Floyd was elected sexton for the sum of two dollars per month. On August 21, 1887, the first delegates to the Reedy River Baptist Association were elected as follows: L. W. Redd, J. E. Crosby, C. W. White, R. E. Rhoden, J. C. Rhoden, and J. T. Setzler, Brother C. W. White was licensed to preach. A committee of two was appointed to see how much money could be raised to get a preacher. This committee was J. T. Setzler and R. E. Rhoden. September 4, 1887, the first church letter to the Association was read and approved by the church with several amendments. The church was admitted to the Reedy River Association in September, 1887. The church raised some money to help pay for the minutes. January 1, 1888, the church called Rev. J. D. Huggins as its pastor. Brother Huggins accepted the call. February 3, 1889, a resolution was adopted to use the envelope system to raise the pastor's salary. May 11, 1889 a resolution was adopted to appoint a committee to see two members for non-attendance at church. August 3, 1889 the church withdrew fellowship from one brother for drunkness. November 3, 1889, Rev. J. C. Rhoden was called to supply the church as pastor until January 1, 1890. July 6, 1890, Rev. J. S. West was called to the pastorate of the church. January 4, 1891, Rev. T. W. Smith was called to the pastorate of the church. December 4, 1892, Rev. G. S. Dorrity was called to the pastorate of the church. January 14, 1894, Rev. S. J. Riddle was called to the pastorate of the church.

143

January 30, 1895, Rev. Thomas A. Campbell was called to the pastorate of the church. February 9, 1896, Rev. J. P. Mahon was called to the pastorate of the church. January 8, 1899, Rev. W. S. B. Ford was called to the pastorate of the church. April 9, 1899 a building committee was elected as follows: Rev. W. S. B. Ford, J. M. Taylor, J. R. Leavell, Jacob Senn, J. M. Foster, W. R. Jones, E. Cavannaugh, E. B. Wilbur, G. Y. Dickert, R. E. Rhoden and Theodore Danielson. September 10, 1899 the name of the church was changed from the Senond Baptist Church to the West End Baptist Church of Newberry.

On September 10, 1899, a resolution was passed to borrow money to finish building the church. October 22, 1899, the new church building was dedicated. September 2, 1900, Rev. W. M. Penson was called to the pastorate of the church. December 1, 1901, Rev. N. N. Burton was called to the pastorate of the church. March 1, 1903, a committee of five was appointed to organize a church at Mollohon. December 4, 1904, a committee was appointed to arrange for the building of Sunday School Rooms. January 31, 1906, Rev. L. B. White was called to the pastorate of the church. September 30, 1907 Rev. J. F. McGill was called to the pastorate of the church. Between 1907 and 1909 the Sunday School rooms were blown away during a storm. On May 9, 1909 a committee of ten ladies was appointed to raise money to rebuild the Sunday School Rooms. January 1, 1910 Rev. T. T. Todd was called to the pastorate of the church. At this time the pastor's salary was four hundred dollars a year. On May 22, 1910, a resolution was passed to call a pastor for full time at a salary of fifty dollars per month.

July 2, 1910, Rev. J. R. Green was called to the pastorate of the church. June 4, 1911, Rev. L. B. White was recalled to the pastorate of the church. October 1, 1912, Rev. N. A. Hemrick was called to the pastorate of the church. October 5, 1913, Rev. J. N. Booth was called to the pastorate of the church. January 1, 1916, Rev. H. W. Stone was called to the pastorate of the church.

On Tuesday, June 6, 1916, the church was struck by lightning and burned down. A protracted meeting had been arranged to begin the following Sunday. Dr. R. G. Lee, then of Chester, South Carolina had been engaged to do the preaching in this series of meetings. The meeting was held in the pavillion in what is now known as Willowbrook Park. On Thursday, June 8, 1916, the church met in conference in the O'Neall Street Methodist church building and committees were appointed to make arrangements to rebuild the church. The Mayer Memorial Lutheran church offered the use of their building for two Sundays a month and this offer was accepted. The Sunday School was held in the West End School building. November 1, 1916, the present building being completed, regular services were resumed, all bills being paid. October 14, 1917 a committee was appointed to raise funds to buy a bell. January 1, 1918, Rev. G. M. Sexton was called to pastorate of the church. June 2, 1918, a committee was appointed to see if they could get day current for the church, on July 2, this committee reported that they could not get day current.

January 1, 1919, Rev. J. A. Anderson was called to the pastorate of the church. On January 12, 1919 a committee was appointed to receive voluntary gifts to help rebuild Mayer Memorial Lutheran church which had been burned down. June 6, 1920, Rev. J. E. Meng was called to the pastorate of the church. September 2, 1922 Rev. C. E. Thomas was called to the pastorate of the church. December 2, 1923, the church licensed Brother H. P. Powell to preach the gospel. In 1926, Mr. and Mrs. J. M. Davis presented the church with a bulletin board. January 15, 1927 a committee was appointed to get plans for building fifteen Sunday school rooms. This committee was Rev. C. E. Thomas and J. M. Davis. In May 1927, the church bought the pipe organ which was formerly in use in the First Baptist Church of Newberry, and had it installed re-arranging the baptistery at the same time.

November 1, 1927, Rev. E. E. Hite was called to the pastorate of the church. January 19, 1928 the church adopted the rotating plan for the board of deacons. April 9, 1928, the heater was bought and installed for the heating the water in the baptistery. On Mothers Day, May 12, 1929, the church and Sunday school raised enough money to build four new Sunday school rooms and installed sewerage in the church. The total cost was three thousand dollars. June 1, 1932, a new roof was put on the church at a cost of six hundred dollars. February 20, 1934, Rev. E. O. Edwards was called to the pastorate of the church. April 2, 1934, the church decided to beautify the church grounds and plant shrubbery. June, 1935, the pulpit platform was enlarged, a new carpet was laid on the floor and a new curtain hung around the choir loft.

September 20, 1935, Rev. and Mrs. E. O. Edwards presented to the Sunday school a Sunday school register. July 11, 1936, Rev. B. F. Rogers was called to the pastorate of the church. February 28, 1937, the church decided to partition off another Sunday School room and paint three other rooms and the tin roof of the Sunday School rooms.

In the beginning, and for a number of years, the church was a mission church and was under the State Mission Board holding only part time services. For thirty years only one, two and three services a month were held. The church finally worked out from under the State Mission Board and for the past twenty years has been a self-supporting, full time church. The church has contributed to all the causes fostered by the denomination and during the five year period of the Seventy-five Million Dollar Campaign gave over seven thousand dollars to this campaign.

The church has at several times during it's history had all of the church auxiliaries organized and working. There are at present a live Sunday School, B. T. U., Women's Missionary Society, G. A.'s, and Sunbeams. Plans are on foot now to make the Sunday school more progressive by grading all the classes. This church has furnished the Reedy River Association with an officer continually for the past thirty-three years. The church started with twenty-two members and has at present three hundred and ten members and a plant including church auditorium, Sunday School rooms, pipe organ, pianos and heating plant that cost approximately twelve thousand dollars.

The Newberry Cotton Mills has been a generous contributer to the church for the past fifty years.

(Sketch in Newberry Observer, April, 1938).

FAIRVIEW CHURCH.

Fairview Church which is thirteen miles North west of Newberry, was organized August 22, 1859 by Revs. A. C. Stepp, W. D. Mayfield. This church succeeded the old Mt. Olive Church which stood on land owned by Charley Davis and later owned by Frank Kelly. There is a rock horse-block standing near the site of Mt. Olive church, the kind used in those days. On August 22nd, 1859, Fairview church was dedicated. Miss Rachel Davis, (later Mrs. Dr. Johnson) was attending boarding school near Union with the Teagues. She and Miss Billie Teague rode horse-back to Fairview on this occasion to attend the dedication.

Messrs. Isaac and Johnson were the first deacons.

Three acres of land was given to the church by Mr. Joe Smith, (Grandfather of Ida Smith).

Mr. J. R. Connelly, a carpenter, was the first person buried in Fairview Cemetery. The membership has never been large, having at one time, 1865, reached one hundred and twelve, but after ten years it had dropped to sixty-one. Today there are sixty-six members. Its Sunday school was organized in 1875 with J. W. Scott, as Superintendent. The old church was moved to its present location in 1869. The building was a log building. It was bought by Chesley Davis and moved to his residence and made into a cow barn. Later was destroyed by fire. Every piece of this church was cut in the woods and hewn by hand. There wasn't a saw mill in this county at that time. The new building was built in 1859. It was a more modern building. Timber was cut and sawed and the interior was of dressed material, not tongue-engroved. It was not a large church; but sufficiently large to accommodate the congregations who attended services up to this time.

In 1932 the old church building was torn down and a new, modern building was erected in its place. Captain M. M. Buford left in his will the sum of four hundred dollars to be used by Fairview church as a memorial to members of his family who are buried in Fairview Cemetery. The four hundred dollars was to be used provided the church would raise a like sum. So through the untiring efforts of their pastor and the members, together with contributions from Mrs. Walter Hunt, Mr. Billy Meetz and his daughter, Amelia Mills Lowmas Blalock, Will Riser, John Riser, James Duncan, and Clarence Johnson, they were able to build the present building.

(Sketch from Newberry Observer, April, 1938).

SOME NEWBERRY COUNTY WOMEN WHO HELPED TO MAKE HISTORY.

MRS MARGARET DUGAN-wife of the Rev. War patriot, and Officer, Major Thomas Dugan, lived in that section of Newberry County, near Gilder's Creek, where many of the sturdy Scotch-Irish pioneers and their families had settled before the American Revolution. All of them were Presbyterians and were instrumental in organizing Gilders Creek Presbyterian Church (many of these later dissented and joined the Associated Reformed Presbyterian Church), a church now disbanded, some of whom went over to other Presbyterian Churches. Nothing is left at the spot except the old discarded church cemetery with it's many old markers, situated in the midst of large trees and brush.

Mrs. Dugan, like many of the women of that period, bore the hardships of the war with a stout heart. A woman of courage, she kept a vigil at her home, and being in sympathy with her husband's work and the cause of liberty she gave her full cooperation in all the movements of the Whigs.

The particular incident in Mrs. Dugan's life, which has come through tradition and is well related in Judge O'Neall's "Annals of Newberry", which showed her strong character and courage, was when the Tories came to her home, killed her older sons and mutilated their bodies, her husband being away fighting for the American cause. These two older sons who had joined the American Army were at home on a short visit. They had to steal home at night, because of the hatred of the Tories. On this night as on other nights the mother stayed awake keeping watch while her sons slept. About two o'clock in the morning she heard a slight noise, a rap on the back door, which was followed by like signals from all the doors. Over a dozen Tories came into the house; but she kept her presence of mind. She put one son up the chimney, another jumped out of the window, fracturing his leg-bone which kept him from escaping. The Tories suddenly filled the house, found both sons. They then set fire to an outhouse, hanged the sons in the yard before the mother and her babies. Not satisfied, they took their swords, hewed the bodies, cutting off their legs and arms. They then skulked away, leaving the mother alone with her babies and the mutilated bodies of her sons. After the quiet torture had finally left her mind, she gathered the parts of the bodies, placed them together, and on a nearby hillside she buried them quietly.

One tradition is that the bodies are buried in old Gilders Creek Cemetery, the church having located the cemetery where the Dugan graveyard was located. Whether the young bodies of these patriots were taken up and re-interred, is not known. The home of Major Dugan was not so far away.

Some of the Tories who participated in this killing, according to tradition, were hung at the Crossroads, a site which was near the home of Mrs. Henry Whitmire.

MRS. MARY GOLDING LEONARD COLE-a Rev. War heroine, On Sunday, November 13, 1938, a memorial service was held at Bush River Baptist Church, Newberry County. A bronz tablet had been installed in the church to the memory of this heroine, the wife of Rev. John B. Cole who was the pastor of this church over thirty years. At this meeting there was also displayed the wedding dress of Mrs. Cole, it's length and general size indicating that she was rather a small woman.

Mrs. Cole, as Miss Mary Golding, was born in Virginia and came to Newberry County with her family and other families, including the Coles, Leonards, and others, which was several years before the beginning of the Rev. War. She was first married to Lochlin Leonard, of Virginia, and after his death, she married Rev. Cole who was then pastor of Bush River Baptist Church. She outlived both of her husbands, dying at the age of eighty-two years, at the home of her granddaughter.

Her part in the Rev. War struggle was in connection with the massacre at Hay's Station, and at another time when she warned the patriots of the coming of the Tories. Her first husband, Lochlin Leonard, lost his life at Hay's Station. In February, 1781, Mary Golding Leonard learned that the Tories under the leadership of Major William (Bloody Bill) Cunningham, were planning to surprise the patriots who were living on the West side of Little River; so she set out to give them warning; arriving at Little River, she crossed the river on horseback, where there was neither a bridge nor a ford. "From that time until her death about fifty years later, she was never able to recall just how she made the Crossing."

In November of the same year the massacre at Hays' Station occured. Lochlin Leonard lost his life there. After the house was burned, completely destroyed, Mary Leonard went there with only a slave girl, found the body of her husband. They walked three miles to the place. She, with the help of her slave, made a rough sled from some boards, put the body on it and hauled it home. One tradition is that Lochlin Leonard had on his shoulder a small trunk which was filled with gold and silver pieces, and other relics, and when he, apparently, was shot in front, he fell on the trunk. The trunk was afterwards discovered with it's contents; and in later years it was in the possession of a family of that community.

HANNAH GAUNTT--lived with her parents in the vicinity of Bush River, Newberry County; they were Quakers. Israel Gauntt, the progenitor of the family, was the father of Hannah, who was in a dramatic incident during the Rev War. This is related in Mrs. E. F. Ellett's "The Women of the American Revolution".

The incident refers to a time which Hannah Gauntt defended her father against two robbers who had entered their home, and physically overcame them, by sheer strehgth.

EMILY GEIGER--The story of Emily Geiger, a young eighteen years old girl during the time of the Rev War, is well related in several histories, including the " Annals of Newberry", and early newspapers. How she rode , alone, through Tory settlements with a message to General Sumter from General Greene; the result of which saved the Americans from defeat.

MRS. SOPHIA REDUS--a niece of Mrs. Cynthia Mower, of Newberry, was born in Maine. She came South on a visit to relatives after the War Between the States, and afterwards made her home with them.

Becoming associated with Mrs. Mower in her business she was, also, active with Mrs. Mower in community work. Her husband having died she lived with her aunt. She became active in church work, also in the work of the W. C. T. U. in Newberry and in the State. She worked for many years for prohibition reform. The habit of drinking of whiskey had become a social menace, and showed it's demoralizing effects among the families of the poor and among men in public offices.

MRS. CYNTHIA ALLEN MOWER--born in the State of Maine on December 22, 1829; the daughter of Mr. and Mrs. Allen of that State. She married Duane Mower, of Maine, and before the War Between the States they came to South Carolina, locating in the town of Prosperity, Newberry County. They established a small mercantile business there, and moved to Newberry about 1867. Her husband having died in that year, she continued the business, very successfully, until her death in 1892.

Mrs. Mower did not confine all her activities to business. She was, also, an influential worker in her church, the Associate Reformed Presbyterian Church, and was head of several church organizations. She organized, too, the fir st Band of Hope and the first local W. C. T. U. in her community, and several branch societies in various communities throughout the county. She, also, became associated with the State organization of the W. C. T. U.

The death of Mrs. Mower is related by the late Rev. E. P. McClintock, who was at that time pastor of the church in Newberry, in Part two of the " Annals of Newberry".

She was the mother of the late George S. Mower, a distinguished lawyer and philanthropist in Newberry for many years; and who represented his county in the State Legislature several terms, was State Senator, and was appointed special judge of the State Circuit Courts.

MRS. J. W. HUMBERT--widow of Rev. J. W. Humbert, a well-known Methodist Minister of the State, was a Miss. Kinard before her marriage. She gave her energies and active interest in many good services of her church and community. She was the first President, as well as the organizer, of the Mission Work in her church. Also, for several years she acted as Secretary of the Woman's Missionary Society of South Carolina. She died at Newberry.

MRS. HAL KOHN, SR.--born in Newberry; daughter of John Harrison and Hulda (Cromer) Summer. After her graduation from the Newberry High School she attended Elizabeth College, Charlotte, N. C. , from whch she graduated B. S. in Music, having studied under well-known masters in that institution. Returning to Newberry, she organized a large music school which she taught for several years.

Mrs. Kohn (Verna L. Summer), began with her husband's large book and supply business in Newberry, later converting it into an art store; and operating a florist business in connection with it, maintaining a large plant near the city. She never gave up her music school while operating her business, having assistants in this work, until later years.

She has been interested, too, in community work, serving on several committees in the different civic organizations.

MRS. E. S. HERBERT-born in Newberry County, S. C. She was Miss Goggans, a sister of the late John C. Goggans, Sr., of Newberry, one-time Clerk of Court; a descendent of Daniel Goggans, the Rev War patriot in a scouting troop of that section.

Mrs. Herbert was an active worker in many local and civic works; also, she was at one time appointed Post Master of Newberry and served several years.

One of her chief hobbies in her public services, was that of the work of the W. C. T. U. She was at one time head of the State organization, and represented this organization in many conventions. She was, also President of the Newberry Auxiliary Society of the Methodist Episcopal Church, South.

She and her husband moved to the city of Orangeburg many years ago, and died in that City.

MRS. JAMES THOMAS MAYES-born in Newberry, S. C in 1861; daughter of Dr.O. B. Mayer, Sr. and Caroline Nancy De Walt of Newberry. She attended the local schools, including the once famous Newberry Female Academy which was under the direction of the late Capt. A. P. Pifer.

She married James Thomas Mayes, of Newberry. She was active in many civic and patriotic organizations in Newberry; one of the organizers and charter members of the local Chapter of the D. A. R. (Jasper Chapter); served in Red Cross work. As a member of the Lutheran Church of the Redeemer, she was President of several church societies, and active in many movements for public service in the community.

Two of her sons were active soldiers in the first World War; one, Lieutenant William M. Mayes, being wounded in battle in France, in which he lost a leg, and later died in California, and another, a Sargeant in the Coast Guards, moved to Greensboro, N. C.

Mrs. Mayes died in Newberry in 1922.

MRS. MARIA BEARD LEITNER-was born, probably, in Pennsylvania; married Major Michael Leitner, son of Christopher Leitner.

Her husband having organized one of the scouting companies in the upper Dutch Fork, and being an active fighter against the tory element, was sought for continously by the tories and the English Troops She was a sister or close relative of Col. Jonas Beard, another famous American Officer in the Rev War. It was at her home that her husband and brother often met to discuss their war problems, and where Major Leitner, with the aid of his wife, wrote a famous address which he delivered to the Grand Jurors at Jacksboro.

On one occasion, the tories having heard Major Leitner was at home, went to his house to capture him; but the rumor was false as he was away on an expedition. The disappointed band of tories endeavored to make his wife tell where he was, but she would not, even though they punished her severely, beat her, and threatened her life. She did not disclose his whereabouts and, no doubt, saved the lives of many young patriots that were on the same expendition.

MRS. HENRY L. PARR-born in Newberry County, S. C.-a daughter of Calhoun F. and Elizabeth (Wilson) Boyd. She attended the local schools; later completing her college course. She married Henry L. Parr of Fairfield County, S. C. They moved to Newberry where both she and her husband became identified with many public service improvements. He was the promoter of the Parr Shoals Dam project, and later was President of the old Newberry Exchange Bank.

Mrs. Parr was active in church work, the Associate Reformed Presbyterian Church, an officer in several of it's societies. She was active in the establishment of the Newberry County Memorial Hospital, and a member of it's first Board of Directors.

MRS. OLA CLARK FLOYD—was born at Jalapa, Newberry County, South Carolina, on September 10, 1869; the daughter of Dr. Richard Pinckney Clark and Adeline Piester Clark.

After being educated in local schools, and at college, she returned to Newberry and married Lou Washington Floyd. They moved to the city where her husband later became prominently identified with large business interests. He built a large and attractive Colonial home on the corner of Johnstone and Calhoun Streets in Newberry (home now owned by E. A. Carpenter of Newberry).

Mrs. Floyd was actively interested in community work in her town, and served in various capacities in civic and committee work, as well as in church work. She began and completed several new movements for local community developments; organized the Newberry Civic League and the Parent Teachers Association, becoming their first President. As a Director in the Newberry Chamber of Commerce she performed effective services; then as a member of the City Board of Health. For sometime she was President of the Newberry County Library Association. During the World War I, she was active in organizing the Newberry Red Cross unit, and served on it's Executive Committee. As County Chairman of Child Welfare Work, she was an energetic worker; as a member of the Council of Defense; on the Liberty Auxiliary, Post 24, and was it's first President. She was appointed temporary Chairman of the American Legion Auxiliary to perfect a department organization in September, 1927; then was elected State Chairman and served one year. Active in U. D. C. work; President of Drayton Rutherford Chapter U. D. C. at Newberry.

In her church, the First Baptist Church of Newberry, she was a leader in the Womans Missionary Society, a teacher of a large class of young women in the Sunday School.

She died at her home in Newberry on December 6, 1928, and is buried at Rosemont Cemetery, in Newberry.

MRS. O. B. MAYER—was born in Laurens, S. C. the daughter of W. W. Jones (she was Harriet Fleming Jones). She is a graduate of Converse College, of Spartanburg, S. C. After a short residence in Laurens after her graduation, she married Dr. O. B. Mayer, Jr. of Newberry, and has since been a resident of that city.

Mrs. Mayer has been active, before her declining health a few years ago, in all local civic, religeous, and community affairs in the city. She was the organizer of the Jasper Chapter, DAR, and was it's first Regent; served as a State Officer in D. A. R. work; and in reference to the work of Tammassee School for young girls, which is located in the Piedmont, she served on several committees. A member and officer of the Newberry County Hospital Auxiliary, of the Newberry Civic League, and other community organizations in the City and the State.

MRS. J. H. SUMMER—was born at Little Mountain, Newberry County, S. C., a daughter of George and Jane (Sheely) Swittenberg. She attended the schools of Little Mountain; after the removal of her parents to near the city of Newberry, she attended schools of her home community, then Newberry College, where she graduated with the A. B. Degree.

Mrs. Summer (as Miss Mayme Swittenberg), taught in the county schools for several years; then Principal of the Little Mountain School, and of the Prosperity High School; during which she pursued post graduate work in Columbia University, of New York City.

She became the second wife of John Harrison Summer, of Newberry. Since then she became active in civic, religeous, and welfare works in the city and county. She was a member of the National Board of Trustees of Synodical Relief of the United Lutheran Church in America, whose headquarters are in New York City. Active in D. A. R., U. D. C., work in the city; President of the Newberry Civic League, being most active in the organization and construction of Margaret Hunter Memorial Park. During World War I, she was local Director in the National Youth Administration, and later District Director. Also, she served in the work of local Re-employment and Unemployment Compensation Offices of the City.

MRS. WALTER H. HUNT—a daughter of James H. Baxter, prominent lawyer in Newberry before the War Between the States, was born in Newberry. Her mother was a daughter of Col. Drayton Nance, also a prominent lawyer in Newberry during it's early period, and a sister of Col. James D. Nance, the distinguished Confederate War Officer who lost his life in battle.

Educated in the local school, then at the academy of Miss Kelly, Charleston, S. C. she later married Col. Walter H. Hunt of Newberry, a prominent lawyer in Newberry and the organizer and first President of Oakland Cotton Mills.

Mrs. Hunt has performed signal services in her county and State, by her activities in patriotic, civic, and religeous work. During the first World War she was Chairman of Food and Conservation in the county, Chairman of the local Red Cross. She was head of the Newberry County Hospital Auxiliary, President of the Organization for Crippled Children; served as President of the local U. D. C. Chapter, Regent of the local D. A. R. Chapter; Trustee of Anderson Female College, having given her talents to help the college in it's growth and development. For over thirty years, she was President of the South Carolina Baptist Mission Board.

MRS. EMILY WEST-was born in Spartanburg County, S. C.; daughter of Marion J. and Elizabeth Scott who moved to Newberry. She married to James Henry West (his first wife) of Newberry, on September 19, 1897. Mrs. West was active in civic, patriotic, and church works. She was State Historian of the United Daughters of the Confederacy, President of the Newberry Chapter, U. D. C., the Drayton Rutherford Chapter, State President of the Daughters of the War of 1812, and member of the Daughters of the American Revolution. Her name is inscribed on one of the memorial pages of the memorial book which was published for that purpose, a memorial of Robert E. Lee's birthplace. Mrs. West acted as Chairman of the Red Cross Auxiliary of her U. D. C. Chapter during World War I. Also, Secretary of the local branch of the Womens Committee of the National Council of Defense. In church work, she organized the first Baraca Class of the First Baptist Church in Newberry, and taught the class for many years. It is now known as the Emily West Baraca Class.

Mrs. West attended the schools of Newberry, then Winthrop College from which she graduated. She taught school for five years, previous to her marriage.

She died in the City Hospital at Newberry on July 24, 1926.

MRS. MARGARET LAND KINARD-was born in Augusta, Georgia, October 12, 1870; daughter of Robert Henry Land and Elizabeth (Griffin) Land. Her mother's parents were Richard Clark Griffin and Mary McMahan Carwile Griffin. She attended the public schools of Augusta, and also the Augusta Female College. She was married to John Martin Kinard of Newberry, South Carolina, on June 5, 1895.

Mrs. Kinard has been active in community work and social work of Newberry. She served as a member of the Newberry Civic League, and as it's Treasurer; a member of the Newberry County Hospital Auxiliary, and at one time as it's President. She has always been active in the service of patriotic organizations. As a charter member of the Drayton Rutherford Chapter, UDC., she has served in various capacities and offices. As a member of the DAR, Jasper Chapter, in Newberry, she has served in various offices, having been at one time it's Regent. Also, a member of the American Legion Auxiliary. For three years she served as State Genealogist in the State D. A. R. Organization; and two years as Corresponding Secretary of the State U. D. C. Organization.

Mrs. Kinard has always been interested in church work, serving as Secretary of the Womans Missionary Society of the First Baptist Church of Newberry for about seventeen years or longer.

MRS. ROBERT D. WRIGHT (ELOISE WELCH WRIGHT)-was born in Newberry, October 4, 1874; daughter of Dr. Spencer Glasgow Welch and Cordelia (Strother) Welch, of Newberry.

Mrs. Wright has served actively in all State and local Women's organizations for public service; as active officer in local patriotic societies; and known as a good public speaker.

She is descended from several Colonial families of Virginia and South Carolina. Her Welch ancestors were Quakers; her paternal grand-father, Williams Welch, having migrated to South Carolina from Iredell County, North Carolina to which place the family had previously moved from Virginia. Though reared a Quaker, and the family having broken up when the Quaker migration to Ohio started, he joined the Presbyterian Church. He was too old for service in the Confederate Army, but gave four sons to the Army.

He married Mary Crozier Glasgow, a member of a Newberry County family, the ancestors of whom came from Ireland, and belonged to the old Scotch-Irish Presbyterians of the Gilders Creek section of Newberry County.

Mrs. Wright was educated in the public schools of Newberry, and at Columbia Female College, Columbia, S. C. from which she received her A. B. Degree, winning the first honor of her class. She taught several years in the public schools in Newberry, during which time she pursued during the summer months, courses at Winthrop College, Rock Hill, S. C.

On December 22, 1900, she married Robert D. Wright, of Newberry, S. C. He was a native of Laurens County, S. C. but had lived in the city of Newberry many years. He was a son of Zaccheus F. and Isobel Jane(Byrd) Wright.

Mrs. Wright has long been identified with public organizations work in the city and the State. A member of the D. A. R. and a former officer; member of the U. D. C. and one time Vice-President General of the National Organization; member of the State W. C. T. U; member of the Newberry County Hospital Auxiliary, and a former officer; member of Columbia College Alumnae Association, and a former President of that organization. She has served, too, as President of the Newberry Public Library Association, and aided materially in the enlargement of the county library in Newberry; as a U. D. C. officer she had charge of the two thousand dollar fund of the General U. D. C. Educational Trust Fund. In addition, she has served her church, the Central Methodist Church, of Newberry, in many capacities.

Mrs. Wright was the principal speaker over the radio on September 17, 1938, in celebration of Constitution Day.

MRS. MARGARET HUNTER-was born at Prosperity, Newberry County, South Carolina, the daughter of John L. and Mary (Dominick) Hunter. Her father's home was near St. Luke's Lutheran Church. She married Frank B. Hunter, distant cousins, of near the same community.

She attended the schools of that section; then went to Lenoir College, North Carolina, and later to Elizabeth College, Charlotte, N. C., from which she graduated.

Mrs. Hunter and her husband moved to the city of Newberry, where he became engaged in business. She became actively interested in local community work. For several years she was the President of the Newberry Civic League, President of Drayton Rutherford Chapter, U. D. C., Chairman of the City Board of Health, active officer in the D. A. R., and State Chairman of Conservation and Thrift, under the D. A. R. State Society. A member of the Newberry Tree Commission. As an active member of the local Red Cross unit she performed much effective service during and after World War I. Mrs. Hunter was a devoted and active member of her church, the A. R. P. Church in Newberry. Also, she initiated many movements to have passed State laws for the betterment of the community, one of which was the Standard Milk Ordnance.

She died March 17, 1934, at her home on Caldwell Street, Newberry. As a memorial to her the municipal park was constructed and named for her, known as the "Margaret Hunter Park."

MRS. ELIZABETH LAND MCFALL-was born at Augusta, Georgia, on April 7, 1874; daughter of Robert Henry and Elizabeth P. (Griffin) Land. Her father's parents were Alexander James Wofford Land and Margaret Black Reid Land, of Virginia. Her mother's parents were Richard Clark Griffin and Mary McMahan Carwile Griffin, of South Carolina.

Mrs. McFall was educated in the schools, including the Tubmen High School, of Augusta, Georgia. She pursued special work in music and voice, having had sixteen years training under Mrs. Nathaniel L. Willet (Mrs. Willet was a graduate of Boston Conservatory of Music). She also received Secretarial training in Augusta, Georgia.

Mrs. McFall has served the State and Local Chapters of both the D. A. R. and the U. D. C. as Vice-President, Gleaner, Historian. She also served as Director of Children for Confederacy, Chairman of several important Committees of the South Carolina Division at the Convention held in Newberry in 1923; also Chairman in Decoration Committee for the South Carolina Confederate Reunion in Newberry in 1929. Served on the first Committee in South Carolina, Division U. D. C. 1923-24, of the Ex-President's Service Pin presented to all past Presidents. As State Chairman of the Southern Magazine, official organ of the U. D. C. 1935-36-37, wining for the State a silver trophy, second prize in the General U D. C. organization. She served on various Committees of the State D. A. R. In the local Chapter, D. A. R., she has served as Registrar 1910-1913, Second Vice-Regent 1920-21, Recording Secretary 1922-26, Corresponding Secretary 1927-29, Regent 1932-35.

She compiled, with the assistance of Mrs. O. B. Mayer (the organizing Regent), a Silver Anniversary Year Book, containing a condensed history of twenty five years work of Jasper Chapter D. A. R., which in 1935 won the first prize at the D. A. R. State Convention. She has served as Chairman of Decorations at State Conventions or State Conferences. In the State work, as Chairman of Ellis Island Committee, 193—32-33, State Chairman of National D.A.R. approved school's committee, 1934-35-36; and several other important committees. She has served on the D.A.R. Tammassee School Board; and as a member at large of the Executive committee of the State D. A. R. She has served as a member of the Newberry County Hospital Auxiliary, both as Vice-President and Secretary; Secretary of the Newberry Civic League; active member of the Newberry Garden Club; and as Chairman of the Committee for unveiling exercises of the World War Memorial, November 11, 1928; also on the local Tree Commission.

Mrs. McFall served as Assistant Clerk of Court during the term of the late John M. Kinard, for a short time, and one year as Secretary in the law offices of Hunt and Hunter, of Newberry.

She is a member of the First Baptist Church of Newberry; and for several years she was counselor of the young women's auxiliary of that church; and as an officer in the Woman's Missionary Society.

MISS. CAROLINE KILGORE-born near Newberry Court House in the year 1884; the daughter of Andrew J. and Mary (Wyse) Kilgore. Her father was for many years a Steward in Ebenezar Methodist Church, about two miles from the city. Her grand-father, Dr. James Kilgore, practiced medicine near Newberry; also for a time acted as local preacher in his community. In the year 1837, it was through his efforts that the original church of Ebenezar was enlarged and improved.
She attended the schools of her community; and being quite young when her parents died, she spent sometime at Thornwell Orphanage, Clinton, S. C.. Later, she attended Winthrop College, Rock Hill, S. C., from which she graduated with the degree of A. B. in 1908. After a short time as a teacher in the public schools, she attended the Summer Sessions at Columbia University, New York, N. Y. Then, she went into special training for missionary service, and was assigned as her field of labors to Brazil, South America. In that country she has served her church for many years.

MRS. JOHN B. MAYES-born near Pomaria, Newberry County, S. C. in 1882; daughter of Charles E. and Nora (Sease) Summer. She attended Summer Schools, and the City schools of Newberry; then Newberry College from which she graduated with degree of A. B. Her post-graduate work was in Columbia, University , New York City, and then at Paris, France, specializing in French.
Returning to America, she became Professor of French and French Literature at Luther College, near Baltimore, Maryland. After a short period of that work, she married John Bernard Mayes, of Newberry; and had three children: John Bernard, Jr., Agnes and Nancy. John B. Jr., served in World War ll, as a Lieutenant in the Air Forces, and was killed in North Africa.
Mrs. Mayes was interested in all civic and community work; acted as County Director in government relief project, library work. After the death of her husband, she became Hostess and Associate Professor at Winthrop College, Rock Hill, S. C. At the present time she is with the University of Maryland, Baltimore, Maryland.

MRS. J. WILLIAM HALTIWANGER-born near Pomaria, S. C. in 1884; daughter of Charles E. and Nora (Sease) Summer. She attended the public schools in Newberry, graduating at Newberry High School; afterwards she graduated at Elizabeth College, Charlotte , N. C.,with special in Music, with B. S. Degree. Attending studios in New York City ; then, at the London, England, conservatory where she specialized in music under well-known masters of the day.
After her return to America, and to Newberry,she organized a large music class which she taught for several years; during which time she served as organist in the Lutheran Church of the Redeemer, of Newberry.
Removing to Columbia, where her husband estlablished a large business, she became asscoiated with the music organizations of that city. She became organist for the Ebenezer Lutheran Church of that City; also, at the Church of the Good Sheppard, of Columbia. She became active in the S. C. Music orgabizatoon; an active worker in the D. A. R., the U. D. C., and other local organizations.

MISS. EUPHEMIA McCLINTOCK--born in Newberry, S. C.; daughter of Rev. E. Pressley and Elizabeth (Young) McClintock.   Her father was pastor of the A. R. P. Church in Newberry for over thirty five years (church at that time was called the Thompson Street A.R.P Church), which was located on the corner of Thompson and Main Streets.

Rev. McClintock and his wife had two daughters, Euphemia and Mary Law McClintock, both of whom became prominent educators.   The latter went to Boston, Mass. and became head of the seminary for girls in that city, which she established.   Later, her sister, Euphemia, joined her in the project.

Miss. Euphemia McClintock received her education in the schools of her community, and the Woman's College, Baltimore, Maryland, where she graduated with the degree of A. B. in the year 1893; later she pursued post- graduate work at other universities, including Columbia University, New York City,   Then, she went to Paris, France, to complete her post-graduate work.

Her first educational work in South Carolina was at the South Carolina Presbyterian College, Columbia, S. C.   While at that institute she became Assistant to the President, Dr. R. P. Pell; and when Dr. Pell resigned the Presidency, going to Spartanburg, S. C. as President of Converse College, she succeeded him to the Presidency of the S. C. Presbyterian College.   This was in the year 1908.

One of her first plans as President was to inaugurate a higher standard of study; and the college flourished under her leadership.   In 1910, a self-perpetuating Board was organized, which purchased the college plant and had the name changed to The College for Women . During her administration many new improvements were made, including two new halls, the Alumnae Hall and the McClintock Hall.   Also, she put forth every effort to raise again the standard of the college; and endeavored to make it a part of the State University system, but failed to get the bill through the State Legislature.

In the year 1915, when the college was consolidated with Chicora College that had been moved to Columbia, she resigned as President.   In 1930 Chicora College was moved to Charlotte, N. C. and consolidated with Queen's College of that city.   In 1915 Miss. McClintock went to Boston, Mass. and joined her sister in her seminary work.

After the death of her sister, she established and became the head of the Erskine Seminary for Girls, of that city, in which capacity she served until her death some years later.

During Miss. McClintock's administration as President of the College for Women in Columbia, South Carolina, Woodrow Wilson, then Governor of New Jersey, visited Columbia, his old home, and was the principle speaker at a meeting of the South Carolina Presbyterian Association, on June 2, 1911. A large reception was given Governor Wilson and his party at the College on the same evening.

Always interested in her students, individually, she helped many in getting started on the road to a college education.

SOME STREETS IN NEWBERRY AND FOR WHOM THEY WERE NAMED.

MAIN STREET (formerly called Pratt Street, for the late Thomas Pratt, merchant of Newberry).

COLLEGE STREET—on which is located Newberry College. (Formerly known as Adams Street, for Dr. Freeborne Adams, a native of Massachusetts, physician of Newberry, who lived in a large house that was located where is now the Hotel Wiseman).

BOYCE STREET—for Kerr Boyce, merchant of Newberry, who owned all the land where is now the Newberry Hotel and the other buildings on that block. This land came from John Johnstone, his father-in-law.

CALDWELL STREET—for Chancellor James J. Johnstone, lawyer and jurist of Newberry.

NANCE—for Major Frederick Nance, one of the first settlers in the village, and who held many public offices in the city, and was at one time Lieutenant Governor.

O'NEALL—named for Judge John Belton O'Neall, author, lawyer, jurist, of Newberry.

CROSSON—for David Crosson, one of the early Covenanters who located in Newberry before the War of Seccession.

McKIBBEN—for James McKibben, lawyer; said to have been the first lawyer to locate within the village. He was a member of the State Legislature from Newberry County.

THOMPSON—for Dr. Thomas W. Thompson, a physician of Newberry, who gave the land for the street and the lot on which the first A. R. P. Church was built.

COATE—for John Coate, who owned the lands whereon the street was made; and conveyed the land whereon the first court house was located, now the public square.

DRAYTON—for Governor Drayton who was Governor of South Carolina about the time the street was opened up.

FRIEND—for the Society of Friends, members of which church owned most of the land through which the street was made.

JOHNSTONE—for Chancellor Job Johnstone, lawyer, jurist, of Newberry, who owned the lands through which the street was cut, from Holman Street to the town limits.

MAYER AVENUE—for the late Dr. O. B. Mayer, Jr., prominent physician of Newberry, who was one of the principle stockholders and an officer in the company which gave the land for the street when the organization developed the Jones property, between Main Street and Scott's Creek and between Gleen Street and the city limits.

POPE TERRACE—for the late Chief Justice Y. J. Pope, lawyer, jurist, of Newberry, who owned the land where the street was built, donating it to the town for that purpose.

CHAPMAN—for the late John A. Chapman, author, business man, and father of J. W. Chapman, the City Clerk and Treasurer.

CALHOUN—for John C. Calhoun, the Vice-President of the United States; lawyer, advocate of States's Rights; native of Abbeville District.

CRENSHAW—for Charles Crenshaw, well-known planter; Tax Collector of Newberry County; who, then living in Newberry, contributed land for the street's construction.

CLINE—for the late W. A. Cline, large builder and contractor, who owned Cline Shops, located on what is now Cline Street, and who gave land for building the street.

CROMER—for the late Dr. George B. Cromer, lawyer, mayor, educator; President of Newberry College.

HARRINGTON—for Dr. William H. Harrington, physician of Newberry; or for his father, Young John Harrington, who owned some of the lands through which the street was built.

GARLINGTON—for the late General A. C. Garlington, of Newberry, an officer in the U. S. Army.

GILDER—for the late Dr. James K. Gilder, of Newberry, who owned the land on both sides of the street.

GLENN—for the late Dr. George W. Glenn, physician of the county; one of the first officers in the Newberry County Fair Association.

SUMMER—for George W. Summer and John H. ("Hack") Summer, brothers, who owned the lands on both sides of the street, having donated the land for the street, from Main to Johnstone Streets, the extension being made when the Jones property was divided into lots and sold.

SPEERS—for the late Leland M. Speers, merchant, undertaker, in Newberry for many years.

FAIR—for the late Simeon Fair, lawyer, State Solictor, whose son, William Y. Fair, owned the land through which it was built.

EVANS—for the late H. H. Evans, member of the State Legislature, Mayor of Newberry, and who owned some of the land through which the street was built.

FLOYD—for the late Lou Wash Floyd, Manager of Newberry Cotton Oil Mill; who owned much of the land through which the street was constructed.

HUNT—for the late Walter H. Hunt; distinguished lawyer; business man; industrialist; President of the Oakland Cotton Mills; and stockholder and officer in the company that developed the property through which the street was built.

BOUNDARY—(formerly known as Higgins Street, for Francis B. Higgins, lawyer, Commissioner in Equity, of Newberry). When the street was extended beyond the Grammar School, the name was changed, since at that time this was about the boundary line of the town.

BURTON—for the late James A. Burton, a large property owner; business man; planter; who aided in the growth and development of the town.

LINDSEY—for the late John Lindsey; planter, business man; who owned the lands through which the street was built, donating it to the town for that purpose.

GREEN—for the late Jordan Green; business man; who helped in many improvements in the town.

LANGFORD—for the late George Langford, who owned the lands through which the street was built.

JONES—for the late Lambert J. Jones; lawyer, Commissioner in Equity; member of the State Legislature; who owned the lands that were developed after his death, including the land through which the street was made.

HUNTER—for Joseph Y. Hunter; business man; banker; who owned lands through which the street was built.

McCRARY—for the late Thomas J. McCrary; banker; industrialist; President Newberry Cotton Mills for several years, until his death.

McMORRIS—for Dr. William W. McMorris, who was a physician in Newberry; owned much of the land in what is now the city business section.

PELHAM—for the late Dr. William E. Pelham, Sr., who was a prominent druggist in Newberry; member of the Board of the Newberry City Schools; owned the lands on what is now Pelham Street.

PURCELL—for the late Charles J. Purcell; merchant; cotton broker; owned land through which the street was built.

SENN—for the late John Senn, merchant, city councilman; and interested in the town's development.

McSWAIN—for the late William A. McSwain; insurance and business man; State Insurance Commissioner for several years; owned the property where the street was built.

MILLIKEN—for Seth M. Milliken, of New York, first selling agent for the Mollohon Cotton Mills, and a member of the company's Board of Directors.

PLAYER—for L. M. Player, a merchant in the village of Mollohon Mill.

MOON—for the late Dr. Peter Moon, of the County.

SILAS—for Silas McCaughrin, who owned and operated a large dairy on what is now the new village of Mollohon Mill; and interested in the development of the plant, having sold all the lands to them.

SHELLY—for the late Captain Shelly, one time large merchant in Newberry, and owned land there.

BRANTLEY—for Dr. J. J. Brantley, a former pastor of the Newberry Baptist Church.

DAVIS—for the late J. Marion Davis; Superintendent of the Newberry Cotton Mills; Mayor of Newberry; Chairman Board of Trustees of City Schools; member of the Governor's Staff.

DAVIS AVENUE—for the late C. C. Davis, contractor and builder, owner of Davis Shops; who owned the land where the street was built.

DOUGLAS—for the late Charles Douglas, member of the Board of Alderman; merchant; former Magistrate of the City.

BAXTER—for the late Frank Baxter, alderman, merchant, and funeral director.

BOOZER—for the late Thomas Q. Boozer, merchant in Newberry.

HARPER—for the Rev. Harper, a former pastor of the ....Church in Newberry.

HATTON—for the Hatton family who lived on that lot adjoining the street.

HAVIRD—for the late Ben A. Havird, merchant, live-stock dealer in Newberry.

HILL—for the late Tabor Hill, Sr. of Newberry, who owned lands in the vicinity.

HARRIS—for the late Pink Harris; operator of shops in the town.

MONTGOMERY—for the Montgomery family who once lived nearby.

REASE—for a well-known colored barber in the city, who owned property nearby.

SCOTT—for Patrick Scott who owned land in the vicinity.

RHODELSPERGER—for E. L. Rhodelsperger, one time alderman of the city; former chief of police.

WERTS AVENUE—for late Michael Werts who owned property nearby; or for Joseph Werts, who was supervisor of streets several years.

SNOWDEN—for the family of that name who lived in the vicinity.

TARRANT—for the late William T. Tarrant; merchant; owned lands nearby.

WHEELER—for late Daniel B. Wheeler; merchant; sheriff; owned land where street was made.

WRIGHT—for the late Z. F. Wright, or his father, Robert Wright.

SOME REMINISCENCES BY THE AUTHOR

Going back to the time, as a small boy, I remember riding with my parents and baby brother to the country and spending Sunday. I recall the two-seated buggy with high seats, and the high steps by which we climbed up into the buggy. The hubs and spokes of the wheels were large and heavy; and the two horses seemed to have a hard time holding up their wide leather collars. We rode sixteen miles in three hours over soft mud or deep ruts, and sometimes crossed creeks that had no bridges over them, once allowing the horses to drink by loosening their check reins. At this time we can go by automobile about two hundred miles in three hours.

Another thing that impressed me, which was in the year 1886, was the Charleston earthquake. I remember our house on College Hill shaking, many trees limbs falling to the ground, and some of the smaller trees falling down. My mother came into my room and said it was an earthquake. She had always taught us to kneel by our beds and say our prayers before retiring; so she asked if I had said my prayers, and stayed in the room until the quake stopped.

From 1886 to 1895, the town was a small village, with many one-story frame stores on Main Street, then called Pratt Street. All the streets in the business section were narrow, (much as they are at this time), with sand or mud; some of the side walks being paved with boards, brick or stone blocks, and the sides being held up with two-inch boards. Trees lined the side-walks, even in the business section; so that it was common to see a merchant sitting in a chair under the tree in front of his store, talking with some friend or playing a game of checks, or crowds sitting under the trees discussing politics. The street in front of the Newberry Hotel was hub-deep in mud when it rained, so that it was often difficult for wagons or buggies to get through it. The side-walks were about on a level with the street, the one on the opposite side being about six inches above the door entrances and floors of the stores and barber shops that were in their one-story frame buildings.

The stores on Main Street have changed materially, especially since the great fire of 1907, when nearly all the old wooden buildings, from the Newberry County Bank Building going East, were destroyed. Starting at the bank building, then a small one-story brick store operated by Eddy Brothers, then by J. T. Dennis, and going East were several small one-story frame stores, a vacant lot (where is now the fruit store), and the one-story frame bakery (about where is now Langford's Store), operated by a German named Crede. He lived in the back of his store, where he baked his bread. Next to this place was a vacant lot extending to Thompson Street. In the rear of this lot was a long brick building, and on the front corner was a small frame house used as a clinic by Dr. Thompson. Dr. Thompson lived in the house which was on the lot where now is the Hotel Wiseman, this long building having been the dining room and kitchen to the dwelling. Later, the long building was used as a meeting place for the W. C. T. U., also as a kindergarten school.

Across Thompson Street was the A. R. P. Church, a long white frame building, with green blinds and a front entrance with narrow vestibules on either side of which were winding stairs to the balcony where the ex-slaves sat during church services. The walk to the street from the church was high, a declivity on each side of it; on the right a path leading down to a spring of bubbling water, which was walled with stone. The church lot covered a space about where is now the Remnant Store (formerly the cafe) and W. Frank Lominick's Hardware store. It is believed the spring is under the present Dixie-Home (Colonial) store. Next to this was Blease's Hotel which was operated by Henry H. Blease (father of former U. S. Senator, Cole L. Blease, and former Chief Justice of the State Supreme Court, Eugene S. Blease). The Blease garden was where is now the Ritz Theater and the Davis Motor Company. In the back part of the garden was a large spring.

The changes have been many on either side of Main Street. The corner store at College Street, East side, where there was a small frame store of one-story, was operated by Orlando Wicker as a candy shop. Later, the store was worked over, bricked up on each side, and occupied by Robert McCarty as a retail grocery. After McCarty's death, John T. Cromer and Hub McGraw operated a grocery business in it for a short time. The next stores were one-story frame buildings. Paul Johnstone, son of Silas Johnstone, operated a grocery in one; and in the corner of it "Jock" Ramage operated a small retail book and stationery business. "Jock" was a cripple. The next store was that of J. William White who operated a tin-shop and store. The next one was Luther Riser's dry goods store which was built high above the side-walk, with wide front steps leading up the porch of the store. This was where is now the Western Auto Store.

Next to this was a two-story frame dwelling occupied by the family of J. Wm. White, about where is now the Fashion Department Store. Next to this was another two-story frame dwelling with the front porch touching the side-walk, about where is now the Belk's Department Store.

Across Coat's Street, where is now the bakery (formerly the A. & P. Store occupied it), and the Spinks Clothing Store (now Clamp's Clothing Store), was a large two-story home, white, with large green shutters, of the colonial style, with narrow porches and large square columns, the front porch touching the side-walk and entrance steps on the side. In front of the steps was a very large and old walnut tree. The home was said to have been built by John Coate, Sr. for his son, John Coate, Jr., who lived in it with his family for many years. All of this block or square belonged to this lot; in rear of which was a brick slave house with several apartments or rooms.

The Post Office occupies the lot where was the home of Richard Chapman who made coffins. Where is now Paysinger's Filling Station was the home of Proctor Todd, a retail grocery merchant on Main Street (where is now Hagood Clary, Sr. clothing store). This house was once the home of Dr. David Ewart who had a small store adjacent to his house and sold medicines that were mostly compounded by him. In front of the home across the street, where is now Eden's Grocery Store, was a tall frame building once used as an inn, which was torn down and the lots used as gardens for the small one-story frame cottages facing College Street (where is now the Copeland Building, occupied upstairs by the Central House). The old board walks stretching from the street to the steps of each cottage were thick wide planks.

Going back to the Street in front of the Hotel (Newberry Hotel), the stores were one-story frame structures. A saloon was on the corner of Friend and Caldwell Streets, South side, over which was a quaint sign showing a beer-barrel lying on it's sides with beer running out of a long faucet into a beer-mug, a white foamy liquid.

Where is now the Scott Building were two one-story frame dwellings of the old type, with wide front porches and chimneys at each side of the house. Setting back some distance from the side street and from the front street were small trees and evergreen bushes. On the corner of Friend and Caldwell Streets, South side, (where is now the Federal Re-employment Office), were two small cottages, adjoining, one occupied by Blatz Shoe Shop and the other occupied by Dr. .... Thompson, a dentist.

Where the Central Methodist Church is now located was once the Methodist parsonage, the church then being where is now the new brick Sunday School building. Next to the old parsonage, and facing Caldwell Street, running back parrellel with Friend Street was a long wooden building which was once used as a print shop by the Grenekers, but about that time used by young boys as a bowling alley. A tradition is that this building was put up by Richard Chapman who moved his coffin shop into it, but after discontinuing his coffin business, it was used as the print shop.

Lower Main Street had frame store buildings, mostly, except the Klettner store, which was brick; and on the corner of McKibben and Main Streets, was a brick store operated by a Jew named Mittle as a dry goods and notions store. I believe this store was rebuilt and bricked up outside when it was, later, sold. It has been occupied in recent years by the Stokes Drug Store (formerly the Way Drug Store), and now by Dr. Dickert as a drug store. Further down, next to Timmerman's Store, where is now the Farmer's Hatchery and R. D. Smith & Son Wholesale grocery, was a one-story frame building which was destroyed by fire. The lots were purchased by Summer Brothers, of Newberry, and the present brick buildings constructed, about four or five stores. In front, across the street, was the buggy and wagon factory of John Taylor, who made and repaired vehicles. He sold his plant to a newly organized corporation, the Carolina Manufacturing Company, who improved the buildings, adding new ones, and installed new equipment; and changed it to a coffin factory, which was destroyed by fire a few years afterwards.

On Boyce Street, between College and Caldwell Streets, were several small one-story frame buildings, the only brick store on the block being that of the one now occupied by G. B. Summer, and Sons. S. B. Jones had an ice-house in one of them which was about the middle of the block; and between it and the furniture store, where is now C. T. Summer grocery store, was a small bottling plant that was owned and operated by a German from Charleston, S. C. He, later, sold the plant to W. Smith Langford who established a Coco-Cola Bottling plant there. On the corner of College and Boyce Streets was a buggy and wagon warehouse, owned and operated by Summer Brothers, whose three main stores at that time were located on the corner of Main and Caldwell Streets, North side, where is now Hal Kohn's Store and Bergen's Clothing store, including the store where the Central Drug Store is located.

Previous to this, Robert T. Caldwell operated a coffin shop on the corner of College and Boyce Streets.

The many changes that have come about during the past sixty years in buildings—if one were to sketch them all—would require much space. The new court house occupies the lots where were then two-story dwellings. One on the corner which was occupied by a Whaley family, and the other nearer the hotel building is the house now occupied by Mrs. C. D. Weeks as a residence, it having been moved to it's present location when the new court house was built. Up until about 1896 the Lake family lived in it, and it was known as the Montgomery home.

Wicker's Livery Stables were located on both sides of Caldwell Street, where is now the warehouse of G. B. Summer & Sons. On both corners of Nance and Harrington Streets (where is now the firehouse)were frame dwellings. All of these and the livery stables were bruned a few years before the great fire of 1907.

Some of the pr vate schools taught in Newberry just before the beginning of the graded school system were those of Miss. Emma Havird (later she became Mrs. J. B. Haigler, Lutheran minister) Miss. Sallie Metts who had a school in small house in backyard of her father's home on College Street; and Miss. Mattie McIntosh, daughter of late Dr. James McIntosh, who had school in a building constructed by her father for that purpose, located on Bundary Street(lately the home of Judge Neal Workman).

The first grade school under the State sytem was held in 1888 in the old Newberry Female Academy building, a one-story brick building on College Street, which later was bought by Dr. W. G. Houseal and made into a medicinic and office, with an apartment upstairs.

Before the Mollohon Cotton Mills were built, all the space in that area were woods and fields, over which, the boys of the neighborhood huntedd many rabbits and doves and partidges. The single-barreled shot-gun which my father gave me served for several years. Between this place and "Graveltown", on Scott(s Creek was the"first culbreth", under the railroad, where a deep pond was used as a swimming pool for the youngsters. At that time it was secluded, not being visible to any passersby. Another swimming pool was the " second culbreth", about one mile below , under or near the railroad.

Another popular swimming place was the old mills pond, then called Langford's Pond, wide and long with good depth. Another swimming place was Wilbur's pond, where later the country club was constructed; but few were allowed to swim in it except by permission.

When Boundary Street Grammar school was built some of grade pupils planted shade trees in the school yard. The author's grade, the fourth, planted a water-oak which is the second from Boundary Street, on right side of building . At that time, the Superintendent, Prof. Frank Evans, lived in a small cottage behind the school grounds and a short distance from Coat Street.

Some of the young boy's fishing places were Scott's Creek, from Jeff Lane's farm (later Dr. Boyd Jacob's place),on down to Livingstone's pasture at the edge of town, near the road going towards Neal's farm (now the Neal Dairy, owned by a grand-son of Thomas Neal). The best places, however, were Crotwell's Pond and Bush River, from which many red perch were caught.

Some incidents of the author's school days stand out clearly; for they were impressive though usual to boys of that day. I remember that at one time I was asked to stay in after school and failed to do so. One of my school mates who lived in the same neighborhood stopped at my father's house and warbed my mother she had better have me"put some strong paste-board in my breeches" when I went to scool the next day, as I was going to get a whipping; but I did not use the paste-board nor do I remember the consequences.

One of the boys' games in school or outside was to form a line with hands clasped; then, to run across the yard in a line, one end swinging around while the other end remained stationary. This was called "swinging the rope". Many boys received a good fall this way. " Leap-frog" was, also, a popular game. The grounds were too small for baseball games, but in the afternoon the boys would assemble on the college grounds or on the grounds of some neighbor's house for a game. One of the latter was on the Leavell grounds where are now the homes of Judge Eugene S. Blease and Clarence T. Hutchinson. Foot-ball, too, became a favorite sport, the old rush game being used, when often the boys received bruises or were shinned, but without a doctor being on the premises.

The Opera House building was not completely finished in those days, it having been erected a few years previously. The same old bell was in the tower, with no town clock, so that it could be seen plainly through the round holes of the tower. Sometimes the boys would climb up the tower from the inside, to the upper windows, then climb out so that they could get through the round holes to the bell. There they would inscribe their names on the bell. I can remember when writing my name on it there were many names of fellows older than I who had climbed up there probably three or four years earlier. But after a lapse of over fifty years all of them are probably obliterated by time and exposure. It was not until a few years ago that the town clock was put in.

The old Court House in those days was a scene of many colorful trials. I remember some of the criminal lawyers whose oratorical powers were well known and were sometimes heard for several blocks around. Some of them were Col. George Johnstone and Y. J. Pope. Some of the younger criminal lawyers at that time, who were, when inspired in certain cases, were equally as oratorical in their speeches. They were Col. Walter H. Hunt, Col. O. L. Schumpert, Dr. George B. Cromer, Cole L. Blease, Thomas S. Sease, Robert H. Welch and I. H. Hunt. Col. George Johnstone served in the State Legislature and one term as U. S. Congressman. Col. Schumpert served as Solicitor of this District, as did Thomas S. Sease who later served in Spartanburg District as Circuit Court Judge for many years. Col. Walter H. Hunt was the organizer and first Prest of Oakland Cotton Mills. Dr. George Cromer, a well known Lutheran Layman served as President of Newberry College for about seven years. Cole L. Blease served in State Legislature and other political offices and also was Governor of the State and U. S. Senator. Another well-known lawyer was George S. Mower who with his law partner, Frank Bynum, served in many important Civil actions; Mr. Mower being, too, both an industrialist and a philanthropist.

Another highly competent lawyer in Civil Actions was Lambert J. Jones, who was succeeded by his son, Dr. Lambert W. Jones who became well-known as a painstaking office lawyer and an efficient analyist. Mr. J. Y. Culbreth practiced a few years and died comparatively young, as did his partner, "Hoot" Merchant, (his brother-in-law). Most of their work was office work, though occasionally Mr. Culbreth took on criminal cases.

The present contingent of lawyers in Newberry are: Honorable E. S. Blease (one-time legislator, Associate Justice and Chief Justice of the State Supreme Court), Steve Griffith (legislator, then Circuit Judge), Eustis St. Amand (a young attorney recently located in Newberry as partner of Judge E. S. Blease). John F. Clarkson (former associate of the late I. H. Hunt, then with Aubrey Harley, and now with William Hunter). B. V. Chapman (former legislator, State Senator, and Acting Solicitor), Henry C. Holloway (former law partner of the late Col. O. L. Schumpert), who has a reputation as being highly competent in office practice and civil actions, Thomas H. Pope (legislator), who served overseas in World War II as Major and Lieutenant Col. and saw action in different sections of Africa and Italy. Col Pope is now associated with Felix Green, a young lawyer recently from Columbia. Fred H. Dominick, who served as legislator, Assistant District Attorney General of the State and later as U. S. Congressman. Neal W. Workman was former law partner of Fred H. Dominick; served in World War I; member of State Legislature; was Probate Judge of Newberry County for over twenty years, and died in office. Alan Johnstone, Jr. has served as legislator, and as U. S. Director in several Federal Unemployment projects both in South Carolina and in Washington. Aubrey Harley, who came from the section of Barnwell, has served several terms in the State legislature; is well known as a careful lawyer in all civil actions.

Some of the druggists at that time, as I remember them, were: Dr. Peter Robertson, who had come from Charleston, and operated the corner drug store in partnership with Dr. James K. Gilder, a physician, under the firm name of Robertson and Gilder. Dr. Robertson married a Prosperity lady, Miss Alice Hunter. Later after the death of Dr. Robertson, Dr. C. D. Weeks, who was then pharmacist in Dr. William E. Pelham's drug store, bought the interest of Dr. Robertson, and the firm became known as Gilder & Weeks. After the death of Dr. Weeks a few years ago, his legatees operated the store for a short time, then sold the store to Dr. James Burgess who now operates it. Dr. Gilder had died several years previous to the death of Dr. Weeks.

Dr. William E. Pelham, Sr. operated a drug store about where is now the Martha Park dress shop. Later, he bought the store across the street, where is now the Smith's Drug Store, and for many years operated a successful business there. After his death, which was after the death of his son, Dr. Wm. E. Pelham, Jr., (a physician), the business was sold to Dr. Neal Miller and Dr. J. Edwin Stokes, who operated it unitl the death of Dr. Miller. Sometimes afterwards Dr. Stokes bought the business he now runs, at the corner of Main and McKibben Streets, from Dr. George Way who had operated it for several years. (Dr. Stokes recently sold out to Dr. E. J. Dickert).

Dr. William G. Mayes owned and operated the Mayes Drug Store at the corner of Main and Nance Streets (now the present location of J. H. Summer Clothing Store), for over thirty years.

Dr. Van Smith, a physician, owned and operated a drug store on lower Main Street for several years. Later, he sold out and moved to Beaufort, South Carolina, where he resumed his medical practice.

One of the newer drug stores is that of Dr. Lominack, who operates a business on upper Main Street, near the Ritz Theater.

Some of the physicians at that time were: Dr. O. B. Mayer, Sr. (he died about 1892), his son, Dr. O. B. Mayer, Jr., Dr. Sampson Pope, and others. Dr. W. G. Houseal and Dr. James M. Kibler, who were cousins, were young physicians then, who first practiced together and also operated a drug store for a short time, which was located where is now the Newberry Hotel Dining Room. After discontinuing their drug business they began to practice seperately, and each soon became known as fine practicioners and diagnoticians. Other young physicians soon located in Newberry, as, Dr. P. G. Ellesor, Dr. Thomas W. Smith, and Dr. J. H. McCollough. Dr. W. E. Lake, who practiced in a section of the county known as New Chappells, moved to town and became known as a fine physician in treating fevers.

Within the past twenty years, many young physicians have located in Newberry, as: Dr. Frank D. Mower, son of Honorable George S. Mower, Dr. William E. Pelham, Jr., Dr. V. W. Dehimes, Dr. Arthur Welling, Dr. Raymond Lominack, (son of W. Frank Lominack), and others. Dr. Grant, colored physician, has built up a good practice; he was interested in improving the Peoples Hospital, and in getting the new housing project for colored people in Newberry.

Some of the Dentists about 1890-95 were: Dr. E. C. Jones, Dr. Theodore Johnstone, son of Honorable Silas Johnstone, and grand-son of Chancellor Job Johnstone. Later, came Dr. Young Brown, Dr. Haskel Kibler, Dr. R. M. Kennedy, and E. M. Anderson who has lately located in Newberry; as also, Dr. F. A. Truett.

Newberry never had an Optometrist until about 1890-95, when Dr. G. W. Conner located here. He married a Newberry lady, Miss Lola Lake, daughter of Thomas M. Lake, one-time Clerk of Court of Newberry County. After Dr. Conner's death, Dr. H. M. Bigby came and practiced over thirty years when he sold his business to Dr. Myron Rones. Dr. Rones sold out to Dr..........

Dr. Cecil Lynch also has recently located in Newberry.

160

Family Folklore.

Some family names (capital letters)
in early period in Newberry County—

The folklore of this section of South Carolina may be fairly representative of most parts of the State during the early period of their settlements. The early families from Europe, whose names are typically significant, at first used their original spellings but gradually changed to the phonetic form of spelling.

Many families in the rural sections still retain much of the wholesome traditions of their forbears, living in many cases on the land their forefathers settled. Perhaps the churches and schools that were planted among them, and have grown along with them, are the foundations for a cultivated spirit, and enables them to observe that the Sun and the trees are parts of God's universe.

From the first settlements through each generation there have been gradual changes in customs, schools, roads, enterprise, and even in the churches—a general growth and development. With all of it there has been it's humorous side.

The first roads were small, narrow drives or paths, rough, in which frequently the rains washed gulleys. Many CANES and plumb trees, and BERRY bushes grew in large patches by the side of the RHOADS and often around the FOOTE of the HILLS, and the SHORES of the RIVERS and LAKES.

Wagons that were made with large, heavy BODIES, shaped like a boat with a BOX attached to the rear, had large, heavy wheels with large hubs and spokes, and were driven to the village for supplies. The FARMERS would bring some products from their farms to sell or exchange for goods they needed at home. On account of the roughness of the road and the slowness of travel sometimes they spent the KNIGHT, sleeping in canvas-covered wagons on the lower public square. The WAGONER had to be GOODE, for he was kept busy.

They lived independent lives, economically, producing nearly everything they needed to eat; making their own clothes, with the cards, the spinning wheel, and the loom. In the Colonial and Rev. War times clothes for men and women were made in varied colors, the cloth soaked in home-made dyes that were made from tree barks, berries or other wild PLANTS. Walnut barks made a BROWN dye. These tasks were performed by the women while the men worked the fields, fathers and SONS.

Few fields were fenced in, the cattle being allowed to roam wherever they wished. Occasionally a rail fence came into use, which was built from SMALL, long STRIPLINGS (now spelled Stribling), placed in a zig-zag manner in order to hold the ends that were placed one on another.

When a girl would WED-A-MAN the male attendents sometimes wore BEARDS, had on short REDD pants tied with BUCKLES, and GREEN shirts, or maybe a GRAY shirt. When a later style caused the pants to be worn a LITTLE longer, though not LONG enough to reach the ankles, the men began to wear WHITE shirts that had RUFF sleeves that were fastened with large BURTONS, Their COATS were short, of a color to blend with the pants, making a NEW-MAN of him.

One of the principal sports at that time was going on a HUNT. When the YOUNGHUSBAND became a HUNTER he would strap his HIPPS with a leather band, and with nerves of STEELE, get his dogs and HITT the trail—and HOWE he felt his OATS! Game was plentiful, including the deer, the FOX, HARE, KOONS, and wild turneys, LARKS, and BYRDS of AULL kinds, even the MARTINDALE which often made it's nest in gourds that were hung on tall sapling poles in the yards; while the BUZZARD calmly floated in the breeze and the WOLFE moaned in it's den or would PACE the WOODS. Hunting was an all day job with them. In the early morning as the COCKS (COX) would CROW, so the FELLERS would face the DRAFTS, trail their prey to a GLENN or MEADOW, and like the KNIGHTS of OULD bring home the BACON. They wasted no SHELLS and no CANNON, for nothing was better than their aims.

Another sport was fishing. FISH was plentiful in the WATERS of the RIVERS; HOPE was high in his YOUNGBLOOD as he made a WEBB that would HOOK his game. SUMMER days were always eventful, going SINGLY down some LANE, and never DUNN; and he would never WELCH in his purpose. Such a young FARMER could in his sports as well as in his WORK, REID the signs of WRIGHT to the WEST or to the EASTLAND; and when the RAINES were coming, like an Indian WORTHY of his

161

tribe, he would NEAL and listen.

Many families from Germany and France besides making good wines from their own grown VINES, (FRENCH wines were especially in demand), had the art of making CROUT; using a HOPPER (now spelled Harper) or large pork barrel. They had the KEYS to many ways of economical living. They produced MOORE vegetables, CORN, or MAYS, and FOWLES of AULL kinds than their NEIGHBORS. The Irish families, too, had many of these early customs that they brought from the old country, that were acquired through intermarriages with French and German settlers in their country.

At the earliest time there were no BANKS, and the people often hid their gold and silver in holes of the WALLS of their HOLMES, or buried it in the yard. The planter would HOARD his money, and like the MANN who was WISE he laid up for a RAINEY DAY; for the GAINES were mostly in NICKLES and PENNYS. Many a FARMER yet COUNTS his money in small change; and when the dreary, BLACk days come to keep his HEAD quite LEAVELL and WAITS for a FAIR day to come.

Another custom was to build MILLS on the creeks and RIVERS, in which to grind their own WHEAT and make their flour and cattle feed. If any FLOWERS grew WILDE around the place, they were soon gone, for the HOGGS and other cattle were allowed to eat in the STUBBLEFIELD after the grain was gathered for the MILLS. They were early RISERS and always arrived at the Mill house in time for early WORK, even though some were WALKERS. AULL the FOLKS were not MILLERS, however, often one operator serving others in his community.

Like the ENGLISH they had their other occupations. There were BAKERS, COOKS, SHEPHERDS, SMITHS, TAYLORS, STOCKMANS, MOWERS, or a BISHOP or a TAYLOR in some places; but like the ancient SPEARMAN or BOWMAN they were ever alert, as a true WORKMAN.

WELLS were not at first dug on the farms, but SPRINGS usually on the sides of BANKS and walled with STONE, or near BROOKS beneath the BOWERS of some weeping willow, furnished the WATERS for drinking and for the family washing. They knew nothing about DERRICKS then with which to draw water or lift heavy loads.

The family washing was done on the streams, usually by servants, or slaves, before the War Between the States, and since that time by servants. The women had a FARR distance to carry their loads, but it was near the water. The servants carried their washing on their HEADS. If there were no BRIDGES they would FORD the streams to get to a suitable POOL or SPRING, which was, perhaps, under a ROUNDTREE. The slaves worked almost STARK naked; they would wring the wet clothes by twisting, one at each end; and good RINGERS were rare.

Few farm implements were available, except those that were made in their own blacksmith shops. They went about their tasks, though, in good GRACE and would never TERRY in their work.

In some HOLMES were large, tall MERRYMANN clocks which had DIALS as long as a CHILDS hand; and at night when the tick of the clock could be HEARD the family would sit by the wide-open fireplace. As the old man smoked his pipe, MARS or the MOON would cast it's beam through the window; then perhaps, he would play his fiddle or HARP for the amusement or pleasure of his family. It is doubtful if the MAYER of any TOWNE could boast of better citizens than were these pioneers.

Some of HOLMES were kept in unique STILES, too, with wide HALLS, and large rooms. They were built with HART WOOD and the shingles were HART, making LEAKS a rare occurance. GUNNS were hung over the doors of the rooms, for quick action if attacked. This was not a superstition but an enforced habit since the days of the Indians and the TORIES. There was a superstition, though, in handling certain tools, as BROOMS that were stood up in corners the straw pointing the way it grew—often WHEAT straw. It was believed that this WAY it would WARD off sickness. The WALLS were painted or papered in colors of GARNETT, and sometimes the KITCHENS they would GARNER. The tables and beds of the wealthy were made of mahogany or oak. In the GARRETTS were sometimes old trunks or cedar chests, behind which would CROUCH a yellow CATT with it's head LOW; reposed in which would be some relics of by-gone DAYS or maybe an old COBB pipe. But, TUTT, it's just a plunder room; for on the walls hung GREEN corn with a CLAMP of CORD around them, with CRISP, yellow ears. In the middle of the floor, perhaps, a wide, white cloth was spread on which were RICE or peanuts to dry, or fruit. In the kitchen, too, or the dining room could be seen pewter plates, of the Colonial period, and BOWLES of pewter; china coming into style at a later period. Many people yet carry out old traditions about planting in certain seasons, according to the signs. Planting Irish potatoes and other root vegetables " in the dark of the MOON; and those that mature above ground had to have a RAY of sunshine—planted on a BRIGHT day. Of course they would FARROW the soil, much as they do now. Major crops were gathered at anytime after maturity, but vegetables were gathered EARLY, as their MEANS would warrant. Enough tobacco was raised to supply the workers on the farms.

There were many other superstitions, too, that, no doubt, were brought over with some families from the old country or were imparted by early Indian lore or by negro slaves. One was if a rabbit ran across your pathway at night or would SCURRY across the road, or a dog would bark while running around the HOUSE, meant that somebody in the family would soon die. Then, some believed in witches, like the early Puritans of New England; so they thought that a horse-shoe had to be nailed over the front door to keep the witches out. This custom was used for several generations; and then gave way to a later sign over the front door or within the house, with the words, "Good Luck" or " In God We Trust". Many of these people retained this idea from the fact that when a horse became ill a horse-shoe was nailed over the stable door, or it was kept there all the time to prevent "distemper" or other horse ailments. A rare, fanatical case was when a young man believed he was being ridden by a witch; so he made a dummy woman who, he thought, was riding him, and standing it up in his yard he shot it " in effigy", thus getting rid of the witch.

Some phases of humor are shown in instances where some of the old land conveyances disclose peculiar situations. When Lewis HOGG who lived on a large plantation on Enoree River, near Broad River, bought another tract that was further WEST, towards DUNCAN'S Creek, one Betsy BUGG sold her small farm and disappeared into fields where the SPEERS were plentiful. Down near Broad River lived Levi FISH, an old man when he died there, content to spend his life near the big stream, even though the BATES thrived a few miles further South, just below the PEAK of the County line. Over near Heller's Creek one John PARROTT lived and died, and some of his descendants "flew the coop" as it were, going to other sections. These HARDY men worked their own LAND, never split hairs with anyone. If they committed a SENN they QUICKLY sought a pardon.

When slavery was built on a large scale, the plantations became larger, and few opportunities came to the small farmer. But they all had gardens and many things to eat for themselves and their slaves. Some of the best slaves and their families were allowed a HALFACRE on which to plant anything they wished to PLANT; HENTZ, they were kept busy. They cured their own HAMM for the WINTER'S use, and sold their surplus products in the village markets. A WORTHY people

Turning back the pages of time we note that at the earliest, and on up to recent years, methods of community cooperation prevailed. Log-rollings, corn-shuckings, cotton pickings, pender-pullings, quiltings were held, common forms of cooperative enterprises among the peoples of the various communities. The NEIGHBORS would help one another. If one got behind in his work or wanted to gather grain quickly when rain approached, each neighbor would bring some slaves and all would work until the task was done. Then the host and hostess would serve something good to eat, which, while the work was in progress was being cooked by the hostess and the wives of the neighbors who had come to help. Sometimes this supper included home-brewed wines or persimmon beer (often called "SIMMON beer"). Sometimes straight whiskey was offered. At the quiltings, participated in by the women, the quilts were made with large square blocks, patches of different colors in checker form, and in each corner square was embroidered a design emblematic of the hostess, or her initials. On that occasion, too, the hostess served good things to eat.

The women darned and knitted socks and stockings, and made many laces. They were very adept in these feats. They yet LOVELACE to-day and embroider much. The less physically ABLE worked around the house, making BASKETTS, WICKER chairs with WOOD bottoms, or FISH nets. Some were SHOEMAKERS who made shoes from hometanned raw HYDE leather which was tacked around the wood soles, and which had to be greased with homemade tallow each morning before the shoes would slip on the feet.

Games played by the children and grown-ups were different from what they are at the present time. They knew nothing of GOLF and tennis, football, basketball, or soft-ball, nor even ROOK. They did have a kind of BALL game which they called "paddle-cat", having bases and using barrel staves as bats. The balls were made at home with a heavy string wound around a small piece of cork or rubber. After the War Between the States "roly-poly" came into styles, which was played by rolling balls with staves on the ground and endeavoring to roll it into a hole. Then came croquet which was popular for several generations; nearly every front yard or backyard being used with wire wickets STUCK in the ground, and played by striking wooden balls with wooden mallets to put them through the wickets. These may be called easy GOING, as compared with the present DAY games. Slaves always looked up to their MASTERS as a kind of KING or KYZER. The master may have been a church or community leader, and like the POPE he , generally , governed affairs in his community. He may have been a JUSTICE of the PEACE, rode a fine horse, with his KITT by his side. His system was thorough, with his COOPER and foreman. At the first BEAM of morning when the JAY began to sing, his yard BELL would ring or BULLS horn sound for the hands to go to WORK. Each had his duty to perform. His SMITH or Shop workers, SAWYER, FIELD workers, and maids were some of them. They had FEW of the HOLIDAYS that are now observed; perhaps CHRISTMAS DAY, but never GOODE FRIDAYS nor Easter, nor VALENTINE day.

The MASTERS allowed no CROOKS among the slaves, if he could help it. If one was caught violating rule he was promtly whipped. The LAW never allowed killing them, and there was no LYNCH law. The POWERS of slave-owners were large outside this realm. Sometimes stockades were made in which to fasten and punish them, or a PITT dug in which to imprison them. Slaves could never leave the plantation unless they had a"pass" (a written one from their master). If one ran away without a written pass and were caught by the " Patrollers"(this was a committee appointed in the community to ride around and catch runaways), they were whipped. Slaves called these "patrollers" by the name of "Bush-whackers" because they often rode in the fields or woods striking BUSHES with heavy sticks to find runaways.

Few Masters allowed their slaves to learn to REID and WRIGHT. It was considered demoralizing to them. If they were caught with a book or piece of paper, writing, they were promptly whipped. Many were sold " on the block", much as horses were sold in recent years, to the highest bidder; and such SALES usually brought buyers from long distances.

Brides and grooms after their wedding ceremonies always stayed with the party and indulged in the "frolic"; and unlike the present time, they immediately after the seremony disappeared. On such occasions the man with the largest BEARD always "took the cake"; but the wedding cake was not so popular as the flask of wine which was offered the one who could ride the fastest or to the bride's parents' home the quickest.

The YOUNG men liked trapping, until the shot-gun and rafe came into vogue. Even yet many catch their game in home-made traps, as the "Rabbit-gum", a long boxlike trap with an opening at one end. Early trapping of WILDE CATTS, LEOPARDS, KOONS, and FOX, in what was known as a "dead FALL" is not used at this time. Wild turkeys, too, were trapped; but the HUNTER'S call in imitation of the turkey's mate, was a common decoy to approach within GUNN shot distance.

As for the churches and schools the first ones were made of logs, small one-room huts, with chimneys made of rough hand-hewn boards and plastered on the inside with thick mud. If the mud fell away and the boards caught fire it was instantly put out with a bucket of water which was kept handy for that purpose. Many of the first homes, and some later ones, made their chimneys that WAY. These churches were called chapels, or CHAPPELLS. After the War Between the States, the negroes, who had been forced to attend the white peoples's churches and sit on the back seats or in the gallaries during slavery time, (many did this several years after the war), built their own churches, which, for sometime, were known as "Brush-harbors", and made with pine poles stuck in the ground and covered and ceiled with brushes.

The wide fire-places in the houses, usually about five feet wide, burned four-foot logs. This was the cooking place, too, skillets being hung suspended over the blaze, or covered pans placed on a bracket held by the wall of the fireplace. Some of the families later built rock or mud ovens in the back yards, in which all food was cooked. The ovens were shaped like a turtle's back, with two doors at the front end for the food and the fuel. Many of the oldest people say that they have never eaten as good bread or pies since the time of the old oven.

During Rev. War times the Tories and many sections were active against the Whigs and would even go to their homes or to churches to attack or capture them. One record states that a certain minister who preached the doctrine of liberty always carried his gun to church; while conducting services his gun would standing close by; and preached his serman with his powder-horn swung around his neck.

When freedom of the slaves came many old slaves stayed on with their former masters, working as wage hands; later, they became renters, in many cases, and a few later owning their own farms. The period of the Ku Klux, which terminated "scalawag" rule among the masses,brought with it soberness. Not until after the days of the " Red Shirts" did South Carolina and other southern States come into a period of development and growth.

HISTORIC OLD HOMES IN CITY AND COUNTY.

"COATSWOOD"-known as the old Chancellor Job Johnstone home, located at 1700 Johnstone Street, in Newberry. It was built by Chancellor Job Johnstone about 1833-34, and occupied by him and his family until his death, when it came into the possession of some of his descendents.

A large house painted white, with three stories and an attic, it is a combination of the English country home and early American colonial architecture. It has a wide porch with granite flooring, which encircles the house. The first story is of brick, plastered over, and two upper stories and attic of frame structure. The walls are thick and the windows and doors are larger than generally is seen in this type of house. There are fourteen rooms with large dimensions. All the winding stairway is made of mahogany rails. The stair cases, the door trims and the mantels are hand-carved from native heart pine wood. Most of the house is put together with wooden pegs; but where nails were used they were hand-wrought. The brass knobs and brass hinges on the doors were imported from England. Some of the door-knobs are nickle-plated. The second story has a veranda across the back, enclosed on three sides by walls of the house and on the open sides by built in Venetian blinds.

A grand-son, Alan Johnstone, Jr., bought the home a few years ago, and remodeled it throughout, but retained most of the original design and architectural style.

The old furniture that was in the old home consisted of many antique mahogany pieces; many of them, later, being divided among the heirs. Originally, four-posted beds, a French bed, silver coffee and tea services; other mahogany pieces; were included among it's furnishings.

The home sets back some distances from the street, surrounded by large red oaks, native cedars, magnolias, holly, and native flowering shrubs. In the rear of the home was the old brick slave quarters, used in later years as a storage house. It is said that Chancellor Job Johnstone used the building as an office during war times, and that he signed in this house a famous document pertaining to the Confederate cause.

MOWER HOME-located at corner of Johnstone and McKibben Streets, once owned by the grandfather of the late Dr. Frank D. Mower, whose name was Duane Mower. It is said to be much over one hundred years old, having been built about 1799 by Phillip Schoppert, a contractor, who erected the first brick court house about that time. One tradition being that when Philemon Waters, the Sheriff of Newberry, bought the house, he had it improved with some additions, and lived in it until his death in 1811. Later owners were Thomas T. Cureton, James McKibben, David Gunn, and then Phillip Schoppert; another tradition being that George Schoppert and not Phillip built it, and that his son, Phillip, lived in it until 1842; that George Schoppert died in it. Phillip Schoppert made additions to the house, in the rear, before he sold it to Dr. Benjamin Waldo. Finally it came into the possession of Dr. George W. Glenn, whose estate being settled in 1867, it was bought that year by Duane Mower.

The house has two stories, with chimneys at each side, a piazza on the first and second stories. It has some of the style of later colonial architecture. The hall is wide and square, mantels wide, with some hand-carved designs. The doors are large, with an old English style, having been imported from England; with their brass knobs, on which are patent engravings showing the English Royal insignia. There are eleven rooms in the house as it is at this time, the late Duane Mower having made some improvements on it.

Large evergreen trees surround the building.

CALDWELL HOME-which has been owned by the Hornsby family many years, is located on the Southeast corner of Johnstone and McKibben Streets. The house was built by Major Frederick Nance for his son—in-law, Patrick Caldwell, a lawyer in Newberry, and son of a distinguished Rev. War officer in the American Army, Major William Thomas Caldwell. A tradition is that Major Nance built the house about 1805-15, and afterwards sold it to Patrick Caldwell.

After the death of Patrick Caldwell it came into the possession of Joseph McMorries; then W. B. McKellar lived in it from 1859 to 1863, when Jacob Bowers lived in it. In 1879 Jesse Hornsby bought the home, while John A. Chapman and family were living in it.

It is a large, two-story house, with wide chimneys at each end or side. The front porch is narrow, with square columns. Thus the usual colonial effect is carried out, as in other homes of that period. It is constructed of heart lumber; the interior showing smoothly finished ceilings, mouldings, and wide fireplaces and mantels. It is close to the street. Large trees around the house.

HENSON HOUSE--located about six miles North of Newberry, just above Jalapa, and two miles to the right at Cromer's Cross Roads. Commonly known as the Gilliam place, having been owned by Robert Glenn Gilliam, a son of Dr. Jacob F. Gilliam. A typical old colonial house.

It was built by Robert Glenn Gilliam about 1830, who lived in it until his death; then his widow and only daughter lived there for awhile. His daughter, Mary Elizabeth, married H. O. Henson, who occupied it several years after the War Between the States. Since their deaths, several different families have lived in it; until it was sold about 1930 to T. B. Amis. Mr. Amis renovated the house, without changing any of it's original design and shape, and made it into a typical Colonial home, tending towards the early New England style.

A small front porch at front entrance with small square columns that stand against the building. A wide chimney at each side; and the side-porch of unusual width, with larger square columns. The house is weatherboarded with thick boards that are of heart lumber. Most of the interior finish is new.

DR. JAMES EPPS HOME--located about twelve miles North of Newberry Court House. It was built by the pioneer of the family, who had come from Virginia before the Rev War. It remained as the Epps property until about 1890 when it was sold to one Abrams (Thomas Abrams) and later occupied by his son, Thomas J. Abrams.

The exterior of the house is of colonial design, two stories high, with large, round columns in front that are constructed of brick and plastered. The windows are wide, the front ones reaching from the floor to the ceiling. A stairway in the back hall leads to the basement, which the earliest families used for a kitchen. The wide hall has double doors that divide it in the center, and a spiral stairway from the first floor to the attic above the second floor. There is a servants's stairway in the back. The living room is finished in white. Many of these improvements were made by Dr. James Epps.

The original landscaping was attractively placed; in front of the house a wide lawn and long walk to the road with broad-leaf cedars on each side, and shrubbery. The flower garden extended to a wide walk on the driveway, bordered with rows of spin trees that extended to the road; and in the rear of the home were elm trees, spin trees, on both sides of the house.

J. C. S. BROWN HOME--located about ten miles East of Newberry Court House on the highway to Blairs. It is about one-fourth mile to the left of the present highway, a private driveway leading to the home. This was the home of the son of Sims Brown, the Rev War patriot, and occupied by the grand-son, Col. J. C. S. Brown, who had the house improved so that it gave a modern appearance but retaining much of it's orginal design. One tradition is that Sims Brown, the patriot scout, also lived in the orginal house.

Col. J. C. S. Brown had some of the house remodeled about 1860, and after his death, one of his sons, John C. Brown, lived in it.

A large two-story house, high off the ground, with long front porch having large square columns down stairs, and on the upstairs porch. The front cornices around the porches are designed with uniform style. The doors are heavy and large, with a double front door. The windows are large, with green blinds, and the house painted white. The stairs are in the rear of the hall. The wall papering present a variety of designs ; and modern base-boards and moulding. The frame work is morticed, and held together with wooden pegs.

There are few magnolias remaining in the yard, some evidence of having been evergreens, crapemyrtle and other shrubbery scattered around the yard; and large oaks surround the house.

"BELFAST"--The old Wallace home at " Belfast" is located near the Laurens County line. It was built by a pioneer of the Simpson family; of solid brick; very old home. Sometime later it came into the possession of the Wallace family, John Wallace, the father of the later William H. Wallace, founder and first Editor of the Newberry Observer.

It is said that the lumber in the house was shipped, mostly, from England after it had been sent there to be specially dressed and finished; it is pure heart lumber. The interior, however, is walnut finish, with hardwood floors, and is plastered. The mantels that are large, with unique designs on them, the stairs, and the wainscoting are all made of walnut lumber. The designs on the mantels seem to represent an oakleaf and ancient Greecian keys. One tradition is that the brick used were made from the soil on the place and kiln-dried on the plantation.

A two-story building with large chimneys at it's sides, constructed of heart pine lumber; much of the base work being hand-hewn. A large front porch with square, boxed wooden columns, and banisters.

There is a large front yard with large shade trees, and evidences of it having much shrubbery at one time.

CALDWELL HOME-located nine and one-half miles from Newberry Court House. It was built by John Caldwell, pioneer settler from Ireland, father of John and James Caldwell of the same community. The home became a central place for congregations of live-stock growers in early times, and the place of lodging for many live-stock dealers who came there to buy new livestock. Also, it was a home for many social gatherings in early times for the young people of that neighborhood.

When John Caldwell came into the community he built, first, a small log-house, which was about one-half mile from this home, which was later destroyed by fire. Then, he built in 1855 the present house, though one tradition is his son, John, had built it. Later, Dr. John Caldwell (the son) left it to his daughter, Caroline Caldwell, who lived there until her death.

The house is built of heart pine lumber, hand-dressed, morticed, tongued and pinned with perfect joints, and fittings. The doors and sash were hand-made, by the contractors, and are of unusual size and beauty. The home is finished with unique interior work, showing handcarvings, large mouldings, beadings, and modernly attractive papering. There are eleven rooms, each sixteen by sixteen feet in size, except the kitchen. An attic above the second story is constructed to give well-built rooms.

CROSSON OLD HOME-located about seven miles East of Newberry Court House, on the old Blair Road. It is the original home of the Irish settler, Alexander Crosson, who was one of the early Covenanters who came to South Carolina just before the beginning of the Rev. War. He came about 1770 from Virginia with his father, Thomas Crosson. One tradition is that his father did not come until a few years after his son came, and landed at Charleston, S. C.

The house was built about 1772, and occupied by the Crosson family for several generations; and in later years was occupied by tenants. It is built of large logs, well constructed for perfect symmetry. The logs are hewn straight and notched accurately for perfect fitting, in the place of using nails; which is said to be more substantial. After completion, the house was ceiled, floored and weatherboarded with hand-planed heart pine lumber. All of the work was done in a seven-foot hole in the ground under the house. One carpenter would enter the hole while another stood on the logs; hence, they were able to saw the boards to fit. The interior shows a wide hall and very large rooms, all made from heart pine lumber.

The last descendant of the Crosson family who lived in the house was Mrs. S. J. D. Price, who was of the sixth generation.

FAIR HOME-located about four miles South of Newberry Court House, on the road to the town of Prosperity; about one hundred yards to the right of the present highway. The first main road ran in front of the home.

The house was built by James Fair, an uncle of the late Col. Simeon Fair, of Newberry. It was in possession of the Fair family many years; then was occupied by Joseph Hunter and his family; then by others at different times. Sigmund Ruff bought the place about 1918, and lived in it.

It stands well back from the highway, a large front yard which shows evidence of having once a variety of shrubbery. There are some shade trees around the house. A two-story building, with an annex at each side; a front piazza with square columns to support it's roof. A chimney at each side of the building, fronting slightly at each annex. The front porch of the main part of the house is narrow, with the square columns both upstairs, and downstairs, supported on large rock bases that reach two feet from the ground. The hall is narrow and short, with mahogany finished beadings, and much of the other interior work of heart pine lumber. Originally, there was much walnut finish in the interior work, but after tenants came into possession, and before it was bought by Mr. Ruff, the walnut was torn away. The doors leading from the hall to the rear have high arched transoms, with triangular shaped panes. The living-room mantel is wide with handcarved designs, and fluted. Other mantels have handcarved designs. The wainscoting is as high as the window sills. The walls show an earlier style of painted or figure papering.

WELLS HOME—located on Nance Street; built by the late Os Wells, a brick contractor in Newberry; and occupied by him and his family. The house was constructed probably just after the War Between the States.
Built of brick that were made on the lands surrounding the place. The walls are solid brick, that have been plastered. The front steps lead from the ground to the porch of the second story; the front porch of the first story lying near the ground. The two rear rooms are lower than the front part of the house. Concrete floors down stairs. The wood work is of pure pine heart lumber. Trees and attractive shrubbery surround the house.

HIGGINS HOME—located on Boundary Street, East of Boundary Street School. It was built between 1810 and 1825 by William Caldwell, whose daughter married Francis B. Higgins, lawyer and Commissioner in Equity in Newberry. Francis B. Higgins and family occupied it for several years. After his death his widow, Mrs. Higgins, lived in it for many years with her daughter, Mrs. James McIntosh. After the widow's death and that of her daughter, Dr. McIntosh married the second time to a widow, Mrs. Burt Rook Boozer, of Newberry; then after Dr. McIntosh died, his widow lived there several years, rearing her two children whom she had by Dr. McIntosh.
The house still stands, some distance from the street, among large oaks, with flowers and shrubbery around the yard. It is a large frame building, white, with old-fashioned green blinds, a narrow porch supported with large square columns. The size and style of the house was not changed when some remodeling of the front porch was made. The interior was decorated at the time the McIntosh family lived in it. The wide mantels with carvings, the wainscoting high, and wide top moulding specially designed, give the interior of the rooms the appearance of early American style. The staircase is hardwood. The many old pieces of furniture at that time were mahogany; an attractive piece was a drop-leaf table with pineapple legs, of solid mahogany; the side-board to match in design; the old secretaire of plain rubber finish; a large grand-father's clock standing on the floor; hand painted family portraits; and a gilt-framed mirror of empire design.

SPEARMAN HOME—located just North of the town of Silverstreet, Newberry County, was built about 1854, by James Spearman who lived in it until his death. He was the father of William Spearman who later lived in it, and of Walter Spearman, who moved to Charlotte, N. C.
A two-story frame house with wide roofs that cover the front porch, supported by large, round columns, giving a colonial effect. The columns stand on a brick base near the ground, the edge of the porch almost touching the columns that extend to the roof. There are ten rooms, large wide windows. The wood is all heart pine lumber. The interior is of heart pine finish; plastered, with attractive beadings, plainly furnished mantels; the wainscoting is modern in style, low, and made of heart pine boards.

"RIVERSIDE"—located in the Maybinton section of Newberry County, about eighteen miles Northeast of the Court House, near Broad River. It was built by John Henderson about 1780, and occupied by him and his family. He was the son of David Henderson who had come from Virginia with his father's family.
John Henderson operated a ferry boat across Broad River, known as Henderson's Ferry. There is a tradition that Theodocia Burr, daughter of Aaron Burr, stayed all night in the home at the time she was traveling from the North to Charleston, the stage road running past the home. She was on her way to catch a boat at Charleston for New York City to see her father who was returning from Europe. This was in the year 1813.
About eighty years ago the house was improved, but retained it's original size and style. It has always been occupied by some descendent of the Henderson family.
A large two-story house with seven rooms. A long piazza stretches across the back of the house, and a wide front porch supported with wide columns. Much of this improvement was made when the house was repaired. There is a large living room with over-high mantels showing designs and beautifully carved ends. A wide staircase leads to the second story. There are many old English styled brass knobs and locks on wide, thick doors. The cellar was plastered. The early furniture consisted of many mahogany pieces, but not now preserved.
There was at one time an old flower garden, bordered with boxwood and roses, with ever-green and cedar trees; but little of these can now be seen.

JOHN EICHLEBERGER HOME-located on County highway leading to Pomaria, one mile North of that town, in Newberry County. A tradition is that the first Lutheran Theological Seminary was established in the home; later, it was moved to Lexington, S. C. and combined with the Lexington Classical Institute. The institute was consolidated with Newberry College when it was established in the city of Newberry about 1856.

It is said that one John Caldwell, an Irish settler, first lived in a small house on the same lot of land, about 1790; and when he later moved further up in the county, the house was made a part of the main house which was built about 1870-75, by John Eichleberger who had bought it in 1832. After Col. Eichleberger's death, Henry Gallman lived there awhile; and about 1871-72 John L. and Patrick Derrick bought it, and lived in it until 1890; then it was occupied by Ludie Shealy, who in 1930 sold it to Dr. Z. T. Pinner, of Pomaria.

At one time the house was attractively styled, the interior having been in mahogany finish that was done by Col. Eichleberger, no doubt, when he remodeled it. The stairrails, mouldings, beadings are of mahogany finish. All of these parts were torn out and carried away by tourists many years ago. A two story house, with wide chimneys at each side; a narrow front porch, with colonial columns at one time could be seen. A delapidated place now, being badly treated by tenants in recent years.

THE SUMMER HOME-located about seventeen miles Southeast of Newberry Court House, just South of Pomaria; built by John Summer and occupied by his son, William Summer, Esq., the Horticulturist, about the year 1838.

It is a large two-story house with ten rooms; it shows old English in style. The original home was improved but retained most of it's size and style. The sills are large, handmade, and wooden pegs bind them together. The rooms are large, with high wainscoting showing panels of walnut finish. The stairway banister rails are walnut, and the arch over the hallway of attractive design. The mantels are wide and variously designed, with handmade panels. The floors and ceilings are wide and high, made of heart pine lumber. The large doors are made with wooden pegs in place of nails, compactly fitted.

The furniture includes an old grand-father clock standing on the hall floor, a mahogany console with folding top, a hepplewhite table of walnut, four poster beds, an old walnut secretary, a walnut side-board; all handmade. Some of the old relics yet in the family are the old spinning wheel, an old sounding board once used in the first Lutheran Church in the neighborhood, old pictures and steel engravings, one engraving typifying an early Charleston scene. An interesting old library, filled with very old books, most of which are rare volumes, on subjects of law, history, science, philosophy, and other subjects. It was the property of the late Henry Summer, an Attorney of Newberry and a brother of William Summer, the horticulturist.

ROCK HOUSE-located about four miles of the court house, Southeast, to the left at Boozer's (now Long's) place. This is past the old Hartford School site.

A tradition is that the house was built before or during the time of the Rev. War by an early settler as a protection against the Indians. About that time one Joseph Hoffman owned lands thereabouts; then in 1788 Daniel Smith owned the house and the land around it. Smith conveyed it in 1841 to John M. Kinard who willed it to his daughter, Rhoda, who was the wife of John Le Gronne. John Le Gronne and wife conveyed it to H. A. Bailey in 1866. William Boozer was the heir of H. W. Bailey, and came into possession of it later, living there for many years.

The house is built of large pieces of rock, mortified together, with very smooth outer surface. The small windows, and the attic end windows that are small holes, indicate it was built for the purpose of using the attic windows in which to place their guns. The chimneys at the side are also used at the present time, built of solid rocks. The side indicates that at one time a small frame room was built to it but afterwards torn away. There are two rooms down stairs and two upstairs, narrow winding stairway leading on the side to the second story. All the floors and other wood-work show thick, heart pine lumber used in it's construction. The window frames are carved, with double frames, and the joists about three by six inches, hewn with a broadaxe. The wainscoting is very high. Wooden pegs are in all buildings.

At one time an oak grove was around the place, but all the trees have been cleared away. Some old Indian relics have been found nearby, stone axes and arrow heads.

JACOB KIBLER HOME—located about one mile from city limits of Newberry, an the old road leading to the left at Caldwell Street extension, South. It was said to have been built by Jacob Kibler of Newberry and occupied by him and his family for many years.
The date of construction was about 1855-60. After the death of Jacob Kibler, and his family moving to other parts of the county, it was rented to various tenants from time to time. The late U. S. Congressman, Col. George Johnstone, once lived in it. Then, Charles A. Bowman, Assistant Post Master of Newberry, lived awhile in the house. Later, Antoine Buzhardt purchased the place and lived there with his family. The present owner is .... Westwood.
A large two-story house, with double chimneys at each side, a wide front porch, with six large square columns and high banisters, and the upstairs porch being similarily constructed. The porch roof is an extension of the house roof, surrounded with fluted cornices, which gives the old Greek architectural effect. The hall is wide, ceilings high, and rooms large. There is a wide stairway in the hall. In all, though, the design is that of the old South. In the rear is an extension which was added after the house was built, which gives eight rooms and a dining room and kitchen.

PEGGY WILLIAMS HOME—located about sixteen miles West of Newberry, near Mudlic Creek, about a mile to the right of the town of Chappells. It was built by a Mr. De Loach, and later owned by Hopkins Williams, a pioneer from Virginia, but who gave it to his son, William Williams to occupy with his family. Mrs. Peggy Williams, widow of William Williams, lived in it several years. It was built about 1839, the year of it's construction being carved on the side of one of it's chimneys.
The only son of Mrs. Peggy Williams, Belton Williams, was killed in a fight with Jesse Scurry of the same community, near Saluda River. Young Belton never married. After the death of the widow, tenants occupied the home; until it was sold to E. L. Dominick.
It is a two-story house with wide chimneys at each side, painted white, with old-styled green window blinds. The front porch is narrow and square, with small square columns that support the roof of porch extending from the first story. The narrow hall or vestibule shows narrow stairway in the rear, and the side entrance into the living room or parlor. In this room is seen a wide mahogany finished mantel with hand-carved designs on it. All the beadings and the mouldings are wide, with high wainscoting around all the walls. All the lumber is made from heart timber.
Standing some distance from the private roadway, it is seen surrounded with large oaks, evergreens, crepe-myrtle, and other shrubbery.

"HOLLYWODD"—located on the highway going East from Newberry Court House, about seventeen miles, and near Broad River. This home was said to have been built by Walter Goodman, an Irish pioneer from Dublin, Ireland. He built it about 1770, and lived there with his family until his death. Later, it came into the possession of Micajah Suber who lived in it with his family. When the Suber estate was settled the place was sold to Miss. Annie Ruff, of Newberry. Dr. James Ruff and his wife, who was Williameta Henderson, had lived in the house for several years.
A large two-story building with eight rooms; originally built as a small house with a store in front of it which was used, also, as a living room. Dr. Ruff made additions to the house, and discontinued the operation of his store. There are large front and rear rooms, large front and rear piazzas, just as the orginal house had; the building not having been changed in style and frame structure. It has the original hard finish and plastering in the rooms, the old beadings and mouldings of plaster.
A large flower garden and an orchanrd were at one time near the house, but little remaining can be seen.

RENWICK OLD HOME— located about eight miles Northeast of Newberry Court House, on or near the old Whitmire Road. It was the home of Col. John S. Renwick, a prominent planter of his day, and who, according to tradition, originated the idea of changing Due West Female Academy into a regular college. Col. Renwick was a grand-son of Rev. John Renwick, a Scotch Presbyterian Minister who came to America with the Cavenanters.
The house was built about 1846 by Col. John S. Renwick who lived in it until his death in 1889. Later, his son, Dr. M. A. Renwick lived there until his removal to Newberry Court House.

THOMPSON OLD HOME- was located on Caldwell Street, two blocks South of the public square, near the corner of Caldwell and Johnstone Streets. The house was torn down two years ago. It was built about one hundred years ago, probably first used as an inn. It's nearness to the sidewalk and it's large wine-cellar, indicate it's age, that it was built before the streets were widened.

It was said that the DeWalts lived in it a while, and the Webbs, the Thompsons, and others at various times.

A two-story frame building, with narrow front porch, chimneys at each side; and the front steps leading to the ground from the side of the porch. A wide front door and wide hall, with steps under the stairs that lead to the wine-cellar.

MONTGOMERY HOME-located, at first, on College Street, between where is now the new Court House and the Wiseman Hotel (originally called the Crotwell Hotel). About the time the new court house was built, in 1906, the house was moved to it's present location on Harrington Street, and occupied by Dr. C. D. Weeks and family.

The earliest known occupant was the family of John Montgomery, a Jewelry merchant in Newberry, before the War of Seccession. Some of the Montgomery family moved to Arkansas and other States of the Northwest. A Lake family occupied it for a few years; and some of their descendants moved to Florida.

The house has a hall which runs the length of the building, with six rooms on the first floor and bath room, and three rooms, hall and bath room on second floor. It retains much of it's original design and style, though some additions were made by Dr. Weeks. The front porch, both upstairs and down stairs, has the same iron banisters, and same columns of square design, with arched cornices, double windows. Much of the old English style is seen in the building.

THE "L" HOUSE-located on South Main Street, shaped like the letter "L". A very unattractive place now, though with some historical interest. It was built by George Schoppert, a Contractor, who built it for Thomas Waters. It was built out of the lumber that was left over from building the first court house in 1799- about the year 1800 or 1801.

The building is now used as a store on Main Street, it's other "L" extension being on McKibben Street.

Originally, Thomas Waters used it as a store which faced on Main Street, and his home was in the part which faced McKibben Street. After him, the McCreless family lived in it; three of whose sons, John, George, and Lewis moved to another State. At one time, Dr. Long lived in it.

GUSS DICKERT HOME-located about eighteen miles Southeast of Newberry Court House, near Broad River. A typical plantation home of slavery days.

The house was built about 1860 by Hardy Suber. After the death of his wife, Hardy Suber and his brother occupied it a while. Sometime after the war, D. A. Dickert bought it, and lived there. When Col. Dickert moved to Newberry different families occupied it at various times.

The house is located in the midst of large oak trees, which shows evidence of having been at one time surrounded with shrubbery. It had fourteen rooms, a large basement with four rooms being part of it. A solid concrete base is seen in the basement where there are brick walls, plastered, and concrete floors. The first floor hall is wide, and rooms and hall plastered. In the living room (parlor) the ceiling is plastered with attractive beadings and mouldings, in the center of the ceiling an attractive circular design which represents a large flower, and in the center of this a large light globe hangs, typifying a flower-bulb. These designs are moulded in the plastering. The mantels are all wide, made of walnut or heart lumber, having unusual designs on them. The stair-rail is walnut. A long, wide porch is around the house, with boxings that border the roof, similar to the ancient Greek style. The rear entrance has two wide solid stone steps. The hand-made oak sills and put together with wooden pegs, and support the base of the two upper stories. The many columns on the front porch are octagonal in shape and about eight inches at the widest point either way.

"FOREST HILL"-located about thirteen miles from Newberry Court House, near the county highway leading to Jalapa. A very old house almost fallen down for lack of upkeep. It was said to have been built before the year 1800, or about the time of the Rev. War, with large hand-hewn logs.

Andrew Turner moved to this house in 1835, which was probably inherited from his people. His only daughter, Mary Elizabeth Turner, married in 1853 to William Clement Gilliam, and resided there until his death in 1854. His son, William Clement Gilliam, became a practicing physician and settled in Spartanburg, S. C. Later, he located in New York City. Andrew Turner died at this home in 1864. Sometime afterwards, Wallace Riser lived in the house; but after his election as Sheriff of Newberry County and moving to the County seat, other families lived in it from time to time.

The house has two stories, with wide chimney at each side of the house. A small narrow front porch with small square columns that are put together with wooden pegs, is seen. Notwithstanding the present delapidated condition of the house, it shows evidence of having at one time a large back piazza. It is ceiled and weatherboarded, which hides the frame work of hewn logs. The evenly matched lumber of heart pine, and smoothly planed, can yet be seen in some parts of the house.

It is situated on a sloping hill, at one time surrounded with large oaks and some shrubbery; but all have disappeared.

SATTERWHITE OLD HOME—located about 15 miles Northwest of Newberry Court House, near Mudlic Creek. The house was built by a Virginia pioneer, John Satterwhite, who served in the American forces during the Rev. War. This is near the site of the settlement of the first Caldwell family from Virginia. Tradition is that this is part of the original lands of the Caldwells and that William Caldwell at one time lived in a house where this home is located. However, the old Satterwhite home was what is now the rear section of this house, which was later added to. It then went into the possession of Dr. Peter Moon; then the Garlinton's occupied it,(one of Dr. Moon's daughters having married General Ernest A. Garlinton, of the U. S. Army). Whether Michael Satterwhite, son of John, renovated the first house, or Dr. Moon, it is not known.

It is a large fourteen room building, two-stories high. A long porch in the back of the house, now used as a front entrance since the change of the road. The original front porch had a small narrow entrance leading into a small hallway. In the hallway is seen the stairs with dark colored finished railings or banisters, built from heart pine lumber. A door leading into the living room (parlor) shows the interior to have wide vari-colored beadings and mouldings around the walls all of plaster mould of smooth design, representing an ancient Greecian vase upheld by an eagle on either side and filled with flowers and vines falling gracefully to the floor; all of smooth plaster mould. The mantels are wide, uniquely designed and finished in a dark color.

Surrounding the house are evidences of a once attractive flower garden, and the large cedars and evergreens still to be seen. The dense small trees that border the driveway give an impression of it's seclusion.

"LIBERTY HILL"—was the old Rutherford Home, now long since has been burned down. The site of this home is about ten miles Southeast of Newberry on County Highway leading towards Broad River.

The original home was destroyed. The present house was built by former Governor Gist for his son, Richard Gist, the original having been bought by Governor Gist for his son, and thereafter burned.

The original home was a large two-story house, with eight rooms, a narrow front porch and large square colnmns, it carried out the old English Style of Colonial times. The back of the home had two wide porches running the width of the house, one on first floor and other on second floor. They opened into a flower garden which was surrounded by a high iron fence; and there were gravel walks in the garden, leading from the garden. A short distance away were two roads that forked, one going in direction of Strethers and the other towards Maybinton, presumably the old Buncombe Road. On one side of the fork was a flat-iron shaped space, containing an abundance of beautiful shrubbery, large hedges trimmed with arched shapes, and other flowers.

In the home was a velvet carpet and an old and beautiful piano; beds and other furniture; all made of mahogany. A specially carved design on one bed roses at head and foot, was used in guest rooms. The floors were all hardwood.

WEST HOME—located on Calhoun Street, Newberry, near Aveleigh Presbyterian Church. It was built by Samuel P. Boozer about the time of the War Between the States, or just afterwards, and was occupied by him and his family during his life-time. He was a merchant in Newberry, after his retirement from the mercantile business, he was in the insurance business. He married a daughter of Rev. Archibald Montgomery, pastor of the Aveleigh Presbyterian Church. When the home was sold to settle the estate of Mr. Boozer, the late James H. West purchased it, and lived in it until his death.

The house has eleven rooms, being two stories high. The interior work is of poplar, and much of it finished in mahogany, with mahogany beadings, wainscoting, and stair bannisters. The stairs are circular. The floors are all oak. Sliding doors from the wide hall to the front living room. A wide front porch with four large colonial columns of Doric design, with base friezes to match, reach up to the second story roof. This outward appearance gives a colonial style which resembles early American.

The front yard is attractive with large trees, with two magnolias and a tea-tree, and attractive shrubbery. The back yard leads into a private park which extends the length of the lot to the other street. It is attractively laid out, with native trees, and shrubbery.

WRIGHT HOME—located now on Coats Street, near the corner of Boundary. The house was moved from the head of College Street where is now the palatial home of Z. F. Wright.

The old Wright home was owned by Robert Wright, father of Z. F. Wright. Originally, the house was built by John Caldwell, son of William Caldwell, the Rev. War patriot and officer. John Caldwell was a distinguished lawyer in Newberry. He organized the South Carolina Bank, Columbia, S. C., gave up the practice of law, removed to Columbia to take over the position of Cashier of the bank. He erected this house about 1825. After his death some of his children lived in it. In later years it was bought by Robert H. Wright who was the first Cashier of old Newberry Savings Bank.

A two-story house with eight rooms, and a narrow front porch having square columns. The old green blinds to all it's windows, and wide chimneys at the sides of the house, are indicative of pre-Civil War styles. The interior shows a narrow hall or vestibule, with large rooms on each side. The flooring and ceiling are made of heart lumber. All the doors in the house are large. In the living room an unusual design of wall paper attracts the eye, with many brightly covered pictures of different shades, with a dominantly blue shade. The figures in the pictures show old Greecian life, with the Athaenian and it's mountainous background, the fount surrounded with beautiful shrubbery, the Greecian maids, and the great palisades by the sea on which stand the statutes of the ancient goddesses. The paper is said to have been imported from France, and is, evidently, over one hundred years old. The mantels are built with panels that have some hand-carved designs.

CENTRAL HOUSE—once the Pratt home, has been torn down within the last few years. It was a large frame three-story building on the corner of Nance and Friends Streets, and used as a hotel.

It was built by Major Frederick Nance for his daughter who was the wife of Thomas Pratt, a merchant in Newberry; and Thomas Pratt and family later moving into the old Langford home on Boundary Street (now Nesley home), which he built. The rear part of old Central House was the dining room and kitchen of the old Nance home which was burned before 1800. The site of the old Nance home was where it is now the left wing of the Newberry Cotton Mill plant.

In the rear of this old home was once a large vegetable garden which extended all the area of the square except the few frame stores then fronting on Main Street, then called Pratt Street.

About sixty years ago or longer, William A. Fallow lived in it and operated a boarding house. Then, P. A. Lovelace moved into it and, also, operated a boarding house.

PRATT HOME—now the Nesley home, was originally built by Thomas Pratt or his father-in-law, Frederick Nance, and was occupied by Thomas Pratt and family. After the death of Thomas Pratt and his wife, the Rev. John J. Brantley and his wife occupied it during his residence in Newberry; then, in 1875, it was sold to William Langford. When William Langford died his son, Andrew Langford and his family lived there awhile.

A large two-story house, which while the Langfords were living in it, was remodeled. It retains much of the original style and design, however, and the same size. The original house had round post bannisters around the roof; the front porch supported by large columns that were replaced with style columns. The wide front windows, and wide front door, are all constructed with heart lumber.

The magnolia trees in the front yard, other trees, the shrubbery, much of which was planted during the lifetime of Mrs. Pratt, still grows. In the rear of the home, some distance from the house, and to the right, was once a large lake or pond that was built by the Pratts. It was used as a fish pond; and was surrounded with many flowers and a lawn. These have all disappeared, and over the pond-site now is a home.

OLD GRAY HOME-is located about seven miles Southeast of the Court House, on or near the old Pomaria Road, and to the right of Ruff's Store. This is near the first settlement of George Gray, Sr., father of the Rev. War patriot and officer, Major Frederick Gray. After the death of George Gray, Sr. his son, George Gray, Jr. lived in it. It is now called the "Jeff Wicker Place".

A large two-story building with wide chimneys at the sides, a narrow front porch, with medium sized columns, and the rooms unusually large; such was a description of the original house.

DE WALT HOME-located on Main Street, Newberry, has been occupied by the family of Dr. O. B. Mayer, Jr. for several years. Dr. Mayer renovated the old home, building a second story in place of the half-story which was in the original house.

The home was first built by Daniel De Walt, son of Daniel De Walt, Sr. who came from Pennsylvania before the Rev. War. He was a planter and merchant. It was built about 1832. Daniel De Walt died there, and his daughter, Caroline, who married Dr. O. B. Mayer, Sr., lived in it until her death. The original home was Colonial in design, with wide roof, a narrow front porch, square columns; one story and attic rooms. The front porch roof was an extension of the house roof. The original sizes of the rooms have been retained, also the frame work and the hardwood floors. On each side of the wide hall are two large rooms.

The original furniture has been retained by the present occupants who are descendants in the third generation. These include old mahogany pieces, the dining room table, side boards, that were considered the best of that period. The tables were made in banquet style, with wide extensions. The card tables (all mahogany) are located on pedestals, now used as console tables; an old wide "grand-father's clock"; brass fenders and andirons; several steel engravings; a highboy; four-poster beds of solid mahogany. All are a part of the original De Walt furnishings. A sword hangs on the left of the hall near the center, which was worn by John Benedict Mayer, when he was sixteen years old young man in the American Army during the Rev. War. Tradition is that it was taken from a wounded Englishman who, knowing he was going to die, asked young Mayer to get him some water. He got a bucket of water and a gourd for the wounded man who rewarded him by giving him his sword.

HALFACRE HOME-located about five miles East of Newberry Court House. It was built about 1845 by David Halfacre, and is near the old home-site of the Gray family. After a few years, it came into the possession of David Ruff, and after his death his daughter who married Fred Gallman has lived in it.

It is a large two-story house with wide sloping roof. In the front of the home is a flight of steps leading from the gound to the second story piazza, underneath which is the first story piazza. The first story is constructed of brick, and the second story of wood, a heart pine lumber. A basement is bricked and plastered, with concrete floor. The very large sills and other frame work are of heart pine lumber. The doors are wide and heavy, and the windows large.

The large oak trees, the pines, that surround the home and other shrubbery, add to the attractiveness of the place. Originally, there were many cedar trees on each side of a long walk leading to the vegetable garden, and which has disappeared.

HARRINGTON HOME-now occupied by the widow of the late J. William White, is located about two blocks from the public square, on Caldwell Street, and in front of the Central Methodist Church. It was built before the War Between the States by Judge J. B. O'Neall for his son-in-law, Dr. William Henry Harrington.

Before the house was completely remodeled, after the war, (originally built in 1830), it presented many of the early colonial designs both the interior and the exterior. The wide chimneys are yet seen at each side of the building, the wide windows and the large sloping roof. The doors retain their original width and thickness, with many of the early English styles of brass door-knobs and locks. The stairway is mahogany. The moulding around the ceilings are of plaster; the hall ceiling still possesses the original circular design of plaster mould. The high arched windows at the rear of the hall, at top of the first stair-landing, is one of the original designs.

The front yard which is now a level green lawn, was once shaded with large trees.

CHAPMAN HOME-located on College Street, was formerly occupied by John A. Chapman, and later by his son, John W. Chapman and family. It is owned by Frank Sutton who has converted it into an apartment house (1847).

Originally, the house was a two-story structure, setting on a lot where is now the Speer's Street School. It was built by Young John Harrington about the year 1818, who never occupied it, but sold it to Dr. Burr Johnstone who lived in it until his removal to Alabama in 1840. Dr. Johnstone sold the house in 1841 to Robert Harrington, who, in 1851, sold it to Col. Simeon Fair. In that year Col. Fair moved the house to where it is now located, raising it off the ground and building a brick first story under it, thus making it three stories high.

At it's old location Col. Fair erected a large two-story stone building which was occupied by his son-in-law, Col. William Drayton Rutherford. After the death of Col. Rutherford, in the Confederate Army, his widow married again to Young John Pope, a lawyer of Newberry, who, later became Chief Justice of the State Supreme Court. This building is now the Speer's Street School.

The three-story building on College Street has wide fireplaces and mantles. The large square columns without reaching up to the third floor, indicates the orgininal Gothic style even though the columns support each floor of the piazzas.

A few remaining oldtime shrubs can be seen in the yard, with large trees.

ROBERT STEWART HOME-is located at the corner of Johnstone and Wilson Streets. It was built about 1835, by Robert Stewart, a merchant in Newberry, and occupied by him and his family. After the death of Robert Stewart the home was sold, and has been occupied by many families since that time.

The house is a frame structure, two stories high, with six rooms on the first floor and four rooms on the second floor. The hall is very wide, the front is used as a reception room. All rooms have large windows, much like the old English style. The interior is finished with heart pine lumber, with few unusual designs. The front porch is narrow, giving a square appearance, with four large square columns reaching from the base of the porch to the roof of the second porch, but connecting with second floor porch. A small alcove or room projects from left side of the first-story, which originally had steps leading to the large flower garden.

He owned all the land on the square, his home at that time being the only one on it; so that the flower garden extended from Friend Street and back to Holcombe Street, to Johnstone Street. The barns were located on Holcombe Street, where he kept many fine race horses; his large vegetable garden being in the rear of his home. The flower garden was made with circular walks that were bordered with small evergreens around the beds of a variety of shrubs and flowers. A terrace was built about one-half way to Friend Street, with grass, and a walk leading down into the "Sunken Garden", which, too, had a variety of flowers, water-lillies, jonquils, daffodils, and others. In the center of the whole garden plot was a Summer House with shaded seats, the shade being produced by overhanging vines and tree limbs. (This description was made by an elderly widow who remembered the place as a young girl).

A near tragedy occured in this home in 1853. A mulatto slave girl who was a servant in the home, became enamoured with a white man from the North, who was staying with the family.

The young man in turn was attracted to the girl. She consented to runaway with him; but the affair was broken up by members of the family. The mulatto girl became enraged and tried to poison the family by preparing a poison and putting it into the drinking water. All the family became extremely ill; but they all got well except Mrs. Stewart's sister who died as the results of the poison. The girl after a brief trial was hanged on the outskirts of town.

LEAVELL HOME-located some distance from Boundary Street, in the western part of the city, in "Gilder's Crest", is now owned by Otto Armfield, Editor and owner of The Sun paper in Newberry. Previous to this, the late James R. Leavell owned it and lived there. In the settlement of the estate of Mr. Leavell, the late Dr. James K. Gilder bought the property.

The house was built about 1860 by William Nance, son of Major Frederick Nance, of Newberry; then after his death it is said that his brother, Robert Nance, lived in it for a while; then it was owned and occupied by Mr. Joiner, of Charleston, S. C., who sold it to James R. Leavell.

Originally, the property included all the square, having a large frontage with a large shaded grove of pines, oaks and much shrubbery, on a gently sloping hillside. When lots were sold on Boundary Street frontage and a new street was cut through running just in front of the home much of the shrubbery disappeared.

The house has eight rooms, two stories, with four large Colonial columns in front extending from bases on the ground floor to the roof of the second floor. In all, it has a distinct Doric style of architecture. The front door is double with colored glasses that represents a variety of flowers showing large round pedals. The hall is wide, the stairs circular, with attractively finished mahogany bannisters. The reception room is large with plaster mould beading.

WICKER HOME-is located on Boundary Street, just over the concrete overhead bridge. Has been occupied by the J. H. Wicker family for many years; prior to which at least two families occupied it: Mr. Randle, a relative of late Silas Johnstone, and Mr. H. C. Robertson who was General Manager of the Newberry Cotton Mills (he came to Newberry from Charleston in 1884).

The house was built by Dr. Pressley B. Ruff, a distinguished physician in Newberry before and during the period of the War Between the States. This would make its date of construction sometime between 1850 and 1855.

A large two-story edifice, of solid brick, it has fourteen rooms. All the interior of the house has been plastered, a new basement built by Mr. Wicker. The exterior is attractive with it's large Colonial columns of Doric design that extends from the base to the roof of the second story. A balustrade is in front of the upstairs front door, with black iron railings of unusual designs. The iron railings were put there by Mr. Wicker who bought them from the Moses estate. (The old Moses home had them, which was torn down in order that the new Floyd Home could be built on the same spot).

It is said that the brick in the house is of the best quality and were made from soil on the same lot.

Attractive shrubbery surrounds the house, with large oaks on each side of the concrete walk. Elms and magnolias covered with green ivy, around which are also circular concret walks, which adds to it's attractiveness.

SOME BIOGRAPHIES OF NEWBERRY CITIZENS—
PAST AND PRESENT—WHOSE RECORDS ARE ABSENT OR INCOMPLETE
IN OTHER HISTORIES.

HUGH KING BOYD- born in Newberry County, South Carolina, on July 7, 1878; son of Calhoun F. and Elizabeth (Wilson) Boyd, of Newberry County. His father was for many years County Treasurer of Newberry County; and his grand-father, for whom he was named, was the County Ordinary for several terms.

After attending the schools in his neighborhood he attended the City Schools, and graduated at Newberry College in 1899, with the degree of A. B. After completing a Business Administration course at Eastman Business College, he attend Tulane University of Medicine, New Orleans, Louisiana, where he received the degree of M. D. in the year 1906.

Returning to Newberry he located at the town of Whitmire and practiced his profession for several years. In 1914, his health becoming impaired, he retired to his farm where he remained until 1919. Being offered a position with the Glenn-Lowery Company in it's clerical department he worked with them until 1923.

In 1924 he was elected Clerk of Court for Newberry County, and has been elected since then for each consecutive term. In 1926-28 he was Chairman of the County Democratic Committee. He was an Elder in the A. R. P. Church, and Clerk of the Board.

He married February 1, 1908, at Greenwood, South Carolina, to Miss. Elizabeth Child, daughter of Dr. R. A. and Essie (Holcomb) Child.

DR. THOMAS C. BROWN—born in Newberry County, at the Brown home on the Buncombe Road, opposite the old Joseph Caldwell home, on May 29, 1836; son of Thomas Jefferson and Anna (Chapman) Brown. He was educated at Mount Bethel Academy, and later graduated at Erskine College, Due West, S.C. After completing his course in medicine, he volunteered his service in the Confederate Army, and was appointed Surgeon of his regiment.

After serving through the war, he settled on his farm in Newberry County. After the days of misrule during the reconstruction period, he was elected to the State Legislature from Newberry County. Later, about 1880, he was elected State Senator. During his term as Senator he became stricken with paralysis; but his condition did not keep him from his active interest in public life.

Dr. Brown was a Ruling Elder in King's Creek Presbyterian Church. After years years being stricken he died at his home on June 26, 1891, and was buried at King's Creek Cemetery.

DR. WILSON CALDWELL BROWN—born in Newberry County in the Mount Bethel community on February 3, 1861; son of Col. J. C. S. Brown. The old Brown homestead, originally owned by the Rev. War patriot, Sims Brown, is still standing, on the left of the highway leading to Strother's Station on Broad River. He was educated in the schools of his community, and in 1877 he entered Erskine College, Due West, S. C., where he graduated in 1882, with the A. B. Degree.

During the reign of the carpet-baggers in the State, and at the age of 14, he became a member of the local rifle club, a vigilant organization, the duty of which was to suppress disorder and maintain peace. This required great activity at night time, for it was then that the fiends perpetuated the most intolerable deeds, such as attacks upon homes, burning them, stealing livestock, and various other thefts. John C. Brown, brother of Wilson C. Brown, was the leader in the organization which included such young men as J. C. Brown, C. D. Buzhardt, Joseph Goree, W. A. Chalmers, William Sondley, "Big" John Wilson, Wilson C. Brown, and S. S. Cunningham.

After graduating from College he clerked awhile at the store of Edward Scott, in Newberry, until December 24, 1882; then he went to his father's farm and worked until October 1, 1883; when he took charge of Mount Bethel School and taught there until June, 1884.

He studied medicine under the late Dr. O. B. Mayer, Jr. in Newberry until October 1, 1884, when he entered the South Carolina Medical College, Charleston, S. C., and graduated there in 1887 with the degree of M. D.

He began to practice in his county, but practiced only seven years, when his health failed and he was forced to give up his practice. During the next four years he farmed and gradually regained his health; but continued work on his farm, giving up altogether his career as a physician

Dr. Brown has filled many public positions of trust in his county and community: for several years he was President of the Southern Cotton Association, President of the Farmers's Union, President of the Farmers's Alliance, and the State Cotton Holding Association. For sometime he served as Chairman of the County Equalization Board-about sixteen years-and of the Township Board for thirty four years. During the construction of the new Bethel-Germany School he was Chairman of the Board of Trustees and Acting Chairman of the School Building Committee. He has served, too, as Township Commissioner. During the years that followed, he served for sometime as President of the Farmers' Mutual Fire Insurance Company, of Newberry County. He is a member of the Associate Reformed Presbyterian Church.

JAMES FITZ JAMES CALDWELL—born in Newberry County on September 19, 1837; son of Chancellor James J. Caldwell and Nancy (McMorris) Caldwell, of Newberry. He received his early education in the Newberry schools, and then attended the South Carolina College, Columbia, from which he graduated in 1857. He studied law under General James Simons of Charleston, S. C., and was admitted to the Bar of South Carolina in 1859. Later, he went to Berlin, Germany, and studied several months.

When the War Between the States started he volunteered for service in the Confederate Army; served as an Officer; and wounded in battle. After the war, he returned to Newberry and began the practice of law.

He soon became recognized as a well informed Constitutional lawyer in the State. He served as Attorney for the old National Bank of Newberry; Chairman of the County Democratic Executive Committee from it's organization in 1860 until it's reorganization in 1876, and then as Chairman from 1877 to 1880. He became special Attorney for the Richmond and Danville Railroad Company, and for many large civil cases in the State and County Courts.

He married in 1875 to Rebecca C. Conner of Abbeville District. He died on February 5, 1925, in the city of Newberry; and is buried at Rosemont Cemetery.

He was a man of letters, too, being the author of several articles and books. He wrote the "History of McGowan's Brigade", (Snowden's History of South Carolina, under the caption, "Rem. of the War of Seccession" Chap. Llll, p. 822, refers to this work).

MILTON ANDERSON CARLISLE-born September 7, 1841; son of Thomas A. and Kitty F. (Teagle) Carlisle, and grand-son of Rev. Coleman Carlisle, a pioneer Methodist minister of South Carolina.

He attended the Union County schools; entered the South Carolina College, Columbia, S. C., but left in his Senior year to joing the college cadet corps in the Confederate Army. He was sent to Charleston, S. C. ; then returned to college after Fort Sumter surrendered. In the Spring of 1862 he joined Company E. , Palmetto Battalion, and became it's Agent, then Ordnance Officer.

After the war was over he studied law in Mississippi, and was admitted to the bar in that State, 1868. He returned to South Carolina in 1874, where he was admitted to the bar, and set up a law office in Newberry, becoming a leading lawyer. He was, too, interested in farming, having owned and operated a large farm near the city.

He was actively interested in the growth and development of the city; gave his time to much of it's improvement. He served several years as President of the National Bank of Newberry, a director of the Board of Newberry Cotton Mills, and other organizations.

He married April 26, 1874 to Mrs. Rosa (Renwick) McMorris, of Newberry County. They had four children.

DR. RICHARD C. CARLISLE—born in Union County, South Carolina, on December 5, 1835; son of Thomas A. and Kitty F. (Teagle) Carlisle. He married to Elizabeth Renwick on September 18, 1869; she was a daughter of John Simpson Renwick of Newberry County, and wife, Mary (Toland) Renwick.

After attending the schools of his Community , he attended South Carolina Military Academy, at Charleston, S. C., where he graduated. Then, he attended the New York Medical Institute, of the New York University, and graduated in medicine.

Returning to his home in Union County, he was appointed Assistant Surgeon in the Confederate States Army; sent to Richmond where he served in the Thornbury and Bonner Hospital. His assignment was with the Seventh S. C. Regiment of Infantry of Kershaw' Brigade. Later, he was promoted to Surgeon of that regiment, and served until the surrender at Greensboro, N. C. At the reorganization of General Johnston's army he was appointed Surgeon of the Seventh and Fifteenth Regiments. He engaged in twenty eight battles and fights, from Gettysburg to Chicamauga; left in charge of a military hospital in Maryland, captured by the enemy, and imprisoned at Baltimore, until he was released through exchange of prisoners.

After the war he pursued his practice of medicine, successfully, in Newberry County. Also, he became interested in many enterprises in and near Newberry. He was a director in the old National Bank of Newberry, in the Newberry Savings Bank, the Newberry Cotton Mills, and the Newberry Cotton Seed Oil Mill. He never sought political office, though often taking an interest in politics; a member of the Newberry County Democratic Club. He was an active member of the Associate Reformed Presbyterian Church.

He died at his home about eight miles from Newberry County Court House, on August 19, 1906.

LEVI CASEY—born sometime before the Rev War; served in that war, first as Lieutenant in militia, in which he commanded the capture of General William Cunningham(" Bloody Bill") and his tory troops in their retreat towards Enoree River. He became a Captain, and then a Brigidier-General in the American Army.

He was one of Commissioners to lay off the new counties that were cut from the old districts, in the year 1783. He and Col. Philemon Waters were appointed from the territory which then included Newberry County. He was one of first Justices in the county, in 1?65. In 1792 he was elected a member of the House of Representatives from Newberry County, and in 1800 he was elected State Senator. In the year 1802 he was elected to the United States Congress from this district, where he served several terms.

He died at Newberry Court House; the date of his death and the his burial place are not known. He left a family.

ANDERSON CRENSHAW—born in Newberry District, South Carolina; son of Charles and Eunice (White) Crenshaw, who had moved from Virginia, and settled near Kings Creek, in Newberry District. His basic education was obtained from old Mount Bethel Academy, near his home. Later, he attended South Carolina College where he graduated in 1806, being the first graduate of that College (now State University). He studied law with Judge Nott, and admitted to the bar of South Carolina.

In 1815 he married Mary Chiles of Abbeville District; and continued to live at Newberry until 1819 or '20 when he moved to Alabama, where he practiced law. In 1821 he was elected Circuit Judge of that State; then, when the Chancery Court of that State was established, he was elected Chancery of the Equity Court there, serving ssveral terms. " He displayed by his deliberateness in drawing conclusions a keen sense of justice and powers of discrimination."

One of his hobbies or pleasures was the reading of the classics; he was a good shakespearain scholar and reader, and delighted in it's characters; loved all classic literature.

He died in the year 1847, after having served twenty six years in judicial positions.

DR. GEORGE BENEDICT CROMER—born Newberry County, in Cromer Township, near Duncan's Creek, on October 3, 1857; son of Thomas Hoard Cromer and Mary M. (Rhiddlehuber) Cromer, of Newberry County. His father was a planter and merchant, four of whose sons served in the Confederate Army.

After receiving his preliminary education in the schools of his community, and in the preparatory school taught by Thomas H. Duckett and Rev. L. K. Glasgow, he attended Newberry College. He graduated from Newberry College in 1877, as first honor student, with the degree of A. B. From 1877 to 1881 he was a member of the faculty of Newberry College, during which time the degree of M. A. was conferred on him by the College. Then, he studied law under the late George Johnstone of Newberry, and was admitted to the bar of South Carolina in December, 1881. The next fourteen years he was the law partner of Col. George Johnstone, a well-known Civil and Criminal lawyer of the State and former member of the United States Congress.

In January, 1896, he was called to the Presidency of Newberry College, which position he filled with distinction for eight years. In June, 1904, he resumed the practice of law at Newberry, and was appointed District Counsel for the Southern Railway Company. He was elected Mayor of Newberry for several terms; from 1915 to 1919 he was Chairman of the State Board of Charities and Corrections; and 1917-18 he was Chairman of the Red Cross Drive in Newberry.

He was the first Chairman of the Board of Trustees of Newberry County Hospital, and was one of the active workers in getting the hospital started. For many years a Deacon and the Chairman of the Council of the Lutheran Church of the Redeemer. Dr. Cromer never sought political office, though he was often asked to do so.

In the year 1901, while President of Newberry College, Wittenberg College and also Muhlenberg College conferred on him the honorary degree of Doctor of Laws.

Dr. Cromer was married twice: first, to Carolyn Julia Motte, of Newberry, on October 11, 1883, who died April 26, 1888; his second wife was Susan Bittle, of Virginia, whom he married on November 27, 1890, who died December 1, 1911. He died at his home in Newberry on September 25, 1935; and is buried at Rosemont Cemetery.

J. MARION DAVIS—born at Newberry, S. C. about 1874; son of George and .... Davis, of Helena, S. C. He attended the local schools a few years, which was the extent of his education. As a very young man he applied for and got a position in the Newberry Cotton Mills as a "Bobbin boy". Possessing unusual ambition, and aptness, he studied at home while holding down his mill job, and received training in English, Mathmatics and textile manufacturing work—basically a self-made man.

He was rapidly promoted in his work, becoming a Second Boss, then Foreman, in one of the departments of the mill. Later, when the Superintendent resigned he was appointed to that position which he held until his death.

He was honored many times by the people of the city. He was elected Mayor, in which he served several terms. He was, also, a member of the Board of Trustees of the City Schools, and Chairman of the Board. Active in civial and fraternal works in the city. A member of the Board of Trustees of the Newberry County Hospital; appointed a member of several committees that were for the good of the community. President of the Newberry Chamber of Commerce for several terms. He was a Deacon in the West End Baptist Church, Superintendent of the Sunday School, and Chairman of the Church Council. Member of the Newberry Country Club, the Kiwanis Club. He was appointed Colonel on the Governor's Staff.

He died at his home in Newberry on April 14, 1933; and is buried at Rosemont Cemetery.

DR. PETTUS GRAY ELLISOR—born at Newberry on June 2, 1869; son of Thomas and Elsie Susan (De Walt) Ellisor, of Newberry County. He received his schooling at Newberry, then Newberry College. After leaving college he entered the drug business in Newberry, where he worked for three years. In 1890 he attended the University of Virginia, and later the South Carolina Medical College, Charleston, S. C., where he graduated with the degree of M. D., fourth in his class, in year 1892.

He began his practice of medicine in the city of Newberry, and continued until until his death on August 14, 1922. He married in January, 1903, to Janie Farrer Vance, of Clinton, S.C

He was a member of the South Carolina Medical Association, and one time it's Vice-President; a member of the Newberry County Medical Association; member of the County Board of Health; and Chairman of that Board for several years.

He was interested in Civic affairs, and community development, including that of the health of the people. He was appointed local Surgeon for the Southern Railway Company, which position he held during his lifetime. A member of the Sons of Confederate Veterans, he served on the staff of Col. Walter H. Hunt, the Commander of the Division of Confederate Veterans, in 1891.

SIMEON FAIR—born Newberry County on his father's farm near Prosperity, on November 17, 1801; son of William Fair and wife; he being a son of Samuel Fair, a settler from County Antrim, Ireland, about 1772.

After receiving his education in the local schools he prepared for law and was admitted to the bar of South Carolina in 1824. He became a law partner of John Caldwell, Esq. He became known as a highly esteemed lawyer, and much of his time devoted to court pleadings.

When the Seminole Indian War started in Florida, he volunteered for service, made Lieutenant, and served until the end of the war. Returing home he resumed his law practice; was elected a member of the State Legislature, serving two terms. In 1846, he was elected Solicitor of the Middle Circuit Court, and held that office until 1868.

He was a Democrat of the Jeffersonian type and of the Calhoun School, a friend to the Union as long as State's Rights were recognized. In 1850 he was inclined towards many union opinions, opposed the breaking up of the union; but in 1860 he became a secessionist, and was one of those who signed the Ordnance of Seccession.

Col. Fair was one of the promoters of the Columbia and Greenville Railroad. He was , too, one of the promoters of and organizers of Newberry College; and the land on which the college stands was conveyed by him to the Trustees of the College.

In the year 1870, he became conspicious in the State in the reform movement in South Carolina, being, also, active in the Presidential campaign of 1872.

He was married December 23, 1840, to Mary Butler Pearson, of Newberry. She died December 31, 1867. Col. Fair died at Glenn Springs, S. C. on July 15, 1873. Both are buried at Rosemont Cemetery, Newberry.

DR. J. WILLIAM FOLK—born Newberry County, near Pomaria, on January 1, 1852; son of Levi and Elizabeth (Counts) Folk. He attended the schools of that section, then Newberry College and Wofford College. He graduated at the South Carolina College of Medicine, Charleston, S. C. in 1874. He located in his home county of Newberry where he practicied for a short time; then, he was appointed Assistant Surgeon at the United States Marine Hospital, Georgetwon, S. C., where he served over twenty five years. He resigned his commission and returned to Newberry, and began practice at his home at Jalapa. Soon thereafter he retired from active practice, devoting his time to farming.

In 1918 he was elected a member of the State Legislature; active member of the Democratic Club, and member of the County Democratic Committee. He was interested in all affiars that affected the cotton planter.

He married, first, to Hattie Fogle, and, second, to Beulah Smith. He had the unique distinction of being the father of fourteen children, ten girls and four boys.

DR. ELI GEDDINGS—born in Newberry District in 1799, about two miles North of the Court House. He was educated at the schools in Newberry; largely reared by his protege, Major Frederick Gray. No doubt he attended the old Mount Bethel Academy. After completing his school work, he studied medicine at the Charleston Medical College, from which he received his M. D. Degree in 1825. He located, first, at Abbeville, S. C.; but soon afterwards removed to Charleston, and parcticed. He studied in Paris and London. In 1828 he opened a private medical school at Charleston, S. C. in which he instructed in Anatomy and Surgery. In 1831 he was elected Professor of Anatomy and Physiology in the Medical Department of the University of Maryland, at Baltimore. During his services there he edited the Baltimore Medical Journal. In 1837 he was called to the Charleston Medical College, Charleston, S. C., to fill the chair of Anatomy and Medical Jurisprudence. In Charleston, he continued to teach and practice until 1858, when he resigned temporarily.

He was appointed Surgeon in the Confederate where he served until the end of the war. After the war he resumed his work as Professor at the Charleston Medical College. He was a frequent contributor to Medical Journals.

DR. EDWIN O. HENTZ—born near Pomaria, Newberry County, June 12, 1864; son of William R. and Ann (Cromer) Hentz, of Newberry County.

He attended the Pomaria Schools, then Newberry College where he graduated in 1885, with the degree of A. B. After graduation he went to the South Carolina Medical College, Charleston, S. C., where he received his M. D. Degree in 1889. He returned to Pomaria, where he practiced for several years.

He was active in church and school works in his commmnity; a member of the Board of Trustees of Mt. Zion Academy; Deacpn in the St. Matthews Lutheran Church. He was elected a member of the Board of Trustees of Newberry College, in which capacuity he served for several years.

Dr. Hentz married in 1890 to Frances Caldwell, daughter of Edward Caldwell and ....(Mars) Caldwell. (she was a native of Abbeville County). They moved to the City of Newberry in 1920, where he continued his practice until his death a few years later.

EDWARD R. HIPP-born near Pomaria, Newberry County, August 29, 1855; son of George and Martha (Summer) Hipp. He received a good grammar school education from the schools of his section. Early in life he started work as a salesman, later establishing a mercantile business of his own.

He married March 1, 1886 to Mary Holloway, daughter of Col. Thomas W. and Martha (Folk) Holloway, of Pomaria. Later, he moved to the city of Newberry and started a business. He was interested in civic and industrial developments of the city; active in Chamber of Commerce work; a director in the Exchange Bank of Newberry; member of the City Board of Health. He was elected President of the Exchange Bank, which position he held until his death at his home in Newberry on June 24, 1910.

He was an active member of the Lutheran Church of the Redeemer, and a member of the Board of Deacons; active for many years in fraternal organization work.

WALTER HERBERT HUNT-born in Newberry on April 16, 1861; son of Walter Herbert and Susan (McCaughrin) Hunt of Newberry. His mother was a daughter of Thomas McCaughrin. He attended Newberry Male Academy, then Newberry College where he completed the Sophomore class; left college to study law in a private law office in Newberry. He was admitted to the bar of South Carolina on May 29, 1883; began the practice of law at Newberry.

He soon became recognized as a lawyer of ability. He never sought public office. He was Attorney for several large coporations, including two Newberry Banks, the Newberry Cotton Mills, the Oakland Mill, and three Building and Loan Associations.

From 1882 to 1888 he was Secretary of the Newberry County Democratic Executive Committee. Afterwards, he served as a Director on the Boards of the Commercial Bank, the Security Loan and Investment Company, the Newberry Cotton Mills, the Oakland Mill, and the Mollohon Manufacturing Company. As one of the principle organizers of the Oakland Cotton Mill plant, (now a unit of the Kendall Mills Corporation), he was elected it's first President and Treasurer, and served in that Capacity until his death. Meanwhile, he had organized and established the law firm of Hunt, Hunt and Hunter (his brother I. H. Hunt, and James B. Hunter.)

Col. Hunt served on the staff of Governor Hugh Thompson as Lieutenant Colonel. He was appointed Special Judge in several Circuit Courts in the State.

He married February 23, 1887, to Lucy W. Baxter, daughter of James M. Baxter, a Lawyer of Newberry. He died in Newberry and is buried at Rosemont Cemetery.

ALAN JOHNSTONE, SR.-born in Newberry August 12, 1849; son of Job Johnstone and Almira Amelia (DeWalt) Johnstone. He attended the schools of Newberry, then Newberry College and the University of Virginia. He married Lilla R. Kennerly, daughter of Dr. Thomas B. and Martha Kennerly, of Newberry District, on November 25th, 1875.

He devoted his life to agriculture and to public service. He was elected a member of the Board of Trustees of Clemson College on it's founding in 1892; elected a member of the State Legislature from Newberry County in 1807, and served several years; from 1909 a member of the State Senate, serving until his retirement in 1928. He became Chairman of the Board of Trustees of Clemson College in 1917; elected President Pro Tem of the State Senate in 1918.

He served as an Elder in the Aveleigh Presbyterain Church in Newberry for several years. He died at his home in Newberry on January 5, 1919, and is buried at the Johnstone Cemetery near Newberry.

DR. THOMAS B. KENNERLY-born in Lexington District, near Dreher Shoals, November 19, 1821, he was educated at the schools in his neighborhood and at Cokesbury Institute in Abbeville District. He read medicine in offices of Dr. Wells and Dr. Fair, Columbia, S. C.; then he graduated in medicine from the Medical University of the City of New York in 1845. He settled in Newberry District, in the Long Lane section, where he married Martha Brown, daughter of Richard Samuel and Margareta (Law) Brown, in December, 1850. He practiced medicine in Newberry County until his death in October, 1884. Children: S. Edward Kennerly; Lilla R. Kennerly; Samuel B. Kennerly; Margaret Law Kennerly; James L. Kennerly; Amelia K. Kennerly.

He was a member of Mt. Tabor Methodist Church, Newberry County. He is buried at King's Creek Cemetery.

ALAN JOHNSTONE, JR.-born at Newberry, S. C. on July 11, 1890; son of Alan Johnstone, Sr. and Lilla (Kennerly) Johnstone. He attended the public schools of Newberry, then Newberry College, from which he received the A.B. Degree in 1910. After two years of post-graduate work at the University of South Carolina, he received both the A. M. and the LL. B. Degrees, year 1912. From 1912 to 1913 he pursued special course at Harvard University. He was admitted to the bar of South Carolina in 1912.

He located for the practice of law at Columbia, S. C. He was elected a member of the State Legislature from Richland County. He acted as Commissioner or representative of the Commission on Training Camp activities of the War and Navy Departments, 1917-1919. From 1919 to 1929, he was Director of the Baltimore Criminal Justice, Baltimore, Md. From 1932 to 1934, he served as State Director of Federal Relief; then, as Field Representative of the FERA, the CWA, and the WPA.

He was admitted to the bar of Georgia in 1918; to the Maryland bar in 1920; and to the bar of the United States Supreme Court in 1918.

While still holding a responsible Federal Position at Washington, he maintains his home in Newberry, the old Colonial home of his grand-father, Chancellor Job Johnstone.

He married Lalla Rook Simmons, daughter of the late J. W. M. Simmons and Lalla (Rook) Simmons.

JOHN MALCOLM JOHNSTONE-born at Newberry in November, 1847; son of Chancellor Job Johnstone, and his wife, Almira Amelia (DeWalt) Johnstone; lived in Newberry. He was educated at private schools in Newberry, and at Newberry College and the University of Virginia. He was First Lieutenant in the Confederate States Army, 1861-1865. Elected to the State Legislature from Newberry County, 1890-'92. He was appointed Consul to Brazil at Paramaribo, 1894-'97. He never married; died at Newberry on February, 1904; buried at old Johnstone Family Graveyard.

GEORGE JOHNSTONE-born at Newberry in April, 1845; son of Chancellor Job and Almira Amelia (DeWalt) Johnstone. He was educated at Newberry College and at the South Carolina Military Academy, Charleston, S. C. He served as a soldier in the Confederate Army, 1861-'65. He attended the University of Edinburg, Scotland, where he graduated in 1870. He was admitted to the bar of South Carolina in 1870. Member of U. S. Congress 1890-'92. He practiced law in Newberry until his death in April, 1921. He is buried at the old Johnstone Family Graveyard.

LAMBERT JEFFERSON JONES-second son of Elijah and Anne Jones; was born July 17, 1813, in Newberry. He was a Quaker, his ancestors coming from Philadelphia.

After the death of his parents, when he was about five years of age, he was reared by a guardian, Judge John Belton O'Neall, also a Quaker, and a noted Judge and Chief Justice of the Supreme Court of South Carolina, in the latter's home at "Springfield", two miles West of Newberry Court House.

He was educated at the academies in Newberry and Greenville Counties, and at Charleston College; then, at Brown University, Providence, Rhode Island, graduating from the latter in three years (1837), with distinction. He was a member of the Phi Betta Kappa Society, which was introduced into the College by Thomas Jefferson, third president of the United States.

After graduation, he studied law for two years under Hon. Thomas H. Pope and Judge J.B. O'Neall, and was admitted to the bar of South Carolina. He held the office of Master in Equity for three years; twice a member of the State Legislature; Trustee of the Newberry Male and Female Academy; Trustee of Newberry College; a Director and Attorney for the Newberry National Bank (then known as the Newberry Bank), for several years.

He married March 16, 1842 to Mary Eliza McHardy, daughter of Robert McHardy and Carolina E. (Williams) McHardy, of St. Augustine, Florida, in the home of Judge John B. O'Neall. Judge O'Neall was, also, the guardian of Eliza McHardy, who was born August 10, 1822, in Newberry County. She was 20 years old and her husband 29 when they married. They had five sons and three daughters.

Shortly after their marriage, he bought the old Colonial home of Chancellor Caldwell, which was located on what was later known East Main Street, Newberry. He acquired considerable wealth and property. When the Confederate War started he owned 35 slaves, personal property and real estate.

Lambert Jefferson Jones practiced law in Newberry for 54 years, from the year 1839. He confined his practice chiefly to Civil cases, but at intervals took on Criminal cases. During these 54 years he was the senior member of the firm of Jones, Jones, and Mower, (these were his eldest son, Benson M. Jones, and his Son-in-law, George S . Mower). Later, after the death of his son, Benson Miles Jones, and the withdrawal of George S . Mower, the firm consisted of Jones and Jones (Lambert Jefferson Jones and another son, Lamber W. Jones), which partnership continued for seventeen years, from the time Lambert W. Jones was admitted to the bar in 1877 until the death of Lambert Jefferson Jones in 1894.

In 1860, Major Jones made an extended visit to England, Ireland, and Scotland, visiting the family brother-in-law, Admiral John Bonnemaison Bunch McHardy, of the English Navy, at Chelmsford, near London, spending considerable time with them.

Lambert Jefferson Jones was appointed "Major" in the Calvary of the State Militia by Governor A. G. Magrath, of South Carolina, and served about ten or twelve years before the War Between the States started. During the war, he was aid-de-camp to Governor McGrath. Although being over age for active service(48 years), and not accepted, he later volunteered and was assigned to the Coast Guard Defense opposite Charleston, South Carolina. He was given the Confederate Cross.

Major Jones and his wife celebrated their Golden Wedding Anniversary on March 16, 1892. They entertained nine daughters and sons and daughters-in-law and sons-in-law, together with nine grandsons and nine granddaughters in their home for one day and one night. One of the most interesting happenings (related by a memmer of the family) was the distribution among the children and grand-children, of a Golden Wedding Badge, made up a golden yellow ribbon having a gold dollar fastened to the center and the name of the husband and wife, with the date of the wedding printed on the badge streamers. A number of the old family mementoes were also distributed.

Major Jones died July 15, 1894, and was buried on his 81 st birthday, July 17, 1894, in the family plot in Rosement Cemetery, Newberry.

JESSE YOUNG JONES-born in Jack's Township, Laurens County, South Carolina, on October 31, 1876; son of ...., and grand-son of Lewis D. and Susannah (Dalrymple) Jones. He attended rural schools; after he removed to Newberry, he received private instruction to improve his education . His parents moved in 1885 to the Newberry Cotton Mills, and there he got his first job, in year 1886.

He married Sarah De Vore, of Ninety Six, S. C., on January 30, 1901; and had several children. He was promoted from time to time in the mill, to second boss, then to overseer in the spinning department. Under an appointment by the civil service he served few months as rural letter carrier at Newberry, but returned to his old job. He was appointed overseer of the spinning department in 1906, which he held until June 1, 1933, at which time he was elected Superintendent of the mill. In 1940, when the plant was sold to northern interests and his health began to fail, he resigned.

In 1914 he was elected a member of the Board of Trustees of the Newberry City Schools, being a member over twenty two years, serving during the latter years as Chairman of the Board.

As a member of the West End Baptist Church, he served as a member of the Board of Deacons. In 1914 he was made Clerk of the Reedy River Baptist Association, and served in that capacity for eighteen years; and served as Moderator of the Association.

He was elected President of the Newberry Chamber of Commerce on April 1, 1936. A member of the Odd Fellows Lodge, having been Grand Master of South Carolina, and a representative to the Sovereign Grand Lodge at Philadelphia in 1926, and at Indiannapolis, Indiana, in 1930. A member of the Amity Lodge of Free Masons; he was elected Master of the lodge in 1921; and member of the Oriental Council, the Newberry Commandary No. 6, the Knights Templar, and Hajez Temple, Nobles of the Mystic Shrine. He never offered for any political office.

ARTHUR KIBLER-born in Newberry County, November 28, 1859; son of Jacob and Frances E. Kibler. He attended the schools of his community; and entered Newberry College, from which he graduated in 1884 with the degree of A. B. Later, the college conferred on him the A. M. Degree. After teaching in the County schools awhile he taught at Newberry College as principal of the Preparatory Department. Previous to that time he had served as County Superintendent of Education, from 1889 to 1893.

He served as Trustee of the Newberry City Schools, also Trustee of the Negro College at Columbia, and Trustee of Summerland Female-College. For several terms he was a member of the City Board of Health of Newberry. In 1897 he was elected a member of the State House of Representatives, and reelected several terms for over a period of fifteen years. At the time of his death he was a member of the Legislature and of the Ways and Means Committee.

For the greater part of his life he took active interest in church work, as Sunday School teacher, Superintendent of the Sunday School, and member of the Church Council.

He was the organizer and first President of the Sons of the American Revolution, the Philemon Waters Chapter of Newberry.

A merchant over twenty years, as a member of the firm of The J. W. Kibler Company, of Newberry, wholesale grocery merchants.

He married October 17, 1908 to Mamie E. Salter, of Newberry, and left one child, a daughter who married James H. Talbert, of Laurens, S.C.

He died in Columbia while in attendance upon a session of the Legislature, on February 3, 1931.

JAMES CAMPSEN KINARD—born in Newberry, S. C. on October 1, 1895; son of George Mauney and Rena De Saussure (Campsen) Kinard. He received his education in the Newberry City Schools, then at Newberry College from which he graduated in 1916 with the degree of A.B. He received the A. M. Degree in 1917 from the same institution. In 1918 he studied at Columbia University, New York City. In 1928 he received the honorary degree of Litt. D. from Erskine College, Due West, S. C. In 1931 the degree of LL. D. was conferred on him by the South Carolina University.

He married Katherine Efird of Lexington, S. C. on June 17, 1920.

He began his teaching career as instructor in Newberry College, in mathematics, in the year 1916; from 1918 to 1930 he was head of the Department of Natural Sciences. He was Dean of the College from 1924 to 1930; Director of the Summer Sessions of Newberry College from 1920 to 1930. He was elected President of Newberry College in 1930, and has served in that capacity since that time.

During his teaching work at the college, he studied law under Dr. George B. Cromer, Attorney of Newberry and former President of the college. He completed the course, with supplemental Summer work, and was admitted to the bar of South Carolina.

His memberships include several organizations, some which are: A.A.A.S., American Chemical Society, South Carolina Academy of Science, Rotary Club, Newberry Country Club, Luthern Church of the Redeemer, in which he served as Deacon, Superintendent of the Sunday School, and Chairman of the Church Council.

JAMES NEWTON MARTIN—born February 14, 1832; son of William Martin. His father was a merchant for whom he clerked for sometime; later succeeding his father in the business.

In 1861, he volunteered for service in the Confederate Army, in Company E., Third S. C. Regiment, and was sent to Virginia, assigned to the Commissary Department in General Bonham's Brigade. He served until the battle of Gettysburg. In 1863, he was elected Lieutenant of his old Company, and served until the end of the war.

After the war he returned to Newberry, and again started in business; and in 1865 sold a partnership interest to William G. Mayes. After a few years he bought the interest of his partner, and continued alone until 1896 when he was elected President of the National Bank of Newberry. He served in this position until his death a few years afterwards in Newberry.

During his business career he was a director in Board of Directors of the Newberry Cotton Mills, also a member of the Board of Directors of the Piedmont Manufacturing Company, at Piedmont, S. C. During the last years of his life he was President of the Newberry Cotton Mills.

He married, first, to Sarah Blair, of Newberry County, on November 8, 1866; his second wife was Bernice Russell whom he married on November 12, 1884. He and both of his wives are buried in Rosemont Cemetery, in Newberry.

DR. ORLANDO BENEDICT MAYER, SR.–born near Pomaria, Newberry County, February 24, 1818; son of Adam and Mary (Counts) Mayer. He attended the schools of his neighborhood, then the Lexington Classical Institute, Lexington, S. C., to which town his family had moved. After completing his course there, he attended South Carolina College, Columbia, S. C., where he graduated in 1837 with the Degree of A. B. He learned medicine under local physicians, and then attended the South Carolina Medical College, Charleston, graduating with Degree of M: D.
He practiced his profession a few years at Pomaria; then pursued post graduate work in European Universities, studying at Paris, France, and at Berlin, Germany, thence to Edinburg University, Scotland, spending three years abroad. He returned home in 1847; and began practicing in Newberry. He became a distinguished practicioner and surgeon.
Dr. Mayer was married three times. First, he married in 1839 to a Miss Davis, of Fairfied District, S. C. but who, then, was living in Mississippi. She died less than a year after their marriage and left no off-spring. His second wife was Caroline De Walt, of Newberry, whom he married in 1851; she died in 1861, leaving one son and four daughters. His third wife was a widow, Mrs. Louisa Kinard of Newberry, by whom he had no children.
Being a good English Scholar, a reader of the classics, he could, also, speak and converse in several different languages, including French, German, Latin, and Greek. After his retirement from active practice, he wrote many character sketches for the newspapers, stories for popular magazines of the day, and author of several manuscripts and books. Some of those that were published are, "Malladose, the Britain; his Wanderings from Druidism to Christianity"; "The Voice, The Hand, and The Silhouette"; and "The Music Girl of the Rue de La Harpe". In the last named book he predicted the invention of the telephone. Some of his original poems were preserved but never published in book form.
Dr. Mayer was Professor of Physiology and Hygiene at Newberry College, until it's removal to Walhalla in 1868, and for a short time after it's removal back to Newberry.
During the later years of his active life his son, Dr. O. B. Mayer, Jr., was his partner in medical practice. He died in Newberry on July 16, 1891.

WILLIAM GLENN MAYES, SR.–born in Union County, S. C. in the year 1819; son of James and Mary Ann(Glenn) Mayes. He was educated at the schools of his community, then attended the Male Institute at Spartanburg where he completed his education. After teaching awhile in Spartanburg County, he returned to Union County, where he married Nancy Jones.
He and his wife came to Newberry where he taught the Jalapa School; afterwards moving to the City of Newberry where he became a partner in the business of James Newten Martin. Later, after selling his interest to his partner, he moved to his farm near Long Lane, in the county, where he died, his wife having already died, leaving a large family.
During his residence in Newberry he took an active interest in local affairs. He was the prime mover in the reorganization of the local Masonic Lodge, becoming it's first Worshipful Master. He was an alderman (then called town warden), and later elected Mayor of Newberry, serving for several terms.

WILLIAM GLENN MAYES, JR.–born in Newberry in 1864; son of William Glenn Mayes, Sr. and Nancy (Jones) Mayes. He was educated in the schools of Newberry, then attended Wofford College, Spartanburg, S. C. two years.
On his return to Newberry, he began a business career, first as drug clerk; and after practical training in that business, he purchased the old Reeder Drug store and built up a large business in the city. He first employed his brother, Dr. Robert L. Mayes, as pharmacist, who was a graduate in Pharmacy at the Charleston Medical College (after his graduation at the S. C. Military Academy, of Charleston). Dr. Robert Mayes gave up this work to complete a medical course at Jefferson Medical College, Philadelphia, where he graduated, then practiced in Newberry for several years, until his death at the age of 53 years, unmarried.
Dr. William G. Mayes married Mary Wright of Newberry; they left no children. He gave his life to the care of his widowed sister and her two small children whom he reared and educated. He was a Steward in the Central Methodist Church for many years, and Chairman of the Church Council. He was Chairman of the Board of Trustees of the Newberry City Schools for several years; President of the Newberry Chamber of Commerce. He and his brother, Dr. Robert, were two of the organizers of the Newberry County Hospital. He died in March, 1937.

DR. JAMES McINTOSH-born at Society Hill, Darlington County, South Carolina, on February 27, 1838; son of James Hawes and Martha (Gregg) McIntosh, of that county. He attended the village school at Society Hill, then South Carolina College, Columbia, S. C., from which he graduated in 1856. Later, he graduated at the South Carolina Medical College, Charleston, S. C., in 1861, with distinction. Ten years later he supplemented his studies in gynecology and therapeutics of the throat and lungs, in New York.

He volunteered for services in the Confederate Army; appointed Assistant Surgeon in Company F, 8th Regiment of S. C. Volunteers; resigned, but rejoined the same company when it was ordered to Virginia as a part of the regular army. He was in Kershaw's Brigade and was at the battle of First Manassas on November 1, 1861. Afterwards, his services being needed in the Medical Corps he was appointed Assistant Surgeon of the C.S.A. with headquarters at Richmond, Virginia; and served until the end of the war.

When Columbia was destroyed by General Sherman's Army, he was ordered to that city, after which he established a temporary hospital at Newberry to care for soldiers, which operated until the volunteers had passed through to their western homes.

He began the practice of medicine at Newberry in June, 1865. In 1876-'77 he was President of the South Carolina Medical Association. He was about that time elected a trustee of Furman University, Greenville, S. C. Upon his retirement from active practice, he became interested in the business and industrial life of Newberry; elected President of the Newberry Savings Bank, and of the Newberry Building and Loan Association; a director in the Board of the Mollohon Manufacturing Company, of Newberry, and other industries; Chairman of the Board of Commissioners of Public Works of Newberry.

He married, first, to Fannie C. Higgins, of Newberry, on November 25, 1862, and had four children. His second wife was Mrs. Sarah B. (Rook) Boozer, whom he married June 13, 1893, and had two children by her. His first wife died on September 25, 1890.

Dr. McIntosh died at his home in Newberry on February 26, 1919. He lived in the old Higgins Home (originally Caldwell Home)on Boundary Street.

DR. FRANK DUANE MOWER-born in Newberry March 17, 1880; son of George S. and Fannie D. (Jones) Mower. He was educated at the city schools of Newberry, and at Newberry College from which he received his A. B. Degree. He graduated at Tulane University, New Orleans, La. with the degree of M. D. After serving an internship at Tulane University, he came back to Newberry and began the practice of medicine.

When the First World War started he volunteered for service; served through the war as Surgeon, with the rank of Major of Medical Corps, U. S. A., the most of which time he was in France.

After the war he returned to Newberry and resumed his practice, which he rapidly built up, gaining the reputation as a distinguished physician. He was for sometime a member of the Newberry County Board of Health; and Chairman of the Board; member of the Newberry Country Club; aided materially in the Newberry County Hospital work; member of the State Medical Society; member of the Newberry County Medical Association; and held memberships in several fraternal organizations; and member of the Associate Reformed Presbyterian Church.

He married on October 19, 1910, to Nina E. Seay, daughter of J. R. and Rachel E. (Stack) Seay. He died in Newberry in 1937.

MAJOR FREDERICK NANCE-born in Amelia County, Virginia, August 13, 1770. He came to Newberry, S. C. after the Rev War, and was soon followed by his brothers, Clement and Robert. He was said to have the first settler withing the village limits, at the time the county was laid off.

He served, first, as a Deputy under William Malone who was the first County Court Clerk in 1791, serving from May, 1791 to February, 1794. At the May term of court in 1794, William Maoone resigned and Fredercik Nance was appointed Clerk in his place. When the County Courts were abolished about 1800 and the Circuit Courts established, he was appointed by the Governor of the State as Clerk of Court of Newberry County. He served until his resignation in 1807.

He assisted Captain Craig to raise a company of militia, ad was appointed a Lieutenant of the company. When Captain Craig abidcated and the left the State, Fredetick Nance as commissioned as Major under Colonel Creswell. Protestations by Captains Henderson and Williams caused a court of inquiry to reverse it; then both Major Nance and Captain Henderson resigned, leaving James Williams to be appointed as Major. (Sources: " Annals of Newberry", and newspapers).

In the year 1808 Major Nance was elected Lieutenant Governor of South Carolina, and qualified with Governor Drayton. In 1812, he was elected State Senator, and served two terms.
In 1816 he was appointed National Presidential Elector from his Congressional District, then consisting of the counties of Newberry, Laurens and Fairfield; he voted for James Monroe for President and Daniel A. Thompkins for Vice-President. On account of a growing deafness, he declined to offer for any other public office; and in 1820 he retired to private life. His wife died in 1829. In 1831 he married Mrs. Theresa Ruff, a widow, who survived him. By his first marriage there were several children; and a daughter by his second marriage.
Major Nance is buried in the old Nance family graveyard, near the western end of Boundary Street.

DR. SAMPSON POPE-born in Newberry, S. C. in 1837; son of Thomas Herbert and Sarah (Strother) Pope. His father was a native of Edgefield District, but came to Newberry to practice Law.
Sampson Pope was educated in the private schools of Newberry, and at the State Military College, Charleston. He went to Arkansas with Col. James Glenn, where they surveyed the boundaries of that State. Returning home, he decided to study medicine. Accordingly, he entered the Jefferson Medical College of Philadelphia, completing the required course in 1857, but too young to receive his degree. He, then, served one year as Interne at Pennsylvania General Hospital, Philadelphia. In March, 1858, Jefferson Medical College conferred him the degree of M. D., after coming of age; and the hospital gave him a certificate as Interne.
Dr. Pope came back to Newberry where he practiced until the War Between the States started. He volunteered for service in the Confederate Army; commissioned as First Lieutenant in Company B., First S. C. Regiment under Captain Whitfield Walker. He rose to the rank of Captain. Later, he was transferred to the Hospital Division and was appointed Senior Surgeon in Wright's Brigade (later known as Sorrell's Brigade). Then, he was transferred to the 22nd Regiment, in Georgia. This brigade saw much active service in Virginia. At the end of the War, Dr. Pope had attained the rank of Major in the Medical Corps.
After returning home, he became interested in reading law, and was admitted to the bar. He joined the firm of Fair, Pope and Pope, he being the Junior partner. The partners were his brother, Y. J. Pope, and Col. Simeon Fair. Afterwards, he decided to locate in Texas, in the year 1878; but in the year 1881, he came back to Newberry.
In 1884, he was elected to the S. C. Legislature from Newberry County, and re-elected in 1886. In 1890, he was elected Clerk of the State Senate and re-elected in 1892. In 1894, he ran as an Independent candidate for Governor, being defeated by the nominee of Benjamin Tillman, who was John Gary Evans.
Dr. Pope was a Mason; member of the Newberry Baptist Church. He married Helen Harrington, daughter of Dr. William H. And Sarah Strother (O'Neall) Harrington, of Newberry. (Mrs. Sarah Strother Harrington was a daughter of Chief Justice, John B. O'Neall, of Newberry). They had two children, Dr. Thomas H. Pope, and Sarah Pope (she married Paul Anderson).
Dr. Sampson Pope died in Newberry in 1906.

DR. THOMAS HARRINGTON POPE-born in Newberry July 7, 1876; son of Dr. Sampson and Helen (Harrington) Pope, of Newberry. He was educated in the City Schools of Newberry, and at Newberry College, leaving College before completing his course; later, he attended the S. C. Medical College, Charleston, S. C., where he graduated in medicine, 1908, with the degree of M. D.
Returning to Newberry he began the practice of medicine at Kinards, later moving to Newberry, where he built up a fine practice.
Dr. Pope volunteered for service in the Spanish-American War, and was appointed first Sargeant in Company B. under the command of Captain W. Smith Langford, of Newberry. He was discharged on account of physical disability (bad eyesight). During World War 1, he was commissioned as Captain in the Medical Corps, but was never called into active service. For several years after the war he was Captain of Reserves in the Medical Corps.
Dr. Pope married October 1, 1912, to Marie Gary, daughter of Chief Justice Eugene B. Gary, of the State Supreme Court, and his wife, Eliza (Tusten) Gary. Dr. Pope and his wife had one son, Thomas H. Pope Jr., who graduated from the S. C. Military Academy, and the State University in Law. (the son was active in World War II, being made Colonel in a Regiment which was in southern Europe).

Dr. Pope has held several positions of trust in various organizations. He was President of the Newberry County Medical Society, 1918-1919; and again in 1925-26; President of the District Medical Society, 1933; member of the State Medical Association; also of the American Medical Association. He has served as a member of the Board of Trustees of the State Medical College, Charleston, S. C., 1924-28; a member of the Phi Chi Medical Fraternity; a charter member of the Newberry Country Club. He was a delegate to the Newberry County Democratic Convention several times.

Dr. Pope died in Newberry a few years ago.

REV. JOHN RENWICK, SR.-born in County Antrim, Ireland, about 1735. He came with the Covenanters to America, and settled near Cannon's Creek. He was the first A. R. P. minister that came to upper South Carolina.

His first pastorate was of that denomination, though he was never installed. He administered the members of that denomination, his congregation, the Lord's Supper in Patrick Carmichael's barn, near Boyds Crossing (this was about one-half distance from Newberry to Prosperity). This occured sometime before his church was built, which was completed in 1771.

In 1772 and 1773, Cannon's Creek Church and King's Creek Church were built; and, jointly, they called Rev. Renwick to be their pastor; who had been with them since 1770. During his brief pastorate of five years the member-ship grew, so that the buildings became too small for each of the congregations.

Rev. Renwick died August 20, 1775, and is buried in the cemetery at Cannon's Creek Church.

REV. JOHN RENWICK, JR.-born December 31, 1770, at sea, while his parents were on their way to America. He was the son of Rev. John Renwick, Sr. and his wife, Jane Bothwell (widow).

He studied in his neighborhood schools. He was licensed to preach January 1, 1807; missionated for two and one-half years; then he settled near Gilders Creek Church, becoming it's first pastor. This church had dissented from the Presbyterian Church. He, also, supplied other churches. On account of declining health he was superannuated before his death which occured on November 20, 1836. His wife was the widow of Rev. David Bothwell, who had come from Ireland. She died December 1, 1847. Both are buried at King's Creek Church Cemetery, about ten miles North of Newberry Court House.

DR. MARCELLUS ADOLPHUS RENWICK-born April 30 1846, in the Long Lane section of Newberry County; son of Col. John Simpson Renwick and wife, Mary (Toland) Renwick. His mother was a sister of Dr. Hugh Toland, the distinguished physician and surgeon who located in California and started the first public institution for the study of medicine in that State.

Dr. Renwick's twin sister, Malissa Jane, died January 24, 1849.

Marcellus Renwick was a small boy when his parents moved from the old Renwick home to one his father had built, the present old Carlisle home, in the neighborhood. The late Dr. R. C. Carlisle had lived in it, with his family, since that time.

During the War of Secession Dr. Renwick left Erskine College, at Due West, S. C., to enlist with the sixteen year old boys in Company M. of Mounted Rifles, of the 20th Regiment, S. C. V., which was commanded by Col. E. S. Keitt. After the surrender he came home, riding an old white horse, accompanied by the family servant, "Daddy Dick", who had cared for him throughout his campaigns.

After the war, he studied medicine at the State Medical College, Charleston, S, C., then at Jefferson Medical College, Philadelphia, Pa. Later, he went to Europe to complete his studies, with postgraduate work in Paris, France. He specialized in eye, ear, nose, and throat diseases. Being forced to leave France on account of the Franco-Prussian War, he returned to America and to Newberry. His aim was to open an office in New York City; but to gratify his parents wish, he located in Newberry County where he practiced for several years.

On account of ill-health he was forced to give up his practice; then moved to Newberry, where he started a mercantile business. Some years later, suffering financial reverses, he removed to his farm where he spent the remainder of his life.

Dr. Renwick always took an active part in church work, in local civic and school activities. He was Chairman of the Board of Trustee of Long Lane School.

His first wife was Mary Erwin of Hendersonville, N. C. His second wife was Kitty Jones. He died July 6, 1918, and is buried at King's Creek Cemetery, by the side of his forbears.

DR. JOHN CLAUDE SEASE-born at Little Mountain, S. C., on July 7, 1892; son of Dr. John Marion Sease and Margaret (Months) Sease. He received his primary education in this schools of his community, then graduated from Newberry College in 1913, with the degree of A. B. He attended the South Carolina Medical College, at Charleston, S. C., from which he received the degree of M. D. in 1917. After serving two years internship at Roper Hospital, Charleston, he returned to Little Mountain and began the practice of medicine with his father. After the death of his father, he succeeded to his practice .

In November, 1918, he volunteered for service in the First World War, and was appointed Lieutenant in the Medical Corps, U. S. Army. After the war he returned to his home and resumed his practice, until July 1, 1934, when he was elected County Health Physician for Newberry County, in which capacity he since worked.

He is a member of the following organizations: Masons, Royal Arch Chapter, Knights Templar, Shrine, the Kiwanis Club, The Newberry County Medical Society, the State Medical Association, the American Medical Association; and a former member of the Board of Directors of the old Little Mountain Bank. He is a member of the Trinity Lutheran Church of Little Mountain, having served as one of it's Deacons.   He is not married (1947).

ROBERT STEWART-born Newberry County February 7, 1803; son of Robert Stewart, Sr. and wife. He married Eliza R. Ward, of Laurens County, S. C.

He moved from his father's farm in Newberry County to Newberry Court House, and started life as store clerk. After a short time he started a mercantile business of his own, which grew, gradually, to a very large business. He accumulated a large estate, but during the War of Secession and the post-war period, he lost most of it.

His son, John Stewart, was a Lieutenant in the famous Palmetto Regiment that went to Mexico in 1847; and lost his wife in Mexico. His father delegated a friend, Dr. Daniel Dobson, to go to Mexico and bring back the body; which he did, taking his wife with him.

Robert Stewart served one term in the State Legislature from Newberry County.

He died June 13, 1879, and is buried in the family plot at Rosemont Cemetery, Newberry.

ADAM G. SUMMER-born near Pomaria, Newberry County, on August 22, 1818; son of John and Mary (Houseal) Summer; brother of John, Nicholas, and Henry Summer. He received his primary education in the schools of his community, then at Lexington Classical Institute, at Lexington, S. C. , from which he graduated. He , then, studied law, and was admitted to the bar of South Carolina in 1840. He began his practice of law at Newberry.

During his short career at Newberry he became liked as an orator, an effective and versatile speaker.

He soon gave up the practice of law and moved to Columbia, S. C., taking over the work as Editor and Manager of the State weekly newspaper, " The South Carolinian". After a short time he sold his interest in the newspaper and returned to his farm, " Ravenscroft", in Lexington County,(Near Pomaria), and devoted his life to agriculture.

In 1850 he was elected to the State House of Representatives from Saxe-Gotha Township, Lexington County,and served several terms.

In 1857 he sold his farm and moved to Florida, purchasing a large estate there. Later, desiring to come back home, he sold the Florida property and returned to the town of Newberry where he resumed the practice of law.

When the War Between the States started, he volunteered along with others for service in the Confederacy. He was sent to Virginia , being appointed Judge Advocate under General Magruder. Later, he was commissioned Commissary Officer with the command to go to Florida, in which service he reamined until the close of the war.

He married September 22, 1865, to Margaret J. Starke, a daughter of Major Thomas Starke, of Fairfield District, S. C. A few months after his marraige he made a visit to Charleston, S. C., where he became quite ill; but thinking himself to be better, started home to meet his wife at her father's home in Fairfield District(her grmother's home in Camden District), He became ill before reaching his destination , and died on the way on July 6, 1866. He left his widow, and a daughter who was born soon after his death.

He was the author of several articles in newspapers and magazines; also, agricultural magazines, as a emember of the Newberry Agricultural Society. He was a contributor to the Southern Quarterly Review, Southern Literary Messenger, and other periodicals. Also, author of character sketches in New York papers. He is buried in Summer family graveyard, near Pomaria..

CLARENCE THOMPSON SUMMER—born near Pomaria, S. C. April 4, 1880; son of Charles E. and Nora (Sease) Summer. His parents moved to Newberry in 1888, where he attended the city schools; later, he attended Newberry College from which graduated with degree of A. B. in 1898.

He accepted position with the firm of Summer Brothers (his father being a member of this firm), of Newberry, as salesman. Later, he became Assistant Buyer, then Buyer for the firm. His father having purchased the interests of his brothers in the firm, and the business incorporated, Clarence T. Summer was made Vice-President of the company to succeed J. H. Summer who had sold all his stock of the company to his brother, Charles E. Summer.

Later, when the firm of Summer Brothers, Inc., were liquidated, he started a business of his own, which he has since operated.

He was for several terms City Alderman, during which time he was Chairman of the Finance Committee. He was a charter member of the Newberry Chamber of Commerce, when it was reorganized. As Chairman of the Finance Committee on the city council he aided in having the City Bond records systemized. He has served at various times in the city's community work program.

He married Eoline Wertz, daughter of David B. and Harriet (Smith) Wertz, of Newberry County. They have one daughter, Martha-Nuell, who is a graduate of Randolph-Macon College, Virginia, and of Columbia University, New York, with degrees of A. B., A. M, and Ph. D. She taught school until she married.

HENRY SUMMER—born at Pomaria, Newberry County, S. C. on April 11, 1809; son of John and Mary (Houseal) Summer, of Pomaria, and grand-son of Captain William F. Houseal, of the Rev War He received his preliminary education in the schools of his neighborhood, where he was prepared for the Junior Class of South Carolina College, and graduated in 1833, with the degree of A.B. After graduation he read law and was admitted to the bar in 1833. He began practice at Lexington Court House, but after a year he moved to Alabama, where, in Talledega, he started to practice. His brother, Nicholas, who was a practicing attorney in Newberry and who had been killed in the Seminole Indian War in Florida, left his valuable library to him under the condition that he return to Newberry; which he did, and practiced in Newberry until his health failed and he removed to his farm.

He married December 22, 1846 to Frances Mayer, daughter of Major Adam Mayer, and sister of Dr. O. B. Mayer, Sr. of Newberry. He was elected to the State Legislature from Newberry County in 1846, and reelected in 1848. In 1851, he with Dr. J. J. Wardlaw, of Abbeville District, were elected to represent the Congressional District (Abbeville, Edgefield, Newberry, and Lexington), in the Southern Congress, to consider the attitude of the Federal government as to the slave-holding States and to recommend a course of action. This came under a special Act of the General Assembly passed in December, 1850. They were the candidates for the Cooperative Party. This convention never asseembled.

During the War of Seccession Mr. Summer suffered great hardships from the Kilpatrick Raiders, a part of Sherman's troops who marched through Columbia, burned the city, and then proceded northward, pillaging and burning as they marched.

After the war, he was elected a member of the convention which met in Columbia, under a proclamation by the Provisional Governor, B. F. Perry, for " the purpose of altering and amending the Constitution of South Carolina, or remodeling and making a new one, which would conform to great changes that have taken place in the State."

He was an ardent friend of Newberry College, a member of the first Board of Trustees and Secretary of the Board; an instructor in the College during the illness of one of it's professors from 1862-to 1863.

He died on his plantation near Pomaria, and is buried in the Summer Family graveyard, just South of the old home.

COL. JOHN ADAM SUMMER—son of John Adam Summer, Sr. and Margaret(?) (Jostin) Summer. He was born in Pennsylvania in 1744. His parents came to South Carolina about 1750.

There were no schools when they came, until the Lutheran minister became instrumental in having a school started. Some of the first Dutch Fork settlers were educated people when they came, as Rev. Gasswell., Major Michael Leitner, Dr. Heinrich Schmitz, and others. Some taught private schools in their homes.

He married Mary Reese. He aided his father in the operation of a large plantation which had been granted as a bounty under the English Royal Decree.

He was interested in the welfare of his section; a Justice of the Peace, Justice of the Quorum, and early became a Whig. He was elected as delegate to the City of Charleston on the eve of the beginning of the Rev. War, which council was held to determine the stand of the people of the State. At first he was criticized by some delegates for his stand against going into the war against England—a stand he assumed to fully represent the will of his people at home. However, the meeting closed with the aim of having speakers travel throughout the northern section of the State, and convince, if possible, the people of the necessity for going into the war for liberty. The speakers were successful to a large extent, so that the people of the upper Dutch Fork became Whigs, most of them fighting on the side of Washington.

When war was declared, John Adam Summer, Jr., was one of the first to organize a militia company, and became it's Captain. The first election having been held at his home, he was instrumental in getting many on the side of liberty. He served in many campaigns in the war; and his father gave much time in aiding the cause by acting as Quarter Master, as Major. At a later time, John Adam, Jr. was made Major in the Quartermaster headquarters.

After the war, he was elected a member of the House of Representatives of South Carolina, from upper Orangeburg District. Later, he was elected Colonel of the Eighth Regiment of State Militia (after it's reorganization it became the Thirty Ninth Regiment).

During the early part of the war, he was one of the men who, in face of fire, brought off an American field piece from the battlefield, which had been abandoned by the Americans.

He died at his home on Crims' Creek in the year 1809, and he and his wife are buried in the old family graveyard, about two miles Southwest of Pomaria, to the right of the old Buncombe Road. This was the homeplace of his father and mother, whose graves are not marked.

JOHN ERNEST SUMMER- born in Newberry, S. C. on September 2, 1887; son of John Harrison and Hulda Ann (Cromer) Summer. He attended the Newberry City Schools, then two years at Newberry College; later graduating at Bliss Electrical School, Washington, D. C. Desiring to get into Architectural work, he became connected with a large firm at Jacksonville, Florida, where he worked for several years, then opened an office of his own at Jacksonville; then removed to Greenwood, S. C.

His work at Greenwood was highly successful, having acted as Architectural Engineer for many large buildings in that area, including the Greenwood High School building, the Carnegie Public Library, several churches, the new jail building at Laurens, the new jail building at Newberry, the Exchange Bank building at Newberry, and many others. In Florida are many buildings by him, New Court Houses at West Palm Beach, and other places, and new court house annex at Jacksonville.

He returned to Newberry to organize the Newberry Lumber and Construction Company, Inc., becoming it's general manager. During his time there, he also maintained an Architectural Office, and was Engineer for several new homes in Newberry, the Newberry Country Club building, and others, including the new jail.

He was elected Alderman of the city of Newberry, and served one term, 1922-24. Active member and officer in the Newberry Chamber of Commerce; a charter member of the Newberry Rotary Club; charter member of the Newberry Country Club; charter member of the Sons of the American Revolution Chapter in Newberry; and active in many civic and community works.

After several years as Manager of the Newberry Lumber Company, he sold his interests in the company, and accepted a flattering offer from an organization in Georgia, assuming the managership of a large organization at Cordele, Ga. When the Second World War started, he was offered a position with the Federal Housing Administration, with headquarters in Atlanta, Ga. This being the home of his wife's people, he accepted and removed to that City. After the war, he established a business of his own as Architectural Engineer, employing several men on his staff.

He married Linda M. Miller, a daughter of Dr. Royal J. and Belle (McClendon) Miller, of Atlanta, on June 2, 1914.

MARVIN O. SUMMER–born in Newberry County on December 13, 1892; son of Guss B. and Trannie (Schumpert) Summer of Newberry County. He attended the schools of the county, and after his parents removal to the city, he attended Newberry College for two years.
Desiring to go into business with his father, he accepted an interest in his father's retail furniture business. After the death of his father, he and his two brothers, Adrain and Gurnie, took over the business.
He served in World War I; and after returning home, resumed his work with the business. He has been active in community development; has served as a director in the Newberry Chamber of Commerce; and for four terms was alderman of the city, 1922-36. A charter member of the Lion's Club; member of the Central Methodist Church, serving on the Church Council; member of the Board of Directors of the Newberry Federal Savings and Loan Association.
He married Louise Kinard, daughter of B. L. and ....Kinard, of Ninety Six, S. C.

THOMAS ROY SUMMER–born in Newberry, S. C. on September 10, 1889; son of John Harrison and Hulda Ann (Cromer) Summer, of Newberry. He received his education in the City Schools of Newberry, and at Newberry College where he received the degree of A. B. He, then, attended the Eastman's Business College, Poughkeepsie, N. Y. and graduated in Business Administration.
He returned to Newberry and accepted a position with his father in the clothing business; later, becoming Assistant Manager and receiving a partnership interest. They operated twenty eight years, when in 1936, he established his own clothing business in Newberry, which is now operated by him and his son, T. Roy Summer Jr.
Always taking an active interest in community work, he served over twenty years as Sec-Treas. of the Newberry Bond Commission. Also, a member of the Newberry Chamber of Commerce, and an officer; charter member of the Newberry Rotary Club; member of the Newberry Country Club; a Mason, Royal Arch, Knights Templar, and Shriner; member of the American Legion, formerly their Finance Officer, and head of the local Chapter. He is a member of the Lutheran Church of the Redeemer, having been a Deacon in the Church.
He married in 1920 to Florence Bowman, daughter of the late Charles A. and Kate (Ewart) Bowman, of Newberry.

HUGH HUGER TOLAND–born April 16, 1806, on Gilder's Creek, Newberry District, S. C.; son of John and Mary (Boyd) Toland, both of Irish families who settled in Newberry area before the Rev. War.
He received his early education in the county schools of his section, and under private tutorship; then sent to other schools of higher learning, and prepared for the study of medicine. He studied under Dr. George Ross, and in 1828 he graduated at Transylvania University, Lexington, Ky. in medicine, at the head of the class of 160.
He returned to Newberry and practiced in the county about two years, going to the Transylvania University in the winters and working in the dissecting rooms there. Then, he spent two and one-half years in Paris, France, under such distinguished surgeons as Guillaume, Jacques, Listvanc, and Philibert Joseph Boux.
He returned to America and settled in Newberry County for practice; but soon thereafter moved to Columbia, S. C. to practice, where he married his first wife, Mary Goodwin. She lived but a short time. He became a recognized physician of that city, his success in relief of the club-foot and strabisms, in the use of the lithotomy forceps, spread beyond the State and arrested the attention of the celebrated surgeon, Dr. James Marion Sims, of Montgomery, Ala.
He married again to Mary Avery of Columbia, in the year 1844, who bore him two daughters. In 1852, after the discovery of gold in California, he went to that State. Within three days after his arrival at Stockton, California, his wife died. He became interested in mining, some mines of which he bought, and brought some of the first quartz mills into that State. He moved to San Francisco, gave up mining, and resumed the practice of medicine and surgery.
He was appointed Chief Surgeon of the Marine Hospital. Four years later he founded the Toland Medical College in San Francisco and became it's first President, acting as Professor of Surgery. For twenty seven years he was known as "the great surgeon of the Pacific Coast". He married again in 1860 to Mrs. Mary B. (Morrison) Gridley, of San Francisco, and had one son.
He placed the college in 1873 in the hands of Regents of the University of California, and it became, thereafter, a part of the State University system. He died in 1880, leaving a widow, a son, and step-son, and was buried in that State.

Dr. Toland was the author of many published articles and essays on surgery, also he published a text-book. He was a good diagnostician as well as a good surgeon—a capable and rapid operator. He operated many times for plastic surgery, it was said, and for bone regeneration, that were unusual operations for that period. He wrote many papers on those topics, that were said to be illuminating and important documents. (Sources: "Annals of Newberry" and newspapers).

DR. SPENCER GLASGOW WELCH--born March 12, 1834, in Newberry County; son of Williams and Mary (Glasgow) Welch, of Newberry County. Williams Welch had moved from Iredel County, North Carolina.

He was educated at Furman University, Greenville, S. C. He studied medicine at Castleton, Vermont, and at Jefferson Medical College, Philadelphia, Pa. from which he graduated with the degree of M. D.

He began his practice of medicine at Newberry, until the War of Secession came on and he volunteered for service in the Confederate Army. He was assigned to Company D., Thirteenth Regiment, S. C. V. Appointed Assistant Surgeon of that Company, and later promoted to regular surgeon in the regiment. He served in this capacity until the end of the war.

Returning home he resumed his practice of medicine; and after a few years, retired from active practice and devoted much of his time to his farming interests.

Dr. Welch married in 1861 to Cordelia Strother, of Edgefield County. His wife died in 1915, after 54 years of marriage. There were two children, Williams Welch and Eloise Welch (she married Robert D. Wright of Newberry). Williams Welch was a noted landscape painter and an artist of recognized ability; he died a few years ago.

Dr. Welch died at his home in Newberry on January 5, 1916, and is buried in Rosemont Cemetery, Newberry.

GENEALOGIES OF SOME PIONEER FAMILIES.

On the following pages are some genealogies of early families of Newberry County. This data is incomplete, as it is impractical to obtain all data in a family; some are more complete than others. After over twenty years genealogical researches on different families in Newberry County and nearby counties, much of the information was found in old court house records, old library records, family records, and other sources, including oldest cemetery markers, etc. Some genealogies furnished by families.

ANDERSON

William Anderson died in Newberry District about 1805. He left a widow, Elizabeth, and four children: Killis, Elizabeth Pitts, Mary Motes, and William. The son, William, died in November, 1841, leaving widow, Elizabeth, and children: Moses, Killis, Mary (wife of Abner Pitts), Hiram, Sarah (wife of Wade Dalrymple), Matilda (wife of William Satterwhite). Wade Dalrymple died in 1842. William and Matilda Satterwhite had children: Eliza Jane (10 years old in 1841), and Matilda C. (8 years old in 1841).

Abraham Anderson, Sr. died about 1790, in Newberry District. His legatees included: Elizabeth (wife of Thomas Gordon), Abel, Jesse, Nathan, Gabriel, Abraham, and George Gordon.

Abraham Anderson died about 1800, left children: Henry (oldest son), Elijah, Jane, Enoch, William, Abijah, Abraham, Levi, and others. William moved to Maurey County, Tennessee. Elijah died in 1816, leaving widow, Elizabeth (mother of his children), and children: Jane, Perminah, Elizabeth, Richard, Elijah.

Joshua Anderson, Jr. (son of Joshua and brother of Abraham), died about 1769, leaving one son, Benjamin, who moved to Georgia. He was living in Green County, of that State, after the Revolutionary War.

Gabriel Anderson married Miriam Smith, daughter of Jerad Smith and wife, Esther (Lindsey) Smith.

Henry Anderson married Ruth Gordon; sold his land in 1778, where he was living on Second Creek. He was a brother of Abraham Anderson, Sr.

One Elijah Anderson died in Union County in 1824. He left a widow, Nancy, and children: Caroline, Polly, Elizabeth, Silas, Martha, Eliza, and Dashana.

James Anderson made will dated June 25, 1816, which was proved in court June 14, 1827. He died about 1826, left widow, Elizabeth, and children: James, William, Ann Alany (wife of John Brown), John, and Mary (wife of William Brown).

William Franklin Anderson made will in 1861, in Fairfax County, Virginia, where he died in 1862, in army service. He left his property to his father, Moses Anderson, and his nephew, Milledge Quitman Chappell, an infant son of James B. Chappell, all of Newberry County.

Mrs. Jane Anderson died in 1848, leaving children: Sarah, Elizabeth, Laura, Whitfied J., Richard S. Executors of her will were: Hamilton Plunkett and W. C. Wiseman.

John Saxon Anderson married Elizabeth Miles, daughter of Thomas Miles. They moved to Georgia.

Mrs. Molly Anderson died in Laurens County about 1810, and left children, Andrew and Molly.

John Anderson, of Greenville County, S. C., died about 1837, leaving widow, Mary, and children: James and William, Ervin, Thomas, Anna (wife of Hewitt Chapman), John, George W., Robert, Mary Jane, David Q.; James left South Carolina before 1852.

David and George Anderson were in Pendleton District before 1803.

Robert Anderson settled on Keowee River, in Pendleton District, S. C., about 1786, on 350 acres of land. His son, Robert, Jr., was given this land in 1812.

Captain George Anderson, son of James, married Anne Coker They lived in Laurens County. As a Revolutionary War patriot, he was wounded at the battle of Kings Mountain. His son, David, served in the Revolutionary War at the age of 12, during last part of war. Captain George was born 1740; married (1) Miss Anderson, (2) Miss Lewis, and (3) Molly Saxon. (See above reference to her).

Dr. Wade Anderson died in December, 1823, in Laurens County. He left a widow, Maria S., and children: Jane R., David Lewis, and Maria W.

BARRE

Jacob Barre, the ancestor of the families of this section, was born about 1753 and died 1800 in Newberry District. He married Mary Christina Quattlebaum, daughter of Matthias Quattlebaum. After his death the widow married Martin Shealy.

He served in the American forces during the Revolutionary War, first as Lieutenant, then as Captain in the militia. The names of his children (by his only wife, Mary Christina) were: Michael, John, Jacob, Matthias, Mary Christina, Susan. The daughter, Mary Christina, married John Kibler in 1816; she died in 1817, and left no children. The mother, who had married Martin Shealy, died about 1817 or 1818.

Michael Barre was born in 1790; buried at Barre Cemetery near Leesville, S. C. He married Mary Minnick about 1815. Their children were: William, Caroline, Hepsibah, Elizabeth, John Wesley, Mary, James M¡chael, John, Daniel Thomas, Sarah Matilda, Henry, and Susan, Amanda, and Frank. William married Leah Bouknight, Caroline married Henry A. Spann, Hepzibah married Henry A. Smith, Elizabeth married Joseph Leophardt, John Wesley married Margaret Catherine Edison, who died in 1851, and he married second time to Sally Quattlebaum; Mary married Walter Quattlebaum; James Michael married Rebecca Dowling; John died when about 14 years old; Daniel Thomas married Rodella Elizabeth Rawl; Sarah Matilda married Dr. S. D. M. Guess; Henry married Anna Reid; Susan married Joseph Guess; Amanda married D. Walter Barre; Frank died in infancy.

John Barre died about 1820, left widow, Catherine, and children, John Phillip and Caroline ("Happy") Barre. The widow, Catherine, who was a daughter of John Phillip Sligh, afterwards married Andrew Cromer, Jr.

Jacob Barre married Elizabeth Hope, and had a daughter, Mary Magdelene, who married David Buzhardt.

Matthias Barre married, first, to Mary Magdelene Werts, and after her death in 1841, he married Jane Berley. He was born in 1800 and died in 1873. Children by first wife were: Elisa, who married W. W. Houseal; Jacob; D. Walter; Julia; William; and Martha; Harriet; Catherine; Frances; Mary L. Children by second wife were: Sallie, John, and Lilly. Jacob married Elizabeth Houseal, sister of William Walter Houseal, and had children: Martha (married Dr. D. L. Boozer, of Columbia, S. C.), Eugene, William Walter, James Matthias, Charles, Erm (married Ben Rawls), Elvira (married William B. Aull). D. Walter married three times - - no children by second wife (second and third wives were sisters, Mary and Kate Workman), William W. Houseal and wife, Elisa Barre, had: John S., Mary, Cornelia, James Emlon, Martha, William P., Edward Julius, Walter Gustave. Julia Ann (1831-1911), married Drayton W. T: Kibler (1825-1901), and had: John Calhoun, Frances T., Mary Eugenia, Walter Alonzo, Elizabeth Caroline, James Matthias, Emma Lillian, Alma Estelle, Florence Augusta, Robert Lee, Rufus W., Lawson Barre (latter two were twins); Eulalie (died in infancy). Martha married Robert Holman. Harriet and Frances each married Michael Bowers and each had one child, Olivia and James Matthias, respectively. William A. married Huldah Gonel - - had two children, Alice and Olive. Mary Lavania married Jesse Rawl.

Matthias Barre's children by his second wife, Jane Berley, were: Sallie, John (killed in Florida in 1872), and Lilly. Lilly married Blufford F. Griffin, of Newberry.

The children of D. Walter Barre by his first wife, Amanda Barre (his first cousin) were: Walter M., Minnie, Ronnie, Eloise, Veda. Eloise married Eugene L. Leavell, of Newberry, children by third wife were: Oswald, Walter, Nellie.

BOOZER

The pioneer of this family was Ulrich Boozer, Sr., who first settled in lower section of old Camden District; later some of his sons moving into Lexington County, others into Newberry County. He had by h/s first wife, a son, George, and a daughter, Catherine. By his second wife, were the following children: Jacob, John, Frederick, Henry, Ulrich, Gasper and Rudolph. The family came no doubt with the German and Dutch emigration from Pennsylvania.

Of the sons, Jacob settled in Lexington County, Henry and Frederick in Newberry County, Ulrich probably in Orangeburg County, as also did Gasper and Rudolph. The families of the lower section still retain the original spelling, "Buser" . . . Frederick and Henry settled on Cannons Creek, in Newberry County; but Henry sold his lands and moved over into the Bush River section of the County.

Frederick married Barbara Gray, a daughter of George Gray, Sr. (sister of Major Frederick Gray, of the Revolutionary War), and had children: Frederick, George, David, John, Daniel, Henry, Adam, Elizabeth Morrow, and Margaret Piester. A son-in-law, James McDill, was executor of his will. The sons, Frederick, Henry, John, and Daniel, moved to the section of Campen Creek, south of Prosperity, on lands owned by their father, Frederick, Sr.

Henry Boozer, brother of Frederick, Sr., made a will in 1828, and died about 1837, leaving widow, Elizabeth (she died in 1845), and children: David, Henry, Frederick, John, Sarah (wife of Jacob Cappleman), Daniel, George, Elizabeth (wife of Daniel Senn), Adam, and Rebecca Hendrix. Sarah Cappleman died and her share of the estate reverted to Mary Ann Cappleman, Henry Cappleman, and Timothy Pugh. Adam died 1840, and left widow, Mary (she died in 1859), and children: Sarah Caroline Lake, John C., Thomas N., Adam P., and George N., and granddaughters, Elizabeth Lake, Mary C. Lake, and Sarah A. R. Lake. John C. married Mary Ann Caroline Floyd, a daughter of Jefferson Floyd, in the year 1844 (she was born before 1822, or before the birth of Witt Floyd) . . .

Henry Boozer, Sr. (son of Henry), died February 22, 1859. His legatees were twelve children and three sets of grandchildren. Children: Samuel, Timothy, Rebecca (wife of William McCormick), Henry, John A., Daniel, William A., Frederick, David W., Andrew, Adam P., and Matthias Pinckney. Adam P. moved to Smith County, Miss. Grandchildren: Lodoska (wife of David Merchant), daughter of a deceased son, George; Allen, George, Amanda Lester - - - children of a deceased daughter, Elisabeth Lester; Thomas and Permelia, children of a deceased son, Edward Boozer.

Thomas N. Boozer married October 8, 1850 to Mary Jane Reid, daughter of Daniel Reid. Frederick Boozer married October 16, 1851, to Elizabeth Stewart (widow). She died April 14, 1857 and left children: (by a former marriage): Sarah Elizabeth Stewart and Ursula Frances Stewart.

David Boozer, known as "Big Dave", son of Frederick and Barbara Gray Boozer, married, first, to Sarah Suber, on September 17, 1813; and second to Amelia Burton, widow of Peter Burton. He left no children by either wife; but left an adopted daughter, Mary, whose escapades were the subject of several colorful articles in local papers during the time of the War Between the States. He had accumulated much property, and having had many reverses, killed himself on February 10, 1850.

Timothy Boozer married Nancy Bridges, daughter of William Bridges, of Prosperity.

John Pinckney Boozer died November 17, 1855, left widow, Elizabeth, and children: Frances E., John D., Samuel L., and a posthumous daughter, Mary, who died on August 14, 1857.

John Boozer died in 1855, left widow, Mary C., and children: Daniel T., Frederick A., Simon D., Benjamin F., and a few minor children whose names were not known at the time of settlement of the estate.

Stanmore V. Boozer died in 1864, left widow, N. C. Boozer, and children, James and Marietta.

David Boozer died in 1857; left widow, Caroline, and children: Sarah Anne Cappleman, Lavania L. Teague, John P. (he died about 1855). John P. left widow, Elizabeth, and four children: Frances E., John D., Mary C. (she died early) and Samuel L.

John A. Boozer died March 13, 1864, left widow Elisabeth, and children: Henry M. (age 19), Benedict M. (age 14), Permelia E. (age 9), Mary J. P. (age 4), and Jefferson David (age 2) . . . .

John C. Boozer died in June, 1865, left widow, Nancy C., and children: Thomas P., Jefferson, George A., John S., Sallie C., Newton.P., Henry M., and Mary D. He owned lands in Stoney Batter section of the county.

BOOZER (continued)

Jacob Boozer, son of the pioneer, married Elizabeth Senn, about 1770, and settled in Lexington County (then upper Saxe-Gotha Township of Orangeburg District). Their children were: Henry, David, William, and Jacob. Jacob married Catherine . . . . and died in 1817 in Lexington County, leaving children, Lemuel, Thaney, Jacob, and Eliza. Henry and William moved to Alabama. David married Catherine Rawl and had children: David L, Wesley, and Jacob H. Jacob H. married, first, Elizabeth Enlow, and second, to Happock Lindsey. Children by first wife were Matthew and Luther, and children by second wife were Lindsey and Jacob. Dr. David L. Boozer (son of above David and Catherine Rawl Boozer), was a well known dentist of Columbia, and for many years, several of his sons following in his foot-steps.

Jacob Wesley Boozer made a will in 1861, and died about 1863. He left three sisters as legatees, viz: Margaret, Rosannah, Nancy Caroline. The executor of his will was a brother, William Washington Boozer.

Frederick Boozer made will in 1849, and died about 1857. He left widow, Nancy, and children: Margaret, Rosannah, Caroline, Henry, Frederick W., George, John, David, William Washington, Daniel and Jacob. Frederick W. died about 1860, and left widow, Eve, and children: Lemuel L. and Harriet.

(Note: Some of the family sketches were written from time to time by the author for the Newberry Observer, Newberry, S. C. and The State, Columbia, S. C. in 1829-30; hence, the apparent overlapping of genealogical data in some of them.)

BOYD

During the fifteenth and sixteenth centuries many of the Scotsmen of the Northland came down upon Ireland, settled among the Irish people and formed a race famous for their vigorousness and for their thrift. At a later time, some of the descendants of these people, having felt the grossness of King William II of England and constant turmoils under William III when the Prince of Orange harassed him in war from 1689 to 1697, came to America where promises of land grants were made. One of these hardy Irish who came was James Boyd who received a land grant from King William III in 1696 for 4,000 acres of land "on the Santee", below Orangeburg.

The Boyds were a wide and prominent family of Londonderry and Ballemena, Ireland; and we find that at later periods other families of the name came over to America and settled in Virginia, North and South Carolina. John Boyd of Bellemena came over before the Revolutionary War and received a land grant from King George III of England for lands in Ninety-Six District on a tributary of Saluda River, which was in the vicinity of Bush River in Newberry County. He had married in Ireland and had three sons at the time he came over, John, Hugh, and David. There was another, Archibald Boyd, who lived on Cannon's Creek. He may have been a son or a near relative. Each of the three sons received land grants from King George III in the same section.

Reference is made in Carwile's "Reminances of Newberry" to one Thomas Boyd, who was a patriot soldier in the war between William of Orange and his father-in-law, James II. He evidently took an important part in this struggle as is indicated by the role played during the war. He was the maternal grandfather of David Johnstone who was the grandfather of Chancellor Job Johnstone of Newberry. "As Presbyterians, they took sides with William of Orange, and a sword is still in the family, in this country, which was worn by Thomas Boyd, the maternal grandfather of David Johnstone, at the siege of Londonderry - - - -." "The wife of John Johnstone was Mary Caldwell, daughter of Job Caldwell of the County of Londonderry, Ireland. David Johnstone's wife was Sarah Meek."

The immigrants were Covenanters or "Reformed Presbyterians" and were eventually absorbed by the Associate Reformed Presbyterian Church in America. The beginning of the organization was in the year 1638 when the Scottish Presbyterians met in solemn form and declared that all nations, as such, are bound to the worship of God and that a constant practical protest should be made to all nations against founding governments on purely civil principles. Thus, the Puritanical idea and rigidness of purpose were their cardinal points. Therefore, when the commissioners met on a certain day, a "Covenant" was written out, deliberately examined and corrected from time to time and finally adopted by the association as their bond of union with each other and their "Covenant with God". "The solemn League and Covenant" as it was called was agreed to by both the commissioners from Parliament and the Reformed Church of Scotland, with its aim for the "reformation and defense of religion, the honor and happiness of the king, and the peace and safety of the three kingdoms of Scotland, England and Ireland."

It is not known who are the descendants of James Boyd "on the Santee" nor of Robert Boyd of "Long Lane" and William Boyd who lived on "Fishing Creek". John Boyd who lived in Union District, having received a land grant in 1773 from King George III was a Revolutionary war soldier. He died in Union County in 1815 and left widow, Jane, and children, Joseph, Nathan, David, Elizabeth, Samuel and John. Reverend Nathan Boyd moved to Newberry County and settled in the neighborhood of New Hope Methodist Church. The family became Methodists and furnished several preachers of that denomination. He died in 1825 and left a widow Elizabeth, and children, John, Joshua, Aaron, Caleb, George B., James, Mark M., Wesley G., and Lewis M. Two of his sons, Reverend Mark M. and Reverend Wesley G., were ministers in this and other sections, and did effective service for their church in the communities in which they worked. Reverend Mark Boyd was the father of the late Reverend Pettus Boyd who served the Methodist churches in this section for many years, making three generations of ministers.

BOYD (continued)

It was probably between 1760 and 1770 that John Boyd of Bellemena, Ireland, came to America and settled in this section, in Newberry District, then Ninety Six District. When he died in 1806, his two sons, John and David, administered on his estate which was a valuable property on Bush River (the son, Hugh, had died in 1799). John, Jr. served in the American Revolution in Colonel Philemon Water's regiment of state militia. David Boyd was a patriot in the Revolution in Colonel Hammond's regiment of state militia and in 1780 was in General Sumter's cavalry.

John Boyd, Jr., married Margaret _____, and he and his family moved to the state of Kentucky, but he returned to South Carolina in 1814 and died in Newberry County in 1827. Some of his children remained in Kentucky. His wife had previously died and he left a large estate consisting of land on both Bush River and King's Creek, to his children and grandchildren: Elizabeth (wife of Hugh Park), and their children, John B., James, Agnes, Margaret, Mary, Hugh, Elizabeth and Nancy Park; Jane, wife of Anthony Hall, and their children, John, Wilson, William, Joseph, Elizabeth, Anthony Hall, Jr., John Boyd (married 1797 to Nancy _____) and children, Margaret, Sarah, Jeanette, James, Nancy, Elizabeth, and Mary; Janette, wife of Joseph Campbell, and their children, Jane, John, Mary, Wilson, Elizabeth, Agnes and Rachel Campbell; Hugh (he died in 1814, had married Anna Caldwell, daughter of William Caldwell, Esq.) and children, John (married Jane Farr), Elizabeth, William, and Jane Boyd (these lived in Bedford County, Tenn.); Wilson (married _____) and children, Martha P., Margaret, John Kennedy, Benjamin, and Hugh M. Boyd; Margaret (wife of James Dick) and children, Janette, Hugh, Alexander, John, James, William and Joseph Dick; James (married Anne _____) and children, Mary, Spencer, and James Boyd. Executors of the estate were James Clark Boyd, a nephew, and Dr. Andrew Todd. Others who received small shares of the property were, David S. Wilson, Ira Corbin, Thomas Bell and wife, Harrison I. Crenshaw and wife, James Caldwell and Wilson Spence and wife.

David Boyd, Sr., son of John Boyd of Bellemena, received a land grant from King George III of England for 550 acres of Beech Creek (Bush River), a tributary of Saluda River, in 1773 and 1774. He married Eleanor Crosson, daughter of Captain Thomas Crosson, a prominent Irish settler of Virginia, who had moved to South Carolina from that state. Many prominent descendants of this family lived and died in this section and in other states, one of whom was the late Judge Crosson of Texas. He had represented Newberry County in the legislature several terms and was a lawyer of fine practice, but moved to Texas and there became judge and district attorney. They, too, were Covenanters and many are buried in the old Covenanter cemetery. David Boyd and Eleanor Crosson Boyd had children, Jane (married David Chalmers), James Clark, Thomas, Nancy (married Robert Butler relative of General Butler of the Revolution), David, Jr., Mary (married Samuel Redd), and Hugh King Boyd. David and Jane Chalmers Boyd and James Clark Boyd moved to Xenia, Green County, Ohio, and have many descendants in that state. A son, Thomas Chalmers, remained in Newberry. The eldest son, James Clark Chalmers, married Susan Summers (she was a relative of Judge J. B. O'Neall and a descendant of Reverend Joseph Summers, a Quaker preacher of this section). Their children were: Thomas Belton, Helen O'Neall, Harvey, Sarah Jane. Belton died in California. Helen married Jeremiah Parkhill, a nephew of Ex-Governor Morrow of Ohio, and had one child, Louis. Harvey died unmarried, as did Sarah Jane. The other children of David and Jane Chalmers were: Jane Allen, William and Nancy. Jane Allen married Samuel Kyle and had two children, David Chalmers Kyle and Margaret Mitchell Kyle. David C. Kyle is a graduate of Miami University and a national surveyor of note. Margaret Mitchell married Reverend Robert White, a Presbyterian minister who labored for many years in the north and north-west as an able and conscientious minister of his church. They had two children, Chalmers Clindering and Amy Kyle. William Chalmers moved to Green County, Ohio and has descendants in Xenia. Nancy died young and is buried in the old Covenanter cemetery in Newberry County.

Robert and Nancy Butler had three children, David K., James S., and Jane C. M. Nancy died in 1830 and Robert married Emily _____ and had one daughter, Elizabeth. Thomas Boyd and his family moved to Holly Springs, Miss.

One of the principles of the Covenanters was opposition to slavery, and they were forbidden to accept slave-holders as members of the church, so they set free all of their slaves. Reference is made in the "Annals of Newberry" that David Boyd set free all of his slaves but was forced to take them back again because they were unable to take care of themselves. This

BOYD (continued)

rule of the church was adopted in 1800, and it is stated David Boyd had gone to a meeting of the church communion at Chester and on being asked if he would promise to free his slaves, he said that he would free them which he did. Afterwards, it was found they could not support themselves, so the authorities compelled him to take them back and become their guardian.

Samuel Redd and his wife, Mary Boyd Redd (sixth child of David Boyd, Sr., and his wife, Eleanor Crosson Boyd) lived on Bush River. He was a man of ideal principles - a just and good man. They had one son, Dr. George C. Redd, and several daughters, Elizabeth, Nancy H. K., Rebecca and Jemima. One of the daughters married Thomas Henderson of Abbeville district. Samuel Redd and his family moved to Texas and one of their descendants, Reverend George W. Redd, is a distinguished Presbyterian minister of that state.

Hugh K. Boyd, son of David Boyd and Eleanor Crosson Boyd married Louisa E. _____. Their children were: Minor Pitts, Calhoun Fair, Cornelia Dalles, Rosalie Worth, Pressley McMorris, Ellen King, and Josephine. He reared a niece, Jeane McConnell (afterwards Mrs. Jane Sloan), and gave her a large tract of land and a mill. Her son, Reverend James Sloan, was a well known Presbyterian minister, served for forty years in different sections and at one time preached at Long Cane. Hugh K. Boyd was tax collector for Newberry County (called county treasurer now) from 1836 to 1844. Judge O'Neall writes of him as one of the best county officers Newberry County ever had, and "of him, as one of the surviving incumbents, Newberry has great cause to be proud, and in pointing to their officers and lives she may, like the mother of Gracchi, say 'these are my jewels!'". He was also county ordinary from 1844 until his death in 1851. Minor Pitts Boyd moved to Georgia and then to Texas where he died. He was a Confederate soldier in Company E., Third regiment of South Carolina Volunteers.

Calhoun Fair Boyd was in the Confederate service in Company E., of the Third South Carolina regiment of Volunteers and was First Sargeant under Captain James D. Nance. After the war, he married, first, Eliza Wilson, second, Ella Duncan Bell. He was a prominent planter in Newberry and for many years held the office of county treasurer. He was a man of large moral force and character, a Christian gentleman and one who had the confidence of his fellow citizens during the whole of his public administration and during his life. He is well remembered as a man with an optimistic manner and seemed to radiate a congenial atmosphere around the young as well as around the older people. The children by his first wife were, Henry Wilson (died in early manhood), Mary (wife of Captain Henry L. Parr, president of the Exchange Bank of Newberry), William Calhoun (he died young), Sarah (died in infancy), and Hugh K. There was a son of the second marriage, Calhoun D. Boyd, who lives in Florida. Henry L. Parr and his wife, Mary Boyd Parr, had children: Henry Wilson (died young); Eddie May (wife of Ralph Baker, a wholesale merchant of Newberry), children, Ralph Parr, Henry Parr, and Mary Boyd Baker; Azile Jane, married Andrew Johnson Patrick and have one child, Henry Lewis; Callie Boyd Parr married Mary Nance and had, Callie Boyd, Jr., Henry Larkin, James Nance, and William Wilson Parr and Henry Wilson Parr who died in infancy.

Dr. Hugh K. Boyd is the efficient and popular clerk of court of Newberry County. He married Elizabeth Child of Abbeville and they have one son, Hugh K. Boyd, Jr.

Cornelia Dalles Boyd married James Reid but left no children. Rosalie Worth Boyd married M. Girardeau, who lived in Newberry several years ago, died and left one daughter, Beaulah, who married Wylie Draffin. Ellen King Boyd married James O. Weston and had, Dalles, John, Daisy, and Sudie. They live at Fort Worth, Texas. Josephine died unmarried. Pressley McMorris was a soldier in the Confederate army and was killed in action, he left no family.

Hugh Boyd, son of John Boyd of Bellemena, and a Revolutionary war patriot, lived and died in the vicinity of Gilders Creek and Indian Creek. He left widow, Janette and children, John, Matthew, Rosa, Jane, Hugh and Robert. Matthew died in 1835 not married. Hugh died in 1824 and left widow, Frances, and children, Isabella, James C., Matthew, Jane H., (wife of John Williams), Jesse, John T., and Mary. John T. married Margaret Frances Dugan, daughter of Colonel Thomas Dugan, an officer of the Revolutionary War, who is favorably mentioned in the "Annals of Newberry". Jesse Boyd and James C., moved to Laurens County and have descendants around Clinton, some of whom moved to Spartanburg. Robert Boyd married Floretta Gray, daughter of Major Frederick Gray, a distinguished Revolutionary war officer, who moved to Abbeville district and is buried on Gray's Hill, overlooking the Savannah River. John Boyd died in 1850,

BOYD (continued)

left widow, Martha Kelly, and children, William M., Gideon, John, and Matthew.

Archibald Boyd lived on Cannon's Creek, Newberry County, and in 1812 became heir to one half the estate of John Barlow who owned lands on Campen Creek below Prosperity, and moved there. About 1814, he sold his lands on Campen Creek and moved up to a farm between Prosperity and Newberry near "Boyd's Crossing". His wife died very soon after his removal and he died in 1830, left children; Archibald, Jr., (married Esther Young, daughter of a pioneer Irish settler, Abram Young), John (married Mary Wilson), Robert (married Margaret _____), Thomas (married Elizabeth I. _____), Jane (married John Gregg), Mary (married Christopher Waukle), James (died 1829, unmarried), Archibald, Jr. and his wife, Esther, moved to Williamson County, Tenn. Their children were James (died in 1825, unmarried), Eliza (married George Thompson), Sarah (married Nathan Young), Mary Alfred, and Joseph Young Boyd. John and Mary Boyd had a son, Kinard Boyd, who married Elizabeth Schumpert and they moved to Fayette County, Tenn.

Many of these families have located in other states, Alabama, Georgia, Tennessee, Mississippi, Texas, Ohio, and Kentucky. Like many of the old pioneer South Carolina families, they have been prominent and influential citizens in their respective localities, some of their descendants going as far as California where they have upheld their family records and have given to the country lives of service as ministers of the gospel, physicians, lawyers, and other professions.

There were other families of Boyds. Some of whom first settled in Laurens County before the Revolutionary War. James, Samuel and William Boyd were given land grants under King George III in the vicinity of Rabun's Creek and Reedy River in that County. They have many descendants in various sections of this state and Georgia. John, son of James, died in 1827 and left children (wife probably had previously died), Abraham, John D., William, Edney, (wife of Woodson Seay), Patsy (wife of Joel Allen), Polly (wife of John H. Boyd), Nancy (wife of Frank Ross), Sallie (wife of Raymond Fuller), Rebecca (wife of Walter D. A. Dean). Joel Allen (a descendant of Charles Allen of the Revolution) and his wife Patsy, had children, Charles, Samuel, Susan, Lydal, Rebecca, Minema, Drury Bacon, William and Milly.

William and Samuel Boyd, sons of John Boyd, lived on Quaker Creek of Little River. Bradford Boyd, a son of John or of William, moved to Georgia and has descendants in that state. He married Margaret Watkins. Samuel Boyd, brother of Bradford, married Nancy Henry of Laurens County and had David, John, Bradford, Sanford and Harrison. David had a son, Bradford, who moved to Texas and died in that state.

Captain Thomas Boyd, a prominent planter of Lexington district, and living near "Spring Hill", was born about 1750. He was a patriot in the Revolutionary War. For several years he held the office of Justice of the Quorum for that district. He married Eve Anne Summer, daughter of Frances Summer, a soldier of the Revolution in the South Carolina Continentals and a son of the pioneer, John Adam Summer. Their children were: Esther (married David Richardson), Margaret (married Jacob Lindler), Janette (married Dempsey Busby), Jane, Robert C., and Thomas, Jr. James C. married the widow of John George Houseal (Mary Margaret Summer, daughter of Colonel John Adam Summer, Jr.). Robert C. moved to Georgia. Thomas Boyd, Jr. married first, Miss Houseal, and second, Miss Kleaser. There were no children from either marriage.

Reverend James C. Boyd was the pastor of Head Springs Prosperity and Cannon's Creek Churches for several years. He was a graduate of Erskine College, and married first, a Miss Pressly and second, Fannie McClintock, sister of the late Dr. E. P. McClintock, who was pastor of the A. R. P. Church in Newberry for so many years. There was a daughter, Fannie, by his first wife, and several children by his second wife: Bessie (married a Bruce), Edward (living in Statesville, N. C.), and others.

David Boyd, of Laurens County, died about 1839, left widow, Margaret, and a child, Jane, who became the wife of Samuel R. Todd.

James Boyd of Laurens County, married Abigail Hunter, daughter of Laughlin and Esther Hunter, and had children: James H., John H., Lucinda (wife of Benjamin Blakely). James Boyd died in 1816, and his widow died in 1857.

BOYD (continued)

James Boyd, son of William, (of Laurens County) died about 1847, leaving widow, Elizabeth, and children: David, William B., Isaac P., Sara K. (wife of Robert K. Simpson), Nancy (wife of John Ballentine), Catherine (wife of Leroy L. Pitts), Jane (wife of T. A. Peden), Elizabeth C. (wife of Joseph Hipp), James F., and Margaret E.

John Boyd made will September 7, 1818, died in Edgefield County in 1822 (will recorded in that county April 10, 1822). Legatees: Children - - Henry K., Maria, and John Boyd; brothers - - Robert and Hezekiah; a sister, Ann Boyd.

Samuel Boyd of Laurens County married Nancy Henry and had children: David (married Margaret Ross), John, Bradford (he moved to Georgia), Sanford, Harrison, and Katherine. David had a son, Bradford, who moved to Texas and died.

John Boyd, of Union County, a Revolutionary war patriot, died about 1815, left widow, Jane and children: Joseph, Nathan, David, Elizabeth, Frederick, Samuel and John.

Benjamin Boyd, Jr. died in Union County on May 19, 1819. He left a widow, Sarah and children: Mary W., Jane H., and Louisa E.

Where are the many families who once lived here and helped build a state now developed into an important unit of our commonwealth? They laid the foundation for this growth by their strict principles of justice and strict observance of the laws of their God, and effective influence upon successive generations. When we observe the great changes that have come about in a few years, the families who have become scattered in different sections, the new people who have moved and settled among us, there is no conception of a human mind deep enough to visualize any of the things that will happen in the future. Like Benjamin Taylor we thing that - -

"A wonderful stream is the river of Time,
As it runs through the realms of Tears.
With a faultless rythm and musical rhyme,
And a broader sweep and a surge sublime,
As it blends with the Ocean of years."

BURTON

The Burtons were at one time numerous in the Counties of Newberry, Laurens and Abbeville. Later, many moved to other States.

There was a Thomas Burton (born 1678, died 1757), who lived in or near Charleston, South Carolina. He married Mary Keeler (born 1665, died 1750). Their daughter, Sarah, married Thomas Potts, Sr.

Another Thomas Burton who died in Laurens District about 1810, left widow, Lillian, and the following children: Robert, Samuel, Benjamin, Rebecca Ward, Anna and Judah. The last two named children were minors at the time of his death.

William Burton, Sr., who lived on Beaver Dam Creek, in Newberry County, married Phoebe _____. He made a will in 1812, but revoked it and made a new will in 1823. He died about 1826, leaving widow, and the following children: Gibeon, William G., Aaron, Cynthia (wife of Daniel Towles), Phoebe (wife of William Reagan; she died early). Cynthia Towles died October 17, 185_ and her husband died soon afterwards. They left children: Edney (wife of John Stephens), Phoebe (wife of Martin Longshore), Sarah (wife of Patrick Lynott), William, Oliver, Jane Pitts, and Peter.

William Burton, Jr., son of William, Sr., made will in 1828, and died in 1829, leaving widow, Lucretia, and the following children: James G. (he died July 25, 1841), not married; William (died 1834, not married), Henry, Phoebe (wife of Christopher Griffin), Lura (wife of Reuben Pitts), Elizabeth (wife of John A. Partlow), and John G. Phoebe was married three times, first, to Cary Williams by whom she had James Pinckney Williams and Lucretia Williams (she married William Y. Dorroh). Her second husband was Christopher Griffin, and after his death, she married Richard S. Cannon who died January 30, 1844. Another son of William, Jr. was Douglass who died before the death of his father.

Mrs. Lucretia (Davenport) Burton, widow of William, Jr., died June 10, 1855. Of the children who shared in her estate, the daughter Phoebe, is shown as wife of Bennett Wallace (this indicates probably Phoebe was married four times) . . . . The daughter, Elizabeth, who married John Partlow was living in Abbeville, and had children: Lura A., John E., Susannah L., and Emma C.

Joseph Burton made a will dated September 5, 1809, and died in Abbeville County about 1811. Children named in his will were: John, William, Mary (whose daughter, Edney, received her share), Elizabeth, Sarah, Catherine, Mahatobel, Josiah, and Douglass.

CALDWELL

During the latter part of the 14th and early part of the 15th centuries, many French Huguenots were expelled from their native land by the revocation of the Edict of the Nantes. Some went to England, and Ireland, then to America. There were three brothers named John, Alexander and Oliver Cauldwell, who first went to England, then settled in Scotland. They purchased an old bishopric estate and the name "Caldwell" was given it by the English King.

Some descendants of these brothers went to Ireland with Oliver Cromwell (whose grandmother was a Caldwell), their names being Daniel, Joseph, John, Andrew and David. They settled in Counties Antrim and Kent. When Cromwell was called to the protectorship of England and the crown restored to Charles II, three of these brothers, John, David and Andrew, fled to America. Joseph died in Ireland, while Daniel continued there though some of his children later went to America, and settled in Pennsylvania, Rhode Island, and Virginia.

William Caldwell and his wife, Rebecca Walkup, came from County Antrim, Ireland, to Pennsylvania, and settled near his cousins who were living in that State in 1740. In 1749, he and his family moved to Charlotte County, Va., where William died, leaving his widow and ten children. The children were: John, William, David, James, Margaret, Martha, Eleanor, Elizabeth, Rebecca, and Sarah. Later, about 1760-65, the widow moved with her children to South Carolina, and settled in Ninety Six District, through the influence of her son, John, an eminent surveyor, who had been doing work in that part of South Carolina.

John Caldwell located much land in the district for the early settlers at a time when the country was not much more than wild brush. He settled near Mudlic Creek, above Little River.

CALDWELL (continued)

He married Margaret Davidson; later was killed by Tories, near the end of Revolutionary War, in his own yard. He left no children. During the War, he was a Captain of militia, the first company of Rangers in the district. He was a member of the Provincial Congress which met in Charleston in 1776. During the war, he was promoted to major.

William Thomas Caldwell, brother of Major John (above), first settled in Abbeville District, where his sister, Martha, was living as the wife of Patrick Calhoun (these were parents of the famous South Carolina statesman, John C. Calhoun). Later, he went to Newberry District and settled near his brothers on Little River. He, too, became a surveyor. He was a patriot in the Revolutionary War; joined his brother John's regiment of Rangers, served until he was captured and sent to St. Augustine, Florida prison for several months. After his release, he came back home, and joined the company of his brother James who was Captain of Infantry. He married Elisabeth Williams and had children: John (married Elizabeth _____ and then Abigail O'Neall), William, Williams, James (some of his children were Sarah, Cataline, Ferdinand), Patrick C. (he married Fannie Nance, daughter of Major Frederick Nance), Elizabeth Ann (she married Francis B. Higgins and had John C. and Elizabeth), Joseph (married Nancy _____).

Patrick Caldwell was a graduate of South Carolina College, studied Law and practiced in Newberry. He served two terms as U. S. Congressman from this district.

James Caldwell, brother of Major John and William Thomas, as a Captain of Infantry in the Revolutionary War, was in the battle of Cowpens under General Pickens. During the battle, he was severely wounded and left for dead on the battle field. After the battle, his brother William Thomas, sought his body, and when he was found alive, the brother brought him into camp, dressed his wounds. He was incapacitated for further service in the war. After the war, he became one of the first members of the State Legislature; then he served one term as Sheriff of Newberry County, refusing to offer for re-election. He married Elizabeth Forrest and had children: James; William Thomas, (he married (1) Matilda Creswell and (2) Harriet McDowell) -- children by first wife being James C. and William E.; George F. (married Edna _____ and had James, Charlotte, George R., Rebecca, and Amy), John H. (left no family), David Robert, Samuel (married first to _____ and second to Rosannah Waters Cothran) and had children (by first wife) -- Samuel, Hugh, Leonard, Hamilton, Lenny, Nancy, and (by his second wife) -- Francis D., Anthony G., and Elisabeth A); Frances E. (she married Hugh Dixon); Rebecca W. (she married James Sprowles and had children: Frances, who became wife of Wade S. Cothran, James C., Mary Ann who married J. L. Pearson, Charles W.); Polly (she married James Young). The son, James, became a lawyer and moved to Sumter, S. C. He married Elizabeth Miller and subsequently moved to Alabama, where he died, leaving five children. One of the children, James Miller Caldwell, became a prominent merchant at Charleston, S. C., where he married Annie Fresail, and they left many descendants.

One Robert Caldwell, probably a son of David or of Robert Caldwell, Sr., married Elizabeth Spence and had children: William, James, and Robin. William married Catherine Davenport and had William W., Elizabeth, Mattie, Nancy and Fannie. James married Jane Davenport, and had Robert, Wilson, John A.; Robin married Miss Sloan, and had William and Calvin.

John Caldwell, a descendent of Daniel who remained in Ireland, came to South Carolina about 1765-68. He first settled in the North section of Dutch Fork (in Newberry section) then in Ninety Six District. He married Janett Helen Peden, in Ireland, and brought his wife and one or two infant children. His oldest son, Joseph, (died 1808) married Margaret Wilson and had James, Dan, and Samuel, and a minor son, Joseph at time of his death, and a daughter, Rebecca, who afterwards married Robert Redd. His wife was the daughter of Francis and Sarah Wilson. A son, John, married Rose Ann _____ and had children: William, Mary P., Margaret, James, Janett, Daniel, Samuel, Archibald. A son, Daniel, married Janette McMaster, and had children: James J. (he married Nancy McMorries, daughter of James McMorries); Eleanor (she married Archibald Fair and had James, Jane, and Calphemia); Mary Ann; Margaret; Rosannah (she married James Brown). A son, James, married Mary Wilson, daughter of "elder" James Wilson, and had children: Joseph, James P., Jane (she married William W. McMorries). There were two other sons, William and Robert, and probably a son, Samuel. Mary Ann probably married Andrew Russell.

The second son of the pioneer, John, was James, who died about 1848. He married Eliza Wilson who died in 1842. She was a daughter of "Elder" James Wilson. Their children were

CALDWELL (continued)

James (he married Sarah B. Chapman); Joseph (he married, first, Margaret Wilson, and second, Angelina Turnipseed). There were two children by Joseph's first wife, Thomas Wilson Caldwell, and George Caldwell. There was a daughter by the second wife who married Joseph Hunter. Other children were: Thomas, John, Eliza and Jane.

There was another pioneer, named John Caldwell, who settled in Spartanburg District before the Revolutionary War. He came from Ireland with his wife, Mary Young. He had a son, William, who married Margaret Crawford, and another son, John. William and Margaret Crawford had children: John C., James, Patrick, William, Polly (she married John Miller), Jean, Kate, Elizabeth, Ann (she married _____ Anderson), Margaret (she married _____ Gaston), Eleanor (she married _____ Wright). John C. married California Coan and had children: Mary C., Andrew J., Sarah Ann, Amanda, Adolphus Leland. Jean married Robert McCorley.

Those who died in Abbeville County were:
John Caldwell, who died about 1795, leaving widow, Elizabeth, and children: William, James, David, Anne Rolfe, Isabel Pickens, Mary Black, Andrew and Jean. The last two named were 21 years old in 1795. The widow died in 1815.

Another John died about 1798, leaving widow, Nancy, and brothers and sisters, Charles, Henry, James, and Joseph.

James Caldwell, Sr., died about 1804, leaving a widow and children: John, David, Rebecca, Elizabeth Wilson, Mary Davis, James, William, Ezekiel, Thomas. (James was son of John - another James the son of David). Other legatees: James Caldwell Pickens, James Wilson, James Davis, Elizabeth Harris Caldwell, Eliza Harris Caldwell, William Leslie, and Elizabeth Harris Kerr.

CANNON

John Cannon, the progenitor of the Cannons of Newberry District, was the son of an Irishman, who settled in the southern part of the State. He died in Charleston District about 1763, leaving the following children: Ephriam, Mary (wife of Jacob Pennington), James, Susannah (wife of Christopher White), Margaret, Rebecca, and Agness (wife of George Smith). It is thought there were two other sons, Samuel and John.

Ephriam Cannon came from Colleton District, settled on a creek in Newberry County, called Cannons Creek, where he received a grant of 200 acres. John Cannon had already settled in the vicinity, for whom the creek was named. He was a brother of Ephriam. Ephriam died about 1803, leaving a widow, Eleanor (she later married John Ulmer), and children: Ephriam (he died about 1818-20, left no family), Samuel, David, John, Rachel, Rebecca Suber, Jane (wife of Samuel Maffett); and a deceased daughter's children (wife of George Martin), Solomon and Mary Martin. The son, John died early, but left several children to share in his father's estate, viz: Jane (wife of John Sligh), David, Ephriam, Anna, Barthdamew, and James. James settled in Anderson County. John Sligh and Jane had a son, Henry. Jane Sligh, after death of John Sligh, married James Hutchinson by whom she had a son, John W. Hutchinson. Another daughter of John was Mary who married Jacob Cromer.

John Cannon received a grant of 100 acres of land on south side of Broad River, on Cannons Creek, in 1774. Land was bounded by lands of James Cannon.

David Cannon (son of Ephriam) was a Revolutionary War patriot, Quartermaster in Colonel Phil. Water's Regiment of militia since the fall of Charleston. After the war, he married Nancy _____ and had children: George J., David M., Thomas V., Sarah (wife of George Setzler), Mary (wife of John Adam Wicker), Samuel D., Anna (wife of Jerry Hutchinson), Mahala (wife of Martin Riser), and William. The son, David, married Mary Magdelina Folk, daughter of John Folk. She died in 1830, left children: John A., Margaret, William, Eli E., Elizabeth, Martha A., and George M. Cannon.

Samuel D. Cannon married Christina _____, and had children: Elizabeth (wife of George A. Sligh), Nancy B., David Albert, Samuel D. Preston, and Jacob Harrison Cannon.

Samuel William Cannon married Lavania E. Gallman, daughter of John G. and Susannah (Gray) Gallman. (See Gray-DeWalt Family).

Samuel Cannon died in Newberry District about 1791, left widow, Lydia, who was the daughter of Isaac Pennington. Their children were: John, Isaac, James, Mary, William, Lydia, Kisiah, and Elizabeth. John died in 1828, and left widow, Eleanor, and children: Isaac, Mary, Gideon, Daniel, and Jabes. William died in 1815, left widow, Elizabeth, and children: Mary Ann, Henry, Nancy, David R., and Elizabeth. Isaac, son of Samuel died about 1808, left widow, Sarah, and children: William, Richard, Mary, and Isaac Pennington Cannon.

CANNON (continued)

There were Cannons in Darlington District, who came originally from the section around Charleston. The Cannons in Spartanburg District were of two sects, one from the Darlington family, and the other from North Carolina.

John Cannon who died in Spartanburg County about 1788, left a widow, Sarah, and children: Ellis, Mason, Jesse, and Lydia.

One Robert Cannon and a Henry Cannon died in Spartanburg County.

CHANDLER AND GILBERT

The Gilbert family was of English descent. One Thomas Gilbert having come from England about 1625 to 1650, settled in the vicinity of Wethersfield, Conn. This was just after Sir Humphrey Gilbert, an English nobleman, brought a colony to Virginia and attempted a settlement in that state in the year 1578 and again in the year 1583. History states that his step-brother, Sir Walter Raleigh, came with a colony in 1587 at which time he discovered the Chesapeake Bay. Neither of these two succeeded in planting a colony that endured the hostile attitude of the Indians. It was not until Captain John Smith settled with his colony at Jamestown in 1606 that the first permanent settlement was made.

It is stated that Sir John Gilbert of Devonshire, England, came with the Plymouth colony in 1638 and settled in Taunton, Mass. This Sir John was the father or brother of William Gilbert who had five sons, one of whom was Thomas Gilbert, who removed to Wethersfield, Conn. In the next generation was Josiah Gilbert, whose son, Caleb, removed from Connecticutt to South Hampton, Long Island, in 1694. This Caleb Gilbert married Elizabeth _____, and had Caleb, Jr., whose first wife, Phoebe, is buried at South Hampton, Long Island.

Just what time Caleb Gilbert, (he was probably a son of Caleb who moved to Long Island) came to South Carolina is not known, but it was just before or just after the Revolutionary War. It may have been he, who along with his brother, Samuel, was captured by the British in 1782 and sent to Mill Prison, at Plymouth, England. They were subsequently released and sent back to America.

The Chandler and Gilbert families were intermarried after their settlements in South Carolina, and belonged to that thriving and well-to-do class of people, who with their courageous and undaunted spirits, helped to build a new country offering glowing opportunities, though in the face of hostile opposition by the Indian tribes.

There were living in Newberry County, two brothers, natives of Virginia, William Chandler, Sr. and James Chandler. Each received a land grant in 1772 from the king, George the Third of England, for lands on the Enoree River. Their descendants moved to other sections. A son, John, moved to Greenville County about 1785. His wife was named Reta. Another son, Jesse, died in 1822 and left his widow, Mary, and children, Franky, Nathan, and Anna. Another John Chandler and his wife, Katherine, also lived on Enoree River. Some of these moved over into Union and Laurens Counties.

Jacob Chandler, born in 1725, came to South Carolina from Pennsylvania and received a grant of land on Bush River. His wife, Anne Chandler, came to this state with him. Their children were Elizabeth, Jonathan (married Rebecca _____), Israel (married Lydia Gilbert, daughter of Caleb Gilbert), and Lydia. Jacob Chandler was too old for active service in the Revolutionary War, but he furnished provisions for the army and manifested his patriotism to the Whig cause, and is, therefore, listed as a patriot. His son, Jonathan, who married Rebecca _____, had Jonathan, Jr., Elizabeth and Charles, and probably others. The other son, Israel and his wife, Lydia Gilbert Chandler, had children: Elizabeth (she married first, a Zeigler, and second, William Inman), Israel, Jr. (he died young, not married), Anna (married Reuben G. Case), Eunice (married Carey Gilbert), Haney (married John Davis), Thomas, and Dorothy (married John Reagin). Several of these moved to the state of Tennessee, viz: Carey Gilbert and his wife, Eunice, John Davis and his wife, Haney, John Reagin and wife, Dorothy.

Caleb Gilbert, who lived on Bush River, died in 1805 and his widow, Anne, died in 1806. They lived in a progressive section of the county and not far from the home of Hugh O'Neall, the father of Judge John Belton O'Neall, whose record as a state supreme court judge is well known. Some of the relatives of Judge O'Neall migrated to the state of Ohio, and I have no doubt but that some of the Gilberts and Chandlers also went to that section; for many living in the vicinity moved. The families of Inman and Pemberton, who lived in the same vicinity, went to the Northwest during this exodus to Ohio. The children of Caleb and Anne Gilbert were Caleb, Jr., Thomas, Lydia (wife of Israel Chandler), Joseph, Sara (wife of a Mr. McNary),

CHANDLER AND GILBERT (continued)

Synthia (married a Mr. Reagin), and Anne (she died young, not married). Thomas Gilbert married Rebecca _____, and they moved to Limestone County, Tenn. He died at Gilbertsboro, Ala., in 1835, having removed from Tennessee to that section. One of his sons, Carey, who had married Eunice Chandler, daughter of Israel Chandler, Sr., also lived in that section. One of their daughters, Elizabeth, is the wife of Prof. J. D. Sandifer, President of Simmons University, at Abilene, Texas.

Caleb Gilbert, Sr., and his brother, David Gilbert, were active soldiers in the Revolutionary War. They both served in the South Carolina militia, David during the years 1780 to 1782. David married Catherine Eichleberger, daughter of Col. John Eichelberger, Sr., and they moved to Lauderdale County, Alabama.

Caleb Gilbert, Jr., died in 1815. He married Kerziah _____, and had a son, Josiah, and other children. Dempsey Gilbert was probably a son who lived on adjoining lands.

Jonathan Gilbert lived in the Bush river section. There is a record of a conveyance of land in the year 1788 by Jonathan and his wife, Hanamiel Gilbert. He is listed as a patriot in the Revolutionary War, having furnished supplies for the army.

In the "Annals of Newberry" there is a reference to one Mordecai Chandler who was in the Revolutionary War in the company of Captain James Lyles. He, (Chandler) and one Reddin were made prisoners after a fight with two men who had professed to them to be Whigs, but afterwards proved to be English or Tories. While Chandler and Reddin were asleep their guns were taken and Chandler was wounded in the head, hence they were taken prisoners to Ninety Six and delivered to Colonel Cruger, the English commander, and were kept prisoners until the fort was evacuated.

Thomas Chandler, son of Israel Chandler, married twice. His first wife was Elizabeth Halfacre, daughter of Captain Henry Halfacre, great grandfather of J. B. Halfacre, county auditor of Newberry) and had children: Margaret Lavania, Drayton Israel Jacob, Mary A. E., (she died young) Lambert H. C., Whitfield G. S., Thomas Chandler's second wife was Dorothy Suber and had one child, Dorothy E. Chandler. Lambert H. C. Chandler who lives at "Beth Eden", Newberry County, married Della Maffett who was a relative of Lieutenant Colonel R. C. Maffett, a distinguished Confederate officer who died in the war. They had one son, Thomas, who died a few years ago, leaving a widow and two small sons. The widow afterwards married Fred Cromer.

Lambert H. C. Chandler has in his possession two interesting heirlooms and relics. One is an old clock now nearly two hundred years old which was brought from Pennsylvania by his colonial ancestor, Jacob Chandler, before the Revolutionary War. It is one of those very tall and wide clocks with double doors, almost large enough for an average man to stand in. The other is an old Bible which has been in the family about one hundred and fifty years, having been first used by Jacob Chandler about the period of 1760-75, and it is still in good state of preservation.

Many descendants of the old families have moved from time to time to other states and sections. The Chandler and Gilbert names are almost extinct in Newberry County. William Gilbert settled in Laurens County, died there and left children: James, Sarah(married John Dean), Elisabeth (married a Collins), Mary (married a Wilson), William, Jr., John, Nancy (married an Austin), Jeremiah, Rebecca (married a Burchfield), and Joshua. Joshua and his wife, Jincy, had a son, Samuel. Jeremiah died in Laurens County in 1855, left a widow, Leah, and children, Nancy (wife of M. A. Hunter), Elizabeth (wife of John T. Bennett), Hosuit (wife of Sterling Smith), Mary (wife of Thomas Hopkins), William, Joshua, Jeremiah, Hannah (wife of John Baldwin), Silas, and Amelia (wife of John Childress).

Alexander M. Gilbert removed from Laurens County to Rutherford County, North Carolina, in the year 1797. He was a brother of William Gilbert. He has descendants in that state. Booker Gilbert left Laurens County and moved to Clark County, Alabama, about the year 1815.

There is another branch of the Connecticutt family of Gilberts, who came to South Carolina several years before the Civil war and lived in Sumter. He was the father of the late Rev. Gilbert, Methodist minister whose last wife was a Newberry lady, Miss Bushardt, sister of Captain Cornelius Bushardt, and by whom were three children, Fred, Mary and Buford. Buford saw service in France during the World War and was captured by the Germans and was for several months prisoner behind the German lines.

During the colonial period and since the Revolutionary War, many descendants of old pioneer families of the North, as well as those of Virginia and North Carolina, came to South Carolina and chose to settle among people, who had already shown the varied opportunities offered in the state. Maybe the apple blossoms bloomed earlier, and the peaches were more attractive; for the season is most always right. At later times some may have moved from

CHANDLER AND GILBERT (continued)

from South Carolina to other states, but not until they had gathered the peaches were they willing to seek new fields of opportunities. However, South Carolina passed through a critical period before and after the Revolution (probably not as bad as just after the Civil war) and many families left her borders on account of the Indians who molested the settlements frequently, and sometimes massacred small settlements.

The Gilberts who lived in Laurens County moved away but we find that two brothers, Jeremiah and Joshua, owned lands in that section at a later period, after the Civil War. There were two other brothers, Abram and Lovinski Gilbert, sons of Abram Gilbert, Sr., who lived in Laurens County, but in the year 1820, they were residents in the town of Newberry and were merchants. They operated a large general store for several years, in the rear of which they operated a billiard room, a "red brick store" owned by Henry Coate. Abram Gilbert, Jr., married Elizabeth West. He left Newberry after assigning his interest in the firm to his brother, Lovinski, and moved to Columbus, Georgia, about 1830. In the year 1840, he moved to Texas and bought up some large ranches but becoming dissatisfied, he and his family were returning to Georgia when he died on the way, in East Texas. The family then moved up into Green County, Alabama, where relatives were living. One of his sons was a gallant officer in the Confederacy, Captain of a company of Alabama volunteers.

CHAPMAN

When the English first settled the Southern section of South Carolina, around Charleston, there were Chapmans who came over from England and helped build the state in that section. Later, some of these moved into the interior. While the name is primarily English, there were two different families that settled in Dutch Fork before the Revolution.

One Giles Chapman came from Bridlington, England, though of Welsh descent, about the year 1725, with his wife Sarah Jackson, and settled in Virginia. They had six children in Virginia, viz: Elizabeth, Samuel, Rachel, Joseph, Sarah, Giles. The family moved to the province of South Carolina and located near the village of Newberry. The son, Giles, became a minister and preached the Dunker faith (this sect originated in Germany and at one time was called German Baptists, the word Dunker or Tunker, meaning "Dippers" - they baptized by having the person kneel and then dipped his head under the water). The Dunkers never shaved their beard nor cut their hair. He preached around Newberry for several years, the church being located near his home about three miles east of Newberry. Afterwards, the Tunkers were combined with the Universalists and he became a Universalist preacher. During the American Revolution, he served as chaplain, in company of Captain William Frederick Houseal and regiment of Colonel Philemon Waters. Reverend Giles Chapman married Mary Summers, daughter of Reverend Joseph Summers, a Universalist preacher who moved to Newberry from Maryland and settled on Bush River. They had the following children: Joseph, Elijah, Elizabeth, who married an Elmore; Nancy, who married a Mills; William, Giles, John, David B., Samuel, and Lewis. Lewis married Rhoda O'Neall, and had one son, Reverend James K. P. Chapman, who moved to Appleton City, Mo. Some of the others moved to the Northwest. (Ref.: Annals of Newberry, Part 2).

The Reverend Giles Chapman was the grandfather of the late John A. Chapman, co-author with Judge O'Neall of the "Annals of Newberry", and was the great-grandfather of the late John W. Chapman, city clerk and treasurer. He has other descendants in this section, some of whom are Reverend A. J. Bowers and former Mayor Z. F. Wright.

Two of the Revolutionary war patriots, Joseph Chapman and William P. Chapman, served in Winn's Regiment of South Carolina militia from Fairfield district. What relation these were to the Newberry County families I have been unable to ascertain. Presumably, some of their descendants moved across the river into Newberry County.

Samuel Chapman died June 1, 1790, leaving a widow, Nancy. He married twice, having married second time February 9, 1775. Children by his first wife were: Giles (died 1792), William (died 179_), Samuel, Rachel B., Alsia, and Sally. Children of the second wife were: Marmaduke, Archibald, Polly (married Joshua Griffith), Nancy (wife of Thomas McConnell), Robert (died without issue), Joseph, Elijah, and Jane. Joshua Griffith died 1812, and left four small children; his widow married a McCollough. Samuel, the father, received a grant

CHAPMAN (continued)

of land in 1772 from King George III, of England, for 100 acres on Cannon's Creek.

William Chapman, brother of Samuel, died about 1790, and left three daughters, viz: Mary (wife of John West Grissam), Lydia (wife of John Douglass), and Delila (she was living in Pendleton District in 1797).

Giles Chapman, son of Samuel, died about 1792, and left two daughters: Charity (wife of James D. B. McCooly), and Abigail (wife of Isaac Collins). They moved to Virginia in 1810.

Joseph Chapman died about 1818, left widow, Penelope, and children: William, Samuel, Sarah. They were children by a former marriage.

William Chapman, son of Joseph, died about 1824, and left children: Jacob, David, Polly (wife of George McCollough), Amos, Elizabeth (wife of Elijah Lynch), Moses, Elijah, William, Joseph, and Giles.

Samuel, son of Joseph, died about 1820, and left several children, some of whom were: John, Elizabeth, Joshua, and Mary.

John Chapman made will in 1849, and died in Spartanburg County in 1854. Children: Edward Wilson, John, Elizabeth, Richardson, Lorenzo D., M. H. (a deceased son), Beverly R., Ann Evans, Mahala Turner, and Polly Legge.

Mrs. Mary Chapman, widow, died about 1844, leaving the following legatees: Children: Mary Ann Glenn, Anna L. Brown, Sarah B., wife of James P. Caldwell; sisters: Anne Laramore, Eleanor Douglass, Sarah Burch, Bridgett Scott; granddaughters: Mary E. Caldwell, Jane H. Caldwell, Mary S. Glenn, Mary Sophia Chapman, Mary Susan Logan.

John Chapman died 1854 in Spartanburg County. He left widow, Rosea, and children: Warren D., Marcus B., Chevis M., John N., Margaret Ann, Nancy C., Octavia C., and Perry E.

Giles M. Chapman married Mary Ann Mobley, daughter of Thomas Mobley of Union County.

B. M. Chapman married Louisa T. Mobley, daughter of Thomas Mobley of Union County.

Abraham Chapman, who settled in the "Dutch Fork", in Newberry County before the Revolutionary War, according to tradition, was an Englishman, and came from Pennsylvania with the colony of Germans, Dutch, and Irish to Newberry County.

Abram Chapman lived near Pomaria before the American Revolution. He married about 1770 to Anna Elizabeth _____, and had the following children: John, William, Catherine, Mary Elizabeth, Margaret, Christina; Catherine married a Fulmer and after his death married George A. Summer. Mary married Frederick A. Kinard, son of Martin Kinard. Margaret married a Fulmer. Christina married John Houseal and after his death, married a Leitzsey.

John Chapman, son of Abram, married Anne Mary _____, and both are buried in the churchyard of the historic church, St. John's (Lutheran), about two miles south of Pomaria. The names of their children were: David (married Elizabeth Summer, Jr.), Elizabeth (married Captain George Epting), Abram (married Mary Addy), Adam (married Elizabeth Fulmer), Polly (married Michael Summer), David had Paul, Adam, Victoria, Augusta. Abram moved to Edgefield County. John had William, John G., John A., Henry H., Walter N., David F., Martha Ann (married John W. Wilson), Polly Katherine (married Joseph L. Haltiwanger), Susan Frances (married Jacob Setzler), and Melvina C. Chapman.

William Chapman, son of Abram, married Mary Elizabeth _____, and had the following children: Mary Elizabeth who married an Abrams, George Henry, Catherine, who married David Koone, Jr., William Robert, Franklin, William Etta, and a daughter who married John Miller. Captain George Henry Chapman married Annie Kibler, granddaughter of Major William Summer, and were parents of the following: Jane, who married Charles Counts, Susan, John, Noah, whose daughter, Anna (now of Albuquerque, N. M.), married the late Reverend George A. Riser. Cummings who married George Swygert, and Dr. James K. (married Mary Summer, daughter of Henry Summer, Esq.). George Swygert and his wife, Cummings Chapman, were parents of the wife of W. W. Berley of Pomaria. William R. Chapman married just across the line of Lexington County.

There were three sons of William Chapman (the son of John), and his wife Christina Wicker, viz: John, David and J. Lemuel. John and David moved to Edgefield County. Lemuel Chapman married, first, a Miss Swittenberg, by whom were, William M., who lives near Little Mountain; John J., who lives at Ward, S. C.; Jane, who married Noah Shealy, and were parents of Albert, Frank and Darr Shealy, the famous baseball stars at Newberry College a few years ago. Albert Shealy was once a pitcher for the New York Yankees in the American League. Mary, another daughter, married John Miller. Martha married Henry Black of Saluda, S. C., Elvira married Richard Stoudemire of Saluda. The second wife of J. Lemuel Chapman was a Miss Dreher, by whom were three daughters and two sons. The sons are B. V. Chapman, attorney

CHAPMAN (continued)

and state senator of Newberry, and Reverend H. D. Chapman, Lutheran Minister, now preaching at Sharpsburg, Md.

Franklin Chapman, son of William, Sr., was the father of Franklin, Jr. and grandfather of Owens Chapman of Peak, S. C.

There is a record of an old deed of land made in the year 1803, in Newberry County Court House, a clerk of court, showing that one Joseph Chapman transferd title to lands on Broad River to David Chapman. This land was originally granted to Joseph Chapman in the year 1771. His wife's name was Catherine.

Elisabeth Chapman, who married Frederick Kinard, had five children, viz: Sarah, Katherine, Elizabeth, William and Frederick.

It is said that the German for "Chapman" is "Kaughman", meaning "Cheap-man". In the early times, probably in the time of the Crusades, or just after the war of the Crusades, when many family names were adapted from names of occupations, this name was given. He was a man who sold small articles cheap and thus became known as the "Cheap-man".

The Chapmans are very numerous in this state now, some moving from other states. There was a Chapman family living in Columbia about 25 years ago who came from a New England state. Very likely they have descendants living in that section at the present time.

COUNTS

One of the early Germans who came to South Carolina and settled in the "Dutch Fork" was Johannes Kounts. He came about 1750 and like many of the old German pioneers,must have first settled in Pennsylvania before coming South. He was married when he came, had three sons, John, Jacob and Henry, when he settled on Crimm's Creek where he received a land grant from King George the Third of England in the year 1751 for 350 acres of land. The English spelling of the name is "John Counts".

The German empire was feeling a disturbance of its economic position when so many of its best citizens were immigrating to America, due primarily to a religious intolerance, incompatible with the views of the Reformed church which by this time was exerting a large influence among the people. The attempted reforms from 1450 to 1500, and again in the year 1515 when one Ulric Zuingle began a strong effort, in the North of Switzerland, to break away from the power of Catholicism by the organization of a Reformed church but with no successful result, brought about a determined effort on the part of Martin Luther. He had come to the people admidst the moral earthquake then permeating the country, with a courageous spirit and that of a martyr, and proclaimed the reformation.

The German settlers in South Carolina, and the Swiss, were people of the highest type, seeking religious freedom and opportunities for personal liberty. Having aided in developing an unknown and barren country by their thrift and industry, for which they were widely known, they felt keenly the extreme restrictions put upon them by the English government in high taxes and enforced measures taking away their personal liberty, so that when the Revolutionary War came on, practically all of them were patriots.

John Counts, son of the pioneer, was a lieutenant in Beard's regiment of state troops during the Revolution, in company of Captain John Adam Summer. His brother, Henry, is listed as a patriot in the state historical commission's office, having furnished provisions for commissioners during the war.

John Counts, patriot, married Mary _____, and had several children. He lived on Crimm's Creek on part of the lands originally granted his father. John Counts or Johannes Kounts. A son of the patriot, also named John, married first, Elisabeth Eichleberger and second, Eva M. Koone. Another son, John Adam, married Margaret _____. The children of John and Elizabeth Eichleberger Counts were, William (married Rebecca Ruff), John Henry (married Kate Dreher), Elisabeth (married John Nicholas Summer). Susannah Margaret (married John Rhiddlehuber), Mary M. (married Jacob Fulmer), Eve Margaret (first wife of Joseph P. Summer), Anna Mary (first wife of General Henry H. Kinard) and John (married Catherine Eichleberger, second wife, Sally Ruff).

William Counts and his wife, Rebecca Ruff, had: Henry (married Miss Gibson), Junius (he died in the Confederate Army), Elizabeth (wife of Levi Folk), Mollie (wife of Job Swygert), Florence (wife of Artemus Bouknight), Charles (married Jane Chapman). Job Swygert and Molly Counts Swygert had, Elizabeth, Martha and Sallie. Charles Counts and Jane Chapman Counts had Anna, James, John, and Rebecca. Levi Folk and Elizabeth Counts Folk had Dr. J. William

COUNTS (continued)

Folk, Christian, Charles and Minnie. Dr. J. Wm. Folk, aretired physician and planter, is a former member of the state legislature. Christian Folk moved to Texas.

John Henry Counts and his wife, Kate Dreher Counts, had several children, one of whom, Mrs. Thomas W. Holloway who died in Newberry recently, leaving a son, Henry Counts Holloway, a well known lawyer of Newberry. and a daughter, Ruby, who married Ernest Thorpe, and lives in Aiken.

John Nickolas Summer and his wife, Elizabeth had Jacob (married Elizabeth Kinard, daughter of Captain Martin Kinard), Alfred (married Martha Boyd), John Nickolas (married Nancy Hill), Mary M. (married John Henry Epting), Susannah (married David Sligh). Jacob and Elizabeth Kinard Summer had Catherine Louise (married John Drayton Smith), Dr. Bluford M., (died in Civil War), Mary (married Thomas F. Harmon), Reverend Walter W., (married first, Nora Hammet and second, Lavania Meadows) who died in 1912, leaving children by each wife. John N., and Nancy Hill Summer had Emily, Oscar, Baxter and William Drayton, some of whom moved to the state of Mississippi.

John Houseal and Eve Margaret Counts Houseal had Walter W., Elizabeth (married Jacob Barre), and Frances (married George P. Summer). After the death of John Houseal, Eve Margaret married Joseph P. Summer and had Dr. William J. (married Jane Aull), Martha (married George Hipp), Ella (married Captain Charles D. Orley), and John C. Summer (he was captain of a company of militia in the Confederate army and was killed in action in 1862 - never married). George Hipp and his wife, Martha, were the parents of the late Edward R. Hipp, a prominent merchant and banker of Newberry, and the late John C. Hipp, Mrs. Nellie Mackey and Mrs. Means of Greenville. Edward R. Hipp married Mary Holloway, daughter of the late Thomas W. Holloway by his first wife, and had Edna (married Dr. Jesse O. Wilson of Spartanburg), Louise (married Homer W. Schumpert of Newberry), Earl, Dr. Edward R. Hipp, Jr., a prominent physician and surgeon of Charlotte, N. C., and Rosalyn (married A. J. Bowers, Jr., a former member of the South Carolina legislature). John C. Hipp married Alice Wheeler and had George C., (married Belle Swittenberg), Hattie (married Roland Fulmer), John C., Jr., W. Frank (married Eunice Halfacre - lived in Greenville), Grady, Everette, Lois (married Dr. Kennedy), and J. Edward who died young just after his graduation from Newberry College. James Mackey and his wife, Nellie Hipp Mackey, were the parents of James, Charles, Arthur, George, Alice, Nellie May and Margaret. W. Frank Hipp was organizer and first president of the Liberty Life Insurance Company of Greenville, South Carolina.

General Henry H. Kinard was the sheriff of Newberry during the early part of the last century. He married first, Anna Mary Counts by whom was one son, John Martin. John Martin Kinard was an officer in the Confederate service, captain of Company F, the Twentieth regiment of South Carolina volunteers. While acting in the capacity of lieutenant colonel, he was killed at the battle of Strassburg in 1864. He had married (1) Mary A. Ruff, daughter of Dr. P. B. Ruff and had one daughter, Alice, who married Elbert H. Aull, and married, second, Lavania E. Rook and had two sons, John M. Kinard, late president of the Commercial Bank of Newberry, and Dr. James P., late president of Winthrop College.

John Counts, Jr., and his wife, Catherine Eichleberger Counts, had Eleander, George A., Elizabeth, (married J. B. Nelson), and Polly who died early, unmarried. John Counts, Jr., died in 1822 and his widow married David Gilbert who moved to Alabama. George A. Counts, familiarly known as "Big George Counts", married Harriet Cromer, daughter of David Cromer, and had children: Elizabeth (married John W. Monts). Fannie (married Isiah Haltiwanger), Mary (married A. D. Haltiwanger), John A., Leonora (married A. H. Wheeler), Texana (married Captain John F. Banks), Janie (married G. Burton Reagin), Walter P., Ernest, Henry R., and William A. Counts. Prof. Ernest O. Counts was for several terms superintendent of the Prosperity High School (he is father of Miss Ethel Counts, Newberry County Demonstration Agent). William A., was a well known school principal in the county. Rev. Henry P. Counts was a prominent Lutheran minister, serving pastorates in this section and in Georgia. Walter Counts, a prominent planter living near Prosperity, died a few years ago. He was the father of two or three children, one being Arthur ("Box") Counts.

Jacob Counts, son of the pioneer, lived on part of the lands of his father on Crimm's Creek, in the vicinity of St. John's Lutheran Church. He died in 1816, having married when near middle age, to Susannah Le Gronne, the widow of John Frederick Le Gronne. They had

COUNTS (continued)

three children, Jacob, Adam and Mary Magdelina. Adam married Sarah Ruff and had Elizabeth (married David Suber), Sallie (married Adam F. Cromer, and they moved to Anderson), John, Walter, Louisa, (second wife of General Henry H. Kinard), J. Benson, Henry H., and Benedict. Mary Magdeline married Adam Mayer (it was Adam Mayer who accompanied General Marquis De La Fayette on the occasion of his visit to South Carolina from the North Carolina state line to Columbia); and they had one son, Orlando Benedict, and three daughters, Susan, Frances, and Elvira. Dr. Orlando Benedict Mayer, the first (born in the year 1818) was an eminent physician and surgeon in Newberry. David and Elizabeth Suber had Fannie (married Proctor Todd), Carrie (married William Lane), Ida (married Monroe Harris), Emma and Anna. Adam F., and Sallie Cromer had Adam C., John S., James H., and Elizabeth Cromer. John Counts died unmarried. Walter Counts married _____ and had Adam, Forest and Effie (wife of Jacob Dickert of Newberry). General Henry H. Kinard and his second wife, Louisa Counts, had Katherine (widow of the late Bishop A. Coke of the Methodist Church) and a son, Henry, who married Annie Smith. Adam Counts, son of _____ Counts, had two sons, Charley and Ben Counts.

In the days of the stage coach road, from Newberry to Pomaria and thence to Columbia was traveled frequently by tourists. It was the main road from Charleston to Charlotte, connecting with the old Buncombe Road near Pomaria by way of Spartanburg. Many old land marks can be seen on this route, many homes of distinctive design and other evidences of culture and development. Beyond the town of Pomaria and past the old home of Captain William Summer is the old Counts place. Captain Adam Counts lived there; and it joins Crimm's Creek and the "Leitner Bounds", lands formerly owned by Major Leitner. Crimm's Creek takes its course through these fields where is seen in secluded spots peculiarly attractive growths of evergreen, dogwood and cedar, with a hint of a once cultured field of flowers and plants. Then old St. John's Church on the left, a short distance from the road, is surrounded by large trees of beautiful growth.

Jacob Counts, brother of Captain Adam Counts, married Polly Ruff and lived near Bethlehem Church. Their children were Harrison (died unmarried), Mary (married William Riddlehuber), Martha (married John J. Dreher), Caroline (married Christain Suber), and David who married Miss Rikard. William and Mary Counts Riddlehuber had Margaret, Louise, Counts, Minnie (married first, David Suber and second, Jacob Leitsey), and Amelia (married Orlando Wicker). John J. Dreher and Martha Counts Dreher had Julius D., (married Emoline Richmond), Rufus (died young), Thaddeus (married Margaret Miller), William Charles (married Sara Huffman), Ernest (married Caroline Hyde), Heber and Edward. Dr. Julius D. Dreher, a prominent educator and statesman, was for many years president of Roanoke College, Salem, Va., and United States consul to Panama and Jamaica. Dr. Ernest Dreher was superintendent of the city schools of Columbia for several years, traveled extensively, and was once connected with Winthrop College. Christian and Caroline Counts Suber had John, David, Jacob Benson, George Benedict, Isabella, and Rebecca. Isabella married Captain Philander Cromer, an officer in the Confederate Army who was killed at the battle of Gettysburg; the widow afterwards married Sanford Eleaser and had a son, Robert Eleaser. Rebecca married James A. Welch and had Anna, Christian (married Julia Hunter), Robert (married Mabel Day and after her death to _____), Amelia (married Thomas Stack), and Mary (married Dr. Henry Eleaser). Robert H. Welch was a lawyer in Columbia. Christian Welch was a school teacher and moved to Texas. John David Suber married first, Sue Reagin, and second, Miss Leitsey. J. Benson lived and died in Newberry, had married Anna Koone, daughter of General Henry Koone, and had children: Mary (married Charles S. Suber), William (married Claudia Coleman), John (married Miss Nance), Annie (married James Duncan), George (died young), and Lucy (married William Elmore).

Henry Counts, son of the pioneer, married Catherine Fellers (daughter of Johannes Feullo, spelled in English "John Fellers"). Their children were: Henry Jr., John, Jacob, Mary, Margaret, Elizabeth, Catherine and Frederick. Henry married Sallie Hair, died early and left a widow and two small children, Peter Wesley and Simon P. Simon P. died young. Peter Wesley married Martha Harmon and had John Henry, J. Calhoun, Walter I., and George. Rev. J. Calhoun Counts was a Methodist minister in this section. J. Henry lived in Lexington and was a member of the state legislature from that County. Catherine married Standiver Hayes. Margaret Counts married James Singleton whose descendants moved to other sections. John Counts (known as "Carpenter" John) married Mary Magdelina Summer, daughter of William Summer, Sr.; they had no children. Elizabeth married Robert Rikard. Frederick married Rosie _____.

Peter Wesley Counts was magistrate in the county for many years, before and after the

COUNTS (continued)

Civil War. He was the only magistrate on record who ever pronounced the death sentence on a murderer, and the murderer was hanged at the appointed time. ("Annals of Newberry", page 641).

David Counts, probably the son of Jacob, had three brothers, George A., Andrew J., (married Doretha C. _____), and Joseph. David married Elisabeth Houseal (daughter of John Adam Houseal and his wife, Mary Summer) and they had Adam (married Polly Ann Setzler), Orlando Benedict (married first, Elizabeth Cummings Setzler, and second, Frances Bushardt), Jacob (married Jane Summer), Francis (married Nannie A. Hinnant), Preston (married Florence Clark), and Fannie H. (married J. A. W. Stoudemire). John Adam and Polly Ann Counts had Antoinette E., Ernest Calhoun, and Houseal. Orlando Benedict and Elizabeth Cummings Counts had Eloise Blanche, Forest S., Hammett B., Junius E., Emily and Fannie. Jacob and Jane Summer Counts were the parents of James Andrew, Carro Amelia and Alice Lavania. Francis and Nannie A. Counts had children, Emma C., William Gage, Thomas B., Minnie Maude and Peter. Peterson O. and Florence Clark Counts had David C., Francis Marion, Zeana S., George Holland, and L. S. Counts. J. A. W. Stoudemire and his wife, Fannie H. Counts, had children: Flora Eugenia, Mary Caroline, Rudolph, Susan S., Gary, Killian and Joseph. George A. Counts, Sr. (familiarly known as "Little George" Counts married Susannah Singley, daughter of the Rev. Martin Singley and his wife, Sophia Bedenbaugh, and had children: Caroline (married a Long), Mary (married a Miller), Louisa (married a Shealy), Jacob C., Andrew M., and J. Luther.

Some of the Counts families moved to Alabama and became prominent citizens of that state. In a book, "Southern Historical Association", by Thomas M. Owens, is given a history of the Counts family in that state. Many have moved to other sections of South Carolina and are energetic workers in their professions. Some are teachers, preachers and business men, while others have remained on the lands of their foreparents and are content to live the "happy life" and enjoy the sunshine and fresh air as nature's free gift to mankind.

CROMER

John Michael Cromer came to America from the State of Baden, Germany. In his petition for a bounty grant dated November 4, 1752, for 200 acres of land, he states that he came from Rotterdam in the Ship Crimless which was commanded by Captain Joseph Cleator, and landed in Philadelphia; that he had three children, viz: Frederick (age 20), Jacob (age 19), Charlotte (age 11). His grant was given for 200 acres on Camping Creek, a branch of Saluda River. From this information it appears that his wife had died before coming, but he may have married again after his arrival and settlement.

Frederick Cromer (1732-1798) married Sybella _____, and had children: Elizabeth, Christian, George, Margaret, Jacob, Godfrey, Michael, and John Frederick. Elizabeth married Henry Wicker, Sr. - - being his second wife - - and had children: Syble, and others. (See Wicker family sketch). Syble married Christopher Singley. Christian (Frederick Christian) married _____ Koon, and had sons, Adam and Simon, both of whom moved to North Alabama, after a few years living in Union County. Adam married Cassandra _____ and had children. Simon married Catherine Wicker and had a son, Thomas, and other children. Margaret married John Koon, and have descendants in Alabama. Jacob died or was killed in the American Army during the Revolutionary War, leaving a widow, Sophia. Godfrey also died or was killed in the Revolutionary War. Both were dead before 1784. Michael (1770-1844) married Hannah Suber and had children, Elisabeth (she married Daniel Minger), William E. who married _____. Daniel Minger and wife left a son, John Samuel Minger. William E. and wife left two daughters, Lavania and Marcella. John Frederick (1775-1851) married (1) _____ and (2) to Barbara _____, and had children: Catherine (who married Jacob G. Leitsey), Mary M. (who married Elijah Wedaman), Susan (who married Simon P. Dickert), Jacob L. (he died 1864) who married Rebecca _____, Sarah (who married George A. Koon), Emannuel, and Frederick. Simon P. Dickert and wife, Susan had John, Melvin, Mary Martha, Thomas, Elvira, Elizabeth. Jacob L. Cromer and wife, Rebecca, had : Amelia, Julius Job (died 1869 unmarried), Anne, Margaret, Elmira, and John Balus. George A. Koon and wife, Sarah, had children: Susan (married William R. Wildeman), George, Richard, John C. (All of this Koon family moved to Tuscaloosa, Alabama, and lived near Moore's Bridge, that state). Emmanuel (1811-) married Nancy Suber (she died in

CROMER (continued)

1850), his second wife being _____; having by his first wife children, Susannah (married _____ Bailey), George Henry, John Frederick (he died 1872), John H. Preston, Enoch Sligh; and by his second wife had a son, Jacob, who married a Dickert. John Frederick married Elisa Crosson (1832-1927), and had children: Silas Joseph, Anna Henrietta (she married Pink Adams), John Frederick, and Fannie Jane (she married Willie Job Hentz).

George Cromer (1767-1825), son of Frederick Cromer, married Margaret _____ (1763-1841), and had children: John George (1797-1867) (married Agnes Wicker), Henry (married Elizabeth _____), Mary (married Daniel Wicker), Catherine (married Andrew Campbell), Elizabeth, David (married Katherine Koon). David and wife, Katherine, had a son, Hilliard Francis Cromer. David married again to _____, and had son, David Derrick who was killed in the Civil War, unmarried. David Cromer was born about 1795 and died in 1858. His son, Hilliard Francis (1822-1860), as a young man went to Tuscaloosa, Alabama, with Solomon Lake, where other Cromers had settled shortly before. After a few years, he returned to his old home in the "Dutch Fork", where he married Nancy Singley (1825-1869), by whom were four children: Mary Catherine (1853-1911), Martha Rebecca (1855-1859), Thomas Henry (1857-1932), and Hulda Ann (1860-1917). Mary Catherine married Walker W. Wicker and had children: Thomas, Clara (she married Harry Stone), Elizabeth (married John Robertson), Mary (not married), Lora (married Albert Schumpert). Thomas Henry Cromer married Mary Summer, a daughter of Joseph P. and Catherine (Glymph) Summer, and had children: John Herman, Laura (she married Dr. Theodore Hemingway, of Kingstree, S. C.), Ethel, and others who died young. Hulda Ann married John Harrison (Hack) Summer, and had children: (George Leland (1881-) Elbert Hugh (1884-1944), John Ernest (1887-), Thomas Roy (1889-), Verna Louise (1892-), Mary Delila (1894-), Ann Julia (1897-), James Harrison (1900-1932). George Leland Summer married Caroline Mayes (1884-), and had children: George Leland, Jr. (1907-), Harry Thomas (1908-), William Mayes (1909-), and James Elbert (1911-). Elbert Hugh married Vera Summer (descendant of John Henry Summer), and had children: Robert, Elbert (died young), Frances, and twin sons, Hugh and Jack, who served in Air Corps during World War II. John Ernest married Linda Miller of Atlanta, Georgia (daughter of Dr. Royal Miller and wife). Thomas Roy married Florence Bowman, daughter of Charles and Kate (Ewart) Bowman, of Newberry. Verna Louise married Hal Kohn. Mary Delila never married, and has served over 30 years as teacher in City Schools of Newberry. Ann Julia married Jacob Wise. James Harrison (who served in World War I), married Margaret Spearman and had two children: James Harrison, Jr., and Margie (she married Charles Forkner and lives in Washington State).

Another son of John George and wife, Margaret, was Michael (1797-1866) who married (1) Mary Boyd and (2) to Celia Kinard. He was a twin brother of John George, Jr. Children by his first wife were: William David (who married Susannah Hipp) who was born in 1818 and died in 1881; George Lemuel (born 1828) who married James L. (1822-1865) who married Louisa Catherine Rhiddlehuber; Caroline (b. 1822), who died unmarried; children by his second wife, Celia Kinard, were: Backman (married Fannie Adams),Susannah (married Lambert Moore); Mary (married Wallace Koon); Katherine (married John C. Wilson); Martha; Jane (1849-1878). George Lemuel Cromer and wife had children: John L., William, and Martha; James L. and wife, Louisa Catherine, had children: Mary Catherine (she was first wife of Col. D. A. Dickert).

Jacob Cromer, Sr., second son of the pioneer, John Michael, was born 1733; married Elizabeth Yost. He had a son, George, who moved to Abbeville District and became an itinerant Methodist preacher, while he farmed. He married Elizabeth (Gray) Ruff, widow of Christian Ruff and daughter of George Gray, Sr. of Newberry District; had two sons, Phillip and Wesley. Phillip married Dorothy Ann Keller and had children: Mary Elizabeth (she married, first, James Tolbert, and second, Robert Wardlaw; had two children, Mary who married G. Washington Dacus and had daughter Isabel who married Reverend Leon Keaton, and Dr. Robert H. Dacus who married Florence Werts of Newberry); George, who died in the Confederate service in Virginia in 1861; Phillip, who died aged 5 years, blind from infancy; Asbury Fletcher, who died in the Confederate service, unmarried; Sarah Virginia, who married Curtis M. Ritchie and had daughter, Eola, who became the wife of Dr. Huntley; Jane Amanda, who married Pinckney Travers Boyd, of Newberry, who died in 1900, leaving children, John Phillip, Dugan, Dorothy, Lucia, Frances, Marion, (they moved to Arkansas); James Augustus (1864-1903) who married Emma Carlton; Samuel Foster who died unmarried; William Oscar (1850-1920), who married Ella Cox; Lindsey Harper (1853-) who married Annie Stevens; Lucia Victoria, who married G. Washington

CROMER (continued)

Dacus; Thomas Thomson, who married Ella Hunt. John Phillip and wife, Rosa Barnes, had children: Mary (married Charles Ray), Martha, Frances (married Archibald Keaton), Jane died in infancy, and probably others. William Oscar and wife, Ella (Cox) Cromer, had children: Waldo Oscar, Daisy Ann (married W. F. Nichols), Maude St. Claire (married James G. Bowers), Marie Samuella (married Cecil H. Seigler), Phillip Sidney, Charles Forrest, Hugh Wilson, William Oscar, Waldo Augustus, Cecil R., and Helen Calhoun Cromer. Thomas Thomson Cromer and wife, Ella Hunt, had children: William (married Sara Dominick), Georgia (married Hovey Smith), Archibald Keaton and wife, Frances, had children: Rev Leon (married Isobel Dacus), Cora (married a Jones), Helen (married Ernest Cheatham), Mary Law (married Prof. Fulmer), Winton, Althea, Fay and Carlisle Keaton.

George Wesley Cromer (son of George), married (1) Susan Keller, and (2) to Anna Keller -- sisters -- and (3) to Mrs. Charlotte Erwin. Children who were probably by first two wives, were: Eugenia (married James Young), no children; Frances (married David Davis) and had children, Anna, Jennie, Tena (she married Joe Eddy); Florence (married George W. Collins) -- left no children; John W. (married, first, to Louisa Cannon, and, second, to Anne Edwards), who left four children by his first wife; James Isaac who married _____ Golding, -- left no children; George Andrew (married Martha Rhodes and left several children); Cornelia (married David Miller), who left children, Susie (married Ezekiel Clinkscales), Jennie (married Augustus Norton Tolbert), Carrie (married Edward Thompson); Annie (married Bonner Hadden), and Eugene (married Willie Clamp), John, and David Miller.

Rev. Phillip Cromer, son of Jacob Cromer, Sr., and wife Elizabeth Yost, married Mary Ruff (daughter of Christian Ruff), and had children: Sarah (married Henry Kelsey), John, Susan (married Langston Lyles). They moved to Tennessee, having first located in North Alabama.

Jacob Cromer, probably a son of Jacob, Sr. and wife Elizabeth Yost, married Elizabeth Folk, his first wife and mother of his children. His second wife was Tina Suber. Children: James, David (married, first, to Elizabeth Wicker) had two children by his first wife, viz: Andrew (1812-1889), Harriet (she married George A. Counts), and by his second wife whom he married in Georgia where he had located down on Flint River, he had, Mary (married David M. Kelly), David, Jacob (he married Margaret Meeks), Hilliard (married May Meeks). Other children of Jacob and Elizabeth (Folk) Cromer were: Elizabeth (married John Keller); Rebecca (married David Keller); Adam (1792-1865 -- married (1) to Fannie Hoard and (2) to Susan (Boyd) Suber, widow of Michael Suber; Matthias (married Catherine _____; Abram (married Maria _____); Saloma (married William Suber); Mary (married A. A. Cody); Hannah (married _____ Peaster).

Adam Cromer (1792-1856) and wife, Fannie (Hoard) Cromer, (1787-1849) had children: Adam Francis (1824-1898) who married Sarah Counts, and had children, Adam C. (1861-), John S. (1866-1938), James H., and Elizabeth. John S. (1866-1938) married Dora Alice Boleman; Ann Louise, who married William F. Hentz; Nancy; Thomas Hoard (1816-1870) who married Mary Ann Rhiddlehuber (1819-1909) and their children were: Elizabeth (married Dr. George A. Setzler); Fannie L. (who married, first, _____ Glasgow, and second to _____ Briggs, and third, to Dr. George A. Setzler (his second wife); children by Glasgow being, John and Bachman Glasgow; John Adam (son of Thomas H. and wife, Mary Ann) married (1) Mary L. Gilliam and (2) to Drucilla _____. James L. (son of Thomas Hoard and Mary Ann) died December 16, 1870 -- he married Carolie Dawkins and had one son, Dr. James Dawkins Cromer, who was a physician in Atlanta, Georgia for many years before his death. Other children of Thomas H. and Mary Ann Cromer were: Wallace who married (1) to Sallie Riser, and (2) to Sue Pratt; Charlton who married (1) to Orella S. Briggs (sister of his brother Backman's wife), and (2) to Mary S. Moseley; Dr. George B. who married (1) to Caroline Motte and (2) to Hattie Biddle; Bachman who married Nancy Briggs; Captain Philander who was killed in the service of the Confederacy leaving widow but no children. Charlton Cromer and first wife had children: Robert (died in Alabama), Drucilla (married William A. McSwain), Sallie (married William Hentz); and children by his second wife being Mary (married Ab Sligh), Hattie, Bertha, Lou Ellen, James, Philander, Joseph, Wallace. John Adam Cromer and wife, Mary L. (Gilliam) Cromer, had children: John, Andrew, Gaston, Sallie, Robert, Maggie, Thomas, Frank. Wallace Cromer (son of Thomas H. and Mary Ann Cromer) had children by his first wife, viz: Lilla (married John A. Eddy), Neena (married Richard Swittenberg), Charlton (married Mary Buford). Wallace Cromer and his second wife had a daughter, Anne, who married a Threatt.

CROMER (continued)

Dr. George B. Cromer, a prominent attorney of Newberry, was Mayor of the city, served as President of Newberry College about seven years. He had two children by his first wife, viz: Margaret and Carolyn. By his second wife he had two sons, George and Beale; George died young, not married; and Beale married in Newberry to _____ Dunston.

Backman Cromer and his wife, Nancy (Briggs) Cromer, had children: Orella (wife of Thomas Chalmers), Iola (wife of Clyde McCarley), Arthur, Elmer, John Wallace, Haskell (he was killed in World War I), Bachman, and Walter.

Martin Cromer, a Revolutionary War patriot, lived on Second Creek, in Newberry County. He is supposed to have been a son of John Michael Cromer, Sr., the pioneer, by his second wife whom he married in America. Land conveyances indicate close relationship to Jacob Cromer, Sr., no doubt a half-brother. He died in 1823, leaving a widow, Mary, and children: John George, David, Henry, William C., Martin, Jacob, Lewis and Mary. John George married a _____ Heller and had Uriah, Langston, Miles (he married first to Adeline Wedaman in 1869, then to Agnes Wicker), Stephen (he was killed in the Confederate service in 1862, leaving a daughter, Eugenia, and widow, Emoline). David died in 1860 leaving widow, Mary, and children: Delila (married Peter Felker), Belinda (married Samuel Prentiss), David Adam, Isaac (married first to Mary Cates and second to Rebecca Singley), Ivey, Franklin, Elizabeth (married, first, to Miles Singley and second, to George Welch and third, to Joseph Lominick), Louise (married Edward Campbell). Miles Cromer and wife, Agness (Wicker) Cromer, had a son, Camillus (1847-1903). William, son of David, married Elizabeth Singley, and he died before the death of his father. Henry, son of Martin, Sr.,died in 1862, leaving widow, Anna, and children Franklin (1837-1862) who died in Confederate service; Harrison P.; George; Mary Elizabeth. William C. Cromer (familiarly known as "River Bill"), lived near Broad River and died in that section in 1862, his wife having died before his death, and left children: Drucilla, Ellen (she married Samuel Wicker), Frances, Robert R., (he died unmarried), George (married Elizabeth _____ who had Henry and William Julius), Ezekiel (called "Eketh") died in 1855, leaving widow and children who were Twiller (she married Thomas McCollough), James Calvin, and Texana. Martin Cromer, Jr. married Mary _____. He died in 1850. Their children were: Jane, Samuel, and Ann. Jacob (son of Martin Cromer), died in 1868 in Anderson County, S. C., leaving widow, Nancy, but no children. Lewis Cromer (son of Martin, Sr.) was born in 1809 and died in 1882. He married Anne Kate Dickert (1817-1897) and had children: Mary (married Dr. Silas R. Heller), Ezra (married Amanda Weathers, and were parents of Jacob Jasper Cromer who married Sallie McLesky, Nancy who married a Meredith, Edrew, Jacob, Hezekiah, Ellen who married _____ Heller, Lewis, Wesley who married and had Milly Ann and Texana. Mary (daughter of Martin Cromer, Sr.) married (1) to John Ringer and (2) to John Heller. All of Lewis Cromer's descendants live in Anderson County.

Isaac Cromer and his first wife, Mary Cates, had children: John Fielding who married and had several children, two of whose sons are Jeff and James Cromer of Newberry County. Isaac Cromer and his second wife, Elizabeth (Singley) Cromer, (she was a daughter of Christopher Singley and wife, Elizabeth (Cromer) Singley), had children: Andrew (married _____ Cromer), Neely (married _____), Ella (married William Lee and moved to Texas), William, and Pinckney (married first to _____ Nance and second, to _____ Crompton).

Henry Cromer (1781-1847) married (1) to Phoebe Yeldell, and (2) to Henrietta Burts. He was probably the son of Jacob Cromer, Sr. In 1830, he was living on Beaver Dam Creek in Newberry County; and in 1838, he and his family moved over into Georgia and settled in what was then known as Franklin County. From old deeds, he was closely related to both Martin Cromer and John George Cromer (father of David Cromer who died in 1858). Children by his first wife were: George (1804-1882) who married Sara Ann Atkins in Newberry County, and had two sons, Jerome Derrick Cromer and Henry Rush Cromer; Sarah; Barbara; Phillip, who married in Georgia and later moved into Anderson County, S. C.; Hiram (1812-1900), who married (1) Sallie Gober and (2) to Anne Letheridge. The children of Phillip were: George, Martin, John T., Edrew, and one called "Bub". Hiram lived in Georgia, had a daughter, Ethel Ann, who married a Roach (she was by his first wife), and by his second wife were two children, William Hiram and Bettie (she married _____ Argo).

Henry Cromer had by his second wife, children: David (1820-1904), who married Susie Fowler (1823-1899); James, who was killed in the War Between the States, and left children living in Arkansas; Thomas (killed in the War Between the States); Samuel, who died when young, leaving no family. David had children: James Franklin Cromer, who married Patsy

CROMER (continued)

Gaines, and had Thomas, William and Lafayette.

Barbara, a daughter of Henry Cromer and his first wife, Phoebe Yeldell, married William Henry Kesler, one of whose sons was George Kesler. They lived in Georgia.

One Daniel Cromer died in Fairfield County about 1820. There were living in Lexington County about 1842 brothers and sisters as follows: Daniel, James, Nancy, Mary, Polly, Adam Cromer (probably the children of one Adam Cromer, son of David, son of Andrew). Settlement of an estate that year included 188 acres of land on a branch of Twelve-Mile Creek, South of Saluda River. Daniel was the father of the late Rev. James A. Cromer, a Lutheran minister who served churches in both North Carolina and South Carolina. One of his sons, Rev. James L. Cromer, also was a Lutheran minister, and was the builder of the present Mt. Tabor Lutheran Church in Newberry County. The children of Daniel Cromer (he died 1865) were Rev. James Albert, Alice (married Henry Shull), Elleg G., Emily married _____ Kaminer), and Anna Ruff. Rev. James L. had a son who has recently been elected President of Lenoir Rhyne College, Hickory, North Carolina.

John George Cromer, the other pioneer, came from the vicinity of Baden, Germany, to Holland and sailed from Rotterdam, the Netherlands, to Philadelphia in the ship, Elizabeth, commanded by Captain Ross. After his colony had been delayed at Rotterdam, by being held under a contract with a merchant there, they came to America. Following his friends to the South, he settled in South Carolina, locating on Camping Creek near the settlement of the pioneer, John Michael Cromer, who was probably a brother. His petition for a bounty grant is dated February 14, 1753, for 250 acres of land on Camping Creek. He had a wife and three children. The children were: John Michael (age 10), George (age 6), Andrew (age 15 months). John George died shortly before October 1st, 1768. His second son, George, died sometime between 1769 and 1772, leaving a widow, Mary Margaret (Seigler) Cromer, but no evidence of leaving any children; she later married Michael Dickert, Sr. In 1773, John Michael (the son) deeded to his brother, Andrew, the one-half part of the original tract of 250 acres.

John Michael (1742-1815) married Susan Hair, and lived on Camping Creek. They had a daughter, Anna Marie, who married George Henry Leber (Lever) and their son was George Henry Leber, Jr. No other children.

Andrew Cromer (son of pioneer) who was born 1751, probably died about 179__. He married Mary Catherine Minnick, a daughter of William Minnick. His widow later married Phillip Gruber. Her children by Andrew Cromer were: Andrew, Jr., David, Mary (wife of Fred Davis), Christina (wife of John LeGronne), and Elisabeth and Jacob. Andrew, Jr. married (1) Mary Wicker who died in 1817; and in 1821 he married to Catherine Sligh, widow of John Barre; David married Elizabeth Ruff, daughter of Christian Ruff; Jacob who was born about 1774, died in year 1800, unmarried.

John George Cromer, after his settlement, and after year 1755, may have had other children; but the records indicate only one, (from the grants made May 1, 1774), a daughter named Kuniguntha.

Jacob Cromer, Sr. died without leaving a will, nor is a settlement of his estate recorded under administration. It is assumed that he gave his property away to some of his children before he died, and died without any property. The deeds and judgments give some clues as to the names of his children. He gave to his son, George, in 1792, all his lands and personal property. Later, it is shown that this George deeded to his brother, Henry, part of the lands. Jacob, Sr. probably married a daughter of Phillip Yost from whom he received part of his land; for a son of Jacob was named Phillip, and a son of George was named Phillip.

George Cromer, shown as son of Frederick Cromer, Sr. and wife, Syble, is probably correct as George signed his name in German script, as Frederick and his other sons did. Jacob, Sr. only made his mark and his sons, either signed in English script or made their marks, not using the German letters. It is said that a large number of early Dutch Fork families retained their mother tongue, the German language, after their arrival, and spoke and wrote in that language. Many old German Bibles were brought over or soon after their arrivals were ordered from Germany.

EICHLEBERGER

George Eichleberger, Sr. made will in 1796 and died about 1805. He left widow, Maria Ursula, and children: George, Martin, Michael, Christian, and John. His first wife was Catherine Sheely who was mother of his children. Maria Ursula was the widow of Henry Kuhn (Koons) when she married George Eichleberger.

Michael Eichleberger married Roasannah Catherine Summer, daughter of Col. John Adam Summer, and had children: George A., Mary Elizabeth (wife of Dr. William Irby of Laurens), and Adam. Michael died early and the widow married his children, John. George A. married Mahala Eigner and had George, Wade, and Phillip. Adam married a Miss Long and had Kate (wife of Reverend Mickell), Andrew, John and Walter. Wade Eichleberger married Fanny Hill. Phillip married Margaret Hobbs.

John Eichleberger and his wife, Rosannah Catherine Summer, had children: Louisa, Caroline, and William Henry. Louisa married Rev. J. C. Hope and had, James (married Mattie Miller), Mary (wife of Dr. L. L. Hobbs). Caroline married Eff. Henry.

John Eichleberger, Sr. (probably a brother of George Eichleberger, Sr.) lived in Newberry County near Pomaria on Cannons Creek. He died in 1827 and his widow, Sarah, married C. H. Smith. He left the following children: George, Catherine (wife of David Gilbert), Susannah (wife of David Ruff), John, Anna Mary (wife of John Kibler), Elizabeth (wife of Phillip Sligh), Christina (wife of Samuel D. Cannon), and Jacob Comanda. John Kibler died in 1835 and his widow, Anna Mary, married in 1848 to David Gilbert who was then living in Limestone County, Alabama. David Gilbert's first wife, Catherine had died. Children by John Kibler were: Permelia, Angelus (wife of David Folk), Elizabeth (wife of Claiborne Dickert), and Jacob Belton Kibler.

Col. John Eichleberger (son of John Eichleberger, Sr.) died in 1844, leaving widow, Maria Elizabeth Ruff (she afterwards married Ephriam Suber), and children: Dr. H. Melvin, Dr. John B., Adam L., William Thomas, Jacob W. F., and Haselius B. Dr. Melvin married Elizabeth Caldwell and they settled in the State of Mississippi. William Thomas, the youngest son, moved to Florida, volunteered in the Confederate Army and was mortally wounded in the battle of Williamsburg, Va. Adam Luther moved to Ocala, Fla., and served in the Artillery of the Confederate Army. Jacob W. Franklin also was a Confederate soldier.

Col. Eichleberger's old home, built over one hundred years ago part of which still stands in a good state of preservation, was rebuilt by his son before or just after War Between the States. It is a two story structure of old Colonial style, the interior being finished in very quaint designs. A few years ago the interior decoration in the reception room was torn down and the parts shipped to New York City where some person had purchased them - - the wainscoting, the door and window facings, the mantle, and the mouldings near the ceiling which extended eighteen inches down the wall and eighteen inches on the ceiling.

EPTING

John Adam Epting, pioneer, came with a colony of Palatines about 1749, and settled on Crims Creek, then a part of old Saxe-Gotha Township. A man of high standing in his homeland, a freeman, he was given a grant of land by King George, the Third, of England, dated October 20, 1749, including 250 acres. The exact location of this tract seems to have been opposite the upper section of Saxe-Gotha Township.

These families came as a result of many changes in Europe about the middle of 18th Century. Under the Haphsburg reign then, in Germany, that country had become an empire of loosely bound states, without the free government of a democracy and individual liberty of it's citizens. A religious change had gradually come about for the past two hundred years, so that about this time the people began to long for less restrictions on their religious freedom, especially those of the Reformed Church, and came over to America in large numbers.

During the early years of the Dutch Fork settlement there were no churches in the communities, but the Rev. Christian Theus, the first Lutheran minister in the section, was induced to make trips from Granby to the upper Dutch Fork, occasionally, and preach to the people in their homes. There were few families in 1750, but they were then coming down from Pennsylvania and from other states in large colonies. In 1760, a reformed church was organized which was established about 1762 as St John's Lutheran Church; and in 1763, a grant of 100 acres was made to the congregation by King George, the Third, "to John Adam Epting and Peter, Dickert, Elders of a Dissenting Congregation (in Trust for a Glebe and Building, a Meeting

EPTING (continued)

House, to the Minister of the said Congregation for the time being), said lands bounded on lands of Melchoir Loyner and Rev. John Gassert, and others". At that time Rev. John Gassert was pastor of the congregation.

The first Lutheran Church, called St. Johns, was started sometime before the establishment of St. Johns in Upper Dutch Fork. It was located on Saluda River, the pastor, Rev. Christian Theus, being persuaded by John Adam Summer, Sr., to come to his community and preach. After preaching among the colonists awhile, St. Johns was started.

John Adam Epting, pioneer, was born about 1715, in Germany and died about 1767, in upper Orangeburg District (now Lexington County), in the Dutch Fork. He had gone back to Germany, and brought back to the Dutch Fork several new families, about 1762, all from the vicinity of Heidleberg. Tradition is, he had so many daughters, and being unable to get husbands for them here, made the trip to get husbands for them. Be that as it may, many of these daughters married into families who had come over about 1752 and 1753. At his death he left widow, Barbara, and the following children that are known (all daughters names not found); Jacob (eldest son), John, Adam Frederick, Anna Mary, Margaret, Elizabeth. Tradition is that a son, George, died at sea, on the way to America, and was buried at sea. He was not married.

Jacob Epting, Sr. (son of John Adam Epting), lived in the lower section of Upper Dutch Fork, Lexington County. He married _____ and had a son, David, and a son, probably named Adam. David (1783-1849), married Elizabeth Rhinehart (1791-1871), and had children: William (1804-   ), who married Rosa Fulmer; John; Eliza; Polly; Kesiah; Betsy. William and Rosa Fulmer were the parents of Drayton (he married Kissie Sulton), John (he married Ella Cook), James (married Susan Wyse), Leophart (married first, Ledocia Fulmer and second, Elisabeth Derrick), Dina (married Grantland Rice), Mahala (married Joshua Amick), John Adam (died unmarried).

John Epting (son of John Adam Epting), married Anne Lohner, and had children: Adam (married Elizabeth Counts, sister of "Carpenter" John Counts); John (1778-1856), married (1) Eve Zeigler, and (2) Elisabeth Werts (1786-1847); George (1790-1846), married Margaret _____, Jacob (1780-   ), married _____. The children of Adam and Elizabeth Counts Epting were: William, Ephriam, Sarah, Christina, Adam. (Christina married Andrew Summer). The children of John and Eve Zeiglar Epting were a daughter, Sarah, who never married. The children of John and his second wife, Elisabeth Werts were: George (1809-1894), Mary Catherine (1808-1808), Eve Christina (1811-   ), George Henry (1813-1813), Anna (1816-1864), Jacob (1820-   ), Mary Eliza (1822-26), John (1814-   ), Catherine Caroline (1818-   ) and Harrison Ezra (1826-   ). George married Elisabeth Chapman (1811-1884), daughter of John Chapman. Anna married George A. Epting (1812-1867), a cousin, and were the parents of Harrison ("Hack") Epting who was killed near Spartanburg, in front of his home. Jacob married Margaret Summer, daughter of John Andrew Summer - - she lived to be over 90 years of age; left large family, one son and several daughters. The son, G. M. B. Epting, lived in Newberry and was for many years manager of the Newberry Bonded Warehouse Company. Harrison Ezra was a practicing physician, who, after few years service in the Dutch Fork, his first wife having died and without issue, he moved up into Anderson District at Williamston, and practiced his profession for many years. He married again there and left a large family. George and Elizabeth Chapman left a large family, their eldest son, Adam, being killed in the War Between the States, leaving a son, James. A daughter, Elizabeth, married William Dickert, whose descendants live in Georgia and other states. A daughter, Martha Delila, married George W. Summer who died in the Confederate Hospital near Richmond, Va. in the year 1862, leaving widow and three small infant sons, Charles Edward, John Harrison ("Hack"), and George W. Summer.

George Epting and his wife, Margaret _____, had children: Jacob (1820-   ), Susannah (   ) who married John Sheely, Mary and Evaline.

Jacob Epting (1780-   ) left a son, George and grandson, Jacob.

Anna Mary (1744-   ), married John Windle Shealy, and had children: Christian, Adam, John, Jacob, Martin, Matthias, Wendle, Henry, David, William, Margaret, Catherine, Mary.

Adam Frederick (son of John Adam, Sr.) was born about 1752 and died in 1786. He married Anna Christina Setzler, who survived him, and mother of his children, viz: John Adam (1773-1801), Jacob (1775-1816), John (1777-1820), and probably daughters whose names are not known. John Adam, Jr. married Eve Christina Leitner, daughter of Major Michael Leitner, and left two infant daughters, Elisabeth and Mary. The widow afterwards married Martin Kuhn (Koon) and had one daughter by him, Katherine; she (the wife) haveing died soon after the birth of their daughter. Jacob married Mary Cannon and had children: Sarah (married Jacob Setzler); Adam (married, first, Eve Koon, and second, to Harriet Swittenberg) had children by first wife - - he was born 1804 and died in 1871; William who married Elvira Glymph; Nancy; John Henry (1808-1881), who married (1) Mary Summer, (2) Lucinda Hoard, (3) Harriet Lane; Elisabeth

EPTING (continued)

(1813-   ), who married Rev. Mark Boyd, and left several children, some of the sons being Methodists Ministers; Anna (1816-1878) married Jabez Lake. John (son of Adam Frederick), born 1777 died in 1820, married Katherine Koon (1782-1826), and had children: Jacob, who died about 1868; George A. (1812-1867), who married Anna Epting (1816-1864), both buried at Beth Eden Lutheran Church Cemetery; Henry, who died in 1837, unmarried; Eve, who married Andrew Campbell; John (1804-1878), who married in 1825, (1)to Elizabeth Felker, daughter of Peter Felker, and (2) to Malina Stewart; and Lewis, who died young, unmarried. John Epting was killed in year 1820, in a duel with a man named Lyles, at the old mustering grounds above Duncans Creek, called, "Goshin's Hill".

Margaret (daughter of John Adam, Sr.) may have been the first wife of Francis Summer; she died young; and may have been the mother of the eldest son, Abraham (of Francis Summer).

Adam Epting (above) and his first wife, Eve Koon, had children: Jacob (183_ - 1893) who married Elizabeth _____; Jasper, who moved to another state; John A. who moved to Scott County, Mississippi and left children, Emma, Ada, Harriet, William, Melanehm; Frances Martha who married John Counts on January 30, 1868; Polly C. who married Felix D. Graham; Thomas L. who moved to Hill County, Texas; Samuel A. (died 1879) who married December 20, 1866 to Molly Derrick, two sons being Joseph and Samuel; Alice A.; Walter J.; Hadessa A.; and Warrens T. (the last four named were by his second wife).

Jacob and wife, Elizabeth _____, had children: Nancy (married Muller Able), H. Irasmus (married (1) Biddie Belleutiut and (2) _____ Cleland) had several children by first wife; Dr. H. Berley, a practicing physician of Greenwood, S. C., where he married a widow; Reverend Monroe J., a prominent Lutheran Minister of Savannah, Georgia, who married _____ Cline, of Newberry, S. C.; Julius J., who married a cousin, Martha Ann Epting and had several children; Charles and Thomas, who married _____ Kibler, and left several children.

FEAGLE

Laurens Feagle died in Newberry County about 1847. He married Rachel Quattlebaum, daughter of Matthias Quattlebaum. She died about 1850. Their children were: John, William, Eve (wife of Martin Koone, Jr.), George, Saloma Ables, and Mary Monts. Saloma Ables children were: Loretta (wife of Robert Bryant), Amytes, Anson, J. L. Penander, and Ethelbert Ables. Mary Monts children were: Sarah (wife of Henry Shealy), Polly (wife of Daniel Harmon), Levi, Mary (wife of Henry A. Long), Susannah (wife of Samuel Sheppard). Samuel and Susannah Sheppard were parents of James H., William, and probably others. Ethelbert Ables died early, and left sons, James and John.

George Feagle (son of Laurens) married Margaret Ann Houseal. They had children: Martha Elizabeth, Sara Catherine, Susannah Josephine, Mary Jane, Frances Pauline, John Nicholas, Warren Madison, Laurens Irving, and Loretta Rachel.

Martha Elizabeth married Aaron Hamilton Kohn, and had two sons, Arthur Hayne and Ernest Houseal Kohn. Arthur Haynes married Mary E. Birge and had five children. Reverend Ernest H. Kohn married Catherine Ehrhardt, of Philadelphia, and had five children.

Sarah Catherine married G. Michael Monts and had children: Margaret Agnes, Mary Eleanor, and Catherine Elizabeth Monts.

Margaret Agnes married Dr. John M. Sease, of Little Mountain, S. C. They had four children.

Susannah Josephine married Captain U. B. Whites (C.S.A.), and had four children, viz: Iola, Mamie E., Robert Lee, and Constance Lenore. Robert Lee married Maggie Sheppard. Constance Lenore married Dr. Karl Markt.

Mary Jane married, first, to W. W. Kohn, and left one child, Sid J. Kohn. After death of her first husband who was killed at the Battle of Gettysburg, she married Francis Bobb, and had five children: Leona Marie, Gertrude, Maggie, George, and Olin Bobb.

Frances Pauline married Nathan B. Wheeler, and had eight children: Eugene (married Anna Shealy), Anna Mae (married Vernon Bickley), Malcy, Forrest, Lauetta, Estelle, and Ruby, Corrie (married John Fulmer).

John Nicholas Feagle married Fannie M. Sease, and had children: Inez (married J. L. Fellers), George (married Annie Lee Saul), Haskell (married Rose Glover), Mattie (married B. L. Miller), May (married E. E. Fellers), Frank (married Nellie McFall) and after her

FEAGLE (continued)

death, he married Myrtle Brown; Joe (married Ernestine Wicker), Varina (married W. R. Betsill), Bess (married J. T. Stewart), Lamar (married Lillie Dell), Robert (married Dallys Watts), John Arthur (not married).

Warren Madison Feagle married Alice Finetta King, of Waxahachie, Texas. They had four children: Ethel, Fay, Balfour, and Arthur.

Laurens Irving Feagle married Dora E. Riser, and had children: Olive, Albert L., Thomas Oscar, Edgar, Aiken, Carl, Rhea, Hugh. Olive married a Halfacre, Albert married Lillie Crough. Oscar died, unmarried. Edgar married Ethel Halfacre. Carl married Jennie Haddock. Rhea married Edna Halfacre.

Loretta Rachel married Jacob I. Wheeler, and had children: Blanche, Frances Iola, Catherine J., Claude R., Bennia A., Roland E., Claire Marguerite. Frances Iola married Harrison S. Cannon. Catherine J. married R. M. Civil. Bennie married C. R. Parnell. Claude married Frances J. Edens. Roland married Kate Stammel. Claire married T. O. Blair.

FLOYD

When Virginia was first settled in the Sixteenth century, the Indians killed large numbers of the people, completely wiping out several colonies. The Jamestown expedition was an instance of such hardships. In the face of this condition many hardy men and women continued to come over to America and take their chances against such odds. The English, Scotch, Irish and Welsh composed the first colonies to Virginia. Among the Welsh was a family named Floyd, who came about 1650, probably a little earlier. This family played no small part in developing country of an unknown wilderness. Many of their descendants were prominent citizens of the State of Virginia, North Carolina and South Carolina.

One of the first governors of Virginia, under the English proprietorship was John Floyd, and Floyd County in that State is named for him. At a later time he had a grandson, who was governor. These two were prominent figures in Virginia politics during the pioneer days.

At a later period, just prior to the Revolutionary War, William Floyd, a son of John Floyd of Accomac, married Obediah Davis, daughter of an Indian princess and her English husband. This William had several brothers and sisters. One brother, John, had three children, viz: Charles, John and Elizabeth. Charles went to sea, but later came to South Carolina. Becoming dissatisfied in Carolina he moved over into Georgia where he reared a large family. He married a Miss Fendor, one of their descendants being William Gibbes McAdoo, statesman and former Democratic candidate for President. The other son, John, is supposedly the Captain John Floyd, who moved into Cumberland County, North Carolina, and later came with his widowed mother and brothers and sisters to Union District, South Carolina.

When Captain John Floyd volunteered for service in the American army he was living in Cumberland County, North Carolina. He probably moved to South Carolina before the end of the war, for the records show he was serving under General Sumter from Union District, in the latter part of the war. He was made first lieutenant and on one occasion during the absence of his captain, he acted as captain and led his company in one engagement against the British. He married in 1783 to Miss Nancy Andrews, whose family also came from North Carolina. Later they moved into Newberry District and settled in its northwestern section.

Captain Floyd and his wife, Nancy Andrews, had 14 children. He died in 1836 at the age of 73. His widow died in 1857 at the age of 100 years. The children were: Eustacia, who married John Jones and moved to Tennessee; Elizabeth, who married Nathan Pitts; Joseph who died early but left a widow, Elizabeth, and two daughters; Susan and Eustacia (Susan was the wife of Henry Burton and Eustacia was the wife of Israel Chandler); Charles, who married Margaret Spearman; Cornelius, who married Nancy _____; Edna, who married James Workman; Rebecca, who married Charles Jones; John Floyd, Jr., who married Francis Tinsley; Naomi, who married William Johnson; Andrew, who married Lucinda Biggs, moved to Spartanburg; William; Robert, who married Mahala Spearman (she was sister of Margaret, wife of Charles); Jefferson and Washington, who married Nancy Shepperd.

According to the Newberry County records, the widow, Ann Floyd, owned large tracts of land in 1795, made transfers to the following children: William, Robert, Temperance (wife of Thomas Liverette), Catherine (wife of Bartlett Satterwhite), John, Rebecca (granddaughter and daughter of son, John), Charles, Gilliam, a grandson (son of daughter Rebecca and her husband, Harris Gilliam).

FLOYD (continued)

Three of the sons of Captain John Floyd moved to Alabama and have descendants in that state, viz: Cornelius, John, Jr., and Robert Joseph and his wife lived and died in Newberry County. Susan married Henry Burton and had Bettie (wife of John Hair), Douglas (married Amelia Floyd, granddaughter of Charles), Joseph married Sallie Dorroh, William died young. Eustacia, who married Israel Chandler, had Joseph, Susan, Elizabeth and Sarah. Elizabeth married Jefferson Davenport and had nine children, viz: Jefferson Davis Davenport, who died unmarried; Charles S., who married Miss Reese; Thomas J., who married Fannie Smith; Emma, who married Harris Reese; Ophelia; Sallie Matilda, who married N. C. Livingstone; Amelia, who died young; Corrie Lee, who married William P. Montjoy of Clinton; Joseph, who married Lucy Floyd; Elizabeth, who married Dwight Smith and Williams.

Charles Floyd, second son of Captain Floyd and his wife, Nancy Andrews, married Margaret Spearman and had the following children: Nancy, who married A. K. Tribble; Barney, who married Annie Williams; Eustaca, who married four times - John Coleman, a Mr. Grier, John Abney, and Wesley Chappell; Elizabeth Anne, who married James P. Williams; Amelia, who married Dr. Rush Gary; Jefferson, who died early; Thomas A., who married Anna Brooks; John S., who married Sue Coleman, and after her death, he married Josephine Peterson, sister of the late Warren G. Peterson. Barney Floyd and Annie Williams had Lancy, Barney, Jr., Maggie, Amelia, and Eula. James P. Williams and wife were the parents of four sons and five daughters: Charles Montgomery (died in North Carolina), John Henry (died near the home place), Thomas Griffin (died in Newberry two years ago), Douglas B. (now living at Ardmore, Okla.), Della (married the late D. B. Wheeler of Newberry - now living in Philadelphia with her son-in-law, the Rev. J. Henry Harms, D. D., former president of Newberry College), Constance (married J. H. Crisp) both now of Fender, Georgia. Three of the daughters: Katharine (married Thomas Neel), Phoebe (married Mansfield Perry), and Lucretia (married Benjamin Perry), died a number of years ago. Thomas A. and Anna Brooks had Mattie, Maggie and Ella; John S. Floyd and wife had John S. ("Jack"), who married a Miss Clary; Thomas A., Ada, Mary Annie; John S. Floyd, Sr. and his second wife, Josephine Peterson, had John S., Mary Sue, Warren Stuart, Charles, and Richard.

John S. Floyd, Jr., ("Jack") lives very close to the place where Captain Floyd located and in the house built by his grandfather, Charles Floyd, over one hundred years ago. It is a quaint old place with its large portico and windows, manifesting early century days. The very large oaks surrounding the place give a serene atmosphere that is inviting to the wayfarer.

The youngest son of Captain Floyd and his wife, Nancy Andrews, was Washington Floyd. He married Nancy Shepperd and had one son, John Napoleon and one daughter, Lurie. John Napoleon married, first, Louisa Anderson, by whom he had one son, the late Lou Washington Floyd, a prominent business man of Newberry. His second wife also was a Miss Anderson, by whom he had one son, Claude, who moved to another state. The daughter, Lurie, married Dennis Lark. The widow of Lou Washington (who was Ola Clark, youngest daughter of the late Dr. R. P. Clark, an eminent physician of Newberry County) died in Newberry in 1928. She was very prominently identified with several women's organizations and was head of the American Legion Auxiliary in the state.

Jefferson Floyd, son of Captain John Floyd, who married in Newberry County, had a son, Leonard, who moved to Arkansas, and a daughter, who married a Boozer. They have descendants in Laurens and Newberry Counties. Anderson Floyd married Lucinda _____ and moved to Spartanburg, William Floyd moved to either Alabama or Tennessee.

Captain Floyd's daughter, Eina, married James Workman. Among their children were: Asa, Hugh, James M. and the second wife of the late D. Walter Barre; half-brothers are Charles and Calvin Workman. Descendants are living in Newberry, Laurens and Greenwood Counties.

FOLK (FULK OR FOULQUE)
(Compiled by a descendant in Washington, D. C.)

The Folk family is traditionally descended from the Fulks (or Foulques), Counts of Anjou, of ancient France. They are directly descended from a French Huguenot family who fled from France to Germany and Holland during the reign of Louis XIV, King of France, as is born out by French, German, and Dutch records of the family. In 1740/1 Jacob Folk and several brothers (probably with their parents) came to this country (America) from Wenningstedt (?), Germany, or from Willemstadt (?), Holland, and settled in the Dutch Fork of Newberry County, S. C. (Annals of Newberry; and Family Tradition). Jacob later went to the place at Pomaria, S. C., where he died on 6/20/1774. He married _____ Epting (daughter of Adam F. Epting) (I believe she was the daughter of John Adam Epting, Sr. - G. L. S.), and was the father of —

  I. Henry Folk (Fulk) — Eldest son, died in the Revolutionary War. He is listed on the payroll of Captain Henington's Company for August, September and October, 1779 (S. C. Histl. & Gen. Mag., Vol. 5).

  II. George Folk (Fulk) — Second son, appears to have settled in Berkeley County (census of 1790) and was the father of a number of children. He was killed by a falling tree.

  III. John Adam Folk — Third son, was born on 3/7/1770 and died on 12/21/1844. He married — 1. Eva Margaret Dickert (born in 1780 and died on 9/3/1811), — 2. Mary Elizabeth Parker (born on 8/30/1797), and was the father of _____ (by first wife):
   1. John Adam Folk, Jr. — Was born on 2/5/1799 and died on 7/5/1855. He married — 1. Catherine Hentz (died at the age of 33 years; daughter of David Hentz), — 2. Christiana _____ (born about 1804), and was the father of _____ :
     (1). Lernia Elisabeth Folk — Born 10/21/1823 and died before 1855.
     (2). John David LaFayette Folk — Born 5/15/1825 and died 5/6-8/1858.
     (3). Dr. Henry Middleton Folk — Born 4/26/1827 and died 3/28/1892. He married Julia Ann Long (born 12/21/1834 and died 12/31/1909) and the father of — William Hayne Folk (father of Julia Elisabeth Folk), Clara Annette Folk (married Dr. Edwin F. Strother), C. W. Folk (died young), and Edwin Henry Folk (father of Ida A. Folk, Edwin Henry Folk, Jr., William Hayne Folk, and James Raymond Folk).
     (4). Wm. Orlando C. Folk — Born 10/13/1829 and accidentally killed 8/5/1852.
     (5). Caroline Christina Folk — Born 9/19/1831 and died before 1855.
     (6). Captain Hamilton Hayne Folk — Born 5/31/1833 and died subsequent to 1890. He married Catherine Adelaide Buzhardt (born about 1839) and was the father of M. Hayne Folk (married a Miss Setsler and had 8 children), John A. Folk (married a Miss Stack and had 4 children), William H. Folk (married Lula M. Cromer and was the father of Dr. Robert H. Folk, Olive Iola Folk, Catherine E. Folk, Andrew W. Folk, Clarence D. Folk, Nellie M. Folk, and Carrie Lee Folk), Ada L. Folk (married Robert C. Perry), Thomas W. Folk (married a Miss Dickert and had 5 children), Christian M. Folk (married Mrs. Lily May(Caldwell) Brown and had 4 children), Julia A. Folk (married John C. Crapps), Mamie Belle Folk (married S. W. Derrick, and J. J. Brown), and Eugene C. Folk (married a Miss Caldwell and had 5 children).
     (7). Martha Harriett Folk — Born 12/15/1835. She married Thomas W. Holloway.
     (8). Lemuel Capers Folk — Born 8/15/1838 and died prior to 1855.
     (9). Ustatia Aubonette Folk — Born 5/21/1841. She married John David Wideman. (Daughter of second wife). By second wife, Elizabeth Parker, were:
  2. Mary M. Folk — married Dr. David A. Cannon. Mary M. Folk died 1836 and left children; John Adam, Eve Margaret, William, Noah Eli, Sarah Elisabeth, Martha Ann and George Martin Cannon.
  3. Sally Folk — was born in 1806 and died on 9/2/1811.
  4. Elias Folk — was born in 1814 and died in 1822.
  5. John Wesley Folk — was born on 8/3/1816 and died on 8/2/1892. He married —1. Polly Aull (daughter of Rev. Herman Aull), —2. Anne Catherine Suber (born 8/19/1819 and died 5/3/1877; daughter of Jacob Suber), —3. Mahala Carter (Native of Colleton County, S. C.; had no children) was the father of —
     (1). Florence Folk — died when about 12 years old.
     (2). J. D. Herman Folk — born 1839 and accidentally killed when about 18 years old.
     (3). Samuel Henry Folk — born 1844 and killed in the Civil War.
     (4). Jacob Asbury Folk — born 11/28/1850 and died 5/8/1866.

FOLK (FULK OR FOULQUE) (continued)

    (5). Dr. Luther Bachman Folk — born 1855 and died on 12/12/1922. He married Ida Hendricks and they had no children.
    (6). Rebecca Eleanora Folk — born 1852. She married Andrew Jackson Bedenbaugh.
  6. Dolly Elizabeth Folk — was born in 1818. She married John Hilliard Graham.
  7. David Folk — was born in 1819. He moved to Fairfield, Freestone County, Texas.
  8. Eve C. Folk — was born in 1821. She married Benjamin C. Busby.
  9. Martha Folk — was born in 1824 and died in 1834.
  10. Eli Folk — was born in 1825 and died in 1826.
  11. Levi Enoch Folk — was born in 1830. He married — 1. Elizabeth Counts, — 2. Mrs. Lou (Neel) Gilder, and was the father of —— (by first wife):
    (1). Dr. William J. Folk — He married, — 1. Harriett Adelle Fogle, — 2. _____ and was the father of a number of children.
    (2). Charles Folk.
  By second wife:
    (3). Christian J. Folk
    (4). G. Ernest Folk — Moved to Texas.
    (5). Everett Folk.
    (6). Otis Folk.
    (7). Neal Folk.

  IV. Jacob Folk — Fourth son, was born on 12/24/1772 and died on 11/10/1845. He married Mary Elizabeth Howard, in 1797, and moved to Colleton County, S. C., in 1803, after first living in Barnwell County. He was the father of —
  1. John Adam Folk — born 1/1/1798.
  2. Elizabeth Folk — born 3/17/1799.
  3. Jacob Folk, Jr. — born 3/7/1802 and died 3/16/1881. He married Olive Brabham Kearse and was the father of —
    (1). John Francis Folk — born 10/19/1822 and died 3/11/1861. He married Mahala Elizabeth Platts and was the father of 8 children.
    (2). Anne C. Folk — born 9/8/1824 and died 4/14/1837.
    (3). Jacob Calvin Folk — born 2/2/1827 and died 9/3/1888. He married Martha C. Riser and was the father of a number of children.
    (4). Dr. William W. Folk — born 1/19/1829 and died 8/25/1893. He married Henrietta R. Grimes and was the father a number of children.
    (5). Nancy E. Folk — born 4/25/1831 and died 6/4/1914. She married John Adam Lightsey.
    (6). George W. Folk — born 12/24/1833 and died 2/24/1860. He married Mary A. _____, and appears to have no children.
    (7). Henry Nimrod Folk — born 2/5/1836 and died 11/28/1916. He married, — 1. Mary Rebecca Weissinger, and 2. Elizabeth Ann Felder, and was the father of 7 children.
    (8). Rebecca A. Folk — born 10/10/1838 and died 6/10/1927. She married, —1. William H. Lightsey, —2. Charles J. Owens.
    (9). Adam L. Folk — born 9/14/1843 and died 8/4/1902. He married Catherine Bell and was the father of 7 children.
    (10). Oliver Perry Folk - born 8/22/1846 and died 10/13/1909. He married, — 1. Julia Lalla Bell, — 2. Mary A. Varn, and was the father of a number of children.
    (11). Polly Folk — married a Mr. Dowling.
  4. Henry Folk — born 9/9/1804 and died prior to 1840. He married a Miss Hemiter and was the father of —
    (1). Dr. Henry Capers Folk — married Mary Lightsey and was the father of 4 children.
  5. Anna Katherine Folk — born 9/21/1806 and died 8/14/1876. She married a Mr. Roberts.
  6. George Folk — born 9/4/1808 and died prior to 1860. He married, — 1. _____ 2. Margaret Rents, and was the father of —
    (1). Susanna Folk — born about 1831. She married Christian McMillan.
    (2). John J. Folk — born about 1833. He married Adelle A. _____ and was the father of a number of children.

FOLK (FULK OR FOULQUE) (continued)

  (3). William Calvin Folk — born about 1839
  (4). Charles Levi Folk — born about 1843.
  (5). Simeon P. Folk — born about 1848.
  (6). Benjamin Franklin Folk — born about 1850.
  (7). Laura Catherine Folk — born 2/19/1853 and died 10/16/1910. She married John T. Mears.
 7. Eve Margaret Folk — Born January 1811.
 8. Susanna Folk — Born 12/16/1812.
 9. Levi Folk — Born 3/14/1815 and died 2/27/1848. He married, — 1. Sarah Copeland, — 2. Susan Catherine Grimes, and was the father of —
  (1). Jacob Levi Folk — born 11/21/1837 and died 7/6/1885. He married Elizabeth Ann Weissinger and was the father of 6 children, one of whom was Mildren Zemina Folk (married Henry Spann Steadman, father of Joseph E. Steadman).
  (2). John Wesley Folk — born 3/18/1840 and died 10/12/1840.
  (3). Jesse Cornelius Folk — born 8/20/1844 and died 7/9/1930. Married Susan Preacher Riser and was the father of 10 children.
  (4). Ella Zenobia Folk — born 2/9/1846 and died _____. Married Dr. Benjamin S. Ray.
  (5). Rebecca P. Folk — born 9/6/1847 and died 6/23/1854.
 10. William Folk — born 8/5/1817.
 11. Mary Folk — born 3/12/1819.
 12. Eve Folk — born 6/1/1821.
V. _____ Folk married Levi Kibler and was the mother of J. D. A. Kibler.
VI. Elizabeth Folk married Jacob Cromer and was the mother of Abraham Cromer, Adam F. Cromer, and David Cromer.
VII. _____ Folk — A daughter.

GARY

The pioneer of this family was William Gary, Sr., who settled near Enoree River, north of Indian Creek, in Newberry County, about 1760. He came with his family from Virginia. He left no will, and no record of his estate other than deeds is found, since he died about 1767 or 1768. His sons were: Thomas, Charles, John, James, William. James (born about 1740) married Rebecca Lee of Virginia and had children: Mary (married Charles Mathis), Hartwell, William Lee Gary (born 1790 and married Elizabeth Rutherford). James moved with his family to Georgia, and settled in Hancock County about 1792.

Thomas (son of pioneer) died about 1797 near Bush River. His wife, Uriah (she was daughter of Samuel Newman), died in January, 1796. Executors of his will were Thomas Gary, Jr. (son), and Providence Williams (son-in-law). Children: Martha (married a Williams), Charles, Thomas, Nancy (married a Williams), Anne (married a Williams), William, Millie (wife of Abner Teague), John, Rebecca, Elizabeth, Newman (married Elizabeth Reeder), Sarah and Samuel. Elizabeth died in 1803, not married.

Thomas Gary, Jr. (son of Thomas) died 1802, leaving a widow, Sarah, and children: Lucreacy, Sarah, and a posthumous daughter, Rebecca, who was born 1802. Sarah married a Teague. Lucrecia married a cousin, Marvel Gary. Rebecca married Martin Gary, a cousin.

William Gary (son of John) moved with his wife, Ruth, to Georgia.

Newman Gary (son of Thomas, Sr.) died about 1850; left widow, Elizabeth (Reeder) Gary, and children: Mary R. (wife of Thomas McDowell), Jesse R., Permelia C. (she married a Pyles). The widow died about 1857. Jesse R. died before death of his father, and left daughter, Louisa, who married Dr. H. H. Huggins.

Charles Gary (son of pioneer) died about 1808, and left children: Thomas, John, Sarah Jones, Mary Williams, West, and William.

Thomas Gary (son of Charles) lived near "Gary's Lane", in Newberry County. He died in 1818, in Alabama, to which state he had gone to live with some of his children. He left widow, Rebecca, and children: Jesse, Linney Gordon, Absalom, Sarah (wife of Charles Davenport), Arthur, Martin J., Marvel, Charles F., Thomas, Isaac, William. In the settlement of Isaac's estate, his children are named as follows: Rutha A., Ranslaer, Isaac Newton, Abner, Pernecia, Elizabeth and Elcy M. His (Isaac's) widow was Mary _____. Thomas's widow, Rebecca (Jones) Gary, was daughter of Charles and Elizabeth Jones.

William Gary (son of Charles) died 1800, left widow, Elizabeth (Jones) Gary, and children: Matthias, Patience, Isaac, David, William, Henry (in Miss.). Matthias married Sarah Melton (daughter of Thomas and Elizabeth Melton) and had several children, viz: West Melton Gary (born 1823 died 1841). Matthias Gary's second wife was Amanda White, whom he married in Sumpter County, Alabama on December 17, 1841. His third wife was Rachel Seal Anderson. They had all moved to Alabama.

Dr. Martin J. Gary died about 1827, left widow, Rebecca, and children: Mariah L., Thomas Rush, and Randolph. The widow later married Allen Vance.

Dr. William D. Gary died and left widow, Jemima, and his father and mother, Jacob and Sarah Gary.

Jacob K. Gary died 1837, left widow, Sarah, and a daughter, Martha.

David Gary died in 1806, and left widow, Elizabeth, and mother, Elizabeth, and two children: Malinda and William Bluford Gary.

Elizabeth Gary died in 1844, and left property to her sister, Naomi Gary who later died in 1849, after which the property reverted to a half-brother, Washington Neel, under condition that William Neel live at the homeplace.

Dr. William D. Gary's widow, Jemima, was previously married to a Griffin — she was daughter of William Mangum. The brothers and sisters of William D. were: Martha, Abigail (wife of J. W. Crouch) Linney, and Sally (wife of Samuel Reeder).

Dr. Charles F. Gary died July 14, 1851, left children: Phoebe, D. F., Arthur T., M. C., and the wife of O. E. Edwards.

Samuel Gary died in 1851, leaving widow, Lucy, and children: George W., Mary E., Nancy A., Permelia E., Thomas D., Louisa F. (wife of William Bailey), Charles M., John E. W., Harriet (wife of John W. Smith). Thomas D. and John E. W. moved to Shreveport, La.

Mrs. Anne Gary died about 1816, and left: Elizabeth Forbes, John Leopard, James Gary, Isaac Gary, William Gary, Saluel Summers, Jesse Gary, Naomi Gary, John Gary, and Elisabeth Gary.

West Gary (son of Charles, Sr.) died about 1814, leaving widow, Frances, and some children.

GARY (continued)

Another David Gary died in 1833, leaving widow, Sarah, and children.
William Gary (son of Thomas, Sr.) died April 20, 1816, leaving widow, Rachel, and children: Thomas Joshua, Mary Ann, Benjamin, Darreta, and William.
Dr. Thomas Reeder Gary (borther of Martin C.) died in Abbeville District. He left widow, Mary Ann, and children: S. M. G., and a daughter Atlanta (she was six years old in 1854) and probably other children.
Hillary W. Gary died July 18, 1861, leaving a widow, Sarah, and children: John S., Sally, Linda, Ida, Eva, and Jesse.
John Gary died in Newberry District about 1802, left widow, Katy, who died in same year. A son, John, Jr., had died about 1789, leaving widow, Anne. John, Sr. was son or grandson of the pioneer William. His widow and children moved to near Anderson, South Carolina where she died. Some of those living in same section in Anderson District (then Pendleton District) were, Thomas Gary, Asa Gary, Jacob Gary. They were brothers and sons of John. They moved from the Bush River section of the county.
Jesse Gary sold to James Gary in year 1800, land on Bush River, bounded by lands of Thomas Gary and others. A one-half tract that was originally granted to William Gary, the pioneer, in year 1767, and conveyed to his son, Charles, and by Charles to his son, John, Jr. (this John was nick-named "Jacky"), in year 1786.

GILLAM

Major Robert Gillam came from Granville County, North Carolina about the year 1770 and received a grant of land of two hundred fifty acres on Pages Creek in Ninety Six District, S. C. in the year 1771. Though he was born in North Carolina, he was descended from Virginia pioneers who helped to explore the Shenandoah Valley many years before.
During the Revolutionary War, he was a brave and patriotic soldier and officer of the American Army. Even before the war began, he was Major of Militia and fought against the Cherokees under General Williamson. About 1780, he retired from active service on account of his age, but his son, Robert Gillam, Jr., was a soldier and saw service, first as a private, then sargeant, and Captain of militia. The son was in the battle of Stono, Musgroves Mill, Blackstocks, and Cowpens. He narrowly escaped capture by the Tories in October, 1781. ("Annals of Newberry", Part I. and S. C. Hist. Com.).
Major Gillam was Sheriff of Newberry County for one term in 1786. He died at his home on Pages Creek in January, 1796, leaving widow, Mary, and children named in his will as follows: Joshua, Robert, Susannah Martin, Martha Smith, and Frances. Also, two grandchildren were named, James Finley and Colley Martin. Susannah's first husband was a Finley.
Joshua Gillam and his wife, Alice, located on lands near Pages Creek that his father had given him. Later it appears that he sold the lands, and nothing more is known about him, except he may have gone to Greenville County or Spartanburg County.
Robert Gillam, Jr., after the Revolutionary War, married Elizabeth Caldwell, and settled on lands his father gave him, on Pages Creek. He was born in Granville County, N. C. in 1760 and died at his home in Newberry County, S. C. in 1813. His widow, Elizabeth Caldwell, a sister of Major James Caldwell, a brave Revolutionary War patriot and officer, lived to be ninety six years old, and died on December 29, 1851. She is buried in the old Gillam family grave yard on Pages Creek by the side of her husband. She was the daughter of William and Rebecca Caldwell who had first settled in Pennsylvania with their parents, coming from Ireland, and later settled in Charlotte County, Va. Her brothers, William, James, and John Caldwell, were brave and distinguished patriots and officers in the Revolution. Their children were: William, James, Sarah, all living to be grown and have families, the other children having died young. (See Caldwell family sketch elsewhere in this record).
William Gillam moved to Surry County, North Carolina and died there February 8, 1862, leaving widow, Theresa, and a son, Dr. Lewis M. Gillam who died in Abbeville County, S. C. There may have been other children. Dr. Lewis M. Gillam married Meredith Moon, daughter of Dr. William Moon. She was little more than sixteen years old in February 1854, when she eloped with Lewis Gillam at the end of a school term, and they were married February 7, 1854.
General James Gillam (son of Robert Gillam, Jr.) lived in Abbeville County. He was born in Newberry District March 5, 1791 and died July 25, 1878. He married, first, Sarah Satterwhite,

GILLAM (continued)

daughter of John Satterwhite; and his second wife was Mrs. Louisa L. Caruth. The children by his first wife were: 1. Cornelia, who was second wife of Dr. John Holland and had children, Edward Payson (married Eoline Olive Powers), Emma Jane (married Robert Marshall Anderson), and Sarah Caroline (married Hugh Lide Law of Darlington, S. C.). 2. Elizabeth, who married Marshall Smith and had children, Robert (married, first, Sarah Carter, and second, Sarah Crisp), James G. (married a Higgins), Eugenia (married Hugh Leaman), Sallie (married George Thomas Anderson), Charles Mason (married, first, John Hamilton and second, John Giradeau Legare). 3. Sallie, who married Mason Anderson and lived near Reidsville, Spartanburg County, S. C., and later moved to Florida. 4. Robert C., who married Mary Glenn and had children, Mary Ann (married Hugh Aiken), Sophia (married Manier Lawton, a son of Rev. W. H. Lawton, a Methodist Minister), Caroline (married John Lawton, a brother of Manier Lawton), Jessie (married James Williams of near Chappells, S. C.). 5. Susan who married Daniel Rudd and is buried in the Rudd Graveyard near Vaughanville, Newberry County. She died in 1856 in her 43rd year, leaving children surviving as follows: W. G. Rudd, G. H. Rudd, and S. C. Owens. 6. James M. who died and left daughters, Lille B., and Annie J. Browne, who were living at Arredonda, Fla. He had married Fanny Donnelly, daughter of Rev. Samuel Thomas Donnelly. Mrs. Elizabeth Smith married a second time to Mitchel Hill of Cross Hill, S. C., and had no children by this marriage.

One John Gillam married Polly Ruff, and had a son, John.

Sarah Gillam, daughter of Robert Gillam, Jr., married Philemon B. Waters and had children: Bary B. (wife of Phillip Schoppert), Robert B., and Philemon. Mrs. Caroline Waters afterwards married Bennett Perry. Phillip Schoppert and family moved to Alabama.

Sampson Gillam died in Union County about 1838. His wife, Drucilla, had died in 1835. Their children were: Robert, Ruth (wife of William Huff), Mark, Siam, Cicely, Sally Scota, and Mariam.

Mrs. Rebecca Gillam died in Newberry County in May 1837, survived by two children: John H. Gillam and Ann W. (wife of John M. Allen of Richland County).

Charles Gillam died in Abbeville County about 1783. He left widow, Jemima, and children: Harris, David, Cicely Rodgers, Mary Goodman, and Martha Goodman. A grand-son, Charles Gillam, was a son of Harris Gillam. A grand-daughter, Jemima Nichols, was a daughter of _____. David died on February 10th, 1842, and left four children: Harris, Rebecca, wife of Abram Poole, and the wife of Samuel G. Cook. Executors: James Gillam and Robert C. Gillam. Charles, Jr (grandson) lived in Laurens County. He married Patsy Wood, daughter of Mrs. Eleanor Wood.

The following In Memoriam was written on the death of General James Gillam (author unknown):

"In the providence of God we are called upon to report the death of General James Gillam, a Ruling Elder in Rock Church.

He was born in Newberry District, S. C. on March 5, 1791. Died in Greenwood, Abbeville County, S. C., July 28, 1878. Age eighty seven years, four months, and twenty three days.

He received a good education, considering the times in which he grew up. He taught school for some years -- then turned his attention to farming and also to merchandise, in both of which he was very successful. He married a Miss Satterwhite, by whom he had fourteen children, only three of whom survive him. His wife died about 1849. A few years after he married Miss Louisa Caruth of Pendleton, who also died in the year 1871, December 18.

General Gillam became a hopeful subject of grace during an interesting revival in and around Greenwood in 1838. He united with Rock Church, which prior to that time had been in a weak and languishing condition. Several other prominent men also united with this Church about the same time. In February 1839, General James Gillam, Dr. E. R. Calhoun and John McClellan, Esqs., were ordained Ruling Elders in Rock Church by Rev. E. Cater, who in June 1838, had been invited to supply the church for one-half of his time. In 1839 for the whole of his time. General Gillam was chosen Clerk of the Session. His first appearance in Presbytery was at Upper Long Cane in March, 1839. He often represented the church, and more frequently in the Synod. The first written narrative from a church session to Presbytery was prepared by General Gillam, the custom had long been for the minister and Ruling Elder, one or both, to give a verbal statement of the spiritual condition of the church. The plan had become very objectionable. The Presbytery called for all the churches to send written narratives, which course has continued to the present time. For many years quarterly collections were taken up for benevolent purposes. In May, 1866, General Gillam submitted to the session

GILLAM (continued)

the question of taking up a weekly collection, as giving was an act of divine worship and the Apostle Paul in Cor. 16: 1-2 gave an order to the brethern in Corinth as he had previously to the churches in Galatia to contribute to the cause of Christ on the first day of the week.

The session decided that the pastor preach a sermon on the subject of weekly contributions and then to introduce the scripture rule. The Presbytery soon urged the duty on all the churches under its care.

Our deceased brother was remarkably attached to the church and was never absent if able to attend. His piety was not sensational, but uniform and steady. He often said to his pastor that he had no excited frame of mind, yet he had peace of mind and joy in the Holy Ghost. His last illness was long and lingering. He was calm and composed and spoke of his submission to God and his implicit faith in Christ. On the third Sabbath in July, the Communion was administered in the church. He expressed a desire to participate in the privilege. The session met at his house at 5 o'clock P.M. and he received the emblems of the Saviour's broken body and shed blood, after which he expressed his thanks for such attention from the church. He grew worse on Tuesday and about five o'clock on the next Sabbath (28th of July) he calmly fell asleep in Jesus. His funeral was preached on Monday afternoon, a large audience being present. His remains were committed to the grave in the Greenwood Cemetery. In the death of such a decided and efficient Ruling Elder, the church is sorely bereaved.

'Help, Lord, for the godly man ceaseth; for the faithful fall from among the children of men.'"

GILLIAM

William Gilliam, a native of Virginia, came to South Carolina and settled on Bush River in Ninety Six District, about the year 1760. He died in the year 1789, leaving children: John, William, Ann, Hannah, and Mary.

John Gilliam died in 1801, leaving mother, Mrs. Dorcas Richey, and a sister, Mrs. Frances Griffin.

William Gilliam (son of William) lived on Enoree River. He made a will dated in 1816, which was proven in Court, November 18, 1822. His widow, Ann (Sims) Gilliam, and the following children survived: James S., Elizabeth (wife of Clement Nance), John Taylor Gilliam, Jacob F. Gilliam, William (he died early and left widow, Rebecca, and two children, John and Nancy), Reuben G., Robert Glenn Gilliam, Nathan Sims Gilliam, Drucilla Ann G. Gilliam, and Sarah Thompson Gilliam. The widow died in 1832. Drucilla A. G. married John P. Neel and had one son, William G. Neel. Sarah T. married Thomas Noland and had John and Frances Noland.

Dr. Jacob F. Gilliam died in October 1836, leaving widow, Mary, and children: Drucilla (wife of James B. Wilson), Sarah (she died young, not married), William Clement, and Pettus Wales Gilliam. Mrs. Mary (Massey) Gilliam died on September 9, 1843.

James S. Gilliam died March 20, 1865, leaving widow, Lucy, and a daughter, Martha Lake. Mrs. Martha Lake died soon after her father and left three small children, Leonora, Miles P., and Robert G. Lake. Mrs. Lucy Gilliam died in 1886 and left a daughter, Elizabeth A. E. (wife of Thomas B. Hatton, living in Texas).

Reuben G. Gilliam died in 1858 and left children: James Thomas and wife, Frances; Ann (she died and left husband, P. P. Hamilton); R. S. Gilliam as Agent for D. M. E. Gee; and William T. Gilliam. Children of Mrs. Ann Hamilton were: Ophelia, Leonora, Parkins, Robert, Joseph, Jane and Bradford. Nephews of Reuben G. Gilliam were: James Goree and Thompson Goree. His wife was Mary Sims, daughter of Patrick Henry Sims.

William Clement Gilliam died August 9, 1854, and left widow, Mary Elizabeth, and one child: William C. Gilliam, Jr. (he was born October 30, 1854).

Robert Glenn Gilliam married Euselia Blackburn. They resided on Indian Creek in Newberry County. They had one daughter, Elizabeth, who married a Hinson.

Pettus Wales Gilliam married Harriet Caldwell Wilson, sister of James B. Wilson. They lived at "White Oak", seven miles north of Newberry, near the present station of Jalapa. They had a son, William Clement. He and his son were both in the Confederate Army. William Clement and his family, with his sons, Roscius Atwood Gilliam and his family, moved to the state of Arkansas.

Mrs. Mary Elizabeth Gilliam, widow of William Clement Gilliam, made a will in 1897 and died about 1903. She lived in Spartanburg, S. C. at the time of her death, to which city her

GILLIAM (continued)

son, Dr. William C. Gilliam, had moved to practice his profession. She was the daughter of Andrew Turner and his wife, Maria Dugan Turner, and lived to a good old age. She was a graduate of Limestone Female Academy and a woman of many attainments. She had travelled extensively, toured Europe on two different occasions, and had in her possession many rare and beautiful articles that were brought from the old country. These she left, in her will, to the members of her family and other relatives.

Dr. William Clement Gilliam, who practiced medicine in New York City and in Spartanburg, is buried in Oakland Cemetery in Spartanburg. He left a widow, Frances (Blake) Gilliam.

Mrs. Drucilla Ann Gilliam Wilson (wife of James B. Wilson) died and left children: Mary Rosalie, William Clement, Sarah Caroline, Gilliam Sims, Josephine Caldwell, and Pettus Wales Wilson.

GLENN

There were several different Glenn families living in the States of Virginia, North Carolina, and South Carolina, during Colonial times. Governor James Glenn of North Carolina and Governor Glynn of the Province of South Carolina were descendants of the Virginia families. During the American Revolution, Virginia furnished several soldiers by that name. South Carolina furnished the following: James Glenn, John Glenn (pension roll), John Glenn, Joseph Glenn, Col. Robert Glenn, and Col. David Glenn. The Smiths, even in Colonial times, had nothing much on the Glenns when it came to family name. In fact, I would not be surprised if Captain John Smith who settled Jamestown, did not have a Glenn in his Colony.

Col. David Glenn, a Lieut. Col. in a South Carolina regiment of militia, came from Ireland. He first landed at Savannah, Georgia, and then moved up into South Carolina, finally settling in Newberry County before the War. After the War, he was a member of the South Carolina Legislature from Newberry County. On page 191 of the "Annals of Newberry" is an interesting history of Col. Glenn's dealings with the English, his escape from two British troopers, and how some of the Tories troubled him. His wife's name was Elizabeth and she came with him from Ireland. They were the parents of children as follows: Anna, Rebecca, Elizabeth, Jane, James, Dr. George Washington, Col. John, and David Glenn, Jr. Col. John Glenn has descendants in Laurens County. Dr. George W. Glenn lived in Newberry County, near Beth Eden Church. Some of his descendants lived in the old Henry Kinard home a few years ago, which was where is now a block of stores, including the Shealy Motor Company.

There was another family of Glenn who came down from Virginia soon after the Revolutionary War and settled in Union County. While none at that time came down as far as Newberry County, there are descendants of the name now living in this section. William Coleman Glenn, a member of a Continental Regiment from Cumberland County, Virginia in the American Revolution, and his brother, Captain Bernard Glenn, an officer in the same regiment, came to Union County. They were sons of Nathan Glenn who came from Scotland. This Nathan Glenn was a son of Nathan Glenn, Sr. of Loch Lomond, Scotland. Nathan Glenn, Jr. married a Miss Wright of Virginia, who was said to be a descendant of the Indian Princess, Pocahontas.

William Coleman Glenn is buried near Fish Dam Ferry, near Carlisle, S. C. in the old Glenn Cemetery. On his monument is seen the following inscription:

"He was engaged in the Revolutionary Struggles for his Country.
The morning sun begins the day,
So soon the night passeth away.
The weary seek for rest,
And in slumbering, sleep and blest.
Youth begins the man to rear,
Age with trouble and with care.
Death doth bring him to rest,
And he in Christ are blest."

He married Elizabeth Bowles, in Virginia. His sister, Louisa, married James Glenn of Mecklenberg County, North Carolina, and were ancestors of Governor James Glenn of that State.

William Coleman Glenn and his wife, Elizabeth Bowles Glenn, had children as follows: Lucy, Elizabeth, Patsy, Nathan, William, Mary Ann, Sarah, Rev. Thomas O., and Jane. Sarah married the Rev. J. B. Shands and moved to Florida; Jane married John F. Glenn, her first

GLENN (continued)

cousin and a grandson of Nathan; Patsy married John B. Glenn, a cousin, and had one son, James, who was the first proprietor of the famous Summer Resort "Glenn Springs" in Spartanburg County; Mary Ann married, first, James Mayes, and second, to Jesse Briggs. By her first husband were several daughters who married and moved away, and sons, Dr. Thomas Mayes who went to California; William G. who settled in the City of Newberry several years before the Civil War, taught school awhile and afterwards was a merchant there. William G. Mayes married a Miss Jones of Laurens County, and had several children. (See Mayes family sketch elsewhere in this book).

At the old Briggs home, about seven miles north of the town of Whitmire, in Union County, is a very old cemetery where some of the Glenns are buried. A very old and peculiar headstone stands at one of the graves, and it faces squarely the setting sun, the foot-stone facing the east. There are undicipherable letters around the top of the head-stone, and near the bottom is the following inscription: "Hoc monumento Sodalium amor gratitudo disciplorum memoriam caluit obiit - May 15, 1815". (Translated: "The love of comrades and gratitude of scholars has cherished his memory by this monument. He died May 15, 1815"). He was evidently a soldier and a teacher, having been one of the many French soldiers who came over and aided the Americans in their cause for liberty. After the war, he was probably a school teacher in that section. The name is almost worn away and could not be read.

GOGGANS

The Goggans family came from Virginia about twenty five years before the beginning of the Revolutionary War. Daniel Goggans and one or two brothers, all Revolutionary War patriots and soldiers in South Carolina militia, were sons of the pioneers from Virginia who settled in the northern section of Ninety Six District. Daniel was killed by the Tories during the latter years of the war and his older sons, who were old enough to fight, were also killed.

George Goggans died about 1815, having made a will in the year 1803, naming the following children: William, James, John, Jesse, Elizabeth Newman, Daniel, George, Nancy Dominy, Cary, Josiah, and Elizabeth Anderson. George died and left no family. William died in 1824.

Daniel Goggans (son of George) died in 1802, leaving widow, Neomi, and two children: Lucinda and Matilda. The widow married John Glenn who died in 1835, and she died in 1843. She had the following Glenn children: Mark, Mary (wife of Joseph Nelson), Elizabeth (wife of John Floyd), James C. (he died unmarried), Cooper N., and John F. Glenn. Lucinda Goggans married, first, John Galloway, and second, Jesse Speer. Her children were: Elizabeth Caroline, John, Matilda, Robert, Frederick, Joseph Jasper, and Balsonia. Matilda Goggans married Robert Williamson.

Bailey Goggans died in October, 1851, leaving widow, Rebecca, and children: Sally (wife of Stephen H. Johnston), Amy (wife of Ross Bonham), Silas, Joseph, Elizabeth, Rachel (wife of William Pulman), Matilda (wife of M. C. H. Davis), Amanda (wife of James L. Davis). Mrs. Rebecca Goggans died Dec. 18, 1851.

Mrs. Phoebe Goggans (widow) died November 1st, 1848. She left children: Nancy (wife of Pleasnt Cox), Thomas, Susan (wife of Isaac Kelly), Phoebe (wife of Wm. Watkins), Lucy (wife of David Stephens), William, Sally, James H., Margaret (wife of _____ Lake), and Martha (wife of David Moate). She was the widow of William Goggans who died September 18, 1824.

James Goggans died in 1864, leaving legatees as follows: Elizabeth Hinson, Susan Thrift, and a brother, Samuel Goggans, Mary Aiken, the daughter of Mrs. Campbell. James M. Davis in a letter written in 1868 from Goldville, Tallapoosa County, Alabama, and in a letter from Abraham Goggans (son of Thomas who was brother of James) from Marion County, Alabama, show Mrs. Rebecca M. Stephens was a daughter of Thomas Goggans. The heirs of Samuel Goggans were: Matilda J. (wife of J. M. Davis), Lucinda T. (wife of J. P. McCrackin), and Emily G. (wife of A. W. W. Hammock in Alabama), and Sarah A. (wife of T. J. Swann in Alabama). Children of Thomas Goggans, brother of James and Samuel, were living in Randolph County, Alabama, viz: Nancy Teague (her son James), John, Hannah Reeder, Elihu, Dicey McCoy (her children: John T., Nathaniel, Nancy Faulkner, William and H. S. McCoy).

Joseph Goggans made will August 23, 1866 and died same year. He left widow, Eustacia, who died November 24, 1883, and children as follows: Elizabeth Jones, Catherine Leitsey,

GOGGANS (continued)

Mollie E. Langford, Nora E. Langford, Talula E., Burr F., and Gibbs J. Goggans.

Jerry Goggans (son of Daniel) moved to Ohio and died in that state. His widow returned to Newberry County, South Carolina, with their only son, Daniel, and lived in the County near "Goggans Store". Daniel died on October 26, 1875, leaving a widow, Emily, and children: E. Jerry, Elizabeth Herbert (of Orangeburg), Mary Frances Dantzler, James K. P., and John C. Goggans. He also left a grandson, William C., who was a son of a pre-deceased son, William D. Goggans. William C. Goggans was a grandson of Elijah P. Lake.

GOREE

The Goree family came from either Pennsylvania or from Charleston, and are supposed to have been of French origin — from the territory of Alsace-Lorraine. They settled in the northeastern section of Ninety Six District, near Tyger River (county lines of Newberry and Union), some moving over into Chester District. Several were soldiers in the American Army during the Revolutionary War.

John Goree (Gorey) made a will in 1795 and died the same year. His widow, Sarah, and the following children survived: John, Joseph, Cladius, Joice (married a Lyles), and Molly (married a Ferguson). Executors: John Goree and Josiah Goree. Cladius died about 1822 and left no family.

William Goree died in the year 1801, left widow, Rebecca, and children: Britten, Amos, Israel, Elizabeth, Selah, Patsy, Mildred, Polly, and Clarecy.

Daniel Goree died in 1801, left children as follows: Alice Kelly, Clara Hogge, Mildred Lyles, Mo Kelly, Selah Parrott, Jane Johnson, William, and John O. Executors: William Goree and John O. Goree.

Josiah Goree died 1816 and left widow, Leana (she afterward married Wm. N. Noland), and nine children: John, Ephriam, Silas, James, Redden, William, Micajah, and Polly. Polly died young, unmarried. John died before 1816, leaving widow, Drucilla, and children, one of whom was a daughter, Nancy, who was under 21 years old when she died in 1822. The widow, Drucilla, married James Lyles. Several members of this family moved to Alabama.

Mrs. Elizabeth Goree (widow of James Goree), died in year 1789 and left children living in Chester District, viz: Jarner Marmon, Clement, Michael, John Ashford, Joshua, Eleazer, Mary Sanders, Easter Wood, Elizabeth Knowling. She left the following granddaughters: Fallinda Goree, Elizabeth Sanders and Sarah Wovnell.

Clement Goree died in 1802, left widow, Charity, and children: Michael, Davis, Clement, Elizabeth Lidy.

Joshua Goree who had bought land in 1785, conveyed with his wife, Fanny, a tract of land in 1798 to Allen De Graffinreid. He died in 1841 in Union County (name sometimes spelled "Gore"), and left his widow and children: Ralph, William G., Katherine, Hannah, Sarah, Elizabeth, Thomas, Joshua, Rebecca, and Frances.

Thomas Goree and his wife, Elizabeth, sold lands in Spartanburg County in year 1820.

John Goree died in 1827, leaving widow, Martha, and children: Sallie McKinnie, John, Daniel, Claiborne, Nancy, Thomas, Isham, Nathan, and Eli.

Redden Goree died February 8, 1843, left widow, Sarah, and children, Robert G., James, and Thompson Goree. The widow had two other children by a former marriage with G. S. Noland, viz: Frances Noland and John Noland.

James Goree died in Chester County about 1818 and left widow, Anna, and a son, James Goree, Jr., and grandsons, G. W. Goree and Isham Goree (sons of Elisha Goree). Other children were, Susannah (wife of Jeremiah McWhorter), William Goree, Mary Darby, and Dorcas Darby (wife of Asa Darby).

John Ashford Goree owned lands in Chester County and died in that County.

Joseph Goree, Jr., died in 1816, leaving property to his sisters and brothers, viz: James L., Lucy (wife of Samuel E. Kenner), Langston, Polly (wife of Simon Ashford), and the wife of William Woodard. Their mother, Mrs. Lucy (Lyles) Goree, was widow of John Goree.

Micajah Goree (son of Josiah) married Laura E. Thomas and had Ellen T. and Joseph H. Goree. He died in 1857 and his widow married William H. Knight about 1860. Joseph H. married Iler Maffett and had children.

GOREE (continued)

Edward Goree died in 1823 and left children: James, John, Sarah Irvin, Mary McKee; and a granddaughter, Sarah McKee.

There were many of the family who went to Alabama and other states. James Lyles Goree settled in Alabama, as did Ephriam and Celia Goree, and Silas Goree. The following is taken from the University of Alabama Alumni Register:

"Goree, Edwin, planter, Marion, entered University of Alabama, 1860, son of John Rabb Goree, Marion, and Sarah Elizabeth King; b. March 15, 1844; Private, C. S. A.; married Bettie Lowry, Marion."

"Goree, Joseph Alexander, (Soph), retired, Tuscaloosa; entered University of Alabama 1841 from Marion; son of James Lyles Goree, Marion, and Martha Rabb; born April 1st, 1825; planter and teacher; married Emma Robertson, Indianapolis, Ind.; died Dec. 30, 1896."

"Goree, Robert Thomas (Soph), planter, of Marion, entered the University of Alabama from Marion 1839; son of James Lyles Goree, Marion, and Martha Rabb; Private, Mexican War; Lawyer; married (1) Caroline Nelson, Greensboro; (2) Mrs. Mary Frank Pritchett (nee Harrison), New Orleans; died 1859."

The following is from "Memorial Record of Alabama", Vol. 1, page 937:

"James L. Goree, lumberman and farmer of Deatsville, Elmore County, Alabama, was born in that county in 1853, the son of Hon. Langston F. Goree, born in Montgomery County, in 1821, who was the son of Ephriam and Celia Goree, natives of Newberry District, S. C. They came to Alabama in 1816 and settled in Montgomery County, afterward removing to what is now Elmore County. He died in the latter county in 1836 aged about fifty two years, and his wife died in 1872. He was of French origin, a self-made man, and devoted all his life to agriculture. They had eleven children, only three of whom lived to maturity and only one now survives. Langston F. Goree was a man of limited education. He was reared as a farmer. He was married in March, 1844 to Mary Barrow of North Carolina, who came with her parents, James and Permelia Barrow, to Autauga, now Elmore, County and later moved to Arkansas, where he died. Since his marriage, Mr. Goree has lived in Elmore County, where he has at times engaged in the saw-mill business, but his general and more proper occupation has been that of planter. He served in the twenty-fourth Alabama battalion as an orderly sargeant and was with the army in Tennessee from 1863 until the close of hostilities. He served through the Georgia and Atlanta campaigns and on to the sea. In South Carolina, he was promoted to the Captaincy, and wounded. He served six years as County Commissioner from 1873. In 1880 he was elected to the Legislature, and served on the committee on corporations. He is a member of the F and A. M. Deatsville Lodge No. 475, and affiliates with the Methodist Protestant Church. Mrs. Goree died October 7, 1885."

GRAY AND DE WALT

(Based on genealogical data compiled by Mrs. T. J. McCrary and Miss Fannie Johnstone)

The pioneers of the Gray and De Walt families came to South Carolina from Pennsylvania, probably 25 years before the Revolutionary War, at a time when many were moving to Carolina from that section. They landed at Philadelphia from the old country.

There were several attempts to settle South Carolina or the southern section of Carolina, before it was divided into two provinces about 1730 (the name "Carolina" was given by King Charles IX of France. Charles in Latin being "Carolus"). Both the Germans of Palatine and the French Huguenots had settled on the coast, and about 1730 to 1735 permanent settlements began to grow, and new settlements were established near Columbia. About 1750 the general influx of emigrants had shown a rapid growth of the section.

The general setting of the Gray family is laid in the old and cultured city of Hesse Cassel, Prussia, in that territory of Germany where the King had his home amid buildings of Gothic beauty and imposing appearances. In this city lived an old family by the name of De Grau. One of the descendants of this family, Frederick De Grau, removed to Potsdam and became a member of the Kings Guards and later was made an officer in the Royal Army. He married a German lady and had Frederick.

When Frederick De Grau came, whit his family, to America, he first went to London where many of the German colonists had assembled preparatory to sailing. He appeared at the Court of King George III, in behalf of the colonists and himself in order to get good passage over

GRAY AND DE WALT (continued)

and to secure Land Grants in America. It so happened that the Queen of England was Charlotte Mecklenburg, daughter of the German Emporer, and she recognized Frederick De Grau as one of the German officers in her father's guards. Through her influence, therefore, he and some of the colonists were given Land Grants in South Carolina. When they sailed, each lady of the colony was given a calico dress by the Queen. Among the colonists was a De Peyster and his wife, Eve Margaret Egmont, and a small son, Gasper De Peyster. The dress given Mrs. De Peyster by the Queen was preserved in the family of Mrs. Rebecca Gray De Walt for many years. Mr. De Peyster died on his way over to America and later the widow married George Gray, Sr., son of Frederick Gray (name changed from De Grau to Gray). She had, also, in her possession silver knee buckles and silver buttons that were worn by Frederick Gray on the occasion of his appearance at the Court of King George III. After the Civil War, during a time of extreme need in the South, the buckles and buttons were converted into silver tea spoons to preserve the metals as well as to serve a need.

When Frederick Gray and his family came to America, and on to South Carolina, the family of De Walt had landed in Pennsylvania. They were two brothers, Daniel and David De Walt, who hailed from the north of France and had lived in Alsace or in Lorraine which was then German territory. They were Huguenots and had sailed the waters of the Rhine and on the ocean as seafaring men. Seeing the exodus of people to the new country, they gave up their sea-faring trade, secured Land Grants from King George III, and began life in a New World with new hopes of religious freedom and a new future. David came to South Carolina, but Daniel remained in Pennsylvania. One of the sons of David had been a paymaster in the English Navy prior to the Revolutionary War, and for this reason he did not join the American Army when America declared her independence. He also felt the imposition of the English Laws on the Colonists and did not want to fight against his friends and countrymen. Therefore, he resigned his Commission in the English Navy, and removed to the Island of Honduras. While living there, he recognized the advantages in the various kinds of timber grown in the section and he began dealing in mahogany, logwood, and other timber, and massed a comfortable fortune. He had made for himself a massive mahogany side-board, later in possession of Mrs. Lucy Caroline Craig of Orrville, Alabama, a great granddaughter. Another relic in the possession of this family is a very large old trunk which was carried by the family in their journeys. It was made of hide with the hair left on it and was tacked to a frame with large brass tacks, and the name "De Walt" written with the tacks.

When Daniel De Walt (son of David De Walt and his wife, Miss Grabill) came back to South Carolina from Honduras, his daughter, Rebecca was born in the vessel coming over. Tradition is, the name of the vessel was the "Rebecca", so the name was given the daughter. This child in later years became the wife of Major Smyley who lived in Newberry but moved to Dallas County, Alabama. The children of David De Walt and Miss Grabill were, Daniel (married Nancy Gray), Catherine (married George Gray, Jr.), a daughter who married a Heller, and another who married an Asbill, and two sons, Daniel and David.

Frederick Gray had a daughter who, probably, married a Gallman. He had two sons, Peter and George, Sr. George Gray married Eve Margaret Egmont Depeyster (widow). Their children were: Nancy, George, Frederick, Elizabeth, Barbara, and John Peter. Nancy Gray married George De Walt and had Rebecca, Daniel and David Dewalt. George Gray, Jr., and Catherine DeWalt had Casper, Mary, Simon Peter, Benjamin, Rebecca, and Susannah. Major John Smyley who had married Rebecca De Walt, was a brave officer in the War of 1812. Their children were: John De Walt, Margaret Ann, Samuel, Dan Caldwell, Nancy Caroline, Susannah, Adeline Rebecca, James John. James John Smyley was in the Confederate Army under General Bragg.

Daniel De Walt (son of Daniel De Walt and Nancy Gray) married Sara Waters of Newberry District, daughter of Philemon Waters, the son of Major Thomas Waters of the Revolution. He was familiarly known as "Ferry Phil" because he operated a ferry on the Saluda River. He was a nephew of Col. Philemon Waters, an officer of the Revolutionary War, and was in the battle of Eutaw under the command of his uncle. After the battle, he said to his uncle, "Uncle, do you call this a battle or a scrimmage?" The children of Daniel De Walt and Sara Waters were: Ker Boyce, Thomas Waters, Napoleon Boneparte, Nancy, Caroline, Sara Elizabeth, Harriet Herbert, Laura Eliza, Amelia, Liberty Victoria, Catherine Rebecca, David and Daniel. Ker Boyce De Walt was a colonel in the Confederate Army. He married Mary Hair and had Lucien, Waters, Daniel, Caroline, Frances Fry (married H. Matthews). Thomas Waters De Walt was a soldier in the Mexican War. He married Charlotte Brown and they moved to Texas,

GRAY AND DE WALT (continued)

died there, and left children in that State, viz: Daniel C., Thomas W., and Susannah. Napoleon Bonaparte De Walt was a Confederate soldier, was in Hood's Brigade and died in service at Richmond, Virginia. He had married Sara Caroline Harris of Newberry and left two children, William Boyce and Magnolia. William Boyce De Walt served in latter years of the Civil War at the age of 16. He married Mary R. Jones and they removed to Falls County, Texas. Their children were: Lelia, Royce, Hasten N., Clyde, Sara, Caroline, Clara, Rita Eleanor, Magnolia, Ivey and William. Nancy De Walt (daughter of Daniel and Sara Waters De Walt) married James K. Adams who was killed at Richmond, Virginia in the Civil War, but left two children, Ida and Lelia. Lelia married a Brandon and died in New York City. Caroline De Walt married John W. Barrett of Mobile, Alabama, and had, Corrine and J. William. Sarah Elizabeth De Walt married Henry William Waters (her first cousin). He was the son of Col. Philemon Waters and his wife, Eleanor Clary Summers. He graduated at the South Carolina College, studied law, but later deciding to study medicine, he became an eminent physician in the State of Texas to which section he had moved. Harriet Herbert De Walt married William C. Wilson of Newberry and had Walter Herbert, Clara Waters. Laura Eliza De Walt married Dr. Jacob S. West of Edgefield County. Their children were: Inez, Sara Rebecca, Arthur De Walt (married Octavia Clarke), Mary Frances (married Blakely Taylor), Thomas De Walt, Ella Kate, Pinckney Ezekiel, and Cora Amelia (married Silas Keeters). Amelia De Walt never married. Liberty Victory De Walt married O'Bryan B. Hughes of Brenham, Texas, and had Edward, Julia, Willie, Henry, Lelia, Annie, Kate, and Herbert. Catherine De Walt married Dr. Fred H. Albert of Houston, Texas.

David De Walt (son of Daniel De Walt and Nancy Gray) married Rebecca Gray (daughter of George Gray and Catherine De Walt). He served in the War of 1812. Their children were: George Gray, Almira Amelia, Daniel, Mary Catherine, Rebecca Adeline, Caroline Nancy, David, Eugene, Eliza Susan. George Gray De Walt married Elizabeth Jane Caldwell and lived at Prosperity, S. C. Their children are: Carrie (wife of Dr. George Y. Hunter), David (died young), and Eugene (died in infancy). Almira Amelia De Walt married Chancellor Job Johnstone, so well known in South Carolina as an eminent lawyer and jurist before the Civil War, and had children: George, John Malcome, Alan, Adeline Rebecca, Frances Alice, Clara Mabel, and Emily Pauline. The late George Johnstone was a prominent lawyer in Newberry and former U. S. Congressman, married Kate Rutherford, daughter of Col. William Drayton Rutherford, a distinguished officer in the Confederate Army. John Malcome never married. Alan Johnstone was a large planter in Newberry and prominent in state affairs for many years; was a member of the State Legislature and the State Senate and President of the Board of Trustees of Clemson College. He married Lilla R. Kennerly, daughter of the late Dr. Kennerly of Newberry County and had Amelia De Walt, Lilla Kennerly (wife of Prof. George McCutcheon of University of South Carolina, Margaret Law (wife of Laurence T. Mills of Camden), Thomas Kennerly (married Jeane Pelham, daughter of the late Dr. Wm. E. Pelham of Newberry), Martha Brown (wife of William Wroton Coleman of Aiken County), Adeline (wife of Walter J. Rountree of Georgia), Alan, Jr. (married Lallah Rook Simmons, daughter of the late J. W. M. Simmons of Newberry), John Malcome (now with the Lexington Power Company of Columbia), and two sons who died in infancy. Adeline Rebecca Johnstone married John Newton Fowles of Columbia and had James Henry Fowles, Job Johnstone Fowles, Matilda Maxcy, and Frances Johnstone. James Henry Fowles married Sophia Stewart Clarkson. Matilda Maxcey Fowles married Edmund Rhett Taber of Montgomery, Alabama. Frances Johnstone Fowles married William Francis Harrity.

Daniel De Walt (son of David De Walt and Rebecca Gray) married Jemima Livingstone. They moved to Tennessee. Their children were: David, Rebecca, Adeline, and George Martin. David volunteered for service in the Confederate Army while a student at Newberry College. He has descendants in Tennessee.

Caroline Nancy De Walt (daughter of David De Walt and Rebecca Gray) married Dr. Orlando Benedict Mayer, Sr. of Newberry. He was recognized as an extraordinarily skilled physician and surgeon throughout the state and in other states, and a man of varied talents and attainments. Their children were: Mary Margaret (wife of William A. Martin), Orlando Benedict, Eugene Adam (died young), Catherine Frances (wife of Dr. Edward C. Conner of Greenwood), Alice Amelia (died young), and Caroline Victoria (wife of James Thomas Mayes of Newberry). William A. Martin and Mary Margaret Mayer had, Caroline, Rebecca (married Henry Chandler), Catherine Watts (married Claremont Rutledge Copeland): they live in Florida. Dr. Orlando Benedict Mayer, Jr., was a practicing physician in Newberry for many years, greatly esteemed and beloved like his father, widely known throughout the section as a painstaking, trust-

GRAY AND DE WALT (continued)

worthy, and exceedingly skilled physician. He was a great friend to Newberry College. He married Harriet Jones of Laurens and had Cornelia Fleming, Orlando Benedict (now in Columbia, Representing the third generation of skillful physicians), and Harriet Rebecca (wife of William Reid, Jr., of Newberry). Dr. Edward C. Conner and Catherine Frances had, Alice Mayer (wife of Henry F. Jennings, lawyer of Columbia), Caroline Louise (wife of William O. Ballentine of Greenville), Katherine Gray (wife of Captain Charles Kirkland Dunlap of the U. S. Army, Coast Artillery), and Mary Clare. James Thomas Mayes and Caroline V. Mayer had, William Mayer (married Sarah Cockrell of Birmingham, Alabama, moved to California), Caroline Nancy (wife of G. Leland Summer of Newberry), Orlando Benedict (died young), James Thomas (married Eleanor Douglas of Birmingham, Alabama). Jesse Barnard (married Lucile Wallace), Bennie Mayer (married Lucy Wallace), and Catherine De Walt (married William Parham of Latta, S. C.). William Mayer Mayes volunteered for service in the First World War, became Lieutenant in the American Expeditionary Forces in France and was severely wounded in action. He was connected with the Third Division, Third Infantry, Company G., A. E. F.

Eliza Susan De Walt (daughter of David De Walt and Rebecca Gray) married Thomas Ellesor and had, John De Walt (died young), Dean Scott (died in young manhood), Pettus Gray and Caroline Amelia. Dr. Pettus Gray Ellesor was a practicing physician in Newberry for many years, a man of successful practice and skill. He married Janie Farrow Vance of Clinton, S. C. Had one daughter, Martha Vance Ellesor of Converse College, Spartanburg, S. C., now with Red Cross work. Caroline Amelia Ellesor married William J. Moore of Greenwood and had, Catherine Rebecca (wife of John Durst Tolbert), William Andrew, Margaret Wardlaw and Gray Ellesor.

One of the daughters of George Gray, Jr., and Catherine De Walt Gray, Susannah, married John George Gallman. Their children were: Mary Magdeline, Rebecca, Elisha, Susannah, Lavania, and Ruth, George Gray, John Peter and Simon Gray Gallman. Mary Magdeline Gallman married Micajah Harris (son of Revolutionary war officer, Captain Micajah Harris, Sr., and his wife, Sara Sheppard). Micajah Harris, Sr. was a son of Burr Calvert Harris of Virginia who was in the war with the Cherokees under Col. John Lyles during General Williamson's campaign of 1776. He was made a lieutenant in 1780 by Governor Rutledge, of South Carolina, and later promoted to captain. He and his wife's brother, James Sheppard, were taken prisoners by the Tories. The children of Micajah Harris, Jr. and his wife, Mary M. Gallman were: Caroline (married Thomas J. Price), Susan Catherine (married first, John Schumpert and after his death, to S. C. Derrick), Rebecca (died young), Mary (married Augustine H. E. Scheck, son of a Lutheran minister of Newberry County), Lavania Frances (married first, Thomas Sloan and after his death, to John B. Martin), Eliza (died young), James Pressly (married Katie McCollum), Thomas Jefferson (died in Civil War at Winchester, Va.), George (killed at the Battle of Vicksburg, Miss., in 1863), Burr Calvert, and Oliver P. (married Amanda Stilwell). Augustus H. E. Scheck and Mary Harris Scheck are the parents of Miss Lois Scheck, now Mrs. Pitts of Newberry.

John B. Martin and Lavania Frances Harris Martin were the parents of the late Curtis Burr Martin of Newberry, who died a few years ago leaving his widow, Mrs. Maybelle Stewart Martin, who later married Samuel B. Jones.

Samuel Reid and Susan M. Gallman had Elizabeth, John, Susan, Newton, Alexander and Mary. Newton Reid married John Price, Alexander married his brother's widow, Joan Price Reid, and had one son, Alexander Reid. Mary Reid married John Jefferson Gallman (a confederate soldier), and had Nathaniel George, Henry, Frederick, Holland and Lewis. Nathaniel George married Annie Tate. Frederick married Christina Ruff (the daughter of the late Col. David Ruff), and Lewis married Maggie Lindler.

Lavania E. Gallman (daughter of John G. and Susan Gray Gallman) married Samuel William Cannon and had Sara Victoria, Ruth Caroline, Alonzo Butler, Benjamin Franklin, Mary Josephine, Adeline, Henry, John Milton and Alice Cleopatria. Sara Victoria married Alfred Crotwell and were the parents of Clara Belle (married Bud C. Matthews, one time President of the National Bank of Newberry), and Samuel Phillip Crotwell, who married Henrietta Neel of Newberry, (but later died in South Georgia where he and his family moved). Alonzo B. Cannon married Fannie Chalmers. They both died on the same day and are buried together at Head Springs cemetery, Newberry County. Their children were: Janie (wife of late Sims G. Brown), William, living in Florida, and Frances, who died young. Benjamin F. Cannon married Henrietta Buzhardt and had Olin B. (married Mary Gibson, daughter of the late Albert Gibson, of Newberry), Henry

GRAY AND DE WALT (continued)

Thompson (married Myra Mower, daughter of the late George S. Mower, a prominent lawyer of Newberry), Samuel (married Sara Schiller, and they live in Columbia), Calhoun (married Nell Lorgin, of Madison, Wis.), Caleb (died young), Roy, and a daughter, Mary (married Frank Wearn). Mary Josephine Adaline Cannon married Thomas W. Gallman, and had Vassey LeRoy, Samuel Thurston, Ralph Aubry, Alice Blanche, James, Bernard, Thomas, Ray, Bertha Gray. Professor Olin B. Cannon was Superintendent of City Schools at Newberry until his death in 1946.

Thomas J. Price and Ruth Gallman had John, William, Caroline and Lewis. William married Lula Brooks, Lewis married Elizabeth Crosson.

Ruth Gray (daughter of George Gray, Jr., and Catherine De Walt), married William P. Johnston of Charleston. They moved to Mississippi about 1815. Their children were: Abigail, Jane (married Henry Lee), Ruth, Amelia, Simon, William and Bulow. The descendants of these live in Mississippi and Texas.

Simon P. Gray (eldest son of George Gray, Jr. and Catherine De Walt) graduated at South Carolina College in 1811, studied law with Judges Mott and De Saussaure, of Columbia, and was admitted to the bar in 1813. He practiced a short time but gave up his practice and devoted all his time to business. He moved to Alabama in 1819, married Leah Rachel Dellet, and had Mary Catherine, George Hampton, Leah Rachel and Simon Peter. They have many descendants in Alabama.

Benjamin Gray (son of George Gray, Jr. and Catherine De Walt) married and moved to Mississippi.

Major Frederick Gray (son of George Gray, Sr. and his wife, Eve Margaret Egmont De Peyster Gray) married first, Floretta Dawkins, of Newberry. He was an officer in the American army during the Revolutionary War, major of a battalion of state troops. He had twelve children by his first wife; and none by his second wife, Mary Geddings. He moved to A beville district when an old man where some of his children were living. He owned an estate near Calhoun Falls, familiarly known as Gray's Mills. His grave is on the summit of Gray's Hill, a familiar spot to the citizens of the surrounding section, and overlooks the Savannah River, where its waters take an unceasing course to the sea. He was buried there at his own request. It was a scene of a Revolutionary War engagement in which he took a part, probably the battle of Cherokee Ford. The estate afterwards became known as the John C. and Patrick Calhoun property.

The children of Major Frederick Gray were: George (married Charity Patterson), William (married Elizabeth Tench), Frederick (married Martha Summer Aiken), Henry (married Elvira Flannagan), Thomas Jefferson (married Dorcas Cunningham), Washington (married Lucinda Haddon), Jane (married David Thomas), Mary (married John Marshall), Floretta (married Robert Boyd), Dorothy (married Pascal Klugh). Henry Gray has descendants in Mississippi. Many of the descendants of Major Gray moved West.

Elizabeth Gray (daughter of George Gray, Sr., and his wife, Eve Margaret Ebmont De Peyster Gray) married George Penny, Nancy (married a Ruff), and had Sarah (wife of Cannon), Victoria (married and moved to Florida), Christina (married Lucretia Clark), and five sons who settled in Florida. The second husband of Elizabeth Gray was the Rev. George Cromer, a Methodist minister who moved from Newberry County to Abbeville County where he died in 1822. Their children were: Phillip and Wesley. Phillip married Dorothy Anne Keller (daughter of John Keller and Elizabeth Cromer of Newberry) and had Elizabeth (married first, James Tolbert, and second, Robert Wardlaw), George (died in Civil War), Phillip (married Rosa Barnes), Franklin (died young), Asbury F., Sara Virginia (married Captain Curtis M. Richie), Jane Amanda (married Pinkney M. Boyd, of Newberry), James Augusta (married Emma Carton, of Georgia), William Oscar (married Ella Cox, of Abbeville), Lindsey Harper (married Annie Stevens), Lucia Victoria (married G. Washington Ducas, and had one child that died in infancy), Thomas T. (married Ella Hunt of Anderson County). James Tolbert and Elizabeth Cromer had two children, Mary and Lucia Victoria. Mary married G. Washington Dacus and after her death, he married her sister, Lucia Victoria, and had two children, Isobel and Robert. Dr. Robert Dacus married Florence Werts, of Newberry. William Oscar Cromer and his wife, Ella Cox, had Waldo Oscar, Daisy Ann (wife of W. J. Nichols), Maude St. Claire (wife of James Barnes), Marie (wife of Cecil H. Seigler), Phillip Sidney, Charles Forrest, High Wilson, William Oscar, Waldo Augustine, Cecil R., Helen Calhoun. Lindsay Harper (he had been blind from birth), and his wife, Annie Stevens, had four sons and four daughters, some of whom live at Kingstree, South Carolina.

GRAY AND DE WALT (continued)

George Wesley Cromer, son of the Rev. George Cromer and Elizabeth Gray, married (1) Susan Keller, and after her death, to her sister, Anna Keller. His third marriage was to Mrs. Charlotte Erwin, by whom were no children. Children by second wife, Anna Keller, were: Eugenia (married Captain David Davis and had three children, Anna, Jannie and Lena; Lena married Joseph Eddy, of Ninety Six, S. C.), Florence (married George W. Collins), James Isaac (married Miss Golden), George Andrew (married Martha Rhodes, had three daughters and two sons), Cordelia (married David Miller) and had Susie (wife of Ezekiel Clinkscale), Jennie (wife of A. N. Tolbert), Carrie (wife of Edward Thompson), Annie (wife of Bonner Haddon, of Abbeville), Eugene (married Willie Clamp), John, and David. (See Cromer family sketch elsewhere in this book).

Barbara Gray (daughter of George Gray, Sr., and his wife, Eve Margaret Edmont De Peyster Gray) married Frederick Boozer. Their son, Henry Boozer, lived in Greenwood County. They had a daughter, Margaret, and another son, David. David married Sara Suber and after her death, he married Mrs. Peter Burton. There were no children by either marriage. Margaret Boozer married Casper Peister (note change from "De Peyster" to "Peister"). Casper Peister was the son of the first Casper De Peyster. Their children were: Simon R., Elizabeth, Benjamin, Milton, David, Jefferson, James Spence, Laura, Sara Adeline. Elizabeth Peister married Nathaniel George Gallman and had, Ann Lavania, Henry Casper, David Frederick, John Jefferson, Sallie, Mollie, Thomas W., Della, Ann Lavania (married Col. R. C. Maffett, an officer in the Confederate Army), Sallie (married Jacob Fellers, a Confederate soldier, lost an arm in battle. He was judge of probate for Newberry for many years). John Jefferson Gallman also lost an arm in battle in the Civil War. The children of Judge J. B. Fellers and his wife, Sallie Gallman, were: Essie Viola, Curtis Ambrose, Lizzie Eugenia (wife of Ernest Luther of Columbia), Rufus G. (living in Columbia), Holland (married Rose Harris), Vernon Bernard, Lucile Inez (wife of Richard C. Neel, of Silver Street, S. C.

Mary Elizabeth Peister Gallman married Samuel Levi Bowers, of Prosperity, S. C., and had Ernest, F. Gertrude, Bessie Margaret, Minnie Lee (she married Thornwell Haynes, son of the Rev. Hilliard and Sara (Lee) Haynes of Union, S. C.), Emma Adela (wife of Prof. Joseph E. Hunter, of Clemson College), and Samuel Bushnell.

David Peister, son of Casper and Margaret Boozer Peister, married Eliza Neel and had, John (married Nora Martin and moved to Texas), Adaline (married James Aull), Lucy (married Montgomery Williams), Banna (married L. W. C. Blalock), Martha (married Henry Aull, now in Florida), Caroline Emily (married Jordan Green), Gertrude (living in Florida). Jordan R. Green and Caroline E. Peister had Annie, Banna, L. William, David P., and Tench Poole Greene.

James Spencer Peister was a lieutenant in the Third S. C. Volunteers in the Civil War and was killed at the Battle of Fredericksburg, Va. During the battle, and at a time when there was a lull in the fighting, his faithful colored servant, Ned Gilliam, bore the body of his master from the field and buried it at a secure spot and marked the place. This insured recovery of the body and it was brought to Newberry and buried in the old Gray graveyard.

Sara Adeline Peister married Richard Pinkney Clark, a practicing physician in Newberry County for several years. Dr. Clark lived at the old Clark place at Jalapa. Their children were: Margaret Catherine (married William Swittenberg), Martha (married William Spearman), Sarah (married William Spearman, after the death of her sister, Martha), Lilla (married Clark Smith), Alma (married Ernest Merchant), Talula (married S. B. Aull), Ola (married L. W. Floyd of Newberry).

About six miles east of Newberry on the highway to Pomaria and just beyond Cannon's Creek, a large rock mound stands out on the left, and on the right can be seen the stone walls of the Gray graveyard, with its heavy iron gate, seemingly locked to prevent promiscuous trespassing upon the grounds of a quiet spot. There are several old tombs to the memories of a once well known and popular family. The grave of the pioneer, the first Frederick Gray, who came from Hesse Cassel, Germany, is near the entrance and unmarked by any monument or slab.

Henry Gray (son of Frederick Gray and Floretta Dawkins) married Elvira Flannagan, daughter of Dr. Ruben Flannagan, of Newberry. They had a son, Dr. Ruben Gray, who moved to Louisiana. Thomas Jefferson Gray had a son, Dr. Frederick Gray, by his wife, Dorcas Cunningham. After her death, he married again and had several children. Mary Gray and John Marshall had a daughter, Silvira, who married Samuel A. Coy. Dorothy Gray and Pascal Klugh had a daughter, Eliza, who married William Norwood. Dr. John Gray married Laura Howard and had Laura,

GRAY AND DE WALT (continued)

Henry, Ben, and William.

The shifting scenes in a community become apparent to older residents, and often it is seen that many old families who, in the past, formed an important element in a cultural community, have moved away and have become scattered in other sections; but their influence is felt, even for generations, and the high character of the descendants yet remaining can be found in every walk of life, giving to their communities effective service, maintaining the ideals of their forbears. New families have moved in from other sections to take their places, and there is a continual removal from time to time.

"Life's but a dream at best;
A strange bewildering scene,
In magic colors drest; -
What is said and what hath been,
All mingled like a gorgeous show
That flashes, moves and passes, but don't go."

GRIFFIN

The first settlers of the family of Griffin came from Virginia before the Revolutionary War, and settled in the Counties of Abbeville, Laurens and Newberry ---- some later moving over into old Edgefield District. There were three brothers, Richard, Anthony, and William (sons of a Welshman) who came from Virginia and settled in the southern section of the present County of Laurens (then Ninety Six District). James and William Griffin were brothers or cousins, and came directly to Newberry County from Virginia (Newberry County was then a part of Ninety Six District).

Richard Griffin was born in Virginia or in Wales in the year 1734. His first wife was Nancy Ann Clarke (she was born 1739 and died 1792), whom he married in 1754. Their children were: Nancy (b. 1756), Mary (b. 1757), Elizabeth (b. 1759; and married William Pickens), Margaret (b. 1761; married Reuben Golding), William (b. 1762; died in Miss.), Lucy (b. 1765; married 1784 to William Watson), John (b. 1767; married Sarah Williams, the daughter of Col. James Williams of the Revolution), James C. (b. 1769; married, first, Miss Goodman, and, second, a Miss Chase), Reuben F. (b. 1771; married Jane Griffin, a cousin), Adino (b. 1773; died in Miss.), Ira (b. 1775; married Susan Wilson), Sarah (b. 1778; married Washington Williams), Richard (b. 1780; married, first, Miss Lipscomb, and second, Rebecca Wilson), Joseph (b. 1782; married Parthena Coleman), David (b. 1786; married Matilda Golding), Anthony (twin brother of David) married Mary Simpson, Larkin (b. 1788; married Jemima Coleman). Ira died in 1830 and left widow, Susannah, and several children. Richard Griffin's second wife was Eleanor whom he married in later life. They had no children.

Reuben Griffin, son of Richard, died 1826. His wife, Jane, a cousin, was the daughter of William Griffin. They had children: Benjamin, Peggy Teague, Kitty Young, Elizabeth Teague, Patsy, and Elihu. Executors: Captain Anthony Griffin and John K. Griffin.

Benjamin Griffin, son of Reuben and Jane, died in Laurens County in 1817. His distributees were his brothers and sisters.

Robert Griffin made will dated Feb. 19, 1809, and died in Abbeville County March 9, 1809. He left widow, Margaret, who died September 10, 1821, and children as follows: Robert F., Ezekiel P., Elizabeth McMillan, Jane (wife of Edmund Stephens). The children of Elizabeth McMillan were: Wiley, Luana, and Peggy. Edmund and Jane Stephens and Robert F. Griffin moved out of the state.

Owen Griffin died in Abbeville County in 1807 and left children: James and Elizabeth.

Charles B. Griffin, of Abbeville District, married Jane Mathis, daughter of Arabella Mathis who died in February, 1854.

Thomas C. Griffin died in Abbeville County in 1875, leaving two sons, Wesley and Joseph.

Anthony Griffin made will in 1797 and died in 1809 in Laurens County, leaving widow, Mary Ann, and children: Asa, Abia, James, Elizabeth Butler, Katy Cook, and Suky. Administration was granted to John Cook. Abia died in 1814. James died in 1801.

William Griffin, brother of Anthony and Richard, died in Laurens County in year 1791. He lived on the west side of Carson's Creek. He left widow, Rachel, and children: William, James, Joseph, Jane, Peggy, and Katy. His son, James, was executor of his will. James married

GRIFFIN (continued)

Miss Chandler, and died 1828, leaving children: Richard T., Matilda, Mary B., Lucinda (wife of Daniel Shell), Kitturah (married first, James Leak, and second, Mr. Harrington), Wade H. (b. 1800), and John B. James' wife was Martha Chandler.

James Griffin, of Virginia, moved to Ninety Six District before the Revolutionary War. He was born 1731 and died in 1781, leaving widow, Frances (she was born 1730 and died 1799), and children as follows: Charles, John, Mary, and others. John and Charles were large landowners in Newberry County. The daughter, Mary, married a Mr. Leavell.

Charles Griffin (b. 1763 and died 1820), married in 1783 to Mary _____ (she was born 1763 and died ____). Their children were: Frances (b. 1784 and d. 1848), who married (1) West Gary and (2) John Williams; James (b. 1787 and d. 1795); John King (b. 1789 and d. 1841); Hetty (b. 1792 and d. 1861); William C. (b. 1794 and d. 1820); Archibald (b. 1797 and d. 1807); Bluford F. (b. 1802 and d. ____); Hetty married in 1807 to Absalom Gary and after his death, she married in 1818 to a Mr. Rabb. William C. married in 1818 to Mary _____. Bluford F. married (1) Agnes Lipscomb Young and (2) Elizabeth Gary.

John Griffin (son of James), made a will dated 1805 and died same year, leaving widow, Anne, and children: Mary (died, not married), Hester (married John Stephens and left son, Daniel Stephens), Rebecca (married John Stephens, widower of her deceased sister), Clary (married Elijah Alberson, and moved to Alabama), Frances (married William Alberson and lived in Laurens County), Nancy (married Obediah Pitts, and moved to Alabama), Susan (married Samuel Plant), Charles (married Jemima Mangum), Sarah (married a McTeer). Obediah Pitts and family settled in Texas. Charles died and his widow, Jemima Mangum, married Joseph Johnston.

Bluford F. Griffin (father of the late Bluford Griffin of Newberry) died and left widow, Agnes. His first wife was the mother of his children.

Captain Anthony Griffin (son of Richard) made will in 1849, died 1850, and left children: Frances Amanda, Dr. William H., Richard F., Jane T. (wife of William A. Fuller), Martha S. (wife of C. C. Higgins), Mary W. (married a Watts), and Sarah A. (wife of Charles H. Phinney). A relative, John D. Williams, was appointed Administrator of his estate. His wife was named Alyan who died about 1815 to 1820.

Christopher Griffin died in Newberry County in 1832, leaving widow, Phoebe, and children: William B., and Hillary Mangum or Griffin. His sisters were: Elizabeth Pitts, Sarah Griffin, Martha Barksdale, and Lucinda Griffin.

Daniel Griffin died in Newberry County in 1799 and left widow, Milly Griffin.

General John K. Griffin who is favorably mentioned in the "Annals of Newberry", was a member of the United States Congress. He died about 1841, left widow, Sarah, who afterwards married Daniel Wallace. He left property to his widow and to the children of a deceased brother, Charles B. Griffin, viz: Charles B. , A. I., John F., and the wife of Dr. Charles Gary.

Charles B. Griffin died in 1845 in Newberry County, and is buried at Bush River Church Cemetery.

William Griffin (cousin of Anthony and Richard), came from Culpepper County, Virginia, before the Revolution. He married and had children: Isaac, and others whose names are not known. His sisters were: Nancy (married a Sims), Frances (married Wm. McTeer of Laurens County). He moved to Edgefield County, and later to Georgia. In his old age, he returned to Virginia where he died. He was pensioned as a Revolutionary War soldier in the Continentals.

William Griffin (of Edgefield) died in January 1812 and left widow, Rebecca, and a son, James. His brothers were: James and Vincent Griffin who were executors of his estate.

Jesse Griffin died in Edgefield County about 1807. His children named in settlement of his estate were: Mary, Eleanor, Elizabeth, William, and Beverly Allen. Executors: William Griffin and Allen Griffin.

William Griffin, of Pendleton District, made will October 5, 1800 and died in 1800, leaving widow, Elizabeth, and children: John, Henry, William, Serjeant, Oswell, Rebecca Breazell, Rosannah, Blocker, Haskey Breazell, Martha, and Elizabeth. His second wife had children who were not named in his will, except as to a "balance of estate to be divided among them".

John Griffin, of Pendleton District, died about 1810 to 1820, leaving widow, Anna, and children as follows: Kennon, Elijah, Joel, John, Heska, Isiah K., and Sarah Rebecca White.

William E. Lawson Homer married Sarah Rebecca and they moved to Marion County, Alabama.

HOUSEAL
(Collaborator: William P. Houseal)
Written 1929

In the ancient kingdom of Wurttemberg, a part of that great territory in Germany where education and culture played a large part in the growth of an imperialistic commonwealth, there lived a family in the 16th century whose name was known at that time as Hausihl. The home of this family was then in Heilbronn, long an imperial free town, situated beautifully on the Neckar, also chiefly notable for its finest edifice, the old Gothic Church of St. Killian. It was also the seat of a Protestant Theological Seminary. It is still quite medieval in its older parts, but has modern suburbs and before World War I, with about 30,000 population, was noted for its flourishing industries.

This early historical setting of the Hausihl (later changed to Houseal) family had not so modern coloring and shading at the time when its founders were first known as dwellers in Heilbronn.

The kingdom of Wurttemberg, in which Heilbronn was one of the chief towns, was one of the three other provinces (Baden, Bavaria and Hohenzollern) of Suabia. Among the inhabitants of that region were the Alemanni, a confederacy of several German tribes which at the commencement of the third century after Christ, lived near the Roman territory and came then and subsequently in conflict with the imperial troops. It is a significant fact that the warlike predecessors of the Alemanni were never subdued by Julius Caesar in either of his campaigns (B. C. 55 and 53), when he twice crossed the Rhine and conquered Gaul and certain German tribes.

The battle-axe was the main weapon of warfare of these tribes, together with a huge wooden shield covered with rawhide which protected their attack of the enemy and repulsed them as they wielded their long handled axes to hew down the foe. Always amazing in their warlike efficiency, the Germans had first introduced themselves to the Romans in 114 B. C., by invading Italy over the Alps, sliding down the snow-clad mountains on their huge shields.

Professor George W. Hauschild of New York City, former member of the Newberry College faculty (1908-1910), is authority for the etymology of the surname Hauschild (or Hausihl), similar to his own, consisting of two German words, "hauen", to hew, and "schild", shield, this Hauenschild, (literally Englished, "hew-shield"), signifying "defender" or "protector". Similar significance, denoting the occupation or profession of the bearers of surnames, being common in Germany — derived in the case of Houseal from the reputation of their ancestors in handling the battle-axe and the shield.

The Alemanni successfully resisted the efforts of three Roman emperors to subjugate them during 150 years (213-360 A. D.) when the Emperor Julian defeated them at Strassburg and drove them across the Rhine, which 100 years previously they had crossed and overran Gaul. Clovis, King of the Franks, finally broke their power in 496, but it remained for the great Charlemagne (800 A. D.) to change the German tribes into civilized people.

Suabia eventually gave to the Germans of a later period the Hohenstaufen dynasty, which produced a number of rulers from 1138 to 1254, among the most illustrious of whom was Friedrich Barbarossa, whose father, Conrad III, took an active part in the Second Crusade, the object of which, as in the first attempt, was to wrest the Holy Land from the dominion of the Saracens.

Thus the ancient line of ancestors of the Houseal family emerged with the progress of modern civilization from the former tribal and primitive environment and took their place along with other peoples in Germany in the march of education and the cultivation of the arts and sciences.

Early in the 18th century there was a citizen of Heilbronn, a man of culture and education, the Rev. Bernard Hausihl, D. D., who became the progenitor of the Houseal family of America. He was a professor in the Protestant Theological Seminary in Heilbronn, being a minister of the Reformed Church. After laboring in the home land, he later moved to England, where he preached the gospel as interpreted by Martin Luther. It is more than probable that he was also court preacher of George II while he lived in London and was chosen for that office because of quite close kinship which he bore to the House Of Hanover, the family coat-of-arms being yet very similar in design to the royal insignia of Great Britain (since the First World War, being changed to the House of Windsor). The Lutheran Chapel was maintained in

HOUSEAL (continued)

London throughout the reigns of the Georges and even until the succession of Edward VII to the throne. Queen Victoria authorized stated services in the chapel and in 1881, she issued an order that the hour-glass on the pulpit should be so gauged that the sermon should not be longer than 20 minutes.

The ancestors of the Houseal family in America were two sons of the Rev. Bernard Houseal. The eldest, Bernard Michael Houseal (born in Heilbronn in 1728), before sailing from Rotterdam, in the spring of 1752, was married in that city to Sybilla Margaretha Mayer, the daughter of an eminent citizen of the city of Ulm, kingdom of Wurttemberg, where she was born August 4, 1733. The bridegroom was ordained by the Lutheran consistory of Holland, having been a student of the University of Strassburg. Upon his arrival in America he became pastor of the Lutheran Church at Fredericktown (now Frederick), Md.; then in December, 1758, pastor of Trinity Lutheran Church at Reading, Pa. It is said in the history of that church he remained there only five years and that "as he and his wife were of superior education and culture, it may be that they became dissatisfied with life in a quiet inland town as Reading, then was . . . confirmed by the fact that he remained in Easton only one year, next finding him (1765) in Philadelphia and in 1770 in New York, where he became pastor of the old Hollandish Lutheran Church, preaching in three languages, Hollandish, German, and English".

Here he and his family found congenial society and he became quite prominent. He was governor of the board of trustees of the College of New York (now Columbia University), and also trustee of the New York hospital. His troubles began with the Revolutionary War, his sympathies being with Great Britain and the Royalist Party. As long as the British held New York, he was protected, but after Cornwallis surrendered and the city was evacuated, he had to flee for his life, and sought safety with his family on a British vessel. It is said that many of the congregation of his church regretted to lose so talented a preacher and faithful pastor. As the vessel was sailing for Halifax, Nova Scotia, the vestry gave him a letter of recommendation to the Lutheran congregation of that city, regardless of the circumstances under which he was leaving. He received but meager support there on account of the small membership. Being advised to apply for aid to the "Society for the Propagation of the Gospel", the name under which missionary work among the colonists was conducted. In order to secure help thus necessary, he was required to go to London and receive reordination at the hands of the Bishop of London, which he did in 1785, and returned to Halifax in the double position of pastor of the Lutheran congregation and also German missionary of the English society. After his death (March 9, 1799), he was buried in a vault beneath his church, the Lutheran Congregation soon afterwards passing under the jurisdiction of the Episcopal Church.

The ten children of Doctor Houseal attained to positions of eminence. Two of his sons, the eldest and the youngest, John Bernard Houseal and George Houseal, became surgeons in the British navy; the second son, Michael Houseal, served on the staff of the Duke of Kent with the rank of Captain. The daughters were Eva Margaretha, Sophia Elizabeth, Anna Elizabeth, Sybilla Sybina, Mary Dorcas Salome, Amelia, and Wilhelmina, two of whom married officers of the British fleet and four others, officers of the British army; the youngest, Wilhelmina, became the wife of Captain W. Seymour, a nephew of the Duke of Kent. A Lutheran doctor of divinity, who furnished this data to the author of the history of Reading (Pa.) Lutheran congregation, laconically said that "the family had no cause to regret that they had cast their lot with the Loyalist Party".

Certain members of Doctor Houseal's family located subsequently in New York and Charleston. The records of the Medical Society of South Carolina show that one son, Dr. John Bernard Houseal, was a member in 1803. He married, a second time, Mary Talbird of Beaufort in 1808, after which he practiced medicine there. Dr. George Houseal also practiced medicine in Beaufort and died about 1824. The family name has entirely disappeared from Charleston and Beaufort, and is now represented by the Cunningham family (some of whom recently lived in Columbia) in Beaufort, and in Savannah by the Thompson family.

William Frederick Houseal, the younger brother (born in Heilbronn in 1730), did not locate in Maryland, where he and his brother, Bernard Michael, went after landing at Philadelphia, nor did he remain very long there, but came at once to South Carolina; thus induced doubtless by the fact that he was intimately acquainted with the family of John Adam Summer, the first settler of the Dutch Fork, who, with a group of Germans from the Palatinate, first sought homes in Pennsylvania, but proceeding southward through the Cumberland Valley, and thence by way of the Shenandoah Valley of Virginia, passing by the ridge section of Fairfield

HOUSEAL (continued)

County, this state, arrived at Broad River at the present location of Parr Shoals, then known as Cohees Falls. Here they crossed the river into Newberry County, doubtless attracted by the prospect of its well watered territory and the extensive forests that reminded them greatly of the Fatherland.

Captain William Frederick Houseal, ancestor of the (present) Houseal family of South Carolina, was a patriot and officer in the Revolutionary War, having chosen a very different course in this respect than his brother, Dr. Bernard Michael Houseal, who had visited him about ten years before the war and preached in St. Paul's (and also no doubt in St. John's) Church near the Houseal home. Captain Houseal served first in command of militia companies in the regiments of Colonel Lyles and Colonel Jonas Beard of Ninety-Six District and was captain of a cavalry troop in the regiment of Colonel Philemon Waters of Newberry County, in which unit the Rev. Giles Chapman (ancestor of the Chapman family of Newberry) was chaplain. Captain Houseal was a gallant officer and was in many engagements during the whole period of the war. The roster of his troop of horse, in his own bold, even handwriting, a fine specimen of script — the chirography characteristic of his brother and their children — is among the Revolutionary records in the South Carolina Historical Commission in Columbia, South Carolina.

Captain William Frederick Houseal first married Mary Elizabeth Stroman of Orangeburg and had two children, Mary Magdalene, who married John Adam La Gronne, and Annie Marie, who married Thomas Ebeneezer Glass, a Scotchman. John Adam Le Gronne (son of Lorentz Le Gronne, a Frenchman) and his wife, Mary Magdalene, had several children, one of whom, John George Le Gronne (now LaGrone), moved to Alabama. Ebeneezer Glass and his wife, Annie Marie, had two children, Thomas Glass and Elizabeth Glass who also moved to Alabama. Thomas Glass' first wife having died, he moved to Abbeville and was married again to Susan Roberts before going to Alabama. Frank P. Glass of Montgomery, Alabama, editor of the Montgomery Advertiser, is a member of the Glass family.

Captain William Frederick Houseal's first wife died early and he married next Anna Margaret Geiselhardt of Newberry County and had four sons and a daughter, John Adam, John, David, William Frederick, Jr., and Mary Margaret.

John Adam, eldest son of Captain Houseal, married Mary M. Summer, daughter of Colonel John Adam Summer. David Houseal married a Miss McRae and left no children. William Frederick, Jr. married Elizabeth Setzler, daughter of George A. Setzler and his wife, Ann Margaret Leitner, daughter of Major Michael Leitner, of the Revolutionary period. Mary Margaret Houseal married Captain John Summer, near Pomaria, who erected a large, imposing residence of Colonial design, now nearly 100 years old and standing amid lovely magnolias and cedars, a monument to Captain Summer's enterprise and civic taste. The home was later occupied by his grandson, John Adam Summer, whose daughter, Mrs. Marie Huggins, now occupies it. Among the valuable treasures of its library is a copy of that rare publication, Audubon's "Birds of America". (It is not known whether Captain John or his son, William, built the home. - G. L. S.).

The children of John Adam Houseal were three daughters, Eve Margaret, Catherine and Mary Elizabeth, and two sons, John George and John. Margaret Eve married Jacob (grandparents of Captain John Swygert of Peak) and they have other descendants living in Laurens and in Newberry County. Catherine married William Rawl and no data of their descendants is available for this sketch. Mary Elizabeth married David Counts and they had John Adam, Rufus O., Orlando Benedict, and Francis Hammett Counts.

John George, eldest son of John Adam Houseal, married Elizabeth Ridlehuber and had one daughter, Herselia Frances (married the late Wallace A. Cline of Newberry), who had one son, Benedict Houseal Cline (died 1899), and five daughters, Alice, eldest (died 1909); Kate (married the late Jacob Ehrhardt of Ehrhardt, died 1918); Caroline (married the late Rev. Monroe J. Epting, D. D. of Savannah, Georgia). Two daughters, Mary and Margaret (wife of J. D. Wicker) lived in Newberry.

John Houseal, Jr., only son of John Houseal, married Eve Margaret Counts and had three children. William Walter (married Eliza Caroline Barre), Elizabeth (married Jacob Barre) and Frances (married George P. Summer). The children of William Walter, who established his home in Newberry as a merchant in 1851, numbered five sons and three daughters. Those living are James Emlon (first graduate of Newberry College) of Cedartown, Georgia, Mattie Virginia (married first, the late Rev. Joseph Q. Wertz, now the wife of the Rev. W. A. Lutz, D. D.) of Charlotte, N. C., William Preston (the "Dutch Weather Prophet") of Columbia, Walter Gustave,

HOUSEAL (continued)

a practicing physician of Newberry. The eldest child, Mary Elizabeth (wife of the late David Julius Hentz of Pomaria), died in 1906; John Irving, second child, moved west in 1875 and died in Memphis, Tenn. in 1908; Frances Cornelia, third child, died in young womanhood in 1867; Edward Julius, fourth son (graduate of Newberry College, class of 1882) died in 1883. William Walter Houseal was honored a number of times by the people of Newberry with public office — first as sheriff in 1855 (this officer could not succeed himself in those days for a second term) and again in 1863; county tax assessor in 1868; three successive terms as auditor, 1884-1886-1888. His death occurred in 1889.

Frances, eldest daughter of John Houseal, Jr., married George P. Summer, who died early thereafter, leaving one daughter, Nora, who died (1865) in young womanhood. Frances Houseal Summer then married Jeremiah Hopkins, and they moved to Mississippi, where during the Confederate War, he was murdered by negro slaves while supervising the clearing of new ground on his farm. The negroes, in felling a tree, caused it to fall upon him and attempted to conceal their crime by burning his body, which, however, not having been entirely consumed, was brought to Little Mountain and buried there, the widow at tthe same time returning to her farm in Newberry County; but her health soon became enfeebled, and removing to the home of her brother, William Walter, she died in Newberry in 1866, survived by two daughters of her second marriage, Mattie (wife of S. M. Ball of Laurens) died in 1926; Ella (wife of G. H. Rawl) who lives in Columbia.

After the death of John Houseal, Jr., his widow married Captain Joseph P. Summer and their children were: Martha (married George Hipp), whose sons, Edward R. and John C., were prominent citizens of Newberry, and two daughters, Alice, wife of George Means (several terms representative from Greenville County) and Nellie (wife of the late J. F. Mackey) of Greenville; Ella (married Charles W. D(Oyley) and then moved to Greenville where she died December, 1927, aged nearly 93; William Jefferson, who died at the age of 26; Captain John Summer, who commanded a company in the Third Regiment of South Carolina volunteers in the Confederate War and died during that period. Dr. William Jefferson Summer deserves special mention here. Reading medicine when quite a boy in the office of Dr. J.A. Berley, he then attended medical lectures at Petersburg, Va., and Worchester, Mass., and was graduated with high honors at the latter school. After he had practiced nearly a year, desiring to fit himself more skillfully in his profession, he attended lectures at the Charleston Medical College. However, even then his health seemed quite impaired and continuing to decline, he was not enabled to gratify his ambition, only practicing about two years and dying at the age of 26, December 21, 1854; when his pastor, the Rev. William Berley of Pomaria in a memorial tribute to him said that "he was a young gentleman of the very first order of talents and had practiced his profession in the midst of flattering success to himself and full satisfaction to the community". (Capt. Joseph P. Summer next married Mrs. Elizabeth Vance, and their children were G. B. Summer of Newberry, Mrs. Emma Stoudemayer, Mrs. Mary Cromer, Mrs. Bray Livingston, Mrs. Nora Kempson and Pinckney Summer).

The numerous descendants of William Frederick Houseal, Jr. (youngest son of Captain William Frederick Houseal) and his wife, Elizabeth Setzler, are scattered over many states, and it is a large family connection, although most of their 13 children died young. Ann Margaret married George Feagle and have children and grandchildren living in Newberry, Greenville and Columbia. Some of them moved to Texas. The eldest daughter, Martha Elizabeth, married Aaron Hamilton Kohn, whose two sons (only children) were Arthur Hayne Kohn, Secretary of the Carolina Life Insurance Company of Columbia, and the Rev. Ernest Houseal Kohn, D. D., Lutheran pastor at Mount Holly, N. C. Sarah Catherine married George Michael Monts, whose children were Margaret (widow of the late Dr. J. M. Sease), Mary (wife of W. A. Counts) and Elizabeth (wife of W. B. Shealy). Susannah Josephine Feagle married Captain U. B. Whites, who took an active part in ousting the carpetbaggers in 1876and was mainly instrumental in having the Negro Republican, Bridges, of Newberry, join the Wallace House. He was Treasurer of Newberry County afterwards, and moved to Atlanta, where two of his children, Robert Lee and Constance Lenora (wife of Dr. Karl Markt) then lived. Two of his daughters Iola and Mary, died in young womanhood. Mary Jane Feagle married W. W. Kohn and he is survived by a son, Sidney J. Kohn. (She next married Francis M. Bobb of Prosperity). Pauline Feagle married Nathan B. Wheeler and had four sons and four daughters. John N. Feagle, eldest son, lived at Little Mountain; married Frances M. Sease, their children being seven sons and five daughters. Warren Madison Feagle moved to Texas and married Alice Finetta King of Waxahachie. Lawrence

HOUSEAL (continued)

Irving Feagle married Dora E. Riser and had seven sons and a daughter. Loretta R. Feagle (married Jacob I. Wheeler) and lived in Columbia, their children numbering two sons and five daughters.

Henry Laurens Pinckney Houseal, son of William Frederick Houseal, Jr., graduated at the South Carolina Military Academy in 1849, and later at the Charleston Medical College. He was located in Columbia for a while, where he was associated with his uncle, Adam G. Summer, in the editorial department of a weekly newspaper, the South Carolinian. Later he moved to Florida and was practicing his profession of medicine when the Confederate War began. He volunteered and was made captain of a militia company, but died in 1862 before he could render much service. He married Mary Lucas before removing to Florida and at his death left three children. Ida, married Thomas Cordes in Florida; Esdail and Mary Ann, the latter two dying early.

Louisa A. Houseal, youngest daughter of William Frederick Houseal, Jr., married J. Walter Stockman. One son, William Franklin, and two daughters, Mary Elizabeth and Susannah, never married. The two latter lived to be nonogenarians.

The children of Captain John Summer and his wife, Mary Margaret Houseal, were Nicholas, Henry, Mary Margaret, John Adam, William, Adam G., George Washington, Catherine and Thomas Jefferson. Nicholas was an outstanding young lawyer in Newberry and at one time the law partner of Judge John Belton O'Neall. George Washington and Catherine died young.

When the Seminole War in Florida began, Nicholas Summer, like many young men with an adventurous spirit, volunteered and went to the scene of hostilities. He never came back, having been mortally wounded in battle at the Everglades and died. His brother, John, went to Florida to bring back his body and was himself taken ill and died. Both of these brothers lie under Florida soil. Henry graduated at the South Carolina College in 1831, and having been admitted to the bar, was first associated with his brother, Nicholas, of Newberry, but later moved to Alabama to practice his profession of law. When his brother, Nicholas, died in Florida, he left Henry his valuable law library under the condition that he would return to Newberry and practice his profession, and this he very soon afterwards did, having his law office there before and during the Confederate War. He was a member of the South Carolina legislature two terms (1846 and 1848), and held many other important public positions, being the first secretary of the board of trustees of Newberry College and supplied gratuitously any chair in its faculty during the Confederate War when no one else was available for such duties. He married Frances Mayer, sister of Dr. O. B. Mayer, Sr. Two of their children lived at Pomaria, John Adam and Kate (first, married to the late Rev. J. F. Kiser), wife of J. B. T. Scott. One son, William, died in early youth. Henry Summer was recuperating his health on his farm near Pomaria in February, 1865, when his home was burned by Sherman's troops, who were in the act of hanging him in his barn in an effort to force him to show where he had concealed certain money, which he did not possess, when their plans were interrupted by a superior officer who appeared upon the scene and ordered Mr. Summer released. This thrilling experience served to hasten his decline in health and he died several years afterwards.

Adam Geiselhardt Summer, one of the younger sons of Captain John Summer, was born at Pomaria in 1818. He received a good academic education at Lexington, but was not the graduate of any college. He was admitted to the bar and began the practice of law at Newberry in 1840. He was a man of unusual mental power. Judge O'Neall, in his "Annals of Newberry", speaks of him as "a polished and versatile speaker". He gave up the practice of law and moved to Columbia, where he published and edited The South Carolinian, a weekly newspaper. Subsequently he disposed of his newspaper interests and moved to his farm "Ravenscroft", in Lexington County, and devoted himself chiefly to agriculture. He was a member of the legislature in 1850. In 1855, he was one of the organizers for its second time of the State Agricultural Society and was elected secretary and treasurer (1855-57). He was also editor of the Southern Agriculturalist (published in Laurensville by R. M. Stokes) before he removed to Columbia. He had a refined and cultivated literary taste and his production of literature was readily accepted for publication by the Southern Quarterly Review, the Southern Literary Messenger and other Southern periodicals, and his humorous sketches and stories in the New York Spirit of the Times attracted considerable mention. In 1864, he married Margaret J. Starke, daughter of Major Thomas Starke of Kershaw District, having moved to Florida in 1857. He died in the prime of life in 1886 while on a visit to Charleston.

HOUSEAL (continued)

William Summer was a horticulturist of Pomaria, a well educated man (graduate of S. C. College) and a writer of some note, but he preferred the life of a planter and at the same time was associated with his brother as editor of The Southern Agriculturist. Both of the brothers were ardent supporters and members of the Newberry Agricultural Society in antebellum days. He was founder of the Pomaria nurseries, which for a long period before the Confederate War and even so thereafter was one of the most reliable enterprises of the kind in the entire South. Mr. Summer imported many rare plants from Europe and shipped his products to many states. He was the first postmaster in his section during the stage coach days in the early '40s, establishing the office in the ancestral home and giving it the name of Pomaria, the etymology of which is a Latin-English combination of "poma", plural of "pommum", fruit, and "area", land, signifying, "Land of Fruit". The name was adopted for the station by the Greenville and Columbia railroad when it was built through that section in 1850, and the post office located there, Mr. Summer continuing to conduct it until his death in the latter '80s.

George Washington and Mary Margaret, son and daughter of Captain John Summer, both died in their youth. Thomas Jefferson, another son, attended West Point Military Academy and then went to Europe to pursue his studies further in some German University, but died before finishing the course.

Many of the pioneers of the Dutch Fork stood by General Washington in the time of the Revolutionary War, for they were a patriotic people who had come to America seeking personal and religious liberty; and they would not have been true to their convictions if they had not had the courage to show the world that they intended to secure what they were seeking. These same principles and the dauntless spirit of them, inherent in their descendants, were shown in other wars, including the World Wars, when many young men of this section fought in France and many died on French soil, having made the supreme sacrifice for American ideals with the effort "to make the world safe for democracy".

KIBLER

John Kibler, who came from Germany, made petition for 350 acres of land in the Dutch Fork, Ninety Six District, dated October 3, 1753; it shows that he came in the ship, Anne, Captain Orr Commanding; that he had a wife and four children, viz: Jacob Weymouth Keibler (age 17), Purcha Keibler (age 13), Jacob Keibler (age 12), Hans Erick Keibler (age 6), and a servant.

It is probable other children were born after petition was filed.

John Kibler (spelling changed) who died 1829, may have been a son of one of the above named sons, Jacob or Jacob Weymouth Kibler, or even Hans Erick. However, it is probable that two went to North Carolina, and Jacob only remained in the county and became father of John and Michael.

John Kibler, who died in October, 1829, left widow, Nancy (Farr) Kibler, and children: Polly (wife of Adam Bedenbaugh), Jacob J., John, Catherine (wife of John Fellers), Daniel (died October, 1829), Levi, Anna, and William. Mrs. Nancy Kibler died 1840, and in the settlement of her estate her daughter, Anna, is named as wife of Ivy Busby. John, Jr. married Mary Summer, daughter of William Summer and had children: Susannah (wife of George Long), Eliza (wife of John Schumpert), and Anna (wife of George Chapman), John, Andrew, and Mary Ann

Michael Kibler married Margaret Kinard, daughter of Martin Kinard, and had children: John, Michael, David, Adam, and Jacob. Tradition is that he used the first cotton gin ever used in Newberry County.

Michael Kibler, Jr. married Elizabeth Koone, daughter of Henry and Eve Catherine Koone, and had: Levi, Henry, Jacob, Adam, Harriet (wife of Adam Sheely), Sally (wife of Anderson Wicker), Catherine (wife of D. Middleton Griffith), Mary (wife of Christian Wicker), Elizabeth (wife of Paul Troutman), Frances (wife of Levi C. Sheppard), Margaret (wife of G. M. Singley).

John Adam Kibler married three times. His first wife was a Miss Fellers. He next married a Miss Maffett, and his third wife was Nancy C. Kinard, a sister of John Middleton Kinard.

Jacob Kibler married Frances Chapman, daughter of Samuel Chapman, Esq., and had children: John, Arthur, William, Elizabeth, Alice, and Sarah. Jacob Kibler was Tax Collector of Newberry from 1848 to 1852.

KIBLER (continued)

David Kibler married three times. His first wife was a Miss Fellers, his second wife a Miss Suber, and third a Miss Hair. He had nine children, many of whom died early in life. His sons were: Drayton, Amos, Godfrey, Middleton, and Calvin. Drayton lived in Newberry many years, married Julia A. Barre, and had children: Calhoun (died soon), Mary (wife of William Johnson), Elizabeth (wife of William A. Kinard), Alma (wife of Robert F. Bryant), Dr. James M., Trannie (wife of Dr. John Simpson), Lilla, Gussie, Robert, and Lawson.

KINARD

The Germans who came to South Carolina about 1745-60 were many. John Kinard, Sr. and Martin Kinard, Sr. came with their families about this time. They were of that thrifty and industrial class of immigrants from the vicinity of Baden in the Palatinate, and left their native country on account of economic distrubances due to an upheavel in religious organizations and the intolerant attitude of the mother-church, the Catholic. The name was originally spelled "Kynnard".

About three miles north of the town of Pomaria, on the main top-soil road from old Bethlehem Church to Broad River, can be seen an old Kinard graveyard. It is on a small hill overlooking a stream to the South that shows evidence of having given an attractive picture in the Spring and Summer when the dog-wood flourished and in the Fall when the leaves put on their many colors. Now the place is covered with tall pines and bushes and the one-time attractiveness has disappeared.

Martin Kinard married Mary _____ and lived in this section, dying there in 1803. He, like many of the pioneers, was a staunch, up-right citizen of his adopted land, accumulating property, and he became a leader in his Church and community. When the Revolutionary War began, he joined the forces of the American Army and served through the war in the regiment of Colonel Philemon Waters. When he died he left a widow and the following children: Frederick (married Elizabeth Chapman), Margaret (married Michael Kinard), Sibella (married Jacob Singley), Martin (married Katherine Kuhn), Christina (married Phillip Sligh, Sr.), Mary (married Michael Kibler), and John (died in 1808, unmarried).

Frederick Kinard settled in the Ruff Community (John Henry Ruff owned lands for several miles on the main road from Phillips Church to Bethlehem Church). He was the father of Frederick, Jr., William, Sarah, Elizabeth and Katherine.

Phillip Sligh, Sr., and his wife, Christina Kinard, had several children, one of whom was Phillip Sligh, Jr., who married Elizabeth Eichleberger, a daughter of Colonel John Eichleberger. They had no children, but reared and educated several orphans, and at their death left considerable property. A large share of their property was left for the organization of a church in the community in which they lived. This church became known as Phillips Church named in honor of its benefactor. Another son, Jacob Sligh who married a Miss Piester (she was probably a descendant of Gasper Piester, an early settler in this section) and they had a son, George P. who married Josephine Maffett.

Martin Kinard, Jr., who married Katherine Kuhn (she was a daughter of the Revolutionary patriot, Henry Kuhn) lived in the Pomaria section for several years. He was a man of vision, and having the spirit of self-reliance and possessing determination, he moved to the county line of Newberry and Laurens Counties, bought lands, and eventually became a wealthy land owner in the vicinity. It was due to his efforts that the first Baptist Church was organized in that community, known as Sharon Church, and it was here that the village of Martins, named in his honor, began. When the first railroad was built through there, it was called Martin's Station and afterwards changed to Kinards. The children of Martin and Katherine Kinard were, John P. who was Sheriff of Newberry County and died in 1890, Henry H. who was, also, Sheriff of Newberry County, Middleton T., Mary, Hulda, Elizabeth, and Martha.

There is much interesting tradition and historical facts, together with early romantic careers of many old pioneers, builders of the different sections of South Carolina, but none quite surpasses those of old Edgefield, Lexington, Newberry and Fairfield Districts during the early part of the last century.

The first wife of General Henry H. Kinard was Anna Mary Counts, daughter of Captain John Counts, and after her death, he married Mary Counts, daughter of Adam Counts. He was the father of Captain John M. Kinard by the first wife. Captain John M. Kinard was Captain of

KINARD (continued)

Company "F" Twentieth Regiment of South Carolina Volunteers in the Confederate Army, and was killed at the Battle of Strasburg in 1864. His successor in command was William M. Kinard, son of John P. Kinard, who after the war became a practicing physician in Newberry, but died early. General Kinard and his second wife had a daughter, Katherine, who married the late Bishop A. Coke Smith, and a son, Henry, who married Miss Annie Smith of Baltimore and lives in Newberry. Mary, a daughter of Martin Kinard, married Lemuel Glymph whose daughter married Captain Joseph P. Summer and were the grandparents of Mrs. Laura C. Hemingway, a journalistic writer. Another daughter, Elizabeth, married Jacob Summer and were parents of Dr. Bluford M. Summer, Rev. Walter W. Summer, and Catherine, who married the late John Drayton Smith of Kinards. Dr. Bluford M. Summer, a surgeon in the Confederate Army, was killed in 1863. The other daughters were, Hulda who married John Hinson, Kate who married M. K. Reeder, and Martha who married John Goree. Middleton T., a son, married Sara J. Harmon.

Captain John M. Kinard was well educated and a man of great promise at the time of his death in the Confederate Army. He had married, first, Mary A. Ruff, daughter of Dr. P. B. Ruff of Newberry, by whom he had a daughter who was the first wife of the veteran editor, Colonel Elbert H. Aull, of the Newberry Herald and News, and the mother of John Kinard Aull, a well known journalist and news correspondent. Captain Kinard's first wife having died, he had married again to Lavania E. Rook and they were the parents of John M. Kinard, President of The Commercial Bank of Newberry, and Dr. James P. Kinard, Dean, and later President of Winthrop College.

John Kinard, Jr., son of the pioneer, John Kinard, was a large land owner near Cannons Creek. He was a man of influence in his section. In the settlement of his will (he died in 1800, his wife having already died) the following children shared in the estate: John P., Nicholas, Michael, Christopher, Samuel and three daughters. The daughters married Adam Singley, Jacob Cook, and Peter Wydemann. John P. married Polly _____, Michael married Margaret Kinard, and Samuel married Elizabeth Hall. Samuel died in 1843 and left children, one a daughter, Rebecca Malinda, became the wife of John Philip Barre of Prosperity. They were the parents, I believe, of Mrs. Kenneth Baker of Greenwood and Charles Barre, Esq., of New York City.

Andrew Kinard, son or grandson of John Kinard, Sr., lived in the vicinity of Cannons Creek, and had a son, Solomon, who moved to Newberry and there became its Postmaster several years before the Civil War. Solomon Kinard married a Miss Wertz and were the parents of J. H. M. Kinard, a former proprietor of the "Newberry Observer". The President of Newberry College, Dr. James C. Kinard, is a son of George Kinard and his wife, Rena (Campson) Kinard, and a grandson of J. H. M. Kinard.

Michael Kibler, Sr., who married Mary Kinard (daughter of the first Martin Kinard) had several daughters and a son, Michael, Jr. The daughters were wives of Jacob Sligh, John Barre, W. David Koone (name changed to Kohn).

In the vicinity of the town of Prosperity are very thickly settled neighborhoods of people noted for their generosity and the sympathetic understanding of the needs of their friends. Probably that is on account of the thriving christian churches in their midsts. There has come from this section many good workers in the Lutheran, Methodist and A. R. P. Churches.

There were three brothers living near Prosperity, Michael, Martin, and George Kinard, who were descendants of John Kinard, Sr. Michael married Sallie Quattlebaum and had David, Jefferson, Drayton, Belton, Jacob and a daughter who married a Kibler. There were, probably, other children. David Belton married Mary Ann Long and were parents of the late Rev. M. M. Kinard, a noted Lutheran preacher, who for several years was pastor of Ebenezer Lutheran Church in Columbia. Another is the Rev. James D. Kinard, now a Lutheran preacher in Statesville, N. C. One lives at Columbia and another in Prosperity. Another branch located at Ninety-Six, S. C.

These families have become scattered, like many of the old families. Some have gone to other fields to seek more remunerative opportunities and to fields of wider service to humanity; but wherever they have gone, they had upheld the family records as workers, builders, and possessing an intelligent understanding of their fellowman.

KUHN

In a history of the Kuhn family of Pennsylvania, in the "Ancestry of Rosalie Morris Johnson", whose mother was Elizabeth Kuhn, there is much of interest pertaining to the Pennsylvania and New Jersey families. The South Carolina families may be said to have sprung from three foreign sources. Casper Kuhn came from the parish Rieden, Germany, in the year 1739, Heinrich Kuhn from the parish Dielstorff, in Germany in the year 1744, and there was a Hans Kuhn, who came over but there is no record of his family.

These families came to America during a period of religious antagonism in the old country, the result of development and growth of a country whose government did not sanction personal liberty and religious freedom. The rapid settlement of America offered new opportunities for a people who had learned through educational and cultural surroundings, the advantages in material and intellectual growth.

Casper Kuhn was born in 1713. He came to South Carolina with his wife, Anna Magdelina Mejer, who was born in 1713. They had an infant daughter, Anna, born in 1739. Very soon after their arrival in Carolina, the wife died. There may have been other children, but no record is given of them. They settled in the lower section of Orangeburg District (now Orangeburg and Richland Counties). He married the second time to Anna Barbara Ernst (she was the widow of George Adam Ernst and daughter of _____ Trapp). His third wife was Anna Maria _____ by whom were three sons, all patriotic Revolutionary War soldiers, viz: John Adam Kuhn (born in 1754), Conrad Kuhn (born in 1756), and Lewis Kuhn (born in 1757). (From "German and Swiss Settlers to America", by Faust).

Heinrich Kuhn came to America, and to South Carolina with his wife, Regula Zobelj, and had three small sons when they came in 1744, viz: Heinrich, Jr., Felix, and Peter. They may have had other children. Heinrich, Jr., was born about 1740, was a Revolutionary War soldier, a Lieutenant in Colonel Philemon Water's regiment of state militia. He married about 1760 to Ursula Sheely, daughter of John Sheely and had eleven children: Benjamin, John, Henry, Elizabeth, Jacob, Francis, Rebecca, Mary, Adam, J. Windel, Katherine and Martin. The sons, John and Henry, also served in the Revolution, Henry as a private in Captain Jacob Fulmer's company of militia during the years 1780 to 1782. The name at this time was changed to "Koone". The widow, Ursula, later married George Eichleberger.

John Koone married Barbara _____ and had, David, Jacob, Ephriam, Christian, Elizabeth, Carolina, Henry, Martin, and Adam. Christian married first, Frederick Prysock, and after his death, to Michael Charles. Michael Charles and Christina Koone had, Harriet, Franklin, Anderson, David and Elizabeth. Benedict Koone died about the year 1802. He left two sons, Nicholas and George Koone, Sr. Nicholas and his wife, Mary and young son, George, moved to Rutherford County, North Carolina.

Wiley David Koone, son of John or George, married first, Margaret Kibler, and second, her sister, Mary Kibler. The children by the first wife were: A. Hamilton, a confederate soldier, who died in the war, Christina, Frances L., and William Walter, who died in the Confederate service. Some of their descendants changed the name to Kohn.

A. Hamilton Kohn married Martha Elizabeth Feagle (daughter of George Feagle and his wife, Ann Margaret Houseal) and had A. H. Kohn of Columbia, S. C. and Rev. Ernest Houseal Kohn, a Lutheran Minister.

William Walter Kohn married Mary Jane Feagle (daughter of George and Ann Margaret Houseal Feagle) and had one son, Sidney J. Kohn. After the death of William Walter, the widow married Francis M. Bobb, of Prosperity.

Francis L. married J. M. Sheely of Prosperity.

Wiley David Koone and his second wife, Mary Kibler, had Wallace, Paul, John M., Sara E., and Elivie. Elivie married a Ballentine and had Willie, Lonnie, Walter, Drayton, Mary, Minnie, Sallie, Lillian, Carrie, Sylvia, Ernest.

One John Koone died in 1854 and left his widow, Margaret Cromer Koone, and children John David, Delila, (wife of Henry Kinard), Martha (wife of Hiram Wicker), Elizabeth Caroline, and Elizabeth. John David was the father of Walter and Wesley Koone who lived near Cannons Creek in Newberry County. Walter married Laura Suber (daughter of Chas. Suber) and Wesley married Anna Singley (daughter of John Singley).

Walter Koone and Laura Suber had several children, some of whom are Prof. Rahn Koone, a teacher in the state public schools, Oliver, George, Dr. Thos. Koone, at present mayor of the city of Cumberland, Maryland, and Julius Koone of Pomaria.

Another John Koone died in 1865 and left Solomon, John Henry, Lavania, Harriet, John N.,

KUHN (continued)

Barbara (wife of Simon Frick), Charles, Laura (wife of James Boland), Charlotte, Lavania.

Henry Koone married Eve Catherine _____ in the year 1786 and had Catherine (married Captain Martin Kinard, Jr.), Mary (married John Metts), Margaret (married William Chapman), Sarah (married F. Bird Willingham), Elizabeth (married Michael Kibler, Jr.), Henry (married first Elizabeth (Riser) Cannon and second, Mary Riser), Eve (married Adam Epting.)

Captain Martin Kinard and his wife, Katherine Koone, had John P., Martha (married Ison Goree), Sallie (married Lemuel Glymph), Middleton T., (married Mary Harmon), Elizabeth (married Jacob Summer), Kate (married M. K. Reeder), Henry H. (married first, Mary Ann Counts and second, Louisa Counts).

John Metts and wife, Mary Koone, had Elizabeth (wife of John A. Wicker), Henry, Simeon, George, Martha, Delila, and Margaret. Martha married George A. Setzler, Jr., and were parents of Pickens O. Setzler of Pomaria. Mary married Lemuel Lane.

William Chapman and his wife, Margaret Koone, had Elizabeth (wife of John Miller), George H., William, Franklin, Caroline (married David Koone), Col. George H. Chapman married Annie Kibler (daughter of John Kibler and his wife, Anna Mary Eichleberger) and had, Jane (wife of Charles Counts), Cummings (wife of George Swygert), Noah, Susannah, and James K. Noah Chapman had a daughter who married the late Rev. George A. Riser, a Lutheran minister, who died in Virginia. Dr. James K. Chapman was a practicing physician at Pomaria, S. C. for several years. He married Mary Summer, daughter of Henry Summer, Esq., died, left three children, two sons and a daughter.

Henry Koone, Jr., familiarly known as "General" Koone, was a large planter in the Broad River section, near Pomaria. He married first, Elizabeth (Riser) Cannon, and had one daughter, Louisa, who became the wife of the late Thomas V. Wicker, of Newberry. His second wife was Mary Riser, sister of first wife, and daughter of Martin Riser and his wife, Mahala Cannon; Mahala Cannon was the daughter of David Cannon, Esq. and his wife, Nancy. Henry Koone's children by his second wife were Texana (married Benson Suber, George W., Samuel, John Oliver, and Emma (married Thomas M. Lake). Thomas V. Wicker and his wife, Louisa, had John H. (married Mamie Paysinger) who lives in Newberry, and is manager of the Farmers Oil Mill and Ice Plant, Lawrence (married a Swygert and then a Dominick), William, Thomas (married a Cromer), Dan (married a Cromer). There was an older brother, Alonzo, who died several years ago, but left a large family. Benson Suber and Texana, his wife, had several children: John, William, Mary, Annie, Lucy, and probably others. George W. and Samuel Koone died early. John Oliver died in Newberry but never married. Thomas M. Lake and wife, Emma, had Marvin, Una, Nina, and Lola.

Adam Epting and his wife, Eve Koone, had Jacob, Henry, Adam, Sarah (wife of Jacob Setzler), William (moved to Mississippi), Nancy, Elizabeth, Anna (wife of Jabez G. Lake). Jacob married Elizabeth Kinard (daughter of Frederick Kinard and granddaughter of Martin Kinard, Sr.) and had Julius J., Dr. Berley C., Rev. Monroe J., Bunyan O., L. Iraeneus, Nancy. Dr. Berley O. Epting was a prominent physician in Greenwood for many years. Rev. Monroe J. Epting was a Lutheran minister of Savannah, Georgia (he married Miss Cline of Newberry, a descendant of Captain William F. Houseal, an officer of the Revolutionary War). Henry married Lucinda Hoard and had several children. Nancy married an Able. (See Epting family sketch).

Jacob Francis Koone was the father of several children, most of whom lived at Chapin, and the grandfather of Rev. Samuel P. Koone, a Lutheran minister.

George A. Koone died in Newberry County in 1821, left a widow, Rosanna Barbara, and children, Uriah, John, George, Adam, David, Elizabeth, Barbara, Katherine. Three of his grandsons shared in his estate: Henry and Emanuel. George A. Koone, Jr., was a practicing physician at Pomaria for several years, married Margaret _____. Dr. George Koons died in 1849 (his widow married William David Ridlehuber). His children were: John, David, Henry, William, Jacob, Phillip, George A., Katherine, Mary, Eva, Elizabeth, Martha (married a Hendrix), Polly and Lavania. The son, George A. Koone, married Sara Cromer.

Martin Koon, Sr. (son of Henry Koon, Jr. and Ursula Sheely Koon) married Eve Christina (Leitner) Epting, widow of John Adam Epting, Jr. and daughter of Michael Leitner and Maria (Beard) Leitner. They had a daughter, Katherine, who married David Cromer, Jr., whose son Hilliard Francis Cromer, married Nancy Singley.

Some of the descendants of these families moved to Alabama and Mississippi, and probably to Texas where there are many Newberry County people living. Wherever they are, they are generally a healthy, thrifty people, giving to their communities conscientious services.

LAKE

The bold immigrants of Northern Germany who came to Pennsylvania and Maryland about 1640 to 1650, were a race of people well suited to intermarry with the English and French who had already settled in Eastern Maryland, and make a race of hardy pioneers who began the settlements of New Jersey and Deleware.

When Wilhelm Weser, born in Hanover, Germany, before 1500, moved to England, there was a general movement of people to America. The name was changed to the English form, William Reeder, and two of his descendants came to America, John to Massachusetts in 1656, and Joseph to Long Island in 1650. This family was said to have been connected with the ancient House of Hanover. There were two sons of Joseph: Jacob and Joseph, Jr. Joseph Reeder, Jr. moved to the vicinity of Morristown, N. J., and here became acquainted with two old pioneer families, Gano and Lake. One of his sons, Joseph, married Susannah Gano (a descendant of Francis Gano, of France, who fled to New York to escape papal martyrdom). They had a daughter, Elizabeth, who married Thomas Lake of New Jersey. Thomas Lake was descended from an old English family who had been influential in establishing a permanent footing in Maryland (the section which is now a part of New Jersey) for the Protestant Church when the Catholics ruled the territory under Lord Baltimore, and the territory was considered a palatinate, in which the Governor had power similar to the King in that period.

About the middle of the eighteenth century, before the Revolutionary War, some of the descendants of Joseph Reeder moved to Ohio. One son, Joseph, moved to Virginia. Thomas Lake who had married Elizabeth Reeder must have moved to Virginia before the War was over, for he removed to South Carolina very soon after the War. He served in a New Jersey regiment, the Second Regiment of Hunterdon County, in Company of Captain Daniel Bray (Striker's "Officers and Men of New Jersey in the Revolutionary War"). Many families moved to other sections after the War and Thomas Lake was living in Ninety-Six District prior to 1790.

One Thomas Lake received a land grant from King George, the Third, of England, for 800 acres of land in Williamsburgh Township, Craven County, in the year 1736. He was too old for service in the Revolutionary War. As there is no further record of his family, the inference is that he moved North, as many of the first settlers did during the first part of the Century.

Another Revolutionary War patriot was John Lake, who was a member of Kershaw's regiment of South Carolina militia from Camden District, in the year 1779. He was in Colonel Frederick Kimball's regiment of militia in 1780.

Thomas Lake was born in 1735, died in Newberry County in 1814. He had five sons by his wife, Elizabeth Reeder, viz: Enoch, John, Elijah, David and Joseph. Elizabeth Reeder Lake born in 1741, died after the year 1814, as she is shown as the widow of Thomas Lake in the settlement of his estate.

Enoch Lake died in Newberry County in 1847. He married Elizabeth Buchanan, member of a prominent Virginia family and relative of President Buchanan, and who had come to South Carolina before the American Revolution.

Their children were: Elizabeth R., John J., Enoch J., Jabez G., Martha (she married a Sheppard), Simeon, Mary (she married a Lyles) and Hester A. Hester A. Lake married, first, Burrell Lyles, and had a daughter, Lucy, who married a Hendrix. Her second husband was Daniel Hughey by whom she had one son, the late Job Hughey of Newberry County, who has a son living in Greenville.

Jabez G. Lake, born in 1807 and died in 1870, married in the year 1832 to Anna Epting who was born 1816 and died 1878. She was the daughter of Jacob Epting and his wife, Mary Cannon Epting, the daughter of David Cannon, Sr. and the granddaughter of Adam Frederick Epting, a Revolutionary War soldier in Col. Roebuck's regiment of State militia. Their children were: Mary Ann Elizabeth, Thomas Marion, Sarah Eleanor, Enoch Jacob, John Bailes Earl, Martha Frances, William Asbury, Emma Lavania, David Charlton, and Jabez Brooks. Sarah Eleanor married a Cannon and they moved to Lindale, Texas. Several others, also, moved to Texas, Enoch, Jacob, Martha, Emma L., and David Charlton. Some of the descendants moved to Laurens and later some of these settled in Florida, and were prominent and progressive business men, aiding materially in building up a new section of the Southland.

Thomas Marion Lake lived in Newberry and was prominent in business, also held the office of Clerk of Court for several years. The "Annals of Newberry" states, "there was no more popular officer". He was a Confederate soldier, and during the greater part of the war was a courier for General Longstreet. A romantic incident is related in the "Annals of Newberry" in which Thomas M. Lake was a participant. The incident occurred during the war. One Joseph

LAKE (continued)

Cofield who was also in the War, related the incident which occurred while he, Joseph Cofield, and Joseph Culbrealth, were riding in a fast train from Richmond to the mountains of Virginia. Coefield said, "On we went, through the pitch darkness with the deep valley and hills all about us illuminated often by the bright flashes of lightening, revealing momentarily the wild grandeur of the scenery and making us feel almost as though we were about to rush headlong into the deep, black abysm of hell. And all the while Culbreath was lying on his back in a happy way behind Lake and myself, telling the story of his love and talking of his sweetheart, Sally, whom he afterwards married". Thomas M. Lake married Mary Emma Koone, daughter of the late General Henry Koone and his wife, Mary Riser (she was a descendant of Martin Riser, a Revolutionary War Patriot in the South Carolina militia). There were several children: Una (wife of Prof. E. B. Setzler, Professor at Newberry College), Marvin, Nina (wife of Ralph Wise of Georgia), and Lola (wife of Casper Smith of Greenwood).

Elijah Lake, son of Thomas Lake the Revolutionary War patriot, died in Newberry County in 1824, leaving his widow, Jane Lake, and the following children: Elijah Pearce, Eugene Coulde, Louise, Elizabeth, Benjamin and Thomas. There is a record of an old deed in Newberry County Court House (Book D., page 597), showing that Thomas Lake and his wife, Elizabeth, conveyed to Elijah Lake in the year 1800, 133 acres of land in Newberry County. Elijah Pearce Lake was the first clerk of Court for Newberry County, when this office was separated from the office of Ordinary, he having previously served two terms as the Ordinary. Elijah Lake died in 1855 and left his widow, Rebecca, and four children: Elijah M. and Isaac K., Rebecca I., and William I. Isaac K. married Elizabeth Rachael _____. Rebecca I. married a Reagin.

Benjamin Lake, son of Elijah, lived and died in Newberry County. He married Anne Coate who died in 1874. Their children were: John R., Benjamin D., Enoch M., Rebecca (married a Moore), Elizabeth (married a Swindler), Jane (married Henry W. Dominick), Elijah (he died and left widow, Mary Ann Elizabeth, and one daughter, Rebecca Ann), and William. William died early but left a daughter, Willie Anne. Some of these moved over into Edgefield County. Benjamin D. Lake died in Newberry County in the year 1886. He married Rebecca Conwell and had, Anne Catherine and William E. Dr. William E. Lake, the son, was a practicing physician in Saluda County for several years and afterwards moved to the City of Newberry where he practiced for many years before he died.

John Lake, son of the patriot, died in Newberry County in 1832, left a widow, Mary, and three children: Drucilla Ann who died early and left a husband, James Anderson, and children, James and Jane Anderson; Deruska; Elizabeth, who died unmarried. There is a record of a conveyance of one hundred acres of land by John Lake to John Hunter in the year 1794, said lands situated on Peters Creek, a branch of the Tyger River (Deed Book C., page 264). This was near the line of Union County to which County some of the family moved.

David Lake, son of the patriot, died in Newberry County in the year 1844. His wife, Margaret, had previously died and his estate was distributed among the following children: Fielding Glenn, Lydia, Nancy, Mildred, William T., Missouri, Rebecca. Also, the following grandchildren: R. P. and Thomas Metts. Fielding Glenn Lake married and had children. One of his sons, George B., was the father of Rev. John Lake, a Baptist Minister. William T. Lake married Lettice Dawkins, two of whose sons were Middleton C. and Frank. Middleton C. was the father of William C. Lake. Frank was the father of Kemper Lake whose children were: Lucy, Vannice, and Prof. R. C. Lake. Mildred married a Hill, who died early. Nancy married John George Cromer. Lydia married Maxmillian Hutchinson. Rebecca married Henry Metts, and after her death he married her sister, Missouri Lake. There were two children by the first wife, R. P. and Thomas Metts. By the second wife were, Frances E. (she married a Mr. Lemon), Sarah (married a Buzhardt), William G., George McDuffie. George McDuffie Metts married Sarah Hargrove and were parents of the late Mack Metts, Sallie, and Mary. Mary married the late John P. Fant and had children: Metts who married Genia Wheeler, Mary Butler who married Robert McC. Holmes, Edgar, Sarah who married Oliver W. Holmes of North Carolina, and Pauline who married Seth Meek (of Spartanburg).

Martha Lake died in 1866 (Elijah P. Lake, Administrator) and left children: Broomfield, Miles P., Nora, and Robert G. The widow of Elijah P. Lake, Eliza A. M. Lake, died in 1891. She was very old and lived between Newberry and Prosperity. In the settlement of her estate, the following are some of her descendants who received a part of her property: Susan A. Dennis, a niece, and daughter of James Dennis; Juna Hunter, widow of her deceased brother,

LAKE (continued)

Thomas T. C. Hunter; Susannah Dennis, a sister, and wife of James H. Dennis; children of a deceased brother, James Y. Hunter (Robert T. C., John, Nathan, and Eliza Whitman); a great grandson, Brabham Goggans, son of a grandson, William Goggans.

Robert T. C. Hunter married Rebecca Boozer and were parents of James Hunter Esq., a lawyer of Newberry, Thaddeus, Joseph E. who holds a professorship at Clemson College; Lafayette (now living in Spartanburg), Robert, Allen and Carrie. Robert T. C. Hunter lived near Prosperity, was a prominent citizen of the county, taking an active part in all public affairs, in the up-lifting of his section, and was a member of the South Carolina Legislature.

Henry Lake died in 1887, left a widow, Eliza, and children: Burr, Hampton, Drayton, Bluford, and Elvira. Drayton Lake died in 1906 and left property to his widow, Harriet Lake.

Ivey C. Lake married and lived in Newberry County. He died comparatively young, but left three daughters, Elizabeth J. (she died in 1887 unmarried), Sara A. R. Longshore and Lucy Longshore.

Joseph Lake, son of the patriot, married Jean Hutchinson, daughter of William and Mary Hutchinson of Newberry County. They had several children: Elias, Thomas, John, William, Reuben, Felix, Mary (she married a Mucklan). Joseph Lake and his family moved over into old Edgefield County. Thomas and John became prominent physicians of that County.

Dr. John E. Lake was born in Newberry County in the year 1809. He was educated at Cokesbury Institute in Abbeville and later attended the University of Pennsylvania from which he graduated. He married Sophia A. Blocker. He was prominent in affairs of that County, and was a member at one time of the General Assembly of South Carolina. One of his daughters, Mrs. Robert Mims, was a fine musician, and her daughter, Eliza Mims, is a famous portrait painter. A grandson of Dr. John E. Lake, also named John, was a missionary in some foreign field.

John Lake, who died in Abbeville, married first, a Miss Hobbs, and second, Josephine Sale. He had one son by the first wife, Felix Fletcher Lake, and two children by his second wife, viz: Josephine and Elizabeth. John Reeder Lake died in 1872 and left his estate to his widow, Permelia Lake.

Many of the old families who moved into Edgefield County from Newberry County, were probably seeking better opportunities for more productive service and profits in their various professions; but they came into a section similar to their own in culture, manner, and productiveness. The towns of Edgefield and Newberry have long passed their Century marks, and are pretty in their ancient landmarks and the large oaks seen in the yards of their oldest homes and on their residential streets. However, the shifting scenes are more apparent in recent years. We see many of the old landmarks giving way to modern progress — the old trees being cut down and the newer buildings being erected. New faces can be seen and some of the older ones have gone. No other two Counties in the State have furnished a greater number of statesmen, literary geniuses, and well-known professional men and women than the Counties of Edgefield and Newberry. Truly their early settlers were a God-fearing people, for it is evident they laid the foundation for Christian education and culture.

LANGFORD

After the Teutonic Angles and Saxons of Europe had conquered Britain and feudalism began to rule as a result of barbaric influence among the people, that country began to put on a semblance of progress. The owners of the lands became lords of their individual realms and lived to themselves. The villein was a freeman and a step higher than the serfs who gave liege to the lords. From this condition came local self-government in England which formed the basis for a thousand year struggle for liberty.

The names of some of the early freemen in England were those of Langford; and the names of several Parishes in Bedford and Cornwall Counties being Langford, indicate feudal lords by this name. One Roger De Langford was the high Sheriff of Cornwall in the year 1225. He took his name from the estate of Langford, in the parish of Marham Church.

One of the early settlers of America was Richard Langford who was in the Plymouth Colony that settled in Massachusetts in 1630. Many of his descendants were prominent men of affairs in New England.

The Langfords of South Carolina are descendants of the pioneers who settled near Charleston. When the lord proprietors came to South Carolina and began a government under the English king, many English people came to Carolina and settled on the coast, as well as French Huguenots. About 1680 a colony of Irish and Scotch came over and settled on Port Royal Island, while about twelve years previous, a number of Dutchmen from New Netherlands (New York) settled on the site where now is the city of Charleston, from which began the growth of this city. The Irish and Scotch were driven by the Spaniards from Port Royal Island to Charleston; thus, the Irish, Scotch, English, Dutch and French formed a race of stalwart energetic people as the first citizens on the South Carolina coast.

William Langford received a land grant from King George, the Third, of England, in the year 1765, which included 100 acres on the south side of Lynch's Creek in Craven County. George Langford received 100 acres from King George, the Third in 1770, in St. James Parish, Berkley County. Another George Langford received 300 acres under a land grant from King George, the Third, in the year 1770, in Berkley County. Many of the descendants of these pioneers moved further into the interior before and after the Revolutionary War.

The records of these during the times when the settlements were being harassed by the Indians and Spaniards, and also during the Revolutionary War, show they were all patriots and soldiers, adhering to the principles of justice and willing followers of General Washington. Daniel Langford was a lieutenant in the South Carolina continentals and was with the army on its course from the seashore to the mountains. John Langford, who lived near Charleston, furnished supplies to the Continentals. Later after the fall of Charleston, he joined the state troops and marched with General Sumter to the upper country where began many bloody battles between the British, Tories and the Americans. William Langford furnished food and forage for the Continentals.

Daniel Langford received for his services in the Continental Army, a bounty grant of 200 acres of land in Ninety Six District, on the main Saluda River. He probably has descendants in the northern section of the state.

John Langford received a conveyance of a tract of land in the year 1787, located on the west side of Buffalo Creek, a branch of the Saluda River. When he died in 1796, he left an estate to his children: William, Jacob and Anne. He had another son, Asa, who had previously died and left a widow and small son, Asa, Jr. John Langford's widow was named Winnifred Langford. In the same year William conveyed to his brother, Jacob, 100 acres on Saluda River. Jacob died in 1805 and left no children, his property reverting to the children of his brother, William, viz., John, William, Samuel, and Sara Weeks. John Myrick, son of John Myrick and his wife, Elizabeth Langford Myrick, was also an heir. The brothers and sisters of John Myrick, Jr., were: William, Samuel, Elizabeth, and Sara Myrick.

Asa Langford, Jr., lived on the Lexington side of the Saluda River, near where the big Saluda dam is now being constructed by large New York interests. This place was known at one time as Langford's Shoals and in more recent years as Dreher's Shoals, one Dreher having married the daughter of Asa Langford, Jr., and lived on the property. The first wife of Asa Langford, Jr., was a Miss Cork, by whom were several children. His second wife was a Miss Smith and had seven children: Stanmore, William, Roy (moved to Alabama), Almenia, Susannah, and two that died young. Susannah married Hezekiah Dreher and lived in the old Langford home near the shoals. This home is still standing, one of those old ante-bellum homes with its large and spacious rooms, that was built to stand the test of time and to stand as a monument to its enterprising builder. But, alas! it must make way for the progress

LANGFORD (Continued)

of industry and will soon be inundated by the mighty waters of the Saluda unless it is removed to a distant point. The fertile valleys which in years past have yielded abundant crops to a sturdy people who have manifested their high-toned, Christian character by the churches within their bounds will no more produce these crops. The churches and the graves of their loved ones will, too, be inundated and lost to the world.

Almenia Langford married George Haltiwanger and they have many worthy descendants in that section.

Stanmore Langford married Sarah Sawyer, a descendant of the pioneer, George Sawyer, of Edgefield district. They had children: Jane E., (she married a Boozer and lived in Newberry several years and had one son, John Boozer), Marietta (married the late Robert W. Davis of Newberry), George Asa (married Elizabeth Livingstone, a descendant of Captain Henry Werts of the Revolution), Amanda (married first, Dr. J. D. Cash, a physician of Newberry, and married second, Burr F. Goggans), Stanmore, William J., and Pierce B. Pierce B. Langford went to Witchita Falls, Texas, and became a prominent banker in that city. The children of Robert W., and Marietta Davis are: Marie R., Alfred, Isaac, Walter, and Nelle E.; George Asa and Elizabeth Langford were the parents of Captain W. S. Langford and Mrs. Ida Asbil (both living in Witchita Falls, Texas), Julius J., David (dead), May, Robert (dead), Stanmore (dead), Marietta (married Harry Danna and lives in Bishopville).

Stanmore B. Langford was a Confederate soldier, Company G of the Second South Carolina Regiment. He died in service. Dr. J. D. Cash and his wife, Amanda, had two children, Dr. Stanmore Cash of New York City, and Mabel (died young). By her second husband, Burr F. Goggans, were: Atlee (married E. R. Partridge), Pierce B., J. Terrell, Guy, Lucile (married W. W. Henn).

In the vicinity of the big Dam on Saluda River, on the Dreher lands there was unearthed an old Indian burying ground in the year 1886, just after a freshet, by the high waters of the river. An old paper taken from the cornerstone of the Confederate monument at Lexington court house upon its removal to widen the streets of the town, gave an interesting account of this occurrence, as related in an article in The State paper several months ago. There was a reproduction of the letter found in the monument, which stated, among other things, that "Dr. Langford of Newberry County came down and made a collection of relics including a valuable collection of bones". The burying ground was supposed to have been underground for several centuries. The remains of an old Indian trail was located just a few years ago, leading from above Ballentine to Saluda River and across to the barely visible remains of an old Indian rock fort, another rock mount or fort being discernable at the beginning of the trail, indicating the homes of the chiefs of the tribes, the Cherokees on one side and the Saludas on the other. Their means of communication were by runners through these trails.

William Langford, son of Asa Langford, Jr., moved to Newberry in early life and was a prominent planter near the city. Later he moved to the city of Newberry where he owned considerable property, and lived in a large two-story Colonial home on Boundary Street, an attractive place with its large, square Corinthian columns of the early century. He married Eliza Lewie and had: Edith (widow of E. P. Mathews), Andrew J. (married Mollie Goggans), Laura (married James Henderson), Emma (married James Davidson), Lula (married William Lane and then James Epting), Angela (married a Bodie), Pickens (killed in Civil War). There are many children and grandchildren of these, some of whom are: Mrs. L. G. Eskridge, Mrs. R. H. Wright, Verna Lane, Blanche Davidson, Mrs. James Aull, Mrs. Bertha Boylston, Mrs. Thad McCrackin, Mrs. Pink Smith of Columbia, Dr. O. A. Matthews of Bennettsville, Clarence Matthews, James Henderson and others.

William Langford owned the lands on Bush River and the old Langford mill site. This was a popular swimming place for young folks many years ago. It was a fine spot with its cluster of oaks and poplars below the dam, providing a cool, shady place for its swimmers.

William B. Langford moved to Lauderdale County, Alabama, and later sold his property in Lexington County to James Langford, his father, these lands having been originally granted to John Langford. James Langford died in 1875. He was probably the grandson of William (son of the first John Langford).

Another William Langford moved over into Newberry County from Edgefield County, and his first wife having died, he married Polly Peterson, widow of the Rev. David Peterson. She was a Turner, the daughter of William Turner and his wife, Miss Spraggins. Rev. David Peterson and his brother, Rev. James F. Peterson, were both prominent Baptist ministers of

LANGFORD (continued)

Edgefield County. Their sister, Elizabeth, married Jerry Goggans, son of the Revolutionary war patriot, Daniel Goggans, who was killed by the Tories. The children of Rev. David Peterson and his wife, Polly, were: John T., David, Mark, William Spencer, Mary and Matilda and probably another daughter. Mary married a Gage and had several children. Matilda married George A. Stephens and they moved to Atalla County, Miss. David was the father of the late Warren G. Peterson of Newberry. Captain William Spencer Peterson was killed in the Civil War in the battle around Atlanta in 1864.

LEITNER

Christopher Leitner (born about 1710 and died about 1768), married before coming to the Dutch Fork in Newberry County, as his petition for bounty grant of 250 acres on Crims Creek, dated October 2, 1752, indicates he had a wife and three children at that time. Another grant for 100 acres on Second Creek was made February 12, 1755. On March 20, 1762, his son, Michael, signed a bounty grant which shows that his father died between 1762 and 1769. Shares of property were divided between sons, John and Michael; and since there was another child who may have died before that time or others who were daughters already provided for, only the two dividend shares are given in the grant.

One Leitner descendant has advanced the theory that Christopher Leitner was one and the same as Joseph Leitner who settled in the Sulzburger Colony at Ebenezer, Georgia, about 1733 (his full name being Joseph Christopher Leitner). There is nothing to bear out this theory, so far found, for Joseph Leitner died and was buried at Ebenezer Church, Ga. before 1769. It appears that Joseph may have moved up into the Dutch Fork in South Carolina about 20 years after settling at Ebenezer, Ga., but inconceivable that he used different Christian names in each State, and if he moved back to Georgia resumed his name of Joseph. All of the settlers who located in the section near Broad River called Little Dutch Fork about 1750-55, came from Pennsylvania, except a few who had come up from the German settlement above Charleston; and it is believed that Christopher came from Pennsylvania with the others.

There was a George Lightner (note difference in spelling) who had come from Pennsylvania before 1760, who may have been a son of Christopher or a brother.

Major Michael Leitner (born about 1735 and died about 1789-91) married Maria Beard (supposedly a sister of Colonel Jonas Beard), and had children: John Christian who died 1806, unmarried, and leaving all his property to sisters who were: Anne Margarette who married George Adam Setzler, Sr., Mary who married Dr. Henry F. Schmitz, Eve Christina who married (1) to John Adam Epting, Jr., and (2) to Martin Koone, Sr., and Catherine who married John A. Setzler, Jr. (See Epting and Koone family lines) . . . .

Major Michael Leitner before the Revolutionary War was a Justice of the Peace, Justice of the Quorum, and from 1775-1781 (two terms) a member of the Second Provincial Congress from upper Orangeburg District. During the war, he was Captain, then Major of Calvary Troops.

John Adam Epting, Jr. and wife, Eve Christina (Leitner) had two daughters, Elizabeth and Mary, at time of death of John Adam, Jr. in the year 1800. Her second marriage to Martin Koone, Sr. about 1802, had two daughters, one Katherine who married David Cromer, Jr. (1790-1858) and had a son, Hilliard Francis Cromer. (See Cromer family lines).

John Leitner (son of Christopher) died about 1802, leaving widow, Mary, and the following children: John Christian, Phillip, John, Elizabeth, Kate, Mary, and Barbara. John Christian moved to Wilkes County, Georgia, and died leaving children: John Christian, Charles B., and Henry D.

There was a George Leitner who may have also been a son of Christopher, though tradition is he came from Pennsylvania about the time Christopher came, so he could have been a brother. This George died about 1813, leaving widow, Barbara, and children: Jacob, George, Henry, Christian, Mary Sestrunk, Catherine (wife of George Graddick), Magdeline Graddick. Another daughter, Elizabeth, had married Miner Gibson, but not named in his will. The father, George, according to a descendant, had married first in Pennsylvania to Mary Creighton and had children: Isaac, Henry and William. Now, these three children may have remained in Pennsylvania or had died before his death, for they are not named in the settlement of his estate. He married second to Catherine Swygert and had children: George (married widow of Jacob Turnip-

LEITNER (continued)

seed), Jacob (1775-1845) who married Mary Eve Graddick (1773-1847), Catherine, Magdeline, Mary, Elizabeth (above), also Christian who married Hester Martin.

Jacob Leitner and wife, Mary Eve Graddick Leitner, had children: Jacob (married Charlotte Souter), David Wesley (1797-1862) who married Elizabeth Smith, Margaret, Christina Ann, Mary, Magdeline, Salena, Hilliard, Nancy who married John P. Williams, Daniel who married Martha Lever, and Susan who died in 1902 at the age of 90 years. David Wesley and wife, Elizabeth Smith, had children: John Wesley, who married Charlotte Hamiter, Elizabeth who married Mattison Abell, Harriet who married George Lever, Rebecca who married Hiram Allen, and Hilliard who died young.

John Leitner (son of Christopher) and George Leitner are listed as having been "Regulators" in the year 1771.

Dr. Henry F. Schmitz and wife, Mary (daughter of Major Michael Leitner) had children: Benjamin F., John A., and perhaps others. John A. Schmitz died in Lexington District after 1855, leaving widow, Mary Ann, and children: Henry A., John F., Andrew Thomas, Sarah Caroline, Polly Catherine, and a step-daughter, Rosannah Schumpert. The spelling of the name was changed to "Smith", and we find there died in Lexington County in year 1875, the Rev. Henry Smith who left widow, Hepzibah Ellen, and children: Henry Walter, William Whiteford, Franklin Burr, Elizabeth Harriet, James M., Hepzibah Ellen (she married Conway Black), Nancy Anna (she married James L. Mitchell), Laura H. (married George A. Fink); also, sons-in-law named whose wives had died were, Simeon R. Crouch, James F. Fink, and John J. Sheely.

Another Michael Leitner who died after 1820, lived in the Dutch Fork of Newberry County. It is not known if he was married. He was probably a son of John Christian and nephew of Major Michael.

The Leitner Coat of Arms are as follows:

A quartered shield; 1st and 4th quarter a silver fluer de lis on azure blue; 2nd and 3rd quarter black with a gold lion, rampant, with crown of gold. In center of shield a small silver shield with a red rose. The Crest: a demi-lion, rampant, on Knight's helmet.

The Arms indicate the Leitners were in the Crusades.

The Leitners lived in Hungary, Germany, Switzerland, and Holland, but probably originated in Switzerland or Hungary at the time of Crusades.

LINDSEY

Colonel Benjamin Lindsey, a Revolutionary War soldier lived and died in Edgefield County, though at one time he owned lands in Newberry County. Some of his grandchildren moved to Alabama. He married Sarah King, a daughter of Ethelred King. He made will dated March 24, 1840, and died in September, 1840, leaving widow, Sarah, and children: Mahalaliel, William K., Dorothy (wife of William Charles), Mary (deceased wife of James D. Lester). He left a grandson, Benjamin Lester and a granddaughter, Sophia Lester (she married a Brown). Executors: William K. Lindsey (son) and Amon Lindsey (cousin).

Mahalaliel Lindsey married Missouri Cunningham, a daughter of Jose and Mary Cunningham of Edgefield County.

William K. Lindsey died in Newberry County, September 20, 1863, leaving widow, Permelia, and children: Martha, Louisa (wife of Francis Holloway), Karen-Happock, Harriet, and Amon B.

Other legatees of Benjamin Lindsey were: Susan Long; children of Randolph Murrell, viz: Benjamin L., William, James, Vashti, Martha Eidson, and Sarah Murrell; Children of William Adams, viz: Mariliza (wife of Daniel Lockridge), Frances, Lucinda, Amanda, Elizabeth, Benjamin, Stewart, Martha, and Jesse Adams; Vary Crane; and Vashti Farrow. These were probably children by a former marriage.

John Lindsey, an early settler in Newberry County, came to South Carolina from Pennsylvania several years before the beginning of the Revolutionary War. He made will dated August 9, 1783 and died about 1787, leaving widow, Alce, and children as follows: James, Sarah Speake, John, Abigail Wells, Thomas, and wife of Jared Smith. Mrs. Alce Lindsey died about 1828; she was a daughter of a Crosson. The sons were Revolutionary War soldiers.

James Lindsey made will April 27, 1799 and died 1799, leaving widow, Ruth, and children: Moses, Alce, Louisa, Sarah, Abigail, Rutha, and James.

LINDSEY (continued)

Thomas Lindsey made will May 25th, 1820 and died in Abbeville County in 1821, leaving widow, Grizel, and children: Joseph E., Grizel, Polly, James, John, and Thomas.

John Lindsey made will February 9th, 1841 and died in February of the same year in Abbeville County, leaving children: James, John, Mary (wife of James Martin), Elizabeth (wife of Jos. Fields), Nancy (wife of John Murphy), Jane (wife of Alanson Nash), Margaret (wife of Larkin Latimore), Alley (wife of Daniel Pruitt). He also left a grandson, Abner A. Nash.

Samuel Lindsey (son of John) was father of John, James and Caleb. He married Elizabeth _____. He died about 1828, having been pensioned as a Revolutionary War soldier.

James died in 1840 and left a son, Caleb Williams Lindsey, and a nephew, James Madison Lindsey, also a brother, Humphry Lindsey.

Caleb Lindsey (son of Samuel) died February 1st, 1816 and left widow, Tabitha, who died February 1st, 1818. Their children were: John, Elizabeth, Joseph G., Caleb, James, Fanny and Alce.

Edmund Lindsey made will March 15th, 1816 and died in 1816, leaving widow, Mary, and children: Nancy Hughes, Ruthe Pearson, William, Edmund, and Phoebe Ogilvie. Executor: John Speake.

Keziah Lindsey died about 1816 and left legatees as follows: Lydia, Samuel, Jacob, Charles, John, George Wells, John Gould, Jared Lindsey, Isaac Lindsey, and Alce Lindsey. Isaac married Hester Sherman, widow of Simon T. Sherman of Laurens County.

Samuel Lindsey -- minor children and orphans on January 5, 1818 -- were: Thomas, James, Lydia, and Samuel.

John Lindsey made will September 7th, 1855 and died about 1859, leaving nephews, John Hays and Thomas Hays; also a niece, Amanda Hipp, and her two children, Walter Hipp and Martha Hipp.

Elbert Lindsey of Laurens County, married Behethmiel, widow of a Mr. Cole, in October, 1851. She resided with her only child, the wife of Henry Hunter, who died without issue.

Thomas Lindsey died about 1815 in Newberry leaving a son, John Lindsey.

John W. Lindsey married Lydia King, daughter of Charles and Charity Pennington King.

Mrs. Elizabeth Lindsey died about 1827 and left children: Wade, Esther (wife of Isaac Lindsey), Thomas, John, Alce, Mary (wife of G. W. Johnson), and Drucilla West. The children of Drucilla West were: John, Young L., Elizabeth (wife of Abram Gilbert), and Jacob Herman West. Wade H. Lindsey died about 1831.

LYLES

Three brothers, Ephriam, John, and Williamson Lyles, came from Virginia and settled on Broad River about the year 1745. John was the first settler and owned the place on Broad River known as "Lyles Ford". He was an Indian trader. His brothers came soon after, and they owned much of the lands on both sides of the River.

Ephriam Lyles, the eldest, was shot in his own home by Indians or enemies before the Revolutionary War began. He left a son, James, who was a distinguished officer and soldier in the Revolutionary War; and his other children were Col. Arromanus who was also an officer in the war, William (known as "Big Bill"), Ephriam, Jr. (known as "Big Eph"), Henry and John -- all soldiers in the American Army during the Revolution. Col. Arromanus, after the war, settled on the East side of Broad River in Fairfield County.

John Lyles, the second brother who came from Virginia, served in the Snow Campaign of 1775 and 1776. He became Colonel of a regiment of militia and was in most of the battles in the State, before the Fall of Charleston. He resigned on account of his age before the end of the war, and his nephew, Col. James Lyles, (son of Ephriam) succeeded him as colonel of his regiment. Col. John removed to Georgia and died soon thereafter. ("Annals of Newberry", Part I and S. C. Hist. Com.).

Williamson Lyles, the youngest brother from Virginia, served in the war as Captain of Company of State Militia, but resigned in 1780 on account of his age. His eldest son, Ephriam (called "Little Eph"), was a soldier in the war. Captain Williamson Lyles was married twice, and his widow, Joice Lyles, survived him at time of his death in 1797. His two sons, Ephriam and Williamson, were by his first wife, and children by his second wife were, Henry, Marcus, Lucy Goree, Sabia Vardeman, Drucilla Dawkins, Rebecca Lake, Mrs. Daniel Rivers, and Mrs.

LYLES (continued)

Qualman. Marcus died in 1833 and left widow, Elizabeth (she married in 1845 to a young man James Madison Suber), and children: James Robert (born 1828) and Pressly E. (born 1831 and died 1848). His sister, Charlotte, was a widow with small children at the time of his death. Mrs. Rebecca Lake died and left two daughters, Lydia Ann and Rebecca. Mrs. Joice Lyles died in 1836 and left her estate to the following: Milly Stewart, Charlotte Goree, Polly Lyles, Sarah Wilson, John Vassels (son of Susan Vassels), William Kelly (son of John and Martha Kelly), and a grandson, Robert Wilson who was executor of her will. Polly died unmarried. Two children of Charlotte Goree were, Harriet Hancock and Ann Lyles. Charlotte Goree died in the year 1842. Sarah Wilson died in 1845. Susan Vassels died in 1845 and left children, Phoebe, James, Sammy (wife of Gideon Jackson), Lyles, Ephriam, Thomas, and John. Gideon Jackson and his wife, and James Vassels moved out of the state. Henry Lyles died and left widow, Elizabeth, and children as follows: Patty (wife of Taplow Poole), Burrell, Massey (wife of Miles Ferguson), Ephriam, Joice (wife of Elias Roebuck), Thomas, and James V. Lyles.

Henry Lyles, son of Ephriam, was a Captain in the Revolutionary War, in a Scouting Troop, and served after the Fall of Charleston. His wife was named Anne.

Major Ephriam Lyles, son of Ephriam, was a Revolutionary War soldier. He died in Newberry County in 1820, leaving a widow, Elizabeth (second wife), and the following children: Elizabeth Caroline (widow of David Anderson), Robert, James E., William, John, Ephriam, Susannah, Mary (she married a Vaughan in 1828), Nancy (wife of George Red), Elizabeth (wife of James Padgett), Harrison C., and Permelia. The last two named were minor children at the time of his death and the only children by his second wife.

Burrell C. Lyles, son of Henry and grandson of Captain Williamson Lyles of the Revolution, was married three times; first, to Miss Henry, second, to Miss Lake, and the name of his third wife is not known. He died in Kentucky in 1850 and his family moved back to South Carolina. A daughter, Mary C., married Joseph F. Abrams; and a son, James M. (by the first wife), remained in Kentucky. Two children by his second wife, Burrell and Erskine, returned to South Carolina and were reared by their mother's people. They were both Confederate soldiers, Erskine being killed at the first battle of Manassas. Burrell C., Jr. died early in life and left widow and several small children.

James M. Lyles (son of Burrell C.) was born in 1834 near Pomaria, Newberry County. He was graduated at the Law School of Louisville, Ky. and practiced law at Richmond, Ky. for several years, after which he located in Kansas. During the territorial struggles in Kansas before the Civil War was a time never to be forgotten in the history of that state. In the Confederate Veteran Magazine of February, 1925, page 60, is a copy of a letter by James M. Lyles, written in the year 1855 to his uncle, James V. Lyles of Columbia, S. C., in which is described the terrible conditions prevailing at that time in Kansas. The Kansas Historical Society has aptly stated that this is the best description ever written of those times. His granddaughter, Miss Catherine Moore, of Palmyra, Mo., in a letter written February 15, 1929, gives an account of his death as follows:

"Being a most ardent Southerner, he used his influence in behalf of the Southern people, who were being robbed and murdered by the lawless element sent into Kansas by the North. So great was his influence that the followers of John Brown and Jim Lane employed a man to kill him. He was stabbed in the back while on the street in Leavenworth, Kansas. He was just past his twenty third year, and shown out like a bright star. At the time of his assassination, in addition to his law practice, he was filling the Office of Circuit and County Clerk (they being one office at that time). The night after he was murdered, his law office was robbed, his private papers, including his family records, business papers, etc. were stolen and destroyed".

His wife, to whom he had been married only five months, was Miss Martha Bonnell of Missouri, and a daughter was born five months after he was murdered.

James V. Lyles, son of Henry and Mary Elizabeth Lyles, lived in Columbia, South Carolina. He was a prominent banker and cotton merchant of that City. At one time he was President of the old Exchange Bank of Columbia, which was destroyed by General Sherman's Army in 1865. He married Mary Mickle of Camden.

Ephriam Lyles, son of Williamson, was a Revolutionary War soldier, after the Fall of Charleston in 1780. He was born in 1762 and was, therefore, just eighteen years old when he went into the Army. He married July 1st, 1796 to Margaret Young, and died April 4th, 1854, in Twiggs County, Georgia. His widow was allowed a pension on an application executed November

LYLES (continued)

30th, 1854, while a resident of Twiggs County in Georgia. They had nine children.

Mrs. Mary Lyles (widow of John Lyles, Jr.) died about 1856 and left children: Reuben S., John V., Thomas J., Eliza, and two children who were dead, Benjamin and Mary. Children of Benjamin were: Reuben and George W. Children of Mary Sims were: Frances, O'Nora, and Pickens B. Sims. Mrs. Mary Lyles was the widow of John Lyles who died in 1843.

Col. Arromanus Lyles, son of Ephriam, was a Revolutionary War Officer in State Militia. He died in 1817, leaving widow, Susannah, living in Fairfield County. His children by a former marriage were: Ephriam, John, Arromanus, Voluntine, Thomas, James, and Elizabeth who became the wife of William Moody.

Voluntina Lyles married Drucilla Sims, daughter of Reuben Sims. They moved to Mississippi and afterwards settled in Louisiana. He died early and his widow died in 1835. Her sister, Polly, was the wife of John Lyles.

James Lyles died and left widow, Susannah, who moved over into Union County and died leaving children: Jesse, Susannah, Elizabeth, Rodgezel, Martha Gibson, Rachel Smith, and Sally Hames.

Robert Lyles (son of Major Ephriam Lyles) died in 1847 and left widow, Jane, and children: Thomas W., Jesse W., John M., William M., Sarah A., and Eliza A. Boatner.

Mrs. Celia Lyles (widow of James, son of Ephriam) settled her husband's estate in the year 1844 (Ephriam was living in 1844), he having died in the year 1842.

Charles Lyles died about 1820, leaving widow, Sarah (daughter of Robert Rabb), and children: Nancy, wife of Dr. Lana Hancock, and John, Nathan, and Jemima.

Ephriam Lyles made will in 1853 and died about 1854 to 1858. His children were: Rebecca Glenn and Louisa F. Worthy. Nephew: Thomas J. Lyles. Grandchildren: Ephriam L. Glenn, Thomas B. Glenn, Sarah A. Henderson, Frances R. Bowker. He was, probably, a son of Major Ephriam who died in 1820.

John Lyles, Sr. died and left the following children: Martha, wife of James Richardson; Drucilla, wife of Richard Hilborn; Elizabeth, wife of Nathan Chandler; William, Mark, Simon B. (his wife was Mary _____), John (he had left home and supposed to have been dead), Basil, Warren D., and Lydia. His widow was named Lydia who died soon after his death. James Richardson and family moved to Alabama and were living in Lauderdale County.

MAYER
(Collaborator: Rev. V. L. Fulmer)

Ulrich Mayer came from Germany, sailing from Rotterdam on the ship "Crumliss", and on November 7, 1752, received a grant of land, 250 acres, situated on Camping Creek. In his petition for land he states that he has a wife and three children, viz: Susannah age 21 (born 1731); Anna Barbara age 14 (born 1738); Ursula age 4 (born 1748) (Council Journal Vol. 20, Pages 552-553).

Ulrich Mayer and wife had the following children: Susannah (1731), Anna Barbara Mayer (1738) married a Mr. Shoemaker, Ursula Mayer (1748).

Andreas Mayer - Platt for 400 acres of land on Crim's Creek November 8, 1753. "Land being in the fork between Broad and Saluda Rivers on branches of Crim's Creek bounded by vacant land, and southeast partly by land of Benedict Kuhn, southwest by land of Johannes Kountz and southeast by land of Andrew Rist. (Council Journal Vol. 20, Pages 546-547).

John Mayer got a grant for 50 acres of land on Crim's Creek January 2, 1754. Bounty land. (This shows that he was a single man at the time. Several years later John Mayer sold this 50 acres of land to Peter Beyer. It is probable that John Mayer was the son of Andreas).

The platt for four hundred acres shows that Andrew Mayer had a wife and six children: Bounty Land. (50 acres for husband and 50 acres for wife and 50 acres of each child.)

Andreas Mayer and wife had the following children: John Mayer (1732 ?), Ulrich Mayer (born September, 1734 and died December 14, 1803, age 69 years and 3 months), four daughters (assumed as no record is found of any other sons).

John Mayer (1732) married and had a son: Andrew G. Mayer who was born June 18, 1769, married Mary Ann Maria Morris, who was born April 13, 1773. They moved to Edgefield County; Andrew died February 19, 1839, age 69 years, 8 months and 1 day. His wife died August 10, 1843, age 69 years, 3 months, and 17 days. Children: John, Jacob, Levi, Andrew, Polly,

MAYER (continued)

Mary, Katie, and Mollie Maria. (They moved to the Sandhills in 1825)
    Ulrich Mayer (September 1734 - December 14, 1803) married first, Elizabeth Monts. Children: 1. John Benedict (1761); 2. Ulrich, Jr. (1763).
    Ulrich Mayer married second, Anne Cathen Frick, daughter of Thomas Frick, Sr. Cathen Frick was born February 30, 1755, and died December 30, 1815, age 60 years and 10 months. Children: 1. George; 2. Christopher (1782), never married; 3. Katherine (John Jacob Bowers); 4. Elizabeth (Simeon Wheeler); 5. Jacob Mayer.

```
                                    (1769)           (John
                (1) (1732)         (Andrew G. Mayer  (Jacob
                    John Mayer     (Mary A. Maria Morris (Levi
                    Wife:          (                 (Andrew
                    Grant 1754     (                 (Polly
                    Crim's Creek   (                 ( Mary
                                                     (Katie
                                                     (Mollie Maria


                (II) (1734)              (1761)
                     Ulrich Mayer        (John Benedict Mayer
Andrew Mayer         Elizabeth Monts     ( Ulrich Mayer, Jr. (1763)
Wife:
(Grant 1753)
Crim's Creek
                (II) (1734)              (Katherine Mayer (Nov. 15, 1787)
                     Ulrich Mayer        (M. John Jacob Bowers.
                     Anne Cathen Frick   (
                     1755                (Elizabeth Mayer
                                         (M. Simeon Wheeler (1791-1871)
                                         (
                                         (Christener Mayer (Aug. 16, 1782)
                                         (Never married, died Feb. 11, 1853.
                                         (
                                         (Jacob Mayer (May 1, 1793)
                                         (M. Mary Wertze (July 7, 1799)
                                         (
                                         (George Mayer

                     FOUR DAUGHTERS:
                     No Record.
```

MAYER (continued)

```
                    (  (1761-1817)              (1818-1891)
                    (John Benedict Mayer    (1. O. Benedict Mayer
                    (Eve Margaret Summer    (2. Frances Mayer
                    (They had only 1 child. (Adam Mayer (1797-1834) (  M. William Summer
                    (                       (Mary Counts            (3. Susannah Mayer
(1734)              (                                               (  M. Dr. Bates
Ulrich Mayer        (
and wife,           (
Elizabeth           (
Monts               (
                    (
                    (  (1763)           (John Mayer----     (Katie Mayer
                    (Ulrich Mayer, Jr.  (1st. Katie Wertz,  (Mary Mayer
                    (Wife               (daughter of George
                    (                   (Henry Wertz .
                                        (John Mayer ----        (Susannah (Dan Sease)
                                        (2nd. Christener Wertz, (Martha (Jacob Eargle)
                                        (daughter of George     (George U. (Elizabeth Eargle)
                                        (Henry Wertz.           (Luther (Nora Stoudemire)
                                                                (Mike (Laura Dominick, died)
                                                                (Adam (N. M.)
                                                                (Andrew (N. M.)
                                                                (Jacob ( N. M.)

                                (d. 1838)         (1. Christener Fike
                                (Christener Mayer (2. Frances Fike (Levi Wheeler)
                                (John M. Fike     (   Married 2nd William Wertze, a widower.
                                                  (3. Martha Fike    (John Sease
                                                  (   Leonard Sease  (James Sease
                                                                     (Fannie Sease
                                                                     (Carrie Sease
                                                                     (Eunice Sease
                                                                     (Elizabeth Sease
                                                                     (Ann; Alma; Edward;
                                                                     (Ella and Lillie
```

George Mayer married Nancy Derrick, daughter of Andrew Derrick and wife Catherine Hiller. After George Mayer's death, Nancy married Rev. Emanuel Caughman (1802-1881).

Three men by the name of Mayer signed the petition for incorporation of St. John's Lutheran Church; 1. Ulrich Mayer, 2. Benedict Mayer, 3. Ulrich Mayer, Senn.

Three Mayers signed the petition of Piney Woods; 1. Ulrich Mayer, 2. Andrew G. Mayer, 3. Johanes Mayer.

Hans Ulrich Mayer was a Revolutionary War soldier, and his two sons, John Benedict and Ulrich were also soldiers in the S. C. militia during the Revolution. His wife was named Alice and they had several children.

Dr. O. B. Mayer, Sr., son of Adam Mayer and his wife, Mary Counts, was an eminent physician and surgeon in Newberry before and after the Civil War. He was a graduate of the University of South Carolina, also of the Charleston Medical College, and did post graduate work in both Paris and Berlin, attending lectures under famous European physicians. In addition to his professional work, he wrote many articles for publication. He was a fine linguist, speaking in seven different languages. He possessed literary talent as was shown during his later years, and was the author of several books and poems.

Dr. Mayer married, first, a Miss Davis of Fairfield, who died within the same year he married and left no children. A few years after he married Miss Caroline De Walt by whom he had four children: Dr. O. B. Mayer, Jr. (b. 1852 and d. 1817), Caroline V. (b. 1861 and d. 1922) who married James Thomas Mayes of Newberry, Katherine who married Dr. Edward C. Conner of Greenwood, and Mary who married William Martin and moved to Florida. Dr. O. B. Mayer, Jr. married Harriet Jones of Laurens and had children: Cornelia, Harriet (wife of William Reid, Jr.), and Dr. O. B. Mayer III, of Columbia.

MAYES

The Mayes family began in Virginia with one Rev. William Maese, a Protestant preacher who came over with an early colony to America from the territory of Holland, about the year 1611. There were others of the family who came at later periods. Some of his descendants came to South Carolina before the Revolutionary War and settled in Ninety Six District.

Samuel Mayes and his brother, William, were Revolutionary War soldiers in S. C. militia. One Samuel Mayes was in the War of 1812 and became a Brigadier General.

James Mayes, a native of Virginia, lived in Union County or Spartanburg District, at "Fairforest", before the Revolutionary War. He was given a grant of land on Fairforest in the year 1767. He became a wealthy planter of that section, and owned flour mills where wheat was ground for the planters of his section. Some of his heirs were: Samuel J. (he married Elizabeth Black, daughter of William Black), Mary S. Wofford, Elizabeth Mayes, Hiram Wofford, Jane Mayes, and James Mayes.

James Mayes, Jr. was a contractor in partnership with one Campbell Humphries in Union District. They erected the stone jail at Union Court House in the year 1825, and in the year 1827 completed the first brick Court House at Spartanburg. He died in October 1829, leaving widow, Mary Ann, and children: Elizabeth Jane, William Glenn, Mary Glenn, Sarah Ann, James Edward, Thomas Alexander, John Bernard, and Martha. He left 1200 acres of land to widow, and children, and also the home tract of 485 acres on Enoree River adjoining lands of Dr. Hezekiah Rice. His widow, Mary Ann (she was daughter of Wm. C. Glenn), afterwards married Jesse Briggs and had several children.

William Glenn Mayes moved to Newberry Court House several years before the Civil War, taught school for a short time and then started a mercantile business with Newton Martin.* He was Mayor of Newberry for several terms. Mayes and Martin operated a large general mercantile store for several years. He married Nancy Jones and had several children who lived in the City of Newberry, viz: James Thomas (married Caroline Mayer), John Bernard (married Agnes Summer), Dr. William G. (married Miss Wright who died early and left no children), Mary (wife of Mel. B. Chalmers), Glenn (he was accidentally killed in West Virginia), Nancy (widow of Rev. Junius B. Fox, D. D., a prominent Lutheran Minister), Frank (living in Virginia), Dr. Robert L. (a distinguished physician who died in Newberry, unmarried), Dr. William G. Mayes was a successful druggist in Newberry for many years; was chairman of the Board of Trustees, City Schools of Newberry, for several years.

James Thomas and Caroline V. Mayer had children: William M. (he was an electrical engineer, served in World War I as Lieutenant of Militia, wounded in battle. He died in Cal. in 1948); Caroline Nancy (she married G. Leland Summer, lived in Newberry, and had four children: G. Leland, Jr., Harry Thomas, William Mayes, and James Elbert, all of whom married and had families); James Thomas, Jr. (he married in Alabama, and reared a family, lives in that state in Birmingham); Jesse (he married Lucile Wallace, of Newberry, had daughter, Caroline. He was killed accidentally a few years ago); Ben Mayer (he married Lucy Wallace, sister of his brother, Jesse's wife) moved to Greensboro, N.C. and had one son who served in World War II). Ben M. served in World War I. There were two other children of James Thomas and Caroline V. Mayes, who died when very young.

Dr. William Glenn Mayes, who married Miss Wright of Newberry, left no children, but reared two children of his sister's, Mrs. Nancy Fox, whose names are Junius and Nancy. Mrs. Nancy Fox was the widow of Dr. Junius B. Fox, once member of the faculty of Newberry College and later a Lutheran Minister, serving as pastor several years the Lutheran Church of the Redeemer of Newberry.

John B. Mayes, Jr., brother of Dr. William G. Mayes, was a merchant several years in Newberry; he married Agnes Summer, a daughter of Charles E. and Nora (Sease) Summer, and had three children: John B., who was killed in World War II as a bombadier; Agness who married and moved away; Nancy.

Frank Mayes was an electrical engineer, served many large utilities in Georgia and Virginia. He married in Anderson, S. C., to which place he moved after his retirement.

(* It is said that William G. Mayes, Sr. was first in business with his brother, Barnard Mayes before going in with Newton Martin; Barnard having moved to the West).

NANCE

Major Frederick Nance, a native of Amelia County, Virginia, came to the village of Newberry after the Revolution. He was born about 1770. He is said to have been the first settler in the village of Newberry. His brother, Clement Nance, must have come about the same time or very soon after. He married Elizabeth Rutherford, daughter of Col. Robert Rutherford of Newberry County. Major Nance was at one time the Sheriff of Newberry County, also the County Clerk, and the Clerk of Court when the District Circuit Courts were established. Children by his first wife were: Elizabeth, Frances, Alfred, and Laura. His second wife was Mrs. Theresa Ruff by whom he had a daughter, Martha, who married John McM. Calmes. He died February 10th, 1840. Dorothy B. married Thomas Pratt, Sally married John K. Griffin, and Laura A. married William Butler.

Robert Rutherford Nance was the Sheriff of Newberry about 1832, and Tax Collector for two terms, and a merchant in the town for several years. He was a graduate of South Carolina College. His wife was Mary S. Pope, daughter of Col. Sampson Pope of Edgefield, by whom he had two sons, Rutherford and Frederick, who volunteered in the Mexican War, were in several battles and returned home without ever having received a scratch. Judge O'Neall states that "one who knew Robert R. Nance as the writer of this sketch knew him may be pardoned in saying he deserved more than he ever obtained, prosperity. No purer man ever lived, no better citizen could, in his day, have been found; no more sincere relative and friend has ever been known by me". He died about 1846 and left widow, Mary S., and children: Sarah Rutherford, Elizabeth Shearer, Amelia Sheppard, and Drayton O'Neall Nance.

Drayton Nance was a graduate of the S. C. College, studied law, and practiced his profession in Newberry. He was Commissioner in Equity in Newberry, and also a member of the State House of Representatives. He died early in life, in the year 1856, leaving widow, Ariana B., and children. His children were by his first wife, Lucy Williams, the daughter of Washington and Sarah (Griffin) Williams. (She was also the granddaughter of Col. James Williams, an officer in the American Army in the Revolution and one of the heroes of the battle of Kings Mountain); Martha A. (wife of Dr. John A. Barksdale), Frances C., William F., James D., Laura E., and Mary Williams Nance. His second wife was Ariana B. Livingstone of Florida.

Col. F. W. R. Nance was Sheriff of Abbeville County.

Captain J. K. G. Nance was at one time Auditor of Newberry County. He left several children.

Col. James D. Nance was Captain of Company E., Third Reg. S. C. Volunteers in the Confederate Army, in the beginning of the war. He was elected Col. of the Reg. in 1862, and his brother, James K. G. Nance, became Captain. He was killed at the battle of the Wilderness, May 6, 1864, not quite twenty seven years old.

Clement Nance (brother of Major Frederick Nance) was a native of Virginia. He died about 1843 in Newberry County. His children were: William G., Nancy S. (wife of William B. Shell), Frederick A., Mary (wife of James Russell), Erasmus G., and Robert. Robert died in 1820 and left widow, Sally, who married Edward Stephens. She was a Miss Walker of Virginia and died in 1853, leaving no children. Robert left one-half of his estate to Amelia Nance (daughter of his brother, Frederick A.). Amelia married on January 6, 1824 to Robert Dunlap. She died November 2nd, 1824, leaving no children. Robert Dunlap married in 1828 to her sister, Sally W. Nance; and he died in 1836 leaving his widow and children as follows: Sarah S., Robert N., and Margaret (she died Dec. 1838). Mrs. Sally W. Nance married Col. John K. Griffin whom she survived. Her third husband was Daniel Wallace whom she married in 1843. She died in February, 1849, leaving three children by her last husband, viz: Edward Wallace, Lela Wallace, and Warren Wallace (he died young).

William Nance came from the Parish of Antrim County, of Halifax, Va., and settled in Union District, S. C. He died in the year 1801 and left children: Thomas Vaughn Nance, Zacariah Nance, Elizabeth Palmer, Sarah Tucker, and Martha Vaughn (deceased). Grandchildren named in his will were: William Palmer, William Nance (son of Thomas), James Nance (son of Zacariah), Lavania Frances Bates, Mary Vaughn Winters Tucker, Mary Nance, and Kitty Palmer. Another legatee was James W. Bates, son of James Bates.

O'NEALL

The O'Neall family came to Bush River's settlement in Newberry County, with the Quakers — they were members of the Friends Church. A tradition is that one Hugh O'Neall, a member of the English Navy, when they were in port near Wilmington, Del., ran away from the Navy and lived in that State, about the year 1730. He was born about 1700. A descendant of an Irish family, the son of Brian O'Neill who was descended from the O'Neills of Shane's Castle in Ireland. Brian O'Neill had three sons, John, Henry and Hugh. Hugh settled near Wilmington, Del. and changed the spelling of the name to O'Neal. He married Anna Cox whose father was a Captain of King William's Army at the battle of Boyne. Hugh O'Neal and family moved to near Winchester, Va. about 1740, where he died and left the following children: William (1740-1786), who married Mary Frost; Hugh who married Miss Parkins; James, who moved to Wheeling, W. Va.; Henry, who married Miss Chambers and settled in Laurens County, S. C.; Mary, who married Frederick Jones, of Laurens District, S. C.; John, who married Grace Frost (sister of his brother William's wife); Thomas, who married Sarah Eavans.

William and Mary Frost O'Neal had children: Abijah, Hugh, William, John, Henry, Thomas, and Sarah Foard. Abijah (1762-1823) married Anna Kelly in 1784 — all moved to Warren County, Ohio in 1799 - and had children: William, Hugh, John, Henry, Thomas, and others. Of these, William (1791-   ) married 1816 to Martha Smith, and had children: Abijah T., James, John Kelly, George T. Other children of Abijah and Anne Kelly O'Neal were, Sarah, Mary Ann, Elisha, Abijah, and Rebecca.

Hugh O'Neal (son of William and Mary Frost O'Neal) was born 1767, married Anne Kelly 1792; died 1848; had children: John Belton (1793-   ), Abigail, Rebecca, Hannah, and Sarah. Hugh was living on Mudlick Creek, near Laurens County line, when he married Anne Kelly of the Bush River MM. He was for several terms, the Commissioner of Public Buildings for Newberry County.

William O'Neal (son of William and Mary Frost O'Neal) was born 1773; married Rachel _____ and moved to Tenn. Their children: James, Mahlon, Mary, Sarah. James married Anna _____.

John O'Neal (son of William and Mary Frost O'Neal) was born about 1770; married and moved to Indiana; became a Quaker preacher in that State.

Henry O'Neal (son of William and Mary Frost O'Neal) was born about 1765, married (1) Rachel Eddings, (2) to Catherine Pickering, (3) to Mary Duncan. Children by first wife were, Benjamin, William and Rachel, all of whom moved to Ohio; by second wife were, Mary, Esther, Rachel, and Elizabeth, who went to Ohio; and by the third wife were, John, Sarah Ann, Mahlon, Thomas Coppock O'Neal.

Sarah O'Neal (daughter of William and Mary Frost O'Neal) married Elisha Ford, and settled in Kentucky.

Thomas O'Neal (son of William and Mary Frost O'Neal) was born in 1788, moved to Miami County, Ohio, where he became a school teacher, later moving into Indiana. He married and had 14 children.

Some of the above families who went to other states dropped the "O" and became simply "Neal".

John O'Neill died in Union County, S. C. in 1808; left widow, Nancy, and children: Henry, Hugh, John, Isobel (last three the youngest), and Sarah Starling, Mary Davidson, Dorcas Donaldson, and Nancy Harris. It is not known what relation he was to the Newberry family, but he was probably the brother of William who married Mary Frost.

Hugh O'Neal, a miller of Laurens District, made will dated October 3, 1787 (no proof date) naming the following children: Hugh Neal (note change of spelling) to have part of land on Little River, including mill and dwelling; Thomas Neal to have land on Raburns Creek; Elizabeth (wife of Thomas McDaniel); and to four youngest daughters — Patience, Ruth, Ann, Rachel — to be well schooled. "When son, Hugh, comes of age, etc." indicates the testator was born between 1750 and 1760. He was the brother of William who married Mary Frost, and owned land above Mudlick Creek, but had moved down to Bush River section where he married Miss Parkins.

PEARSON

Benjamin Pearson was a Quaker and lived on Bush River. Some of his descendants migrated to Ohio during the first part of the last Century. There were several brothers who were, probably, sons of an Irish settler, that lived on Bush River, viz: Benjamin, William, Samuel. Benjamin made will December 10, 1784, and died about 1788, leaving widow, Margaret, and children: William, Abel, Samuel, Robert, Joseph, John, Enoch, Rosannah Russell, and Marjory Buffington. His brother, William, had died before his death.

Samuel Pearson, brother of Benjamin, lived on Bush River. He made will dated January 16, 1788 and died 1790, leaving widow, Mary, and children: Benjamin, Samuel, Enoch, William, Mary (wife of _____ Taylor), Martha (wife of Henry Steddam), Hannah, Eunice, and Sarah.

William Pearson (son of Samuel) died about 1800 and left children: Martha, Edney, Mary (wife of Robert Miles), Jesse, Samuel, William, Henry, Anna. His wife was Ann _____.

Enoch Pearson (son of Samuel) died 1790 and left widow, Phoebe, and several children, two of whom were sons, Samuel and William. Executors: Henry Steddam, Abel Thomas, and William Pearson (brother).

Benjamin Pearson (son of Samuel) moved to the State of Ohio.

Enoch Pearson (son of Benjamin) married Hannah _____.

Samuel Pearson (son of Benjamin) married Abigail _____.

John Pearson (son of Benjamin) died before 1802 and left heirs: John, Elizabeth (wife of Isom Langley), Isom Langley, Jr., Jane Langley, Thomas Black, and Mary Black. He conveyed land on Second Creek in Newberry County in year 1774, which was granted to him by Daniel Williams, his uncle. (This was an original grant dated January 1st, 1752, to Paul Williams who assigned the land to Jeremiah Williams, and Jeremiah Williams conveyed it to Daniel Williams).

John Pearson and wife, Jean, conveyed land on Cannons Creek in Newberry County to Terrence Riley on December 24, 1775.

Samuel Pearson and wife, Rebecca, conveyed land to Robert Caldwell, on Beaver Dam Creek, in Newberry District, being part of three hundred acres owned by James Williams, his brother-in-law.

Thomas Pearson and wife, Mary, conveyed to Jonas Pearson, one hundred acres on Muddy Creek, a branch of Bush River, being part of a grant to Thomas Pearson on December 29th, 1767. He gave to Friends and Brothers called "Quakers", two acres on a small branch of Bush River on February 9th, 1796, for their church, consideration being love and affection. The conveyance was made to Samuel Miles and Samuel Teague, members of Rocky Spring Meeting. He had a son-in-law, Abel Insco, who was remarkable for stuttering. The family moved to Ohio.

Mrs. Hannah Pearson, widow of R. R. Pearson, died April 2nd, 1842.

Abel Pearson and wife, Mary, conveyed land to Joseph Hill in 1796, said lands having been granted to him April 4th, 1785.

Isaac Pearson made will December 7th, 1827 and died about 1828, leaving seven hundred acres of land in Union County to the following children: William C., Bird M., Rachel, Elizabeth, Jeremiah, Mary (wife of John Bates), President, Newton, and Independence.

POPE

Sampson Pope came from Virginia and settled in the section of old Ninety Six District which is now Edgefield County, before the Revolution. His willis dated July 22nd, 1788, proven in court October 28th, 1803, and he died about 1800 to 1803, leaving widow, Susannah, and children as follows: Solomon, Jacob, and Henry. Jacob died about 1795 and left children, Sampson, George, and Elisha. Elisha married Catherine Travis and both died before the year 1814, leaving children: Maria (married James Stallworth), and Harriet (married Jonothan D. Williams, son of Davis Williams) — they moved to Alabama.

Solomon Pope (son of Sampson) made will October 19th, 1794 and died in 1794, leaving widow, Susannah (Dawkins) Pope, and children: Mary (wife of Nathan Cook), Elizabeth (wife of Lewis Matthews), Mourning (wife of Drury Matthews), Temperance (wife of John Strother), John Wiley (died 1797, left widow, Elizabeth), Susannah, Charity (died 1796 — no issue), Solomon (died 1798 — no issue), Henry (died, left widow, Sarah, who married John Little), Patience (wife of James Rabb), and Sampson. John Wiley and Elizabeth had children: Rebecca,

POPE (continued)

Wiley M., and John. (Widow, Elizabeth, married Ezekiel Nash). Patience Rabb died in 1809. Henry and Sarah Pope had one son, Solomon Lewis Pope.

George and Sampson Pope (sons of Jacob) lived in Edgefield District. George later moved to Alabama, and became an influential local Methodist preacher. Sampson had several sons, viz: George, who was Clerk of Court in Edgefield and died in office; Thomas H., who moved to Newberry Court House and practiced law in that City; Sampson had, also, several daughters, two of whom were: Elizabeth (wife of Joel Abney), and Mary (wife of Azariah Abney).

Thomas H. Pope, lawyer, served one term in the State Legislature from Newberry County; he was Commissioner in Equity from 1838 to 1840 when he resigned. He died about 1851, leaving widow, Harriet N., and children as follows: Sampson, Thomas H., Young John, Neville, Birt, Strother, and Mary Elizabeth.

Dr. Sampson Pope, son of Thomas H., was a practicing physician in Newberry for several years.

Judge Y. J. Pope, son of Thomas H., was an eminent lawyer in Newberry. He was Associate Justice and then Chief Justice of the South Carolina Supreme Court. He married _____ Fair, daughter of Col. Simeon Fair. (She was the widow of Col. Wm. Drayton Ruthford of the Confederate Army).

Jacob Pope, Jr., died in Edgefield County about 1846, leaving widow, Elizabeth, and a son, Mark F., who married Martha L. _____. The children of Mark F. Pope were: Jacob William, Helen Pauline (wife of John P. Ridgell), Frances Maria, and Mary Josephine. A grandson of Jacob Pope was Jacob Pope Rutherford.

George Pope died in Edgefield County about 1843 or 1844 and left two children: Helen O'Neall and Young Harrington Pope. His father-in-law was Young John Harrington; his brother-in-law was John Belton O'Neall. He was brother of Thomas H. Pope.

William Pope died in Spartanburg County in 1869, leaving two children: Nancy and Elizabeth. Elizabeth married William T. Horton and had two children: William and Amanda. Other legatees in his will were the children of Taylor Pope.

QUATTLEBAUM (QUADDLEBAUM)

Matthew Quaddlebaum, Sr. settled on Campen Creek in Ninety Six District (the section of Newberry County) before the beginning of the Revolutionary War. He had several children, some of whom were: Rachel Feagle, Girtrand Rhinehardt, Matthias, and Peter.

Matthias Quaddlebaum, Sr. (son of Matthew) was a Revolutionary War soldier, serving in the South Carolina militia. He married Rachel Derrin who had received a Bounty grant of land adjoining his land on Rocky Branch, a tributary of Turkey Creek, for patriotic service during the war. He sold this land of one hundred acres on February 9th, 1795 to John Yans. He settled in Lexington District, S. C. where he died and left children as follows: Mathias, Jr., Marie Christine (wife of Martin Sheely), Peter, and others.

Peter Quattlebaum lived in Newberry County and died in 1806, leaving widow, Catherine (she was Catherine Cappleman), who was the mother of all his children (she died on November 4th, 1806), as follows: David (married a Harmon), Peter, Joseph, Catherine, and Sarah. Catherine, who was born July 3rd, 1802, married Oliver Moore of Newberry County, and they moved to Alabama. Sarah married John Michael Kinard.

Joseph Quattlebaum (son of Peter) died in Newberry County January 22, 1848. He married first, _____ Threwett and second, to Margaret Lynch, who survived him, with the following children: Simeon, Caroline, Belton, John, Joseph, and Catherine. Administration of estate was granted to George Gallman in 1848.

John Quattlebaum made will July 17, 1851, and died in Lexington County. His children named in the will were: William, John, Willis, Samuel, Paul, Thomas, Walter, Joseph, and Mary Howard. Walter died about 1863 and left widow, Mary Ann, and several children, one of whom was Mittie Margaret Dowling, a child by his first wife. John's first wife was Mettee

David Quattlebaum (son of Peter) moved to Edgefield County. He left a widow, Rose A. (Harmon) Quattlebaum, and children: William, Henry M. Harmon D., George W., James H. and Nancy C. (A complete genealogy of this family appeared in the S. C. Hist. Mag. Chas.- about 1948).

RAMAGE

Joseph Ramage, the ancestor of the Ramage families of Laurens and Newberry Counties, and Edgefield County, died in Laurens District about 1824. He left a widow, Elizabeth whose maiden name was Roberts, and several children, some of whom were the following: James, John, Robert, Mary, Isiaah, Joseph, Benjamin, Alexander, and Mary.

Robert Ramage and wife, Mary (Coate) Ramage moved to Chambers County, Alabama; had son, Joseph Orren Ramage.

James Ramage died April 2, 1837, in Edgefield County, S. C. He had moved from Newberry County to that county. He left a widow, Elizabeth (Sheppard) Ramage,(she married again to Clark Martin in 1843) and the following children: Laura Ann, Elizabeth, James C., Joseph Orren, and John W. Mrs. Elizabeth Ramage-Martin was a daughter of James and Susannah Sheppard, of Edgefield County. The late Judge Carrol Ramage, of Saluda, S. C. was a son of James C. Ramage.

Joseph Orren Ramage married Mary Vaughn Meadors, of Laurens County, S. C., and moved to Chambers County, Alabama. They had a son, James Blakely Ramage, and perhaps other children. James Blakely Ramage married Carrie Robinson Towles (daughter of Toliver and Sarah Ann Robinson Towles).

John W. Ramage died in Newberry County. He married twice; his first wife being from Edgefield County, by whom was a son, Thomas F. (1812-1852); and by his second wife, Lucy (Kelly) Henderson Ramage (she was widow when he married him), there was a son, Burr J. Burr J. Ramage practiced law in Newberry several years; at one time being the Clerk of the County Court. He had daughter, Fannie, a son, Josh, both of whom died unmarried in the town of Newberry; also two sons who were prominent in educational and religious work in South Carolina and Tennessee. Rev. Bartow B. Ramage, an Episcopal Minister, who once served a large church in Nashville, Tenn., and Burr J., a lawyer who lived in Nashville, Tenn. Burr J., the father, married Sarah Ann Wilson, a daughter of William Wilson, a native of Edgefield County, but at that time was the Judge of the Court of Ordinary in Newberry.

There were three brothers who left Laurens County between the year 1807 and 1812 and settled in Kentucky. Their names were, Joshiah, John, Issiaah. Josiah married Margaret _____ and had a son, Josiah, Jr., who married Lucinda Jessop.

RUFF

George Ruff, a German, or son of a German emigrant, lived just North of Crims Creek above Pomaria. He was a Revolutionary War patriot, and after the war was appointed one of the first County Court Justices in Newberry County. The first Court was held at the home of Col. Robert Rutherford in the year 1785. He died about 1803, leaving widow, Ann Barbara (who was mother of his children), and children as follows: George, John Henry, Elizabeth (wife of William Rutherford), Saloma (wife of John Peaster), and David. Saloma married three times, her second husband being John Eichleberger, and the third a Mr. Smith. Ann Barbara Ruff died in 1826.

George Ruff, Jr. died about 1811, and left widow, Nelly, and no children. His widow afterwards married Jesse Graham.

John Henry Ruff married Elizabeth Summer, daughter of Col. John Adam Summer, a Revolutionary War patriot and officer of the State militia. Their children were: Adam (married Tarsa Hill), Langdon (married Polly Sligh), Walter F. (married Ann Suber), George Oliver, Sarah (married Adam Counts), Martha (married, first, Dr. Jacob King, and second, William Welch), Mary (married Henry Gallman), Elizabeth (wife of John Eichleberger), Rebecca (she married first, William Counts, and second, to Charles P. Howard). Adam Ruff and Tarsa Ruff had one son, Orlando Ruff; Adam died early and his widow married Frederick Nance. Langdon and Polly Ruff had children: Dora, Walter, John Henry, Willie, David. George Oliver Ruff married Lavania C. _____ and had one son, John S. Ruff.

Christian Ruff, brother of George Ruff, Sr., made will October 20th, 1794 and died in 1797, leaving children: Mary Ann, John, Catherine Hiller, Elizabeth, Christian, Hannah, Rebecca, and a son-in-law, David Cromer.

John Ruff died 1819 leaving widow, Frances, and children: George, Polly (wife of John Gillam), and Henry.

Dr. Pressly B. Ruff (born Dec. 24, 1801) was a successful practicing physician in Newberry. About 1845 he and his two brothers, William H. and John Ruff, and his brother-in-law

RUFF (continued)

James A. Graham, formed a partnership for the purpose of buying and selling slaves. The brothers moved to Alabama, where James A. Graham had gone. He was a descendant of Christian Ruff, Sr.

David Ruff (son of George) married Elizabeth Gray and had children: Henry, Jr., John, Christian, Sally (wife of George Penny), Betsy (wife of John Holt), David, and George. George died about 1820 and left children, William, Warren, Hilburn, and George. David Ruff died and his widow married Rev. George Cromer, a local Methodist preacher, and they lived in Abbeville County, on Long Cane. She had two sons by Rev. Cromer.

Walter F. Ruff (son of John Henry) died in April 1857, leaving widow, Ann R. Ruff.

Christian Ruff made will March 1st, 1830 and died in Abbeville County about 1844, leaving widow, Lucretia. He was son of David and Elizabeth Ruff.

John Ruff made will in 1859 in Abbeville County, leaving children: Martha Adams, David P., Mary A. Hutchinson, Joseph H., Thomas J., George W. C., Henry M, Sarah V., and Samuel A. C. He was a son of David and Elizabeth Ruff.

George Ruff (of Georgia) executed a mortgage in 1820, on personal property, to one Frances Ruff.

RUTHERFORD

Col. Robert Rutherford was born in Virginia; married in that state to Dorothy Brooks, and moved to South Carolina, and settled about nine miles East of Newberry on a place known as "Liberty Hill". He was a patriot in the Revolutionary War, and an officer. After the war, he was elected a member of the Legislature, and was one of the first County Judges appointed, presiding at a session held at his home in 1785. He died in 1814. He married (1) to Dorothy Brooks, and (2) to widow Frances Harrington who died 1824. Children by his first wife were: John, Mary Mathias, Joanna Minter, Nancy Slappy, Happy Elizabeth (wife of Major Frederick Nance), Thomas B., William, Sarah (married F. Hardy), Robert (died young). Grandchildren: Robert R. Nance, Drayton Nance. Great granddaughters: Dorothy Ann Wadlington, Elizabeth Wadlington, Polly Brooks Wadlington, and Sarah Wadlington.

John G. Rutherford died 1835, leaving widow, Mary Ann, and sons, John William, Antonio G.

Thomas B. Rutherford died about 1865, leaving widow, and children. A son, Orson Adams Rutherford, died about 1868.

Josiah Rutherford died before 1805, without issue. His mother, Mrs. Elizabeth Pope, and sisters, Mary and Sarah Rutherford, were his legatees.

William Rutherford died about 1845; married Elizabeth Ruff, daughter of George Ruff. She died before he died. He left son, Dr. Thomas B. Rutherford, who was the father of Col. William Drayton Rutherford, an officer of the 3rd State Reg. Confederate Troops, and killed in battle. William Drayton had married Miss Fair, leaving a daughter, Katherine, who later became the wife of George Johnstone, lawyer and one time member of the U. S. Congress.

. . . .

The following sketch of the Rutherford Families was compiled and written by Mrs. Agatha Abney Woodson, of Edgefield, S. C.:

"Rutherfords from Scotland descended from Rutherford of Teviotsdale and are entitled to use the Rutherford Coat of Arms. Following is the history of several who emigrated to America, settling finally, in Virginia, North Carolina, South Carolina and Georgia. In the year 1689, several brothers of the scotch family of Rutherfords joined the army of William III, when he invaded Ireland. They fought in the battle of Boyne. Two were company officers and the third a Presbyterian Minister. They all remained in Ireland, settled there and married, one settling in the County of Tyrone, one in Down, and one in Managhan. Several of the sons of these men emigrated to America during the decade between 1720 and 1730. The name Thomas has been a very popular one among the members of these American Rutherfords, and much confusion has arisen among historians in consequence. One of these was Thomas Rutherford of Paxteny, Penn. who was the father of Robert Rutherford of the Valley of Virginia. He also had a brother named Robert. This man has been called, by Mrs. Seggins White, a descendant of Rutherfords, Thomas Hugh Rutherford, and is said by her to have been married to Susan or Sarah de Montegre. In records secured a number of years ago by the

RUTHERFORD (continued)

family descending from Sir John Rutherford is the definite statement that it was Thomas Hugh Rutherford who settled in North Carolina. However, I will not digress further, but take up my narrative. It is said that Thomas Rutherford of Paxtony, Penn. comes of the family from which the mother of Sir Walter Scott descended, and that the Rutherford Coat of Arms hangs in his hall, and that there was a great resemblance between the members of the family. This is old and first coat of arms without decoration (1260). Three martletts on a field silver, signify that some of the family had been in the warlike expedition to the Holy Land."

ACCOUNT OF ORIGIN

"The traditional account of this ancient family is that a man of distinction on the Border, having conducted Ruther, King of Scotland safely through the river Tweed on an expedition against the Britons at a place, which from that event was called Rutherford, by the King and after his expedition, the king bestowed some lands contiguous there to, on his conductor from which time his posterity assumed the name of Rutherford, as soon as Sir names became used in Scotland. Be that as it may, certain it is, that the family of Rutherfords of that ilk from which several other considerable families have sprung, having that sir name, in the south of Scotland, are descended from that family and they have always been classed among the ancient and powerful families of Teviotsdale Scotland. - (From Burkes Landed Gentry of Scotland and Ireland)."

IN AMERICA

"Sir John Rutherford of Teviotsdale Scotland, later of Ireland, was the father of several sons who emigrated to this country. He was descended from James Rutherford who had married Lady Margaret Erskine a lineal descendant of Charlemange, through the Duchess of Loraine. Sir John married Elizabeth Corncross or Cairncross, and from him is descended the American branch of the family, some of whom settled in New York and New Jersey.

One of these sons, Thomas, ill pleased with New Jersey, started further southward "on his own horse back" (Saunders). While on this journey, on the Nottoway River in Virginia, Colonel Robert Rutherford was born, April 1734.

In after years, Thomas Rutherford, still of a restless disposition, moved further south and settled in North Carolina, where he was intimately concerned with the political movements of the colony, as well as other members of his family. One member of the family, John Rutherford, was a member of his Majesty's council of N. C. On March 1st, 1775, he was present in council and advised Governor Martin to issue his proclamation to inhibit and forbid Whigs to meet at Newberne (Wheeler's History of N. C.). He was Lieutenant General John Rutherford of His Majestys Forces and said to have been killed during the Revolution.

A brother of Thomas Rutherford, named James, came down to North Carolina, but the only record we have of him, is that his property was confiscated during the Revolution in 1777.

Thomas Rutherford, himself, was a member of the Assembly under Royal Government from Cumberland County, N. C. For a while he appeared to side with the Whigs. In 1774, he was elected to the Provincial Congress. In 1775, he was a member of the Whig convention which Governor Martin denounced. In the military organization of the state, he was commissioned a colonel but as he joined the adherents to the crown in 1776, Colonel McAlester displaced him. In 1779, his property was confiscated. He had holdings in Georgia, whither he repaired and stayed until the close of the Revolution, when in accordance with a law passed by the Georgia House of Representatives, known as An Act of Confiscation and Emercement, he again had his land confiscated and he suffered banishment going to Winchester, Virginia, where it is said he had a brother living. There he died and is buried.

It was probably not until after the education of his children that Thomas Rutherford moved to North Carolina. It is stated in O'Neall's "Annals of Newberry" that his son, Robert, was educated at Hobbs Hole, Virginia. The exodus of the family was prior to 1765. I have always been under the impression that Lieutenant General John Rutherford, one of those men who formed the Council of Administration of Governor Dabbs, was a son of Thomas Rutherford, but Mr. A. S. Salley of the S. C. State Historical Commission tells me that I am wrong, that his name was not "Rutherford", but "Rutherfurd". However, that makes very little difference, and none so far as our own line of descent goes.

RUTHERFORD (continued)

I would like to give here a notice of that Continental Congress to which Thomas Rutherford belonged in 1774. This congress met at Newberne and was an assembly independent of Royal authority. This Congress is an epoch in our history. It was not a conflict of arms or force, but it was the first act in that great drama in which battles and blood formed only subordinate parts (Wheelers History). Thus it will be seen that our ancestor himself was one of the first to wish to throw off the yoke of British oppression.

When the Provincial Congress met at Halifax, 4th of April, 1776, we find a name to be later noted in the annals of the nation, Griffith Rutherford. He was the grandson of Samuel Rutherford, the Presbyterian Minister, of whom I have before spoken. His father had stopped in Wales on the way over to America and had married into the Welsh family of Griffith, a sister to my own Griffith ancestor.

He and his wife were drowned coming over and the young son, Griffith, was reared by a family in Virginia, possibly his uncle's family. A history of his military operations is a part of the history of the states of North and South Carolina. He died in Sumner County, Tennessee in 1799.

The emigration of Thomas Rutherford and his brothers must have dated back to about 1730 as his son, Robert, was born in Virginia on his way southward in 1734. We have no positive record that any of the brothers came south, unless it was James whose lands were confiscated, so it is very reasonable to suppose that Lieutenant General John was his son as well as Colonel Robert and James of whom we have positive knowledge. Of his daughters we have a record of Agatha, who married James Beulware of Virginia and came with her brothers from North Carolina bringing with her a large family of sons and one daughter; and Susannah who married Russell Wilson, Esq. and is buried in the Rutherford grave yard in Newberry, S. C. by the side of her brother Robert and sister Agatha.

Colonel Robert Rutherford (1734-1814) married first, Dorothy Ann Brooks, who was the mother of all of his children, then he married Mrs. Francis Harrington, the mother of Y. J. Harrington who survived him. In Colonial days, he moved to Chatham County, North Carolina. He was a member of the first Provincial Congress which met at Hillsboro, N. C. He was a Colonel of the County of Chatham under the Committee of Safety during the war of the Revolution. His son, Colonel John Rutherford, was a gallant soldier and officer during the Revolutionary War. Colonel Robert Rutherford moved to South Carolina in 1780 and here he assisted in establishing the County Court System and was made Judge of the Court, the first session being held in his own house in Newberry. (See Colonial Records of N. C., Wheeler's "History of N. C.", page 84 and O'Neall's "Annals of Newberry", page 212). Of his son, John Rutherford, who was made executor of his father's estate, he is reported to have been killed at the battle of Eutaw Springs, but such was not the case as he administered on the estate of Robert Rutherford in 1814. At that time he was living in Georgia, where so many of the family seem to have gone. He was the ancestor of Miss Mildred Rutherford, our wonderful Historian. The only Rutherford killed at Eutaw Springs, of whom I have positive knowledge, was Major James Rutherford, the son of General Griffith Rutherford. In the office of the South Carolina Historical Commission, I found a receipt given the state for services of this Major James Rutherford, killed at the battle of Eutaw Springs, by General Griffith Rutherford. Until then I had been willing to allow that the James killed there, was not killed at all, but merely wounded, as it is a known fact that Robert Rutherford's brother, James, was wounded at Eutaw.

Robert Rutherford was for many years a member of the Legislature and represented that state in the Congress of the United States. He owned and operated the first Whitneys Cotton Saw Gin. He died in 1814 in his 80th year.

James Rutherford was a prominent soldier during the Revolution who had also been at Eutaw and had been severely wounded. A copy of his will is recorded at Edgefield naming his wife, Drucilla, who was a daughter of old Van Swearingen of Virginia. He died about 1798 leaving a large family, some in North Carolina and some in South Carolina. Many of the Rutherfords in North Carolina today are his descendants. He was born about 1735 or 1736 and died in 1798 in Edgefield County, S. C. His descendants are many of the Colemans, the family of George Huiet who married Dorothy Ann Rutherford, daughter of his son Joseph Rutherford who had married his cousin Micah Griffith, the large family who claim descent through Harriet Rutherford daughter of Joseph Rutherford and who married John E. Foy, a son of Joseph Rutherford. Dr. James Rutherford who married Martha Foy and reared children who intermarried with the Yarbroughs, Thompsons and Pittmans. The large families of Perry of Wake and Nash

RUTHERFORD (continued)

Counties of North Carolina, the Rutherfords of North Carolina descended from his sons Robert and James who did not come to South Carolina, the Phillips family of South Carolina descending through the son and daughter of Joseph Rutherford, Dolly Huiet and Griffith Rutherford. Captain Philemon B. Waters who married Mary Huiett, daughter of George Huiett and Dolly Rutherford, so that through this descent are the families of Dr. John Dawson Waters of Saluda, S. C. and the large and interesting family of Waters living at Johnston, S. C. A daughter of James Rutherford whom he names as Dorothy in his will married James Paul Abney. From this couple are descended a large line of Abneys in Mississippi and Texas.

Agatha Rutherford Boulware (1738-1821). She married James Boulware in Virginia. He is recorded in Spottsylvania records as being from that place. He later moved to Essex County and from there emigrated to North Carolina with the family coming with her brother to South Carolina in 1780. She had several grown sons, two of whom served in the War of 1812. Her children were: William Boulware, George Boulware, Rutherford Boulware, Spencer Boulware, Robert Rutherford Boulware, and Mary Ann. The latter married her kinsman, Joseph Griffith, the son of David Griffith and possibly his first wife, Hannah Middleton, whom he had married in Orangeburg precinct in 1750. Joseph Griffith was born in 1757, served in the Revolution and died about 1814. It is possible that Joseph was a son of the second wife of David Griffith who is named in his will as Micah. It is known that they were married prior to 1764 as they are registered as voters in the Cheraws in 1764. There were three daughters to this union, Mary Ann who married John Prator and moved to Georgia, Micah who married her kinsman Joseph Rutherford and Agatha who became the second wife of John Abney, son of Paul Abney and Eleanor Hamilton. She was the grandmother of this writer. The sons of Mary Ann were John Griffith who moved to Georgia, Henry Wisdom Griffith, Joseph Griffith, James Rutherford Griffith and William Griffith. These were the ancestors of many prominent men and women in South Carolina and other states.

Susannah Willson. - Susannah Willson must have been older than her brothers although we have no dates of her birth or death. It is possible that they may be found in the Court House here. She married Russell Willson, Esq. a very rich man and a man who was very prominent in the affairs of what is now Saluda County. He was a Justice of the Quorum Court, a magistrate under the Crown before the Revolution and served as a Captain during the Revolution in South Carolina. He was the father of several sons who were also prominent. Russell Willson, Jr. served in the Revolution, Simpson Willson was a very rich man who moved to Florida. The daughter of whom we have knowledge, was Nancy who married Andrew Lee who came down to South Carolina from New Jersey and settled in Edgefield County on the Saluda River.

Family of Colonel Robert Rutherford. - 1. Lieutenant Colonel John Rutherford married Polly Hubert and was ancestor of Miss Mildred Rutherford of Athens, Georgia, the Lipscombes, Hutchens, Wells, many of the Cobbs of Georgia and others.
2. Elizabeth married Major Frederick Nance who was a Lieutenant Governor of South Carolina. From this couple descend the large family of Wallaces, Dunlaps, Baxters, Sheppards, all very prominent in the history of South Carolina.
3. Mary who married a Mathis of whom we have no record.
4. Joanna who married Colonel John Morgan Minter of North Carolina who was Colonel of Militia in North Carolina. Col. Minter moved to Georgia and the descendants of this line are the family to which Honorable Minter Wimberly of Savannah belongs and other Minters in Georgia, and Mrs. Orme Campbell of Atlanta, Georgia and Miss Rose Weaver of Selma, Alabama. - State Registrar D. A. R. of Alabama.
5. Sarah married Christopher Hardy who was killed at Hays Station during the Revolution, as is given by some members of the family, but if the family did not come to South Carolina until after the Revolution, this could not have been the same man who was killed at Hays station. I have no other record of this family.
6. Thomas Brooks married a daughter of Maximillian Haynie, a noted mathematician of his day. He moved to Georgia, where he was given land in Oconee River in his father's will.
7. William married Elizabeth Roof of Lexington, S. C.
8. Robert Rutherford, Jr. married, lived and died in Newberry, but I haven't the record of his family, which include many prominent families there.

In his will, Robert Rutherford mentions his grandchildren, Betsy, Dorothy and Polly Brooks Wadlington, children of Thomas Wadlington. There was another daughter, Nancy, who married Frederick Slappy. Evidently the daughter who married Major Thomas Wadlington was named for her mother, Dorothy, as in the settlement of the estate of Major Wadlington, Dorothy

RUTHERFORD (continued)

Rutherford Wadlington and Aaron Cates were the administrators. Major Wadlington was a son of William Wadlington of Newberry. Another grandson mentioned in his will was Robert Rutherford.

It is said of the women of the Rutherford family that they were the most beautiful in the state, one of the most beautiful being Dolly Rutherford, the daughter of Dr. Thomas H. Rutherford who married her cousin John A. Nance. Another beautiful descendant of the Rutherfords was Agatha Griffith Abney whom Governor P. M. Butler said was the most beautiful woman he had ever seen, except one. As she was my own grandmother it does not behoove me to say more except that she was as wise and good as she was beautiful."

SATTERWHITE

John Satterwhite, Sr. was born in Charlotte County, Va., in the year 1734. He married about 1760 to Frances _____ (she was born 1736 and died 1789), came to South Carolina and was granted three hundred acres of land on Mudlick Creek, near Little River, Ninety Six District. He died in 1809 and is buried at the old Satterwhite graveyard on this land. He was Justice of the Peace, and also was Sheriff, of Newberry County. His second wife, Mary _____, whom he married in Newberry County, married again. Children by first wife were: John, Bartlett, William.

Bartlett Satterwhite, Sr. married Catherine Floyd, daughter of Mrs. Anne Floyd (widow) who was the mother of Captain John Floyd of the Revolution. He died about 1815 and left children: Nancy (wife of Frederick Boazman), John, William, Catherine Susan, Bartlett, and Elizabeth.

John Satterwhite, Jr. (son of John Satterwhite, Sr.) was born in 1761 and died 1817. He married in 1789 to Susan McKie (born 1760 and died 1810), daughter of Captain Michael McKie of Virginia. He lived in the fork between Little River and Mudlick Creek. He and his father were both Revolutionary War patriots. Children were: John, Bartlett, Drury, Michael, wife of William Meriweather, wife of Blackgrove Glenn, Sarah Caroline (wife of General James Gillam), Susannah (wife of Dr. Peter Moon).

Drury Satterwhite (son of John, Jr.) died 1812 in Newberry County. His first wife was Nancy P. Poole by whom were children: Thomas, Narcissa, Frances, Eliza (died 1817). His second wife was Susannah Poole (sister of first wife) by whom he had one child, Teresa Caroline. Susannah died 1816. Thomas settled in Livingstone County, Alabama.

Michael M. Satterwhite (son of John, Jr.) died about 1825, leaving widow, Catherine, and three children: John, William, and Richard S. The widow married in 1827 to Andrew Lee Lark.

William Satterwhite (son of John, Sr.) died about 1806. He was Deputy to William Malone, the County Clerk of Newberry from 1798 to 1801. He left no family.

Bartlett Satterwhite, Jr. (son of John, Jr.) died about 1807 and left widow, Rebecca (she died 1817), and children: Elizabeth Bullock, Jemima Glover, and Eliza Glover. He left a niece, Martha Moore (daughter of Elijah and Susannah Moore). Also, he left grandchildren (children of Elizabeth Bullock) as follows: Elihu Bullock, Benjamin Franklin Bullock, Satterwhite Bullock, James Bullock, and Wiley Bullock. Also, he left a grandson, William Satterwhite Glover.

Sarah Caroline Satterwhite (daughter of John, Jr.) was born in 1796 and died in 1849. She married General James Gillam, a son of Captain Robert Gillam, Jr.

John Satterwhite (son of Michael M.) made will Jan. 2, 1875, and died 1877, leaving widow, Elvira, and children: Richard S., and Michael M. Michael M. married _____ Mathews and had children: Dr. Irvin Satterwhite (a druggist in Newberry), and others.

Richard S. Satterwhite married Susan C. Vance, daughter of William M. C. and Elizabeth Vance. She was born Jan. 4, 1805 and died September 15th, 1879. They had four children: John, Bessie, James Lafayette and Pettus.

William Satterwhite was born Feb. 3, 1805 and died Dec. 8, 1883. He left the following children: Calvin A., Eliza J. (wife of Wm. Reeder), Matilda (wife of Asa Davis), Elizabeth (wife of Henry H. Blease), Cordelia C. (wife of James Davis). Calvin A. died Jan. 6th, 1867 and left widow, Nancy E. (McKittrick) Satterwhite. His first wife was Margaret Cannon by whom he had a son, John W. C. Satterwhite. Another son, John F., died July 17th, 1862, leaving widow, Eustacia (she afterwards married Perry Workman), and children as follows: John W.,

SATTERWHITE (continued)

May Jane Smith, and William Franklin Satterwhite. William Satterwhite was a son of Bartlett Satterwhite, Sr. and his wife, Catherine Floyd Satterwhite.

SCHUMPERT
Collaborators: Rev. John Long and B. T. Paysinger
(Written in 1929)

When political Europe boiled in discontent during the period of 1300 to 1500, just after the wars of the Crusades, people began to renew their interest in education and culture, the arts and sciences, that were a part of the existence of the old Roman Empire, the ancestral country of many of the people in southern Germany. This was the age of the Renaissance and prepared the way for a religious upheaval in Europe which came when Martin Luther nailed his 95 theses on the door of the Castle church at Wittenberg. Many attempts had been made to free a regenerated country from under the influence of the Roman church, but until Luther's act and the manifestation of his forceful character did a new power come to the people.

Ambition began to work in the hearts and minds of the people and to avoid the religious persecutions of a dominant Roman church many of them immigrated to England and Wales, and even to Scotland; hence the German names in those countries today. At a later period, about 1620 to 1700, some of these began to colonize America under the English government; and during the period of 1725 to 1775 they came over to America in large numbers and settled in the states of Pennsylvania, Maryland, Virginia, North Carolina and South Carolina. It is said they came to South Carolina from Pennsylvania so fast many returned to Pennsylvania and some of the families became divided.

The political chaos and restrictive measures in Germany for a long time, therefore, forced many of the German Palatines living along the banks of the Rhine, in Baden, Hesse, Wurttemberg and Heidleberg, to seek settlements in America. Among these was the family of Schumpert. When Jacob Schumpert, one of the pioneers of this family, came over (he probably came in the colony of 1762) he received a land grant from King George III of England for 250 acres of land in Craven County, situated on Little River, a branch of Saluda River. The survey was made in 1767 and the grant made in the year 1771. At the same time there were two others, brothers, John Jacob and George Adam Schumpert, who came over. They were either brothers or sons of Jacob. George Adam received a land grant for 100 acres in the year 1768, situated in Berkley County on Campen Creek, a branch of Saluda River; and John Jacob received a land grant for 100 acres in Berkeley County, on Campen Creek, in the year 1768. The localities were very close together and were in the Dutch Fork settlement.

The descendants of the Schumpert pioneers lived mostly within the territory granted to their forbears until about the middle of the past century when some moved farther up into Newberry County and few into Edgefield County, while others removed to the states of Georgia, Tennessee and Louisiana.

Frederick Schumpert, son of John Jacob or George Adam, lived across the line in Lexington County, not far from Saluda River. He had a brother, Peter Schumpert. Frederick married Mary Kinard, daughter of Michael Kinard and his wife, Margaret Kinard (Margaret Kinard was a daughter of the first Martin Kinard, a Revolutionary War patriot in the regiment of Col. Philemon Waters). The children of Frederick and Mary Kinard Schumpert were: Catherine (married a Conwill), Jacob K., Elizabeth, William, Polly (married Jacob Long), Amos, Sara Ann (married James Cureton), John Frederick and Elisha K.

Jacob K. Schumpert was a prominent mill man living on Bush River. He was a man of fine character and physique. There is an interesting sketch in the "Annals of Newberry" about him. He is referred to as "A kind and hospitable gentleman, both he and his wife were very fond of company, especially the company of young people, often having a house full for weeks at a time". He believed strongly in justice and right and manifested this spirit in his life. The wife of Jacob K. Schumpert was Harriet Abney, daughter of Zachariah Abney, son of a Revolutionary War soldier killed by the Tories. They left several children: Dr. John I., a prominent physician who located in Louisiana; Mrs. E. M. Kingsmore, who died in Birmingham, left sons, one of whom married Laura Bowman of Newberry, Mrs. C. T. Wells of Newberry, widow of the late Osborne Wells, parents of Henry, Thomas, Jacob (dead), Amos (living in Minneapolis, Minn.), Harriet (wife of Prof. C. L. Trabert of Newberry College), Mary (wife of Thomas Harrell),

SCHUMPERT (continued)

Ruth (wife of J. L. Welling), Mrs. E. A. Cassidy, wife of the late Rev. Mr. Cassidy, presiding elder of the Methodist Episcopal Church, South; Osborne L. and Frederick A. Schumpert.

Col. Osborne L. Schumpert was an outstanding lawyer in Newberry for many years and solicitor of the Seventh Circuit for several terms. He married Mary E. Pool, daughter of the late Jordan P. Pool of Newberry and had Aumerle, now living in Columbia (married Bessie Morton of Farmville, Va.), who have a son, Osborne Lamar, and Thyra, who married John S. McClure of Knoxville, Tenn., who died early, leaving a daughter, Mary Schumpert McClure. Frederick A. Schumpert was a prominent merchant in Newberry for several years, but retired a few years ago. He married his cousin, Miss Abney of Edgefield, who died, leaving two daughters, Myrtle and Elizabeth, both of whom married and live in Florida.

Amos Schumpert (son of Frederick) moved to Alabama.

John Frederick Schumpert lived at Dead Fall, near Silverstreet, Newberry County. He was a successful planter but died early in life. Dead Fall was a popular locality during the early period, and it is said to have got its name from an incident which occurred at that point when horse races were a part of the afternoons' sport in that section. On a very smooth, straight stretch of road for one mile, from Silverstreet to Dead Fall, the races were held, and during one of the races a horse fell dead at this spot - hence the name.

John Frederick married Rachel N. Welch and had one child, John Frederick, Jr., who lived on the paternal estate. He was the popular sergeant-at-arms of the state senate for many years until his death; married Alice Werts, daughter of Michael Werts of Newberry. (Michael was the grandson of Captain Henry Werts of the Revolution). Their children are: Juanita (wife of W. T. A. Sherard, Iva, S. C.), Homer W. (married Louise Hipp) who is superintendent of the city water and light plant of Newberry; Gilette Pearl (wife of F. W. Webster of Coral Gables, Florida), Alice Frederika (wife of Frank Allen, Rock Hill, S. C.).

Elisha K. Schumpert lived near Prosperity and was also a mill man, owning a large flour and grain mill on Bush River. "Schumpert's Mill" was popularly known all over that section of Newberry and Edgefield Counties (now Saluda). He married first, a Miss Morgan, by whom were several children. His second wife was Mattie Stone. The children were: Harriet (married William A. Moseley of Prosperity, now of Jacksonville, Florida), William F. (married Euphemia Taylor), John E. (married Miss Bland), Sumter Beauregard (popularly known as "Sump", engineer on the Southern railway for many years; never married), Frederick L. (moved to Houston, Texas, married and has descendants there), Frank E. (married Kitty Livingstone), and James C.

A daughter of Frederick Schumpert, Polly, married Jacob Long, who lived within the vicinity of Schumpert's Mill. They had several children: G. Frederick, Elizabeth, Trannie and Luther M. G. Frederick Long married Sallie Fellers (sister of the late Judge J. B. Fellers of Newberry) and had Della (wife of John C. Goggans, former clerk of court of Newberry), Cornelius (married Miss Marsh of Trenton), Fannie (died unmarried), Frederick (married Miss Marsh of Trenton, sister of his brother's wife), Lawson (president of Practical Drawing (publishing) company of Dallas, Texas, married and lives there), Reuben (a prominent electrical engineer, now living in Virginia), Jacob (died in California a few years ago), Maggie (married William Spearman, both dead), Lena (first wife of Walter S. Spearman of Silver Street).

John C. Goggans and his wife, Della Long, had J. Lawson (now a lawyer in Dallas, Texas), Daniel Forest (an electrical engineer of Helena, Mont.), Helen (married John Crosland and live at Bennettsville), Lois (married George Balle of Laurens), Sadie, Grady (a practicing attorney of Dallas, Texas) and Ruby (married William T. Brown, now in Columbia).

Luther M. Long married Anna Schumpert, a daughter of John Schumpert and granddaughter of Jacob Schumpert, Sr. - one of the many instances of "the labyrinthal tie that binds humanity together". Their children are: the Rev. John J. Long, D. D., a prominent Lutheran minister and now dean of Summerland College; Edgar, Robert, William, Rufus, Junius Fox, Ola, Minnie, Mary, Anna and Eula. Dr. John J. Long married first, a Miss Livingstone and had two sons, Olin and Virgil. By his second wife, Bessie Blair, he had two daughters, Anna Mary and Mildred. Edgar Long married Fannie Harman; Robert married first, Mary Abrams, and after her death, he married Ethel Folk, daughter of Dr. J. W. Folk, former member of the house of representatives from Newberry; William married Maggie Bickley, and Rufus married her sister, Nora Bickley; Junius Fox married Nancy Werts; Ola married Carl Heller; Minnie married James Sease; Eula married George Epting; Mary married John Shealy. Anna Long died unmarried.

Jacob Schumpert, who died in 1842, a son of one of the pioneers, was twice married leaving by his first wife, ten children: George Adam, Samuel, John, Peter, Christina

SCHUMPERT (continued)

(wife of John Paysinger), Elizabeth (wife of Kinard Boyd), Mary (wife of Joseph G. Conwill), Sarah (wife of David Werts), John Jacob and Lucinda Harrison (wife of Thomas Carson and mother of the Rev. James Carson, a Baptist minister of Edgefield County for several years). Another legatee in his will was Permaelia A., the wife of Luke Smith. George Adam married Elizabeth _____ and had one son, the late Frank M. Schumpert, who was judge of probate for Newberry County for several years, died and left children by his wife, Lily Merchant: Ora (wife of Reuben Bouknight), Ernest (married Lizzie Whitman), Hugh (lives at Anderson, S. C.), Mamie (wife of Arthur P. Werts of Silver Street), Claude C. (married Myrtle Dennis), Marion (married Drayton Taylor), Lillius E., who married and lives at Anderson.

Samuel Schumpert died near Silver Street. He married Elizabeth G. _____ and left children, Texana J., Peter M., George Frederick, H. Lawson, Samuel P. (died early). His granddaughter, Sammie Ann (daughter of Samuel P.) is mentioned in his will.

John Paysinger and his wife, Christina Schumpert, had: Benjamin, Jacob J., Samuel S., Frederick S., Thomas M., Henry, David, Pamelia, Elizabeth Carolina (called "Callie"). The family of Paysinger is a good, old substantial family of Newberry County, composing an element of thrifty, upright people, including many descendants living in this section and elsewhere.

Benjamin Paysinger married Eliza Fellers and had Emma, Lawson, John, Olivia, Hattie and Benjamin. Emma married Thomas Buzhardt and had the following children: Ida (wife of E. Lee Hayes), Mamie (wife of William W. Hornsby), Lula (wife of Julius J. Langford), Viola (wife of Eugene Werts), Benjamin T., a prominent business man of Newberry (married Lola Swittenberg), Walter (married Eunice Sheely), Olin (married Epsey DeHihns). Lawson married Lily Boozer of Prosperity, and had, Ethel (wife of H. C. Lorick of Augusta, Ga.) and Holland.

John married Emma Kinard of Ninety-Six and had Benjamin and Noel. Olivia married James Derrick (no children). Hattie died young. Benjamin married Julia Strother and had Josie (wife of W. P. McAlhany), Mamie (wife of George Bailey of Greenville), John (married Annie Caldwell), Strother (married Marian Daniel).

Jacob Paysinger married Nancy Chapman (daughter of Samuel Chapman) and had Samuel (died young), Fannie (married Duffie Sligh, no children), Charles T. (married Florence Dennis), Ernest (married Sallie Longshore). Mary, wife of Thompson Young of Prosperity; they moved to Georgia).

The children of Charles T. Paysinger and his wife, Florence Dennis, are: Annie (married a Barnett), James (married a Tompkins), Fannie, Fred (married Leone Swindler), Mildred (married Thomas Setzler), Myrtle, Gerald and other children, some of whom died young. Ernest Paysinger and his wife, Sallie Longshore, had Madison (died young), Ellen (married Claude Abrams of Newberry) and Ernestine (married Osborne Long of Newberry).

Samuel S. Paysinger married Rose Chapman and had John (married a Sligh), Henry (married Lester Bloomer), Albert, Pinckney (married Ellie Cousins), David, Robert (married Sara Summer), Permelia and Bessie (married a Lee and lives in Georgia).

Frederick S. Paysinger married three times. His first wife was Callie McCollum (widow of Milton Buzhardt) and his second wife, Vinnie Maffett (daughter of Robert Maffett), by whom was one child, Ida, the wife of McK. Hutchinson of Newberry. His third wife was Carrie Mitchell (no children).

Thomas M. Paysinger married, first, Adeline Werts and second, Rebecca Buzhardt, and left one child by the second wife, Mamie, the wife of John H. Wicker. Henry M. and David S. Paysinger were killed in the Confederate War. Permelia Paysinger married Z. L. White and had John William, Elizabeth (first wife of R. C. Williams, now of Columbia) and Alma (wife of the late William Taylor).

Elizabeth Paysinger married first, Pinckney Boozer and second, Charles C. Teague. Children by first husband were: Fannie (married George Mills of Prosperity), John, Luther, Fred Thomas, Arthur (a practicing physician at Graniteville), James, Lola, Lucy. John married Jane Langford. Lucy married Dr. Thomas J. Hunter of Trenton, and after her death he married her sister, Lola.

David Werts and his wife, Sara Schumpert, had children: J. Belton (first married Miss Pitts and then a Miss Brown), Jacob L., John A., Frances, David B., and Rosannah. Frances married Thomas J. Maffett. David B. married first, Hettie Smith, after her death, to the widow of the late Calhoun F. Boyd. Rosannah married Dr. Andrew Wicker, had two daughters, and moved to Alabama.

Samuel Pinckney Schumpert died in 1873, left his widow, Malissa Elizabeth, as his only heir at law. He was the son of Samuel Schumpert.

SCHUMPERT (continued)

George Schumpert, Sr. and his wife, Rhoda, lived in the Bush River section. Conveyance of land made by them in 1845 indicating the place of their home.

John Schumpert, son of Jacob Schumpert, Jr., died in Newberry County in 1877, left his widow, Eliza (she was the daughter of John Kibler and his wife, Mary M. Summer), and children: Mary M. (wife of R. W. Whitesides, descendants in York County), Lucinda F. (wife of Pierce M. Hawkins), John C., Anna C. (wife of Luther M. Long), Susan M. Frannie, Robert L., and Ida B. The late Robert L. Schumpert owned the Schumpert roller mills near Newberry. His widow (daughter of the late Rev. Mr. Whitaker) and his children live in Newberry. John Calvin Schumpert died a few years ago. He married a Miss Stewart and had Daniel Edward (married Sue Coleman). Albert (married Lola Wicker), Pearl (married Andrew Nichols). P. M. Hawkins and his wife, Lucinda F., had Bloomer, Jesse Frank, a daughter who married LeRoy Summer and had several children. Susan M. married George Marion Boyd Epting and had several children. Trannie married G. B. Summer and lives in Newberry. J. F. Schumpert and his wife, Anna Barbara, lived in Lexington County, as did Daniel C. and his wife, Eliza.

One John Schumpert died in Lexington County in 1868, and left an estate, including a large tract of land to a son, Jacob A., and two daughters, Sara E. and Anna L. Schumpert.

Another deed made in the year 1801 shows that Catherine Schumpert of Barnwell district, daughter of one of the pioneers, George Adam Schumpert, conveyed lands originally granted to her father under a land grant in 1768.

David Schumpert married Mary Aaron about 1820. He was appointed guardian of his wife, a minor, she having been left property in the same year. The bondsmen were George Schumpert, Jacob Schumpert and George Rikard.

Peter Schumpert, son of the pioneer, was one of the first elders in old St. Peter's Lutheran Church in Lexington County. (This church celebrated its centennial just a few years ago). One of his sons, John, moved over into Edgefield County and died there in 1851. He left a valuable estate of 773 acres on Saluda River. His widow, Mary Smith, daughter of Matthew Smith, survived him with the following children: John W., Peter M., Mary Ann (wife of John Wise), Keren-Happoch (wife of Allen Cook), Jesse, and Thomas L. The minor grandchildren who received shares of the property were: John Wise, Malissa Wise, Perline Wise (children of a pre-deceased daughter, Nancy, wife of Joel Wise).

Jesse Schumpert moved over into Newberry County, married Mary Singley (daughter of Martin Singley), and had Victoria (wife of Michael Long), John M., Benjamin B. (a merchant of Prosperity), Jacob Frederick (died young), and Thomas L. His second wife, Catherine, survived him.

John M. Schumpert lost an arm by the explosion of a portable steam engine. He married Jane Monts and had several children: Ira, now dead, married Mattie Wicker. Levi B. (married Anna McCullough and lived in Newberry), Cyrus (married Kate Livingstone and lives at Prosperity), Perry A. who married and lives in New York City. Benjamin D. Schumpert married Eliza Boland and had children: Leland, Phoebe (wife of Claude Singley of Prosperity), Charley, Frank Ward, and Julia (wife of Doctor Hunt of Saluda). Thomas L. Schumpert, Jr. married Fannie E. Rikard (sister of H. H. Rikard of Newberry, and had Osborne L., Mary Lena married B. L. Wheeler). Georgia (married Arthur Counts), Fred H., and Howell B.

SHEPPARD

James Sheppard married Janette Riddle, daughter of William Riddle, and had children: Frances, Joice (married first, Wm. Strother and second, Benjamin Culpepper), Thomas, Sally (wife of Micajah Harris), Netty (dead), William, James, Lewis (dead), Honorias, and George (dead). Frances married (1) a Gilder and (2) _____ Edwards, and had children: Preston Gilder, Sally (wife of James Dodgen), John Edwards, Lewis Edwards, Nancy (wife of John Lockhart), and Jane (wife of Eli Dodgen). Micajah Harris and Sally had children: Jane (wife of Perry Anderson), Cynthia (wife of Michael Peaster), James, Polly (wife of Govan Gordon), Micajah, Letty (wife of Drury Culpepper), and Taploe. Lewis died and left children: George, Netty (wife of Jesse Grimes), Nanch (wife of Jacob Ruff), and Lewis. James Sheppard, Sr. died about 1791 and his widow died about 1825.

George Sheppard (son of James) married and had children: James, William, Nancy (wife of William Sia), Nann (wife of John Hendrix).

Honorias Sheppard (son of James) married Margaret _____ and died about 1858, leaving his widow, and several children, to wit: Levi C., Nancy (wife of William Garmany),

SHEPPARD (continued)

Harriet (wife of Minereal Livingstone), Simeon, and Young. William Garmany and wife, also Simeon and Young Sheppard, all moved to Cherokee County, Alabama.

William Sheppard, Sr. (son of James) died in Newberry County on November 29th, 1825, leaving children and grandchildren. Children: William T., John, Levi, Thomas T., Sarah Rogers, Lewis, George, a daughter who was the wife of Henry Boozer, wife of Frederick Boozer, Honorias, Samuel R., Stanmore, Janette (dead), and David. William T. died about 1828 and left his widow, Sarah, and children: James G., Benjamin F., Temperance, Elizabeth (married a Black about 1835), Sarah (died 1825). William T. Sheppard's wife was Sarah Gillam, daughter of Robert Gillam, a Revolutionary War soldier. Levi left children, John, Nancy, Sarah, and Levi. Sarah Rogers left children, Temperance, Levi G., and Sophronia.

Thomas T. Sheppard (son of William) died about 1837, left widow, Elizabeth B., and children: Lewis A., Susan, William W., Thomas, James, Daniel, Temperance, and Benjamin F. Benjamin F. died about 1833 not married.

Mrs. Sarah Sheppard died February 19th, 1862, leaving children: Nancy (wife of Moses Coppock), wife of John W. Hatton in Arkansas. John W. Hatton and wife had two children, John and Frances, who shared in estate.

James Sheppard son of James) died about 1823 and left widow, Susannah, and children: Uriah, Maximillan, Nancy (wife of John Jones), Elizabeth (wife of James Ramage), William H. (dead), Henry, Lewis, Joice, and Anna. Anna married William H. Hatton.

Maximillan Sheppard (son of James, Jr.) died about 1848, leaving widow, Sarah, and children: Susan (wife of William Morgan of Coweta County, Georgia), Ruth, Caroline (wife of David Boozer), Nancy, Frances, and John. Dr. Thomas W. Thompson was appointed guardian for the three last named children who were infants.

Honorias Sheppard (son of William) was born August 19, 1807, and died April 11, 1861. His widow, Rhoda Araminta, was born October 10, 1839 and died May 31st, 1862. His first wife was Phoebe Dennis (daughter of James and Prudence Dennis) by whom were two children: Mary E. (wife of Peter Schumpert), and James R. Peter and Mary Schumpert were the parents of Frank M. Schumpert. Children by his second wife were: Addie, and Honorias (he was a posthumous son, born few weeks after the death of his father).

SINGLEY

John Singley (Single) received a grant of land from King George III, of England, in the year 1769, for 150 acres located in Craven County, South Carolina, on both sides of Bush Creek and West side of Wateree Creek. He received another grant in 1771 for 100 acres located on both sides of Wateree Creek.

Martin Singley (Single) received a grant of land in the same section as John Singley. He died about 1790, leaving a widow, who was Fanny Roiser, and children as follows: Jacob, Frederick, Rosannah, Elizabeth, and probably others. The above John may have been a son or brother of Martin. Rosannah married Henry Wertz, Revolutionary War patriot.

Jacob (born about 1760) was a Revolutionary War patriot; served in the State militia under Captain William Frederick Houseal. He married Martha Sibella Kinard, a daughter of Martin Kinard, Sr. and wife, Mary Kinard. Their children were: Rev. Martin (1782-1856), Adam (married Mary Kinard), John, Matthias, and others. A tradition is that Rev. Martin had nine brothers.

Rev. Martin Singley married Sophia Bedenbaugh (1787-1858) and had children: Jacob (married Sarah Wise), Susannah (married George A. Counts), Rosannah (married Joseph Wise), Caroline (married Adam Hartman, Mary M. (married Jesse Schumpert). Jacob and wife, Sarah Wise, had children: George M., Henry M., Levi D., Mary E., Rosannah L., Martha M., Nancy A. Of these, George M. married Margaret Kibler, a daughter of John and Elizabeth (Koon) Kibler -- Elizabeth, the daughter of Henry and Eve Catherine (Epting) Koon. Jacob was born in 1805 and died in 1881, and his wife, Sarah, was born in 1809 and died in 1855. Their children were George M., Guss, Jacob, Henry M., Rosannah.

Christopher Singley, who may have been one of the brothers of Rev. Martin Singley, was born about 1785, married Mary Sibella Wicker, a daughter of John Henry Wicker (Johannes Wilhem Weisker), a pioneer, and his second wife, Elizabeth Cromer, a daughter of Frederick Cromer and his wife, Sybella Cromer. Christopher and his wife, Sybella, had children: John,

SINGLEY (continued)

Elizabeth, Rebecca, Nancy, Eve. John married Margaret _____. Elizabeth married William Cromer and left descendants living in Anderson County. Rebecca married Isaac Cromer. Hilliard Francis Cromer married the daughter, Nancy. Eve died unmarried. John had a son, Miles Singley, who married one Elizabeth Cromer, and died young leaving no children. (See Cromer family sketch).

John Singley, the other pioneer, above named, may have moved from the county as no record of his estate is found.

Matthias Singley, son of Jacob and Sibella (Kinard) Singley, married Margaret Kinard. Some of their children were, G. Melvin, Adam, and John Lewis (he moved to Georgia and married Emily Cole and had children: William Henry and John. G. Melvin married _____ and had children, G. Melvin, Jr., Lee A., James, John H., Malcome and others.

STARK

The Stark or Starke families lived in Newberry, Abbeville, Fairfield, and Union Counties, during and before the Revolutionary War. At a later time we find many living in Camden and Richland Counties.

Major Thomas Stark was one of the earliest settlers in Ninety Six District. He was granted three hundred acres of land on Gilder's Creek in the year 1768. He was a distinguished Officer in the South Carolina militia during the Revolutionary War. Probably it was he who married Ruth King, daughter of Charles and Charity (Pennington) King. His brother, Jeremiah, married her sister, Mary King.

Jeremiah Stark received a grant of one hundred acres of land on Gilder's Creek in 1772. Afterwards he moved to Abbeville District and died there in 1824, leaving widow, Mary, and children: Charles, Benjamin Osborn, Thomas, James, and Charity Vernon. Charles received a large share of the estate of his father before his death, the balance being divided among the other children . . .

Robert Stark, the Sheriff of Ninety Six District, sold in the year 1775, some lands to Charles King, in payment of debts contracted by other parties --- in compliance with the British Law, Act of 1731, under King George II.

Charles Stark (son of Jeremiah), made will dated October 6, 1838 and died in October of same year in Abbeville County, leaving widow, Keziah, and children: Samuel C. (dead), James H., and Mary Madison. Also, a grandson, Samuel J. H. Stark, was a son of Samuel C. Stark. Executors who qualified October 17, 1838, were: Col. A. Rice, and Dr. Abner Fant.

Col. Robert Stark, a Revolutionary War soldier and patriot, was a prisoner for a long time of the British, confined in the "Exchange" afterwards known as the "Old Post Office" at Charleston. A letter written in 1782 at Jacksborough is referred to in the "S. C. Gen. and Hist. Magazines", Vol. 26, page 195.

William Stark and wife, Anne, conveyed to Thomas Stark in the year 1788, land in Newberry District which was originally granted to William Stark in 1786.

Thomas Stark and wife, Rachel, conveyed to Robert Anderson (lately from Ireland), three hundred acres in Newberry District in the year 1788.

Thomas Stark, Sr. made will July 5th, 1806 and died 1806, leaving lands on Little River to his widow, Sarah, and children: Thomas, Elizabeth King, Mary Perry, Fanny Quinney. Other legatees were: George Martin, _____ A son, James, was not mentioned in his will. Qualified executors on August 10th, 1806 were: Captain Reuben Stark and Captain Jesse Harris.

John W. Stark (son of Thomas, Sr.) moved to Hillsborough County, Florida and was living in that place in 1845.

John W. Stark, Sr. made will January 12, 1826 and died in 1828, leaving son, John Malone Stark, his property, with condition that if said son died without children, the property to go to James D. Stark and John W. Stark, "sons of my nephew, Thomas Clark". John Malone Stark died 1837.

Samuel, Reuben and Thomas Stark were brothers living in Fairfield County. They were nephews of John W. Stark, Sr.

Thomas Stark of Fairfield County, graduated at the South Carolina College (now University) in the year 1832.

Turner Stark made will March 12, 1806 and died 1806 in Fairfield County, leaving property to minor children, (his brother, John Stark, as Trustee), as follows: Turner, Jr., Elizabeth

STARK (continued)

(wife of Archibald Hagood), Lewis, Philemon (eldest son), Nancy, Douglas, and Jane. Turner Stark, Jr. moved to Mobile, Alabama. Turner Stark, Sr. left widow, Sarah (probably second wife). Philemon died in 1830.

Reuben Stark (brother of Thomas Stark, Sr.) made will dated October 22, 1805 and died in 1806 in Fairfield County. He left widow, Susannah, who married in 1808 to Sheppard Rickert.

Reuben Stark made will in 1830 and died soon after, leaving widow, Elizabeth G., and children: Wyatt W., and Samuel C. Samuel C. had a daughter, Mary Martin. All lands in Alabama and lots in Pensacola, Florida were left to his wife and children.

Thomas W. Stark, of Fairfield County, died about 1826, and left property to the following: Elizabeth Stark, Jane (wife of Edmund Harrison), and Louisa (wife of a Griffin).

Mrs. Frances E. Stark of Anderson County and her husband, Samuel James H. Stark, were married February 15th, 1852, by the Rev. Mr. Rice at her father's home in Abbeville when he was twenty four years old and she was eighteen years old.

John Stark, of Fairfield County, married Rosannah McMaster, daughter of James McMaster, Esq. He died about 1832, leaving widow and children as follows: Nancy (wife of Thomas Mc-Master), James, Ruth (wife of Joseph Keller), John B., Polly (wife of Archibald Gillis), Jane, Jacob K., and Rebecca (she died 1841). Archibald Gillis and wife moved to Winston County, Miss.

Pennington Stark died about 1833 in Fairfield County, leaving widow, Rachel, and children: Ross S., Rebecca (wife of George Y. Roland), Thomas W., Mary E (wife of H. A. Stephens), Eleanor, John, Nancy Ann (wife of Daniel J. Finger), Elizabeth (wife of George W. Hunter). Ross S. Stark and his mother, Rachel, and a brother, John, settled in Tippah County, Miss. Elizabeth Hunter died in 1844 leaving three infant children: Rachel, Pennington, and Elizabeth.

Mrs. Grace Stark (widow of Thomas Theodore Stark who was son of Jeremiah Stark, Sr. and wife, Mary King Stark) made will dated March 25, 1841 and died 1841, leaving the following legatees: Children of Mrs. Elizabeth Ware (Wier), Theodore Stark, Mrs. Lucy Staunton, Dr. Theodore Stark, and Dr. Rufus Nott. In a codicil, some money was left to Dr. W. T. Mayo. Other legatees named were: Margaret Howell Lykes, Polly Hay, Lucy Hay, Mrs. Rebecca C. Brown and Grace Brown Elmore. Executor named: Franklin H. Elmore. Another legatee was Thomas C. Brown.

STEWART (STUART)

Robert Stewart (1711-1805) married 1732, to Martha Richardson (1717-1793), had children: Robert (married Mary _____)— son, John; this grandson, John, married Lavania _____ and had son, Robert D. Stewart. Robert D. Stewart (1798-1869) married Eliza R. Ward (1803-1879) of Laurens District; they are buried in Rosemont Cemetery at Newberry. Robert D. was a prominent merchant in Newberry; lived in a large house at corner of Johnstone and Wilson Streets, once famous for it's beautiful flower gardens that covered nearly the entire square. A son, John, lost his life in the Mexican War in 1848, only 22 years old. Another son, James E., lived in Newberry.

John Stewart who received a grant of 250 acres of land located between Enoree and Tygar Rivers, in 1774, died in that section in 1823, leaving a widow, Lavania (she died 1838), and children: Robert D., Nancy Sims (wife of Joseph Pearson), John E., James W., Thomas D. Thomas D. died about 1825, leaving widow, Milly, and children: James, Jefferson, John, Mary (wife of John R. Lyles), Elizabeth (wife of Daniel Murphy), Anne. James W. (son of John), was in Lauderdale County, Ala. in 1842. John E. (son of John) was in Madison County, Tenn. in 1842.

Joshua Stewart died about 1806-07, leaving widow, Mary, and his estate to children of his brothers, Robert and William, viz: Daniel, Thomas, Dudley (son of William); and John (son of Robert).

John Stewart died in 1806 in Laurens County. He left children: Francis (eldest), David, Nelly, and others.

Joseph Stewart, Sr. died about 1808. His daughter, Lydia, married _____ Waters; and his grandson, John, who was son of a predeceased son, Robert.

A grant of 100 acres of land on Saluda River was made in 1774 to Joshua Stewart. William Stewart, Sr. received grant of land in 1769 on Beaver Dam Creek. "Little" William Stewart

STEWART (STUART) (continued)

(son of William Stewart, Sr.) moved to Edgefield District and married Mary _____. Mrs. Janette Stewart (widow of William, Sr.) received grant of 250 acres in 1774. Josiah Stewart sold his land on Little River to Mrs. H. P. Scurry in 1855.

Alexander Stewart, shoe-maker, conveyed to Joseph Reagin, blacksmith, 109 acres on Henn-coop Creek, a branch of Rocky River. This was an original grant to Thomas Waters on April 6, 1792, who conveyed it to said Alexander Stewart on December 12, 1792. Alexander left a son, William.

SUBER

Matthias Suber received a grant of land in 1754, bounty grant, in the Dutch Fork, near Broad River. George Suber received a grant of 100 acres in 1774, in the same section, as did Conrad Suber. They were the sons of Matthias. Other sons were, no doubt, those who after-wards served in the American Army in the Revolutionary War, viz: Conrad, John, Ulrick, and George.

George Suber married Christina Folk, who, after his death in 1823, married again to Jacob Cromer in 1831 (she was the second wife of Jacob Cromer). George's children by Christina Folk were: Henry, Hannah (wife of Silas Koone), Nancy (wife of Enoch Cromer), Mary (wife of Samuel Harmon), Elizabeth (wife of David Eargle), Anna (wife of John P. Livingstone), Enoch, George Aaron (he died 1843), and Alfred (a posthumous son, born 1823) . . . . . Children of Silas and Hannah Koone were: George A. and Andrew T. Koone; there may have been others. Children of David and Elizabeth Eargle were: Mary Ann, Jacob, who settled in Pickens County, Alabama.

Conrad Suber, Sr. married Rebecca _____ and had children: Conrad, Jr. (married Lucy Wicker), Uriah, John, George, Leonard.

Conrad Suber, Jr. and wife, Lucy, had children: Jacob, Elizabeth, Rebecca, George, Henry, Martin and David. Jacob died 1852, left children: David F., Jacob H., Elizabeth (wife of Alexander Edrington), Anna C. (wife of J. Wesley Folk), and Laura Lavania. Henry died in 1853, left widow, Susan, and children: Jacob, Mitchell, and others.

Uriah Suber died about 1832, leaving children: Sarah (wife of David Boozer), David, Ephriam, John, Rebecca (not married), Mary (wife of Michael Buzhardt), Elizabeth (wife of William Welch), Hannah (wife of John Glymph), Viney, Christian (he married Caroline Counts), Solomon (married Elizabeth _____), Uriah, Jr. (died unmarried), and Lavaniah (married Lemuel Boozer).

Solomon and Elizabeth Suber had children: Anna, Viney, John W., and Christian H. Major Christian H. Suber was an officer in the Confederate Army; a lawyer in Newberry for many years; he never married, but helped his sister rear her children, and helped, financially, many of his nieces and nephews.

Anna B. married Walter F. Ruff, Lavania C. married George O. Ruff. Ephriam died and left widow, Elizabeth, and children: Thomas Jefferson, Elvira Elizabeth.

Michael Suber died about 1813, left widow, Elizabeth, and children: John George, Abraham, Emmanuel, John Thomas, Susannah (she married an Eigner), and Rebecca.

Several descendants of these pioneers have moved to other states.

SUMMER
The Summer Family in Europe.

The name has been spelled different ways -- Sommer, Summer, Sumer, Sohmer -- and is thought to have been spelled in the time of the Crusades, "Sumer" or "Sumrer", which means in the German or Tuetonic language of that time, "grain measure" ..... Another meaning during that time was "Drummer" or "Tamborine Beater". The name is not derived from the season.

The Emmental family of Summer can be traced from the year 1426, at which time a famous Cloister living in Sumiswald had extensive possessions. In 1539, according to tax records, one Benedict Summer owned the estate called, "Eichols"; also Hans Summer and Ulrick Summer owned large estates in the valley of "Hornbach". All of the above refer to families of Switzerland, from where they originated, as did many early German families who later had migrated from that country into Germany and other countries.

In the year 1711, many people from the Canton Berne wandered to Holland, in part they were Menonites who were compelled to emigrate. Others who had gone previously to Germany, left that country for America. In 1723 Ulrich Summer was in Germany. In 1707 Jacob Summer renounced his home rights in Sumiswald; settled in Durlach (the State later situated in Germany, called Baden). Odenwald is in that neighborhood. In this district the neighborhoods were governed by the First Bishop of the Catholic Church; hence many families sought refuge in America so that they not only could receive land grants, after their lands were confiscated, but also that they could worship according to their own Reformed Church's principles -- the Lutheran Church.

Hans Adam Summer was a native of Odenwald, in the Oberland District; and in seeking a new home in America, he sailed up the River Rhine and joined a colony of people at Rotterdam where, it is stated, he married a young lady in his colony just before sailing. That was in the year 1743.

The Summer Coat of Arms is very much like that of the Summers who lived in England. The English families added the letter "s" which is a contraction of the old English form of "Summer's Son", meaning the eldest son came into possession of the father's estate by law, and the estate was called by that name. These Summers were and are descendants of German families named Summer who had come to England just after the crusades. The Coat of Arms is the following:

     Vert: A fesse daucette erm
     Crest: On a Globe of the World, Winged ppr.
       an eagle, rising, or.

Another source gives it thus:
     Arms: Vert (green) a fess daucette ermime.
     Crest: On a globe winged proper
       an eagle rising (gold)

     From "Houseal and Summer Families",
     Archives of Library of Gettysburg Lutheran
     Theological Seminary, Gettysburg, Pa.

"Oberland -- the upper country in Switzerland, comprising Canton of Berne, Sembeythe Lake of Thum, with adjacent parts of Unterwald and Uri-Umrechdeseine, it is applied to the Valles of Haste Srundenwald and Lemtrbrume."

"The Odenwald is a mountaineous region in Germany, in southern Hesse and the adjacent parts of Baden and Bavaria between the neck on which separates it from the Spessart, which includes various small tributaries of the Rhine, Kockes, and Maine. A beautiful region known as 'Bergstrasse'.

JOHN ADAM SUMMER, SR., PIONEER

The pioneer of this family came from Odenwald, in Germany, a section of the Oberland which stretches along the border of Northern Switzerland and bounds on the edges of Baden and Hesse (the old lines).

He sailed from Rotterdam to the United States about 1743; said to have married a young lady of his colony at Rotterdam, named Miss _____ Jostin. They arrived in the ship, St. Andrew, at Philadelphia on October 7, 1743. The Council Records in the S. C. Archives states that he came in Captain Russell's Ship, "and waited on ye God in Council where he was directed to go unto the country to look for the land whereon he might settle, and then to apply for a warrant. The Petitioner accordingly fixed on a plot of land near Broad River; that he had a wife and three children, the children's names being Adam (age 8), Henry (age 6), and Magdelina (age 4); and humbly prays his Excellency and Honors to order the Surveyors General to lay off to ye Petitioner of 250 acres of land on Crim's Creek ....". "Dated at Charleston, 31st August, 1752."

Since he is said to have lived about seven years in Pa. before coming South, the date of his exploration and land grant corresponds with the records in Pa. as to his arrival at Philadelphia.

The following is a part of a letter written by William Summer, Esq., Horticulturist, of Pomaria, S. C. in year 1878, to Col. Brantz Mayer, of Baltimore, Md.: "John Adam Summer migrated from the Oberland, in Germany, ... and remained in Pennsylvania where he lived for about seven years....... He came to America to better his condition ...... After his term of service was up in that State he set out on a trip of exploration, leaving his wife and children with the family who had given him employment. After a trip through Virginia he returned to his family. Later, he obtained a horse from his former employer, set out on a second trip of exploration, extending this trip down into the Carolinas, and was pleased with his discoveries. He returned to his family in Pennsylvania and brought them to the place of his selection for a settlement. This place proved to be near Broad River, in the "Dutch Fork", (in Lexington County near Newberry County line)."

"On his second trip through Virginia while reviewing his first observations and passing through one of the Indian Tribes, he turned his horse into a small stream to drink, discovered a young Indian in great agony. He offered the Indian the assistance he could, when he made signs by his fingers that he had been three days there and had been bitten by a rattlesnake, and by signs comprehended the course he wished to go — and he laid him across the back of his horse, walking by his side and holding him on, brought him to the Indian Camp, a distance of several miles, where there was great rejoicing as he was the son of the Chief and they had been searching for him for three days. They at once gave him (Summer) an unbounded welcome, settled him in their midst, and heaped around him piles of dried venison beef and everything they had to subsist upon, and embracing him urged him to remain with them; that his wishes would be supplied. He remained with them about three days, and begged them to suffer him to depart, that he had a wife and family he wished to return and see. They then began to pile on his horse more than he could carry — he took a small part."

"As he went on his way and he came among other Indian tribes, they received him with unusual welcome, making him understand he had relieved one of their people." Runners had been sent on ahead of him to tell other tribes of his coming so that he would not be molested.

"When he came to Esvapadeena (Indian name for Broad River), the Indians showed him a ford which they said had been made by Buffaloes, originally, and then used by them; and crossed over and came into the forks of Broad and Saluda Rivers where he chose to make a settlement... He said that this reminded him of Oberland, and here he was content to make his home. He found the whole country overrun with the wild pea, the bottoms of the streams and valleys overlined with cane, affording abundant food for his cattle and horses."

"............after he was settled, and in his journeys to Granby he met Rev. Christian Theus, of the Reformed Church, the pastor of the people there, and in conversation with him, he and his wife wished to join his church (having been reared in a Catholic community) and have their children baptized. He had him to visit his family and to preach in his neighborhood; and he encouraged the people of his section to come and attend to these duties. Here was established one of the first churches, known as St. Johns Lutheran Church. A grant of 100 acres was made by King George II, to the German Society, then Reformed and Lutheran." . . .

"He was a man of firm will and purpose and gave no encouragement to the idle, but was ever ready to assist and aid those who desired to make a home in his settlement." . . . . He brought several families with him from Pennsylvania to the Dutch Fork. Churches and schools

SUMMER (Continued)

soon sprung up, and in due time the cause of education received encouragment, and culture and good society and liberal education prevails among the citizens of this community. While many of the citizens have sought homes in other portions of the State and the United States."

As a leader in his community, he at first was a Loyalist as were many others in his neighborhood. But later, when his adopted country formed their own government on the side of liberty which seemed the only salvation for the people, he took the side of General Washington. The others of that community also changed and became patriotic citizens. During the Revolutionary War he was Manager of the Commissary of that section and gained the title of Major. Of his six sons who became grown and had families, all were patriotic citizens and soldiers in the Militia during the War. He died sometime in the early 1790 s. His sons who had families were:

    John Adam, Jr. (b. 1744 and died 1809),
    Henry (b. 1746 and died after 1800),
    Nicholas (b. 1754 and killed at battle of Granby 1781),
    Francis (b. 1756 and died about 1810-12),
    George Adam (b. 1760 and died 1833),
    William (b. 1764 and died 1832),
    Mary Magdelina (only daughter) was born 1748 and died _____ married Bartholemew Minnick.

John Adam Summer, Jr., the eldest son, was a Lieutenant, then Captain in State Militia during the Revolutionary War. He commanded a company in the Regiment of Col. Philemon Waters. An incident is related in O'Neall's "Annals of Newberry", of how he carried off an American field piece on the battle-field in the face of fire, at the risk of his life, after it had been abandoned by soldiers in their retreat at the battle of Stono. After the war he became an active and progressive citizen in the upper "Dutch Fork"; a Justice of the Quorum, Justice of the Peace, and a member of the State Legislature.

Before the War, he was delegated as a member of the Committee to meet in Charleston to formulate plans for the safety of the community.

About 1770, he married Mary Reese, by whom he had four daughters, and probably a son who died young. His wife was born in 1744 and died in 1818. They are both buried near the highway about two miles below Pomaria, near Crims Creek, on land that was originally the plantation of John Adam Summer, Sr. The daughters were: Eve Margaret (b. 1775 and died _____), who married John Benedict Mayer (b. 1761 and d. 1817, a Revolutionary War patriot in Waters Reg. of Militia); Elizabeth (b. 1772 and d. _____) who married John Henry Ruff (b. _____, d. _____); Mary (b. _____, d. _____), who married (1) John Adam Houseal, (2) Solomon Sligh, and (3) Robert Boyd; no children by two last named husbands; Katherine (b. 1782 and d. 1852), who married (1) Michael Eichleberger, (2) his brother, George Eichleberger, and (3) David English; no children by third husband.

John Benedict Mayer and Eve Margaret had descendants: A son, Adam Mayer, an only child. After death of John Benedict, the widow married Alexander Stewart but had no children by him. Adam Mayer (1797-1834) married Mary Counts, and had children: Dr. Orlando Benedict Mayer (1818-1891) who married (1) Miss Davis, and (2) Caroline DeWalt (1829-1861); Susannah, who married Dr. G. M. Bates, and moved to Florida; Frances, who married Henry Summer, Esq.; and Elvira, who died when quite young. Dr. O. B. Mayer, Sr. and Caroline DeWalt had children: Dr. O. B. Mayer, II (1853-1918) who married Harriet Jones, of Laurens, S. C.; Caroline V. (1861-1922) who married J. Thomas Mayes, Sr. (1858-1935); Katherine who married Edward C. Conner, of Greenwood, S. C.; Mary, who married William Martin, and moved to Florida. Dr. G. M. Bates and wife, Susannah, had two children, Newton and Orlando. Henry Summer, Esq. and wife, Frances, had several children (see Nicholas Summer line). Dr. O. B. Mayer, II and wife, Harriet, had three children, as follows: Dr. O. B. Mayer, III (b. 1898 _____), Cornelia (1894 _____), Harriet (b. 1901 _____). Dr. O. B. Mayer, III is now a practicing physician in Columbia, S. C.; served in the Second World War, as Major in the Medical Unit. Harriet married William R. Reid, Jr. of Newberry, S. C. Cornelia was for several years a teacher in the City Schools of Columbia, S. C.

Dr. O. B. Mayer, Sr. was a prominent physician and surgeon before and after the War Between the States. Also, a writer. (See Mayer Family Sketch). Many of his books and poems were burned in the great fire in Newberry in 1907.

Dr. O. B. Mayer, II, like his father, a prominent physician and surgeon of Newberry, was a leader in the business and civic affairs of the City. He accumulated a nice competency; was a director in the Commercial Bank and other industrial organizations. For several

SUMMER (continued)

terms he served as Mayor of Newberry. A member of the Board of Trustees of Newberry College; serving also as a Lecturer on Hygiene and Physiology for several terms, as did, also, his father.

Adam Mayer, father of the first Dr. O. B. Mayer, was a prominent planter near Broad River, in the "Dutch Fork"; for a short time was in business at Lexington Court House, but removed to his plantation where he died and was buried in the family graveyard. When General Lafayette visited our State, Adam Mayer was delegated as Captain of a local Militia Company, to meet the General at the State line and escort him as far as Columbia, on his way to Charleston.

The children of James Thomas Mayes, Sr. and wife, Caroline V. Mayes, were: William Mayer (1883-1948), who married (1) Sarah Cockrell, of Birmingham, Alabama, and (2) Catherine _____ (widow); no children by either wife; Caroline Nancy (b. 1884 _____), who married George Leland Summer (b. 1881 _____) married in the year 1906; (See Francis Summer line) -- James Thomas, Jr. (b. 1889 _____) married Eleanora Douglass (1892 _____) of Alabama and had two children, James Thomas and Mary Elizabeth; Jesse Bernard (1891-1932) who married Lucile Wallace and had one child, Caroline; Bennie Mayer (b. 1893 _____) married Lucy Wallace (sister of his brother Jesse's wife), and had one son; Katherine (1895 _____) who married William Parham, and had children; and Edward Glenn (1897-1898) - (See Mayes Family Sketch).

Edward C. Conner and wife, Katherine, had four daughters, viz: Alice who married Harry Jennings of Columbia, and after his death to _____; Caroline Louise who married William O. Ballentine, of Greenville, S. C.; Katherine who married K. Dunlap; and Claire.

John Adam Houseal who married Mary Summer, had children (he was born 1773 and died 1816): John George (1808 _____) who married 1830 to Eliza Rhidlehuber, and had children, Frances, who married in 1849 to Wallace Cline, of Newberry; Katherine (1799-1821) who married William M. Rawls, and had children, two of whom were Bennie and Bernard. Bernard died young. Bennie married Sarah Hatiwanger and had children: Henry J., Bernard H., E. H., and Haltiwanger, also a daughter who married Samuel J. Derrick; Elizabeth (1815 _____) who married in 1832 to David Counts, and had children: Adam (1838 _____) who married 1867 to Polly Ann Setzler, Francis (1842 _____) who married 1861 to Nancy Hinnant, Orlando Benedict (1844-1927) who married (1) Elizabeth Setzler — died 1887, and (2) Frances Buzhardt, Fannie H. (1847 _____) who married 1866 to J. A. W. Stoudemire, Preston (1849 _____) who married 1869 to Florence Clark (1849-1929), and Jacob (1852 _____) who married 1872 to Jane Summer; Eve Margaret (1797-1867) who married Jacob Swygert and had children: Anderson Harrel (1816-1841), Louisa (1818 _____) married 1842 to George Moyer, Catherine E. (1824 _____) who married 1843 to James Milton Wilson, Frances (1825 _____) who married 1846 to William R. Chapmen, Mary who married Anderson Bundrick, Ozro H., who married Mary Ann Fulmer, and George A. (1829 _____) who married Nancy M. Wilson.

John Adam Counts and Polly Ann Setzler had children: Houseal, Antoinette Eulilia (1868 _____) who was second wife of William M. Wilson — no children, and Ernest Calhoun (1870 _____) who married

Orlando B. Counts and Elizabeth Cummings Setzler had children: Enoise Blanche (1870 _____) she died young; Forest Setzler (1872 _____); Hammet Bates (1874 _____); Junius E. (1876 _____); Emily ( ), and Fannie ( ).

Jacob Counts and wife, Jane Summer, had children: James Anderson (1872 _____), Corra Aurelia (1874 _____), and Alice Lavania (1878 _____).

Francis Counts and wife, Nannie A. Hinnant, had children: Emma Cora (1863 _____), William Gage (1868 _____), Thomas B. (1874 _____), Minnie Maude (1876 _____), and Jeter.

Preston O. Counts and wife, Florence Clark, had children: David C. (1871 _____), Francis Marion (1872 _____), Zeanah S. (1874 _____), George Holland (1877 _____), and L. S. Counts.

J. A. W. Stoudemire and wife, Fannie Herselia Counts, had children: Flora Eugenia (1867 _____), Mary Caroline (1869 _____), Rudolph (1871 _____), Susan E. (1876 _____), Gary, Killian, Joseph.

George Moyer and wife, Louisa Swygert had children: Jacob A. (1846 _____) married 1867 Mary Jane Moore; Elizabeth C. (1851 _____) married _____; Margaret A. (1854 _____) married 1877 to Jacob Bedenbaugh; John Lawson (1860 _____) married

---

William R. Chapman and wife, Frances Swygert, had children: Junius Elmore (1847 _____)

SUMMER (continued)

married 1870 to Eliza A. Hiller; Mary Lenora (1849-1849); Jacob Wm. S. (1851-1867); Alice Ansonia (1853 _____) married 1877 to Alexander Singleton, of Newberry.

Anderson Bundrick and Mary Swygert had children: Ida who married Jacob J. Sease, Mary who married George Fulmer; Kate who married Charles Summer, Isadore who married John Frank Corley.

Ozro H. Swygert and wife, Mary Ann Fulmer, had children: John C. (1847 _____) married Anna Swygert, and had children, Margaret, John C., Mary, Ozro; Brooks (1856 _____) who married (1) Alice Sease, and (2) to Agnes Rice, and had sons by first wife and a daughter by second wife — sons were, Thomas Irvin, Darcey, and Shell, and the daughter, Sara Eliza; George A. (1849 _____) married Lula Stuck; Malissa (1854 _____) who married in 1872 to James H. Shell; Mary Alice (1851 _____) who married _____.

George A. Swygert and wife, Nancy Wilson, had children: Mary Alston (1851 _____) who married _____ Kramer, James Jacob (1852-1868), Mary Emma (1854 _____) who married Dr. Sandel.

The third daughter of John Adam Summer, Jr, Elizabeth, who married John Henry Ruff lived North of Pomaria, and is buried at the old Ruff family graveyard. John Henry Ruff was an extensive landowner, his lands stretching for several miles North of the village of Pomaria. Their children were: Adam who married Tarsa Hill, Langdon who married Polly Sligh, Walter F., who married Ann Suber, David who married Susannah Eichleberger, George Oliver who married _____ Sligh, Sallie who married Adam Counts, Martha who married (1) Dr. Jacob King, and (2) to William Welch; Mary (Polly) who married (1) Jacob Counts and (2) to Henry Gallman, and Rebecca who married William Counts.

Adam Ruff and Tarsa Hill had children: Orlando and Adam. Adam died young. The father, Adam, Sr. died also at young age and his widow married Fred Nance.

Langdon Ruff and Polly Sligh had children: Dora who married Robert L. Caldwell, and had children, Henry, Mamie, Marie, and Julia; (Julia married Wm. H. Eddy, of Newberry); Walter who married Mollie Leitsey, and had children, Tarsa (1874-1920), Hampton (1876 _____), and Vinne (1878 _____) who married Wm. Kibler, Anna Dora (1883-1885), Holland who married Talu Lominack, and Leon who married Lucy Stone; John Henry who died unmarried; Willie who married Ella Shealy; David who married (1) Fannie Caldwell and (2) to Elizabeth Halfacre — had children by first wife, James (married Foley Banks), Ambrose (married Leila Sease), Hampton — not married, Caldwell (married Pauline Nance), Laomus (married Clara Lominack), Blanche (married Walter Long), Biddie (married Hampton Sease). David Ruff and his second wife, Elizabeth Halfacre, had the following children: David (married Mannie Lominick), Crissie (married Fred Gallman).

Walter Ruff and wife, Ann Suber, had children: _____.

George O. Ruff and wife, Mary Sligh, had one son, John S. Ruff (familiarly known as "Snib" Ruff) who married and had several children.

Adam Counts and wife, Sallie Ruff, had children: Elizabeth who married David Suber, Sallie who married Adam F. Cromer (they moved to Anderson County, S. C.), John, Walter who married a Miss Suber, Louisa who married (1) Henry H. Kinard, and (2) to Dr. O. B. Mayer, 1. — had two children by first husband, Henry H. and Katherine (Katherine married Bishop A. Coke Smith, of the Methodist Church); Rebecca and William Counts had children: Henry, Junius, Elizabeth (she married Levi Folk), Mollie (she married Job Swygert), Florence (she married Artemus Bouknight), Charles who married Jane Chapman, Henry H., Jacob Belton, and Benedict. Jacob Belton married (1) a Miss Metts and (2) to Mary Oxner, and by second wife had sons, Ben and Charlie, and a daughter who married _____ Lominick.

Levi Folk and Elizabeth Counts were parents of the following: Dr. J. William Folk (1852 _____) who married (1) Hattie Fogle, and (2) to Beulah Smith; Christian, (married Della Squener); Charles who married Fannie Bouknight; and Minnie who died young. Dr. J. William Folk graduated at Newberry College and at the S. C. Medical College, Charleston. He was Asst. U. S. Surgeon at the Port at Georgetown, S. C. for about 25 years. Returning to Newberry, he located on his farm at Jalapa; served as a member of the State Legislature from Newberry County. He had 14 children - 10 girls and 4 boys.

In listing the children of John Henry Ruff and wife, Elizabeth, the name of a daughter, was left off. This daughter married Col. John Eichleberger who died 1844, and had children: Dr. H. Melvin who married Elizabeth Caldwell and moved to Miss., Dr. John B. who moved to Florida, Adam Luther who went to Florida, William Thomas who was killed in Civil War, unmarried, Jacob W. F., who moved to Floida, George, and Hazelius Bookman Eichleberger.

SUMMER (continued)

Charles Counts and wife, Jane Chapman, had children: Anna who married J. Cal Singley, Elizabeth who married John Jacobs, Belle who married _____ Eleazer, James, John, Rebecca.

Jacob Counts and Polly Ruff had children: Harrison, Mary (married William Rhidlehuber), Martha (married John J. Dreher), Caroline (married Christian Suber), David (married Miss Rikard). William Rhidlehuber and Mary Counts had five children, viz: Maggie, Louise, Counts, Minnie (married David Suber), Amelia (married Orlando Wicker). The second husband of Minnie was Jacob Leitzey. David Counts and Miss Rikard had children: Henry, Louise, Laura, William H.

John J. Dreher and wife, Martha, had children: Backman who married Anna Nunnamaker, Dr. Julius D. who married Emoline Richmond, Rufus (he died young), Thaddeus who married Margaret Miller, William, Charles who married Sena Huffman, Ernest who married Caroline Hyde, Heber, and Edward.

Dr. Julius D. Dreher was a graduate of Roanoke College, Salem, Va. and after serving a Professorship at that Institution, became it's President in which he served for over 20 years. After his retirement he was appointed U. S. Consul to _____ Jamaica, Tahiti, and then to Toronto, and to Panama.

Ernest Dreher was Superintendent of the City Schools for several years at Columbia, S. C. After extensive travels in many foreign countries, he returned home and was appointed Burzar at Winthrop College, at Rock Hill, S. C.

Christian Suber and wife, Caroline Counts, had children: John David who married (1) Sue Reagin, and (2) to _____ Leitzey; Jacob Benson who married Anna Koon and had children: Mary (married Charles S. Suber), John (married _____ Nance), William (married Claudia Coleman), Annie (married James Duncan), Lucy (married William Elmore), George (died young) ....; George Benedict who married _____ Lominick; Isabella who married (1) Capt. Philander Cromer who was killed in the Confederate War, and (2) to Sanford Eleazar — had one son, Robert Eleazar; Rebecca who married James A. Welch and had children: Anna (not married); Christian (married Julia Hunter); Robert (married first to Mabel Day and second to Nettie Heath; Amelia who married Thomas Stack; Mary who married Dr. Henry Eleazar.

Robert Welch was a lawyer in Newberry, thence moved to Columbia where he practiced his profession, and was appointed Attorney for the Federal Land Bank, in which capacity he served for many years.

The youngest daughter of John Adam Summer, Jr, Katherine, had the following children by Michael Eichleberger: George who married Mahala Eigner and had children — George, Wade, Phillip; John Adam who married a _____ Long and had children - Kate (married Rev. Mickaell), Andrew, John, Walter; Mary Elizabeth who married Dr. Wm. Irby, of Laurens, S. C. Phillip Eichleberger married Margaret Hobbs. He was Captain of State Volunteer militia company in War Between the States.

George Eichleberger and wife, Katherine, had children: Louisa Caroline who married Rev. James C. Hope, who had, James and Mary; Mary who married Eff Henry; William Henry Eichleberger. James Hope married Mattie Miller and had children: James, who married (1) Maggie Swygert, and (2) to _____; George who married Beatrice Bedenbaugh; Mary who married Richard Hipp; and John J. who married (1) _____ Thatchine, and (2) to Ruth Digby. Mary Hope married Dr. L. L. Hobbs and had children: James, Jefferson, William, and John F. Col. John F. Hobbs, a graduate of Newberry College, traveled extensively; and in the South Pacific Islands he was captured by natives and compelled to live with them for a time, as a kind of god or king, ruling over the tribes until he could escape from them. Eff Henry and his family moved to Mississippi. James Hope, Jr. was a teacher for many years, as Superintendent of several large schools in the State, and served for over 25 years as State Superintendent of Education.

In the year 1850, Rebecca Ruff, daughter of John Henry Ruff and Elizabeth Summer Ruff, married a second time to Charles P. Howard, her first husband, Wm. Counts, having died.

Henry Summer, the second son of the pioneer, was a First Lieutenant in the State Militia during the War of the Revolution, serving in Col. Philemon Water's Regiment, in the Company of his brother, Captain John Adam Summer. He married Christina Dominick, daughter of the pioneer, John Dominick. Little is known of his descendants, except one son named George lived

SUMTER (continued)

in Lexington District. A daughter, Barbara, married John Koon (1762-1847), and had children: David, Jacob, Ephriam, Christina (married Michael Charles), Elizabeth, Caroline, Henry, Martin, Adam. Another daughter, Maria, also married a Koon.

Abram Fulmer married Elizabeth Summer who was probably a daughter of Henry Summer One of their daughters, Mary Ann, married Ozro Swygert. (See John A. Summer, Jr. line) ......
Another daughter, Rosa, married William Epting and had children: Drayton and others (see Epting line). Five of their sons moved to Alabama, viz: William, Michael, John, Joel, David, Mary. Joel married Mary Fulmer, a cousin, daughter of Matthias Fulmer. David married Ona Wessinger. Joel returned to the old home and died there.

There were three brothers who moved to Tennessee about the year 1818, viz: John Summer, Nicholas Summer, and David Summer. David named his eldest son, Henry, which seems to indicate they were sons of the above Henry Summer. However, others of David -- named Michael and Anderson -- seem to indicate that there is a possibility they were sons of William Summer, Sr. as these names seem to be in several generations of that line .

David Summer lived about two miles South of Pomaria, the old home known as the "David Summer Home" was owned and occupied by several different families, some of those living there at different times being the families of Sease and Fulmer. David Summer married a Miss Fulmer, and this place no doubt was originally her father's plantation. Their children were (some born after their removal to Tennessee): Henry (married a Miss Stonicpher), William (1812-1901) who married Clerissy C. Staples, Michael (1818-1914), Jackson, George, David, Lemuel, Levi, Anderson (1828-1912) who married Phoebe Jones, Katherine who married Nathan Blake, Sallie who married Levi Blake.

William Summer and Clerissy C. Staples had children: Lucinda who married R. A. Davis, Rev. Benjamin T. (died 1923), William (died 1863), David, and Sallie (1851-1862).

Michael Summer had the following children: David, James Edward, John Robert, Mattie, Hettie, Susie, Jennie.

Anderson Summer and wife, Phoebe Jones, had children: Michael E. who married Sarah Drew, Edward R. who married 1875 to Geneva Drew (she died 1918), George Nicholas who married Ida Clark, William A. who married Hattie Ford, Ralph (died 1875) who left sons David, John, Joseph; Lucinda who married G. W. Mitchell.

Ida May (died 1920) who married W. H. Rhodes; Mary Jane who married Joe Detherage and had a daughter, Edith, Katherine who died young.

Michael E. Summer and wife, Sarah Drew, had children: Ben N. (b. 1887 _____) who married Emma Lester, Gussie C. (b. 1895 _____) who married J. G. Clawson, Norris (b. 1897 _____) who married Kate Clark.

Edward R. Summer and wife, Geneva Drew had children: Frank A. (b. 1879 _____) who married Kate Dunn; Edith (b. 1881 _____) who married Steve Fowler; Ethel M. (b. 1884 _____) who married David E. Stone; Walter R. (b. 1888 _____) who married Bessie Heady; Maude D. (b. 1890 _____) who married Orin Reid, Phoebe M. (b. 1893 _____) who married John C. Cooper; Vernie (b. 1898 _____) who married Charles Maury; J. Dolphin (b. 1901 _____) who married Opal Cornwell; Nellie Gertrude (1882-1885); Leitia Louise (1895-1896) and J. Anderson (1903-1905).

George Nicholas Summer and wife, Ida Clark, had daughter, Mary Jane (b. 1883 _____) who married O. G. Atkinson.

William A. Summer and wife, Hattie Ford, had children: Flossie (b. 1887 _____) who married John Calvin Cooper, Florence F. (b. 1889 _____) who married Herbert Jarvis, Olive May (b. 1893 _____) who married Conroy Christianson, Servyle Sylvester (b. 1898 _____) who married Daisy Parker.

G. W. Mitchell and wife, Lucinda, had a son, Robert Earl (b. 1891 _____) who married Frankie Miller.

W. H. Rhodes and wife, Ida May, had children: Edna (b. 1882 _____) who married William Carrol Hurt, Charlie (b. _____ d. 1920) who married Dolly Toner.

Nicholas Summer, the third son of the pioneer, was born about 1752; married in year 1777 to Eve Margaret Sease, and had one child, a son, John. He was killed in 1781 at the battle of Granby in the Revolutionary War while fighting as a private in the militia. He lived a few miles South of Pomaria, near what was later known as the "Cross Roads".

The son, John Summer (1779-1855), accidentally lost a leg and walked with a peg-leg, becoming familiarly known as "Peg-leg" John Summer, to distinguish him from his cousin,

SUMMER (continued)

"Yellow-leg" John Summer who wore yellow leggins. He married Mary Houseal and became a well-to-do planter of his section. About the year 1832, he built a large two-story home near St. Johns Lutheran Church, which still stands and is occupied by some of his descendants. It is a typical anti-bellum house, with many antique designs on the interior.

The children of John Summer and Mary Houseal were: John (1812-1836) not married; Nicholas (1604-1836) not married; William (1815-1878) not married; Henry (1809-1867) who married in 1846 to Fannie Mayer, a sister of Dr. O. B. Mayer, I; Adam G. (1818-1866) who married in 1865 to Mary Starke; Thomas J. (1826-1851) who died unmarried. William and Nicholas were both graduates of the S. C. College, at Columbia, S. C., both studied law and were admitted to the bar of South Carolina, and practiced in the town of Newberry. Nicholas was a young man of great promise, but volunteered for service in the Army, in a regiment formed at Newberry, and as a Sargent, fought in the Seminole Indian War in Florida where he was killed. His brother, John, went to Florida to bring home the body but took sick and died there. William never married. He was a well-educated man but preferred life on his farm where he built a large nursery business, importing some rare specimens of plants from Europe, and shipping his products to other Counties and States. He was known as the "Horticulturist". He started the first Post Office at his home (his fathers home at its present location), and called the place "Pomaria", which name was formed from some Latin derivatives meaning fruits and plants.

Henry Summer, Esq. was a lawyer in Newberry before the War Between the States. He accumulated a very large and valuable library which was said to be one of largest private libraries in the State. He was a constant worker for Newberry College, the Institution he served both as Instructor and then as a Trustee for many years; having been one of the prime workers in having the College removed from Walhalla after the War back to Newberry to its original location. He held many positions of honor and trust; and was one of the members of the Sesession Convention; and a member of the State Legislature. He and his wife, Fannie Mayer, had children: Thomas Nicholas (1847-49); John Adam (1851-19__); Mary; Catherine.

John Adam married 1874 to Alice Efird and had children: Jessie (1878-_____) who married Rev. Y. Von A. Riser; William Carl (1881-_____) who married Louise Carter; Rosalyn (_____) who married Dr. Virgil B. Sease, and lived in Parlin, N. J. Marie (_____) who married Dr. Herman H. Huggins, and they live at the old Summer home near Pomaria. Dr. Huggins lately died. Mary Summer married Dr. James K. Chapman in 1877, and had three children: Louise (1878-1923) who married George Swygert; Henry who married and lives at his fathers old home place near Pomaria; and Ben Chapman. Catherine Summer (1858-_____) married (1) to Rev. Kiser, a Lutheran minister, and after his death, she married a widower, J. B. T. Scott.

Adam G. Summer who married Mary Starke was, also, a lawyer in Newberry, who was said to have been a very intelligent man and a versatile speaker. He died when very young leaving a widow and an infant daughter, Mary Margaretta, who later married a Mr. Gamble, and they lived in Jacksonville, Florida.

Francis Summer, fourth son of the pioneer, was born about 1756 and died about 1810-15, in Lexington District, near Newberry County line. He married Margaret Epting, a daughter of John Adam Epting, Sr. After her death, he married Christina Hipp. He received a grant of 300 acres of land on Penny's Creek in 1786, for service in the Continentals during the Revolutionary War. He also served in the State militia as a private in Col. Philemon Waters' Regiment. Since Penny's Creek is located in Abbeville District, near the old French-German settlement, it is supposed he moved there and lived a short time; then returned to his native section at the time many of the German settlers in Abbeville District moved to the Dutch Fork to be with their friends who spoke the same language.

He was a member of the first Grand Jury formed in Newberry in 1785, just after the formation of the new county from old Ninety Six District. In the same year he was appointed one of the members of the first Road Commission formed just after the Revolutionary War and after the establishment of the new county. He was a large planter, operating a store in connection with his farm, as did his son, John, at the same place years later.

The eldest children who may have been by the first wife, Margaret Epting, were: Abram who married Magdelina Addy; Eve Ann who married Captain Thomas Boyd, Sr.; Catherine who married a Mr. Stone; and the others who were by a second wife, Christina Hipp, were, Sarah (1793-_____), Mary M. (1795-1880) who married (1) John LaGronne and (2) Silas Merchant;

SUMMER (continued)

John (1797-1867) who married Cynthia Ray. A grandson, Joseph, who was reared by him as his own son (1804-1871) married (1) Eve Margaret Counts and (2) to Catherine Glymph (widow Vance). Another son named in his will was John Adam.

Thomas Boyd, Sr. died 1835 leaving his widow, Eve Ann, and three sons and three daughters, viz: Thomas, Jr., Peggy (wife of Jacob Lindler), Esther (wife of David Richardson), Janette (wife of Dempsey Patterson), James (died young), Robert C. He left grandchildren: Elizabeth Boyd (wife of Robert C. Boyd), and Mary M. who lived with her son, John George Houseal. Thomas Boyd, Jr. married (1) to Caroline Ellen Eleazar and after her death to Elizabeth Houseal.

Mary M. Summer and John La Gronne (he died about 1830) had six children: John who married a Minick, Katherine who married a Minnick, Susan who married George Boozer and had Drayton Boozer and Rev. Cornelius P. Boozer, a Lutheran Minister, who served as a Trustee of Newberry College for several years; Mary who never married; Elizabeth who married a Feagle; Christina who married an Enlow; and Sarah. John La Gronne, Jr. moved to Alabama, as did Drayton Boozer. Silas Merchant and Mary M. Summer had sons, Nicholas and David. David moved to Florida. Nicholas married Louisa Bedenbaugh and lived near Newberry. Their children were: George (married Ella Lester), Alice (married James Vaughn), Mary (married a Long), Frank (married Beatrice Cousins), Langdon (married Emma Miller), Kate (married Wylie Taylor) Flossie (not married), Henry Wingard (married Alberta Cook), Edward (married Mary Minnick), Roberta (married W. Elisha Schumpert).

Some of the children of Rev. C. P. Boozer were: Lee, William, Dr. Hugh T. (in N. C.), Ruth (married Dr. Nickleson), Maxcey, and Luther.

Abram Summer who married Magdelina Addy had one child by her, Rebecca, who married Daniel Jacobs of the "Dutch Fork". Abram left his wife, and went to Alabama where he lived. It is said that he married again in that State one Nancy Seigler who was, also, from the Dutch Fork section. His wife in South Carolina, after his 20 years absence from the State, filed a petition to the State Legislature to make her marriage to George Monts a legal one, which was granted. Daniel Jacobs and his wife, Rebecca, had children: William, Joseph, Rebecca, Mary, and John. John married Ellen Eleazar and had children: Walter, John, Elizabeth (she married _____ Huff). John, Jr. married _____ Counts. (See John A. Summer, Jr. line).

John Summer was familiarly known as "yellow-leg" John (he wore, habitually, yellow leggons) to distinguish him from his cousin, "Peg-leg" John Summer, who had a wooden leg. He ("Yellow-leg" John) married Cynthia Ray who had come to this section from Tennessee with her widowed father and a small sister. She was about five or six years old when they came. John Francis (he was killed in 1863 in Confederate Army) married Louisa Swittenberg, and left children, Martha, Preston, Mary, and Thomas E. Martha married John Barrett and lived in Augusta, Georgia. Preston never married, died in Columbia, S. C. Mary married James Lever and had several children. Thomas E. married Mary George, and moved to Cherryville, N. C., where he had the following children: a son who married Bessie Kendrick, Loyd who married Mary Toppins, Dewey who married Acie May Dellinger, and another son who died young; Annie Belle who married Lewis Bowling, Nellie who married Otto Dellinger, Allene who married Carlisle Browning, and a daughter who died young. John Summer and wife, Cynthia Ray, had other children, viz: Emmanuel who was a jeweler in Augusta, Georgia, but ill health forced him to sell his business and retire to his home in South Carolina where he died, unmarried; Amelia (she married Jacob Lucas); Anna (she married Henry Miller); Henry (died young, unmarried); Andrew (died young, unmarried); George W. (married Martha Epting); and Jacob (1846-1942), who married twice, and left no children by either wife. Children of Jacob Lucas and Amelia Lucas were: Francis B. (1856-1890), who married Kate Fulmer, Martha who married William Haltiwanger, Emma who married one John Summer, Mary who married an Eargle, and John who married, first, a Stuck, and then Alewine. Children of Henry Miller and wife, Anna, were: Walter (married Martha Bowers), Kate (died unmarried), Julia Ann (died unmarried), Luther (died young, unmarried). George W. (1838-1862) who married Martha Epting (1838-1925) had children: Charles Edward, John Harrison ("Hack"), and George W. Charles Edward (b. 1858 d. 1947); John Harrison ("Hack") (b. 1860 d. ____); George W. (b. 1861 d. 1944). Jacob married, first, to Caroline Eleazar, and second, to _____ Chapman. Another daughter of John and Cynthia (Ray) Summer was Martha Ellen (1841-1896) who married, first to William P. Freshley, and second, to P. B. Lever.

SUMNER (continued)

George W. Summer, fifth child of John and Cynthia (Ray) Summer, was a planter living about two miles South of Pomaria. As a member of the local Guards of which he served as Sargeant, ne volunteered for service in 1861 in the Confederate Army. He joined the Company of Captain Phillip Eichleberger as a private — Company H, 13th Regiment, SC. V. Col. D. A. Dickert, the author of "Kershaw's Brigade", spoke of him, verbally, as a brave and impetuous soldier on the battle field. He died in Winder Hospital, near Richmond, Va. on July 13, 1862. He had been promoted to Corporal just before his death. He left three small children and his widow who took over the operation of the farm, completed the construction of a large two-story dwelling they had started together, and with unusual Christian character and strong purposes reared the three sons to become wealthy, leading and influential citizens in the City of Newberry. The sons, John Harrison and George Walter, just after they married, moved to the City, in year 1884, and they were later, in year 1888, joined by their brother, Charles Edward, in business. They built up a large business under the firm name of Summer Bros.

Charles Edward Summer (b. Nov. 1858-1947) married (1) Nora Sease, and (2) to Jane Sease, sister of his first wife. Charles Edward and Nora Sease had children: Clarence Thompson (1880-_____), Agnes I'Cora (1882-_____), Susan (1884-_____). Charles Edward and Jane Sease had children: Elmer Sease, Charles Forrest, Ruby, Kate, Rosa Lee, and another daughter who died young. Clarence T. Summer married Eoline Wertz, daughter of David Wertz, and have a daughter, Martha Nuel. Agnes I'Cora married John B. Mayes and had children: John Bernard, Agnes, Nancy. John Bernard was a Lieutenant in Second World War, served in North African Campaign as a bombadier, where he was killed. Susan who married William Haltiwanger had two sons, James and Charles Edward, now merchants in the City of Columbia. Elmer Sease married Annie Griffin, of Atlanta, Ga. and had children: Elmer, Jr. (he died young) and Evelyn. Charles Forrest married Mittie Young and had two sons, Thomas and Forrest (both served in World War Two, one as a Lieutenant), and two daughters. Ruby married Robert Hanna and had a son and daughter. They live in Chesterfield, S. C. where Robert Hanna is a practicing attorney. Kate who married David Caldwell of Newberry, have no children. Rosa Lee who married (1) Karl Gustafson and (2) to Robert Moore — no children.

John Harrison Summer (b. March 16, 1860-_____) married (1) Hulda Ann Cromer (b. March 3, 1860 d. 1917), daughter of Hilliard Francis and Nancy (Singley) Cromer (see Cromer Family line); and (2) to Mamie Swittenberg. Children by first wife were: George Leland (b. 1881 _____) who married Caroline Nancy Mayes (1884 _____); Elbert Hugh (b. 1884 d. 1944) who married Vera Summer (see George Adam Summer line); John Ernest (1887 _____) who married Linda Miller of Atlanta, Georgia; Thomas Roy (1889 _____) who married Florence Bowman, of Newberry; Verna Louise (1892 _____) who married Hal Kohn; Mary Lila (1894 _____) unmarried — for many years a teacher in the City Schools of Newberry; Annie Julia (1897 _____) who married Jacob Wise; James Harrison (1900-1932) who married Margaret Spearman, left a son, James Harrison and a daughter, Margaret. Children of George Leland Summer and wife, Caroline Nancy Mayes: George Leland, Jr. (1907 _____) married Sadie Smith; Harry Thomas (1908 _____) married Evelyn Mills; he served in Army Engineer Corps during World War II; William Mayes (1909 - _____) married Sarah Swittenberg; James Elbert (1911 _____) married (1) Juanita Lefler and (2) to Ollie Denton (one daughter, Jean, by first wife); he served in Army Headquarters - Base Depot - as Sargeant, two years in France. Children of Elbert Hugh Summer and wife, Vera Summer, viz: Robert (he served in Navy during World War II); Frances Hulda; Elbert (died young); Hugh and John Henry (last two twins who both served in Air Corps during World War II, the first as a bombadier in the South Pacific and the latter as a paratrooper — both were Lieutenants). Children of John Ernest Summer and wife, Linda Miller: Hulda Cromer who married a Roebuck and lives in Georgia; Linda; Royal; Marion. Children of Thomas Roy Summer and wife, Florence Bowman: Roy, Jr. (who served as Lieutenant in the Aircorps during World War II), and Claridge Walter (who served in Air Corps as Sargeant). Children of Hal Kohn and wife, Verna Louise: Hal, Jr. (who served in World War II — Lieutenant in Photographer Division); Mary Birge; and Verna.

John Harrison Summer and his second wife, Mamie Swittenberg, had one daughter, Jane (b. 1922 _____) who married Lieutenant Charles Ragland, who served in World War II, and in in Army several years after war. Resigned from Army and located in Newberry.

George Walter Summer and his wife, Polly Long, had children: Delila (1882-1883); Eugenia (1884 _____) married Clarence R. Wise and had children, Summer, Clarence, Jr., William

SUMMER (continued)

and Pauline. George Walter, Jr. and his wife, Ollie Smith, had children, George and William; Homer D. (died young); Gilbert — not married, died in 1947; Oscar who married Vinnie Eleazar had son, Oscar, Jr., who was a soldier in World War II; Junius Fox (died young); Grace (not married); Carrol who married _____ of La.; Robert Earl who married Lucile Beam, of North Carolina. Carrol is a graduate of Newberry College and of Tulane Medical College, New Orleans, La. He is a practicing physician in La., holding the position of State Health Physician. He served in World War II, as a Major and Lt. Col. in the Medical Corps.

Charles Edward Summer, merchant, planter, was at one time City Alderman, member of Board of Public Works, Director in the Newberry Savings Bank, President of Summer Bros. Company when the firm became incorporated, and a Director in the Mollohon Mfg. Company.

John Harrison Summer, merchant, was formerly Vice-President of Summer Bros. Company, later becoming principle owner and manager of the J. H. Summer Company. Formerly a Director in the Newberry Real Estate Company, and a Director in the Newberry Handle and Shuttle Factory. At this writing (year 1947) he is said to be the oldest merchant in the City of Newberry, having operated his business over 64 years. Also, a Director in the Newberry Bonded Warehouse Company, before it was sold to the Standard Warehouse Company.

George Walter Summer, merchant, manufacturer, planter. He was formerly a Director in the Summer Bros. Company, Director in the Commercial Bank of Newberry, President of the Newberry Bonded Warehouse Company, Vice-President of Oakland Cotton Mills, Vice-President of the Security Loan and Investment Company, President of the Newberry Lumber Company. For several years he served as Trustee of Newberry College. He was active in the organization of the Mollohon Cotton Mills of Newberry, became its first President, serving in that capacity 25 years, when it was sold to the present owners, Kendal Corp.

All three of the above brothers were at different times active in civic work in the City, members and officers in the old Newberry Chamber of Commerce and other organizations.

Clarence T. Summer who served as Vice-President of Summer Bros. Company during its latter days, was alderman of the City, and also President of the Carolina Auto Company. He is now (1947) a merchant in Newberry doing a large business.

John Ernest Summer was the organizer of the Newberry Lumber Company when it was purchased from the C. C. Davis Estate, and acted as manager for several years, building its present plant many years ago. He is an Architectural Engineer, and served as a Government Architect during the Second World War. He designed many large buildings in Newberry, Greenwood, and other cities. At this time (1947) he operates his own office in the City of Atlanta. At one time he served as Alderman in Newberry, member of several Civic Clubs, helped organize the Newberry Country Club, designing its first Club House.

George Leland Summer, Sr. a graduate of Newberry College, with postgraduate work in Economics, Law and Business Administration — degrees A. B. and A. M., is a Tax Consultant. His hobby has been in historical research, being the author of several articles in magazines and daily papers along the lines of both history and economics. At one time he served as a Director in the Mollohon Mfg. Company, and as Secretary and Assistant Treasurer; as Assistant Cashier and Acting Cashier of old Newberry Savings Bank; as Secretary-Treasurer of the Mayes Company, Inc., member of old Newberry Chamber of Commerce, S. C. Historical Society, and one-time active officer in the Knights Templar.

Thomas Roy Summer, a graduate of Newberry College, has served as Assistant Manager of the J. H. Summer Company for several years; then in business of his own, operating a clothing store in Newberry. He has served in several civic organizations; has served for several years as Treasurer of the Newberry City Bond Fund; member and officer of the Newberry Chamber of Commerce, the Newberry Country Club, and other organizations.

Joseph P. Summer and his first wife, Eve Margaret Counts, had children: Dr. William J. (1829-1854) who married Jane Aull — he was a graduate of Brown University, Rhode Island, practiced medicine short time until his death; Martha (1832-1865) who married George Hipp and had children, Nellie (married James Mackey, of Greenville, S. C.); Dan who married a Means; Edward R. who married Mary Holloway; John C. who married Alice Wheeler; and Charles; Ella who married Charles D'Oyley June 23, 1853; John C. (1840-1862) was not married, having been killed in the War Between the States while serving as Captain of a Company of Militia.

Joseph Summer and his second wife, Catherine Glymph, had children: Pinkney who married Mary Huffman; a daughter who married Bluford Stoudemire; Mary (1857-1926) who married Thomas Henry Cromer (1857-1933), lived in Greenville, S. C.; Guss B. who married Trannie Schumpert and had children, Marvin, Eugene, Weeda, Adrian, Curnie, Geneva; Nora, who married Luther

SUMMER (continued)

Cousins. Edward R. Hipp and wife, Mary Holloway, had children: Edna (married Dr. J. O. Wilson, of Spartanburg, S. C.); Louise who married Homer W. Schumpert, of Newberry; Earl, who served several years in the U. S. Navy as Officer — a graduate of the S. C. Military Academy; Dr. Edward R., a physician and surgeon, now in a hospital as Surgeon at Charlotte, N. C.; Rosalyn who married Andrew Jackson Bowers, Jr., Newberry. Thomas H. Cromer and wife, Mary Summer, had children: John Herman (1880-1940) who married _____ and had children, Thomas, Louise, and Mildred; Laura who married Dr. Theodore D. Hemingway of Kingstree, S. C. whose son, a graduate of the S. C. Military Academy, served as an Officer in the Second World War; Ethel who is unmarried, and a teacher in the City Schools at Greer, S. C. Marvin Summer married Louise Kinard; Eugene died in Florida; Weeda Summer married Robert L. Lominick; Adrian Summer married Dempie Coleman; Gurnie married Estelle Stewart; Geneva married _____ Eargle.

Edward R. Hipp, Sr. was a prominent merchant in Newberry several years, and was at one time President of the Exchange Bank of Newberry.

John C. Hipp and wife, Alice Wheeler, had children: George C. (1880_____) who married Belle Swittenberg — whose children are, Harold and Mary Alice; Hattie who married Roland Fulmer and had children, Edward, Harriet, and Albert; John C., Jr. a graduate of Newberry College, and an Architectural Engineer; J. Edward (died young); W. Frank (b. _____ d. 1943) who married (1) Eunice Halfacre (daughter of Dr. John C. and Lula Neel Halfacre) and (2) to _____; Grady, Everett; Lois who married _____ Kennedy.

James Mackey and wife, Nellie Hipp, had children: James, Charles, Arthur (married Gladius Harbug), George, Alice (married _____ Perry), Nellie May (married Earl Stahl), and Margaret.

W. Frank Hipp, a graduate of Newberry College, was the organizer and first President of the Liberty Life Insurance Company, of Greenville, S. C. After his death, his son succeeded him to the Presidency.

John Adam Summer who is named as a legatee in the will of Francis Summer, may have been the ancestor of George Henry Summer who moved to Georgia, as many of the pioneers' sons and grandsons named their sons, John Adam.

George Adam Summer, Sr., the fifth son of the pioneer, was born in 1760. He was pensioned in 1832 and died 1833, having served as private in the State Militia during the Revolutionary War. He served a while in his brother, John Adam Summer's, Company, afterwards in Company of Captain William F. Houseal. He married Susannah Henry and had about six children, whose names are known, viz: John Nicholas, George Adam, Jr., Andrew, Susan, Elizabeth, and Polly.

John Nicholas (1783-1868) married Elizabeth Counts (1786-1847), and had children: Jacob, Alfred, John Nicholas, Jr., Elizabeth, Susannah, and probably others. Jacob (1817-1880) married Elizabeth Kinard (1816-1887) and had children: Catherine Louise (b. 1840 d. _____) who married John Drayton Smith; Dr. Bluford M. (1839-1863) died in Confederate service, not married; Mary who married Thomas F. Harman of Newberry; Rev. Walter W. (1850-1912) who married (1) Honora Hammett (1852-1878), and (2) to Lavania Meadors. The known children of John Drayton Smith and wife, Catherine Louise, are Dr. Thomas W. (b. 1869-d. 19__) who married Lillian E. Mahon in 1891; John B. (b. 1872 _____) who married Lillian Estelle Roland (b. 1871 _____); and probably others. The children of Thomas F. Harmon and wife, Mary, were: John Middleton - died age 21, not married; Minnie who married Robert T. Reagin; Sallie who married W. O. Goree; Nora who married Rev. J. E. Rushton. The children of Rev. Walter W. and wife, Lavania Meadors, were: Claude who married and lived in Union, S. C.; Elizabeth who married H. I. Horton, Jr.; Kate who married James Whitlock; M. Bluford who married Helen Gross; and Aileen. Children of Rev. Walter W. and his first wife, Honora Hammett, were: Nora who married B. F. McKellar, Sr., Hammett who died young, and Mamie who died young. Afred married Martha J. Boyd and moved to Mississippi. John Nicholas married Nancy Hill and moved to Mississippi, had children, Emily, Oscar, Baxter, William. Elizabeth Harriet married (1) William Swittenberg and (2) William Epting; had children, John C. Swittenberg and Albion M. Swittenberg, Christina and Susan. Susannah (b. 7-22-1807, d. 12-31-1881) married David Sligh (b. 11-8-1801, d. 3-28-1884) - both buried at Lutheran Church Cemetery at Walhalla, S. C. Dr. Thomas W. Smith and wife, Lillian E. Mahon, had children: Lillian Gertrude (1892 _____) who married Frank G. Wright (1888 _____); Mahon (1895 _____) who married Juel E. Paddon; Catherine Louise (1899 _____) who married James Epting, Jr. (1897 _____); Thomas W. (1904-1924) died unmarried. John B. Smith and wife, Lillian E. Roland, had children: John B., Jr. (1894 _____) died in First World War, in France;

SUMMER (continued)

Luicile Octavia (1896 _____); Gerald Harper (1897 _____); Lucas Walker (1899 _____); Drayton Edgeworth (1904 _____).

George Adam Summer, Jr. married Miss _____ Penny, and had children: George Penny who married Frances Houseal, had nine children and rearing only one, daughter, Nora, who married Jeremiah Hopkins. Jeremiah Hopkins and wife moved to Mississippi, where he was afterwards murdered on his plantation. His widow found his body after it was burned, but only the heart was saved and she brought it back to South Carolina, along with her two daughters, Nora and Ella, and buried the heart in the family plot near Pomaria. Other children of George Adam, Jr. and Miss Penny were: Margaret, James Andrew, William, Henry, Mary, John. Margaret married Rev. John Epting and had children: Jane who married (1) Fred Ballentine and (2) to George Dickert; Olivia who married Frank Addy; Sudie who died unmarried; Boyd who married Sue Schumpert; Rebecca who married Adam Luther Summer. James Andrew (1825-1916) married Mary Stoudemire (1832-1901) and had children: Charles (1852-1908) who married Kate Bundrick (1859-1921), John who married Salinda Lucas, James (1857-1927) who married Elizabeth Buzhardt, Tulle W. (1858-1903), Susannah who married (1) George Moss and (2) to George Epting, Willie who married Henry Busby, Carrie who married John Summer, Pluma who married Ed Wessinger. William married Christina Hipp and had children: Thomas (1834-1924) who married (1) _____ and (2) to Martha Mayer, Walter P. (1850 _____) who married _____, Henry, James P. (1855-1938) who married Mary Counts Epting. Henry (son of George Adam, Jr.) was born about 1818; married (1) Caroline Epting and (2) a Miss Sheely, widow of John Bickley — he had children by first wife, viz: John Henry (1849 _____) married Frances Elizabeth Riser (they moved to Florida, thence to Atlanta, Ga.); Martha who married (1) Joe Matthews and (2) to Dr. R. C. Kibler; Marilla who married Jack Matthews; Caledonia who married Hampton Kinard; Mary who married Adam Rikard, November 11, 1869; Ella who married Benjamin Kempson; Cincinnatti ("Natti") who married Bunyan Epting; Caldwell who married Banks Hiller. Mary (daughter of George Adam, Jr.) married James Wilson and had children: John William who married Martha Chapman, Milton who married Kate Swygert, Dr. Pinckney — died young, in Confederate service, Henry, and A. Ogilvie who married Mary Chapman, Walter who married Alice Harvey, Willis May who married (1) Eugenia Minnick and (2) to Eulilla Counts, Pettus who married Ann Rice, Nancy who married George Swygert, Missouri who married _____, Marilsy who married Dr. Harrison ("Hack") Epting, Narcissus who married (1) J. T. Setzler and (2) to _____ Lemon. John Summer and wife, Nancy Fulmer (1821-1893) had children: Elizabeth who died young, unmarried; Mary who married a Sims; Martha who married Melvin Ellesor; Sudie who married Alex Dumas; George who married Sunie Sparks; Frank who died in Confederate Service. Boyd Epting and his wife, Sue Schumpert, had children: Belle, Ida, Robert L. (married Mary Brown), Ben and Jessie. John Henry Summer (familiarly known as "Jack") and his wife, Frances Elizabeth Riser, had children: Carrol, Robert (1881 _____) died in California, Alma who married George Snead, Sidney, Vera who married E. Hugh Summer (see Francis Summer line). Willis May Wilson and wife, Eugenia Minnick, had children: Margaret who married Rev. James D. Kinard, a Lutheran Minister, whose son, Rev. Carl Kinard, is now President of the S. C. Lutheran Synod; James P. died unmarried; Bennett Earl who married Minnie Patrick; Milton Gaines _____ ; Bunyan, Job, Mary, Anne, and Kate all died when very young.

Andrew Summer (son of George Adam Summer, Sr.) married Christina Epting and had children: William Anderson, Jacob, John Adam, Mary. Mary married William Rister. Andrew had two daughters by a former marriage, viz: Elizabeth who married Jacob Eargle, Susan who married Simpson Patterson. Jacob married Ann Addy and had children: John, Henry, Walter, Nicholas, Frank.

Susan Summer (daughter of George Adam, Sr.) who married John Hipp, had children: Adam who married (1) Catherine Setzler and (2) to Eve Setzler — had children, George (see Francis Summer line), John who married Elizabeth Miller, David who married Martha Hipp, Elizabeth who married John Sease. John Hipp and wife, Elizabeth Miller, had children: Pickens who married Hattie Koon, Nora who married L. B. Dreher, Minnie who married _____ Metts, Mattie, and Lula. John Hipp and family moved to Mississippi. David Hipp and his wife, Martha Hipp, had children: Richard who married Mary Hope, Annie who married William Hatton, Sr. John Sease and wife, Elizabeth Hipp, had children: Ida who married Job Koon, Mary. Adam Hipp and his second wife, Eve Setzler, had a son, Adam who married Narcissus Epting, and had several children — a daughter who married a Sparks and lived in Columbia, S. C. and a son, Adam, who moved to North Carolina.

SUMMER (continued)

William Summer, the sixth son of the pioneer, was born in 1764 and died in 1832. He married his brother Nicholas' widow, who was Eve Margaret Sease, in the year 1782. They lived southwest of the place now called Pomaria, just across the Newberry County line, in Lexington County. The same place in which her son, John (by her first husband), lived, near the "Cross Roads". William Summer was a member of the Road Commission after it was first surveyed, in 1786, succeeding his brother, Francis, who in the same year had moved to Abbeville District, but later returning to Dutch Fork.

Their six children known to live to be grown were: Anna (1785 _____); William, Jr. (1787-1818) who married Elizabeth Fulmer; Henry (1790_____) who married Molly Counts; Mary Magdelina (b. 12-28-1782, d. 1849) who married John Counts — known as "Carpenter" John (b. 9-14-1777, d. 1838) — they had no children; Susan (1793-1833) who married Michael Wertz (1790-1853); Margaret (1798-1823) who married John Kibler.

William Summer, Jr. and Elizabeth Fulmer had children: Mary Margaret (1812-1856) who married (1) David Chapman and (2) to John Minnick; Anderson (1814 _____) who married Susannah Setzler; George Michael (1815 _____) who married Polly Chapman, daughter of John Chapman; Eve (_____) who married John Fulmer; Katherine (1817 _____) who married William Epting; Sally (_____) who married _____ Rice. The widow, Elizabeth, married John Addy.

David Chapman and wife, Mary Margaret, had children: Paul Calvin (1833-1860) who married Mattie Eison; Adam C.(1834-1853) died unmarried; Mary C. (1842-1921) who married A. O. Wilson; Paul Chapman and Mattie Eison had a daughter, Mary, who married Allie Clark, and they had children: William Arnold Clark, Stuart Clark, George Henry Clark who died in 1923. A. O. Wilson and Mary C. Chapman had children: Harriet who married (1) James Davis and (2) to Charles Duncan; Anna B.; Mary Jane who married Edward Moyer and had, Auburn, Homer, and Clevie (Clevie married Waddy McGirt); Bessie who married David Denny; Alice; John who married Blanche Red.

John Minnick and wife, Mary Margaret, had children: Georgiana (1849_____) who married Jacob L. Dominick; Eugenia Rebecca (1851-1892) who married W. M. Wilson; Alice Idora (1853 _____) who married Milledge Lindler. Jacob L. Dominick and wife, Georgiana E. Minnick, had children: Cora Lee — not married; Mary Elizabeth — not married; Aurelia Belle — died young; Frederick Haskell who married _____; James Claude who married Miss _____ Boozer; Harry Wicker — not married; Geneva — died young; Mazie — not married. Frederick Haskell Dominick was a lawyer in Newberry many years; represented his County in the State Legislature; Assistant Attorney General of the State; and represented his district in the U. S. Congress.

Milledge Lindler and wife, Alice I. Minnick, had children: Lola who married _____ Younginer; Mamie who married _____ Eleazar; Eva who married Joseph Ballentine; Arlie who married _____; Jessie who married Arthur Monts; Maggie; Mildred who married _____ Metts; John who married _____; Janet; Haskell who died in infancy.

Anderson Summer and wife, Susannah Setzler, had children: Pink (185_-_____) who married Mary Summer (see George A. Summer line), and had Susanna, Frances, Dola, Elizabeth, Bennett Y., and Thomas; John who married (1) Frances Koone and (2) to Nancy Epting; Lavania who married James Davenport; Cornelia who married _____ Hollingsworth; Mary Jane who married Jacob Counts (see John Adam Summer, Jr. line).

George Michael Summer and wife, Polly Chapman, had children: Elizabeth (1836-_____) who married Thomas Huffman; George Michael who married and had James E., and probably others; Pink who married _____. Thomas Huffman and Elizabeth had: Pink who married Mary Summer, his first wife, and after her death married Frances _____; John who married _____; Kate who married Pickens Setzler; Vassie; Mary who married Pink Summer (see Francis Summer line). Other sons of George Michael and Polly (Chapman) Summer were: William ("Uncle Willie") born 1842 and died 193_, who married (1) Elvira Setzler and (2) _____ Epting — children by first wife, Susan, Lula, John Adam, William Pinckney; and Frances C. by second wife; Adam Luther (1840-1898) who married Rebecca Epting and had children: Caroline, Aurilla, Lonia, James E. Susan, daughter of William and wife, Elvira Setzler, married a Boland. John Adam, son of William and wife, Elvira Setzler, married Sims Graham. William Pinckney married Frances Cole and had children:Statona, Louise, Willie D., Ollie T.

SUMMER (continued)

Eve Margaret Summer who married John Fulmer, had children: Elizabeth who married Walter Bush, Polly Ann who married Hart Chapman, Eugenia, Fannie, Ella, Frank, Adam, Kate who married Francis Benson Lucas, George who married Mary Bundrick, James who married Kaus Epting, Mattie who married Jackson Counts and had, Boozer and Winfield Counts.

John Kibler and wife, Anna Margaret Summer, had children: Eliza who married John Schumpert; Anna who married George H. Chapman; Susannah who married in 1839 to George Long (he died May 8, 1862). George H. Chapman and wife, Anna Kibler, had children: Jane who married Charlie Counts, John, Cummings (1843-1925) who married George Swygert, Dr. James Kibler Chapman who married Mary Summer (see John A. Summer line). Dr. Chapman practiced medicine for many years at Pomaria, S. C. Charlie and Jane Counts had children: Anna who married J. Cal Singley, Elizabeth who married John Jacobs, Rebecca, Belle who married _____ Eleazar, James, John. George Swygert and Cummings Chapman (1843-1925) had children: Anna who married William W. Berley; Joel; Robert; George who married Louise Chapman and had daughter, Helen. (see John Adam Summer, Jr. line). The family of John Jacobs were all burned to death at their home at "Spring Hill", in Lexington County.

Henry Summer, third son of William Summer, Sr. and wife, Eve Margaret (Sease) Summer, married Molly Counts and had three sons, all of whom moved to Coweta County, Georgia, about the year 1846. They were: John Nelson (1814-____) who married and has descendants in the section of Barnesville, Georgia; Elias (1816-____) who married Elizabeth Beavers; and John Adam (1821-____) who married _____ Martin. Elias and Elizabeth Beavers had children: William Franklin, Mary M., James Henry (1844-____), Edward Elias, John, Martha, Monora, Sarah who married a Puckett, Charlie (1854-____), "Doc S", Beulah M. (1859-____) who married _____ Ragland, and another who died in infancy. John Adam and his wife, Miss Martin, had children: John Christian (1837-1918); William Harrison (1843-____) who married _____; Henry who was killed in War Between the States, at battle of Fredericksburg. John Christain and wife had children: Henry H.; a daughter who was wife of Dr. M. A. Foil, living at Mt. Pleasant, N. C.; Rev. John Ernest who married and lived at Macon, Georgia; Lille Belle (1876-1899) — unmarried; and three daughters who were wives of D. G. Bardin, Willard Gaulding, and Jack Cole. Children of Rev. John Ernest Summer and his wife are: David Bardin (1902-____) and Lillie Belle who married F. L. Minnix.

Michael Wertz and wife, Susan Summer, had children: William (b. ____ d. 1858) who married (1) _____ and (2) to Elizabeth Suber; Henry who married Drucilla Spearman; Michael (1829-1907) who married Elizabeth Stephens (1840-1910); Jonothan who married Nancy Spearman; Eliza who married (1) John Taylor and (2) to John Elmore; Caroline who married William B. Reagin; Susan who married George Long.

William Wertz (son of Michael and Susan) had by his first wife the following children: Burr, Sallie who married a Walton, Henry, Susan, Rebecca, Mary Jane. He had by his second wife a son Daniel who married and lived in Newberry; afterwards, moving to Georgia.

Henry Wertz and wife, Drucilla Spearman, had children: William who married Lucretia Hendrix whose children were Henry Edward (he married Annie Lake), William, Eloise (she married Dan Dehardt), Walter (he died young), Minnie Lee who married William H. Eddy and had son, Henry.

Michael Wertz and wife, Elizabeth Stephens, had children: Ida (1859-1862); Alice (1861-____) married J. Fred Schumpert; Emma (1863-____) who married Dr. James M. Kibler, a practicing physician in Newberry for many years; Addie (1866-1872) Fannie (1869-____) who married James L. Moorhead; Maggie (1872-____) who married Prof. F. L. Eyer, of Limestone College, Gaffney, S. C.; Ernest (1874-1879); Rosa Belle (1876-1889); Clarence (1878-____) who married Maude Chisholm; and Florence (1880-____) who married Dr. R. M. Dacus, of Greenville, S. C.

Jonathan Wertz and wife, Nancy Spearman, had children: Michael who married Clementine Nance and had son, Frank Moon Wertz; Ella who married Dr. Brooks and lived in North Carolina — with large family; Alice who married _____ Bozeman (they moved to Texas); Drucilla who married Yancey Floyd and had Guy, Ruth, and another daughter who married Grover Davenport; Leila who married Thomas Bryant, at Orangeburg, S. C.; John who married Lee Hentz Huff; Samuel who married a Mathis; Rufus who married Sally Wertz and had John, Broadus, and Nancy (wife of Junius Long); Lula who married Latimer W. Long.

Caroline who married William B. Reagin had children: James B. who married Tranquilla Long and had, Elizabeth (wife of Elisha Cureton), Mary (wife of William Beatty), Sallie (wife of Clark Abrams), Phoebe (wife of Warren Abrams), Rose (wife of Ben Sease); John W.

SUMMER (continued)

who married Cordelia Golding and had, Robert, William, Maggie, and Dorothy; Robert T. G. who married Nina Harmon; G. Burton who married Jane Counts and had, Marie (wife of Allen Crosson), and Grace; Elizabeth; Henry — killed in War Between the States — not married; Susan who married J. David Suber.

George Long and Susan Wertz had children: Latimer W. who married (1) _____ and (2) to Lula Wertz; George M. who married Anne Davis; Elizabeth who married Herbert Boulware; Frances Ellen. Latimer W. Long and his second wife, Lula Wertz, had children: Latimer who died young; George Wren who married Elizabeth _____ and lived at Greenville, S. C.; Nora who died young; Frank (moved to Florida); William who married Nancy Holt; Oscar who married Toche Cobb; Bessie; Nancy who married Drayton Ham; and Horace. George M. Long and wife, Annie Davis, lived in Florida; had children: Eugone, Ethel, Rose, Georgie. Herbert Boulware and wife, Elizabeth, had children: James who married Madeline Davenport; Sudie; Cynthia who died young; George P. who married Alda Patterson; and Herbert L. who married _____ Eleazar.

Dr. James M. Kibler and wife, Emma Wertz, had children: Bessie who married Frank W. Chapman who live at Greenwood, S. C. — their children, James Kibler and Francis, Jr.; Julia; Lillian; Annie who married Vernon Wheeler, of the U. S. Army; Mary who married Henry E. Holley and had, Elizabeth and Henry E., Jr.

James L. Moorhead and wife, Fannie Wertz, had children: Paul who married Helen Snead; Lucile who married George Harris; Douglass who married Ida _____; Claude who married Louise _____; Frances who married Hugh Moorhead; Fred; Margaret; James; Florence.

Clarence F. Wertz and wife, Maud Chisholm, had children: Margaruete, Mary and Frances.

Dr. Robert M. Dacus and wife, Florence Wertz, had children: Robert Mabry Dacus, Jr.

J. Fred Schumpert and wife, Alice Wertz, had children: Juanita who married W. T. A. Sherard, of Iva, S. C.; Homer W. who married Louise Hipp; Gillete who married F. Wingfield Webster (live in Florida); Fredna. Children of W. T. A. Sherard and wife, Juanita Schumpert: Alice Virginia, Ethel, Juanita, Laura.

The daughter of John Adam Summer, Sr., pioneer, Mary Magdelina, married George Bathalomew Minnick. It is said they had seven children and at one time owned 100 acres of land in Greenville District, S. C. A brother, John Adam Minnick, died in 1785 leaving by will some of his property to his brother's (George Barthalomew) seven children. In that year John Adam left a daughter, Mary Catherine, his mother, Rosannah Minnick, his widow, Barbara Minnick, and a sister named Mrs. Mary Catherine Freind. Another brother was, probably, John Minnick, Sr., who lived down on Crims Creek, Lexington District, who gave his son, John Minnick, Jr., 100 acres of land in same section.

Copy of Original will of Francis Summer, Revolutionary War Patriot, and son of the pioneer, John Adam Summer, Sr.

THE STATE OF SOUTH CAROLINA.

"In the Name of God, A men — I, Fra^s Summer, of the State aforesaid, and Lexington District, being sick and weak of body, but of perfect mind and memory, do make and ordain this my last will and testament, that is to say, —"

"First - I recommend my soul to Almighty God that gave it and my body to be buried in Christian-like manner, according to the Holy Rights of our Church — and as touching such wordly estate, wherewith it has pleased God to help me in this life, I give and bequeath in the manner following:

"Firstly, I give and bequeath to my beloved wife, Christina Summer, one hundred acres of land to be taken off of a tract of one hundred fifty called Heuber's Tract, to begin at a pine station on the East side of the Barn, thence across the plantation to a White Oak on the public road, then strait on to the Creeke a small distance below the mouth of the Cool Branch, thence as the line will direct, to one hundred acres the upper part of S. Tract, also one mare, saddle and bridle.

"Secondly, I give to John Adam Summer and Jacob Long to one share out of my estate, viz: after the remainder of my estate is sold and equally divided, the two above named to draw one share between them.

SUMMER (continued)

"Thirdly, I give unto my beloved son, Abram", Summer, one hundred and fifty dollars, to be had out of my estate for the purpose of purchasing land —

"Fourthly, I give unto my beloved daughters, namely, Sarah and Mary Summer, each of them one cow and a feather-bed; then the remainder part of my estate to be sold at auction at a reasonable amount, then all my heirs to stand back until my two sons, John and Joseph Summer, receive four hundred dollars each (extra), then the remainder to be equally divided between my wife and all my children, except the above named J. A. Summer and Jacob Long, to have but the one share between them as above mentioned. Also, my desire is that my two sons, John and Joseph, to have sufficient schooling to be levied out of their portion.

"I, also, do nominate Major William Summer and Benedict Mayer my sole Executors of this my last Will and Testament, and do hereby utterly disallow, revoke, and disannul all and every other former testament, will and legacy bequeathed and executed by me in any wise. Before this time named, willed, and bequeathed, verifying and confirming this and no other to be my last will and testament.

""In witness whereof, I have hereunto set my hand and seal this 27th day of Jan'y. in the Year of Our Lord, 1810 — and in the Thirty Fourth year of the America Independence.

Signed, Sealed, Published, pronounced and   Fr$\underline{d}$ Summer (L S)
Delivered by this F. Summer, as his last
will and testament in the presence of
        Peter Dickert,
        Rob't. Glen.

Those of the name Summer who served in the Confederate Army, in the 13th Regiment, Company H, S. C. V. (From records of the S. C. Historical Commission)
     Adam L. Summer, 3rd Sargeant.
     George W. Summer, Corporal, died 1862,
     George Michael Summer,
     James H. Summer,
     J. Franklin Summer,
     W. Thomas Summer,
     John Henry Summer,
     John George Summer,
     William L. Summer

SUMMERS

Rev. Joseph Summers, a Quaker preacher came from Maryland to Ninety Six District about the year 1760 and settled on Bush River. He was twice married, his second wife, Eleanor, was the daughter of Major Thomas W. Waters, a Revolutionary War patriot and Officer, in the S. C. militia. His children were: William, Ellen Waters (married a Lee), Cassendra (married a Briggs), Anne (married a Wells), Dorcas (married a Coleman), John (married Rose Waters), Jesse (married Sarah Coate), and James, and Mary (wife of Rev. Giles Chapman).

James Summers (son of Rev. Joseph), made will June 7, 1826, proven in court Aug. 7, 1826, and died 1826 in Edgefield County. He left widow, Elizabeth, and children: Allen, William, John, James, Ruth (wife of Isaac Arnold), Elizabeth, Eleanor, Mary, and Rebecca Black.

William Summers, Sr. (son of Rev. Joseph), died in 1816, leaving widow, Susannah who died in 1829, and children as follows: Joseph W., William, Alce (wife of Robert Worthington), Eleanor (wife of Henry Cooper), Hezekiah, Tabitha (widow of Thomas Worthington), Samuel, Elijah T., and Mary (wife of Robert Pitts). His wife was Susannah Teague whom he married in 1777.

Hezekiah Summers (son of William, Sr.), died about 1823 and left children: Susan (wife of James Chalmers), Amanda, Sampson, Jacob, Elizabeth, and Henry. His wife was Helen Pope.

Elijah T. Summers (son of William, Sr.), married in 1807 to Margaret Peaster. He died and left widow, Margaret, and children: Susannah, Mary Ann, and Rebecca. He died aged 96 years in the State of Alabama. Mary Ann married a Hunter and lived in Alabama.

John Summers (son of Rev. Joseph) married Rosannah Waters, daughter of Col. Philemon Waters, a brave and distinguished Revolutionary War soldier and Officer of the South Carolina Militia. He made a will in year 1832 and died about 1836, leaving widow, and children: Nancy C. (wife of Peter Hair), Eleanor C. Waters, Rhoda W. Kilgore, Rosannah C. Gary, William, John W., and Mary B. Leavell. Children of Mary B. Leavell were: Larkin D. Griffin, William C. Griffin, and Permelia C. Kilgore (wife of Warren J. Kilgore). Mrs. Nancy Hair died Feb. 7th, 1836, just previous to the death of her father, and left children as follows: Rosannah F. (died 1836), Mathias (died Feb. 7th, 1847), John S., Nancy C., and Mary Frances (wife of William Chapman). Mrs. Rosannah Waters, widow, married Stanhope H. Harris.

John W. Summers (son of John), died January 13th, 1852, leaving three sisters: Ellen C. Waters, Rhoda W. Kilgore, and Nancy Caroline Hair. Rhoda married James Kilgore.

William Summers (son of John), died about 1847 and left children: John, Philemon, Benjamin Franklin, Mickeal, Rosannah, Drayton, Henry Clinton, William, and Permelia.

John Summers (son of James who was the son of Rev. Joseph) was born in 1805 in Edgefield County. He married Tabitha Spearman of Newberry County. They moved to Alabama. Their children were: Edmund, Margaret, Laura, Thomas, George, John, Joseph, William, James, and Amanda -- all lived in Alabama.

Joseph W. Summers (son of William, Sr.) moved to Georgia, remained there a short time, and then located in Texas before the Civil War. He married Elizabeth Lynch.

Mrs. Eleanor Worthington, after the death of her husband, married John Edmundson and moved to Giles County, Tennessee. Mrs. Alce Worthington, after the death of her husband, married Allen Fuller who was a Universalist preacher. She had a daughter, Harriet Worthington, who married a Mr. Williams in 1838, and had two daughters.

Samuel Summers (son of William, Sr.) married in 1803 to Delilah Gary, daughter of John and Anna Gary. They moved to Georgia about 1835. They had two sons and a daughter, one of the sons being a young married man when they left South Carolina.

WAITS (Wait)

John Wait was a Revolutionary War soldier, serving in the Continental Army in Virginia. He was pensioned April 17th, 1834, aged 77 years, while a resident in South Carolina.

John Wait made will dated March 28, 1829 and died about 1835 leaving widow, Frances, and children: Mariah (wife of James Sims), Phillip, Franklin, Peachy, Polly, and Fanny. Mariah Sims died early and left children: John Sims and Rhoda Sims. Polly married William Graves and had children: Nancy S., Elizabeth M., Joseph F., James T., Phillip H., Peachy K., Obed W., William, and Polly F. Graves. Franklin Wait died in 1838 and left widow, Sarah, and two minor children, John Travis Wait and Ludy Wait. Fanny Wait married James Anderson. Peachy Wait married William Crocker, then they moved to Alabama, and afterwards to Tenn. Mrs. Frances Wait died in 1844.

Philip Wait married Rhoda Powell, daughter of William and Nancy (Bobo) Powell. She died before he did, and he died between the years 1840 and 1850, leaving children: P. C., Belinda (wife of Robert Todd), Peachy (wife of J. Richard Tenney), Maria (wife of James Clardy), Rhoda Frances (wife of a Hamilton), John C., and Lilly F.

John Wait made will Sept. 7, 1805 and died 1805 in Abbeville County, leaving widow, Ann, and children: Henry, Thomas, Sophia, John, Robert, Netty, Betty, Peggy, Francis, and Aaron.

Aaron Wait (son of John) died about 1833 in Abbeville County, leaving widow, Nancy, and six children: John, David, Henry, Samuel, Catherine, and Ann.

John T. Wait died about 1860 in Anderson County. He left widow, Rutha.

William Waits and Samuel Waits (brothers) lived on Saluda River in Newberry County. They were, probably, sons of John Waits who was granted land in 1786 on Hamblin Creek, branch of Saluda River. John Waits and his wife, Sarah, conveyed lands on the North side of Saluda River in 1808 to Philemon Waters.

William Waits made will dated September 9th, 1841 and died Sept. 2nd, 1843 leaving widow, Mary, and children: John (his wife, Amy), James (his wife, Lydia), Simeon (his wife, Judy), Simpson (his wife, Rose Sealy), Benjamin (his wife, Sarah), Drucilla (wife of William Langford), Vincent (his wife, Martha), Silas K. (his wife, Martha Anne).

Simeon Waits moved to Franklin County, Ala. James Waits and wife, William and Drucilla Langford, moved to Lauderdale County, Ala. Silas K. and his mother, Mrs. Mary Waits, went to Coosa County, Ala.

James Waits (son of William) married Lydia _____ and had children: Simeon (in Louisana), Kathrine (married first to a Beard, second to a Buckingham), Martha (died unmarried at Florence, Ala. in 1901), Caroline (married Frank Hewett), Belton (killed at Gravelly Springs early in the Civil War), Drayton (married and moved to Texas), Elizabeth (married a Boone), Lee B. (married Henrietta Turner), Shelton (married Stella Wood and died in Dallas, Texas), Amelia (married C. C. Stribling) died at Clifton, Tenn.

Samuel Waits died in 1858 and his widow, Rosannah, died soon after, in the same year. Their children were: Nancy (wife of Allen Ballentine), Sarah, William, Emmanuel, Rosannah (wife of Jesse Free), Mark, Martha (wife of Jacob Fulmer), Levi, John, Mary Ann (wife of John Fulmer), Samuel T. Levi and Samuel T. moved to Alabama. John went to Georgia. John and Mary Ann Fulmer moved to La Feyette County, Miss. Drayton Waits was the son of Rosannah Free.

Levi Waits (son of Samuel) was born 1800 and died in 1886. He married Elizabeth Fulmer and had children as follows: Eliza Ann (died young), William Ivey (he had six children, Patrick, John, William, Belton, Susan, Viola who married Hunter Shaw), James Wesly (he had children, Joseph, William, James, Wesly, John and Levi), George Pinkney (he was born in South Carolina in 1832 and died in Alabama in 1917), Rosa Ann, Mark (he had children, George Belton, Elizabeth who married a Shaw), Albert (he had children, Stanley, Walter, Annie who married a Pope, Ada who married a Harmon, and another daughter who married a Perry).

WATERS

The earliest record of the Waters family goes back to the Fifteenth century in England. At a later period, about 1626, one John Waters of Eastcote, in the County of Northamptonshire, England, made will in which he named five sons: Thomas, Joseph, Ambrose, James, and Samuel. Also, two daughters: Elizabeth and Ann. He named six grandchildren: John Waters, William Waters, Judith Waters, Esyer Waters, Richard Pinchard, and John Pinchard. His wife, Alice, is also mentioned.

WATERS (continued)

Samuel Waters (son of John) was born in 1616 and died 1665, leaving widow, Anne, who died in 1700. They lived in St. Sepulcheres Parish, London, and had issue: John, Samuel, Elizabeth, Thomas, and a daughter who married William Goodwin. John came to America and settled in Gloucester County, Va. where he received patent for land in Sept. 1678. He removed to Rappahanock County, Va. His wife was Arabella _____. He died in 1694, and administration was granted to John Waters Dec. 10th, 1695.

Samuel Waters (son of Samuel) married Margaret _____.

Elizabeth Waters (daughter of Samuel) married William Overton and they moved to Virginia. Their daughter, Barbara, married John Winston.

Thomas Waters, the tobacco merchant of London married Anne _____.

Edward Waters (of England) married Grace O'Neil. He died in 1630. Their children were: Margaret, William (he was born 1624 in Va. and died 1685). William married Mrs. George Clarke, a widow, in Virginia, and had children: Richard, John, Edward, Thomas, Obediance, William, Jr. William, Jr. had sons, Thomas and James. (Above data furnished by a descendant).

The first settlers of this name that came to Ninety Six District, South Carolina, were Thomas Waters and Philemon Waters, brothers. They came from Virginia before the Revolution, and were brave soldiers and officers in the S. C. militia during the war.

Philemon Waters was a member of Capt. George Mercer's Company (Washington's Regiment) from May 29th to July 29th, 1754, and of Capt. Andrew Lewis' Company of detachments from July 29, to Sept. 29, 1754, in Virginia. He was born in Prince William County, Va. Sept 1st, 1734 and died in Newberry County, S. C. March 29, 1796. He was first Capt. of company of State militia in South Carolina during the first part of the Revolutionary War, and afterwards was promoted to Lieut. Colonel of Militia. He had several children, some of whom were: Rose (wife of John Summers), Philemon B., and others.

Major Thomas Waters was a Major of a battalion of State troops during the Revolutionary War. One of his daughters, Eleanor, married Rev. Joseph Summers. He had a son Philemon who died March 4th, 1818 leaving widow, Ruth, and children as follows: Jonothan D., Thomas, Harriet, and Eliza. His widow married Starling Baldree.

Fleming Waters died in 1847 in Anderson County, S. C., leaving widow, Rebecca, and children: Ilzan, Williford, Macklin, Sarah E. (wife of Thomas J. Davis), Ida (wife of Willis Stack), Mary R. (wife of F. M. Moss), wife of E. J. Giles, F. A. (wife of Y. T. McAllister), Martha (wife of a Mitchel), and John A. Children of Willis and Ida Stack were, Fleming Stack and Thomas Stack.

Mrs. Mary Waters made will dated July 4th, 1792 and died about 1798, leaving children: David, Rachel Beel, Elizabeth Lombes, Sarah Porter, Martha Burne, and Janett.

Langdon Waters married Margaret Musgrove, daughter of Edward Musgrove. She and her brother William Musgrove, and her sisters, Rachel, Leah, and Linney, sold lands at Musgrove's Mills, at a Sheriff's sale in year 1796.

Thomas Willoughby Waters was appointed Tax Collector in Newberry County in year 1788, in October.

Wilkes B. Waters and his wife, Anna (she was daughter of Levi Manning) made suit in equity in year 1812.

Bordwin Waters and wife, Jean, of Spartanburg District, conveyed land to Benjamin Byrd of Laurens District, on Warrior Creek, in year 1794.

David Waters died in Feb. 1819 in Newberry County. He left widow, Elizabeth, and children: Mark, David, Daniel M., and Mary Ann Elizabeth. The widow married Edward Stephens.

Philemon B. Waters died in 1807 leaving widow, Sarah, and children: Mary, Robert and Philemon B. A brother was Wilkes B. Waters. Mary married in 1825 to Philip Schoppert. Philemon B., Jr. died soon after the death of his father.

WERTS

In the Parish Dielstorff, Germany, there lived about the period of 1650 to 1700 a family of Wirtz, who were prominent in affairs and a people of some influence. At a later date, in the year 1744, one of their descendants, the Rev. Heinrich Wirtz, came to America with a colony of Germans and Swiss. He was a preacher of the Reformed Church and it was his desire to aid his people in their trip to the New World, to lands that had been painted in glowing words, relieving them of the religious persecutions that still prevailed in the old country. This colony embarked from Rotterdam and landed at Philadelphia, came directly to South Carolina, their determined location before leaving.

The section to which they first came and settled was Orangeburg District, probably near old Granby in Lexington County, where many of the Germans and Swiss were settling. They lived there a short time and some moved up to the section of Pomaria. According to the records, one George Henry Werts (he was probably the Rev. Heinrich Wirtz as the locations of settlements are the same) received a land grant from King George II of England, including 150 acres on Crimm's Creek, a tributary of Broad River and between Broad and Saluda Rivers. This was in the year, 1753. In the same year Catherine Werts (the wife or sister of Henry Werts) received a land grant from the English government covering 50 acres adjoining that of Henry Werts.

One reason given for moving farther up was that they were having trouble with the Indians and were informed the tribes in the Upper Fork were not giving the people as much trouble. However, they did not have any bed of roses as some of the letters written back home indicated. One Boni wrote to the people in Pratteln: "South Carolina is hot, sandy land, where only Welsh corn and rice grow. Good bread is so expensive that poor people cannot buy it." The Rev. Mr. Wirtz received a letter from friends in the old country wanting to come over and join them. His reply was that they were all keenly disappointed as they did not come into the land of Caanan as they expected, and he advised against coming. Another wrote to the homeland that "Carolina is a foul land, no good fruit grows and wheat has to be bought from Pennsylvania, otherwise there is no bread but pimpernickle."

The Rev. Heinrich Wirtz (Henry Werts) was probably the father of the two settlers in the Dutch Fork, John and George Henry. These two brothers are mentioned in the "Annals of Newberry" as Revolutionary soldiers, serving as Captains of state militia. A story is related of their near capture by a band of Tories when they were at home one day in the summer of 1780. The band surprised them at their home but they escaped to the tall, thick bushes of Crim's Creek. While there in hiding the band would go up and down the creek searching, and thrusting swords through the bushes in close proximity to them. They afterwards did valiant service in the army. (S. C. Hist. Com. lists the two brothers as privates in the American Army during the Revolutionary War).

George Henry married Molly Singley (daughter of the pioneer, Martin Singley, Sr.). They lived and died near Prosperity within a mile of Kibler's Bridge. Their children were: John, Michael, David, Adam, Mary Elizabeth (married David Sheely), Mary (married Jacob Mayer). Mary Magdaline (married Matthias Barre), Christina (married John Mayer) and Catherine. There was an older son, who died unmarried, named Henry. The other sons moved to the northwestern section of Newberry County and located near Bush River and Saluda River. Many of the descendants of these four brothers form an industrious citizenship around the town of Silver Street and some have moved to other sections.

Michael Werts (son of Henry) died 1853, in Newberry County. He left widow, Louisa, and children: Eliza Taylor, Caroline Reagan, Susan Long, Jonothan, Michael, Henry, Martha and Adelaide.

Mrs. Eliza Taylor (widow) married John Elmore, 1856, and left children: Susan C. Taylor, Calvin S. Taylor, and Susan Long (wife of George Long).

John, son of George Henry Werts, Jr., married Eve Riser and had Elizabeth, Christina (wife of Peter Rikard), Sarah (wife of Michael Fellers), John, Susan (wife of Solomon Kinard), and William. William married, first, Elizabeth, daughter of Samuel Bowers, and second, the widow of Levi Wheeler. William and his first wife were parents of James, Samuel and William and Lavinia (wife of John Mathis), Leonora Alice (wife of John W. Hartman), Sallie Eve (wife of A. M. Counts) and Bettie.

Michael, son of George Henry, Jr., married Susan, daughter of William Summer, and had Michael, Jr., Henry, Jonathan, Elizabeth, Carolina and Susan. Michael Jr. married Elizabeth Stephens and were parents of the following children: Alice (widow of the late J. Fred Schumpert, sergeant-at-arms of the state senate), Emma (wife of Dr. James M. Kibler of Newberry),

WERTS (continued)

Fannie (wife of James L. Morehead of Gaffney), Margaret (wife of Prof. J. L. Eyre (director of music department, Meredith College, Raleigh, N. C.), Clarence (lately living at the Werts home in Newberry, but at present in Greenville, S. C.), Florence (wife of Dr. R. M. Dacus of Greenville).

Henry and Jonathan married sisters, Nancy and Drucilla Spearman. Elizabeth married John Elmore. Caroline married William B. Reagin and had James B., John W., Robert T., G. Burton and Elizabeth C. One son, Henry W., was killed in the Confederate War. Susan married George Long and had several children, two of whom were Latimer W. and George M. Long (later moved to Florida). Michael Werts, Sr., was married three times. By his second wife he had a daughter, Adelaide, who was the wife of Thomas M. Paysinger.

David Werts, son of George Henry, Jr., married Mary Lever and had J. Belton, Jacob L., John A., Frances, David B. and Rosannah. Jacob L. (married Alice Maffett), John A. (married Nora Kinard), Frances (married T. J. Maffett), David B. (married, first, Hettie Smith and had Eugene (formerly County Superintendent of Education of Newberry), Eoline (wife of Clarence T. Summer of Newberry) and two other daughters, who married and moved away. Rosannah married Dr. Andrew M. Wicker and had two daughters, who married and moved to Alabama.

Adam, son of George Henry, Jr., married Elizabeth Hope and had David (married Mattie Blair but had no children), Andrew (married Mollie Noble and left one son), Katherine (who married John M. Livingston and were parents of Dan Livingston of Silverstreet and the grandparents of Julius J. Langford and Mrs. White Fant of Newberry and of Capt. W. S. Langford, now of Wichita Falls, Texas). Captain Langford was an officer in the Spanish-American War as captain of a company of South Carolina troops.

Jacob Werts married Rebecca _____ and died in 1873. No children are mentioned in this will, and David Werts, Sr. is named executor.

John Werts, patriot of the Revolutionary War, married Anne Catherine Hair, daughter of Peter and Anne Hair. They lived and died in the same section as the brother, George Henry. He died in 1842 and his wife, Anne Catherine, died in 1827. According to the will, which is filed in the probate judge's office in the Newberry courthouse, he left his property to the following children: Henry, John, Mary (wife of J. W. Sheely), Barbara (wife of John Berley), Elizabeth (wife of John Epting), Mollie (wife of William Sheely), Christine (wife of William Kinard), and grandchildren of a deceased daughter, Adam and David Minick. Another son, Elias, died in 1836. The "Annals of Newberry" mentions a son, William, who is the father of the Rev. J. H. W. Wertz (surname changed to Wertz), a Lutheran minister who died in 1883 while pastor in Orangeburg County. The name in "The Annals" was probably intended for John, as William is not mentioned in the will and several of the children of John located in Edgefield County. The Rev. J. H. W. Wertz was the father of the Rev. Joseph Q. Wertz (married Mattie V. Houseal of Newberry, 1881), a Lutheran minister who preached at Lexington, also at Orangeburg and in his father's former pastorate in Orangeburg County, and then in North Carolina, where he died at China Grove, in 1908. Other children of the Rev. J. H. W. Wertz included: Jesse, Mary (married the Rev. Joab Edwards), Elizabeth (married an Etheridge), Georgia (married Edward Derrick), Hassie (married Leppard Nichols). Two of the sons, Preston S. B. Wertz and Noah W. Werts, lived in Orangeburg.

Henry, son of Capt. John Werts, married Elizabeth Lever and had Dr. D. Henry, who was a practicing physician near Slighs; G. Paul, who is the father of Johnnie Werts, the famous baseball player; Edward, W. Anderson, Henry M., and Wesley (killed in the Confederate War). Elizabeth and John Epting were the parents of the late Capt. George Epting of Pomaria and of Dr. Harrison Epting, who died at Williamston; the grandparents of the late G. M. Boyd Epting of Newberry, son of the Rev. John Epting. Barbara and John Berley were the parents of Susan, who was the wife of A. M. Bowers. Christina and William Kinard were the parents of Elizabeth, wife of Major Jacob Epting of St. Paul's, and a daughter who married Capt. H. H. Riser of Edgefield. Major Jacob Epting and his wife, Elizabeth, had Dr. Berley Epting, who died in Greenwood; the Rev. Monroe J. Epting, a Lutheran minister, who died in Savannah, Ga.; L. I. Epting of Newberry, Bunyan Epting, who now lives in Georgia; Julius, who died in past few years, Charles and Thomas Epting, who died near St. Paul's Lutheran Church.

Several of the descendants of the Rev. Heinrich Wirtz were ministers of the gospel, some were physicians, merchants and planters. Wherever they were living and are now, they have shown that same spirit of service and leadership manifested in their pioneer ancestor.

WICKER

There were two pioneer settlers who came from Germany to South Carolina: Matthias Weisker and Johannes Frederich Weisker. Matthias Weisker received a Royal Bounty Grant for 200 acres of land near Broad River, in year 1755. This indicates he had wife and three children in that year. Johannes Frederich Weisker received a Royal Bounty Grant for 100 acres on Second Creek, in year 1763. This shows he was married but had no children in that year. Using the English phonetic spelling they changed the spelling of their name, to Matthias Wicker and John Frederick Wicker. John Frederick later signed his name, John Henry Wicker.

Matthias Wicker who married Mary Sebla _____ died about 1785-88, having made a will dated 1778, in which he named four children, as follows: John Adam, Simon, Mary and Katherine. John Adam died about 1827, leaving widow, Katherine (she died 1834) and children, viz: Mary (wife of Michael Dickert), Elizabeth (wife of David Cromer), Sally (wife of Henry Dickert), Katherine (wife of Simon Cromer), Anna (wife of Jacob Setzler), Christina (wife of Jacob Fulmer), John (died young), Abram, and Matthias. Simeon Cromer (son of Christian) and wife, Katherine, had children: Elizabeth, Susannah, George, Thomas and Adam. Simon Wicker died about 1845, leaving children: John Adam, David, Margaret (wife of Abram Chapman), Christina (wife of William Chapman). John Adam (son of Simon) married Elizabeth Metz, daughter of John Metz and his wife, Mary M. (Koone) Metz. Mary M. Metz was the daughter of Henry Koone, Sr. and wife, Catherine Eve (Epting) Koone. It is probable that this John Adam was a son of Simon Wicker, Jr., the son of Simon, Sr. Simon, Sr. was the son of Matthias Wicker, Sr. whose son, Matthias Wicker, Jr. died about 1788, leaving widow, Mary Sebla.

John Adam Wicker, Jr., son of Simon Wicker, Sr. married Mary (Cannon) Epting, widow of Jacob Epting, and had children: George Adam and Andrew Middleton (twins), born 1817; John Adam, b. 1820; David L., b. 1822; Thomas V., b. 1824; Jacob Lemuel, b. 1827.

John Henry Wicker died about 1819, in Newberry County. Children by his first wife were: Rachel (wife of George Moyer), Christian, Lucy who married Stewart, Kate (wife of Joseph Turner), Magdeline, Henry, and probably others who died young. A tradition is he had 12 children by each of his two wives. His second wife was Elizabeth Cromer, daughter of Frederick and Syble Cromer, who died about 1824; their children were: Syble (wife of Christopher Singley), Elizabeth (wife of Jaurele or Jacob Richmond), Barbara (wife of John Hall), Rosana (wife of John Morris), Agnes (wife of George Cromer), Daniel (married Mary Cromer), Elias, Uriah, Abram, John (he married _____ Cline), Waldrod, Michael, Henry, Magdeline. The two youngest were Abram and Uriah. the son, Henry, died in September, 1805, leaving two minor children, Elizabeth (wife of Daniel Keller), and Mary (wife of Andrew Cromer). Jacob Richmond and wife, Elizabeth, had children: John, Missouri (married Dec. 17, 1868 to Nathan Mars), Frances Eugenia (married December 17, 1868 to James Hubbard.

John Uriah Wicker died in 1808, and his widow, Catherine, married John Peter Kinard. She was the daughter of Mrs. Christina Sligh. He left no children. John Peter Kinard died in 1828, and his wife, Catherine, died in 1826.

Uriah Wicker (son of John Henry), died about 1824. His distributees were brothers and sisters.

Michael Wicker (son of John Henry by his second wife) died about 1861. His widow having already died, he left children: Fannie (wife of Levi Livingstone), Anderson, and Peter T. J. Anderson left children: David W., Melvina L., Martha F., Louisa E., Sarah C., and William P. Peter T. J. Wicker was father of Drayton T. and others.

Hiram Wicker, son of Christian Wicker, married Martha Koone, daughter of John and Margaret (Cromer) Koone. He died in March, 1874, and his widow died in same month and year. They left children: Lavania Frances who married Jacob Richardson, Elizabeth C., Daniel C. and Walker W.

Christopher Singley and wife, Syble Wicker (daughter of John Henry), had several children. (See Singley Family line).

John Uriah Wicker (above) who died in August, 1808, left his property to his brothers and sisters, viz: Magdeline who married George W. Rhiddlehuber who died young leaving two children, Sarah (married Adam Fulmer) and John; (Magdeline, the widow, married Matthias Hentz); Lucy who married Conrad Suber and died leaving children, Elizabeth Halfacre, Henry Suber, Martin Suber, David Suber, Jacob Suber, Rebecca Suber, George Suber; John Wicker who died young and left widow, Elizabeth, and children, Matthias, John, Andrew, and David; Agnes who married Charles Bundrick and had children, Elizabeth (wife of David Hentz), Polly (wife of George Sligh), Nicholas, Sally, David. David Bundrick died early and left widow, Polly, and two minor children, Alfred and Anne; Gasper Wicker who died and left widow, and children: Hannah (wife of Craven Lane), Polly (wife of William Kelly), Elizabeth (wife of Henry Rickard), Andrew who had

WICKER (continued)

died previously but left son, Andrew, Jr.; and Ruby Wicker who never married. Matthias Wicker, son of John, died about 1883-84, leaving widow, Rachel, and children: James Monroe, Thomas Jefferson, and Henry Pinckney. Gasper Wicker died about year 1813.

Isaac Wicker died August 4, 1850, leaving the following brothers and sisters: Sarah (she died 1852), Jacob, Andrew, Samuel, Henry, and Mary (she married John Lominick). All were children of Waldred Wicker.

Jacob Wicker died about 1890, leaving widow, Ann Elizabeth, and children: Henry Monroe, John P., Thomas L., Nancy Suber, Sarah Felker, and Margaret C. Harmon.

There were two Wickers who moved to Mississippi — Enoch G. and Peter. Enoch G. married Barbara, daughter of Adam Metts.

WILSON

Francis Wilson died 1816 leaving widow, Jane, and children: David, Francis, John, Hugh, and William.

John Wilson made will Oct. 16, 1795 and died 1796 leaving brother, James Wilson, and sisters, Janett Alexander, Elizabeth Wilson, and Sarah Walker. Other legatees were: Martha Figs, John Moore (a cousin). Executors: Daniel Clary, William Summers, and John Smith. He left all his lands and tenements in Ireland, County Antrim, Barrantre of Tome, Townland of Cloughan, to be sold and proceeds divided among the legatees.

John Wilson made will April 7th, 1794 and died same year leaving widow, Elizabeth, and children: Sarah and Mary. He also left brothers: Thomas and James Wilson.

George Wilson died about 1790. His widow, Mary, made will October 4, 1794 and died 1796 leaving children: Hester Denton, Mary, Margaret McClelland, Elizabeth, John, and Andrew.

Archibald Wilson died in Ireland in 1792, left as legatees, his six sisters, viz: Jane, Rachel, Margaret, Anne, Elizabeth, and Susannah. Another sister who was dead, was the mother of Mary Glasgow, wife of James Glasgow.

James Wilson, Sr. was a native of Ireland, and came to South Carolina after the Revolutionary War. He died in Newberry County on Dec. 29th, 1841 in the 99th year of his age. His wife, Janett, had died in Nov. 1826. Their children were: Elizabeth (wife of James Caldwell), James, Francis, and Thomas.

Francis Wilson (son of James, Sr.) died March 29, 1836, leaving children: James B., Jane (wife of William Martin), Sarah (wife of Thomas Chalmers), Elizabeth (wife of David Clary), Margaret (wife of Joseph Caldwell), Mary (wife of Dan Caldwell), Martha Caroline (wife of Wilson Caldwell), Thomas Edward, Harriet, and Anne (wife of John C. Higgins). Dan and Mary Caldwell moved to Chambers County, Alabama.

Thomas Wilson, Sr. made will June 5th, 1834 and died about 1838. He left widow, Mary, and a son, John, by a former marriage, and the following children by the second marriage (widow was 2nd wife): Elizabeth (wife of John Reid), Sarah (wife of George Boozer), Mary (wife of Adam Boozer, deceased), George, James R. (dead), and Thomas, Jr. Thomas Wilson, Jr. died on Dec. 11, 1831 and left no family. The children of James R. Wilson were: Young Thomas, Martha, Sarah, and Charlotte. Another legatee named in will of Thomas Wilson, Sr. was Lyda Nesbitt of New York.

John Wilson (son of Thomas) made will July 31, 1848 and died in December, 1848, leaving widow, Jane, and children: Martha Jane, John Caldwell, Thomas Robinson, Rosa Elizabeth Wilson, and Nancy Livingstone. Executor: James Maffett.

John Wilson made will dated Oct. 31st, 1821, proven in court Dec. 24th, 1821. He left widow, Mary, and four children: Elizabeth, Maria, Janett, and Marmaduke.

James Wilson (son of James, Sr.) known as "Elder James" Wilson, died on October 23rd, 1868, leaving the following children: James R., Thomas B., Maria (wife of Henry Cappleman), Amelia Hunter (dead), Thompson (dead), William C., Mary Jane (wife of Daniel Buzhardt), Eliza (wife of Calhoun F. Boyd), John (dead). He left one great grandchild mentioned in settlement of his estate, viz: Thomas Davis, son of Sarah Davis who was the daughter of Amelia Hunter.

James R. Wilson (son of "Elder James") married Susan A. and had children: Emma E., James E., Carrie E., Thomas B., and Frank. Carrie E. married a Buzhardt.

James B. Wilson (son of Francis), was born in 1805 and died 1864. He married first, Drucilla Ann Elizabeth Gilliam, by whom were several children. His second wife was Mary E. Wright by whom was a son, Frank Z. Wilson. He and his two wives and several children are buried

WILSON (continued)

at old Tranquil Graveyard.

William Wilson was born in Edgefield District and died in the town of Newberry on Nov. 15th, 1845. He held the office of Ordinary of Newberry County, and was an able and efficient officer. His wife died early, and at his death, there were two children who survived him, viz: James H. Wilson, and Sarah Ann. Sarah Ann married Burr J. Ramage, Esq. of Newberry. James H. Wilson was appointed trustee for Nancy Anderson (then Nancy Gent, wife of Daniel Gent). Her children by a former husband were: Mary A. Anderson and James W. Anderson.

Robert Wilson died in November, 1838 leaving widow, Elizabeth. Elizabeth was the widow of Clough S. Amos of Virginia, before her marriage with Robert Wilson.

Samuel Wilson died about 1820 and left widow, Sarah, and five children: John, Samuel, Elizabeth, Hugh, and Jane (wife of John Spence). John and Jane Spence had a son, James Spence.

Thomas Wilson (son of James, Sr.) died left children: James L., William, Jane (wife of Anthony Greer), Sarah (wife of Abner Hutchinson). Anthony Greer and wife, Jane, and Abner Hutchinson and wife, Sarah, moved to Chambers County, Ala.

James Wilson died 1812, in Abbeville District. He left widow, Tabitha, and children: Mary Robinson, Elizabeth McCrackin, James Henry, Nancy, and William.

Rutherford H. Wilson (of Jasper County, Miss.) was appointed attorney to represent Thomas and Christina (Dickert) Nelson, of the same County and State, in the settlement of the estate of Michael Dickert of Newberry County, year 1853.

Francis Wilson died in 1862 and left widow, Melvina, and children: Emma, Eliza, and Clementine.

James M. Wilson died October 24th, 1874, and left a child, Matilda Eva (about eight years old), and widow, Katie E. Wilson. Also, there were two other children, Maria P. and Lillian G. Wilson.

One James Wilson came from Abbeville County and settled in the Dutch Fork section of Newberry County where he died about 1850 to 1855. He left widow, Mary, and children as follows: George P., John W., James M., Mariliza Jane (wife of Dr. Harrison J. Epting), Mary Narcissa (wife of Jacob G. Setzler), Nancy (wife of George A. Swygert), Andrew A., Henry C., Walter S., Willis M., and Pettus C.

D. L. Wilson sold property to Thomas Lake in year 1854. He died about 1855 to 1860 and his widow, Hannah B., died within the same year. Their children were: L. Pauline, Rebecca, William Onston, De Lancy, George, and Herbert.

David Wilson (son of Francis), married Elizabeth Wilson. They moved to Anderson County from Newberry County, where his wife died in year 1828. They had a son, Francis A. The father afterwards married Lucretia Dollar and had a son and a daughter. They moved to Hamilton County, Ill. in 1832 where his wife died in 1834. Francis A. Wilson married Hadessah Boyd of Fayette County, Tenn. She died in 1879. He married again in 1883 to Cordelia Boyd.

One John Wilson died about 1783-85 in Abbeville District, leaving a widow, Catherine, and children, Ann and Jean, and a step-daughter, Sarah Lockhart.

Another John Wilson died about 1797 in Abbeville District, leaving a widow, Ruth, and children, John, James, Jacob, and Betsy.

Henry Wilson died about 1808 in Abbeville District. He left a widow, Betsy, and children. Robert Wilson died 1798 in Abbeville District. Michael Wilson died about 1790-94 in Abbeville District, and left a widow, Margaret, and children: John, Charles, and others.

Charles Wilson died 1811 in Abbeville District and left children: James, Michael, John, Andrew, Elizabeth, and Margaret.

WORTHINGTON

Samuel Worthington died about 1784 in Abbeville District. Children: Mary, Martha, Robert, John, Sarah, Benjamin, wife of Samuel Coat, wife of Isaac Toland, and Elijah.

Elijah (or Elisha) Worthington died in Edgefield District. He had married Milly Davis, daughter of Mrs. Mary Davis (widow), before 1797. Children: Samuel, Chesly, and others.

John Worthington (son of Samuel) married Elizabeth Davis (daughter of Mrs. Mary Davis and sister of Elisha's wife, Milly). He died about 1825, leaving the widow, Elizabeth, and children: Polly (wife of George Hunter), Margaret (wife of Francis Spearman), Betsy (wife of Samuel Chapman), Sarah (wife of Joseph Griffith), Fanny (wife of Isaac Herbert), Thomas,

WORTHINGTON (continued)

Chesley, John, Samuel, Rhoda (wife of Graves Spearman) — Rhoda died before 1825; Reuben (d).

Benjamin Worthington (son of Samuel) married Judith Steadman about year 1795; they moved to Hopkinsville, Ky. Children: John, Robert, Hepsibeth, Samuel, Mary, Rhoda, Elizabeth, George Pinckney, Sarah, Margaret, and Benjamin Pickney. About 1817 they moved from Ky. to Alabama.

Reuben C. Worthington (son of John) died 1825, same year father died. He was graduate of South Carolina College in 1818. He married Harriet B. Lorick (daughter of Jacob Lorick). He made will dated March 25, 1825. He left widow, and one son, Jacob Augustus Worthington.

Thomas Worthington (son of John) died about 1829, in Newberry District, leaving widow, Tabitha, and children: Harriet, John R., Amelia, and Marcus.

Jacob Augustus Worthington died 1844, leaving as heirs: his aunt, Esther Ruff (wife of Dr. P. B. Ruff); Mary (wife of S. L. Heller, Esq.); cousins, Eliza Lorick and Harriet Lorick (children of Claiborne Lorick) . . .

Dr. Benjamin R. Worthington died in November, 1859, in Newberry County, leaving widow, Almeda; brothers, Chesley and Samuel; sisters, Margaret Caldwell and Emily Leavell.

WISE AND WYSE
Collaborator: Fred Wyse (Written 1929)

In the valley of the Saluda River, soon to be flooded by the impounded purposes, are the original home places of many of the early settlers of that section known as the Dutch Fork of South Carolina. Among the early pioneers is the family of Weiss, now variously spelled Wise and Wyse, hailing from the archbishopric of Merseburg, Prussia, and tracing its ancestry through a one-time numerous and old knightly family dating back to 1293 when Conrad Wayse first came to notice in a record of a Naumburg bishop. Soon after 1740 it appears that the later members of the family lost their landed estates and became practically extinct in Germany.

The port records of Philadelphia register the names of Frederick Weiss and John Jacob Weiss as arriving August 31, 1750, on the ship Nancy, sailing from Rotterdam and later from Cowes, England.

The tradition runs that these two brothers decided to separate and reconnoiter their adopted country and at an appointed time to meet again in Charleston. After John failed to keep the appointment, Frederick Weiss decided to cast his lot with the Germans then beginning to occupy lands in the fork of Broad and Saluda Rivers.

Ernest Frederick Weiss was granted land in 1752 on the north side of Saluda River in Orangeburg District, where the highway now crosses from Chapin to Lexington, and until recent years this crossing had always been known as Wyse's ferry. There was another Wyse's ferry about 18 miles farther up the river where Capt. Joseph W. Wyse lived at a later date. Beyond the river in the Hollow creek section Michael Wise settled but if there was any relation between the two it was not known. However, it is probable that he was some relation of the Michael Weise of Harkerode in Mansfield, Germany. Also in Edgefield District a John Wise was an early settler and another John Wise in Spartanburg District. The descendants of this latter John Wise now spell their name Vice, thus using the phonetic German for the English spelling of the name. When the first census was taken in 1790, Frederick Weiss' name, and his son, George's, were listed as Vice, the census taker evidently writing it as pronounced to him.

Frederick Weiss (1752-1821) married Anna Barbara Bickley (1749-1837), daughter of John Jacob Bickley of Germany, and to them were born 13 children, according to the obituary of Barbara Weiss, who is credited with a progeny of 182 souls at the time of her death. One of the daughters married a Unger, the father of Jacob Under, and grandfather of Dr. Henry Unger; another married a Hiller, the father of elder John Hiller; one daughter married Thomas Wingard; another became the wife of Christopher Wiggus, now generally spelled Wiggins; a daughter, Crate, married Christian Harmon. Sophia Jane married the Rev. James Stingley, a Lutheran minister. George married Margaret Kelly, John married Elizabeth Kelly and Frederick married Julia Kelly. The three brothers marrying three sisters, daughters of George Kelly of Ireland.

The effort to anglicize the name at this time is doubtlessly responsible for the differences in spelling. It seems that the Irish spelling of Wyse was adopted by George and Frederick

WISE AND WYSE (continued)

due possibly to the influence of their Irish wives and the then prominence of the Irish wives in Waterford, but John adopted the English spelling of Wise, and the branches have since been distinguished by this variation of the name.

George Wyse (1781-1847) was the father of Keziah, who married Jesse Bates. Elizabeth and Sarah married brothers, Jacob and Fred Harmon, and moved to Attala County, Mississippi, and later to Guadalupe County, Texas. Mary married Dr. Patrick Todd and moved to Ocala, Fla., in 1858, and whose descendants later lived in McIntyre, Ga. Barbara never married, but lived with the Todds. Henry married Eliza Caughman and they had two children, George marrying Louisa Sutton and Margaret marrying James Hamilton. The other son of George, named Joseph, married Sarah Cayce of the old family of that name beyond the river from Columbia. Both Henry and Joseph moved to Mississippi. Joseph, who died in 1878, was the father of James, Harriett, Emanuel, Sarah (who married W. T. Kendall), Archibald, Margaret (who married E. F. Shuler and lived at Sallis, Miss.); Silas (married Mary Mitchell), they having one daughter, Elmer, and living in Meridian; John (married Lillian Wade) and their daughter married B. H. Bacon, and Joseph whose wife was Elizabeth Hayden.

The second Joseph's children were Mannie, who married Annie Belle Allen; Lagrove married Cora Robertson and their children are Frank and Zelda, Mary married W. D. Leslie, Cooper married Ditte Teague and their child was named Doris; Waldo, Maggie, Augustus and Wray died young.

John Wise (1779-1860) was the progenitor of most of the Newberry family. He was granted land in 1799 in Lexington, (this section at one time being a part of Newberry District) but later he moved to Newberry County, about 1841 for at that time he obtained an additional grant of 546 acres at McNary's ferry on the Saluda. John and his brother, George, were founders of St. Michael's Lutheran Church (in 1816), which split off from old Bethel on account of a disagreement over the question of the language in which the services should be held, the English or the German. The elder George Weiss and his father, Frederick, were members of Bethel Church, the first Lutheran Church in this section, as was also George Kelly, the father of the girls marrying the three Weiss brothers. On a Sunday during the sessions of an ecclesiastical meeting held in St. Michael's Church in 1816, the services were transferred for the day to old Bethel Church and it is related that while services in German were in progress within the church, other services were held outside in English and in the rear of the church still other services were being conducted for the slaves. Just what language was used for the Negroes is not recorded!

The Wises and Wyses appear to have been Lutherans from the very first and today they are strong in this denomination. In close proximity of their old homeplaces is the town of Little Mountain, where James Wise now lives, and it is said that all of the inhabitants are of this faith with but one exception. Another Lutheran Church founded by the members of this family is Corinth in Saluda County, which was organized and built by Capt. Joseph W. Wyse.

John Wise was the father of 12 children: David married Rosa Etheridge, Levi died young. Joel, who died in 1895, married first, Melissa Schumpert, and then Mary Jane Moore. Sallie married Jacob Singley, George, who died in 1877, married first Mary Roberts, then Mary Shealy. Nancy married John McNary, the owner of the ferry by that name. Jesse, dying in 1867, married Martha Etheredge, then Jensie Etheredge. Elizabeth married John Derrick, then Jacob Caughman. Christina married Frederick Kinard. Margaret married Michael Shealy, Jemimia married George Addy, and Jeremiah married Dot Jennings then Elizabeth Fellers.

Of these David and Joel moved to south Georgia where a large colony of Wises center around Plains. David was the father of Tyre, who lost his life in the Confederate War, Philip married Louise Chappell and their children were Leland, Arnold, Philip, Alonzo, Elmer, Georgia, and another daughter who married L. W. Addy. Joseph married Josephine Derrick and their children were Luther, Tyre (married Arine Livingston), Annie married Luther Moore; Irene, Fannie, Florence, Minnie, Cora and Samuel; William was killed in the Confederate War, Fannie married George Hiller. Calhoun married first, Adella Etheredge and by this union one son, Allen, was born and he married Hattie Cobb and their children were William and Lillian; Fannie Coogle was the second wife of Calhoun and by this union were the following children: Walter, George, Rosa (married Capt. A. Murray), Hattie, William (married Alma Clark), Melly Mae, John (married Eola Anderson), and Daniel. Clara, a daughter of David, married a Christie, and Luther married first Lilly Dean and their daughter was named Ethel. Luther's second wife was Addie Lunsford. David also had another son, Pickens, who died young.

WISE AND WYSE (continued)

Joel Wise's children by his first wife were Melissa, who married Phil Jennings. John lost his life in the Confederate War. Perlina married D. S. Derrick. By his second wife were Dr. Burr T., who married Laura Addy and they have three sons, Burr, Samuel, and Bowman, two or possibly all of whom are doctors and operate a large hospital at Americus, Ga. Fannie married C. Forest, Samuel married Camilla Addy and their children were Ralph, who married Nina Lake, and they have a son named Hilton, and Fletta married W. J. Smith, Emma married J. T. Stapleton, Laura married Wesley McGill and Louise married Samuel A. Markett.

George Wise's children by his first wife were Solomon, Charlotte, Elizabeth (who married Jacob Derrick then Michael Shealy); Margaret (who married Henry Jennings); John, who married Martha Shumpert, and their children were, Mary, who married George Shealy; Savannah, who married J. J. Epting; Adlla, Pickens and James, who married Elvira Garrett, and they have a son named Patrick. Major Patrick E. Wise who was the head of the Prosperity family, was another son of George, and he married Christina Aull, daughter of the Rev. Herman Aull. His sons, Allen Garlington, J. Lawson and Bachman, have lived throughout their lives at Prosperity. Allen G. married Rebecca Birge and by this union were born Birge, who married Ellen Werts and their son is Birge, John Patrick; Annie Belle, who married J. P. Brown; Walter married Jessie Lorick; Lillian married C. M. Harmon; Mary married C. Taylor; George married Moss Fellers, and Robert K. Allen Wise's second wife was Wilhelmina Hussung. Elizabeth, daughter of Patrick, married John B. Lathan of Little Mountain; Sallie married F. N. Calmes, a member of an old Newberry family; Lawson married Laura McFall and their children were McFall, Willie Mae, George, Tena, Patrick, Margaret and Nellie. Bachman Wise died only recently at Columbia.

George Wise (1851-1909) married Melverda Ramage and located in Saluda. He was the father of Dr. Oscar Wise, who married Allie Witt, and their son is Allen; Herman married Etta May West, and their children are George Herman and Beatrice; Lucile married W. N. Padgett; Clarence married Eugenia Summer and their children are Summer, William, Clarence and Pauline; Jacob married Julia Summer; Allen was killed in the World War, and the other daughters were Martha, Edna, Christina and Jimmie Leah.

James, son of Patrick, married Nora Miller and their sons were Burke and Harold.

William Wise was the son of Jeremiah and his second wife. He married Elizabeth Banks and by this union was a son, Roland, who married a Werts, and their son was named Julian; another son of William was named William, who married Bertha Stevens, then Eula Whittle; Samuel married Mary Stevens and their children were Samuel and William; Menta married Ben Holstein; Clyde died young; John married Sarah Holstein and their children were Vernon, Frank, David and Sarah; a daughter of William married a Long; Blanche married Pinckney Bodie; Columbus married Tiny Whittle and they had a son named Ernest. Columbus' second wife was a Blomb and by this union were Columbus, Elizabeth, Vance and Cleo.

Christine, daughter of Jeremiah, married Wilson Derrick, then Michael Dunovant, and her third husband was a Hallman. Other daughters of Jeremiah were Lucy, who married David Addy, then David Charles; Mary Ann married J. A. Caughman, then _____ Husband.

By his second wife, Elizabeth Fellers, Jeremiah Wise's children were: Eugenia, who married a Bauknight; Victoria married Rufus Shealy; then there were Ella Alice, Julia, Mamie and Frederick. Frederick's first wife was Lavinia Bodie and their children were: Lutie, who married William Smith; Kate who was the second wife of Smith; Daisy married William Drafts and Claude married Lucy Crouch. By his second marriage to Chatty Smith, Frederick's children were Bernice, Smith, Lucile, Calhoun, Louisa, Gary, Eliza and Eula.

Jeremiah's son, Mid Wise, married first Nancy Kinard and their children were Nancy Hiller, who married a Coleman, and Lila, who married Daniel Gunter. By his marriage with Eula Oxner, Mid Wise's children were Avis, Ernest and Robert.

Gregg Wise was another son of Jeremiah, he marrying Nancy Trotter, and was the father of Nancy, who married Sheppard Merchant; Nertie, who married Leaphart, and Lillian.

The third and youngest son of the oldest George Weiss was Frederick Wyse (1790-1854), who married Julia Kelly and by this union all of his children were born, his second wife being Charlotte Shull. He lived on the old home place of his grandfather who first settled in this country.

Edwin J. Scott, in his "Random Recollections of a Long Life", says: "From Granby I returned home, and proceeded next week (year 1824) to collect (taxes) in the Fork at _____ and Frederick Wyse's on Saluda. Mr. Wyse's mother and his mother-in-law, both very old women, lived in the house with him, his wife and a large family of children, thus showing three, if not four, generations under the same roof, and they all seemed to be quiet and peace-

WISE AND WYSE (continued)

ful. Here I saw the last flax wheel turned by a treadle by the feet of the old ladies, and he kept up the practice of having one of his children stand by the table and ask a blessing before meals."

Of Frederick Wyse's daughters, Keziah married Martin Caughman, who was the father of Banks L. Caughman, who was for years prominent in state politics, and Elizabeth Caughman, who married Walter Barre of Lexington. Barbara married Godfrey Harmon, Martha married Malachi Lowman, Mahala married Calvin Fellers, Charlotte died young, Mary Ann married Doctor Compton and Rebecca married Herman Lowman.

Of the sons, Allen, died young, Dr. Benjamin Wyse married Charlotte Eleazer and their son, John H., who became a Lutheran minister, married Grace Hinderlite of Virginia and their children were Annie Belle, Frederick, Virginia, George, Hardenia, John and Emaline. Benjamin's other children were: Ada, who married John Hiller; Adella, married George B. Green; Frederick, who died in Virginia, and Joseph and Robert.

Capt. Joseph W. Wyse (1818-1886), son of Frederick, married Rosannah Singley, daughter of Martin Singley, and lived at the upper Wyse's Ferry on Saluda, which was the crossing from Prosperity to Batesburg before the bridge was built a few miles down the stream. His son, Adam Logan, married Rebecca Wilson, sister of the late Rev. J. Herbert Wilson, and by this union were born: Rosa, Adella; Maude, who married Robert Bass; Colin, who married Martha Black, then Feagle, and by his first wife were Colin, who married J. R. Payne, Heber married Emma Ackers, Bessie married R. T. Blease, Bartow, son of Logan, married Lavada Dowling and moved to Florida and is the father of Bartow, Heber and Robert Wilson. Benjamin, another son of Logan's married Mary Crout and has a son, Benjamin Delaney.

Allen M. Wyse, son of Joseph, married Marilla E. Riser, daughter of Capt. H. H. Riser, and their children were: Wyman, Allen, Estelle, who married the Rev. V. Y. Boozer, a Lutheran minister; Joseph H. married Nellie Peck and lives in Virginia, Rosa married John T. Burton and moved to Mississippi, Frederick C. married Elizabeth Hennies and their children are Frederick, Elizabeth, Barbara and Joseph Allen; Lottie married the Rev. C. E. Norman, and they live in Japan as Lutheran missionaries.

Joseph Wyse's daughters were: Sophia, who died young; Sarah, who married J. C. H. Rauch; Mary Ann, who married Andrew J. Kilgore of Newberry, and Rebecca, who became the wife of Judge Ira B. Jones, chief justice of the supreme court.

John Harrison Wyse, youngest son of Frederick married Henrietta Barber of Orangeburg, and lived at the old home place of the first Weiss. Later his son, James, who married Della Fulmer, fell heir to the place and only recently the title has passed by James' children to the company now developing a large power project on Saluda River. This place has been owned and occupied continuously by members of the family for nearly 180 years. James' descendants are: John H., Mary, Rosa, Frederick and Eloise (who married Winfred Shealy). Viola, a daughter of John married Lonnie Harmon and their present home is on lands originally occupied by George Weiss and wife, Barbara Bickley.

Not many miles from the old home places of the Weisses is, or was, an object of peculiar interest the presence and purpose of which having never been explained.

When Robert Mills prepared in 1826, his statistics of South Carolina, he mentioned a work of great labor existing on the south side of Little Mountain, in the shape of a huge well walled with rock to a height of three feet above the surrounding ground and sixteen feet thick. In his time, a hundred years ago, no man then knew the purpose or the date of such a work and Mills suggested it to be the work of the Indians or some enterprising miners. One can readily discard the 'aborigine" idea for it is well known that he did not exert himself to any such extent, - he did little profitable work and buried his dead in a mound above the ground, some of these mounds having been found along the river. On the other hand it is said that the surrounding ground did not indicate mining operations though the residents claimed that at one time virgin lead was obtained from the mountain, but this doubtful _____ was generally attributed to _____ which had been stolen from the _____ stores in Charleston and hidden in the caves on the mountain. Can it be possible that the discovery of the secret of this work, great labor will lead to the unearthing of a prior civilization in Carolina?

OTHER EARLY COLONIAL PIONEERS AND THEIR FAMILIES.

AARON—Jacob Aaron lived in Edgefield District, and died there in the year 1800. He left property to his widow, Margaret Aaron, and the following children: Mary (she married David Schumpert), and perhaps others whose names are not known. The widow afterwards married Thomas West of the same district and had children: William (he moved to the West), Elizabeth, Sarah, Thomas. Mrs. Marga West died in 1817.

ABERNATHY—John Abernathy married Rhoda Davis, a daughter of Mrs. Mary Davis, widow, before the year 1800.

ABERCROMBIE—James Abercrombie of Laurens County, made will dated November 29, 1819, which was proven in court February 9, 1820, in which year he died, his wife having already died. His children named in the will were: Mary O'Daniel, Isabella Blackwell, Susannah Matthews, Hannah Brooks, Margaret Buckner, Elizabeth, and James. A stepson was Archibald Daniel, Jr. A grand-son was James Abercrombie. Other legatees were: Rebecca Gosnell, wife of Gabriel Gosnell. Executors named were: Elias Brooks, and James Abercrombie(his son).

ABLES—John Ables married Saloma Feagle, a daughter of Laurens and Rachel (Quaddlebaum) Feagle. Their children were: Loretta (wife of Robert Ryan), Anytes, Anson, J. L., Penander, Ethelbert. Ethelbert died early in life, but left two children, James and John.

ABNEY—John Abney made a will dated June 20, 1812; died about 1818-20; left widow , and several children as follows: Lark, Charlotte, Polly, Isabella, and Ann. Charlotte married _____ O'Neall. Another legatee was Arthur Dillard. The widow to have guardianship of her own children who were Isabella and Ann.

Azaraih Abney died about 1844 in Edgefield County, and left children: Mary Elizabeth(she marr: Elijah Lake after 1844), Susannah (married David Peterson whom she survived, but she died same year), Ann Augustine(she married after 1844 to Cooper B. Glenn, and died about 1849), Nathaniel, Azariah, Joel(he died before the father), Matthew, Elizabeth, and ......

Joel Abney died about 1815 or '16 in Edgefield County, left widow Elizabeth, and the following children: Elmina, Narassi, Elijah P., Mark M.,Charlotte, Azariah (his son Joel shared in estate) He left , also, a sister-in-law, Miss. Charlotte Pope, as a legatee.

Paul Abney died about 1820, left children: John, Jane Barnes, Martha Peterson(her son , Paul Abney Peterson), Mary Babbs, Tabitha Hicks, and Elizabeth Black.

ABRAMS—William Abrams married Martha, daughter of George Whitmore, before the year 1800. Georg widow was Elizabeth Whitmore, having been the widow of William Gary when she married him.

Mrs. Mary Abrams died about 1830-35 in Newberry County. She left children: Alexander, James, John, Annie, Elizabeth, and Mary. He left, too, a son-in-law, William Marrs.

ADAMS—Several different families. William Adams died about 1834 in Newberry County, left child Behethland (wife of Robert Gillam Wallace), Nancy, William, Archibald, Fields, George, Martha, Frances, Susan, Robert, Silas, and Mary. George died about 1845 and left widow, Nancy, and child Susan, Frances, Thomas, William H., and Lyda. They lived on Saluda River, near Chappells.

William(son of above William) died in November, 1836, leaving 188 acres land on Saluda River t his widow, Deboroh, and five children: William F., Thomas, Lucinda P., Zacariah, Elijah, and Louisa Frances.   The widow, Deboroah, married James H. Goggans. William F. and his family, with his sister, Lucinda, moved to Chambers County, Alabama.

George Adams died about 1807 in Newberry County, left widow, Sarah, and children: Mary (wife George Wells), William, Edward, Phillip, James, and Patsy Winningham. A son, Robert, was named Executor of his will, but not named as a legatee.

John Adams, Sr., died in 1822 in Edgefield County, and left children: William H., Barthomew S. Elizabeth Tompkins, Susannah Tompkins, Mary Stolesworth, Rebecca Holloway, James, John, and Sara (she married a Gibson).

Dr. Freeborn Adams died about 1816 in Newberry village. He is buried at the old cemetery near Kings Creek known as the Crenshaw-Finch graveyard. He was a native of Newburyport, Mass., and ca to this section when a young man. He was a practicing physician when he came; married in the section of King's Creek; moved to Newberry Court House, where he lived in a large colonial home located where is now the Hotel Wiseman. Later, the home burned . At his death he left no will, but left a widow, who was the daughter of Edward Finch, also left children: A son, Ossian, who died young and left no family; the wife of Dr. John W. Simpson; and the wife of Thomas B. Ruther

Other Pioneers (continued)

Mrs. Margaret Adams died in Union County, about 1806, and left children: John, William, Ann Martha, Martha Woolbright, James, and Margaret.
John A. Adams, of Union County, S. C., who was twenty-one years old in 1815 at time of death of his grand-mother, Mrs. Jane Hope, left a family. A daughter of Mrs. Jane Hope, Rebecca, married William Adams and had children: Robert, William, Susan, Jane M., James W., Margaret E., and John A.
AIKEN-George Aikin (originally spelled, "Akin") made a will dated July 7,1810, which was proved in Court on March 31, 1817. He died in 1816, left widow, Sumner Aiken, and three gr-children, as legatees, George, Joseph, and Sumner (they were children of a pre-deceased son, and his wife, Nancy. James Aiken died about 1804, left widow, Mary, and children: John, Sally, William. Executors of his will were Hugh Aiken and Robert Bankhead.
ALLEN-Charles Allen, Sr. married Lucy Bacon, daughter of Lydall Bacon and Mary Allen Bacon. Their children were: Drury, Mary Barksdale, Joel, Richard, Charles, Sabra (she married Joshua McNeese), Lydall, Sarah (she married Lewis Saxon), Cynthia (she married John Williams). Charles Allen, Sr. was born ib 1744 and died in 1805. A son, Charles, Jr., married Susan Garner. He was pensioned as a Rev War soldier and veteran, the record showing he was born in Charlotte County, Virginia, in 1764, died in Laurnes County, S. C., in 1860, nearly one hundred years old. They had children: Joel, Sarah (wife of John Crisp), Sophia (she married Rev. Samuel Lewers), Millie (wife of Daniel Hooker), Namima (married a Davis). Joel married Patsy Boyd, daughter of John Boyd, Sr., of Laurens County, S. C. Charles, Jr. is buried at the old family grave-yard, about four miles North of Laurens Court House.
Josiah Allen died in Efgefield County, S. C. before the year 1784. He was a son of one Charles Allen who lived in Abbeville District, S. C.
ALBERSON-Elijah Alberson married Clary Griffin, daughter of John and Anne Griffin, and moved to Alabama before the year 1805. William Alberson married Fanny Griffin, daughter of John and Anne Griffin, and were living in Laurens County in the year 1805.
ALEWINE-Henry Alewine died in Newberry County in the year 1830. The administrator of his estate was John B. Miller. Thomas Alewine made will January 17, 1856, which was proved in Court on February 12, 1856; left children: Elisha, Jane Mosier, William, Caroline (wife of Joseph Abrams), and Dorothy (wife of Benjamin Abrams). Dorothy died before the death of her father.
ALEXANDER-Rev. Joseph Alexander made will July 19, 1809, and died same year. He left children: Martha Byers(her two children were Baldwin and Joseph Byers), Sarah (widow of Joseph Barnett), Samuel David, Editha (wife of Robert S. Walker), Esther (married a King), Josephine (the youngest daughter), George Baldwin, Juda (she married a Bankhead), Anne (wife of James Garrison), and Margaret (wife of Abner McJunkin). Executors : Joseph McJunkin, Sr.,Colonel Joseph Hughs.
AMOS-Clough S. Amos made will dated November 13, 1837, and died in November, 1838, leaving a widow, Elizabeth, and one child, Mary, who married Allen Cates. The widow left six gr-children: Allen Scrugs, Clough Scrugs, Elizabeth Scrugs, Sarah Scrugs, Janes Scrugs, James Scrugs. All gr-children named were children of Mary Cates. Executor: Robert Wilson.
ANDREWS-Ephriam Andrews made will February 20, 1822, which was proved in Court September 2, 1822. He died same year, leaving widow, Frances, and children: Ephriam, Nancy, Young, Elizabeth, Edney, Allen, William, Polly(she married John Fetts). Executor: John Fetts.
ARDIS-Matthias Ardis lived in Edgefield District, in a section which was called " New Windsor Township." He made and executed a will dated October 29, 1774, and died in 1779 or 1780, leaving his widow, Christina, and the following children: Mary (wife of John Bradley),Elizabeth (wife of Francis Carlisle),Isaac, Jacob, Sarah, Abraham, Daniel, David.   John and Mary (Ardis) Bradley had three sons: .... After his death, the widow married John Devenport who died early leaving children, Polly Ann and Luscius. Mrs. Christina Ardis died 1795. Her daughter, Sarah, had a daughter, Mary Ardis, who married Benjamin Bowers. Mrs. Christina Ardis was a sister of Voluntine Zinn, whose son, Henry Zinn, lived in Edgefield County. Abraham Ardis, of Beech Island, made will December 20, 1816, and died soon afterwards. He named two children in his will, David and Matthew. Abrham, Jr. died in 1837, left widow, Sarah, and one child, Sarah Maria.
ARICK-John A. Arick made will dated June 3, 1808, and died in Fairfield County in 1810. He left widow, Mary, and several children, three sons being John, Lee, and William. Two gr-daughters, Ann Dugan, and Mary Dunklin (daughter of Richard Dunklin) are name in the will. Mrs. Mary Arick

Other Pioneers (continued)

died in 1831, and in her will is mentioned a son, Lee, and the following other children: John Adam, Mary Elizabeth, Thomas Lewis, William. A witness to the will was Cynthia Dugan.
Thomas Arick died in Brooksville, Florida. John Aris died in Ocala, Florida. William and Lee moved to the State of Louisiana. Lee D. Arick made will February 10, 1862, and died same year His legatees were: Ann Waring (daughter), Beam, and Christian McCay Nevett(latter two in Flor: Mary Gaza(daughter). Executor; James B. Beam(son-in-law). William, son, had alread; died. His wife had died—Mrs. Sarah Arick—in year 1842, the Executor and Trustee of her estate being Robert Cathcart.

ARNOLD-Zacariah Arnold died in Laurens County, S. C. about 1829, and left widow, Mary, and si: children: Mary (wife of John West), Rebecca (wife of William Flinn), Sarah (wife of Lewis Savage), Lewis Q., William A., Nancy E (wife of William H. Pulley). He left a gr-son, George Berry West. His widow died about 1835.

Hendrick Arnold died in Luarens County soon after making his will which is dated July 15, 179! He married Ruth........, and children named in will were: Mary, William, Nancy, and Ira.

Anderson Arnold died about 1814 in Laurens County. He left widow, Mary, and children whose names are not known; but she married again, about 1816, to Drury Boyce.

ASHFORD-George Ashford ,ade will dated October 3, 1810, proved in Court September 14, 1814. He died about 1813-14, and left children: Sarah, Simon, William, Ann Rent, Mary Fag, Michael, Elizabeth Hutchinson, George, Sibbie Schockley, Moses, Jane Morgan, Leana Goree, Micajah, James Bennett William Simon, and Constant Hogan. Moses Ashford died about 1825, in Union County, S. C. He left children: Anna, George, and Polly.

ATKINS—John Atkins and wife, Margaret, were living in Moore County, North Carolina, before 17 Soon afterwards, he sold his lands and moved to Laurens County, South Carolina.

Another John Atkins lived in Newberry County, where he died in 1806, leaving a widow, Sela, an a son, John. One John Atkins and his wife, Sarah, sold 100 acres land in Newberry County, which lands had been granted to him in year 1768.

Abner Atkins died in Newberry County in 1826, leaving widow, Sarah Ann(she was the widow of Phillip Gilder who had died in year 1808), and children: Jermome, Selina, Jane, Robert, Luther and a daughter who had married John Clark. Robert died young, unmarried.

Benjamin Atkins lived in Newberry County over 30 years. He married Eve........; and sold hi land about 1797.

Francis Atkins died about 1856 in Abbeville County, South Carolina. He left widow, Elizabeth and children: Robert, Margaret(she married a Dale), Ravenna(a son), and James.

AUGHTRY-David Aughtry married Elizabeth McGraw, and lived in Union County, South Carolina.

ATKINSON—John Atkinson made will dated June 14, 1799, which was proved in Court on October 2, 1799. He left children: John, Thomas, William, Gracy Spearman, Mary Blason, Martha Lewers, Ann Spearman, and Elizabeth. One Thomas Atkinson made will December 2, 1830, and died January, 1831, leaving widow, Tabitha, all of his estate. After the widow's death, certain trac of land to go to the following legatees: Tabitha F. Meek, daughter of John and Sarah Meek, lat of Laurens County; and a nephew, Beaufort Atkinson Wallace.

AULL-Rev Herman Aull, a Lutheran preacher, came to the southern section of Newberry County. farmed and preached in the upper Dutch Fork section, in Newberry County. He married, first, to Christina Rikard, and his second wife being Eve Riser, (widow of ...... Wertz).

AULTON—James Aulton made will dated October 12, 1798, which was proved in Court July 4, 1799. He died the same year, leaving widow, Phoebe, and children: Sarah Waldrop, John, Amelia, James William, Jemima, Spencer, Elizabeth, Margaret. The last five named were minors in 1799, under guardianship of the widow.

BABB-Mercer Babb lived in Newberry County at time of making his will, in year 1794, which nam his legatees as follows: Wife, Rhoda Babb; a brother, Thomas Babb; a sister, Margaret Wadlingt nephews, Henry and Mercer Babb (sons of Thomas); and Mercer Wadlington (son of Margaret Wadli

BACON-The Bacon family first settled in Laurens County, the pioneer, Lydal Bacon, having come from Virginia. He was descended from Captain Edmond Bacon who received patents for land in th State , Kent County, in 1687, where he married Ann Lydal, daughter of Captain George Lydal and gr-daughter of Sir Thomas Lydall of England. Lydal Bacon was born 1717, died in ...... He marri Mary Allen and had children: Ann, Lydal, Lucy, Edmund, Elizabeth, Sarah, Langston, and Drury.

Other Pioneers (continued)

BAKER-Caleb Baker died in Abbeville County, in year 1803. In his will is named his wife, Margaret, and left children. John Baker died in Abbeville County. He left widow, Rebecca, and no children named in his will. One John Baker made will May 3, 1823, and died same year. He left widow, Elizabeth, and children: John, Elizabeth, William, Joseph, Faithy, Other legatees, who received $1.00 each, were: Mary Wallace, Keziah McClellan, Rosannah Wallace. Jacob Baker married in Newberry County to Eve M. Kinard, daughter of Christopher and Mary Kinard. Their children were: John, Milton, Edward, Harriet Ann, Samantha, Margaret (she married John W. Crompton), Christina (married to James Dawkins).

BAIRD-Thomas Baird died in 1797, leaving widow, Jannett, and several children. He had a brother Alexander Baird. John Botts Baird died in Abbeville County about 1803; left widow, and a son, James. Mrs. Mary Biard died in 1819, and left children: James R., Rebecca Rowe, and William P. Raiford.

BAILY-James Baily died in Pendleton District about 1818, He left widow, Mary, and children: Elizabeth (wife of John P. King); Wyatt, Frances (wife of John Fleming); Martha (wife of...); and ....   Zacariah Baily died in Laurens County about 1834, and left children: Rebecca Notes, Zacariah, Absalom, William, John, Coleman(d), James Polly Chandler, Winnifred Walker, Sarah Chandler.   Coleman Baily, son of Zacariah, died in Newberry County about 1836, and left children: James A., William L., Laura, and Ann F.

BANKS-Charles Banks married Elizabeth King, daughter of Ethelred King. He died in 1825. Children were: Albert Banks, Mary E. Banks, Charles A. Banks.

Randal Banks died in 1857, in Newberry County. His legatees were: Mother, Drucilla Banks; brother, James C. Banks; sisters, Rhoda Dominick (wife of Henry Dominick), Marcella Sheppard and her children, Mary and Frances Sheppard.

BARKSDALE-Beverly Barksdale married Anna, daughter of Joseph Terry, of Pittsylvania County, Virginia, before the year 1785. He moved to South Carolina, but left that State.

BATES-Michael Bates made will in 1800, and died in January, 1801. He lived in the Dutch Fork section of Newberry County. Children: Catherine Bowers, Jacob, Elizabeth Heirs, Nancy Bowers, Andrew, George, David, and John. George Bates (son of Michael) died in 1804 in Newberry County, leaving legatees: Catherine Bates (his mother), Julia Bates (daughter of Andrew Bates), and two brothers, David and John.

Henry Bates died in 1806, leaving children: James, Sarah, Nancy Barrentine, Jenny Baldree, Rebecca Taylor, William, Henry, Christopher, and Zacariah. Christopher before 1806, and left widow, Keziah, and two small children, John and Henry.

Farr Bates died about 1840, leaving widow, Catherine, and children, Farr and Thomas.

Humphry Bates died about 1805, in Union County, S. C. He left widow, Mary Bates.

Fleming Bates died 1808, in Union County. He was a son of Isaac Bates, and of Mary Ann Bates.

BALDREE-George Baldree died about 1820, leaving widow, Mary, and children: Robert, William, Starling, Hosea, Rhoda (she was wife of William Davis). Starling Baldree married Ruth Waters, daughter of Philemon Waters, Jr.

BALDWIN-Eli Baldwin died in Greenville County, S. C. about 1838, leaving widow, Elizabeth, and children: Abner, John, Sylvanus, Hiram, R. B., Cynthia, and Eli. Other distributees named in settlement of his estate were: Robert Holland, J. W. Clark, E. B. Cantrell, Jarratt Yeargin, and G. W. Phillips. John died in 1843, in Forsythe County, Georgia.

BARRETT-Henry O. Barrett lived in the Quaker settlement of Newberry County, on Bush River. He married Lydia Jenkins, daughter of Isaac Jenkins, Sr. and wife, Rebecca (Harbert) Jenkins. A daughter, Hannah Barrett, born about 1816, married Dr. DeLaney Lane Wilson, of Edgefield County, S. C. (Dr. D. L. Wilson was born about 1813); they moved to Abbeville County, S. C.

BARTON-Thomas Barton died in Greenville County about 1823. In the settlement of his estate, his widow, Bethear, and the following other distributees are named: John, William, Benjamin, Elisha (probably moved to another county), wife of Roland Suggs, wife of Arthur Barrett, wife of Cheaton Merritt.

Thomas Barton died in Edgefield County about 1840, leaving widow, Dicey, and children: Joshua, Benjamin, John, Timothy, William, Elizabeth Burkhalter, Mary Kirkland, Thomas, and Andrew.

One Benjamin Barton died in Anderson County, S. C. in 1808, leaving widow, Darcus, and children: Bailey, Joshua, Sela Cannon, Jean Brown, Benjamin, Vashti Kirksey, James M., Thomas, Eliza, and others.

313

Other Pioneers (continued)

BAUSKETT—John Bauskett came to Newberry County from Orange County, North Carolina, about the time of the Rev. War. His son, Thomas Buaskett, came with him. They settled ten miles East of Newberr County Court House, near what was afterwards known as "Bauskett's Church". John died in 1813. Thomas married a daughter of John O. Daniel. James Bauskett died about 1800, left mother, Yourath Bauskett, and brothers and sisters, as follows: Frances Reid, John, Daniel, Ann Middleton, Baby Williams, Elizabeth Perdue, Pleasant, and Margaret. (Much data on this family in the " Annals of Newberry").

BEARD—John Beard died in Newberry County in 1798. He left widow, Drury, and children: Adam, John, Andrew, and Simon. Simon died in 1802, and left widow, Margaret. Adam died in 1807, and left two daughters, Jean Vickery and Mary. Mary Beard died in 1813. They lived in Abbeville County.

William Beard died in Union County, leaving widow, Eleanor, and children: William, Eleanor, John, Margaret, Susannah, Anna, and another daughter who married a Landrum. He moved from the Enoree River section of Newberry County.

Stephen Beard died in Newberry County on July 2, 1856. His children were: Mary Ann (wife of Charles Wilson), Katherine (wife of George Griffith), Henry, Carwile, William L., John J., Adeline, Samuel, Spencer. (Spencer, a daughter, was born September 17, 1837.

Col. Jonas Beard, a patriot officer in the Rev. War, came from old country. He was a member of the Provincial Congress, 1775-1779, from Saxe-Gothe Township. Alos, he was Colonel of a Regiment of the American Army during the Rev War. According to family tradition, he was one time captured and held in prison at Ninety Six; but esacped and rejoined his troops. He married about 1768 to Katherine Kirchner, and had children: Frederick, Mary Grace (she married Capt. John Strobel), William , and Dorothy. He died at Columbia, S. C. July 7, 1796.

James Beard died in Newberry County in 1799, leaving widow, Elizabeth. Other legatees were: Elijah Dawkins (wife's son by a former marriage), Barbara Beard (his sister).

William B. Smith Beard was born about 1825, and died in 1847. He was a son of Josiah Beard, and a maternal gr-son of William B. Smith.

John Beard died in Newberry County about 1817, leaving widow, Elizabeth, and children: Jane (wife of David Montgomery), Agnes (wife of James Gordon), Jennett (wife of .... Richey), Margaret (wife of ...... Campbell).

Clough Beard moved from Newberry County to Spartanburg County. His brothers, William P. and Wesley J. Beard, moved to Pickens County, Alabama, about the year 1850. Jane Beard, John F. Johnson and wife, Nancy, moved to Mississippi.

BEASLEY— Thomas Beasley died in Laurens County in 1832; left children: Polly Ferguson, Nancy Holland (wife of Abraham Holland), Elizabeth Ferguson, Dorothy Chalmers, Jincey (wife of John Williams). A gr-son, Edmund Holland; and gr-children (children of Dorothy Chalmers), Martha A., Permelia, Elizabeth J., William S., Thomas B., and Frances Chalmers. Dr. Alexander Chalmers was appointed Trustee for Jincey Williams.

George Beasley died in Fairfield County, S. C. about 1833, He left widow, Molly, and Children: Rachel (wife of John Conder), Elizabeth, Margaret (wife of Benjamin Conder), and Jacob.

BECKETT—John Beckett (Bicket) made will May 19, 1862, in army camp at Massaponax, Virginia. A Confererate sooldier in Company G., 14th Reg. of S.C.V. He died or soon afterwards killed, leaving widow, Sarah, and children: Andrew W., John H., and tow others. His father-in-law was Andrew J. Weed.

Mrs. Jane Beckett (Bicket) made will Feb 8, 1862, which was recorded in court March 24, 1862. Her devisees were: Sarah McComb(wife of Andrew Brown), and John Becket, a son. John Hamilton Young received balance of estate after settlement of estate to above named .

Dr. James M. Beckett married Juliet Margaret Johnston, of Fairfield County, S. C. (she is burie in Rosemont Cemetery, Newberry, S. C.) She was the daughter of John and Mary Johnston; and she died July 31, 1835, aged 26 years. They were the parents of Mary Rebecca Donnelly(wife of Rev Samuel D. Donnelly), Susan (wife of Thomas N. Brown, of Virginia), Thomas N. and Susan Brown moved to South Carolina, and were the parents of James Beckett Brown whose wife was Anna........

Samuel Beckett and wife, Rebecca, of Laurens County, S. C., moved to Marshall County, Tennessee She was the daughter of Timothy Swann, ot Laurens County.

Other Pioneers (continued)

BEAM-Sarah Beam died in Fairfield County after 1838. She left a niece, Susannah Beam, and brothers, Albert and William. William died young, but left a widow, and the following children: Jesse, Thomas, Mary, Sarah, and Elizabeth. She left, also, a nephew, Jacob Feaster.

BEATTY-Robert Baetty died in Union County about 1800. He left widow, Mahala, who was his second wife. Children by his first wife were: Cyrus, Margaret, Mary, Robert, Elizabeth, James, and Eleanor Phillps. Curus was living in White County, Tenn. when he sold 75 acres land on Padgett's Creek in 1817. Robert, Jr. gave his son, Samuel, 275 acres on Tucker Creek, in Union County, in year 1820. Mahala Beatty gave to her ste-children land in year 1804—Cyrus, Margaret, Mary, and Rhoda.

BEDENBAUGH-Adam Bedenbaugh, a Rev War patriot, married a Miss. Werts, in Newberry County, and had children: Adam, Henry, Jacob, Michael, Abram, Christian, David, John, and William. William moved to Georgia. Jacob married Rebecca Hair, a daughter of Matthias and Fanny Hair, before the year 1817.

BELTON-John Belton and wife, Charity, lived near Bush River, Newberry County. They moved from Camden District. Members of the Bush River Friends Meeting from 1792-1804, included the names of Jesse Belton, Anna Belton, Elizabeth Belton, William Belton, and Susannah Belton.

Samuel Belton died in Camden District in 1793, leaving widow, Rachel, and children: John, Samuel, Martha, Ann, and Charity. Jesse Belton and his wife sold land in Laurens County in 1807. William Belton died in Laurens County in 1830.

Abraham Belton, brother of John Belton, Sr., was a surveyor in Richland County. He married Sarah, daughter of John and Mary Toland of Newberry County. John Belton, Sr. was, also, a surveyor in Richland County. He made a will February 17, 1790, which was proved in court and recorded September 15, 1790. He left children: Ann, Mary, Rebecca, Elizabeth, Martha, Christian, and James English Belton. His son, John, died before death of the father and left a widow, Mary. His brother-in-law, Joshua English, is named in his will, as was his brother, Abraham.

BERLEY-Gasper Berley died in Newberry County about 1804. He left a widow, Mary, and children: John, Elizabeth, Frederick, Margaret, Martin, Magdeline, Gasper, Sibert.

Adam Berley married Elizabeth Riser, daughter of John Riser, Sr.

Gasper Berley married twice(" Annals of Newberry"), four sons by first wife were, Gasper, Martin, Sibert, Harman.

BICKLEY-Thomas Bickley lived in Lexington District. He came from Germany about 1750, when a small boy, his father having died on the way over and was buried at sea. Thomas married Ann Oak, and had children: John, Thomas, Elizabeth (married Michael Sutton), Anna (married ...Hamiter), The children of Ann Hamiter were: Fanny (age 17 in year 1820), John (age 16), David (age 15), Joel (age 12), Harriet (age 10). Anna Hamiter and her sister, Dorothea, died before the beginning of the year 1820. John Bickley married before 1800 to Rachel Nichols, a daughter of George Nichols. Rachel died in 1801.

BISHOP-Joseph Bishop married a daughter of William Hutchinson, before the year 1805.

BLACK-John Black lived in Newberry County. His will is dated December 25, 1796, and proved 1797. His wife having already died, he left children: Joseph, Robert, Francis, Andrew, Oliver, Mary A., Ann, and Susannah.

Daniel Black lived in Newberry County, but moved into Edgefield County. Henry Black moved to Georgia. John Black died in Laurens County about 1841. He left widow, Sarah, and children: Agatha, William E., Elizabeth (wife of John S. Henderson), Oscar, John Blair Black, Tranmore F., and Harriet Melinda Black. Mrs. Sarah Black was Sarah Conway before her marriage.

BLAIR-Samuel Blair died in 1815, in Abbeville District. He left children: John, Thomas, William, and Abigail.

William Blair, weaver, lived in Newberry County. He sold lands to Patrick Carmichael on July 3, 1786, including 194 acres on Campin Creek, the conveyance being made by David and James Blair.

BLACKBURN-William Blackburn lived in northern section of Newberry County, where he died prior to 1790, leaving family. Two of his sons, Daniel and William, lived in Newberry County.

John Blackburn lived on Indian Creek in Newberry County, as did Stephen Blackburn. John was born June 30, 1760, and died in Perry County, Alabama, December 24, 1853. His wife, Nancy, was born

Other Pioneers (continued)

September 22, 1769, and died Novemmmber 30, 1830. They had a daughter, Nancy(born 1805), who married James McLaughlin (born 1800), of Laurens County. They moved to Perry County. Alabama . Stephen lived a place called "Rich Hill"; his widow married Dr. William Rook. His sister was Mrs. Robert Glenn Gilliam.("Annals of Newberry").

William Blackburn made will September 15, 1817, and died 1819, leaving widow, Mary Ann, and children: James, Sibella, Susannah, Stephen, and Sarah. He was a son of William Blackburn, Sr. who lived on Indian Creek.

Mrs. Mary Blackburn died about 1868, leaving legatees: Daughters-Elizabeth T. Kennedy and Nancy Bobo; gr-children-Mary Ann Elizabeth Gilliam, William Wesley Gilliam, John Robert Gilliam, Margery Rose Ann Gilliam, and McSwain Blackburn Gilliam.

BLALOCK—John Blalock, carpenter, lived in the Northwest section of Newberry County. He left a will dated August 5, 1790, which was proved in court May 16, 1791. His son, Lewis, inherited a large part of his lands. Other legatees named in his will were: Reuben, Roland, Micajah Bennett, John Blalock Bennett, John Blalock Roland, Sabard Oglesby, Sr., and his seven children. John Blalock's wife was named Alidia. He served in the Rev War in Captain Zacariah Brook's company of State Militia. One of his daughters, Mary, married Pennington King.

One ...... Blalock married Margaret Johnson, daughter of James Johnson, of Edgefield County. Their children were: James, John, Hugh, and Catherine.

BLEASE—Thomas W. Blease, Jr. was born in Edgefield County on November 22, 1822. and died in the town of Newberry on May 31, 1880. He was the son of Thomas W. Blease, Sr. and wife, Bethany Blease. Mrs. Bethany Blease moved to Newberry with her sons, Thomas W. Jr. on April 13, 1865.

Henry H. Blease was born May 11, 1832, at Edgefield Court House. He was married twice. By his first wife, he had children: Cole L., Harry, Corrie, Ella, Leila. Cole L. and Harry were lawyers in Newberry . Cole was elected Govenor, then U. S. Senator. Henry H. Blease's second wife was Miss. Satterwhite, of Newberry County, by whom were three children: Eugene S., Bertha , and Cannon G. Eugene S. represented his county in the State legisltaure, was Associate Justice, then Chief Justice of the State Supreme Court. Cannon G. was Sheriff of Newberry County for over twenty years.

BOAZMAN—Cooper Boazman married Catherine........ and had children: William W., Fannie (she married Frank G. Spearman), Edmund, Washington, Grant, Joseph, Elizabeth, Winnie, and Ida. William W. married Sarah Smith and had children, Walter and Nellie.

David G. Boazman married Catherine Payne, daughter of Edmund Payne.

BOBB—Francis Bobb died in Newberry County about 1849. In his will, his wife, Mary, and a son, William , are named. He had other children who were under age in 1836, the date of his will. Francis Bobb, Jr. died in Newberry County in 1853, leaving widow, Sarah, and children: Mary Ann, Frances Elizabeth, William Berley, John Sligh, George Lawson, and Simon Washington. Simon was under 21 years old in 1853.

BOBO—Absalom Bobo came to Laurens County from Culpepper County, Virginia, before the Rev War. He married Mary Sims in Virginia, a daughter of Thomas Sims, of Culpepper County. He made will July 8, 1808, which was proved February 11, 1813; died in 1812. His widow, and children named in will as follows: His predeceased daughter, Nancy Powell (wife of William Powell), whose childre were named. Children of Nancy Powell: Betsy (wife of Larkin Gaines), Rhody (wife of Phillip Waites), Peachy (wife of David D. Posey), Polly (wife of Robert R. Delph), Fannie (wife of Robert B. Norris), Sarah (wife of Reuben Powell), Amy S. (wife of Nathaniel J. Rosemond), Belinda (wife of Adam Crane Jones), Milly W. and Virginia(last two minors in 1813).

Sampson Bobo was born 1738 and died in 1804; married Sarah Simpson, who was born 1743 and died in 1816. They lived in Laurens County. His son, Barham, father of Dr. William J. Bobo, lived in Union County, S. C.

BOGAN—John Bogan and his son, Isaac Bogan lived in Union County. John died in 1803, and left children: Isaac, Elizabeth, Rebecca. Elizabeth married a Kilpatrick. Rebecca married a Brandon. Isaac died in 1805, leaving widow, Easter, and children: John, Easter, Jannah Jones, Isaac, Jam William, Charles, Marshall, and Caswell. He left a gr-son, Giles Sumner. Mrs. Easter Bogan was a daughter of ..... Farrar.

BOGGS—John Boggs and wife, Nelly, sold land in Newberry County in year 1805.

Other Pioneers (continued)

BOLAND- John Boland came to the Dutch Fork section, in what is new Newberry County, before the termination of the Rev War. He first married a widow, Mrs. Counts, by whom he had one son, Abram. After her death he married a Miss. Feltman, by whom were children: John, Henry, Adam, George, David, William, Jacob, Barbara and Mary. Most of these children, if not all of them, moved West, some locating in Alabama and Texas. Abram married a Miss. Sease and had children: Frederick, William, Adam, Joseph, Levi, Walter, Middleton, Mark and Ozra. (Most of this data from the " Annals of Newberry", Part 11).

BONDS-Thomas Bonds died about 1837, leaving widow, Rebecca, (she died in 1853), and children: Frances (wife of Eli Goree), Nancy M. (wife of Nathan F. Johnson), Louisa (died 1853, not married), Hugh K. T., and Laura F. Frances Goree died in 1843, leaving two children, Rebecca and Salina. Nancy M. Johnson died in 1851, leaving children, Rebecca F., Susan Mary, Thomas L., and .... Hugh King Toland Bonds married Rachel Hunter and lived in Laurens County. Laura F. Bonds married Dr. Robert Hunter, of Laurens County.

Richard Bonds made will Sept 4, 1786, and died 1787. He left widow, Joice, and children: Minah, Richard, William, Sally, Reta, and Betty.

Noah Bonds died about 1811 in Newberry County. He left a widow, Fanny, and children: James, William, Hampton, Ezekiel, Reuben, and Rebecca. William died in 1814, and left no family.

Ezekiel died in 1824, left widow, Esther, and children: Esther (wife of William Page), Silas, and another child who died before estate was settled.

Dudley Bonds died in Newberry County in 1815, leaving widow, Frances, and children: Jean, Nancy, William, Meredith, Thomas, Dudley, Martha, Elizabeth. Dudley, Jr. moved to Jackson, Georgia.

Mrs. Nancy Bonds died in Newberry County in 1850, and left children: James, Thomas, Rebecca (wife of William S. Birge), John C., Mary B. (wife of Lemuel Dillard), Kezia W. (wife of S. L. Davis), and a daughter, Rachel, who married Washington Meadors and moved to Alabama about 1840.

BOUKNIGHT-Daniel Bouknight made will 1850, and died in October, 185.... leaving widow, Mary, and children: Reuben, Caleb, William, James D., Mary Ann Norris, Leah C. Barre, Caroline E. (married J. R. Eidson), A son, James D., died before the death of his father, leaving widow, Martha, and a daughter, Laura M.

BOULWARE-Isaac Herbert Boulware lived in Newberry County. Robert Boulware died in Newberry County in 1813. He left a widow, Nancy, and children: Andrew, James, Mary, Caty, Elizabeth, and Tabitha, Executors of his will were: Spencer Boulware (brother) and Edmund Spearman.

BOWERS-Benjamin Bowers lived in Edgefield County, leaving a widow, Mary (Ardis)Bowers. David Bowers died in 1834 in Edgefield County, leaving widow, Martha, and children: Catherine Barnes, Anna McCarey, Eliza (her son, Thomas Bowers, shared in estate), Mary (wife of John Hatfield), Susannah (wife of Henry Starr), Sarah (wife of George Dunbar), John . David Bowers had a brother, Philemon Bowers.

Stephen Bowers lived in Newberry County, in the Stoney Batter section. He married a Miss. Bates and had children: David, Samuel, Andrew, Jacob, Levi, John, Sallie,(she married a Wheeler), Elizabeth (married a Fellers), Nancy (married a Maffett), Vina (married a Young).

BOX- Abraham Box lived in Laurens County. Joseph Box was in Laurens County before 1825, and Robert Box was in that county about 1844. Robert married Patsy Burgess (she was widow of William Chandler who had moved to Tennessee about 1810). She was the daughter of Joel Burgess.

BOYCE-John Boyce came from Virginia to Newberry County before the Rev War started. He had sons: James, Robert, John, David, Alexander, and Kerr. James died about 1814, left no family). John died in Laurens County June 22, 1843, leaving children: Hannah, Robert, Sarah, and another daughter who married a Henderson and left children, William T. Henderson, Robert H. Henderson, Sarah C. Henderson(she married Randolph Adams), and a daughter who married John B. Craig(their daughter, Jane, was wife of Dorsey Gary)

BRADLEY- John Bradley lived in Edgefield County. He married Mary Ardis, and had three sons. James Bradley served in the American Army during the Rev War.

BRASWELL- William Braswell died about 1816, leaving widow, Susan, and children: Allen, David, Rutherford, Arthur, Polly, Betsy, James, William, Aaron, Nancy.

BRIDGES-George Bridges married Nancy Edwards and moved in 1806 to Kentucky. Later, they went to Indiana or to Illinois. They had eight children: Allen, William, George, Joseph, Charles. Charles was born April 11, 1802. Other children: John, James, Nancy.

William Bridges died in Newberry County in 1855. He had a daughter, Nancy, who married Timothy

Other Pioneers (continued)

Boozer (son of Henry Boozer, Sr.). Another daughter, Temperance, married Mr. Hussey. A granddaughter, Nancy C. Bridges, married a Mosely.

George Bridges and wife, Anne, conveyed to Robert Drennan, one hundred fifty acres land in Newberry County on September 2, 1797.

BRIGGS—Jesse Briggs, of Union County, married Mrs. Mary Ann (Glenn) Mayes, widow, and had several children. She was the daughter of William Coleman Glenn and Elizabeth (Bowles) Glenn, both from Virginia. Her father served in the American Army during the Rev War, in Va.

BRIGHT—John Bright died about 1808, and left legatees: Barbara Prisock (wife of George Prisock), Elizabeth Bright, and Jacob Bright.

Jacob Braight and wife, Barbara, deeded to Jacob Havacre one hundred acres land on Cannon's Creek in 1787; said lands originally garnted to Matthias Bush, alias Bright or Braight.

William Bright married Polly Fulmer, daughter of Abram and Elizabeth (Summer) Fulmer; they had a son, Dr. George H. Bright. Dr George H. Bright was a physician in Newberry County few years, then moved to Richmond, Va. His son, Dr. Fulmer Bright, also practiced medicine; and was Mayor of the city of Richmond, Va. for several terms.

BROCK—James Brock married Mary Hunt. He died about 1847, and his widow about 1856. Their children were: Aaron, Andrew, Elizabeth, Meredith, Patsy, Malissa, Emoline, Lucinda, Frances, Edna, and Polly. One Elias Brock settled on Reedy River in Laurens County about 1774.

BROOKS—Elisha Brooks lived in the northern part of Newberry County. He died in November, 1807, leaving widow, Nancy (Butler) Brooks, and children: Wesley, Matilda, Lavania, Elizabeth, Edney, Polly, Stanmore, William Butler.

Jesse Brooks married Ann..... about 1778. They left Newberry County before 1800 and settled in Kentucky. Their children were: Ivey, Lavania, William H., Betsy, Thomas, Bird, Patsy. His brother, Elisha Brooks, remained in Newberry County.

Zacariah Smith Brooks died about 1845 in Edgefield County. He left children: Whitfield, Lucinda Bird(she died before the death of her father), Behethleland Bird (she died before her father died).

BROWN—Nathan Brown was born 1731, and died June 28, 1779; buried at King's Creek Church Cemetery. Grissel Brown settled above Indian Creek before the Rev. War. He was born about 1742 and died May 30, 1810; buried at King's Creek Cemetery.

John Brown, native of Scotland or Ireland, first lived near Philadelphia. Pa., where he married Sarah Sims. They came to this section and settled near King's Creek Church. They had a son, Sims, and three daughters. The son served as a patriot in the Rev. War.

Sims Brown married Miss. Baldreck, and had children: James, John C., Richard S., Sims E., and Alexander, Thomas Jefferson, and Sarah. James died January 8, 1813.

One Thomas Brown made will May 8, 1797, and died same year. He left wifow, Winifred, and children: George, Thoms,Netty, Elizabeth, Hannh. Netty married Joseph Goodman. George died in 1806, and left widow, Sarah, and several small children.

James L. Brown married Margaret Law, daughter of James and Martha Law. He left children: James L., Martha E., and Sims E. He was the son of the patriot, Sims Brown.

One Robert Brown was born in County Antrim , Ireland, on May 20, 1762. He came to South Carolina and settled in Newberry County, near where is the town of Prosperity. He maarried Nancy Young on April 8, 1794. Their children were: James, George, Young, Mary Russell, and Elizabeth Moore.

Dr. Jacobs Roberts Brown, a patriot officer in the Rev. War, was one of the County Judges of Newberry when it was first established. He had come from Amherst County, Virginia, his native State; he served in the State Militia of Virginia as Lieutenant and Captain. (See: " Annals of Newberry", Part 1, by Judge J. B. O'Neall).

BROWNING—John Browning came from Virginia to South Carolina before or during the time of the Rev. War. He married twice, his second wife being Susannah......... He had a daughter, Clara (by his first wife) who married David Culbertson, of Pendleton District, S. C.

BRYSON—William Bryson of Laurens County, married a daughter of John Kirk before the year 1799. They had children: James, Sarah, Robert, John, and Jane.

BUCHANAN—John Buchanan came from Virginia and settled in Newoerry County before the Rev War. He died 1793, the date of his will being June 12, 1785. He left widow, Elizabeth, and children: John, Nancy Turley, Micajah, William, Mary Hutchinson, Anna Hoard, Susannah, and Jesse.

Other Pioneers (continued)

James Buchanan died in Abbeville County in 1805, leaving widow, Frances, and the following children: Mary, Rebecca, Frances, and Robert. James Buchanan, son of Robert, is mentioned in his will. Robert died about 1845, left widow, Elizabeth, and children.

Micajah Buchanan died in 1831, left widow, Jane, and children: Thomas G., Clary (a daughter), Drucilla (wife of James Fant), Mildred (wife of Thomas C. Crooks), and Elizabeth (wife of George Souter). Thomas G. died in Union County May 19, 1845, leaving widow, Christina, and children: Franklin, Martha, Jesse, and George.

BUFFINGTON- Peter Buffington died about 1826 in Edgefield County, S. C. William Hester Buffington married Polly Clark, daughter of Henry Clark, of Edgefield County. Their children were: Matilda, Hester, James, Joseph, Henry, Polly. Abner Clark was a brother of Polly (Clark) Buffington. Matilda married James Jones.

BUFORD-Henry Buford married Elizabeth Tucker, in Union County, before the year 1817. She was a daughter of .... and Lucy Tucker.

Leroy Buford moved to Chester District from Virginia after the year 1790. He is buried at Fish Dam Cemetery. He married Frances Ragsdale and had children: Priscilla (married William Gaston), and other children.

BULLOCK- Mrs. Elizabeth Bullock was a daughter of James and Rebecca Williams of Newberry County. She died and left children. A daughter of Bartlett Satterwhite, Elizabeth, married .... Bullock, and had children: Elihue, Benjamin, Satterwhite, James, and Wiley.

BUNDRICK-David Bundrick made will December 24, 1823, and died January 5, 1824, leaving widow, Magdeline, and children: Anna Cabune Bundrick and Alfred Wallis Bundrick.

Jacob Bundrick died 1840, leaving widow, Ruth, and children: James Nathan, Jacob Ivy, John Andrew, Henry A., D. Hamilton, Elizabeth, and Martha. The widow married in 1845 to Benjamin Barrett.

BURKE—James Burke died in Laurens County about 1850. He left widow, Barbara. Mrs. Burke had been married before to a Briggs, and had a son, Jesse Briggs. Her children by James Burke were: James (moved to Alabama), Martin (moved to Texas), Mary (wife of John Templeton), William (moved to Georgia), Sarah Puckett, Jemima (wife of James Foster), Delila Morrell (moved to Texas), Levi (moved to Mississippi). John and Mary Templeton had children: James, Barbara, John, Mary (wife of Joseph Garrett), and William C. Templeton.

BUTLER-Robert Butler married Nancy Boyd. His wife died in 1830, and left children: David K., James S., Jane C. M. Her brother, Hugh K. Boyd, was appointed Administrator. Robert Butler died in 1833 and left widow, Emily(his second wife), and children: David, James, Jane C.M., and Elizabeth A. C.

Rhesa Butler married Elizabeth Dalrymple, a daughter of Thomas Dalrymple, Sr.

BUZHARDT—Jacob Buzhardt made will in 1809 and died soon afterwards. He left widow, Margaret, and children: Phillip, Jacob, Gasper, Elizabeth Wright, and Mary. A gr-son, Thomas Wright. The widow, Ann Margaret, died in 1817.

John Buzhardt married Anna Mary Hair (widow of Peter Hair). Her children by her first husband were: Matthias, John, and others. By John Buzhardt were seven daughters: Mary, Catherine Veits, Rachel Charles, Agnes Stockman, Margaret McCallie, Molly Thomas, Barbara Maffett. Other legatees: Barbara Buzhardt, Anna Mary Buzhardt.

John Buzhardt died about 1816, leaving widow, Elizabeth, and children: Abner, James, Cyrus, John S., Anne C. The widow afterwards married Waldrod Wicker.

BYNUM— Samuel Bynum of Newberry County, married Cinderilla, daughter of Peter and Jane Lester. Jesse Bynum died in Abbeville County about 1790. Turner Bynum was killed in a duel at Hatton's Ford, on August 17, 1832, aged 28 years. He was killed by Benjamin F. Perry who, afterwards, became Governor of South Carolina. His father, Turner Bynum, Sr. was born 1777 in Southhampton, Virginia, married in South Carolina to Elizabeth Miller, daughter of John Miller, of Charleston, and Catherine (Long) Miller, of Newberry, S. C.

BYRD—Solomon Byrd died in 1810 in Edgefield County. He left widow, Nancy, and children: Esther Smith, Eborn, Sally, Elijah, Frank, John, Rachel Jordan, Mary, Billion. The son, Billion, was under age in 1810.

CAIN—Alexander Cain made will September 26, 1805, and died in Union County in year 1806. He left widow, Rhoda, and children: Jemima, Isaac, John, Launcelot, Vardry, Naomi, Polly, Lucy Ann, and Edward Sanders Porter Cain. Isaac died in 1833, left widow, Polly, and children:

Other Pioneers (continued)

Amos, William, Isaac, Elvira, James, and John.

Jonothan Cain lived in Union County. He had children: Abner, Abijah, Hardy, Harold, Elvira (she married a Townsend), Delila (wife of Mahlon Pearson), Rebecca (wife of Jacob Pearson), Barbara (wife of John Pearson),Sally Burgess, Celia (wife of Captain Dawson Hull who died in Spain), John, Abner, Delila, Rebecca, Barbara and Elvira moved to Wayne County, Indiana.

CALHOUN–The pioneer ancestor of the Calhouns of old Abbeville District was Patrick Calhoun who died in Pennsylvania, leaving a widow, Catherin, and several children, who later moved to Virginia. They then moved, about 1760, to Abbeville District, South Carolina. Her three sons who came were, Ezekiel, James, and William.

James Calhoun died about 1843 in Abbeville County, leaving a widow, Sarah, and children: James M., Sarah, John A., and William H.

William Calhoun died about 1840, in Abbeville District, leaving children: James L., Thomas J. Lucretia A. Townes, Martha C. Burt.

Alexander Calhoun, who had come from Ireland, settled in Pendleton District, where he died in 1825. He left a widow, Susannah, and children: John, David, a daughter (wife of George Campbell), a daughter (wife of Abner Ledbetter), daughter (wife of William Bell), a daughter (wife of James Gilmer), Alexander arrived in the United States about 1795, and he received his naturalization papers in 1813.

John Calhoun died in Laurens County about 1838; left a widow, Sarah, and children: Polly Adkins, Matilda, Posey, Squire, Margaret (wife of James Kenman), Clarissa (wife of Hiram Pitts) Lucinda (wife of Barnes Walker), Keziah (wife of Russell Brigs), Nancy (wife of Washington Henderson), Harriet, and Emoline.

Samuel Calhoun (1788--1873), moved to Texas about 1840. His first wife and two sons died in South Carolina before he left. He married again and had children: Martha (wife of James W. Cabiness), William, John H., Catherine, and Lucy.

CALMES–William Calmes was born in Winchester, Virginia, about the year 1761. He came to South Carolina with his father when about twelve years old. His father bought lands on Enoree in section of Newberry County and settled; but, becoming dissatisfied, returned to Virginia, and at the outbreak of the Revolutionary War, William volunteered in the militia of that State, and was soon promoted to Lieutenant in which position he served under the French General Marquis De La Fayette.

After the war he returned to the farm his father had bouth in Newberry County, which had been willed to him. He resided there until 1806 when he bought a place near the town of Newberry, and moved to it for the purpose of educating his children at the Newberry Accademy. He was a member of the House of Representatives, served one term and refused to be a candidate for re-election. He died January 8, 1836. His children were: Nancy (wife of Young John Harrington), Harriet Neville (wife of John T. Swann), Elizabeth (wife of _____ Kincaid), Marquis, William B., Francis F., and George B.

George B. Calmes made will February 3, 1844 and died in March of the same year. His legatees were: John Swindler and his mother, Joicy Swindler, and his brothers and sisters.

CAMERON–James Cameron made will November 18, 1852, and died in Edgefield County in 1858. He left widow, Malinda, and children: John Pressly, Mary Lodoska, James Strong, Margaret Roasannah, Frances Rhydonia, and Randolph Butler Cameron. Executor, and guardian of children: John S. Renwick.

CAMPBELL–Joseph Campbell married Jeanette Boyd, daughter of John Boyd, Sr., and had children: John, Jane (wife of Davis S. Wilson), Mary, Wilson, Elizabeth, Agnes, and Rachel.

Joseph Campbell, Sr. and his wife, Sarah, sold lands in 1787—an original grant to him in 1770. He died in 1791, and left his widow, Sarah, and the following children: Jariat, William, He left a grand-daughter, Betty Anderson.

Mrs. Elizabeth Campbell (widow of Thomas Campbell), died in 1819, and left a son, George, and a daughter, Mary Hare. She left grandchildren: William Hare, and Deborah Hare (children of her son-in-law, Earl Hare).

Robert Campbell and his wife, Mary A. E. (Dugan) Campbel lived in Newberry County. They left a family.

Edmund F. Campbell died in 1849; left a family. His widow, Charlotte, and the following

Other Pioneers (continued)

children: George M., Edmund, Newton, S. A., Hannah, Stephen, James, Ansel, Jefferson, Lucinda, Mary (wife of James Aiken).

Andrew Campbell married Eve Epting, daughter of John Epting and his wife, who are all buried in the Beth Eden Cemetery, about 5 miles north of Newberry Court House.

Abraham Campbell and wife, Frances, lived in Abbeville District before year 1800.

Hugh Campbell married Elizabeth Buchanan and lived in Abbeville District. Their son, Robert, married Virginia Kyle.

CAPPLEMAN—John Cappleman died in Newberry County in 1830. He owned five hundred acres of land on Cannon's Creek, which was divided among his children as follows: Jacob, Margaret (wife of Jacob Chapman), Elizabeth (wife of Peter Taylor), Rebecca, Henry, John, Sarah, Mary Ann, Daniel B., Dolly Ann, and Prussia Ann. The first four named were of full age. Adm. granted to Daniel Boozer.

CARMICHAEL—Patrick Carmichael died in Newberry County about 1802; left a widow, Elizabeth (Thompson) Carmichael. (She was born 1749 and died in 1835)...

William Carmichael died in Newberry County in 1820; left widow, Mary, and children: Arthur, Abraham, and Robert. He willed some of his property to Abraham Young, of Newberry County.

Arthur P. Carmichael was born December 18, 1814, and died in Illinois. He was son of C. A. Carmichael, both having moved to Henderson County, Ill. about 1840. Arthur P. married Jane Henderson, whose family, also, moved to Illinois.

Charles A. Carmichael, Jr., died October 21, 1849, in Newberry County. He left as his legatees his brothers and sisters, viz: James, Ebenezer, William, Arthur, Margaret (wife of William Walker), Jane (wife of James Henderson), Mary Ann, Elizabeth (wife of Franklin Arthur).

Robert Carmichael died about 1855, in Newberry County. He left a widow, Elizabeth, and children Patrick T., Joseph D., Caroline E., Lucinda E., Hannah P. (wife of William M. Davis), Mary Ann (wife of Abram Carmichael), William T., and Oliver B.

Abram Patrick Carmichael died in Coweta County, Georgia, about 1873. He left a widow, Mary J. (Young) Carmichael.

CARTER—Richard Carter and wife, Margaret, were living in Laurens District, in 1773, when he purchased land, and later sold, about 1777, to his son, George Carter. Richard received a grant in year 1769, for 200 acres on Cane Creek in Laurens District. He deeded to another son, Robert, land in 1777; and land to third son, Joseph, in 1784.

George Carter and wife, Naomi, sold their land in Laurens District in year 1771.

Robert Carter, of Camden District, was a Revolutionary War patriot.

Zimri Carter died in Laurens District about 1840. He left a widow, Mary, and children: James, Thomas, William, Henry N., and Jane (she became wife of John Strain). Gr-children were: Mary (wife of Bennett Wallace), Martha M., Jane P. (these were the children of a pre-deceased son, Robert), and James M. and Samuel (children of a pre-deceased son, Richard).

CASEY—General Levi Casey lived in Newberry District, and was one of the first Justices of the County Court in 1785 and 1786. He was one member of a committee to settle the question of the location for the first court house of Newberry County. He served in the Revolutionary War as patriot officer, first as Captain, then as Lieutenant-Colonel; and after the war received the honorary title of Brigidier-General by his government. When he died, about 1807, his widow, Elizabeth, and Josiah Duckett administered on his estate. His children were: Nancy (she married Jacob Rhoads), John, Levi, James D., Samuel O., and a daughter who married Thomas Johnson, and another daughter who had married Thomas Davis.

One John A. Casey married Katherine Shell, daughter of William Shell, of Newberry District.

CARWILE—Zacariah Carwile who lived to be over 90 years old, came to Newberry District from old Abbeville District. He was a patriot in the Revolutionary War. His son, John S. Carwile, was a school teacher; but later he became the Tax Collector of Newberry District, and in 1820 he was elected Sheriff of Newberry County. He (the son) married on December 20, 1809, to Elizabeth Williams, and reared seven children, viz: Mary (wife of Dr. Richar C. Griffin), Zacariah, Sarah (wife of Hilliary Gary), John B., Richar C., Elizabeth, and Caroline.

CARSON—John Carson died in 1808 in Edgefield District. He left a widow, Helen, and several children.

James Carson, Sr., died about 1820 or 21 in Edgefield District, and left children: James,

Other Pioneers (continued)

Robert and Sally Abernathy. He left grand-children: James Warren Carson, Randal and Drucilla De La Laughter, Harmon Bozeman Carson, Thomas Abernathy Carson, R. A. Carson, and James W. B. Carson.

Thomas Carson died about 1790. He came to America from North Ireland. At his death he left a widow, Margaret, and several children, among whom was a daughter, Elizabeth (she was born in North Ireland about 1764); who married John McGough.

CASON-William Cason, Sr. and his wife, Ann, lived in Laurens District. He had a brother, Benjamin Cason. His son, William Cason, Jr., lived in his father's plantation near Bush River, and married Mary ....; afterwards moving into Edgefield County, before the year 1800. They had first settled near Bush River in Newberry District, before 1780.

Thomas Cason was in Laurens District about 1800. At his death he left four children: John, James, William, and Samuel. His sister, Mary, died between 1812 and 1820. Another sister, Sarah, married ..... Miller, and died about 1828, leaving a step-son, John Miller, a step-daughter, Rebecca Cason, and brothers, Thomas and William.

William Cason had children, Thomas and Elizabeth (she married ..... Burkhalter), and, probably others.

Joseph Cason and wife, Rebecca, (she was the daughter of John Miller),lived in Laurens County. John Miller had married Sarah Cason (his second wife) who was not the mother of his children.

CATES-Aaron Cates made will February 7, 1816, and died in same year. He left property to his daughter, Dorothy Wadlington, and her three daughters, who were: Dorothy Ann (wife of Jefferson L. Edwards), Polly Brooks Wadlington, and Sarah Susannah Frances Wadlington. A nephew, Aaron Cates (sone of a brother Robert Cates), is named in will. Other legatees were: Aaron Cates, a cousin (son of John Cates living in Tennessee).

Robert Cates died about 1820, leaving widow, Sarah, and the following other distributees: Asa, Aaron, Elizabeth (wife of Robert Cooper), Sarah, Robert T., and John S. Cates.

Ezra Cates, surviving Executor of the will of Thomas Cates, deceased, is named in settlement.

Allen Cates married Polly Amos, daughter of Clough and Elizabeth Amos.

Isiaah Cates died about 1800, leaving widow, Jane, and children: Ezra, Nancy, Aaron, William, Elizabeth, and Susannah.

CAUGHMAN-Jacob Caughman married before the year 1830 to Elizabeth, daughter of Frederick and Elizabeth (Chapman) Kinard. He died early, left son, Noah Caughman. His widow married John Rhinehardt.

Among those named in the first U. S. Census, 1790, are: Andrew Coafman, Martin Coafman, and Elizabeth Coafman. They were in Lexington District.

CHALMERS-William Chalmers died about 183... and left children: David, James, Jane (wife of John Clary), Alexander W., Nancy (wife of James P. McCrackin), Elizabeth (wife of .... McDill). David and Jane Boyd moved to Green County, Ohio.

Alexander Chalmers married Dorothy Beasley, daughter of Thomas Beasley of Laurens District. They had children: Martha A., Permelia, Elizabeth J., William S., and Frances.

Thomas B. Chalmers married the widow of Hugh K. Boyd and afterwards left the State, supposedly to the Northwest.

Thomas A. W. Chalmers and Martha A. W. Chalmers, Frederick Boozer and Eliza P. Boozer, John R. Leavell and Elizabeth J. Leavell, William S. Chalmers, Thomas B. Chalmers(by Thomas Chalmers, Guardian), were complainants in equity court in year 1843.

CHAMBERS-Alexander Chambers died about 1795 in Newberry District, leaving widow, Jane, who died in 1820. Their children were: Alexander, Jane (wife of John Martin), George H., Elizabeth Paul, Grace (wife of John Johnson), Margaret (wife of William Waldrop), Frances M (wife of William Mangum), and Matthew. Matthew Chambers married Jane Harper and had son, Alexander Chambers.

Thoroughgood Chambers made will March 10, 1809, and died same year. He left one-half of his estate to his widow, Ann, and the other one-half to Elizabeth Briton Kelly.
Executor: Samuel E. Kenner. Mrs. Ann Chambers died about 1814. Spencer Wadlington married in 1817 to Ann B. Kelly.

Other Pioneers (continued)

Stephen Chambers died in Abbeville County about 1809.

Benjamine Chambers died in Abbeville County in 1827, and left a widow, and a daughter, Arabella Crawford.

CHAPELL-Henry Chapell died 1820, left a widow, Mary, and children: Martha Caroline (widow of Phil B. Waters), Samuel M., Elizabeth Frances (she died young). His brother, William Chapell, had died a few years prior to his death. They both lived across the river, in old Edgefield County (now Saluda County). The widow, Mary, afterwards married Oliver Towles.

COBB-John Cobb died in Abbeville District about 1782.

Nathaniel Cobb died in Union District about 1814, leaving a widow, Elizabeth, and children: Mary, Sarah, Fanny, Nancy, and Betty. He may have had sons, also, as part of his will is missing.

James Cobb and wife, Elizabeth, sold lands in Union County in 1796.

Howell Cobb died in Newberry District about 1812-13, left widow, Abigail, and children: Delton and Sarah.

Benjamin Cobb died in Newberry County about 1808, left widow, Elizabeth, and Children: James, Howell, Susannah (married a Tate and had Children: Robert, Samuel, Anne, William) (all were minors in 1808).

Ransome Cobb died in Greenville District about 1835, and left a widow, Matilda, and children: Maria, William, Emily, William T., James H., Judith Caroline--all minors in 1835

Robert Cobb, Sr. died in Pendleton District about 1827; left children: Robert, Catherine (wife of William Kirksey), Penelope (wife of William Moore), Tobias (died before death of his father and left children: Elizabeth, Penelope, and Leah). Gr-sons: Jesse G., Pressly G., Samuel P.—— all sons of Robert, Jr. and wife, Jemima (Garner) Cobb.

Edmund Cobb, of Union District, gave house and lot to the Elders of the Presbyterian Society, which they occupied as a Meeting House. He died about 1806, leaving a widow, Margaret.

CLAPP-Jacob Clapp died in 1815 in Newberry County. He left widow, Susannah, and the following children: Adam (aged 22), John (aged 21), David (aged 19), Henry (aged 16), Elizabeth (aged 11), Sarah (she died in 1822), and Rebecca (aged 9). These were ages of children in year 1824, at the time bill in equity was filed.

CLARK-The Clark families were many in the counties of Newberry and Abbeville, and some lived in the counties of Edgefield and Laurens, during the early days. They were of Presbyterian stock and came from Scotland or Ireland before the Revolutionary War.

William Clark made a will July 3, 1790, and died in 1791 in Abbeville County. He left a widow, Mary, and children: David, Alexander, Jane, Mary, Susannah, Robert, William, and John Huston. Mary (the daughter) died in 1805, and her will names her brothers and sisters as legatees, also James Bates, James C. Hemphill, and Margaret Hemphill. William, Jr. died in 1809, left no family. John Huston Clark died in 1803 and left widow, Sarah, and brothers and sisters as legatees.

Dr. Benjamin Clark died in 1796, left brother, Ebenezar Clark, and two children, Elizabeth and Jean N. He left some personal property to the children of his mother-in-law, Mrs. Agnes Cochran, whose names were John, James, and David Cochran.

Samuel Cochran died about 1805 in Abbeville County, and left widow, Rosannah, and children: John, Leving, Moses, George, Permelia, Aaron, Elizabeth, Cassa, Peggy, Samuel, Mary, and Thomas.

John Clark died about 1840 in Abbeville County. Legatees: John Clark Scott (son of William Scott); sisters, Nancy Clark, and Hannah Goodman; daughters of John Boyd, deceased, Celia D. Boyd, and Esther C. Boyd; children of James Wilson, deceased, Katherine, Joseph, Samuel, and James Wilson. Executors: Thomas Dubose and Thomas Cunningham.

William Clark died 1842 in Abbeville County and left propery to his nephew, William Clark, and to children of a deceased nephew, Patrick C. Clark. Other distributees in settlement made in 1843 were: Jane A. Clark (wife of Stephen C. Neel), Sarah K. Clark (wife of Alexander McAlister), John A. Clark, deceased; edmund P. Clark, deceased; and Mary Ann Clark (wife of William Kelly and niece of William Clark).

Thomas Clark made will in year 1790 and died in 1793. He left widow, Mary, and children: John, Thomas, George, James, Robert, Mary (wife of John Lewis), Jean (wife of Joan Reese), Elizabeth, Priscilla, and Ann. John died in 1795 and left no family. Thomas died in 1808.

Other Pioneers (continued)

George Clark died March 12, 1838, in Newberry County, and the following persons shared his property: Mrs. Mary E. Hardy, George I. K. Clark, William Maybin, W. T. Holleyman, and W. S. Clark. A daughter, Harriet, married Herman Holleyman December 19, 1838; she died November 6, 1840, and afterwards he married her sister, Jane E. Clark.

John T. Clark died about 1850 in Laurens County. Adm. granted to Allen W. Clark.

William Clark and wife, Judith, filed a bill of complaint against estate of Edmund Craddock, father of Judith Clark. Edmund Craddock died October 27, 1791. His wife was Ann Elmore, daughter of Thomas Elmore of Amelia County, Virginia. Ann Craddock (widow) married James Saxon of Virginia.

John Clark died January 15, 1821, and left widow, Sarah, and children: William, Thomas, James, Ann Foster, Martha, and Sarah (wife of Edward Johnson).

One George Clark died in 1834, leaving widow, Catherine, and children: Margaret Neel, Thomas L., Richard P., John H. (died young and left no family), and Sarah M. (wife of Dr. Thompson Wilson). He lived on Bush River.

CHILDS (CHILES)-James Chiles who lived a short time in Newberry County, where he married Elizabeth A. Caldwell (daughter of James and Elizabeth Forrest Caldwell), moved to Green County Alabama. His wife died in Newberry about 1830. They had a son, William C., and a daughter, Elizabeth A. Chiles.

Robert Child was born November 6, 1791, in Culpepper County, Virginia, and died in old Abbeville District, (this section which is now in Greenwood County), South Carolina, about 1815, to which place he had moved from Virginia. His wife, Sarah E. (daughter of Richard M. and Elizabeth Todd, of Abbeville District), was born October 27, 1823, and died March 31, 1847. They are both buried in the old Child Cemetery, in the southern section of Greenwood County. J. W. Child is, also, buried in the same cemetery. He died August 11, 1858, aged 57 years; and his wife, M. F. Child, died November 20, 1837, aged 33 years.

CHUPP-Joseph Chupp died in Newberry County about 1852. He left a widow, Elisabeth, and a son, Jesse, who received his lands on Beaver Dam Creek. A provision in his will that the lands to go to the children of his brother, David Chupp, if his son should die without issue.

CLEMENTS(CLEMMONS)-Obediah Clements died in Egefield County about 1802, leaving widow, Sarah, and Children: (names not given in his will). Witnesses to will were Simon Clements, George Clements, Stephen Clements. Exrs: Captain John Terry, Stephen Terry.

William Clements and wife, Elisabeth, conveyed lands in Edgefield County in year 1825.

Jacob Clements and wife, Fanny, lived in Laurens County, S. C. They moved to Green County, Kentucky, before the year 1820.

Stephen Clements and wife, Mary, sold land in Laurens County in 1853.

Abraham Clements lived in Spartanburg County, S. C., but moved to Rutherford County, N. C. before the year 1779. Edmond and Edward Clements, brothers, were in Spartanburg County in 1816.

COATE-John Coate (known as "Little John" Coate), was the original settler on the lands on which the town of Newberry is located. He gave to the town and the county two acres on which to erect a court house and other public buildings, and it is the same where is now the public square and old court house. This grant was made September 8, 1789, seven years after the county was formed, to James Mayson, Philemon Waters, Robert Rutherford, William Caldwell, and Jacob Roberts Brown, who were then the county judges, " a lot of two acres lying on a small hill West of the new dwelling house of John Coate....." John Coate's wife was named Susannah. He died about 1802. Two sons, Marmaduke and Henry, lived in the village. Henry married Elisabeth Long, daughter of Benjmain Long, and after her death he married her sister, Polly Long.

Another John Coate died about 1803, his will being dated May 25, 1799. He left widow, Mary, and children: Samuel, John, William, James, Mary Pemberton, Katy Cassells, and Rebecca.

Thomas Coate made will October 6, 1799, and died in the year 1800; He left widow, Sarah Ann, and children: James, Ann, Katy, Mary, William, Jesse, and Sarah.

John Coate(of Georgia) died about 1803, and left widow,Mary, and children: Mary (wife of Robert Ramage), Rebecca (wife of Thomas Morgan), Anna (wife of Benjamen Lake).

Other Pioneers (continued)

One John Coate died about 1802-1803, left widow, Rachel, and children: James, Sampson, Wright. Wright Coate made will November 19, 1808, and died in same year. He left widow, Mary, and children: Frederick , Daniel, and Susan. Exr: John Belton O'Neall.
Mrs. Rachel Coate was the widow of John Wright when she married Jon Coate.

William Coate, Elisabeth Coate, Jesse Coate, and Sarah (Coate) Summers, Hardy Fluker and his wife, Sophia (Coate) Fluker, of Edgefield County, were some of the heirs of " Little John" Coate.

One William Coate made will July, 1816, and died about 182-22. He left widow, Mary, and children: John, Mary (married a Taylor), Sarah (wife of Patrick McKennan), Margaret, Ann, Dorothy, William, Reuben, Jesse.

James Coate died in 1806, leaving widow, Rebecca, and children: Nancy (she died young), and Mary (married Joseph Hall).

Mrs. Ann Coate made will March 20, 1805, and died same year. Her legatees were as follows: Daughters, Jean, (she married a Vardaman), Nancy Cannon, Sarah Cannon; sons,by a former husband, George Johnson and Levi Johnson; grand-daughter, Mary Koone; grand-son, Daniel Johnson.

Samuel Coate died in 1807, and left widow, Mary, and other legatees as follows: James Wilson, James Reeder, James Steadman, John Williams, John Taylor, Jesse Neel, Deliliah Coate.

Captain Henry Coate(son of " Little John"), died January, 1828, and left widow, Polly (Long) Coate, and children: Amelia(wife of John Lindsey), Elizabeth (wife of William G. Nance who died just before death of her father),John , James M., George R., Benjamin F., Amanda (she married Benjamin F. Cochran), William H. , and Barbara. Benjamin F. and Amanda Cochran moved to Richmond, Va. Amelia Lindsey was the only child by his first marriage to Elizabeth Long. The widow, Polly, afterwards married John Gaskins, and descendents moved to Mississippi.

COCHRAN-Andrew Cochran died in 1796 in Abbeville County. He left children: Andrew, Rachel (wife of Samuel Patterson), Jean (wife of John Beatty), Eleanor (wife of ...... McCreary),Hugh, John, and William. Samuel Glasgow, a grand-son, received part of his estate.

James Cochran, Esq., died in Abbeville County in 1822, leavinga widow, and the following children: Martha, Nancy, Sarah, James, and Reuben.

David Cochran died in Abbeville County about 1825. His three youngest children were: Alexander Porter, Sarah Shaw, and Hanna F. Cochran.

John Cochran died about 1860 in Abbeville County, leaving widow, Elisabeth (Lee) Cochran, and children: Wade E., Elisabeth P., Samuel G., and Mary R. (wife of Samuel F. Stephens).

COCKERILL- Sanford Cockerill made will January 31, 1818, and died about 1820. His wife had previously died. He left children: Thomas and Elisabeth W. Grand-children: Amos Jenkins, John Jenkins, Craven Jenkins, Elizabeth Vant (they were children of a deceased daughter, Cynthia, wife of Aaron Jenkins).

COFIELD-Dr. James Cofield moved from Union County to Newberry County. He was born in 1844, and died in 1888.

COHE-Joseph Cohe made will September 16, 1807, and died in Newberry County about 1808. His daughter, Elizabeth, married Samuel Jenkins. His two other daughters were: Mary (wife of John Conrad Ream), Margaret (wife of George Cherry). A grand-son, Joseph Cherry, shared in his estate.

COLE-James Cole, Sr., died about 1805 in Newberry County. He left widow, Jeanor (she died in 1823), and children: John B., Thomas, James, Gabriel, Bailey, Rchard, Jeanor. Jeanor, the daughter, amrried Jacob Gary; she died in 1822 leaving two children, William Bailey Gary and Jeanor Gary(Jeanor Gary died shortly after the death of her mother). Exr: William C. Griffin. In the will of Mrs. Jeanor Cole is named her daughter-in-law, Rebecca Steadman, whose former husband was her deceased son, Thomas Cole. Sons named in her will were: Bailey, Richard, John B., James, and Gabriel Cole. Thomas Cole's three children were, James, Equilla, and Providence.

William Cole died about 1804, in Newberry County. He left widow, Rachel, and children: David, Betsy(wife of Chesley Davis), Jesse, Mary (wife of William Muckles), The widow, Rachel, afterwards married Providence Williams who died in year 1816.

John Cole, Sr., died in 1805 in Newberry County. He left widow, Mary, and children: Jesse G., William, Mason G., John, Reuben, Elisabeth, Mary, and Crawford.

Other Pioneers (continued)

COLEMAN-Robert Coleman died 1783, and Phil Coleman died in 1785, both in Abbeville District. Daniel Coleman died in Edgefield District about 1802, leaving widow, Lucy, and children: John, Ann, Thornton, Parthena, Barbara, and Patty.

Daniel Coleman died aboult 1819 in Abbeville District, leaving widow, Edney, and a son, Thomas Jefferson Coleman, and sons-in-law, Joseph Griffin and Larkin Griffin.

William Coleman died about 1825 in Abbeville District, leaving widow, Nancy, and children: James Wells Coleman, Frances Cookson Coleman, Nancy Wells Coleman, and John Thornton Coleman.

John Coleman died before 1829, and his widow, Mary, died in that year. Their children were: Dorest, Sarah, Martha, Mary, Richard, John, William, Edward, James, and Matthew W. Matthew W. died in 1840, leaving brothers and sisters as legatees. Rchard died about 1809, and left widow, Martha.

George Coleman died in 1857 in Abbeville District, leaving widow, Margaret, and children: Jane (wife of William Childs), Silas T., Thomas E., James H., Mary K., Margaret A., Albert A., Robert A., and William S. Coleman. All were by his second wife, the widow. Children by his first wife were: George, Samuel, and Elizabeth.

COLLIER-Benjamin Collier made will July 2, 1797, and died same year, in Newberry District. He left widow, Elizabeth, and children: John, Joseph, William , Anne, Benjamin, and Audrey. Some of the children moved to Georgia. Joseph died in 1819 in Edgefield District; left widow,Amy, and children: Amy Farrow, Hillary, Polly (wife of Samuel Boyd), Albion, Thomas, Sarah G. Coombs, and Nancy Talbert. Samuel and Polly Boyd had children: John, Joseph, Amy, Augustus, Sarah, and Cynthia Boyd. Other grand-children were: Mary Madeline Chasteen Garrett, Amy Welborn, Joseph Collier, Anna Collier, Edward Collier.

COLLINS-John Collins died about 1801 in Abbeville District. Charles Collins, Sr. died in 1836 in Abbeville District, leaving widow, Sarah (she died 1837), and the following children: James, Charles, Ceala Graham, Esther Pope, Mary Pope. Charles, Jr. died about 1836, after his father's death, and left widow, Jane, and children: Nancy, Mahala, Elizabeth, Franky, Charles, Ephriam, Noah, Manessa, Gabriel, Louvania, Lucinda (last three were minors in 1836).

Moseley Collins died about 1797 in Fairfield District. He left a brother. Michael, and sisters: Ann, Elizabeth, Ruthy Drake, and Sally Kirby.

Daniel Collins made will February 7, 1815, and died in Fairfield District, leaving widow, Eleanor, and children: Cynthia, Jane, and Polly.

CONWELL-Joseph Conwell died about 1817 in Newberry District, leaving widow, Sophia, and children: Daniel G., Joseph, and others. Joseph is named as the youngest child.

John Conwell died in 1816, left mother, Rachel, and the following brothers and sisters: Hosea, Bailey, Benjamin, Wilkes, Elizabeth (wife of John Rikard). Hosea died in 1829. Bailey died about 1845, leaving widow, Catherine, and children: Rebecca (wife of Benjamin D. Lake), Ellen, Mary, Drayton, and Amos.

Joseph G. Conwell married Mary Schumpert, daughter of Jacob and Eleanor Schumpert.

Yates Conwell died about 1816. William Conwell died about 1802, leaving widow, Hetty, and children, including a son, Joseph, who died about 1817.

COOK-Henry Cook, of Brunswick County, Virginia, was the father of John and Drury Cook. Drury settled in North Carolina, while John went to Ninety Six District, South Carolina. John lived near what is known as Cook's Ferry before the Rev. War. He married his first wife in Virginia, and his second wife was the daughter of General John Pearson—Martha Pearson. John was a Captain and patriot in the Rev. War. After the death of his second wife, Martha, he moved to Hancock County, Georgia, and married a third time. He died there about 1812. Sons by his second wife were: John (married Ellen Hampton), Burrel who married Mary Pope, (daughter of Solomon Pope), Phillip (married Martha Wooten), Henry who never married, Isaac who married Elizabeth Rivers, Mrs. Thomas Hutchinson, Mrs. Gundest, Mrs. McCreless, Mrs. Bellamy, Mrs. Herbert, Mrs. Battle, Mrs. Daniel.(The above data compiled by Mrs. Mary Laurence Cook Woodson in 1870).

Jacob Cook died about 1834 in Newberry District, leaving widow, Margaret (she his second wife was not mother of children), and the following children: John, David, Jacob, Henry, Michael, and the wife of Samuel Bowers, the wife of William R. King, Levi, ames G., Sarah D.

Other Pioneers (continued)

Allen A., Samuel J., Phillip, Caleb, and Anderson Alford. The minor children of Samuel Bowers were: Jacob, Rebecca, and Elizabeth.

George A. Cook died January 6, 1856, leaving widow, Nancy C., and children: Sallie L., Drayton B., Texana E., Ebenezar M., and Nancy Y.

Phillip Cook died in October, 1862, and left as his only distributees the following: Sarah D., his sister, (wife of John A. Bedenbaugh); and the children of his brother, Allen, who were, George, Nancy, Ellen, Emma, John; and the children of his brother, Samuel J., who were, Drayton, Sallie, Texana, Ebenezer, and Nancy Y. (as above).

COOPER-William Cooper made will December 7, 1800, which was proved in Court January 4, 1801. He died in December, 1800, leaving widow, Elizabeth, and children: Joseph, Daniel, William, John, Stephen, Abigail, Hannah, Robert, Henry, and George. Henry's daughter, Anne, married James K. Anderson, and they moved to Giles County, Tennessee. Henry's widow, Eleanor, married John Edmondson and moved to Giles County, Tennessee.

Powell Cooper died about 1834, leaving widow, Martha, and the following children: Eliza (wife of Henry G. Sibley), Elizabeth (wife of Isaac Jenkins, the son of John Jenkins). Elizabeth and Isaac Jenkins married in 1835.

COPPOCK-Joseph Coppock was a Quaker and lived on Bush River. He left a will dated October 11, 1799, and died about 1801. He left widow, Jane, and children: John, Thomas, Benjamin, Joseph, Elizabeth Coate, Margaret, Jane, Samuel, William, and Jesse. Joseph, Jr. died about 1815 to '20, leaving widow, Esther, who died in 1826. Their children were: Sophia (wife of James Divver), Rhoda (wife of Elihu Julien), Sampson, Young Joseph, Philadelphia, Esther, and Patterson.

Joseph Coppock died 1801, leaving will which was proved same year. He left widow, Abigail, and children: Aaron, John, the wife of Benjamin Weeks, Susannah, Abigail, Mary, Isaac, Anne, Prudence and Samuel. Isaac Coppock died about 1817, leaving the following children: Mark, Isaac, Mary, and Eleanor. Executor: John Jenkins.

COTHRAN-Alexander Cothran lived on Beaver Dam Creek, but moved to Abbeville District where he died. Dempsey Cothran married Rosa Waters, a daughter of David Waters, of Newberry District, in year 1815.

Samuel Cothran moved to Abbeville District where he died in 1826, leaving widow, Polly, and children: Dempsey, John, Charlotte Stephens, Wade S., and Dolly Ann. He left a grand-son, Franklin Stephens, who is named as one his distributees .

COTTER-William Cotter was an American soldier in the Rev. War, in a Virginia Regiment. He married Catherine Vance and settled in Union District, South Carolina. They had several children, one of whom was a son, John Vance Cotter.

COWAN-Andrew Cowan died about 1788 in Abbeville District, leaving widow, Ann, and children: John, Isaac, William, Ann, Elizabeth, Mary, and Leany. John Cowan died about 1790-93, in Abbeville District; left widow, Margaret, and children: James, John Archy, Samuel, Susan, Mary, Eleanor, Nevil, and Elizabeth Walton. William Cowan died about 1810, leaving widow, Margaret, and children: .... His brother, Isaac, died about 1831, leaving widow, Jane, and children: James, John, Annie Hawthorne, Elizabeth Lyons, Polly Evans, Jane Ellis,......; and grand-children, Isaac C. Richey, Elizabeth D. Rcihey, and Jane T. Hawthorne.

David Cowan died about 1826, in Laurens District. His legatees were: James, John, Francis, Celia, Anne, Rebecca, Magdeline. Magdeline married Joseph McCollough.

William Cowan died in Laurens District about 1840, leaving five children, three of whom are named in the settlement of his estate, as follows: William A., Mary A. G., and Sarah.

CRAIG-William C. Craig, of Laurens District, married before 1832 to Elizabeth Boyce, a daughter of John and Sarah (Robertson) Boyce, of Newberry District.

CROTWELL-Alfred Crotwell married Sarah Victpria Cannon, in Newberry County.

CRUMPTON-Thomas Crumpton, Sr., died in Spartanburg District in September, 1816. He left widow, Rachel, and children: Matthew and Thomas. Matthew died and left widow, Elizabeth, and two children: Thomas and Rachel.

Other Pioneers (continued)

CLARY—Daniel Clary lived in Edgefield District. He died in November, 1824, leaving widow, Frances, and children: Matthew, William, Martha, Wesley, Ivey E., Nancy. William moved to Gallatin, Illinois. Martha married Jordan Hunt, and moved to Epson County, Georgia. Wesley, too, left the State. The son, Matthew, lived and died in Edgefield District. Daniel Clary was a Tory in the Rev. War, and is referred to in the " Annals of Newberry".
David Clary was son of a pioneer from Ireland, who came to America after the end of the Rev. War, and settled near Indian Creek in Newberry District. David married Elizabeth, daughter of Francis Wilson, before the year 1836. They joined the Covenanter Church. Some of the family are buried at old Head Springs Church Cemetry.

COX—Andrew Cox (Opcks)was granted land on the North side of Saluda River on March 21, 1768, including one hundred acres.
Cornelius Cox made will 1784, and died about 1788-'89. He left widow, Ann, and children: John, William, George (he died in 1791), James (he died 1794), Mary(she married Joshua Stewart), Elizabeth (wife of William Stewart), Margaret (wife of John Van Lew), Sarah (wife of Francis Higgins). Mrs. Sarah Higgins died in 1799, leaving children: Francis B., Charlotte (wife of William Wilson), and Dorothy.
Allen Cox, Sr. died before the year 1798. His heirs and legatees named in a deed executed in 1799 were: James Cox, Allen Cox, Jr., Robert Cox, Henry Hazel, George Gothard, Lewis Watson, John Watson, Zebulon Savage, and Daniel Cox. Allen, Jr. made will 1831, and died October 15, 1831, leaving widow, Mary, and children: Abraham Allen (cripple),Sidney (she married.......Todd), and the wife of Lewis Plant, the wife of James Bearden, Pleasant Cox, and Behethlehand C. Phillips. Some of these moved to Georgia, as did the widow, Mrs. Mary Cox. William Cox made will November 28, 1804, and died 1805, leaving widow, Eliza, and children: James Pressley, Elizabeth, Cornelius, William. Mrs. Eliza Cox married, later, to a Mr. Webber. William, the youngest, was born after the will was made. The father, William Cox, Sr., was a son of Cornelius Cox, Sr.

CRENSHAW—Charles Crenshaw was born in Virginia, married Eunice White of that State, and moved to South Carolina, settled on King's Creek. He was a son of William Crenshaw, of Amelia County, Virginia, and wife, Miss. Carr. Charles was one of the founders of old Mount Bethel Academy. He had a large family but many of his children died young. He died in 1814, leaving his widow, Eunice, and children: Archibald, Abner, Anderson, Walter, Willis, and Phoebe. Archibald died about 1863, leaving some property to his daughters. Dr. Abner Crenshaw married Charlotte Elmore, daughter of John A. Elmore, and moved to Alabama. His first wife is buried in Laurens Cemetery, Laurens, S. C. Walter died in Newberry County, unmarried. Willis married Amanda Chiles, daughter of Walter Chiles, of Abbeville County. Phoebe died young, unmarried.
Anderson Crenshaw(son of Charles), practiced law in Newberry few years, then moved to Alabama where he became a distinguished Judge. He was the first graduate of the South Carolina College (now South Carolina University), at Columbia, S. C., in the year 1806, the only member of his class. He married Mary Chiles, of Abbeville County, a daughter of Thomas Chiles; and two of their sons, Thomas and Walter, were born in the town of Newberry, another son, Rev. Charles Edward Crenshaw, was born in Alabama.

CRESWELL—Col. James Creswell died in November, 1800, in Newberry District. He owned land near the line of Newberry and Laurens Counties, known as the "Island Ford Plantation". His widow, Jeanette, married about 1802 to Major Richard Watts. She had one child by Col. Creswell, a daughter named Matilda who married William Caldwell, Esq. Matilda died in 1817, leaving two children, James and William Caldwell. Her husband, William Caldwell, died on January 11, 1826, leaving a widow, Harriet (his second wife), and the two children named above.

CRISP—John Crisp lived in Laurens District. He married Sarah Allen, daughter of Charles Allen, a Rev War patriot. They had children: Allen, Lucy, Joel, Edwin, Margaret, John, George, Susan, Manima, Lemuel, Millie (she was sometimes called, " Bettie"), John, Jr. married in 1848 to Jane Bryson who was his first wife. His second wife was Isabella Davis. Children by his first wife were: Sarah Allen, Mary Elizabeth, and Matthew Bryson. Children by his second wife were: William Roger, John Headley, and Ida Mason.

Other Pioneers (continued)

CROSSON— Thomas Crosson came from Ireland, first settled in Virginia before coming to South Carolina. He and two sons, Alexandre and John, settled in Newberry County before the Rev. War. One of his sons, Thomas, lived in Newberry County. Another, Robert, moved to Abbeville County.

David A. Crosson died about 1831, leaving widow, Isabella, and children: James M., Sarah A., and Mary. The children were by a former marriage.

John Crosson lived in Newberry County; died about 1829, leaving a son, David A. (above). They belonged to the Covenanter Church.

A descendent, Judge Crosson, a distingusied lawyer and jurist, moved to Texas.

CROW—William Crow died before the year 1800, left widow, Sarah, and children: Charles, and others. Charles made will April 6, 1802, and died same year, leaving widow, Elizabeth, and children: Charles, Jr., ...

CRUMLEY—James Crumley lived on Bush River in Newberry County, and died on his plantation in 1816. He left widow, Margaret, and children: John, Samuel, Russell, and Ira. His widow married Thomas Waters in 1820.

John Crumley, probably the pioneer of the family, bought land on Bush River in year 1770. He made will June 19, 1794, and died same year, leaving widow, Hannah, and children: Charles, Thomas (he married Ruth......), Samuel, James, Benjamin, Rachel Barrett, Catherine, Jemima, Sarah. Charles married Rebecca Heaton and they had a son, Benjamin, who married Joan Gregory. Benjamin and Joan were the parents of William Smith Crumley who married Elizabeth (Jones) Monroe of Laurens County. They moved to Georgia.

CUNNINGHAM— John Cunningham died in Newberry District about 1799. He left land in Pendleton District, which was originally granted to James Cunningham. to his widow, Mary, and two children, William, and Kate Tinsley (she married David Thompson). Children of David and Kate Thompson were: Bryant, Lucretia, and Sarah.

Patrick Cunningham, came from Virginia to Laurens District before the Rev. War. He was a Tory, and abrother of the celebrated Tory leader, "Bloody Bill" Cunningham.

Arthur Cunningham came from Ireland, and settled first in Greenville District, about 1768. He died in Anderson County about 1798, leaving widow, Jane, and children: James, John, Samuel, Sarah Fleming, Jane Carson, and a daughter, Margaret, who died young. Samuel and his family moved to Illinois. John and James were patriots in the Rev. War; they moved to Georgia. John Married Ann Davis.

CURETON—Captain John Cureton was an American Officer in the Rev. War; commanded a company in regiment of Col. Williamson. He lived in Newberry County, and died not many years after the war. His widow, Hannah (Thrweatt) Cureton, died 1821, leaving a will dated November 5, 1816. Their children were: Thomas T., Susannah K. (married a Hunter), Daniel T., Elizabeth B., and George W. George W. Cureton died in 1824. Thomas T. made will May 7, 1827, and died same year. He left one-third of all his property to his widow, Mary A., and his children to receive their shares as they becameof age. The will was made in Newton County, Georgia—or Newnan County. While in Newberry he served as Sheriff in 1812-14. In 1810 he was elected Major of the upper batallion of the 39th regiment. Elected Ordinary of Newberry District, resigned in 1827, and moved to Georgia.

John Moon Cureton lived in Laurens County, but died in Greenville County. He left widow, Nancy, and children: Robert, Pleasant, Nancy Ligon, and Polly Kilgore.

Daniel T. Cureton, son of Captain John, married March 8, 1811, to Sybel Matthews.

James Cureton died in Newberry County January 29, 1866, (killed by negroes). He left widow, Sarah, and children: Malissa, Harris, Cebilla (wife of George Brown), Fred S., Elisha A., Mary E., and Sarah A.

DALRYMPLE— George Dalrymple received a grant og two hundred acres land on Bush River on November 14, 1754. He was granted, also, three hundred acres on Carson's Creek on Saluda River, April 2, 1773.. John Dalrymple received a grant of one hundred fifty acres on Bush River, July 8, 1774. Thomas Dalrymple received a garnt of one hundred acres on Bush River, November 19, 1772. Samuel Dalrymple received a grant of one hundred acres on Bush River, July 8, 1774.

John Dalrymple was a private in South Carolina Militia during the Rev War. His wife, Susannah, survived him. Their children were: Thomas, Elizabeth, John, Mary, Rebecca, and Sarah.

Other Pioneers (continued)

Thomas Dalrymple made will February 26, 1844, and died about 1845, leaving widow, Nancy, and children: Stephen M. (he married Eleanor.......), Elizabeth (wife of Rehesa Butler), Susan (wife of Wiliam Satterwhite), Nancy, Wade, Thomas W., and Sarah Ann (she was the only child by second wife). A grand-son, Thomas Butler, and a grand-daughter, Sophronia Caroline Dalrymple, are named in his will.

Thomas W. Dalrymple made will April 30, 1855, and died October 26, 1856. His legatees were his brothers and sisters. At this time Nancy was married to James E. Peterson. Sophronia Caroline was twenty one years old on December 5, 1851. They moved to Cass County, Georgia.

John Dalrymple (son of John), married Ann Dalrymple, a cousin. Their children were: John, Henry, Lucretia, Mahala, Benjamin, Susannah, Lucinda, and Ephriam. Rebecca, daughter John Dalrymple, Sr., married Jesse Jones, and their children were: John, Ephriam, Samuel, Lewis D., and Eleanor. Lewis D. Jones married his cousin, Susannah Dalrymple, daughter of John Dalrymple, Jr., and had children: Samuel, Jesse, John D., Anna, Ephriam, E. Pinkney, Willis, and Rebecca. E Pinkney Jones married Elizabeth Goggans, and had children: Susie, Barney, Thomas, Josephine, and Sue.

Mrs. Nancy Dalrymple (widow of Thomas), married Elijah Teague on February 4, 1849. She died March 18, 1852. Mrs. Sarah Ann Dalrymple died July 1, 1850, and left children: Mary Elizabeth, Emmaliza, William H., and Regina Alice.

DANSBY-Ivey Dansby made will in February, 1858, and died in Newberry County, leaving widow, Elizabeth, and children: Mary Ann Stoddard, Josephine Glenn Dansby, David Drayton Dansby, Elizabeth Evaline Dansby, and Susan Emma Dansby.

DARBY-John Darby made will June 20, 1825, and died same year. He left widow, Susannah, and several children. His wife's oldest son, Benjmain, to share like the balance of the children. Richard Darby died in March, 1826, leaving widow, Elizabeth, and children: Stephen, William, Thomas, Barthalomew, Nancy (wife of Samuel Hall), Polly (wife of Bird Roberts, of Laurens District), Clara (wife of John H. Hancock), Betsy, Mahala, and John. John died before the death of his father, and left children: Margaret (wife of Jacob Alewine), Ivey, John, Eve, James, and Barthalomew. The last three were under twenty years old in year 1826.

DARLINGTON-David N. Darlington and Gabriel D. Darlington married Mary Edwards, and after her death to her sister, Margaret Edwards. They were daughters of Edward Edwards and his wife, Mary. They moved to Adams County, Ohio, before the year 1820.

DAUGHERTY-James Daugherty made will November 15, 1794, and died in 1795. He left widow, Mary, and children: George, Charles, and James. The children of James, Jr. were, James and George.

DAVENPORT-Isaac Davenport lived near Beaver Damm Creek, in Newbery District. He left a will in 1806, and died same year. He was married twice and had, probably, a baker's dozen of children. Some of his children and grand-children by his first wife were: William (married Ann........) and his children, Patsy, Stephen, George, Isaac, John, Sally who was wife of George Wilson, Betsy who was wife of William Pitts, Moses, James, William, Ann, Lucinda, Catherine; Betsy, who married James Murdock; Willis; Sally, wife of James Gibson; Rachel, who married Manassa Mann; Hetty, widow of John Golding. Children of Manassa and Rachel Mann were: John, Eve, William, Armen, Sally, and Hettie (wife of Moses Mathis). Isaac Davenport's second wife was Eve........who was his widow, and their children were: Francis (he married Patsy........and had children, Burle, Pinkney, Carey, Matilda, Isaac); Edney (she married ..... Lewis); Stacey (she married ...... Mitchell); Patsy (she married Russell Gibson); Isaac (he married Anne ......); James (he married Nancy ....); Willoughby (he married Phoebe.....) Burle Davenport moved to Butler County, Alabama. Isaac and Anne had children: Joseph, James, David, and the wife of James G. Burton. James and Nancy had children: Eve, Elizabeth, Tabitha, James Madison, and an unknown child. Willoughby and Phoebe had children, Jonothan, Cicely (she married Charles Scott).

Joseph Davenport made will August 5, 1788, and died about 1791, leaving children: Rebecca (wife of Bartlette Satterwhite), Anny (wife of John Phillips), Jemima (wife of Samuel Goode), and David.

David Davenport (son of Isaac and Ann), died October 23, 1803, and left seven hundred acres land on Little River, one-third to his widow, Hannah, and twethirds to his children, Joseph and Edna (she was wife of Robert Malone).

Other Pioneers (continued)

Thomas Davenport made will September 14, 1812, and died about 1815-16. He left widow, Lettice, and certain legatees. The following clause is noted in his will: "In respect to a legacy bequeathed to my first wife, Sally, by John Partlow, of Spottsylvania County, Virginia, one half of such legacy to go to Lettice Davenport and the other half to my son, Burkett Davenport, and my daughter, Lucy Harris."

William Davenport made will November 22, 1803, and died in August, 1805. Settlement was made in Equity Court in 1833. His widow, Sarah, died in 1823. A daughter, Anne, married John Kelly and had children: Isaac, Wiley, Mary (wife of William Stewart), Sarah, Elizabeth Abigail. Another daughter, Jemima, had married Charles Neel, who had died, and had children: John, Milly, Sarah (wife of Allen Pitts), Nancy (wife of Julian Westmoreland), Isaac, Matthias, Rebecca, Mary (wife of Ransome Wells), Elizabeth (wife of John Mann). All of the children of John and Elizabeth Mann moved to Green County, Tennessee. Mrs. Anne Kelly died January 1, 1816.

John Gillam Davenport died about 1860 or '61. His will is dated March 17, 1860, and proved 1861. He named a son, Napoleon B. Davenport, and a cousin, Henry Burton, as Exrs. of will. He willed to his son, N. B.,"a gold-lever watch and a Merriman's clock, also all his jewelry, mahogany washstand, trunk, silk dress of his late wife, an iron safe, and fourty-four slaves." The following clause is in his will: "..... and that my body be buried in a metallic case, if such can be had, and buried in the burying ground known as the 'Isaac Davenport Burying Ground', by the side of my mother, or if that be impractical, at the feet of my deceased brother, James M. Davenport." Other legatees named in his will were: Louisa McClure, Annie W. Hill of Texas, my sisters; James M. Young, son of my sister, Catherine S. Young, and Jonothan D. Rudd of Texas, my nephews; Lucy C. McKeener (daughter of James M. Davenport, decd), my niece; Theresa Williams, my sister-in-law; and John Hopkins Williams, my father-in-law.

DAVIS—Harmon Davis, Sr. received a grant of land on Dunlap's Creek, in what is now Newberry County, in year 1766. He married Phoebe .... and had children: Reason (died 1831), Harmon (died 1816), Rachel (married John Davis), Sarah, Ruth, Nancy, William, Hannah Fontaina, and the wife of Henry Steadman. Reason died in Newberry District, left widow, Elizabeth, and children: John, Van, Daniel G., Harmon, Joshua, Catherine Taylor, Stacey. John and Rachel moved to Pendleton District, where they sold lands in 1814, to Van Davis, of Newberry District, being their undivided shares of estate of Harmon Davis, Sr., deceased. Reason, Jr. died in 1852, leaving two sons, Abijah and Van, and a daughter, Hannah. John died in 1804, or 1803, leaving widow, Mary, and children: Nancy (wife of Cornelius Floyd), and wife of John Mitchell, and wife of Ezekiah Eastland.

Another John Davis died January 26, 1833, in Newberry County, leaving children: John, William, Susannah. The son, John, married Mary ..... and had children: John Thomas, Mary, Elizabeth, William, and the wife of Mordecai Chambers.

Mrs. Mary Davis died before the year 1797. The joint heirs of her estate were: Chesley Davis, Samuel Davis, Fanny Davis (wife of Thomas W. Waters), Elizabeth Davis (wife of John Worthington), Milly Davis (she married Elisha Worthington), Thomas, Molly, Jesse, Rhoda (she married John Abernathy), Nancy (married Joseph Jones). Chesley Davis had a son, William C. who married Sarah Loftus and had daughters: Mrs. Pinckney Johnson, Mrs Wallace Riser, and others.

Van Davis died in Pendleton District in year 1810, and left widow, Lucy, and children: Abigail, Hezekiah, Nathan, Jesse, Eliphas, Van, Martha, Rachel, Hannah, Miles, Jean, Rhoda. A grand-son, John Davis, is named in his will. Legatees receipts show following: Ameriah Felton, David Tate, Joseph Hall, Thomas Burris who married a daughter.

Mrs. Mary Davis, widow of one Van Davis, of Newberry County, (he had died October 1, 1839), died December 15, 1853, leaving children: Francis, Nancy, Martha, (she married Charles Franklin after year 1859), Rachel, James A., Jane, and Caroline. A daughter, Margaret, who died before 1860, had married Henry Moore. Henry Moore left his family, moving out of the State, leaving his wife with two small children, James Moore and Ellen C. Moore.

William Davis died in Newberry County about 1823, leaving widow, Elizabeth, and children: John, William, Samuel, Mary (wife of William Saxon).

Other Pioneers (continued)

DAVIDSON-Thomas Davidson died in Newberry County about 1799. He left widow, Molly, and children: Nancy (wife of Henry Newton), Sally, John, Jenny. A daughter, Betsy, who was not of age in 1802, and a son, Samuel, who was under age in that year, shared in certain property.
Nathaniel W. Davidson died in Newberry County in 1854, leaving a widow, Martha H., and no children named as legatees. Samuel N. Davidson died June 13, 1862, in the Confederate Army. His property was given to his sisters, Mary F. Reeder, Sarah A. E. Reeder.
John Davidson died December 22, 1847, and left no legatees except the children of his brother, Alexander, who were: John J., William A., Nathan W., Reuben S., James W., Elizabeth J., and Jennett.

DAWKINS-George Dawkins made will which was proved in Court June 4, 1788. He died same year, leaving children: Susannah Pope, Mary Ann Lane, Elizabeth Pope, Mrs. Grigsby (widow), George, Jemima Herbert, Nancy Barrett. Grand-children: Ellen Hampton, Thomas Barrett, William Dawkins Lane. Newphew: Thomas Dawkins.
Thomas Dawkins, Sr. died about 1782, in Abbeville District, leaving widow, Elizabeth.
One George Dawkins died in Abbeville District about 1781, leaving widow, Chloe, and children: George, Joseph, Thomas, Hannah, and Polly.

DE GRAFFINREID-Baron De Graffinreid or Christopher De Graffinreid, was a native of the Canton, Berne, Switzerland. He came with a colony of Swiss and Germans to America before the Rev. War. His two sons, Christopher and Allen, first lived in Virginia, and afterwards moved to Union District, South Carolina. Allen was the father of John and Terzevant De Graffinreid.

DERRICK-John Derrick made will September 15, 1825, and died same year, leaving widow, Elizabeth, and children: Jesse, Kersey, Caroline. Exrs: Andrew Derrick, George Wise, and Elizabeth Derrick. His land joined that of Jacob Derrick. Andrew Derrick married Catherine Hiller.

DENNIS-John Dennis bought 50 acres land on Buffalo Creek, in Newberry District in year 1799. James Dennis married Susan Hunter, one of their children being Susannah.
Mrs. Prudence Dennis died about 1847, in Newberry County, She left children: Martha Lester, Phoebe Sheppard, Jesse, Rebecca, and P. H. Dennis.

DESECKER-Peter Desecker, Sr. settled at Purysburg about 1734. He had a son, Peter, who located near Broad River, about 1773. Another son, Jacob, settled in Fairfield County, and was father of William Desecker of that County. Jacob is listed as a Rev. War patriot. Peter, Jr. died about 1810 or 1819. Jacob died 1833, left widow, and children: Grace Howell, Rebecca M., Joel, William (William had died and left two children, John and Grace).
Michael Desecker died January 31, 1830, in Newberry County. He left widow, Catherine, (she was a Rikard before her marriage), and children: Mary (wife of James T. Lane), John, Anna, Martha, Elizabeth, and Sarah. Martha married Jesse Beam who had lived in Fairfield County.

DIAL-Jeremiah Dial lived on Second Creek in Newberry County. He made will April 1, 1805, and died same year. He left widow, Margaret, and children: Jeremiah, William, Margaret (wife of George Ingram), Jane (wife of John Boyd), Sally (wife of Hugh Harper). Grand-children: David Montgomery Dial and Margaret Dial, and Jeremiah Dial.
Alexander Dial died about 1803, in Laurens County, leaving widow, Mary, and following legatees: Thomas Hitt, James, Dermillion, Lemarius, Alexander.
Isaac Dial died about 1835 in Laurens District. He left widow, Polly, and children: Isaac, Garlington C., Polly (wife of William Henderson), James, Hastings, Henry, Franklin, Harriett, Drury, Isabella, Nancy, and Martha.

DILLARD-James Dillard, of Laurens County, married Mary Ramage.

DICK-James Dick married Margaret Boyd, a daughter of John Boyd, of Newberry District. Their children were: Hugh, Jeanette, Alexander, John, James, William, and Joseph.

DICKERT-Peter Dickert was one of the earliest German settlers in the "Dutch Fork" of Newberry County. He was a Justice of the Quorum, a Justice of the Peace; and was one of the first Elders of St. John's Lutheran Church. He had a son, Michael, and others. Michael married Margaret Seigler (she was the widow of George Cromer). He made will October 1, 1808, and died about 1811, "old and stricken in years." His children were: Michael, Peter, Christopher, Margaret (wife of John Folk), and Hannah (wife of George Stockman, Sr.).

Other Pioneers (continued)

Christopher Dickert died about 1817, and left widow, Christina, and children: Michael, Elizabeth (wife of Reuben Reid), Adam and Henry. Mrs. Christina Dickert married Simon Wicker. Michael married Mary Wicker, daughter of John Adam Wicker, Sr. and wife, Katherine.

DICKEY-John Dickey received a grant of one hundred acres land near Broad River, in 1774. In 1787 he and his wife, Jane, were living in Laurens District. He died in Fairfield County after the year 1820, and left children: John, William, Sally, Nancy (wife of William M. Crymes), Susannah (wife of Stanley L. Westmoreland), and Craddock. John Garlington was Executor of his will, and Guardian of the minor children who were: Rebecca, Mary, Parthena, Patsy.

DIVVER-James Divver located at Newberry Court House as a teacher about 1819, coming from New Brunswick. He was a native of Scotland. He worked for a college education; then he attended and graduated at the South Carolina College. After graduation he was appointed tutor of mathematics in that institution. He came back to Newberry in 1828, and became head of the Newberry Academy. He married Sophia Coppock in 1828. Later, they moved to Charleston where he died leaving widow and nine children. (Some of the Divvers are buried in the old Baptist Church Cemetery at Anderson, S. C.)

DOBBINS-Washington Dobbins married Kiziah Keller, daughter of George and Elizabeth Keller, before 1830. They moved to Perry County, Alabama.

DOBSON-Dr. Daniel Dobson came to Newberry from North Carolina. He died 1848, when yet a young man.

DODGEN-William Dodgen lived on Little River, in Newberry District. He received a grant of three hundred acres land in 1771. After his death, his widow, Elizabeth, married a Vaughn. His two sons, James and Ollemon, were given one hundred acres, each, by their mother, Elizabeth Vaughn, in year 1790.

DOMINICK-John Dominick, pioneer of the family, came to Newberry District (then a part of old Ninety Six District), about the year 1750. He received a grant of land located in the Dutch Fork. A deed made in 1797, showing certain grantors, indicates the following were legatees in that year: John Dominick, Andrew Holman, Henry Summer, William Fulmer, Elizabeth Dominick, all of Lexington District, conveyed one hundred fifty acres of land to Jacob Dominick, Christian Dominick, and Margaret Dominick; said land having been originally granted in 1752 to John Dominick.

Henry Dominick, probably one of the youngest sons of the pioneer, served in the Rev. War. He married Agnes Fellers, a daughter of Michael Fellers, and had children: Henry Christian, and others. After his first wife's death he married Margaret Fellers (sister of his first wife), and had children: David, Andrew, Mary, Noah, George, Catherine, and Frances.

DONNELLY-Rev. Thomas Donnelly was born in County Donegal, Ireland, in May, 1772; educated at the University of Glasgow. Tradition is he came to America when a young man; attended college where he studied Theology; and was licensed to preach about 1799. He died December 27, 1847. He was the father of Rev. Samuel D. Donnelly who lived in Newberry at one time. Rev. Samuel D. Donnelly was living in Florida when he died in 1879. He was born in old Chester District on February 14, 1808. They were Covenanters; but later Rev. Samuel D. preached in the Presbyterian Church, having served churches at Greenwood before going to Florida in 1873. He died at the home of his daughter, Mrs. F. D. Rice. He had a daughter, Fanny, who married James M. Gillam, son of James Gillam, who lived near the old Star Fort, at Ninety Six, S. C. They had, also, two daughters, Anne and Lillie.

Rev. James Donnelly made will April 4, 1855, and died same year, leaving children: Francis, Olin, George Summerfield, Andrew Emory, John David Fletcher, Margaret Kezia Jane, and Hamilton Harriet Elvira Louisa. Executors: John Brownlee, James C. Harper.

DORN-Peter Dorn died in Edgefield District about 1826. His son, John Dorn, died March 13, 1826, and left widow, Mahala, and the following heirs: James Parkman, Jane C. Turner, Frances Dorn and Adeline Dorn.

John Dorn, Sr. made will in 1846, and died soon afterwards, leaving widow, Sarah, and children: William B., Robert, John, Rebecca Smith, Benjamin Jones, Mary Turner, Demsley, and Solomon. A son-in-law was Robert M. Smith. William B. Dorn died leaving widow, Mattie, and small children.

Other Pioneers (continued)

DOYLE—John Doyle died about 1791 in Newberry District. His estate was administered by Mary Dail; and property sold in settlement for Jeremiah Dial and others.

Jesse Doyle lived in Edgefield District, from where he moved to Alabama about the year 1795.

DRENNAN—Robert Drennan died in Newberry District about 1802. He left a widow, Betty (she w was the mother of all his children), and children: John (oldest son), Fanny Sloan, Martha, Robert and William.

DUCKETT—Thomas Duckett made will July 18, 1822, and died in 1824. His children were: Susannah (wife of Andrew Gibson), James (dead), Thomas (dead), Jacob, John, Baruch, Joseph, Sally (widow of Josiah Fowler), Patsy (widow of Levi Fowler), Polly (wife of Daniel Reeder), Betsy (wife of Edward Jeans), and Rachel (wife of Baruch O'Dell).

Thomas Ducket, Jr. died about 1800, leaving widow, Lydia, and probably some children.

Another Thomas Duckett died April 20, 1835, leaving widow, Nancy.

DUGAN—Thomas Dugan made will July 13, 1822, and died 1822. He was a patriotic officer in Rev War. He left six hundred seventy acres land on Indian Creek to his then living children who w ere: Mary (wife of James Murry), John J.(he died before his father), James, William, Thomas, George, Hiram (he died in 1823, unmarried), and Park Dugan. The children of John J. were: Lucy L., Mary J., Robert, Elizabeth Ann, Martha E., Margaret Caroline, and William H. The children of Park Dugan were: Mary, Jane, and Eliza. Lucy L. married William Davis. Mary J. married Francis Asbury Shell and moved to Mississippi. The widow of Thomas Dugan was Mary......... Robert died early but left widow and small son, Robert, who lived at the home place of his father, John J. Dugan. William Dugan died in 1831, and left widow, Elizabeth Lemmon (Wright) Dugan, and children: Lucinda C. (wife of Meredith Freeman), Maria M. (wife of Andrew Turner), Margaret Frances (wife of John T. Boyd), Mary A. E. (wife of Robert Campbell), Kucinda Freeman had children who were minors in 1858, viz: Martha M., Ernesta S.F., William D., and Sarah L. F. Freeman. Sarah L. F. married Jefferson McMinn. All left the State.

DUNCAN—John Duncan, Sr. received bounty grant of lands in what is now Newberry District, as early as 1755, located on what is now known as Duncan's Creek. James Duncan received grant in 1768. George Duncan received grant in 1774. Robert Duncan, Jr., received grant from his father, Robert Duncan, Sr., in Union District. He died about 1825, leaving widow, Susannah.

Amos Duncan died In Newberry Districtm left will dated March 31, 1801, which was proved in court August 5, 1805, in which year he died. He left widow, Elizabeth, and children: Amos, Isiaah, Sarah Ann, William, George, John, Elizabeth, Hannah, and Eli Johnson Duncan. Some of these children moved to Ohio, along with the Quakers. Elizabeth married Charles Inman. Hannah married Obediah Winters. Amos, Jr. died before 1830, leaving widow, Margaret, and children: George, Sarah, John, Hannah, Matilda, and Elizabeth. John (son of Amos, Sr.), moved to Indiana, as did Obediah Winters and his wife. Sarah Ann (daughter of Amos, Sr.), married (1) Samuel Taylor, and (2) Henry Fletchall; she had by Taylor a daughter, Elizabeth Mills, and by Fletchall the following children: John, Sarah, Mary, Hannah. The name was changed "Fletcher".

Robert Duncan, Sr. made will January 12, 1801, and died 1802. He left a widow, Betty, and children: John, Robert, William, Martha, Fanny Sloan, Betsy Lavania Stewart, Nancy Freeman, Jane, James, and Sarah. Martha married a Kelly. Sarah married a Massey.

James Duncan made will August 26, 1816, and died same year. His legatees were: Lavania Nonitt, Nancy Stewart (daughter of his sister), Elizabeth Hill (daughter of Maragret Hill),

John Duncan died in Edgefield District about 1805, leaving widow and children. His first wife was Rachel...... and second wife, Margaret........ who survied him 1809. He left nine children by his first wife, as follows: Abel (he moved to Perry County, Alabama), Lydia, William, Jeremiah, Patsy (wife of John Williams), Rebecca (wife of Humphrey Prior), Catherine (wife of Isaac Parmer), Rachel (wife of Henry Hilburn-she died previously), Polly (wife of Thomas Dean-she died before 1809), He left two children by his second wife, the wife of John Edmundson and the wife of Daniel Stewart.

DUNLAP—Robert Dunlap married Sara W. Wallace (widow of Daniel Wallace), of Newberry. She died in 1849, and left husband, and the following children: Sara S. (wife of William H. Wallace), and Robert N. Dunlap.

DUNN—James Dunn died at an advanced age in 1805, in Abbeville District, leaving widow, Agnes, and children: Robert, Samuel, William. Robert died in 1844, leaving widow, Jane, and children: Andrew, John, William, Elizabeth, Phoebe, (she married Hodges), Polly Richey.

Other Pioneers (continued)

DURRETT- Thomas Durrett died in Newberry County in year 1789. His children were: Benjamin, William, Lucy (wife of Edmund Price), Francis. His estate was settled by James and Agnes Kelly. He died in 1799; and his widow, Agnes, married James Kelly. Benjamin married Margaret Hogge and they left several children. One son, Thomas, married Rebecca Alewine, and had children: John A. J., Joseph, Reuben, Bejamin, Thomas J. All of them moved to Alabama. Margaret Hogge had a brother, Thomas Hogge, Joseph H. Durrett married Caroline Browne, in Alabama.

DYSON-Abraham Dyson died about 1836, in Newberry County. He left children : Thomas (he married Margaret............), and Margaret Dyson. He left nephew, John B. Wilson, part of his estate, and a niece, Nancy C. Williams.

EASTLAND-Thomas Eastland lived on Little River, Newberry County. He died about 1815, and named in his will the folowing children as legatees: Joseph, Wiliam, Sarah, Susannah (she married Jeme..Davenport), and Ezekiah. A grand-daughter, Rugia Eastland, received one-third of Sarah Eastland's share. A grand-son, Thomas Bevine Eastland, received a share of the estate. Ezekiah was a Deacon in the Bush River Baptist Church, a man of sterling qualities. He served as Tax Collector in Newberry in year 1812, to fill the unexpired term of Charles Crenshaw who had resigned or died. Later, Ezekiah moved to Tennessee.

EDENS (EDDINS)-Abraham Eddins made will January 8, 1792, and died about 1801 or 1802, leaving widow, Sarah,and children: Anne Burdin, Frank Kelly, Mary Burdin, Joseph, Lucy(she married a Johnson), Judith Renels(Reynolds), Sarah Chandler. Exrs: Josiah Chandler, William Wilson, William Dunlap.

William Eddins, Sr.,a Rev War patriot, was probably a brother of above Abraham; but he had, too, a son named Abraham.

Theophilus Eddins died in Edgefield District. One of his sons, Benjmain, had a son , William.

EDMUNDSON-Caleb Edmundson received a grant of 450 acres in 1772, located on Enoree River, in Newberry County (then Nine ty Six District). He died about 1791, left widow, Judith, and children: Caleb, Thomas, William, and Jospeh. Another son, Isaac, had died in 1790.
Isaac married Eleanor Counts, had children. Caleb, Jr. died in Pendleton District in 1800. He left a widow, Margaret, and children: Ann. Elizabeth, Hester, and Joseph. Thomas died about 1809 in Pendleton District. He left widow, Ann, and children: James, William, George, Benjmain, and Elizabeth Boulware.

Captain William Edmundson , of the United States Army, died after 1818, leaving an estate to his brothers and sisters.

One Michael Edmunston and his wife, Susannah, moved to Cass County, Georgia, from Pickens Cpunty, S. C., about the year 1830.

EDWARDS—The Edwards families were once numerous in this, Newberry County, and in Laurens County. Like many of the early pioneers, many of them caught the western fever, and moved to Ohio, Indiana and other western or northwestern States, some going to Alabama and Mississippi. The pioneers came from Maryland or Virginia to South Carolina before the Rev War, except Robert Edwards who came about 1781.

John Edwards married Mary Turner, a daughter of William Turner of the Little River section of Newberry County, He died probably before the year 1800. His widow, Mary Edwards, made willJune 26, 1813, and died about 1816, leaving children: Elizabeth Cotton, Letesha Watts, Rutha Turner, Mary Darlington, Margaret Darlington, Edward, Patty, John S., Patsy, Katy Turner, and Alexander McMillan.

One Edward Edwards returned to Virginia, died and left widow, Margaret, and children, Polly and Sally. He must have returned to Newberry County, or there was another Edward Edwards, for there is an old deed made 1824 showing he was in Newberry County, and his daughter, Mary, was living in Adams County, Ohio.

Patsy Edwards married .... Thomas, and had children: Edward, Polly, and Elizabeth McCool. Gabriel D. Darlington and David N. Darlington were in Adams County, Ohio, who were, probably, sons-in-law of John Edwards.

Robert Edwards who had come from Maryland just after the Rev War, had wife, Margaret, and children: David (married Margaret Bridges),Margaret (married George Bridges), Isobel (married William Silvers). George Bridges and family and that of William Silvers moved to Georgia about 1804. They were killed by Indians, as was supposed.

Other Pioneers (continued)

David Edwards moved from Camden District to Newberry District about 1777, and lived near Broad River. He married Jane.......... Children's names not known; but it is supposed that David and Samuel were sons. David, Jr. married Sarah ..... and lived on Cannon's Creek, near Broad River. Samuel sold one hundred ninety acres land on Hall's Branch, near Bush River, to David Edwards in 1791; and moved to another county.
One David Edwards, brother of Robert, married Mary Patty about 1786, and had children, the most of whom moved to Indiana. A son, Charles, died in Newberry District.
John S. Edwards died in Jefferson County, Alabama, about 1840. The distributees named in settlement of his estate were: George Robinson and wife, Sinkler Lathan and wife, Rhoda, and John M. Edwards.
Captain Edward Edwards died about 1821, in Union District, S. C. He left widow, Catherine, and children: Daniel Cannon Edwards, Edward Henry Edwards, Mary Wakefield Edwards. He left to his widow a house in the city of Charleston, S. C., which was located on the corner of Meeting Street and Smith's Lane. In 1820 Edward Edwards paid $2,000.00 for some slaves, bought from Charles and Lewis Pressley, other consideration being love and affection for Catherine Pressley (daughter of Cahrles Pressley) whom he was about to marry. His first wife, Mary, was the mother of his children, except one. They were: John A., James Fisher, and George Washington Edwards. He married Catherine C. Pressley on August 29, 1820, and left and infant son by her, Charles W. Edwards.
ELLIMON-John Ellimon, Sr. married Mary Johns and were parents of Enos Ellimon. Enos made will April 27, 1787, and died about 1788, leaving widow, Catherine (Collins) Ellimon, and children: John, William, Elizabeth, Amy, Hannah, and Mary Bonds. John married Susannah Coppock (daughter of John and Abigail Skilken Coppock), Their daughter, Elizabeth, married Isaah Pemberton. They were Quakers and lived on Bush River, members of the Bush River Monthly Meeting. William married Jane Jay; and one of their sons, Isaac, married Mary Jones, a daughter of Wallace Jones, Jr. and wife, Rachel (Patty) Jones,(Rachel was his first wife and mother of his children).
ELLISON-Robert Ellison died about 1806 in Fairfield District. He left widow, Jane, and children: John, William,(oldest), Robert, James, Joseph, and Sarah. Grand-children: Elizabeth (oldest daughter of William), and Robert (second son of John). Executors: William Ellison, nephew, and ....
One William Ellison died in Fairfield District about 1833, leaving widow, Mary, and children: William, and the wife of Alexander Chambers, and the wife of Alexander W. Yongue.
ELMORE-This family came from Virginia to Newberry. Afterwards, some of the descendents moved to Georgia and Alabama, while a few migrated with the Quaker Colony to Ohio or Indiana. Thomas A. Elmore died 1825. He married Elizabeth Chapman (1784-1839), a daughter of Rev. Giles Chapman, Chaplain in the American Army during the Rev. War. Their children were: Giles, Eleanor (wife of John Wilson), Ruth (wife of Lewis McCollough), Elijah, William A., Mary (wife of John Elmore, a cousin), Nancy (wife of Henry O. Wilson), Elijah moved to Georgia. William A. conveyed land in 1874 to his nieces, Ruth Morgan, wife of Butler Morgan, and ......
William Elmore died about 1792 or '93, leaving will dated January 31, 1780. He left widow, Abigail, and children: Ridgeway, Joseph, Sarah, Mary, Rachel, John, Stephen. Ridgeway died in 1805, leaving widow, Prudence, and two daughters, Abigail and Mahala.
EMBREE-John Embree was a son of Conrad Imrick who was granted a bounty of land located on Bush River,in 1771. Later, Conrad gave five acres , in 1772, to the Friends Society, Bush River Monthly Meeting, on which to erect a church building. He was one of the Trustees of the church; that is, John, who with his wife, Mary, moved to Georgia at the time many of the Quakers moved into that State and into the Northwest. His brother, Moses, remained in Newberry District; who had sold lands in 1787.
Jacob Embree, member of the Bush River Monthly Meeting, moved to East Tennessee. His son, Jesse, married Mary, daughter of Drury Jones, son of Wallace Jones, Sr.
ENGLISH-John English died in Newberry District about 1803, leaving widow, Rachel (Cannon) English, and children: Joshua, Edward, Thomas. Rachel was the daughter of Ephriam and Eleanor (Ulmer) Cannon, of the Broad River section of Newberry District.
David English died in Newberry District about 1832. He married Rosannah Catherine (daughter of John Adam Summer), widow of George Eichleberger, and left no children.

Other Pioneers (continued)

ENLOW—John Enlow lived in Newberry District. He married before 1808, to Margaret Hallman, daughter of Andrew Hallman.
Jacob Enlow married Elizabeth, daughter of Christopher and Mary Margaret Kinard, before the year 1845. Their children were: James D., William F., Louisa, Eliza, Lydia, Mary Jane, Quincy, Thompson, Elizabeth (she married Jesse Taylor).
EPPS—John Eppts came from Virginia to Newberry District (then Ninety Six District), before the Rev. War, or about the time of the end of the war, as one tradition states. His will is dated June 3, 1824, and he died same year, leaving children: Daniel, William, James Baugh, Martha Shell, Nancy Shell, Polly Abernathy. Also, a grand-son, John Epps, who was son of William. Daniel made will September 13, 1834, and died same year, leaving widow, Mary, and children: James and George. His will is recorded in Mecklinberg County Court House, Virginia, October 20, 1834. William (son of John), made will May 24, 1843, and died September 17, 1843, leaving widow, Henrietta, and children: John W., Samuel J., Eliza L. (she died early), ... Eliza L. married John D. Huston by whom were the following children: William W. or William M., James R., Daniel E., John W., and Thomas E. James Baugh Epps married about 1798 to Sarah Finch, daughter of Edward and Martha Finch, of Newberry District; they moved to Mississippi. He was born in 1772, and died 1834. James Monroe Epps married Elizabeth H. Law, sister of Dr. John A. Law.
ETHERIDGE—Samuel Etheridge and his father settled in old Edgefield District. He bought land on the South side of Saluda River in year 1789 from Dougal W. Dougal.
Elijah Etheridge moved from North Carolina to Newberry District, and soon after moved to Georgia.
EVANS—The earliest family of this name in the section of what is now Newberry County were Quakers. They lived near Bush River, having settled there before the Rev War. Many of the family went to the Northwest with other Quakers. Robert Evans moved to Tennessee. His brother, Joseph, moved to West Milton, Ohio. Isaac died in Newberry District about 1825, and left children: Netty, Unity, Joseph, Isaac, Huldah, and Eleanor. His sister, Elizabeth Evans, was Guardian of his orphan children, his wife having died before his death.
EWART—James Ewart came from Ireland and settled in Ninety Six District, on Long Cane Creek. On September 22, 1767 he recived a bounty grant of two hundred and fifty acres land.
Andrew Ewart received a bounty grant of three hundred acres on Reedy River on March 8, 1768. He was, probably, a brother of James. James died before 1820, left a son, James. James, Jr. was a merchant in Columbia, S. C. for several years; and died in 1835. His widow, Mary, died when she was not yet 36 years old, and left children: James, John, Samuel,....David. David married Nancy........ who died June 21, aged 21 years. Afterwards, David married Magdeline........ who died October 25, 1822, aged 22 years. Children by the second wife were: Mary Ann (died aged 15 years), and James (born in 1821).
James Ewart (son of James, Jr.), died August 15, 1857, leaving children: James B. and Juliet. James B. Ewart moved to Kershaw District; was graduated at the South Carolina College, Columbia, S. C. in 1848. James (son of James, Jr.), after the death of his wife, married again to Rebecca Beckett, daughter of Dr. James M. Beckett. After his death, his widow married Rev. Samuel Thomas Donnelly, a Presbyterian minister.
David Ewart, brother of James, was in partnership with his brother in Columbia, S. C., as merchants. He was the father of Dr. David E. Ewart, who lived in the town of Newberry.
FARROW—William Farrow made will May 28, 1792, and died 1793, leaving widow, Lenny, and children: Thomas, William, Samuel Jackson, Sarah, Jean, Elisabeth. A grand-daughter, Edney, (oldest daughter of son, Thomas,) was a legatee. The widow, Mrs. Lenny Farrow, died about 1795. Langdon Farrow died in Spartanburg District about 1800. Samuel Farrow died in about 1825 in Spartanburg District.
Mrs. Christia Farrow made will November 6, 1815, and died 1816, leaving husband, Samuel, and children: John G. Brown (son of a former husband), Sarah arrow, John Farrow, Willis Farrow, and Caroline Farrow.
Thomas Farrow died in Union District, leaving widow, Patience, and children: ....
John Farrow, Sr. died before 1856, in Laurens District. He left children: Rebecca Bogan, Hannah Higgins, Thomas F., Jane (wife of John F. Moss), Another son, John F., had died and left children: Jane (wife of Samuel Woodruff), Julia (wife of Thomas Hickson), Elizabeth (wife of Joshia Mitchell), John (he moved to Texas).

Other Pioneers (continued)

FAIR-Samuel Fair came from Ireland about 1772, and settled in Newberry District, near Stoney Hills. He died about 1776, leaving children: Samuel, William, Margaret, and probably others. William married Elizabeth Young, and had children: James (moved to Abbeville County), Archibald (moved to Florida), Simeon, Dr. Samuel (he lived in Columbia, S. C.), Gen'l. E. Y. (moved to Montgomery, Alabama), Dr. Drury (he moved to Selma, Alabama).
Col. Simeon Fair was a lawyer in Newberry, represented that county in the State Legislature, and was District Solicitor for several terms. He made a tour of Europe in 1842. He served in the Seminole War in Florida. He married Mary Butler Pearson, and had children: John S., William Y., James I., and a daughter who married, first, to Col. William Drayton Rutherford, of the Confederate States Army, and, second, to Judge Y. J. Pope.

FANT-Ephriam Fant died about 1851, in Chester Distict, S. C. He left widow, Sarah, and children: Abner (he died young), Sarah J., Ephriam F., David, Jane, Mary Wright, Catherine Castles, and Samuel.
One James Fant married Drucilla Buchanan (daughter of Micajah Buchanan), before the year 1829.
Dr. Samuel Fant operated a drug store in Newberry several years. He made will March 4, 1882, which was proved in Court November 1, 1886, and left widow, Fanny, and minor children.

FARLEY-John Farley and wife, Mary, came from Scotland and settled in North Carolina before the Rev. War. Later, some of the family moved to Laurens District, S. C. His widow died in Laurens District 1830 or '31. Her only surviving child at time of her death was Thompson Farley.
William H. Farley died in Laurens District (then called Laurens County) about 1850, leaving widow, Phoebe, and several children, the eldest child being Eunice J. Farley.

FARR-William Farr lived in Union District, where he died sometime before the year 1810, leaving widow, Elizabeth, and children: William B., Titus G., John P., Robert G., James and Rchard. James died and left widow, Frances, and children: William B., Regina P., and Cicely. Rchard died and left widow, Lucy, and children: William B., Waites, Nancy, (wife of John Sanders),Thomas G., and W. G. Farr.

FELKER-Jacob Felker settled in the Dutch Fork of Newberry District. The original spelling of the name was, "Furgar", as shown in oldest deed records. He married Barbara............ and had children: Elizabeth (married John Suber), Polly (married Conrad Suber), Jacob and Peter. Polly Suber died before 1815, and left husband, and children; some of children, John, Peter, and Sarah Suber. Jacob , the pioneer, died about 1819, naming above as legatees, together with a garnd-daughter, Elizabeth Heller. The widow, Barbara, died about 1828 or '29, leaving will dated August 31, 1821; in which a grand-daughter, Elizabeth Oxner, is named, also William and John Bishop to receive the share of their deceased mother, Mary Bishop.
Peter Felker, Sr. died September 24, 1844, about one hundred years old. He left widow, Lodoska, (she was his second wife),and the following children: Elizabeth (wife of John Epting), Caroline (wife of G. W. Seigler), Polly Suber (she died before 1847, the year of settlement of his estate), John A. (he died before 1847), Ellen, Nancy Metts (she died before 1847), Samuel D., Isaac A., William P. (he died before 1847).
John A. Felker died before 1838, leaving widow, Mahala (she died in 1842), and children: Mahala (wife of William Lowe), Mary Ann, Emma S., and Wiley H.

FELLERS- John Fellers (the name originally spelled, "Fello"), made will July 12, 1793, and died about 1800. His wife having already died, he left legatees, his children as follows: John George, Catherine (wife of Henry Counts), Anna Maria (wife of Jacob Utz), Margaret (wife of Henry Dominick), and Christina. John George lived and died in Newberry District; but many others moved to other States.

FIKE-George Fike made will April 16, 1821, and died same year. He left widow, Christina, and children: Martin, George, Mary, Christina. Some of the descendents moved to Spartanburg District.

FINCH-Edward Finch came from Virginia to South Carolina, and settled on King's Creek before the Rev. War. He was one of the founders of the well-known school, Mount Bethel Academy, and gave land whereon the school building were erected. He made will May 3, 1821, and died about 1823, leaving widow, Martha, and children: Lucretia Tucker, and the wife of Archibald Crenshaw, and Judith (wife of Dr. C. B. Atwood), Sarah (wife of James Baugh Epps), Nancy (wife of Frederick Foster. Grand-children: Edard B. Finch(son of Dr. Ivey Finch), Martha Crenshaw(daughter of Archibald), Eliza Crenshaw(daughter of Archibald), Quincy (daughter of Dr. Ivey Crenshaw).

Other Pioneers (continued)

FINLEY-John Finley received a grant of one hundred fifty acres land on North side of Saluda River, October 12, 1770, which he sold to Elisha Brooks on February 7, 1780.
    James Finley made will September 1, 1787, and died in Newberry County about 1795. He left widow, Ann, and the children of his brothers, Hugh and Robert, received some of his personal property. Mrs. Ann Finley died 1802, leaving property to the children of her sister, Mrs. Mary Glasgow.
    John Finley, Sr. died in Laurens County about 1852, leaving widow, Polly, and children: James, Hampton, Elizabeth (wife of Larkin Coleman); and grand-children, Mary Frances Finley (daughter of Hampton Finley), Sarah Frances Pyles, and James F. Coleman, and Nancy Elizabeth Coleman.
    Paul Finley died in Laurens County about 1843, leaving children: Hampton, Margaret M., Nancy Funk, Annie Coleman, Lettice Coleman, Jane Houlditch, Elizabeth Cargile (deceased), and John. Sarah Wait, daughter of Nancy Arnold, received share of estate.
    John Finley, of Fairfield County, S. C., died about 1820, leaving widow, Elizabeth, and children: Charles, Isom, John, Judith, Martha (wife of Abel Gibson), Susan, Nancy, Elizabeth, and Daniel D. Finley.

FISH-John Fish died about 1799 in Newberry District, leaving widow, Mary, and children: Mary (wife of Jesse Smith), Hannah (wife of John Johns), Ruth (wife of John Barrett).

FERNANDEZ-James Fernandez was born in Union District, S. C. He came to Newberry about 1810. He was elected Ordinary of Newberry in 1815. ("Annals of Newberry", Part I). He died in Mississippi about 1843, leaving widow and five children; the children were: John, Henry, Caroline, Mary, Sarah.

FLANNAGAN-Reuben Flannagan lived on Bush River, Newberry County. His widow, Arbrilla Flannagan, made will June 6, 1814, and died same year, leaving children: Reuben, Fanny. (Fanny married an Owens). Mrs. Arbrilla Flannagan had children by a former marriage, as follows: Bruce Prather, (he died and left widow, Martha), Basil Prather, Josiah Prather, Cassandra Williams. Also, a grand-daughter, Dicey Prather.

FLANNARY-David Flannary was living in Spartanburg County before the year 1793. He lived on Brushy Creek. After that year he moved to the Northwest, where Abraham, Joshua, and Thomas Flannary had moved before the year 1786.

FLEMMING-The Fleming families were in Pendleton District, S. C. And in Laurens County, S. C. in early times. Moses Fleming moved from Pendleton District to Georgia.
    Rose Ann Fleming who was born about 1790, married John Albright, and was removed to Louisiana.

FORD-James Ford made will May 13, 1787, and died same year. He left children: Rebecca Anderson (widow), Elizabeth Lindsey (wife of Samuel Lindsey), Rachel Ford, James Ford (he died before his father). He left a grand-son, John, who was a son of James Ford.

FOSTER-John Foster lived in Union District, S. C. He made will dated March 13, 1821, and which was proved in Court June 11, 1838. He left widow, Hannah, and children: Nathaniel, Pleasant, Edmund, George, Betsy (wife of Pleasant Sneed), Sally (wife of Jesse Hughs), Polly (wife of John Roberts), Nancy (wife of William Page), Juliana (wife of John Nichols), Temperance (wife of John Golding), Susannah (wife of John Stokes), Sibby (wife of William Blackley). Sally Hughs had a daughter, Morning, and other children. Exrs: Edmund Hames, John Pridmore, Sr., and Nathaniel Foster.

FOWLER-Richard Fowler died about 1798, leaving widow, Ruth, and children: Nathan, Levi, Elijah, Ruth, Josiah, and the wife of Josiah Duckett. Elijah died in 1802, leaving a widow, Isabel.

FRAZIER-William Frazier died 1793, in Fairfield District, S. C. He left children: John, William, Ezekiel, Samuel, and probably others. Exrs: Jacob Gibson, Sr., Wm. Frazier, Jr. (son)

FREAN-Rev. Thomas Frean was born 1793, in Ireland, came to South Carolina and settled in Newberry District, after a short stay in Charleston, S. C. He was the son of Patrick Frean of Ireland. He is buried at old Quaker Cemetery on Bush River.

FRESHLEY-William Freshly lived in Lexington District, S. C. He married Martha Ellen Summer, a daughter of John Summer, Jr.

FREY(FRY)-Jacob Frey died 1800 in Newberry District. He left a widow, Elizabeth, and children: Jacob, Elizabeth, Cynthia, Fredericka, Ursula, Madelina, Hannah Keller, Louisa Wicker, and Maria Rikard.

Other Pioneers (continued)

FRITZ—Nicholas Fritz married Naomi .... and had children: Elizabeth (she married Wallace Jones, Jr.), and others.

FULMER—Everard Folmer and George Folmer (brothers) came from Germany. They settled in upper Orangeburgh District (now Lexington County) before the Rev. War.
Captain Jacob Fulmer was a patriot officer in the Rev. War.
Abram Fulmer had a large family, some of whom moved to Alabama.

FURNAS—Joseph Furnas moved to Ohio about 1805. He died in that State in 1812, leaving widow, Sarah, and children: John, and others. Mary Pearson Furnas was a daughter of Joseph Furnas, and she married a Mr, Jay.

GALLAGHER—William Gallagher lived in Newberry District. He married Mary Grove and had children: Permelia, Martha, James Franklin Gallagher. Permelia married a McCollough. Martha married a Swittenberg and moved to Mississippi.

GAINES—Thomas Gaines made will July 17, 1800, and died same year, leaving widow, Delilah, (she was previously married to Richard Strother), and the following children: Sarah Fort Strother, Nancy R. Strother, James Gaines, Thomas Boykin Gaines, Mary Pendleton Gaines, Isabella Gaines, Peggy Gaines, Katy Gaines, Sally Gaines.

GALBRAITH—John Galbraith came to Newberry District with the Quakers. He died 1802, leaving four children: Joel, James, John, and Charity. In his will is, also, named a sister-in-law, Mariam Sanders, who was to live in his home with his children, and have active charge of his property. Executors: Samuel Gauntt and Joseph Furnas. James and his brother, John, moved to Columbus County, Ohio. James's wife was Jane........
Nathan Galbraith lived on Bush River. He, too, moved to the Northwest.

GALLOWAY—Peter Galloway made will 1774, which was proved in Court September 3, 1787. He left widow, Margaret, and children: Peter, James, John, Mary (wife of John Douglass), Elizabeth, Jean, Anna, and Martha. Executors: Robert Speer, William Wilson.
Jonotha Galloway, of Abbeville District, married Martha Speer, daughter of John Speer and wife, Mary L. Speer.

GALLMAN—George Gallman lived in the eastern section of Newberry District, near Cannon's Creek. He married a daughter of George Gray, Sr. John G. Gallman married Susannah Gray, a daughter of George Hray and Catherine (De Walt) Gray; and had children: Mary Magdeline, Rebecca, Elisha, Susannah, Lavania, Ruth, George G., John Peter, Simon G. Gallman.

GALPHIN—George Galphin received a grant of one hundred acres land near Savannah River, February 10, 1775. He married Rachel Du Pre.

GARLINGTON—A Laurens County family, though some later descendents lived in Newberry County.

GARMANY—John Garmany died in Newberry County before the year 1850, leaving widow, Mary, and children: Margaret (wife of John Maffett), James, William, Hamilton, George, Mary (she married Henry Brown). The son, George, moved to or near to Savannah, Georgia.
John Garmany came from Ireland about 1785, the date of petition for naturalization being October 31, 1808, after twenty years residence in America.

GARNER—James Garner died in Newberry District before the year 1805, leaving widow, Mary, and children: Elizabeth (wife of John Pemberton), Mary (wife of Joseph Jones), John (he married Sarah........), Robert (married Jemima........), Sarah (wife of Charles Crow), James, and Katherine. The son, James, died about 1842, leaving widow, Maria, and children: John (died before 1842), Joseph, Robert, Charles, and James C. Robert died before 1847; left no family.

Thomas Garner made will July 13, 1791, and died about 1792, leaving widow, (widow not named in will-she may have been dead), and children: John, Sarah Safford, Molly Roberts, Benjamin, Elizabeth; and a neice, Sally Garner. Benjamin married Elizabeth..........

Joseph Garner married Eliza Teague, daughter of Abram Teague, of Newberry County; they moved to Mississippi. His children, who shared in the property of their grand-father, Abram Teague, were the following: James Pinckney Garner, Abram Teague Garner, both of whom were, in 1858, in Pontotoc County, Mississippi.

Thomas Garner died in Union District, S. C. about 1778, leaving widow, Elizabeth (Chapman) Garner, and children: Sarah, William, Anne, John. John married Anne Kern, and died 1803, leaving children: Andrew, William, James. James married Mary Brice.

Other Pioneers (continued)

GARRETT-Levi Garrett died 180.., and left widow, Mary, and children: Joseph, Narcissa, Priscilla, June, Nathan, and Levi. He was a son of Silas Garrett who had two other sons, Jesse and Moses.

GASKINS-John Gaskins married Sarah Long (daughter of Benjamin and Priscilla Turner Long). Their children were: Albert G., Elmira, and Sarah, and perhaps, others. They moved to Mississippi.

GAUNTT-Israel Gauntt made will December 5, 1798, and died about 1800, leaving widow, Hannah, and children: James, Joseph, Jacob, Hannah, Rebecca (she married .... Gilbert), and Mary Coate.

GEIGER-Harmon Geiger lived in Lexington District. He made will October 15, 1778, and died 1779. His widow, Margaret, who afterwards married James Slappy, was left part of his estate. Children were: Randolph, Magdeline (she died young), Elizabeth Ann, Margaret. James Slappy and his wife, moved to Georgia.

Jacob Geiger lived in Northeastern section of Newberry County, near Tyger and Broad Rivers.

GEDDINGS-The Geddings lived near old "Gum Springs", in a home which has been burned down. Some of the family moved away. A son, Dr. Eli Geddings, practiced medicine in Newberry a short time, then moved to Charleston, S. C., where he practiced many years.

GEORGE-David George died in Abbeville County (then part of Ninety Six District). He left a widow, Rebecca, and children. In 1778 he was in Union District, where he sold six hundred acres of land.

John George died in Union District in 1791, leaving widow, and the following children: John, Mary, Thomas. John Jasper (son-in-law) and John George (son) were Executors of the will.

GIBSON-Abraham Gibson conveyed land to his son, Isaac, in Fairfield District, in year 1787.

Jacob Gibson died in Camden District in 1794, leaving widow, Sarah, and children: Abel, James, Jacob, Joseph, David, Stephen, Benjamin, Lucy, and Judith.

GILBERT-Caleb Gilbert was living in Newberry during the time of the Rev. War. He was a Rev. War patriot; captured by an English ship, sent to an English prison, Plymouth, England, in 1782. After the war he was returned to the States; and he came back to his home in Newberry County. He married Ann Chandler, and had children: Thomas, Joseph, Lydia Chandler, Sarah McNary, Syntic Reagin, Ann and Caleb. Thomas moved to Alabama where he died in 1835; he married in Newberry County to Rebecca Gauntt; after her death, he married again to Mary ......

Jeremiah Gilbert lived in Laurens County. He died about 1855, leaving widow, Leah, and children.

Abram Gilbert, born about 1800, was a merchant in Newberry, with his brother, Lovinski Gilbert. They were said to have built the first brick store in Newberry. Abram sold his interest in the business and moved to Georgia, near Columbus. He married in Newberry to Elizabeth West (she was born 1811; the daughter of John West and wife, Drucilla Lindsey West).

GILDER-Gilbert Gilder sold lands in Newberry County in 1790 to Jeremiah Williams, located near King's Creek.

Phillip Gilder died about 1808, left widow, Sarah, (she afterwards married Abner Atkins), and children: Eliza, James, Phillip (all under 21 years old in 1808). James died about 1853 or '54, leaving widow, Laura, and children: James H., Phillip N., Laura Jane, Sarah Tabitha, Caroline Julian, Susan Cornelia. James attended medical lectures under Newberry physicians, and also attended courses at medical college at Cincinatti. His son, James, also studied medicine, but died young, leaving a son, Dr. James L. Gilder, who practiced in Newberry.

GILREATH-William Gilreath lived in Newberry County and died in 1795, leaving widow, Mary, and children: Jesse, Mary, John, William, Alexander, Sarah Thompson, George, Nancy Turner.

GILLILAND-William Gilliland lived in Abbeville District, where he died in 1785.

Robert Gilliland lived in Laurens District where he died, leaving widow, Nancy, and children: John, Samuel, Robert, Jane (wife of Samuel Taylor), Ann (wife of Samuel Stewart), Martha, Nancy, Rachel (wife of Robert Stewart).

GIST-William Gist died 1802, leaving children: Joseph, Nathaniel, William Thomas, and Francis F. Gist. Nathaniel lived in Union District, as did Joseph. One Mordecai Gist married Mary Cattell in January, 1784.

Other Pioneers (continued)

GLASGOW—James Glasgow came from Scotland before the Rev. War, and settled on Indian Creek, Newberry County (then Ninety Six District). He brought with him his wife, Mary, whom he had married in Scotland. He made will October 17, 1775, which was recorded in Court November 26, 1793. He died between 1785 and 1793, leaving his widow, Mary, and children: Robert, John, Archibald, Wilson, Margaret, and Rachel. Margaret married John Kinard and Rachel married Robert McCrackin. Robert died in January, 1835, leaving children: Mary (wife of Zaccheus Wright), Ann (wife of James Fair), James (died young), Rachel (dead). James left four children, Archibald C., Robert, James, Spencer. Rachel married James Thompson and left children: Robert C., Elizabeth Louise and Glasgow Thompson. James Thompson moved to Tennessee after the death of his wife.

GLYMPH—John Glymph died about 1807, leaving widow, Elizabeth. John Glymph, Jr. married Hannah Suber, daughter of Uriah Suber. Her brother, Ephriam Suber, married Elizabeth Glymph, sister of John, Jr.

Emmanuel Glymph married Mary Kinard, daughter of Martin Kinard, Sr. who had moved from the Dutch Fork to near Kinard's Depot.

GODDARD—Daniel Goddard died 1868, in Laurens District. He left widow, Elizabeth, and children: John E., Thomas W., Lucinda, George, Polly Smith (all children by his first wife). By his second wife he had, Daniel and Henry.

GOLDING—Elisha Golding died and left children, William and Washington. Robert Golding had daughter, Nancy, who married Bela R. Mangum. Thomas Golding had children: Parthena (wife of John Floyd), Lucinda (wife of Abner Pitts). Reuben C. Golding died October 26, 1857, aged 15 years. He was a son of Elisha Golding.

GOODE—Garland Goode made will October 2, 1792, which was proved in Court in October, 1795. He left widow, Sallay Robertson, and children: Lydia Garner and Elisha Gill Robertson (the youngest son), and probably other children who were not named in the will. He left, also, a grand-son, William Elliott.

GOODMAN—Timothy Goodman made will March 21, 1802, and died same year. He left widow, Nancy, and children: Rebecca, Sarah, Wiley, James, Duke, and Buford.

GOODWIN—John Goodwin sold lands in Newberry District in 1791. Joseph Goodwin married in Newberry District to Eliza Hargrove, daughter of Solomon Hargrove.

Sampson Goodwin died in Union District in 1805, leaving children (all under 21); John, Mary, Betsy, Wytes, Nancy, Sandel. John died in Union District in 1823, leaving children: Elizabeth, Cassey Hayes, Delila, Anna, Polly, Sally.

GORDON—John Gordon received a grant of four hundred sixty acres land in both Union and Newberry Districts, on Enoree River (then part of old Craven County), in year 1754. Major Thomas Gordon (son of John), served as a patriot officer in the Rev. War. He was the first Sheriff of Newberry County when the county was established in 1782. He was, too, a Justice of the Peace. He married Elizabeth Anderson. Some of his children were: Ruth (married Major Thomas O'Hearon), Eli, Jesse, Elizabeth, John, Eli married Miss Voluntine (or Valentine), of Newberry County, and had children: Voluntine, Thomas, and others. Jesse married and left the county.

Nathaniel Gordon died and left two small daughters, Jane and Elizabeth. Jane married in 1813 to Alexander Barber; she died in 1848, leaving no children.

GOULD—William Gould lived in Newberry District, near Saluda River. John Gould lived in the village; kept store and tavern. He taught school in the Beaver Dam section of the county. He married Charity Lindsey, daughter of Thomas Lindsey, and had children: ...... After the death of his wife he moved to Georgia, then to Louisiana. (Ref: "Annals of Newberry" p. 94).

GRASTY—Thomas Grasty made will September 1789, and died same year. His sister, Martha Grasty, was given his lands on Beaver Dam Creek, which joined those of his brother, John Grasty They were, probably, sons of Sashel Grasty who was an old man during the Rev. War.

GRAHAM—James Graham married, first, to ..... and, second, to Nancy .... By his first wife were children: Polly Suber, Elizabeth (wife of James Parks), George, Joel. Children by his second wife were: Harriet (wife of John Ruff), James A., John H., Sarah Ann (wife of James L. Bowers), Julia Ann E. (wife of Isaac Felker), Martha (wife of Allen Scruggs). James died May 26, 1850, and his wife, Nancy, died in February, 1837.

Other Pioneers (continued)

GRAVES—James Graves died about 1790-91, in Fairfield District. He left widow, Mollyson, and children: Mary, Sarah, and William.
William Graves married Polly Wait, of Laurens District. She died before 1845, leaving children: Nancy S., Elizabeth M., Joseph F., James T., Phillip H., Peachey K., Obed W., Polly F., and William.
GREENWOOD—Daniel Greenwood received a grant of one hundred acres land on Manchester Branch, of Little Saluda River, in the year 1767. John and Frank Greenwood were in Pendleton District as early as the year 1800.
GREGG—William Gregg, Sr. was born in 1745, in Ireland, and died in Newberry District on November 10, 1816. He married Jane...... whi died September 14, 1823, aged 84 years. A daughter, Mary, married Samuel Spence, who was her second husband.
GRENEKER—Thomas Ferguson Greneker was born about 1827, in Newberry District, and died 1889.
GREEN— Thomas Green died in Newberry District in 1787. He left his property to his brother, John. John Green made will in 1790, and died 1791. He left his estate to his nephew, William Green, and to his neice, Green Green. (They were children of a deceased brother, William Green.)
GREGORY—Isaac Gregory died 1797. He left property to his wife, whose name was not given in the settlement of his estate, then to his children: Jared, John, Benjamin, Robert, Elizabeth, Isaac, and Jeremiah. Isaac, Jr. died about 1824, leaving children: Alce Lowery, Levi, Jerry, Allen, Wesley, and Isaac. John died 1843, and left widow, Elizabeth, and children: Thomas, Levi, Isaac, James M., Mary, Letty (wife of Joseph Lyles).
GRIFFITH—Joshua Griffith made will February 24, 1797, and died same year, leaving children: David, Joseph, William, Joshua, Sarah, Osaac, and Joel. Executors: Giles Chapman, Jospeh Chapman. Joshua Griffith, Jr. died about 1809, leaving widow, Mary, and four children: John, Katy, West, and Joshua. Mrs. Mary Griffith was a daughter of Samuel Chapman and his second wife, Nancy. The widow, Mrs. Mary Griffith, afterwards married ..... McCollough.
GRIGSBY—Enoch Grigsby came from Virginia to Edgefield District. He married Susan Butler. When he died about 1790 he left widow, Mary (his second wife), and children (all by his first wife), as follows: James, Rhydon, Nancy, Susannah (she married .....Hill).
GRIMES—Dillon Grimes died about 1854 in Newberry District, leaving widow, Isabella, and six children: Albert, James, William, Lucinda, Eliza, and Sarah.
GUNN—David Gunn, John Gunn, Elizabeth Gunn, who were brothers and sister, lived in Newberry. David d ed January 24, 1823. John and Elizabeth moved to North Carolina.
HAIR—Peter Hair made will August 24, 1772, and died about 1790. His children were: John, Matthias (or Mathew), Mary, Catherine, Rachel, Margaret, Milly, Agunk, Baeber. Matthias Hair made will April 1, 1817, and died April , 1817. He left widow, Fanny, and children: John, Peter, Barbara (she married ...Nichols), Sarah Counts, Elizabeth Hiller, Rebecca (wife of Jacob Bedenbaugh), Mary (wife of John McCart), and Nancy.
HAMPTON—Benjamin Hampton made will March 4, 1801, and died in 1804. His wife, Anna, had died previous to his death. Their children were: Elizabeth Malone, George, Edwards, William, Sarah Malone, Mary Johnson. Executor: Major Lewis Hogge.
John Hampton and wife, Joice, lived on Enoree River; sold lands in that section to John Sparks in year 1785. Joseph Hampton and wife, Rachel, lived on King's Creek; sold their lands in 1789 to Peter Brazzleman.
HALL—James Hall, in Newberry District, had sister, Jane, who married Andrew Speers; and other sisters and brothers, John, Joseph, Nancy Stone, Rebecca Fleming.
Samuel Hall married Nancy Darby, and later moved to Pleasant Grove, Pickens County, Alabama.
Anthony Hall married Jane Boyd, daughter of John Boyd, Sr., and had children: John, Wilson, William, Joseph, Elizabeth, Anthony, and, perhaps, others.
Matthew Hall lived in Newberry District. His will is dated January 17, 1817, and died 1819-'20, leaving widow, Margaret, and children: Thomas (dead), John Alexander, James (dead), and .... The children of Thomas were: Matthew and Thomas. The children of James were: Agnes and John. He left property to the Associated Reformed Presbyterian Church at King's Creek.
HALLMAN—Andrew Hallman died about 1808, his wife having previously died. Their children were: John, Margaret, (wife of John Enlow), Susannah (wife of Arna Hutchinson), Mary (wife of Michael Bedenbaugh), Elizabeth (wife of Samuel Kinard), Catherine (dead), Catherine had married (1) John Minnick and had child, George; then she married(2) Daniel Mickler.

Other Pioneers (continued)

HAMITER--Jacob Hamiter lived in Lexington County. He married Nancy Bickley. Mrs. Ann Hamiter, daughter of Thomas Bickley, of Lexington County, left children: John, David, Fanny, Joel, and Harriet. Mrs. Anna C. B. Hamiter died about 1867, leaving children: John A., Anna Bush, George W., and Christina.

HAMM--James Hamm sold two hundred acres land on Bush River, Newberry District, in 1788. He and his wife, Avarilla, signed the deed; land having been originally granted to Jeremiah Hamm by Letters Patent, as a bounty, on August 28, 1772, at Charleston, S. C.

HANCOCK--Dr. Zana Hancock lived near Broad River, Newberry District; he married Miss. Lyles, and settled later in Mississippi.

Joseph Hancock conveyed land in Edgefield District to Benjamin Ryan Rillman; located on Gap Branch, and containing ninety six acres; being part of an original grant of five hundred acres to John Hancock, Sr.

HARDY--Thomas Hardy, Sr. died about 1814, in Newberry District, leaving children: James, Thomas, John W., Pheobe Reynolds, Elizabeth, Freeman, Mary Gordon, Nancy Clark, Susannah Crenshaw, and .... His wife died between 1810 and 1814. Freeman Hardy moved to Alabama, and died in Dallas County, that State, on March 20, 1848. He was born March 20, 1771, having died on his birth-day. He married Sarah Rutherford, and had children: Freeman,Jr., John. Freeman, Jr. married Keziah Lanier on August 15, 1816, and had children: Susan F. (married a Fleming), and Robert M. (1817-1857).

John Hardy died about 1799 in Edgefield District, and left children: Richard, Sarah Cunningham, Daniel, Robert, John, William, Covington. Executors: Charles Hardy, Richard Hardy. Other legatees named in his will were: Fanny Ingram, Betsy Ingram (daughters of his widow by her first husband).

Thomas Hardy, Jr. made will February 20, 1823, and died same year. He left widow, Anna (Powell) Hardy, and children: Catherine, and Frances Jeter Hardy.

John W. Hardy made will July 2, 1806, and died same year. He left widow, Nancy, and children: Hamblin E., James F., and William. His widow, afterwards, married a Shell.

HARMON--John Harmon lived near the Laurens County line; died in that county. He made will on July 25, 1789, and died sometime in year 1794. He left widow, Mary, and children: Godfrey (he married Charity........), Sophia (wife of Daniel Taylor), Thomas, William, Samuel, James, Jacob, Peggy, David, and George. George was born just after the will was made. The testator's widow died about 1817. William died in July, 1808, leaving children: Jean, Margaret, Jennett, and probably others, who were, John, James, Samuel, and Sally Clary. James (son of John, Sr.), died about 1835, leaving widow, Mary, and children: Matthew S., Wesley, Jethro, Elizabeth, Harriet (wife of Rchard Simmons), Abbiness (wife of Isaac K. Jenkins), Cannazza, Rachel, and Amanda. David (son of John, Sr.), died in January, 1845, leaving widow, Martha, to have property; after her death, all lands to go to William Irvin Marchant, son of Harriet Marchant.

John Harmon, known as " Big" John, lived on Bush River. He made will in 1849, which was proved in Court on February 1, 1853; he died 1852. Children were: Mary Marie (wife of George Morris), Keziah (wife of William Lever), Nancy (wife of John H. Stockman), Rachel (wife of James Z. Connelly), Elizabeth (wife of David Nunnamaker), Margaret (wife of Godfrey Dreher), Martha (wife of P. W. Counts), John W. William P. Wesley Franklin, son of Mary Marie Morris, is named as a legatee.

William Harmon (son of John, Sr.),was born 1779, and died 1843. He left widow, Bridget, (she was a daughter of Rev. Thomas Frean), and children: John L., Mary (wife of Rev. John Watts), Jesse, Elizabeth Spearman, William P., Leila or Delila Lindsey, Nancy, Sarah I., and Thomas F.

HARP--John Harp married Abigail Mills, a daughter of Mrs. Sarah Mills, and they lived in the Quaker settlemnet on Bush River.

HALFACRE (originally spelled "Havaker")--John Halfacre made will September 1, 1795, and died about 1796. He left children: Jacob, Elizabeth, Barbara, and Henry. Executors: Henry Halfacre(son), George Gray, Jr.(son of his wife by a former husband). He came from Virginia before the Rev. War and settled near Cannon's Creek. The son, Jacob, moved to Tennessee. Henry married Elizabeth Suber; she died about 1857. He was born in Virginia about 1773, and died 1828 in

Other Pioneers (continued)

Newberry County. Their children were: David, Jacob, Daniel, Henry, Rebecca, and Elizabeth. Jacob moved to Mississippi. Henry was the father of Dr. John C. Halfacre.

HARRIS—Burr Calbert Harris was born in Virginia, and came to South Carolina with his first wife, Mary Haynie. An old land conveyance gives his name, then, as Burr Calvert (alis Harris). He made will August 26, 1783, and died about 1786 or '87, leaving widow, Jean, and children: Obed, George, Thomas, and Micajah. Micajah served under Col. John Lyles in General Williamson's campaign against the Cherokees. He was, also, active in the American Army in the Rev. War. He was promoted to Lieutenant of a militia company, later Captain. He was taken prisoner by the Tories, but escaped. He married Sarah Sheppard, and had children: Taplow, Janette, Anderson, Micajah, Lillie Culpepper, Mary Gordon, Cynthia Peaster, and James. He died about 1814, and his widow, Sarah, died about 1819. Micajah, Jr. married Mary Gallman (daughter of John George and Susannah Gray Gallman). He died May 12, 1867, and left children: Caroline, Susannah Katherine, Rebecca (died young), Mary Ann, Lavania Frances (married Thomas G. Sloan), Eliza (died unmarried), James Pressley, Thomas Jefferson (died 1862 in Confederate service), George (killed at battle of Vicksburg, Miss.), Burr Calvert (died at age 55), Oliver P. (died at Columbia, S. C. May 20, 1915).

Nathaniel Burr Harris came to Newberry Distruct before the Rev. War. He died about 1788, leaving widow, Mary, and children: Mosiby, Rebecca Ann, Rchard, and the wife of Samuel Harris

Abram Harris died in Newberry District about 1819, leaving widow, Catherine, and children: Michael, Emmanuel, and Anna Elizabeth.

HATCHER—Seth Hatcher died about 1812, in Newberry District. He left widow, Linley, and children: Daniel, Nancy, Linley, and two other daughters.

HATTON—David HATTON made will December 1, 1842, and died same year. He left widow, Jane, and children: Anne Catherine Blandenburg, John, and William. His widow married Peter Mozier.

HAWKINS—Peter Hawkins came to Ninety Six District before the Rev. War. He was born in Virginia, married there, and settled in the Stoney Hills of Newberry District. Children were: Edward, Jacob, Peter, William, Prudence Dennis, Elizabeth Rankin, and others. His wife was named Prudence. He died about 1800-1802. Jacob married Jane Hunter and had children: George, Peter, Eliza, Sallie Young.

HAWORTH—George Haworth lived on Bush River; belonged to the Bush River Monthly Meeting (Quaker Church). He received a bounty grant of one hundred fifty acres land located on Beaver Dam Creek, a branch of Bush River, in year 1773. He sold his land in 1814, and moved to Clinton County, Ohio.

Nathaniel Haworth lived on Bush River. Some of his children were: John, Sampson, and others. James Haworth was the father of Jemima (Haworth) Wright, wife of John Wright.

HAYES—Joseph Hayes and wife, Alice, lived on Bush River. They conveyed one hundred acres land in 1775 to John Richardson.

James Hayes made will December 18, 1799, and died about 1800, leaving widow, Frances, and children: James, Isabella, and Sarah.

Standiver Hayes married Catherine Counts; conveyed land in year 1812.

HAYNIE—William Haynie made will in 1801, and died in same year, leaving widow, Catherine, and a brother, John, as sole legatees.

Maximillan Haynie came from Prince William County, Virginia, to South Carolina about 1772. He located in what is now Newberry County. He married, first, in Virginia, and had two daughters. His second wife was Elizabeth Buchanan, a Virginia family that had located in Newberry District, and had ten children: Mary (wife of Burr Calvert Harris), Sarah Courtney (in Virginia), Susannah Stephens, Nancy Rutherford, Frances Ruff, John, and Anna. A grandson, Aaron Haynie, also shared in his estate. He died in 1814.

HEATON—Benjamin Heaton made will June 25, 1790, which was proved in Court June 29, 1791. He left estate to grand-children, as follows: Wiliam Weeks, John Weeks, James Weeks, Benjamin Weeks, Hannah Weeks. A nephew, Clorata Weeks, is named in will—nephew of children. His great-grand-daughter was Ctharte Weeks.

HENDRIX—William Hendrix died before the year 1800, leaving widow, Margaret, and children: John, Isaac, Thomas, Rebecca, Mary Kelly, and the wife of Henry Mills, and the wife of Anthony Swarnes.

Other Pioneers (continued)

HENDERSON—Thomas Henderson who died in Luise County, Va. about 1768, leaving widow, Elizabeth, were the progenitors of most of the Hendesons in South Carolina. His children were: John, Thomas, William, David, Mary Sison, Elizabeth Kerr, Anne, Gr-children: Charles Kerr and David Kerr.

Thomas (son of Thomas), died about 1795, He left widow, Polly, and children: Nathaniel, William, Polly, Elizabeth, Nancy, Fanny, Sicely, David. Nathaniel died about 1803, leaving widow, Rebecca, and children: Thomas, Richard, William, Nathaniel, Eli, and Martha. Nathaniel, Jr. who died about 1810, left widow, Nancy, and children: Matthew, Richard, Jemima G., William D., and Martha. William D. died in 1829.

David (son of Thomas, of Va.), was born about 1744 and died in 1805, His wife having died, he left children: John (1766—1816), David Sims, Jemima, Nancy (she married Nathaniel Gordon). John married (1) Katherine Harden, and (2) to Elizabeth Lyles—children by first wife: David Watland, Thomas, John, James. Thomas married Hannah Noland, and they were the parents of Stouton Henderson, who lived near Broad River. John married Elizabeth Black. James married (1) Martha Atwood, and (2) to Sallie Glenn— a son by Martha Atwood named, "Jack", and children by Sallie Glenn, James and Lidie. David (son of Thomas of Va.), had other children: Polly who married a Wadkington; Sibella who married a Lyles; Mamie, Sarah, and Elizabeth who married a Littleton. Other children by John and his wife, Katherine Harden, were: Charles Hardin, Nancy Hardin (she married A. W. Thompson, of Union District), Hannah, and Anne who married Wallace Thompson. Children by John and his second wife, Elizabeth Lyles, were: James, Lucy, Sarah, and Caroline. Other children by Nathaniel, Jr. and his wife, Nancy, were: Hannah (wife of Allen Lyles), and Drucilla (wife of Archilles Lyles).

One Nathaniel Henderson died in Fairfield District about 1780, and left children: Richard, Nathaniel, Edward, John, Anne Wilson, Tyre, William, Patience, James, Sherod, and Elizabeth.

One Robert Henderson died in Pendleton District about 1802, leaving widow, Isabel, and children: David, Nathaniel, James, John, Robert, and William.

One William Henderson died about 1830 in Abbeville District. He left as his legatees the following: Nathaniel, James, John, Shadrack, Nathan, Samuel, and Elizabeth (wife of John Marshall), and Sarah (wife of William McDill). The children of Wm McDill and Sarah McDill were Robert and Thomas, and probably others.

Some of daughters of Thomas Hendreson who died in 1795 in Union District were: Polly who Married Henry Mills, Fanny who married Thomas Ward, Cicely, Nancy who married Owen Jenkins, and Judy Waltt.

HEAD—James Head, of North Carolina, moved to Edgefield District, S. C. He married Effany..., and had children: Jane (wife of Thomas Youngblood), and others.

Richard Head died before 1823, leaving widow, Nancy, and children: Tabitha C. Clara (wife of Joseph Tripp), James N., Hannah N. Wimpey, Rebecca S., William P., Lucinda (wife of James Barrett), Nancy (she afterwards married John C. Williamson).

HELLER—John Heller lived near Second Creek, Newberry District. He married Sarah, daughter of ...... Glymph.

Jacob Heller died in Newberry District. His will is dated Dec. 12, 1835, and proved in court Oct. 16, 1839. He left four children, named in will: David, Elizabeth, John, and Mary.

HALFACRE—Jacob Halfacre (originally spelled "Havaker") made a will dated Sept. 1, 1795; and died in Newberry County in 1796. He left children: Jacob, Elisabeth, Barbara, and Henry. Exrs: Henry Halfacre (son), and George Gray, Jr. (son by his wife who was a widow when he married her). He came from Virginia before the Rev. War, and settled about five miles East of "Coats Shop" (now Court House), near Cannons Creek. The son, Jacob, moved to Tennessee. Henry remained in Newberry District, and lived on part of original land of his father during life, where several generations of the family lived. He married Elizabeth Suber who died in 1857. He was born in Virginia about 1773, and died in Newberry District in 1828. Their children were: David, Jacob, Daniel, Henry, Rebecca, and Elizabeth. The son, Henry, was the father of the late Dr. John C. Halfacre, of Newberry. The son, Jacob, settled in Mississippi.

HENRY—William Henry made a will dated March 9, 1795, and died 1796, leaving a son, George. James Henry lived in Laurens County, and in Union County about 1800. There was a William

Other Pioneers (continued)

Henry in Chester County in 1786.

Thomas M. Henry died in Chester County about 1844, left widow, Catherine, and children: Francis, Elihu, John S., James, and wife of Nicholas Curry, the wife of Joseph, Herndon, the wife of S. G. Miller.

In Pendleton District about 1800-1810, there were living Thomas Henry, John Henry, and William Henry.

In Newberry County was James Henry and descendents. He died August 13, 1845, and left children: George, James A., Barbara Jane, and Hugh P. Henry. His wife, Nancy, died about 1836. A daughter, Catherine, died in 1833.

James A. Henry (son of James), died 1893, and left widow, Sophia Elizabeth (Boozer) Henry, and children (by widow), viz: James Matthew and Walter Samuel, both of whom became Methodist ministers.

Hugh P. (son of James), married Martha H. Boozer (sister of Elizabeth who married James A. Henry), and were parents of Prof. Howell M. Henry, graduate of Newberry College and for many years holding the chair of History in a college in Virginia.

HERBERT-Isaac Herbert settled in the Bush River section of Newberry County. He was a Quaker and attended the old Quaker Meeting House on Bush River. He married Frances........ One of their sons was Captain Chesly Herbert who graduated at the S. C. University at Columbia in year 1855, married Elizabeth Goggans, daughter of Daniel and Emily Goggans. He volunteered for service in the Confederate Army, was wounded twice in battles, and after the war returned home a cripple for life. He was murdered "by a Negro who had stolen his horse, and had been arrested by him, and who was sharing his bread with the culprit by the roadside." (From "Annals of Newberry", page 589).

George Herbert made will Feb. 9, 1807 and died in the same month and year. His widow, Elizabeth, survived, and their children: Hillery, Martha, Nancy, George B., and Thomas E.

Mrs. Ann Herbert (widow) made will April 12, 1814 and died same year. Her daughters were: Elizabeth Corll, Rachel Dunn, and Charity Galbreath.

The sons were: Walter and Peter Herbert. Grand-daughters named were: Ann Batten, Ann Teat, Ann Barett, Ann Corll, and Ann Dean.

HERNDON-Col. Benjamin Herndon, a distinguished patriot and officer in the S. C. militia during the Rev. War, lived in Newberry District. He made will June 9, 1814 and died December 29, 1819, leaving widow, Patience Terry, and children: Joseph (moved to Tenn.), Mary B. (married John M. Lewis and moved to Tenn.), Stephen, Frances (wife of Daniel McKie), Elizabeth M. (wife of Samuel Farrow), Benjamin (dead), Nancy Coke (wife of John Rice), Rebecca Ellis (wife of Zacariah Reid), Zacariah P., Barbara Asbury (wife of David Johnson), Sally (wife of William Rice), Patsy M. Harriet, John Newton, and Lucy Boswell. Benjamin, Jr. left a widow, Sarah P. The last three children were infants, under 14 years old, and were left in charge of Patience Terry Herndon as Guardian. He left four thousand acres of lands on the North side of Duck River in Tennessee where Mary B. Lewis lived. Executors: Wm. Rice, David Johnson, and Spilsby Glenn.

HENTZ-Matthias Hentz was son of a pioneer of the Dutch Fork of Ninety Six District (now Newberry County). He married and had two sons, David and Michael. Michael moved to Georgia. David died about 1850, in the Dutch Fork, leaving children: David R., Rebecca (wife of George Sondley, Sarah C., Virginia, Susannah C. Noyd, Narcissa (wife of George Anderson), Another son, Henry M., died before death of his father, about 1850. He left widow, Elizabeth. Sarah Catherine married John A. Folk, and had children: John D. L., Henry M.. Wm. O., Hayne H. Martha, Augusta K. Children of Rebecca Sendley were: David, Susannah, William, Sarah, Virginia, and Narcissa. Susannah married second time and had children: Hayne H., Nancy, William, and Backman.

HICKS-Charles Hicks died 1808 in Edgefield District. He left widow, Susannah, and children: Martha, Polly, Nelly, Susannah, Rebecca, James, and Edward.

HEWETT(or Huitt)-Jacob Hewett made will March 4, 1809 and died in 1810, leaving widow, Christina, and children: Jacob, and Mary Elizabeth (wife of Adam Rish).

HIGGINS-Francis Higgins married Sarah Coxe, daughter of Cornelius and Anne Coxe. She died 1799. Their children were: Francis B., Charlotte (wife of Wm. Wilson), and Dorothy (wife

Other Pioneers (continued)

of Henry Edrington), Sarah Ann, Mark, John, and Mary.

Francis B. Higgins, a graduate of S. C. University, was an eminent lawyer in Newberry. He filled many public positions of trust, among them being that of Commissioner in Equity. He was State Senator for several terms and did effective work while in that body. He married Elizabeth Caldwell, a daughter of William Caldwell, a Rev War patriot and Officer of the American Army. Her mother was Elizabeth Williams, daughter of Major John Williams who was a member of the South Carolina Provincial Congress during the Revolution and an officer in the state militia.

HIATT(HYATT)—Francis Hayett was living in Newberry District in 1790, in which year he conveyed 50 acres land to his son, Jacob Hayett. Some of descendents moved with Quakers to Ohio about 1810—20.

Daniel Hiatt married Fanny White in Union District befor 1804. She was a daughter of Thomas White. David Hiatt married Fanny White, widow of Thomas White.

Thomas Hiatt died in 1843 in Union District, leaving widow, Martha, and children: Jesse, Nancy Callman, Milly Ward, Elizabeth Balew, Sarah Ann Jackson, James Hiatt, William Hiatt, Mary Ann, Amanda, Harriet, and Caroline.

Jesse Hiatt died in April, 1858, in Union District, leaving widow, Elizabeth, and children: James, Mary (wife of Wm West, Jr.), Thomas, John, Amanda, and Sarah.

HILBURN—William Hilburn belonged to the Bush River Meeting—Quakers—and lived in Newberry District. He married Jane ...... and had children: Levi, William, Robert, Israel, Nathaniel, and others.

Levi Hilburn died about 1827, in Newberry District. He left widow, Jane, and children: Henry, Hugh, Richard, Matilda Jay, Melinda Wright, Mahala Heget, Matura Rogers; Gr-ch: Hillery and Hannah Hilburn. Mrs. Jane Hilburn was daughter of Joseph Thompson. Melinda had married Wright. Henry married Rachel Duncan, and had children: Thomas B. (he married Nancy Wilson), Harriet, Rhilly, Reasy, Maddy, Rutha, Conrodia, and Orcathia. Henry died in 1828, and Rachel died after 1837.

HILL—Lodowick Hill lived in Ninety Six District, S. C. before the American Revolution in which struggle he participated, first as a private and then as a sergeant in General Sumter's brigade. He married Susan Grigsby in 1785 (daughter of Enoch and Susan (Butler) Grigsby). Their children were: Mary, Teresa, Theophilus, James, Sarah, Henry Hampton, Rhydon and Jonothan. They were all born in Edgefield District.

Theophilus Hill married Susannah Richardson and had children: Lodowick, Mary, Henry, Rhydon, James R., Martha, Elizabeth, William. They have many descendents in the counties of Newberry, Abbeville, Edgefield, and other sections.

Stephen Hill lived in Northern section of Newberry County and owned 1137 acres land on both sides of Duncan's Creek. He died in May 1849, leaving a widow, Elizabeth, and children: Sarah Jones (wife of Jesse Jones), Joseph, Hollaway, John W., Calvin, and Mary Cummins Hill. These have many descendents in Newberry, Union, and Spartanburg Counties and in other states.

Thomas Hill died June 29, 1823, leaving widow, Elizabeth, and a son, Travis, by a former wife, who was an only son.

HINTON—Thomas Hinton died in Abbeville County. His daughter, Mrs. Martha Turner, died about 1849. His other children were: Mary (wife of George W. Paul), Rebecca (wife of Aquilla F. P. Douglas), Jeremiah, John, Elizabeth (wife of J. I. Hamilton), Nancy A. and a deceased daughter who had married Nathaniel Jeffries.

HIPP—John Hipp, one of the pioneer German settlers of the upper Dutch Fork, was granted land about 1750. He had a wife and children when he came. George Hipp came from Germany about 1752, and had no family when he came.

John Hipp, Jr. (son of John), married Susan Margaret Summer, a daughter of George Adam Summer, Sr. He died about 1845 and left widow, and children: Syble Livingstone, Christina (wife of William Andrew Summer), John Adam, William A., Elizabeth, Mary Margaret (wife of John H. Fulmer), Anna (wife of J. Adam Boland), and John. John Hipp died about 1846, and left widow, Amanda, and infant children as follows: Walter, Susannah, and Martha.

Other Pioneers (continued)

John Hipp, Sr. made will dated in 1786, and died about 1800, leaving widow, Susannah, and children (as named above). His widow afterwards married John Kinard, Sr.

Andrew Hipp married Nancy....... and died leaving widow, and a son, Andrew, and several daughters who were wives of the following: James Duckett, Ralph Hughs, Labon Rhodes, John Neighbors, Elisha Rhodes, Hiram Rhodes, William Odell, and John Wallace.

George Hipp, Sr. (a gr-son of the pioneer, George), died about 1855, leaving widow, Eliza Elizabeth, and children: Sarah Anne (wife of James Gordon), John David.

HOARD—James Hoard belonged to the Virginia imigrants who came with the families of Buchanan and Haynie to South Carolina before the Revolution. He died in Newberry County in 1797, leaving his widow, Ann, and several children. One son, William, is named in settlement of his estate. The widow, Ann, died about 1809 and Nancy Lane and Frances Hoard were appointed Administratrices.

HODGES—James Hodges made will May 19, 1786 and died in same year. He left widow, Martha, and children: Joseph Hodges, Jesse Hedges, Christina Hodges, Robert Shaw, Hailey Shaw, Rebecca Shaw, and Patty Shaw.

HOGGE—Major Lewis Hogge was a pioneer settler on Indian Creek in Ninety Six District (Newberry County).

John Hogge came from Virginia. He had a son, Thomas, who married Martha Chandler, and a daughter, Margaret, who married Benjamin Durrett. Some of this family moved to Alabama and Georgia.

Zacariah Hogge made a will dated December 12, 1811 and died in 1812, leaving widow, Talla, and children as follows: Ona, Mahala, Leonora, and Elmo. Executor: Lewis Hogge, Sr.

HOLDER—Daniel Holder died in Union District before 1850, leaving widow, Ruth, and ch: Amy (wife of Wm Walker), Matilda (wife of David Vaughn), Ruth, Sally, Beardin, Berryman S., Gr-ch: Berryman E. Beardin, Elizabeth Vaughn, Daniel Holder (son of Berryman S. Holder), and Samuel Vaughn.

HOLLAND—Abraham Holland came from the southern section of the Shenandoah Valley of Virginia before the Rev War. He died about 1800 in Laurens District, leaving widow, and following children: Reason, William, Richard, Jeremiah (his widow),Nancy Simpson, and a daughter who had married Richard Fryer.

Reason Holland settled in Abbeville District. He made will dated 7-30-1802 and died same year in Laurens District. He left widow, Mary, who died Dec. 13, 1802, and children: John, Thomas, Jeremiah, Sarah, Elizabeth, Rachel, Maria (married Matthew McCary), Anna (married Roebuck Wilder). Of these, John married Mary....., Jeremiah married Mahala.....; Sarah married Robert Young; Elizabeth married Henry Tucker: Rachel married Charles Simpson;

John Holland died about 1824. His widow, Marry Ann, Survived him. They had seven ch: George W., Lucretia, Malinda, Lucinda (wife of Jeel T. Foster), M. D., and John P.

Thomas Holland died about 1815, leaving widow, Jane.

Abraham Holland was living on Duncans Creek in 1816; had wife, Nancy. He was son of Thomas Holland, brother of Asanor Holland.

Weyman Holland, Brother of one Abraham, bought lands from Wm Shaw who sailed for England and never returned.

John Holland died March 17, 1835, in Laurens District. He left widow, Mary Ann, and ch: Geo. W., John P., Lucretia (wife of H. R. Shell), Lucinda (wife of John T. Foster), Mary Ann (wife of Wm Fowler), Louisa K., and Malinda.

Abraham Holland died in Laurens District about 1860, leaving ch: Reason, Richard, and a pre-deceased son, Jeremiah. Jeremiah's wife was Nancy Langston who afterwards married a Simpson.

Thomas Howard died 18.. in Laurens District, leaving widow, Mary, and ch: Elizabeth Jane (wife of Thomas D. Young), Thomas, A. F., G. R., R. W., Bluford, Rusk, May Ann, Martha K., All were minors except Mrs. Young.

HOLLINGSWORTH—The Hollingsworths were Quakers on Bush River in Newberry District. Isaac Hollingsworth married Susannah Wright, daughter of John Wright. They moved with the Quaker migration to Ohio. At that time, they had five daughters and three sons. The sons were Jeel, John, and William, who later moved from Ohio into Indiana. The daughters were Rachel,

Other Pioneers (continued)

Ruth, Keziah, Sarah, and Susannah. They all married in Newberry District before moving, except Susannah who married Elisha Jones, twin brother of Elijah Jones who died in Newberry.
James Hollingsworth died in Edgefield District. His will is dated Nov. 13, 1818, proved in court in 1822. Children: John, Sarah Carson, Polly Harrison. Gr-ch: James, Alexander, James (son of James, Sr.), Quincy Miller, John Walton (his wife Polly), John Walton and Polly had a son, Enock Walton. Other legatees were: James Carson and James Harrison. (From "Edgefield County record of wills and Deeds").......

HOLLOWAY-Lewis Holloway came from Pennsylvania to Virginia, then to Edgefield District, S. C. arriving in S. C. after the Rev War. He married in Va. In Dec. 1786, to Rachel Williams, widow of Thomas G. Williams, of Brunswick County, Va.

Jordan Holloway died in Edgefield District. His estate was given to the following distributees in 1837: Daniel, Elijah, Wiley, Martin, Matilda (wife of John Dunn), and wife of Geo. Reams.

John Holloway died about 1845, in Newberry District. He left children: Thomas W., And Helen, both quite young when parents died. Thomas W. settled in the Dutch Fork, at Pomaria, Newberry County. He married twice, having children by each wife.

HOLMAN-John Holman was one of the first settlers in upper section of Newberry District. He was granted 250 acres land on Big Saluda River in year 1767.

He was, probably, the father of Andrew Holman who married a daughter of John Dominick; Windel Holman, Richard Holman, William Holman, John Holman, Jr., and David Holman. They were all living on Saluda at a later date (about 1780 to 1790). J. Windel Holman married Christina ..... William married Mary........., and they had a son, William, Jr.

HOPPER(HARPER)-John Hopper died about 1826-27 in Newberry District. He left widow, Mary, and children: Hugh, Anne (wife of John Boyd), James, Nancy (wife of Hugh Boyd), and William (he died before death of his father and left children).

William Hopper (son of John), died 1818, left widow, Sarah, and children: John, Hugh, Alexander, Sarah, Ann Grymes. The widow was a daughter of Jeremiah Dial, of Newberry District.

Another William Hopper died about 1800, and left following legatees: George, Elizabeth, Jane, and a daughter who married John Martin.

HOPE-Rev. J. C. Hope married Louisa Caroline Eichleberger, daughter of George and Katherine (Summer) Eichleberger, of the Dutch Fork of Newberry District. Their son, James, married Mattie Miller, and a daughter, Mary, became wife of Dr. L. L. Hobbs, parents of John L Hobbs, traveler, adventurer, author.

HOUGH(HUFF)-Martin Hough deeded land in 1798 to George Leitsey, his nephew. He died in 1816 and left widow, Margaret (she died in 1830), legatees: George Leitsey (cousin), George Long, Jr., and a sister, Maria Vanderburgh who was living in Fairfield County.

John Huff died in Edgefield Dist. about 1815-16. He left widow, Sarah, and ch: Allen and Jylius (to have lands in Granville County, N. C.), Daniel, Anne Edwards, Mary Edwards, Sally Cogbrom, Fabtha Rainsford.

HOUSTON-John Houston, Sr. made will june 1, 1778, and died about 1785 to 1790, leaving widow, Else, and children: John, Robert, Joseph, Alexander, Benjmain, and Catherine. John Died and left widow, Mary, who later married Joseph Le Master.

John Houston made will December 26, 1802, and died same year, leaving widow, Jean, and children: John, William, Elizabeth, Samuel, Nancy, James, and Jenny. A nephew, Hugh Houston, and two sons-in-law, James Armstrong and Robert M. Mann.

James Houston died in November, 1802, and left a daughter, Mary Houston, and a son-in-law, William Sample.

Benjmain Houston (son of John Houston, Sr.), died about 1815 ot '16, leaving widow, Elizabeth and children: Alice, James, and Benjamin. Exrs: John Gray and Alexander Houston (brother).
William Houston (son of John Houston, Sr.), made March 18, 1808, and died same year. He left widow, Anne, and children: Peter, Jane Brown, James, Agnes Martin, John, William, and Thomas. Alexander Houston (son of John Houston, Sr.), made will August 11, 1855, and died 1855. He was married twice. His second wife, Jane, died before his death. Children by first wife were: Robert H., James A., Matilda C. Nobles, Elizabeth A. Cowan, John A. , Joseph B., Susan A. Nobles. and William J. Children bu first wife were: Armstrong R., Cornelius B., Alice, Jane Scott, Cornelia A., and A. R. Houston.

Other Pioneers (continued)

HORSEY-Daniel Horsey was granted land on Second Creek before year 1775. His widow, Sarah, sold this land to Josiah Rutherford in 1789. Samuel Horsey was living on Second Creek after the year 1800.

HOWARD-John Howard died about 1819 in Newberry District. He left widow, Avis, and children: Joseph, Betsy, Susan, William, Sarah, Edward, John, Avis, Stephen, and Samuel. Charles Howard lived in Newberry County, married Counts.

HUGHES-James Hughes lived on Indian Creek, in Newberry County. He was said to have lived to be one hundred ten years old. ("Annals of Newberry", p. 44)

HUGHEY-John B. Hughey made will December 1, 1833, and died about 1833 in Abbeville District. He left widow, Ruth R., and children: John Thomas, Jane C., Frances A., Laura C., Albertine E.

HUNT-Michael Hunt came from North Carolina to Ninety Six District before the Rev. War. He married Elizabeth Abernathy (widow) and lived on Bush River, Newberry County. He died soon after his settlement, and his widow lived on the land until her death in 1797. In her will she names her daughter, Isabel, and also two sons by a former marriage, James and John Abernathy. Also, a grand-son, James, a daughter-in-law, Rhoda, are named.

Jacob Hansel Hunt married Sarah Morgan, a daughter of Rueben Morgan, Sr., and wife, Elizabeth Morgan. A son, Hulet Hunt, married Rebecca Kelly, daughter of John and Anne (Davenport) Kelly.

Jacob Hunt came from North Carolina to Newberry after the Rev. War. He married a daughter of Walter Herbert, of Newberry County, and lived on Bush River. They had sons, Walter Herbert Hunt, Isaac F. Hunt, and James Hamilton Hunt.

HUNTER-Nathan Hunter came from Ireland to Newberry District after the Rev. War, or about 1780 He married Mary Young in Ireland. They had children: Joseph, William, George, Nathan, James, Elizabeth Drennan, Jane Thompson, Mary Devlin. Some of their descendents moved to the States of Indiana, Illinois, Texas, Florida, and other States.

John Hunter died about 1834 in Laurens County, leaving widow, Nancy, and children: William, Nancy, Isabella, Elizabeth, John C., James O., and the wife of O. Richardson.

HUTCHINSON-Alexander Hutchinson died about 1801, leaving widow, Elizabeth, and children: John, Arnat, James, and Jenny. John Hutchinson died 1830, leaving widow, Elizabeth, and children: James, Janette, (married Frazier); and a gr-son, James, son of a deceased son, Arnat. William Hutchinson died about 1806, leaving widow, Mary, and children: John, William, Thomas, Jarem, Jean (wife of Joseph Lake), and the wife of Joseph Bishop, and the wife of Jacob Felker.

INMAN-Benjamin Inman made will November 4, 1798, and died 1799, leaving widow, Elizabeth, and children: Ahab, Arthur, Benjamin, Jehu, Ferrely, Charles, Elizabeth, and George.

John Inman died about 1803, leaving widow, Mary, and aged mother, Mrs. Jemima Inman.

Joshua Inman made will in 1810, and died about 1814, leaving widow, Ann, and children: .... (no names given in will). Widow named as Trustee for children. Exr: Thomas Gilbert.

INSCO-Abel and James Insco, brothers, lived on Bush River, and moved to Ohio with a colony of Quakers. James married in Ohio and had daughters.

JACKSON-Frederick Jackson, Sr. died in Union District before 1835. He left a widow, Letitia, and children: Sarah (wife of Benjamin Holcombe), Susan (wife of Abram Walker), Elizabeth (wife of Samuel Bullington), Mary (widow of Thomas Harris), Edith (wife of Joseph D. Murphy); and to Z. Hooper, as Guardian for minor children, Amy, Nathaniel, Ralph, John, and William Jackson.

JACOBS-Johannes Jacobs died about 1784. Administration of estate granted to his widow, Cynthia Jacobs.

JAY-This family lived on Bush River, and most of them moved to Ohio with the Quakers. The following were on Bush River before 1800: John, William, Thomas, James, David, Robert, Alexander, and Jesse Jay.

William Jay made will January 7, 1797, which was proved in Court February 28, 1797. He left widow, Margaret, and children: Mary, Sarah, William, David, James, Elizabeth, Charlotte Layton, Ann, Deborah, and Susannah. Exrs: John Jay and David Jay. Most of the family moved to the Northwest between 1810 and 1830.

Other Pioneers (continued)

JENKINS—David Jenkins died about 1810. Isaac Jenkins died before 1798; left widow, Rebecca(Kirk) Jenkins. David Jenkins, Jr. died about 1823.

Mrs. Elizabeth Jenkins, widow of Isaac Jenkins, died about 1836. One Isaac Jenkins married Mary Davis and had children, Marcus and Edwin.

JENNINGS—John Jennings sold land in Newberry District in 1803 to James Brady; then moved to Chrleston, S. C. Robert Jennings lived in Edgefield District, where he sold land on Bird Creek, in "Cuffetown". Phillip Jennings died in Edgefiedl District before 1850. His estate which was settled in 1850 showed the following distributees: Lucy Jennings (his widow), John Coleman, Thornton Coleman, Anna (wife of John Deharise), Batheny Chapman(he died before settlement and his children shared), Mary Parton (deceased sister, whose children were named), John Jennings, William Jennings, and the children of a deceased sister, Lucy Parton.

JOHNSON—James Johnson was living in Newberry District in 1790. John Johnson made will October 20, 1794, and died about 1799, leaving children: Samuel, Robert, James, William, Rebecca, John. John Johnson made will October 6, 1796, and died same year. He left children: Michael, Eleanor, Mary, John, Margaret, James, Katrin, Charles.

Mrs. Mary Johnson (widow of John Johnson) married John Caldwell in 1821. John Johnson had died about 1820. She was a daughter of Peter Kerr and wife, Susannah (McQuerns) Kerr. Mrs. Winnifred Johnson , widow, died about 1805, having made will dated Feb 23, 1805, and proved in Court same year. She left children: Richard, Stephen, Martha,(married Griffin), Sarah, and William Pitts Johnson.

JOHNSTON—John Johnston, Sr. made will June 19, 1795, which was proved in Court March 10, 1800. He was a planter and distiller. He left children: Robert, Rebecca, Samuel, William, James, Elizabeth, and John (John was the oldest son).

John Johnston died in 1802, leaving widow, Haney, and children: Davis, Thomas, John, Mary, Daniel, Abraham.

Samuel Johnston died in Fairfield County(brother of John of Newberry District), He was born about 1769 and died in 1853. He left widow, Elizabeth, and children: John, Samuel E., Margaret (wife of James P. Adams), Madison, William D., Charlotte A. (wife of Dr. David Means), Juliet C. (wife of John C. Johnston), Rebecca (wife of Harry Adams), Jane, Burr, Harriet (wife of Birt Harrington), Sarah (wife of .... Randell). His grand-children named in will were: Rebecca Chambers,daughter of sylvamus and Caroline Chambers.

Alexander Johnston made will September 4, 1815, and died about 1816. He left widow, Margaret and children: James, William, John, Margaret, and Jennett. He owned land on Second Creek.

Andrew Johnston died about 1819, leaving daughter, Nancy Lee, and a half-brother, Dr. John Johnston; and sisters, Martha McDow, Frances Lee(both in Camden District). Joseph Lee, son of Thomas Lee, Esq., is named as a legatee.

JONES—Lewis Jones was born near County line of Newberry and Laurens, and is buried at old O'Dell Cemetery. He was born 1787 and died 1855. Holloway Hill married Sarah Jones who was born January 13, 1833 and died August 5, 1903. Lewis married Lydia Hill who was born 1802 and died 1873; and had children: Jesse (1818-1856), Nancy (married William G. Mayes, Sr)?, and other children.

Jesse Jones,(of Laurens County) married Rebecca Dalrymple, a daughter of John and Susannah Dalrymple. They lived near Bush River in that county.

James Jones , of Newberry County, and his wife, Hannah, deeded lands on Beaver Dam Creek to George Gibson and Richard Gibson, in year 1773.

Joseph Jones made will September 13, 1814, and died about 1816 or '17, leaving widow, Mary, and children: John, Mary (wife of James Garner), Sarah Busbee, Fanny Busbee, Susannah, Nancy, Delphia, and Katy. One Joseph Jone married Nancy Davis, a daughter of Chesley and Mary Davis.

Elisha Jones made will December 16, 1843, and died 1844 in Fairfield County, leaving widow, Judith, and children: Dorcas (wife of.... Hall), Jemima (wife of ..... Crankfield), He left grand-sons: Elisha Hall, John Thomas Hall, and othe children of Dorcas Hall. Exrs: William Jones (brother), Dr. Wm. E. Hall (son-in-law), Ralph Jones (nephew).

Captain Thomas Jones, an officer in the American Army during the Rev. War, died before 1787, leaving widow,Catherine, and children: Thomas, and other children, that moved to Hancock County, Georgia. Other children: Joseph, John, Litter, and others.

Other Pioneers (continued)

Wallace Jones, Sr. moved from Newberry District to Greenville District; later, he moved to Ohio with the Quakers, about year 1808. He was known as "Cap" Jones on account of services as a patriot in the Rev. War. He was born 1742, married Elizabeth Fritz, who was born 1744. He died 1823 and his widow in 1830. He was a son of Henry Jones. Their children were: Wallace, Jr. (1773-1854) who married Rachel Patty (1774-1828); and others.
Wallace Jones, Jr. and wife, Rachel, had children: Philemon (married Naomi Tucker), John (married Susan Tucker), Jesse, (married Susannah Embree), Mary (married Isaac Ellemon), Wiley Smith Jones (married Adelia McConnell), Dorcas (married Benjamin H. Pearson), Henry (he died 1811 aged two years).
JULIEN-Peter Julien lived in Newberry District on Bush River. He married twice, his second wife being Sophia...... (a widow). He was a patriot in the Rev. War. He died in 1808, leaving the following grand-children: Azariah, Eli, Jesse, Stephen, William, Susannah, and Hannah Julien. A son, Peter, Jr., lived on Bush River. Sarah Julien died 1823.
George Julien and wife, Mary (Walls) Julien lived in Chester District at the time they moved to Wayne County, Ohio, about 1815.
KELLER-Joseph Keller lived in the Dutch Fork section of Newberry County. He married Ruth Stark, the daughter of John Stark, Sr. and wife, Susannah (McMaster) Stark, before the year 1830. George Keller died before 1830, leaving widow, Elizabeth, who, after his death, married Jacob Lohner. She died in March, 1830. Children by her first husband were: Mary (wife of Henry Oxner), Sarah (wife of William J. Connelly), Imry, Redempsy (wife of Lent Hall), Keziah (wife of Washington Dobbins), Anna (wife of John J. Ulrick). Lent Hall and wife moved to Anderson County. William J. Connelly and wife moved to Lauderdale County, Tenn. Washington Dobbins and wife moved to Perry County, Alabama.
John Keller and Daniel Keller were twins, who married sisters. John married Elizabeth Cromer and Daniel married Rebecca Cromer, daughters of Jacob Cromer, of the Dutch Fork section.
KELLY-John Kelly, Sr. made will August 26, 1775, and died same year, leaving widow, Mary, and children: Isaac, Samuel, and probably others.
James Kelly married Agnes Durrett, of Newberry County, widow of Thomas Durrett.
Joseph Kelly died about 1796, leaving widow, Mary, and brother, Thomas Kelly.
William Kelly made will 1798, and died same year, leaving widow, Susannah, and children: Penelope and William.
Mrs. Mary Kelly made will April 1, 1798, and died same month and year. She left children: John Ryan and Margaret Head. William D. Kelly married Matilda Thomas, daughter of Stephen Thomas of Little River.
Samuel Kelly (son of John Kelly, Sr.), was a native of Kings County, Ireland. He and his family came to South Carolina before the Rev. War, and first settled in old Camden District. They came to Newberry District, settled on Bush River, before the Rev. War (then called part of Ninety Six District). They belonged to the Quaker Church. Mrs. Hannah Kelly made will April 22, 1817, and died about 1820, leaving children: Rebecca Elmore, Anne O'Neall (wife of Hugh O'Neall); and children of a deceased son, John Kelly. Her grand-children were: John Belton O'Neall, Samuel Elmore, Hannah Frean, Rebecca Elmore, Abigail Caldwell, Rebecca O'Neall, Sarah O'Neall, and Karen-happock Evans.
James Kelly was a Rev. War patriot, Lieutenant in State Militia. His brother, Edmund, was a patriot soldier; died when over one hundred years old. James Kelly died January 24, 1824, leaving children: Thomas G., Edmund B., Edward, Greenwood. Edmund B. Kelly died and left children: Ivey, Isham, Elizabeth, Thomas, Priscilla. His widow, Frances, married .... Alewine
John Kelly married 1792 to Anne Davenport, daughter of William Davenport. Mrs. Anne Davenport died January 1, 1816, leaving children: Isaac, Willy, Sarah, William D., Mary (wife of William Stewart), Elizabeth, Rebecca (wife of Hulet Hunt), and Abigail.
Jacob Kelly died about 1808 in Union District, S. C. He moved from Lexington District.
Jacob Kelly died in Lexington District, leaving widow, Nancy, and children: Rebecca (wife of Noah Roberts), Catherine Sophia (wife of Job Russell), Sarah (wife of Reuben Wingard), Mary Magdeline (wife of Robert Ferguson), Elizabeth Ann (wife of .....), Barbara Louisa, Susan Matilda. Elizabeth Ann married .... Snyder. Barbara Louisa married .... Corley. Susan Matilda married ...... Kaminer.

Other Pioneers

KENNEDY-Dr. Joseph Kennedy died 1796 in Abbeville District. He left widow, Mary, and children: William E., Mary Boir, Josiah N., Andrew, Elizabeth, Joshua, Joseph.

David Kennedy died 1814, in Abbeville District, leaving widow, Hannah, and ch: Elizabeth, Martha, Jane, Hannah, John, James Morrow, and David. Also, a gr-son, David Elmer.

Roddy Kennedy died 1831, in Laurens District, leaving as his hiers: William Kennedy, Elijah Reeder and Wife, John L. Reeder, Bernard Curley and wife Rebecca (all of whom were living out of the state); and Mary A. Glasgow, James L. Kennedy, and P. H. Felker and wife. Samuel Kennedy died 1842, in Laurens District. Admr. of his estate: Nathaniel Kennedy.

James P. Kennedy died 1851, in Laurens District, He left heirs: Samuel Bolt and wife, John M. Franks and wife, T. L. Budgett and wife, and Leannah Kennedy.

Andrew Kennedy died about 1857, in Laurens District, leaving widow, Anne (Moore) Kennedy, and children: John, Cunningham Moore Kennedy.

KENNERLY-Dr. John B. Kennerly came to Newberry District from Lexington District. He died 1884. He married Martha Brown, daughter of Richard Samuel Brown, of Newberry District; and had children: James L., Lilla R., Edward, Samuel, and Amelia K.

KERR-Samuel Kerr was first lawyer in Newberry to locate in the town. He was there before 1804. In 1806 he moved to Louisiana.

Peter Kerr married Susannah McQuerns before 1800, and had children: Mary, who married (1) John Johnson, and (2) to John Caldwell in 1821.

KENNER-Samuel E. Kenner died in Newberry County on Feb. 28, 1844, an old man. His widow, Lucy, died in September 11, 1873. His first wife was Elizabeth Grasty who was the mother of five children. His second wife was Lucy Goree who was the mother of nine children. Children named in his will were: Robert R., Joseph D., James L., Lawrence L., Howson Calhoun, Martha Bishop, Frances M. Caldwell, and Mary L. Moorman. His grand-children were: Samuel E. Kenner, Frances Kenner, Anna Thompson Goree Kenner, Lodoska A. Bishop, Samuel K. Gudelock, Thomas S. Moorman, and wife of John S. Bates. Great-grand-children: Augusta C. Bates and Hame Glenmore Bates.

KESLER-Henry Kesler died about 1802, in Newberry District. He left children: Henry, David, Abraham, Paul, Elizabeth, Barbara, Margaret, Catherine (wife of Christian Sitz), Susannah (wife of Fred Farr), Christina (wife of Christopher Dickert).....

KEY-Henry Key made will dated April 25, 1779, and left three sons named in will, viz: Henry, William, and Tandy C. also, three daughters, Mary, Naomi, and Martha. Henry died 1810, leaving widow, Phoebe, and ch: John (eldest son), Polly Martin, Lucy Cabeness, Elizabeth Thurmond, Henry, Barsilia (son), James, Mary Ann, Tandy, Permelia. Two gr-ch: Henry Martin and Elizabeth Martin.

William Key died about 1800 in Edgefield District. He was son of Henry Key.

William Key (son of William), died 1802, in Edgefield District. He left widow, Fanny, and ch: Gabriel, Samuel, Tandy M., William, Patsy, Nancy, and Sarah. Sarah married Archibald Griffin.

KILGORE-Mrs. Rhoda W. Kilgore died about 1859 in Newberry District. She was widow of James Kilgore, who had moved from southern section of state to Newberry District. She left children: Andrew, Harriet, Caroline, Mary Ellen. Andrew died in Newberry District about 1892, son of above, Dr. James Kilgore,

KINCAID-William Kincaid died and left children: Mary Glenn, William, Anne Hall (died 1836—no children), Rebecca Davis (wife of Jonothan Davis), Jane Pope (wife of James Pope), Elizabeth Vance, Margaret McMahan (wife of Daniel McMahan, Sr.). William, Jr. died 1830 and left widow, Elizabeth, and children: Elizabeth (wife of Edward Anderson), Nancy, Rebecca, William, James, John, and Bolivar. Mrs. Jane Pope died early and left one child, James S. Pope. Mrs. Elizabeth Vance died and left children, Nancy (wife of Thomas Furman), William Armstrong, William K. Vance, and Mary P. Vance. Mrs. Margaret McMahan had children: Daniel, John, Margaret, Nancy Hill (wife of William R. Hill), Frances Ervin (wife of Dr. Ervin), Elizabeth, and James who died early.

KING-Charles King lived in Newberry County, and died about 1790, the date of his will being January 21, 1789. His wife, Charity Pennington, died before his death. Their children were: Jacob M. (married Kerzia.......), Pennington, Lyda (wife of John W. Lindsey), Mary (wife

Other Pioneers.

of Jeremiah Starke), Ruth (wife of Thomas Starke), Charity (wife of ..... Gordon), Rebecca, and Kerzia. Pennington married Mary Blalock and had children: Jacob, Rebecca, Kerzia, Mary, and Butler. His widow married Bailey Bell about 1810. They moved to Jones County, Ga.

Ethelred King made will August 30, 1825, and died soon after. His children were: Sarah (wife of Benjamin Lindsey), Martha (wife of William Langford), Elijah, Elizabeth (wife of Charles Banks).

Pendleton R. King married Janette Sheppard, daughter of William Sheppard.

KIRK-Isaac Kirk was a member of the Quaker Church on Bush River. He died about 1815, leaving widow, Rebecca, and one child, Phoebe, who afterwards married Dr. Marmaduke Thomas Mendenhall, an eminent and skillful physician of Newberry.

Mrs. Rebecca Kirk made will November 2, 1834, and died in year 1837. Her first husband was Isaac Jenkins by whom she had children: Rebecca (wife of Thomas Lake), Isaac, John, David (living in Ohio), Anne (married Thomas Barrett and moved to Ohio), Lydia (widow of Henry Barrett, deceased), She also named a grand-daughter in her will, Hannah Barrett, daughter of Henry and Lydia Barrett. She had one child, Phoebe, by her second husband, Isaac Kirk.

KNOX-John Knox lived in Newberry County. He probably had no sons, for his heirs were children of a deceased daughter, named on January 4, 1802 in an old deed, as follows: Janette Steel, and John Knox Steel.

KYSER-George Kyser, Sr. made will August 26, 1807 and died in Edgefield County the same year, leaving widow, Elizabeth, and children: Philip, George, Jeremiah, Elizabeth, and Nancy.

George Kyser, Jr. married Emily .... and had children, one of whom was Malichi B. Kyser (born December 25, 1811). They moved to Alabama.

LANDERS-Michael Landers made will March 2, 1804 and died 1804 leaving widow, Jane, and one other legatee, John Lemony.

LANE-Alexander Lane lived in York County. His son, William Lane, a Lieutenanct in State militia during Revolutionary War, married Margaret McDowell of Spartanburg County.

Craven Lane died about 1837 in Newberry District, leaving widow, Hannah, (she died 1838), and left ch: John, David, James, Ledford, Lemuel. David died 1844, when young, unmarried. James J. volunteared for Mexican War, in Co. L., Palmetto Reg—died in Hospital at Jalapa, Mexico, on June 7, 1847, unmarried. He was a son of Lemuel Lane, and gr-son of Craven. Lemuel died July 27, 1866, and left widow, Mary A. and ch: John C., Amassa Ann (wife of Adam B. Counts), James J., and William H.

James T. Lane died Feb. 15, 1842, leaving widow, Mary, and ch: Armina A., James D., Laura E. (wife of Leander B. Ramage), Sims B., Hoard W. Mrs. May Lane was daughter of Michael and Catherin Descoker.

William Dawkins Lane died in Union District in 1795.

Mrs. Nancy Lane died about 1845, in Newberry District, leaving children: Maria Cromer, Elvira (wife of Wm Epting), William R., Franklin R., James T., Harriet (wife of Henry Epting), Nancy (wife of David Wicker). Maria Cromer after death of her first husband, married Chesley Davis.

LANGSTON-Caleb Langston died 1800, in Union District, leaving widow, Elizabeth, and ch: John, Absalom, Jesse, Nathan, Samuel, Christian, His brother, Nathan, was named Exr. of will. Absalom died in Nevada, 1845, left widow, Minta, and 10 children.

Daniel Langston died 1822, in Union District, leaving widow, Martha, and ch: Sarah (wife of James Corley), Rebecca (wife of John H. Holland), Mary (wife of Elijah Eubanks), Rhoda (wife of Daniel Chandler), Delila, and Isaac.

William Langston died 1854, in Union District. He left widow, Martha, and ch: Calhoun, and Theodore A. Langston.

Solomon Langston died 1823 in Laurens District, leaving widow, Sarah, and ch: Henry, Solomon, Bennett, Amy Christopher, Sarah Miller, Leodocia (wife of Thomas Springfield), Patty Jones, Selah (wife of Samuel Stiles), Henry died befor 1855, leaving widow, Sarah, and nine distributees.

Henry Langston died about 1844, in Laurens District. He left ch: John, William, Thomas,

Other Pioneers.

Sarah (wife of Wm Murphy), James, wife of Jeremiah Holland, wife of James Hardin, wife of James Toland, and wife of James Mason. William and Sarah Murphy had ch: J. M., H. L., wife of James Rodgers, wife of Robert Smith, wife of James Cooper.

LARK-Cullen Lark lived in Abbeville District. He died in year 1805 and left widow, Elizabeth, who afterwards married Thomas Cobb. He had one son, Andrew Lee Lark, by a former wife. His second wife, Elizabeth, was a sister of Samuel Savage.

Andrew Lee Lark died near Chappells, in Newberry County, on May 8, 1878, aged 84 years. His wife, Catherin (born May 16, 1801 and died March 2, 1870), was a daughter of .... They are both buried at Cross Roads Baptist Church, two miles East of Chappells. Children: Cullen, Dennis, Sarah Blakely (wife of Jeter Mitchell), Ellen (wife of E. L. Gunter), Ellen Gunter died before death of her father and left children, Wm E. Gunter, Ellen P. Gunter. Dennis Lark died 1874, left children: Pawnee (age 16), Cullen (age 7), Nancy (age 5). James W. (son of Andrew) died 1862, in Confederate army and left no family. Mrs. Laura C. Lark (wife of Dennis Lark), died Jan. 15, 1873; her son, John, had died before her death.

John Lark, of Abbeville District, died about 1783, leaving widow, Rachel.

One John Lark died in Edgefield District about 1824; leaving widow, Precious, and ch: Elizabeth Raiford, and John Lark.

LAYTON-George Layton died in Laurens District. He married Adaline Todd, on Jan. 1, 1857.

Charlotte Layton, daughter of William and Margaret Layton, married in 1797, or before. They belonged to the Quaker Church of Bush River, and moved to Ohio about 1810.

Stephen Layton of Spartanburg District, married Martha Smith, daughter of William and Anne Smith, Before 1796.

LATHAN-Sinkler Lathan married Rhoda Edwards in Newberry. She was the daughter of John S. Edwards who had moved to Jefferson County, Alabama.

LAW-Samuel Law, Sr. lived in the King's Creek section of Newberry County. He had children: Samuel (died 1808), James (died 1836), William, wife of a McClintock, and wife of McTyre or McTeer. Grand-children: Elizabeth McClintock, Margaret McClintock, Agnes McClintock, and John McClintock, Elizabeth McTyre, Mary McTyre, and Tenny McTyre. He died about 1813.

Samuel Law, Jr. died about 1808 and left widow, Margery.

James Law died 1836 and left widow, Martha, and children: John A., Elizabeth H., Margaret Brown, and H. (a daughter). Grand-children: James L. Brown, Sims E. Brown, and Martha E. B. Brown. Mrs. Martha Law died December 19, 1848. Elizabeth H. married James M. Epps.

Dr. John A. Law died Oct. 2, 1843, leaving widow, Rosannah S., and children: Harriet L., and James W. Law.

LEAVELL-Robert Leavell made will October 6, 1787, proven in court, July 28, 1797. He left widow, Sarah, and children: Edward, John, Frances Ryal had a daughter, Betsy Ryal.

James Leavell made will August 16, 1810 and died 1810, leaving widow, Elisabeth, and children: James, Addie, Peeby, and Betsy.

Noah Leavell died about 1810 to 1815 and left minor children: Noah, Edward, and Nelly.

Isaac Leavell died about 1815, in Newberry District, leaving widow, Dellilah, and children: Noah, Nelly, Edward, and Timothy (he died before 1821).

John Leavell died 1826, leaving widow, Frances, and ch: Betsy; Katy (wife of George Clark), Polly, Richard, Charles, Martha, Peggy, James Teague Leavell, Robert Griffin Leavell, John Roland Leavell, and William Page Leavell.

LEE-Michael Lee died in Union County in November 1807, leaving widow, Drucilla, who died in 1814. Their children were: Michael (dead), Sarah Lamb, Jane Little, Thomas (dead), Catherine Roebuck, Mariam Kershaw, and two helpless children, Joseph and Polly. Children of Michael, Jr. were: John, Asbury, Robert, Sarah (wife of Nathaniel Rogers), Elizabeth (wife of Felix Jenkins), Frances (wife of Thomas Little), Evaline, and Mariam. The children of Thomas were: Moses, Nancy, Lucinda, and Sarah (wife of Isaac Stroud).

William Lee made will Sept. 12, 1796 and died in 1796, leaving children: Michael, Thomas, John, Joseph, William, Catherine Breed, Jane Howel, Olivia Frazier, Sarah Bates, and Nancy Jackson. He owned lands on the Tyger River.

John Lee died in Union County in 1823, leaving widow, Hannah, and children: Sarah Rochester,

Other Pioneers.

Lydia, Hannah, Priscilla, Elizabeth, William C., John, Jonothan, Jeremiah, and Sampson.

Joseph Lee died in Union County and left widow, Franky, and a daughter, Mary, and a brother, Thomas Lee.

Stephen Lee died in Fairfield County in 1807, leaving widow, Mary, and children: Elizabeth, Rebecca, John, and Stephen. All children were by a former marriage.

Captain John Lee died in Lexington County on October 6, 1829, leaving widow, Elizabeth Eleanor, and children: John W., Mary (wife of William J. McMillan), Richard H., Junius Edward, Andrew, Patrick H., Benjamin F., Thomas C., Elizabeth E., William H., Joseph A. L. Lee.

Robert Lee died in Union County.

William Lee died in Union County about 1839, leaving widow who was pregnant at time of his death. His father was Thomas Lee.

Mrs. Frances Lee (widow of Joseph Lee, son of William Lee) left property to Mary Lee, the daughter of Joseph.

Amos Lee died in Union County in 1843.

Thomas Lee of Union County, conveyed lands, through love and affection, in year 1832, to the following: May Lee, Margaret Lee, Lavania Lee, Massa Sally Lee, and John Lee. He gave $10.00 in note to each heir, as follows: Green Lee, William Lee, and Katy Hopkins.

Robert Lee died about 1798 in Spartanburg County. He left widow whose name is not given, and children: John, Annie, Milly, James, and Richard.

John Lee, Sr., died about 1850 in Spartanburg County. He left widow, Elizabeth, and children James, William F., Dorcas (wife of John Pierce), Susan (married a Lindsey), Anna (wife of Aaron Shurbert), Mary (married a Gore), Elizabeth (wife of Hugh Pearce), Jerry, John, Nancy (wife of John Thompson), Richard, and Willis.

Mrs. Selah Lee died about 1837 in Newberry. He was, probably a native of either Fairfield County or of Union County. He left widow, Mary M. (Setzler) Lee, and children: Eve Margaret, William D., John C., Honarias Pl, Frances Elizabeth, and Lavania E. His widow died June 18, 1852. William D. Lee moved to Rutherford County, North Carolina. He was appointed Guardian for the following children, December 9, 1871: Henry M., William B., and Elizabeth Lee.

Andrew Lee made will in 1796 and died in 1807 in Edgefield County (now Saluda County). He left widow, Nancy, and children: Garphon, John W., Wilson, Hannah Patrick, Susannah, Nancy, and Sarah.

Thomas Lee died in Edgefield County in 1805, leaving widow, Mary Ann, and several small children. Executors: Randal Lee, and Samuel Gilbert.

Thomas Lee, Sr. died in 1816 in Abbeville County, leaving widow, Anne, and children: Margaret (wife of William McCullough), Anne, William, John, and Andrew, Sr.

LE GRONNE (LAGRONE)-Lorentz Le Gronne, a native of the upper section of France, probably Alsac-Lorraine, came to South Carolina in an early colony. He was given a grant of land on Cannon's Creek, in the Dutch Fork, in year 1752.

John Adolph Le Gronne (probably a son of Lorentz) was given a grant of one hundred acres land on Cannon's Creek on October 31, 1765. He had a son, John, and grand-sons, John Jr. and Frederick.

Tobias Le Gronne (son of Lorentz) lived on Cannon's Creek. Some of his children were: John Jacob, Tobias, and John Frederick.

John Le Gronne (son of John Adolph) and wife, Mary Christina, and Frederick Davis and wife, Mary, conveyed land in year 1809 to Ulrick Mayer.

John Le Gronne died about 1830 and left widow, Mary M., (she afterwards married Silas Merchant), who was a daughter of Francis Summer (Rev. War soldier). Their children were: Susannah, Christina, Sarah, John, Catherine, Elizabeth, and Mary.

LEAK-George Leak died about 1809, and left ch: Anna, William, Samuel, Jincey (wife of William Brown), James (died a minor), Margaret, Alzira (wife of Adam Braddock), Malinda (who married 1833 to Middleton W. Cobb). Mrs Malinda Cobb died in 1835, leaving an only son, James W. Cobb, who was born Jan. 15, 1835, and died Jan. 26, 1835.

LEITSEY-George Leitsey died 1816 in Newberry District. He left a widow, Elizabeth, and ch: George, Jacob, John, Eve Margaret, Mary Elizabeth, Mary, Mary Magdeline. An aunt,

Other Pioneers

Margaret Hough, is Named in his will. Exr. George Long.
Jacob Leitsey moved to Colleton District.
LEAPHART-Gasper Leapart died in Lexington District. He married Elizabeth Sex who was born 1778, near Charleston, S. C. One of their sons, John, lived in Lexington District.
LEWIS-Stephen Lewis made will dated Aug. 11, 1788, and died about 1789, leaving widow, Mary, and children. One a son, James, and a son, Richard.
David Lewis died about 1822 in Pendleton District. He married (1) Ann Benson who died 1812; and (2) to Penelope.........
John Lewis lived in North Carolina; married Sarah..... and left ch: David, Stephen, Jacob, Richard, John, Sarah (she married John Hendrix) in 1780, in N. C.).....
- Richard Lewis and Jacob Lewis lived in Newberry District. Jacob married Mary (McCowan) Floyd, a widow.
LESTER-James Lester came from Virginia, of English or Scotch descent. He received a grant of three hundred fifty acres land on Saluda River, by Letters Patent at Charleston, June 9, 1735, under the hands of Hon. William Moultrie, Esq., Governor and Commander-in-Chief of the State of South Carolina. It is not known who were his children but the earliest records show that the following (probably sons) were living in the section of Saluda River before the Revolutionary War: Peter, James, Samuel, and Charles.
Peter Lester died in 1808, leaving widow, Jane, and children: Patsy (wife of George Thomas), Peter R., Willis D., Sarah (wife of George Harmon), Mary (wife of Thomas Morris), Rhoda (wife of Julius Williamson), James, Cinderilla (married Samuel Bynum), Jane (married Abner Bozard), Vincent, and Simpson. George Harmon and wife, Sarah, had son, George. Mrs. Jane Lester moved to Indiana with some of her children.
James Lester, Sr. (father of Peter) died after 1808 and left the following children as legatees: James, John, Isaac, Joyce (dead), Charles (out of state), Abner (out of State), and Samuel (out of state). Joyce married James Beaumont, died and left a son, James Beaumont, Jr. Samuel died in 1817 unmarried.
William R. Lester made will in 1817 and died same year, leaving legatees: Marha Darby, Elizabeth Leste, George D. Lester, Cynthia Dawkins, Rosannah Lester, and Simon B. Lester.
Charles Lester died in Newberry County in 1827. He married a Miss Musgrove and had children: Allen, Smith (he moved to Alabama),Alfred (moved to Alabama), Millbury(wife of Dempsey Gilbert),Maria (wife of George Boozer), Susan (wife of Lacy Havird). A brother, Alfred M. Lester, is named as a distributee of the estate.
Allen Lester married Martha Dennis and had children: James, Charles, William, George, Alfred, Martha (wife of Atwood Connelly), Prudence Rogers (she died, left daughter Mary Jane Rogers), Phoebe (wife of Warren Kirkland), Rebecca, Jane Rikard.
LIPSCOMB-John Lipscomb married Rebecca Williams, daughter of James and Rebecca Williams. They had two sons, James and Thomas. Col. James N. Liscomb was born in Abbeville District, 1827, graduated at the South Carolina College in 1847.
LITTLE-David Little died in Laurens District, left widow, Cahrity, and several children.
Charles Little died in Laurens District, leaving widow, Anne, and children.
Moses Liddle died in Abbeville District about 1802, leaving widow, Elizabeth, and children: Moses, Jr., James, Tarsus, Elizabeth, Esther, Isabella, Jean.
Jonas Little died in Union District in 1821, leaving widow, Rebecca, and children: Ames, Jonas, Thomas, Adam, Ruth(wife of Aaron Springer), Mary (wife of Jerome Miller), Benjamin, Hannah (wife of Lawson Swink).
LITTLEJOHN-Some of the early Littlejohns were in Spartanburg County, viz: Charles, Francis, Henry, Thomas, Samuel, William, Marcellus, and Felix Littlejohn.
LIVINGSTON-Martin Livingston was granted two hundred fifty acres land on Campin Creek in 1767. His son, John, sold this land in 1785 to Nicholas Sligh. He was the only heir of his father. John had sons, John, Martin, and others.
John Livingston, Jr. gave to his son, Martin Livingston, Jr. a tract of land in Newberry District.
Martin Livingston, son of Martin , Sr., was born about 1770 and died 1837, leaving widow, Jane, and children: John, Sarah, Martha, Elizabeth, Martin Henry, and McC. Mynard Livingston.

Other Pioneers (continued)

LOFTON—John Loften made will December 26, 1799, and died 1800, leaving children: Ezekiel, Thomas, Rachel Barlow, Abigail, Cathron, John, William, and Anne Johnston. A grand-son, John Lofton, also shred in his estate. He lived on Indian Creek, in Newberry District.

William Lofton died about 1812, the date of his will being May 6, 1803. His will was proved in Court November 3, 1812. He left children: Eli, Daniel, Eleanor, Sarah, Elizabeth, William, and Abigail.

LOHNER—Michael Lohner received a bounty grant of two hundred acres land on a branch of Owen's Creek, a tributary of Broad River, in the year 1774. He died and left widow, Mary Magdelina, and children: Jacob, John, Susannah Setzler, Eve, Barbara, and Magdelina.

John Lohner (son of Michael), was born February 2, 1765, in the Dutch Fork, Newberry District (then Ninety Six District). He volunteered for service in the American Army in the Rev War, in March, 1782, aged 17 years. He was a private in Company of Captain Jacob Fulmer, Regiment of Col. Jonas Beard, and was discharged in September, 1782. He was pensioned September 26, 1832, while a resident in Lexington District, South Carolina.

LOMINICK—Michael Lominick made will January 14, 1806, and died in same year, leaving widow, Polly, (she was the mother of all his children), and the following children: David, John, Henry, Jacob, George, Daniel, Benjamin, Rebecca, and Katy.

LONG—Jacob Long received a grant of one hundred acres land on Cannon's Creek, in year 1768. His sons, Adam and Bathlomew, lived on his homeplace. His widow, Elizabeth, lived on place. There were other children.

Thomas Long, Sr. (son of Jacob), and his wife, Mary Magdelina, deeded lands on Campin Creek to George Michael Long in year 1825. He deeded to his nephews, Jacob, Barthlomew, and Thomas, all claims to a tract which was part of the original two hundred acres granted to Jacob Long.

Bathlomew Long, Sr. died in year 1800, leaving widow, Catherine, and children.

John Jacob Long died about 1835 in Newberry District, leaving widow, Mary, and children: John, Beulah. He was a son of Thomas Long.

Mrs. Elizabeth Long died in 1817, and left daughters: Rosannah Barbara Koon, and Susannah (wife of John Michael Koon).

Mrs. Elizabeth Long died about 1855, leaving property to her son, George Abram Long. Her brother, Christian Long, and her nephew, Dr. John Long, are named in will.

Captain William Long made will September 18, 1815, and died same year, in Union District. He left widow, Elizabeth, and children; James, John, William, Benjamin F., Henry (had died), Letitia (wife of John Ezell), Caroline (wife of Amaza Ezell), Elizabeth (wife of James Flannagan), Mary (wife of Daniel Mabry), and Sarah (wife of Smith Wills). Benjamin F. Long moved to Newberry District, where he married Priscilla Turner, a daughter of William and Elizabeth Turner. Their children were: Sarah (wife of John Gaskins), Polly (wife of Henry Coate), Benjamin F., and others. Benjamin F.,Jr. had one child, Caroline M., who died in 1834. Children of John and Sarah Gaskins were: Albert G., Elmira, Sarah, and perhaps others. Mrs. Priscilla Long died in 1833. Major Benjamin F. Long, Sr., was a Rev War patriot, having served in Brandon's Regiment of South Carolina Militia. For a short time he was the Sheriff of Newberry County. He died in 1816. Some of his grand-children moved to Mississippi

George Long, Sr. married Elizabeth Catherine Stearley, and had children: Jacob, George, Jospeh, Mary, Elizabeth, Catherine, Sarah.

Adam Long died August 27, 1852, leaving children: William D., Henry A., Thomas C., Nancy (wife of Simeon Schumpert), Mary, Samuel J., Sarah, Jacob A., Christina, and John A. Long.

LONGSHORE—Levi Longshore died in Newberry District about 1818. Admx. of his estate was Mrs. Sarah Longshore, and Admr. was Euclides Longshore. Distrubtion made in 1831 to the following: John, Levi, Sarah, wife of George Davenport, and the children of Euclides Longshore. John Longshore died about 1820, leaving children and widow. His widow was Sarah Longshore, and the children as follows: Euclides, John, Levi, Polly, Wade, and Sarah. The son, Euclides, died about the same time and left widow, Elizabeth, and children: Levi and Charlotte.

LORICK—Jacob Lorick died about 1826 , and left widow, Mary, and children: Claiborne, Harriet B., Mary, and Esther. Harriet B. married John T. Young. Esther married Dr. P. B. Ruff , in Newberry, who was his first wife.

Other Pioneers (continued)

LOWE-Isaac Lowe died in Fairfield District in 1792, leaving a family. His son, Isaac Augustus Lowe, was born 1792, about three months after the death of his father. He died in Georgia. A son, George, was under age in 1792.
James, William, and Obediah Lowe lived in Laurens District. Obediah died before year 1839.
LYBRAND—John Lybrand lived in Lexington District. His wife was Elizabeth Fulmer, a daughter of Abram Fulmer. They had a son, West Allen Fulmer, who married Sallie Derrick.
LYNCH-Rev. Elijah Lynch died in Newberry District, and is buried at old Chapman Graveyard. He married Elizabeth, a daughter of William and Elizabeth Chapman. Their children were: Polly (wife of Jacob Bowers), David, Elijah, Giles C., Harriet (wife of John L. Morgan), Margaret (wife of Joseph Quattlebaum). Grand-children: Elijah Elmore, John E. Summers, Harriet Hesterly, Appleton Elmore, Elizabeth Elmore. Mrs. Elizabeth Lynch (his widow), died about 1855, leaving children as above named, except that Elizabeth had married Elisha K. Schumpert. Some of these moved to Coweta County, Georgia.
MACKEY-Daniel Mackey purchased five hundred twenty acres land in Newberry District in 1787.
MAFFETT-Robert Maffett was born 1765 and died 1837, leaving widow, Barbar (Buzhardt) Maffett who was born 1767 and died 1844. Their children were: John, James, Samuel, Robert, Elizabeth (wife of John McCollum), Sally Luther, Bethsheba Kibler, and Margaret Livingstone.
Samuel Maffett died about 1810, leaving as his legatees: John, Ephriam, Margaret, William, Sarah, Elizabeth. His wife was Jane Maffett. She survived him and was the Guardian of their minor children in 1820, Ephriam, Margaret, William, Sarah, Elizabeth.
John Maffett married Rebecca Gallman, a daughter of John G. and Susannah Gallman. Children: Martha (wife of John Ector, of Georgia), Susan (wife of William Blalock), Caroline, Mary (she moved to Georgia and thence to Texas), and Samuel.
The following shared in the estate of Matthew Boyd who died about 1834: Silas Maffett, Sarah Maffett, Elizabeth Maffett, Mary Maffett, who were children of William Maffett, deceased; William Hill and wife, Sarah D. Hill who moved to and settled in Pontotac County, Mississippi.
MALONE—William Malone lived in Newberry County prior to 1800, then moved to Georgia. His son, William Malone, Jr., lived on his father's land on Enoree River, which had been conveyed to him in 1787. William Malone, Jr. was the first county clerk of Newberry.
William, Jr. made will June 13, 1826, and died 1843, leaving widow, Elizabeth (Hampton) Malone and children: Dorothy Brooks (wife of Daniel B. Chapman), Mary Davis (wife of Isaac Jenkins) and Eliza Emily. Dorothy B. Chapman had children: Elizabeth (wife of Jacob A. Hill), and Mary E. Chapman. Mary Davis Jenkins had children: Marcus, Edwin, and, perhaps, others.
John Malone was granted land on Second Creek in year 1775. His son, John, Jr., lived on the land until 1790 when he sold it to Andrew Russell and moved away. John Malone, Sr. came from Virginia about 1770 with his family. His son, John, Jr., was born in Virginia about 1761.
MANGUM-William Mangum made will in 1827, and died July 5, 1827. He left widow, Ann, and children: Daniel, John, William, Edney (she was wife of John F. Glenn in 1831), Rebecca, Nancy (wife of William Peterson), Peggy (wife of James Neel), and Jemima (wife of Charles W. Griffin); and children of a deceased son, James, who were, James Franklin Mangum, Edney Allen Mangum. James left a widow, Edney. William Mangum married Frances M. Chambers, a daughter of Alexander Chambers
Hillary Richmond Mangum married Frances Davenport, and died February 1, 1874, leaving widow, who was a sister of Jefferson Davenport, and the following heirs:_____
MANN-Robert Mann made will March 27, 1782, and died about 1785 or ' 86, leaving widow, Susannah, and children: James, John, Robert, Jean Nix, and Susannah. He left, also, a grand-son, Manassa Mann. The widow died about the year 1800. John Mann made wil September 26, 1805, which was proved in Court November 4, 1805. He left widow, Anne, and four children: Henry, Robert, James, and Joseph.
MANNING-Levi Manning made will March 22, 1796, and died few days afterwards, in Newberry District. He left widow, Elizabeth, and children: Levi, Luke, Jethro, Elizabeth (wife of John Threweatts), Anna (wife of Wilkes B. Waters), Margaret, Polly, Sally, Sally married Rhydon Griggsby.

Other Pioneers (continued)

MARS—Robert Mars lived on King's Creek, and is buried in old King's Creek Cmetery, about ten miles North of Newberry Court House.
John Mars made will October 16, 1812, and died about 1813, leaving children: John, Mary, and the wife of John Hall who moved to Ohio. He, also left a grand-son, Robert Mars.
MARPUT—John Marput died in 1823 in Newberry District. He left a widow, Sarah, and children: John, Joshua, Matilda Hendrix, Daniel, Phillip, Elizabeth, Michael, Sarah. John moved to Tennessee and was living in Giles County in 1836. Elizabeth married David Boozer. Sarah married George Gibson. Martha M. married Henry Hexdrix. Mrs. Sarah Marput, the widow, was a daughter of Joshua Inman, a member of the Bush River Monthly Meeting (Quaker Church). Phillip (1797-1889) married Oda Thomas (1800-1858), and lived in Missouri; and had children: Polly, Patsy, John, Matthew, Washington, Titha Ann, Becky Ann, Andrew, Nathan Thomas, Houston, Lucinda, Carolina.
MARTIN—Patrick Martin died about 1813 and left two sons, John and Alexander. Alexander died in Abbeville District about 1830, leaving widow, Agnes. John died in Abbeville District in 1822, leaving widow, Nancy, and children: Betsy Rebecca (married .... Thompson), William, John, Polly Thurman, Sally, David, Molly Edwards, Phares (a son), Caroline Matilda, Katy, Sylvia Lee, Edmund Carthage, and James Hill. Charles Martin was born 1745 and died 1808, in Abbeville District. He married Patsy Moon, daughter of Jacob Moon, and had children: Jacob, Sucky Moore, George W., and William. Grand-children: Patsy Bibb, James Cobb, and Thomas Cobb.
Thomas P. Martin died about 1830, left son, John. In case son died without issue, his will stipulates that the following shall be legatees: Thomas S. Martin, Washington B. Martin, and Charles Martin (all were nephews); and Elisha, Indiana (nieces); a brother, Jaurole Martin. Thomas S. and Eliza were living in Augusta, Georgia, in 1830.
Reuben Martin died about 1812 in Laurens District, leaving sons and daughters, as follows: Reuben, Henry, Joseph, Benjamin, John, Samuel, Stephen, and ....
Edmond Martin died about 1795 in Edgefield District. He left a widow, Catherine, and children: Milly Tutt Martin, Benjamin Martin.
Mrs. Elizabeth Martin died 1797 in Edgefield District, and left children: James, George, Barkley, Matt, Marshall, John. He left grand-children: Benjamin Martin, Milly Tutt Martin (children of son, Edmond); and Mary Ann Edwards.
MARTINDALE—William Martindale came to South Carolina from Pennsylvania about 1770. He married (1) Martha.......... and had children: John, James, William, Joseph, Thomas, and three daughters (two of the daughters married Youngs and one married Norman). His second wife was Elisabeth .... and had children: David, Martin, Miles. Martin married Elizabeth Pearson, daughter of John and Barbara (Cain) Pearson, of Newberry District. They were Quakers and all moved to Ohio.
John Martindale married in Union District where he lived about 1788. His wife was Racle.....
William Martindale, Jr., married Martha Bishop, and had children: James, John, Moses, and six daughters.
Joseph Martindale lived in Laurens District, but moved to Louisiana about 1816. He married Mary..........
MASSEY—The Massey family lived above Indian Creek, Newberry District. One married a Miss. Duncan and had daughter, Mary, who married Dr. Jacob F. Gilliam.
William M. Massey, Jr. died about 1790 in Union District, shortly after selling a two hundred acre tract of land located in Newberry District.
MATTHEWS—Victor Matthews made will December 21, 1795, and died about 1796 in Abbeville District, leaving widow, Isobel, and children: John, James, Isaac, Esther, Ann, Elizabeth, and Rebecca. Exr: Joseph Matthews.
Isaac Matthews, of Virginia, married his cousin, Mary Matthews, and moved to South Carolina about 1768. He had a son, Moses. One Isaac Matthews died in Edgefiled District about March 25, 1791, leaving widow, Anna, and children: Moses, Lewis, Hardy, Micajah, Daniel, Cabelle, and Elizabeth. Cabelle married Thomas Pace. John Matthews (brother of Isaac) made will October 25, 1793, and died 1794, leaving son, Isaac, and other children. His widow, Agnes (Calhoun) Matthews received part of his estate.

Other Pioneers (continued)

MATHIS—This name is a contraction of the name, "Matthews," for names undergo changes in spelling, sometimes, in some branches of a family.

Moses Mathis married Hetty Davenport, and were living in Newberry County in 1835.

Mrs. Susannah Mathis made will September 23, 1839, which was proved in Court October 21, 1839. She left children: Lewis, Timothy, Alcey, and others. Timothy died previous to the death of his mother, and left children: John and Leizabeth. Alcey married a Crouch, and left two children: Hillery Hardy and Nowell Crouch.

MAXWELL—Andrew Maxwell made will November 9, 1815, which was proved in Court July 29, 1821. He left brothers and sisters as follows: John, Jenny (wife of James Stephens), Susannah (wife of George Boozer); and a nephew, Robert Maxwell, son of John Maxwell.

Robert Maxwell, Sr. (son of John Maxwell, Sr.) died in 1797, leaving widow, Mary, and the following children: Anna (wife of Andrew B. Moore), John, Elizabeth (wife of Thomas B. Williams), Robert (he died settlement of estate), William (had died), and Charles. Robert, Jr. left a son, Hugh. The widow, Mrs. Mary Maxwell, married Adam Caruth.

MAYBIN—William Maybin and his brother, Matthew Maybin, lived in Newberry District, near Broad River, when the Rev. War started. They were both patriots in the war. William married Jane Duncan, and was killed at the battle of Hanging Rock in 1780. Matthew was taken prisoner and sent to Charleston, then to St. Augustine, Florida. William left children.

MAYES—Thomas Mayes, of Union District, left children: John, Thomas, Edward, Jane, Margaret, Elizabeth. Edward died about 1838, leaving widow, Rachel, and children: Dorcas, Sarah, Samuel, John, Monroe, and Sarah Ann.

Andrew Mayes died before 1819, in Union District. Some of his heirs were in Jasper County, Georgia, when they filed a petition for settlement of the estate. They were: Samuel Mayes, Mary Mayes, John Reid, Elinor Ricks, John Thompson, Andrew Reid, Robert Mayes, Rutherford Mayes, Andrew Mayes, John Mayes, James Mayes, Thomas Mayes, Samuel Davidson. James and Thomas were in White County, Illinois, in year 1817. Joseph died about 1840 in Green County, Alabama, leaving widow, Nancy, and seven children.

MAYS—Col. Benjamin Mays came from Pennsylvania to Edgefield District before the Rev. War. he was a priot officer in the war. He died and left a large family.

MEADORS—John Meadors died 1824, leaving widow, Lucy, and children: John, William, Polly, Permelia (wife of Samuel Miller), Joseph, James W., Alice, Lucretia, Elizabeth, Harriet, Frances, and Minerva.

James Maedors died about 1826, leaving widow, Jane, and son, Willis.

James Meadors died in Laurens District about 1804, leaving widow, Susannah (she died 1826), and children: Jason (he married Mary Vaughn), Reuben, John, Ann (wife of James Saxon). Reuben died about 1829, leaving widow, Hannah, and children: Susannah Prather, Rachel, Oney Polly,(married.... Pearson), Martha, Reuben, and James A. Mrs. Hannah Meadors was a daughter of James Adair, Sr. and Hannah Adair.

Washington Meadors (son of Jason and Mary Bonds Meadors), died 1842, in Chambers County, Alabama. He left widow, Rachel, and children: Nancy (wife of Dr. J. F. Leak), Mary (wife of Thomas H. Brown), John E., Camilla R., James C., Hercelia A., and Jason S. Meadors.

MELTON—Nathan Melton died in Edgefield District, leaving widow, Susannah, and children: Nathan, Jr., Susannah, Nancy, William, and Naomi. Nathan, Jr. married and had children: Austin Phillips, and Robert Audwell Melton. Naomi married .... Smedley. Nancy married ..... Crouch. The first wife of Nathan, Sr. was Nancy Allen.

William Melton signed a declaration in 1775 to fight as a ptriot in the Rev. War.

William Melton (son of Nathan, Sr.), died about 1831, leaving widow, Hannah, and children: Clem, William,   He had another son, who had died and left the following children who are named as heirs of William Melton: Stephen, Martha, Charles, Sarah Williams, Lucinda, and Louisa Melto

William A. Melton (son of William), died about 1836. He married, first, to Mary Gary, and, second, to Lucy Allen Williams (widow), and, third, to Rebecca Thompson Boren (widow). He died in Walton County, Georgia.

MENDENHALL—Dr. M. T. Mendenhall, a native of Guilford County, North Carolina, lived near Bush River, in Newberry District, before he moved to the town. He married Phoebe Kirk, a daughter of Isaac Kirk.

Other Pioneers (continued)

MERCHANT—Silas Merchant married Mary Margaretta (Summer) Le Gronne, widow of John Le Gronne, in Newberry District, and had children: David, Nicholas, and, probably, others. David moved to Florida.

METTS—Adam Metts, Sr. and wife, Margaret, conveyed land on Campin Creek to John Metts in 1829. John Metts died in January 1835, leaving children: Henry, Martha, Elizabeth (wife of John A. Wicker), Delila, Simeon, Mary, George, and Silas (Silas died unmarried). John Metts left widow, Mary M., who was a daughter of Henry Koon. Henry Metts died about 1855, and left widow, Missouri, and children: Thomas (moved to North Carolina), Frances E. (wife of Robert Lemon), Sarah G. (wife of Lemuel Buzhardt), David G. McDuffie, William G., and Roderick (he died previous to his father's death). Phillip Metts died May 16, 1842, leaving widow Rebecca, and children: Martha C. (wife of Giles Finch), L. P., Susannah, M. A., Elizabeth G., Rebecca A., and David W.

MILES—Samuel Miles lived on Bush River, and was a member of the Quaker Church. He made will February 11, 1807, and died same year. His wife was already dead. He left children: Rhoda Frost, Elizabeth Marshall, Mary O'Neall. A niece, Jane Miles, is, also, named in his will; and John Abbott and Mary Geddings who were living with him when he died.

Mrs. Sarah Miles made will December 23, 1820, and died 1821, leaving children: John, Haswell, and Elizabeth McDonald.

MILLER—Jacob Miller died about 1841, leaving widow, Zina, and children: George, John, Christina (wife of Thomas Buchanan), Susannah (wife of William Cromer), Mary (wife of ..... Alewine), Anne, Jonothan, Elizabeth (unmarried), Hannah (wife of ..... Wedaman), Hannah Wedaman died and left children: Andrew, Sarah Ann, Lucy. John died and left children: Jacob, Louisa Dawkins, John, Elizabeth, Jane, Zacariah, Cecily, and Thomas Drayton.

John B. Miller lived in Newberry County. His children in 1840 were: Elizabeth, Cicely, Zacariah, Jane, and Thomas.

MILLS—William Mills, Sr. received a grant of three hundred acres land on Youngs Fork, branch of Bush River, in year 1767. His wife was Rebecca....... Their son, John Mills, and his wife, Mary, sold this land in year 1774 to Joseph Scott, as the father had died about that year. Other children were: Isaac, William, Thomas.

Mrs. Rebecca Mills died about 1806 and left children: Robert, William, Elizabeth Cauntt, and Charity Downes. Adm. granted to Major Frederick Gray.

Robert Mills, Sr. died in 1791, leaving widow, Charity, and children: William, Robert, and others.

John Mills, Sr. (son of William) married (1) Elizabeth Edwards and (2) Mary Pearson. Children by first wife were: William, Alexander, Jemima, Elizabeth, Mary, John, Marmaduke. Children by second wife were: Enoch and Elijah.

Marmaduke Mills married Patience O'Neall Dec. 31, 1789, at Bush River Meeting House (they moved to Ohio before 1804). Their children were: Rachel (married William Jay), Anna, and Patience.

Matthew Mills received a grant of land in Craven County, in Feb. 1760. His heir-at-law, Joseph Mills, Sr., received this property in year 1806

Mrs. Susan Mills died 1837, leaving children: Abigail (wife of John Harp), Sarah (wife of Joshua Hendrix), Polly (wife of Archibald Todd), John (moved to Warren County, Indiana), Nehemiah Thomas (moved to Carthage, Leake County, Miss. in 1840), Jacob (moved to Warren County, Ind. about 1840), and Fatima (wife of Jerome Atkins).

Thomas Mills and wife, Jean, lived on Bush River.

Nehemiah Thomas Mills and wife, Ann, sold lands on Indian Creek January 1, 1817. They also sold land on Bush River in 1814, which he inherited from Nehemiah Thomas Mills, deceased, (he was probably his father).

John Mills (of Anderson County) made will August 1, 1825 and died about 1830, leaving widow, Elizabeth, and children: Lucinda (wife of Evil Williams), and Berry Beasley (called Mills). Executor: Sampson Pope.

Archibald Mills died in Newberry County. His wife, Christina, died July 24, 1881, and left children: Archibald B., Mary Nichols, Julia Taylor. She was a widow, Paysinger, when she married Archibald Mills, and had a son, Martin Paysinger.

Other Pioneers

MITCHELL—Isaac Mitchel first settled in Newberry District; then he moved to Abbeville District, where he died about 1789. His will is dated June 29, 1789, and proved in court Oct. 6, 1789. He left widow, Mary, and ch: Ursula, Mary, Catherine, Sarah, and Isaac. Isaac Mitchell, Jr. was not yet 21 years old when his father died but all the daughters were married.

Isaac Mitchell, Jr. made will dated Oct. 29, 1811, proved in court 1812, the year of his death. He left widow, Sarah, and a daughter, Dorcas Ritchey, also several gr-children who were children of deceased sons and daughters, viz: Jemima Mitchell, David Crews, Jacob Crews, Susan Mitchell, Sarah Humes, Sarah Golding, Sarah Swards, Polly Langsdale, Catherine McKie, Kerzia McKie, William Newton, Isaac Newton, Henry Newton. His son, Isaac, left widow, Anna, Children of Dorcas Ritchey were: Jane, Robert, Ruth, Sarah, Rachel, and Tabitha. The following gr-gr-children are named in his will: Susan Griffin, Mary Griffin, Frances Griffin, John McKie, Anna McKie, Exrs: Ezekiel Eastland (a nephew), John Eastland (a nephew), and James Caldwell (a friend). In a letter dated May 25, 1822, the following heirs signatures appear: Moses Stephenson, Ruth Stephenson, Kerzia McKie, Sarah Humes. Isaac Mitchell conveyed six acres land where stood the old Cross Roads Meeting House on Goose Ond Creek, in year 1802, to the Baptist Cross Roads Congregation and other religious societies, for no consideration than love, goodwill and affection. Trustees named in the conveyance were: John Satterwhite, Sr., Bartlette Satterwhite, Sr., Robert Gillam, Elisha Brooks, and Daniel Dyson.

Rev. William Alexander Mitchell (born 1779 in Scotland) married Frances McCollough, in Virginia. They moved to Charleston, S. C. Daniel Mitchell was Sheriff of Union District, S. C. about 1827.

John S. Mitchell who first settled in Edgefield District, then came to Newberry, where he taught school, moved to Bristol, Hartford County, Conn. He deeded on acre of land in the village of Newberry in 1816 (consideration $600.00), to Samuel Benham and Lyman Benham, of Burlington, Hartford County, Conn.

John B. Mitchell, a Rev. War patriot, lived in Newberry District; taught school; and died in Edgefield District. He was also a Methodist preacher.

MINNICK—John Adam Minnick died 1785, in Newberry District. He left widow, Barbara, and brother, George Bartholomew Minnick, a sister Mary Catherine Friend, and his mother, Rosannah Minnick, also a daughter, Mary Catherine Minnick.

William Minnick died in Lexington District, leaving the following heirs: John Minnick, Anne Mary Monts (a widow), Mary Margaret (wife of George Aull), Mary Catherine (wife of Phillip Gruber), Mary Magdeline (wife of Thomas Long), Mary Elizabeth Leitsey (a widow), Rosannah Barbara (wife of Andrew Rish), Eve Margaret (wife of John Hartman).

John Minnick and wife, Anne Mary, of Lexington District, conveyed 100 acres land in Newberry District to their son, John Minnick, Jr. in 1811, located near Thomas, Wm, and Barthlomew Minnick's places.

John A. Minnick, Jr. married daughter of John and Anne Catherine Werts, and had children: Adam, David and others, before year 1827.

MITCHUM—Joshua Mitchum died in Abbeville County about 1845, and left a brother, James Mitchum and two sisters, Martha Lenham and Margaret Jones.

Thomas Mitcham married Elizabeth Jones, daughter of Wallace Jones, Sr., who moved to Ohio.

MITCHEN—E. B. Mitchen died about 1819, in Edgefield District. He left no legatees.

MICKLER—Christian Mickler, Descendent of an old Teutonic family, died about 1879.

MONROE—John Monroe (of Virginia) lived in Laurens District. He made will dated year 1808 and died about 1821, leaving widow, Sarah, and children: Jennett, Betsy, Sally (wife of James Case), Robert Alexander, John Sheppard, Andrew, Larkin, Cathron, Nancy, and Mary T. (wife of John Sheppard). Mary T. was born after the death of her father (a posthumous child).

Robert Alexander Monroe died in October 1828 and left widow, Elizabeth, and children: John, William, Frances, Margaret, and Adaline.

Mrs. Sarah Monroe (widow) died in August 1835.

Larkin Monroe died in June 1849, leaving widow, Rebecca, and small children. Nancy married a Black. Janett married a Monroe, and died 1847, leaving children: Margaret, Daniel, and

Other Pioneers.

John H. Daniel married Elizabeth Morgan and had James, William, and Jesse.

John H. Monroe died April 6, 1858 in Laurens County. He was the son of Robert and Janette Monroe. He left widow, Martha C., who afterwards married John McCants of York County.

MONTGOMERY-William Montgomery made will September 21, 1795, which was proven in court October 11, 1800. He left children: Samuel, Andrew, Jennett, and William. He also named a grand-daughter, Eleanor Montgomery. Jennett married a Caldwell.

David Montgomery died about 1831, leaving widow, Jane, and children: Margaret, Mary Ann, John David, and Jane (married to J. G. McCrackin). David's widow was Jane Beard.

William Montgomery, Sr. made will September 21, 1795; proved December 9, 1800; children: Janet Caldwell, William, Samuel, and Andrew. Gr-child: Eleanor Montgomery.

Andrew Montgomery received a grant of 100 acres on Scotts Creek, near Newberry, in 1773; originally granted in 1768 to Wm. Montgomery, Sr.

David Montgomery died 1808(son of Hugh, Sr.), in Fairfield District. Brothers and sisters were: Charles, Hugh, Martha Ford, Elizabeth Reynolds, Margaret, and Jean Rice.

Hugh Montgomery died 1804, leaving widow, Margaret, and children: David, Charles, Margaret, Elizabeth, Martha, Hugh, Jane.

Charles Montgomery, Jr. died 1820, leaving widow, Margaret (she was pregnant), and children: Charles, William, David, Hugh, Margaret Bell, Nancy Thompson, and Martha Curry.
Gr-ch: Nancy, Peggy, Jane, Wm(children of Sarah Bell, died),
Peggy, Nancy, Wm, James, Sarah Benjamin, Rebecca (children of Jane Warick, died).

MONTS-Gasper Montz, native of Germany, came to Ninety Six District (the Dutch Fork of Newberry County), before the Rev. War. He married a Minnick, and had children: John, William, James, Adam, and probably others. William married a Miss Shealy. John married (1) to ...., Feagle, and (2) to Polly Kinard, and had children by both wives.

MYRICK-Dr. Samuel Myrick practiced medicine in Newberry County where he died about 1819. He is buried at the old "Village Grave-Yard".

MOON-Dr. Meridith William Moon came to Newberry County after the Rev. War, from Ireland, and lived in the fork between Little River and Saluda River. " He was a physician of much eminence and practice. He was an able and acceptable Methodist preacher". ("Annals of Newberry"). His wife died before his death and he died in the year 1828, leaving children as follows: Peter, Sarah (wife of William T. Jones), Maria (wife of Elisha Hammond), Meridith William, Jr. Dalton Lark, Dennis Fletcher, and Elizabeth Ann, and Francis Asbury. Francis Asbury died in 1834, unmarried.

Dr. William Meridith Moon, Jr. died 1836, leaving widow, Susan, and children: Caroline and Martha. He practiced for a short time. His widow married Thomas G. Gillam in 1839.

Dr. Peter Moon practiced medicine in Newberry County a few years, gave it up and put his attention to his farming interests. He married Susan Satterwhite, a daughter of John Satterwhite, and lived near Little River. His wife died January 12, 1852, leaving four children: John S., Susan (wife of Frederick A. Nance, her first husband having been Jesse Scury who had died), Sallie Lark (wife of A. C. Garlington), and Octavia who married (1) Wm. K. Griffin and (2) Col. Wm. Y. Fair of Newberry.

Jacob Moon lived in Abbeville District or Edgefield District before the Rev. War. One of his daughters, Patsy, married Charles Martin. Allen Moon, probably a son or grand-son, moved to Georgia. His sister, Susannah, married David Richardson about 1790.

MOONEY-Israel Mooney died before 1820. His widow, Charlotte, who was a sister of Andrew Cromer, administered on his estate.

MOORE-William Moore received a grant of two hundred fifty acres land in 1768 in Ninety Six District (Newberry County), South Carolina. Some of his sons were: William, Robert, and Samuel. Several of the Moores served as patriots in the Rev. War. Robert was in regiment of Col. Philemon Waters.

Robert Moore married Hannah .... and had children: James, Abraham, Oliver, Daniel, William T., and wife of Robert Carmickael. He died about 1824.

James Moore, Sr. died May 6, 1849, leaving widow, Rosannah, and children: Nancy (wife of Samuel Sloan), William, Rosannah, James, and Margaret (wife of Samuel Bowers). Mrs. Rosannah Moore died about 1863, and in her will, dated Dec. 20, 1860, is mentioned a daughter,

Other Pioneers.

Jane Ann Huntington, and a grandson, Thomas P. Huntington, and a granddaughter, Rose B. Huntington.

William Moore (son of William) lived on Cannon's Creek in Newberry County.

Samuel Moore died August 21, 1841, leaving widow, Mary, and children: Robert T., Elizabeth (wife of George W. Yarborough), Abraham E., Andrew J., Nancy (wife of J. Walter Stockman), Samuel W., Mary Jane, Deborah Ann, and Hiram W. Mrs. Mary Moore moved to Texas with some children and died in Lear County, of that state, on March 28, 1859, leaving children: Deborah Ann (wife of Drayton Nolly), Elizabeth Yarborough, Mary Jane (wife of Joel Wise), Nancy Stockman; also grand-children, D. Langdon, Samuel, Pressly, Frances, Mary Jane, Caroline-children of a deceased son, Robert T. Moore; and Samuel, Martha, and Deborah Ann—children of a deceased son, Andrew J. Moore.

Oliver Moore (son of Robert Moore, Sr.) was born June 30, 1799, married Katherine Quattlebaum who was born July 3, 1802. One of their daughters, Hannah (b. May 8, 1828 and d. May 6, 1885) married John McCreless (b. May 8, 1825 and d. Feb. 12, 1873) of Edgefield District. The moved to Pike County, Ala. Three of their sons served in the Confederate Army, viz: Daniel, Robert C., and G. F. C. Robert C. was in Co. G. 1st reg. Fla. Infantry. G. F. C. was in Co. G. 1st reg. Fla. Infantry. Both were paroled at Greensboro, N. C. May 1, 1865. Robert C. was a Third Sergeant.

William T. Moore (son of Robert Moore, Sr.) died on a Sunday, July 9, 1848, leaving widow, and three minor children.

Benjamin Moore lived on Mudlick Creek in what is now the Western section of Newberry County, near Saluda River. He sold two hundred acres land on Pages Creek on February 8, 1774, to Thomas Burden.

William Moore died about 1824. lived on Pages Creed and Saluda River. He left widow, Esther, and small children.

John Moore (of Saluda River) died about 1827 or '28, and left children: Catherine, Alexander A., Sarah T., and Henry. His wife was a daughter of Mrs. Phoebe Williams.

John A. Moore died about 1856. He was Trustee for Meridith Gillam, the wife of Dr. Louis M. Gillam.

MORGAN—Thomas Morgan was granted three acres land on King's Creek on February 17, 1767. John Morgan was granted four hundred acres land on Sargum's Creek, a branch of Tyger River, on August 19, 1774. Joshua Morgan received a garnt of two hundred acres land on Two-mile Creek, on Enoree River, on December 24, 1772. He died in 1799, leaving widow, Diana.

Thomas Morgan and wife, Isobel, sold lands on King's Creek November 25, 1774. They were, probably, the parents of Reuben and Thomas J. Morgan, the latter of whom moved to Alabama.

Reuben Morgan, Sr. died about 1822 in Newberry District, leaving widow, Elizabeth, and children: Thomas (in Alabama), Sarah (wife of Jacob Hausel Hunt), John (died), Rachel (dead), Daniel, David, William, Ezekiel, Reuben, Elizabeth (wife of Francis Price). John left widow, Elizabeth, and children: Nancy, Tabitha, Susannah, Luke, Mark, Mary, and John L. Rachel married William Watson and left children: Humphrey, William, Wiley, Elizabeth (wife of William H. Logan). David Morgan and wife, Nancy; Thomas Morgan and wife, Rebecca; sold lands on Bush River to James Wood in 1817. Thomas' wife was Rebecca Coate, daughter of John Coate. Mrs. Elizabeth Morgan (widoe of John) was mother of children; she died 1834. A daughter, Mary, married Levi Harmon. Tabitha married John Mathis. Nancy died in 1837, unmarried. Susannah married in 1839 to James Bushardt. Levi Harmon and wife moved to Fayette County, Mississippi.

Mark Morgan died August 5, 1850, leaving widow, Matilda, and children: Narcissa and Shields Buther Morgan. Butler Morgan was a Confederate veteran, lived in Newberry.

Isaac Morgan was granted land on Second Creek, near Broad River, in 1769. His wife, Anne, died before he died.

MORRIS—John Morris married Rosannah Wicker, a daughter of John Henry Wicker, and wife, Elizabeth (Cromer) Wicker, before the year 1816.

MORROW—Christopher Morrow and wife, Anne, lived in Newberry District in 1772. Mrs. Elizabeth Morrow died in Abbeville District about 1816, leaving children: Mary Cooper Stuart, Elizabeth(she died leaving daughter, Elizabeth Cooper), John Arthur, and three other daughters whose names are not known.

Other Pioneers (continued)

John Morrow died about 1802 in Abbeville District, leaving widow, Sarah, and his father, to whom he left a slave, and a brother, William, who lived in North Carolina.

Another John Morrow died about 1828 in Abbeville District, leaving children: James W., Jane, Thomas M. The widow, Jane, died in 1835.

Hugh Morrow died 1837 in Abbeville District, leaving widow, Jane, and children: Jane, Sarah (she married John Richardson soon afterwards), Eleanor, Mary, Robert, John, Samuel, David and George.

William Morrow died about 1828 in Abbeville District, leaving widow, Sarah, and children: Andrew, James, Nancy Haslett, Polly Buchanan,(Polly died before settlement of the estate and left a son, John). Grand-children: Mary (daughter of son, John), William (son of son, James), William (son of son, John), Sarah Buchanan(daughter of Polly).

MOSELEY-Absalom Moseley married Mary Richardson and had children: William, Mason, Wiley, Daniel, Sallie, Winnie, and Nancy Burkhalter. William, Mason, and Wiley moved to Arkansas. Daniel married Caroline Bridges, a daughter of William Bridges, and had children: Hanson C., William A., Nancy C. Nancy C. married George D. Brown. ("Annals of Newberry", p. 635).

George Moseley died about 1824 in Laurens District, leaving widow, Polly and children: George, Betsy Moore, Robertson, Fleming, Nancy, Tulley E., Sophia, Thomas H., Eliza A., Austin C., Fontaine, John, Frances Belcher, and Polly Young.

James Moseley died about 1828 in Edgefield District, leaving widow, Mary, and children: John, Sally, Frances, James, Harriet, Patsy, Eliza, Clement, and Middie.

MUSGROVE-Edward (or Allen) Musgrove lived near what was later knowne as " Musgrove's Mill", in Spartanburg District. He was the grand-father of Philemon Musgrove Waters. He had children bi his first wife, as follows: Beaks Musgrove, and probably others; and children by his second wife were: Mary and Susan; and children by his third wife were: Margaret, and probably others.

MURDOCK-Jesse Murdock died in 1836 in Newberry County. He left widow, Matilda, but no children named in his will. Exr. of will: Samuel Davidson.

MURPHRY-James Murphry made will March 27, 1787, and died 1787, in Newberry County. He left widow, Sarah, and children: John, Dowdell, Jemima (married..... Roland), Ann (married .....Marfrin), and Rebecca.

Mark Murphry died about 1830 in Union District. He left widow, Holly, and children: Sarah (wife of Thomas Cooper), Mariam(married Thomas Cooper), Damaris Jackson, Simon P., Jeremiah B., Emmanuel, Lemuel, John M., Joseph P., and William P. (After death of Mariam Cooper, her sister, Sarah, married Thomas Cooper).

McADAMS-Robert McAdams made will August 8, 1820, and died about 1822, leaving children: Sarah, Katy, Thomas, Providence, Henry, James, Linney, and John.

McAMIE-William McAmie made will February 5, 1816, which was proved in Court January 1,1817. He died in Twiggs County, Georgia, about 1816, leaving widow, Sarah (mother of children), and three children: John Braden (age 10), William Johnston (age 8), and Martha Brooks (age 4).

McCAIN-James McCain made will August 5, 1786, and died about 1787, leaving two children named in his will, John and Maty, and his wife, Elizabeth.

McCARTY-John McCarty married Mary, daughter of Matthias and Fanny Haire, before the year 1817.

McGRAW-Matthew McGraw died in Newberry County, his will dated November 28, 1848. He left his property to Mary Ann Lorick, widow of Jacob Lorick.

McCLELLAND-William McClelland settled in Newberry District before the Rev. War. Some of his sons were: David, John, George. His wife, Margaret, was mother of his children. John McClelland died about 1817, leaving children: William,John,James, and Isabel, and Jane (wife of James Boyd). Isabel married David McCollough. James and Jane Boyd had Jane and Thomas. John McClelland, Jr. (son of John), died about 1825, leaving his part of his father's estate to his brothers and sisters, including the heirs of Jane Boyd, decd.

Another John McClelland died July 30, 1836, leaving widow, Elizabeth, and children: Anna, Pergy, Margaret, William (he died about 1839, and left no family), and Elizabeth. This John was a son of William McClelland.

McCLINTOCK-Robert McClintock lived near Enoree River. He was a Minister of the Gospel; and died about 1803. His sons were: James, Robert, Matthew, and, perhaps, other children. James died in 1804, leaving widow, Catherine. John died about 1803, leaving widow, Jane, and children: John, Martha, Mary Mills, Betsy Fleimg, and Nancy.

Other Pioneers (continued)

McCLINTON—Samuel McClinton died about 1807 in Abbeville District, leaving children: James, Robert, Samuel, Margaret Gilmer, Mary Gilmer, and Susannah.

McCLURE—Robert McClure and wife, Margaret, lived in Newberry District, where they bought land in 1787. She was Margaret Pearson Buffington. Carey McClure and wife, Maria Louise, sold land on Little River in 1835.

David McClure died about 1816. James McClure died 1816. William McClure died about 1822, leaving widow, Ruth, and children: John, James, William and others.

McCOLLUM—James McCollum married Elizabeth McCollum, a cousin, about 1812 or '14. Many of their descendents live in Georgia and Mississippi. John McCollum married Elizabeth Maffett, a daughter of Robert Maffett, Sr., and had a son, James, and other children.

McCONNELL—William McConnell made will May 30, 1803, and died same year. He left widow, Mary, and children: Nancy, Mary, Andrew, and John.

McCRACKIN—William McCrackin made will December 1, 1784, and died about 1785, leaving his property to his father, Arthur McCrackin, his brother, Thomas McCrackin and heirs, and to other brothers and sisters, who were, Arthur, John, James, Robert, and Ruth.

James McCrackin died on Indian Creek after year 1820. Robert McCrackin died about 1817. Jesse McCrackin died about 1820; and administration granted to James McCrackin, Sr., James McCrackin, Jr., and John Glasgow. Thomas McCrackin died about 1804, leaving widow, Elizabeth. James G. McCrackin died in September, 1842, leaving widow, Susan E., and children: Nancy J. Fowler, John P., David J., and William A. McCrackin.

McCRELESS—John McCreless died in Edgefield District in 1806, leaving a widow, Sarah, and children: James, John, George, and three daughters, the youngest being Leodocia. The son, James, had died and left three sons, George, Surles, and James. George (son of James) was born in Edgefield District May 31, 1792, and died in Alabama February 3, 1872. He married Elizabeth Dorn and had children: James and John(both were soldiers in the Confederate Army), and James died 1862 .

Captain George McCreless lived in Newberry District. He and his brother, John, came from Virginia. He died about 1830, leaving widow, Elizabeth, and children: Mary C. (wife of Dr. Thomas H. Shell), Maria T. (wife of Dr. Nathan Renwick), Sarah C., and Nancy E. Dr. Nathan Renwick and wife moved to Georgia.

McDOWELL—Patrick McDowell owned lands in Newberry County. He sold his lands and moved to Charleston County, South Carolina, and died in the city of Charleston in year 1813. His surviving children were: James McDowell, Alexander Sinclair, James McCrackin.

McCRARY—Thomas McCrary died about 1790 in Laurens District, leaving widow, Lettice, and children: Charles, Thomas, Matthew, Jane(wife of John Greer), Moses, George, Christopher, Andrew, Mary, Catherine. Moses died in 1807. Dr. George McCrary died about 1837, leaving widow, Elizabeth.

Alexander McCrary died in Edgefield District about 1844, leaving widow, Ann, and children: John, Thomas, Samuel, and Margaret Head.

Robert McCreary doed about 1850 in Barnwell District, leaving widow, Ann, and children: Joshua, Robert, Jesse, Eliza (wife of M. L. Moseley). His wife, Ann, was a daughter of James Harley. Grand-children named in settlement of estate were: Jesse, Ovlivia, Sarah, Onelia (children of Loren and Mary Ann Mosley). Loren died and his widow, Mary Ann, married John Noland.

McGILL—James McGill made will February 8, 1779, and died about 1782, leaving daughter who was wife of Anthony Golding, and other children. Sons of Anthony Golding were: James, William , amd Anthony. The testator owned land in Frederick County, Virginia, from where he moved. He left a nephew, William Lowery, certain property, with the condition if he die without issue, the property to be sold and the money divied among nephews living in Ireland.

Samuel McGill died about 1815 in Newberry District, leaving widow, Lucy, and children: Mary Bradford, Margaret Kerr, Andrew, Charles, James, and Nancy.

John McGill died about 1785 in Abbeville District, leaving widow, Margaret.

Daniel McGill married Margaret McLain and lived in Florida.

McGOUGH—John McGough died about 1805 in Abbeville District, leaving widow, Sarah, and children: John, William, James, Samuel, Mary, Agnes, Sallie, Moses, Josiah, Benjamin.

Other Pioneers (continued)

McKIE-Thomas McKie made will October 20, 1796, which was proved in Court March 26, 1798. He died in Abbeville District and left widow, Martha, and children: Jean, Thomas, William, John, and James. Exr: Samuel Reid.

Michael McKie died November 1, 1814, in Newberry District, leaving children: Daniel, Micahel (he died previous to father's death), Alexander, Rebecca (wife of Major William Craig, she first married William Satterwhite), Susannah (she died about same time, wife of John Satterwhite, Jr. who had died September, 1817). The only child of Michael McKie, Jr., was Martha, who married William Powell. Children of John and Susannah Satterwhite were: Michael, Susannah (wife of Dr. Peter Moon), Sarah (wife of James Gillam), and Elizabeth. William Powell moved to , or was living in Brunswick County, Virginia.

Daniel McKie lived in Edgefield County; but later he or a son went to Spartanburg, S. C.

McKITTRICK-John McKittrick married Mary Susan Dalrymple, a daughter of Thomas Dalrymple and Nancy, his wife. Their children were: John J., James, William, and Nancy.

McLAIN-John McLain died 1824, left widow, Jane, and children: Francis, David, Margaret (wife of James McDaniel), Jane (wife of James Forbes), Janette, Maria (she married John Penny after the death of her father, when she was seventeen years old, in year 1824).

John McLain made will February 24, 1837, and died about 1838, leaving widow, Polly, and children: John, James, and some younger children.

McLAUGHLIN-John McLaughlin was bonr in 1752, in South Carolina, and died after the year 1850, in Alabama. He was a Rev. War patriot.

James McLaughlin received a garnt of land in Ninety Six District in year 1786.

John McLaughlin was bonr 1771 in Laurens District, and died in 1856. He married Sarah..... and had children: James, George, Charles, Samuel Goode, and a daughter. The son, James, married Nancy Blackburn in 1821; he died April 30, 1858.

McLEAS-Andrew McLeas lived in the northern section of Newberry County. He made will September 11, 1794, and died about 1795, leaving widow, Jean, and children: Andrew, Robert, Martha, and Janette.

McMASTER-James McMaster died about 1819, and left children: Thomas, Mary Conrad, Anne McCravey, Janette Caldwell (wife of Dan Caldwell), Rosannah (wife of John Starke).

McMORRIES-John McMorries made will December 28, 1823, and died January, 1824. He left widow, Nancy, and children: Spencer J., Harriet (wife of .... Calmes), William W.W., Daniel M., John B. F., Frances A. E., Joseph S., Edward R., and Jonothan M. Exrs: Fielding F. Calmes, Spencer J. McMorries. His wife was Nancy Morgan, daughter of Major Spencer Morgan of the American Army in the Rev. War. John McMorries was born in Fairfield District 1769. Spencer J. married Patsy Herndon, daughter of the Rev War patriot and officer, Col. Benjmain Herndon. They had a daughter, Martha H. McMorries. Dr. William W. McMorries was born 1803, and died in Union District August 22, 1883, leaving children: Mrs. Johnson, of Alabama, Mrs. Grier of Due West, Mrs. Cofield of Union, and four sons. Edward R. was born 1818, and died 1854. He was a merchant in Newberry. He married Frances............

McNEES-Robert McNees died in Laurens District about 1800. James McNees received a grant of land in Laurens District in 1772(then Ninety Six District). His wife was Rachel..... John McNees sold two hundred acres land in Newberry District in 1797 to James McNees. They were then living in St. Marks Parish.

Robert McNees died about 1840 in Laurens District, leaving widow, Sarah , and chilren: Samuel, Susan (wife of John Milner), Margaret Babb(she died soon afterwards),Richard, James (he had died),Agnes (wife of Joshua Teague), and Sabra White. Mrs. Sarah McNees died 1854; was formerly married to Lewis Saxon and by him had children; she was a daughter of Charles Allen, Rev War patriot.

McNEILL-James McNeill died about 1828 in Newberry District. He married Nancy......., and had children; Jane Eliza, Polly Anne, and Robert Nealy McNeill.

James McNeill died about 1835 in Newberry District, and left as his legatees: Gasper Buzhardt and wife, Peter Black and wife, Samuel Chapman and wife, and John T. McNeill.

McPHERSON-James McPherson died in Laurens County about 1851. His heirs were: Madison, Sarah, Elihu, E. G. Nelson, L. K. Teague, Sally, Monroe. Elihu died 1852, unmarried. Burgess McPherson died in Laurens County about 1825.

Other Pioneers (continued)

McQUERNS—Samuel McQuerns died about 1820, and left children: James, Alexander, Samuel, Esther (wife of Francis Wilson), Margaret (wife of Alexander Willey), and Elizabeth.
Mrs. Susannah McQuerns had children: Mary (wife of John Johnson), Elizabeth (wife of John Caldwell).
McTEER—Mrs. Frances (Griffin) McTeer died 1803, and left children: Elizabeth, Frances, Mary Vance, and Margaret Alton. Her grand-sons were: Samuel Vance, William Vance. Her brother was James Griffin. The daughter, Frances, married John Speer; and daughter, Elizabeth, married William Speer (brother of John Speer).
William McTeer died about 1829, leaving widow, Mary, and children: Elizabeth (wife of Frederick Whitmire), Sarah, William, John, Margaret, and Rebecca. N. C. Vance was guardian for his minor children. Other children were: Samuel, Nancy (wife of John Stewart), and Mary (wife of Elisha Hipp).
NATES—Jesse Nates died in Newberry County about 1848, leaving the following legatees: Zacariah Nates (brother), Rebecca Sophia Duncan (wife of George Duncan). Exr: Jacob Cook. He was preparing to go into the Mexican campaign when he died.
NEALLY—George Neally made will June 8, 1818, and died about 1819, leaving widow, Mary, and son, Samuel.
NEEL—Robert Neel died about 1796 in Newberry District, leaving widow, Elizabeth.
John Neel died on November 16, 1836, leaving widow, Elizabeth, (she was the mother of his children), and the following children: Margaret (wife of Robert Wright), Joseph, (he died and left no children), Elizabeth, Jane, Rosannah, Robert, Sarah Caroline, and Lavania.
George Neel married Margaret Clark, daughter of George Clark, and had children: Margaret (wife of Maxcey McMorris), Thomas L., Sarah A. K., and Louisa A.
NESLEY—Martin Nesley died about 1822, leaving widow, Mary, and children.
NEWMAN—Samuel Newman made will November 12, 1770, which was proved in Court March 7, 1779. He died about 1778, leaving widow, Martha, and children: John and Samuel; and other children, Uriah (wife of Thomas Gary), and Mary Crow. He gave his son, Samuel, his land in Georgia. A grand-daughter, Phoebe Bartram, received a share equal with his two daughters.
NEWTON—John Newton was living in Newberry District in 1784. In 1784, he was in Edgefield District. He married Naomi Mitchell and had children: Isaac, William, and Henry Newton.
Mrs. Naomi Newton was a daughter of Isaac Mitchell who died in Newberry District about 1812.
NICHOLS—Solomon Nichols lived on Indian Creek, where he married the widow, Elizabeth Renwick. He was formerly married. He died September 29, 1793, and his widow died September 15, 1796. He had children by his first wife, and his widow had children by her first husband, John Renwick. His step-children named in his will were: Agnes Renwick, Mary Ann Renwick.
George Nichols died about 1801, leaving widow, Elizabeth, and children: Allen, William, Sally (she died unmarried), Rachel (wife of John Bickley), and Luke. The widow married in 1804 to Isaac Haithcock; and she died in year 1805. William Nichols married Barbara Hair, daughter of Matthias Hair, before the year 1817.
NIMMONS—William Nimmons died about 1805, in Newberry District. He left widow, Margaret, and children.
NOBLES—Hezekiah Nobles died about 1830-31, in Edgefield District. He left widow, Alcey, and children: John, Mark, Luke, Sally Bolger, Elizabeth Holloway, and Rhoda Beam.
NOLAND—Aubrey Noland died about 1814, and left a son, Phillip, who lived near Enoree River. He left widow, Edy, and children: Thomas, George, Betsy, Hannah, and the above named son, Phillip. Betsy married Micajah Suber. His father-in-law was Major Lewis Hogge who lived in the same section.
Sampson Noland died about 1828, and left children: Phillip, Samuel, Thomas, Mary Hughs, William, and Elizabeth Ferguson. The children of Elizabeth Ferguson (in 1828) were: Sampson Oland Ferguson, James Washington Ferguson.
Stephen Noland lived in Fairfield County, but died in Georgia. He left widow, Mary, and children: Stephen, who married Mary Addison,(she was a daughter of Christopher and Agnes Addison). Christopher Addison was a patriot in the Rev. War.
Thomas J. Noland died about 1823, left following legatees named in settlement of his estate: Redden Gorse and wife, Sarah; John Noland, and Frances Noland.

Other Pioneers.

PEASTER—Gasper Peaster (originally spelled De Peyster) was a German. He married Eve Margaret Edgemont of Switzerland, and they started for America in one of the early colonies but he died on the way over. His widow, by whom he had several small children, among them, Adam, and Gasper, afterwards married George Gray in South Carolina.

Gasper Peaster, Jr. died in Newberry District about the year 1833, leaving widow, Margaret, and children: Elizabeth (wife of N. G. Gallman), Simon, Spencer, David, and Adeline.

Mrs. Rachel Peaster made will May 14, 1817, proven in court Dec. 13, 1819, and died about 1819, leaving daughter, Rachel Boatner (alias Eigner), and four sons, Leonard Suber, Conrad Suber, John Suber, and George Suber. There was another son, David Eigner, who had two children, George Eigner and Eliza Eigner. She was married three times, (1) an Eigner, (2) a Suber, and (3) a Peaster.

Adam Peaster made will Nov. 9, 1821, proven in court Jan. 9, 1822, and died about 1821. He left wife and children whose names are not given, but a brother, Casper, is mentioned.

PEMBERTON—Richard Pemberton made will 1805 and died 1805, leaving widow, Lyda, and children: Isaac, William, Rachel, Elizabeth, Sarah, Anne.

Isaac, Robert, and John Pemberton (brothers) went to Ohio and settled in Miami County.

Isaah Pemberton died July 13, 1794, and his wife, Elizabeth, died Dec. 28, 1795. They left ch: George, William (twins)—born 1753; (William died 1777); Isaah (born 1756); Elizabeth (born 1785); Richard (born 1760); Hannah (born 1762); Ann (born 1764); Judith (born 1765); Thomas (born 1766); John (born 1769); Sarah (born 1772); Ruth (born 1775).

PENNINGTON—Jacob Pennington died about 1775—79. He left widow, Mary, and ch: Mary Noble, Abigail Cafey, Sarah Bright, Charity, Elizabeth, and Deliah. Son-in-law, James Bright. Brother: Abraham Pennington. Widow: Mary Pennington (after his death she married Abram Gray, of Laurens District)... Charity married Charles King who died in Feb. 1789.

PENNY—George Penny married Sarah Ruff, daughter of Mrs. Elisabeth (Gray) Ruff. (Mrs. Ruff afterwards married Rev. George Cromer and moved to Abbeville County). Their children were: John W. Penny, James P. Penny, Thomas H. Penny, Martha G. Penny, and Henry H. Penny.

PERRY—Thomas Perry made will 1797 and died about 1798, leaving two daughters, Delilah and Sarah. Sarah married Moses Hunter, and she died and left two children, Delilah Hunter and James Hunter. (Delilah never married.) He received grant of land in 1768, on Enoree River.

Nathan Washington Perry was born 1755, in Maryland. He married (1) Dikando Walls (born 1756), and (2) to Reba Chandler, of Newberry District. He had a brother, Thomas, who also moved to Newberry District. He died 1800. Children by first wife were: Sarah (married Robert Leavell in 1803), Robert Leavell and wife moved to Ohio: they were Quakers. Nathan's other children probably were: James, John, Margaret, and Zadoc.

Thomas Perry, of St. Helena's Parish, died 1766. He married in 1758, to Martha Ladson.

Benjamin Perry died after 1780 in Camden District, leaving widow, Mary.

PETERSON—David Peterson died about 1827 in Newberry County, leaving widow, Mary (daughter of David Turner), and children: Eliza (wife of Andrew McConnell), Matilda, John, Mary, David, Mark, and Spencer. The widow of David Turner, Frances, married Jesse Jay.

Wm. Peterson married Nancy, the daughter of Wm. and Ann Mangum.

PHILLIPS—Gabriel Phillips made will Nov. 28, 1808 and died in 1809, leaving children: Edward, Susannah Starkey, Peter, Gabriel, Hannah (wife of .... Cuper), and John.

John Phillips died about 1827 or 1828 in Edgefield District. He left as his legatees: Three brothers—Martin, Thomas, and Joseph Phillips; and sisters—Deliah (wife of Joseph), Mary (wife of Martin). Father: Thomas Phillips.

James Phillips sold his land in Chester District about 1795.

Micajah Phillips died about 1811 in Edgefield District. He left widow, Sally, and ch: Thomas Phillips, and Martha Purcell (wife of Zacharias Purcell).

PITTS—Henry Pitts made will dated June 4, 1803, proven in court August 1, 1803. He left widow, Hannah, and children: John, Sarah Deas, Elisabeth Dodgen, Jane Butler, William, Mark, Henry, Joseph, Charles, Sarah, and Nancy Slaughter.

John Pitts made will November 8, 1820 and died 1821, leaving widow, Henrietta, and children: Jonothan, Charles, Bluford, Carwile, James, and Rebecca.

Joshua Pitts made will Feb. 4, 1825 and died in Feb. 1825, leaving widow, Matilda, and three children: Dalton, Pinkney, and a small infant not yet named.

Other Pioneers (continued)

O'CONNER—William O'Conner married Miss Young. One of their daughters, Helen, was a distributee in settlement of estate of John T. Young who died in 1842.

O'DELL—Baruch O'Dell made will Oct. 29, 1832, proven in court June 7, 1837. He left widow, Rachel, and brothers and sisters: John, Rignal, Polly Duckett, and children of a deceased sister, Peggy Smarts (Mary Dillard and Thomas Smarts); and children of a deceased brother, Thomas O'Dell (Nancy and Sarah Emily). Thomas Smarts, Joseph Ducett, John O'Dell, and Baruch Duncan, received balance of property after all debts and legacies paid. Joseph Duckett died before settlement and his share lapsed.

OTTERSON—Dr. Samuel Otterson married Narcissa, daughter of .... and gr-dau. of Wm. Thompson. Mr. Thompson died 1822.

Samuel Otterson married Ruth Gordon, in Newberry Co. He was a Rev. War patriot and officer in the State Militia. He was father of Dr. Samuel Otterson.

OUTZ—Diedrich Utz lived in Newberry District (then part of old Ninety Six District), where he received a grant of 200 acres on Cannons Creek in 1768. This was in the upper Dutch Fork, and he was probably one of the members of the colonies of German and Swiss and Dutch who came from Pennsylvania to that section. He sold this land in 1783.

Peter Outz, Sr. died about 1829, in Edgefield District. He left a widow, Elizabeth, and children: David, John, Henry, Elizabeth, Martin, George, Peter, Abram, Aaron, Daniel, and Benjamin.

Jacob Outs (spelled Euts) died about 1825, in Newberry District, leaving his mother, Mary Euts, sister, Christina Euts (she married Solomon Dowman), and a nephew, Hohn Dowman.

OWENS—William Owens made will September 23, 1820, proven in court October 9, 1820. He left widow, Nancy, and sons, James and William.

OXNER—Henry Oxner died about 1792. Adm. granted to Jacob Oxner.

Emmanuel Oxner died in 1871, leaving widow, Nancy B., and several children. A son, William B., was Administrator of the estate. A son-in-law was William D. Lee.

Mrs. Nancy B. Oxner died in 1882, leaving property to her grand-children, William Bowman Lee, Henry Moostb Lee, and Mary E. Lee; also to her daughters-in-law, Elizabeth (wife of William B. Oxner), Susannah (wife of John Z. Oxner). A daughter married Wm. D. Lee and lived in North Carolina, in Rutherford County.

Henry Oxner died and left children: Louise (wife of D. S. Brown), Catherine (wife of J. D. Cannon); and a grand-daughter, Jane McLain. Henry married Mary, daughter of George and Elizabeth Keller, before 1832.

Jacob Oxner, Sr. made will dated Jan. 27, 1806, proved in court Feb. 12, 1807. Children: Martin, Elizabeth (wife of Henry Fish), Barbara (wife of Michael Fellers), Jacob, Nancy (wife of Jacob Miller), Rachel, Molly (wife of John Lominack), Michael, George, Joseph, Manuel, Susannah, Christina, Rebecca, and Elizabeth Oxner.

PAGE—William Page, Sr. died about 1827, in Newberry District. He left children: Berry, Sarah, William, Thomas G., Benjamin, Elijah, and wife of Clackston Mize. Another son, Pendleton, had died before death of father.

William Page, Jr. married Hester Hancock, of Newberry District, and moved to Georgia.

PARR—John Parr died in Fairfield District about 1823, leaving a widow, Nancy.

James Parr died 1824 in Fairfield District, leaving widow, Elizabeth, and a son, Henry.

Claiborne Pair made will dated April 25, 1818, proved in Court August 21, 1830; in Union District. He left widow, Martha, and children: James and others.

Dorcus Pair made will dated August 5, 1840, proved in court Sept. 28, 1849. He left ch: Harvey, Richard, and Margaret (she married Absolom Ivey). There may have been other children.

Allen Pair, Sr. died 1849, in Union District. He left heirs: Andrew, James, Roland, Mary, and Viney Pair.

Andrew Pair (1813—   ) married Nancy Davis (1815—   ), in Union District. They left Ch: Nancy, Elizabeth, Robert L., Joseph D., and Samuel A. Pair.

James Pair made will dated May 31, 1857, proved in court Dec. 5, 1864, in Union District. He left widow, Nancy, and ch: William P., Mary M. (wife of Benj. Seigler), Martha (wife of Wiley Aney), Amanda Savage (widow), Ann(wife of Andrew Nance), Sallay (wife of James Robinson).

Other Pioneers.

PARKINS-Capt. Daniel Parkins came from Virginia to Newberry District, He lived on Bush River, and owned "Parkins Mill" on Saluda River. He was born 1758. A member of the Quaker Church, the Bush River Meeting. He married Jane Carradine, daughter of Abraham Carradine. He served awhile as Justice of the Peace, Capt. of a militia company, and a member of the Board of Commissioners of Public Buildings, in Newberry District. His sons, Abraham and John, died young. He and his wife, also, died early in life. Other sons, Charles, Isaac, Allen R., and Mark all died young, unmarried, except Allen R. who moved to Greenville District. There was a nephew, Daniel Parkins, Jr. Allen R. married about 1816 in Greenville to a Miss Paul. He died there in 1837, leaving his widow and several small children. His eldest son was named Daniel.   ("Annals of Newberry", pp.171-172).........

PARK-Anthony Park was one of the first settlers in Newberry District. He was a Rev. War soldier. He lived beyond Indian Creek, near the home of his half-brother, Col. Thomas Dugan, an officer in S. C. militia during the Revolution.

Hugh Park married Elizabeth Boyd, daughter of John Boyd, Sr., and had children as follows: John, James, Agnes, Margaret, Mary, Hugh, and Elizabeth,

Mrs. Mary Park (widow) of Chester District, deeded to her son, Robert Park, land in Newberry County in the year 1806.

PARMER-Isaac Parmer made will March 31, 1787 and died in 1788, leaving widow, Sarah, and children: William, and four daughters.

PARROTT-John Parrott died in Newberry County. He married before year 1812, to Nancy Buzhardt, a daughter of John and Elizabeth Buzhardt.

PATTERSON-James Patterson made will April 23, 1806, proven in court May 4, 1819. He died about 1819, leaving widow, Eleanor, and sister, Nancy Mann and her five children, viz: George McFarland, John McFarland, James McFarland, Judith McFarland, and Summer McFarland. These were children by a former marriage, the last two named being daughters.

PAYNE-Elihu C. Payne died in Newberry County on November 1, 1864, leaving widow, Elizabeth A. and a son, John W. Payne.

Richard Payne made will March 22, 1803, and died 1803, leaving widow, Elizabeth, and children Edmund, John, James, David, and Katy.

John W. Payne died in 1857 in Newberry County, leaving widow, Lucinda, who afterwards married Rev. William B. Boyd. He had brothers, James and David Payne, and a sister, Katherine Payne. Nephews were, John Satterwhite and Richard S. Satterwhite.

Another brother was Edmund Payne. They lived in Newberry District. Katherine married Andrew Lee Lark. Edmund had a daughter, Catherine, who married David C. Boazman. He (John W. Payne) had a half-sister, Satira, wife of Stanmore Holston, who moved to Chambers County, Ala.

Richard Payne's first wife was Elizabeth Manning, After his death she married John Grigsby, of Edgefield District.

PAYSINGER-John Paysinger married Christina Schumpert and had children: Benjamin, Thomas M., Elizabeth, Jacob, Samuel S., Frederick S., Henry, David S., and Permelia. Benjamin married Eliza Fellers. Jacob married Nancy Chapman. Samuel S. married Rose Chapman. Frederick S. married (1) Callie McCollum and (2) Vinnie Maffett. Callie McCollum was the widow of Milton Buzhardt and Vinnie Maffett was the daughter of Robert Maffett. His third wife was Carrie Mitchel. Thomas M. married (1) Adeline Werts and (2) Rebecca Buzhardt. Henry Mock Paysinger and David Paysinger were both killed in the Civil War. Permelia Married Zed White of Newberry, and they were parents of John William White.

Frederick Paysinger died about 1822. Adm. granted to John Paysinger, Jacob Schumpert, and John Bickley.

PATTY-James Patty married Margaret Motes (she was born 1753), in Newberry District and had ch: Rachel (1774—1828) who married Wallace Jones (1773—1854); Sarah (wife of William Spencer); Mary (wife of David Edwards); James, Charles, David, and Dorcus Motes. James Patty died about 1795, and his widow, Margaret, died in 1803. They belonged to the Quaker Church, and some of children moved to Ohio.

PEAK-Isaac Peake of Union District married Sarah Edwards, daughter of Repps Edwards who died in 1840. Sarah Edwards died before the death of her father. They left one son, Isaac E. Peake (brother of Sarah)....

Other Pioneers.

Allen Pitts married Sarah Neel, daughter of Charles and Jemima Davenport Neel, Mrs. Jemima Neel was a daughter of William and Sarah Davenport.

Amasa Pitts died in Newberry County, leaving widow, Catherine, who died in year 1857. Their children were: Abner, Hillery, Sanford, Ira, Reuben, Drayton, Permelia, Frances Ann, Susan Jane (she married John Belton Werts), and Rachel. Hillery, Ira, and Sanford, moved to Pontotac County, Miss. Abner, Drayton, and Permelia went to Russel County, Miss. Permelia married Joshua Pitts, of Alabama. Rachel married .... Owens.

Abner Pitts died in Newberry District, leaving widow, Mary (Waldrop) Pitts, and ch: Caleb (he died 1826, leaving no family).

Abner Pitts died about 1850, leaving widow, Mary, and ch: Elizabeth (wife of James H. Adair), Matilda, Caleb, Frances (wife of Andrew Workman), Stacey, Newton, Ephriam.

Joseph Pitts died in Newberry District about 1816, leaving widow, Ann, and ch: Amasa (eldest son), Nancy (married .... Aiken), Hannah Anderson, Asa, Joseph, Celia. Gr-ch: Ann Aiken, Joseph Anderson, Peggy Anderson. Other legatees (settlement of 1835) were: children of Michael Toland.

William Pitts died 1838 in Laurens District, leaving widow, Sarah, and ch: Reuben Griffin Pitts, Nellie, William, Daniel, David, Jesse, Thomas, and John Pitts.

Reuben G. Pitts died Nov. 3, 1854, leaving widow, Lura (Burton), Pitts, and ch: John D., William Henry, and James B. Pitts.

Lucinda Pitts died 1855, left legatees: Aaron B. Pitts, Wesley S. Pitts, James W. Pitts, Chesly H. Pitts, Moses Pitts, and Mary Cook (wife of Zion Cook)...

PLANT-Robert Plant died about 1835, and left widow, Sarah, and children: Elizabeth, Lucinda (wife of David S. Glenn), Williamson, Davidson (he died January 18, left no children), and Robert J., Mary A., and Jefferson. (Davidson died January 18, 1832).

Samuel Plant, of Laurens District, married Susan Griffin, daughter of John and Anne Griffin.

PLUNKETT-Robert Plunkett lived in Newberry District, on Beaver Dam Creek. In the year 1815 his heirs sold his lands to Hamilton Plunkett. Heirs were: Elizabeth Hguhen, Benjmain Crumley, Hannah Crumley, Charles Plunkett, William Plunkett, Robert Cleland, Jane Cleland, David Murdock, Agnes Murdock, James Cleland, Ann Cleland. The wife of Charles was Mable; wife of robert, Jane; wife of David Murdock, Agnes; wife of William Plunket, Sarah; and wife of James Cleland, Ann.

POOLE-Abram Poole married a daughter of James Williams, and had children: Eugenia Poole, Mary Coleman, and others.

Adam Poole, Sr. , a Rev War patriot, lived in Union District. His son, Adam, Jr., married Miss. Crosby and lived in Chester County.

William Poole made will April 22, 1796, and died same year, in Newberry County. He left widow, Frances, and children: Edward, Patty Ragsdale, Nancy, Richard, Frances, Sukey, Sabon, and William P. Mrs. Frances Poole died in 1812. William P died in 1816, leaving properyy to the following brothers and sisters; Richard P., Fanny Moseley, Susannah (died), Nancy (she was dead at time of settlement). Nancy married Drury Satterwhite and had children: Thomas, Narcissa(wife of Richard Griffin), and Frances. After the death of Nancy , Drury Satterwhite married her sister, Susannah Poole, who , also, died early and left two infant children, Emily and Theresa. They moved to Madison County, Alabama.

POWELL-William Powell died in Laurens County , leaving children: William Wesly, Nancy (both these children by his second wife); and Elizabeth Gaines, Peachy, Rhoda, Polly, Fanny, Sally, Amy, Belinda, Milly, Virginia ,(these were by his first wife). Exrs: Phillip Wait (son-in-law), and James Powell (brother).

Samuel Powell died 1824, leaving children: Samuel, Thomas, Elizabeth (wife of Zacariah Bailey). Thomas Powell died about 1834 in Laurens District, leaving widow, Lucinda, and children: Samuel,Thomas, Marietta (wife of David Goodman), Elizabeth, Nancy Bailey (her children, William , Robert, Margaret Delilah).

PRATER(PRATHER)-Middleton Prater bought land on Saluda River, in Laurens County, in 1790. Brice Prater and Jesse Prater, each bought land on Duncan's Creek, Laurens County, the former in year 1797, and the latter in year 1822. John Prater died in Laurens County about 1825, leaving legatees: Martha Prater, William Dollar, Daniel Owens, James Prather, Archibald Prather.

Other Pioneers (continued)

Zacariah Prater died about 1814, leaving widow, Ruth, and children: John, Daniel, William, Hezekiah, Nancy, Ruth, Mary, Zacariah. The widow died 1825, and the following received shares of her estate: Christopher Whitman and wife, John Watts and wife, William, John, Daniel, Zacariah, Hezekiah, and Maximillan Sheppard and wife.

PRATT-Thomas Pratt lived in Newberry many years, a successful merchant from 1813 to 1837, the year of his death. He maried in 1816 to Dorothy Brooks Nance, daughter of Major Frederick Nance, and had children: William F., Robert, Simeon, Priestley, Amelia, Mary, Carolina, Virginia, and Angela. Amelia married J. B. F. McMorries. Prestley died at Pueblo, Mexico, during the Mexican War.

James Pratt died about 1828 in Abbeville County. His wife had died before his death. Children: John, Robert, William.

PRESNAL-William Presnal, living in Lexington District, owned land in Newberry District, located on Hawlick's Creek, a tributary of Saluda River. He sold this land in 1807. He married Sarah Clark, daughter of William Clark, in year 1784. Jacob Presnal sold land in Newberry District in year 1819.

PRESSLEY-Charles Pressley died 1837 in Abbeville District, leaving widow, Elisha, and children: Levi, William, Catherine Edwards, Adam, Lewis, Jane, Elizabeth (she was wife of Joseph Phillips). John Pressley died 1809 in Abbeville District, leaving widow, Nancy, and children: John E., and others. David Pressley died about 1819, leaving the following legatees: Joseph Lowery, George Brown, Samuel Pressley, John T. Pressley. John B. Pressley died about 1833. Rachel Pressley died about 1839 in Pendleton District, leaving following legatees: Mother, Anne Pressley; sisters, Jane M. Pressley, and Elizabeth Porter of Alabama; brother-in-law, Elijah Wilbanks.

PRICE-John Price died about 1804 in Newberry District, leaving widow, Dicey, and children: John, William, Elizabeth Anderson, James, Nancy, Hugh, and Thomas.

Mrs. Susannah Price made will March 9, 1818, which was proved in Court March 16, 1819. She left a daughter, Mary Dyson, whose son, John Dyson, was made Executor of her will.

PRISOCK-Frederick Prisock lived in the Dutch Fork of Newberry County. He died March 25, 1817, leaving widow, Katy, and children: Margaret (wife of John Le Gronne), Frederick, John, Adam, Sally, Molly, and George. George died just previous to his father's death, and left children, David and Rosannah.

PROCTOR-Samuel Proctor made will October 24, 1794, which was proved in Court May 19, 1795, the year he died. He left the following children named in his will: Samuel, Phillip, Jean McCall, Sarah Adams, Mary Winningham, and the wife of Joseph White. Phlip married Margaret........ and had a son, Henry, at the time of testator's death. A grand-son, Samuel Adams, is , also, named in his will.

John Proctor made will April 6, 1824, and died same year. He left widow, Susannah, and children: Debby Adams, Thomas, Lucinda, Daniel, Zacariah, Elizabeth,(these were children by a former marriage). His widow's children by a former marriage were: James Bearden, and Eli Bearden.

PUGH-Azariah Pugh died about 1794 in Newberry District, and left children: Jesse, Ellis, Thomas, Azariah, and William. A daughter married Peter Julien.

Richard Pugh died in 1796, leaving widow, Mary, and grand-daughter, Nancy Cochran; four step-children, John W. McClannahan, Margaret Cochran, William McClannhan, and Samuel McClannahan.

Edward Pugh died in Newberry District. Some of his children were: John, Azariah, and Elizabeth Gilbert. John Pugh died about 1815, and left widow, Mary, but no children named in his estate settlement. Another John Pugh who lived on Bush River moved to Harrison County, Indiana.

PURCELL-John Purcell died about 1794 in Edgefield District. He left widow, Barbara, and children: William, Zaccheus, Mary, Elizabeth Hearon, and probably others. He left, also, a small shre of his estate to Edmund Purcell. William died in Edgefield District between 1830 and 1837, leaving the following distributees: Edmund, Alexander, and Tappenus.

PYLES-Nicholas and Anne Pyles lived in Pendleton District, but moved to Kentucky before the year 1800. Children: John, Moffett, J. E., Abner, Hans, Jehu, Hiram, William, Nicholas, Thompson, Byrd, Alfred, David, Samuel, Edith Husband, Nancy Crabtree, Jane, Susannah, and .....

Other Pioneers (continued)

Dr. Lewdy Pyles died about 1826 in Laurens District. He left widow, Agatha, and children (their names shown in returns and not in will): Newton, Madison, Susannah, Jefferson,   His brothers were: Abner, Addison, Milton.   A brother-in-law: Jesse Teague.   Newton had children: Laura and Marion. Dr. Abner Pyles married, second,to Frances........ in May, 1822, and they were seperated in October, 1822. Addison married Martha Crenshaw, daughter of Archibald Crenshaw of Newberry District.

QUARLES-Richard Quarles married Sarah Middleton, daughter of Hugh Middleton, and lived in Abbeville District. He moved to Edgefield District , where he died about 1818, leaving widow, Sarah, and children: John, William, and others.

James Quarles died in Edgefield District, (his will is dated September 21, 1812), leaving widow, Sally, and children: Susannah B., Robert G., Mary Ann, and Richard. He left a brother, Richard, and a brother-in-law, Edmund Belcher.

John Quarles died in Edgefield District before 1843, leaving the following legatees: Amos Bush and wife; Susan, William, Adeline, Sarah, Jane Quarles.

William Quarles died , leaving widow, Sarah, and children: John, David, Sarah Jane (wife of William W. Thompson).

Another William Quarles died and left children: Samuel, Sterling, William (he died 1821), Frances Collier, Elizabeth Butler, Mary Ann (wife of George Boswell), Louisa. The widow, Nancy, died after year 1848, the date of a bill of partition.

QUAY-Alexander Quay died in Union District before 1850, leaving widow, Catherine, who died about 1851. A daughter, Ann, married Clough Sims, and had children: William A., Sarah E., Alice C., Elizabeth C., and Margaret M. F.

RAWLS-Benjamin Rawls made will August 15, 1865, and died about 1866, in Columbia, S. C. He left the following children who are named in the settlement of his estate: Marie L. (wife of George S. Bowers), James S. (he had died), John I., Benjamin F., Thomas I., and Mary S. Bullard.

RAY-Both the Rhea and the Ray families (sometimes spelled " Wray"), lived in Pennsylvania and Virginia in early Colonial times. Later, many drifted down into the Carolinas, to Tennessee and other States. Rev. Joseph Ray , or Rhea, a grand-son of Matthew Rhea, came to America in 1769, with his wife, Elizabeth,   They had the following children: John, Matthew, William, Joseph, Samuel, Margaret, Elizabeth.

Turner Ray came from Virginia to Ninety Six District before the Rev War. He married Nancy......., and had children: John, James, Mary (wife of David Hill), Anne (wife of John Lee), Sarah (wife of Alfred Miller), Cynthia (married Severand Wesson), and Nancy. John (son of Turner), died about 1830, leaving widow, Polly, and children: John, Samuel, Elizabeth (wife of John Johnston), Nancy (wife of Balis Gist), Patsy (wife of Nathan B. Chisolm), Charles, Eleanor (wife of John Anderson).   James (son of Turner) died and left no family.

Margaret Ray married John Barrett, and had children: Abigail (wife of Daniel Marchant), John M., and Jane.

Thomas Ray made will September 19, 1788, and died about 1792, in Abbeville District, leaving widow, Susannah, and some small children.

REAGAN-William Reagan died September 11, 1830, leaving widow, Phoebe, and children: John E., Gideon B., James I., William D., Robert L., Elizabeth D., Burton, Phoebe Ann, Kerr, and Cynthia.

Reason Reagan died 1825, leaving widow, Anne, and children: John, Cary, and others.

John Reagan married Dorothy Chandler, daughter of Israel and Lydia (Gilbert) Chandler. Israel and Lydia Chandler were married July 25, 1793. (From an old family Bible), They moved to East Tennessee about 1825.

REDD-George Redd made will August 15, 1827, and died about 1828, leaving widow, Nancy, and children: Maria (wife of Robert D. Gray), Ephriam L., James W., David J., Samuel W., Mary S., and William C.

James Redd made will May 21, 1850, which was proved in Court March 27, 1858. He left children: Eleanor (wife of Andrew Cromer), Jane Margaret (wife of ..... Reid), Nathaniel Davidson was appointed Trustee for the two daughters.

Other Pioneers (continued)

REEDER-Thomas Reeder died about 1822, and left several children, one of whom was a son, Thomas C. Reeder. Thomas C. was born April 9, 1798, and died September 4, 1834. He married Mary Teague Fowler on March 31, 1825. Their children were: Richard Franklin (born August 7, 1827), Isaac Newton Teague (born July 11, 1830, and died December 30, 1892). Isaac Newton Teague Reeder married Martha Catherine Webb on October 25, 1849. She died on December 25, 1919. Simon Reeder died about 1797. Samuel Reder died about 1858, leaving widow, Sarah, and children: William D., James J., Abner W., Adeline (wife of J. Frank Wheeler) and John H. Reeder.

REPLOGLE-Jacob Replogle made will November 28, 1795, which was proved in Court February, 28, 1796. He left widow, Judith, and the following step-children: George Long, Jacob Long, Michael Long, Catherine Miller, and Ann May Reeder.

REESE-David Reese, son of John Reese, moved to North Carolina from Newberry District.

REID-Hugh Reid was one of the early settlers of old Ninety Six District, living in Abbeville District. He was born 1746 and died 1829. His wife, Margaret, was born 1754 and died 1818. They are both buried at Long Cane Cemetery, in Abbeville County.

David Reid came from Ireland and settled about four miles East of Newberry Court House, about the year 1790. His son, Daniel, was in the War of 1812, as Captain of a Calvary Troop. Another son, Samuel, was a Justice of the Peace, and was Lieutenant in the Calvary during Nullification times. (Reference: " Annals of Newberry").

REIGHLEY-Henry Reighley lived in Newberry, owning a tract on Scott's Creek, near the town, including one hundred acres land. He sold this land to John Coate on February 23, 1779, and moved to Camden District.

REISINGER-Feight Reisinger came from Germany, and settled in the Dutch Fork, Ninety Six District. He received a grant of one hundred fifty acres on Second Creek about the year 1760. He and his wife, Susannah, conveyed this land in 1768 to William Dawkins.

RENWICK-Rev. John Renwick, Sr., a Covenanter Minister, came from Ireland, and settled near King's Creek. He died in 1775 and left widow, Elizabeth, who, later, married Solomon Nichols. Mrs. Elizabeth Nichols died 1796, and left property to her sons, John Renwick, James Renwick(alias Miller), and to her daighter, Agnes Renwick, A daughter, Ann, had married John Cary Royston, and she died in 1802. Another daughter, Elizabeth, made complaint in an equity suit, in the year 1813.

Rev. John Renwick (son of Rev. John Renwick, Sr.), died 1836. He married Jane Bothwell, widow of Rev. David Bothwell, a native of Monaghan, Ireland. In the settlement of the estate of Mrs. Jane Renwick, the following children are named: Ebenezer Bothwell, John W. Bothwell, James J. Bothwell, David E. Bothwell, William W. Renwick, Mary Ann Eliza Renwick, Rosannah H. Renwick, Martha J. Renwick (wife of James Clary). William W. married Elizabeth Abrams about 1810. He died about 1816, and left widow, and children: James A., and John S.

Dr. Nathan Renwick, also a descendent of the first John Renwick, at one time lived on Indian Creek, but moved to Georgia, thence to Alabama, Benton County, where he died.

RICHARDS-William Richards sold eighty five acres alnd in Newberry District in 1796 to Jonothan Pratt.

Joseph Richards died about 1804, in Newberry District. In the settlement of his estate no heirs are named.

RICHARDSON-Robert Richardson died in Newberry District about 1798, leaving widow, Mary, and children: James and Benjamin. James died 1815, not married. The widow, Mary, married John Reese who died in 1817. John Reese had a son, David, by a former wife.

Amos Richardson was a Rev. War patriot. He had a son, David Richardson. Benjamin Richardson married Sarah R. Vaughn, daughter of T. Drury Vaughn, and had a daughter, Elizabeth, and other children.

Peter Richardson died about 1812, leaving widow, Frances, and eleven children. The widow doed about 1816, leaving the following legatees: John, Sarah, Denominy, Keziah, Elizabeth. Administration was granted to George Smith. Peter had a son, Jonah, who died 1803, leaving widow, Lavania, and three small children, John, Hiram, and Jonah.

Daniel Richardson died 1813, and Administration was granted to his father, Daniel Richardson, Sr.

Other Pioneers (continued)

RICHEY—William Richey died in Abbeville District about 1782, leaving his father, Robert Richey, and his mother, Margaret Richey, a sister, Mary Richey, as his only heirs.
Robert Richey died in Abbeville District, leaving widow, Mary, about year 1825, and the following children: Margaret Seawright, William (died-his son Robert), Janette Seawright, Amy Brownlee, Elizabeth, Nancy Pousley, James, and Robert.
George Richey died in Newberry District, on Enoree River, February 15, 1852. He left widow, Melvina, and three children: Mary Jane, Melvina, Martha E. (all under 21 years old). The widow married Franklin Wilson on March 23, 1853; she was a daughter of Robert Hardy and Caroline Eliza Hardy (she died 1822). Robert McHardy was living in St. Augustine, Florida, when he made marriage contract with Caroline Eliza Williams, his second wife. (Note name is spelled, " McHardy" and place of " Hardy").

RIDDLE—William Riddle died in Lexington District about 1815, leaving widow, Janette, and children: Joice Sheppard, Honorias, Dicey G., Mahaliel, Jahajah, Napoleon B., Mary M., Drucilla, Simon P., Lewis. Lewis died in 1816, unmarried.

RIDDLEHUBER(RHIDLEHUBER)— William L. Rhiddlehuber died June 17, 1863, leaving widow, Mary M., and children: John J., Mary C., Amelia L., Martha J., Leonora, Mary M. The widow had an interst in the estate of her mother, Mary Ann Gallman.
Thomas Rhiddlehuber and wife, Elizabeth, sold land on Big Creek to Adam Bedenbaugh in year 1816.
John Rhiddlehuber made will October 13, 1849, which was proved in Court January 30, 1850. He left children: Elizabeth (wife of John G. Houseal), Polly (wife of Thomas Hoard Cromer), Louisa (wife of James Cromer), William L., Mary, Henry Walter, and Susannah Fulmer.

RHODES—Elisha Rhodes died in Newberry District about 1820 to 1823. The following distributees relinguished right of administration to Michael Rhodes on September 16, 1823: Eleanor Rhodes, T. Rhodes, Anne Rhodes, James M. Kilpatrick, Margaret Kilpatrick, and Temperance Kilpatrick. Jacob Rhoes died 1817, in Newberry District.
Absalom Rhodes died 1823 in Augusta, Georgia, leaving widow, Eleanor, and children: Aaron, Hiram, Nicholas, and Temperance.
William Rhodes doed about 1824 in Edgefield District, leaving widow, Elizabeth, and children: Jacob, John, and Elizabeth.
Laban Rhodes, Jr., died September 3, 1850, leaving widow, Margaret (Hipp) Rhodes, (she died November 7, 1857; was a daughter of Andrew and Nancy Hipp). His father was Jacob Rhodes, and his grand-father was Laban Rodes, Sr.

RHODLESPERGER (RIDDLESPERGER)— Peter Rhodlesperger, Sr. lived and died in Newberry District. He had a son, Peter, Jr., and, probably, other children.

RIKARD—Thomas Rikard (originally spelled, "Rathurst̄y̆) died about 1770, leaving the following heirs: William , Michael, Peter. They made a divison of their father's estate on June 3, 1771. Peter died soon after and left his share of the estate to his brother, Michael. Michael Rikard and wife, Elizabeth, convyed land on Cannon's Creek in 1778 to Michael Rikard, Jr.
George Rikard died about 1825, leaving property to children: Henry W., Christina (wife of David Halfacre), George A., Elizabeth (wife of John Riser), Peter (dead), Catherine (wife of Daniel Storie).
Mrs. Anastasia Rikard (widow of Laurence Rikard), made will April 9, 1810, and died same year, leaving children: John, Sr., Andrew, Jacob, Elizabeth Edwards, Ann, Mary Griffith, Barbara Setzler, Magdeline Williams, Anne Morgan, Catherine, Christina Riser, and Šarah Dailey.

RILEY—John Riley made will June 24, 1794, and died 1795, leaving widow, Rachel, and children: Zacariah, Jeremiah, Hesekiah, and Keziah (wife of ..... Thompson). Grand-sons named in will were: John Riley and William Riley (sons of Jeremiah Riley).
Mrs. Hannah Riley made will November 10, 1788, and died in 1790, leaving son, Thomas, and othe legatees, as follows: Jesse Graham, James Graham, John Graham, Joel Graham.
Andrew Riley made will 1847, and died about 1848, leaving widow, Mary, and children: John Rutledge, Dan Talbert, James Harvey, Robert Russell, William Newton, Mary Elizabeth, and Martha Jane.

Nicholas Ringer and wife, Sarah, were appointed administrators of the estate of David George, deceased, in the year 1797. John Ringer married Elizabeth, daughter of Martin Cromer, before the year 1820.

Other Pioneers (continued)

RISER—George Riser came from Germany before the Revolutionary War. His children were: Martin, John, George, Adam, Jacob, and, probably, others. Adam and Jacob moved to Mississipi. Martin Riser, Sr. was a soldier in the Rev War. He was married three times. His first wife, a Miss. Sease, had children: John, Martin, Eve, Christina, Elizabeth. His second wife, Christina Rikard, had children: Adam, George, Jacob, Mary, Harriet, Sallie, and Susan. His third wife, a widow, Mrs. Summer, had no children by him.

John Riser married Barbara Ann Zeigler, and had children: Lavania (wife of J. B. Kibler), George A., Ann C. (wife of A. W. Bundrick), Elizabeth (wife of Adam Berley), Adam, and James A.

RISH—Adam Rish sold two hundred and twenty nines cares land on Crim's Creek in 1810 to John Chapman, which was originally granted to Andrew Rish and Peter Stockman. His wife was Elizabeth..........

RIVERS—John Rivers died in Edgefield District about 1790. Some of his descendents, probably moved into Lexington District.

Nathaniel Rivers married Sucky Robertson, daughter of James Robertson, and had children: Irvin, Nathaniel, and others. They were living in Chester District.

ROBERTS—Thomas Roberts died about 1787 in Edgefield District, leaving children: William, Mary Justice, Elizabeth Upton, Thomas, Amon, John, Rebecca Nobles, Rachel Nobles, Absalom.

Thomas Roberts died about 1787-90 in Edgefield District and left widow, Mary, and sons, Jeremiah and Lee.

ROBERTSON—John Robertson, of Newberry District, married .... Bushardt. He died December 25, 1832, and left children: John B., William H., Warren, Sarah (wife of John Boyce). Children of Mrs. Sarah Boyce were: Elizabeth (wife of William G. Craig), Martha (wife of John Henderson), Nancy (wife of John Whitmore), Margery, Sarah, Robert, Harriet, and Lucinda Boyce.

Samuel Robertson died 1831, leaving widow, and the following children: John, Eliza, William, Rosa Ann (wife of James Burnett), and a daughter had died and left daughter, Jenny.

William Robertson (Robinson) died about 1808, in Laurens District, leaving widow, and the following children: John, Thomas, Isom, and Robert.

ROGERS—Daniel Rogers died about 1809 in Edgefield District, leaving widow, Mary, and children: Daniel, Hannah Melton, Elisabeth Nelson, and Susannah Reid.

Jacob Rogers, Jr. (of North Carolina), sold land in Newberry District in 1787. Stephen Rogers (of Cheatham County, North Carolina), sold land in Newberry District in 1785. John Rogers (son-in-law of William Sheppard), made a ten-year lease of land in 1824.

William Rogers, Sr. died about 1822, in Union District, leaving widow, Sibby, and children: Amy, Henry, Betsy (married.....), Ledford, James, Jesse, Joseph, William, Robert, Thomas, Magdelina(Molly) Jenkins. James Rogers died in 1836 in Union District, leaving widow, Martha, and children: Adam, John, James Dean, Sarah Jane, William Andrew. William Rogers died about 1838 in Union District, leaving thirteen legatees: Levi Rogers, William B. Stribbling, William M. Rogers, John Robinson, Green B. Rogers, Mary M. Rogers,(she was a minor).

Patrick Rogers died May 27, 1805, in Laurens District. He left children: John, Polly, Pollonas, and others. John Rogers died in Laurens District about 1828, leaving widow, Sarah, (she died 1832), and children: James L., Lucinda (wife of Thomas Brownlee), Tabitha Martin, and Jane.

ROOK—James L. Rook died July 8, 1850, in Newberry District, leaving widow, Mary, and one child, (the child was born after his death, named James).

ROPP—John Ropp lived in the Broad River section of Newberry County.

Henry Ropp died March 11, 1847, leaving widow, Polly, and children: Mary Anne, Arthur, Nancy (all under 21 years old).

Peter Ropp died in July, 1851, in Newberry District. His wife had, probably, died. The legatees were: Children, William, H., John W., George J., Anna (wife of John Koon), Mary (wife of David Rhiddlehuber), Jacob L. A deceased son, Henry, left children: Mary Ann, Samuel, and Nancy. Mrs. Winatha Ropp (wife of George J. Ropp), died April 11, 1856, leaving husband, and four small children, Nancy, Frances, Mary L., and George A. Ropp.

Other Pioneers (continued)

ROSS—Thomas Ross made will November 1, 1800, which was proved in Court March 25, 1801, and died in 1801. He left widow, Hester, and children: Thomas, Susannah, Mary, Elizabeth, and Jane.

James Ross made will October 12, 1822, which was proved in Court December 20, 1822. He left widow, Dorothy, and children; Nancy Rushton, Mary, Sarah, Willis, and Wiley. Exrs: William Rushton, Thomas Ross (brother), and Lewis Gwyn.

ROUNTREE—Dudley Rountree lived in Edgefield District. Jesse Rountree died about 1815 in Edgefield District, leaving descendents.

RUBLE—Peter Ruble made will October 24, 1789, and died about 1790. Children were: Samuel, Susannah (wife of William McDowell), Mary (wife of William Murdock), and Jane (wife of .... Lester). His father, whom he named in his will, was living in Frederick County, near Winchester, Virginia.

RUDD—Daniel Rudd made will March 22, 1856, and died in same year. His wife, Susan, (she was a Gillam), married, first, to Dr. William M. Moon, and had a daughter, Meredith E., who eloped in 1854 at the age of sixteen years, at the end of her school term, with Louis M. Gillam , a cousin.   Children by Susan Gillam were: Jonothan D., Wallace G., Sallie C., George H., and Robert B.   Robert B. was about five years old in 1856. Some of the Rudds moved to Texas.

RUSSELL—Andrew Russell, Sr. died May 26, 1832, in Newberry District, leaving widow, Jane, and children: Joseph (died October 18, 1836), Robert, William, Mary (wife of John Tolbert), Caroline (wife of ..... Spurlock), John (died before his father),and left children, Ersamus, Caroline, Andrew, James, Margaret. Some of these moved to Mississippi. Andrew Russell, Jr. died 1858 in Newberry County. His legatees were (children of his brothers and sisters): William, James, Ann (wife of R. Y. Brown); children of Robert; children of John; children of Mary Tolbert; Sarah Jane Blair, daughter of Jane Blair.

Robert Russell died in Abbeville District about 1825, leaving widow, Jane, and children: John, Robert, Jane (wife of John Brown); and other legatees, James and Margaret Smyley, Jane C James, William, Alexander, and John Richey. Mrs. Jane Russell died about 1833, leaving husband, James Russell, children: E. C., E. A., Mary, James C. Russell. Her husband died just previous to her death.

Matthew Russell died about 1813, leaving widow, Malinda, and children: Josiah, Osborne, Thomas, Elizabeth, David, Martha, Matthew, Sarah, James, Jane, and Linney.

SANDERS—William Sanders died in Edgefield District about 1816, leaving widow, Joanna, and one child. He had a sister, Martha Williams.

John Sanders, of Union District, conveyed to David Sims, of Newberry District, one hundred acres land between Broad and Tyger Rivers, being one-half of a tract which was granted to John Sanders and Nathaniel Henderson on May 28, 1798.

Michael Sanders, of Union District, died before 1805, leaving widow, Jane, and children.

Andrew Sanders died about 1841, in Newberry District, leaving widow, Temperance, and six children: Arnold, Jacob, Elizabeth, and others.

SCHAFFER—Frederick Schaffer came from Germany to America about 1750; landed at Savannah, Georgia, and later came to the Dutch Fork, in Lexington District, where he was granted fifty acres of land. He married Elizabeth............, and had children: Elizabeth (she married Peter Schumpert), and other children. He was a patriot in the Rev. War.

Phillip Scaffer died about 1793 in Camden District. He lived on Little River, in Fairfield County. He left widow, Maria Margaret, and children: Mary Scott, Maria Margaret Polick. MichaelScaffer received a grant of one hundred fifty acres land on Sleepy Creek, a branch of Savannah River. Later, he bought land in Newberry County, and removed to that section.

SAVAGE—Samuel Savage made will 1805, and died in same year, in Anneville District. He left widow, Frances, and children: Samuel, Frances Hearon, Elizabeth Lark, (she was the second wife of Cullen Lark).

SAWYER—George Sawyer deeded land in 1812, in Edgefield District, to his children, viz: William Early, Easter, Sebinah, Rachel, Elizabeth, Hellender, Nancy.

One George Sawyer , of Newberry District, left his wife, Elizabeth, and their children about 1807, and went to Alabma; children were: Elizabeth, William , Mary,   His wife was Elizabeth Stone before marriage.

Other Pioneers (continued)

Another George Sawyer, of Edgefield District, conveyed lands in 1832 to his wife, Mary; after his death, she deeded this land to their children: John V., Mary, George R., Lucinda, Deborah, Matilda Kinard, Stanmore, Hepsebah.

SAXON—Samuel Saxon was the Sheriff of Ninety Six District about 1780 to 1792. Altha Saxon died about 1817 in Laurens District, leaving widow, Susannah, and children: Noah, Lurana, Mary, John, Altha. He was a Rev. War patriot, and was pensioned as a Continental soldier.

Lewis Saxon died about 1813, leaving widow, Sarah, and children: Hugh, Allen, Polly, Joshua, Lydal, Tabitha, Susannah, Samuel, and Harriet. All were minors that year. Samuel died in 1831. He was Sheriff of Laurens County about 1800.

Benjamin Saxon made will January 4, 1784, and died 1785, in Abbeville District. He left widow, Elizabeth (Perry), and children: James, William, Samuel, John, Benjamin; and had a deceased son, and a deceased daughter who had married a Barksdale. Grand-children: Samuel Barksdale, Mary Saxon.

Charles Saxon, Sr. died in Abbeville District, but had moved to Laurens District. His will is dated June 2, 1816, and he died same year. His children were: Polly (wife of George Anderson), Sarah Rodgers, Lewis (his widow, Sally McNees), and probably others. Grand-son was Charles Saxon, Jr. who was named Executor.

SCHMITZ—Dr. Henry F. Schmitz was a German physician, and came with a colony to the Dutch Fork about 1750-60, and practiced his profession. He married Mary Leitner, a daughter of Major Michael Leitner, a distinguished patriot officer in the Rev. War.

John A. Schmitz lived in Lexington District. He and his wife, Mary Ann, conveyed land to their children in the year 1855. Children were: Henry, John F., Andrew Thomas, Sarah Caroline, Mary Catherine; and a step-daughter, Rosannah Schumpert.

Benjamin Schmitz died in Lexington District, left widow, Anna Katherine, and children.

William J. Schmitz executed a real estate mortgage in 1854 in favor of Andrew Sheely and John Sheely.

The name is supposed to have been changed to the English form , "Smith."

SCHOPPERT—George Schoppert lived and died in Newberry . The date of his death was about 1825. He left widow, Catherine, and a son, Phillip, and several daughters. George was a brother-in-law of Thomas W. Waters, and built the court house and jail (the first brick and stone edifices—now gone). He came from Maryland just after the Rev. War. Phillip moved to Alabama.

SCRUGGS—Jesse Scruggs was granted land in Edgefield District in 1786; and in year 1807 he and his wife, Easter, sold the land to Daniel Reid.

Allen Scruggs married Martha Graham, daughter of James and Nancy Graham. His brothers and sisters were: Clough, Sarah, Jane, James. His children: Joseph B., Micajah Suber, Allen Benjamin, Elizabeth, Caroline, Nancy, Gertrude, Francis B., Seth Ward, Annie Laurie(she married E. D. Andrews, of Greenwood, S. C.), These were children by his second wife, Mary Elizabeth Suber.

SEASE—John and Leonard Sease lived near Lexington and Newberry County lines. They sold lands in Newberry District about year 1795.

SEIGLER—Carrol Seigler arrived in America in year 1752, and settled in the Dutch Fork of Ninety Six District, where he received a bounty grant of two hundred fifty acres land. He had wife and three children in 1752, the children's names having been: Mary Margaret (age $5\frac{1}{2}$ years), Eva Elizabeth (age 4 years), John Carrol (age 2 years).

George Seigler married Caroline, daughter of Peter Felker and his first wife.

SENN—Matthias Senn died about 1827 in Newberry District, leaving widow, Christina, and children: Emmanuel, Rebecca, Harriet (wife of John Coppock), Martha, James M., John, and probably others. John died just before death of his father, leaving children. Emmanuel died February 8, 1843, leaving following brothers and sisters: Rebecca Boozer, Martha Dobbins. Rebecca Boozer's children were: Lemuel, David S., and Lavania. Martha Dobbin's children were: Francis S. and others.

John Senn, Sr. died May 2, 1845, leaving widow, Mary, and children: Jesse, David, Daniel, Zacariah, John M., William A., Mary J., Frederick, Selina Crumley. David died 1849, leaving widow, Margaret, and children: Rebecca (daughter by first wife, Sally), John Drayton (son by second wife), Sarah, Cornelia and Thompson, (children by thrid wife, Margaret).

Other Pioneers (continued)

SETZLER-George Adam Setzler, Sr. was born in Erbach, Germany, about 1760. He married in the dutch Fork of Newberry District to Ann Margaret Leitner, daughter of Major Michael Leitner, and had an only daughter, Elizabeth, who married Wiliam Frederick Houseal, Jr. George Adam was, probably, a son of John Adam Setzler, Sr. who came to the Dutch Fork from Erbach, Germany, about 1765, and received a grant of land located on Second Creek. His widow, Catherine, received the bounty in 1766. Another son, John Adam Setzler, Jr.lived in the same section.
John Adam Setzler, Jr. married Catherine Leitner, a daughter of Major Michael Leitner, and had children: Elizabeth (wife of Martin Suber), Eve (wife of John A. Hipp), Mary A. (died, unmarried), George A. (he married, first, Margaret Suber, and , second, to Shartel Suber, and, thrid, to Martha Metts), George A. and Margaret Setzler had children: Sarah E. and Mary Ellen.
Jacob Setzler died in 1812 in Newberry District, and left three children: John, Mary, and William.
John Setzler, Jr. died February 3, 1844, left widow, Mary, and children: George A. and Martha C. His wife was Mary Fike, of Newberry District.
SEYMOUR-Isaac Seymour, Sr. made will August 24, 1817, which was proved in Court August 2, 1819. He had a son, Isaac, Jr. who married Anne......... and had the following children: Robert Williams Seymour and Mary Anne Margaret Seymour.
SHEELY-John Sheely came to the Dutch Fork from Germany about year 1752. His son, John Windel Sheely, came with him, and other small children. John Windel married a daughter of John Adam Epting, one of the pioneers of the Dutch Fork, about 1770. They had several children. John Sheely, the pioneer, had children on his arrival in the Dutch Fork as follows: Barbara (age 14), Catherine (age 12), Ursula (age 9), Mary Ann (age 8), Windel (age 7), Marharet (age 6). John Windel Sheely had children: Adam, Christian, Matthias, David, Henry, William, John Wendel, Martin, Andrew, and, probaly, others.
SHELL-Stephen Shell was born in North Carolina ...., and died in Newberry District Sept 11, 1822. He left widow, Jane (Ellis) Shell, and children: Mary E. (wife of Daniel Lofton), George, Ira, Milly,(wife of David Yeargan), Susannah (wife of William William Brown),Daniel, Francis Asbury, and Lemmon . Exrs: Francis Asbury Shell (son), Herman Shell (brother). George married Sarah Lee Hearn. Ira married Nancy Heller. Milly married david Yeargan in 1808. Susannah married William Brown in 1812. Daniel married Mrs. Griffin. Another son, Stephen, Jr., married Elizabeth Howell. William and Susan Brown moved to Georgia; and had children: William, Lemmon Meredith, Stephen, Thomas, Ann Eliza, Susan, and Coleman.
Francis Asbury Shell married Mary J. Dugan, daughter of John J. and Nancy Dugan, and moved to Mississippi. Martha E. Dugan, sister of Nancy, married Coleman Bailey in 1817, and after his death she moved to Mississippi. They settled in Aberdeen,County of Monroe, Miss.
John Shell made will December 12, 1817, which was proved in Court on February 5, 1818. He left widow, Elizabeth, and children: John Ellis, Isham Malone Shell, Edmond, Sophia, and Drury I. Shell.
SHIRLEY-Thaddeus Shirley lived in Newberry District, on Enoree River, about 1790. He assigned all his interest in one hundred acres land which he inherited from John Roberts and wife, Sarah, in 1791.
SHOCKLEY- The Shockleyswere , originally, from Laurens District
SHULL-The Shulls were in early times in Lexington District. Henry Shull married Anna Roof, of that District.
SIBLEY-Joseph Sibley lived on Bush River, Newberry District. He died before the year 1828, and left children: James W., Harriet Henretta, Henry, Abigail. James W. Sibley since his father's death, and before year 1829, leaving widow, Nancy, and children: James, William , Martha. Harriet Henrietta married Reuben Watkins since the death of her father. Abigail married James R. Crispin.
SIEG-Samuel Sieg married Amanda E., daughter of George A. and Anna (Epting) Epting. He died 1871, leaving widow, Amanda, and the following children: Anna Rebecca, George David, Carlisle Samuel, (the last an infant child).

Other Pioneers (continued)

SIMPSON-William Sims died March 17, 1814, in Union District. He left two sisters to share his property: Isabella Means and Nancy Mayes (wife of Joseph Mayes); and two nieces, Margaret H. (wife of Pleasant Harris), and Mary Simpson Davidson (daughter of sister, Polly Davidson).

Perry Jackson Simpson died about 1861, and left widow, Rebecca, and son, John Alexander Simpson. His brother, Thomas Chaney Simpson died before his death.

SIMS-Matthew Sims died about 1795 in Newberry District, leaving widow, Jemima, and children: Hannah (wife of David Henderson), Drucilla (wife of ....Backley), Mary (wife of.....Sanders) Ann (wife of ..... Henderson), Charles, Matthew (married Mary......),Nathan (had died), James (had died), David, Reuben. Grand-children: William Sims and Sarah Shelton (children Charles), ... He left some of his land to children in Hanover County, Virginia, which had been given to his son, Nathan. The son, James, left widow, Elizabeth, who died in 1820, leaving children: Matthew, Nathan, Reuben, Drucilla Brazzleman; and whose grand-children were: Elizabeth, Dricilla, James, Nancy. James, the father and grand-fther, had died on November 27, 1794.

David Sims (son of Matthew,Sr), died about 1831, leaving children: Nancy (wife of Joseph Reid), Jemima Glenn (wife of Jethro Reid), David G., and James M. Sims.

Reuben Sims (son of Matthew, Sr.), doed about 1817, leaving widow, Nancy, and children: Drucilla (wife of John Lyles), Cicely, John S., Mary (married John Lyles after death of her sister, Drucilla), Elizabeth (wife of .....Crenshaw), Nancy (wife of .... Maybin), Charles (had died), and Jemima (wife of ....Thomas).

John Sims was living in Newberry District (then Ninety Six District) in 1770. He conveyed a tract of land in 1772 to Henry Butler.

Nathan Sims(son of James), died in Abbeville District in year 1803, leaving widow, Mary, and children: Amelia (wife of ....Griffin), Leonora (wife of ....Calhoun), Sarah (wife of ......Smith), Susannah (wife of .....Bond), Agnes (wife of ......Smith), Downes, Martin, John, George, Starling, Leonard, and William.

Patrick Henry Sims died about 1821, leaving widow, Lucy, and children: Mary (wife of Reuben Gilliam), Elizabeth (wife of William Kelly); and other children who were minors at time of his death, William, Anna G. (wife of Samuel O. Gordon), Bernard, James, Reuben T., and Jenny.

SLIGH-Ulrich Sligh (Sleight) came to America in the ship Crimless, sailing from Rotterdam in 1752. He brought with him his wife and four children. Children were: Creda (age 15), Eve Catherine (age 18), John Jacob (age 5), Margaretta (age 3), He received a grant of three hundred acres land in the Dutch Fork.

Nicholas Sligh settled on land in Newberry District (then Ninety Six District) before the Rev. War, located on Cannon's Creek. He made will September 27, 1790, died about 1791, leaving widow, Catherine, and sons, John and Jacob. Exrs: Phillip Sligh, John Livingstone, Jr. and Jacob Buzhardt.

Phillip Sligh, Sr. lived on Cannon's Creek. He married Christina Kinard, daughter of Martin Kinard, Sr. He was born 1755 and died 1818. His wife was born 1761 and died 1846. Children : Phillip, Jacob, Mary (wife of Phillip Buzhardt), Elizabeth (wife of Jacob Buzhardt), Catherine, Sarah, and David; and George who had died in 1816, leaving no family.

Phillip Sligh, Jr. was born 1792 and died 1883; married Elizabeth Eichleberger who was born 1800 and died 1883. They had no children but reared an adopted son, George A. Counts.

Jacob Sligh was born 1812 and died 1846. He married Miss. Peaster, and had children: George P., and others. George P. Married Josephine Maffett.

SLOAN-Samuel Sloan made will December 11, 1851, which was proved in Court January 26, 1852. He left widow, Agnes, and children: Archy, James, Mary Caldwell, Jane Franklin, John, Samuel, (the last two were his youngest sons).

SMITH-George Smith received a garnt of land on Second Creek in year 1769. He left widow, Mariam, and children: John (married Jane.....), Susannah, and others.

Thomas Smith lived in the Dutch Fork of Newberry County. In 1807 he conveyed lands to his sons, George and William; and in 1812 , lands to his wife, Mary. He died about 1812, leaving to his widow, Elizabeth, and children certain property. Children: Margaret (wife of Obediah Jones), Elizabeth (wife of Joshua avis), and William.

Other Pioneers (continued)

Matthew Smith died about 1819, leaving children: Karen-Happock (wife of Daniel Livingstone), Mary (wife of John Schumpert), Rachel (wife of......Singleton), Littleton, and Luke.

Nathaniel Smith died about 1833, leaving widow, and following children: John, Elizabeth, and Littleton,

Jesse Smith and wife, Mary (Fish) Smith; John Johnson and wife, Hannah (Fish) Johnson; John Parrott and wife, Ruth (Fish) Parrott; conveyed lands in 1801 to John Graham.

William B. Smith lived in the Saluda River section of Newberry County. He had a daughter who married Josiah W. Beard, whose son, William B. Smith Beard, died about 1847.

Laurence Smith died about 1797 in Newberry District, leaving children: Nancy. Elizabeth (wife of John Cole), Linney, Susannah, Thomas, John, Mary, and Fanny.

Robert Smith died about 1817, leaving widow, Stacey, who died in 1818, and a son, William R. Smith.

Mrs. Esther Smith (widow), made will September 19, 1818, and died about 1822, leaving children: Sarah (wife of John Speake), Alcey (wife of Joseph Smith), Elizabeth (wife of Killian Allen), Mariam (wife of Gabriel Anderson), Jared, John, Sarah. Jarded Smith, Sr. made will November 16, 1825, and died December, 1825, leaving widow, Mary, and a daughter, Sarah, and a sister, Alcey, as his legatees.

Mrs. Ursula Smith, widow of Robert, married James C. Vaughn who had died in 1868 leaving one child by her, Pope B. Vaughn.

William Smmth, of Union District, died about 1796, leaving widow, Anne, and children: John, Patsy, Solomon, Catherine (wife of Nathan Langston), Polly (wife of Bennett Langston), Milly (wife of William Edwards), Elizabeth (wife of William Parker), Nancy (wife of John Smith), Nancy Ann (wife of William Smith), Martha (wife of Stephen Layton).

One Archibald Smith and his brother, John Smith, came to Laurens District about 1800 or few years later from Somerset County, Maryland.

SMYLEY-John Smyley, Sr. came to Newberry District from Colleton District. His son, John, was born near Cannon's Creek on July 16, 1783, and died September 7, 1849, at Pleasant Hill, Alabama. He is buried in the Presbyterian Churchyard at Pleasant Hill. The son married Rebecca DeWalt, daughter of Daniel and Nancy (Gray) De Walt, who, too, moved to Alabama.

SMYTH-Andrew Smyth died in Newberry District about 1798, leaving widow, Elizabeth Ann Smyth. They probably had children.

SONDLEY-Richard Sondley made will November 3, 1823, which was proved in Court October 13, 1828. He left widow, Sarah, and children: George, Richard, Betsy McCollom, Sarah (wife of Robert Anderson). George died November 13, 1847, leaving widow, Martha, and children: Narcissa (wife of George Anderson), Susannah, William, Sarah. Virginia, David. George and Narcissa Anderson moved to Talledega County, Alabama.

SOUTER-Martin Souter died about 1802 in Newberry District, in the Dutch Fork section. He left widow, Anna Katherine, and children: Henry, Jacob, George, Anna, Catherine, and Elizabeth.

SPARKS-George Sparks made will in 1796, and died same year, leaving property to the use of his sister, Rachel Bicknell, in North Carolina; until his son, Reuben Sparks, became of age.

SPEAKMAN-William Speakman made will February 15, 1786, which was proved in Court September 6, 1790. He left widow, Mary, and children: Margaret (wife of John Callahan), Elizabeth (wife of John Welch), Robert, Christiana, Mary, William, Thomas.

SPEARMAN-Thomas Spearman made will October 23, 1794, and died about 1800, leaving widow, Margaret, and children: William, Elizabeth (wife of William Powers), John, James, Mary wife of Samuel Yeargan), and Edmund. They were children by his first wife. Children by his second wife, the widow, were: Sara Rutherford Spearman, Robert Smith Spearman, Samuel Dishman Spearman. Other legattess named in settlement of estate were: Ann Shelton, Wesley Spearman, Thomas W. Spearman, John Atkinson, Jane Spearman.

Edmund Spearman died about 1827, and left widow, Susan, and children: Peggy (wife of Charles Floyd), Mahala (wife of Robert Floyd), Thomas, John, Edmund, Nancy, Laurence. Mrs. Susan Spearman moved with some children to Alabama.

SPEER-William Speer, Sr .(1747-1826), married Martha........ and had children: Alexander, John, William, and Margaret Rucker. The widow died about 1835 in Anderson County, S. C.

Other Pioneers (continued)

Robert Speer (or Speers) lived on Little River, Newberry County. He married and had the following children: Andrew, David, John, William, and Robert.

David Speer married Margaret Gillam and had children: Robert, Jane, John, Andrew, David. He died about 1815, and his widow married about 1816 to Thomas Archibald.

Robert Speer (son of Robert), of Newberry District, died October 19, 1822, possessed of much property, of which Mary Wagner, of Monroe County, Alabama, was entitled to a share. She appointed Robert Evans of Newberry her lawful attorney, year 1827. Robert had married Mary Barton and had children: Elizabeth (wife of David Stephens), Samuel, Jesse, Mary Wagner, John, and Nancy. Samuel married Lydia Evans and had son, John. Jesse married a young lady of the Quaker section, near Bush River, and moved to Alabama, then to Ohio. Nancy married Alexander Jay and moved to Ohio. Mary Wagner had a daughter, Malinda, who married ..... Garner.

John Speer (son of Robert Speer, Jr.), was born about 1796, and died in Tennessee about 1826. He married Frances McTeer who was born 1781, and died in 1847. They went, first, to Shelby County, Alabama, then to Wayne County, Tennessee.

Samuel Speer (son of Robert, Jr.), married Lydia Evans.

SPENCE—William Spence, native of Ireland, came to the eastern section of Newberry District (then Ninety Six District), before the Rev. War. He brought with him his father, Andrew Spence, and two brothers and two sisters. ("Annals of Newberry", Part 11). The brothers were, James and Samuel. Samuel married Mary Gregg. James was a patriot officer in the Rev. War, a Captain of a militia company. He married Elizabeth Cannon after the war, and had sons, William Harrison Spence and Milton Spence, and, probably, other children.

James Spence, Jr. died about 1820 in Newberry District, leaving widow, Martha, and children: Elizabeth (wife of Robert Caldwell), Agnes (wife of Hugh Wilson), William, John, and Wilson. Wilson Spence married Mary.......... His wife died in May, 1836, leaving children(by a former marriage with John Rhame); Elizabeth (wife of Samuel McKie), Margaret (wife of Halditch Hipp), and John Rhame, Jr.

STEADMAN (STEDOM)—Henry Steddom conveyed land in Newberry District about 1798, which was, originally, granted to Mrs. Mary Steddom on April 9, 1768. Henry married Martha........ Mrs. Mary Steddom, the widow, married Samuel Pearson, a Quaker on Bush River.

John Steadman died about 1797 in Abbeville District. Judith Steadman married Benjamin Worthington about 1795.

STEARLEY—George Stearley lived in the Dutch Fork of Newberry District. He died soon after the Rev War, leaving widow, Mary Ursula, and children: George, Jacob, Elizabeth Catherine. The widow afterwards married Rev. Frederick Joseph Wallern, a Lutheran Minister of the Dutch Fork. George Stearley died about 1835, leaving widow, Permelia, and children: Benjamin, Elizabeth, and Joseph. The widow married William Robe in 1839. Catherine Stearley, daughter of George Stearley, Sr., married George Long, Sr., and had children: Jacob, George, Jr., Joseph, Elizabeth, Mary, Catherine, and Sarah.

STEEL—John Steel owned lands on Cannon's Creek in 1776. He and his wife, Ann, sold their home tract to Patrick Riley in year 1801.

Samuel Steel came from North Carolina before the Rev. War; lived short time in Newberry District; then moved to Ohio where he served as a patriot in the Rev. War. One of his sons, Joseph, who was born in Ninety Six District (Newberry County section). moved to Buncombe County, North Carolina. He had married Janette Taylor in Newberry.

Mrs. Janette (Knox) Steel, daughter of John Knox, conveyed land, with her son, John Knox Steel, to James Dixon on January 4, 1802.

STEEN—John Steen married Margaret Vance and lived in Union District before year 1800.

Gideon Steen married Neomi Townsend and lived in Union District.

STEPHENS—John, David, and Edward Stephens lived in Newberry District. Mrs. Elizabeth Stephens died about 1822, the wife of John Stephens. Edward Stephens and wife, Elizabeth, conveyed land in 1820. David Stephens and wife, Elizabeth, conveyed land in 1813. Elizabeth Stephens conveyed land to her son, David, in year 1804.

STILL—John Still died about 1797 in Edgefield District. He left widow, Jane, and children: John (married Susan Malone), Thomas, Dorcas De Loach (he died before his father), Hannah Flannagan, Sarah Youngblood, Mary Cockroof, Lettice, David, Benjamin, Joseph, Jolly, (the last four named were under 21 years old in 1797.)

Other Pioneers (continued)

STOCKMAN—Henry Stockman made will Spril 4, 1828, and died same year. He left widow, Nancy, who died in 1833. Their children were: John Peter, Elizabeth (widow of Henry Kinard), Anna (wife of David Kinard), George A., John H., Mary (wife of Thomas Rikard), Margaret (wife of John Zeigler, both dead). Thomas and Mary Rikard left children: Elizabeth (wife of Sherard Smith), Anna (wife of Andrew Calhoun), Susan, Martha, Levi Harris, and Mary Ann. John Zeigler and wife , Margaret, had a daughter, Margaret.

STODDARD—Robert J. Stoddard married Frances Du Pre (she was born 1847). Mary Ann Dansby married ...... Stoddard (she was twenty three years old in 1858). She was the daughter of Ivey and Elizabeth Dansby, of Newberry District.

STONE—John Stone died about 1828 in Edgefield District, leaving widow, Elizabeth, and children: Elijah, Lydia, and Edy (a daughter)....

Chaney Stone married before the year 1832 to Elizabeth, daughter of Nathan and Catherine Langston, of Spartanburg District. They had children: Sarah Ann, Simpson, Eliphas, and Martha.

STRIBLING (STRIPLING)—William Stripling married Mary Taylor, daughter of Benjamin and Elizabeth Taylor, of Newberry District. They were married previous to the year 1820, and lived on Little River.

STROTHER—Jeremiah Strother married in Virginia to Eleanor......... Their son, George, married in South Carolina to Catherine Kennerly. Their grand-son, William Strother, married Joyce Sheppard.

William Strother made will May 16, 1779, which is recorded in Richland County Court House. He left children: Kemp T., and Catherine (only children named in will). Catherine married in September, 1783 to Andrew Lester. Andrew Lester having died in 1795, his widow married in 1798 to Samuel Nelson.

John Strother , of Edgefield District, married Temperance Pope, daughter of Solomon Pope, before the year 1794.

SULTON—Michael Sulton, who lived in Lexington District, married Elizabeth Bickley. Their children were: Kezia (married Drayton Epting), Nancy (married Henry Metts), and others.

SWANN—John Swann made will March 7, 1796, which was proved in Court March 28, 1807. He left widow, Rebecca, and children: Mary, Timothy, Ann, and Barbara.

SWINFORD—Samuel Swinford died about 1809 in Newberry District. He left widow, Sarah, and children. Isaac Swinford died in Newberry District, leaving legatees: Levi and Sarah Swinford. Legatees receipts show the following: Rachel Swinford, John Swinford, Sarah Swinford, and Sevier Swinford.

John Swinford, Sr. gave his son, James, in 1814, about fifty one acres land ; also, to his son, Isaac a tract of land; and to a son, Levi, and his wife, Betsy, a tract of land.

Phillip Swinford and his wife, Dorcas, lived in Newberry District. After his death, his widow married ....Richey.

SWITTENBERG—Abraham Swittenberg and wife, Anne Catherine, conveyed land on Crim's Creek in year 1792 to Peter Stockman.

John Swittenberg made will November 9, 1867, and died November 22, 1867, leaving widow, Nancy P., and children: William C. (born May 3, 1851), Ellen O (wife of William J. Waters), Mary C., and Lilla B. Executor: John Hillery Sligh.

TAGGARD (TAGERT)—William Taggard, Rev. War patriot officer, a Second Lieutenant in the Regiment of Colonel Thompson, lived in Newberry District, near Broad River.

John and James Taggart (probably sons of William) moved to Abbeville District.

Moses Taggart was the Ordinary of Abbeville District about 1840-46.

TARRANT—Leonard Tarrent first settled in Greenville District, having come from Virginia. His will is dated February 23, 1791, in which is named his wife, Mary, and children as follows: Benjamin, Leonard, Samuel, Nelly, Roalnd, Elizabeth Kirby, John, and James.

Rev. Benjamin Tarrent, Jr. (1767-1820), had son, John Robert, who lived in or near Greenwood, South Carolina. John Robert married Elisabeth Mitchem Marion and had sons: Rev. Benson R., Marion, and Sumter. Sumter was killed in the War Between the States.

Leonard Y. Tarrant moved to Marion, Alabama, with his wife, Elisabeth (Griffin) Tarrant, whom he had married on September 16, 1835.

Other Pioneers (continued)

TALBERT-William Talbert died about 1789 in Edgefield District. He left a family. Michael Talbert was born 1799 in Edgefield District, and died 1822 in Tennessee. He married Mary Truett who was born in 1807 and died 1877.

TATE-Henry Tate married Celia, daughter of Reps Edwards and moved to Indiana.

TAYLOR-William Taylor (1747-1836) lived in Newberry District; married Janette...... and had children: Janette who married Joseph Steel, and others.

William Taylor, who lived on Bush River, made will Ovtober 10, 1781, whith was proved in Court March 4, 1789. He left widow, Mary, and children: Samuel, Jonothan, Martha, and Prudence. Jonothan made will 1795, and died same year, leaving widow, Mary, and children: William, Richard, Jonothan, Isaac, with wife of John Thomas, Ann Chandler (her sons, Jonothan and Israel Chandler), the wife of Richard Leavell, and the wife of Joshua Reeder.

Benjamin Taylor died about 1819, leaving widow, Elizabeth, and children: John, Anthony, George, William, Elizabeth, Fanny, Nancy (wife of John Edwards).

John Taylor married Lucy Hill, daughter of Thomas Hill. He died 1824, leaving widow, Lucy, and four children: Milton, Thomas Jefferson, George William, and John Travis Taylor.

TEAGUE-Joshua Teague made will May 12, 1804, which was proved in Court May 2, 1808. His children were: Elisha, Israel, William, Abner, Isabel Mason, the wife of William Gray, Sophia Lyon, James, Susannah Major, and Mary M. Adams.

Abram Teague died November 20, 1831, in Newberry District, leaving widow, Nancy, and children: Lucinda (wife of James Leavell), James, Eliza (wife of Jospeh Garner), Hannah (wife of Daniel Buzhardt), and Charles. Lucinda Leavell had children: Sarah (wife of Hillery Pitts),Rebecca (wife of William Souter). Eliza Garner had children: James Pinckney and Abram Teague Garner. Hannah Buzhardt died and left one child, Mary E. James E. Teague moved to Anderson County, Texas. James P. Garner and J. J. Garner moved to Pontotac County, Mississippi. James Leavell moved to Pontotac County, Mississippi.

Joshua Teague (son of Elijah, Sr.), died about 1817, leaving children(or legatees); Isaac Teague, Hannah Teague, Jehue Pitts, Elijah Teague, Abram Teague, Thomas Goggans, and James Smith.

James Teague died 1817 in Newberry District, leaving widow, Elizabeth, and children: Dorothy G., Davis, John W., William J., and Ann M.

TEMPLETON-David Templeton ,Sr. died in 1817, in Laurens District. He left children: James, David, John, Robert, William, and probably others. Some of his grand-sons were: David and Robert Hanna.

Aaron and James Templeton owned lands in Luarens District before year 1810. John Templeton lived in Luarens District, and married Mary Burke, daughter of James and Barbara Burke, and had children: James, Barbara, John T., Mary (wife of Joseph Garrett), and William C. Templeton.

James Templeton died in Luarens District about 1824, leaving widow, Jane, and children: John, Samuel, Mary, Jane (wife of John McDowell), and David C. Templeton.

TERRY-Joseph Terry', of Pittsylvania County, Virginia, died about 1785, leaving children: David, Thomas, Joseph, Anna (wife of Beverly Barksdale), Lucy Williams, Elizabeth Oliver, and a son, Champness. Grand-sons: Thomas (son of David), Dr. Crawford Williams (son of Lucy Williams),and .... (some of these lived in Greenville District).

Stephen Terry died in Edgefield District in 1837, leaving children: Stephen, Jr., James, John, Susannah. Children of James were: Rchard E., William, Thomas, Ann (wife of James Meggs), James, Hilliard J., Samuel C., Susana,Frances A., and Moses.

THOMAS-Nehemiah Thomas made will May 15, 1796, and died same year, leaving widow, Abigail, and other legatees as follows: Nephews, James Dobbins, John Dobbins, Edward Thomas (son of brother Edward in North Carolina), Thomas Johnston, Nehemiah Mills (son of Thomas Mills, the blacksmith), Nehemiah McKensey (son of George McKensey), Sarah McKensey (wife of George McKensey), Sarah Mills (wife of Thomas Mills).

James Thomas, Sr. died 1825 in Newberry District, leaving widow, Polly, who died in 1840, and left the following children: David Betsy Justice, Sucky Adams, Polly Toland, William (he died in 1827, not married),Stephen (he died in November, 1828, leaving widow and one child), Olive Long, James (he died in 1836).

Other Pioneers (continued)

James Thomas, Jr. died about 1836, leaving widow, Elizabeth, and children: Francis, Laura, Sarah. The widow married Samuel Sheppard about 1838.

Edward Thomas died August 9, 1840, leaving widow, Elizabeth, and children: Precious,(wife of Franklin Fuller), Timothy, Mary Ann, Sally (she died unmarried), and John.

David Thomas died about 1828, in Abbeville District, leaving the following distributees : Thomas, William, John Thomas; Jane (wife of Moses Hughs), Peggy (wife of Samuel Thompson), Elizabeth (wife of Daniel Malone), Harriet (wife of William McCree), Karen-happock (wife of Henry Ammons).

THOMASSON-George Thomasson died in Laurens District before 1835, leaving widow, Elizabeth, and children: Sally (wife of William Willis), James, Washington, George, Nancy, John, William, Polly, Mahala, and Elizabeth.

THOMPSON-Joseph Thompson died in Newberry District about 1795. Charles Thompson died about 1817, leaving widow, Nancy (Gray), his second wife. Children by first wife were: James, Abram, Joseph, George, Charles, and Esther. Henry Thompson died about 1850, leaving widow, Catherine, and their children: Thomas Jefferson, Mary Jane, (wife of George Boyd), Jacob, , Lavania, Sarah C., and John G. John Thompson made will August 24, 1817, and died 1817, leaving widow, Sarah, and children: Henry, Baker, William, Jason J., Samuel, Elvira, and Julia Ann.

John Thompson made will December 28, 1780, and died about 1782. He left widow, Ann, and children: Richard, Ephriam, Andrew, John, William, Mary, Margaret, and Ann.

Joseph Thompson made will September 21, 1813, and died in Miami County, Ohio, leaving children: Richardson, Jane, (wife of Levi Hilburn), Mary (wife of William Jenkins), His grand-children named in will were: Ann, Mary,Sarah (daughters of a deceased son, Jospeh, Jr.); and Sarah McKensey, who married ..... Mills.

James Thompson married Rachel Glasgow in Newberry District. She died leaving three children: Elizabeth Louisa, Robert C., and Glasgow, who inherited part of the estate of their grand-father, Robert Glasgow, deceased. James Thompson moved to Tennessee about 1837.

Robert Thompson, of Virginia, married Cynthia Merryman, of Cumberland County, Virginia, in year 17.... (she was a daughtter of Jesse Merryman). They came to Union District, South Carolina, and settled. Their children were: Nancy (wife of Robert Tate), Henry, Hobson, Elizabeth (wife of Joseph Slappy), William, Mary, Nathaniel, and Martha (wife of Ellis B. Gresham).

THORNTON-Abraham Thornton died about 1797 in Edgefield District, leaving widow, Elizabeth, and children: Samuel, Thomas, William, Eleanor, Rachel, Abraham. Thomas died in 1822.

TIMMERMAN-Jacob Timmerman died about 1826 in Edgefield District, leaving widow, and several children.

TINNEY-William Tinney made will November 29, 1807, which was proved in Court December, 1807. Matsilvia, and sons, Isaac and Ricahrd.

Richard Tinney made will May 10, 1812, which was proved in Court November 27, 1820. He left widow, Ruth, and son, Isaac, and others.

TINSLEY-James W. Tinsley , son of James Tinsley, a Rev War patriot, was Tax Collector in Newberry several terms. He was a grand-son of Col. James Williams, who was killed at the battle of King's Mountain, in the Rev War.

TODD-David Todd died about 1816 in Newberry District. He left widow, Grrissey Todd. William Todd died in Abbeville District about 1822, leaving widow, Elizabeth, and children: Archibald, William, Tirzia, Mary Ann, and Sereny. The widow, Elizabeth, died about 1855, leaving the following children as her legatees: Mary Ann Eddings, Elizabeth Eddings, Harriet Eddings, Rebecca McCrackin, James McCrackin. Grand-sons: William Childs(son of a deceased daughter, Sarah Childs).

TOLAND-Mrs. Mary Toland died in October , 1858. She was the widow of John Toland. She left children: Joseph, Dr. Hugh H., John S., James J., Sally Belton, Malinda Cameron, Mary Renwick (wife of Col. John S. Renwick), Elizabeth Boyd, Caroline Price. John S. Toland left the State. Dr. H. H. Toland attended Medical Lectures, Louisville, Kentucky. He studied, also, in Paris, France. He became a successful physician in Newberry County, then moved to Columia, S. C., thence to California, where he died about 1885 or '86.

Other Pioneers (continued)

TOWLES- One genealogical record gives the name, Stokely Towles, who died in Virginia about 1765, and that three of his sons, came to South Carolina, who were: Oliver, John, and Stokely.
John Towles was a Rev War patriot. He lived on Tyger River, Newberry District, where he received a grant of two hundred acres land in 1768.
Stokely Towles (son of Stokely), died in Abbeville District about 1784, leaving widow, Martha, and small children: John, and others.......... He received a grant of one hundred acres on Turpin's Creek, branch of Saluda River, in 1774.
Oliver Towles (son of Stokely), was killed in the Rev War, in 1781. He was in the Third South Carolina Continental establishment as Lieutenant, then as Captain. He was prisoner for fourteen months, after the Fall of Charleston, before he was released. He left widow, Jane, (she was mother of his children), who died in Newberry District in 1826. Their children were: Daniel (oldest son who served as a private in the Infantry during the Rev. War), John, Elizabeth, Tabitha. John died early and left two sons, James and John. Tabitha married ..... Goodman, and left children: Daniel Goodman, and Tabitha Lindsey (wife of Caleb Lindsey). Elizabeth married Rutherford Boulware of Edgefield District. Daniel Towles (son of Captain Oliver Towles), married Cynthia Burton, daughter of William Burton, Sr. and wife, Phoebe Burton.
Seth Towles died in Edgefield District. Oliver Towles, Jr. died in Edgefield District, and left widow, Mary, and children: Susan E. (wife of R. M. Scurry), Mary O. (wife of Pickens B. Weaver), Eliza, and Ralph. He was the Ordinary of Edgefield District about 1840. He left to his heirs eight hundred fifty acres land, called "Half-way Swamp". His widow died in 1857.
TUCKER-Joseph Tucker died in 1803 in Union District. His widow, Lucy, made will August 6, 1817, and died about 1820, leaving children: Robert, Joseph, Lucy Wright (she had died), Peter, Polly Wright, Frances, Elizabeth (wife of Henry Buford), and Oliver Hardy Tucker. Exrs: Samuel Hardy and Nathaniel Sims. Joseph Tucker died about 1826, leaving widow, Fanny, and children: James A., Mary, Nancy Brock Tucker, George Buford Tucker. The widow died about 1858. George Buford Tucker died about 1804, leaving widow, Elizabeth. Captain William R. Tucker (son of Joseph and Lucy Tucker), died about 1815, leaving widow, Mary, and bhis mother, Mrs. Lucy Tucker. His widow died in same year.
TURNER-William Turner came to Newberry District about 1752, and settled on Little River, where he received a grant of land. His death occured about 1776; and his widow died about 1811 leaving children: Edward, Mary Edwards, Elizabeth Stephens, Deborah Cook, and Priscilla Long(wife of Benjamin Long). Three sons had died before she made her will in 1811.
John Died in 1809, leaving widow, Fanny, and children: Polly (wife of David Peterson), John (died 1809, soon after his father),William who left a widow; and Mary (Houston) Mitchel Richard left a widow, Mary(she later married .... Barrett), and two small children. Another daughter married Michael Abney. A grand-son, William Turner, lived in Edgefield District, where he married Susannah..........
Thomas Turner made will November 9, 1793, which was proved in Court April 24, 1798. He died 1798, leaving widow, Sarah, and children: William, Absalom, Jesse, Jeremiah, David, John, Paky, Elizabeth, and Patsy.
William Turner made will December 30, 1789, and died 1790, leaving children: William, Rebecca, Rhoda, Edward, Basalom, David, Susannah, and Ann. David died about 1825, and left no familly.
William Turner, of Newberry District, died December , 1825, leaving widow, Mary, and children (by his only wife): Rebecca, Nancy, and another daughter who was the wife of James Williams, Wesley, William, and Thomas.
Thomas Turner, of Luarens District, made will January 13, 1807, which was proved in Court October 20, 1823. His widow, Abby, survived, with following other legatees: Elizabeth Reynolds as Administratrix of estate, Chambres Turner, of Green County, Alabama: a nephew, Tandy Griffin, who was to receive all property after death of widow, Abby.
ULRICK—John J. Ulrick lived awhile in Newberry District, He married Anna, daughter of George and Elizabeth Keller. His wife died before 1835, leaving her husband and the following children: Hiram B., William, and Elizabeth Keller. Mrs. Elizabeth Keller , widow, married Jacob Lohner; and she died in March, 1830.

Other Pioneers (continued)

USERY—Thomas Usery came from North Carolina to Newberry District, where he died about 1830. He left a daughter, Elizabeth, who married Williamson Baker, and, probably, other children.

VANCE—Samuel Vance, of Ninety Six District, South Carolina, was born about 1753, and died in Laurens County, South Carolina. He married Mary McTeer, daughter of William and Frances (Griffin) McTeer. Their children were: Samuel, William, and others. Samuel, Jr. married Sally Hampton, and had children: Lucinda (born 1810, married 1837 to Thomas J. Wilhoite, in Culpepper County, Virginia), and others.

William M. C. Vance died April 7, 1836, leaving widow, Elizabeth, and ten children as follows: Carr E., Caroline (wife of Henry Meetze), Frances (wife of Elihu Alton), William L., Martha A. (wife of John J. Hill), John B., Eliza A. (wife of Thomas A. Rudd), Jane E. (wife of Archie Clark), Susan C. (wife of Richard S. Satterwhite), and Washington (he died 1839, not married).   Carr E. Vance died in April. 1850, and left widow, Elizabeth, (she married later, to Joseph P. Summer), and the following children: Sarah E., Samuel K., and Carr E. Samuel and Carr E. moved to Louisiana. Eliza A. Rudd died about 1850, and left children: Carr F., Elizabeth, and Eliza A. (she died when young). Another son, Nathaniel Vance, had died about 1812, leaving widow, Mary Vance.

VARDEMAN—William Vardeman came from Pennsylvania with his family before the Rev. War. He settled near Hunting Fork, between Enoree and Tyger Rivers. He made will February 4, 1783, and died about 1788, leaving widow, Bridget, and children: John, William, Peter, and James. James inherited the home plantation at Hunting Fork. Some of the other sons moved to Georgia and Alabama.   James sold his lands later, so it is, probably, he, too, went to Alabama.

VAUGHN—John Vaughn (Vann) died about 1779 in western part of What is now Newberry County, near Saluda River, leaving his widow, Elizabeth, and children. His widow died 1792, and left property to the following children: William Dodgen, Ollimon Didgen, James Dodgen, Elizabeth Cole, and a grand-daughter, Ann Noland. These were the widow's children by a former husband.

Nicholas Vaughn came to Ninety Six District about the time of the Rev. War. He was a tavern keeper, and was afterwards elected Sheriff of Newberry District. He had sons by his first wife, as follows: James, T. Drury, and Wlater. His sceond wife was Nancy Lee, widow of Andrew Lee, of Lee's Ferry on Saluda River. Nicholas died about 1803 and the following were his distributees of his estate: T. Drury Vaughn, James Vaughn, Walter Vaughn, Russell Vaughn,....

T. Drury Vaughn made will 1844, and died about 1845, leaving children and grand-children. The children were: James C., Sarah R. (wife of Benjamin Richardson), Behethlehand (wife of .....Hill), Elizabeth C. (wife of James Richardson),   Grand-children were: Walter, Nancy (children of James and Elizabeth Richardson),Frances (daughter of Behethlehand Hill), Drury V. Scurry, Drury T. Vaughn (won of James C. Vaughn). T. Drury Vaughn's wife was Elizabeth.......

James C. Vaughn married Ursula Smith (widow), and died about 1868, leaving one son by this marriage,(his second wife,) Pope B. Vaughn. He had by his former marriage two sons, Edward P. and Drury T.   Edward P. died June 6, 1858, leaving widow, Frances H., and children: James T., Drury T., and Mary E.

VESSELS—Charles Vessels , Rev. War patriot, at one time lived near Augusta, Georgia. His son, Shadrach Vessels, was killed at the battle of Fishing Creek, leaving two sons, James and Shadrack; and another son, Charles. Charles Vessels, Rev War patriot, had another son, Charles; his wife having been a daughter of William Farr, of Union District.

James Vessels married Susan Lyles , in Newberry District, and had children : James, Phoebe, Sammie (wife of Gideon Jackson), Lyles, Ephriam, John, and Thomas. Some of these children located in other States.

VOLUNTINE (VALENTINE)—John Valentine was in Newberry District during the time of the Rev. War. He had four sons and four daughters, as follows: John C., Benjamin, Dr. Thomas, Rebecca (she married (1) .... Stack, and (2) .... Johnson), a daughter who married .... Whitmire, another daughter who married ...... Hatton, and a son, Zacariah, and another daughter.
Benjamin married Martha........   John C. was born 1780; married Ruth Rebecca Gordon, a grand-daughter of Major Thomas Gordon, an officer in the State Militia during the Rev. War. Zacariah died about 1828, leaving legatees: Thomas L., Sarah F., John S., and Margaret C.

Other Pioneers (continued)

VOSS—Joseph Voss made will August 1, 1812, which was proved in Court November 2, 1812. He left widow, Rebecca, and children as follows: John, William, Charlotte.

WADLINGTON—Thomas Wadlington, Sr. moved from Virginia to South Carolina about 1767; he settled on Enoree River, with four sons: Thomas, William, Joseph, Edward. William left a son, James, who married 1820 to Ann Bauskett, daughter of Thomas Bauskett. James died 1831, leaving one son, Thomas B., and a daughter, Caroline.

Thomas B. Wadlington marriet Harriet Sondley who died early, leaving no children; and died 1882. His sister, Caroline, married Col. Ellison S. Keitt, of Orangeburg District in 1853. (Ref: "Annals of Newberry",)

Edward Wadlington made will December 24, 1790, which was proved in Court May 16, 1791. He died about 1791, leaving widow, Frances, and children: Sarah Ann, Jesse, Bailey, John, Spencer, and Nancy.

WALDROP—John Waldrop made will June 27, 1794, which was proved in Court October 20, 1794. He left widow, Tabe, and children: Ezekiel, David, Esekiah, Stephen, William, Isaac, John, Ann, Elizabeth, Tabe, Judey, Christina (she married .... Pitts), and Sarah (she married..... Campbell).

James Waldrop made will May 25, 1798, which was proved in Court July 30, 1799. He left widow, Mary, and children: John, David, Solomon, Samuel, Richard H., James, Elijah, Elisha, Abraham, Isaac, Mary (married.... Pitts),Nancy (married .... Pitts), and Reta.

Samuel Waldrop (son of James), made will August 7, 1799, which was proved in Court 1799. He left widow, Susannah, and a child, Patsy. His wife was pregnant at time of his death; she was a daughter of James Davenport.

Elisha Waldrop (son of James), made will July, 1809, which was proved in Court 1809. He left widow, Phoebe, and chilren.

Elijah Waldrop (son of James), made will February 1, 1813, and died about 1820, leaving widow, Jemima, and several children.

WALKER—Joseph Walker died about 1818 in Newberry Districtm leaving widow, Sarah, and children: John G., Robert C., Mary (wife of William Morris), and Mararget Ann who went to Bedford County, Tennessee.

Mrs. Janette Walker, of Newberry District, died about 1795. She made will June 6, 1775, leaving a legatee, John Kinard (and his heirs).

John Walker, Sr. died 1810; and John Walker, Jr. died 1806; both in Edgefield District.

William Walker died about 1817 in Laurens District, leaving widow, Elizabeth, (she died about 1819), and children: Ann (wife of Beufort Powell), Elizabeth (wife of Jacob Otter), John, Elijah, Elisha,William South, Jr., Daniel Ford, Samuel Phifer, Robert Freeman. All of above named as widow's legatees in 1819, except Ann Powell and Elizabeth Otter, who are named as daughters of testator.

John Walker, of Laurens District, made will May 23, 1829, which was proved in Court February 2, 1840. He left widow, Kitturah, and children: Allen, Francis B., Hogan, Azariah. Elizabeth Shaw, Patsy Milam, Deborcah Wilcox, Emily Langston, and Emoline Walker.

WALL—John Wall died about 1840, in Edgefield District. Some of his family moved to Laurens District.

WALLACE—John Wallce, Sr. died about 1800 in Newberry District, leaving widow, Amy, and children: Elizabeth Payne, John, James, William, Joseph, and Frances. He lived on Goose Pond Creek, near Mudlick Creek.

William Wallace made will January 25, 1813, which was proved in Court August 2, 1819. He left widow, Mary, (she died about 1822), and children: Henry (married Tabitha.......), Howell, John, Ruth, Hugh, William. Henry died July 8, 1820, and left widow, Tabitha, and children: Allen, William Robert, Roderick, Benjamin, John, and Martha Elizabeth.

Hugh Wallce (son of William), died March 6, 1825, and left no family. His property was bequeathed to his brothers and sisters and their children. Ruth is named as wife of John Jamison. William was dead, but his children were,. Robert, Mary, and Margaret (wife of George Foster Wells). Howell was dead, but his widow, Elizabeth, and children, Mary and Howell, shared in estate. Other children of William Wallace not mentioned in his will, but named as sisters of Hugh, were: Winnie (wife of David Boazman), Mary (her children, Hugh Wallace, Catherine Brown, Winnie Brown), Margaret (her child, John Lindsey), Elizabeth (her child, Willis Wallace), Frances (her children, Edmund Brown, Lucinda Brown, Matilda Brown).

Other Pioneers (continued)

John Wallace (son of William), moved to Green County, Tennessee. Winnie Brown (daughter of Mrs. Mary Brown), married February 4, 1830 to Henry Thompson while living in Newton County, Georgia. A certificate of marriage is filed in Newberry Court House, dated Feb 1, 1830 or '39, signed by Rev. Jesse Stanselle, Minister of the M. E. Church, of Newton County, Georgia.

William Robert Wallce (son of William), died about 1816, leaving widow, Frances (Gillam) Wallace. The widow married John Jamison about 1818. She had four children by William R. Wallace, and one child (Francis Wallace Jamison) by her second husband.

Joseph Wallace (son of John), died Janury 25, 1825, leaving widow, Rebecca, and children, Sarah and Willis. The widow married Daniel Williams in 1827. She died 1829, leaving husband and child, Sarah Wallace. Willis was a son by a former marraige.

Elizabeth Wallace married David Boozer, and died leaving folloing legatees: Mary E. Wallace, John P. Boozer, Frances Caroline Boozer. (Frances Caroline died June 9, 1834).

Jonothan Wallace was born in Virginia, moved to the sectoon of what is Luarens County before the Rev. War. His son, General Daniel Wallace, a lawyer of Union, S. C., was famous during the "Wallace House" regime in the South Carolina legislature. General Daniel Wallace married Elizabeth Davis of Greenville District. Their son, William Henry, was Judge of the Circuit Court and member of the State House of Representatives. He (William Henry) married Sarah Dunlap of Newberry, a daughter of Robert Dunlap, Sr. Her brother, James, was appointed Governor of Florida by President Andrew Jackson. (Ref: "Encyclopedia of Eminent and Representative Men in the Carolinas".)

WARD-Samuel Ward, of Amelia County, Virginia, died December 25, 1806, leaving widow, Susannah, and children: Patsy (wife of Peter Ligon; married 1808), Seth (age 17 years in 1813), Sally (age 15 years in 1813), Judah (age 13 years in 1813), Susannah (age 13 years in 1813), Prudence (age 11 years in 1813), and Eliza (age 8 years in 1813). The widow, Susannah, moved with her family and her brother, Thomas Ligon, to Laurens District in 1809.

WARDLAW-Many of the family lived in Abbeville District. John Wardlaw, Sr. died about 1791 in that district, leaving widow, Lydia, and children: James, Samuel, Hugh, Mary, Lydia Heard, Peggy, Hannah, Nancy, Betty, Isobel,(she married ..... Heard), Andrew.

Joseph Wardlaw died about 1795 in Abbeville District, leaving widow, Agnes, and children: John, William, Alexander, James, Mary, and others. The widow, Agnes, died 1795.

One Joseph Wardlaw and his wife, Mary Ann, moved from Laurens District to Lauderdale County, Tennessee.

WARE-The name is sometimes spelled, "Wier". Robert Ware died in Edgefield District about 1818, leaving widow, Peggy, and children: Nicholas, Sarah Harris, Lucy Bacon, Robert, Thompson, George, Susannah Barksdale, Joseph (he died before 1818), Henry (married Amelia Jones), Peggy Merriwether, Lucinda Carson, (she was a widow in 1829).

Mrs. Jane Ware died about 1832 in Abbeville District, leaving children: James, William, Robert, Nancy. Grand-daughter: Jane Ware.

WATKINS-Andrew Watkins died in Newberry District about 1824, leaving widow, Katherine (Adams) Watkins, and children: Daniel, Louisa (wife of John Wiseman), Lavisa, Andrew, and Margaret (she died unmarried). Mrs. Katherine Watkins died about 1836.

James Watkins married Nancy Taylor, daughter of Benjamin and Elizabeth Taylor. They moved to Georgia in 1827.

Robert Watkins died about 1828 in Abbeville District, leaving five children: George, Alfred, Robert, Augustus Lyric and Augustus Peyton. George was granted land in Lauderdale County, Alabama. His brother, John, was an executor of his will.

WATSON-John Watson died about 1791 in Edgefield District, leaving widow, Anne, and children: Jacob, Arthur, William, Charity Anderson, Ceale, Martha, John, Lucretia (she married ...Jones) Willis Murphry. His lands included part of the lands of Captain Michael Watson, deceased. Arthur died 1806, leaving widow, Richmond, and children: Hezekiah, Abner, Fanny, Patience (wife of John Eidson), Lyda Warren, Abraham, Arthur P., and Absalom.

John Watson, Sr. died in Newberry District about 1849, leaving a son, Thomas.

Elijah Watson, Sr. died about 1841 in Edgefield District, leaving widow, Chloe, and children: Chloe Ann (eldest, not 21), Michael, Artemus, Tillman, Stanmore, Elijah, Sophia, Sarah Raiford.

Other Pioneers (continued)

WATT—Samuel Watt, Esq. died about 1802 in Abbeville County, leaving widow, Janette, and children. He sold to Peter Perkins of Pottsylvania County, Va. two hundred fifty acres land on Woolney Creek, South fork of Saluda River, in year 1797, which was granted to him on July 16, 1785.

Mrs. Janette Watt, of Abbeville County, made will dated 1805, and died same year leaving children: Samuel Lesly, Nancy, Jane, Rosa Anne Bowie, Polly, and Elizabeth. Her nephews were: John Bowie, and Samuel Watt Bowie. Other legatees named were: Janette Lesly Miller, and Peggy Miller. Executors: James Wardlaw, Esq., James Kyle, and Andrew Bowie.

Samuel Watt (born Aug. 22, 1787 and died May 14, 1823), married Mercy Rice on Jan. 28, 1808. They moved to Alabama.

James Watt, of Anderson County, died about 1835. He left widow, Mary, and children: Thomas, Samuel, Robert, John (dead), and William (dead). John left widow, Molly, and children: Peggy (wife of Kelly Sullivan), and others. James died and left widow, Rachel, and children: John, James, Andrew, Dudley, Nancy, Peggy (wife of John Stephenson), Samuel, Thomas, and William. William died and left widow, Jane, and children: Peggy, Joseph, Rachel, Jane, Martha (wife of William, Henderson), James, and Mary.

James Watt, Jr. died about 1830 in Anderson County. Nancy Watt made affidavit in Murray County, Ga. appointing Andrew W. Watt her attorney in fact.

WATTS—Major Richard Watts made will dated Nov. 15, 1813, and died in Feb. 1814, leaving widow, Janette M., and brothers and sisters as legatees, viz: George, James, John (dead), Nancy Carson, Fanny Whitworth, Children of John Watts were: Buford T., Braxton, John P., Louisa, Narcissa, Cornelia, Elvira, Margaret, Matilda Vaughn, Eliza (wife of John C. Waters). Fanny Whitworth died and left children: Nancy (wife of John Smith), Elizabeth (wife of John Craddock), Sindney (wife of Willis Brown), Isaac, Higgerson, Cynthia, Susan (wife of Sidney Craddock), John T., and Richard.

Mrs. Janette Muir Watts (widow of Major Richard Watts), died in April 1827, leaving property to her nephews, Patric McDowell and James McDowell; and to her nieces, Sarah C. Black, Harriet Caldwell, Charlotte McDowell, and Agatha McDowell. Also, property to her two grand-children: James Caldwell and William Caldwell.

Major Richard Watts was Sheriff of Newberry County from about 1790 to 1795.

John Watts (brother of Major Richard), died in Laurens County in 1812, leaving widow, Peggy, and children (see names above),

James Watts died in Laurens County in 1843 and left legatees: Elihu C., Priscilla (wife of Robert Griffin), James, John, Narcissa (wife of Samuel Goodman), Elizabeth (wife of J. Chapman), William D., wife of T. Spearman, and wife of C. Sprowles.

Richard Watts married in 1826 to Mrs. Mary Chappell, widow of Charles B. Chappell.

Robert Watts died in Edgefield County in 1839. He left legatees as follows: Benjamin Watts of Chatham County, Ga. Jane W. Joyner (a niece of Wilkes County, Ga.), and another niece, Mary Roberts. He was buried, at his request, in his native town, Savannah, Ga. in the family grave-yard.

William Watts died about 1836. His legatees were: Temperance Watts (his widow); and his children: John, James, Eliza (wife of Thomas D. Howard), and Thomas. The widow and her son, Thomas J. Watts, were living in Columbus County, Alabama, in year 1855.

David Watts and wife, Latisha, deeded land to John Edwards, including two hundred fifty acres on North side Saluda River, in the fork of Little River and Saluda, originally given by will of William Turner, to his daughter, Mary Edwards.

Mary F. Watts married about 1846 to John I. Watts. She was under age, and Benjamin F. Paysinger was appointed her guardian in 1848.

WEDAMAN—Peter Wedaman made will dated April 15, 1837, proved in Court, May 1, 1837. He left ch: Christopher, Rebecca (wife of William Elmore), Elizabeth (wife of John Boozer), Mary (wife of Joel Griffith), Nancy (wife of David Morgan), Barbara (wife of Peter Walden). Gr-daughter: Dolly Chapman. Daughter-in-law: Margaret Wedaman.

Elijah Wedaman, of Dutch Fork, Newberry District, married Mary M. Cromer, daughter of John Frederick and Barbara Cromer.

WEEKS—William Weeks died about 1792 in Newberry District. Exr. of his will was Mercer Babb.

Other Pioneers.

He left ch: John, Hannah, William, Benjamin, and James. There may have been other children. He left no will—only legatees receipts for shares in their father's estate.

James Weeks died about 1815. No distributees named in settlement of his estate. Some left Newberry County.

WELCH-Isham Welch (A Quaker) moved from Frederick County, Va. to Iredell County, N. C. He married Sabriah Williams, of N. C. Their son, Williams Welch was born in N. C. in 1802. The son moved to Newberry District, S. C. and died. Williams married 1827 to Mary Crozier Glasgow (1812--1851), and had four sons to serve in the Confederate Army. Mrs. Mary Crozier Glasgow was a daughter of Archibald and Mary (Spencer) Glasgow.

WELLS-Humphrey Wells lived in Newberry District, between Little River and Saluda River. He married Rebecca Goodman, daughter of Timothy Goodman. They had children. A son, Daniel (he was nephew of Thos. Stark), owned land on Headley's Creek, Newberry District.

Mrs. Abigail Wells conveyed land in 1813 to her gr-gr-daughter, Rebecca Wells, daughter of Humphrey Wells. She died same year, leaving ch: George, Samuel. Left sister: Esther Smith.

David Wells was born in 1772, and lived to be 100 years old. He married Barbara Hiley.

George Wells, Sr. died 1839, leaving widow, and following ch: Abner, George Foster, Sarah Payne, Livingston, Horatio N. Wells. gr-ch: Julia Ann, Elijah, Mary Lockhart, George, Susan, William, John W., and Margaret.

George Foster Wells died 1867 leaving widow, Margaret (she was daughter of William Wallace who had died before 1825), and a son, George Foster Wells, Jr.

Livingston Wells died 1836. He was son of Geo. Wells. He left his estate to brothers and sisters, viz: George F., Sarah Payne, Horatio N. (to his dau. Fanny). Sarah married Elihu Payne. Horatio had two daughters, Frances, who married John B. Boazman and Mary Teresa who died in Jan. 1835.

John W. Wells died March 2, 1854, leaving property to his brothers and sisters, as follows: Julia Ann (wife of Joseph White), Mary (wife of James E. Lockhart), Susan (wife of Daniel Procter), Margaret (wife of Wilford F. Peterson), George Foster, Elijah, and William A. Wells.

Joseph Wells married Margaret.......... (probably in Pa.) A daughter Rachel married John Wright and moved with Quakers to Camden District, thence to Newberry District where they joined the Bush River Meeting. Some of their descendents later went to Ohio.

WEST-William West was the earliest known settler in Ninety Six District, S. C. He lived in the section of Edgefield and died in 1780, leaving widow, Mary, and children as follows: William, Thomas, James, Martha Cox, Nancy, Sarah Leopard, Elizabeth Allen, Betty, Priscilla, Patience, John, Joseph, Jacob. Executors: Jesse Allen and Charles Leopard.

Isaac West (son of William West of Va.), came to South Carolina and settled in Laurens District, married Mary Payne. Their children were: Isaac, James, Jacob, Jonothan, William, Thomas, Annie, Prudence, Susan, and Mary.

Joseph West (son of William), made will April 17, 1821, and died 1821 leaving widow, Sarah, (who died in Nov. 1828), and children as follows: Arthur, William, Nancy (married Andrew Jones), Elizabeth (married Stanmore McDaniel), Martha (married Thomas E. Norris), Sarah (married Andrew H. Patrick), Joseph, and Mary. Other legatees were: Andrew H. and S. S. Patrick (sons of Andrew and Sarah Patrick), Adam Le Gronne, and a nephew, John West.

William West (son of Joseph), died about 1833 in Edgefield County. Adm. granted to Arthur West.

John West married Mary Arnold in Laurens County.

Berry West died about 1825 in Laurens County, leaving children: George Berry, Sarah, and John. They moved to Monroe County, Miss.

Thomas West died anout 1816 in Edgefield County. Adm. granted to Daniel Arnold.

Jacob West died about 1818 in Edgefield County. Adm. granted to Joseph and Rachel West.

Walter West made will dated March 27, 1807, and died March 29, 1807, in Newberry County, leaving widow, Elizabeth who died in Nov. 1823. Their children were: Benjamin, John, Joseph (he died early), James, Elizabeth (wife of Sampson Wood), Katy, and Walter (he became 21 years old in 1822). Executors named: James Johnson and Benjamin Johnson.

Benjamin West died about 1820 to 1823 and left widow, Eleanor, and children: Polly, Elizabeth, Dennis, and James T. All children died young except Polly.

Other Pioneers.

Thomas West married Margaret Aaron (widow of Jacob Aaron of Edgefield). She died 1817 and left children by Thomas West as follows: William, Thomas, Sarah, and Elizabeth--all minors.
John West (son of Walter), married Polly..............
Alexander West, Jr. died about 1817 leaving widow, Sibella, and children: John R., and Rachel R. Rachel R. West married about 1835 to James Busclark of Anderson County. Mrs. Sibella West, widow, relinquished her right of Administration to John King.
Sibby West died about 1829. Adm. granted to Dr. James Kilgore.
Alexander West and wife, Hannah, conveyed lands on Beaver Dam Creek, Newberry County, to William King in year 1806, said lands bounded by lands of Robert West, John O'Neall, and Henry O'Neall. He sold sixty acres on Hall branch, Bush River, in 1823, to Peter Hawkins.
Robert West and wife, Elizabeth, conveyed land to Jesse Dobbins in year 1809, on South side of Bush River.
Jacob Sherman West, an orphan not yet 14 years old in year 1819, Geral W. Johnson was appointed guardian of his person and estate.
Almerian West died in Newberry County May 17, 1855. Adm. was granted to Josiah Stewart. His wife, Olive West, died in 1849. They left two infant daughters, Nancy Amanda and Susan Frances.
Dr. Jacob S. West married Laura De Walt, daughter of Daniel De Walt, and they moved to Polk County, Texas— were living there in year 1859.
Mrs. Drucilla (Lindsey) West died and left children: Young L., John, Elizabeth (wife of Abram Gilbert), and Jacob Sherman West.
Robert West died 1827, in Newberry District. Left widow, Mary, and ch: Sion, Arthur, Dicey, Cornelius, Elizabeth (wife of Solomon Smith), Kittrena (wife of Mathias Vaught), Robert, Mary (wife of Wm. McClaney). Gr-son: Simon West.
WHIPPLE-Dr. Israel Whipple lived in the Indian Creek section of Newberry County. He made will dated September 11, 1825, proven in court Sept. 19, 1825. He left property to the following legatees: Elizabeth Harrison, on condition she will not marry a oree, a Pearson, nor a Mann; Elizabeth Oxner; Letty Dawkins: Catherine Oglesby; and Charles Rabb.
WHITMAN-John Whitman died about 1825, in Newberry District. Adm. of his estate was granted to Christopher Whitman on Feb. 24, 1826. Distributees named: John, Elizabeth, Eliza A., Temperance, Nancy, and children of a deceased son (Elizabeth Spearman, Sarah Oxner, and Margaret T. Whitman).....
WHEELER-George Wheeler, Rev. War patriot, was born in the Dutch Fork, Newberry District. He married Barbara Addy and had ch: John, George, Simeon, Jacob, Polly. John and George died young. Simeon married (1) Elizabeth Mayer, and (2) to Elizabeth Shealy. Children by first wife were: Mary (wife of Levi Boland), Elizabeth (wife of Frederick Fulmer), Children by second wife were: Michael, D. Henry, Simeon, Jacob, Levi, and George.
WHELCHEL-Francis and John Whelchel, brothers, lived in Edgefield District. Francis married Judith David, and John married her sister, Abigail David. They both served as patriots in the Rev. War. After the war they moved to what is now Cherokee County, South Carolina. Their father, Francis Whelchel, Sr., and their mother, Mary (Waters) Whelchel, both died in Cherokee County.
WHITE-Isaac White died 1801 in Union District, leaving widow, Mary, and ch: Sarah Smith, Elizabeth Jane, John (dead), Hannah Palmer, Isaac, Thomas, Isbell Cooper. Isaac, Jr. died 1826, leaving widow, Juley, and ch: Jeremiah, George, Hulda, Elvay, Nutty, Sophia.
William White died Jan. 22, 1819 in Union District, leaving widow, Nancy, (she died about 1818—20), and children: Coleman, William, Polly (wife of Zepheriah Holes), Nancy (wife of Allen Warnock), Sarah (wife of Aaron McCollum), Susan (wife of Thomas Hart), Isaac, Hannah (wife of John Stribbling).
William W. White (son of William who died 1819), died March 9, 1862 in Union District, leaving widow, Sophia, and ch: Francis M., Adolphus C., O. P., Henry R., Margaret M. (wife of Charles E. Fowler), Orrie (wife of David Orr— she died Oct. 1862); R. M. (died, not married); Elliot (died July 21, 1854) who left widow, Mary, and children: Shelton, Elizabeth, and California. Elizabeth (daughter of Elliot), married James Lancaster. Shelton died before 1864. Mary (wife of Elliot) died Nov. 19, 1867. California was 15 years old in 1854.

Other Pioneers.

William White, Jr. died 1830 in Union District, leaving widow, Elizabeth, and ch: Sarah, James, William, Lucy (wife of Javan Barnett), Samuel, Jane (wife of Johnson Coggins), Susan (wife of William F. Coggins), Rachel (wife of Javan Barnett), and Elizabeth.

Thomas White (son of Isaac), died 1804 in Union District. He left children: Meadow (born 1804), Fanny (she married since year 1804 to David Hiatt), and Jane Haynie.

John White died about 1805 in Union District, leaving ch: Henry, David Smith, Ann, Mary, and Elizabeth.

John White died about 1833 in Union District, leaving widow, Sarah, and ch: Mabry, John, Thomasson, and others. His widow died 1838.

David White died about 1834 in Newberry District. Admr. of his estate was John Plant— granted Jan. 26, 1835. His widow was Lovinsky White. Brothers and sisters: Robert White, Wm. White, Jane (wife of John Phillips), Catherine (wife of James Brown). Son, William, died before 1844, leaving widow, Frances, and several children, on being son William G. White.

James White died in Laurens District about 1817, leaving widow, Elizabeth, and several children, whose names not given in settlement of estate.

Richar White, Jr. died after 1847, in Union District, leaving widow, Mary (Fowler) White, and a brother-in-law, Stephen Fowler. His widow died in Dec. 1861, leaving brother, Stephen, and three sisters, viz: Sarah Hames, Milly Millwood, Elizabeth Bently. Her other legatees were: Children of Ellis Fowler, decd—Henry, Elbert, Julia (wife of Wm. Sprouse), Mary (wife of Newton Lipsey); Children of John Fowler, decd—Thomas, Charity (wife of Wm Fowler), Rebecca (wife of Felix Burgess); children of Lydia Hames, decd—Coleman, Frank, WilliamP., Joshua, and Mary Dunoway.   (From Court Citation dated 1865)......

William White died 1799 in Edgefield District, leaving widow, Susannah, and ch: Henry, Betsy Pollard, Mary Lilley, Patty Wilson, George, Sukey, William, Sarah, Tabitha, Charles, Richard M.

William White, Jr. died 1806 in Edgefield District, leaving widow, Sarah, and ch: Alexander, Fuby Sims, Joseph, Mary, John, Amos, and Anthony.

Nathan White died about 1816 in Edgefield District, leaving widow, Rebecca, and ch: Nathan, Mary, and Jacob Miller White.

Burgess White died in Edgefield District about 1830.

Stephens White died 1803 in Union District, leaving widow, Agnes, and ch: Catherine (wife of Thomas Hanna), Hugh, Alexander, James, John, and Margaret (wife of James Gaston).

WHITMIRE-William Whitmire lived in Newberry County. He made will dated Aug. 20, 1831, proved in court Feb. 1, 1841. He left widow, Sarah, and ch: Nathan, Charity, Jesse, Ruth, Joseph, Henry, Jackson, and Thomas.

Frederick Whitmire, pioneer, lived on land where town of Whitmire is located.

Mrs. Phoebe Whitmire died about 1836. She made will dated Sept. 6, 1835, proved in court Oct. 19, 1836. Her brother, John, and a sister, Caroline, (both under 21 years old), were named in her will.

John Whitmire married Nancy Boyce, a daughter of John and Sarah (Robertson) Boyce, of Laurens District, before year 1832.

WHITTEN-Robert Whitten was granted 320 acres land on Duncan's Creek, Newberry District in 1789. He conveyed 175 acres of this tract to John Whitten in 1793.

Moses Whitten died Sept. 1, 1823, leaving widow, Martha, and ch: Stephen, Mary (wife of Reuben Rogers), Tina (wife of John Davidson), Sarah (wife of John Whitten), Martha (wife of Thomas Jeans), Basdel, Rachel, Netty, and Elvira. Stephen moved to Tennessee. John Davidson and wife, Tina, moved to Kentucky.

Mrs. Sarah Whitten (widow of John), died June 23, 1838, in Newberry District. She left a daughter, Nancy Whitten.

Ambrose Whitten died about 1791 in Newberry District. Admr. of his estate was Elijah Whitten

WILKINS-John Wilkins died about 1818 in Laurens County. Adm. granted to Alexander Wilkins.

Robert Wilkins, Esq. died about 1848 in Spartanburg County, leaving widow, Tempy, and children. A daughter, Mary Roland, had died. Executors: William M. Wilkins and J. R. Wilkins

William Wilkins and wife, Elisabeth, of Spartanburg County, sold lands in year 1803 including two hundred acres on the ridge between Thickety Creek and Pacolet River.

Other Pioneers.

William Wilkins, of Union County, moved to Rutherford County, North Carolina, and died there about 1850, leaving widow, Jane, and children as follows: Sophia, Elizabeth, Mary, Minerva, William, Lamont, Lewis, Martha, Robert, James, Charles, and Eugenia.

WILKINSON-John Wilkinson, Sr. made will May 13, 1795, and died same year, leaving children as follows: John and Sarah.

WIMBERLY-William Wimberly died about 1802-04 in Edgefeield District, leaving widow, Elisabeth, and children: John, William, Sarah, Elizabeth, and Ezekiel Winn.

WILLIAMS-Daniel Williams who died in Hanover County, Virginia, about 1732, and his wife, Ursula (Henderson) Williams, were said to have been ancestors of the familiy of Col. James Williams who moved to South Carolina. Col. James Williams, an officer in the American Army during the Rev. War, was killed at the battle of Kings Mountain, N. C.

Some of the children of Col. James Williams were: Daniel, Joseph, John, James, Mary, (she was wife of James A. Williams), Elizabeth, (wife of James Tinsley), Sarah, (wife of John Griffin).

John Williams, brother of Col. James, moved to North Carolina, and then to Laurens District, South Carolina, where he became a member of the S. C. Provincial Congress.

James Williams, of Newberry District, died about 1832, leaving widow, Rebecca, and children: Permelia (she was an only child by his first wife, who died unmarried); and children by his second wife (the widow), were, George W., Mary Ann (wife of Weeks Pippin), Patsy (wife of Hillery Tolbert); and grand-children were, James Bullock and Rebecca Bullock (children of a deceased daughter, Elizabeth Bullock), Mary Coleman, Eugenia Poole(these two were by a daughter, Sarah, wife of Abram Poole), James Lipscomb and Thomas Lipscomb (children by a deceased daughter, Rebecca, wife of John Lipscomb).

Daniel Williams, Sr. made will December 15, 1823, and died in 1825, leaving widow, and children: Frances Leavell, Anne Neel, Daniel, Sarah, and others.

(Daniel Williams, son of Col. James, was killed in the Rev. War).

Daniel Williams, of Edgefield District, died about 1822, leaving widow, Permelia, and children: Reames M., William B., Anderson J., John, and James.

Washington Williams made will April 19, 1829, and died same year, leaving widow, Sarah (Griffin) Williams, and children: John D., James Griffin, Margaret, Lucy (wife of Drayton Nance), Nancy (wife of John Watts, Jr.), Caroline (wife of James Creswell), and another daughter.

Mrs. Katy Williams died on Bush River about 1820, leaving children: John, Polly (wife of Richard T. Cannon), Caroline, Elisabeth (wife of John S. Carwile), Nancy (wife of James W. Tinsley), Katy (wife of Thomas Gary). A grand-son, John W. Cannon, son of Sarah, the first wife of Richard Cannon. Mrs. Katy Williams was the widow of Stephen Williams who died 1803.

Nathan Williams made will March 31, 1795, and died 1796, leaving widow, Sarah, and children: John, Patience, and an unborn child.

Joseph Williams died about 1803 in Laurens District, leaving brother, Davis Williams, and Nephews, Williamson Williams (son of Samuel), Takey Williams, (son of Nancy), Joseph Farrow.

Mrs. Frances Williams (widow of one John Williams), had previously married a Gary, and had a son, George W. Gary who died in August 16, 1840. George W. Gary left widow, Lucrectia, and no children named (his widow was seventeen years old). Her husband, John, died about 1825, leaving his widow and two children: Catherine (she married John G. Burton), and Elizabeth Frances.

Providence Williams, Sr. made will February 2, 1813, and died about 1817-'18, leaving widow, Rachel, and children: Sarah Neel, Elizabeth Dalrymple, Abigail, John (he had died before father), Stephen, Rebecca Cole, Patience McAdams, Mary Gary, Obedience, Aquilla, Job, James, and Eleanor. These were bu a first wife, Anne or Elizabeth Gary, daughter of Thomas Gary, Sr. The son, John, left children: Ephriam, Providence, Thomas, Blanche. Mrs. Rachel Williams was the widow of William Cole when she married Providence Williams.

Providence Williams, Jr. died about 1837, leaving widow, Mary, and children: Elizabeth P., John, Rebecca, Drucilla A., George. The widow, the mother of the children, died 1847.

Mrs. Phoebe Williams died about 1827, leaving children: James, Delilah Parham, Sarah Rogers, and a deceased daughter who was wife of John Durham, Fanny (she had already died), who was the wife of John Moore. John Moore and wife, Fanny, had children : Alexander, Catherine, Sarah, and Henry W. Moore.

Other Pioneers (continued)

Davis Williams died about 1853 in Laurens District, leaving children: Elizabeth A. Miller, Samuel M., Henry R., Joseph H., Leonard, Robert H., Ephriam, Williams A., James H., Frances (wife of R. W. Clary), Mary (wife of William F. Metts).   Cildren of R. W. and Frances Clary were: Nancy E., Mary Alice, Jane Emoline, and James Clark. William A. Williams had graduated at the South Caolina Military Academy at Charleston, S. C. James H. Williams was a student in medicine at the Charleston Medical College.

Cary Williams died about 1826 in Newberry District, leaving widow, Phoebe, and children: Cary (he was born after his father's death), and other children (named above).   The widow married Christopher Griffin in 1828.

Hopkins Williams died about 1800, in Newberry District, leaving widow, Nancy,(she died soon death of her husband), and left two children: John Hopkins and William. William died 1829 leaving widow, Margaret, and three children, Frances, John Belton, and Nancy Clementine. William had an older child by a former marriage, named Sena Williams.   John Hopins Williams(son), made will April 3, 1871, and died about 1874 or '75, leaving children: James W. (married Kitty Marshall), Robert G., and probably others. He left grand-children named in will, as follows: William A. Williams, Eliza Foster Williams; and a great-grand-son, John William Davenport(son of a grand-son, Napoleon B. Davenport).

WILLIAMSON-John Williamson was granted land in Ninety Six District (now Newberry County) before the Rev. War, which he sold in 1797 to James Williamson; one hundred acres on Saluda River.

Robert Williamson married Matilda Goggans, daughter of Daniel Goggans.

Humphrey Williamson made will March 31, 1812, which was proved in Court September 11, 1812. he died about 1812, leaving widow, Elizabeth, and children: Humphry, Neely, Henry.

Thomas Williamson died about 1841 in Laurens District, leaving widow, Jane (she died next year), and children: John, Sanders, William, Mary (wife of Ira Gambrell), and the wife of .... Swinle or Swinler.

James Williamson died about 1836, in Laurens District, leaving widow, June, and children: James, William, Harmon, J. H., Thomas, and Anne Taylor.

WILLINGHAM-James Willingham, of Hanover County, Virginia, sold a slave in 1786 to George Montgomery, of Newber y District, S. C.

Thomas Henry Willingham died about 1799 in St. James-Santee Parish, leaving widow, Sarah, and a son, Thomas; who reveived all of his property.

Aves Willingham, of Fairfield District, left property to his nephew, Aves Ellis, in 1796.

Joseph Willingham died about 1854 in Fairfield District, leaving widow, Mary, and children: Martha (wife of William F. Elkins), Sarah, John, James, Joseph, William E., Mary A., and Margaret E. (the last four children named were under age in 1854).

F. Bird Willingham died in April, 1842, in Newberry District, leaving widow, Sarah (Koone) Willingham, and children: William, Pleasant, Frances, Henry W., Mary Ann, Amanda (wife of John Harmon),and probably others.   The widow was the daughter of Henry and Eve Catherine Koone; she died 1830.

WINDLE-Mrs. S. Windle lived in Newberry District. She was a widow when she married .... De Walt.

This is an Abbeville County and a Fairfield County name.

WINN-Thomas Winn died about 1797 in Abbeville District, leaving widow, and children: Abner, Lemuel, Thomas, Elijah, Richard, Sarah, Elisabeth, Lettice, and Robert. His widow was Lettice..........   His brothers were: William, Washington. His widow died about 1824, leaving legatees as follows: Elisabeth Graves, Lettice Walker (wife of N. G. Walker), Robert Winn, (he was pensioned as a Rev War veteran), Abner Winn, Lemuel Winn, Elijah Winn; and her sisters, Elizabeth Thompson and Mrs. Littleton Hunt.

James Winn died in Fairfield District about 1793.

William Wynn died in Edgefield District, leaving widow, Charlotte, and children:......... his grand-children named in settlament of estate were: Louisa Wynn, Susannah Wynn, Martha A. Wynn, William Wynn, Robert Wynn.   His brother, Thomas Wynn, is named.

John Winn (Rev. War patriot) died about 1827, in Pendleton District.

Another John Win had died about 1782 in Camden Districr (now Fairfield County), leaving children, John and Peter; and nephew, Joseph Winn; and grand-child, Thomas Bacon.

Other Pioneers (continued)

WISEMAN—John Wiseman sold lands in Newberry District about 1801, to Hugh Wilson. Robert Wiseman sold land in 1786 to Alexander Cross. Hugh Wiseman sold one hundred acres land located on old Charleston Road, in 1813, to Henry Ruff.
Mrs. Louisa Wiseman died in Bell County, Texas, November 2, 1856, leaving husband, John S. Wiseman, and children: Frances, John T., William F., Louisa Jane. Silas Johnstone, of Newberry, S. C., was Administrator of her estate.
WITT—Michael Witt lived in Newberry District. He sold his lands and moved to Florida. He had children: Andrew, Michael, John M., Catherine (wife of John Glaze), Christina (wife of Mark Lyles), Mary M.(wife of John Feagle), All were children by his first wife, Elizabeth. After her death he married Matilda......., and had children: Jacob, Rachel, William, Jane, and Hamilton Witt.
WOOD—Samuel Wood died in Newberry District about 1819, leaving widow, Elizabeth, and children Ambrose, Silas, Anna, Nancy, and probably others.
John Wood died in Newberry District about 1800, leaving widow, Grace, and children: Elizabeth and others.
Thomas Wood died in Newberry District, leaving children: Samuel, John, Benjamin. Benjamin married Judith.........
One Thomas Wood died in Union District, leaving widow, Anna.
William Woods, Sr. died in Laurens District about 1800, leaving children: Hugh, Harvey, Martin, Clarissa, Nancy, Martha Boyd, Kellet, Susan Curry, Mary Gray, Larisa Mahon, Abner. Abnner died nefore the death of his father, leaving children: Hastin, Clara, and Spencer.
WOOTEN—Joab Wooten died about 1808 in Edgefield District.
Aaron Wooten, Sr. died in Camden District (now Fairfield County). He left a will dated October 1, 1814, and widow, Mary, and children: Moses, Ruth Miles, John, Aaron, and Joseph.
WORD (WARD)—James Word died in Laurens District, leaving widow, Elizabeth, and children: John, William, Thomas, Sarah, James, Charles, Robert, Elizabeth, and another daughter who was the wife of Voluntine Harlan.
WORKMAN—Daniel Workman died in Newberry District about 1805, leaving widow, Janett, and children: William and Mary, and probably others not named in estate settlement. The widow married ..... Leonard. She died before 1816, about that time. A daughter, Mary, married in 1821 to Abraham Alewine.
WRIGHT—John Wright, who had come from Camden District with the Quakers, lived on Bush River. He died about 1790, leaving children: John, Joseph, Nathan, the wife of Isaac Cook, the wife of Isaac Hllingsworth, William Thomas, Isaac. The son, John, died before his father's death, leaving children, one being Jesse Wright. Joseph had a son, John, Nathan was the father of William Wright. Isaac Cook and wife had son, Joseph and a duaghter, Rachel. All of these families moved with Quakers to Ohio, some going to Indiana, those that were living at time of mirgration. Nathan Wright (son of John, Sr.), died in Newberry District about 1805, leaving a family, his widow being Sarah Wright.
James Wright, a native of Ireland, settled in 1825 in Newberry District; where he died on January 3, 1825. His wife, Lucy, died 1824. They are buried at old Tranquil Cemetery, seven miles Northeast of Newberry Court House. Their children were: William, Zaccheus, Elizabeth (wife of William Dugan), Mary (wife of Isham Shell), Lucy (she married ..... Shell), The Shells moved to Newton County, Georgia. Children of Mrs. Lucy Shell, as named in the will of James Wright, were: Henry W. Shell, Martha Ann (wife of William B. Hodges).
Zaccheus Wright (son of James), was born in Newberry District 1783, and died 1862. His wife was Lucy........ They were parents of Robert H. Wright.
Alexander Wright (son of ....), died about 1825 in Newberry District, leaving widow, Jenny, and children: Mary (wife of Thomas Boyd), Anna (wife of James Henry), Jane, Nancy, Elizabeth. Mrs. Ann Henry had children: James A., George R., Hugh P., and Jane B. Barnett.
YANCEY—Benjamin Yancey died about 1817, in Edgefield District.
YARBOROUGH—John F. Yarborough died in Abbeville District before 1830, leaving legatees: Sarah, John W., R. T., Mary E.(wife of Henry Ruff).

Other Pioneers (continued)

YEARGAN—Mrs. Mary(Spearman)Yeargan was a daughter of Thomas Spearman by his first wife, before the year 1794. Edward Yeargan married a daughter of Thomas and Ruth Stark before year 1808.

YELDEL—Robert Yeldell and wife, Phoebe, lived in Newberry District. The family moved to Abbeville District after his death in 1789. Children were: John, Robert, Jane, Mary Harrison or Hairston, Martha, Anthony, and Phoebe. Jane married Francis Atkins. Another daughter was Sare White. Phoebe married David Adams. A son, James, died before death of his father, and left children: Robert, and others. Anthony died about 1826—1827. A son-in-law was Joseph Dennis.

YOUNGBLOOD—James Youngblood died in Edgefield District about 1792.

Peter Youngblood died 1794 in Charleston District, leaving widow, Mary, and ch: Peter Edmund, William, Thomas F., Richard, and Elizabeth.

Lewis Youngblood died in Edgefield District about 1822.

Thomas Youngblood died in Edgefield District about 1822.

Samuel Youngblood, one of sons of Peter Youngblood, Sr., who moved to Richmond County, Ga., served in the S. C. Militia during the Rev. War.

Land Grants: Thomas Youngblood—Colleton District—1770
Henry Youngblood—on Blufftown Creek—1767
Peter Youngblood—Colleton District—1773

YONGUE—Martin Yongue married Sarah Ann Martin about 1775 to 1785, and lived in Fairfield District. They had a son, Martin Yongue, Jr. who died in year 1867 aged 83 years.

Martin Yongue, Jr. married Julianna L. Cameron who was born in 1790 and died Oct. 2, 1874. Their children were: Cynthia (born Jan. 17, 1810 and died June 15, 1888), who married John M. Milling; James, who married Frances Crosby Estes; Andrew, who married Nancy Robinson; Jane, married, but died young; Jennie; and Malinda. Martin Yongue and wife are buried at Salem church in Fairfield County.

YOUNG—William Young came from Ireland before the Rev. War began and settled in the Southern section of Ninety Six District (the Stoney Hills section of Newberry County). The earliest record of him is the year 1776 when he and his wife, Elizabeth, conveyed a tract of land to John Reyley, originally granted to him in year 1772.

George Adam Young was granted land near Broad River in year 1770 (Newberry County). He conveyed this tract of one hundred acres to Jacob Young (spelled "Youn") in 1797. Jacob and his wife, Margaret, sold it to Simon Wicker in 1797. Jacob died 1800 and left the following legatees: Elizabeth Balderee, John Young, Catherine Balderee, and Jacob Young.

Jacob Young, Jr. and wife, Sarah, sold land in the Dutch Fork to Martin Kihard in year 1821.

James Young came from Ireland before the Rev. War and was granted land in the Stoney Hills of Newberry County in year 1768. He lived on Bush River in 1790. In 1796 he and his wife, Mary, conveyed three hundred four acres on Bush River to Patrick Carmickael. He died about 1810 leaving his widow, Mary, and children, 898 acres land between Broad and Saluda Rivers. The children who sold all their rights and claims to these lands to the widow, Mary Young, were the following (sale made 1812); Elizabeth (wife of William Fair), Mary (wife of Charles Thompson), Joseph Young (married Marianna......), Hannah (wife of Robert Carmickael), Anne (wife of Robert Brown), Abram Young (married Sarah........), Esther (wife of Archibald Boyd), James Young (married Isabella .....), Robert and Hannah Carmickael had a daughter, Hannah P., who married William W. Davis.

Joseph Young died about 1820, left an estate to his widow, Sarah (she was probably a second wife), and to his mother, Mary Young. His son, Jacob H. Young, was named as Guardian for his other children who were: James, George, Jane, Archibald, and Elizabeth Anne. A son, Arthur Young, died about 1825, leaving one child, Mary Anne Elizabeth Young.

James Calender Young and wife, Teremiah, sold in year 1800 one hundred ten acres land between Enoree and Tyger Rivers, Newberry County, to John Young.

James Young (of Abbeville District), owned land on Reedy Branch, on Long Cane, which he conveyed to his son Samuel who sold it to David Cannon of Newberry County in year 1821. He came from Guilford County, North Carolina, to Abbeville District in Year 1786, locating on McKennelly Creek, ten miles West of Abbeville Court House. He married Jane Caruthers,

Other Pioneers.

daughter of Mrs. Martha Caruthers, and sister of James and John Caruthers and Mrs. Benj. Terry. Their children were: Francis, John, Samuel, and Joseph, Isabella, Mary, Jane, Margaret, Martha, and Susannah. Francis married Nancy Little. Samuel married Emma .... Isabella married a Magill. Margaret married Elihu Beard. Martha married a Mitchel, and died before 1822 leaving children, Francis, Thomas, Samuel, and Jane. Susannah married a Kerr, died prior to 1822, and left children as follows: Martha Valendingham, Rachel Sims, Francis Kerr and John Kerr. Jane Young married John Baskin in 1800.

Samuel Young died in Abbeville County in Oct. 1817, leaving widow, Elizabeth, and children: Robert, William, James, Lucinda Ellen, and Amiline.

James Young (of Laurens County), died 1807 and left children: Elizabeth Carter, Polly Medley, John, James, Lucy, Sally, and Kitty.

James Young, Jr. (of Laurens County), died in 1824, leaving widow, Mary Ann, and small children.

Robert Young (of Laurens County), made will dated October 27, 1824, and died in 1824, leaving widow, Sarah, and children: Joseph, Reason, Jeremiah Madison, Elihu, Newton Sprous, Mary Rachel, and Elizabeth Low. Elizabeth Low married a Mr. Holland.

Joseph Young (of Laurens County), died in 1861 leaving children: Robert (he was dead, his wife, Martha, surviving), Andrew, and Anne E. (she married a Hudgens).

John Young (of Newberry County), by the approbation of his mother, Elizabeth Disher, and his step-father, Lewis Disher, put himself out as an apprentice in year 1815, to one Thomas Pratt, merchant of Newberry, until he became twenty-one years of age.

John T. Young (of Newberry County), died about 1842, leaving an estate to the following: Helen O'Conner (daughter of William O'Conner), Frances Shell (daughter of Dr. Thomas Shell), and William O'Conner.

Thompson Young, Sr. died in Newberry County in year 1865, leaving widow, Martha, who died in 1874. They had children as follows: Hannah (wife of William Lester), Martha (wife of David Crosson), Mary I. (wife of Henry S. Boozer), and James. A son, Joseph, had died and left a daughter, Alma, living in Ocala, Fla. about 1870.

James Mason Young, Sr. died about 1849. His wife, who was Catherine Davenport, died in 1846. They had one child, James Mason Young, Jr.

James Young and wife, Molly, had one child, George M. Young, who died early and never married. James Young died and his widow, when she died, left her property to George Myers (he was probably a brother of father).

ZEIGLAR-Nicholas Zeiglar was granted land in Newberry County in 1754, one hundred fifty acres on a small branch of Cannon's Creek. (then Ninety Six District). He conveyed this land to his son, Hans Adam Zeiglar, who deeded it to Peter Stockman. Peter Stockman gave the land to his daughter, Catherine.

John Zeiglar Married Margaret Stockman, daughter of Henry Stockman. They both died before 1828, leaving a daughter, Margaret Zeiglar.

ZIMMERMAN-Phillip Zimmerman made a will dated December 7, 1792, which was recorded in January, 1797, in Edgefield County Court House. He left widow, Ann Aphelona, and children: Henry, Peter, Mary, and Elizabeth.

Henry Zimmerman made will dated June 20, 1798, which was recorded in 1799, in Edgefield County Court House. He left widow, Mary Entrin, and children: Henry, Samuel, Mary, Nancy, Elizabeth, and Sarah.

SOME OLD CEMETERY MARKERS IN CITY AND COUNTY.

Rosemont Cemetery in the City. At the two main entrances to the cemetery are two columns at each, constructed of stone and with bronz tablets. The first reads:

Ola Clark Floyd
First President Civic League
Erected by
Civic League
In grateful remembrance
of her loyal service.

On tablet on other column of this entrance reads:

Walter Herbert Hunt
First President Cemetery Association
Erected by
the association
in acknowledgment of
his faithful service.

The remains of members of Judge John Belton O'neall's family were first entered in the old Village Cemetery, but later were removed to Rosemont Cemetery. The following are markers over the graves:

In Memory of
..........O'Neall
who was born 14th March, 1799,
and died 22nd December, 1815.

Sacred
To the memory of
Miss. Bathsheda Pope,
fifth daughter of Sampson
and Sarah Pope. She was born
November 2nd, 1807,
and died January 23rd, 1836,

This marble raised by the hand of Conjugal affection covers the mortal remains of John Belton O'Neall, late Chief Justice of the State of South Carolina.
He was born April 10th, 1793, and died December 27th, 1863, aged 70 years, 8 months, and 17 days.
"Thy dead men shall live, together with my dead body shall arise"..Isa. 26-19.

"I will ransom them from the power of the grave. I will redeem them from death. I will by thy plague, O, grave. I will by thy destruction."
Hos. 13-14.

Here lies the body of
Henry Miles O'Neall, who was
born 23rd December, 1808,
died 31st December, 1843.

Here lies the body of
John Caldwell, Esq., who
was born 9th September, 1785,
and died
15th January, 1856.

Sacred
To the memory of
Helen O'Neall,
daughter of Sampson and Sarah Pope,
and wife of
John Belton O'Neall,
born
November 19, 1797,
died
November 10, 1871.

Sacred
To the memory of
Rebecca O'Neall, fourth
daughter of John B. and
Helen O'Neall.
She was born March 26th, 1827,
and died March 10th, 1834.

Here
lies the body of
Elizabeth O'Neall, wido
and relict of Henry Mi.
O'Neall, who was born
30th Sept, 1815.
died
20th January, 1844.

Here
Lies the body of
Hugh O'Neall.
He was born 10th June,
1767. He died 18th
October, 1848.

Here
Lies the body of
Anne O'Neall.
She was born 12th August,
1767. She died 4th October
1850.

Sacred
To the memory of
Elizabeth Albright O'Neall,
Sixth daughter of John B.
and Helen O'Neall.
She was born November 3rd
1831, and died March 21st,
1834.

CEMETERY MARKERS (continued)

Revolutionary War Patriots:

Sacred
To the memory of
William Thomas Caldwell, a
native of Charlotte Co., Va.,
who was born March 10th, 1748,
and died December 16th, 1814,
and his wife, Elizabeth Ann Caldwell,
a daughter of Major John Williams, of
Laurens District, S. C. who was born
May 28th, 1759, and died January 3rd,
1815, only fifteen days after the death
of her husband.
The bodies of both were entered in
this grave.

Sacred
To the memory of
Captain James Caldwell
who departed this life
Jan 11th, 1813,
in the 58th year of his age.
He was an affectionate
husband, a kind parent,
and an indulgent master;
a devoted friend to his country
and to the Church of Christ.
" Mark the perfect man, and
behold the upright, for the
end of that man is peace."

Sacred
To the memory of
Mrs. Elizabeth A. Caldwell
who died on the third
day of October, 1822,
in the 58th year of her age.
" She lived a life to be admired,
And died a death to be desired.'
" Blessed are the dead who
die in the Lord".

Mexican War Soldier:

The Bereaved Parents
Lieut. John W. Stewart, late of
Company L., Palmetto Regiment,
S.C. Volunteers, to perpetuate his
memory, have placed this stone above his
mortal remains.
He was born on the battlefield,
near Liberty Spring, Laurens District,
25th August, 1826,
and died in Mexico,
on the 2nd November, 1847.
He was among the first who devoted himself
to the call of his country, when in the
Summer of '46 a requisition was made for
volunteers. His services brief and painful
as it was, afforded to him few opportunities
for deeds of daring or heroic bravery. The
fatal march to Alvarado, consigned him and
many others of the Newberry boys to sick beds.
He with a portion of his command was left sick
in Vera Cruz when the Palmettoes began their
toilsome march on Perote, Puebla, and Mexico.
As soon as his health permitted he and they
began on their march to join their comrades.
On the way he showed the true metal of a son
of Carolina, that sickness could not make him
unmindful of his duty.
When a sentinental unfortunately killed himself
and the guard refused to turn out he seized a
musket and called on the men to follow him,
marched to the spot.
When at the National Bridge, the party was assaulted
by Guerillas, he seized the gun of a fellow soldier
and pushing forward used it to good purpose.
Sickness, wasting, fatal sickness, prevented him from
sharing in the glories of Contreras, Churubusco,
Chapultepec and the garita Del Belin.
(continued above)

After the capture of the City,
he was allowed to turn his face
homeward, but in two days the spirit
of the young, the brave, and the
beloved one, was forced from his
wasted tenement of clay, and was
borne in the peace which expected
to the bosom of his Father
and God.

" Rest dear departed one,
Thy Father bids thee rest.
Rest in endless glory, dear son.
Thy Mother blesses thee, and thou
art blest!"

CEMETERY MARKERS (continued)

Confederate War Soldiers:

Rev. George William Holland, D.D.
July 16, 1838
Sept 30, 1895
A faithful Minister of Christ,
Gentle unto all men, apt to teach.
The Beloved Grand Reporter of the
Knights of Honor of South Carolina.
1877-1895.
"Spectemur Agendo."
President of Newberry College
1878-1895.
  Our Beloved President,
  Newberry College is his monument,
  The Alumni of the College
  are his living epistles.

A small gray stone monument with double base on which is a small stone cross, with simple design, has inscription:
" At the foot of this cross, the sign of our redemption, are deposited the mortal remains of
  my beloved wife,
  Emile Boue,
  Born in France Oct 10, 1820,
  Died in Newberry, Jan 24, 1867.
          ---- T. Gouin.
     (Note: The name of cutter is
      evidently French name)

About one hundred yards in rear of the Farmers Oil Mill plant, located to left from Boundary Street, in Newberry, S. C., is a small flat gray stone indicating the spot where Calvin Crozier, a Confederate War hero, was killed and left buried for a day and a night. Then, the body was transferred to the Village Cemetery where it was buried for several years before it was again placed in a grave at Rosemont Cemetery. The inscription reads:
    Calvin Crozier
  was murdered here by the
  33rd U.S. Regt. of Negro Federal
  Soldiers, Sept 8, 1865.
    This stone was placed by
    Calvin Crozier Chapter,
    U. D. C.

Under the base of one side of the Crozier monument is the following inscription:
"Rest on embalmed and sainted dead,
Dear as the blood you gave.
No impious footsteps here shall tread,
The harbage of your grave,
Nor shall your glory be forgot
While fame her records keep,
Or honor points the hallowed spot
Where valor proudly sleeps."

Hedwig Wickman
Born in Germany
Fe 14, 1844
Died in Columia,
S.C. Fen 2nd, 1901.

E. L. Bradley
Born
May 20, 1820
Died
Jan 3, 1864.

Young John Pope
April 10, 1841—March 29, 1911.
Soldier, Jurist, Statesman, he rests
  from his labors.

" And the dead thus meet the dead,
While the living o'er them weep.
And the men by Lee and Stonewall led
And the hearts that once together bled,
Together still shall sleep."

S. Burt Higgins
1st Regt.
S.C. Volunteers,
Greggs Brigade
He fell in the Seven
Days battle near Richmond,
Va. At Cold Harbor,
June 27th, 1862.
Aged 23 years, 7 months,
and 17 days.

Calvin S. Crozier
Born
at Brandon, Miss.
August, 1840,
murdered at Newberry, S.C.
** Sept 8, 1865 **
****
CROZIER
****
After the surrender of the Confederate Armies, while on the way to his home in Texas from a Federal prison, he was called upon at the railroad station at Newberry, S. C. on the night of Sept 7, 1863, to protect a young white woman temporarily under his charge, from gross insults offered by a negro Federal soldier of the garrison stationed there. A difficulty ensued in which the negro was slightly cut, the infuriated soldiers seized a citizen of Newberry upon whom they were about to execute savage revenge, when Crozier came promptly forward and avowed his own responsibility for the deed, thus refusing to accept safety from allowing a stranger to receive the violence intended for himself.
****
He was hurried in the nighttime to the bivouac of the regiment to which the soldier belonged, was kept under guard all night, was not allowed communication with any citizen, was condemned to die without even the form of a trial and was shot to death about daylight the following morning and his body mutilated.

CEMETERY MARKERS (continued)

Rosemont Cemetery:

Spanish-American War soldiers—
James K. Weeks
March 19, 1879
Sept 8, 1902

S.G.(Pet) Merchant
B. April 27, 1866
D. Jan 26, 1921

William M. Griffin
Boy SCL
S.C. Navy
Aug 21, 1911
B. Sept 9, 1862

William Jackson Smith
Oct 11, 1865
Jan 27, 1926

Edmund Laylan McIntosh
1872—1906

William Divver
B. April 28, 1868
D. Jan 16, 1903.

Harry T. White
B. Sept 19, 1869
D. Sept 8, 1900

Lois Lovelace
Co. B.
S. C. Inf.

E.H.Kingsmore
Died Feb 10,1937
aged 75 years.
(No marker over his grave)

James Gregg Miller
Nov 14, 1862
May 18,1933

Frank W. Fant
Co. G.
2nd S. C. Inf.

James Guy Daniels
Jan 18, 1877
Oct 31, 1916

Worls War 1 soldiers—
Leumas Dunbar
Died Jan 20, 1936

Owen McR. Holmes
1895—1930

Walter G. Franklin
S.C., U.S. Army, Pvt.
D. Jan 5, 1933
(killed in auto accident)

John D. Davis
Sept 29, 1883
Nov 29, 1934

Robert L. Neal
S.C. 53 Inf. Cook
6 Div.
D. March 12, 1928

O. Newell Haigler
Corp. U. S. Army
Medical Dept.
Jan 9, 1895
Sept 13, 1920

Earl Bullock—no marker.
(Killed accidentally in 1937)

Ensign Joshua Ward Motte
Simmons,
son of
J.W.M. and Lalla R. Simmons.
Born Sept 1, 1886
Died March 14, 1919
He died in the service of his country.

Robert I. Gilliam
Mar 17, 1901
Apr 15, 1932

Ernest M. Sweet
April 17, 1898
August 3, 1935

Curtis T. Morris
Feb 3, 1894
Nov 1, 1933

Dewey Sease Addison
July 9, 1898
Jan 17, 1923

Dr. Frank D. Mower
Surgeon U. S. Army
Died 1937 (No marker)

Elbert Jackson Dickert
July 6, 1895
Nov 19, 1926

Buster Harris
April 14, 1907
Dec 17, 1927
(one of heroes of the
S—4, U.S.N.)

Fred S. Mayfield
August 1, 1893
May 16, 1934

(An unmarked
grave in new
section)

William L. Miller
Aged 26 years-no marker

Carl Henry Albrecht
Sept 17, 1896
March 9, 1934

Eugene Summer
(no marker)
(Another unmarked grave here)

James Harrison Summer
(no marker)

(An unmarked grave in
Bishop Square)

George C. Vines
Oct 19, 1891
Jan 1, 1931

Bennie James,
son of
T. W. and Mary G. Folk.
April 29, 1896
Oct 17, 1918.
" Blessed are the pure in he
for they shall see God."
(Killed in France)

CEMETERY MARKERS (continued)

Old Village Cemetery (copied Jan 28, 1930)-

Edward Y. R. McMorries,
son of
John and Nancy McMorries,
born Oct 28, 1818,
died Nov 3, 1854.
For many years he was an active merchant in Newberry. First in every noble and benevolent enterprise and first in the hearts of those who knew him best, his manly deportment, his amiable disposition, gentle manners, and noble impluses commanded the esteem and admiration of all his acquaintenances. He was, indeed, one of the excellent of the earth.
" Blessed are the pure in heart,
for they shall see God."
His wife was Frances McMorries.....

In Memory of
Mary B., wife of Jacob Hughes, daughter of R. & M. Hammond, of Kershaw District, S. C. Born 28th Dec. 1807, and died 21st July, 1835. As a wife she was faithful and affectionate, as a mother, kind and intelligent.
Though not publicly attached to any church, her principles were those of the Gospel, viz: Faith in Jesus Christ, and in her last illness she was quietly patient and resigned.
" Her flesh shall slumber in the ground,
'Till the last trumpet joyful sound;
Then burst the chains with sweet surprise,
And in her Savior's image arise."

In Memory of
Mrs. Sarah Ann Moore,
Born Nov 21st, 1813, and died May 23rd, 1844. She had been a member of the Methodist Church, Episcopal, eleven years previous to her death, and died in the full possession of the Christian hope. This stone is erected to her memory ob her husband, William Thompson Moore.

In Memory of
Caroline Hammond Hyde, Consort of Rev. E. K. Hyde,
Nat. April 20, 1810,
Ob. Nov 11, 1847.
She was an accomplished lady, Adorned with every Christian Virtue.

Louisa M. McMorries
died Feb 14, 1835,
aged 28 years, 11 months,
and two days.

Benjamin Thomas Saxon, a member of the Church of Aveleigh, Commissioner in Equity for Lexington and a member of the Bar of Alabama and South Carolina. He was born in Madison County, Ala. the 22nd Feb 1819, and died at Newberry Court House, S. C. the 7th April, 1842. The members of the Bar of Newberry consecrate this slab to the memory of their beloved Associate.

Here lies the body of George Tracey who was born in Northumberland County, Va. May 1st, 1789, and died at Newberry Court House, Sept 15th, 1824.
He died without-------- but lamented by his friends who have erected this stome to his memory.

Sacred
To the memory of
Mrs. Permelia Moore, Consort of William T. Moore and daughter of William and Elizabeth Fair, who was born Aug 28, 1816, and departed this life Oct 7th, 1838, aged 22 years, 1 month, and 9 days, leaving a husband and two small children and numerous other relatives and friends, to mourn their irreparable loss.
"I leave the world without a tear,
Save for my friends and children dear,
To bear their sorrow, Lord, descend,
And to the friendless, prove a freind."

Sacred
To the memory of
Mary B. Chapman who departed this life Nov 18th, 1854, in the 32nd year of her age.
"Living an humble Christian and consistent member of the Methodist Church, she died in peace and rests with God."

D. R. Lathrop
was born Sept 2,
1811,
and died March 12,
1848.

Emily R. Lathrop
Born April 25,
Died Sept 2, 1897

Sacred
To the memory of
Dr. Samuel T. Myrick, son of John and Eliza Myrick. He was born on the 27th Feb 1819,
and died 21st March, 1849,
aged 30 years,
and 26 days.

Sacred
To the Memory of
Joanna Seybt, Consort of George L. F. Seybt daughter of .....Hatch of Charleston, S. C.

CEMETERY MARKERS (continued)

Village Cemetery (continued)-

Here lies the body of
Mrs. Eliza M. McLemore, who was
born on the 26th March, 1806, and
died on the 10th April, 1840.
She was the daughter of James and
Fanny McMorries, and a relict of
Dr. John McLemore who died in the
campaign of 1836 in Florida,
She was a member of the Church of
Christ, enjoyed it's consolations
amid the sorrows of life, and died
full of hope of a happy immortality
beyond the grave. May her children
long remember and imitate her example.
Great God prepare..(illegible).

Sacred
To the Memory of
John B. Davidson, a native of
Burlington, N. J., but for 25
years previous to his death a
citizen of the village of Newberry,
S. C. He was born 21st Jan 1762, and died
21st June, 1826.

" ....Ye good distressed!
Ye Noble few ! Who here unbending
stand ....
" Beneath life's pressure, yet bear up awhile,
And what your bounded view, which only saw,
A little part, deemed evil is no more.
The storms of wintry time will quickly pass,
And one unbounded Spring encircle all."

(This stone is placed here in obedience to
the will of his widow, Mary Ann Davidson,
decd, by her Executors.)

To
The Memory of
John H. Carter who departed
this life March 4, 1859, in
the 41st year of his age.
This tomb was erected by his wife
to his memory.
"Jesus, My All."

Permelia Ann,
wife of
Z. L. White, and daughter of
John and Chrsitiana Paysinger,
died Oct 25th, 1865, aged 30 years.
" She's gone. Forever gone.
The Ling of tenners
Lays his wide hands upon
her lovely limbs,
And adjusts her beauties,
With his icy tenorth."

Sacred to the Memory
of
Nancy Boyce, wife of Ker Boyce,
merchant of Charleston, S. C.
She was an example of all that is
lovely in the female character,
discharging her duties. A child,
a wife, mother, and a member of Society.
A cheerfulness, zeal, and assiduity which
could only spring from a sincere heart
full of religious obligation. She was a
Christian, diligent, devout, humble, through
life, triumphant in death. Her bereft
husband prays this humble tribute to her
memory.
Nat. Oct 9th, 1795,
Ob. Aug 30th, 1823.

Sacred to the Memory of
Mary Ann Davidson, widow and relict
of John B. Davidson. She was a native
of Maryland but for the past 28 years
of her life resided in the Village
of Newberry, S. C. She was born
24th Oct 1773, and died 21st Sept 1829.

" Farewell pur spirit!. Vain in the
praise we give,
The praise you sought from life's
Angelic flows;
Farewell, the virtue which deserve
to live,
Deserve an amplier bliss than
life bestows."

(This stone is erected to the memory
ôf the deceased , was placed here
in obedience to her will , by Thomas
Pratt and Pressly B. Ruff, her
Executors.)

Mary Brown
Born
Jan 16, 1864
Died
May 11, 1882.

Elvira C. White
wife of
Z. L. White, and daughter
of J. H. and Catherine Counts,
Died
Oct 23rd 1882,
In the 52nd year of her age.

In Memory of
Five Unknown Confederate
Soldiers, Erected by
Drayton Rutherford Chapter,
U.D.C. 1916.

Sacred
To the memory of
Ogeechee,
wife of J. J. Whitener,
born July 4, 1853,
died Sept 24, 1873.

Sacred To the
Memory of
Sarah A. Summer Boyd,
who was born May 5th,
1810,
and departed this life
Nov 22nd, 1811.

CEMETERY MARKERS (continued)

Village Cemetery(continued)-

Sacred
To the Memory of
Hugh King Boyd who was born
March 29th, 1806, and died
March 11th, 1851,
Educated in the faith of the
    Ancient Covenanters,
He exhibited in youth their
meekness and self-denial,
And forsook not in manhood their
rigid virtue and unbending
    integrity.
In all relations of private
life, he was benevolent and kind,
    In
those of a public character, he was
    upright and just.
" Why should we moan departed friends,
Or shake at death's alarms?
' Tis but the voice that Jesus sends,
To call them to his Arms."

In Memory
of
Mrs. Louisa M. McMorries
who died Febry 4th, 1835,
aged 28 years, 11 months,
and 2 days.

Harriet Rebecca Johnston,
    wife of
Burr Johnston and daughter
    of
John and Sabella Foote,
Born 20th Jany 1800,
Died 19th Oct 1834.

Gen. H. H. Kinard,
March 29, 1806
June 17, 1869.

Dr. James P. Kinard,
Sept 15th, 1829,
Sept 21st, 1854 (in Paris).

Capt. John M. Kinard,
July 3rd, 1833,
Oct 13th, 1864 (killed battle of
            Strasburg, Va.)

Louisa F. Kinard,
Dec 29, 1866,
Nov .... 1872.

In Memory of
Bethany Blease
Born
Sept 17th, 1797,
Died
April 13th 1865.
She survived her husband, Thomas
W. Blease, Sr., late of Edgefield County,
seven years, ten months, and twelve days.
She was a woman of superior mind and of
earnest piety.

In Memory of
Frances A. Blease,
wife of
Thomas W. Blease,
who died Oct 8th,
1872, aged 44 years.

Inscription on marker over grave of the
first Volunteer from Newberry in the Confederate
Army:
    Captain Basil Manley Blease,
        Co. B.
    Born Edgefield C. H., S. C.
        Dec 11, 1826,
    Died at Newberry, S. C.
        Jan 2, 1877.

Catherine J. Johnston,
Born 1st Jany 1819,
Died 15th August 1835.

Sacred
To the memory of
Mary Ann Kinard,
    wife of
Gen'l. H. H. Kinard, and
daughter of Capt John and
Elizabeth Counts;
who departed this life March
19th, 1851, aged 42 years and
    17 days.

Sacred
To the Memory of
Major Charles Wesley Shell,
who was born May 8th, 1810,
and died Dec 25th, 1831,
aged 21 years, 7 months, and
    16 days.
His youth, his virtue and his talents
have caused his numerous friends and
relations to feel most seriously and
deplore sincerely their loss.
But in the language of Job: " The Lord
gave and the Lord hath taken away;
blessed be the name of the Lord."

John J. Whitener,
Born
July 2, 1848,
Died
May 7th., 1888.
The dread Angel of death
has visited our once happy
home, and took from
us our loved one. A
devoted husband and
father has passed fr
death to eternal life
Thomas W. Blease, Jr.
born at Edgefield Court Hou
S. C. Nov 22nd, 1822,
Died
May 31st, 1880,
Aged 57 years,..... months,
    and ..... days.

Mary Alabama,
wife of
John M. Kinard,
and daughter of
Dr. P. B. and E. A. Ruf
was born March 31s
1839, and died March 15
    1860.
My Jesus has come for m

CEMETERY MARKERS (continued) 409

Village Cemetery (continued)-

Pressley B. Ruff, M. D.
Born
Dec 21, 1801,
Died
Dec 28, 1890.

Sacred
To the memory of
Anne E. Ruff, daughter of
Dr. P. B. and Esther Ruff,
who died July 22nd, 1849,
aged 1 year, 1 month, and
25 days.

Sacred
To the memory of
Claiborne M. Ruff,
son of
Dr. P. B. and Esther Ruff,
who departed this life
July 18th, 1849,
aged 13 years, 8 months,
and 13 days.
Intellectual and studious,
he gave promise of much usefulness, but God took him.
He died at Mt. Amon Academy,
in Edgefield District.

To
The memory of
Harriet Catherine Ruff,
wife of
Dr. P. B. Ruff,
daughter of Christopher
and Sophie (Harrison)
Thompson.
Born Fairfield, S. C.
27th July, 1819,
Died in Newberry, S. C.
23rd March, 1887.
" With every excellence refined."

Sacred
To the memory of
Frances Harriet Ruff,
was born August 19, 1842,
and died August 11, 1879.

In Memoriam:
John J. Ruff, son of
Dr. P. B. and E. A. Ruff,
was born
April 25th, 1845.
At the age of 16 he entered
the Confederate Army, and was
engaged in many hard fought
battles, receiving four wounds,
the last at the battle of
Spottsyvania C. H., which proved
fatal; he died June 2nd, 1864,
at Winder Hospital, Richmond, Va.
He died in the hope of a blessed
immortality.

Sacred
To the Memory of
Esther A. Ruff,
Consort of Dr. P. B. Ruff,
and daughter of Jacob and
Mary Lorick. She departed
this life Dec 4th, 1850,
aged 34 years, 10 months
and 27 days.
For years a faithful member of
the Methodist Church, and a
consistent Christian. She died
in peace, and rests with God.
Abounding in the virtues, just
and kind, in all the relations
of life; she is embalmed in the
hearts of the surviving family
and a large circle of relations
and friends.

Confederate Soldiers' graves at Smyrna Presbyterian Church Cemetery(about 5 miles from Newberry Court House):

I. Z. Abrams   1846-1919,
S. S. Abrams   1843-1923,
R. W. Atchison 1832-1895,
Dr. D. W. Patton 1829-1885,
J. J. Amick 1826- 1891,

M. M. Coppock 1827-1884,
T. R. Wilson 1838-1871,
H. D. Boozer 1841-1920,

Gillam Pitts, T. P. Pitts .
(no markers)

Little River Presbyterian Church Cemetery—
Sacred
To the memory of
Col. John Simpson,
who was born on the 13th
of November, 1751,
aged 63 years, 10 months,
and 6 days.

Sacred
To The Memory of
Reuben Griffin, Esq.,
who was born the 19th
December, A.D., 1762,
and departed this life the
28th day of June, 1826,
aged 63 years, 6 months,
and 9 days.

There were many other markers at this old cemetery, but some have been torn away or removed . The site of this spot is where the old church was once located, about 17 miles Northwest of Newberry Court House, across from the old Griffin home, on the highway leading to " Belfast". The above two are graves of Rev War patriots.

CEMETERY MARKERS (continued)

Old Village Cemetery, Newberry, S. C.-

The Marble
is erected to the memory of
Joseph Kerr
who was born in Rowan County,
North Carolina,
August 16, 1797.
(inscription four sides of
tall monument)

On the fourth side:
Possessed of solid talents,
upright views, an amiable temper
and obliging manners, he gave
his able and useful life; but
his sun went down in the morning
and the day, mysterious Providence
of God disappointed the fairest hopes.
Yearly man's........ is best estate
is altogether..... vain.
(stone broken in places)

Rosemont Cemetery- Newberry, S. C.-
Sacred
To the memory of
Major John Waters Summers,
son of
Col. John & Rosannah Summers,
(she was the daughter of
Major Philemon Waters, of
the Revolution),
Born
Oct 29th, 1814,
Died
Jan 13th, 1852.

In Memory
of
Mrs. Harriet Summers,
the wife of
John W. Summers,
the daughter of
Major James and Mary Graham,
She was born
on the 13th of Oct. 1821,
and died
on the 15th of Dec. 1844,
aged 23 years,
2 months and 2 days.

On second side:
After receiving a regular
educational at Yale College,
and the public honors
of that Institution,
he was trained in the school
at Litchield
to the profession of Law.
in the practice of which he
was afterwards established
at Augusta, Ga.

Springwood Cemetery, Greenville, S. C.-
Graves of some former Newberry, S. C.
citizens-

Curtis B. Atwood-

In memory of
Mrs. Judith Atwood,
born
in Newberry County,
March 4th, 1790,
died
in the city of Greenville,
April 29th, 1871.

Sacred
To the memory
of
Mrs. Elizabeth Williams,
wife of
Col. James Williams,
who died on the 15th of
July, 1812,
aged 60 years.

On the third side:
Induced by feeble health
to travel towards his
native State, he was
arrested by death, while
on his journey, at this
place, June 25, 1823.

In
Memory of
Dr. Burrell Chick
who was born
Jan 15, 1776,
and departed this life
Jan 25, 1847.

Erected
By Conjugal
affection
in memory of
Mrs. Massey Chick,
who was born June 29,
1781,
and died May 9, 1845.

Sacred
To the memory
of
Mrs. Elizabeth Thompson
Williams,
wife of Thomas B.
Williams,
who departed this life
on the 2nd of March,
1832,
aged 38 years and 8 days
(This grave has an odd angle
head stone placed so that
grave in direction of set
sun).

CEMETERY MARKERS (continued)

Quaker Cemetery-located about 3 miles Southwest of Newberry Court House, near Bush River, where the Bush River Meeting House was located. The markers in 1932 were:

In Memoriam
Lucy Gilliam
Born Oct 5, 1800
Died Feb 2, 1886

Mary Gilliam
Born Nov 17, 1824
Died Feb 13, 1847

Jane Lake
Sept 2, 1777
Died Dec 2, 1831

Mary M. Lake
Born Feb 23, 1806
Died Aug 26, 1821

To The Memory of
Elizabeth Lake
Born Feb 10, 1809
Died January 9, 1835

Elijah Lake
Born Feb 1, 1768
Died Feb 1, 1824

Phebe Ann Lake
Daughter of I.K. and
E. R. Lake
Died Nov 14, 1853
Aged 20 years

Rebecca Gilbert
Died Sept 9, 1816

George Blair
Born Nov 22, 1831
Died Feb 27, 1834

Janet Rogers
Died Oct 10, 1825

John Blair
Born Oct 15, 1799
Died July 21, 1848

George Latham
of New York.

Mrs. Sara A. Earle
Wife of Major Thompson
Earle
Departed this life June 9,
1817, aged 16 years, 11 months, and
21 days.

Lewis Spillars
Born May 10, 1803
Died December 12, 1830

J. B. Hunt
1834

Walter Herbert
Born June 13, 1773
Died Dec 15, 1851

Ann Herbert,
wife of
Walter Herbert,
Died March 3,
1847.

Jesse Ruk.....
(stone broken)
Died Oct 2, 183..
Aged 29 years.

I. D. Herbert

Isreal Chandler
Born March 25, 1770
Died March 13, 1829
Aged 58 years, 11 months,
18 days

Lydia Chandler
Died Jan 24, 1832,
Aged 56 years, 5 months,
and 15 days.

W. J. Hunt 1829.

William McP. Herbert
Died April 1, 1842
Aged 7 years, 8 months.

Frances Herbert
Born Oct 3, 1803
Died Jan 4, 1845

Timothy Pugh
Born July 5, 1808
Died October 13, 1849

Catherine Pugh
Born December 25, 1806
Died May 23, 1859.

Sarah Pugh
Born May 18, 1775
Died May 29, 1859
Aged 84 years, 11 days.

Rebecca Jane,
Wife of R. B. Reagan
Born Aug 3, 1830
Died June 17, 1866.

An old granite stone
with only the year:
"1786".

HERE
Lies the body of
Samuel Kelly.

Margaret Parham
Died July 27, 1836
Aged 73 years.

Isaac Kirk
Died June 17, 1815
Aged 53 years, 5 months,
A native of Pennsylvania.

Rebecca Kirk
Died 8 day of 5
month, 1837,
Aged 70 years, 1 month,
and 20 days.

Mary Jenkins
Died Sept 2, 1833

Sarah Jenkins
Died May 2, 1852

Mary Jenkis
Died Aug 26, 1834

Thomas Lake
Born Oct 11, 1797
Died Dec 27, 1854
Aged 57 years, 2 months,
and 16 days.

Rebecca Lake
Wife of Thomas Lake
Born Aug 21, 1795
Died Oct 30, 1855
Aged 60 years, 2 months,
and 20 days.

Elisha Lake
Born March 5, 182...
Died Dec 8, 1834

Thomas John Lake
Born June 11, 1827
Died Feb 22, 1829

Isaac Jenkins, Sr.
Died 3rd day of the 4th month,
1798
Aged 40 years, 7 months,
and 2 days.

Maris Jenkins
Died 12 of 1st month, 1801.

Mrs. Phebe K. Mendenhall, daughter
of Isaac and Rebecca Kirk,
wife of Dr. M. T. Mendenhall,
Born June 1807, Died Oct 21, 1874.

CEMETERY MARKERS (continued)

Quaker Cemetery (continued)-

HERE
Lies the body of
John Kelly
Who was born the 3rd of
April, 1758, and died
the 20th October, 1817.

E. M. 1809

HERE
Lies the body of
Hannah Kelly
who died the 18th of
June, 1820, in the
83rd year of her age.

Nehemiah Thomas,
was born the 10th day of
the 8th month, 1790, and
deceased the 8th day of the
5th month, 1795.

Mrs. Hester B. O'Connor
Consort of William O'Connor and
daughter of Joseph and Esther
Coppocle, who was born Feb 7,
1819,
And departed this life on
June 13, 1840.

On a square tapering stone, about 10 feet high, there is the following:

MY
William Harmon Frean, Born January 20, 1834;
Died July 6, 1855.

Hannah Kelly Belton
Daughter of Thomas and Hannah Frean,
and widow of Dr. Belton, deceased of
Mississippi. Born November 29, 1826,
Died November 15, 1858.
(Above on West side of stone)

On the East side of stone:

Dead
Hannah Frean,
The wife of Thomas Frean and daughter of
Matthias Elmore and his wife, Rebecca Kelly.
Born October 25, 1795; Died June 29, 1859.

Thomas Frean
A native of the County Tipperary, Ireland.
Born June 15, 1793; Died April 7, 1861.
To awaken his fellow citizens to a sense of their
degradation, he wrote and published a pamphlet
" TEN YEARS IN THE TREASURY OFFICE."

THE
Last Tribute of affection which a HUSBAND and A FATHER
can bestow.
(This is on the North side of the stone)

On the South side of stone:

Beloved
John Francis Frean
Born December 16, 1821
Died October 3, 1827.

Patrick Frean
Born July 1, 1824,
Died September 1, 1829.

Rebecca Ann Frean
Born April 30, 1818,
Died December 25, 1831.

John Belton O'Neall Frean,
Born September 14, 1832,
Died October 6, 1832.

CEMETERY MARKERS (continued)

Helena Church Cemetery-

Joseph H. Davis
Born
July 31, 1842
Died
August 10, 1874

Mother
Amanda Davis
Born
Feb 18, 1846
Died
May 8, 1897

To the Memory of
Willie and Lannie,
sons of
A. A. and S. I. Davis.

(several unmarked
graves)

In an iron enclosure are the following:

In
Memory of
Frances Darby
who died
December 28, 1863,
aged 60 years.

In
Memory of
Mattie,
daughter of W. B. and S.E.
Lowe,
was born Oct 7th, 1862,
and died Sept 29th, 1863.

William Zobel
Born
in Wurtemberg, Germany,
June 5, 1830,
Died
in Helena, S. C.
March 9, 1892.
Aged 61 years, 9 months,
and 4 days.
(He was a Confederate Soldier)

Louisa A. F.
Zobel,
Born
Heilbron, Germany,
July 23, 1834,
Died
Helena, S. C.
April 28, 1920.

OLD KADESH CHURCH SITE CEMETERY-
Located 10 miles Northwest of Newberry
Court House.

Sacred
To the memory of
Dr. James K. Gilder, M.D.
who was born Nov 17th, 1832,
and departed this life
Sept 7th, 1856,
leaving a bereaved wife, one
child, and a large circle of
friends............

(Other graves here
with no markers)

In Loving Remembrance of
Henry Paul Zobel,
Born March 21, 1875,
Died Feb 24, 1891.

Christian Rudolph
Born
in Wurtemberg, Germany,
March 3, 1803,
Died
Feb 21, 1868.

Pauline Louisa
Zobel
Born Helena, S.C.
July 1, 1863,
Died July 14, 1869.

Another grave with
small stone but no
inscription.

Sacred
To the memory of
Sarah T. Neal,
who was born
April 4th, 1836,
and departed this life
March 2nd, 1856.

Sacred
To the memory of
Col. James Gilder,
son of
Capt. Phillip & Sarah
Gilder.
Born Jan 1st, 1802,
Died Jan 27th, 1856.

Oscar Perry
son of
C. J. & M. C. Zobel,
Born
Nov 22, 1898,
Died
Jan 12, 1902.

Infant child
of
C.J. & M.C. Zobel

Infant child
of
C.J. & M. C. Zobel

The grave of Capt. Jphn Williams, an officer
in the Confederate Army, is in this graveyard;
said to be close the the edge of the highway,
a small ditch having been washed out near it.
At this time(1935) the whole area is covered
with pine trees..

CEMETERY MARKERS (continued)

Beth Eden Lutheran Church Cemetery— located about 4½ miles North of Newberry Court House, on or near the old Whitmire road. Some of the markers are:

In Memory of
Andrew Campbell
who died
Jan 8th, 1869,
in the 77th year of
his age.

Asleep in Jesus
Louisa F. Cromer,
wife of
George E. Campbell,
Born
April 15, 1836,
Died
June 26, 1923.

Dr. William M. Kinard,
son of
J. P. & E. M. Kinard,
Born
Feb 11, 1842,
Died
April 3, 1877.
(Confederate soldier)

In
Memory of
J. N. Summer,
Born
Dec 15th, 1783,
Died
Sept 6th, 1870,
He was for 71 years a
consistent member of the
Lutheran Church.

Mary A.,
daughter of
G. E. & L. F. Campbell,
Born
October 2, 1866,
Died
September 18, 1875.

In Memory of
Eve Campbell,
Born
June 2, 1809,
Died
Dec 19, 1879.

Sallie Baker Campbell
January 22, 1881,
December 15, 1938.
Edward F. Campbell,
Sept 12, 1871,
....
(Above two on one stone)

Sarah Kinard,
wife of
Dr. Wm. M. Kinard,
Born
Aug 29th, 1847,
Died
July 20th, 1885.

Sacred to the memory of
Mrs. Elizabeth Summer,
who was born in Newberry
District, 22nd of June,
1786, and died Dec 21st, 1847,
aged 61 years, 5 months,
and 21 days.
She was the wife of Mr. John
Nicholas Summer for the past
41 years, 9 months,
and 8 days.

Willie Coleman,
son of
G. E. & L. F. Campbell,
Born
July 14, 1878,
Died
April 23, 1896.

David P. Campbell,
August 23, 1875,
August 13, 1919.

Frances Lavania,
daughter of
D.P. & M. M. Campbell,
Aug 20, 1915
Dec 19, 1934.

Sacred
To the memory of
Anna Epting,
Consort of
George A. Epting,
who was born
June 2nd, 1816,
and died
August 26, 1864.

Here
lies the remains of
Maj. John P. Kinard,
Born
Dec 22, 1820,
Died
Nov 1, 1882.

George E. Campbell
Born
Dec 10, 1821,
Died
Oct 12, 1896.

Sacred
To the memory of
Jacob Epting
who was born
Oct 19, 1849,
and died
Jan 30th, 1868,
aged 18 years, 3 months,
and 11 days.

Sacred
To the memory of
George A. Epting,
who was born
Jan 12th, 1812,
and died
Nov 15th, 1867,
Aged 55 years, 10 months,
and 3 days.
(Confederate soldier)

Here rests
the mortal remains of
Bluford M. Summer, M. D.
son of
Jacob and Elizabeth Summer,
who died at Fort Deleware,
September 13th, 1863,
aged 24 years, 9 months,
and 1 day.
(Confederate soldier)

Confederate Soldiers with no marker
Capt Philander Cromer, Officer,
killed at Fredericksburg, Va.
Elijah Whitmire,   J. G. Fulmer
Henry Werts,   Bill Clamp,
John R. Wicker,

Two not proved to be Confederate soldiers:

Thomas Hoard Cromer,
Born 1816,
Died 1870.

John Swittenberg,
Born April 25, 1818,
Died Nov 22, 1867.

Confederate Soldiers:
Jesse Cornelius Dickert,
Born July 8th, 1828,
Died May 14th, 1877.

J. William Caldwell,
Born Dec 6, 1843,
Died Nov 19, 1905.

Robert Henry Burton,
Born Aug 4, 1848,
Died April 30, 1913.

H. H. Folk,
Born May 30,
Died May 13,

CEMETERY MARKERS (continued)

Beth Eden Church Cemetery (continued)-

Confederate Soldiers:

William P. McCollough
Born Oct 18, 1843,
Died June 1, 1924.

W. Langdon Waters
Born Dec 6, 1833
Died Sept 9, 1914.

George A. Sligh
Born Oct 22, 1822
Died Nov 22, 1913.

James L. Cromer
Born Aug 2, 1838
Died Dec 16, 1870

Thomas W. McCollough
Born July 20, 1846
Died May 18, 1929.

OLD COVENANTER CEMETERY-located about 8 miles Northwest of Newberry Court House, above Jalapa, to right of highway, near Gilders Creek.

In
Memory of
Mary Red
who was born
March 15th, 1797,
and departed this life
June 28th, 1836.

Sacred
To
The memory of
Samuel Red,
Husband of
Mary Red.
He departed this life
on April 1st,
1835,
Aged 50 years.

Sacred
To the memory of
David C. Red
who departed this life
August 28th, 1834,
aged 4 years, 8 months,
and 6 days.

In
Memory of
Harriet Jane Chalmers
who died
April 4th, 1839,
aged 1 year.

In
Memory of
Eleanor Boyd,
who departed this life
14th day of November,
1820,
aged 61 years.
She liv'd belov'd,
And died lamented.

In
Memory of
David Boyd, Sen'r.
who departed this life
Dec'r 5th, 1833,
aged 75 years.

In Memory of
Nancy C. Chalmers,
who departed this life
Nov 1st, 1815,
aged 4 years.

D. B.

Sacred
To the memory of
William H. Clary,
who was born
June 27th, 1821,
and died October,
1825.

Sacred
To the memory of
Nancy Clary,
who died June 4th,
1822,
In the 10th year of
her age.

Sacred
To the memory of
Alexander C. Clary,
who died
September 25th,
1823,
In the 9th year
of his age.

Sacred
To the memory of
Mary Ann Clary,
who departed this life
the 28th Oct, 1820.
Aged 5 years.

In
Memory of
Jane Henry,
Who departed this life
March 13th,
1821,
To her left are 2 sons,
D. B. and J. C., and to
her right, A.M.

Sacred
To the memory of
Thomas B. Chalmers,
who departed this life
September 23rd, 1842,
aged 24 years,
4 months, & 26 days.
He left a wife and 3
children to mourn his
loss.

Old Ebenezar Methodist Church Cemetery- located 15 miles North of Newberry Court House. Some markers:

Sacred
To the memory of
Joseph Caldwell,
who was born
31st Dec 1769,
and departed this life,
Feb 27th, 1838.
" Blessed are the pure in heart,
For they shall see God."

In Memory of
Mrs. Ruth Caldwell,
who departed this life
7th June, 1844,
aged 64 years, 4 months,
and 1 day.

Christina Hancock,
B. May 17, 1791
D. June 6, 1862.

CEMETERY MARKERS (continued)

Prosperity Cemetery- some of markers- Rev War patriot, Archibald Boyd-

Menta Memori
Here lieth the body of
Archibald Boyd who
departed this life the
4th day of December, 1802,
aged 44 years.

Sacred
To the memory of
Jane Boyd,
A native of Ireland, who
came to the State in 1772
as the wife of Samuel Fair.
After his death she married
Archibald Boyd whom she also
survived, and died
November, 1807.

Sacred
To
The memory of
Capt. Archibald Boyd,
who departed this life
August 20th, 1816,
in the 36th year of his age,

Mt. Bethel Church Site and Cemetery (second church)-located about 10 miles East of Newberry Court House, on old Buncomb Road, between old Caldwell home and Enoree Baptist Church- In a small square enclosed with an iron picket fence are a few graves, but only one of the box-like type of marker with the following inscription:

In
Memory of
Mrs. Elizabeth Boozer,
wife of
George B. Boozer,
and daughter of
James & Elizabeth Caldwell,
Born Jany 1821,
Died August 7th, 1857,
Aged 36 years, 7 months.

Other markers:
George Turnipsee,
Born
Nov 6th, 1800,
Died March 20, 1866.

(A small showing flag of
Confederacy, with name:
W. J. Buzhardt)

Frances A. Turnip
wife of
J. O. Turnipseed,
Born
Oct 10th, 1847,
Died
May 28th, 1887.

Sacred
To the memory of
Mrs. Susan L. Moody,
of Sumter, S. C.
who died
at the residence of
Mrs. T. W. Caldwell,
Newberry, S. C.
March 23rd, 1864.

In
Memory of
Cornelia O. Paysinger,
daughter of
F. S. Paysinger,
who was born
May 24th, 1841,
and died
Dec 11th, 1867.

In
Memory of
Arthur W. Paysinger,
son of
F. S. & C. O. Paysinger,
who was born
Dec 23rd, 1867,
and died
Feb 9th, 1869.

(These two inscriptions are on same stone)

St. Paul's Lutheran Church Cemetery-located above Pomaria about two miles-two markers of the many there-

Henry Summer,
Born
Oct 4th, 1815,
Died
June 21, 1892,
Aged 76 years, 8 months,
17 days.

In Memory of
Mrs. C. C. Summer,
wife of
Henry Summer,
who was born
Feb 25th, 1818,
and died
Sept 10th, 1874,
Aged 56 years, 6 months,
and 17 days.

St. Matthews Lutheran Church-located Northwest of Pomaria, about six miles, near Broad River- only three markers of the many there-

Henry Cromer,
Died
February, 1862,
Aged 69 years.

John Heller,
Died
Feb 26, 1887,
Aged 86 years.

Mary,
Wife of
John Heller,
Died
Sept, 1874,
Aged 71 years.

CEMETERY MARKERS (continued)

Bush River Baptist Church Cemetery-located about 10 miles Northwest of Newberry Court House, some of the oldest markers as follows:

John Satterwhite
Born Oct 16, 1818
Died Dec 1, 1877
Aged
59 years, 1 month,
14 days.
" Beneath this sod now lies the form
That to us was dear and lovely,
Whose sparkling eyes increased our joys,
But now they are gone and we are lonely."

Elvira Satterwhite
wife of
John Satterwhite
Born
Nov 29, 1828,
Died
Nov 26, 1894.

CROW,
died Sept 22nd,
1802- age 86.

In
Memory of
William Cole,
who died
March 23rd, 1802,
aged 33 years.

Sacred
To the Memory of
Jesse Gary,
Born Oct 22nd, A.D. 1782,
Married May 5th, A.D. 1800,
Died Jan 30th, A.D. 1843,
The monument, the bereaved
children of the much lamented
deceased, have raised as a feeble and
lasting tribute to his departed
worth; bearing a faint emblem of the
love and veneration they mutually bore
to him while living, and humbly
wish to extend through time.
" It is not the tear at the moment shed,
When the cold turf has just been laid
o'er him;
That can tell how beloved was the
soul that fled,
Or how deep in our hearts we deplore him."

In
Memory of
Capt. West Gary,
who died
the 16th April,
1814.

Sacred
To the Memory of
Mary Gary,
wife of
Jesse Gary,
Born June 14, A.D. 1782,
Married May 5, A.D. 1800,
Died Oct 11, A.D. 1842.
While living she was devoted to
her family.
Her death was a sad bereavment,
Her children considering their
loss was her gain,
Are ready to exclaim,
" The Lord is good."
And with due respect do erect
this monument to her memory.
May her walk in life be a guide
to lead us all to God.
" My living friends, weep not for
me,
While you on earth remain;
Tho' I am called to leave you
here,
With Christ we will meet again."

In
Memory of
Charles Gary,
Deceased July, 1808,
aged 75 years.
(Rev War patriot)

In Memory of
Mrs. Martha Williams,
daughter of T. & R. Gary,
who married July 20th, 1803,
and departed this life
Feb 20th, 1807, aged 27 years.

Sacred
To the memory of
John Armstrong,
who departed this life
the 27th April, 1815,
in the Thirty fifth year of
his age. His disconsolate wife erects this
marble as a testimonial of the affection
which having borne him while living, she yet
feels now he is dead.

In Memory
of
Hettie Gary,
who was born
May 7th, 1814,
and died
Feb 24th, 1831.
"Welcome that death whose
painful strife
Bear us to Christ, our
better life."

In Memory of
Christopher Griffin
who was born on the
26th day May, 1793,
and departed this life
on the 13th day of
Feb 1832.

In Memory
of
Frances Williams,
Relic of
John Williams,
first of West Gary,
who was born
Sept 25, 1784,
and died
Sept 4th, 1848.

Sacred
To
The Memory of
Elizabeth Griffin,
wife of
Gen. C. B. Griffin,
who was born Aug 19, 1809,
and died Oct 21st, 1845,
aged 36 years, 2 months,
and 2 days.

CEMETERY MARKERS (continued)

Bush River Baptist Church (continued)-
Elizabeth Griffin
(continuation from previous page)
The monument her bereaved husband has
reared as a feeble token of the love
cherished towards her while living,
and would humbly desire to endure
through life.
"Here lies my dear and loving wife,
My only bosom friend.
I hope in heaven to see her face,
When I this life do end."

Sacred
To
The Memory of
James Gary,
who was born Feb 25th,
1777,
and died Jan 17th,
1832,
aged 54 years, 10 months,
and 22 days.

Mary Elizabeth,
wife of J. W. Smith,
and daughter of
W.P. & Letty Gilliam,
Born
Nov 23rd, 1843,
Died
August 1, 1876.

Ruth Cummings,
wife of
J.W. Smith,
and daughter of
W.P. & Letty Gilliam,
Born
Feb 13, 1852,
Died
Nov 11, 1874.

In Memory of
John Suber,
Honest integrity, accomplished by
great simplicity of character and
unobstrusive acts of neighborly
kindness, attended his foot-steps
through life.
He died October 11, 1859,
aged 62 years, 7 months,
and 6 days.
His two surviving sons erect this
tablet to perpetuate his memory.

Sacred
To
The memory of
Catherine Gary,
wife of
James Gary,
who was born
Dec 17th, 1779,
and died April 7th,
1824,
aged 44 years, 3 months,
and 20 days.

Sacred
To
The memory of
Elizabeth Vance,
Consort of Samuel Vance,
who departed this life
Nov 29th, 1827, and
the 44th year of her age.

Sacred
To The memory of
Stephen Blackburn
who was born 29th July
1798,
and died 13th Dec 1834,
Whose private virtues were many
and whose loss loss his relatives
and acquaintenances deeply deplore.
"Relations all who read this stone,
You know that I have undergone
consumption sore decay.
My dust doth speak to you behind,
See ye the one thing needful mind,
Lest you be called away."
T. G.
Dec'd. Decemb'r
the 28, 1800.

Beneath this tablet
Repose the Mortal remains of
Lavania Suber,
Consort of
John Suber,
and daughter of
George and Ann E. Gallman,
Born 1805,
Died April 16, 1855.
Her charms of gentleness,
her tender solicitude for
the welfare of others, her
kindness and uprightneousness
endeared her to all who knew
her. Idolized by her husband
and children, and reverenced with
affection by a large kindred,
only the God who took her could
love her better than they. (cont above)

Sacred
To the memory of
John Reeder
who was born
Oct 27, 1788,
and died
March 13, 1845.

Sacred
To
The Memory of
Malinda Gary,
who was born
Feb 19, 1807,
and died June,
29th, 1827,
aged 20 years,
4 months, and
10 days.

Sacred
To the memory of
Mary Reeder,
Consort of
John Reeder,
who was born Dec 5,
1790,
and died March 21,
1855.

Sacred
To The memory of
William Satterwhite,
Born
Feb 3, 1805
Died
Dec 8, 1883.

In
Memory of
Susan Satterwhite,
wife of
William Satterwhite,
and daughter of
Thomas & Elizabeth
Dalrymple,
Born
Jan 4, 1805,
Died
Sept 15, 1879.
"Blessed are the dead wh
died in the Lord."

Her care of the poor
and the sick was highly
exemplary, and many a
widow and orphan shall
rise up and call her
blessed.
"Friend after friend dep
That finds not here an e
Were this frail world o
final rest,
Living or dying none
were blest,
The memory of the Ju
is blessed."

CEMETERY MARKERS (continued)

Duncan's Creek Presbyterian Church Cemetery-located about 5 miles East of Clinton, S. C., in Laurens County and near the Newberry County line.

Sacred
To the memory of
William Craig (D.O.)
who departed this life
Oct 9th, 1824,
in the 64th year of
his age.

In
Memory of
Margaret Fairbeirn
who departed this
life August 3rd, A.D.
1830, aged 60 years,
5 months, and 9 days.

Sacred
To the memory of
John Bouland
who was born the 5th
of May, 1760,
and departed this life
the 2nd February,
1820,
In the 60th year of
his age.

Sacred
To the memory of
Robert Long
who departed this life
January 20th, 1840,
Aged 80 years.

Mrs. Charity Little,
wife of
David Little, Sr.
From 1770 to
Nov 6th, 1826.

In Memory of
Alex, Fairbeirn
Died 15th June,
1798,
aged 76 years.
Also, Catherine, his wife,
died 16th July, 1781,
Aged 41 years.

Here lies the body of
George Young, Sr.
who departed this life
on the 13th October,
1833,
In the 78th year of his age.
This is erected to his memory
by his son, George.

In Memory of
Thomas Murdough
who died 15th August,
1809,
aged 81 years.

David Little, Sr.,
From Nov 11, 1767
to Nov 17, 1812.

Sacred to the memory
of
Rev. John B. Kennedy
who departed this life
December 12th, A.D. 1846,
in the 81st year of his age.

Sacred
To the memory of
Rebecca Kennedy
Consort of
Rev. John B. Kennedy
who departed this life
July 29th, A.D. 1846,
in the 70th year of her age.

Sacred
To the memory of
Elizabeth Young,
who departed this life the
2nd November, 1800,
aged 45 years.

Leonard Beasley
Va. Line
Rev War.

Joseph Adair, Jr.
Der. Com.
S.C. Mil.
Rev War.

In Memory of
James Afair, Sr.
who was born
May 15th, 1752,
and died
Aug 18th, 1818.

In Memory
of
Hannah Adair,
wife of
James Adair, Sr.
who was born
Sept 28th, 1750,
and died
Nov 10th, 1826.

Enoree Baptist Church Cemetery-located about 10 miles East of Newberry Court House, near Keitt's Crossroads. The following are some of the markers:

In
Memory of
John A. Keer,
who was born
June 17th, 1790,
and departed this life
March 25th, 1832

In Memory
of
Capt. Andrew Suber,
who died
Dec 13th, 1843,
aged 34 years, 2 months,
and 11 days.

In Memory of
Eliza A. B. Suber,
Consort of
Capt. A. Suber,
who died
Dec 8th, 1843.

Sacred
To the memory of
Sarah Thompson Goree,
who departed this life
March 3rd, 1813,
aged 33 years,
11 months & 15 days.

In
Memory of
Our precious father,
Dr. John W. McCants,
Born
Jan 25, 1819,
Died
July 9, 1871.

In
Memory of
Our precious mother,
Fannie E. McCants,
Born
October 13th, 1830,
Died
August 4th, 1859.

In
Memory of
Henry Swindler,
Born October 11th,
1785,
Died October 22nd,
1843,
Aged 58 years,
and 11 days.

Sacred
To the memory of
Redden Goree,
who departed this life,
Febry 8th, 1813,
aged 41 years,
4 months & 1 day.

CEMETERY MARKERS (continued)

Enoree Baptist Church Cemetery (continued)-

In
Memory of
Margaret Swindler,
Born March 18th,
1790,
Died January 23rd,
1849.

Charles F. Sligh
was born July 11, 1810,
and died
December 4th, 1860,
aged 50 years, 5 months,
3 weeks and 1 day.

Elizabeth Sligh,
wife of
Charles F. Sligh,
born
May 27th, 1817,
died
May 20th, 1884,
" Asleep in Jesus."

Bauskett Graveyard- located near Enoree Baptist Church-

Maj'r.
James Wadlington,
Born April 10th, 1782,
and died October 31st, 1834,
In his last illness he sought
and obtained the consolation
of religeon. He died trusting
in the Lord. His surviving friends,
therefore, are not without hope that
they shall see him again in a more
glorious and beautiful form.

Sacred
To the memory
of
Elizabeth Ann Wadlington,
who departed this life
May 20th, 1834, aged
15 years, and 2 months.

Thomas Bauskett Wadlington
May 25, 1821,
Dec 10, 1882.

(Other graves here with
no markers)

Old Tranquil Cemetery- located about 8 miles North of Newberry Court House, to right from Jalapa.

Sacred
To the memory of
Sibella,
wife of
Robert G. Gilliam,
and daughter of
William and Mary Blackburn,
who was born Jan'y 4th,
1796,
was married May 4th, 1826,
She professed conversion and
joined the M. E. Church in the
Fall of 1838, and departed
this life August 9th, 1857,
She was a consistent member,
and died in peace.

Sacred
To the memory of
John K. Hinson
who was born March 16th,
1816,
and died September 29th,
1854.
He was for many years a
member of the M. E. Church,
and died in Great Peace
and triumph.

James B. Wilson,
Born
Dec 25th, 1805,
Died
Oct 8th, 1864.

James William Wilson
Born
December 24, 1840,
Died
October 13, 1864.
(Confederate soldier)

To
The memory of
Mary E. Wilson,
wife of
James B. Wilson,
Born
March 13th, 1821,
Died
August 20th, 1889.

Jacob Gilliam
Wilson,
Born
Dec 9, 1844
Died
Oct 7, 1864
(Confederate soldi

A Tribute
of respect
To the memory of
George Herbert,
By his
children.

Sacred
To the memory of
Pettus Ward,
son of
James B. & D.A.E. Wilson,
who was born
Nov 21st, 1852,
and departed this life
August 22nd, 1859.

Sacred
To the memory of
M. Josephine,
third daughter of
James B. & Drucilla
Ann Elizabeth Wilson,
who was born
February 16th, 1843,
and departed this life,
October 22nd, 1857,
She lived beloved and
died lamented.

Sacred
To the memory of
Sarah C.,
second daughter of
James B. & Drucilla
Ann Elizabeth Wilson,
who was born
May 11th, 1839,
and departed this life
Sept 17th, 1857,
She lived beloved and
died lamented.

Sacred
To the memory
Mary R.,
first daughter
James B. & Druci
Ann Elizabeth Wi
who was born
Oct 4th, 1836,
departed this li
August 17th, 185
She lived belove
and died lamente

CEMETERY MARKERS (continued)

Old Tranquil Cemetery (continued)-

Sacred
To the memory of
Drucilla Ann Elizabeth,
wife of
James B. Wilson,
who was born
Nov 4th, 1815,
and departed this life
March 14th, 1858.
She died in peace and
rests with God.

Zaccheus F. Wright
Born
Sept 25m 1825,
Died
Oct 9, 1885,
"Blessed are the dead
which die in the Lord."

To
The memory of
Sarah Wright
Died
Oct 20, 1865,
aged 75 years.

Sacred
To The Memory of
Van Davis
Born December 11th,
1791,
departed this life
October 1st, 1839,
aged 48 years, 10 months,
and 10 days.
"Mortal, reflect as you pass by,
As you are now so once was I.
As I am now, soon you must be,
Prepare through Christ to follow me."

In
Memory of
Jane Chambers,
wife of Barnette F. Chambers,
and daughter of
Van and Mary Davis,
who was born Dec 21st, 1820,
and departed this life
July 12th, 1865.
"To where this silent marble weeps,
A friend, a wife, a sister sleeps,
A Heart within whose peaceful cells,
Affection, virtue, loves to dwell."

In Memory of
Franklin Wilson
who died at Camp near
Charleston, S. C.
Feb 1st, 1863,
in the 44th year of
his age.
(Confederate soldier)

Sacred
To the memory of
James Wright
who departed this life
Jany 3rd, 1825,
aged 79.

Sacred
To the memory of
Mary Wright
who departed this life
Sept 6th, 1841,
aged 56 years.

Sacred
To
The Memory of
Rev. Stephen Shell,
who departed this life
Dec 11th, 1822,
aged 68 years.

Sacred
To the memory of
Mary Davis,
wife of
Van Davis,
Born July 12th, 1796,
departed this life
December 15th, 1853,
aged 57 years, 5 months,
and 23 days.
"Mortal, reflect as you pass by,
As you are now so once was I.
As I am now soon must you be,
Prepare through Christ to follow me."

Sacred
To the Memory of
Barnette Chambers
who was born August 29th, 1823,
and departed this life
Jan 4th, 1862.
(Confederate soldier)

Sacred
To
The memory of
Jane Shell
who departed this life
July 12th, 1822,
aged 68 years.

Sacred
To the memory of
Lucy Wright
who departed this life
September 27th,
1824,
Aged 67.

Sacred
To the memory of
John Yeargin, Sr.
who died
Jan 29th, 1816,
aged 59 years.

Sacred
To the memory of
Sarah Shell,
wife of
J. E. Shell,
who departed this life
May 15th, 1828,
aged 33 years.

Richey Wilson
Died
Feb 18th, 1924,
in the 56th year
of his age.

Lucy,
daughter of
Rich'd & Mary Wilson
and wife of
Eugene Glasgow,
Born Jan 30, 1902
Died Dec 5th, 1923

Mary Wright
Born
Sept 17, 1785,
Died
Sept 6, 1841.

Zaccheus Wright
Born
January 9th, 1783,
Died
March 21st, 1862.

In
Memory of
Frances E. Davis,
Born
Dec 23rd, 1824,
Died
Nov 2nd, 1867.
" But why repine? 'Twas
Heaven's will. 'Tis best.
We hope she's happy now
amongst the blest."

In
Memory of
Nancy Davis
Born
March 18th, 1818,
Died
July 31st, 1868,
"Sleep on, sister,
and take thy rest,
God willed thee hence,
he thought it best."

In
Memory of
Thomas B.B. Gilliam,
son of
Jacob F. & Mary
Gilliam.

CEMETERY MARKERS (continued)

Old Tranquil Cemetery(continued)-

Sacred
To the Memory of
Jacob F. Gilliam,
who departed this life
August 6th,
1836,
aged 48 years, 1 month,
and 10 days.

Sacred
To the memory of
Mary Gilliam
who departed this life
Sept 19th, 1843,
aged 55 years.

Sacred
To the Memory of
Sarah J. L. Gilliam
who departed this life
April 28th, 1837,
aged 12 years, 2 months,
and 27 days.

In
Memory of
Newton H. Gilliam,
son of
Jacob F. & Mary
Gilliam.

In Memory of
James M. Moore,
Born April 25th, 1852,
Died Jan 5th, 1862,
aged 9 years, 8 months,
and 10 days.
Jamie is not dead but sleepeth.

Sacred to the Memory of
Margaret Moore
who departed this life
Oct 11th, 1855,
aged 27 years,
4 months, and 12 days.
She leaves 2 children to
mourn their irreparable loss.

Sacred
To the memory of
Sarah Massey
who departed this
life
March 18th, 1848,
aged 35 years.

Sacred
To the memory of
Lieut. Thomas F. Hunter
who was born
Dec 3rd, 1835.
He united with the Lutheran
Church at Beth Eden, and fell
while defending his country,
June 8th, 1863.
" Blessed are the dead who die
in the Lord."
(Confederate soldier)

Sacred
To the Memory of
James Hunter
who was born
Oct 24th, 1829,
He united with the Lutheran
Church at Beth Eden, and died
while defending his country,
June 16th, 1863.
" Blessed are the dead who die
in the Lord."
(Confederate soldier)

Here
lies the body
of
Lucy Wright
who departed this life
the 28th June A.D.
1817,
aged 29 years.

Wilson Family Graveyard-located 4 miles East of Newberry Court House on old Blairs or Maybington road.

Our Mother
Mary Wilson,
wife of
James Wilson, Sr.,
Born in the year 1800,
Died
August 2nd, 1868,
in her 68th year.

To
The memory of
Henry Wilson
who was born
January 14th, 1826,
and died
November 24th, 1862.
(Confederate soldier)

Caleb Wilson
who was born
April 15th, 1840,
and died
December 13th, 1862.
(Confederate soldier)

(By the grave of
the mother is a bu
dark gray slab with
no inscription—
probably grave of
James Wilson, Sr.)

Cross Roads Church Cemetery-located near Chappels- some of markers-

Sacred
To the memory of
James Wallace Lark,
Born June 5, 1840,
and departed this life in
the service of his country,
January 23rd, 1862.
(Confederate soldier)

Andrew Lee Lark
Died May 8th, 1878,
aged 84 years.

Catherine Lark,
Consort of
Andrew Lee Lark,
Born May 16th, 1801,
Died March 2nd, 1870.

CEMETERY MARKERS (continued) 423

Cannons Creek A.R.P. Church Cemetery-some of the markers-located Southeast of Newberry Court House, about 5 miles.

Here
lies the body of
The Rev'd Mr.
John Renwick
who died August 20th,
A.D. 1775.
Aetatis Suae 40.

Here
Lies waiting for the
resurrection the body of
John Caldwell,
son of John & Rosannah Caldwell,
who departed this life
on the 8th of August in the
year of our Lord 1831,
aged 26 years.

Here
Lies the body of
Alexander Johnston
waiting for the resurrection,
who departed this life
March 25th, 1816,
aged 70 years.
(Rev War soldier)

In
Memory of
Rosannah Moore,
Consort of
James Moore,
who was born in
County Antrim,
Ireland,
and died on the
13th of Nov, 1831,
in the 83rd year
of her age.

In
Memory of
Robert Maffett
who died
Sept 17th,
1837,
aged 72 years.

In
Memory of
Barbary Maffett,
who departed
this life
July 31st, 1844,
aged 77 years,
3 months, & 19 days.

Here lies the body of
Mrs. Mary Ann
Royston
who died Jan'y 18th,
A.D. 1801.
Aetatis Suae 28.

James Sloan
died 1860,
aged 62 years.

Jane Sloan
died 1867,
aged 75 years.

Sacred
To
The Memory of
Robert Moore
who departed this life
March 23rd, 1834,
in the 75th year of
his age.
" Mark the perfect man
and behold the upright;
for the end of that man
is peace."
(Rev War soldier)

To
The memory of
Daniel Reid
born
March, 1785,
died
August 29, 1849.

Sacred
To the memory of
Rev. Charles Strong,
son of James Strong, Esq.,
of Chester District,
and Pastor for eight years
of the Congregations of King's
Creek, Cannon's Creek, and Prosperity.
He lived beloved, and died lamented
by all who knew him, on the
20th of July, 1824,
in the 36th year of his age,
his life of usefulness ended.
He was distinguished for his vigorous
intellect and amiable manners, his
unassuming and dignified deportment,
his solid and extensive learning, his firm
attachment to evangelical truth,
his fervent and constant piety.

Short grave here—
no marker.

In
Memory of
Robert Drennan
who departed this life
15th Sept 1802,
aged 77 years.

James Sloan
born
Sept 8, 1795,
died
Jan 15, 1868.

In
Memory of
James Moore
who was born
March 1st, 1769,
and departed this life
May 7th, 1849,
in the 81st year of
his age.

To
The memory of
Jane Reid,
Died
April 14th, 1850,
aged 71 years.

Robert Maffett
Born
Oct 30th, 1797,
Died
Sept 18, 1870.

In
Memory of
Elizabeth Drennan
who departed this life
5th May, 1815,
aged 78 years.

James Cameron
died
Sept 27, 1858,
aged 59 years,
11 months, &
16 days.

In
Memory of
James Moore
who was born
March 17th, 1793
and died
Sept 12th, 1867

In
Memory of
Samuel Smyley
Died
March 14th, 1819,
aged 23 years,
left wife and
small children.

To The
Memory of
Samuel McCalla, Esq.
a native of County
Down, Ireland,
who departed this life on
the 6th of September,
in the year of our Lord
1824,
in the 51st year of his
age.

In
Memory of
Samuel B.
Maffett,
son of
Robert & Nancy
Maffett,
who was born
March 9th, 1832
died
July 19th, 1841.

CEMETERY MARKERS (continued)

Cannons Creek Church Cemetery (continued)-

In
Memory of
James Wilson, Sen'r.
who departed this life
Dec 29th, 1841,
In the 99th year
of his age.

In Memory of
Jennet Wilson
who departed this life
Nov 1826,
in the 7..th year
of her age.

In Memory of
Thomas P. Wilson
who departed this life
December 11th,
A.D. 1831,
In the 29th year
of his age.

In
Memory of
James Wilson,
son of Thomas and
Mary Wilson, who
departed this life
April 17th, A.D. 1830,
In the 31st year
of his age.

Here
lies waiting for
the resurrection of the body
of John Caldwell, who departed
this life on the 29th of
Nov. 1844,
aged 70 years.

Here
lies waiting for the
resurrection the body of
Rose Ann Caldwell
who departed this life the
17th day of Oct, 1837,
aged 57 years.

Sacred
To
The memory of
James McNeill, Sr.,
a native of County
Antrim, Ireland,
who departed this life
Nov 13th, A. D.
1836,
In the 68th year of
his age.

Sacred
To
The memory of
Mary McNeill,
wife of James McNeill, Sen.,
native of the county
Antrim, Ireland, who
departed this life Oct 16th,
In the year of our Lord, 1827,
In the 15th year of her age.

Sacred
To
The memory of
James McNeill, Jr.,
son of James & Mary McNeill,
a native of the county Antrim,
Ireland, who departed
this life August 17th, in the
year of our Lord, 1828,
In the 40th year of his age.

To the
Memry of
Ann Spence,
a native of the County
Down, Ireland,
who departed this life
on the 19th January, in
the year of our Lord,
1828,
In the 19th year of her age.

Sacred
To the memory of
Samuel Fair,
who was born in County Antrim,
Ireland, and removed to America
in 1772, losing at sea a son and
and aged father. He died in September,
1775, leaving two sons and one
daughter, William and Samuel and
Margaret, and lies buried in or near
the spot marked by this stone.
" One generation passeth away and
another generation cometh, and
the earth abidith eternal."

Here
lies waiting for
the resurrection of the body
of Dan Smyley,
son of
John and Margaret Smyley,
who departed this .life
9th June, A.D. 1817, in the
23rd year of his age.
" In pride of youth in
life's most flattering
bloom,
With every generous
sentiment inspir'd,
He sunk, regretted, to an
early tomb,
And from his Brothers and
Sisters dear, expired.

In
Memory of
William Maffett,
son of
Samuel and Jane Maffett,
who departed this life
Oct 8th, 1831,
aged 26 years.
"O life, frail off-spring of a day!
'Tis puff'd with short gasp away,
Swift as the short-lived flower, it flies,
It springs, it blooms, it fades, it dies.
The sun that makes your violets bloom
Once cheered his eye now dark in death,
The wind that wanders o'er his tomb,
Was once his vital breath."

In
Memory of
Leonora E. Maffett,
daughter of
Robert and Nancy Maffett,
who was born
February 21st, 1850,
died
September 28th, 185...

Sacred
To the memory of
Lt. Dan S. Maffett,
Co. O. 3rd S. C. Reg't.
Born
July 29th, 1838,
wounded in battle at Knoxvill
Tenn. Nov 13th, and died
Nov 20th, 1863.
Nobly he fell whilst fighting for
liberty.

CEMETERY MARKERS (continued)

Cannon's Creek Church Cemetery(continued)-

Sacred
To the memory of
Mrs. Nancy Maffett,
wife of
Robert Maffett,
Born
July 5th, 1805,
Died
Oct 12th, 1876.
"Jesus said unto her, I am the resurrection, and the life;
he that believeth in me though he were dead, yet shall he live."

To
The memory of
Sarah Wright,
Died
Oct 20, 1865,
Aged 75 years.

Maffett Family graveyard-located 6 miles Southeast of Newberry Court House, near Phillips Church-

Sacred
To the memory of
James Maffett
Born
March 18, 1795
Died
Jan 20, 1880.

Sacred
To the memory of
Rebecca Maffett
who departed this life June 25, 1848
in the 50th year of her age.

Sacred
To the memory of
H. B. Maffett
who departed this life
June 26th, 1846,
in the 16th year of his age.

Betty,
daughter of
James & E.C.Maffett,
Born May 5th, 1865,
Died Oct 23rd, 1871.

Livingston Family Graveyard-located about 10 miles Southeast of Newberry Court House, past old T. J. Wilson home-

D. M. E. Wicker,
Died 1862.
(Confederate soldier)

Erected
By Husband
To the memory of
Margaret Elizabeth,
wife of
Daniel M.E. Wicker,
daughter of
John and Rebecca Kinard,
who was born Wednesday,
March 9th, A.D. 1831,
died Sunday,
June 18th, A.D. 1854,
duration in life
23 years, 3 months, & 9 days.
Duration in marriage,
4 years, 5 months, & 17 days.
She was for several years a pious member of the Evangelical Lutheran Church, a benevolent woman, a kind parent, and an affectionate wife.

Belton Levi,
son of
D.M.E. & M. E. Wicker,
Born Sunday, June 11th, 1854,
and died Friday,
June 30th, 1854.
Duration in life
19 days.

Rebecca Florence Maffett
was born April 12, 1856,
and died Oct 5th, 1865.

T.P.J.Wicker,
Born
Sept 10, 1820,
Died
Aug 20, 1896.
(Confederate soldier)

Lavania,
daughter of
N.G. & Elizabeth Gallman, and wife of R.C.Maffett,
was born October 2nd 1834,
and died July 5th, 1860.

Martha Wicker,
wife of
T.P.J.Wicker,
Born
Oct 11, 1819,
Died
Jan 12, 1879.

Sacred
To the memory of
George F. Sligh,
who was born
Sept 5th, 1833,
and departed this life,
March 29th, 1871.
(Confederate soldier)

Sacred
To the memory of
Rebecca Caroline,
daughter of John and Rebecca Kinard,
who was born
Sept 17th, 1837,
and died
July 21st, 1857,
aged 19 years, 10 months, and 4 days.
The deceased was a pious member of the Lutheran Church at Bethlehem.

Sacred
To the memory of
Elizabeth P. Kinard,
Consort of
George A. Kinard,
and daughter of David and Sarah P. Livingstone,
who departed this life
Nov 25th, A.D. 1847,
aged 27 years, 11 months, and 22 days.

Taylor Family Graveyard-located in forks of Saluda and Little Rivers, left of Sanders place-evidently the Benjamin Taylor place-

E. T.
Deceased March 4th, 1827,
aged 59 years.

B. T.
Deceased March 29, 1811,
aged 53 years.

CEMETERY MARKERS (continued)

Coate Family Graveyard-located near site of old Coate's Meeting House, above Dead Fall- near site of old Turner's Fort, on Little River, about 6 miles from Newberry Court House-

In Memory of
Benjamin Mayer, Third,
son of John & Thompson
Coate.
Born Dec 18, 1853
Died Dec 15, 1854.

Betsy Coate,
wife of Capt. Henry Coate,
Deceased Oct 7, 1806,
Born Oct 29, 1786.

In Memory of
William H. Coate
Born Aug 24, 1806,
Died Sept 24, 1806.

Thomas Coate,
son of
John & Thompson Coate,
Born June 2, 1843,
Died Sept 3, 1849.

(Evidently other graves not marked)

Stripling Family Graveyard-located near the Benjamin Taylor Graveyard, near Little River- William Stripling, Sr. was owner of original grants there, in the fork between Little River and Slauda River- site shows remains of old home, with graveyard about 200 yards to left- but no markers other than small rough stones or rocks with no inscriptions- except one which shows, " J.E.--1778".

Head Springs ARP Cemetery-located about 4 miles North of Newberry Court House, South of Jalapa-

In Memory of
Williams Welch,
son of
Isham and Sobriah Welch,
of Iredell County, N.C.
who was born Sept 1st,
1802,
and died Feb 18th, 1874.

In
Memory of
Elizabeth Welch,
wife of
William Welch,
who died Feb 8th, 1833,
aged 39 years.
She lived beloved and died lamented.

Sacred
To the memory of
Dickson Caldwell
who departed this life
on the 15th of June,
1837
aged 45 years, and
8 months.

Elizabeth Jane,
daughter of
Col. G. S. & S. L. Cannon,
and wife of
Thompson Connor,
Born
June 18th, 1842,
Died
December 28th, 1915.

In Memory of
Mary C. Welch,
wife of
Williams Welch,
and daughter of
Archibald and Mary
Glasgow,
who was born
January 12th, 1812,
and died
January 7th, 1851.

In memory
of
William Welch,
who died
November 11th, 1853,
aged 60 years.

Sacred
To the memory of
Robert Caldwell
who died
Feb 17th, 1860,
in the 79th year
of his age.

Thomas E. L. Chalmers,
Born
May 31st, 1863,
killed by a train
Sept 7th, 1895,
aged 32 years, 3 months,
6 days.

In Memory of
Isaac Welch,
son of
Williams & Mary C.
Welch,
born
May 5th, 1843,
died
June 22nd, 1857,
aged 14 years, 1 month,
and 17 days.

In Memoriam,
Thomas A. W. Chalmers,
Born
Sept 21st, 1806,
Died
March 25th, 1866.

Sacred
To the Memory of
Priscilla Chalmers
who was born
Feb 18th, 1824,
and died Dec 22nd, 1848.
She has left a husband to
lament her loss. Also, by
her right side rests her
infant son, Z. Taylor,
aged 7 weeks.

Sacred
To the memory of
Nancy McCrackin
who was born in 1790,
and departed this life
August 18th, 1846.

In
Memory of
Cornelia C. Welch,
daughter of William
and Mary C. Welch,
who was born Dec 28,
1850,
and died Oct 2, 1863

Martha A. W. Ch..
Born
Nov 2nd, 1820,
Died
Oct 25th, 1898.
"Blessed are the d..
who die in the Lo..
they rest from th..
labors and their
works do follow t..

In Memory
of
Richard Chalme..
Born
Nov 9th, 1836,
Died
in the servic..
Culpepper C.H.,
on the 15th of
1863,
Aged 26 years,
months, & 6 d..
(Confederate so..

CEMETERY MARKERS (continued)

Head Springs Cemetery (continued)-

Capt. Thompson Connor
Born
April 8th, 1832,
Died
Sept 23rd, 1895.
(Served in Co. B-3rd Reg. S.C.V.)
(Confederate soldier)

In Memory of
Rebecca Means
who was born 3rd March, 1756,
and died the 3rd December, 1832,
in the 77th year of her age.
A native of Boston, Mass.
At an early age removed to this State,

Abel Connor
was born
August 28th, 1803,
and died
June 30th, 1863.

Our Father
J. A. Caldwell,
Born
August 7th, 1809,
Died
September 3rd, 1885.

In Memory of
Elizabeth Caldwell,
who was born
April 15th, 1788,
and died
August 15th, 1862.

In Memory of
Rhoda Connor,
wife of
Abel Connor,
Born
Jan 22nd, 1805,
Died
May 13th, 1884.

In Memory of
Mary Caldwell
Born
Jan 28, 1815,
Died
Feb 3rd, 1867.

Margaret Rosanna,
daughter of
John & Rosa Caldwell,
May 6, 1821,
May 21, 1883.

J. D. Connor
was born
Oct 14th, 1828,
and died
June 16th, 1842.

Our Mother,
Jane Davenport,
wife of
J. A. Caldwell,
Born
April 15, 1820,
Died
January 26, 1883

Here lies awaiting for the resurrection, the body of
Robert Caldwell
who died
June 21st, 1856,
aged 45 years, 6 months, and 15 days

Halfacre Graveyard-located 4 miles Southeast of Newberry Court House- on old Pomaria Road-

In Memory of
Henry Halfacre,
a native of County
Shanlove, Va., who
died July 12th, 1828,
in the 53rd year
of his age,
leaving a wife and six children to mourn their irreparable loss.

Sacred
To the memory of
Jacob E. M.,
son of
James M. & Rebecca Crosson,
who was born
14th day of April,
and died the
5th day of December 1837,
Aged 7 months and 19 days.

Elizabeth Halfacre,
wife of
Henry Halfacre,
was born
April 17th, 1779,
and departed this life
Febry 1st, 1857,
aged 77 years, 9 months, and 24 days.

To
The memory of
Lydia Elizabeth
Chandler,
daughter of
Thomas & Elizabeth
Chandler,
who was born September
7th, 1833, and died
Dec 16th, 1835.

Sacred
To the memory of
Henry Halfacre
Born
August 25th, 1811,
Died
April 3rd, 1882

Carrie Leticia
daughter of
Jane & Henry Halfacre,
Born
April 7th, 1845,
Died
August 19th, 1884.
" At Rest".

Luther Calvin,
son of Henry
and Jane
Halfacre,
Born April 7,1845,
Died Nov 30th,1886.
Christ hast said,
" What I do ye know not now, but ye shall know hereafter."
(Confederate soldier)

Other graves- with no markers.

In Memory of
Thomas Jefferson,
son of
T. & E. Chandler,
who was born
Dec 5th, 1835,
and died March 1st, 1837.

Summer Family Graveyard-located near Crims Creek, on road leading from right from St Johns Lutheran Church-

Evidently several graves without markers, only two being marked- probably John Adam Summer, Sr., pioneer, buried here-

CEMETERY MARKERS (continued)

Summer Family Graveyard (continued)-

In
Memory of
Col. John Adam Summer, Esq.
Born
September 29th, A.D. 1744,
Deceased
October 1st, A.D. 1809,
Aged
65 years and 1 day.
May he rest in peace.
(Rev War soldier)

Sacred
To The
Memory of
Mary Summer,
the wife of
Col. John A. Summer,
was born
Anno Domini 1744,
Died August 3rd, 1818,
Aged 74 years, 6 months,
3 weeks, and 3 days.
" Here lies a mother fond and dear,
May children drop a silent tear."

Another Summer Family Graveyard, located near site of old " Cross Roads" School, a short distance from road leading from private road, South, from highway to Little Mountain-

William Summer,   (Another grave, that of his wife, is marked)
Born 1764,
Died 1832.
(Rev War soldier)

Ruff Family Graveyard-located about 12 miles Southeast of Newberry Court House, on left of highway to Pomaria-

Here
lies the body of.
John Henry Ruff, Esq.
who was born
August 12th, 1773,
and died December 25th, 1835.
He discharged all the duties
of life well. The tears of his
wife and children, grand-children,
enighbors, and slaves, bedew his tomb;
and his memory cherished by them
with lasting affection.
He died in the hope of
everlasting life,
through the promise of his
Lord and Redeemer.
" Blessed are they that have not
seen and yet have believed."

In Memory
of
John Adam Counts,
who was born
Oct 26th, 1797,
and departed this life
January 7th, 1844.

In
Memory of
Margaret Elizabeth Ruff,
who died
July 1st, 1848,
aged 76 years.
She was the daughter of
Col. John Adam Summer,
and was married to
Henry Ruff
Sept 18th, 1792,
This slab is placed here by her
children, not to conceal her faults
and publish her virtues, but simply
to serve as a guide to her posterity,
in their pilgrimage of affection ,
and to record their hope that both
this shrine has been fulfilled, the
promise of immortality and of
incorruptibility.

In Memory of
George O. Ruff,
Husband of
Lavania Ruff,
Born December 31st,
1817,
Died December 7th,
1855.

In Memory of
Christiana Ruff,
daughter of
George O. & Lavania Ruff,
Born January 5th, 1847,
Died June 2nd, 1855.

Jacob Belton Counts,
Died
June 23rd, 1875,
Aged
54 years, 5 months,
& 5 days.

Sacred
To the memory
George Langdo
son of
Henry & May M.
Gallman,
aged 8 months,

CEMETERY MARKERS (continued)

Ruff Family Graveyard(continued)-
Here
lies the body of
Col. John Eichleberger
who was born September 13th,
1794,
and departed this life
Febry 3rd, 1844.
Aged 49 years, 7 months,
and 10 days.

William Thomas Eichleberger,
Born
April 15th, 1838,
and died
from wounds received in
battle,
Williamsburg, Va.
June, 1862.
(Confederate soldier)

Beneath this marble
lies all that was mortal of
Henry Gallman,
Born August, 1794,
Died April 8th, 1845,
aged 51 years.
"Mortal, reflect as you pass by,
As you are now, soon must you be-
Therefore, prepare to follow me."

In Memory of
Maria Elizabeth,
wife of
Col. John Eichleberger.
She was born October 12th,
1802,
Died
September 23rd, 1849.
This tomb is erected by her
sons as a token of
Respect and Love.

Walter Franklin Ruff,
Born
August 14th, 1812,
Died
April 16th, 1857,
He was a good husband, and
in his domestic relations,
sincere in all his attachments,
and a warm and devoted friend.

This tablet
is erected by the children
of Mary Gallman,
as a tribute to the memory
of a devoted mother,
who was born Feb 11th,1794,
and died
October 30th, 1863.
"The memory of the just
is blessed."

Sacred
To
The memory of
George Langdon,
son of
Col. John Eichleberger
and Elizabeth Eichelberger.
Born December 25th, 1834.
Died Febry 20th, 1839.

In Memory
of
Elizabeth Eichleberger,
wife of
Dr. H. M. Eichleberger,
who was born
December 27th, 1827,
and died
September 12th, 1849,
aged 21 years, 8 months,
and 16 days.

" Thou art gone to the grave,
but if it were wrong to deplore thee
When God was thy ransom, their
guardian and guide,
We gave three and took three and
soon will restore thee,
Whose death has no sting since
the Savior hath died."

DeWalt-Gray Families Graveyard- located about six miles Southeast of Newberry Court House, on Pomaria highway-

This slab
is erected by
The Trustees of Aveleigh
in memory of
John Peter Gray,
a pious and beloved
member of that Church,
whose
cordial attachment
to
his brethern, to the
Presbyterian Faith,
and to
The Gospel of Christ,
was manifested
by
His life
and by
A liberal Free Will Offering
in
His last will.
Nat. Sept 14, 1768,
Ob. Oct 18, 1844.

Here
lies in the expectation
of a happy resurrection the body
of Mr. George Gray
who was born on the 16th of
Aug. 1756, and
departed this life on the 27th
of Jany, 1826.
He was a tender husband and
affectionate father,
and a good Christian.

In memory of
Mrs. Susannah Gallman,
wife of
John Gallman,
and daughter of George &
Catherine Gray,
who was born December 28th, 1787,
and departed this life April 6th,
1852.
She was the mother of nine children,
—above

Here lies the body
of
Mrs. Catherine Gray,
wife of
George Gray,
who was born
on the 8th of October,
1764, and died
on the 22nd of April,
1848.
This slab was erected to
her memory by her children

and the subject of desease
and pain for the last 15
years of her life, and a memb
of the Associate Reformed Chu
for more than 25 years.
As a mother she was kind and
....

CEMETERY MARKERS (continued)

Gray-DeWalt Graveyard(continued)-

In Memory
of
John P. Gallman,
who was born
July 8th, 1816,
and departed this life
June 30th, 1852,
"Remember, Lord, how short a
time I shall on earth remain."

Here
lies waiting for the
resurrection of the body
of John Gallman
who
died Feb the 12th, A. D.
1826,
aged 50 years.
Leaving a wife and
eight children to mourn
their irreparable loss.

In
Memory of
Nathaniel George Gallman,
who was born
Oct 21st, 1800,
and died
August 16th, 1865.

Sacred
To the memory of
Rebecca DeWalt,
wife of
David DeWalt,
and daughter of
George and Catherine Gray,
Born
Nov 23rd, 1802,
Died
April 6th, 1880.

Here
lies waiting for
the resurrection of
the body of
David DeWalt,
born September 11th,
1794,
and departed this life
October 28th,
1834,
after an illness of ten hours.
He was a tender husband,
an affectionate father, a kind
Master, and a sincere friend.
He has left a wife and seven small
children to lament their
irreparable loss.

Riser Family Graveyard-located South of Pomaria, on road to Little Mountain-

M. Riser
Died October 4th,
1844.

Sacred
To the memory of
Sarah Fellers
who departed this life
July 1st, 1837,
aged 29 years, 9 months,
and 15 days.
She has left a husband and
three small children
to mourn their
irreparable loss.
As a wife, she was kind
and benevolent,
As a mother she was tender
and affectionate.

Another Riser Family Graveyard-located
West of Pomaria, near Adam Aull home-

In
Memory of
John Riser
who died Dec 3rd, 1851,
aged 64 years and 22 days.

Sacred
To the memory of
Barbara A. Riser
who was born
March 6th,
1794,
and departed this
life Feb 27th, 1860
aged 65 years, 11
months, and
21 days.

Rikard Family Graveyard-located on private road leading from rear of "Caldwell Ruff" home,
about 12 miles from Newberry Court House- some of the markers-

Sacred
To the Memory of
Michael Rikard
who departed this life
the 2nd of May A. D. 1846,
aged 82 years, and 8 months.

Sacred
To the memory of
Margaret Rikard,
wife of
Michael Rikard,
and daughter of George
& Elizabeth Eichleberger,
who departed this life
Febry 23rd, A.D. 1842,
aged 79 years and 14 days.

CEMETERY MARKERS (continued)   431

Bethlehem Lutheran Church Cemetery-located about 14 miles Southeast of Newberry Court House-
left of Pomaria Highway at old Suber place- some of the markers-

Sacred
To the memory of
Col. Samuel Cannon
who departed this life
22nd July, 1849,
in the 76th year of
his age.

In
Memory of
John Cannon
who departed this
life the 29th
August, 1836,
aged 69 years,
8 months & 23 days.

In
Memory of
Ellen S. Riser,
daughter of
Col. S. Cannon,
who departed this life
Oct 4th, 1829, aged
22 years, 5 months,
& 2 days.

Here
Lies the body of
Nancy,
wife of
David Cannon, Senior,
the mother of 13
children, who departed
this life the 3rd of
Jan 1825, aged
59 years.

Sacred
to the emory of
John Eichleberger,
who was born
Jan 21st, 1758,
and died April 9th,
1827.
(Rev War soldier)

Sacred
To the Memory of
Thomas V. Cannon,
son of
David & Nancy Cannon,
who departed this life
April 26th, A.D. 1843,
aged 35 years, 1 month,
and 16 days.
Possessed of all those
qualities of mind which
ennoble humanity, discharging
with strict fidelity, regularity,
and propriety, all the duties
incumbent on HIM as a husband,
father, citizen and friend. Cut
down in the vigour of manhood and
in the zenith of his usefulness,
He died lamented by all who knew
him, but ..... by his disconsolate
Relict by whom(as a memento of the
purest joy and affection), this
humble monument is erected.

Here
Lies the body
of
David Cannon,
Senior,
who departed this life
March 26th, 1826,
aged 67 years.
He was the father of
13 children.
He was much respected and
lamented by the poor
and needy.
(Rev War soldier)

In
Memory of
John A. Cannon,
Born
Dec 28th, 1820,
Died
Sept 16, 1878,
aged 57 years, 8 mos.,
& 19 days.

Sacred to the Memory of
George Johnson Cannon,
An affectionate husband, a faithful
friend, a kind Master, and honest man,
and an humble Christian,
departed this life on the 13th of
January, A. D. 1848.
aged 43 years, 9 months, and 8 days.
He left no children to mourn for him,
but his active and unwearied kindness
to the fatherless, has often bedewed
his grave with orphans' tears.
His bereaved widow erects
this monument to his memory.

Sacred
To the Memory of
Samuel D. Cannon
who departed this life
Jany 26th, 1839,
aged 38 years and 7 months.
He left a wife and 5
children to mourn their
irreparable loss.

Here
Lies the body of
Captain William Cannon,
son of David and Nancy
Cannon,
departed this life the
17th October, 1815,
in the 28th year of his
age.
Well respected and much
lamented.

Here lies
awaiting for the
Resurrection the
body of Rebecca Red,
daughter of Jospeh &
Margaret Caldwell,
who departed this life
August 14th, A.D. 1815,
in the 22nd year of her age.

Annie C.,
wife of J. W. Folk,
Born August 19, 1819,
Died May 3rd, 1877,
"Blessed are the dead which
died in the Lord, from
henceforth: Yea, saith the
Spirit, that they may rest from
their labours: and their works do
follow them."

Samuel Cannon,
Dec 24th, 1818
July 26th, 1883.

Lavania E. Cannon
Feb 13, 1820,
May 27, 1894.

Sacred
To
The memory of
Sarah Cannon,
wife of
Col. Samuel Cannon,
who departed this life
Nov 15th, 1827,
aged 49 years, 7 months,
and 2 days.

In Memory
of
Sarah E. Cannon,
Consort of
J. A. Cannon,
who died
Nov 8th, 1853,
aged 28 years, 10
months, & 6 days.

CEMETERY MARKERS (continued)

Bethlehem Lutheran Church Cemetery (continued)-

Sacred
To the memory of
Rev. Jacob Moser,
who was born March 6th, 1795,
and died December 26th, 1865,
aged 70 years, 9 months, and 20 days.
"Servent of God, well done,
Rest from thy lov'd employ,
Enter thou Master's joy."

In -
Memory of
Mary A. Moser,
who was born Jan 15th, 1830,
and died April 17th, 1865,
aged 35 years, 3 months, and 2 days.
"Farewell, sister, 'till we meet in glory."

Sacred
to
the
Memory of the
Rev. John G. Schwartze,
ordained to the work of the Ministry,
and elected professor of Theology in 1830,
and ceased to be mortal on the 26th August, 1831, having just attained his 24th year. He was meek, humble, full of Charity, and devoted to God; he esteemed his life not dear to himself, so that he might finish his course with joy. His talents, his zeal, his sincerety, and piety, rendered him the delight of his friends, the ornament of Society, the joy and the hope of the Church.

Gilder's Creek Cemetery-site of old church- located 10 miles North of Court House, on county highway leading to the Mollohon section of the county, just across Gilder's Creek-

Here
Lies the body of
Mary Hipp
who departed this life
October 30th, 1817,
aged 24 years.

Isaac Keller
Born
December 7th, 1790,
Died
June 2nd, 1871,

John L. Glasgow;
Born
June 6th, 1824,
Died
June 17, 1868.

William Kirkpatrick
who died June 1st, 1787
Martha Kirkpatrick
died Dec 20th, 1792.
(Above two on one marker)

Sacred
To the memory of
John Boyce, Sr.
who departed this life
3rd April, 1806.
aged 61 years.
(Rev War soldier)

Here
lies the body of
Elizabeth Boyce who
departed this life
9th April, 1797,
aged 70 years.

In
Memory of
David Montgomery
who died Dec 30th, 1831,
aged 65 years.

In
Memory of
Jane Montgomery,
the wife of
David Montgomery,
who died
December 26m 1831,
aged 58 years.

Heare
Lyeth the body
of James Beard who
departed this life 7th day
of Feb aged 20 years- also
Jean Beard who
departed this life 16th Febry,
aged 55 years.

In Memory of
Jane McCrackin,
who departed this life
June 4th, 1833,
aged 35 years, 6 months,
and 12 days.

' Mary J.,
daughter of
J. A. & Mary Speers,
Died
Feb 23rd, 1827,

Leroy Dodridge,
son of
J. A. & Mary Speer
Died
Dec 7th, 1832,

Sacred
To the Memory. of
John Richey
who died
June 22nd, 1840,
aged 80 years.

John B. Richey
Born
April 15, 1791,
Died
March 7th, 1862.

Sacred
To the memory of
Mary Jane Richey
who departed this life
November 7th, 1856,
aged 15 years, 1 month, and 18 days.

Sacred
To the memory of
Samuel Richey
who departed this life
the 9th day od Dec
in the year of our Lo
1836, aged 31 years,
months, and 10 days

CEMETERY MARKERS (continued)

Gilder's Creek Cemetery (continued):-

Sacred To the memory of George Richey, who was born the 13th April, 1811, and died the 15th March, 1852.

In Memory of Jennett Richey, wife of John Richey, Died May 8th, 1859, aged 90 years.

Sacred To the memory of Mary R. Glasgow, who departed this life November 11th, 1846, In the 17th year of her age.

Sacred To the memory of Samuel Glasgow, Consort of James Glasgow(?) Who departed this life February 24th, A.D. 1847, aged 58 years, 8 months, and 19 days.

Sacred To the memory of Mary Glasgow who departed this life Oct 10th, 1822, aged 85 years.

Sacred To the memory of Robert Abner Glasgow, who departed this life on the 30th October, A.D. 1844, Aged 24 years, 9 months, and 24 days.

Mrs. Eleanor Patterson, who died 20th September, 1837, Aged 74 years.

Sacred To the memory of Rachel Keller, Consort of Isaac Keller, and daughter of Archibald & Mary Glasgow. Born Feb 1st, 1801, and died March 6th, 1855, aged 54 years, 1 month, and 5 days.

Sacred To the memory of Absalom Glasgow who departed this life Feb 6th, 1834, in the 35th year of his age.

Sacred To the memory of Neomi Glasgow, daughter of Archibald & Mary Glasgow, who departed this life September 23rd, 1831, aged 34 years.

Sacred To the memory of Wilson Glasgow who departed this life September 11th, 1817, aged 45 years.

Sacred To the memory of James Wilson Glasgow, who died 20th July, A.D. 1841, Aged 22 years, 2 months, and 25 days.

James Patterson, who died A.D. 1816, ... and Constant Ruler of the Presbyterian Church.

Sacred To the memory of Hiram Glasgow, who died Feb 20th, 1847, In the 37th year of his age.

Sacred To the memory of Rosanah L. Glasgow who died December 28th, 1848, in the 7th year of her age.

Sacred To the memory of John Glasgow who departed this life on the 11th December, 1826, In the 70th year of his age.

Sacred To the memory of Mary Glasgow, who departed this life April 1st, 1844, aged 71 years.

Maria McCrackin, Born March 27, 1804, Died November 20, 1861, aged 51 years, 8 months and 24 days.

Sacred To the memory of James Glasgow, Consort of Sarah Glasgow, who departed this life A.D. 1831, aged 44 years.

Sacred To the memory of Elizabeth Glasgow, Spouse of Robert Glasgow, who departed this life on the 10th November, 1823, aged 69 years.

Sacred To the memory of Mary R. Glasgow, who died Jany 2nd, 1841, in the 10th year of her age.

Sacred To the memory of Charles Hargrove, who departed this life the 29th of October, 1849, aged 25 years.

Sacred To the memory of James Glasgow, son of Archibald & Mary Glasgow, who departed this life November 27th, 1831 aged 18 years.

Sacred To the memory of Archibald Glasgow, who departed this life September 22nd, 1818, aged 49 years.

Sacred To the memory of Mary Glasgow, who departed this life March 23rd, 1835, aged 61 years.

Sacred To the memory of Robert Glasgow, who departed this life 17th Jany 1885, aged 72 years, and three months.

Here lies Mary Toland, Born August 20th, 1773, and died...........

CEMETERY MARKERS (continued)

Gilder's Creek Church Cemetery (continued)—

Sacred
To the memory of
Mr. John Toland,
who was born
Febry 1st, 1776,
and died October 14th,
1849.

Elizabeth Toland,
wife of
James Boyce,
who departed this life
September 27, 1823,
aged 25 years.

Sacred
To the memory of
Rachel Thompson,
wife of
James Thompson,
who departed this life
on the 18th day of
December, 1852,
In the 35th year of
her age.

Robert McKee
who departed this
life January 4th,
1831,
Aged 11 years.

Here
lieth the body of
Robert McKee,
who departed this life
May 8th, 1835,
aged 13 years.

Here
lies the body of
Mary McKee,
who departed this life
December 8th, 1801,
aged 45 years.

........McKee,
Died Dec 9th,
1843,
Aged 60 years.

Rutherford Family Graveyard—located about 12 miles Southeast of Newberry Court House, on old Buncombe Road (now Highway), to the right from Keitt's Cross Roads—

Here
lies the remains of
Col. Robert Rutherford,
who died
the 25th January, 1814,
in the 79th year of his age.
He has left a numerous family
to lament the loss of an
affectionate and provident
father. He was a friend to
the Orphan and the Widow.

Here
lies interred
Dorothy Rutherford,
wife of
Robert Rutherford,
who departed this life
5th November, 1795,
in the 60th year of her age.
She was 38 years
An amiable example of
conjugal virtue, and an
affectionate mother.

Sacred to the memory
of
Abel Harrington
who departed this life
the 30th of October,
1804,
aged 23 years.

Sacred to the memory
of
Frances Rutherford,
who departed this life
the 16th of October
1823,
aged 79 years.

Sacred To The
Memory Of
William Rutherford,
son of
Robert & Dorothy B. Rutherford,
who departed this life
July 21st, 1845,
aged 71 years, 7 months,
and 14 days.
Benevolence, hospitality and
Charity without ostentation to
all within his sphere of usefulness
Characterized his life.

Sacred
To the memory of
Elizabeth Rutherford,
who departed this life
July 26th, 1839,
A member of the Lutheran
Church.
Aged 63 years.
" Blessed are the dead which
die in the Lord."
The stone erected by her husband,
William Rutherford.

To The
Memory of
Capt. John Rutherford,
who departed this life
February 8th, 1835,
aged 27 years
and 3 months.
He has left a widow and
two children to mourn
their irrecoarable loss,
"Unvail thy bosom, fruit
tomb,
Take this new treasure t
thy trust,
And from these sacred
relicks room
To seek of slumber in t
dust."
" ....

Sacred
To the memory of
Maj'r. Anteoine Gilbal,
who departed this life
June 4th, 1842,
A native of France and one of
Bonaparte's Majors, who on
Bonaparte's surrender,
he sought a home in America;
and as his last request his remains
now rest by the side of his
particular friend, Capt. John G. Rutherford.

CEMETERY MARKERS (continued)

Rutherford Family Graveyard(continued):-

Here lies the Remains
of
Dorothy Brooks
Calmes,
the affectionate wife of
Thomas Berry Calmes,
who was born June 1st,
1799,
and departed this life
February 27th,
1819.
Disease invades the chastest
temperance;
and alarm through thickest shadow
pursues the sound of peace.

Here
Lies the Remains
of
Dorothy Henrietta
Calmes,
daughter of
Thomas B. & Dorothy B.
Calmes,
who was born July 24th,
1818,
and departed this life
July 15th, 1819,
Bright, transient, as
morning dew,
She sparked, was exhaled,
and went to Heaven.
(above)

Also, the remains
of the first born of
Thomas B. & Dorothy B.
Calmes,
who passed from it's
primevous abode to
mansions of happiness,
without calling to
taste the bitterness
of earthly things.

King's Creek (A.R.P.) Church Cemetery- located about 12 miles North of Newberry Court House-
about 100 yards to right of old Whitmire highway-

Sacred
To
The memory of
Col. Thomas Dugan,
who departed this life
on the 8th of Dec 1822;
aged 74 years and
6 months,
and
Mary, wife of Thomas Dugan,
who departed this life
Dec 30th, 1819,
aged 69 years, 7 months,
and 24 days.
"With length of days unto their
mind,
I will them satisfy,
I also my salvation
Will cause their eyes to see."
(Rev War soldier)

Sacred
To
The memory of
John Dugan,
who departed this life
June 29th, 1822,
aged 46 years, 6 months,
and 23 days.
" Ye righteous in the Lord,
rejoice.
It comely is and right
That upright men with
thankful voice
Should praise the Lord of might."

Sacred
To the memory of
Nancy Dugan
who departed this life
July 22nd, 1855,
aged 83 years, 8 months,
and 22 days.
" Ye righteous in the Lord, rejoice,
It comely is and right,
That upright men with thankful voice,
Should praise the Lord of might."

Sacred
To The
Memory of
Capt. George Dugan,
who departed this life
March 25th, 1827,
aged 37 years
& 25 days.

Sacred To the memory
of
Elisabeth L. Dugan,
wife of
William Dugan,
who departed this life
March 13th, 1856,
aged 69 years and 1 month.
" The languished head is at rest,
It's thinking and aching are o'er,
This quiet immovable breast
Is heaved by affliction no more.
This heart is no longer the seat
Of trouble, and tortouring pain,
It ceases to flutter and beat—"
" It never shall flutter again."
....

Sacred
To the Remains of
Park Dugan
who departed this life
October 20th, 1817,
aged 30 years, 7 months,
and 6 days.

In
Memory of
William Dugan,
who died
Sept 20th,
1831,
in the 50th year
of his age.

Sacred
To the Memory of
Robert Dugan
who departed this life
June 7th, 1823,
aged 30 years, 11 months,
and 23 days.

Sacred
To The
Memory of
Thomas Dugan, Jr.
who departed this life
on the 24th September,
1839,
aged 54 years, 11 months,
and 27 days.

CEMETERY MARKERS (continued)

King's Creek (A.R.P.) Church Cemetery (continued):-

Sacred
To the memory of
Robert Dugan
who departed this life
April 1st, 1822,
aged 48 years, 1 month,
and 24 days.

In
Memory of
Mary Brown
who departed this life
7th of November, 1810,
aged 48 years, 9 months,
and 18 days.

In
Memory of
James Brown,
who departed this life
8th of January, 1813,
aged 28 years, 11 months,
and 25 days.

In Memory of
Matthew Hall
who departed this life
the 11th October, 1820,
aged 85 years, 1 month,
and 2 days.
Agnes, his wife, lies at
his left hand,
who departed this life
the 8th September, 1813,
aged 80 years, 2 months,
and 13 days.

Sacred
To the memory of
Robert Mars
who departed this life
the 3rd of December,
1846,
aged 57 years.
" Blessed are the dead which
died in the Lord, saith the Spirit,
that they may rest from their
labours, and their works do
follow them."

To
The Memory of
Margaret Erskin
who died Aug 16th,
1843,
aged about 76
years.

Sacred
To the memory of
Rebecca Chambers
who died October 17th, 1815,
aged 25 years.
" The law brought forth
her precepts ten,
And then dissolved
in grace this vine three
boughs, and then in
Glory too her place.'

Here lies
Hannah Mars,
Died Nov 1,
1775.

In
Memory of
Margaret Hall,
wife of
Thomas Hall,
who departed this life
the 10th December, 1826,
aged 39 years 1 month,
and 20 days.
Henry, aged 1 year and
12 days.
A still-born child lies
on her left hand.

Sacred
To the memory of
John Mars
who died
the 12th day of
Nov, 1828,
aged 54 years.

Sacred
To the memory of
Sarah Mars
who died the 16th day
of June, 1819,
aged 52 years.

To
The memory
of
Samuel Pearson,
who departed this life
Feb 1843,
aged 73.

Sacred
To the memory of
Alexander Chalmers
who departed this life
16th Febry 1816,
aged 30 years.

Sacred
To the Memory
of
Dr. Samuel Pearson,
who departed this life
the 13th October, 1853,
aged 32 years.
" Blessed are the dead which
die in the Lord from
henceforth, Yea, saith the
Spirit, that they may rest
from their labours and their
works do follow them."
Those that knew him best
loved him most.
That noble, generous heart
has gone to rest.

Mrs. Jane McMorries,
wife of
Dr. W. W. McMorries
Born
March 6th, 1805,
Died
January 28th, 1870.

Sacred
To the memory of
Mary Chalmers
who departed this
life 8th Feb. 1816,
aged 68 years.

Sacred
To the memory of
Hannah More,
wife of
D. V. Scurry,
and daughter of
Wm. W. & Jane McMorries,
Born Oct 2, 1836,
Died Aug 15, 1860,
The righteous triumph
in death.
On the opposite side of above
marker is the following:
Willie, son of
D. V. & H. M. Scurry,
Born July 30, 1860,
Died Oct 8, 1860.

CEMETERY MARKERS (continued)

King's Creek (A.R.P.) Church Cemetery(continued)-

Sacred
To the Memory of
Sarah Mars
who died Oct 1st, 1842,
aged 51 years, 6 months,
and 9 days.
" Lord, now lettest thou thy
servant depart in peace,
according to thy word;
For mine eyes have seen
Thy Salvation."

Sacred
To the memory of
David Chalmers
who departed this life
11th Febry. 1816,
aged 62 years.
" An honest man is the
noblest work of God."

Menta Memori
Here lyeth the
body of Nathan Brown
who departed this life
June 28th, 1779,
aged 48 years.
" Remember, men, as you pass by,
As you are now, so once was I;
As I am now, so must you be,
Prepare for death and follow me."

Sims Brown
1760-1822.
was a Scout in the
Revolutionary War; put
into service at the age
of fifteen, on Snow Hill
near the bridge over
King's Creek by his father,
John Brown,
the original settler of
Newberry County.

In
Memory of
Rev. John Renwick,
who was born
December 31st, 1770,
and died
November 20th, 1836.

To
The memory of
Robert Mars, Senior,
who departed this life
5th of June 1813, aged
84 years.
"Remember, man, as you pass by,
As you are now, so once was I;
As I am now, so you must be,
So prepare for death and follow me."

Scared
To the Memory
of
Robert S. Mars
who departed this life
April 2nd, 1843,
aged 49 years.
And must this body die,
This mortal frame decay?
And must these active
limbs of mine
Lie mouldering in the clay?

In
Memory of
Grissel Brown,
who departed this life
May 30th, 1810,
aged 68 years.

Mary Baldrick,
wife of
Sims Brown,
native of
Orangeburg County.
" One generation passeth away,
and another generation cometh:
but the earth abideth forever."
(This inscription on same
monument as Husband)

In Memory
of
Mrs. Jane Renwick,
who was born
in Monaghan, Ireland, 1773,
and died the 14th December,
1847,
The deceased in early life
married the Rev. David
Bothwell, and with him
left country and friends
to further the cause
ever dearest to her heart.

437

Sacred
To the Memory
of
Cahrles W. Mars,
who died
May 10th, 1840,
aged 25 years, 4 months,
and 10 days.
He has
"Gone to the resting place
of man,
His long, his silent home;
Where ages past had gone
before,
Where future ages come."

Sacred
To the memory of
Mary Chalmers
who departed this life
8th Febry 1816,
aged 68 years.

Here lyeth the
body of Jane Brown,
who departed this life
the 15th Sept , 1785,
aged 74 years.
Joseph Brown who was born
the year 1777, died the
10 th year of his age.
" Be ye ready, also."

In
Memory of
Margaret Caldwell,
wife of
Joseph Caldwell,
and daughter of
Francis & Sarah Wilson,
who was born
December 2nd. A.D. 1813,
and died
May the 3rd, A.D. 1856.

To
The Memory of
Sarah E. M. Caldwell,
daughter of
Joseph & Margaret Caldwell,
who was born December 8th,
1834,
and died October 2nd.
1843.

CEMETERY MARKERS (continued)

King's Creek (A.R.P.) Church Cemetery(continued)-

In
Memory of
John S. Wilson,
son of
Francis & Sarah
Wilson,
who died
Sept 25th, 1821,
in the 5th year
of his age.

In
Memory of
Francis Wilson,
son of
Francis & Sarah
Wilson,
who died
Sept 5th, 1831,
in the 7th year
of his age.

In
Memory of
Sarah Wilson,
wife of
Francis Wilson,
who departed this life
Jany 12th, 1833,
in the 45th year
of her age.

In
Memory of
Rebecca Ann Wilson,
daughter of
Francis & Sarah
Wilson,
who died Oct 11th,
1821,
aged 6 months

In
Memory of
Francis Wilson
who departed this life
March 29th, 1836,
in the 58th year
of his age.

In
Memory of
Thomas E. Wilson,
son of
Francis & Sarah
Wilson,
who died December
20th, 1843,
in the seventeenth
year of his age.

In
Memory of
Martha C. Wilson,
daughter of
Francis & Sarah
Wilson,
who died Oct 5th,
1821,
in the 3rd year
of her age.

In
Memory of
An infant son of
R. R. & M. S. Nance,
who was born Oct 8th,
1826,
and died on the same day

Satterwhite Family Graveyard-located 16 miles Northwest of Newberry Court House, about 100 yards from old county highway, near Chappells, S. C.-

Beneath
these wall are
deposited the mortal remains
of
Mrs. Susan Moon,
daughter of John & Susan
Satterwhite.
Born on the 16th Nov. 1792,
Married the 10th of Dec. 1817,
Deceased the 12th of Jany, 1852,
aged 59 years, 1 month,
and 27 days.
In every relation of life a pattern
of filial, conjugal, maternal and
social vurtues.

Sacred
To the
Memory of
Michael M. Satterwhite,
Born
March 24th, 1794,
Died
April 5th, 1825,
aged 31 years,
and 12 days.

Sacred
To The
Memory of
John Satterwhite,
who was born
on the 12th day of
Sept. 1761,
and died on the ....
day of Sept. 1817.
(Rev War patriot)

William Theodore Satterwhite,
son of
Michael & Catherine Satterwhite,
Born Oct 17th, 1821,
Died Oct 9th, 1859.

Sacred
To the memory
of
Susannah Satterwhite,
who departed this life on the
17th day of July, 1810, in
the 60th year of her age.
She was Consort of
John Satterwhite,
and daughter of
Michael McKie of Virgnia.

Sacred
To the memory of
Elizabeth Simpson,
Consort of John W. Simpson,.
and daughter of John & Susannah
Satterwhite.
She was born on the 3rd day
of May, 1803,
and departed this life on the
2nd day of September, 1824,
aged 21 years, and 4 months.

CEMETERY MARKERS (continued)

Nance Family Graveyard-located about 100 yeards to the left of Boundary Street, rear of old Nance place (now the Havird Home)-

Sacred
To The Memory of
Thomas Pratt
who died on the 26th
of Febry, 1857,
aged about 51 years.
He was a man of integrity,
patience and industry, in his
dealings with men, honest and
indulgent, and as a husband,
Father, Master, affectionate,
tender and humane.
He was a Christian in the hour
of affliction and death.
His confidence in the Savior
of Sinners was firm and unshaken,
and even after the Soul had
fled from the body, his
countenance was the index that told
his bereaved family and friends
that his was the death of the
righteous, and his
last end like theirs.
" Blessed are the dead who die in
the Lord."

Here
are sleeping
Wm Burns Brantly
and
Sophia Louise Brantley.

In Memory of
H. P. McMorries
who was born
March 6th, 1847,
and died May 24th,
1848.

Sacred
To the memory of
Carrie Frances,
infant daughter of
Joseph S. & Angelina
McMorries,
Born May 15th, and
died June 3rd,
1851.

Elizabeth S. Nance,
born March 11th,
1784,
died April 4th,
1835.

In Memory
of
Our Mother,
Mrs. D. B. Pratt,
Born 9th October,
1798,
Died 6th August,
1854.

An
Infant son of
Washington & Virginia
P. Calmes,
1849.

In
Memory of
Dora A. Calmes,
Born
August 11th, 1851,
and died
Jan 26th, 1855.

In
Memory of
Edwin Calmes,
born
January 25th, 1851,
died
March 21st, 1856.

Sacred
To the Memory of
Mrs. Amelia D. McMorries,
Consort of
J. B. F. McMorries,
and eldest daughter of
Thomas & Dorothy B. Pratt.
She was born on the 7th
June , 1825.
and died
on the 13th May, 1853.
"Many waters cannot quench love,
Neither can the floods drown it."—
—Solomon.
"Rejoice and be exceeding glad for
great is your reward in Heaven."—
—Matt. V. 12.—

Sacred
To the memory of
John R. Nance,
born March 10th,
1819,
and died 2nd Oct,
1836.

In
Memory of
Sarah F. Pratt,
who was born
19th May, 1827,
and died 9th Dec.
1828.

Infant
son of
R. R. & C. E. Pratt,
born and died
the 5th of July,
1845.

Fielding Calmes Pratt,
son of
R. R. & C. E. Pratt,
Born 9th October,
1846,
Died 9th July,
1847.

Dr. William F. Pratt,
Born
October 7th, 1818,
Died
July 11th, 1878.

Francis W. Caldwell.
son of
P.C. & F. E. Caldwell,
was born
Febry 15th, 1832,
and died
March 3rd, 1834.

My Husband.
Here
lie the remains of
Alfred Nance,
son of
Frederick & Elizabeth Nance,
born in Newberry, So. Ca.
26th July, 1812,
died on his plantation in
Dallas County, Ala.
19th March, 1855.

In
Memory of
Eliz'h R. Pratt,
who was born
April 20th, 1817,
and died
January 13th, 1818.

Infant
Daughter of
R. R. & C. E. Pratt,
born 28th and died
on 29th of October,
1842.

Sacred
to
Frances Amelia
Griffin.

Sacred
to
The memory of
the infant son of
J. A. & S.W.
Griffin.

Sacred
To the memory of
Eliza P. Butler,
who was born
Febry 25th,
and died
June 3rd, 1838.

CEMETERY MARKERS (continued)

Nance Family Cemetery(continued)-

In
Memory of
Patrick C. Caldwell,
who was born
March 10th, 1801,
and died
November 22nd, 1855.
He graduated in the South
Carolina College in 1820,
and later preparing himself
for the practice of Law, he
followed that profession for
several years. He represented
his native district, at different
times, in both branches of the
State Legislature, and he also
represented the State in the
27th U. S. Congress.

In Memory of
Henry Priestly Pratt,
who was born June 7th, 1825,
and died October 26th, 1847,
He volunteered in Company L.
raised in the district under
Capt. Williams,
for the Mexican War, and on
the 13th of January, 1847,
he left his home and friends
destined to return no more.
He fell prey to a disease in
a strange land and an enemy's
country, and died in a Military
Hospital. His friends made the
utmost exertion to obtain his
remains, but without success.
He sleeps at Puebla in Mexico.
This monument is here erected to
his memory in the burial place
of his Fathers.

Sacred
To the memory of
Lucinda Ann,
wife of Frederick Nance, Jr.,
daughter of John & Rebecca Bullock,
Born October 31st, 1811,
Died October 8th, 1829,
aged 17 years, 11 months, & 8 days.
In the morning of life, while just
entering upon the discharge of those
duties wherein she was calculated
to be most useful,
she has been called to another and
a different world, we trust to be
more happy and more useful. Those
who knew her can bear testimony that
as a wife she was loving and affectionate,
as a child, filial and obedient, as a friend
and neighbor, open, frank, and disinterested.
---above

Sacred
To-the memory of
Frances E.,
wife of P. C. Caldwell, Esq.,
and daughter of Major Frederick
Nance. She was born May 13th, 1816,
and died March 3rd, 1832,
leaving her husband and an infant
son, with numerous friends and
relations to mourn their loss.
Her career in life was short but
whilst she remained she discharged
it's various duties with honor to
herself and satisfaction
to her friends. This marble
is placed over her remains
as a tribute of respect
by her Husband.

Sacred
To the memory of
Margaret Ann, daughter of
Robert and Sarah W. Dunlap,
Born 9th March,
1835,
Died the 12th December,
1838,
Aged 3 years, 9 months,
and 3 days.

Beneath this cold Tomb
lies
the remains of
Robert Nance,
a native of Virginia,
born
10th January, 1776,
and
died 17th November,
1822.

A large number of friends
and relations, together with
a disconsolate Mother and bereft
Husband, are left to deplore her
untimely loss. This monument is
erected by her Husband as a
tribute of respect to her memory.

Here
lies the body of
Drayton O'Neall Nance,
the youngest son of
Robert R. & Mary S. Nance.
He was born Nov 15th, 1835,
He died July 2nd, 1854.

Sacred
To the Memory of
Mrs. Amelia Dunlap
wife of
Robert Dunlap, Esq.
daughter of Major
Frederick and Elizabeth
Nance,
of Newberry; born 21st
March,1803, and died
2nd November, 1824.
Whilst her friends most
sincerely deplore her
untimely loss, the
recollection of her virt
and examplary life, and he
confidence and resignation
death, afford them comfort
and consolation.
This monument, an humble
tribute of respect to her
memory, is erected by her
Husband.

Sacred to the Memory
of
Erasmus G. Nance,
third son of
Clement and Elizabeth S.
Nance,
who was born
8th January, 1814,
and died
8th January, 1855.
aged 41 years.

Sacred
To the
Memory of
Elizabeth Dunlap,
eldest daughter of
Sarah W. & Robert Dunlap,
who died on the
6th August, 1834,
Born 25th January,
1831,
aged 3 years, 6 months,
and 11 days.

Sacred
To the memory of
Thomas Pope,
second son of
R. R. & M. S. Nance,
who was born March 4th,
1824,
and died Oct 7th, 1826

CEMETERY MARKERS (continued)

Nance Family Graveyard (continued)-

Mary E. Caldwell,
daughter of
P. C. & F. E. Caldwell,
Born
Aug't 29th, 1829,
Died
June 9th, 1830.

Sacred
To the memory of
Frederick Nance, Sen'r.
a native of Amelia County,
State of Virginia,
who died February 10th, 1840,
aged about 70 years.
He came to this State a youth
without means or friends, but by
a course of industry and prudence
and a correct deportment, among those
with whom his lot was cast, he
acquired wealth.
As a parent he was affectionate,
and solicitous for the welfare
of his children.
As a Master, humane and liberal.
In his intercourse with men he was
influenced by the principal that
others had rights as well as
himself, and therefore respected
them.
His children, among the many frailties
incident to human nature, saw his many
virtues, and mourned, in him, the loss of
a Parent and Benefactor.
Out of the patrimony which he left
them, this monument is erected
to his memory.

Sacred
To the Memory of
Elizabeth Nance,
wife of Frederick Nance,
Senior,
who was born March 29th, 1772,
and died October 14th, 1829,
Leaving a husband, eight
children, and a large family
connexion to mourn her
irreparable loss.
This monument is erected by
a fond Husband as a small
tribute of respect to the
many virtues that adorned
her while living; and will
crown her with joys unspeak-
able and full of glory
to which she has gone.
For thrity five years she
exemplary in the important
relations of wife, mother,
and mistress, and
although she was strictly
attentive to the
duties which devolved
upon her in this life,
she was not unmindful of
the promise held forth in
the words of,
" Come unto me all ye that
labour and are heavy laden,
and I will give you rest."

White Family Graveyard-located near Vaughanville, to the
left of road from school house- near Cahppells, S.C.-

Martha E. White,
wife of
Robert W. White,
born
December 6th, 1844,
died
May 15th, 1879.

Joseph White,
Born
Sept 9th, 1817,
Died
Oct 13th, 1873.

Julia A. White,
wife of Joseph White,
Born
August 31st, 1818,
Died August 29th, 1886.

Magnolia Cemetery, Greenwood, S. C.-copy of marker over grave of soldier of War of 1812,
who was a native of Newberry County, S. C.-

Sacred
To the memory of
Gen. James Gillam,
Born March 5th, 1791,
Died July 25th, 1878.
" Whoever liveth and believeth
on me shall never die."

CEMETERY MARKERS (continued)

Chapman-Summers Graveyard, also known as the old Tunker Church Cemetery- located about 4½ miles Southwest of Newberry Court House, near the old Paysinger home-

John Abney Chapman,
born March 9, 1821,
died Sept 9, 1906,

John Jacob Paysinger,
born Jan 16, 1825,
died Sept 7, 1896.

Rev Giles Chapman,
Born June 21, 1748,
Died April 15, 1819.

Samuel Chapman, Esq.,
son of Rev Giles Chapman,
and Mary, his wife,
Died August 6, 1876,
in his 80th year.

Jacob Kibler,
born Feb 3, 1816,
died Dec 21, 1890.

Rev Elijah Lynch,
Died Aug 10, 1842,
aged 69 years, 6 mos.,
and 10 days.

Elizabeth Lynch,
(wife of Rev. Elijah Lynch).
Died Nov 4, 1855,
Aged 80 years, 4 months,
and 18 days.

Capt. Hezekiah Summers,
Born March 11, 1780,
Died Sept 10, 1823.

William Summers, Sr.
Died Oct 12, 1823,
aged 67 years.

Honorias Sheppard,
son of
William and Nancy Sheppard,
Born August 19, 1807,
Died April 11, 1861.

Mary A. Chapman,
born Oct 22, 1820,
died April 16, 1889,
(she was the wife of John
Abney Chapman and daughter of
Samuel & Elizabeth W. Chapman).

Giles Chapman, Jr.
Born Feb. 1791,
Died Sept 1, 1831.

Elizabeth Worthington,
wife of
Samuel Chapman, Esq.,
born August 10, 1801,
died June 10, 1880.

Frances Elvira Kibler,
wife of Jacob Kibler,
and daughter of
Samuel Chapman, Esq.
Born July 27, 1833,
Died August 15, 1875.

Thomas A. Elmore,
Born April 20, 1776,
Died July 15, 1825.

John Summers,
Born June 29, 1763,
Died March 22, 1836.

Mrs. Helen Summers,
Born Oct 10, 1785,
Died Feb 4, 1836.

Susannah Summers,
wife of
William Summers,
Died Oct 7, 1829,
aged 68 years.

Mrs. Rhoda Aromenta,
widow of
H. Sheppard, and
dau. of Mark and Jane
Hawkins,
Born Oct 10, 1839,
Died May 31, 1862.

Samuel S. Paysinger,
Born Dec 2, 1835,
Died Oct 23, 1905.
(Confederate soldier)

John W. Chapman (Lawyer)
died Oct 31, 1851,
mar. Amanda.......

Mary Summers Chapman,
wife of
Rev. Giles Chapman,
Born Oct 10, 1758,
Died Oct 15, 1813.

Rosannah Chapman,
daughter of Samuel
Chapman, and wife of
Samuel S. Paysinger,
born Oct 19, 1839,
died Sept 24th, 1920.

James H. Dennis,
Born Apr 9, 1831,
Died Feb 11, 1910.

Elizabeth Chapman Elmore, (
Born Feb 13, 1784,
Died Feb 22, 1839,
(Dau. of Rev. Giles Chapman)

Rosannah Summers,
(Consort of John Summers),
Died Nov 13, 1840,
aged 68 years.

Phebe Sheppard,
wife of
Honorias Sheppard, Jr.,
Dau. of James & Prudence
Dennis,
Born July 4, 1809,
Married Dec 27, 1827,
Died June 7, 1855.

Mary Ellen Chapman,
born Feb 20, 1831,
died Nov 20, 1888,
wife of J.J.Paysinger,
and daughter of
Samuel & Elizabeth
Worthington Chapman,

Samuel R.C.Chapman
Born July 17, 1837,
Died Feb 21, 1869.
(Confederate soldier,
Law student, but
never completed cou

Susannah Cureton (yo
Dennis,
dau. of Dr. T. Youn
wife of
James H. Dennis,
Born March 27,1838,
Died Feb 2, 1902.

Frances Permelia,
wife of
G. McD. Sligh,
and daughter of
John J. and Nancy
Ellen Paysinger,
who was born Nov 14
1853,
and died Oct 20,
1880.

CEMETERY MARKERS (continued)

Crenshaw-Finch Families Cemetery-located near King's Creek, about 10 miles East of Newberry Court House, one-half mile to right of road crossing King's Creek-

In
Memory of
Edward Finch
who was born Feb 27th, 1750,
and died May 13th, 1823,
in the 74th year of his age.
"This modest stone that for vain marbles can,
May truly say, 'Here lies an honest man.'
For to laud, praise nor friend to slothful ease,
Content with virtue in the vale of peace,
Calmly he looked on either life, and here
Saw nothing to regret or there to fear,
From Nature's rose satisfied
.... that he lived and that he died."

Sacred
To the
Memory of
Dr. Freeborn Adams,
who was born in
Newburyport, Mass.
1773,
and died on the 17th of
September, 1813,
in the 39th year of his age.

Sacred
To the memory of
James M. Henderson,
who was born
July 27th, 1812,
and departed this life
Oct 27th, 1860,
" An honest man, the noblest work of God."

Sacred
To the Memory of
William Crenshaw,
son of
Charles & Eunice Crenshaw,
who departed this life
1794,
Aged 3 years.

In
Memory of
Martha Finch,
relict of Edward Finch,
who was born Nov 5th, 1749,
and died Nov 5th, 1827,
aged 78 years.
" Here rests a woman, good, without pretense.
Blessed with plain reason and with sense,
Passion and pride were to her soul unknown,
Convinced that virtue only is own.
So, unaffected, so composed a mind;
So firm, yet so soft,
So strong, yet so refined.
Heaven, as it's purest gold by loving......
The Spirit sustained but the woman died."

Sacred
To the
Memory of
Ossian Adams,
son of
Dr. Freeborn & Juliet
Adams,
who was born Dec the 18th, 1812,
and died on the 20th of
Oct 1831,
aged 18 years, 10 months, and 2 days.

Sacred
To the memory of
Martha Cleopatria,
wife of
James M. Henderson,
who was born July 5th, 1819,
and died December 31st, 1844,
aged 25 years, & 6 months,

Sacred
To the Memory of
Thomas Crenshaw,
son of
Charles & Eunice Crenshaw,
who departed this life,
1795,
aged 18 months.

In
Memory of
Dr. Ivey Finch,
son of
Edward & Martha
Finch,
died March 10th, 1815,
born 1788,
aged 27 years,
....

Sacred
To the memory of
Charles Crenshaw,
who departed this life
21 June, 1814,
aged 65 years.
(Rev War soldier)

Sacred
To the Memory of
Ann Crenshaw,
daughter of Charles
& Eunice Crenshaw,
who departed this life
1795,
in the 13th year of her age.

Sacred
To the Memory of
Phebe Crenshaw,
daughter of Charles and
Eunice Crenshaw,
who departed this life
21st Sept. 1815,
aged 15 years, 5 months, and 10 days.

In
Memory of
Martha C. Finch
Born Sept 29, 1813,
Died Aug 13, 1814.

In
Memory of
Martha Finch,
Born March 2, 1774,
and died about
17 years of age.

In
Memory of
Wesley Finch,
son of
Edward & Martha
Finch,
Born March 12th, 1784,
and died about 12 years
of age.

Sacred
To the Memory of
Eunice Crenshaw,
wife of
Charles Crenshaw,
who departed this life
24th of September, 1815,
aged 62 years.

Sacred
To the Memory of
Elizabeth Crensh
daughter of Charles
& Eunice Crenshaw,
who departed this
life 1794,
aged 5 years.

Lavania Nance,
wife of
R. V. Gist,
daughter of Dr.
Thomas B.
Rutherford,
Born 8th Nov,1
Married 28th O
1858. Died 7th
Nov. 1883.

CEMETERY MARKERS (continued)

Crenshaw-Finch Families' Cemetery (continued)-

Sacred
To the Memory of
Archibald Crenshaw,
son of
Charles & Eunice Crenshaw,
who departed this life
on the 22nd Febry,
1818,
aged 41 years, 7 months,
and 26 days.

Sacred
To the Memory of
Mary Crenshaw,
wife of
Archibald Crenshaw,
who departed this life
25th January, 1816,
aged 29 years, 9 months,
and 27 days.

Sacred
To the Memory of
Phebe Crenshaw,
daughter of Archibald &
Mary Crenshaw,
who departed this life
16th June, 1818,
aged 6 years, 7 months,
and 1 day.

Sacred
To the Memory of
Charles Crenshaw,
son of
Archibald & Mary
Crenshaw,
who departed this
life on 19th Sept,
1814,
aged 1 year and 8
days.

Sacred
To the Memory of
Nancy Crenshaw,
daughter of Archibald &
Mary Crenshaw,
who departed this life
5th Nov, 1814,
aged 5 years, 11 months,
and 16 days.

Sacred
To the Memory of
Dr. T. B. Rutherford,
who was born
November 5th, 1801,
and died
May 19th, 1865,
" He was an affectionate
husband, a liberal and
loving father, a kind
neighbor, and a true
Christian."

Sacred
To the Memory of
Laura,
wife of
T. B. Rutherford,
who died
June 24th, 1859,
aged 51 years, 1 month,
and 15 days.
She was faithful in all the
relations of life,
and died in the peaceful hope
of Heaven.
She was for many years a zealous
member of the Methodist Church,
and most devoted Christian,
Cultivated virtues, and making
herself happy by contributing to the
happiness of others.

Laura Rutherford,
wife of
James F. Hall,
Born
Nov 14th, 1839,
Died
Nov 25th, 1916,
" Into thine hand I commit
my Spirit, thou hast
redeemed me, O Lord God of
Truth."

John Hopkins Williams Family Graveyard-located about 16 miles West of Newberry Court House-left of Main highway to Chappells, S. C.-   An iron picket fence with large iron gate around graves-

In Memory of
John H. Williams,
son of John and Martha
Williams,
who was born Jany 20th, 1830,
and died March 15th, 1832.

John Hopkins Williams,
Born
Nov. 3, 1793,
Died
June 2, 1876.
" The long day's work is done,
and we must sleep."
From early boyhood a member of
the Cross Roads Baptist Church.

In Memory of
Nancy D. Williams,
daughter of
John and Martha Williams,
who was born
September 17th, 1828,
and departed this life
August 10th, 1856,

In Memory of an infant
daughter of
John and Martha Williams.

In
Memory of
John Williams,
son of
J. G. & S. A. Davenport,
Born December 7th, 1845.

In
Memory of
William Williams,
Born May 29th, 1791,
Died December 2nd, 1829.

In Memory of
Martha Williams,
wife of
John Williams,
who was born
January 20th, 1803,
and departed this life
October 18th, 1838.

CEMETERY MARKERS (continued)

John Hopkins Williams Family Graveyard (continued)-

In Memory of
Betty,
daughter of
John H. & Martha Williams,
Born
September 5th, 1831,
Married June 4th, 1857,
to Major S.T.H. Williams,
Died
September 15th, 1859.

In Memory of
Theresa
daughter of
John H. & Martha Williams,
Born
April 8th, 1835,
Married November 18th, 1860,
to Capt. John G. Williams,
Died
October 30th, 1863.

In Memory of
My Dear Husband,
William A. Williams,
who was born March 25th,
1825,
and died Febry 11th,
1858.
He was a true Christian and a
member of the Presbyterian Church.

Sacred
To the memory of
Richard Davenport, son of
John G. and Sarah Davenport,
(formerly Miss. Williams),
who was born Jan 20th, and
died July 24th, 1843,
aged 6 months, 4 days.

Sacred
To the Memory of
Elizabeth Gillam Davenport,
daughter of John G. and
Sarah Davenport (formerly
Miss. Williams),
who was born Sept 22nd, and
died Nov 16th, 1841, aged 1
month and 25 days.

Sacred
To the Memory of
Sarah Ann Davenport,
daughter of
John and Martha Williams
(formerly Miss. Smith),
consort of John G. Davenport,
who was born April 19th
1824,
and died November 28th,
1846,
aged 22 years, 4 months,
and 9 days.

Rudd Family Graveyard- located near Vaughnville School, on right of
highway leading from Chappells, S. C.-

Sacred
To the Memory of
Susan C. Rudd,
Consort of D. Rudd,
and daughter of
James and Sarah C. Gillam,
was born November 17th,
1813,
and departed this life,
January 19th, 1856.

In Memory of
Fields Rudd,
who departed this life
on 1st October, 1839,
aged 32 years, 1 month,
and 22 days.

Margaret Caldwell
daughter of
John and Frances Rudd,
Died August 13th, 1816.

In Memory of an
Infant child of
A. & E. G. Rudd.

Sacred
To the memory of
Daniel Rudd,
son of
John & Frances Rudd,
who was born 1808 or '9,
and departed this life
July 31st, 1856.

Erected
to the memory of
John Basket.

Erected
to the memory of
Daniel Basket.

Phoebe Burton,
daughter of Aaron &
Elizabeth Burton,
who was born Feb 28th,
1815,
and died August 21st,
1837,
Aged 22 years, 6 months,
and 6 days.

Sacred
To the Memory of
James G. Rudd,
son of
D. & E. G. Rudd,
was born
Febry 18th,
1836,
and departed this life
September 26th, 1855.

In Memory of
Eliz. G. Rudd,
wife of D. Rudd,
and daughter of
Jonathan & Susannah
Davenport,
Born June 6th, 1812,
Died August 28th, 1840.

Elizabeth Burton,
wife of Aaron Burton,
who was born
Febry 21st, 1784,
and departed this life
December 15th, 1836,
Aged 51 years, 10 months,
and 6 days.

In Memory of
Frances Rudd,
Consort of
John Rudd,
who died July 28th,
1827.

In Memory of
John Rudd, Sen.
who was born May 11,
1772, and died
November 11, 1829,
aged 57 years and
6 months.

In Memory of
Frances S. Rudd,
Born Nov 23rd, 1837,
Died Oct 5th, 1840.

Martha Rudd
(on small rock)

CEMETERY MARKERS (continued)

Rudd Family Graveyard (continued)-

Sacred
To the memory of
Cornelia S. Rudd,
daughter of
D. & S. C. Rudd,
was born April 1st, 1843,
and departed this life
October 26th, 1844.

In Memory of
Nancy Cason Rudd,
daughter of
John and Elizabeth Rudd,
Born August 2nd, 1841,
Died August 3rd, 1844,
Aged 3 years, and 1 day.

In Memory of
An infant daughter of
John and Elizabeth Rudd,
Born May 4th, 1843,
Died Oct 31st, 1845.

Oldest son of
M. E. & L. M.
Gillam,
Still born
Nov. 2nd, 1853.

On the Gillam Smith Place, not far from Rudd Garveyard are some graves and markers, one of which is the following:

To
The Memory of
Wesley Smith,
Born
Dec 22nd, 1798,
Died
April 17th, 1868.

In the Magnolia Cemetery, Greenwood, S. C. is the following marker:

Robert C. Gillam
Born
August 13th, 1820,
Died
Sept 18th, 1897.
"My God is the Rock of my Refuge."

Davenport Family Graveyard-located about 10 miles Northwest of Newberry Court House, on left from highway to Silver Street, first going left at site of old Longshore's Store-

Sacred
To the memory of
Jonothan Davenport
(son of James & Elizabeth
Davenport—formerly
Miss. Gillam),
who was born October 7th, 1780,
and died July 5th, 1842,
aged 61 years, 8 months,
and 29 days.

In Memory of
James M.,
son of
Jonothan and Susannah
Davenport,
Consort of M. A. E.
Davenport,
Born April 8th, 1811,
Died Febry 22nd, 1848,
aged 36 years, 10 months,
and 14 days.

Sacred
To the memory of
Susannah Davenport,
daughter of Thomas and
Lucy Eastland,
(formerly Miss. Towles),
Consort of
Jonothan Davenport,
who was born
March 30th, 1781,
and died
January 11th, 1842,
aged 60 years, 9 months and
11 days.

In Memory of
Maria Antoinette
Josephine,
daughter of J. N. and
M. A. E. Davenport,
Born April 18th, 1839,
Died Nov 1842,
Aged 3 years, 6 months.

Sacred
To the memory of
Catherine Susannah Young,
youngest child of
Jonothan & Susannah Davenport,
Consort of
James M. Young,
was born November 21st, 1824,
and died December 28th, 1846,
Leaving an only child, husband,
younger brother, and two younger
sisters, to deplore her loss.
SISTER.

M E M
of Isaac
Davenport.
He departed this life
26th June,
1816,
Aged 63 years and 2 months,
and 23 days.
May he rest in peace.

CEMETERY MARKERS (continued)

Davenport Family Graveyard (continued)-

The Memory of
John Gillam,
son of
Jonothan and Susannah
Davenport,
who was born
Febry 26th, 1818,
married to
Sarah Ann Williams,
December 1st, 1840,
and departed this life
October 12th. 1861.

In Memory
of
Elizabeth Gillam,
daughter of
T. C. and A. W. Hill,
who was born
September 30th, 1841,
and died
August 27th, 1847.

In Memory
of
Thomas Angelina,
daughter of
T. C. and A. W. Hill,
who was born
Febry 28th, 1851,
and died
Febry 15th, 1852.

In Memory
of
William Oscar,
son of
T. C. & A. W. Hill,
who was born
March 25th, 1847,
and died
October 27th, 1847.

In Memory of
Silas,
son of
T. C. and A. W. Hill,
who was born
September 28th, 1845,
and died
October 10th, 1853.

In Memory
of
Walter Scott,
son of
T. C. and A.W. Hill,
who was born
March 3rd, 1854,
and died
August 2nd, 1854.

First Baptist Church Cemetery, Edgefield, S. C. —two of the many markers there, who were American soldiers in the Mexican War-

Sacred
To the Memory of
Pierre La Borde,
born in France,
died at Edgefield
Court House,
November 14th, 1820,
aged about 50 years.

Preston S. Brooks,
Born in Edgefield Village,
August 6th, 1819,
Elected to the State Legislature
in 1844. Elected Captain of
Co. D., Palmetto Regiment, in
1846, and served during the
Mexican War.
Elected to Congress in 1853,
and died in Washington City,
January 27th, 1857.

Charles Allen Family graveyard-located about 3 miles North of Laurens Court House-

Sacred
To the memory of
Charles Allen, Esq.,
He was born
May 3rd, 1764,
Married to Susan Garner,
Dec 12, 1782,
Died
Jany 5th, 1856,
Aged 91 years, 8 months,
and 2 days. He and his wife
lived together 68 years,
and 5 months.

Sacred
To the Memory of
Susan Allen,
wife of
Charles Allen, Esq.,
who died
May 13, 1851,
Aged 86 years, 11 months,
and 8 days.

Other markers at First Baptist Church Cemetery, Edgefield, S. C.-

CEMETERY MARKERS (continued)

First Baptist Church, Edgefield, S. C.-

Thomas Glasgow Bacon,
Born June 24th, 1812,
Died September 25th, 1876.
Colonel of 7th Reg. S.C.V.
" Let me go, I want to go to
my regiment........",
his last words.

John Edmund Bacon,
March 3rd, 1829,
February 19, 1895.

Jonothan H. Carter
Jan 1, 1821,
Mar 7, 1884,
Lieut. U. S. Navy,
Capt. C. S. Navy.

Thomas John Adams,
Born March 12th, 1847,
Died May 30th, 1902,
Confederate Soldier,
Editor Edgefield
Advertsier 33 years....

Saluda, S. C. -Redbank Baptist Church Cemetery-
Confederate Soldiers-

John C. Little,
1847-1922.
C.S.A.

Andrew S. Cromer,
Born
Feb 16, 1828,
Died

Benjamin Lewis,
Co. B. 2 S. C.
State Troops,
C.S.A.

Jesse Turner,
Co. K.
2 S. C. Art.
C.S.A.

Wesley Cockrell,
April 17, 1835,
Oct 28, 1928,
C.S.A.

Lieut. Hudson Watkins, Jan 24, 1903.
Co. F. Palmetto
Sharpshooters, S.C.
Vol. C. S. A.
Born Sept 28, 1838,
Died Aug 18, 1864.

Spencer Jennings,
Co. K.
S.C. Art.
C.S.A.

Zedekiah Crouch,
April 1, 1843,
Nov 7, 1933.

Winnsboro, S. C.--old Cemetery at Methodist Church Site- Some of markers-

Sacred
To the memory of
Michael Moore, Esq.
who departed this life
Sept 8, A.D. 1817,
in the 65th year
of his age.

Sacred
To the memory of
Mrs. Rebecca Moore
who departed this life
Nov 4th, A.D. 1851,
Aged 73 years, and 6 months.

Lieut. Waddy Means,
1st Reg. S. C.
Regular Infantry.
Died Febry, 1865.
(Confederate soldier)

Capt. John Buchanan,
a soldier
of the Revolution.
Died April 1824,
Aged 74 years.
And his wife,
Sarah Buchanan,
Died April, 1825,
Aged 78 years.

Winnsboro, S. C.- Presbyterian Church Old Cemetery-

The just man walketh in his
Integrity.
Major Gen. John Buchanan,
Born August 9, 1790,
Died April 2, 1862/
A soldier of the War of 1812,
an honorable representative of
Fairfield for many years in the
House and Senate.
He was a profound lawyer,
an honest man,
And died sustained by
Christian faith.

Sacred
To The Memory of
Major Joseph Kerr,
Who left this transitory scene
of existence on the 4th day of
January, 1822, in the 70th year
of his age.
He was a native of Ireland, but
emigrated to America at an early
age, and during the War of
Independence, established the
character of a brave man, in the
various relations of private life,
which he sustained; he was distinguished for rectitude and benevolence,
and in his whole conduct, and
covoured to the honorable and useful
without estentation.

Sacred
To the Memory of
Mr. Hugh Barkley, Sr.,
a native of Ireland.
Born
25th December, 1763,
and died
on the 11th Nov. 1811.

CEMETERY MARKERS (continued)

Gillam and Wallace Families Graveyards-located about 17 miles Northwest of Newberry Court House, to right of highway to Chappells, S. C., on Page's Creek-

(Here are two graves with small soapstone markers with no inscriptions—one supposedly that of Major Robert Gillam, Sr., one time member of the State Legislature; having served as Major in State Militia during the Rev War; and probably the other Major Gillam's wife)-

Sacred
To the memory of
Rebecca Gillam,
daughter of Robert and
Elizabeth Gillam,
who was born Jan 17, 1793,
and died December 1, 1800.

Sacred
To the memory of
Robert Gillam, Jr.
who departed this life
on the 7th November,
1813,
In the 56th year of his age.
"Death like an overflowing stream,
Sweeps us away this life a dream."
(Rev War patriot and Capt in
S. C. Militia)

Sacred
To
The memory of
Elizabeth Gillam,
who died
December 29, 1851,
in the 97th year of
her age.

In
Memory of
Catherine Waddell
Gillam,
daughter of
Robert and Elizabeth
Gillam,
Born Sept 13th,
1795,
and died May 24,
1802.

In
Memory of
T. O. Gillam,
daughter of
Wm. & T. H. Gillam,
Born
Nov....,1834,
and died May 20,
1836,
aged 18 months.

Rebecca Gillam,
Infant of
James & S. C. Gillam,
Died Oct 8th,
1849,
aged 5 months.

To
The memory of
Mary E. Gillam,
daughter of
Wm. & T. H. Gillam,
aged 15 months.

Sarah C. Gillam,
wife of
James Gillam,
Died 20th June,
1849,
In the 52nd year of
her age.

Eph. Calhoun Gillam,
Infant son of James
& S. C. Gillam,
Died 22nd Sept.
1836,
Aged 4 years.

Sacred
To
The memory of
P. B. Waters,
Who was born Jan 3rd, 1775,
was married to Sarah Gillam,
April 23rd, 1803,
and departed this life Feb 26th,
1807.
"Ye who have felt misfortune's frown,
Here pause and drop a tear,
And ye who naught but pleasure,
Here learn how vain earth's joy's,
How soon they fade away."

William L. Gillam,
Infant of
James & S. C. Gillam,
Died the 4th August,
1831,
Aged 2 years, and
10 months.

Erected
To the Memory of
Col. Wm. F. Sheppard,
who died the 1st day of
December, 1818,
in the 36th year of his age.

Sacred
To The Memory of
Sarah Sheppard,
daughter of
Robert & Elizabeth Gillam
who was born
March 14th, 1785,
and died August 1st,
1821.

Wallace Family Square-

Sacred
To the Memory of
Mary Brown
who departed this life
December 28th, 1811,
aged 27 years.

Sacred
To the memory of
Francis Jamison,
who departed this life
Feb 20th, 1818,
aged 28 years.

Sacred
To the memory of
Wm. Wallace, Jr.
he died in 1815,
about 40 years of age.

In Memory of
Elizabeth Boozer,
who died
December 26th, 1831,
in the 34th year of
her age.

Sacred
To the memory of
Frances Jimerson,
she died 1825,
aged about 7 years.

Sacred
To the memory of
Frances Wallace,
daughter of
R. G. & Behethland
Wallace,
who departed this life
November 7th, 1854,
aged 22 years,
9 months and 6 days.

CEMETERY MARKERS (continued)

Gillam & Wallace Families Cemeteries (continued)-
Wallace Square-

Sacred
To the memory of
Robert G. Wallace,
son of
William & Frances
Wallace,
who was born Sept 12th,
1810,
and departed this life
Feb 3rd, 1857,
aged about 46 years,
4 months, and 21 days.

Sacred
To the memory of
Mrs. Behetheland Wallace,
wife of
Robert G. Wallace,
and daughter of
Wm. and Susan Adams,
who was born
November 11, 1808,
and died
September 24, 1860.

Martha E. Adams,
wife of
William H. Adams,
and daughter of
Henry & Tabitha Wallace,
who was born
November 6th, 1820,
and died
November 13th, 1855,
Aged 35 years and 7 days,
leaving a devoted husband
and six children. She was
an obedient child, tender and
devoted mother, true as a
friend and neighbor, and at all
times mindful of the wants
of the needy.

Floyd Family Graveyard-located about 12 miles Northwest of
Newberry Court House, on old road to "Belfast", about 100
yards from the new highway-

Sacred to the memory
of
Captain John Floyd, an
active Officer in the
Revolutionary
War.
Born the 15th Feb 1756,
and died in
the 78th year of his age.

Sacred
To the memory of
Mrs. Nancy Floyd,
wife of
Captain John Floyd,
She was born in Mecklenburg
County, in the State of
Virginia,
and died in Newberry District,
South Carolina,
March 22nd, 1857,
aged about 100 years.

This Tomb
is preserved to the memory of
Charles Floyd,
son of
Joseph and Elizabeth Floyd,
who died August 20th, 1847,
aged about 37 years.

Sacred
To the memory of
Charles Floyd, Sr.
who died
August 20th, 1853,
aged 64 years.

Sacred
To the memory of
Susan Frances,
wife of
Maj. Israel & Stacey
Chandler,
Born Dec 7th, 1836,
Died Oct 4th, 1841.

James B. Chappell,
Feb 15th, 1830,
Dec 25th, 1870.

Martha E.,
wife of
James B. Chappell,
Oct 9th, 1835,
July 20th, 1871.

Sacred
To the memory
of
James Workman,
Died March 26th
1844.

Sacred
To the memory of
William Anderson,
who departed this life
Nov 23rd, 1841,
Aged 70 years.

In
Memory of
Elizabeth Anderson,
who was born
Dec 9th, 1774,
and died
Nov 9th, 1849.

Sacred
To the memory of
Edney Workman,
who departed this
life Sept 27th,
1866.

A daughter's tribute to Her Father.
Sacred
To the memory of
Washington Floyd,
husband of Mary M. Floyd,
who departed this life
after a long illness,
Feb 17th, 1871,
Aged about 63 years.

In
Memory of
Mrs. Nancy C., wife of
Washington Floyd,
who was born
March 10th, 1813,
died Dec 2nd, 1868.

Sacred
To the memory of
Mrs. Louisa Floyd,
wife of
John N. Floyd,
who was born Feb 9th, 1840,
and died Jany 4th, 1861.

In
Memory of
Matilda Satterwhite,
Consort of
William Satterwhite,
who was born
March 10, 1804,
and died........
(stone br.

CEMETERY MARKERS (continued)

Floyd Family Graveyard(continued)-

Sacred
To the memory of
Evaline Matilda,
wife of
Moses Anderson,
who was born
Oct 26th, 1818,
and departed this life
Oct 21st, 1867,
She joined the Bush River
Baptist Church July 7th,1832,
possessed of a naturally kind
and gentle disposition, and
maintained her Christian character
through life, and died in full
assurance of a glorious
immortality.

Sacred
To the memory of
William Franklin,
son of
Moses and Catherine Anderson,
who was born
Sept 20th, 1837,
and departed this life
March 26th, 1862,
At the first call of his
beloved State, he enlisted
in the 3rd Regt. S. C. V.
and performed his duty
faithfully,
until he was cut down
by the hand of death,
though just entering
into manhood he had gained
the love and esteem of all
his acquaintenances.

(Some unmarked graves)

Caldwell Family Graveyard-located about 15 miles Northwest of Newberry Court House, just across Little River, and near Mill Creek-

A square rough stone, moss-grown, shows the letter "J" with other letters obliterated by rains over the years—this probably the grave of Major John Caldwell who was killed by a Tory band during the last year of the Rev War-

Sacred
To the Memory of
Charlotte Jane
Sproull,
who departed this life
on the 18th of Sept.
1818.

A small foot stone here, showing
the initials, B. C. C.

(Apparently there are other graves in this
graveyard not marked)

Buzhardt Family Graveyard-located about 4 miles Southeast of Newberry Court House, on right of old Pomaria Highway-

In Memory
of
Catherine Buzhardt,
daughter of
Jacob & Elizabeth Buzhardt
who died March 22nd, 1866,
aged 58 years, 25 days.

David H. Buzhardt,
Born
Sept 1st, 1811,
Died
Sept 19th, 1881,
Aged 70 years,
and 18 days.

Mrs. Mary M. Buzhardt,
wife of
David H. Buzhardt.
Died March 3rd, 1876,
Aged 59 years, 6 months,
" The sorrows of life are now past,
The haven of sweet rest is gained.
Dear Mother, we'll meet thee at last;
And with Jesus forever reign."

Sacred
To the memory
of
John Austin Buzzard,
was born July 18th, 1855,
departed this life
May 31st, 1856,
aged 10 months, and
13 days.
"................."

Sacred
To the memory of
John S. Buzzard,
who was born July 16th,
1819,
departed this lifeJune 14th,
1855,
aged 35 years, 11 months,
and 14 days.
—above

"Prepare to meet the God,
O'Israel,"
" Meet the perfect man and behold
the upright, for the end of that
man is peace."

CEMETERY MARKERS (continued)

Buzhardt Family Graveyard(continued)-

In
Memory of
Beaufort Simpson Buzhardt,
son of Daniel H. and Mary M.
Buzhardt,
a member of Co. E. 3rd Regt. S.C.V.
was born the 26th December, 1838,
A minnie ball in a skirmish before
Richmond, Va. the 29th June, 1862.
Thus passed away a pure Christian
Spirit, who gave his life in defense
of his country.

Sacred
To the memory of
Johnnie Jacob McSwain,
son of
David H. & Mary M. Buzzard,
who was born
June 11th, 1857,
and died
Nov 1st, 1863.

J. B. Traywick,
infant son of
Rev. J. B. & Carrie E.
Traywick,
Born and died
Oct 28th, 1875.
He will bloom again.

Sacred
To the memory of
Harriet Olivia Buzzard,
was born October 11th, 1848,
departed this life April 20th,
1855.
Aged 6 years, 6 months,
and 9 days.

In
Memory of
Samuel Jefferson Buzhardt
who was born
in Newberry District, S.C.
on the 16th May; 1830, and
died at home from desease
contracted in camp on
Sullivan's Isalnd,
on the 17th of Dec. 1862.
"O, for that city fair and bright,
which shall not pass away,
The glory of the Lord, it's light,
The lamb it's cloudless day."

Sacred
To the memory of
Jacob Buzzard,
who departed this life on
the 25th July, 1854,
aged 80 years.

Beaufort Simpson Traywick,
infant son of
Rev. J. B. & Carrie E.
Traywick,
Died July 25th, 1875,
aged 4 years.

Jacob Sligh Buzhardt,
Born
Sept 1st, 1821,
Died
Sept 1st, 1858,
The slab marks the place
of rest.
" Then shall the dust return
to earth as it was and the
Spirit shall return unto
God who gave it."

(O, Hope Buzhardt,
Confederate soldier,
buried here with no
marker)............

Sacred
To the memory of
Elizabeth Buzzard,
who was born on the 27th
December 1781, and departed
this life on the 17th June,
1834,
aged 66 years, 5 months,
and 20 days.

Sacred
To the memory of
Lawson Berley
Buzzard,
who was born Sept 9th,
1853,
departed this life
May 25th, 1855,
aged 1 year, 8 months,
and 16 days.
"God bless an early death,
and take the Spirit unto
himself."

A Confederate soldier's grave near Fish Dam Ferry, Union County, S. C.-

Sacred
To the memory of
Robert W. Gilliam,
Born Union District, S. C.
August 3rd, 1827,
Killed at Malone's Farm, Va.
July 30th, 1864.

ABSTRACTS OF OLD WILLS
NEWBERRY COUNTY COURT HOUSE
Will Book " A "

Page #1-
James Murphry, decd., will 3-27-1787; proved 6-5-1787.
Wife: Sarah (to have homeplace and all movable property during her life).
Ch: John, oldest son (to have 30 acres out of tract of 330 acres on Dry Creek),
Dowdle (to have 150 acres, a part of above tract, and 50 acres to my wife, then to son Dowdle).
Jemima Roland, Ann Maybin, and Rebecca Murphry to have certain property.
Witnesses: Thomas Gordon, William Chandler, and William Hampton Chandler.
Exr: Dowdle Murphry. Exrtx: Sarah Murphry.

Page # 2-
James Hodges, decd. Will 5-19-1787; proved 6-5-1787.
Wife: Martha. Ch: Joseph, Christina, Jesse, and Rebecca Shaw and Patty Shaw.
Other legatees: Sarah Glass and Toby Glass.
Witnesses: Reuben Golding, George Elliott, Haley Shaw, and Joseph Hodges.

Page # 3-
Thomas Green, decd. will 4-30-1787; proved 6-6-1787.
Brother: John Green (to have 250 acres with homeplace and slaves).
Witnesses: Edward Kelly, Edmond Kelly, Mary Ann Smith.

Page #4-
Richard Bonds, decd. Will 9-24-1786; proved 6-6-1787.
Wife: Joice (to have residue of estate during her life). Ch: Minah (son), to have 157 acres on both sides Beaver Dam Creek; Richard, to have land he lives on, also 50 acres that was bought from John Anderson; William, to have 1,000 wt. of tobacco and hogs on Reedy River; Sally, to have certain cattle and personal property; Retter, to have two cows; Betty, to have certain personal property.........
Witnesses: Edward Kelly, Thomas Lake, Ann Johnson.
Exrs: Minah Bonds and Joice Bonds.

Page # 5-
John Glenn, decd. Will 9-20-1784; proved 9-3-1787.
Living near Saluda River. Wife's name not given....
Ch: James, John, William —to have all lands of 300 acres, 200 acres of which is where I live, and 100 acres bought from my brother, Wm. Herbison, decd, and not yet released by his widow, Ann Herbison.
Other ch: Jean, Mary, Margaret, Ann, to have certain property; then residue to my wife during her life.
Exrs: John Douglass and Thomas Brown.

Page #6-
Peter Galloway, decd. Will 10-26-1774; proved 9-3-1787.
Wife: Margaret (to have 100 acres whereon we liv during her life, afterwards to my son, Peter).
Ch : Peter (to have 50 acres, remainder of 150 acres to George Hayworth); John (to have 100 ac that was originally granted to George Hayworth, with 50 acres adjoining it); Mary Douglass (to have the 200 acres surveyed for James Brooks), h husband, John Douglass; Elizabeth, Jean, Anna, a Martha (all four to share in the above 200 acre
Witnesses: Robert Speer, John Douglass, and William Herbison.
Exrs: William Herbison, and Robert Speer.

Page #7-
John Newman, decd. Will 8-16-1780; proved 9-3-178
Wife: Nima. Ch: James (to have 150 acres adjo: ing Joseph Johnson, with it's Patent, to be posse by him at time of his being 18 years of age); Samuel (to have 225 acres, part of an old survey lying next to the river, to be possessed at 18 ye of age); John, youngest son, (to have 150 acres with it's Patent, being the place whereon I live, to be possesed by himat 18 years of age), also to have my silver watch), My brother, Samuel Newman, to have a square barrel gun and a smooth boore. Witnesses: Phillip Phegin, Sarah Inman, and Thomas Burton. Exrs: Nima Newman, Joseph Johnson.

Page #8-
John Lindsey,Sr., decd., will 8-9-1783; proved
Wife: Elce(to have all estate during (9-6-1787. her life). Ch: James, oldest son,(to hav certain property), John, Sarah Speakes, Abigail Wills, Thomas, and Samuel. Son-in-law: Jerrard Smith. Exrs: Elce Lindsey, Samuel Lindsey.
Witnesses: Thomas Dugan, Isaac Morgan, Moses Linds William Hamilton.

Page #9-
Robert Mann, decd. Will 3-27-1782; proved 9-6-178
Wife: Susannah (to have all movable estate during her life, and plantation where she lives).
Ch: James (to have 100 acres adjoining Farr Sprin John (to have 100 acres adjoining above tract), Robert (to have 100 acres where plantation we liv on), Jean Nix, Susannah. Gr-son: Mannasse Mann (to have 50 acres opposite to, or before the door next to Joseph Green's. Exrs: James Mann, Susanna Mann. Wit: Solomon Reese, Elizabeth Reese, Geo. Go

453

Abstracts Old Wills (continued)

Page #10-
James Ford, decd. Will 5-13-1787; proved 9-6-1787.
(of King's Creek)   Wife: not named—to have
my old horse called, "Shoemaker".
Ch: Rachel, oldest daughter,(to have a feather-
bed and such furniture to her, and no more of my
estate); Rebecca Anderson (now a widow); Elizabeth
Lindsey(wife of Samuel Lindsey); James (he died
just before his father);.... Gr-son: John Ford,
son of my deceased son, James Ford. Witnesses:
Robert Brown, George Cray, James Lindsey.
Exrs: Rebecca Anderson, Samuel Lindsey.

Page #13-
At a Court held at Newberry County Court House on
9-7-1787, Letters of Adm. were granted to John
Barlow in right of his wife, Elizabeth, on the
estate of John Johnston, decd. Bondsmen: John
Barlow, Jeremiah Williams, William Young.

Page #14-
Estate of Johnston, decd. Appraisers: Joseph Caldwell,
William Caldwell, William Young, dated 9-7-1787.

Page #15-
John Vaun, decd. Will 1-2-1799; proved 6-2-1788.
Wife: Elizabeth (to have all lands and movable
estate during her life, to be willed as she wishes).
Witnesses: John Waldrop, John Motes, William
Murdock. Exrs: Elizabeth Vaun, George Goggans.

Page #16-
Nathaniel Harris, decd. Will 12-30-1787; proved
Wife: Mary (to enjoy all estate,   6-2-1788.
both real and personal, during her life, and
after her death to be divied among children and
gr-son. Ch: Moseby, Rebecca, Richard, Jemima,
Samuel(Samuel is a son-in-law), Littleberry and
Clough.   Gr-son: David Gillam. Witnesses: Lewis
Mitchell, Moseby Harris, George Elliott, and
Jemima Gillam.

Page #17-
Estate of Robert Maun, decd. Appraisers: Edward
Musgrove,Robert Hannah, Esq., Braswell Prather,
and James Craigh. Under direction of Susannah Maun,
Admx., dated 6-3-1788, James Montgomery empowered
to qualify appraisers. Inventory taken 7-10-1788.

Page #19-
Enos Elliman, decd. Will 4-21-1787; proved 6-2-1788.
Wife: Catherine. Ch: John, William, Elizabeth, Amey,
Hannah, Mary Bonds. Witnesses: Robert Speer, Isaac
Ballenger, Samuel Brown. Exrs: John Ellimon,
 Catherine Ellimon.   ....

Page #20-
Isaac Parmer, decd. Will 3-31-1787; proved 6-2-17
Wife: Saraith (to have 100 acres land).
Ch: William (to have 100 acres); four daughters
to have 51 pounds, 7 shillings, 7 pence, current
money of South Carolina. They to be raised by my
wife and son, William. Witnesses: William Herrin
Robert Brown, Catrin Ryley.

Page #21-
Mathias Wicker, Jr., decd. Will 6-5-1778; proved
                                   (6-2-1788.
Wife: Mary Sibla. Four ch: John Adam, Simon, Mar
and Catherine. Exrs: John Adam Youn, and Michael
Bickert.

Page #22-
George Dawkins, Sr. deced. Will-no date; proved
Taken by the oath of Wm Baluntine, (6-4-1788.
a subscribing witness to said will, and Elizabet
Beard who had the said will in her custody at t
of death of the testator and sometime after,
before said will was destrpyed. Legatees:
Mrs. Jemima Herbert(to have two slaves , and at
her death to go to her children, except Nancy
Barrat to have one slave); Mrs. Mary Ann Lane
(she was lent two slaves during her life and at
her death to be divided among children); Susan
Pope (dau) to have two negroes; Ellen Hampton
(gr-dau) was lent two negroes during her natura
life; widow Grigsby (a dau) was lent two negroe
during her natural life, and after her death to
equally divided among her children; George (sor
to have several negroes; Thomas Barratt(gr-son)
to have a negro boy; Wm Dawkins Lane(gr-son) to
have a negro fellow. Exrs: George Dawkins (sor
and Thomas Dawkins (nephew).

Page #25-
Benjamin Pearson, decd. Will 12-10-1784; proved
(of Bush River)   (6-6-1788.
Wife: Margaret (to have plantation whereon I li
400 acres-during her natural life or widowhood).
Ch:William , Abel, Samuel, Robert, Joseph, John,
Enoch.   Whereas I sold a tract of 200 acres to
brother, William Pearson, now decd, which if my
sons pay the balance due, comes to them.
My daughters, Rosannah Russell and Marjory
Buffington. Witnesses: Zebulon Gauntt, John
Wilkerson, and James Kelly. Exrs: Margaret Pea
(my wife), William Pearson (my cousin), and
Enoch Pearson (my son).

Abstracts Old Wills (continued)

Pages 26-27-
Gerard Smith, decd. Will-none. Adm. granted to Esther Smith, his late widow, on 6-3-1788....
Appraiser: John Lindsey, Esq., Robert Rutherford.

Pages 30-32-
John Gallman, decd, Court held 9-3-1788, letters of Adm. granted to Gasper Piester. Bond: 1,200 pounds sterling. Warrant of appraisment directed to Frederick Gray, Jeremiah Williams, George Ruff, Esq., and James Sheppard.

Pages 33-34-
Jacob Anderson, decd. Adm. granted to James Strother, 9-8-1788. Appraiser: Levi Anderson, John Blalock, Abel Anderson, Sr., and Abraham Anderson, Jr.

Page 35-
James Willson, decd. Adm. granted to James Willson on 9-3-1788. Levi Casey to qualify appraisers, viz: Dudley Bonds, Samuel Cannon, Jesse Brooks, William Blackburn.

Pages 38-40-
William O'Neall, decd. Will 7-15-1786; proved 9-2-1788. Wife: Mary (to have lands we live on, West side of Bush River). Ch: Abijah (to have land whereon he lives), Hugh (to have land with the grist mill, William (to have saw-mill and as much land on North side Bush River), John (to have land on S. side of Bush River), Henry (to have land between John's land and that of James Brooks), Thomas, Sarah Foard, Trustees for children : William Pearson, Henry Steddom. Witnesses: Elisha Ford, David Hollingsworth, and John Sanders.

Page 42-
Daniel DeWalt, decd. Will 10-17-1776; proved 9-2-1788. Adm. granted to George Gray on 3-2-1789.
Appraisers: James Sheppard, Thomas Spearman, William Sheppard, James Sheppard, Jr. Wife, Susannah, as Extrx.
Ch: Mary Magdeline, Catherine, Daniel, Peter, Susannah.
Witnesses: John Gallman, Jr., Martin Levistein, and Michael Dickert.

Page 46-
Randolph Robinson, decd, Estate. Adm. granted to Suffias Robinson(his widow), and Thomas Gordon, Sr. on 3-2-1789. Appraisers: Edward Kelly, John Liles, Sr., Williamson Liles, and Thomas Lake.

Page 49
Jacob Stearly, decd. Adm. granted to Ursley Stearly, widow. on 3-2-1789. ....

Page #51-
Charles King, decd. Will 1-21-1789; proved 3-2-1789. Wife: (no name). Ch: Jacob, Pennington, Lyda Lindsey, Mary Starke, Ruth Starke, Charity Gordon, Rebecca, Keziah, Witnesses: Micajah Bennett, Wm. Ragland, Samuel Ragland. Exrs: Jacob King(son), Jeremiah Starke (son-in-law), Samuel Cannon(friend).

Page #55-
Peter DeWalt, decd. Will 2-21-1789; proved 3-2-1789. Legatees: George Gray (brother-in-law),to have 100 acres that was willed to my father; mother; my four sisters, Catherine, Mary, Susannah, and Ruth.
Witnesses: John Riley, William Moore, Frederick Gray.
Exrs: George Gray, James Boyle. (James Boyle empowered his friend, George Gray, to act in his place

Page #57-
John Gary, Jr., decd. Will 8-29-1785; proved 3-2-1789. Wife and children to have all estate—no names given.
Witnesses: John Cole, Daniel Williams.
Exr: Providence Williams. ....

Page #61-
Hugh Caldwell, decd, estate. Jacob Roberts Brown to qualify the following appraisers: Reuben Golding, Golding Tinsley, John Tinsley, and James Tinsley.
Adm. granted to Samuel Caldwell on 3-2-1789.

Pages 63-64-
Stephen Lewis, decd. Will 8-11-1788; proved 3-3-1789. Wife: Mary (to have one-third of land, where she choses, to her use during her life).
Son: James (to receive above land after death of my wife, also all movable property ; and son's part be sold and monet put out at interest until he is 21 years old). Witnesses: Daniel Johnson, and Sarah Johnson. Exrs: George Goggans, Michael Sanders.

Pages 66-67-
William Gilliam , decd. Will 2-27-1789; proved (3-3-1789.
Wife: (no name). Ch: John, Ann, William. William to have all tenements on Bush River and 165 acres land whereon I now live, and all of my carpenter tools, etc.
My daughter Ann to have one-half of the rents of the messuage or tenements where testator now lives, for the maintenance of my son, John.
Other ch: Hannah and Mary. All cattle to be taken over by my Exrs. Harmon Davis, Jr. and Daniel Perkins.
Witnesses: Samuel Pearson, Sr., Thomas Reid, Sr., William McDowell.

Abstracts of Old Wills (continued)

Page 70-
William Taylor, decd. Will 10-10-1781; proved
Wife: (no name). (3-4-1789.
Ch: Samuel (to have 250 acres whereon I now live);
Jonothan (to have 200 acres); Martha (to have
200 pounds lawful money); Prudence, youngest
daughter,(to have 200 pounds lawful S. C.
Currency). Witnesses: Samuel Kelly, Samuel
Ridgell, Joshua Reeder.

Page 72-
Court held at Newberry on 6-4-1789-
Adm. granted to Gabriel Anderson on estate of
Joseph Hogg, decd. Appraisers: Samuel Lindsey,
James Strother, Abraham Anderson, Levi Anderson.

Page 74-
Cornelius Cox, decd. Will 11-22-1784; proved 1-8-1790.
Wife: Ann. Ch: William , George, James, (James
to have 250 acres, and William and George to have
one-half of it); Margaret, Sarah, Elizabeth
Stewart, Mary Stewart, and John.
Exrs: George Cox (son), and William Cox.

Page 75-
Thomas Grasty, decd. Will Sept, 1789; proved 12-y-
Sister: Martha Grasty, to have 150 acres (1789.
and a slave. Brother: John Grasty, to have
a slave. Witnesses: Edward Kelly, John Liles,
Ann Chandler.

Page 76-
George Cox, decd. Adm. granted to James Cox on
12-10-1789. Appraisers: William Weeks, Joshua
Stuart, Thomas Spraggins, and James Wills.

Page 78-
Giles Chapman, decd. Adm.granted to Sarah Chap-
man, the widow, on 12-18-1789.
Appraisers: Elias Hollingsworth, David Pugh,
Daniel Smith, and Mathias Elmore.

Page 80-
Samuel Pearson, decd. Will 1-16-1788;proved 3-2-1790.
Wife: Mary (to have 300 acres where I live,during
her life. Ch: Benjamin, Samuel, Enoch, William,
Mary Taylor, Martha Steddom, Hannah, Eunice, Sarah.
My share of the mills, which is one-half, to be
sold and the price to be converted to the children
named. My step-father to be properly taken care
of during his life.Witnesses : William Hawkins,
Hugh O'Neall, William O'Neall.
Trustees: Zimri Gauntt, William Jenkins.

Page 82-
William Turner, decd. Will 12-30-1789;proved 3-3-
Wife: Mary (to have plantation we live on durin
her lifetime or widowhood). Ch: William, Davi
Rebecca, Rhoda, Edwards, Absalom, Susannah, and
Ann. Witnesses: Joshua Inman, Rebecca Turner,
Michael Burtz. Exrs: Mary Turner (wife), and
Mercer Babb·(friend).

Page 85-
Jacob Huffman, decd. Adm. granted to Rachel Dunca
on 3-2-1790. Appraisers: Samuel Cannon, Joshua
Reeder, James Cassels, and John Cannon.

Page 87-
Hannah Riley, decd. Will 11-10-1788; proved 6-7-1
Legatees: Jesse Graham(or Riley), James Graham,
John Graham, Joel Graham. My beloved son,
Thomas Riley, to have all personal and other
property, etc. Exrs: Thomas Riley, Jeremia
Williams. Witnesses: George Nolly, Mary Ann
Smith, Chris. Hardgroves.

Page 88-
Enoch Pearson, decd. Will 1-19-1790; proved 6-7-1
Wife: Phebe (to have plantation we live on durin
her life or widowhood. Ch: Samuel (to have one-
half of land I live on, also land I bought from
John Riley for 290 acres); William (to have the
other one-half of land I live on).
Exrs: William Pearson (brother), Phebe Pearson,
Abel Thomas, Henry Steddom.

Page 90-
John Wright, Sr., Will 9-17-1789; proved 6-8-1790
Wife: (no name). Ch: Joseph(dead)-to his son
John; John-to his son, Jesse; Nathan-to his son,
William; and to my son-in-law, Issac Hollingswort
to have my shoe-makers tools and one certain cow
and calf. Other legatees: Joab Brooks, son of
James Brooks; Joseph Cook, my gr-son,(son of Isa
Cook); William Hollingsworth, my gr-son,(son of
Issac Hollingsworth); Isaac Cook (my son-in-law;
to have the price of a cow which he never pai
for; Rachel Cook (daughter of Isaac Cook).
Witnesses: Isaac Hollingsworth, John Coate, and
Charity Cook. Exrs: Joseph Wright, my son.

Page 91-
Thomas Wilson, decd. Admr: Thomas Gordon, Sr.
Admx: Suffias Robinson. Granted 3-31-1790.
Appraisers: John Liles, Sr., Edward Kelly, Thom
Lake, Williamson Liles.

Abstracts of Old Wills (continued)

Page 94-
Catherine Hart, decd. Widow. Adm. granted to James Mayson and Isaac Crowther on 6-7-1790. Appraisers: James Mayson, Jr., James Creswell, Benjamin Glover, Jr., and Richard Grooms.

Page 97-
William Speakman, decd. Will 2-15-1786; proved Wife: Mary. Ch: John, Robert, (9-6-1790. Margaret Kellyhan, Elizabeth Welch, Christina, William, Thomas, and Mary. William and Thomas to have the care of their mother who is to receive support from the plantation whereon she lives during her life. Witnesses: John Lofton, James Kennedy, and John Garriot.

Page 98-
John Blalock, Sr. decd. Will 8-5-1790; proved (Carpenter) (5-16-1791. Wife:(Name not given). Son: Lewis. Other legatees: Micajah Bennett, Reuben Roland, John Blalock Bennett, John Blalock Roland, Sabard Oglesby, Sr. and his seven children. Witnesses: George Bush, John Housen Bush, John Blalock Roland.

Page 99-
Joseph Campbell, decd. Will 9-1-1790; proved (5-16-1791. Wife: Sarah (to have remainder of land located on Spring Branch). Ch: William, Jariat(to have all land on Spring Branch and the orchard). Gr-daughter, Betty Anderson. Other legatee, William Coate. Witnesses: John Waldrop, James Johnson, Benjamin Johnson. Exrs: Jariat Campbell, Sarah Campbell.

Page 100-
Peter Ruble, decd. Will 10-24-1789; proved 6-18-1791. Ch: Samuel (to have 150 acres, the Southwest part of land on branch of Bush River); Susannah McDowell and husband(Wm. McDowell), to have North-east corner of tract to line adjoining William Gillam's land, Zimri Gauntt's, and Walter Harbour's, to have during her lifetime; Mary Mordock (to have 50 acres joining land of Walter Harbour's, Joseph Freeman's, and Samuel Dunkin's), with her husband, William Mordock; Jane Lester (to have 25 pounds sterling money. This estate left to me by my father, in Frederick County, Virginia, near Winchester, and to be equally divided as aforesaid. Exrs: Samuel Ruble, Wm. McDowell, Peter Lestaer, William Murdock.

Page 103-
John Kelly, decd. Will 8-26-1775; proved (no date). Codicil dated 9-1-1775. Wife: Mary (to have plantation whereon I live and one-thrid of all personal property during her natural life, and then to be divided among my children) Ch: Isaac, Samuel, and other children whose names not given. Witnesses: Benjamin Pidgeon, Sarah Major. Witnesses: Benjamin Pidgeon, John Milhouse, Z. Gauntt—to Codicil.
(Affidavit dated at Camden District, S.C. 11-1-1775).

Page 105-
Benjamin Heaton, decd. Will 6-25-1790; recorded Gr-dau: Hannah Weeks. (6-29-1791. Gr-sons: William Weeks, John Weeks, Benjamin Weeks (to have tract on Beaver Dam Creek, branch of Little River, in Laurens County, containing 200 acres). John to have part of land where house is located. Another gr-son, James Weeks, to have 100 acres on King's Creek, which was bought from John Atkins. Gr-Gr-daughter, Charte Weeks. Other legatees: Clorata Weeks (nephew of John), Benjamin, William, and Hannah Weeks. Remainder of estate to be divided between my two gr-daughters, Hannah Weeks and Charte Weeks, to be paid to them when they marry or come of the age of maturity. Witnesses: Rhoda Babb, Sarah Hasket, Jude Stedman.

Pages 107-108-
Joseph Fish, decd. Adm. granted to Ann Fish on 5-16-1791(widow of intestate).

Pages 109-110-
Samuel Cannon, decd. Will- no date; proved 5-16-1791. Wife: Lyda. Ch: John, Isaac, James (three eldest sons), Mary, William, Kiziah, Lyda. Mary named as eldest daughter. Youngest daughter, Elizabeth. My wife, Lyda, to have 100 acres land—original grant in Clement Davis' name—and also all my Movable property. Exrs: John Cannon and Isaac Cannon (sons). Witnesses: Thomas Clark, Kizia Cannon, Elizabeth C. Cannon.

Page 112-
Joseph Davenport, decd. Will 8-5-1788; proved Wife: (No name given). (5-16-1791. Ch: Rebecca Satterwhite (to have 200 acres where she now lives); Amy Phillips (to have certain slaves and personal property); David. Gr-daughters: Jemima Satterwhite (daughter of Bartlett and Rebecca Satterwhite); Edna and Jemima Goode(daughters of Samuel and Jemima Goode) when Jemima arrives to age 18. (next page)

457

Abstracts Old Wills (continued)

Page 112-
Gr-sons: Joseph Phillips (son of John and Amy Phillips), Joseph Davenport (son of David and Hannah Davenport)—to have 250 acres. Adm. granted to David Davenport 5-16-1791. Other legatees: Milot Welch (to have three pounds sterling during her life and also she to have small room and fire-place at East end of my dwelling house, and provisions). Witnesses: John Thomas Satterwhite, Starling Dixon, Alexander McMullen.

Pages 115-116-
Nicholas Slike, decd. Will 9-27-1790; proved 5-16-1791. Wife: Catrina (to have one-third part of my estate). Ch: John Uvey, Jacob. All lands to my sons. Oldest children to have certain slaves. Exrs: John Livingstone, Jr., Phillip Slike, and Jacob Buzzard.

Pages 120-
Christian Houpt, decd. Adm. granted to widow, Mary Houpte, on 3-10-1790. Appraisers: William Houseal, Adam LaGronne, John Livingstone, John Eichleberner.

Page 122-
John Green, decd. Will 11-16-1790; proved 5-16-1791. Niece: Green Green. Nephew: William Green. (Above are children of my deceased brother, Wm. Green). All my lands and other property to go to them. Witnesses: Lewis Hunt, Edmond Kelly, Agnes Kelly. Exr. named by Court on 5-25-1791.

Page 125-
Samuel Chapman, decd. Adm. granted to Joseph and William Chapman at a court held 5-16-1791. Appraisers qualified were: Thomas Smith, Israel Gauntt, William Aspernell, and Francis Atkins.

Pages 129-130-
Edward Wadlington, decd. Will 12-24-1790;proved Wife: Frances. (5-16-1791. Ch: John, Sarah Ann, Jesse, Bailey, Spencer, and Nancy. Extrx: Mrs. Francis Wadlington. Exr: William Wadlington (brother), Wm. Malone, Sr.

Page 132-
James Sproul, decd. Adm. granted to Jean Sproul and John Buyer(Boyer) on 7-28-1791. Appraisers: John Buyer, George Atkins, Edward Goree, Thomas Duckett on 7-28-1791.

Pages 134-135-
Anna Mary Buzhardt, decd. Will 11-13-1790; proved Legatees: John Buzhardt (husband). (7-27-1791. Ch: Barbara, Anna Mary, Matthias Hair, John Hair. Matthias Hair to have 100 acres which was willed to me by my first husband, Peter Hair. (Cont above)

Mary Buzhardt died and her children named were: Catherine Veits, Rachel Charles, Agnes Stockman, Margaret McCallie, Molly Thomas, Barbara Maffett. Exrs: John and Matthias Hair(sons). Witnesses: Lorentz Rigart, John Rigart, and Michael Dickert, Sr.

Page 135-
Peter Hair, decd. Will 8-24-1772; proved 11-25-1 Legatees: Hettie Hair, Jr. (to have 100 acres on Cannon's Creek); sons, John (to have 100 acres Campen Creek), Matthias (to have 100 acres Campen Creek); wife, Mary Hair (to have one-third part of personal estate, also to have 100 acres on Cannon's Creek for use during her life then to the two children as she sees proper). All balance of personal estate to be divied amo my nine children, viz: Mary, John, Catherine, Rachel, Agnes, Margaret, Molly, Matthias, and Barbara.

Page 136-
Elizabeth Vaughn, decd. Will 2-27-1791; proved Ch: William Dodgen, Elizabeth Cole, (10-18-17 Ollemon Dodgen. Gr-ch: Ann Toland, James Dodgen. Exrs: George Goggans, Daniel Pit Witnesses: William Smith, Christian Pitts.

Pages 136-137-
Shadrack Carter, decd. Adm. granted to Elizabeth Carter on 10-17-1791. Peter Julien, Justice of the Peace, qualified the appraisres on 11-28-1 who were: Levi Manny, Charles Banks, Ethelred Ki and David Lindsey.

Pages 138-139-
James Sheppard, decd. Adm. granted Jennet Sheppa on 10-11-1791. Appraisres: George Gray, Frederic Gray, and Daniel DeWalt.

Pages 141-142-
Elisha Brooks, Sr., decd. Adm. granted to Elisha Brooks, Jr. on 7-29-1791.

Pages 142-143-
John Doyle, decd. Adm. granted to Mary Doyle on 10-17-1791. Appraisers qualified same date: Adam Chambers, James McCrackin, George Aubrey, Arthur McCrackin.

Pages 144-145-
Theodoras Feltman, decd. Adm. granted to Jacob buzard on 7-29-1791. Admr. was Guardian of son, Frederick Feltman, and other children. Appraise Wm. Elmore, George Suber, Rudolph Buzard.

Abstracts Old Wills (continued)

Pages 146-147-
Ambrous Whitten, decd. Adm. granted to Elijah Whitten on 10-18-1791. Appraisers: Abner Casey, Robert Wilson, Josiah Duckett, and John Duncan.

Page 149-
John Doyle, decd. Public auction of and sales of property on 1-10-1792. Admx: Mary Dial. Some of sales made to Jeremiah Dial, Mary Dial, and others.

Pages 150-151-
Richard Bartwisle, decd. Will 6-25-1789; proved 3-2-1792. Legatees: Mary Bartwisle Layton (to have five pounds sterling to help having her schooled); Milly Layton (to have one-third part of all my estate as wages for her constant care and service done to me, with one-third part of the remainder to her use for life); balance of estate to Mary Bartwisle Layton, daughter of Milly Layton. Exrs: Henry Steddom, and William Pearson. Court held 3-3-1792- with Judges present as follows: Jacob Roberts Brown and George Ruff. Adm. granted to Wm Pearson.

Pages 153-154-
George Grayham , decd. Adm. granted to Jesse Grayham on 2-9-1792. Some purchasers at sale of property were: Jesse Grayham, James Grayham, Mary Grayham, William Riddle, and David Cannon.

Page 155-
Jacob Gray, decd. Will 1-16-1792; proved 5-22-1792. Ch: Ann Pitts, Agnes Butler, Elizabeth Gray, all of whom were to be Executrices.

Page 156-
Shadrack Carter, decd. Widow: Elizabeth Carter. Sale bill dated 6-12-1792.

Page 157-
John Heller, decd. Adm. granted to Catherine Heller at Court held 3rd Monday in October, 1791— date 10-17-1791. Appraisers: Christian Ruff, Conrad Zuber, Leonard Zuber, Sandford Cockrell.

Page 159-
Henry Oxner, decd. Adm. granted to Jacob Oxner on 5-21- 1792. Appraisers qualified 6-2-1792, as follows: Adam Keller, Michael Zuber, and David Collins.

Page 161-
Robert Johnston, decd. (will)
Adm.granted to John Gates on 7-28-1791. Appraisers qualified and valued property on 9-3-1791, who were: William Farrow, Sr., John Moore, Thomas Farrow.

Pages 163-164-
Martin Singley, decd. Will 3-15-1780; proved 3-1-17 Wife: Zr. Fouring riser (German letters) Ch: Jacob, Frederick, Elizabeth, and others. Wife to have all estate, both real and personal, fo her use as long as she remains single, and pay my debts. After her death my plantation of 150 acres to go to my son, Jacob, by paying my son, Frederick five and twenty pounds in gold or silver value thereof. The said Jacob Singley at the death of his mother to take my youngest daughter, Elizabeth, to keep and maintain her and put her through school, until she is of age. Witnesses: Rudolph LeGronne, Robert LeGronne, Thomas Hughs. Appraisers: James McMaster, Frederick Boozer, Phillip Sligh, John Livingston.

Page 165-
John Buchanan, decd. Will 6-14-1785; proved 2-28-1 Wife: Elizabeth (to have use of two-thirds of land on N. side of Heller's Creek, joining Broad River). Ch: Nancy Turley (to have one-third part of my land Whereon I live, on S. side of Heller's Creek); Jesse, John, Micajah, William, Mary Hutchinson, Anna Ford, and Susannah.
Exrs: James Hord (son-in-law), William Buchanan (son Witnesses: Nimrod Mirris, Thomas Thomley, and Jacob Gibson, Sr.

Page 166-
Samuel Lonam, decd. Will 7-12-1777;proved 5-20-1793 Wife: Olive Lonam (to have 100 acres during her life, which was granted to George Hartley). Ch: Squire (to have all lands after the death of my wife). Every sister of Squire to have five shillings sterling money, each of them , to be paid by Extrx. Olive Lonam. Witnesses: Barnard Mountz, John George Mountz, Barbary Mountz.

Page 167-
Dr. Daniel Haning, decd. Adm. granted to Peter Brazzleman on 2-28-1793. Appraisers: Robert Powell, Charles Crenshaw, William Wilson, and John C. Royst

Page 171-
WilliamTaylor, decd. Exr: Mercer Babb. Adm. granted to Mercer Babb on 2-28-1793.

Page 176-
John Kelly, Sr. decd. Adm. granted to Samuel Kelly, Jr. and Abijah O'Neall on 3-2-1793.

Page 181-
Jannet Walker, decd. Will 6-26-1775; proved 5-20-17 Legatees: John Kinard and his heirs(100 A. Indian

Abstracts Old Wills (continued)

Page 182-
James Johnston, decd. Adm. granted to Ellender Johnston on 2-28-1793. Appraisers: Isaac Evans, Hugh Marshall, Jacob King, Michael Johnston. (All qualified except Michael Johnston).

Page 184-
William Farrow, Sr., decd. Will 5-28-1792; proved 7-26-1793. Exrs: Leony Farrow and Thomas Farrow. Wife: Leony Farrow(to have use of all property during life). Ch: Thomas, William, Sarah, Jean D., Samuel Jackson, and Eli. Gr-daughter, Sydney Farrow (eldest daughter of son, Thomas). Copy of will certified 8-28-1793 by William Malone, Clk. Ct. Newberry, South Carolina.

Page 186-
Appraisers of Wm Farrow, Sr property: Jacobs Robt. Brown, James Caldwell, Wm Caldwell, John Moore.

Page 188-
William Wilson, decd. Adm. granted to James Wilson on 5-20-1793. Appraisers qualified same day: James Burns, Thomas Davis, and Dudley Burns.

Page 190-
William Johnston, decd. Adm. granted to Nelly Johnston on 5-20-1793. Appraisers qualified on 11-22-1793: Ephriam Cannon, Richard Gains, Robert Steel, Alexander Johnston.

Page 192-
William Elmore, decd. Admrs. and Exrs: Abigail Elmore (his widow), John Elmore (son) om 5-20-1793. Will dated 1-31-1780; proved 5-20-1793. Widow to have 300 acres land and all movable estate, located on Bush River, during her life-time. Ch: John, Ridgway, Joseph, Stephen, Sarah, Mary, Rachel. Witnesses: Farrence Riley, John Kinard, Thomas Smith.

Page 194-
James Glasgo, decd, Will 10-17-1775; proved 7-30-1793. (of Gilder's Creek). Wife: Mary (to have one-third of all personal property, also house and 50 acres during her life, which land was formerly possessed by James Cannon). Ch: Robert (to have 100 acres with house which I now live in); Margaret, John (to have 50 acres land), Rachel, Archibald Wilson-Glasgo. Witnesses: James Finley, Ann Finley, and Thomas Dugan.

Page 195-197-198-
William Miles, Sr., decd. Adm. granted to Samuel Miles, David Miles, and William Miles, Jr. on 7-30-1793. Sales bill certified 12-28-1793.

Page 199-
Allen Robinson, decd. Adm. granted 7-28-1793 to Sarah Robinson (his widow). Appraisers qualified 8-7-1793 : Levi Manning, Daniel Parkins, Mark Smi

Pages 201-203-
Peter Galloway, decd. Adm. granted to Mary Gallow his widow, on 7-28-1793. Appraisers: Robert Speer, James Plunkett, Thomas Brown, and John Douglass.

Pages 204-205-
John Curle, decd. Adm. granted 10-21-1793 to Thomas Haskett. Appraisers: James Wadlington, Benjamin Evans, Abijah O'Neall.

Page 206-
Thomas Clark, decd. Will 12-21-1790; proved 10-21 Wife: Mary (mother of children), to have 250 acre plantation during her life, or until her two your sons are 21 years old. Ch: John(eldest son), Thomas (second son), George (third son), James Robert, Mary (wife of John Lewis), Jean (wife o John Rees), Elizabeth, Ann, and Priscilla. Exrs: John Clark (son), Mary Clark (wife). Witnesses: Job Colvin, Charles Gary, Jr., and James Lindsey.

Page 209-
Alexander Buoys, Decd. Adm. granted to John Buoys on 7-31-1793.

Pages 210-213-
Henry Anderson, decd. Adm. granted Jesse Anderso on 2-28-1794. Appraisers: Thomas Gordon, Micajah Harris, Levi Anderson--qualified 3-8-1

Page 211-
Solomon Nichols, decd. Will 4-6-1791; proved 2-28 Confirmation of previous transfers of property to his present wife, Elizabeth, and her childr by a former marriage. Witnesses: William Wils Sims Brown, Robert Brown.

Page 214-
Robert Kennedy, decd. Adm. granted to Lucretia Kennedy and George Herbert on 2-28-1794. Appraisers qualified: Charles Crenshaw, Thomas Hardy, and John Maxifun.

Pages 216-217-
Adam Cloy, decd. Adm . granted James Cloy and' James McMaster on 2-28-1794. Appraisers 3-11-1 John H. Ruff, John Kinard, Ephriam Cannon.

Abstracts Old Wills (continued)

Pages 218-219-
William Campbell, decd. Adm. granted to John Buoys on 3-2-1793. Appraisers: Patrick Lowery, James McMahan, Edward Goree, and William Scott.

Pages 220-221-
James Cox, decd. Adm. granted William Cox on 5-20-1794. Appraisers qualified 7-5-1794, were: Robert Speers, Daniel Richardson, George Arnold.

Page 222-
Henry Dunn, decd. Adm. granted 5-19-1794 to Daniel Parkins. Appraisers 7-30-1794: Daniel Richardson, William Conwell, and William Gould.

Pages 225-226-
John Waldrop, decd. Will 6-27-1794; proved 10-20-1794. Wife: Tobe Waldrop (mother of children), to have all of 200 acres plantation and all movable property during her life or widowhood.
Ch: Ezekiel, Izekiah, Stephen, David, William, Isaac, John, Ann Elizabeth, Tobe, Judy, Christina Pitts, Sarah Campbell.
Part of will: If Ezekiel Waldrop should die before his children marry, and Robert Waldrop should come of age, the money shall be kept by the Exrs. until the said children should come of age. Exrs: Charles Griffin and Stephen Waldrop.

Page 227-
John Harmon, decd. Will 7-20-1789; proved 5-19-1794. Wife: Mary (to have 150 acres where I now live during her life). Ch: Godfrey (to have 250 acres on S. side of Saluda River, on Beaver Dam Creek); John (to have 100 acres on Buffalo Creek, joining John Roof); Thomas (to have 200 acres on Buffalo Creek, joining James Williams); William (to have 39 acres joining Lightner's land). Witnesses: Charles Thompson, Samuel McQuerns, Abraham Thompson. Exrs: Thomas Smith and Jacob Harmon.

Page 230-
John O'Dell, decd. Adm. granted to Ellenor O'Dell on 5-19-1794. Appraisers qualified 6-5-1794, as follows: Rignall O'Dell, Henry Davis, Gassaway Rogers. Sale made at dwelling house on 9-1-1794.

Pages 233-235-
John Wilson, decd. Will 4-7-1794; proved 5-19-1794. Wife: Elizabeth (to have one-third of land during her life or widowhood).
Ch: Sarah and Mary (they to have two-thirds of all property). Brothers: James Wilson, Thomas Wilson, appointed Exrs. Witnesses: H. W. Wilson, Charles Wilson, Mary Wilson.

Page 237-
David Martin, decd. Will 5-4-1794; proved 7-29-1794 (Minister of the Gospel)
Wife: Martha (to have one-third part of the money from estate). Ch: Catron Black and Hester Colley, my two daughters; and sons, David, George, Solomon, Samuel, Deborough, Ruth, (last two daughters, who are to have money from sale of all movable property).
Exrs: David Martin, William Summer.
Extrx: Martha Martin (wife).

Page 240-
Azariah Pugh, decd. Will 4-9-1793; proved 10-20-179
Wife: (name not given). Ch: Thomas (to have plantation I live on, of 143 acres), William (to have 143 acres, a part of the land I live on) All my movable estate to be divided among my other children; and that Peter Julien's children to have one child's share, to be divided among them.
Exrs: Ellis Pugh, Jesse Pugh. Witnesses: Isaac Jenkins, Jesse Jenkins, David Jenkins.

Page 241-
John Crunley, decd. Will 6-19-1794; proved 10-20- (1794.
Wife: Hannah (to have plantation whereon I live and all movable property during her life or widowhood. Ch: Thomas, oldest son,(to have 5 shillings sterling money), Charles (to have 250 acres whereon he lives, originally surveyed for William Caldwell), Samuel (to have 251 acres, being part of two surveys laid out by David Pugh), James (to have 251 acres, being part of a tract originally laid out to James Coats), Benjamin (to have 200 acres on Beaver Dam Creek, surveyed for Joseph Buckman). After the death of my wife, Hannah, Benjamin Crumley to have his choice of two tracts, either the one whereon I live or the one before mentioned. Certain shares of estate to go to daughters, Rachel, Catherine, Jemima, Sarah. There being 300 pounds of money in Virginia, in hands of Robert Bull and Joseph Lupto due next May, and which is to be sent for, all debt to be paid, and remainder to be divided among al my children and my widow. Extrx: Hannah Crumley. Exrs: Joshua Inman, Robert Richardson.

Page 242-
Isaac Pugh, decd. Adm. granted to William Richards on 5-19-1794. Appraisers: George Johnson, James Vardiman, Benjamin Hampton, William Calmes.

Page 244-
Joseph Wright, decd. Adm. granted to Charity Wright on 8-1-1794. Appraisers: James Beatty, etc.

Abstracts Old Wills (continued)

Page 246-
Allen Cox, decd. Adm. granted James Cox on 5-19-1794. Appraisers: John Atkinson, Daniel Dyson, James Hill, and Bartlett Satterwhite, Sr.

Page 248-
John Waller, decd. Adm. granted William Hill on 5-19-1794. Appraisers: Thomas Gordon, Sr., David Ferguson, John Clark, John Maxedeen.

Page 250-
Samuel Chapman, decd. Adm. granted to Joseph Chapman on 10-20-1794. Appraisers: John Coate, Francis Atkins, Benjamin Atkins, John Wilson.

Page 252-
John Mangum, decd. Adm. granted to William Mangum on 10-20-1794. Appraisers: James Waldrop, John Floyd, Daniel McKie, qualified 11-16-1794.

Page 254-
Hugh Creighton, decd, Will 8-5-1793; proved 10-21- Wife: (no name), to have plantation whereon(1794. I live, of 100 acres during her life, and all household effects, etc. Gr-daughter: Mary Dennis to have a riding saddle and the bed we lie on, after my wife's death. When my two gr-children, Joel Dennis and Creighton Ward, are arrived to the proper ages in law, all monies to be equally divided between them. My daughters Mary Ward and Anne Dennis, and other children as they arrive to proper age. Witnesses: Samuel Kelly, Sr., Samuel Kelly, Jr., John Kelly, Sr. Exrs: Daniel Parkins.

Page 257-
Robert Spencer, decd. Adm. granted to Rachel Spencer on 10-20-1794. Appraisers qualified on 10-23-1794: Joshua Inman, Walter Harbour, and Joseph Cook.

Page 261-
William Gilreath, decd. Will 10-2-1794; proved 3-3- Wife: Mary. Ch: Jesse, Mary, John, William, (1795. Alexander, George, Sarah Thompson and her heirs, Nanny Turner. Nanny Turner to have one-third price received for 400 acres of land in Wilkes County, N. C. one-third to son, Jesse, one-third to son, George. Exrs: Mary Gilreath (wife), George Gilreath(son), and Jesse Gilreath (son). Witnesses: Charles Crenshaw, Stephen Pearson, Elizabeth Campbell.

Page 262-
Andrew McLease, Sr. decd. Will 9-11-1794; proved Wife: Jean (to have 100 acres on line (2-28-1795. of John Wilson's land; and after her death to go to my son, Andrew). Ch: Andrew, Robert (to have 100 acres.....), Martha(50 acres...), Jennett,etc.

Page 268-
John Clark, decd. Will 1-7-1795;proved 2-28-179 270 acres to go to my brother, J. Thomas Clark, land located on N. fork of Tyger River. My personal property to be sold and the money to b divided among my three youngest brothers and sisters, viz: George, James, Robert, Priscilla. Exrs: Thomas Clark (brother), Patrick Lowery. Witnesses: Reuben Flannagan, John Williams, Robert Caldwell.

Page 272-
Samuel Proctor, Sr., decd. Will 10-24-1794; proved 5-19-1795. Late of Newberry County but now of Laurens County, S. C. Ch: Samuel, Phillip (to have 50 acres being part of 350 acre to join land of Dr. John Caldwell and that of h wife, Margaret's, decd. land; then the said land of 50 acres after death of Phillip to be prope of my gr-son, Henry Proctor.); Edward (to have 50 acres joining land of Daniel Clark); Jean Mc (to have 15 pounds sterling); Sarah Adams(to 10 pounds sterling). Son-in-law, Joseph White, have the remainder of the above mentioned 350 acres, except 50 acres which I give to my gr-so Samuel Adams. My other daughter, Mary Winningh to have 15 pounds sterling and other certain property. Exrs: Joseph White, Thomas Fakez.

Page 274-
Jonothan Taylor, decd. Will 10-9-1793; proved
(5-18-17
Wife: Mary (to have one-third of all movable estate and one-third of lands during her widow Ch: William (dead), his heirs to have land whe his widow, Mary, now lives; Richard(dead), his widow, Mary, to have 5 shillings sterling; Jonothan, to have land whereon I live; Isaac, t have land on Indian Creek, reserving 50 acres f my son-in-law, John Thomas, and his son, Willia Thomas; Ann Chandler, her property to her sons, Israel and Jonothan Chandler. Trustee: William Miles, Jr. Exrs: Richard Leavell and Joshua Reeder(both sons-in-law), and Jonothan Taylor(s Witnesses: Abraham Large, Rhoda Taylor, Wm. Belton.

Page 275-
Richard Strawther, decd. Adm. granted to Gabrie Jerrald on 2-28-1795. Appraisers qualified on 4-16-1795: Nimrod Morris, James Baird, Landford Cockrell....

Page 279-
John Mangum decd. Admr: Wm Mangum , 6-10-1795

Abstracts Old Wills (continued)

Pages 282-286-
Henry Wilson, decd. Adm. granted to James Caldwell.
Exrs: James Caldwell and Robert Gillam, Jr.
Will 4-6-1795; proved 5-18-1795.
Ch: Nancy, Mary, Tapphenas, Edna(my four daughters),
James and Henry, my two sons.
Witnesses: Phillip Proctor and Margaret Proctor.

Page 287-
John Wilkinson, Sr, decd. Will 5-13-1795; proved
Ch: John, Sarah(she to have 100 (7-28-1795.
acres whereon I now live). Trustee: Edward Benbow.

Page 288-
John Gorey, Sr., decd. (later spelled "Goree").
Will 5-19-1795; proved 7-28-1795.
Wife: Sarah (to have my estate during her life
or widowhood). Ch: John, Joseph, Claudius,
Joice Lyles, Molly Ferguson. Witnesses:
Richard Bonds, Johnson Ferguson, James Waters.
Exrs: John Goree and Joseph Goree (sons).

Page 290-
Alexander Chalmers, decd. Will 7-7-1795; proved
(7-9-1795.
Wife: Jane (to have my plantation and stock
during her life). Ch: David, William, Matthew,
Jane Hopper, and Alexander(last named son to have
two-thirds of said plantation after the death of
my wife). Gr-son: Alexander Chalmers (son of
Matthew) to have remaining one-third of my
plantation.

Pages 291-292-
Mary Ann Lane , decd. Will 11-10-1792; proved
(of Lexington District) (5-19-1795.
4 ch: Thomas, William , James, and Mary Taylor.
Whereas, under the will of my father, George
Dawkins,decd, certain negroes were lent to me
during my life, are to be divided among my heirs.
Guardians for son James Lane: James Baird, William
Dawkins. Exrs: James Baird and Wm. Dawkins.
Witnesses: Barbara Baird, Haney Dawkins, Betty
Baird.

Page 295-
Mrs. Mary Davis, decd. Will 3-19- 1791; proved
5-18-1795. Ch: Chesley and Samuel Davis(these to
have all lands and some of household furniture).
Sons to act as Exrs. Witnesses: Elijah Worthington,
James Black, and David Berry.

Pages 306-307-
John Waldrop, decd. Will(no date); proved Oct.1794.
(not recorded on this page)

Pages 299-301-
Matthew Sims, Sr., decd. Will 4-14-1795; proved
Wife: Jemima (to have all lands (5-18-1795.
remaining in her hands during her
life or widowhood, under care of the Exrs.).
Sons: Charles; Matthew (to his wife, Mary);
James(dead)-to his heirs; Nathan (dead)-to his
heirs; Reuben; David. After death of my wife,
200 acres whereon I live, on Tyger and Broad
Rivers, to be sold and money equally divided
among my four daughters, or their children. The
daughters: Hannah Henderson, Drucilla Backley,
Mary Sanders, and Ann Henderson. If Matthew's
wife, Mary, should take her third part or right
of dower of a certain tract of land in Hanover
County, Va., which land I did purchase from my son,
Matthew, and did give to my son, Nathan, I direct
my Exrs. to stop and detain out of my son's, Mathew,
parts , as much as will fully satisfy my son's,
Nathan, estate; and to pay to Admrs. of estate of
said Nathan, dec. In case my widow does not claim
dower, my Exrs. are not to detain any part of my
son's, Matthew, decd., share. Gr-children:
William Sims and Sarah Shelton (the children of
my son, Charles Sims). Exrs: Reuben Sims (son),
Bernard Glenn (kinsman). Witnesses: John Stewart
, George Wilson, Fanny Stewart.

Pages 304-305-
Henry Lyles, decd. Adm. Granted To Nancy Lyles,
his widow, on 5-18-1795. Appraisers qualified on
7-11-1795, were: John Goree, Thoroughgood Chambers,
and James Kelly.

Page 308-
Archibald McQuerns, decd. Adm. granted to James
McQuerns on 7-8-1795.

Pages 309-310-
James Finlay, decd. Will 9-1-1787; proved 7-9-1795.
(of Indian Creek). Wife: Ann Finlay.
Wife named Executrix and sole heir of property.
Other legatees: Heirs of my brother, Robert Finlay,
to have one shilling; heirs of my brother, Hugh,
to have one shilling; sisters, Margaret, Mary,
and Eleanor, or their heirs, to have one shilling
each. Witnesses: Robert Glasgow, John Glasgow,
and Archibald Glasgow.

Page 312-
James Patty, decd. Adm. granted to Richard
Thomson on 7-8-1795. Appraisers qualified on
9-16-1795: Jacob Beiller, Daniel Parkins, and
Gabriel McCool.

Abstracts Old Wills (continued)

Page 314-
Joseph Thomson, Jr., decd. Adm. granted to Richard Thomson on 7-28-1795. Appraisers qualified 9-2-1795: Edward Benbow, William Jenkins, David Jenkins.

Pages 316-317:
Frederick Le Gronne , decd. Adm. granted to his widow, Susannah Le Gronne, on 7-28-1795. Appraisers qualified 8-12-1795, were: Frederick Boozer, Martin Taylor, John Livingston. Sale bill y Susannah Counts, Admx. on 11-6-1795, indicates idow had married a Counts.

Page 318-
John Wedaman, decd. Adm. granted to John Kinard on 7-28-1795(called "Little" John Kinard). Appraisers qualified 10-10-1795: Laurence Rikart, Henry Boozer, William Stone.

Page 321-
David Cox, decd. Will 6-7-1795; proved 10-19-1795. Brother: James Cox (to have all of my estate, both real and personal). Witnesses: Joseph Towles, John Hill, Darias Sargent. Exrs: James Cox (brother), and James Dyson (friend).

Page 322-
John Riley , decd. Will 6-24-1794; proved 10-19-1795. To my beloved wife, Rachel Riley, I give my plantation of 144 acres whereon I live and all Movable property during her life. After her death, lands to go to my two gr-sons, John and Wm. Riley (sons of Jeremiah Riley). Certain valuable estate to my three sons and my daughter, Zacariah Riley, Jeremmah Riley, Hezekiah Riley, and Keziah Thompson. Witnesses: James Wadlington, Mercer Wadlington, and Catherine Eutes (or Utz). Appraisers qualified on 11-19-1795: Daniel Smith, David Jenkins, and "Georgia" John Coats.

Page 331-
Mary Wilson, decd. Will 10-4-1795; proved 10-19-1795. (widow of George Wilson) Daughters: Mary Wilson, Hester Denton, Margaret McClelland, Elizabeth. Sons: Andrew and John. Witnesses: Samuel McConnell, John Sloan, Hugh Wilson. Exrs: John Barlow, John Stewart, and John B. Mitchell.

Page 332-
James Daugherty, Sr., decd. Will 11-15-1795; proved Wife: Mary (to have one-half of my (11-19-1795. personal property except a black horse known as George's; also, to rent plantation whereon I live except such part bequeathed to her during her life or widowhood; then, to descend to my son, Charles. .... Ch: Charles, George, James, John. (above)—

75 acres land bounded by George Ruff , Uriah Zuber, and Ashford's land, to go to my son, Charl who, when he dies, the land to go to my gr-son, George (son of my son, James). My gr-son, Jam (son of James, my oldest son, I give a large Bib My second son, John, I give a horse, to be purch from money due me by James Hutchinson. My thi son, George, to have 188 acres , being part of t tract whereon I now live; also, 28 acres adjoining Jacob Sligh's and the Setzler lands.
Exrs: George Daugherty (son), David Cannon(frie Witnesses: A. Glazier, Margaret Glazier, John Bo

Pages 334-335-
Jacob Halfacre, decd. Will 9-1-1795; proved 10-19 Wife: (name not given) (1795. Ch: Jacob (to have 20 pounds sterling money), Elizabeth (to have 20 pounds sterling money), Barbara (to have 20 pounds sterling money, and one-half of present year's crop), Henry (to have plantation whereon I live, with wagon, the dist ery, and half the year's crop),
Exrs: Henry Halfacre (son), George Gray, Jr.(s Witnesses: John Peaster, Jacob Bossart, Laurence Rickart. ....

Pages 340-342-
William Gilliam, decd. Adm. granted to John Justis on 10-19-1795. Appraisers qualified: Samuel Brown, Joseph Furnas, William Murdock.

Pages 343-344-
Estate of Richard Strawther, decd. Admr. sale bi shows names of some of the purchasers as follows John Matthews, James Hord, John Long, Delilah Strawther, James Baird, Gabriel Gerrald, John Ra Alexander Bookter, Barthomew Turnipseed, Delaney Carrol, George Radish, Michael Dickert, George Feller, Capt. Cortly, Joseph McMorries, William Lyles, George Montgomery, David Thompson, Thomas Boyd, Frederick Boozer, Jacob Riser, John Baker, Lewis Sheppard, Lewis Coursey, Bartlett Smith, William Vaughn, WilliamStrawther, Thomas Bardf Benjamin Harrison, Johnston McClamie, Adam Hamiter, Ben Gerrald, Christian Graddick, John McClamie, Jacob Felker, M. T. Strawther, Adam Apton, George Ayner, John Walker, Ephriam Lyl Christian Gartman, Peter Stuckman, Simeon Ell Jacob Gibson, John Slike, George Raddish, Jame Liles, Thomas Butler, John Rochell, Bartlett S Gasper Weaker...... Recorded April 7, 1796.

Pages 347-348-
Linney Farrow, decd. Adm. granted to Thomas Farr on 10-19-1795. Appraisers qualified 11-14-1795: Wm Caldwell, John Moore, John Satterwhite, Sr.

Abstracts Old Wills (continued)

Pages 348-349-
Jacob Replogle, decd. Will 11-28-1795; proved 2-28-1796.
Wife: Judith.   Step-daughter: Ann Mary Reeder(she to have my plantation cart in consideration of her love and affection by nursing me in this my sickness). All the remainder of my estate to go to my beloved wife, Judith, during her natural life. After her death, the estate to go to my step-children, as follows: George Long, Jacob Long, Michael Long, Catherine Miller, Ann Mary Reader, all to share and share alike. Exr: Michael Kinard. Witnesses: Martin Hough, John Quaddlebaum, Jr., Frederick James Wallern.

Page 350-
George Gray, Sr, decd. Will 11-9-1795; proved 2-28-1796.
Wife: Eve Margaret (to have a negro slave, and $200.00 cash, and furniture, three books, a German book, a Prayer Book, and a book called, " Truth of Christianity;" also, two cows and calves, two sheep, and two hogs. She is to live on the Plantation where she choses during her natural life. Ch: George, Jr., Frederick, Peter, Christina (she was Gallman's wife). Christina to have 150 acres joining John Gallman's land, and others. Other Ch: Barbara (wife of Frederick Boozer), Elizabeth (wife of David Ruff, Esq.). Remainder of estate to be divided among six children. Witnesses: Michael Dickert, Sr., Frederick Boozer, Michael Long. Exrs: George Ruff, Jacob Buzhard.

Pages 352-354-
Estate George Gray, Sr., deced. Appraisers........

Pages 355-356-
George Sparks, decd. Will 10-20-1795; proved 3-2-1796.
Sister: Rachel Bicknell who was , or is, in North Carolina, to receive estate and use it until my son, Reuben Sparks, is 21 years old. Exr: George Powell. Witnesses: Volentine Braswell, Reason Davis. Appraisers qualified 3-17-1796: John Beard, Harmon Davis, John..........

Pages 359-360-
John Caldwell, Sr., decd. Will 2-5-1796; proved 2-29-1796.
Wife: Susannah (to have use of my dwelling and plantation , stock, etc. during her life). Ch: John (to have 168 acres where he now lives), William (to have 100 acres where he now lives), Margaret Dyson (to have 150 acres , being part of a tract called "Halfway Branch"), Elenor Caldwell, David (to have 150 acres, being balance of tract called " Halfway Branch"), James (to have my dwelling plantation after death of my wife, with all appurtances, and 200 acres , and all estate (above)- his mother leaves), Robert (to have 4 or 5 acres on Saluda River).
Exrs: John Caldwell (son), Daniel Dyson (son-in-law).   Witnesses: William Allen, Phillip Proctor, Henry Proctor.

Pages 362-364-
Robert Gillam, Sr., decd. Will 1-22-1796; proved 2-29-1796.
Wife: Mary (to lend her during her lifetime two slaves women, and remainder part of Edmond Ellisor's land on N. side of Page's Creek. Ch: Joshua (to have land hereon he lives, including small tract Col. Mayson is to make right to); Robert, Jr; Susannah Martin; Martha Smith; Frances. Gr-ch: James Finlay, Colley Martin. Exrs: Robert Gillam, Jr., John Wallace, Isaac Mitchell, Sr. Witnesses: Fields Red, Harris Gillam, Susannah Red.

....

Pages 365-366-
Nathan Williams, decd. Will 3-31-1795; proved 2-29-1796.
Wife: Sarah (to have land and remainder of movable property left to her use during her life or widowhood.) Ch: Patience, John, and one which is expected to be born. Exrs: Thomas Gary, Stephen Williams. Witnesses: Michael Sanders, John Gary, Stephen Hill. Appraisers qualified 3-25-1796: Charles Gary, Isaac Taylor, Robert McAdams.

Page 368-
Dr. John Wilson, decd. Will 10-16-1795; proved 2-29-1796.
Exr: Daniel Clary, William Summers, and John Smith. Witnesses: Giles Chapman, Jesse Summers, Samuel Summers.
All my lands and tenements in Ireland, County of Antrim , Barrentre of Tome, Townland of Cloughan, to be sold and the money for my just debts and reasonable expenses. Then, to give to my brother, James Wilson, one shilling sterling and no more. My sister, Janett Alexander, to have one shilling sterling and no more. My sister, Elizabeth, to have one shilling and no more. My sister, Sarah Walker, to have 50 pounds sterling in fee simple. Also, I give to Martha Figs 100 pounds in fee simpl My sister, Sarah Walker's, children to have 100 pounds sterling in fee simple, to be equally divided among them. My cousin, John Moore, to have 5 pounds sterling in fee simple. To the children of my sister, Martha Figs, I give 40 pounds sterling, to be equalled divied among them.
Appraisers qualified 2-29-1796: Timothy Thomas, John Summers, Elisha Ford, Hugh O'Neall.

Abstracts Old Wills (continued)

Page 371-
James Winningham, decd. Adm. granted to George Adams on 10-19-1795. Appraisers qualified same day as follows: Samuel Proctor, John Caldwell, William Allen, and Elisha Brooks.

Page 372-
January 2, 1796, Estate of Allen Cox, decd. Eleven legatees received each in dividens 16 pounds and 9 shillings.

Pages 372-374-
Edward Kelly, decd. Adm. granted to Mary Kelly, on 10-20-1795. Appraisers qualified 12-9-1795: John Goree, Thorogood Chambers, and John Stewart.

Pages 375-376-
John Goree, Sr. decd. Adm. granted to John and Josiah Goree on 7-29-1795. Will proved in Court 7-28-1795. Appraisers qualified 5-6-1796: David Sims, Thomas Lake, John Stewart.

Pages 377-378-
Samuel Jones, decd. Adm. granted to Rebecca Jones on 2-28-1796.
Appraisers qualified 2-29-1796: James Griffin, Thomas Gary, Isaac Taylor.

Pages 379-380-
Abner Ellomon, decd. Adm. granted John and William Ellemon on 2-29-1796.....
Appraisers qualified: Aaron Mills, Alexander Cothran, and Daniel Richardson.

Page 381-
John Porterfield, decd. Adm. granted to Sarah Porterfield on 10-21-1795.
Appraisers qualified on 10-21-1795:
John Moore, Richard Griffin, John Fifer.

Pages 382-383-
John Langford, decd. Will 6-16-1791; proved 2-2 (1796
Wife: Winnefred.
Wife to have balance of property after shares distributed to children.
Ch: William (to have stock and one-half of land I live on, on the W. side of Buffalo Creek); Jacob (to have movable property and one-half o land I live on, on E. side of Buffalo Creek); Anne (to have certain movable property and 200 acres land, on Carter's line. My gr-son, Asa Langford, to have one shilling sterling.
Exrs: William Langford (son), Winnefred Langfo (wife). Witnesses: Jacob Free, Joseph Cotten, and Jacob Langford.

BIBLIOLOGICAL REFERENCES

Newberry-location, topography, soils, etc. Natural resources, rivers, fauna, etc.
U. S. Dept. of Agriculture; Soil Survey of Newberry County, 1918; traditions of oldest inhabitants, and knowledge of residents; the " Annals of Newberry, the Remininces of Newberry"; McCrady's " History of South Carolina"; Mills' "Statistics of South Carolina"; etc.

Early Settlers-names, families, incidents, etc. Their trials, aims, works, etc.
County Court House records, local library record; the " Annals of Newberry", the " Reminincas of Newberry"; State Historical Cammissions's Office ; Early county newspapers; Mills's Statistics; Newberry Observer, May 6, 1886; letter to Col. Brants Mayer, of Baltimore, regarding first explorations, by William Summer, Esq. in 1878.

Ethnology-Green's Indians of South Carolina; Fairbank's Sociology; U. S. Bureau of Ethnology, 1891-92, 1904-05. History of Villages in Newberry County. Newberry Observer, April, 1938; " Annals of Newberry", Part 2.

Rev. War Patriots-battles in section of what is now Newberry County- State Historical Cimmission; Lee's History of the War in the Southern Department; McCrady's History of South Carolina; Landrum's History of Upper South Carolina; Chapman's History of South Carolina; the " Annals of Newberry"; church histories; etc.

War of 1812-State Historical Cimmission; family traditions; County court house records; etc.

War with the Seminoles in Florida-State Adjutant's Office, Columbia, S. C.; the " Annals of Newberry"; old letters; etc.

Mexican War-Carwile's " Reminincas of Newberry"; the " Annals of Newberry"; Adjutant General's Office, Columbia,S.C.; etc.

War Between the States- Dickert's " History of Kershaw's Brigade"; Caldwell's " History of McGowan's Brigade"; the " Annals of Newberry", Part 2; the " Confederate Veteran's" Magazine, Vol. 22, pp. 408-09.

Women in the Confederacy- " South Carolina Women in the Confederacy"; State U.D.C., Vols. 1 and 2; Confederate march through Newberry and Union; " Military Operations of General Beauragard", Vo.11, p. 412; local public libraries—old letters, etc.

Newberry Confederate Officers killed- " Annals of Newberry"; Military Operations of General Beauragard";"Confederate Military History"(Vol. 5, pp. 125, 177, 265, 12, 13).
Story of Julius Zobel- Dickert's"History of Kershaw's Brigade; Newberry Observer, by Col. Dickert; local traditions; etc.

First Tavern in Newberry- Newberry Observer, January 26, 1884; etc.

Celebration at Liberty Hall, Newberry District-with Rev. War veterans present- Southern Times and Gazette, September 8, 1837; etc.

Reconstruction Period- the " Annals of Newberry", Part 2, pp. 765-66; Miller's Almanac, 1874; Reynold's " Reconstruction in South Carolina", pp. 15,20,74,75, 76; interviews with oldest residents.

Early County Government-Interviews with oldest lawyers in Newberry; Newberry Observer, April, 1938, by G. L. Summer; S. C. Acts of General Assembly, 1832, pp.14,35, 1834, p.24, etc. County Court House records; General Sessions Courts, 1851-52, p. 208; Sessions Court, 1852-58; First Court Minutes; etc.

Early Lawyers in Newberry-O'Neall's "Bench and Bar of South Carolina"; old newspapers; etc.

Early Mayors in Newberry-Old minutes of City Council; old newspapers; etc.

County Jails-Newberry Observer; " Annals of Newberry"; "Remininces of Newberry"; personal interviews; old Court House records; etc.

Members of General Assmebley of South Carolina from Newberry County, 1893-1946- State Library records.

Villages and communities in the county-origins of names-traditions, historical sketches; Remininces of Prosperity, By Matthew Hall, Newberry Observer, September 4, 1884.

Economic and Social Developments- Early Railroads (Newberry Observer, 1938; "Annals of Newberry Part 1; personal interviews with oldest railroad officials; etc. Agricultural developments- S.C.Dept of Agriculture, Annual Bulletins; etc. County Fairs- Newberry Observer, January21, 1886, and 1938; County Fair Bulletins; personal interviews; etc.

Early Industries-State Agricultural Statistics; Columbia Record Industrial Edition, Oct 21, 1916; Tenth Annual Report S. C. Commissioner of Agricultural work, 1913; personal interviews; The Rising Sun, Oct 5, 1859; " Annals of Newberry", pp. 736, 749; Miller's Almanac, 1874; Newberry Chamber of Commerce Bulletins, and County Fair booklets; etc. Newberry Cotton Mill, Newberyy Observer, May 10, 1883, 1938; personal interviews; etc. Other textile mills, Newberry Observer, 1938; etc.

Newberry Fire Department-Newberry Observer, 1938, interviews with oldest residents; City Council records; oldest newspapers; etc.

Newberry County Hospital- Annual Reports of Hospital Board; interviews with Supervisor of Nurses; old minutes; etc. Newberry County Health Unit-interviews with Secretary, old minutes and records.

Public Libraries- Interview with Libratian of Newberry College, and with Supervisor of library work in the County; etc.

D.A.R. and U.D.C Chapters- interviews with oldest members; Newberry Observer, 1938; old minutes; etc.

Parks- data frompersonal interviews with builders and officers. Newberry Country Club-Annual Reports and Minutes; interviews with Architect and with Contractor;

Newberry Electric Light and Water Plant-Newberry Herald & News, July 24, 1900; Intervew with Superintendent of Plant; olf records.

Service Clubs-Bulletins from Officers; personal interviews; etc. Masonic Lodges-Old Minutes; personal interviews; Miller's Almanac, 1874; old newspapers. American Legion-Data from officers; Newberry Observer, 1938.

Old Cemetery Markers- personal visits by author and copies made by him-with few copies made by descendents or transients.

Early Literature in County, and early publications- Some Newberry authors- Waucope's " The Writers of S. C."; Wallace's " History of South Carolina"; the " Annals of Newberry"; Rutherford's " The South in History & Literature"; consultant: Dr. E. B. Sotzler, Professor of English Literature at Newberry College; oldest local newspapers; etc.

Education in City and County-History of Newberry College, (Carwile's " Reminices of Newberry" " Annals of Newberry", Part 2; Newberry Observer, 1938, by Dr. James C. Kinard; County Education Association, Educational Bulletins; oldest newspaper sketches; etc.
   Early education—above references.   County schools-local residents interviews and data firnished, as Crosson Field Scool, by Mrs. Ellis; Cross Roads School, by Dr. J. W. Folk; Pomaria School, Newberry Observer, 1938, and " Annals of Newberry", pp.723-24; Prosperity Schools, Newberry Observer, 1938, and " Annals of Newberry", pp. 12-121; Whitmire Schools, Newberry Observer, 1938, by Mrs. Ann E. Lewis; Mount Bethel Academy, Newberry Observer, 1938, by Dr. W. C. Brown and Mrs. Ann Jeter; the Newberry Herald and News, 1933, by G. L. Summer.

Churches in City and County-Newberry Observer, 1938, contributions by G. L. Summer, and by members of local churches. Hallman's " History of Lutheran Synod of South Carolina"; Letter of William Summer, Esq, 1878; " South Carolina Evangelical Progress", by William P. Houseal; S. C. Department of Agriculture; Old Bounty Grants records, Columbia, S. C.; Personal interviews with pastors; Carwile's " Reminices of Newberry"; " Annals of Newberry", pp. 679, 694, 699; Jones-Mills "History of Presbyterian Church in S. C."p. 962; Hinshaw's "Quaker Genealgies"; " Annals of Newberry" , Part 2, on Quaker migration to Northwest; Sketch on Lutheran Church of the Redeemer, by Dr. E. B. Keisler; Newberry Observer, 1938; St. Paul's Lutheran Church, Newberry Observer, 1938, by Dr. William P. Houseal; Old minutes of Aveleigh Presbyterian Church, and sketch and data furniches by pastors; " History of Methodism in S. C.", by Chrietzberg; Southern Chrsitian Advocate, 1937; Historical sketch of old Little River Church in Newberry County, Newberry Herald, April 9, 1873; Howe's " History of the Presbyterian Church in S. C."(Vol. 1);   Scrap Book with sketch from Greenville News of December 7, 1930; etc.

Music and Art in Newberry-Interviews with local music instructors; the " Annals of Newberry"; oldest newspapers, with references to mmsic and portrait painters in Newberry.

Folklore—Oldest newspapers; personal interviews with oldest citizens in county ; Scott's " Random Recollections of a Long Life"; O'Neall's " Annals of Newberry"; McCravy's "History of South Carolina"; etc.

Women Who Made History in the City and County-Ellet's " Women of the American Revolution", Vol. 12, p.260; O'Neall's " Annals of Newberry", Part 2, pp.505, 507, 547, 615; The State paper, 1929; traditions from oldest residents; Henning's " Columbia, Capital City"; Wallace's " History of South Carolina", Vol. 4; Lutheran Woman's Magazine, of Philadelphia; Newberry County Hospital records; notes from relatives and friends; " Who's Who in America", Vol. 8, p. 1484;"A Confederate Soldier's Letter to his Wifey p. 1; Newberry Observer, September, 1938; Landrum's " History of Upper S. C."; " Centennial History of the A.R.P. Church, pp. 127-131; Waucope's " The Writer's of South Carolina", p. 39; " Noble Deeds of American Women", by J. Clement, pp. 192-194.

Old Muster Rolls—Newberry Artillery, 1883, from Newberry Observer, May 10, 1883; Newberry Rifles, 1887, Newberry Observer, 1887; etc.

Theaters and Amusements—Personal interviews with theater managers; early news paper sketches.
Early Cyclones; hurricanes, etc—Newberry Observer, 1883; " Annals of Newberry; p. 770; p. 189. Newberry Observer, Nov 29, 1883, and Feb 21, 1884; etc.
Historic Homes- Personal interviews with oldest residents; traditions and facts, most of which verified with county court records.
Biographical-Data furnished by local families, some from , " Men of Mark in S. C."; " Emminent and Representative men in S. C."; the " Annals of Newberry"; the " Reminices of Newberry"; etc. (Complete biographies previously published on Newberry citizens —most of these not again written).
Traditions sometimes verified with following; " Johnson's Traditions of American Rev(1851), pp. 423-424; Ramsey's "History of S. C."; Sims's " History of S. C."; Logan's " History ofUpper S. C."; Mills's Statistics";"Memoirs of the War in the Southern Department;" etc.

INDEX
ABSTRACTS OF OLD WILLS

Name	Page	Name	Page	Name	Page
Anderson, Henry	460	Gary, John, Jr.	455	Oxner, Henry	459
Anderson, Jacob	455	Gillam, Robert, Sr.	465	Parmer, Isaac	454
Bartwisle, Richard	459	Gilliam, William, Sr.	455,464	Patty, James	463
Blalock, John, Sr.	457	Gilreath, William	462	Pearson, Benjmain	454
Bonds, Richard	453	Glasgow, James	460	" Enoch	456
Brooks, Elisha	458	Glenn, John	453	" Samuel	456
Buchanap, John	459	Goree, John, Sr.	463,466	Porterfield, John	466
Buoys, Alexander	460	Grasty, Thomas	456	Proctor, Samuel, Sr	462
Buzhardt, Anna Mary	458	Gray, George, Sr.	465	Pugh, Azariah	461
Caldwell, Hugh	455	" Jacob	459	" Isaac	461
" John, Sr.	465	Grayham, George	459	Replogle, Jacob	465
" William(son)	....	Green, John	458	Riley, Hannah	456
Campbell, Joseph	457	" Thomas	453	" John	464
" Josiah	....	Hair, Peter	458	Robinson, Allen	460
" William	461	Halfacre, Jacob	464	" Randolph	455
Cannon, Ephriam	.....	Hanning, Dr. Daniel	459	Ruble, Peter	457
" John (son)	.....	Harmon, John	461	Sheppard, James	458
" Samuel	457	Harris, Nathaniel	454	Sims, Matthew, Sr.	463
Carter, Shadrack	458,459	Hart, Catherine	457	Singley, Martin	459
Chalmers, Alexander	463	Heaton, Benjamin	457	Slike, Nicholas	458
Chapman, Abram	.....	Heller, John	459	Sparks, George	465
" Giles	456	Hodges, James	463	Smith, Gerrard	455
" Samuel	458,462	Hogge, Joseph	456	Speakman, William	457
Clark, John	462	Houpte, Christian	458	Spencer, Robert	462
" Thomas	460	Huffman, Jacob	456	Sproul, James	458
Cloy, Adam	460	Johnson, John	....	Stearley, Jacob	455
Cox, Allen	462,466	Johnston, James	460	Strawther, Richard	462,464
" Cornelius	456	" John	454	Taylor, Jonothan	462
" David	464	" Robert	459	" William	456,459
" George	456	" William	460	Thompson, Joseph, Jr.	464
" James	461	Jones, Samuel	466	Turner, William	456
Creighton, Hugh	462	Kelly, Edward	466	Vaughn, Elizabeth	458
Crumley, John	461	" John, Jr.	457	Vaun, John	454
Curle, John	460	" John, Sr.	459	Wadlington, Edward	458
Daugherty, James, Sr.	464	Kennedy, Robert	460	Waldrop, John	461,463
Davenport, Joseph	457	King, Charles	455	Walker, Jannett	459
Dawkins, George, Sr.	454	Langford, John	466	Waller, John	462
Davis, Mrs. Mary	463	Lane, Mary Ann	463	Wedaman, John	464
De Walt, Daniel	455	Le Gronne, Frederick	464	Whitten, Ambrose	459
" Peter	455	Lewis, Stephen	455	Wicker, Matthias	454
Doyle, John	458,459	Lindsey, John, Sr.	453	Wilkinson, John, Sr.	463
Dunn, Henry	461	Lonam, Samuel	459	Williams, Nathan	465
Ellemon, Abner	466	Lyles, Henry	463	Wilson, Henry	463
" Enos	454	Mangum, John	462	" James	455
Elmore, William	460	Mann, Robert	453,454	" John	461
Farrow, Linney	464	Martin, David	461	" John, Sr.	464
" William, Sr.	460	Miles, William	460	" Dr. John	465
Feltman, Theodore	458	Murphrey, James	453	" Mary	464
Finley, James	463	McLease, Andrew, Sr.	462	" Thomas	456
Fish, Joseph	457	McQuerns, Archibald	463	" William	460
Ford, James	454	Newman, John	453	Winningham, James	466
Gallman, John	455	Nichols, Solomon	460	Wright, John, Sr.	456
Galloway, Peter	453,460	O'Dell, John	461	" Joseph	461
		O'Neall, William	455		

GENERAL INDEX (not complete)

	Page
Abel, Dr. E. G.	5,
Abrams, J. C.	50,
" , J. W.	36,
" L. D.	50,
" M. E.	28,
Abstracts of Old Wills	453-456,
A. C. L. Railroad	39,
Adams, Dr. Freeborne	5,25,
" F. E.	57,
Agricultural Growths	33-36,
Aiken, D. Wyatt	49,
Albrecht, R. Theo.	64,
Aldermen of Newberry	29-31,
Alexander, Rev. James	69,
Allen, Charles,	
Family Graveyard	447,
American Legion, Post 24,	50,56,
American Legion Auxiliary,	50,51,
Amis, T. B.	36,
" Mrs. T. B.	36,
Ammons, John,	19,
Anderson, Ernest,	70
" J. W.	49,
" Mrs. Susan,	69,
Aragon-Baldwin Mills,	44,
Art and Music,	63,
Asbury, Bishop Daniel,	86-87,
Atkins, A. W.,	36,
Aull, Ben M.,	50,
" Carrie E.,	70,
" James H.,	41,
" John L.,	5,
" John P.,	41,
" Mrs. S. B.	53,
Authors of County,	62-62,
Aveleigh Pres. Church,	62-63,
Babb, Rev. Earl,	56,
Bachman Chapel Luth Church,	130,
Bailey, E. S.	5,55,
Baker's Finance Co.,	47,
Baker, Ralph B.,	47,48,56,
Ballentine, Wm.	19,
Banks, John F.,	49,
Barnwell, John G.,	44,
Barre, Matthias,	5,
Bauskett's Graveyard,	420,
Baxter, James M.,	69,
Beard, J. N.,	48,56,
Beauregard, Gen'l.,	13,
Bedenbaugh, Mrs. Addie W.,	53,
" Dr. J. I.,	89,
" J. M.,	71,

Belcher, Mrs. W. E.,	61,
Berley, Rev. J. E.,	5,
" " J. A.,	5,
" Dr. Wm.,	5,
" Rev. Wm.,	69,
Beth Eden Church & Cemetery,	135, 414,
Bethany Luth Church,	126,
Bethel Bapt. Church,	137,
Bethlehem Bpat. Church (Col),	101,
Bethlehem Luth. Church,	129,
" " " Cem.,	431-432,
Bibliological Records,	467-469,
Biographies,	175-192,
Black, S. A.,	56,
Blackwell, Gordon,	48,
Blatz, W. H.,	41,
Blease, Capt. Basil M.,	13,41,
" Cole L.,	14,
" Eugene S.,	56,61,
" Harry,	58,
" Henry H.,	5,49,59,
Boinest, W. B.,	49,
Bond, James,	15,
Boozer, Henry D.,	49,
" Samuel P.,	5,
" Thomas Q.,	5,
Boulware, I. H.,	45,
Bowman, Charles A.,	52,
" Mrs. C. A.,	52,53,
" Florence,	54,
Bowers, Rev. A. J.,	53,
" A. J., Jr.,	47,53,56,71,
" Ethel,	54,
" A. M.,	5,
" Minnie Lee,	53,
Boyce, John,	22,
" Kerr,	5,
" Robert,	5,
Boyd, Archibald,	4,
" B. D.,	42,
" Calhoun F.,	5,
" F. M.,	57,
" M. J.,	49,
Boyles, John,	41,
Bradley, Floyd,	43,
Braswell, Peter,	4,
Brehmer, J. W.,	36,
Briggs, R. P.,	49,
Broad River School,	76,
Broadus, Leonora,	48,
Brooks, Daniel,	5,
" Wm. M.,	69,
Brown, Mrs. A. T.,	61,

Brown, James D.,	36,
" J. Epps,	46,
" Jacob Roberts,	19,
" Ruby G.,	50,
" Sims E.,	5,
" Mrs. Sims W.,	51,
" Dr. Wilson C.,	53,
" Wilson C., Jr.,	56,
" Wm. Spencer,	39,
" R. K.,	65,
" " Jew",	5,
Bruce, J. D.,	5,
Bryson, H. M.,	56,
" Mrs. R.N.,	60,
Buford, M. M.,	50,
Bullock, Mrs. Leila,	50,
" Thomas E.,	56,
Burgess, Dr. J. N.,	48,
Burns, B. Z.,	56,
" Dr. D. J.,	56,
Burr, Aaron,	23,
" Theodocia,	23,
Burton, Henry,	22,
" James A.,	48,
" Mrs. J. A.,	52,53,
" Mary C.,	54,
" Mary L.,	52,69,70
" Richard,	48,
Busby, Nathan,	19,
Bush, A. F.,	41,60,
Bush River Bapt Ch,	136,
" " " Cem.,	417-15
" " School,	76,
Butler, Dr. J. W.,	64,
Buzhardt Family Graveyard,	451-452,
Buzhardt, B. S.,	49,
" Olin L.,	59,
Bynum, Frank L.,	27,
Caldwell, Family Graveyard	451,
Caldwell, Huiett C.,	56,
" James,	19,
" Capt James,	22,
" Mrs. James,	51,
" J. C.,	56,
" James J.,	55,
" J. David,	25,42, 48,51,
" Mrs. Kate S.,	51,
" J.F.J., 13, 53,7
" John,	4,22,26,
" Maj. John,	4,
" Dr. John,	5,51,
" Sarah,	50,51,

473

aldwell, Dr. John,	5,	
" Patrick C.,	26,	
" Mrs. Rebecca,	22,	
" Virginia H.,	50,	
" Maj. Wm.,	4,22,26,	
alhoun, John C.,	.....	
allison, Dr. H. G.,	59,	
almes, F. N.,	49,	
" William,	4,	
alvin Crozier Chap. UDC,	54,	
" " Story,	54,	
ampbell, Dr. Robert,	5,	
annon's Creek ARP Church,	111,	
" " Cemetery,	422-425,	
annon, Ben F.,	45,	
" Dr. David A.,	5,	
" Ephriam,	19,	
" Olin B.,	56,60,70,	
" R. Wright,	48,71,	
apers, Mrs. Ellison,	53,	
arlisle, M. A.,	5,	
arlson, "Swede",	5,	
arpenter, E. A.,	47,56,61,	
" D. O.,	56,71,	
arson, Rev. J. W.,	56,	
arwile, Gertrude,	61,	
" John B.,	5, 15,42,	
" John S.,	5,21,	
" Mrs. Mary J.,	52,	
asey, Abner,	19,	
" Brig. Gen. Levi,	19,	
ash, Dr. J. D.,	5,	
emetery Markers,	402-452,	
entral Hotel, Site,	.....	
entral Meth Church,	114,	
hamber of Commerce,	48,	
hambers, Alexander,	5,	
hapman-Summers Graveyard-		
Old Tunker Ch Cmetery,	442,	
hurches-Old-Gone,	100,	
hurches To-day,	101-144,	
hapman, Agness,	50,	
" B. V.,	27, 28,	
" Mrs. B. V.,	51,	
" Dr. James K.,	5,	
" John A.,	49,	
" John W.,	5,	
" Junius E.,	5,	
Chappell's Depot,	93,	
Chappell, James,	25,	
" M. Q.,	55,	
Chero-Cola Bot Co.,	46,	
Cherokees-Early Indians-	7,9,	
Chick, R. S.,	5,	
" Pettus W.,	5,64,	
Chick's Springs,	.....	
Childs, W. G.,	40,	
City Clerks,	29-31,	
Clarkson, John F.,36,47,48,56,		
" R. H.,	69,	
Clark's Ford, Site,	......	
Clark, John, Sr.,	24,	
" " Jr.,	24,	
Clary Brothers,	47,	
" J. H., Jr.,	51,	
" Mat W.,	47,	
Clayton Memorial Ch,	101,	
Cline, Wllace A.,	5,15,41,	
Coats, Henry,	.....	
" James,	5,	
" "Little" John,	5,14,	
" Marmaduke,	5,	
" Family Graveyard,	426,	
"Coatswood",	....	
Coco-Cola Bot Co.,	46,	
Cogdell, John S.,	15,	
Cole, Mrs. Mary G.L.,	145,	
Cofield, Dr. James,	5,	
Coleman, M. A.,	45,	
" A. L.,	45,	
" Pete,	51,	
" William,	44,	
Colony Luth Church,	129,	
Commercial Bank,	....	
Commercial & Industrial		
Growths,	40-43,	
Confederate Veterans,		
year 1931,	17,	
Conner, Dr. G. W.,	.....	
Colonial Homes—old—	310-401,	
Cooley, T. F.,	56,	
Copeland, O. O.,	56,	
Coppock, E. S.,	5,	
" Joseph,	5,	
Council of Fram Women,	51,	
Country Club,	55,	
Counts, A. H.,	48,	
" Ethel,	34,52,	
County Commissioners,	21,	
" Fairs,	136-138,	
" Farm Agents,	52,	
Covenanters,	415,	
Cozby, Rev. John S.,	70,	
" Miss. Willie,	69,	
Crawford, James M.,	5,	
Crenshaw-Finch Graveyard,	443,444,	
Cromer, Miss. Carolyn,	61,	
" Mrs Ellen B.,	50,	
" Dr. George B.,	56,60,61,70,	
" H. W.,	50,	
" Capt Philander,	13,	
" Wallace C.,	49,50,	
" William W.,	56,	
" Thomas H.,	5,	
Crosson Field School-	80,81	
Crosson, Mrs. Carrie G.	53,	
" James M.,	69,	
Cross Roads School,	83,	
" " Church, &		
Cemetery,	422	
Crotwell, J. A.,5,42,43,		
" Sam P.,	41,	
Crozier, Calvin,	54,	
" " UDC,	54,	
Cunningham, Wm,	22,	
("Bloody Bill"),		
D. A. R. Chapter-		
Jasper Chapt,	52,	
Daniel, Maggie W.,	50,	
Daniels, John W.,	50,	
Darby, William,	64,	
Davidson, Blanche,	54,	
Davenport, J. D.,	5,43,	
" Graveyard,	446-4	
" John G.,	22,	
Davis, C. C.,	5,	
" Eva Jane,	48,	
" Frank G.,	56,	
" J. Marion,	5,56,7	
" T. E.,	36,	
Dean, Henry Lee,	70,	
" J.,	46,	
Dendy, Rev. M. C.,	56,	
Denning, Mrs. Daisy B.,	36, 51,	
Dennis, Carol M.,	56,	
" Sudie,	50,52,	
Denson, P. N.,	50,	
Dentists,	29,	
Derrick, John L.,	49,	
" Dr. J. J.,	48,56,	
	60,61,	
" Mrs. S. J.,	61,	
De Walt-Gray Graveyard,	429-430,	
De Walt, G. G.,	21,	
Dickert, Dr. E. J., Jr.,		
	5,	
" Wm. H.,	5,41,	
" Mrs. Wyche,	48,	
" Yancy T.,	36,45	
Digby, T. J.,	44,	
Divver, James,	69,	
" Wm. D.	.....	
Dodson, Dr.,	5,	
Dominick, Elizabeth,	70,	
" Fred H.,	53,56	
" George K.,	48,6	
" Harry W.,	44,5	

Dominick, H. C., 57,
" J. Claude, 53,
" J. J., 45,
" Grady, 56,
" School, 79,
Dorrity, B. L., 56,
" Benetta, 59,
D'Oyley, W. B., 37,
Drayton Rutherford Chap UDC, 53,
Drive-In Theater, 65,
Duckett, J. C., 50,
" Thomas, 49,69,
Duffie, W. J., 5,69,
Dufford, C. A., ...
" Mrs. C. A., 50,
Dugan, Mrs. Margaret, 145,
" Maj. Thomas, 5, 22,
Duke Power Company, 46,
Duncan, Mrs. Annie S., 50,
Duncan's Creek Pres. Church, 108,109,
Duncan's Creek Pres Ch Cemetery, 419,
Duncan, James C., 50,
" John, Sr., 4,
" " Jr., 4,
" Mrs. Rosa, 53,
" Thad S., 43,
Dunlap Home Site, ...
Dunlap, Robert, 55,
Dunn, Dr. Wm. A., 5,
Early Banks, 42,
Early Business Men, 5,
" Schools, 68,
" Publications, 62,
" Pioneers, 4,
" History-Indians, 6,
Eagles Club, 51,
Earhardt, John W.,Sr., 14,57,
" " Jr., 48,56,
Eastside Bapt Church, 140,141,
Ebenezar Camp Ground, 119,
" Meth Church, 117,118,
" " " Cem, 415,
" " (New), 119,
Economic Developments, 33-48,
Eddy, John A., 5,50,
" Wm. H., 51,
Education—Schools, 67,
Educators of Past, 68,
Edwards, Mrs. Bessie, 50,
" David, 19,
" J. E. Edwards, 50,
" John, 19,
Eichleberger Old Home, ...
Elam, Roy H., 57,
Ellesor, Dr. P. C., 5,

Emery Circle, 52,
Emery, R. G., 44,
Englis, John A., 17,
Enoree Bapt Church,138,
" " " Cemetery, 419,
Epps, John, 56,
Epting, Carl E., 56,
" G.M.B., 5,70,
" Mem Meth Church, 114,
" John C., Jr., 36,
" T. E., 56,
Eskridge, L. G., 7,8,42,48,55,
Evans, E. M., 5,
" Mrs. E. M., 54,
" Benj., 5, 22,
" Camille, 53,
" Herbert H., 5,45,
Ewart, Dr. David E., 5,
" William F., 57,
Ethnology, 7,
Exchange Bank, ...
Ezell, P. B., 52,
" Mrs. P. D., 51,
Fair Grounds-Old Site- ....
Fair, Jefferson, 69,
" Dr. Samuel, 5,
" Simeon, 36,
" Mrs. Octavia, 70,
Fairey, Prof., 71,
Fairview Church, 144,
" School, 74,
Folklore—Family—......
Fant, C. White, 55,
" Frances E., 56,
" John P., 5,
" Lois, 61,
" Mrs. Mary P., 50,
" O.H.P., 5,
" P. Metts, 45,
" William A., 5,
Farm Women's Council, 51,
Farmers' Alliance, 49,
" Mutual Ins. Co., 47,
" Oil Mill, 44,45,
Finch, Edward, 19,24,
Finney, Dr. Roy P., 59,
First Baptist Church, 24,
" " " of Edgefield,447,448,
First Village Academies, 69,
Fischer, L. F., 46,56,
Fish Hatchery, 46,
Fellers, Mrs. Henry T., 50,51,
" F. Raymond, 5, 56,
" Holland O., 5, 57,
" J. B., 5,

Follers, R. M., 5,
" Thos. M., ...
" Mrs T. M., 50,
Fernandez, James, 5,55,69
Floyd Family Graveyard, 450-451,
Floyd, John, 22,
" L. W., 5,44,46,11,71,
" Mrs. Ola, 50,51,52, 53,54,147,
Folk, H. H., 5,44,45,49,
" J. W., 50,
" Dr. J. Wm., ...
" Levi E., 49,
Foote, Mordecai, Sr., 58,59,
" " Jr., 58,
"Forest Hill"—old Turner Home
Fortly Club, 52,
Fox, Rev. J. B., 50,
Freed, Rev. Chas. A., 56,
French, J. D., 45,46,
Friday, L. B., 56,
Friends Society (1M), 102,
Future Progress Society, ...
Gaillard, P. C., 40,
Gaines, C. B., 44,
Garlington, Gen. A. C., 13,
" Octavia, 69,
Garmany, Dr. George W., 5,49,
" School, 78,
Gary, Dr. John K., 5,
" Gen. Martin, 64,
" Dr. Thomas R., 5,
Gates, Dr. Elijah, 5,
Gauntt, Hannah, Jr., 146,
" Isreal, 146,
Geddings, Dr. Eli, 5,23,
Geiger, Emily, 146,
Genealogies-Pioneer Families- 193-309,
Gilbert, Abram, 5,41,
" Lovinski, 41,
" Thomas, ...
Gilder's Creek Cemetery, 432-434,
"Gilder's Crest"—old Nance Home.
Gilder, Dr. James L., ...
" Dr. James K., 5,49,70
" Bessie L., 54,
" P. Fant,
Gillam Family Graveyard, 449,
" Maj. Robert, 4,16,22,
" Capt. Robert, Jr., ...
Gilliam, Claude G., 36,
" Dr. Jacob F., ...
" Wm. C., ...
Gilliland, George, 58,

475

irardeau, Capt.......	5,	Hart, Mrs. Anna K.,	36,50,	Houseal, Wm. F.,	22,
lasgow, George C.,	45,	Hartchett, Mrs. O. H.,	50,	" Dr. W. G.,	5,50, 60
" John R.,	69,	Hardy, W. D.,	37,49,	" W. G., Jr.,	70,
" T. R.,	50,	Hartford School,	75,	" Wm. P.,	62,
lenn, Col. David,	4, 23,	Hatton, Wm,	88,	" Wm. W.,	5,
" Elizabeth,	53,	" Dr. Wm. M.,	5,	Huffman, Waldo C.,	36,
" Dr. George W.,	19, 36,	Havird, C. L.,	5,26,59,	Huggins, Mrs. Herman,	26,
" Lawrence, W.,	53,	" J. Oliver,	......	Hulett, Dr. Moses D.,	50,
" W. G.,	49,	Hays Station Battle Site	.....	Humbert, Rev. J. W.,	.....
lenn-Lowery Mfg Co.,	44,	Hayes, David L.,	48,	" Mrs. J. W.,	146,
oggans, Burr F.,	5,	Hawkins, Effie,	53,	Hunt, Maj. Isaac,	13,
" James K. P.,	70,	" J. Frank,	36,46,	" Isaac H.,	47, 56,
" John C.,	5,	Haynes, Mrs. Minnie B.,	.....	" Jacob H.,	21,
" John C., Jr.,	.....	Head Springs Cemetery,	426-427,	" Memorial Bapt Ch,	141,
" Sadie,	50,51,	Hedgepath, Harry H.,	56,	" Walter H., Sr.,	
" W. D.,	5,	Helena,	92,		5, 43, 44,
ordon, Maj. Thomas,	16, 19,	" Church & Cemetery,	136-413,	" Walter H., Jr.,	56,
overnment-Early-County-	18,21,	" School,	85,	" Mrs. W. H.,Jr.,	
race Lutheran Church,	124-126,	Hemphill, J. C.,	60,		52,53,54,60,61,
racey, John,	5,	Henderson, David,	......		148,149,
raham, L. C.,	48,	" Island,	......	Hunter-Saner Lumber Co.	....
ray, Maj. Frederick,	23,25,	Henry, R. E.,	44,	Hunter, Mrs. Carrie D.,	53,
reen, Jordan R.,	5,	Henson Old Home,	......	" Frank R.,	56,
" Felix B.,	.....	Herbert, Mrs. Charlotte,	50,	" Dr. George Y.,	43,55,
reneker, Richard H.,	5,	" Mrs. E. S.,	147,	" James B.,	48,56,
riffin, John K.,	26,	" Mrs. Susan C.,	50,	" Mrs. Margaret,	52,53,
" Dr. W. K.,	5,	Herndon, Col. Benjamin,	22,		54, 150,
riffith, Steve C.,	27,	" Zack,	22,	" Nathan,	4, 38,
ulf Refining Co.,	45,	Hicks, Thomas L.,	47,	" Robert T.,	47,
unn, David,	5,	Higgins, Francis B.,	13,55,69,	" T. Wm,	27,
uy, James,	5,	" Francis W.,	14,49,	" Mrs. William,	36,
agood, L. K.,	71,	" J.,	43,	" N. A.,	21,
alfacre, David,	49,	" Old Home,	......	Hurd, Stiles,	41,
" Family Graveyard,	427,	Hill, J. W.,	49,	Hutchison, Hiram,	5, 55,
" Henry,	49,	" Lucy,	48,	Hutto, C. C.,	48,56,
altiwanger, Mrs. Susie S.,	151,	Hiller, S. J.,	49,	Indian Creek Church,	.....
ampton, Benjamin,	4,	Hipp, David,	88,	Indian Wars,	9, 11,
arbart, Thomas,	19,	" Edward R.,	5,43,88,	Inman, Benj.	......
ardin, James C.,	69,	Historic Sites,	22,26,	Insurance & Investment	
are, Peter,	21,46,	Historic Old Homes,	163-174,	Companies,	47-48,
" Thomas A.,	56,	Holcomb Legion,	......	Jackson, W. T.,	58,
argrove, J. C.,	50,	Holeman, John,	5, 21,	Jacobs, Dr. T. Boyd,	42,
" Capt. S. C.	....	Holland, Rev. George W.,	71,	Jails of Newberry,	16,
arley, R. Aubrey,	27,	Holloway, Henry C.,	27,	Jalapa Community,	91,
armon, P. K.,	56,71,	" J. B. O'Neall,	71,	" Schools,	68,...
" Mrs. Ruby W.,	53,	" Thomas W.,	37,42,	James, C. M.,	41,
" Thomas F.,	5,	" Dr. W. C.,	5,	" Major George,	69,
arms, Rev. J. H.,	71,72,	"Hollywood"—Goodman Old Home,	..	" Dr. ....,	.....
" Mrs. Sarah W.,	52,	Holmes, Mrs. Butler F.,	51,54,	Jamison, O. M.,	5,
arrington, Birt,	55,	" O. McR.,	56,61,	Jasper Chap DAR,	52,
" Old Home	....	" Mrs. O. McR.,	52,	" Sgt. Wm.,	52,
" Dr. Wm. H.,	5, 26,	Holy Trinity Lutheran Church,	134,	Jenkins, M. J.,	5,
" Y. C.,	5, 69,	Hood, William,	69,	Jolly Street School,	80,
arris, Burr Calvert,	9, 10,	Hornsby, Alice,	61,	Jones, Adam C.,	5,
" C. Monroe,	5,	" J. D.,	41,	" Dr. E. C.,	29,
" Micajah,	9, 10,	" M. P.,	50,	" Mrs. E. C.,	52,
" Victor,	19,	Houseal, Dr. Robert W.,	5,	" Mrs. Gena M.,	52,

476

Jones, G. G., 50,
" Jesse Y., 43,48,56,
" Lambert J., 16,36,
" W., 27,
" Miss. Pawnee, 63,
" Sam B., 5,50,61,
" Capt. Thomas, 9,10,
" C. M., 5,
" Warren ("Hogge"), 59,
Johnson, Mrs. Bessie G.,
" Mrs. Eleanor, 50,
" James W., 36,45,48,
" Pope D., 48,71,
" Thomas P., 5,
" William, 5,
Johnston, John, 5,
" Rev. James, ...
Johnstone, Adeline, 54,
" Alan, 38,45,70,
" " Jr., 25,
" Dr. Burr, 5,55,69, 70,
" George, 27, ...
" Chancellor Job,
  15,16,25,55,69,
" Dr. John Foote,5,
" Job,(Memorial), 16,
" Julia, 59,
" J. Malcome, 5,
" Mrs. Kate (Rutherford),
  52, 53,
" Mrs. Lilla K., 50,
" Martha, 54,
" Paul, 5,
" Silas, 36,
" Dr. Theodore, 29,
" Thomas K., 53,55,56,
Kadesh Ch Site and Cemetery, 413,
Katzberg, Dr. A. J., 5,
Keisler, Rev. E. B., 56,
Keitt, Mrs. Anna Coe, 50,52,
" E. S., 49,
" J. L., Sr., 53,61,71,
" J. L., Jr., 43,48,53,56,71,
" Thomas E., 56,
" Thomas W., ...
" Mrs. Thomas W., 50,
Kelly, Timothy, ...
" John, ...
" Samuel, ...
Kendall Mills, 44,
" Henry P., 44,
Kennedy, Dr. R. M., 29,
Kennerly, Dr. Thomas B., 5,
Kibler, Arthur, 5,47,53,71,
" Dr. E. H., 56,
" Dr. James M., 5,53,69,
" John W., 5,47,

Kibler, Lawson B., 50,
" Julia, ...
" Lillian, ...
" Jacob Old Home, 4....
" William, 47,
Kilgore, Andrew J., 38,
" Caroline 151,
" Dr. James, ...
" Mrs. Mary (Wyse), ...
Kilpatrick's Raid, ...
Kinard, Henry H., 36,
" Henry ("Bud"), 59,
" Dr. James G., 48,56,
" Dr. James P., 69,70,
" Capt John M., 13,
" John M., 5,43,44,53,56,
  60,70,
" John M., Jr., 53,
" John P., 13,49,
" Julian H., 50,
" Mrs. Katherine E., 52,
" Mrs. Margaret (Land),
  50,52,53,149,
" Solomon, ...
" William, A., 51,
Kinards School, 75,
" Station, 91,
King, Dr. Jacob, 5,
King's Creek ARP Church, 112,
" " Cemetery, 435-438,
Kingsmore, E. H., 5,
" C. H., 64,
Kirkland, Randolph, 45,
" Mrs. R. W., 50,
Kiwanis Club, 56,
Klettner, Otto, 5,14,71,
Kneece, Dr. B. E., 59,
" J. V., 71,
Knight, H. S., 49,
Knotts, Dr. Paul E., 59,
Knox, Mrs. Louise, 50,
Kohn, Hal, Rev., 56,
" Mrs. Verna L.(Summer),
  50, 146,
Koon, Rev. Lewis, ...
" P. H., 49,
" Rev. S. P., ...
" Dr. George A., ...
Kuhn (Koon), Henry, Sr., ...
"L" House, ...
La Gronne, Frederick, ...
Lake, E. J., 49,
" Thomas M., 5,
" Dr. Wm. E., 29,
Land, Robert Henry, 5,
Lane, Ben, 58,
" Frank, 58,

Lane, Lemuel, ...
" Wm. J., 5,
Langford, Annie Lee, 53,
" Griffin, 51,
" Herman, ...
" Maude, 54,
" Julius J., ...
" William, 43,
" Capt. W. Smith,
  50,57,60,71,
Lawyers in Newberry, 27,
Leavell, John R., ...
" Robert Y., 5,
" James, ...
Lebanon Methodist Church, 118,
Leitner, Maj. Michael, 19,89,
" Mrs. Maria(Beard)
  147,
Leitzey, Capt. Wm. L., 13,
Leonard, Lochlin, ...
Lester, James, 4,
" Col. Wm., 53,
" Wm, UDC Chap., 53,
Letter, Copy —from Ireland,
  31,
Liberty Hill, 91,
"Liberty Hall", (Old Rutherford
  Home Site),....
Libraries, 61,
Lightsey, Miss. Theresa, 59,
Lindsey, John, 19,22,
" John A., 48,
" Samuel, 5, 20,
" Dr. Wylie, 5,
Lion's Club, 56,
Lipscomb, E. M., 45,48,56,
" James M., 37,
Literary, 62,
Little Mountain, 93,
Little Mountain Schools, 82,
Livingston, D. A., 56,
" D. G., 90,
Livingstone Family Graveyard,
  425,
" Mrs. Hassie, 50,
" Dr. R. E., 5,
" Elford, 5,
" Wm. T., 5, 60,
Locke Construction Co., 42,
Lominack, Dr. Raymond, 5,
Lominick, Dr. Richard, 56,
" Robert M., 57,
" W. Frank, ...
Long, Benjamin, 26,
" G. Fred, 5, 44,
" Henry O., 36,
" Dr. John , 5,

477

ag, Rev, John J.,	......	Mayer, Dr. O. B., Sr.,	5,	Mower, Mrs. Cynthia,		
" O. L.,	5,	" " " Jr.,	5,43,		5,49,146	
" Nora,	53,		44,47,	" Duane,	5,64,	
" Dr. Thomas,	5,	Mayes, Mrs. Caroline M.,	52,147,	" Dr. Frank D.,		
" Dr. Von,	......	" James Thomas,	5,50,		5,60,	
" Wilbur E., Jr.,	57,	" John B.,	56,	" Mrs. F. D, .		
ng Lane School,	74,	" Mrs. John B.,	151,	" George S.,	14, 38,	
ngshore, J.,	50,	" Lieut. John B., Jr.,	....		43,44,58,70,71,	
" J. C.,	56,	" Dr. Robert L.,	5, 60,	" Old Home,	.....	
ve, John,	19,	" Dr. William G.,	5, 71,24,	Mt. Bethel Academy Site, 86,		
velace, B. H.,	5,	" William G., Sr.,	5,26,	" " " Hist.,	86,	
ttle River Pres Church, 109-110,		" Lieut. Wm. M.,	....	" Hermon Luth Church, 135,		
" " " Cemetery, 409,		Mayson, James,	19,	" Pleasant Luth Church,		
theran Church of Redeemer, 121-122,		Mayors of Newberry,	29-31,		135,	
" Theological Seminary,	....	Mayzick, John,	49,	" " Meth. Church,		
les, Col. James,	23,	" N. B.,	70,		119,	
" Col. John,	23,	Meek, Seth M.,	56,	" Tabor Luth Church,	123,	
" Capt John,	4, 23,	Meetze, Rev. George E.,	....	" " Meth Church,	120,	
" Capt Williamson,	19,	" Rev. Yost,	......	" " School,	82,	
ffett Family Graveyard,	425,	Members of S. C. Gen. Assembly,		" Zion Bapt Church,	137,	
ffett, Capt. James M.,	13,		28-	Mudlic Battle Site,		
" Col. Robert C.,	13,	Mendenhall, Dr. M. T.,	5, 22,	Murray, A. W.,	38,48,56,	
" Robert,	....	Mendenhall's Mill,	......		6,71,	
gnolia Cemetery(Greenwood), 441,		Meth Ch C emetery (Winnsboro)		Music in Newberry,	63,	
lone, William,	19,		-448,	Myrick, Dr. Samuel,	5,	
ngum, Rev. Daniel,	136,	Mexican War Soldiers,	11, 12,	McCaughrin, Fannie B.,		
nn, Joseph,	5,	Meyers, J. C.,	49,		52, 53,	
" William S.,	58,	Miller's Chapel Meth Church (col),		" James N.,		
nning, Levi,	19,		-101,		44,53,56,	
rgaret Hunter Park,	57,	Miller, Capt. John,	......	" Lucy W.,	52,53,	
rshall, Robert,	56,	" Dr. Neal,	......	" Robert L.,		
" L. R.,	5,	" A. M.,	36,		5, 42, 43,	
rtin, Curtis Burr,	......	Milliken, Seth M.,	43,	" Capt. Silas,	46,	
" Foster N.,	5, 70,	Mills, Thomas M.,	52,	McCarley, Brice,	58,	
" Mrs. Helen M.,	61,	" William,	.....	" Mrs. Ida (Cromer),		
" J. Newton,	5,43,50,	Mimnaugh, James A.,	5,		50,	
" Lalla,	70,	Mittle, " Jew",	5,	" John,	37,	
asonic Lodges,	55,	Mollohon Mfg Company,	43,44,	McCermick, Anne,	32,	
atthews, Bud C.,	48,60,	Mollohon Section of County,	91,	" John,	32,	
" Mrs. C. A.,	51,	Montgomery, John,	5,	" Maxwell,	31,	
" Rev. Curtis,	.....	" Old Home,	.....	McClintock, Rev. E. P.,	...	
" Matthews, Wm. L.,	56,	" Summerfield,	5,	" Miss. Euphemia,		
axwell, Loyd,	48,	Monts, C. E.,	48,		-152,	
aybin, Col. Benjamin,	.....	" Michael,	19,	" Mary Law,	.....	
aybinton,	94,	Moon, Frank,	49,	" Robert,	.....	
aybry, H. W.,	46,	" James P.,	48, 56,	" Old Home Site,	...	
ayer, Adam,	......	" Mrs. J. P.,	63,	McClure, Mary S.,	52,	
" Andrew,	......	" Dr. Meredith,	.....	McCollough, Dr. J. H.,	....	
" Cornelia,	51,	" Dr. Peter,	.....	" Mrs. L. G.,	51,	
" Adam—Home Site,	.....	Moony, Joseph,	5,	" Robert,	5,	
" E. T.,	45,	Moore, Dr. E. H.,	5,	" W. P.,	50,	
" E. Boyd,	45,	Moorman, Col. Robert, 5,37,43,		McConnell, Mrs. F. H.,	....	
" Mrs. Harriet J., 52,53,61,		Morgan, Maj. Spencer,	32,	McCrackin, Thad.,	......	
	147,	Morris, E. Y.,	5,	McCrary, Thomas,	......	
" John A.,	......	Moseley, H. C.,	40,	" Thomas J.,	5,43,	
" Memorial Luth. Church, 126-128,		Moses, F. J.,	5,	McDaniel, C. P.,	48,	
" Ulrick,	......	Mott, ...,	5,	McDonald, Mrs. Hattie L.,		
					........,	

McFall, Mrs. Elizabeth (Land), 52, 150,
" James Y., 5,
" Jesse Y., 5,13,43,53,71,
" Nellie, 70,
McGraw, James, 5, 43,
McIntosh, Dr. James, 5,.73,.
" Dr. J. H., 5,
" Mrs. J. H., 53,
McKellar, W. B., 55,
McKibben, James, 27,
McLean, Fred, 56,
McMaster, Rachel B., 70,
McMorries, E. Y., 5,
" John, 5,
McMullin, James H., 43,
McQuerns, Samuel, 4,
McSwain, Mrs. Caroline L., 52,
" William A., 47, 71,
McWhirter, George, 5,
Nance, Drayton, ...
" Maj. Fred, 20,26,69,
" Family Graveyard, 439-441,
" Col. James D., 13,
" J. K. G., 49,
Natural Resources, 2,
Neel, Thomas M., 5, 44,
Neel's Dairy, ...
Nealy, Dr. Thomas, 5,
Negro Slaves, 8,
Neville, D.W.A., 45,
New Chapel Meth Church, 119,
" Ebenezar Church, 119,
" Hope Meth Church, 115,
Newberry Bank (1st site), 42,
" Bapt Church, 24,
" Civic League, 54,57,
" College, 71,72,
" " Library, 61,
" Cotton Mills, 43,
" Court House, 14, 16,
" County Education Association, 67,
" County Fair, 36,138,
" " Farm Agents, 52,
" Country Club, 55,56,
" County Health Dept., -59,
" " Hospital, 60,
" " Library, 61,
" Hotel, 45,
" Creamery, 45,
" County Teachers, 67,68,
" Electric and Water Dept., -57,
" Federal Savings & Loan, 47,
" Female Academy, 69,70, -Patrons,

Newberry Fire Dept., 58,59,
" Garment Plant, 45,
" Graded Schools, 40,
" Handle & Shuttle Factory, 41,
" Harmonic Society, 63,
" Hatchery, 45,
" Hosp Ins Co., 47,
" Music Club, 63,
" Opera House, 64,
" Red Cross Assoc., 51,
" Sporting Club, 49,
" Steam Laundry, 45,
" Total Abstinence Society, 49,
" Womans' Club, 51,
Norcross, Paul, 57,
Norris, Houseal, 56,
" John T., 43,
" Robert, ...
Norwood, Mrs. J. E., 53,61,
Newberry Industries, ...
Oakland Cotton Mills, 44,
" Meth Church, 115,
O'Dell, John, 19,
" P. B., ...
O'Neall, Mrs. Abigail, 26,
O'Neall Consolidated School, 84,
O'Neall, Mrs. Helen, 39,
" John B., 16,22,36,69
" Rev. Lewis, ...
" William, ...
" Mill, Site,
" St. Meth Church, 114-115,
Origin of County's Name, 2,
Optometrists in Newberry, 29,
Other Pioneers, 310-401,
Pages Creek, ...
Paine, A. S., 48,
Palmer, J. B., 43,
Palmetto Cotton Co., 45,
Palmetto Guards, 50,
Park, Capt. Anthony, 4,
Parkins Ford, ...
Parkins, Capt Daniel, 23,
Parr, Henry L., 5,16,43,60,
" Mrs. Henry L., 147,
Patterson, Mrs. Martha Orr, 61,
Paysinger, S. C., 36,47,56,
" Mrs. Marion (Daniel), -51,
" Thomas M., 39,
Peak Station, 94,
" School, 82,
Pearce, Rev. George H., ...
Pearsall, Mrs. Mary, 50,
" Vance V., 50,

Peery, Rev. J. C., 56,
Pelham, Dr. W. E., Sr., 70,
" " " Jr., 5,
Pence, Rev. E. Z., ...
Pennington's Fort, ...
Pentecost Holiness Church, -101,
Peoples, John O., 5,52,
" W. C., 5,
Perdue, J. R., 14,
Peterson, Rev. David, ...
" John T., 43,
Phillips, J. M., 55,
Physicians in Newberry, 29, (1936-46)
Pickett, Rev. John R., ...
Pioneers and families, 310-401
Pifer, A. P., 69,
Pitts, D. D., 46,
Pomaria, 88,
" Luth Church, 122,
" Oil Mill, ...
" School, 80,
Pool's Brick Yard, ...
Pool, Tench C., 5,41,42,57,
" Carrie J., 54,
Pope, Dr. Sampson, 49,
" Sarah, 54,
" Solomon, 69,
" Thos. H., Esq., ...
" Dr. Thomas H., 5,50,60,
" Thos. H., Jr., 48,
" Vincent, 5,
" Y. J., 43,
" Mrs. Y. J., 53,
Porter, Georgia, 50,
" Sidney ("O'Henry"),...
Portrait Painters, 64,
Pratt, Mrs. Dorothy, 26,
" Thomas, 5, 69,
" William F., 5,
" Dr........, 5,
Presbyterian Church Old Cemetery (Winnsboro), -448,
Pressley, John, 69,
" Rev. Samuel, 69,
Price, Mrs. Corrie (Black), -53,
" Mrs. J. D. S., ...
" Julian, ...
Prince, Jesse, 58,
Prosperity, 89,
Prosperity ARP Church, 113,
" Bapt Church, 138,
" Cemetery, 416,
" Community League, -51,

Prosperity High School,	73,	
" Oil Mill,	.....	
Pruitt, J. C.,	56,	
Pryor, Wallace,	71,	
Publications in Newberry,	....	
Public Hangings,	21,	
" Nuisances,	21,	
Pugh, A. F.,	.....	
" Sallie,	53,	
Purcell, Charles J.,	5,	
" Edward B.,	48,53,56,57,	
" Mrs. Trent K.,	50,	
" Keitt,	48,	
" Rook,	65,	
Quattlebaum, Jefferson,	49,	
" Matthias,	.....	
Quaker Cemetery,	411-412,	
" Old Church Site,	411,	
" History,	102-104,	
(Bush River MM)		
Racial Elements,	7,	
Railroads throuhg Newberry,	38-40,	
Ramage, John L.,	5,	
" Joseph,	.....	
Raines, Burrell (Col)	5,	
Rast, Dr. L. A.,	5,	
"Ravenscroft",	.....	
(Summer Home Site),		
Redbank Bapt Church Cemetery, (Slauda),	448,	
Red Cross,	50,	
Reeder, Gertrude,	......	
Reedus, Mrs. Sophia M.,	49,146,	
Reid, Hayne,	.....	
Reid, Mrs. Helen (Smith),	50,	
" Joseph,	69,	
" Wm. R., Sr.,	48,	
" " " Jr.,	57,	
Rem. of Newberry, by the author,	155-159,	
Renwick, Hugh T.,	50,	
" Dr. James,	5,	
" Dr. J. I.,	.....	
" James S.,	50,	
" Rev. John, Sr.,	....	
" " " Jr.,	....	
" Dr. M. A.,	5,43,	
" Old Home,	.....	
" Rev. War Patriots,	9,10,	
" " Battle Sites,	12,	
Rhinehardt, Dr. V. W.,	51,	
Rhodelsperger, E. L.,	.....	
" George,	56,	
" Peter,	41,	
Rice, Wm. W.,	64,	
Ridgeway, W. A.,	52,	
Rikard Family Graveyard,	430,	
Rikard, Henry H.,	.....	
Riser, John, (Graveyard),	430,	
" Martin, "	430,	
" Luther,	5,	
" Robert,	21,	
" Rev. Sydney T.,	.....	
" " George,	.....	
" " Y. Von A.,	.....	
Ritter, Rev. H. C.,	56,	
Rits Theater,	64,	
"Riverside"—Old Henderson Home,	.....	
Robertson, Braswell,	19,	
" Henry C.,	43,	
" Dr. Peter,	5,	
"Rock House",—Old La Gronne Home,	.....	
Rogers, John,	26,	
" Old Home Site,	.....	
Roland, Thomas,	50,	
Rones, Dr. Myron,	.....	
Rook, Don,	56,	
Rosemont Cemetery,	402,405,410,	
Rotary Club,	56,	
Rural School-Johnstone Sch-	73,	
Rudd Family Graveyard,	445-446,	
Ruff Family Cemetery,	428-429,	
" Christian,	.....	
" George,	19,	
" Dr. P. B.,	5,	
" " " Old Home,	......	
Rutherford Academy,	76,	
" (Drayton) UDC,	53,	
" Family Graveyard,	434-435,	
" Col. Robert,	14,19,23,	
" Dr. Thomas B.,	19,	
" Col. Wm. D.,	13,25,64,	
Sales, L. M.,	.....	
" George M.,	.....	
Salley, A. P.,	43,48,56,	
Saluda Old Town,	.....	
Sanders, Mrs. C. W.,	51,	
" Frank,	51,	
Salter, J. Z.,	5,	
Sons of Am. Rev.,	53,	
Sanitary Dairy,	46,	
Satterwhite, Bartlette,	19,	
" Family Graveyard,	438,	
" John, Sr.,	22,	
" " Jr.,	....	
" M. M.,	77,	
" Dr. Irwin,	.....	
" Old Home,	.....	
Schaeffer, Col. L. J.,	50,	
" Rev. W. C.,	.....	
Schaver, Michael,	.....	
Scheror, Rev. J. A. B.,	....
" M. G.,	......
Schmits, Dr. Henry F.,	.....
Scholtz, Eduard,	5,
Schoppert, George,	15,
" Phillip,	5,
Schumpert, Fred H.,	542,
" Homer W.,	57,
" Jacob K.,	....
" J. Fred,	.....
" Mrs. Kitty L.,	53,
" O. L.,	.....
" Mrs. O. L.,	53,
Schwartz, Rev. John C.,	.....
Scott, George T.,	5,43,
" John W.,	49,
" Patrick E.,	5,56,
" " C.,	5,
Scurry, B. M.,	56,
" Mrs. B. M.,	36,
" Fred F.,	56,
" John R.,	......
Seabrook, Wm. B.,	.....
" Rev. Wm. L.,	....
Sease, Burton,	36,
" B. Govan,	36,
" Ellerbe,	36,
" Dr. J. Claude,	5,56,
" J. J.,	51,
" Dr. J. Marion,	5,
" Judge Thos. S.,	....
Seawell, Thomas M.,	46,
Security Loan & Investment	-47,
Seigler, John Carrol,	
Seminole Indian Wars,	11,
Senn, Dr. Hugh B.,	5,59,
" John A.,	.....
" Mrs. Texelle,	48,
" Dr. W. D.,	14,45,
" Jacob,	.....
Service Clubs,	56,
Setzler, Dr. E. B.,	.....
" Mrs. E. B.,	.....
" Hubert H.,	.....
" James P.,	.....
" Dr. John B.,	56,
" Dr. Marion,	....
Shady Grove Meth Church & Cemetery Site,	..
Shannon, C. H.,	14,
Sharon Meth Church and Cemetery,	119,
Shealy, Rev. Charles J.,	...
" " J. D.,	......
" Virgil J.,	......
" W. C.,	......

Shell, Allen, ••••
" Dr. Thomas J., 5,
Sherard, W. M., 55,
Shockley Brothers, 5,
Silver Street, 90,
" " School, 85,
Simmons, J. W. M., ••••
" Lalla Rook, 54,
Simpson, Dr. J. W., ••••
" Gov. William, ••••
Sims, David, ••••••
Singleton, Alex., ••••••
Singley, P. Clyde, ••••••
" P. Claude, ••••••
" Martin, ••••••
" Family, 277,
Sirrine, J. E., 44,
Slave Laws, 21,
Sligh, Rev. J. A., 14,38,
" Holland, 56,
" P. B., 50,
" Rev. W. K., 44,45,
Sloan, J. J., 21,
" Rev. T. W., ••••
Smetzler, Rev. J. P., •••
Smith, C. M., ••••••
" C. M., Jr., 51,
" Gillam (Cemetery), 446,
" John, 50,
" Robert D., 5,47,
" " " Jr., ••••
" Robert, 5,
" Julius, 5,
" Dr. Thomas W., ••••
" Dr. Van, 71,
" William R., 5,
Smyrna Pres Church, 110,111,
" " Cemetery, 409,
" " School, 73,
Social Developments, 49-65,
Sons of Am. Rev., 53,
Southern Bell Tel Co., 46,
" Cotton Oil Co., 44,
" Railway Co., 39,
Spanish-American War Soldiers,
Co. B., 1st Reg., 65,
" G., 2nd " , 66,
Spanish-American War Veterans, -50,
Spartan Grain & Mill Co., ••••
Speak, Rev. John W., ••••••
Spearman, John R., 21, 37,
" J. W. L., 49,
" Marcus L., 5,43,57,48,
" Old Home, ••••••
Speers, L. M., 5, 70,

Spence, Capt. James, ••••••
"Springfield", Old Home
Site of Judge O'Neall,..
Sproles, A. J., 5,
Springwood Cemetery,
(Greenville), 410,
St. Amand, C. E., 27,
Starke, Maj. Thomas, ••••••
Standard Warehouse Co., 45,
Steadman, Rev. J. M., ••••••
Stephens, David, ••••••
Stewart, Mrs. Eunice (Shockley), -50,
" Mrs. J. R., 51,
" Mrs. O. G., 53,
" Robert, 5,37,41,
" (Robert) Old Home,•••
" Thomas O., Jr., 50,57,
St. Paul's Luth Church, 131-133,
" " Cemetery, 416,
" James Luth Church, 130,
" John's Luth Church, 123,124,
" " " School, 74,
" Luke's Episcopal Church, 104,
" " Luth Church, 134, 130,
" " " " Cemetery, •••
" Matthews Luth Church, 129,130,
" " " Cemetery, 416,
" " Bapt Church (Col) 101,
" Phillips Luth Church, 133,
Stokes, Dr. J. Edwin, 56,
Stone, W. O., 36,
Stoney Hills School, 77,
Streets of Newberry-names-153,154,
Strippling, Wm.,Graveyard, 426,
Strong, Rev. Charles, 49,
Stuck, Dr. E. E., 56,
Stuckey, W. A., 71,
Suber, Hardy- Old Home- ••••••
" J. M., 45,
" Rev. Thomas F., ••••••
" Ulrich, ••••••
" Charles F., 41,
" Z. H., 45,
Sumner, Adam, G., ••••
" Mrs. Caroline(Mayes), 52,
" C. E., 5,38,41,43,53,57,
" C. Forest, 41,
" Clarence T., 5,
" Brothers, ••••••
" Elmer S., 56,
" Francis, 19,
" E. Hugh, 5,
" G. Leland, Sr., 5,44,53,
" " " Jr., ••••••
" George W., 5,43,44,46,53,
55, 56,60,70,

Sumner, Grace, 50,52,
" Mrs. G. R., 51,
" Guss B., 25,
" Harry Thos.,•••••
" Lieut. Henry,••••
" Henry, 69.
" Mrs. Hulda(Cromer),..
" James E., 51,
" John Adam, 4,23,
" " Jr., 19,
" J. Ernest, 16,53,55,
" John C., 13,
" John A., 26,
" John H., 5,43,
" Jno. A. Family
Graveyard, 427-42
" Mrs. Lavania E., 50,
" Mrs. Mamye S., 50,51,
53,54,147,
" Mrs. Martha D. Epting
 -••••••
" Marvin O., 56,
" Nicholas, ••••
" Mrs. Nora (Sease),..
" Oscar R., 56,
" Robert E., .47,
" T. Roy, 55,56,71,
" William, 37,
" " Family Graveyard
-427-428,
" William, Jr. Old Home, - •••••
" Dr. William, 5,
" William M., 46,
Summers, John, ••••••
" Rev. Joseph, 4,
Sutton, Frank, 56,
" Mrs. Frank, 50,
Swittenberg, Horace O., 46,5(
" John, 19,
" " Jr., 51,
Swygert, George, 19,
" John C., ••••••
Tabernacle Meth Church, 119,
" School, 75,
Tarleton's Tea Table, ••••••
Tanyard Hill, ••••••
Tarrant, Thomas, 5,
" Wm. T., 5,43,70,
Taylor, Benj (Graveyard),
-425,
" John, 41,
" John M., 14,
" Jonothan, ••••••
" John W., 5, 58,
" Thomas, 49,

m, J. C., 44,
gue, Abram, ...
" Elijah, ...
" Joshua, ...
lford, Wm., 44,
aters, 64,
spian Club, ...
mas & Howard Co., 47,
masson, Maggie, 48,
mpson, John R., 49,
" Old Home Site,...
" Dr. Thomas W., 5,
marsh, Charles, ...
merman, W. B., ...
" I. T., ...
id, James F., 5,
" Proctor, ...
" Wilton, 56,
land, Dr. Hugh H., 5,
pography, 1-2,
wles, Capt. Oliver, ...
wns & Villages in County, 88-99,
wnsend,........ 5,
abert, Charles L., 56,
" Mrs. Harriet (Wells), -52,
anquil Meth Church Site, 120,
" " " Cemetery, 420-422,
rinity Meth Church, 121,
ruett, Dr. F. A., ...
unker Church Cemetery, 442,
" " Site, 442,
urner, Howard, 56,
" Thomas, ...
" Thomas F., ...
" William, ...26,
nited Daughters of Confederacy, 53,54,
nion School, 76,
anduslah Spring, ...
illage Cemetery, 406-409,410,
oight, Rev. A. G., ...
" Rev. Gilbert, ...
oss, P. J., 57,
adlington, Edward, 19,
" Thomas B., ...
" William, 19,
aldo, Dr. Joseph, 5,
alker, Capt Whitfield, 13,49,
allace Old Graveyard, 449,
allace, Clarence, 36,
" Dr. D. D., ...
" Robert G., 57,
" " Jr., 56,
" Walter B., 43,48,55,60,

Wallace, W. C., 47,
" Wm. H., 70,
Wallern, Rev. Fred J., ...
Walters, I. W., 50,
" William, 58,
Walton, J. B., 42,
War of 1812, 11,
War Between the States, 13,
Ward, D. M., 5,
Warner, Capt Jacob, 13,
Water's Blockhouse, ...
Waters, Col. Philemon, 4,19,23,
" Philemon B., 5,
" Maj. Thos. W., 15,
Watson, E. L., 50,
" Wm. R., ...
Way, George D., 51,
" Dr. P. E., ...
W. C. T. U., ...
Wearn, G. Frank, ...
" Richard H., 5,50,
Webb, W. H., 5,43,
Wedaman, D. L., ...
Weeks, Dr. C. D., 50,59,
Welch, Eloise, 70, (Mrs Robt H. Wright),
Welch, Dr. S. G., 49,
" Williams, ...
Welling, J. L., ...
" Dr. Arthur, ...
Wolls, Foster, ...
" Henry B., 50,56,58,64,...,
" Old Home, ...
" Osborne S., 5,14,42,
" Match Factory, ...
" W. Fulmer, 56,64,
" Theater, 64,
" Thomas, ...
Werts, C. F., 53,57,71,
" Eugene S., 57,
" J. M., 49,
" Michael, 38,
Wessinger, Rev. J. C., ...
West, Benjamin, ...
" Charles, 56,
" Mrs. Emily (Scott), 53,
" Home, ...
" J. B., 49,
" J. Henry, 47,
" Perry E., 36,
West End Bapt Church, 142-144,
Wheeler, A. H., 49,
" Dan B., 5,
" D. H., 43,
" Mrs. Ethel(Saner), 53,

Wheeler, J. S., ...
" Dr. J. S., 42,
" Mrs. Juliet(Booser),53,
" Eva Jane, 48,
Whitaker, Rev. H. W., ...
White Family Graveyard, 441,
White, Harry T., 58,
" J. Wm., 5, 58,
Whitener, Guy, 41, 45,
" Lumber Plant, 45,
Whites, Mamie, ...
Whitmire, Fred, ...
Whitmire Village, 95-99,
" Schools, 79,
Wicker's Camp Ground Site, ...
Wicker, Andrew, 5,
" John H., 24,44,45,55,56,71,
" Dr. John K., 24,
" J. Monroe, 14,
" Orlando, ...
" Thomas E., ...
" Thomas V., 5, 44,
Wightman Meth Church, 115-117,
Wilbur, E. B., 5,43,44,
" Welch, 55,
Wild Flowers in County, 3,
Williams, Daniel, 24,
" Hopkins, ...
" James, 19,
" Col. James, 24,
" Col. James H., 12,13,
" Jeremiah, 19,
" John D., ...
" Joe (Col), 46,
" Leonard, 69,
" Peggy-Old Home, ...
" John Hopkins Old Cemetery, 444-445,
Willingham, J. K., 57,
" Pauline, 60,
Willowbrook Park, 58,
Wilson Family Graveyard, 422,
Wilson, Frank Z., 543,
" Rev. J. I., ...
" John C., 5, 37,
" L. A., 5, 45,
" Leland, 45,
" Mrs. O. J., 51,
" Thomas J., ...
" Vernon C., ...
" W. O., ...
" William, 69, ...
Winn, Jane, 52,
Wise, Clarence R., 56,
" Rev J. H., ...
" William R., 57,
" Jacob R., 50, 59,

Wiseman Hotel,	45,	Works Progress Administration,	....	Yarborugh, Dr. B. T.,	5,
Wiseman, James E.,	45,	Worthington, Dr. Benjamin,	5,	Youmans, Clem I.,	46,
" W. C.,	5,	" Samuel,	....	Young, Abram,	....
Witt, Rev. E. C.,	....	Wright, Downs,	51,	" George,	....
Women of Newberry—		" Rev. George A.,	....	Zealy, Rev. J. T.,	....
who Made History,	145-152,	" James,	....	Zion Meth Church,	120,
Wofford, J. W.,	....	" John,	....	Zion Bapt Church,	
Wood, James R.,	....	" Jonothan,	....	(see Mt.Zion),	
" Silas J.,	49,	" Joseph,	....	Zobel, Julius,	....
Womans's Club,	51,	" Robert D.,	....		
Woodward, William,	19,	" Mrs. Robert D.,	53,54,61,149,		
Wooten, S. J.,	5,	" Robert H.,	5, 15,43,		
Workman, Herbert A.,	56,	" W. T.,	5,		
" Mrs. J. M.,	....	" R. H.,	53,		
" Neal W.,	27,....,	" Mrs. R. H.,	54, 60,		
" Mrs. Neal W.,	50,51,	" Zack F.,	5,26,43,44,60,61, 47,48,53,55,56,		
		Wyche, C. C.,	....		
		" Dr. C. T.,	....		

www.ingramcontent.com/pod-product-compliance
Lightning Source LLC
Chambersburg PA
CBHW071221290426
44108CB00013B/1252